The IDG Books Bible Advantage

The *Windows NT Server 4.0 Administrator's Bible* is part of the Bible series brought to you by IDG Books Worldwide. We designed Bibles to meet your growing need for quick access to the most complete and accurate computer information available.

Bibles work the way you do: They focus on accomplishing specific tasks — not learning random functions. These books are not long-winded manuals or dry reference tomes. In Bibles, expert authors tell you exactly what you can do with your software and how to do it. Easy to follow, step-by-step sections; comprehensive coverage; and convenient access in language and design — it's all here.

The authors of Bibles are uniquely qualified to give you expert advice as well as insightful tips and techniques not found anywhere else. Our authors maintain close contact with end users through feedback from articles, training sessions, e-mail exchanges, user group participation, and consulting work. Because our authors know the realities of daily computer use and are directly tied to the reader, our Bibles have a strategic advantage.

Bible authors have the experience to approach a topic in the most efficient manner, and we know that you, the reader, will benefit from a "one-on-one" relationship with the author. Our research shows that readers make computer book purchases because they want expert advice on a product. Readers want to benefit from the author's experience, so the author's voice is always present in a Bible series book.

In addition, the author is free to include or recommend useful software in a Bible. The software that accompanies a Bible is not intended to be casual filler but is linked to the content, theme, or procedures of the book. We know that you will benefit from the included software.

You will find what you need in this book whether you read it from cover to cover, section by section, or simply one topic at a time. As a computer user, you deserve a comprehensive resource of answers. We at IDG Books Worldwide are proud to deliver that resource with the *Windows NT Server 4.0 Administrator's Bible.*

Brenda McLaughlin
Senior Vice President and Group Publisher

Windows NT™ Server 4.0 Administrator's Bible

Windows NT™ Server 4.0 Administrator's Bible

by Robert Cowart and Kenneth Gregg

IDG Books Worldwide, Inc.
An International Data Group Company

Foster City, CA ✦ Chicago, IL ✦ Indianapolis, IN ✦ Southlake, TX

Windows NT™ Server 4.0 Administrator's Bible

Published by
IDG Books Worldwide, Inc.
An International Data Group Company
919 E. Hillsdale Blvd.
Suite 400
Foster City, CA 94404

Library of Congress Catalog Card No.: 96-78236

ISBN: 0-7645-8009-4

Printed in the United States of America

10 9 8 7 6 5 4 3 2 1

IB/RV/RQ/ZW/FC

Distributed in the United States by IDG Books Worldwide, Inc.

Distributed by Macmillan Canada for Canada; by Contemporanea de Ediciones for Venezuela; by Distribuidora Cuspide for Argentina; by CITEC for Brazil; by Ediciones ZETA S.C.R. Ltda. for Peru; by Editorial Limusa SA for Mexico; by Transworld Publishers Limited in the United Kingdom and Europe; by Academic Bookshop for Egypt; by Levant Distributors S.A.R.L. for Lebanon; by Al Jassim for Saudi Arabia; by Simron Pty. Ltd. for South Africa; by Pustak Mahal for India; by The Computer Bookshop for India; by Toppan Company Ltd. for Japan; by Addison Wesley Publishing Company for Korea; by Longman Singapore Publishers Ltd. for Singapore, Malaysia, Thailand, and Indonesia; by Unalis Corporation for Taiwan; by WS Computer Publishing Company, Inc. for the Philippines; by WoodsLane Pty. Ltd. for Australia; by WoodsLane Enterprises Ltd. for New Zealand. Authorized Sales Agent: Anthony Rudkin Associates for the Middle East and North Africa.

For general information on IDG Books Worldwide's books in the U.S., please call our Consumer Customer Service department at 800-762-2974. For reseller information, including discounts and premium sales, please call our Reseller Customer Service department at 800-434-3422.

For information on where to purchase IDG Books Worldwide's books outside the U.S., please contact our International Sales department at 415-655-3172 or fax 415-655-3295.

For information on foreign language translations, please contact our Foreign & Subsidiary Rights department at 415-655-3021 or fax 415-655-3281.

For sales inquiries and special prices for bulk quantities, please contact our Sales department at 415-655-3200 or write to the address above.

For information on using IDG Books Worldwide's books in the classroom or for ordering examination copies, please contact our Educational Sales department at 800-434-2086 or fax 817-251-8174.

For authorization to photocopy items for corporate, personal, or educational use, please contact Copyright Clearance Center, 222 Rosewood Drive, Danvers, MA 01923, or fax 508-750-4470.

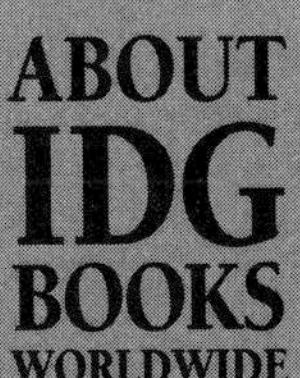

Welcome to the world of IDG Books Worldwide.

IDG Books Worldwide, Inc., is a subsidiary of International Data Group, the world's largest publisher of computer-related information and the leading global provider of information services on information technology. IDG was founded more than 25 years ago and now employs more than 8,500 people worldwide. IDG publishes more than 270 computer publications in over 75 countries (see listing below). More than 90 million people read one or more IDG publications each month.

Launched in 1990, IDG Books Worldwide is today the #1 publisher of best-selling computer books in the United States. We are proud to have received eight awards from the Computer Press Association in recognition of editorial excellence and three from *Computer Currents*' First Annual Readers' Choice Awards. Our best-selling *...For Dummies®* series has more than 25 million copies in print with translations in 30 languages. IDG Books Worldwide, through a joint venture with IDG's Hi-Tech Beijing, became the first U.S. publisher to publish a computer book in the People's Republic of China. In record time, IDG Books Worldwide has become the first choice for millions of readers around the world who want to learn how to better manage their businesses.

Our mission is simple: Every one of our books is designed to bring extra value and skill-building instructions to the reader. Our books are written by experts who understand and care about our readers. The knowledge base of our editorial staff comes from years of experience in publishing, education, and journalism — experience which we use to produce books for the '90s. In short, we care about books, so we attract the best people. We devote special attention to details such as audience, interior design, use of icons, and illustrations. And because we use an efficient process of authoring, editing, and desktop publishing our books electronically, we can spend more time ensuring superior content and spend less time on the technicalities of making books.

VIII
WINNER
Eighth Annual Computer Press Awards 1992

You can count on our commitment to deliver high-quality books at competitive prices on topics you want to read about. At IDG Books Worldwide, we continue in the IDG tradition of delivering quality for more than 25 years. You'll find no better book on a subject than one from IDG Books Worldwide.

John Kilcullen
President and CEO
IDG Books Worldwide, Inc.

IDG Books Worldwide, Inc., is a subsidiary of International Data Group, the world's largest publisher of computer-related information and the leading global provider of information services on information technology. International Data Group publishes over 276 computer publications in over 75 countries. Ninety million people read one or more International Data Group publications each month. International Data Group's publications include: **ARGENTINA:** Annuario de Informatica, Computerworld Argentina, PC World Argentina; **AUSTRALIA:** Australian Macworld, Client/Server Journal, Computer Living, Computerworld, Computerworld 100, Digital News, IT Casebook, Network World, On-line World Australia, PC World, Publishing Essentials, Reseller, WebMaster; **AUSTRIA:** Computerwelt Osterreich, Networks Austria, PC Tip; **BELARUS:** PC World Belarus; **BELGIUM:** Data News; **BRAZIL:** Annuário de Informática, Computerworld Brazil, Connections, Super Game Power, Macworld, PC Player, PC World Brazil, Publish Brazil, Reseller News; **BULGARIA:** Computerworld Bulgaria, Networkworld/Bulgaria, PC & MacWorld Bulgaria; **CANADA:** CIO Canada, Client/Server World, ComputerWorld Canada, InfoCanada, Network World Canada; **CHILE:** Computerworld Chile, PC World Chile; **COLOMBIA:** Computerworld Colombia, PC World Colombia; **COSTA RICA:** PC World Centro America; **THE CZECH AND SLOVAK REPUBLICS:** Computerworld Czechoslovakia, Elektronika Czechoslovakia, Macworld Czech Republic, PC World Czechoslovakia; **DENMARK:** Communications World, Computerworld Danmark, Macworld Danmark, PC Privat Danmark, PC World Danmark, PC World Danmark Supplements, TECH World; **DOMINICAN REPUBLIC:** PC World Republica Dominicana; **ECUADOR:** PC World Ecuador; **EGYPT:** Computerworld Middle East, PC World Middle East; **EL SALVALDOR:** PC World Centro America; **FINLAND:** MikroPC, Tietoverkko, Tietoviikko; **FRANCE:** Distributique, Golden, Hebdo-Distributique, Info PC, Le Guide du Monde Informatique, Le Monde Informatique, Reseaux & Telecoms; **GERMANY:** Computer Partner, Computerwoche, Computerwoche Extra, Computerwoche Focus, I/M Information Management, Macwelt, PC Welt; **GREECE:** GamePro, Multimedia World; **GUATEMALA:** PC World Centro America; **HONDURAS:** PC World Centro America; **HONG KONG:** Computerworld Hong Kong, PCWorld Hong Kong, Publish in Asia; **HUNGARY:** ABCD CD-ROM, Computerworld Szamitastechnika, PC & Mac World Hungary, PC-X Magazine; **ICELAND:** Tolvuheimur/PC World Island; **INDIA:** Information Systems Computerworld, PC World India, Publish in Asia; **INDONESIA:** InfoKomputer PC World, Komputek Computerworld, Publish in Asia; **IRELAND:** ComputerScope, PC Live!; **ISRAEL:** People & Computers; **ITALY:** Computerworld Italia, Computerworld Italia Special Editions, Macworld Italia, Networking Italia, PC Shopping, PC World Italia, PC World/Walt Disney; **JAPAN:** DTP World, HP Open World Japan, Macworld Japan, Nikkei Personal Computing, Open World Japan, OS/2 World Japan, SunWorld Japan, Windows World Japan; **KENYA:** East African Computer News; **KOREA:** Hi-Tech Information/Computerworld, Macworld Korea, PC World Korea; **MACEDONIA:** PC World Macedonia; **MALAYSIA:** Computerworld Malaysia, PC World Malaysia, Publish in Asia; **MEXICO:** Computerworld Mexico, Macworld, PC World Mexico; **MYANMAR:** PC World Myanmar; **NETHERLANDS:** Computer! Totaal, LAN Magazine, LanWorld Buyers Guide, Macworld, Net Magazine, Totaal! Beurskrant; **NEW ZEALAND:** Absolute Beginner's Guide, Computer Buyer, Computer Industry Directory, Computerworld New Zealand, MTB, Network World, PC World New Zealand; **NICARAGUA:** PC World Centro America; **NIGERIA:** PC World Nigeria; **NORWAY:** Computerworld Norge, Computerworld Privat (Datamagasinet), CW Rapport Norge, IDG's KURSGUIDE, Macworld Norge, Multimediaworld, PC World Ekspress, PC World Nettverk, PC World Norge, PC World's Produktguide, Windows World Spesial; **PAKISTAN:** Computerworld Pakistan, PC World Pakistan; Panama: PC World Panama; **P. R. OF CHINA:** China Computer Users, China Computerworld, China Infoworld, China Telecom World Weekly, Computer & Communication, Electronic Design China, Electronics Today, Electronics Weekly, Game Camp, Game Soft, Network World China, PC World China, Popular Computer Weekly, Software Weekly, Software World, Telecom World; **PERU:** Computerworld Peru, PC World Profesional Peru, PC World Peru; **PHILIPPINES:** Computerworld Philippines, PC World Philippines, Publish in Asia; **POLAND:** Computerworld Poland, Computerworld Special Report, Macworld, Networld, PC World Komputer; **PORTUGAL:** Cerebro/PC World, Computerworld/Correio Informático, Dealer World Portugal, MacIn/PCIn, Multimedia World Portugal; **PUERTO RICO:** PC World Puerto Rico; **ROMANIA:** Computerworld Romania, PC World Romania, Telecom Romania; **RUSSIA:** Computerworld Russia, Mir PK, Sety; **SINGAPORE:** Computerworld Singapore, PC World Singapore, Publish in Asia; **SLOVENIA:** MONITOR; **SOUTH AFRICA:** Computing S.A., InfoWorld S.A., Network World S.A., Software World; **SPAIN:** Computerworld España, COMUNICACIONES WORLD, Dealer World, Macworld España, PC World España; **SWEDEN:** CAP&Design, Computer Sweden, Corporate Computing, MacWorld, Maxi Data, MikroDatorn, Nätverk & Kommunikation, PC/Aktiv, PC World, Windows World; **SWITZERLAND:** Computerworld Schweiz, Macworld Schweiz, PCtip; **TAIWAN:** Computerworld Taiwan, Macworld Taiwan, PC World Taiwan, Publish Taiwan, Windows World; **THAILAND:** Thai Computerworld, Publish in Asia; **TURKEY:** Computerworld Turkiye, MACWORLD Turkiye, PC WORLD Turkiye; **UKRAINE:** Computerworld Kiev, Computers & Software, Multimedia World Ukraine, PC World Ukraine; **UNITED KINGDOM:** Acorn User, Amiga Action, Amiga Computing, Appletalk, Computing, GamePro, Macworld, Network News, Parents and Computers, PC Advisor, PC Home, PSX Pro UK, The WEB; **UNITED STATES:** Cable in the Classroom, CD Review, CIO Magazine, Computerworld, Computerworld Client/Server Journal, Digital Video Magazine, DOS World, Federal Computer Week, GamePro, InfoWorld, I-Way, JavaWorld, Macworld, Multimedia World, Netscape World Online, Network World, PC Entertainment, PC World, Publish, SunWorld Online, SWATPro Magazine, Video Event, WebMaster; **URUGUAY:** PC World Uruguay; **VENEZUELA:** Computerworld Venezuela, PC World Venezuela; and **VIETNAM:** PC World Vietnam.

7/16/96

Credits

Senior Vice President and Group Publisher
Brenda McLaughlin

Acquisitions Editor
John Osborn

Marketing Manager
Melisa Duffy

Managing Editor
Terry Somerson

Development Editor
Jim Sumser

Copy Editors
Colleen Brosnan
Katharine Dvorak

Technical Editor
Rob Sanfilippo

Editorial Assistant
Sharon Eames

Production Director
Andrew Walker

Production Associate
Christopher Pimentel

Supervisor of Page Layout
Craig Harrison

Project Coordinator
Ben Schroeter

Production/Page Layout
Tom Debolski
Ritchie Durdin
Elsie Yim

Quality Control Specialist
Mick Arellano

Media/Archive Coordination
Leslie Popplewell
Melissa Stauffer

Proofreader
Mary C. Oby

Indexer
Rebecca R. Plunkett

Book Design
Drew R. Moore

Cover Design
Three 8 Creative Group

About the Authors

Robert Cowart has been writing for computer magazines and book publishers for over 14 years. Specializing in instructional books about computer software, he has a strong background in PC operating systems. He cut his teeth writing 8080 assembler code for CP/M systems in the early 1980s when he built his first personal computer from scratch. After earning a BS degree in digital electronics from Merrit College, he performed technical support, programming, and training services for North Star Computers. Subsequently, he started his own dBASE consulting company, doing custom programming and systems installations for small businesses. He has written approximately 100 feature articles for magazines such as *PC Week, PC Tech Journal, Microsoft Systems Journal, A+, Keyboard, PC World, MacWorld,* and *MacWeek.* While writing for *PC Magazine,* he developed the automated testing programs that benchmark LANs for Ziff-Davis magazines' PC-Labs. For the last 10 years he has specialized in writing computer books only. Robert also holds a BS degree in psychology from Temple University.

Kenneth Gregg writes from his five years of inside experience in the Windows NT product group at Microsoft. For the last two of those years, he was the Windows NT Test Manager, leading a group of 180 engineers responsible for all aspects of the Windows NT product line testing, and directed several large network test labs. He drove the Windows NT testing operation through the release of both Windows NT 3.1 and 3.5.

As the third software design engineer to join the NT test team in 1989, Ken developed test software for the NT kernel and assisted third-party software developers in porting their applications and drivers to NT before its release. Prior to leading the entire NT test organization, Ken promoted multiprocessor hardware designs to computer manufacturers, trained new NT team members, developed application test strategies, and managed the NT kernel testing group. He has since served as a beta tester for both Windows NT Server 3.51 and 4.0.

Ken has been involved with software development for nearly 20 years as a consultant, engineer, and manager. Most recently, he was Senior Director of Software Engineering at Artisoft, which develops the LANtastic network operating system. He has designed, developed, and tested system software at Microsoft, Wang Laboratories, and Texas Instruments for personal computers, networks, factory robotics, and telephony. Ken holds a BS in Computer Science from Michigan State University and an MS in Computer Science from the University of Texas.

To my agents Chris Van Buren and Bill Gladstone, for their attention and dedication to my career amidst a whirlwind of evolving technology.

—RC

To my wife, Theresa, who patiently put up with yet another grueling computer-related project. She's now been a member of the "Widows NT" group not once, but twice.

—KG

Preface

When you read about Microsoft these days, it's often hard to think of it as the underdog in any ring of the software circus. It seems as though the company dominates nearly every area of mainstream PC computing — to the chagrin of many a small software development company. And yet after 13 years of developing network products, Microsoft is still struggling with the elusive goal of dominance in networking — until recently, anyway.

Windows NT Server 3.5, 3.51, and now especially version 4.0, have turned the tide. NT's market share increase, specifically in new corporate network installations, has accelerated dramatically in the last several months. Meanwhile, Windows NT is slowly chipping away at arch rival Novell's installed base, as more MIS organizations are converted to the NT way of life.

From Whence the Inside Stories?

When telling you about Windows NT, co-author Ken Gregg speaks from inside experience. As a member of the Windows NT product test group at Microsoft from July 1989 through September 1994, he helped grow NT from a delicate sapling into a towering redwood. And as the company increased from 4,000 to over 16,000 employees, the NT test group went from three to over 180 people.

During his tenure at Microsoft, Ken personally developed software to test NT's kernel, helped third-party software and hardware developers move their products to NT, and managed the kernel test group to create tests for file systems, fault tolerance, device drivers, and compatibility. He then spent the last two of his five years there as the Windows NT Test Manager. The test team developed and ran over three million lines of test code, to assure the quality of every nook and cranny of the operating system.

Throughout this book, you will be treated to glimpses of what went on inside the NT group as Windows NT gradually became an industrial-strength product. Through these narratives (which Ken often relates in the first person), you'll get a sense of the effort and sacrifice, as well as a few comic moments, that went into the making of Windows NT. Here's a sample:

INSIDE STORY

Coconut milk, spicy curry, hot red pepper, roasted peanuts — the distinctive aromas of the foods of Thailand swirled through my car in nauseating intensity. It was going to be another late night of testing the newest build of Windows NT Server, and to energize the troops, I was hauling dinners for over 60 people from their favorite Thai restaurant. As I unloaded the various brown paper sacks, I noticed that a container labeled Tom Tum Goong had fallen onto its side. Now I had no clue what Tom Tum Goong might be, but I knew that the engineer who hungrily awaited it was going to be Tom Tum Glum. The entire soupy contents had leaked onto the carpet of my trunk, which smelled like it belonged in a Bangkok bazaar.

So did the conference room where several engineers helped me set out the redolent repast. In no time the full test force was milling around the oval table, cracking jokes, exchanging theories about NT bugs, and sharing Thai spring rolls. The pleasure of the camaraderie, along with the pain of another evening spent away from home, typified the general perception of many project participants. To them, the Windows NT group was both the best place and the worst place to be within Microsoft.

In the beginning, the NT group had been a sought-after, almost elite organization, where people had the singular opportunity to help create from scratch the future of Microsoft's operating system technology. The group was run by smart, intensely competitive people with exacting standards of quality. Both the development and test groups were highly respected by other Microsoft organizations. On the other hand, the NT group had deservedly gained a reputation for a killer pace with extremely long hours. As time went on, this reputation offset the attraction of joining the group, making it more difficult to recruit talent from other areas of the company.

Well over 400 development engineers, test engineers, managers, and support staff worked incredible hours for months on end to meet the periodic beta and product release deadlines. Days often stretched to 14 hours or more, workweeks extended to seven days, and team members would sometimes slog on for two days at a time without sleep. Personal lives fell into shambles, and sometimes marriages disintegrated.

Somehow I managed to emerge with my nervous system (and even my marriage) intact. I still reminisce at certain reminders of that time of great challenge and excitement. For example, whenever I'm driving my car on a warm day, the reawakened odor of Tom Tum Goong pungently brings back memories of those nightly NT dinners. And whenever someone suggests that we go out for Thai food, I promptly suggest burgers instead.

Who Should Read this Book

If you're a network administrator who's new to Windows NT Server and you need to get up and running quickly, this book is written just for you. And even if you're new to network administration in general, this book provides the fundamental knowledge you need to jump-start your career. You'll learn how to get the most from your servers and your network, how to plan for the future of your enterprise, and how to harness the powerful tools and techniques that you need to succeed as a Windows NT Server network administrator.

If you're responsible for installing and administering Windows NT Server, you've come to the right place for practical advice on NT's strengths and limitations, keeping your network running smoothly and efficiently, and keeping your users happy and productive. If Windows NT Server is already installed, and you just need to perform certain administrative tasks such as nightly backups or managing user accounts, you can turn directly to the sections that teach you how to use NT's powerful administration features.

We assume you've used DOS and one or more of Microsoft's Windows products — Windows 3.1, Windows for Workgroups, or Windows 95. If you lack basic Windows mouse and keyboard skills, you'll need to consult a beginner's text for the fundamentals. Exposure to PC networking is helpful but isn't required. If you're coming from a NetWare background, you'll find information that will help you relate NT concepts to those that you're used to.

How this Book is Organized

This book is divided into five parts. Rather than covering the features of each Windows NT Server utility from a general perspective, we've focused on specific tasks that you'll need to accomplish as an NT network administrator. Some NT utilities provide a broad range of functions, so you'll see different aspects of the same NT utility covered in different parts of the book.

Part I presents an overview of the Windows NT product line, then delves into the internals of the operating system. If you're new to PC networks, Chapter 3 provides you with the fundamental knowledge you need to get started. Chapter 4 gets more specific as it presents the key network features of Windows NT Server 4.0. You'll find lots of network administrator success secrets in Chapter 5. In Chapter 6, you'll get all the information you need to decide where and when to install Windows NT Server, Windows NT Workstation, and other Microsoft products on your network.

Part II takes you step-by-step through the process of designing your server and your network. You'll then get expert advice as you proceed through each step of installing Windows NT Server 4.0. You'll learn how to organize large enterprise networks, implement TCP/IP, hook remote computers to your network, and integrate NT with other networks you may already have. We'll also walk you through installation of the various network clients offered by Microsoft.

Once you've got Windows NT Server installed, Part III shows you how to use it. You'll learn about the easy Windows 95-like user interface. You'll find out how to share and distribute data among your users. And you'll discover how to use NT to communicate and collaborate effectively across the network.

Part IV digs into the details of day-to-day administration of your Windows NT Server computers and your network. You'll find out how to configure and maintain your servers and your network. You'll learn how to protect your valuable data using NT's backup, security, and fault-tolerance features. Administering user accounts on your network will become a breeze. In Chapter 19, you'll learn powerful techniques for optimizing both the speed and reliability of your NT-based network. You'll find out about the NT registry database, which contains virtually all configuration information. Finally, we'll share some valuable tips, tricks, and troubleshooting techniques.

In Part V, you'll learn how to transform your computer that's running Windows NT Server 4.0 into a World Wide Web server. You'll find out how to install and configure Microsoft's Internet Information Server, use FrontPage and Office to create Web pages, and manage a secure connection to the Internet.

At the end of the book, you'll find handy appendixes. These include an NT command-line reference, a glossary of NT and network terms, and pointers to all sorts of additional sources of information about Windows NT Server.

How to Approach this Book

If you have no experience at all with Windows NT Server, your best bet is to start at the beginning and read the chapters in sequence. Later chapters build on the foundations established in earlier ones. If you'd prefer to skip the internals discussed in Chapters 2 and 4, you can do so and still navigate in later chapters.

If your immediate goal is to get your first Windows NT Server 4.0 computer up and running, you can jump directly to Part II to learn how to prepare your computers and network for installation. If NT is already installed, and you want to leap right into administration tasks, Part III and Part IV will get you started.

Conventions Used in this Book

When we introduce unfamiliar terms, they'll be in *italics*. We define new terms when they're first used. If you encounter an unfamiliar term or acronym, you can always check the glossary in Appendix B to refresh your memory.

The new Windows NT Server 4.0 user interface often uses the term "folder" to refer to what you already know as a directory. The two terms are synonymous. You'll find that NT itself uses both terms in different places within the user interface. In this book, we've also used both terms, matching the NT user interface whenever possible.

When you see the term "SystemRoot" used at the beginning of a directory path, it refers to the directory in which you install Windows NT Server. For example, if you install NT in C:\WINNTS, then substitute C:\WINNTS wherever you see SystemRoot. NT automatically defines SystemRoot as an environment variable that you can use in batch files.

Since the hierarchy of menus in the NT user interface can sometimes get pretty deep, we'll use a shorthand for telling how to navigate menus. If we ask you to "Click Start ➪ Programs ➪ Administrative Tools ➪ Disk Administrator" you should click the Start button, point to Programs, point to Administrative Tools, and then click Disk Administrator.

Throughout the book, you'll encounter text that is set off from normal text. Sections marked with the TAKE NOTE icon contain supplementary material. Sections of text labeled CAUTION are warnings of potential hazards. TIPs give you additional insight and practical techniques that might not be obvious. You'll also find the included Worksheets helpful in planning and designing your server and network. You can copy these worksheets and fill them out whenever you need them. CROSS REFERENCE icons highlight references to other chapters where you will find additional information.

Let's Get Started

You've decided to learn all about Windows NT Server at an exciting time in the network computing industry. NT has been cleared for takeoff in the marketplace, and now it's barreling down the runway. The Windows NT Server knowledge and skills you acquire today will make you more valuable to your organization than ever before.

We know (and you may already know) that the Windows NT Server topic is huge in scope. There's no way to cover every nook and cranny of the product in a single volume. Microsoft's NT Server documentation spans a daunting seven large manuals. However, these pages will give you enough vital information to quickly become a productive and proficient network administrator. And since that's why you picked up this book in the first place, let's cut the preliminaries and get started.

Let's Get Started

Acknowledgments

Creating a book of this size and substance is a considerable undertaking. Tracking the development of an operating system as ambitious as Windows NT Server — not to mention documenting it in a way that is truly useful for the reader — requires enormous attention to detail. Many people are involved in such an undertaking. Bringing such a book to press in relatively short order to meet the demands of the buying public makes the task even more Herculean. There are several people I want to thank for their help in making this process a reality.

First, thanks to John Osborn and Jim Sumser at IDG Books Worldwide. Working with IDG Books on this NT project is particularly exciting due to its timeliness. NT is a milestone product in the history of PC operating systems, certainly a far cry from the CP/M of 15 years ago. In its own way IDG Books is a milestone as well. When so many publishers are mired in doing things by "the book," or "the old school" way, IDG Books remains innovative. Other publishers would do well to sit up and notice, for example, how IDG Books supports its authors and readers by offering excerpts and updates to their books via the World Wide Web.

Certainly without the help of my co-author on this project, Ken Gregg, this book would have involved a sea of writers. Books of this length often involve teams of writers working together, and Ken, due to his broad knowledge of NT, fine writing style, and ability to produce, has reduced that number to three. A significant amount of material was written by Ken, and edited by his colleague Karen Thure. As a consummate team, I thank them both for their energetic and reliable production of high-quality, easily readable chapters.

No book on Windows NT Server these days would be complete without coverage of the Internet. Thanks also to Sanjaya Hettihewa for his contributions to the Internet section of the book. And thanks to Brian Knittel of Quarterbyte Systems for his incredibly quick and thorough treatment of the Internet security chapter.

—Robert Cowart

At the very top of my acknowledgments list is Karen Thure, who brought her writing and editing experience and talent to bear in making this book a much better experience for you. She painstakingly edited my manuscript drafts and breathed new life into potentially parched technical material. Karen was my key partner in making this book a reality.

My hat's also off to Jim Sumser, Development Editor at IDG Books, for keeping everything on course and for being the voice of reason whenever crisis loomed. Jim is a real pro. Thanks to Rob Sanfilippo for his thorough technical editing and feedback. Thanks to Colleen Brosnan for doing such a great job in copy editing the final manuscript.

I owe many thanks to the folks in the Windows NT test team at Microsoft for their willing assistance in verifying product information and in jogging my memory about significant NT development milestones. These ever-helpful test managers and engineers include S. Somasegar, Sanjay Jejurikar, Jonathan Manheim, Arden White, Joe Holman, Mak Agashe, and John Spencer. Their expertise typifies that of the entire Windows NT product group at Microsoft — whom I admire and thank for once again turning out another stellar set of products.

—Ken Gregg

Contents at a Glance

Table of Contents

Part III: Using Windows NT Server 447

Part IV: Configuring and Administering Your NT Server Network 571

PART

Windows NT Server: An Inside Look

✦ ✦ ✦ ✦

In This Part

✦ ✦ ✦ ✦

Windows NT Server and You

The fact that you've picked up this book says a lot about you. You've decided to run Microsoft Windows NT Server 4.0 on your network, and you may be responsible for installing and administering that network. You want the inside story on what the product can and can't do. You want to know how to keep the network running smoothly, how to coax it to perform at its best, and how to keep your users and your manager happy. Or, you might be in charge of performing nightly backups and handling midnight user emergencies, and you want to find out more about the powerful tools you're using and how to get the most from them. Regardless of your role, you're interested in doing a great job and providing stellar support to the network users in your organization.

Your organization probably selected Windows NT Server for some combination of the following important benefits:

- **Reliability** through a solid kernel, isolation of errant applications, and fault tolerance
- **Performance** from a completely 32-bit architecture, highly optimized I/O, and efficient use of resources
- **Scalability** via support for large disks and multiple CPUs within a single computer
- **Portability** through support for multiple CPU platforms, including Intel x86 and RISC
- **Security** for multiple users and resources, both locally and over the network
- **Usability** through easy installation, upgrades, graphical utilities, and the Windows 95 look and feel
- **Maintainability** with powerful, centralized network administration features
- **Compatibility** with a wide range of hardware, software, and networks

Whether you're new to network administration or are an experienced network administrator about to switch to Windows NT Server, this book shows you not only what to do and how to do it, but also why and when. It teaches you how to get up and running quickly, how to get the most out of your servers and your network, and how to plan for the future and avoid painting yourself into a corner. Most importantly, it gives you the knowledge and tools that you need to succeed at providing great service to your organization.

Getting Started with Windows NT Server

Jumping into the administration of a new operating system can be a daunting proposition. If you've administered other servers, based on UNIX or NetWare, for example, you'll find that becoming productive at installing and administering Windows NT Server is more straightforward and much less complex. Don't worry about sacrificing power and flexibility, though. Windows NT Server provides a rich set of features and capabilities that will meet the most demanding needs of your enterprise. On the other hand, no system is perfect. The product isn't without its quirks, traps, and limitations. This inside look clues you in on how to recognize, avoid, and work around these problems. You'll be able to locate and circumvent the tar pits.

In presenting this material, I assume that you have some hands-on experience with DOS and Windows, basic knowledge of the standard hardware components of IBM-compatible PCs, and some exposure to (not necessarily experience with) PC networking concepts.

Complex terms are explained when they first appear, and Appendix B provides a handy glossary to help you along the way. If you're already experienced with networks and network administration, or you already know about the Windows NT architecture, you can skim or skip some of the introductory material on these topics.

Welcome to the Windows NT Family

Windows NT currently represents Microsoft's most powerful and reliable operating system architecture, providing a robust, secure, 32-bit network operating system with the familiar Windows 95 user interface. It's targeted at workstations and servers in the corporate enterprise environment, unlike Windows 95 which is primarily geared to home computers. These workstations and servers can range from Intel 486-based PC desktop computers to multiprocessor computers containing up to 32 processors. However, your choices for Windows NT computers aren't limited to Intel CPUs. Windows NT also supports other CPU architectures, including DEC Alpha, MIPS R4x00, and PowerPC.

The Windows NT family of operating systems consists of two siblings: Windows NT Server and Windows NT Workstation. These two products are identical in terms of their underlying operating system architecture. They differ only in how they're tuned for optimal performance in their intended environments and in several advanced features that Windows NT Server provides.

Windows NT Server Is the Superset

Windows NT Server 4.0, the focus of this book, has been optimized to provide a highly responsive network that's easy to administer. It efficiently uses memory for caching large amounts of data, gives high priority to network users, and offers improved performance of typical 32-bit network server applications. Windows NT Server is a superset of Windows NT Workstation. It adds powerful tools for centralized network administration and security, enables Apple Macintosh computers to connect and use resources, provides higher reliability through fault tolerance features, and offers remote access server capabilities. Windows NT Server can act as a highly reliable server to an unlimited number of network clients. The essence of Windows NT Server revolves around networking, which I discuss more thoroughly in Chapters 3 and 4.

Windows NT Server actually belongs to another product family — Microsoft BackOffice. BackOffice gets its name from the concept that client workstations are typically on desktops in the front office, whereas the server computer and its applications are placed in the back office. In addition to Windows NT Server, Back-Office includes SQL Server, Systems Management Server, SNA Server, Exchange Server, and Internet Information Server. All of these applications run on the Windows NT Server platform.

Windows NT Workstation Is a Subset

Windows NT Workstation is tuned to operate at peak performance in an interactive desktop environment. This version of the operating system has a somewhat smaller memory footprint, gives highest priority to execution of interactive operations such as keyboard and mouse input, and offers higher efficiency for 16-bit and 32-bit desktop applications. The product includes the ability to provide peer-to-peer networking, to be a network server for up to ten client workstations, and to connect as a client to any number of servers.

Throughout this book, I use the terms Windows NT or just NT to refer to the overall system architecture and when discussing features common to both the workstation and server products. I use NT Server and NT Workstation in some cases to refer to the respective products.

INSIDE STORY

Over the years since the NT development project started, I've heard much speculation, often humorous, about what the NT acronym in Windows NT really means. Before the first NT product arrived, many Microsoft competitors and detractors had their own favorite definition. The most common of these definitions was *not there*. One competitive definition that backfired appeared on IBM's Nice Try T-shirts, distributed at a major computer conference, after the parting of the ways between IBM and Microsoft. The *N* and *T* letters were huge, and the remaining letters were extremely small. Unless the shirt was right in front of you, all you saw were the letters NT. These T-shirts created priceless walking advertising for NT and Microsoft, courtesy of IBM's promotional budget.

Internally at Microsoft, as the NT team burned the midnight oil approaching one of its key beta releases, some engineers went through a progression from near term to now term to no time. I later saw one of the most clever and befitting definitions etched on an NT promotional mug: iNdustrial sTrength. As you'll see in the next few chapters, Windows NT, and especially Windows NT Server, can best be described as Industrial Strength Windows.

What's the Meaning of the Name NT?

Microsoft's authentic definition of the NT acronym is *new technology*, although many of the features offered by this product line have existed before in various forms. The real innovation in NT is that it successfully draws the best and most powerful capabilities from the operating system, user interface, and networking worlds. Microsoft succeeded at designing and integrating them into a complete, highly reliable, cohesive product that's easy to install, maintain, and use.

In this and subsequent chapters, I discuss the details of what Windows NT brings to the table and what it all means to you as a network administrator. But first, let's look behind the scenes at some of the origins of the design philosophies and concepts that have evolved into Windows NT.

From Whence It Came

Back in 1988, Microsoft's Bill Gates hired Dave Cutler away from Digital Equipment Corporation, where Dave had been the father of the VMS operating system. His charter at Microsoft was to lead the design and development of another major operating system, this time for the PC and emerging RISC processors. Along with several other experienced players hired from DEC and some key Microsoft engineers, the team set out to create what would become known as Windows NT.

Windows NT 3.1, the first retail version of the operating system, was released in July 1993. It arrived in two flavors: Windows NT and Windows NT Advanced Server. (The word "advanced" was soon dropped, because it implied too much complexity, and the word "workstation" was added to better differentiate the two products.) Windows NT was tuned for high-end workstations, whereas Windows NT Advanced Server was optimized for use as a robust network server.

By the time they released Windows NT 3.1, Microsoft had already invested five years, nearly $150 million, and countless hours of human sacrifice (the kind where people work extremely hard, not the other kind) by over 400 people to design and deliver an operating system containing 5.6 million lines of heavily tested, high quality code. Each subsequent Windows NT release has brought improved performance and enhanced features.

The Mach Influence

In addition to the influence of VMS concepts on NT, the design of the NT operating system was strongly influenced by the Mach operating system, designed at Carnegie-Mellon University. Mach, a variant of UNIX, provided robustness and flexibility by isolating the core operating system, or kernel, from protected subsystems that provided the interfaces to applications. Without affecting the integrity of the kernel, protected subsystems could be altered or added to provide different application interfaces, enabling emulation of multiple operating system environments. This approach lets NT support Windows NT, OS/2, and POSIX applications simultaneously and enables relatively easy addition of other operating system environments in the future.

The OS/2 Heritage

Microsoft Windows NT shares a bit of common ancestry with IBM OS/2. By 1989, Microsoft and IBM had jointly developed 16-bit OS/2 and were working together on the 32-bit version, OS/2 2.0. In parallel, Microsoft had already started design and development on the NT project, believing that a portable, scalable, 32-bit operating system was needed. At that time, the primary programming interface for NT was going to be the OS/2 2.0 32-bit API. (*API* stands for Application Programming Interface. It's the set of system services called by applications.) In fact, at that time, the NT project was internally called NT OS/2.

By the middle of 1990, it was clear that Microsoft and IBM didn't agree on the direction of OS/2 and that Microsoft Windows, after several years of promotion, was finally becoming wildly successful in the marketplace. The two companies ceased their joint development, and IBM took over development of OS/2. Microsoft retained NT, changed the name of the NT OS/2 project to Windows NT, and defined its new programming interface, the Win32 API. Microsoft's new technology operating system had now become a member of the Windows family.

Going Their Separate Ways

Although OS/2 and Windows NT share a common heritage at Microsoft, they're based on completely different source code. At the time of the split between IBM and Microsoft, OS/2 code was highly dependent on the Intel CPU architecture and wasn't easily portable to other processors. Much of the system was written in Intel assembly language, and some of the C code was dependent on the Intel architecture. (Several years would elapse before IBM completed a port of OS/2 to a non-Intel CPU, the PowerPC, but this project was shelved just before release, due to lackluster performance.) Microsoft had to create Windows NT from the ground up, using C, C++, and a very small amount of assembly language, to ensure that NT would meet the product's aggressive design goals. Despite their different source code bases, many of the concepts implemented in Windows NT and OS/2 are similar.

The UNIX Connection

The UNIX operating system was developed back in 1970 at AT&T. Due to a long standing antitrust decree, AT&T wasn't permitted to market UNIX. Instead the source code was made widely available to colleges and universities, to be used for educational purposes. The wide availability of the source code generated a proliferation of versions, tools, features, and incompatibilities in the UNIX world. Several companies modified and marketed their own versions of UNIX.

The Achilles heel of UNIX has been the lack of standardization among its various implementations. Software written for one UNIX version doesn't necessarily port easily to a different flavor of the system. Although the advent of graphical interfaces have increased UNIX's usability and popularity, multiple interfaces compete for mind share among developers and users. All this has resulted in fewer applications, and in spotty support of other environments such as DOS and Windows. Attempts have been made over the years to standardize and unify the UNIX operating system, to put to rest this objection. Indeed, the announcement and release of Windows NT caused at least one of these committees to redouble its efforts toward standardization. Thus far, however, most variants of UNIX remain nonstandard.

One standard has emerged as important in the U.S. government computing marketplace. POSIX, which stands for **P**ortable **O**perating **S**ystem Interface based on UNI**X**, became a procurement standard for government computing contracts in the late 1980s. The POSIX standard, defined in IEEE Standard 1003.1-1990, provides a set of APIs and rules that UNIX operating system vendors should follow to provide better portability between UNIX implementations. The government provides a test suite to verify compliance with the POSIX standard. Although few UNIX products are fully compliant, having POSIX certification can help land government contracts. Windows NT, in an effort to play in this market, includes a POSIX subsystem that has been certified as being compliant.

Windows NT vs. UNIX

Although both NT and UNIX are designed as multiuser systems, they use very different approaches. Windows NT is designed for client-server computing, in which multiple users on PC (or RISC) workstations access servers through a network and often share the computing load among the workstations and servers. UNIX is designed around a host-terminal model, in which multiple users access a host computer through terminals.

A key advantage of Windows NT over UNIX is that, because NT is provided for all platforms by one vendor, there's a guaranteed standard programming interface and set of tools provided with the system. Application code ports easily from one platform to another, with a known set of support functions available on each platform. There's one graphical interface — namely, Windows. There's one primary set of APIs — namely, Win32. Microsoft defines and controls the NT standard. Microsoft assures that any hardware manufacturers who port the system to a new platform or deliver the system preinstalled on their computers, provide all of the standard NT components to the customer.

UNIX Influences

Contrary to what some pundits have said, the UNIX operating system still has a strong following, one that has continued to grow in some sectors since the introduction of graphical user interfaces for the system. UNIX is no longer relegated to university computer science labs, but has found its way into the corporate world. The Mach design, discussed earlier, as well as UNIX's approach to multitasking, multiprocessing, device drivers, and networking (specifically, TCP/IP) have strongly influenced Windows NT architecture and features. If you're already familiar with the UNIX design, you'll recognize in the following sections where Windows NT borrows from the UNIX world and where NT has removed some of the complexities and pitfalls in administering UNIX systems.

How Does Windows NT Do It?

Now that you have some background on the genealogy of Windows NT, I'm going to explain some of the key features of the operating system. First, I'll focus on NT's approaches to dealing with several "multis" — multitasking, multiple message queues, multithreading, multiprocessing, and multiple platform support. These features contribute to NT's robustness, scalability, and portability.

Next, you'll learn about Windows NT's file system support and fault tolerance features, which enhance NT's compatibility, security, performance, and reliability. Finally, you'll be introduced to a powerful feature of NT networking — remote access service.

Windows NT's internal architecture is covered in depth in Chapter 2. In Chapter 6, I will compare and contrast Windows NT with other Windows environments.

Multitasking

Multitasking refers to the ability of the operating system to share the CPU among several tasks. The idea behind multitasking is to provide you with the illusion that, although there's only one CPU in the computer, multiple applications are executing simultaneously. The operating system creates this illusion by quickly switching control from one application to another, providing each with a slice of time on the CPU. Although, operating systems may take any of several approaches to multitasking, two important approaches relate specifically to Windows and Windows NT: *cooperative multitasking* and *preemptive multitasking*.

First, an analogy. Suppose your manager says that you need to improve your ability to multitask. He explains that you need to make progress on each task, spend proportionally more time on the highest-priority tasks, complete the higher-priority tasks sooner, and be able to change direction quickly, switching to another task whose priority is suddenly raised.

Your tasks are big enough that you typically can't complete them in one sitting. You break the large tasks into smaller pieces that can be accomplished in a reasonable amount of time and that represent milestones of accomplishment. I'll call the completion of one of these pieces a stopping point.

Cooperative Multitasking

Your manager doesn't tell you specifically what type of multitasking to use. So you decide to do *cooperative multitasking*, because you're a very cooperative person. You go about your tasks, switching to a different, higher-priority task every time that you reach a stopping point in the current task. If it takes a little longer to get to a stopping point in your current task, you don't alter your plan. If your boss stops by and raises the priority of a different task, you tell him that you'll work on it as soon as you reach a stopping point on your current task. He's unhappy, because he feels that you should immediately drop your current task and work on the high-priority item.

In cooperative multitasking, the tasks themselves control how long they keep your attention. Priorities aren't reexamined until you reach a stopping point. A change in priorities has no effect until you reach a stopping point in the current task.

Cooperative Multitasking in Windows

Windows 3.x uses cooperative multitasking. Each application determines its own stopping points, or points at which it yields the CPU to another application. If an application never yields the CPU and continues executing, it won't allow any other applications to run.

The success of cooperative multitasking is completely at the mercy of the Windows applications that you're running. You see it fail miserably when a buggy Windows application hangs and the whole computer locks. You also see this when an application is legitimately executing for a lengthy period, as you stare at the hour-glass cursor, unable to switch to other applications. For cooperative multitasking to work well, applications must cooperate with each other by periodically giving up the CPU. In reality, they don't always cooperate. As you'll see, Windows NT has solved this problem.

Preemptive Multitasking

After a mentoring moment with your manager, you both agree that you'll try *preemptive multitasking*. This time, you assign a time limit to your current task. If it takes too long to reach a stopping point, you hit your time limit and look again at all your tasks and their priorities. If your boss calls you and raises the priority of a different task, you immediately drop your current task and work on the one with higher priority.

In preemptive multitasking, you determine how long each task keeps your attention. You set limits on how much time that you're going to spend on each task and dynamically alter your plan periodically. You don't get bogged down in one task, to the exclusion of all else. If priorities change, you immediately alter your plan to accommodate the new situation.

Preemptive Multitaking in Windows NT

Windows NT implements preemptive multitasking. In this environment, the operating system controls the length of time that each application has access to the CPU, by providing a slice of time to each one. When the time limit expires, the operating system evaluates priorities and gives the CPU to the appropriate application. An errant application in an infinite loop doesn't prevent other applications from running. If a higher-priority application requires CPU time, control is switched immediately to deal with it.

In the preemptive environment, applications are a bit more complex. They can't make the simplifying assumption that they won't be interrupted during critical operations, as many Windows 3.x applications can. They must assume that control can be passed to another application or to the operating system at any time. Windows NT provides several methods for applications to synchronize with each other to avoid potential problems caused by preemption.

Because many Windows 3.x applications assume that they run in a cooperative multitasking environment, Windows NT simulates this environment for all 16-bit Windows applications. This approach maximizes application compatibility, but unfortunately doesn't prevent one 16-bit Windows application from holding up another. It does, however, prevent the whole computer from locking up. You'll se how in Chapter 2.

Multiple Message Queues

Windows applications rely on messages from the keyboard and mouse to determine what to do next. Every time you move the mouse, click a mouse button, or press a key, a message is sent to the system and is routed to the application. Input events such as these are stored in a message queue, and messages are read from the queue by applications.

The Bottleneck Problem

Windows 3.x uses a single message queue, shared by all applications on the computer. All input messages are funneled into this queue and must be retrieved by the receiving applications in the order that they arrived. In this model, if an application (either a wayward application or a very busy one) doesn't read all of its messages, all other interactive applications must wait. Preemptive multitasking doesn't solve this problem, because the other applications can't continue until they can get to their messages. They can't get to their messages until the errant (or slow) application reads its messages from the queue. Consequently, the single message queue can become a bottleneck for the entire system, as some applications wait for others to read their messages from the shared queue.

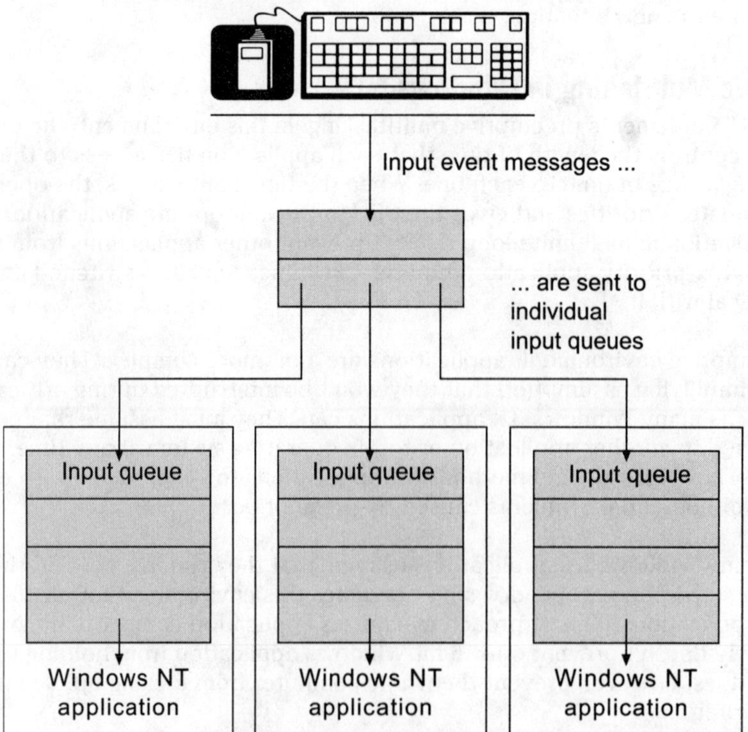

Figure 1-1: Windows NT uses multiple message queues to prevent bottlenecks.

NT's Solution

Windows NT prevents message queue bottlenecks by providing each application with its own message queue, as shown in Figure 1-1. Messages destined for an application are routed directly to its private queue. The speed with which messages are read by one application has no effect on other applications. The bottleneck of the single message queue is removed, increasing reliability of the system even when an application goes astray.

Multithreading

Multithreading refers to the ability of the operating system to support multiple paths of execution within a single process. It enables an operating system process or application process to perform multiple functions simultaneously, without waiting for other functions within the process to complete. This sounds more complex than it is. Let's look at an analogy from television.

Consider an episode of *The Love Boat*. (Bear with me, this *is* going somewhere.) An individual *Love Boat* program typically consists of several story lines, each with its own set of unique characters and conflicts. The crew of the ship is a set of characters that persist through the entire show and appear in all of its story lines. Each story line is presented in short scenes throughout the program, and the order of scenes from different story lines is interwoven during the program. The individual story lines continue to progress to their respective conclusions. When the last story line is complete, the program is over, thankfully. (If you're desperate for a different analogy, *Fantasy Island* is another example of this story line approach. Just substitute Mr. Roarke and Tattoo for the ship's crew. But that's another story.)

How NT Uses Multiple Threads

A process is like an episode or program, and a thread is like an individual story line within that program. A process consists of one or more threads. Each thread is given slices of CPU time (scenes) to execute and make progress until its work is completed. A thread typically has a very specific task (story line) to perform. It has some of its own local data (unique characters within the story line) and has full access to global data (ship's crew), shared by all threads within the process. When the last thread has finished its work, the process has completed (and the program is over).

The NT operating system itself consists of many processes and many threads. Some of these processes execute automatically. Some execute only when invoked by the user or by another process. Each of these processes contains one or more threads. For example, there's a thread that constantly monitors the keyboard for input, another thread that executes whenever data has been read from disk, and another thread that executes every few seconds to flush cached data to disk.

Multithread Applications

The operating system isn't the only benefactor of multithreading. Applications running on NT can also take advantage of using multiple threads. Suppose you're using a spreadsheet application. The application is a process, performing a wide variety of activities. If the application has only one thread, it can't perform any useful work while accepting keyboard input. It must wait idly for your relatively slow keyboard presses. Moreover, the application can't accept keyboard input while it's performing a CPU-intensive function, such as recalculating a large number of values. This can be very inefficient for both the computer and you. Either the computer is waiting for you when it could be doing something useful, or you're waiting for the computer to complete the current step, when you could be moving ahead to the next step.

To avoid this, the application could be designed to use multiple threads. If the application used one thread for accepting keyboard input and another for performing recalculation, less time would be wasted. You could start a large recalculation, and then you could immediately be able to enter additional data if the application were using another thread. You wouldn't have to wait for the recalculation to complete, and the computer would be able to perform useful recalculation work while you enter the next set of data.

Figure 1-2 illustrates four threads simultaneously working on different chores in a multithreaded spreadsheet application. Thread 1 is accepting input from the keyboard and mouse. At the same time, thread 2 is recalculating the spreadsheet. Meanwhile, thread 3 is sending a chart to the printer, and thread 4 is displaying a moving stock ticker at the bottom of the screen.

On a computer with one physical CPU, threads are scheduled and executed in a round-robin fashion. Each thread gets a slice of time to execute based on its priority. On a computer that contains more than one physical CPU, Windows NT dispatches a thread to each CPU, so the threads actually execute simultaneously on different processors. Thus, at a given moment, a four-CPU computer may be executing up to four threads simultaneously.

Multiprocessor Support

As a business expands, as the number of users on the network grows, and as the processing demands increase on individual servers and workstations, there's clearly a need to infuse more horsepower into existing computers without having to change the operating system or applications. The ability to add more CPUs to a computer to increase throughput is a very attractive and effective approach to this problem.

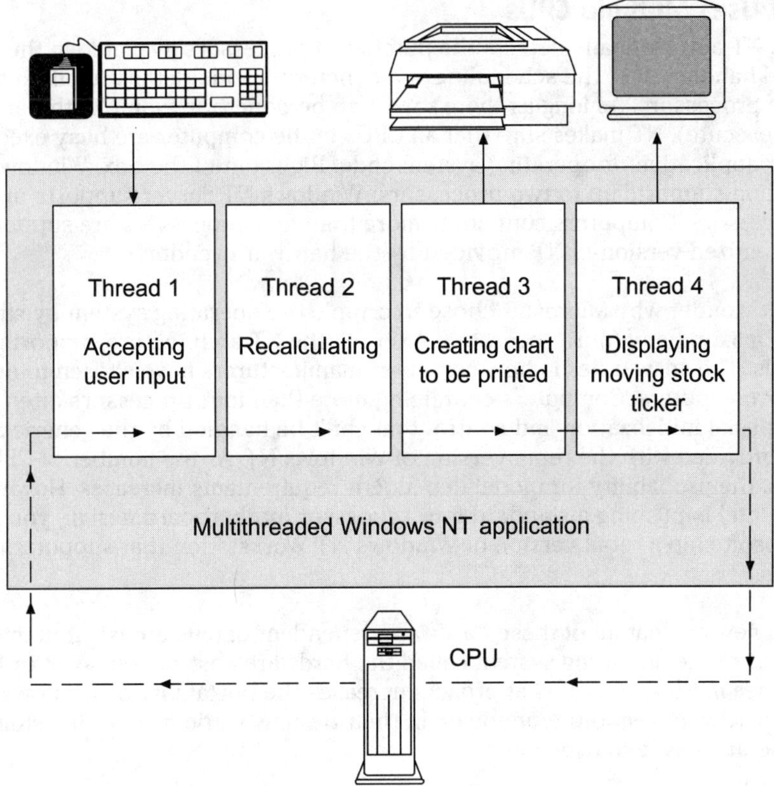

Figure 1-2: Windows NT multithreading enables efficient progress on multiple chores within a process.

The Windows NT architecture provides scalability through built-in support for Symmetric Multi-Processing, or SMP, computers. An SMP computer contains more than one identical CPU. These computers can contain from 2 to 32 processors. Each of these CPUs has equal access to all memory, devices, and other resources in the Windows NT takes full advantage of the increased computing power by evenly distributing the workload among all of the available CPUs. This translates to faster performance, as you add more physical processors to the computer.

How NT Uses Mutliple CPUs

Windows NT automatically detects the number of processors available in the computer and handles all of the scheduling and synchronization details required to share the processors. As long as there's work to be done (for example, threads are ready to execute), NT makes sure that all CPUs in the computer are busy executing either application or operating system code. Right out of the box, Windows NT Worksta-tion supports up to two processors; Windows NT Server supports up to four pro-cessors. Computers containing more than four processors are supported by a customized version of NT provided by the hardware vendor.

You might wonder why Microsoft chose to cripple the operating system by supporting a maximum of four processors. After all, the NT architecture supports up to 32 CPUs. The answer lies in how computer manufacturers have chosen to design their SMP computers. Computers containing more than four processors often require special initialization and control that can't be handled by the generic SMP support provided with the retail version of Windows NT. As the number of CPUs increases, the probability for model-dependent requirements increases. However, now that Intel is pushing a standard four-processor motherboard design, you may see Microsoft ship a retail version of Windows NT Workstation that supports up to four CPUs.

The good news is that all of these hardware-dependent details are isolated into a component of the operating system called the hardware abstraction layer, or HAL. As you'll see in Chapter 2, this approach increases the portability of Windows NT, enabling hardware vendors to innovate in their designs without requiring changes to the operating system itself.

Windows NT takes advantage of SMP computers at several levels. First, if several CPU-intensive applications are running and they aren't competing for access to the same hardware devices, they can run simultaneously across the available CPUs. Second, if a 32-bit application is designed to use multiple threads of execution within a single process, individual threads can run simultaneously across processors. Third, because the NT operating system itself is multithreaded, different portions of the operating system can actually run simultaneously on multiple processors.

Another multiprocessing approach, called asymmetric multiprocessing, or AMP, implements a very different model for CPU usage. In contrast to SMP, AMP computers dedicate specific functions to specific CPUs and typically don't deviate from this assignment. For example, an AMP computer might run operating system code on one CPU and an application on another CPU. This often results in the idling of some of the CPUs even when there's work to do, because the CPUs can't deviate from their assignments.

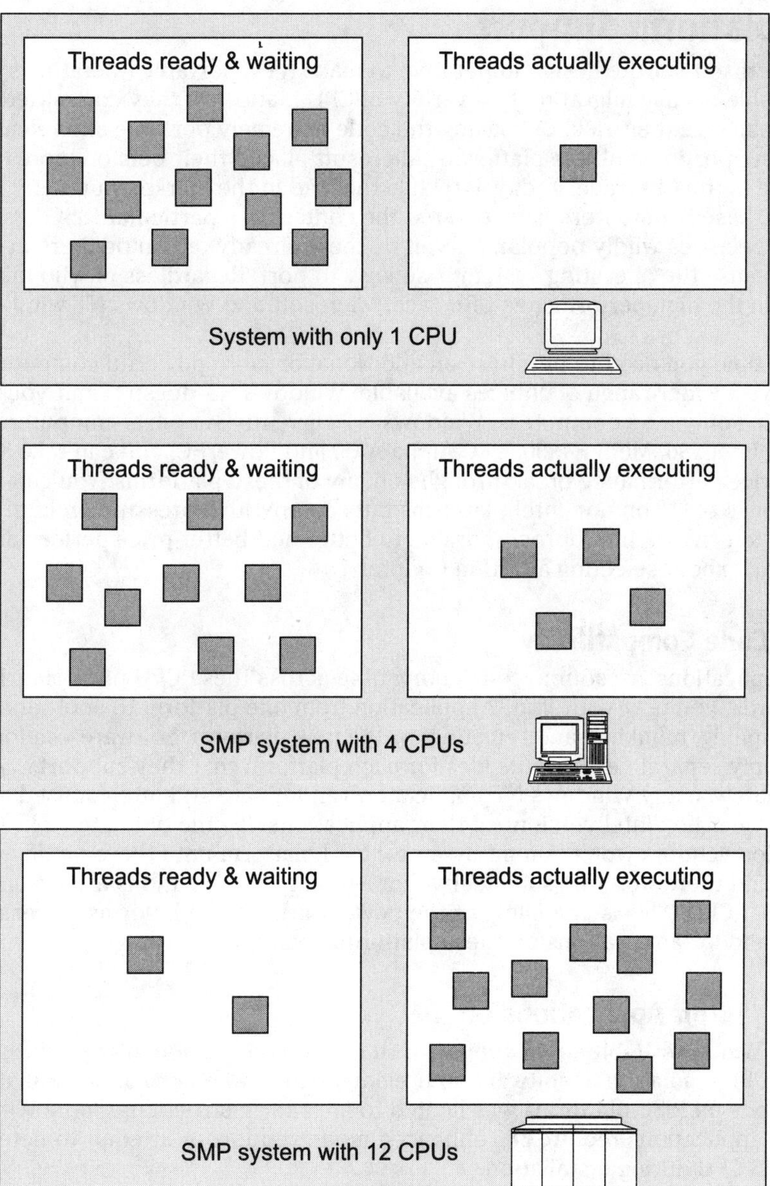

Figure 1-3: Windows NT scales well as you add processors to SMP computers.

Multiplatform Support

When Microsoft set the design imperative to make NT a portable operating system, capable of easy migration to a variety of CPU platforms, they committed to RISC to minimize their risk. By making the code extremely portable and releasing a product supporting multiple platforms, Microsoft placed their bets on more than one horse in the CPU race. Today, Intel has the lead in the market, but many powerful RISC-based computers have entered the contest. If a particular RISC-based platform becomes wildly popular, NT will be there already or can be there in short order, because the operating system is so easy to port. Regardless of who takes the lead in the high-performance CPU race, Microsoft and Windows NT win.

The next time you need to purchase an additional or more powerful computer, you'll have a wider range of choices available. Windows NT doesn't limit you to considering only Intel computers. Windows NT currently supports computers based on Intel x86, MIPS R4x00, DEC Alpha AXP, and PowerPC. You can take advantage of price-performance breakthroughs on any of these platforms. You can bet the presence of NT on non-Intel platforms puts competitive pressure on Intel to continue to drive its microprocessor line to better and better price-performance ratios. I talk about selecting a CPU in Chapter 7.

Source Code Compatibility

Win32 applications are source code compatible across these CPU platforms. In other words, you port your Win32 application from one platform to another simply by recompiling, relinking, and retesting for the new platform. Software vendors must supply separate executable files for each platform that they support. Unfortunately, many Windows NT application vendors are still Intel-focused and don't yet offer non-Intel versions of their applications. It's the old Catch-22. Application vendors won't commit to a new CPU platform until there's sufficient volume, and there won't be sufficient volume until the applications are available to run on that CPU. This is changing, as the power of the RISC platforms increases and demand for applications on these platforms increases.

Running 16-bit Applications on RISC

DOS and Windows 16-bit applications are supported on the non-Intel platforms, through CPU emulation in software. In previous Windows NT releases, emulation of Intel code on RISC platforms was limited to Intel 286 instructions. Some Windows and DOS applications require 386 enhanced mode support or attempt to detect a 386 or 486 CPU during installation.

Creating a Portable NT

To create a truly portable product, independent of a specific CPU, Microsoft had to avoid building any processor-specific assumptions into the operating system. This daunting task was particularly difficult because many of the developers on the team knew the Intel x86 architecture inside and out. It was too easy to slip into the x86 comfort zone when developing the system. To overcome this temptation, Microsoft started by implementing the core NT operating system on a RISC processor, the Intel i860. Although the i860 version of the code wasn't released, it did play a critical role in enforcing a processor-independent discipline within the team, resulting in the creation of a very portable operating system.

386 or 486 CPU during installation. On RISC platforms using 286 emulation, these applications either refuse to install or terminate while running. With the advent of Windows NT 4.0, RISC platforms are now provided with a 486 emulator, removing the 286 limitation. Microsoft has confirmed that this permits at least 30 more commercial applications to run on NT 4.0. Many more applications will benefit from 486 emulation, but they haven't yet been tested explicitly.

In addition to handling details of multiprocessor control, mentioned earlier, the HAL also hides dependencies that vary among CPU architectures. Using this approach, porting NT to a new CPU platform requires the creation of a customized HAL and recompilation of the product for the new CPU, including operating system, drivers, and so forth. The role of the HAL is discussed in more detail in Chapter 2.

File Systems

Windows NT fully supports the FAT file system used in DOS, Windows 3.x and Windows for Workgroups, the VFAT file system used in Windows 95, and the NT file system, called NTFS. In earlier Windows NT releases, OS/2's HPFS was supported, but this support has been dropped in the NT 4.0 release. Microsoft found that few customers dual-boot between OS/2 and Windows NT. Moreover, because NTFS provides superior security and recoverability, many customers with legacy OS/2 applications running on NT have already migrated to NTFS. Removing HPFS support enables NT to use resources more efficiently because it doesn't need to keep an additional file system loaded.

The NTFS File System

NTFS borrowed heavily from the best features of both FAT and HPFS, then added more security, robustness, and capacity. As you'll see, NTFS is the file system of choice for Windows NT servers.

NTFS is recoverable. It takes steps to assure that it can always maintain a consistent state and avoid loss of data on the partition. NTFS uses a transaction-based approach to updating its on-disk data structures, enabling recovery even if the power fails or the computer isn't shut down properly. Recovery typically takes only a few seconds, regardless of the size of the partition. (Although OS/2's HPFS supports file system recovery, the recovery can take hours to run on large partitions, holding the computer in an unusable state during this time.) NTFS keeps redundant copies of its critical data, so that a failure in a particular spot on the disk won't result in the loss of the partition. In contrast, both FAT and HPFS keep vital file system data in specific sectors on the partition, making the entire partition vulnerable to a single disk sector failure. Finally, NTFS supports hot-fixing, so if it encounters a bad sector on disk, it marks the sector as bad and moves the information to a good sector.

NTFS file system recoverability doesn't guarantee recovery of your data. Any data that your application may have been writing at the time of a power or system failure may be lost. NTFS recovery assures only that the rest of the partition is unaffected, because the file system structures are recovered to the last known good state. For redundancy and recoverability of user data files, you need to use NT's fault tolerance features, described in the next section.

NTFS Security

NTFS is secure. Security information is stored on disk with each file and directory. This prevents unauthorized access to the file by anyone who doesn't have explicit permission granted by the file owner or system administrator. NTFS is fully integrated with the NT security model, so access to files is treated just like access to other resources on the system. NTFS is the only file system on Windows NT that enables you to assign permissions to individual files. You will learn all about permissions in Chapter 18.

As you'll see throughout this book, security is pervasive throughout the Windows NT operating system. Using NTFS and other security measures, Windows NT is *C2-certifiable*. This means that the National Computer Security Center, or NCSC, has evaluated Windows NT on specific computer configurations and concluded that it can correctly enforce your security policy up to a C2 level. The amount of security actually implemented on your network and your servers is up to you, as network administrator. C2-certifiability provides the means to implement a highly secure environment, but doesn't force you to do so.

NTFS Disk Efficiency

Because NTFS uses 64-bit disk addressing, it can deal with very large disk drives. It provides for disks and files up to 16 exabytes long. That's 16 quintillion bytes, a number with 20 digits. This is about as close to an infinite amount of data as you want to get. Practically speaking, you'll be hard-pressed to create anything larger than 2 terabytes, or 2 trillion bytes, using today's available hardware. Compare these huge capacities with the maximum 2 gigabyte partition size imposed by FAT under DOS.

Depending on disk sizes and file sizes, NTFS can make much more efficient use of disk space than FAT does. FAT is limited in the number of allocation units, called clusters, on each disk. Thus, as the disk size grows, the size of the clusters must increase dramatically. For example, on a 640MB disk, FAT uses a 16K cluster size. In this situation, a tiny 512-byte file uses up a whole 16K, effectively wasting 15.5K of disk space. Similarly, a 17K file uses 32K of disk space, because it requires one 16K cluster plus another cluster to store the additional 1K. This wasted space because of large cluster sizes is called internal fragmentation. NTFS uses a maximum cluster size of 4K, regardless of the size of the disk. This significantly reduces internal fragmentation (and thus reduces wasted space), especially on large disks.

NTFS provides yet another route to more efficient disk space usage — file compression. Using Explorer or command line utilities, you can compress individual files, the contents of entire directories, or the contents of an entire disk partition. Once a file is compressed on NTFS, compression and decompression are handled transparently by the operating system. Any application can open a compressed file and see the uncompressed data, without the need to run a decompression utility. Note that NTFS compression is done on a file-by-file basis, in contrast to DOS DoubleSpace and DriveSpace compression, which compress an entire partition into a single large file. Note also that Windows NT doesn't support DoubleSpace or DriveSpace compression.

NTFS File Names

NTFS supports long filenames and directory names of up to 256 characters each. These names can include spaces and periods, and both upper- and lowercase letters. When accessed over the network by down-level clients such as DOS, Windows 3.x, or Windows for Workgroups, long filenames are converted to a DOS-palatable 8.3 format. Moreover, 16-bit applications running on NT won't enable creation of long filenames. They'll see NTFS long filenames in the converted 8.3 format. (In contrast, although OS/2 HPFS supports long filenames, these filenames can't be accessed by down-level systems such as DOS.) Windows NT supports long filenames on VFAT, just as Windows 95 does. Thus, files with long names created under either system on VFAT can be seen by either operating system.

Finally, NTFS provides full support for POSIX applications on NT and, on Windows NT Server, access by Apple Macintosh clients.

Fault Tolerance

There's no way to make a computer running Windows NT completely immune to failure. However, Windows NT Server provides several opportunities for you to make it resistant to catastrophic failure and data loss. The operating system offers a number of features collectively referred to as fault tolerance capabilities. These features enable you to implement a server that's highly reliable and can quickly, sometimes automatically, recover from hardware failures without loss of data or the need for lengthy server downtime. Some of these features also improve file access performance and offer convenient ways to use existing disk space.

Disk Arrays

Windows NT has implemented some of the capabilities known as RAID, or *redundant array of inexpensive disks*. The idea behind RAID is to spread or duplicate data across multiple disk drives to improve performance, to recover from hardware failures without losing data, or a combination of both. RAID technology can be implemented in hardware or software. Although NT supports hardware RAID solutions, they're typically expensive. The features discussed here are software solutions that use standard disk hardware components.

The cost of additional drives is well worth the improved performance and data protection offered by Windows NT Server's fault tolerance capabilities. If you've been watching disk storage prices fall in recent days, it should be clear that use of redundant hard disks is fast becoming a cost-effective proposition. It's interesting to note that the RAID approach was proposed back in 1987, when a megabyte of PC disk space cost at least 40 times what it costs today. Keep this in mind as you plan your server hardware requirements.

RAID technology is classified in six levels, numbered 0 through 5. NT Workstation offers only level 0, whereas NT Server provides levels 0, 1, and 5. Refer to Table 1-1 for a listing of RAID levels and their associated Windows NT features and benefits.

Table 1-1
A Comparison of RAID Levels

RAID Level	*Windows Server*	*Windows NT Workstation*	*Windows NT Feature*	*Better Performance*	*Higher Reliability*
0	√	√	Striping (no parity)	√	
1	√		Mirroring/Duplexing		√
2			N/A		
3			N/A		
4			N/A		
5	√		Striping (with parity)	√	√

Mirroring and Duplexing

Disk mirroring, at RAID 1, uses two disk drives to provide duplicate copies of all data written to disk. Everything written to one drive is written to the other. If a read fails because of a bad spot on either drive, the data is immediately read from the other drive. If one of the drives fails completely, the other drive takes over. In a disk mirroring pair, 50 percent of the available disk space is used for the redundant data.

Disk duplexing is exactly the same as disk mirroring from the operating system's perspective. Disk duplexing provides additional hardware redundancy by placing the two disk drives on separate disk controllers. Thus, the redundancy is moved back to the controller. If one of the disk controllers fails, the survivor takes over without skipping a beat. Depending on the hardware involved, the duplexing approach can yield better performance than mirroring, because the redundant data is no longer funneled through a single disk controller.

Striping

Disk striping is a bit more complex. From 2 to 32 disks are combined into a single large virtual disk, called a stripe set. Data is written in equal-sized stripes across all of the disks in the stripe set. The data doesn't reside on any one disk but is spread across all of the disks involved. The thought of how the files are actually stored is downright scary, until you see it in action and realize that all of the details for striping are handled transparently by the operating system.

Windows NT's RAID 0 flavor of striping, stripes without parity, is purely a performance enhancement. No redundant information is maintained, so if one disk in the stripe set fails, data from the entire set is lost and can't be recovered. The RAID 5 version, stripes with parity, requires at least three disks because it dedicates the equivalent of one disk to store parity information. This information is used to regenerate the original data, if one of the disks fails.

Volume Sets

Although not considered a fault tolerance or performance feature, *volume sets* provide a convenient way of combining and using several unused disk areas into a single logical partition. They also enable you to extend an existing NTFS partition to include additional free space.

You'll learn about NT fault tolerance in Chapter 19.

Remote Access

Remote access is often used as a generic term to describe various methods of accessing computers or networks from remote computers over communication lines. The remote computers are typically laptops on the road or desktop computers at home. Two popular approaches to remote access may be used: *remote control* and *remote node* (see Figure 1-4). To fully appreciate what Windows NT offers, it's important to understand the difference between these two approaches.

Remote Control vs. Remote Node

Remote control products, such as Carbon Copy, CoSession Remote, pcANYWHERE, Close-Up, and REACHOUT enable you to connect to a specific computer and control that computer by taking over control of its keyboard, screen, and mouse. Typing keys on the remote computer effectively enters keystrokes into the computer being controlled. Whenever the screen on the controlled computer changes, it's displayed on the remote computer's screen. In a typical scenario, you would control a computer on your desktop at work from a computer at home. If your computer at work were on the network, you could have access to network resources by remotely controlling the computer at work. For each remote user, there must be a complete computer at the other end, waiting to be remote controlled. The bandwidth of the communication line is often saturated with screen data coming back from the controlled computer. For high-resolution screens, this can bring even the fastest modem link to its knees.

Remote node capability enables you to tap into the network from a remote location. Your remote computer then becomes a node on the network, as if it were just another computer connected to it. You have full access to all of the network resources that your network account normally allows.

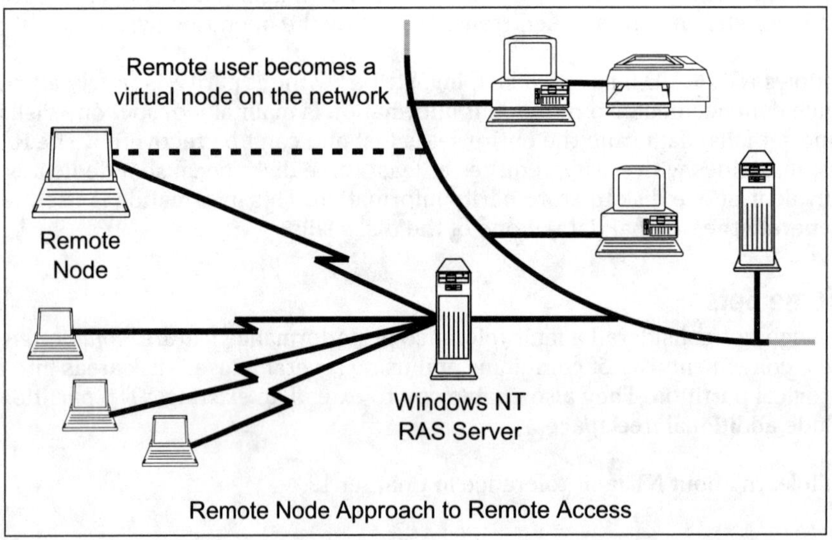

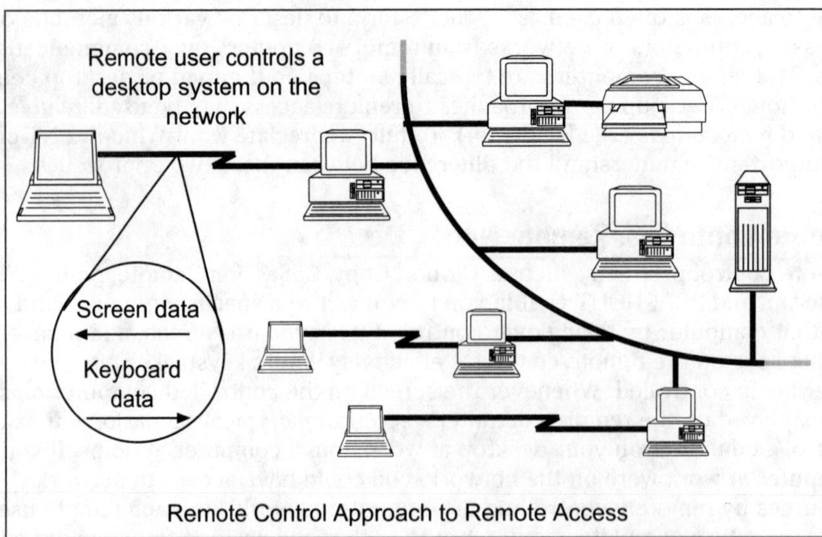

Figure 1-4: Remote control and remote node are two approaches to remote access.

Windows NT RAS

Windows NT Remote Access Service, or RAS, provides remote node capability. Remote node better matches the client-server computing model. Because applications are typically run on the remote computer, network traffic is reduced, and you typically experience better performance. Remote node is also more scalable, as your remote access needs grow. Adding capacity in a remote node situation consists of adding another communication port to the server, and increasing performance typically requires adding more memory to the server. In contrast, adding remote control capacity requires the addition of an entire computer to act as a remote-controlled computer.

The remote node feature provided by Windows NT's RAS gives you a more flexible, scalable, and better-performing solution than remote control. Although Windows NT Workstation provides you with one client and the ability to be a server to one remote user, Windows NT Server extends the capability to simultaneously handle up to 256 remote clients on a single server computer. As an NT network administrator, you'll really appreciate RAS the first time that you have to handle an administration task at 2:00 a.m., and you complete it in minutes while sitting at home in your pajamas. Your network-dependent users will love it when they take their laptops and hit the road. Chapter 11 will fill you in on RAS.

Importance of Compatibility

Although compatibility is mentioned last in the list of benefits presented earlier, it's certainly not the least important. Regardless of any other features that it offers, if an operating system can't run well on a wide range of popular hardware, execute a large percentage of available applications, and communicate well with existing computers over networks, it won't provide customers with a compelling reason to upgrade. Even the best of operating systems is completely dependent on hardware, software, and network compatibility for its very survival in the marketplace. Without this keystone, the rest of the product crumbles. The OS/2 operating system has struggled with this fact for several years and still lags behind other operating systems in some of these areas. The NeXT computer is a prime example of a system that fell primarily due to lack of applications.

Windows NT Server Compatibility

Windows NT meets the compatibility challenges of today's competitive marketplace. Through extensive compatibility testing by Microsoft and hardware vendors, Windows NT now boasts verified compatibility with over 3,600 computer systems and more than 2,200 hardware devices. On the software front, Windows NT provides the ability to run applications written for DOS, Windows 3.x, Windows for Workgroups, Windows 95, Windows NT, OS/2 1.x, and POSIX.

In addition, the ability of Windows NT to communicate over the network with other computers is comprehensive. This is especially true of Windows NT Server. NT networks can consist of computers running combinations of Microsoft operating systems including DOS, Windows 3.x, Windows for Workgroups, Windows 95, and Windows NT, as well as non-Microsoft systems including Novell NetWare, UNIX, and Macintosh computers. I cover networking concepts and capabilities in more detail in Chapters 3 and 4.

16-bit Applications in a 32-bit World

DOS and Windows aren't dead. With literally millions of copies on existing computers and hundreds of thousands of applications running on them, it will take time for complete migration away from 16-bit software. Even after software developers convert their applications to 32-bits for Windows NT and Windows 95, users will have to see strong, tangible benefits before upgrading their applications and hardware.

Microsoft's long-term strategy has been to shift software developers away from 16-bit Windows programming and toward programming to the 32-bit Win32 interface. Win32 provides a simpler memory model, freeing developers from the complexities and limitations of the Windows 3.x world. On one hand, this is an attractive proposition for developers, because they can focus their efforts on innovating application features and spend less effort dealing with the intricacies and attendant headaches of 16-bit programming. Taking the plunge into the 32-bit world has the added benefit of making the applications act more robust, because they're protected from interference by other applications when run on a 32-bit operating system. On the other hand, software developers had to focus their resources where the business volume was — 16-bit Windows. So, achieving Microsoft's goal of 32-bit conversion would take time. They had to provide the ability for customers to run their 16-bit applications on Windows NT.

DOS and Don'ts

Unlike Windows 3.x and Windows for Workgroups, Windows NT doesn't rely in any way on the presence of DOS. Thus, when running NT, DOS is nowhere in the system. To run DOS applications, NT creates a *virtual DOS machine*, or VDM. A VDM is a Win32 application that provides a complete virtual Intel x86 environment running DOS. Each DOS application gets its own VDM, and each VDM runs in its own address space. This prevents the applications from affecting each other or the operating system. In this sense, NT's VDM provides better DOS than DOS.

The Road to 32-Bits

Although Microsoft began evangelizing in order to persuade software developers to convert their products as early as 1990, NT's survival as an operating system couldn't wait for these developers to create new 32-bit versions of their applications. The 1995 advent of Windows 95 acted as a catalyst in the industry shift to 32-bits. However, many Windows applications still haven't yet stepped into the 32-bit world, and users still depend on many popular DOS applications to run their businesses. Microsoft's customers required 16-bit application compatibility. Because of this, Microsoft gave Windows NT the ability to run existing Windows and DOS applications right out of the box.

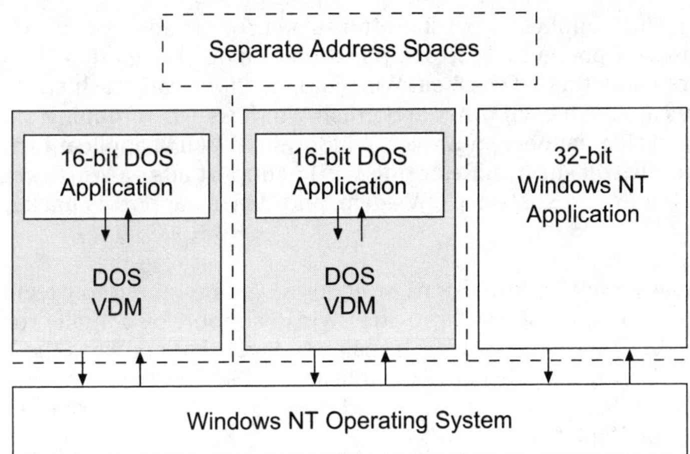

Figure 1-5: Multiple DOS VDMs on Windows NT protect DOS applications from affecting each other.

NT's tolerance of DOS applications is limited. NT provides virtual access to standard PC hardware devices, but it gets angry when DOS applications attempt to deal directly with disk sectors, for example. Unless someone with administrator privileges is running the application, NT prevents direct disk access. This keeps a few applications from running and confuses some copy protection schemes, but it prevents a host of viruses from damaging the system and errant applications from scribbling on hard disks. Windows NT trades off full DOS compatibility in favor of system integrity and robustness. This is the correct tradeoff for a system that's designed to be highly reliable and secure.

WOW, What a Concept!

The term Windows On Windows, or WOW, sounds as if it involves energy-efficient dual-pane glass. WOW actually refers to the mechanism used to run 16-bit Windows applications, which I'll call Win16 applications, on top of Win32. WOW consists of a single VDM to support all Win16 applications (see Figure 1-6). Within this VDM, a thread is provided for each application, and these threads are cooperatively multitasked. While a Win16 application thread executes, all other Win16 application threads are blocked. None of the other Win16 applications can run until the executing application thread relinquishes control.

This approach emulates the Windows 3.x environment, in which the applications are cooperatively multitasked and share the same address space. Because WOW is a VDM, it protects the rest of the system, both applications and the operating system, from the effects of an errant Win16 application.

Because all of the Win16 applications run in the same process address space, the WOW approach doesn't prevent a Win16 application from affecting other Win16 applications or from affecting WOW itself. Win16 applications can crash each other, just as they can crash each other and crash Windows when running under Windows 3.x. Even if this happens, however, Windows NT, Win32 applications, and even DOS applications will survive. Restoring Win16 support after a Win16 crash doesn't require rebooting. Just start WOW again, and Win16 support is back in business.

WOW doesn't actually run Windows 3.x to provide the APIs required to execute Win16 applications. (In contrast, OS/2 provides Win16 support by actually running a copy of Windows 3.x.) WOW provides a translation layer that converts the Win16 interface to the Win32 interface. If a Win16 application spends a large percentage of its time executing in Win16 APIs, it will spend its time on NT in the translation layer and in executing Win32 code.

Everything Has a Price

Windows NT provides support for 16-bit DOS and Windows applications while ensuring system integrity. The costs for this integrity include less compatibility and slower performance. Hardware emulation, trapping I/O operations, and converting Win16 to Win32 in both directions all take CPU cycles away from the applications.

The actual performance difference between running an application in its native 16-bit environment and running it on NT varies widely, depending on the operations that it performs. In general, applications that are calculation-intensive show little performance difference, whereas applications that perform a large amount of API calls and screen operations show more degradation. On average, 16-bit applications run from 5 percent to 50 percent slower under NT.

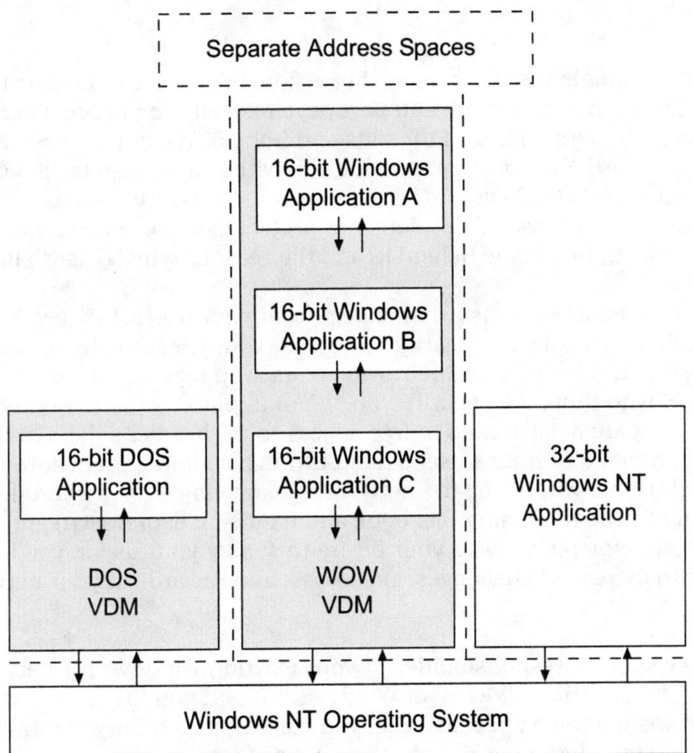

Figure 1-6: The WOW process provides a cooperative multitasking environment for 16-bit Windows applications.

There's no way to get around the additional overhead required to ensure Windows NT's system integrity, other than by running only 32-bit applications. However, some aspects of NT's architecture can compensate for this price. For example, disk-intensive applications benefit from 32-bit disk drivers and large disk caches. Likewise, 32-bit printer drivers and screen drivers help in graphical applications. Win32 itself can be a performance plus, if the application makes few API calls and most of the application's work is performed within the APIs, in 32-bit code. These factors can combine to make some 16-bit applications actually run faster under Windows NT than in their native environments.

Summary

The role of network administrator has many dimensions. You have to be part technical guru, part teacher, part magician, and part psychologist. The insights in this book give you a solid understanding of the nuts and bolts of Windows NT Server. They'll propel you toward NT guru-ship, provide you with the tools to teach your users and teammates, and enable you to be an occasional network magician. The inside stories from the Windows NT development project give you a deeper understanding of the product, the people behind it, and the reasons why NT is what it is.

Although I offer insights on what issues to expect from your users, the development of your psychologist role is primarily up to you. Your users might sometimes blame the network or the servers for their own errors. You may take heat from some of your users who think the security you've put in place is too restrictive, especially if the users are accustomed to free access to each other's data. In the beginning, you might need to hold a user's hand through a simple procedure until they become comfortable with using the network. By knowing your way around NT and networking (through reading this book and hands-on experience) and by applying your interpersonal skills and your desire to satisfy your users, you'll be well on your way to increased challenges, successes, and rewards in your networking career.

You may have very specific responsibilities in your existing Windows NT network. If you don't need or want to swallow all of Windows NT, and you just want to get practical tips and wisdom on a specific topic, you can skip the theory, internals, and installation chapters and jump right to the topics of interest. For example, if you want to know how best to perform nightly backups, you'll find what you need in Chapter 18. Of course, it won't hurt to gain an understanding of other aspects of the system and impress your colleagues, users, and boss with your new-found knowledge.

The market momentum of Windows NT Server is growing rapidly, according to reports from industry leaders, Microsoft, and the press. Expertise in Windows NT Server-based networks is, and will continue to be, an increasingly valuable commodity on the job market. I was fortunate to be in on the ground floor of the development of Windows NT. You're fortunate to be getting involved with Windows NT on the ground floor of its burgeoning acceptance in the world of corporate enterprise networking.

INSIDE STORY

The spring 1993 beta release of Windows NT 3.1 was so stable that National Westminster Bank in the UK used the beta live on their production network, months before the product was released. Imagine betting all of your bank customers' direct deposits on the beta release of a network operating system! And they were successful. Windows NT 3.1, although it had some performance deficiencies, nevertheless gained a reputation for great stability and robustness. This sort of reputation is unheard of for the first release of an operating system. It's a testament to Microsoft's commitment to investing in the quality of the NT product, from hiring a quality-conscious development leader in Dave Cutler, to providing a nearly one-to-one ratio between engineers in the development and test groups, to creating the laboratory infrastructure to beat the living daylights out of the system to find and fix real-world problems before customers ever saw them.

Windows NT 3.5, 3.51, and now 4.0 have maintained a high level of stability and offered significant performance enhancements over version 3.1. This, too, has been a major accomplishment in the operating system world — each tweak to improve performance has the potential of destroying robustness. As Dave Cutler used to ask his developers, "Yeah, it's twice as fast, but does it still get the right answer?" The Windows NT team at Microsoft continues to make sure the answer is "Yes."

In Chapter 2, you get a more in-depth look at the Windows NT architecture, and how it compares to Windows 3.x and Windows 95. If you're new to networking, Chapter 3 provides background on networking concepts and terminology. Chapter 4 introduces you to the specifics of Windows NT networking and designing a network based on Windows NT Server.

Inside the New Technology Architecture

Welcome to Windows NT Anatomy 101. Yes, you're in the right room. And you're about to embark on a fantastic voyage through the internal organs of Windows NT. Along the way, you'll pick up clues and insights that will help you succeed as a Windows NT system administrator. You'll get to know the key building blocks that make NT the powerful system that it is. What's more, you'll be able to use this intimate knowledge to impress your users, coworkers, and boss with your in-depth awareness of what's really going on inside. In this chapter, you get an inside look at the Windows NT operating system architecture. I introduce all of the major pieces of the operating system and explain how they interact.

The Windows NT operating system was developed as a standalone, general-purpose operating system, completely independent of DOS. As you're about to see, NT is an extremely modular and extensible system, capable of serving as the platform for Microsoft's Windows operating system technology for many years.

Although networking is an integral part of Windows NT, this chapter focuses primarily on non-networking components. I discuss networking in depth in Chapters 3 and 4.

Hang on. We're going in. "Scalpel...."

Windows NT Inside Out

In the following sections, I reveal the internal architecture of the Windows NT operating system. Although knowledge of NT internals isn't absolutely required to operate NT servers and networks, the background is helpful in understanding how the system fits together and why it behaves as it does. Don't drop the anatomy course. Read on. The life you save may be your computer's.

In some cases, knowledge of these NT building blocks helps you to troubleshoot problems that you encounter with your NT computers. For example, when your server crashes someday, you'll be able to determine what pieces of NT were executing when the server croaked. And you'll know what those pieces are supposed to do for you. Understanding what NT pieces fit where helps you piece them back together when the time comes.

Kernel Mode vs. User Mode

Most modern processors offer the ability to execute code at different privilege levels. These privilege levels grant varying degrees of freedom to access hardware resources. They're typically used to improve the reliability of operating systems by granting the greatest privileges to the operating system code and running user applications in the most restricted mode. This approach protects the operating system from damage by errant applications.

The Intel 486 CPU provides four privilege modes ranging from Ring 0, the most privileged, to Ring 3, the least privileged. The MIPS R4000 processor offers three modes called kernel, supervisor, and user. Each processor architecture implements privilege levels in different ways and uses diverse terminology for the available modes.

Windows NT uses two privilege modes: *kernel mode* and *user mode*, shown in Figure 2-1. Kernel mode refers to the most privileged processor mode available on the CPU, with completely unrestricted access to all memory, hardware devices, and privileged instructions. User mode refers to the most restricted processor mode. User mode code can only access its own virtual address space and must rely on code running in kernel mode to access any hardware or to perform privileged operations.

Traditionally, operating systems have been designed to run their own code completely in kernel mode and to run all application code in less-privileged user mode. As the following sections show, Windows NT puts its core operating system in kernel mode but also places some of the traditional operating system functionality in user mode.

I begin by discussing the Windows NT operating system components that run in user mode and then delve into the depths of kernel-mode components.

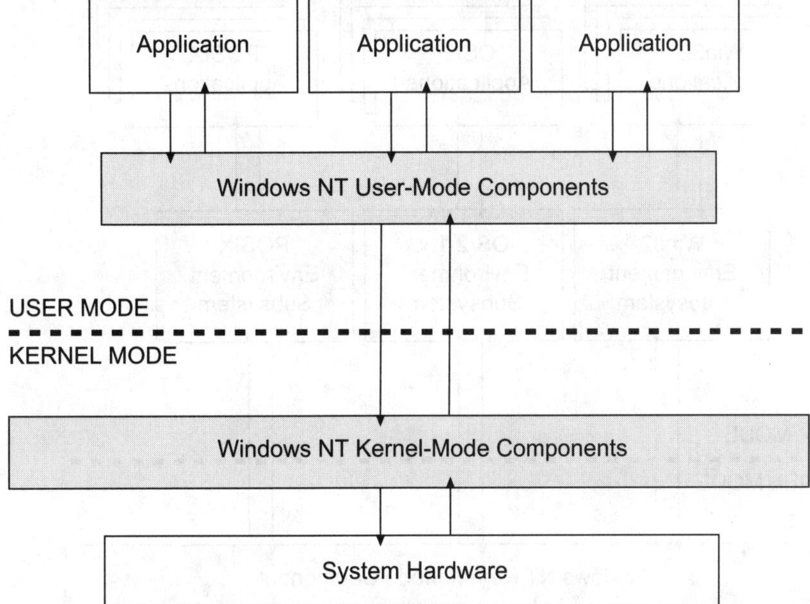

Figure 2-1: Windows NT includes kernel-mode and user-mode components.

Environment Subsystems

Windows NT has multiple personalities. No need to break out the Thorazine, though. In this case, having multiple personalities is a good thing. Windows NT emulates multiple operating system environments, enabling it to run applications written for a variety of operating systems. It accomplishes this feat through the use of *environment subsystems*.

Each environment subsystem is simply a user-mode process that provides services to applications, as illustrated in Figure 2-2. These services emulate the behavior or personality of a specific operating system environment. In a sense, the environment subsystem acts as a sort of translator that converts requests made by an application to requests that the Windows NT kernel-mode components can understand. For some operations, the environment subsystem can perform all of the work internally and doesn't need to make a request of kernel-mode components.

The Client/Server Model

Windows NT uses a *client/server* model to implement its personalities. NT classifies environment subsystems as *servers*, and classifies applications as *clients*. You've likely heard this terminology before, in the context of client and server computers on networks. Although this model has similarities to the networking model, let's concentrate now on how these terms apply to NT's environment subsystems.

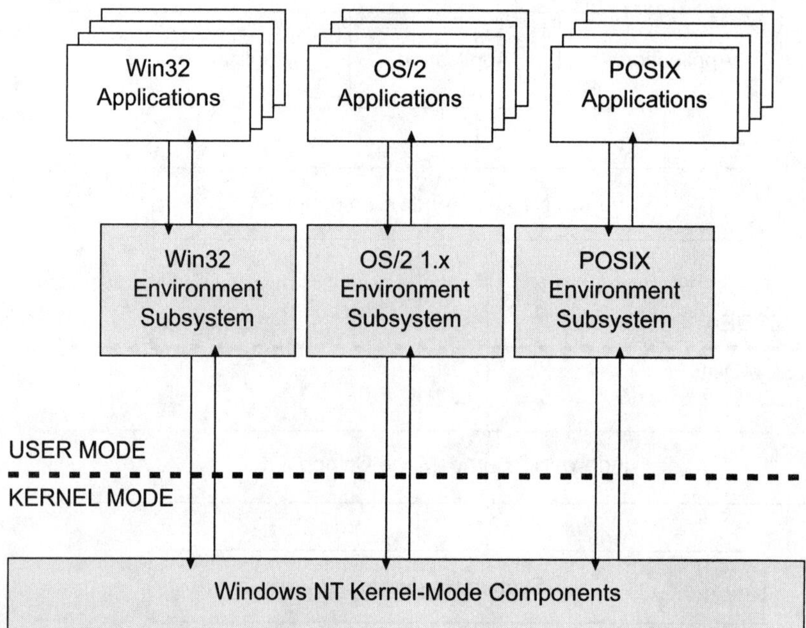

Figure 2-2: Windows NT's user-mode environment subsystems provide multiple operating system personalities.

An environment subsystem server provides services to its client applications. The server can provide these services to any number of clients. The client applications request these services by making API calls. For example, the Win32 subsystem (server) provides services via Win32 APIs to all Win32 applications (clients).

When you invoke an application, Windows NT examines information at the beginning of the executable file to determine what type of application it is. It then hooks up the application with the appropriate environment subsystem for execution.

Windows NT includes environment subsystem servers for Win32, OS/2, and POSIX. Support for other operating environments such as DOS and Windows 3.1 aren't handled by environment subsystems but are dealt with in user mode. The following sections present more information about all of these components.

Win32 Subsystem

The Win32 subsystem acts as the environment subsystem server to all Win32 client applications. Each Win32 application runs in its own address space, separate from other Win32 applications and separate from the Win32 subsystem. You can launch and run 32-bit Windows (Win32) applications from Windows NT Explorer, from a Windows NT command prompt, via the Start button, or from within another Win32 application.

INSIDE STORY

It was now two hours into the marathon NT performance review, and the hot debate had sputtered into a long, uncomfortable pause. Even the slightest movement against the high-backed leather chairs seemed to create deafening noise. The dimly lit Microsoft executive conference room seemed full of these embarrassing leather sounds. Everyone was self-conscious. Bill Gates was getting the bad news about the sluggish performance of an early version of the NT code. And he wasn't happy.

At Microsoft, the client/server environment subsystem design had been a controversial one for many months. Folks in upper management (including Bill) and in other groups at Microsoft felt it might introduce too much overhead to the system, potentially leading to unacceptable overall performance. Typically, this debate boiled down to a tradeoff between performance and reliability, with the decision resting on the side of reliability more often than not.

Nevertheless, the NT team was constantly estimating and measuring the time required to complete a client/server transition cycle, starting with a Win32 API call from an application and ending with returning the result to the application. In one area of the system, this careful scrutiny led to bundling requests together and shipping them across to the subsystem in bulk. This approach reduced the number of client/server transitions among applications and the subsystem. The technique became known as *batching,* because requests were sent to the subsystem in wholesale batches.

After months of measuring, modifying, and several more tense performance review meetings, it became clear that while some overhead was contributed by the client/server environment subsystem design, performance issues lay elsewhere in the system. The performance folks then turned their guns on these other areas. And the dreaded performance reviews continued to hound the harried NT team.

Win32 is Windows NT's pivotal environment subsystem. Although its primary function is to act as the environment subsystem server for Win32 applications, it's also a server process for all other environment subsystems. Why? The Win32 subsystem must manage all keyboard input, mouse input, and screen output for the entire system.

Win32's Central Role

Figure 2-3 illustrates the relationships between the Win32 subsystem and other environment subsystems. On the input side, keyboard and mouse messages are all delivered to the Win32 subsystem. The subsystem is then responsible for immediately doling out these messages to the appropriate threads in other processes. Remember the multiple message queue approach, discussed in Chapter 1? The Win32 subsystem is responsible for implementing this approach as it distributes input messages to application threads.

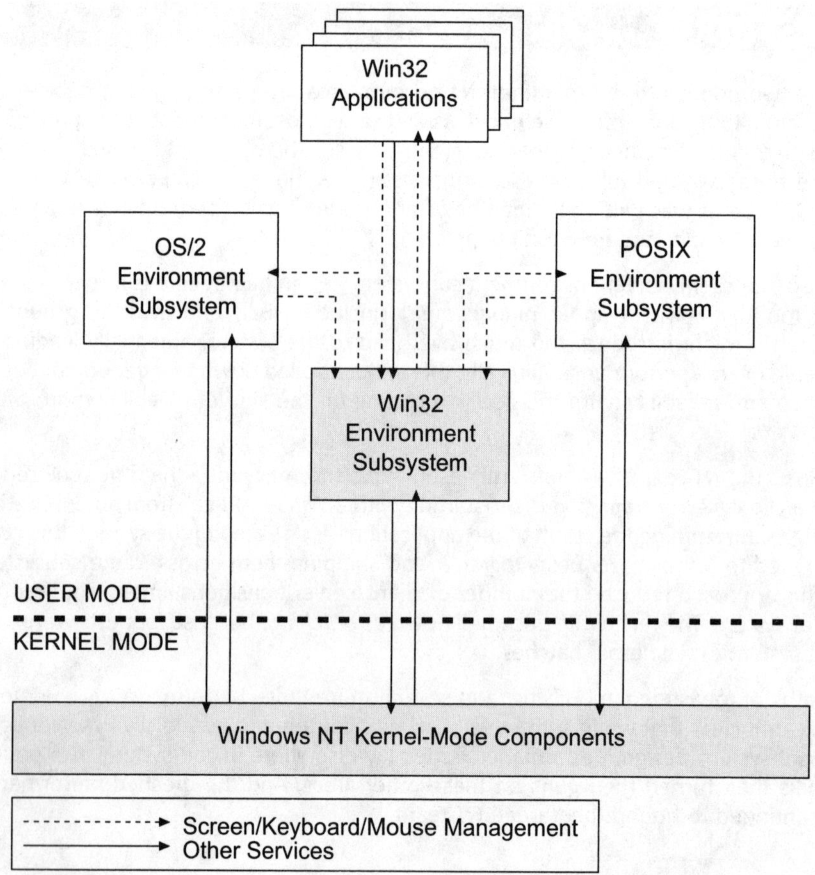

Figure 2-3: The Win32 environment subsystem serves applications and other subsystems.

On the output side, the Win32 subsystem must handle all changes in the state of the screen. Thus, any operation that performs screen output, even output initiated by an OS/2 or POSIX application, finds its way to the screen through the Win32 subsystem.

Another bit of fallout from moving GDI into the kernel is that it requires all new display drivers. The drivers from previous versions of Windows NT aren't compatible with the new architecture in version 4.0. Microsoft supplies drivers for the most common devices as part of NT. If you rely on your hardware vendor for your display drivers, you'll want to check on their support for NT 4.0 to assure that there won't be an availability lag.

THE BIG ADVANTAGES OF CLIENT/SERVER

What are the advantages of this client/server subsystem model?

First, this approach enables Windows NT to provide several different programming interfaces while leaving the core operating system fairly simple and easy to maintain. None of the interface or behavioral details of OS/2, for example, are known by the kernel-mode components of NT. Windows NT captured all of this intelligence within the OS/2 subsystem. Using subsystems to emulate different operating systems also has the advantage of enabling additional environments in the future, simply by creating a new user-mode subsystem. (Actual development of a new environment subsystem isn't a trivial task, but it's much easier than changing the internal design of the system to accommodate the new APIs.)

Second, the model enables extensibility without the need to change anything in the core operating system. For example, if Microsoft needed to add a bunch of new APIs to Win32 (and, believe me, they find themselves doing so on a regular basis), the changes would be limited to the Win32 subsystem. Changes to the kernel-mode components would be required only if the building blocks provided at that level couldn't support the new APIs.

Avoiding changes to the kernel components is important to maintain the stability and integrity of the core operating system. The more complexity you pour in and the more frequently you make changes, the better chance you have of breaking something that was working.

Finally, the client/server subsystem approach contributes to the robustness of the system. It centralizes global information in the subsystems and protects that information from interference by applications and by other subsystems. By placing subsystems in their own private address spaces and by separating them from the core operating system, everyone is protected from everyone else. Any failures that do occur have very limited effects on the overall system.

OS/2 Subsystem

On computers based on the Intel x86 architecture, Windows NT can run 16-bit OS/2 1.x character-mode applications, through version 1.3. You can launch these applications and run them without modification from Windows NT Explorer, from a Windows NT command prompt, via the Start button, or from within a Win32 or another OS/2 application.

The OS/2 subsystem acts as the environment subsystem server to client OS/2 applications. Each OS/2 application runs in its own address space, separate from other OS/2 applications and separate from the OS/2 subsystem. OS/2 client applications make all requests via the OS/2 subsystem. The OS/2 subsystem, in turn, communicates with both the Win32 subsystem and the Windows NT executive to implement its services.

PURITY OF THE WIN32 SUBSYSTEM

Is the Win32 subsystem design really that pure? Is the kernel really protected from problems in the Win32 subsystem code? When you're talking about Windows NT 4.0, the answer is "almost."

The biggest change that Microsoft made to the operating system's internal architecture in version 4.0 was to move the bulk of the *User* (the name of NT's window management component) and *graphics device interface* (GDI) functions from user mode to kernel mode. Applications still call APIs in the Win32 subsystem, but the Win32 subsystem turns around and sends the requests to kernel mode immediately. The good news, and the reason that Microsoft made this change, is that you'll typically see improved performance of applications making heavy use of graphics and window manipulation.

Now the potentially bad news. Recall that one key advantage of environment subsystems is protecting the kernel-mode components from bugs in applications or even in the environment subsystems. Now that the User and GDI pieces have moved into kernel mode, a crash in them could bring down the entire system.

To be fair, I've run some pretty intense work station and server applications and have never crashed the User or GDI components. Before the final product is released, you can bet that Microsoft will have tested the daylights out of this change to assure that it hasn't introduced any new instability.

Presentation Manager

So far, I've addressed only OS/2 character-mode applications, but what about graphical applications for OS/2? The two graphical interfaces provided on OS/2 1.x — Presentation Manager and AVIO (advanced video I/O) — aren't supported by the retail version of Windows NT. However, if you must run these applications on NT, Microsoft separately offers the Windows NT Add-on Subsystem for Presentation Manager.

OS/2 Compatibility

Even in the realm of OS/2 1.x character-based applications, the OS/2 subsystem has compatibility restrictions. OS/2 applications aren't supported on the non-Intel CPU platforms supported by Windows NT. Applications that attempt to access memory or I/O ports at privilege level Ring 2 aren't supported. Moreover, the OS/2 subsystem doesn't support any custom third-party OS/2 device drivers and requires them to be rewritten to use the Windows NT driver model.

When you think about OS/2 1.x compatibility, think in terms of 16-bit legacy OS/2 applications, not the 32-bit OS/2 applications being offered today.

This is because the OS/2 subsystem on NT doesn't support 32-bit OS/2 2.x or OS/2 Warp applications. Although one of the original project goals was to provide the OS/2 2.x interface, this support was dropped in favor of the Win32 interface.

The impetus behind support of OS/2 1.x character-mode applications was to enable a smooth migration path from 16-bit OS/2. By the time Windows NT development was fully underway, many Microsoft customers had already taken the OS/2 plunge. They were now running their businesses using SQL Server and other critical applications on OS/2. In addition, a number of customers had written in-house OS/2 applications and were reluctant to port their applications immediately to Win32. The OS/2 subsystem on NT bought them time and took away a key customer objection for migration from OS/2 to Windows NT.

In Chapter 17, you'll learn how to configure and manage the OS/2 subsystem.

POSIX Subsystem

You can launch and run 32-bit POSIX applications from Windows NT Explorer, from a Windows NT command prompt, via the Start button, or from within another POSIX application. Because the POSIX subsystem provides source code compatibility and not binary compatibility, POSIX applications must be compiled and linked explicitly for execution on Windows NT. POSIX applications supported by NT are character-based and run in a command prompt window, just like OS/2.

The POSIX subsystem acts as the environment subsystem server to client POSIX applications. Each POSIX application runs in its own address space, separate from other POSIX applications and separate from the POSIX subsystem. POSIX client applications make all requests via the POSIX subsystem. The POSIX subsystem, in turn, communicates with both the Win32 subsystem and the Windows NT executive to implement its services.

You'll run into trouble if you run a POSIX application against a non-NTFS volume. And Windows NT won't warn you that you're doing anything wrong. You'll have to take responsibility for assuring this.

Why? POSIX has some quirks in how it deals with files. These aren't bugs. They just reflect differences between UNIX and DOS in their approaches to handling files.

If a POSIX application requires file system access, it must perform its file operations on an NTFS volume. NTFS is the only file system on Windows NT that provides full support for POSIX. If an application uses another file system, the application may not behave as expected.

Of the 12 proposed POSIX standards, each covers a different aspect of operating system functionality. Less than a handful of these dozen proposals on the table have emerged to become actual standards. The POSIX subsystem on Windows NT addresses only one of these standards. POSIX.1, or IEEE 1003.1-1990, is the standard implemented on NT. It specifies the C language API for POSIX.

INSIDE STORY

The final days before releasing Windows NT 3.1 were long and hectic. Development and test managers met every few hours to go over the latest list of bugs, carefully sifting what should and shouldn't be fixed as the team approached the final build. A high level of excitement filled the air, as nearly four years of labor was about to result in the birth of a real product. No one wanted to touch the code to fix any more problems. After all, the system was very stable, beta customers were saying "Ship it," and the team didn't want to make any changes that would put the product's stability at risk.

After more than two days without sleep, I thought that we had finally approved and fixed the last bug before shipping the product. My drowsy gait down the hallway was suddenly interrupted by a frantic test engineer, quickly explaining that a problem introduced in the POSIX subsystem a few days before would prevent NT from passing the POSIX certification tests. After a brief discussion, we decided that we had to change the code.

We took the chance to fix the bug, and the POSIX subsystem in Windows NT 3.1 was later successfully certified POSIX compliant. The POSIX subsystem went down in NT history as the last component that we touched before shipping the 3.1 product. And the team never let the POSIX development engineer hear the end of it.

Other User-Mode Components

Beyond environment subsystems, a handful of other Windows NT components live in user mode. These components perform important functions and are worth understanding. They support DOS and Win16 applications and implement system security.

MS-DOS Environment

Although Windows NT enables you to run DOS applications, it doesn't accomplish this through a DOS environment subsystem. Instead, it surrounds a DOS application with virtual hardware, tricking the application into thinking it's running on its very own PC.

DOS isn't a multitasking environment, so there's no need for centralized management and scheduling of applications, as is necessary in the Windows 3.1 environment. Each DOS application with its associated virtual hardware is treated as an island, separate from all other DOS applications and any other processes running on the computer. In other words, each DOS application lives in its own virtual world.

Insulating DOS Applications

When you invoke a DOS application, the application is immediately enveloped by a *virtual DOS machine*, or VDM. The VDM and the DOS application exist as one

Win32 process. As illustrated in Figure 2-4, each DOS application gets its own VDM, and each runs in its own address space. The VDM's virtual PC provides the DOS application with the following:

✦ Execution of Intel x86 instructions

✦ Simulated DOS INT 21 services

✦ Simulated ROM BIOS interrupt services

✦ Simulated standard PC hardware devices

DOS VDMs communicate with the Win32 subsystem for keyboard and mouse input and for screen output. Because VDMs are Win32 applications, they need to access other Win32 subsystem services as well. Figure 2-5 shows this communication path.

DOS Compatibility

As I mentioned in Chapter 1, the virtual PC environment limits what it enables a DOS application to do. Well-behaved DOS applications perform all of their I/O operations through DOS system calls and shouldn't have a problem executing in the NT VDM environment. A DOS application that attempts to access the hardware directly is detected by the system and summarily killed, and you're informed of its death.

For example, the DOS version of Norton Utilities attempts to read from and write directly to the disk hardware. Enabling any application to do this could compromise both security and stability of the system. To provide broader 16-bit application support, Microsoft has attempted to virtualize some hardware devices that wouldn't compromise the system. For example, their recent efforts have enabled Delrina WinFax Pro to run on Windows NT.

Users of Windows NT are frequently confused about what they're running when they invoke the command prompt, sometimes referred to as the console. This is NT's command line environment, which accepts keyboard commands and displays the text results. The confusion arises from Microsoft's use of the MS-DOS logo as the icon for this application. Microsoft has tied this icon to the command prompt in each version of Windows NT.

You should ignore the MS-DOS icon. When you fire up one of these windows, you're really running a Win32 command processor called CMD.EXE. There's no 16-bit code involved, and DOS isn't associated in any way with CMD.EXE. Almost all of the DOS-like commands that you invoke from the command prompt are 32-bit versions of their former selves. Because Win32 processes can invoke all other types of applications (for example, DOS, OS/2, POSIX, Win16), you can invoke any of them from the Windows NT command prompt.

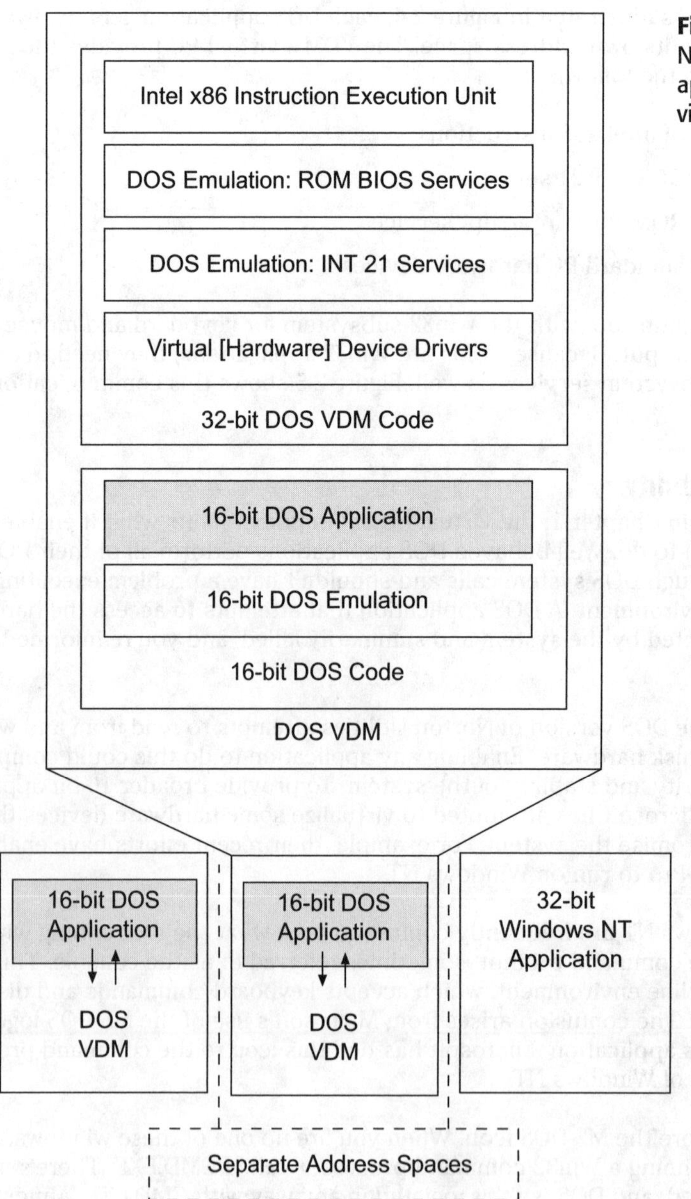

Figure 2-4: Windows NT surrounds a DOS application with its own virtual PC environment.

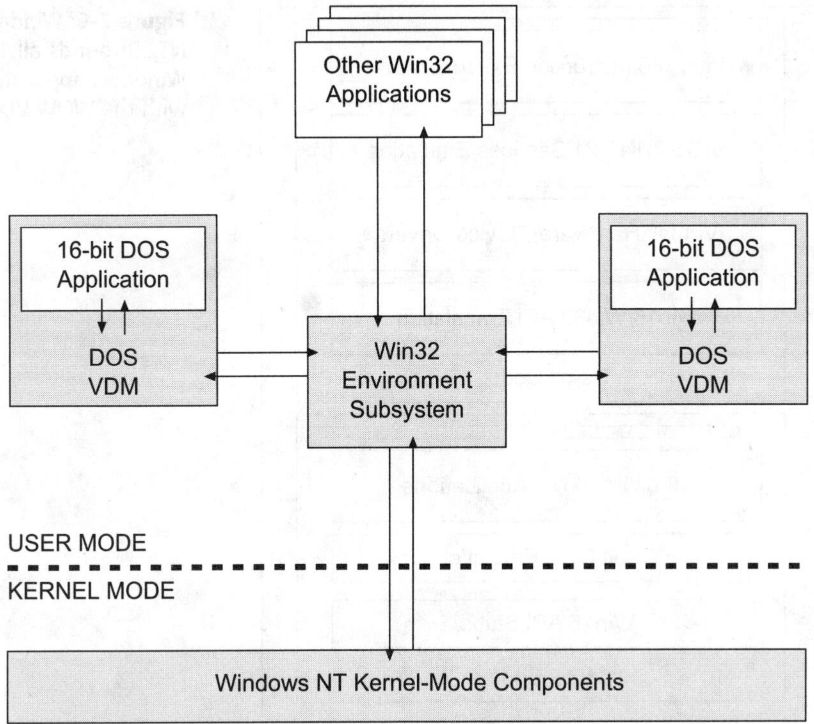

Figure 2-5: DOS VDMs communicate with the Win32 subsystem.

Windows 16-bit Environment

Windows NT supports running 16-bit Windows applications. Similar to DOS support, NT uses the VDM approach and doesn't provide a Win16 environment subsystem server. By default, a single VDM called WOW (Win16 On Win32) is used to handle all Win16 applications. Think of the WOW VDM as a virtual Windows machine.

Because Win16 applications are dependent on DOS services, use of a VDM to surround the applications with virtual hardware is still required. In this respect, WOW is quite similar to NT's DOS support. In addition to a virtual PC, though, WOW adds a translation layer to convert Win16 APIs and messages to and from Win32. You can see this layer in Figure 2-6. WOW uses the Win32 subsystem to execute these translated API calls.

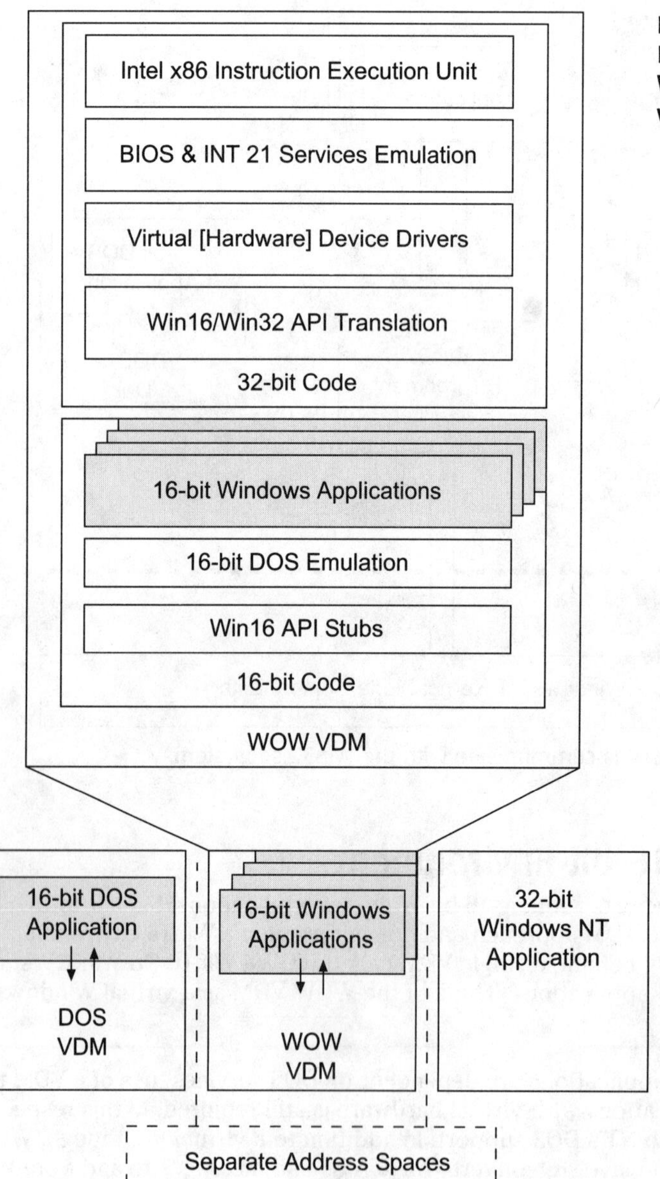

Figure 2-6: Windows NT surrounds all 16-bit Windows applications with the WOW VDM.

Simulating Windows Multitasking

Because Windows 3.1 is a multitasking environment and Win16 applications expect to be cooperatively multitasked, WOW must simulate cooperative multitasking among all Win16 applications. Each Win16 application is given its own thread within the single WOW VDM process, but only one thread is ever permitted to run at any given time, and each thread must yield control before another can run.

Just as in Windows 3.1, all Win16 applications share a common address space and can potentially harm each other or bring WOW itself down. However, WOW is separate from all 32-bit applications and DOS applications running on the system. The worst that a Win16 application can do on NT is to bring down all Win16 applications.

You can optionally run a Win16 application in its own separate address space. Doing this has the effect of protecting other Win16 applications if this one crashes and protecting this application from the other Win16 applications, should they go nuts. Moreover, you may get quicker responsiveness from this application, because it's preemptively multitasked like Win32 applications. See Figure 2-7 for an illustration of this option.

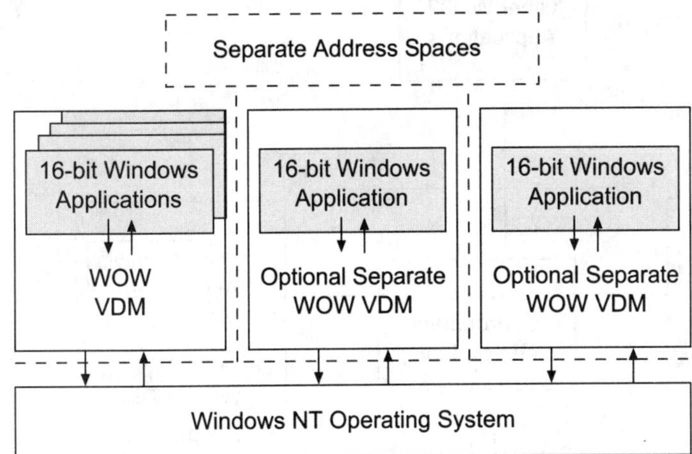

Figure 2-7: You can optionally run Win16 applications with their own separate WOW VDMs.

When you select this option for a Win16 application, the system gives the application its very own WOW VDM when invoked. This yields the one disadvantage of running in a separate WOW. It consumes more memory resources.

Here's what to do to cause a Win16 application to run in its own WOW VDM, and thus in its own address space:

1. Right-click the icon for the Win16 application shortcut, and then click Properties. (If the icon isn't on the Windows NT desktop, use the Windows NT Explorer to find the application shortcut, then right-click the icon in Explorer.) You should see the property sheet for the application.
2. Now click the Shortcut tab and select the Run in Separate Memory Space check box. The next time that you invoke this application via its shortcut, the application will have its own copy of WOW and will execute in its own separate address space.

WOW and Win32

WOW VDMs communicate with the Win32 subsystem for keyboard and mouse input and for screen output. Because VDMs are Win32 applications, they need to access other Win32 subsystem services as well. Each WOW VDM translates between the Win16 and Win32 interfaces and performs the requested operations in the Win32 subsystem. Figure 2-8 illustrates the relationship between multiple WOW VDMs and the Win32 subsystem.

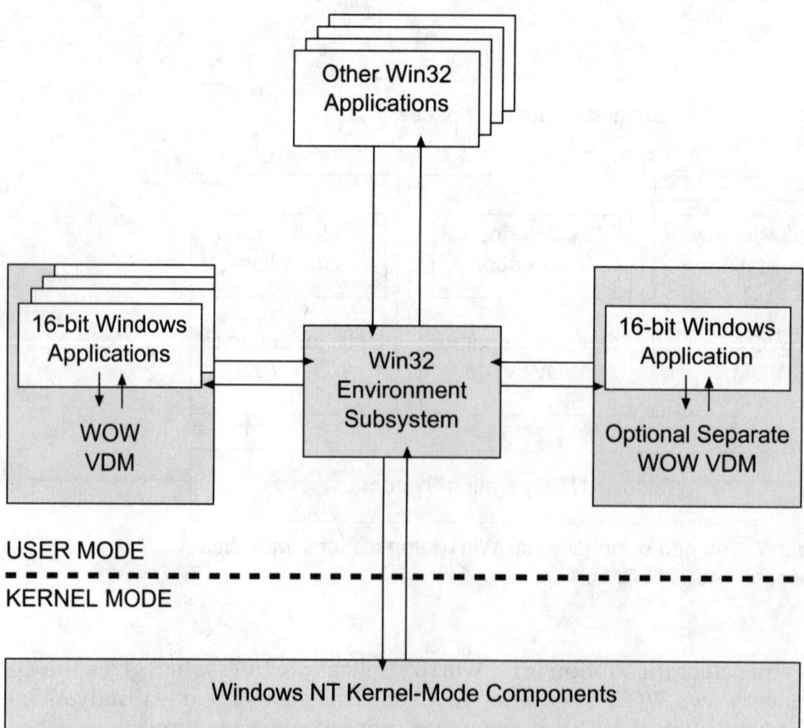

Figure 2-8: WOW VDMs use the Win32 subsystem for API execution and interactive I/O.

Security Subsystem

Three Windows NT components operate in user mode to handle security issues. Collectively, these components are known as the *security subsystem*. They work in tandem with kernel-mode components to implement NT's tight C2 security. These components, shown in Figure 2-9, include the following:

- ✦ Local security authority
- ✦ Logon process
- ✦ Security account manager

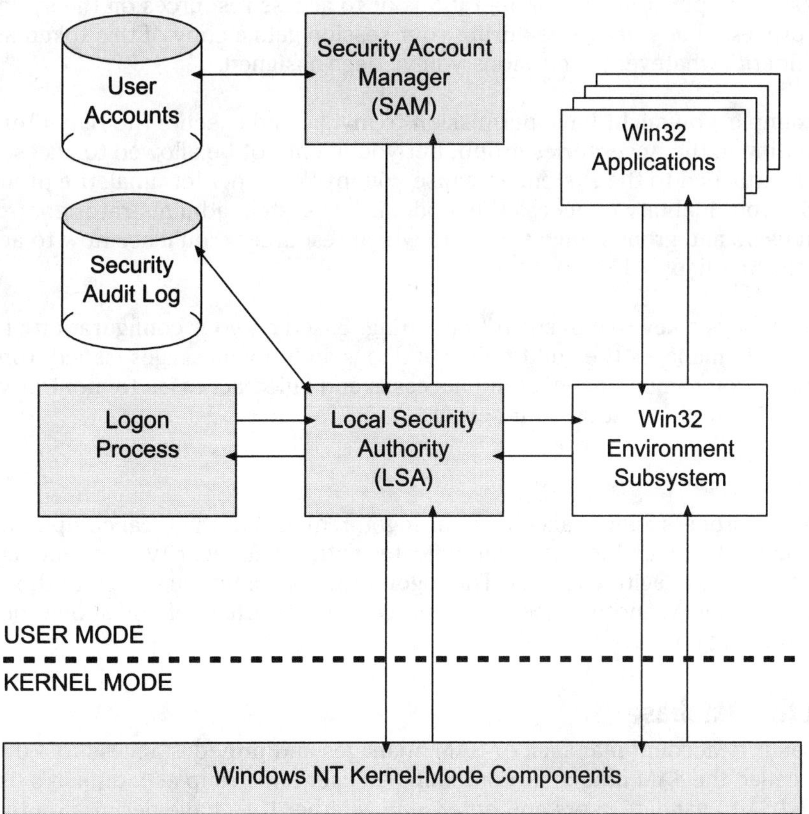

Figure 2-9: Security components in user mode constitute the security subsystem.

LSA's Central Role

The local security authority, or LSA, is the pivotal component of the security subsystem. It acts as a server to the other user-mode processes. LSA's main role is to manage the security policy on the local computer and provide user authentication services to other system components. LSA communicates with the security reference monitor down in kernel mode. Kernel-mode components are discussed in a later section.

LSA generates a *security access token*, each time you or one of your users logs on to the system. The security access token is a chunk of information about you, including your name, your unique security ID, and security information from the various groups to which you belong. The token is used to check whether you have permission to perform certain operations or to access resources on the system. Each process that you invoke during your session gets a copy of this token and thus inherits whatever permissions you've been assigned.

For example, you might have permission to invoke and execute the HyperTerminal application in the Accessories group, but you might not be allowed to access the modem attached to the system. Because you invoke HyperTerminal, the process inherits your inability to access the modem. The system administrator controls which users and groups have access to which resources. You'll see how to accomplish this in Chapter 18.

LSA also plays a key role in security auditing. Based on your configuration of the system, LSA manages the audit policy and logs auditing messages issued from kernel mode. You can audit successful accesses and failed accesses to monitor who's really trying to do what on your server.

Handling User Logons

The logon process simply accepts your logon requests at the local computer. It displays the logon dialog and communicates with other security components to validate you as a legitimate user. The logon process communicates with the local security authority, another user-mode process, to determine if you should be allowed to log on.

SAM the Database

The security account manager, or SAM, manages and provides access to a database, called the SAM database, containing all user and group accounts. It's used by the LSA to validate users and determine whether they have permission to perform various operations.

WHAT'S C2-LEVEL SECURITY?

You've heard me mention C2 security a couple of times now. C2 security is defined by the U.S. Department of Defense in its *Department of Defense Trusted Computer System Evaluation Criteria*, more affectionately known in the security world as the *Orange Book*. This document defines several levels of security, from D (least stringent) to A (most stringent). Several sublevels are defined within the B and C security definitions. Windows NT 4.0 is currently C2 secure. It was designed to support B2 security in a future release of the product.

The Orange Book definition of C2 boils down to a few key requirements. In a C2 environment, if you own a resource (say, a file or a printer), you must be able to control who has access to that resource. The operating system must require that you identify yourself with a unique user name and password before gaining access to the system. The system must be able to keep an audit trail of successful and failed accesses to system resources and must provide this information to the system administrator. Moreover, the system must protect itself from unauthorized tampering of memory contents or system files.

Finally, a C2-secure operating system must take steps to prevent users or processes from randomly or intentionally reusing resources that might contain sensitive information. A simple example involves files. Other users must not be able to access the data in a file after you delete it. A more subtle example involves system memory. A chunk of memory, even after it's freed for use by other processes, might still contain information that other users shouldn't see. NT must assure that contents of memory blocks and deleted files are wiped clean before allowing another process to reuse these resources.

C2 security is important for Windows NT to play in the government market, but many of these features are valuable in the corporate arena as well. Most organizations have data that needs to be protected from prying eyes (for example, source code, product plans, personnel information, salaries). Although you may not manage data that needs to be protected, at the very least you can prevent naive users from damaging their system configurations. Remember, though, that your NT systems will only be as secure as you make them, based on how you configure NT's security features.

Windows NT Executive

The Windows NT executive consists of several operating system components that all run in kernel mode. User-mode processes, such as the environment subsystems discussed earlier, interact with the NT executive by calling system service APIs, shown in Figure 2-10.

Understanding the kernel-mode components of the operating system gives you a better appreciation of how and why NT does what it does (see Figure 2-10). The following sections discuss each of the executive components. Now join me on a journey into the depths of the Windows NT operating system.

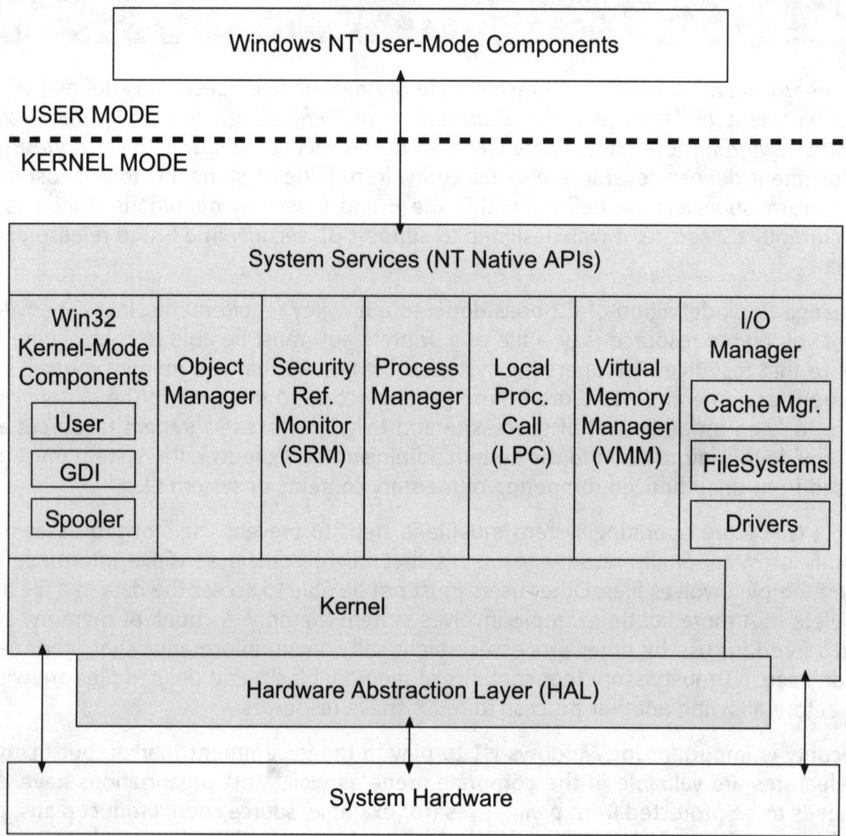

Figure 2-10: The Windows NT executive is the core of the operating system and runs in kernel mode.

System Services

Each component of the Windows NT executive provides a set of APIs. Some of these APIs are designed to be used exclusively by other components of the operating system executive. These APIs are invisible to user-mode processes and are made available only in kernel mode within the executive.

Other APIs supplied by the NT executive are designed to be called from user-mode processes. These APIs comprise the system services layer, sometimes call the *NT native services.* These services are called by environment subsystems and libraries linked to applications to perform operating system functions. In a sense, the system services are the skin of the NT executive. They make up the visible outer layer, hiding the complex guts underneath.

ABOUT SYSTEM SERVICES APIs

The Windows NT executive is a self-contained operating system, missing only the user interface. Before the Win32, OS/2, or POSIX subsystems were developed for NT, the only programming interface available was the NT native API. Initially, Microsoft used only these APIs to write all test software that was used to verify the integrity of the executive.

The NT native APIs, which are virtually all named with the prefix *Nt,* weren't designed to be called by applications directly. They're very general and primitive, often requiring a long list of parameters to specify explicitly what is being requested. If you've programmed using Windows APIs, you know that the Windows API parameter lists are lengthy. Many NT native parameter lists are even longer.

Because the caller specifies every detail, these APIs are flexible enough to implement a wide range of operating system environments. Their flexibility has been proven by the successful implementation of the diverse requirements of the Win32 and POSIX subsystems.

The system services layer is more conceptual than real. There's no separate system services component in the executive. The system services layer is really just the collection of all available system services offered by the components of the NT executive.

User, GDI, and Spooler

In earlier versions of Windows NT, three components now in the NT executive used to live in user mode. In Windows NT 4.0, they've been moved into kernel mode to improve performance.

The *graphics device interface*, or GDI, provides functions that control output to the video displays, printers, plotters, and other graphics devices. It enables applications and system components to display text, draw lines, curves, bitmapped images, and so forth. The *User* component handles the management of windows and their constituent parts including frames, buttons, dialogs, menus, and list boxes. This component makes calls into GDI to perform the actual drawing of these window elements. The *Spooler* component supports printing by queuing up print jobs and managing their distribution to physical printers.

Object Manager

Almost every system service performed in the Windows NT executive is performed on what is called an *object*. An object is a representation of a physical or conceptual entity in the system. For example, Windows NT objects include:

- Files
- Directories
- Processes
- Threads
- Synchronization objects (semaphores, mutexes, events, timers)
- Virtual memory objects

Many other objects exist. The point to remember, as illustrated by Figure 2-11, is that just about everything passed around and processed within the NT executive is represented by an object.

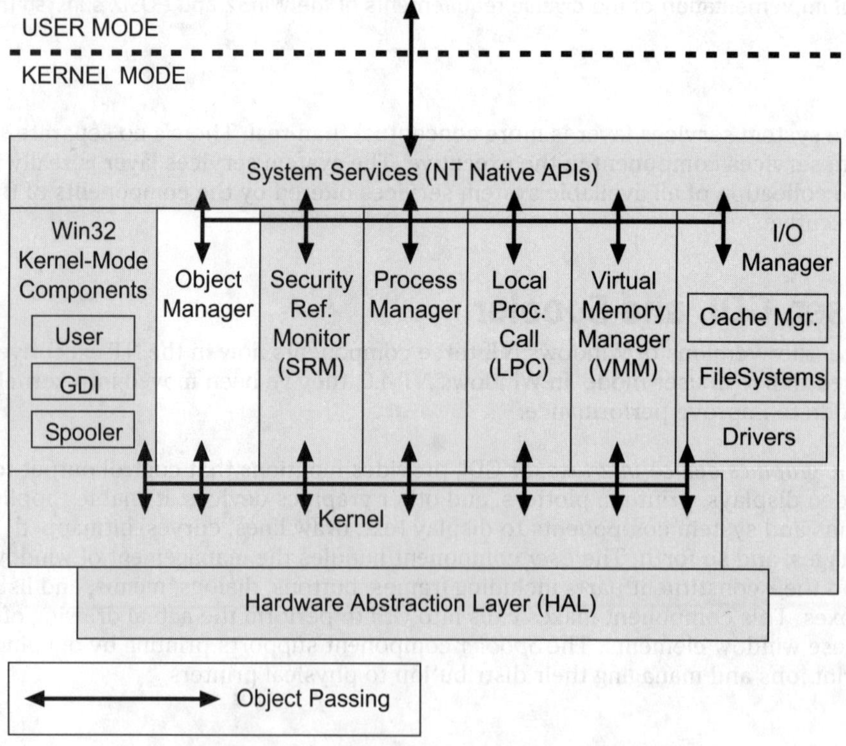

Figure 2-11: Windows NT uses objects for just about everything.

An object is described using a data structure that contains information on its type, the actions that can be performed on it (for example, create, delete, set, clear, and so on), a set of attributes defining the behavior of the object, and its relationship to other objects. In addition, each object includes security information that specifies who is allowed to do what to the object.

ABOUT OBJECT NAMES AND HANDLES

Many of the objects in Windows NT are named, similar to the way in which files are named. In fact, the object manager maintains a hierarchical directory of object names, modeled after the directory structures in file systems.

When an object is created or opened, the system provides the caller with a unique *handle* to the object. Recall that, back in the 1970s, CB radio enthusiasts created unique nicknames for themselves called handles. In NT, a handle is simply a unique way of referring to an object. Once a process has a handle to an object, it uses that handle to manipulate the object with the appropriate APIs. When the operations are complete, the process closes the object, making the handle invalid.

When you use Windows NT Server's Event Viewer to examine security audit logs of accesses to objects, you'll see these names and handles included in the descriptions of the objects. You'll discover how and why to audit object accesses in Chapter 18.

Objects can be opened and accessed by more than one process or by the same process multiple times. In this situation, the object manager performs the vital function of tracking the number of references to the object in the system. When all references are no longer needed, the object manager makes sure that the object is deleted, freeing valuable memory resources for other objects to use.

Some objects are permanent and don't vanish when all references to them are gone. Files and directories on disk are examples of permanent objects. Thank goodness *they* don't disappear until you explicitly delete them.

Security Reference Monitor

The security reference monitor, or SRM, enforces the security of the local system. SRM acts as a guard or gatekeeper. When a user or application requests access to any object, SRM checks for proper authorization before granting access to that object.

As you can see in Figure 2-12, SRM, like other components of the executive, provides services to both kernel and user mode. These services include checking user privileges and verifying authorization to access objects.

As you might have guessed, the object manager is one of SRM's key customers. Every time that an attempt is made to create an object, the object manager asks SRM if the requesting process is authorized to create this type of object. Likewise, when a process attempts to open an existing object with specific access rights, the object manager looks to SRM for validation.

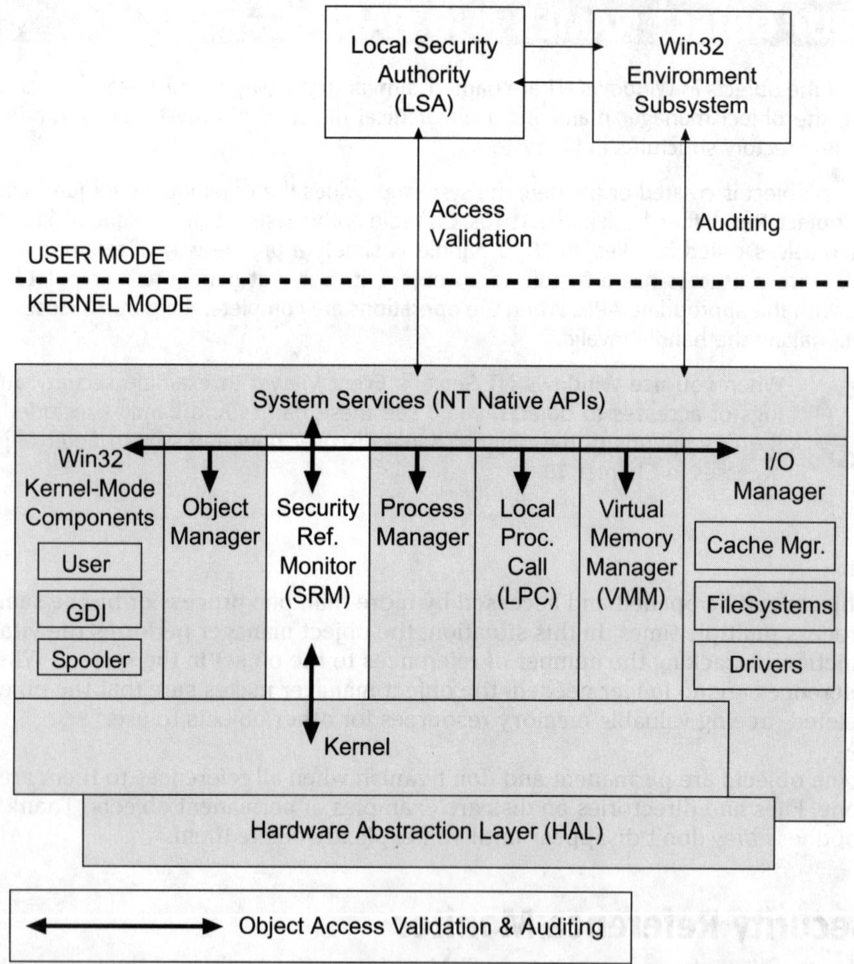

Figure 2-12: The security reference monitor provides security services to kernel- and user-mode components.

The auditing function provided by SRM keeps you on top of what's really happening on your network, security-wise. For example, it can make a record of every attempt to access an object, both authorized and unauthorized. You'll find this useful in understanding what your users are doing and in catching problems with your security implementation. You may discover both intentional and unintentional unauthorized accesses to the resources on your computer. This knowledge of actual security events gives you the power to tighten your security policy in just the right places.

INSIDE STORY

Early in the development of NT, long before its first release, we found a couple of nasty bugs in the process manager. These bugs caused the memory of the process to become corrupted. A few of the test engineers started calling this component the *process mangler*, until the bugs were finally fixed.

Because security is pervasive across all objects in virtually every corner of the system, SRM must work in concert with several other system components.

Process Manager

The process manager has a very simple task. It provides services to other parts of the system that create, delete, and modify processes and threads. The process manager simply supplies these services and doesn't actively dispatch or schedule any work. Scheduling of threads for execution falls in the domain of the kernel component, which is discussed in detail later.

Whenever you fire up an application, the operating system eventually finds its way down to the process manager to create the process and all threads within that process. The process manager gets the application in a state of being ready to run.

A process is represented in the system by a process object. The process object contains information about the process's virtual address space, the set of resources visible to the process, and the set of threads within the process. Similarly, thread objects, which represent threads within a process, contain all of the information required to describe the content and state of a thread.

PROCESS PARENTHOOD

In some operating systems, processes can have hierarchical relationships and may have complex ways of dealing with process termination. For example, some systems always treat the creating process as a parent and the created process as its child. When the parent process terminates, all of its child processes are terminated automatically.

The NT process manager doesn't keep track of any relationships between processes. In Windows NT, it's the responsibility of the environment subsystems to keep track of these rules and relationships, if any, and to do the right things when processes are created and terminated. This is part of the magic that enables NT to provide personalities of various operating systems through its environment subsystems.

Local Procedure Call

The local procedure call mechanism, or LPC, provides an efficient way to communicate between two processes on the same computer. Think of LPC as a sort of very short-distance Federal Express, where the message absolutely, positively has to be next door within a few milliseconds.

Recall that each Windows NT process has its own separate address space. Because the operating system design relies on the client/server model described earlier, it must have a quick and easy way of passing data between client and server processes. LPC to the rescue. It provides functions to create a communication link between two processes and to pass information between those processes.

LPC and Win32

Consider an application that makes a Win32 API call. From the perspective of the application, it does this by specifying a set of parameters and calling the API function. When the function completes, the system passes a return code back to the application. As far as the application knows, all of the work performed by the API was done inside the library to which the application linked. This concept is illustrated in Figure 2-13.

Although some Win32 APIs are indeed fully implemented within the library linked to the application, most are implemented in the Win32 subsystem. How do you get the API parameters shipped from the application over to the Win32 subsystem, make the appropriate API call there, and ship the return code back to the application? For each API implemented in the Win32 subsystem, the library function linked to the application contains a *stub function* that communicates with the Win32 subsystem via LPC.

A stub function simply packages together all of the API parameters with an indicator of which API to call. It then ships this package via LPC to the Win32 subsystem and waits for a reply. Meanwhile, the Win32 subsystem has been listening for requests from applications. When it receives the request, it retrieves the API parameters and calls the appropriate Win32 API to do the actual work. Once the API has done its work, the Win32 subsystem packages the return information, sends it via LPC to the waiting application, and the stub function receives it and returns it to the application code.

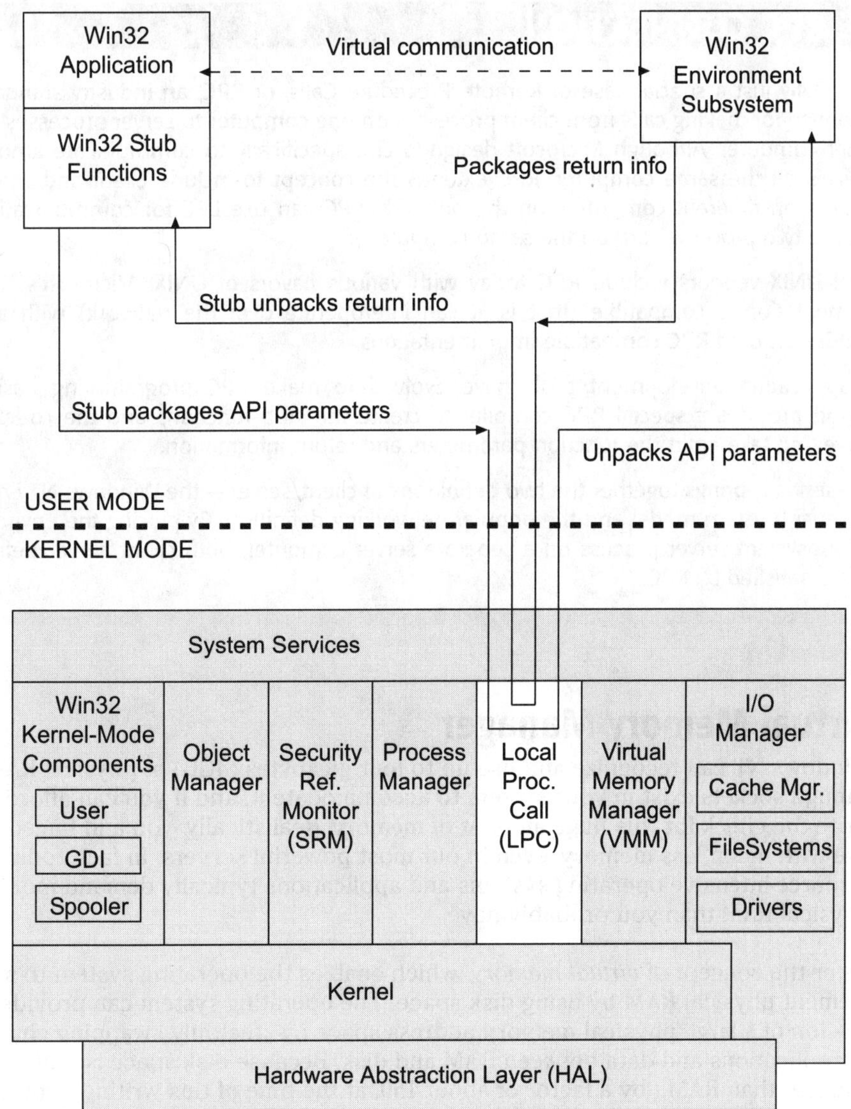

Figure 2-13: Client applications make requests to server subsystems via LPC.

THE RPC CONNECTION

LPC is really just a special case of Remote Procedure Calls, or RPC, an industry standard mechanism for making calls from client processes on one computer to server processes on another computer. Although Microsoft designed LPC specifically to communicate among processes on the same computer, RPC extends the concept to include client and server processes on different computers on the network. RPC can use LPC for communication when the two processes are on the same computer.

Several UNIX vendors include RPC today with various flavors of UNIX. Microsoft's RPC implementation is compatible (that is, it can interoperate over the network) with any OSF/DCE-standard RPC compatible implementations.

RPC application development tools have evolved to make RPC programming easier. Microsoft provides a special RPC compiler to create the stub functions and the code to package and take apart the function parameters and return information.

RPC essentially brings together the two definitions of client/server — the Windows NT environment subsystem model and the popular networking definition. By placing the environment subsystem server process on a separate server computer, both client/server definitions are satisfied by RPC.

Virtual Memory Manager

Windows NT can recognize and use up to four gigabytes (4GB) of physical RAM, if enough sockets exist in your system to accommodate it, and if you can afford to write the check for this huge amount of memory. Realistically, you and I need to live with much less memory, even in our most powerful servers. In fact, today's resource-intensive operating systems and applications typically demand more physical RAM than you probably have.

Enter the concept of *virtual memory,* which enables the operating system to supplement physical RAM by using disk space. The operating system can provide the illusion of a large physical memory address space by stealthily swapping chunks of applications and data between RAM and disk. Because disk space is much cheaper than RAM (by a factor of about 150, at the time of this writing), you can create a large virtual address space for a relatively low cost. The tradeoff is reduced performance, because disk access is considerably slower than RAM access.

NT's Memory Model

Windows NT provides each process with its own 4GB virtual address space. Actually, only the lower 2GB is available to a user-mode process. The upper 2GB is reserved for use by the operating system. The entire address space is divided into 4K chunks called *pages.*

At any given time, a page might be somewhere in RAM, or it might be in a file on disk. The virtual memory manager, or VMM, keeps track of the location of each page of memory. It performs all of the housekeeping necessary to provide a process with access to each of its pages when needed and hides all of the details of where everything really is.

Virtual Memory Paging

All paging activity is handled by the virtual memory manager. A process tries to access a page of memory by attempting to read or write some data or by attempting to execute instructions in that 4K portion of its address space. If the page is currently in RAM, access to the page is provided immediately. VMM provides a translation of the location of the physical page in RAM to the process's virtual address space.

If the page isn't in RAM, but currently resides on disk, VMM starts working for a living. The attempt by the process to access the page triggers a special event called a *page fault*. VMM immediately arranges to read the page from disk into RAM. If RAM has no available slots, VMM must first select the *least recently used*, or LRU, page in RAM and kick it out of memory by writing it to disk. This frees up a slot for the requested page. Once the requested page is in memory, VMM provides the translation of the physical page in RAM to the process's virtual address space. The process is then allowed to continue executing, completely oblivious to all the action that has just taken place on its behalf.

Although the virtual memory manager handles all of the details of virtual memory and paging under the covers, paging activity isn't always invisible to you, especially in a production server environment. If your system has very little physical memory, if it's bogged down with many processes, if a process is hogging too much memory, or if the disk is spending all of its time seeking and not transferring data, paging can become your worst nightmare.

You'll learn in Chapter 19 how to detect, monitor, and overcome excessive paging activity using Windows NT's Performance Monitor.

Memory Protection

Because each process is given its own virtual address space, VMM makes sure that it never gives one process access to another process's memory. As I mentioned before, this approach prevents one process from interfering with another process and is a key reliability feature of the operating system.

YOU CAN'T GET TO PAGE ONE

VMM provides another enhancement to system reliability. The first 4K page in a process's virtual address space is protected by VMM so that any attempt to access it generates an error condition. Why waste a whole page of address space by making it inaccessible?

If you've ever programmed in C (or any other language that uses pointers to memory), you probably know that one of the most common programming errors involves attempting to read or write to memory address zero using a pointer that was never initialized. In some operating systems, this bug can generate random behavior, system crashes, and even physical damage. (An associate of mine once blew out his computer monitor when his program mistakenly read address zero and used the result to drive his monitor at the wrong frequency.) NT always traps these errors, preventing any potential disasters caused by scribbling in low memory.

VMM Services

Thus far, I've told you about what VMM does behind the scenes. Like other components of the Windows NT executive, VMM also provides a set of services to other parts of the system and manages a set of objects. VMM manages shared memory regions used for communication between processes. This feature is used by LPC for efficient transfer of large messages. In addition, VMM offers a feature called file mapping. This facility enables you to perform file I/O operations by simply reading and writing memory locations. VMM provides additional services, including reserving large virtual address ranges, managing pools of available memory blocks, assigning protections to pages, and managing the amount of memory resource allocated to each process in the system.

I/O Manager

The I/O manager provides the physical senses of the operating system. It manages all of the input and output for the system, including all data coming from the keyboard, mouse, disk, or CD-ROM, and all data flowing to the screen, printer, or disk. One of the I/O manager's key functions is communicating among various I/O drivers. Drivers handled by the I/O manager include file systems, hardware device drivers, and network drivers.

To be as simple and as modular as possible, Windows NT uses a layered approach to device drivers. Each type of driver has well-defined interfaces both above and below it, making insertion of another driver between two existing layers relatively easy.

An excellent example of this layered driver approach in action is the fault tolerance driver, ftdisk.sys. This driver implements the fault tolerance features you read about in Chapter 1. Ftdisk sits just below the file systems and just above the disk hardware drivers. It translates write requests into multiple writes to different drives. In the case of disk mirroring, for example, ftdisk accepts each write request from the file system above and sends to the device drivers below two physical write requests, one to each drive of the mirrored pair.

Most NT drivers can be loaded, unloaded, started, and stopped without ever rebooting the system. This characteristic of the I/O manager makes it easier for you to manage the devices on your NT systems. You can add a device to the system, install and start the driver, and use the device immediately. Likewise, if you remove a device from the system, you can stop the driver and remove it without rebooting. You'll see exactly how to do this in Chapter 17.

Device Drivers

The NT team wanted to make driver development as straightforward as possible. Although the NT I/O system model has made progress in that direction, device driver development is still a very complex proposition.

Device drivers on Windows NT are written in C and perform 32-bit addressing, just like Win32 processes. They're safe to run on SMP systems, which means that they perform all of the necessary synchronization required if they find themselves running on a multiprocessor computer. Microsoft requires testing of a driver on multiprocessor computers before it can be added to the NT hardware compatibility list.

Following the I/O Trail

Each I/O operation is described by an *I/O request packet*, or IRP. IRPs are passed down between driver layers, sometimes waiting behind other queued I/O requests at certain layers. Once the IRP reaches the hardware driver level and the IRP reaches the front of the driver's queue, the driver starts the I/O operation on the device.

A TALE OF TWO DRIVER MODELS

The 32-bit device drivers written for Windows NT and those written for Windows 95 aren't currently compatible. The state of the Windows driver world still requires hardware device vendors to develop and ship separate drivers for the two operating systems.

Device driver development is an expensive proposition, so Microsoft is working on a mechanism to provide a single device driver model that enables development of drivers compatible with either environment. This should increase the number of drivers compatible with Windows NT, because some hardware vendors have focused all of their driver development efforts toward the higher-volume Windows 95 product.

INSIDE STORY

Although the acronym IRP was intended to be pronounced as individual letters (the same way that we say IRS), several folks on the NT team started pronouncing it phonetically. Soon, IRP became a verb, and it wasn't unusual to hear test engineers talk about a new buggy driver "IRPing" on the system. You'll probably never look at this acronym the same way again. Hey, these inside stories can't all be pleasant.

After the I/O operation completes, the IRP is passed back up through the layers, notifying each layer that the operation has completed. If an application issued the original request, it's notified as well.

Synchronous vs. Asychronous I/O

The Windows NT I/O manager supports two approaches to dealing with completed I/O operations. The simplest and most common is called *synchronous I/O.* In the synchronous approach, the application execution is synchronized with the completion of an I/O operation. When the application issues the request, its execution is blocked and must wait until the I/O operation is complete. Once the I/O finishes, the application is allowed to continue to execute where it left off.

In contrast, *asynchronous I/O* enables an application to issue the request and continue executing before the request completes. In this mode, the application isn't blocked and can continue to perform useful work while the relatively slow I/O operation progresses. The application and the I/O operation are allowed to progress asynchronously at their own pace. Once the I/O operation completes, the operating system notifies the application by calling a function specified by the application or by otherwise indicating that an event has completed. The operating system itself uses asynchronous I/O in many of its processes and threads.

Caching

The I/O manager performs another very critical function. *Caching* is an approach to improving file system performance by keeping frequently used data in memory for quicker access. The I/O manager includes a cache manager that deals with all of the details of caching data in memory, dynamically growing and shrinking the memory used for caching, and copying data from memory whenever possible to avoid I/O operations. The cache manager works closely with the virtual memory manager to implement its file mapping model as efficiently as possible.

Kernel

The Windows NT kernel is the heart of the operating system. Your heart's main goal is to feed all parts of your body with a continuous supply of blood, to keep it running efficiently. Likewise, the NT kernel's main goal is to feed all available CPUs in the system with a continuous supply of useful work, in the form of executable threads, to operate the entire system as efficiently as possible.

The kernel's primary function is to schedule threads to run. Recall from Chapter 1 that these threads can be in single-threaded applications, multithreaded applications, and part of the operating system itself. Each thread is assigned one of 32 priority levels. The kernel always makes sure that highest-priority threads are handled first.

Changing Priorities

To maximize responsiveness of the system, the kernel continuously manipulates a thread's priority based on the amount of CPU time that the thread has used and on the completion of I/O events for the thread. A thread's priority slowly decreases over time if it's CPU-bound. Its priority increases when an I/O operation completes. This approach gives highest priority to interactive processes or processes that perform large amounts of I/O. The kernel manages the details of raising and lowering thread priorities over time.

Keeping CPUs Busy

In SMP systems with more than one physical CPU, the kernel is responsible for dispatching threads to each of the CPUs and assuring proper synchronization between these threads. Although different threads can execute simultaneously on different processors, two threads that manipulate the same critical data mustn't be allowed to execute simultaneously. Otherwise, the results would be unpredictable. If two threads that are trying to touch the same critical data are ready to run, the kernel assures that one thread finishes its data manipulation before the other is allowed to proceed.

REACTING IN REAL TIME

Thread priorities actually come in two classes — variable and real-time. Most threads run in the variable priority class, enabling the kernel to decay or boost their priorities based on CPU time used and external events.

Real-time priorities are treated as higher priority than the variable class. The kernel leaves them alone. They're designed for use by time-critical threads that require a very specific response time. For example, if your application were monitoring a chemical reaction, you might need to sample the reaction's progress many times per second. When you add real-time priority threads to the mix, the kernel cannot juggle their priorities and thus cannot maximize the responsiveness of the system.

What happens when there's nothing to do? If a CPU is available for use, but no thread is ready to execute on it, the kernel schedules a do-nothing thread, called the *idle thread*, to run on that CPU. The idle thread executes in a loop until a thread with real work to do becomes ready to run. So, all CPUs have something to do even when there's nothing to do. This is one case where busywork is a necessity.

INSIDE STORY

In the beginning of the NT project, there was only one NT kernel, fully enabled for multiprocessor synchronization. And the team saw that it was good. But it came to pass that performance testing revealed multiprocessing overhead incurred while running on single processor computers. And the NT team said, "Let there be two kernels." And there were. – Dave 12:17

Multiprocessor synchronization is a tough problem, especially when your goal is to keep all CPUs as busy as they can be. Situations often occur when two threads are ready to run, and two CPUs are available to run them, but they both need to manipulate the same critical chunk of data.

To avoid random results, the first thread must complete its data manipulation before the second thread is allowed to touch the data. On a single-CPU system, you could solve this by temporarily preventing a switch to the second thread. However, on a multiprocessor system, these threads are actually running at the same time.

The NT team solved this problem using *spin locks*. Each thread that needs to manipulate the critical data first checks to see if any other thread is already doing so. The first thread to check this sees that no other threads are already there, and it proceeds. This thread holds the lock and keeps all other threads out. The second thread, executing on a different physical CPU, waits or spins in a loop until the lock is released by the first thread.

When the first thread is done, it releases the lock. The second thread sees this, stops spinning, and proceeds. In the worst case, if all threads need to access the same critical data at the same instant, only one CPU is doing useful work, and the remaining CPUs are spinning, waiting for the first thread to release its lock.

The good news is that spin locks are typically held for an extremely short time, and the occurrence of multiple threads needing access to the same critical data at the same instant doesn't happen frequently. The bad news is that there's a small amount of overhead associated with checking to see if a thread on another processor is already holding a spin lock. There's no way around this on a multiprocessor system, but computers with a single CPU needn't perform this operation.

So, there are two kernels. Ntkrnlmp.exe contains the spin lock code required for multiprocessor systems. Ntoskrnl.exe contains no spin lock code and is designed to run on single-processor systems.

Kernel Services

In addition to scheduling threads to run, the kernel has a few other responsibilities. It handles hardware interrupts from devices and dispatches them to the appropriate drivers and threads. It deals with exception conditions, caused either by invalid software operations such as writing to nonexistent memory, or by hardware faults such as memory parity errors. The kernel also handles key aspects of gracefully shutting down the system and restoring it after a power failure occurs.

Finally, the kernel manages a set of objects used by other parts of the operating system. Just as each of the other modules within the executive provides services, the kernel provides an API interface used by upper layers of the operating system. The kernel objects are used, as you might guess, to control and synchronize the scheduling of threads on the system. Kernel-managed objects include events, mutexes, semaphores, and timers.

Hardware Abstraction Layer

The hardware abstraction layer, or HAL, is the lowest level and most hardware-dependent layer of the Windows NT operating system. The HAL provides a very thin but critical interface between the operating system and the hardware. It essentially hides the implementation details of the hardware platform from the operating system and device drivers, making them much more portable among different flavors of hardware design.

Why is a HAL necessary, you ask? The answer is increased portability for NT. Recall that one of the design goals of Windows NT is to be easily portable across different CPU architectures. Now extend that concept to include portability between different computer makes and models that use the same processor architecture.

For example, both ISA (Industry Standard Architecture) and MCA (Micro Channel Architecture) systems use the Intel x86 CPU, but operating systems and device drivers must manipulate the hardware in very different ways on these systems. The HAL isolates the hardware variations and *abstracts* them to the rest of the operating system. This enables the operating system and device drivers to run unchanged on a wide variety of hardware platforms. Think of the HAL as virtual hardware.

HAL Services

The HAL exports APIs and data structures to the upper layers of the operating system and device drivers to handle hardware-dependent issues including the following:

- ✦ Processor initialization (especially support for SMP computers)
- ✦ Instruction cache and data cache control

- Device driver support (including bus addressing, interrupt control, DMA functions)
- Timing and interrupt functions (including performance monitoring support)
- Firmware interface functions
- Kernel debugger support
- Low-level error handling and error message display

The operation of the HAL is typically invisible to you, because your interaction with the system takes place through the Windows interface. However, when the NT system hits a fatal exception and stops, and you see the infamous *Blue Screen of Death*, the text is written to the screen by the kernel through the HAL interface. This is one admittedly unpleasant way to see the HAL in action.

The HAL doesn't hide all hardware dependencies from the operating system. For example, the entire operating system has been recompiled to run on each supported CPU architecture. Small portions of the kernel and virtual memory manager contain some code that's dependent on the CPU architecture. Device drivers typically contain device-specific code, but the differences between makes and models of systems using a particular CPU architecture are hidden inside the HAL.

HALs Everywhere

Microsoft provides as part of the operating system several HALs for each CPU platform supported. These files enable shrink-wrapped Windows NT to deal with common variations of system hardware designs. For example, NT includes different HALs for the Intel x86 platform to support standard ISA/EISA/PCI computers, MCA computers, Compaq SystemPro computers, systems based on the Corollary SMP design, and so forth. There's even a HAL that specifically works around an interrupt design flaw in an early version of the Intel 486. Microsoft supplies anywhere from three to a dozen different HALs for each supported CPU platform.

HAL'S SMP ROLE

In SMP systems, the HAL hides the details of how to recognize, initialize, and control the multiple processors. At boot time, the HAL determines if one or more of the processors has failed, and only tells the kernel about the processors that are in good health. For example, if the HAL realizes during the boot process that one processor is broken in a system containing four CPUs, the HAL presents a virtual set of three available CPUs to the kernel.

SMP computers are designed primarily for improved performance, not for fault tolerance. If a processor fails while the computer is running, the operating system halts. If the processor is still dead when the computer is restarted, the HAL hides the dead CPU from the kernel. Thus, SMP doesn't provide fault tolerance, except to the extent that it allows the computer to boot and run after a CPU failure.

HAL'S EVOLUTION

Microsoft originally conceived the HAL concept for NT to provide hardware-dependent support for various flavors of MIPS Rx000-based systems. As the NT team progressed on the port to the Intel x86 processor, they realized that more hardware-dependent details could be moved from other parts of the system into the HAL, making the upper layers of the operating system code more uniform across different hardware platforms. This had the effect of increasing the number of different HALs, while making the rest of the operating system much more hardware-independent.

As a general rule, the original names of the APIs that moved into the HAL didn't change, so if you have a HAL Development Kit, you can see where the functions existed originally by interpreting the API name prefixes. Several HAL function names begin with *Ke*, for example, revealing their original heritage as former kernel functions.

To deal with those systems not covered by the Microsoft-supplied HALs, computer manufacturers must use a HAL Development Kit from Microsoft to create their own customized HALs. These customized HALs are typically distributed with the computer hardware, and are often preinstalled with Windows NT on the systems.

Summary

In this chapter, you've looked into the depths of the Windows NT operating system architecture. Windows NT as a general-purpose operating system provides greater reliability, scalability, portability, security, and maintainability than any other version of Windows. With the release of NT 4.0, its usability and compatibility are close to that of Windows 95. Chapter 6 provides you with an in-depth comparison of Windows NT with other Microsoft Windows products.

I've purposely stayed at arm's length from the topic of networking in this chapter. Networking is central to Windows NT Server, so I cover it separately and in more depth in the chapters that follow. If you're new to networking, Chapter 3 provides valuable background on networking concepts. Chapter 4 introduces you to the specifics of Windows NT networking and designing your network based on Windows NT Server.

Welcome to the Network University

✦ ✦ ✦ ✦

Now that you've been through orientation and have chosen your major, it's time to attend class at the Network University. You already took a tutorial in NT anatomy in Chapter 2 — but that was just the beginning. By the end of this chapter, you'll be well on your way to your degree in computer networks.

If you've been thrown into the deep end of managing and maintaining and perhaps even building your organization's computer network, but you don't have much knowledge of networks, you've come to the right place. In this chapter, I lead you through the fundamentals of PC networks. You get a solid foundation of network basics onto which you can build more specific knowledge and experience in the chapters that follow. Because networks are central to the purpose and operation of Windows NT Server 4.0, you need to understand the key elements of networks up front.

If you already have real-world networking experience behind you, the material in this chapter will probably be old hat. If so, I recommend skipping this chapter to get your teeth into Chapter 4. There I fill you in on more specifics of networking with Windows NT Server. If you encounter unfamiliar terms in Chapter 4, you can come back to this chapter or refer to the Appendix B glossary.

Network Concepts

As you progress through your quest for network knowledge, it's easy to get overwhelmed at times by the complexities and acronyms that you encounter. When you feel as though you're getting stuck in a tar pit of terminology, just remember this. In its simplest form, a network consists of two connected computers that communicate with each other. Although most networks include more than two computers, understanding how two computers communicate goes a long way toward understanding how networks containing thousands of computers work. Keeping this in mind will help you in your journey through networks.

The network concept shouldn't be completely new to you. The telephone system is one network example that you've probably already directly experienced. This complex system creates the illusion of two tin cans connected by a string, albeit a very long string. In reality, the telephone network consists of many thousands of interconnected computerized and mechanical switching systems. Your conversation and the invisible signaling that happens before and after your chat are often routed through many systems in the telephone network. Conference calling, call-waiting, caller ID, and 900 numbers come to you courtesy of this huge, complex network.

What's in a LAN?

A *local area network*, or LAN, is a network of computers that spans a fairly limited area, typically ranging in scope from an office to a campus of buildings. LANs were originally intended to share expensive printers and large disk drives within an organization. This original purpose is still predominant today. Sharing printers and files remains the primary motivation for many businesses to build a LAN. More recently, businesses have started sharing other costly peripherals such as CD-ROM drives and high-speed modems. Figure 3-1 shows a simple LAN.

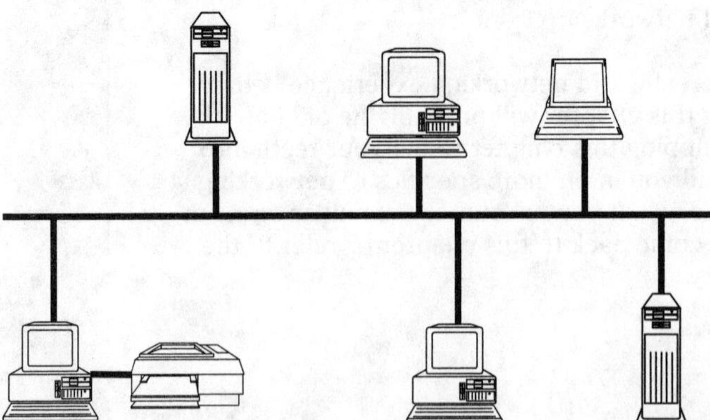

Figure 3-1: A local area network (LAN) connects computers over short distances to share resources and to communicate.

Over the past dozen or so years, the use of LANs has continued to evolve and broaden. Now an enterprise increasingly looks to the LAN to fulfill many of its communication needs. These requirements include

- E-mail
- Group scheduling
- Group project tracking
- Shared databases
- Access to the Internet
- Maintaining hardware and software inventories
- Connecting to mainframe systems

Windows NT Server 4.0, coupled with appropriate network-aware applications, is designed to meet these evolving corporate requirements.

Although a LAN covers a small geographic area, you shouldn't assume that LANs are small. A single local area network can contain two computers or several thousand. The LAN in my office, for example, currently connects three computers. The LAN on the Microsoft corporate campus connects well over 8,000 computers.

Widen the Scope

A *wide area network*, or WAN, is a network of computers that spans a large area, often connecting multiple sites of an enterprise across cities, states, countries, and even continents. Conceptually, a WAN is the same as a LAN. However, because WANs require long-distance connections between sites, often including leased lines and satellite links, they have their own special set of design, maintenance, and cost issues. WANs are sometimes called *long-haul networks*. Figure 3-2 depicts the WAN concept.

You might encounter the acronym MAN. Though it sounds quite sexist, MAN stands for metropolitan area network. The term is intended to cover large campus or city computer networks that span several miles — somewhere between a LAN and a WAN. I prefer to stick with just the LAN and WAN terms to distinguish between geographic scopes and leave the MAN alone.

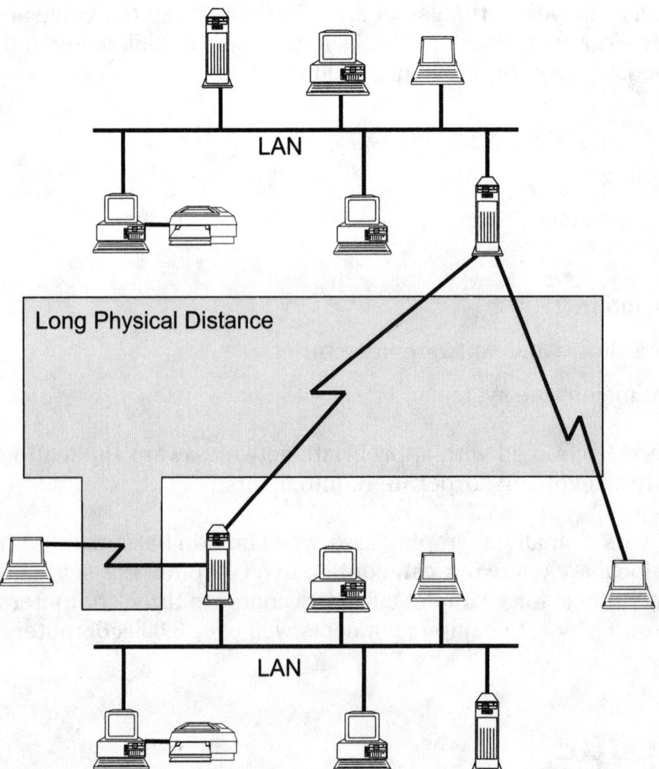

Figure 3-2: A wide area network (WAN) connects computers and LANs over long hauls.

You may have heard about the government project called SETI, or Search for Extra Terrestrial Intelligence. Scientists beam radio signals into the cosmos and listen for a response from the gray guys with the big eyes. Immense distances are involved in this communication. SETI might be considered a wireless WAN, if we were sure there was someone or something on the other end listening. Remember, you need at least two computers to form a network.

WANs often consist of interconnected LANs. Each site of a corporation might have its own LAN, with each site LAN connected by a WAN. Whenever you connect two or more networks together, you form an *internetwork*, sometimes called an *internet*. The term internet (with a small *i*) refers to any large network made up of interconnected smaller networks.

As you'll see in Chapter 4 and in later chapters, Windows NT Server includes support for WANs and internetworking.

Networks Are Everywhere

The largest internet in the world is the *Internet* (with a capital *I*). At the time of this writing, estimates indicate that the Internet connects more than 20,000 networks in 132 countries, with nearly 35 million users worldwide. These numbers have been climbing dramatically in the last couple of years. You'll find out how to get your Windows NT network plugged into the Internet in Part V.

What Are Nodes, Clients, and Servers?

Throughout this book, I use the term *node* to refer to any device directly connected to the network. Thus far, I've mainly talked about computers connected to the network, but other network-ready devices do exist. For example, you can attach certain laser printers directly to the network. HP's JetDirect laser printers are good examples. So, by definition, a JetDirect printer is as much of a node as your networked desktop PC.

The terms *client*, *server*, and *client/server* are often used to mean many different things. This can be very confusing, especially when you're first learning about networks. Let's define them precisely, and I promise to use them consistently throughout the book.

A *client* is a node on the network that accesses resources (files, printers, CD-ROMs) offered by another network node. Typically, your desktop PC is a client that accesses resources shared by another computer. The pivotal piece of software on the client node is the *redirector*, which forwards (or *redirects*) local requests to access shared resources on the network. A client is sometimes called a *workstation*, but this term has other implications that may be confusing. The Windows NT Workstation product, for example, can be both a client and a server, so I won't use the term *workstation* to

WHAT ABOUT INTRANETS?

You might have read or heard recently about the phenomena of *intranets*. This term has been a source of confusion to many. Translated literally from the original Latin and Middle English, intranet means "network inside." But it really boils down to this.

Corporations are using the great new Internet communication tools for internal communications to their employees who are connected to the corporate LAN. MIS departments are taking advantage of these tools to disseminate and gather corporate information in an attractive and effective way. They needn't be connected to the Internet to accomplish this.

mean *client.* Microsoft network clients can include computers running DOS, Windows 3.x, Windows for Workgroups, and Windows NT systems. DOS and Windows 3.x require additional software to enable them as network clients.

A *server* is a node on the network that provides shared resources to clients (see Figure 3-3). The key piece of software in Windows NT Server is the *server driver,* which fields requests received from the network and provides access to the requested resources. A server can be *dedicated* to a specific task, such as sharing a color printer or sharing a database file. A server can also be *nondedicated,* enabling you to use it to run local applications or to act as a network client, while the server functions take place in the background. Computers running Windows NT Server can act as either dedicated servers or nondedicated servers.

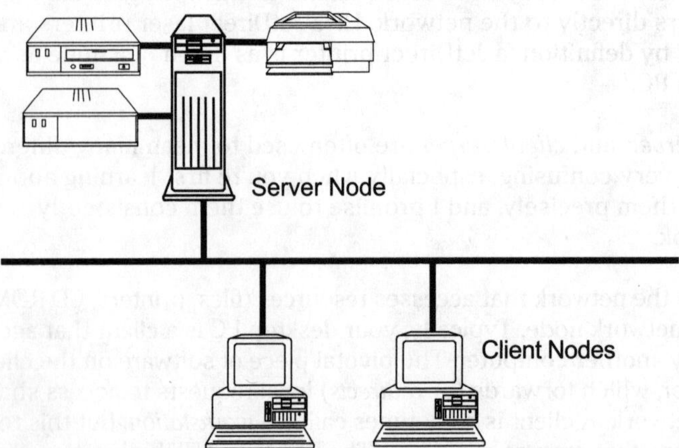

Figure 3-3: Client nodes gain access to server resources and services through server nodes.

Client/Server Defined

The term *client/server* is used for many things today. You saw in Chapter 2 that the Windows NT operating system uses a client/server model to implement some of its internal components. In the network world, client/server is sometimes used to refer simply to a network containing client and server computer systems. In other contexts, folks use client/server networking to refer to networks that contain dedicated servers.

In this book, unless I otherwise qualify it, I use the term *client/server* to refer to the relationship of actually sharing the workload between client and server applications on the network. Client/server applications go beyond simply sharing file and print resources. In this environment, clients ask servers to perform services on their behalf, typically returning results back to the clients. Part of the computing effort takes place on the client (front end), and part takes place on the server (back end). Microsoft SQL Server is a good example of a client/server application.

Enter the NOS

A *network operating system*, or NOS, controls network functions, manages resource sharing, and provides security and administrative tools. Traditionally, a NOS is software that sits on top of a general-purpose operating system, adding network functionality through device drivers, tools, and services. However, the term *NOS* also refers to general-purpose operating systems with network functionality built in, as with both Windows NT Workstation and Windows NT Server. Other examples of network operating systems include Windows for Workgroups, NetWare, LANtastic, Banyan VINES, OS/2 Warp Connect, IBM LAN Server, and Microsoft LAN Manager.

The acronym saga continues. I've seen some network literature call the underlying general-purpose operating system (used by the NOS) a workstation operating system, or WOS. Stay away from it. It's confusing.

Peer-to-Peer Networks

In a *workgroup* or *peer-to-peer network*, every node can be both a server and a client. Each node can share its resources with other nodes. Security and user account information is distributed to each node acting as a server. There's no centralized administration of this information, a limitation that can become a real problem as networks grow large.

A NOS that offers peer-to-peer networking is sometimes called a *peer NOS*. Windows NT Workstation, Windows for Workgroups, LANtastic, and OS/2 Warp Connect all offer peer-to-peer capabilities. Even Windows NT Server optionally offers this approach to networking, as you'll see later in this book.

Dedicated Server Networks

A *dedicated server network* is designed around one or more server nodes dedicated to acting as servers to the client nodes on the network. This approach is often characterized by centralized administration of security and user account information. Because of this, dedicated server networks are typically easier to administer and control, especially in large enterprise network installations. Windows NT Server, IBM OS/2 Warp Server, LANtastic Dedicated Server, and NetWare are all examples of dedicated server network products.

NETWORK CLUSTERING

One of the original design goals of NT was "distributed computing." At the time, this simply meant building networking support into the operating system. Today, truly distributed computing includes a concept called clustering. This approach involves logically tying multiple networked servers together in a cluster, to act as one large server. Workload is distributed across the clustered nodes, and other servers pick up the slack if one of the servers fails. At the time of this writing, both Microsoft and Digital (the folks who pioneered clustering several years ago) are readying clustering products for Windows NT. Watch for them.

In practice, many networks today are a combination of peer-to-peer and dedicated server networks. For example, many of the clients in a dedicated server network have and use the capability of sharing resources with other nodes on the network. Windows NT networks are no exception to this practice.

Start with the Hardware

I'm going to take a bottom-up approach to the discussion of networks. I start with the basic hardware skeleton and build up the layers of software required to create a functioning network.

Interconnection of PCs into a network requires several hardware components. Each PC needs to have a hardware spigot to enable connection to the network. Reliable connections among the PCs are needed, usually using some type of cable, but not always. Additional external components are sometimes needed to connect these computers.

The String

The method of physical connection among the PCs is the first choice that you need to make in planning a network design for your enterprise. Doing this first narrows the field of choices that you need to make for other network hardware components. Several cabling technologies are available, each with its own characteristics of speed, reliability, cost, and flexibility. I discuss them in detail in Chapter 8.

Today, most networks are built using some type of physical cabling, but wireless networks do exist. Compared with cabling, wireless networks are relatively expensive and are sometimes unreliable, slow, or both. I discuss this further in Chapter 8.

The Tin Cans

Once you've selected the network cabling to be installed in your facility, you need to equip each participating PC with a *network adapter*, sometimes called a network interface card, or NIC. The type of cabling that you've chosen narrows your number of choices for network adapters.

Network adapters are now readily available for reasonably low prices. Literally hundreds of choices pepper the market today. Nearly 200 different network adapters have been tested and found compatible with Windows NT Server 4.0, and many others not yet tested are fully compatible with these cards. In Chapter 8, I cover the ins and outs of network adapter selection, installation, and configuration.

The Connection Landscape

Once you have more than two nodes, the number of possible ways to connect them together increases. For practical reasons, you can't typically connect every node directly to every other node on the network. Thus, a handful of connection arrangements has emerged from which you can choose. The arrangement of nodes relative to each other and to the network connections is called the *topology* of the network. The three topologies that predominate today are the *bus*, the *star*, and the *ring*. All of these topologies can be used in a Windows NT Server network, so let's look at each one in turn.

Bus Topology

The bus topology connects each node to a single cable, called a bus, as shown in Figure 3-4. The bus shuttles data back and forth between the nodes connected to the network. Terminators at each end of the cable prevent the data from falling out the ends of the bus or from bouncing off the walls and back into the cable. (If you understand what terminators really do, you know I'm kidding. If you don't, then this is a good way to think of it and will get you laughs when you chat with hardware gurus.) In a bus topology, data transmissions from one PC to another are seen by all nodes on the network. Nosy users can eavesdrop on the raw data as it passes by on the bus.

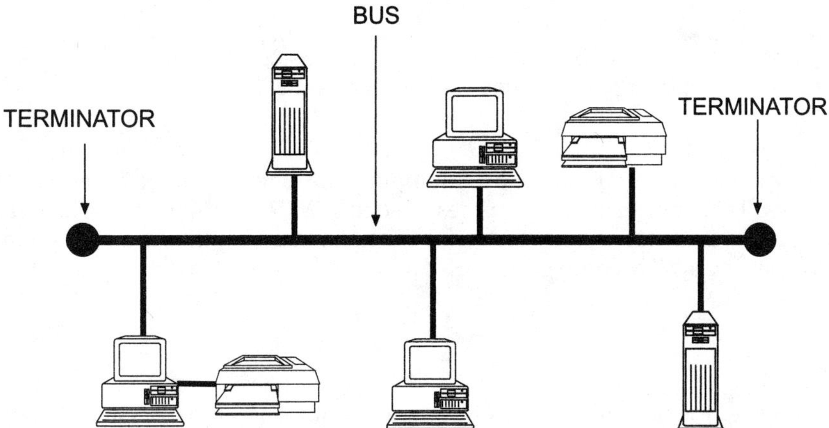

Figure 3-4: The bus topology connects all nodes to a single cable, called a *bus*.

Star Topology

The star topology connects each node to a central device called a *hub*. To continue with the transportation analogy, consider how large airlines schedule their connecting flights. Delta Airlines, for example, uses Atlanta as a hub city, routing most of its connecting flights through this single airport. If you want to travel from Phoenix to Cleveland, you would likely fly from Phoenix to Atlanta, and then from Atlanta to Cleveland.

Figure 3-5 illustrates the star network topology, in which data flows back and forth to each PC through the central hub. Data transmissions between two PCs on the star are seen only by the central hub.

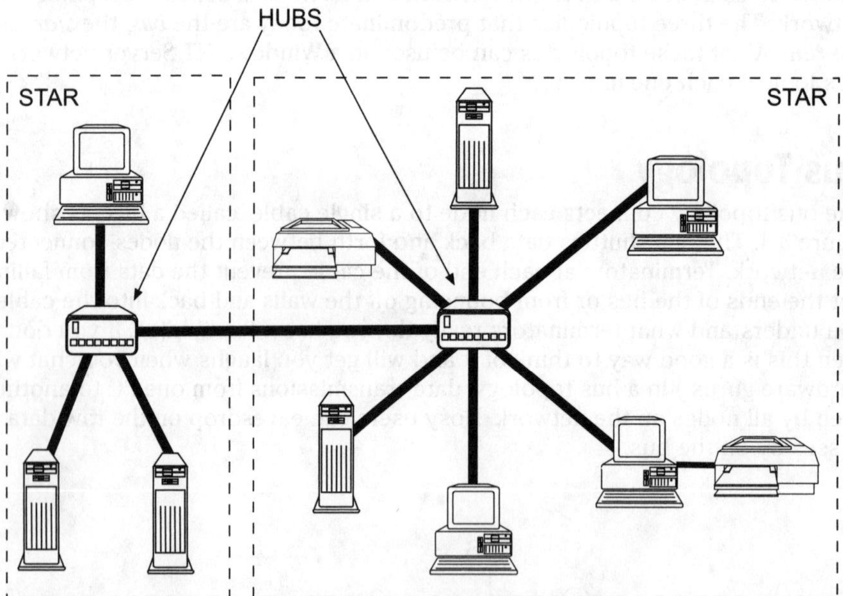

Figure 3-5: The star topology connects nodes to a central hub.

As shown in Figure 3-5, you can use multiple hubs, connect them, and create larger networks. This approach is sometimes used in a WAN environment, where each office has its own star-shaped LAN, and the hubs at each office are hooked up to each other via a WAN connection.

Ring Topology

In the ring topology, the network forms a single data path from one node to the next, with the first and last nodes in the path connected to each other. In other words, the network is an unbroken circle or ring of nodes, as you can see in Figure 3-6. If you start at any node in a ring network and follow the data path in one direction, you sequentially visit all other nodes on the network and end up where you started. Data travels in one direction around the ring, passing from one node to the next. The fact that data is seen by all networked nodes on the ring between the sending and receiving nodes makes the ring topology similar to bus topology, in terms of security.

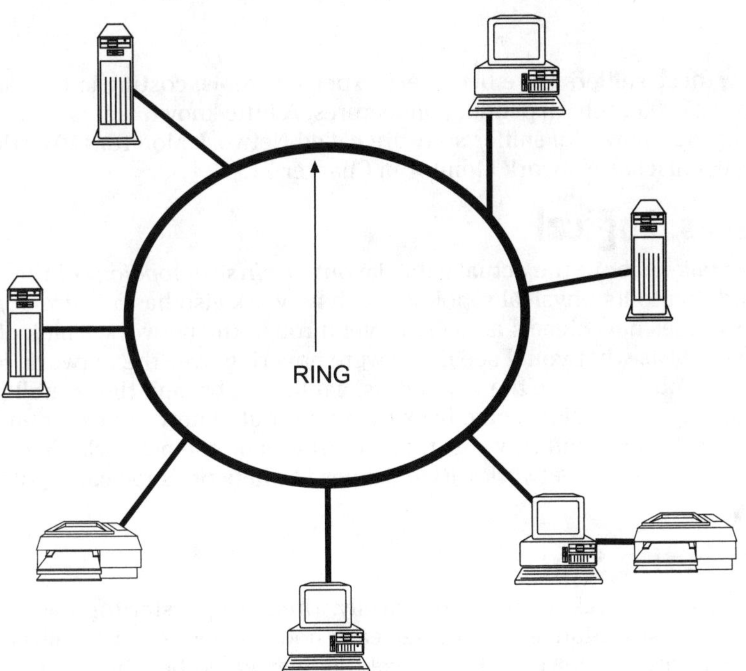

Figure 3-6: The ring topology connects all nodes to a logical unbroken ring.

Legitimate Eavesdropping

I've mentioned the fact that, in some network topologies, data can be seen by each computer attached to the network. A *network analyzer*, sometimes called a *sniffer*, is a special device used to capture and interpret raw data sent over the network. If data passes by a sniffer device, the data can be captured regardless of its intended destination. Network professionals legitimately use sniffers as diagnostic and troubleshooting tools.

INSIDE STORY

Before its release as a product, the internal Microsoft code name for Network Monitor was *Bloodhound*, because it was designed to be "a great sniffer." The bloodhound legacy lives on in some of the Network Monitor's terminology. For example, components of this application communicate using a mechanism buried deep in the product called BONE, which stands for Bloodhound-Oriented Network Entity. Of course, as with all other Microsoft products, the folks in the NT team actually used early versions of Bloodhound to solve real-world problems on their test networks. At Microsoft, this practice of using your own product is called "eating your own dog food." This part of the business sure seems to be dog-eat-dog.

Traditionally, these sniffers have been very expensive tools, costing in the range of $10,000 to $25,000 each, depending on features. A little-known fact is that Microsoft included powerful sniffer software called Network Monitor in Windows NT Server 4.0. I discuss Network Monitor in Chapter 21.

Physical vs. Logical

Thus far, I've talked about the actual cable layout or *physical topology* of these networks. In addition to its physical topology, each network also has a *logical topology*, which describes how signals actually travel through the network. Think of the physical topology as what you'd see if you were hovering over the network, looking down on it. You would see the computers, cabling, hubs, and the overall physical wiring topology used. Now come back from your out-of-network experience, enter the network cable, and travel as the data travels on the network. The path that you take through the network wiring defines the network's logical topology.

The Star is the Star

In practice, most networks today are physically wired using a star topology. If you hover above the installation again, you see each node cabled to a centralized hub device in a star pattern. However, the logical topology could be a bus, a star, or a ring, depending on how the cables and hub are configured. For example, a network with a physical star topology can have a logical bus topology. In this case, all data is transmitted to all attached nodes.

Figure 3-7 shows a physical star topology that is a logical ring topology. Even though the nodes are wired like a star, attached to a central hub, the data travels from one node to another in only one direction, forming a logical ring. Follow the arrows in the Figure 3-7 to prove it to yourself.

As you might have guessed at this point, hubs come in several flavors. A hub can be either *passive* or *active*. Passive hubs simply act as a centralized wiring box and do nothing to the data transmitted through them. An active hub can provide enhancements limited only by the imagination of the hub manufacturer. These capabilities range from simply amplifying and improving weak or distorted signals to sophisticated diagnostic, management, and reporting features.

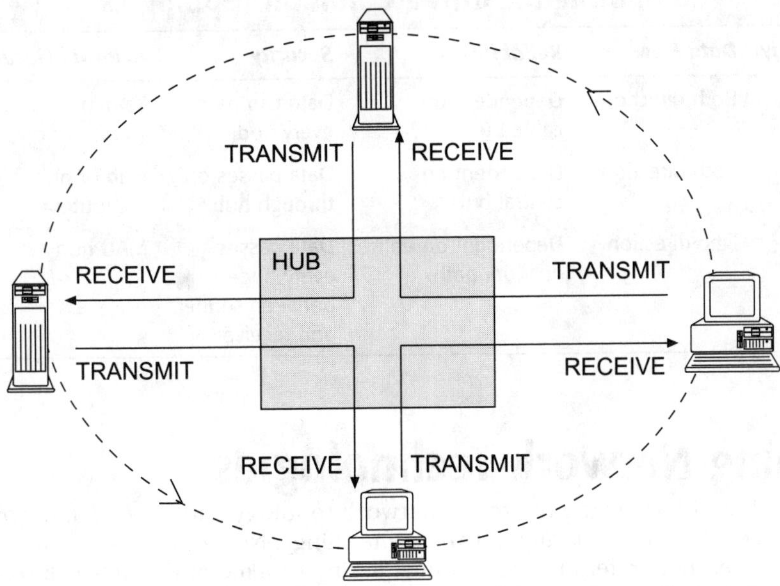

Figure 3-7: A network with a physical star topology can have a logical ring topology.

A bus network is often physically configured as a star, using a simple hub. A ring network is almost always physically laid out as a star. It operates logically as a ring network by using a special hub device called a *multistation access unit*, or MAU. (You might also see the acronym MSAU, which means the same thing as MAU.) This is the type of hub used in Figure 3-7.

Star Advantages

Why is the star the predominant physical topology? First, this approach enables all network cables to converge in a central location. This simplifies troubleshooting, reconfiguring, and disabling misbehaving nodes attached to the network. Second, because each node is connected to the network via its own dedicated cable, it's easy to add, move, and remove nodes as requirements change. Finally, because many manufacturers are now building intelligence into hubs, they can have the advantage of providing centralized management and diagnostic tools.

Table 3-1 summarizes this discussion of the three common network topologies, in terms of the flow of data, reliability considerations, security, and additional external hardware required.

Table 3-1
Comparing the Three Common Topologies

Topology	*Data Flow*	*Reliability*	*Security*	*External Hardware*
Bus	Both directions	Dependent on cable bus	Data can pass every node	Terminators (hubs are optional)
Star	Both directions	Dependent on central hub	Data passes only through hub	Hub or hub computer
Ring	One direction	Dependent on entire network path	Data passes every node between sender and receiver	MAU hub

Examining Network Technologies

I've often heard folks using the terms network topology and *network technology* interchangeably. They're really not the same things. Network topology, as you've just learned, refers to the physical wiring scheme of the network (the physical topology) and the logical path taken by the data within the network (the logical topology).

Network technology, on the other hand, refers to a specific set of standards for addressing, accessing, arbitrating, and transmitting between nodes on the network. The two most common network technologies in use today are *Ethernet* and *Token Ring*. Windows NT Server supports both of these network technologies, as well as others.

Ethernet

Ethernet technology was developed back in 1973 at Xerox's Palo Alto Research Center. Ethernet is very popular and is widely used today. It enjoys broad hardware and software support in the marketplace, and fierce competition has driven hardware prices low. Although market share figures vary with each published survey, most folks agree that Ethernet makes up the bulk of the LAN market today.

Ethernet Rides the Bus

Regardless of how it's physically wired, the logical topology of an Ethernet network is always a bus. Ethernet can be physically configured using either a bus or star topology. The physical bus topology is getting less prevalent, except perhaps in networks of two or three computers. In most cases, if the network is physically wired as a bus, you'll see coaxial cable (similar to cable TV cable) used to connect the computers. If a star topology is used in an Ethernet network, you'll almost always see twisted-pair cable (similar to telephone wire) between computers and hubs. I tell you more about Ethernet cabling alternatives in Chapter 8.

You may sometimes hear or read the terms medium or network medium used to describe the physical network path, which might be anything from cable to radio waves. Although these generic terms are precise, they are a little too abstract for me. I typically use the word cable to refer to the network connections between nodes.

Because an Ethernet network is logically a bus, all nodes are connected to the same cable, and everyone hears everyone else's data transmissions. This approach of sharing a single cable is known as *multiple access*. Because all networked nodes use a single cable for communication, they must learn to share and play nice. Only one node is allowed to transmit at a time, so somehow they have to agree on how to access the shared bus.

Avoiding Collisions

Consider a telephone party line. They're not as common as they used to be, but they still exist in a few areas. If you've never had one, here's how they work. A single phone line is shared by several households, sort of like having phone extensions to your line in several other households. When you want to make a call, you pick up the phone and listen. If you don't hear anyone else using the line, you can go ahead and use it. If you do hear someone using it, you're supposed to hang up and try again later.

Likewise, if you're already talking on the phone line and someone else tries to use it, that person is supposed to hang up immediately and try later. Occasionally, he or she feels that his or her call is more urgent than yours and will ask you to hang up. If your call isn't as urgent, you might agree to hang up and let him or her use the line.

In the Ethernet world, as in the telephone party line scenario, all participants have to be good listeners. Before transmitting data (making a call) on the bus (party line), a node needs to listen to the bus to hear if anyone else is transmitting. This is known as *carrier sensing*.

When two networked nodes attempt to send data on the cable at the same time, a *collision* occurs. Both transmissions fail. The two nodes must each wait for a short, random time period, and then they each try again. The short waiting period is politely saying to the other node, "No, after you." If the waiting time periods weren't random, the same two transmissions would collide again on the next attempt.

After transmitting its data, a node continues to listen to the bus for a collision with its transmission. This is similar to listening for someone else attempting to use the party line and is known as *collision detection.* The difference here is that the node detecting the collision (hearing someone else trying to use the line) always backs off (hangs up) and tries again later. Talk about being polite!

Access Methods

The set of rules used by a network technology to arbitrate the use of the network cable is called the *access method.* Ethernet's access method is known as CSMA/CD, a mouthful of letters which stand for **C**arrier **S**ense **M**ultiple **A**ccess with **C**ollision **D**etection. Based on the preceding discussion, you should be able to see the origins of this access method description. (Don't you just love easy-to-remember acronyms such as this one? I once contracted briefly at AT&T, and on my first day was presented with a huge bound volume containing nothing but acronym definitions. As I looked up the various acronyms that I encountered, I discovered a frightening truth. Most of the acronyms had more than one definition, and some had as many as five. These things caused more confusion than they eliminated.)

A network technology such as Ethernet includes specification of many details including data transmission speed, electrical characteristics of the signals on the cable, amount of data allowed in each transmission, and the access method. Although the other details are important, the access method is typically the most distinguishing factor among the various network technologies. You'll see a dramatically different access method in the next section.

Most Ethernet hubs have collision detection lights that glow red if they detect many collisions on the network. If heavy network traffic starts using up much more than 35 percent of the total network bandwidth, collisions increase dramatically, and your users begin to notice slower network responsiveness. In practice, most networks use less bandwidth than this, and collisions aren't a huge issue.

However, if they do become a problem, you can consider segmenting the network using a bridge, which I discuss in Chapter 8.

Token Ring

Token Ring technology was developed by IBM and introduced in 1984. Although it's now an industry standard, it's still considered by many to be a technology proprietary to IBM. You'll find that it's most popular in "blue" businesses with heavy commitment to IBM equipment, where close integration with IBM mainframes or minicomputers is required. Elsewhere, you'll probably see Ethernet. One reason for this is that the cost of adding a node to a Token Ring network can run anywhere from two to five times the cost of adding a node to an Ethernet network. However, you'll see that Token Ring does have some advantages over Ethernet in certain situations. Token Ring is fully supported by Windows NT, and you can choose from several NT-compatible Token Ring networks.

INSIDE STORY

The misty rain pelted the skylights of Microsoft Buildings One and Two, as test engineers ran up and down dozens of rows of computers in labs to fire up the toughest network stress tests in the history of the NT project. These frantic folk were oblivious to the outdoor weather conditions, since on any given day in Redmond, a guess of misty rain would probably be a correct one. The goal on this particular gloomy day was to have at least 1,000 computers participating in a companywide NT network stress test – the first of what would prove to be many such ordeals.

Stress tests are designed to uncover problems in one day that might take weeks or months to encounter at a real customer site. The idea is to compress as much activity into the shortest time possible, often repeating the same operations over and over. In addition, these tests are designed to have lots of these intense activities happening all at once, to hit as many different situations as possible.

On this particular damp day, the network stress test was designed to pelt several powerful Windows NT SMP servers with data from as many client computers as the team could muster. And, from the servers' perspectives, this test was going to be more like a torrential rainstorm than the half-hearted mist that drizzled down the windowpanes. If a server drowned in the data flood, it meant that we'd uncovered a nasty bug to fix. If a server survived, we'd know that the product was extremely stable. Either way, we'd win.

Earlier that afternoon, Bill Gates had sent e-mail to other parts of Microsoft on behalf of the NT group. He'd asked them to help the NT team reach their goal of 1,000 stress test computers participating that night. This assistance from above was intended to help us achieve our goal. Before people went home that evening, they downloaded and cranked up the NT stress test on their desktop PCs.

A few stalwart volunteer test engineers monitored the test through the night. The number of participating computers climbed quickly to 850, then 927, and then hovered for a time around 980. Managers made the rounds to empty offices, starting the stress test on any idle computer they found. Engineers pulled in a few more lab computers. A team somewhere else in the company finally called it a night and started the tests on their own desktop PCs.

The results? All that company teamwork and cooperation paid off. We got well over 1,000 computers pelting data at the NT servers under test. Some of the servers stayed up the entire time without a hitch, with all of those client computers pounding on them for hours. Others had some problems and provided us with valuable information on what needed to be fixed.

Overall, the test was a success. That night, the team had proved the stability of NT and gathered enough information to improve the product even more. And, as the bleary-eyed test engineers headed for the parking lot, the chilly Redmond mist woke them up just enough to drive safely home.

Token Ring Around a Star

The physical topology of a Token Ring network is always a star, but the logical topology is always a ring, as demonstrated in Figure 3-7. As I mentioned earlier, all nodes are connected to a special hub called a MAU, which configures the logical network topology into an unbroken ring of nodes. Figure 3-7 shows the path that data travels in a Token Ring network. The connection between the node and the MAU hub has two sides. Data comes into the node from the hub on one side, and data is sent from the node to the hub on the other. Whenever you connect a new node to the hub, you effectively insert that node into the logical ring.

As I mentioned in the Ethernet discussion, the major distinguishing factor among different network technologies is the access method used. I also promised you a very different access method. Have I ever let you down? Token Ring network technology uses a very distinctive access method, called *token passing*.

Passing the Token

A *token* is a special little message that constantly circulates around the ring. Remember the Chance card in Monopoly that read, "Advance *token* to the nearest railroad"? In this game, you moved your token (the little shoe, or dog, or thimble) around the board in one direction. This could go on forever until you ran out of money or drove everyone else out of the game. Likewise, the token in a Token Ring sails around the network ring constantly.

If a node has no data to send on the network, it receives the token and passes it to the next node in the ring. This activity continues until someone has something to say. When a node wants to transmit data on the network, it must wait for the token to arrive. At this point, the node seizes control of the token and transmits the data. During this time, no other nodes even attempt to send data, because they don't hold the token. While the data is circulating on the ring, each node briefly peeks at the data to see if it's the recipient. If the data is meant for someone else, the node just forwards it to the next node. When the receiving node sees that it's supposed to receive the data, it reads it off the network. Once the data is transmitted successfully, the sending node releases control of the token by sending it out onto the ring again.

Eliminating Collisons

Notice that no collisions occur in this access method, because only one node ever attempts to send data at a given time. Token Ring technology isn't without its problems, however. For instance, sometimes the token gets lost. (Don't ask me where these tokens go. Theories abound that the lost tokens are in the same place as those single socks that disappear from your dryer.) When the circulating token is lost, no one has permission to send data, and it's very quiet in the network — too quiet. To remedy this and other unusual situations, one of the nodes on the ring, called the *active monitor*, is dedicated to detecting errors. Among other duties, it regenerates a new circulating token when the token has been lost.

The Case for Token Ring

Situations arise in which Token Ring is preferable to Ethernet. In a factory automation project on which I worked at Texas Instruments, we connected a large number of microcomputers on the factory floor to an IBM mainframe. Each microcomputer was attached to several robot devices in the factory, including robotic arms, automated warehouses, ion implanters, and mobile robots transporting material. It was critical to assure immediate communication of any problems encountered by these robotic devices, and this communication had to happen over the LAN.

We selected Token Ring as our network technology for two reasons. First, connectivity to the IBM mainframe was required, and support for Token Ring connectivity to this system was readily available to us. Second, we had to assure that each computer had an equal and periodic chance to communicate on the network. Ethernet couldn't guarantee this, but Token Ring could. Because of the token-passing access method, each computer was frequently given a turn to send data.

Faster Network Technologies

Businesses are placing increasing demands on networking bandwidth, trying to push huge amounts of data over the wire to support real-time imaging, voice, and video. Current networking technologies are often straining under the load. The network cable has, in some installations, become a narrow funnel that's choking the flow of data required for these new applications. Newer network technologies such as FDDI (Fiber Distributed Data Interface), Fast Ethernet, and ATM (Asynchronous Transfer Mode) have emerged to help. Windows NT Server already supports many of these technologies, and support will grow as new technologies emerge.

In Chapter 8, I discuss these other technologies, as well as the nuts and bolts of how to design and configure your Windows NT Server network.

Lay on the Software Layers

Thus far, I've focused only on the hardware concepts associated with networks. But what about the software required to make the data fly among the networked computers? And how do the hardware components I've just talked about work together with the software pieces to transfer data?

In the early years of computer networking, each computer manufacturer defined its own mechanism for communicating between its systems. Their approaches were proprietary. A computer from one manufacturer typically couldn't communicate with a computer from another. In other words, each manufacturer used a different internal language for transmitting data on its network. One manufacturer's network didn't understand the languages that other networks spoke. It was a veritable Tower of Babel.

A Matter of Protocol

The term *protocol* is used to describe the rules and conventions for communicating between computers. In a sense, a protocol is an agreed-upon language, dialect, and set of cultural conventions used on the network. You may be familiar with the protocol term from the world of international diplomacy. Ambassadors and visiting heads of state must follow the local protocol (governing both speech and behavior) to avoid miscommunication and international incidents. The consequences of not adhering to the local protocol can range from simple misunderstandings to all-out wars. On computer networks, the consequence of using different protocols is termination of all diplomatic relations before they even get started.

Setting Standards

Because of the need for different networks to communicate with each other and because of the growing complexity of network hardware and software, some sort of standard was necessary. So, in the early 1980s, a committee of network professionals created a standard for network design called the Open Systems Interconnection (OSI) Reference Model. The OSI model describes the flow of data between the physical network connection and your application. The idea behind this model is to provide an organized, layered description of network communication to be used as the basis for network design. The model is open rather than proprietary. Everyone is encouraged to share its details, create products that are compatible with one another, and add value by building products that extend existing ones.

The OSI Model

Open any mathematics textbook targeted at grades two through eight, turn to its first chapter, and you're likely to see a lesson on sets. (At least, this was true for the textbooks I used in those grades. Your mathematics training may vary.) I recall feeling frustrated at seeing the same lessons on sets warmed over at the beginning of each school year. Now I realize that I still remember what subsets, supersets, unions, and intersections are. Those lessons on sets taught me a model of looking at the world and classifying things that stuck. When I grew up, it even became useful in my computer science career, believe it or not.

My feelings about the OSI model are similar to those that I used to have about sets. When I'd open any book on networking to the first few chapters, I'd find myself painfully plodding through page after page of OSI drivel. However, after I learned more about networking and began to delve into how computer systems talk to each other, that drivel began to take on fresh meaning. At that point, I realized that the OSI model provides a valuable way of looking at networks and understanding the relationships among all of the hardware and software components needed to make them work. Repetition never hurts, especially if you end up with a tool that you can really apply and use. Understanding the OSI model is a valuable part of your networking education.

FROM ISO TO OSI

The folks who created the OSI model started their work in 1977 and completed it in 1984. They began with a proposal originally put forth by the International Standards Organization (ISO). The ISO consists of a huge number of committees and individual country organizations that participate in the creation of worldwide standards. (They haven't generated any galaxy-wide standards yet, due to lack of representation. I suspect they asked the marooned Roswell alien to participate, but this has never been confirmed or denied, except by the *National Enquirer*.)

In networking literature or discussions, you may see or hear references to the ISO/OSI Reference Model. In the interest of cutting down your diet of alphabet soup, I refer to it as the OSI model in this book.

The Ideal Network

The OSI model is just that — a model. It doesn't describe a particular network design; rather, it describes what some would call an ideal network design. Although this model has proven valuable to the network industry, actual products rarely match the OSI model exactly. Thus, the OSI model becomes, for you and me, an excellent tool for analyzing existing network designs. It provides a framework for understanding how these designs operate. In later sections, I'll use this framework to show how several of the Windows NT network protocols work.

Now, let's take a look at the OSI model, what it means, and what it buys you. Figure 3-8 identifies the seven layers of the OSI model for networking.

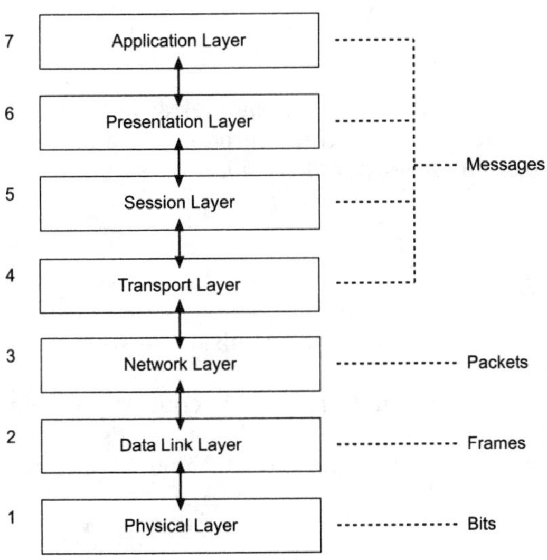

Figure 3-8: The seven layers of the OSI model provide a framework for understanding networks.

Layers upon Layers

Each layer in the OSI model provides services to the layers above and below it. Each layer also hides the implementation details of the lower layers from the layers above it. Thus, a given layer communicates only with the layers immediately above and below it. This approach, even outside of network territory, leads to more modular designs. Recall from Chapter 2 that Windows NT itself uses layered design techniques to provide services and hide implementation details.

You'll see in Chapter 4 how the networking components of Windows NT Server fit into the OSI model. Let's start at the bottom and work our way up through the model's layers.

The Physical Layer

The lowest layer of the OSI model, called the *physical layer*, defines the physical transmission of raw data between nodes on the network. The physical layer includes the specification of the network cable itself, as well as details of how bits are fundamentally transmitted on that cable. For example, the physical layer defines what voltage is used to transmit a binary 1 and what other voltage is used to represent a binary 0. In addition, this layer deals with such issues as how many pins exist in the network connector, what each pin does, what the details of transmission timing are, and so on.

Physical characteristics of data transmission differ among cable types, as well as among the various network technologies such as Ethernet and Token Ring. These physical transmission differences are dealt with in the physical layer. It hides the gory transmission details from all other layers above it. The service it provides to the upper layers is physical transmission and reception of raw binary data on the network cable.

The Data Link Layer

Unlike the physical layer, which deals with data as a meaningless stream of binary data, the *data link layer* begins to put some structure on the information. Rather than dealing with just bits, the data link layer handles *frames* of data.

Frames of Data

Frames are logical chunks that include not only the data to be transferred, but also some additional information. The latter includes the source and destination of the data and information that enables detection of transmission errors.

You should be thankful that I'm using the term frame in this context. The official OSI term for this chunk of data is physical-layer-service-data-unit. It's not much fun to write or read, but you might want to impress (or alienate) your friends with it at your next network administrators' party.

Fundamentally, the data link layer translates an outgoing data frame into a raw bit stream and delivers this to the physical layer for transmission. As data comes in from the network, the data link layer translates the raw bits received from the physical layer into data frames. The format of the frame differs among network technologies. An Ethernet frame looks slightly different from a Token Ring frame, for example. These differences are handled in this layer of the model.

However, there's much more to the data link layer than simply packing and unpacking data frames. This layer is also responsible for implementing the network technology's access method. On an Ethernet network, the data link layer must deal with collision detection on the bus, as you saw earlier in the Ethernet section. Likewise, this layer handles token passing on a Token Ring network.

In addition to managing the access method, the data link layer manages node-to-node communication on the network. It's responsible for assuring an error-free communication path between nodes. This enables all layers above the data link layer to assume that they have a reliable data transmission facility underneath. The upper layers don't need to worry about lost or corrupted data. The data link layer accomplishes all this communication magic using *node addresses* and error detection information in the data frame.

Node Addresses

Consider for a moment your home address, which defines your unique physical location on a particular street. How was your address created? Typically, it was preassigned to your house or apartment by the builder or the city. Having this address makes it easy for Sears to deliver your new refrigerator, for Mom to send you those cookies, or for the cable TV installer to show up three hours late to your door.

Each node has its own address on the network. A node address is typically programmed into the network adapter by its manufacturer. The address provides a unique way of identifying the node on the network. Each frame at the data link layer contains both the source node address and the destination node address.

Avoiding Corruption

External electrical noise can blow away an entire data frame traveling on a network. To guarantee delivery, the data link layer must use some sort of acknowledgment approach to assure the frame arrived at its destination address. Typically, the sending node transmits the frame and waits for a special acknowledgment frame from the receiving node. On the other end, the receiving node pulls the frame off the network. If it arrives intact, the receiving node transmits an acknowledgment frame back to the original sending node. If the sender sees no acknowledgment after a specified period of time, it retransmits the original frame.

In practice, the data link layer doesn't typically wait idly for the acknowledgment. It keeps on sending other data frames upon request from the layers above and continues to receive other data frames and acknowledgments of previous frames that it sent. It keeps track of outstanding frames that haven't been acknowledged.

What if the data frame arrives just fine, but the acknowledgment frame is lost on its return trip to the sender node? If the acknowledgment never arrives, the sender must retransmit the original data frame. Because the frame already arrived at its destination (only the acknowledgment was lost), the retransmitted frame is a duplicate. The data link layer must then take steps to recognize and ignore the duplicate frame.

Noise on the network can also corrupt the contents of a frame. Even though it arrives at its destination, the contents may have been altered along the way. It's critical that the data link layer provides error-free data to the upper layers, so this layer must detect and discard damaged frames. Before sending a frame, the data link layer calculates a special error-detecting code and attaches it to the frame. On the receiving end, the data link layer calculates the code again and compares it against the original code embedded in the frame. If they match, the data arrived intact. If they don't match, the data link layer concludes that some part of the data was damaged along the way and must be resent.

The error-detecting code attached to the data frame is typically called a CRC, which stands for cyclic redundancy code, or sometimes cyclic redundancy check. It's easily calculated based on the remainder of the data in the frame. As a rule, the network adapter calculates and verifies the CRC in hardware. The CRC is an error-detecting code, not an error-correcting code. It enables detection of an error so the frame can be discarded and retransmitted. It doesn't provide the error-correcting information required to regenerate damaged data.

Where Is the Data Link Layer?

The combination of the physical layer and the data link layer is typically handled within the network adapter device driver, the network adapter hardware itself, and the physical connection between the nodes. Moreover, these layers are defined by the network technologies used, such as Ethernet and Token Ring. This makes sense, because network adapters are very different animals for different network technologies.

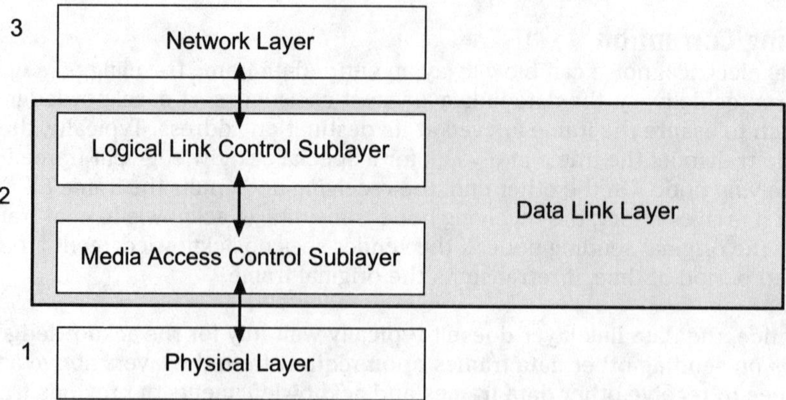

Figure 3-9: The LLC and MAC layers are sublayers of the OSI data link layer.

With these two layers defined, you can transmit small chunks of data between two connected nodes on a network. Each node examines every frame and picks up only those frames that bear its destination address. At a rudimentary level, these two layers provide all of the ingredients for bare-bones communication on a simple network. However, networks are rarely simple for very long.

The Network Layer

How do you send a chunk of data (say, a file) that's larger than the maximum allowed by the data link layer? How do you send data efficiently between nodes that aren't directly connected to each other? These and other questions are addressed by the *network layer.*

Packets of Data

Just as the data link layer dealt with frames, the network layer deals with *packets.* A packet is simply a chunk of information that contains the original data to be transmitted, along with some additional addressing information. If a packet is too large to be transmitted in a single shot by the data link layer, the network layer breaks it into multiple pieces and sends them through the data link layer. It then reassembles the packet at the receiving end.

The additional addressing information in the packet puts the packet on the right path toward its final destination. The network layer performs any necessary translations of names into network addresses, then picks an appropriate route for the data to travel to its destination. Why select a route? In a given network, there might be many possible paths between the source and destination of a transmission. Rather than flood all possible paths on the network with redundant packets, the network layer picks one route.

LAYERS WITHIN LAYERS

Because the data link layer has several responsibilities, it's sometimes further subdivided into two smaller layers. These sublayers have been formally defined as *logical link control,* or LLC, and *media access control,* or MAC. (Just what you needed, more layers and more acronyms.)

As Figure 3-9 illustrates, LLC is the higher of the two sublayers. It manages the node-to-node communication flow. MAC is the lower of the two sublayers and handles, as you might guess, the network technology's access method. It's also responsible for assuring error-free transmission.

Although not part of the OSI model, these sublayers are defined in an IEEE standard, and you'll hear them in networking discussions. The MAC acronym is particularly confusing, as folks easily mistake it for a reference to the Macintosh computer. I stay away from using this acronym for either purpose. When I must use it, I always use the term *MAC sublayer.*

The approach to selecting which route to take varies widely with different network designs. In the simplest case, the route is determined by a static table that rarely changes. In the most complex case, the network layer figures out the best route for each packet to take, based on current network traffic conditions. Either way, the network layer strives to put the packet on the most efficient path possible toward its final destination.

NT's Network Layer

I define and discuss Windows NT Server protocols in Chapter 4, but it's useful to mention a couple of points here. Windows NT Server provides IPX and IP protocols at the network layer. The Microsoft NetBEUI protocol has some components of the network layer, but because this protocol doesn't support routing, its network layer is not complete.

The network layer performs no error checking. It sends the packet on its way toward its final destination and always assumes its safe arrival. On the surface, this is a reasonable assumption given the high reliability of today's networks. However, because errors do occur, the network layer is considered an unreliable service. There's no feedback mechanism in this layer to detect lost or damaged packets. As for guaranteeing safe arrival, the network layer says, "It's not my job."

The Transport Layer

Unlike the network layer, the *transport layer* provides a reliable end-to-end delivery service. Whereas the data link layer assures delivery of frames between two nodes along the data's path, the transport layer assures delivery between the source and destination. It processes *messages,* which, like frames, are chunks that contain the data to be transmitted, along with additional control information. The transport layer accepts messages from and delivers messages to the appropriate processes on the local node. This layer enables processes on two different nodes to converse with each other.

Passing Messages

The transport layer breaks long messages into smaller packets before sending them to the network layer. In some cases, the transport layer takes several short messages and bundles them in a single packet, to transmit the data in the most efficient way possible. On the receiving end, this layer unpacks packed messages, reassembles small packets into long messages, and takes care of acknowledging receipt.

Windows NT Server provides TCP and SPX protocols at the transport layer. Microsoft's NetBEUI provides some transport-layer functionality. I define and explain the NT protocols in Chapter 4.

In the layers I've covered so far, each layer has handled a different chunk of data. From the transport layer on up through all remaining OSI model layers, the chunks of data passed between layers are called *messages.*

The Session Layer

The *session layer* negotiates and maintains connections between processes on different nodes. Rather than focusing on delivering individual messages, this layer handles complete dialogs between processes. Conversations between processes on different nodes are established, maintained, and terminated by the session layer.

Establishing the connection, called a *session,* often involves some sort of security authentication. This might involve a user action such as logging on to the network, or it might involve two processes negotiating over how they plan to communicate.

In addition to establishing connections between processes, the session layer is responsible for supporting transaction-based applications. For example, if a series of commands to a database must be completely carried out to avoid leaving the database in an inconsistent state, the session layer provides a mechanism to assure that this happens. The session layer can also provide data *checkpoints.* Using a checkpoint, a node can say, "I've heard everything in our conversation up to this point." If the network fails, only data sent after the last checkpoint needs to be retransmitted.

REDIRECTORS AND SERVERS

At the session layer, network operating systems typically provide special drivers that perform vital networking functions. In Windows NT, these key networking components are called the *redirector* and the *server.*

A redirector routes, or redirects, requests for network resources from the local computer to the network. (The term *redirector* is Microsoft terminology. Novell uses the term *requester* for its version of this component.) For example, establishing an association between a drive letter and a shared directory elsewhere on the network and transferring files to and from that drive are all activities that go through the redirector.

The server provides the other end of this connection. It processes requests from redirectors and provides access to the shared resources that they request. The request to access a shared directory, for example, comes in from the network and is handled by the server driver.

One way to distinguish the redirector from the server is to remember the source of the requests. The redirector accepts requests from layers above it, on the local computer, and forwards the requests out to the network. The server accepts and handles requests from layers below it. Those requests come in from the network.

In Chapter 4, I cover where these components fit and what they actually do in Windows NT Server.

Finally, the session layer provides for correct ordering of message delivery. In other words, the session layer assures that messages are received in the order that they were originally sent.

Layers 3 through 5 of the OSI model, including the network, transport, and session layers, have a special designation. Together, they form what is called the *subnet layers*. Network protocols are often implemented within these three layers. You'll see in Chapter 4 that some Windows NT protocols follow this rule, and some don't.

The Presentation Layer

Contrary to what you might expect from its name, the *presentation layer* has nothing to do with presenting data. The most accurate way of thinking about this layer is as a set of commonly used services that transform or translate data from one format to another. So, why is it called the presentation layer? Because it defines how the network presents itself to your applications.

The presentation layer sometimes provides data compression services. These services enable application data to be compressed before sending and decompressed on receipt, to minimize the amount of data actually transmitted over the network. Data encryption is another service offered by this layer. Data can be encrypted on its way to the session layer and decrypted on its way from it. Finally, the presentation layer often provides generic methods of converting data, including translating file formats between operating system platforms, converting ASCII to EBCDIC character codes, and so on.

Now I feel guilty, because I've told you about a layer that is almost nonexistent in Windows NT. You'll see the presentation layer's limited role in Chapter 4.

The Application Layer

The *application layer*, contrary to popular belief, isn't comprised of user applications. It's a set of functions offered directly to applications to provide convenient access to network services. These services typically include file transfer, remote program execution, e-mail and chat services, and remote database access.

Peeling the Onion

If you've ever peeled an onion, you've probably noticed two things. First, you cry. Second, an onion has many layers, and you can keep peeling and peeling until you reach a small core. For analogy purposes, I'll leave the tears out of the discussion and stick to the layer phenomenon.

Think of the OSI model layers as adding layers to a data onion. At the core is the application data that you want to send over the network. This could be a file, a customer record, or the line that you just typed into a network chat program. In any case, it's the raw data that you want to transmit, and it contains no information that enables it to reach its destination.

As the data descends through each of the OSI model layers, it picks up a new outer layer of information to help it get where it needs to go. You saw some examples of this information in the previous sections. Network address information is thrown in at more than one level, a CRC is added in the data link layer, and message sequence numbers are likely provided in the session layer.

Each OSI model layer adds an outer layer of information to the previous layer. When the data onion reaches the physical layer, the entire vegetable is sent over the network. When the other end receives the data onion, it pushes it up through the OSI layers, peeling off one layer of information at each step. By the time it finally arrives at the application layer, only the original core data remains. Figure 3-10 shows the journey of the data onion through the network.

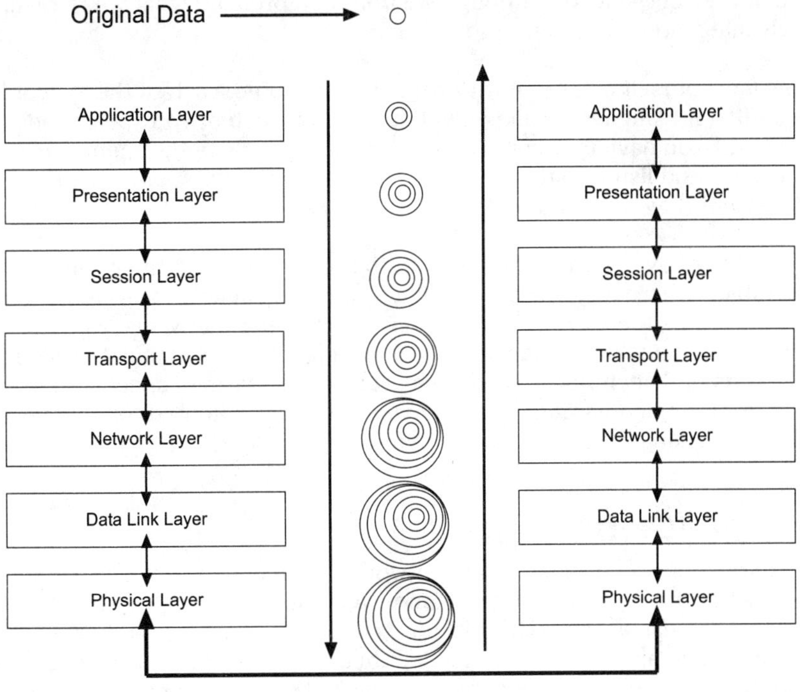

Figure 3-10: Each layer of the OSI model adds a layer of information to the "data onion."

Interconnectivity vs. Interoperability

You'll hear and read the terms *interconnectivity* and *interoperability* fairly often in your network experiences. Both words are a mouthful, and unfortunately both are sometimes used interchangeably when they shouldn't be. To help avoid any confusion, I'm going to present a couple of analogies that should help you learn, remember, and explain the distinction between these two terms.

Think of the differences between the mechanics of reading and reading comprehension. At a very basic level, reading involves the mechanics of looking at the words on the page, moving your eyes through the text, and turning pages. Comprehension, on the other hand, involves actually processing the words and sentences that you've read and understanding what they mean.

Interconnectivity is like the mechanics of reading. Your eyes can see the words on the page, and you can move through the text, but you do not comprehend what the words mean. Interoperability is like comprehension. It involves processing and understanding what you're reading. Keep in mind that, just as there are many levels of comprehension, there are many levels of interoperability. For instance, I might comprehend what I read at the fourth-grade level, whereas you might comprehend at the college level. Although we both comprehend what we're reading, you're gleaning more information than I am.

Now, imagine yourself in a room with three other people. Each of these people speaks a different language, none of which is yours. Each of you speaks, and each of you listens. You have interconnectivity with the people in the room, because you can speak and listen to them. However, you don't understand what the others are saying, and they don't understand you.

Thus, you don't have interoperability with the other people in the room. To be interoperable, either you'd have to learn all their languages, or they'd have to learn yours. Again, there are different levels of interoperability, just as there are different levels of understanding and speaking a language. You might understand several words of French but don't have a grasp of the parts of speech. Thus, you might have a little understanding, but nowhere near as much as you'd have if you'd been speaking the language since your toddler days.

Raw Connections

Now let's bring these concepts back to networks. Interconnectivity means that nodes can physically connect to the network and even talk and listen to each other's data frames. You can accomplish this, for example, by placing an Ethernet card in each of several computers and connecting them with the appropriate cables and hubs. You've achieved interconnectivity, because the computers are connected, but no comprehension of data is achieved.

Useful Communication

Interoperability occurs when nodes on the network actually understand the data being transmitted and can communicate with each other in meaningful and useful ways. Interoperability can happen at several levels. For example, you can achieve interoperability at the physical and data link layers, but because you're running different protocols at the higher layers on different nodes, the nodes can't possibly understand each other. This level of interoperability really doesn't buy you anything.

True Interoperability

Useful communication between nodes requires running compatible protocols in the subnet layers (layers 3 through 5). Doing this enables, for instance, two Windows NT computers to communicate with each other or an NT computer to communicate with a Novell computer. Interoperability at even higher layers enables network applications such as e-mail and group scheduling to work together across the network.

WHAT ARE ROUTERS AND GATEWAYS?

In discussing the interoperability issue, you'll often hear about *routers* and *gateways.* It's important to understand what these terms mean.

If you need to connect two networks that use different technologies, a *router* provides the solution. A router transfers data between networks that typically use incompatible technologies. A router has a node address on the network. Routers are frequently used as intermediate destinations.

A *gateway* is a very generic term that refers to different things. In each case, a gateway plays a role of translator on the network. First, it can refer to a router, exactly as I've just described. In this context, the gateway translates between two different network technologies. Second, a gateway can refer to a translator between two different protocols on a network.

Finally, a gateway can refer to a piece of software that translates between data formats to make applications compatible with each other. The most common type of application gateway translates between different flavors of e-mail packages. Say you send an e-mail message from CompuServe to an address on the Internet. Your message has to go through a CompuServe-to-Internet e-mail gateway, which puts your message in the correct form on the Internet. Any reply that you receive has to come back through another gateway in the opposite direction. Microsoft's SNA Server is another example of a gateway, enabling connection of an entire PC network to IBM mainframes through a single gateway server.

Some operating systems, including Windows NT, enable you to run more than one protocol at the same time. This has the effect of making a single node simultaneously interoperable with several different types of nodes. For example, running multiple protocols on a Windows NT computer can enable it to communicate with a UNIX computer, a Novell server, and a Macintosh desktop system all at the same time. You'll see in detail what protocols are supported in Windows NT Server when you read Chapter 4.

Homogeneous vs. Heterogeneous Networks

So, why all this concern and fuss over network interoperability? Why not just purchase compatible hardware for all nodes in the network and run the same operating system and the same protocol on all nodes? If you did that, every node could interoperate with every other node, and life would be much easier. True enough. You, as a network administrator, would certainly spend less on aspirin.

Simple Networks

Such utopian networks do exist. A *homogeneous network* consists of nodes that all use the same network technology (for example, Ethernet). All of these nodes run the same protocol (for example, TCP/IP) and are completely interoperable with each other. Brand-new, small networks are sometimes homogeneous for the first part of their existence, because all of the hardware and software has probably been purchased and installed in one fell swoop.

Real-World Networks

In the real world, though, situations are typically much more complex, or they become more complex over time. You may want to have a Windows NT Server-based network but have already invested in several UNIX workstations, Macintosh computers, and perhaps a Novell NetWare server. Most of your networked nodes might use Ethernet technology, but one department has a Token Ring that connects to the company's mainframe. Your business might depend on a specific CAD application that runs only on UNIX, and other applications that you need may run only on NT. Your software developers might require PCs, whereas your technical writers might require Macintosh systems.

Although you may find solutions to these problems that could give you a homogeneous network, the costs of these solutions are often far too high. For example, converting applications that depend on a particular operating system platform is typically a very expensive proposition, even if your company controls the application's source code. If you don't control the application code, it may be impossible to convince the software vendor to convert to the new platform. Moreover, converting your entire enterprise to a single network technology might mean ripping out and replacing your existing network infrastructure. This approach can be very costly and may be impossible, if the business can't tolerate the associated network downtime.

You also need to consider the cost of various networking solutions to meet your changing requirements. The cost of converting your users from one operating system to another only begins with the cost of the software. Expenses for associated hardware upgrades and user training can quickly eclipse the software expense. The low cost of a particular network technology might make it the standard for most of your organization, but a faster, more expensive technology might be required by one department.

Thus, most enterprise networks are (or eventually become) *heterogeneous networks.* These networks consist of nodes that may use a variety of different network technologies, with several different protocols running on the network simultaneously. Some nodes are fully interoperable with each other, but all connected nodes don't necessarily interoperate. A variety of operating systems and even processor architectures are present in the various network nodes.

Networks built from existing computers or from existing departmental networks are typically heterogeneous right out of the chute. Homogeneous networks become heterogeneous over time, as new technologies and new requirements are grafted to the network.

INSIDE STORY

The initial networking goals for Windows NT, set back in 1990, were pretty modest. The intent was to design NT to share files and printers with other Microsoft products, including Windows for Workgroups, Windows 3.1, DOS, and Microsoft OS/2 1.x. This simplistic view didn't last long.

NT program managers were responsible for crafting the product feature set to meet customer needs. During the following months, these managers presented NT's proposed feature set to customers and potential customers. The goal was to solicit feedback on what people really needed to run their businesses.

The issues streaming back from customers painted a very jolting picture. Did Microsoft truly think that networks in the real world were 100 percent heterogeneous Microsoft networks? Were they ignoring the huge number of UNIX systems out there? Could they really expect to win corporate enterprise accounts if they couldn't interoperate with NetWare, the network with the largest installed server base in the industry? Windows NT must interoperate with non-Microsoft networks, if it expected to compete in the real world.

Networking in NT became a moving target for the beleaguered team. First, UNIX interoperability was added to the team's plate. Then came a NetWare-compatible client to access NetWare servers. Soon, the team had to create tools to ease migration from a NetWare-based network to Windows NT. SNA Server was moved to NT, to provide access to mainframe systems. All of this required more development and more testing. It seemed to the team like an uphill battle.

(continued)

INSIDE STORY *(continued)*

Scores of people in the network group burned the midnight oil to complete each networking piece. Developers were outfitted with pagers, enabling them to handle network emergencies at any hour. Folks who complained about this arrangement were told to focus on fixing the bugs and to stop whining.

Within minutes after a new network component was released to the group for testing and general use, other engineers invariably appeared at the door of a tired network developer. "The server's down. And you were the last one to touch the code." "It doesn't connect to NetWare anymore. What did you do to it?" "I got a Blue Screen as soon as I started transferring a file. Come to my office and take a look." Or simply, "It's broke. Fix it!"

Such was life in the networking group for months. If lots of hard work and suffering are required to achieve anything worthwhile, Windows NT networking certainly proved worthwhile.

Summary

In this chapter, you've earned your degree at the Network University. You've gained a fundamental overview of the basic networking terminology, the hardware and software required to create a network, and how networking components interact with one another. For the most part, I've purposely stayed away from detailing how these concepts directly apply to Windows NT Server. Most of the concepts here aren't unique to the Windows NT world.

With the background that you've acquired in this chapter, you now have a solid foundation on which to build your Windows NT-specific knowledge of networking.

Chapter 4 teaches you about the details of Windows NT Server networking, how they relate to the concepts that you have just learned, and many of the issues that you need to consider in designing your state-of-the-art network based on Windows NT Server 4.0.

Inside Windows NT Networking

By now, you're probably wondering about the details of Windows NT Server networking. I don't blame you. After all, networking is central to Windows NT Server's existence, and you need to know what it provides on this front.

You're starting this chapter with a foundation of networking knowledge, either from reading Chapter 3 or from your own professional experience. In this chapter, you'll gain a solid understanding of the networking architecture and features that Windows NT Server offers. This knowledge prepares you to make some key decisions as you get ready to install and configure NT.

Is NT OS or NOS?

Windows NT is sometimes referred to as an operating system and sometimes as a network operating system. In fact, you've already seen both in this book. Well, both are right.

As I mentioned in Chapter 3, a NOS is traditionally defined as software that runs on top of a general-purpose operating system to control access to a network and to manage access to resources provided on the network. You discovered in Chapter 2 that Windows NT is a general-purpose, complete operating system whether or not it's networked with other computers. In essence, NT is both an OS with networking capabilities and a NOS that includes a general-purpose operating system. Or, to paraphrase the classic *Saturday Night Live* spot, "It's a floor wax *and* a dessert topping!"

Inside the NT Network

As you saw in Chapter 2, much of Windows NT is designed in layered components, with well-defined interfaces between them to communicate with adjacent layers. The Windows NT networking is no exception to this layered design approach.

Figure 4-1 illustrates the major components involved in the Windows NT networking architecture. At the lowest layer, network adapter device drivers control the networking hardware. Transport protocol drivers implement meaningful data conversations between nodes on the network. Redirectors and servers handle outgoing and incoming requests for shared resources.

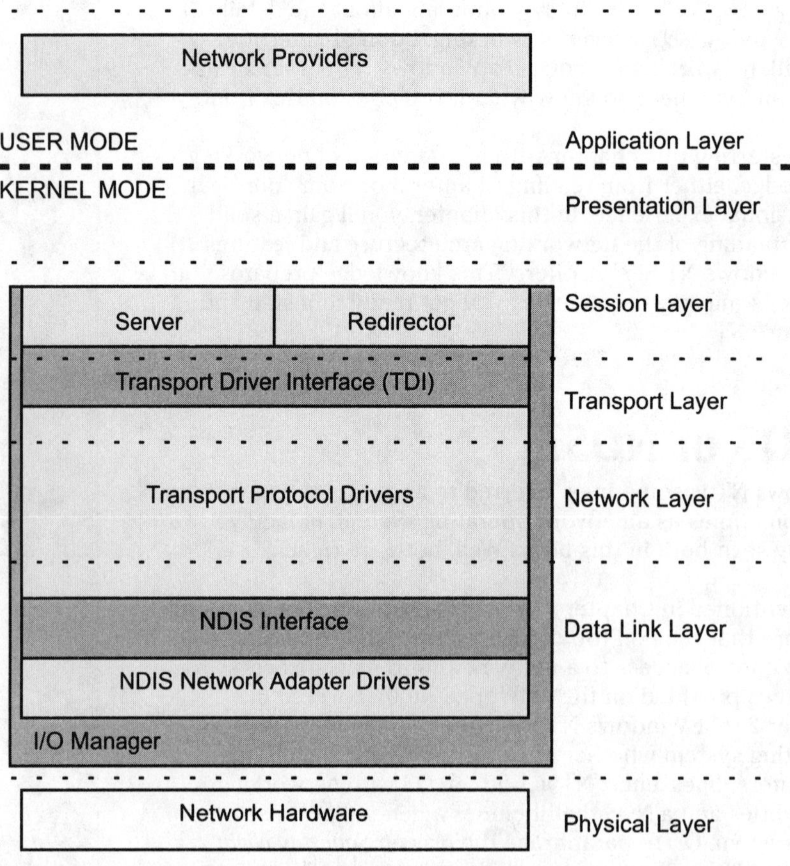

Figure 4-1: The Windows NT networking components are implemented in layers.

I haven't included all of the details of the NT networking architecture in Figure 4-1. As I discuss each area, I zoom in on the nitty-gritty.

Let's look at each of the key components and the roles that they play. In the discussions that follow, I show you how each component corresponds to both the Windows NT system architecture from Chapter 2 and the OSI model presented in Chapter 3. We start from the bottom and work our way up.

Network Adapter Drivers

The lowest layer of the Windows NT networking architecture is comprised of network adapter device drivers. Because these are NT device drivers, they live in the NT I/O manager component and run in kernel mode. These drivers communicate directly with the network adapter hardware.

The Driver Problem

Before 1989, network adapter drivers were very difficult to develop and weren't the least bit portable from one operating system to another. No standard interface existed for writing device drivers or the network communication protocols that sat on top of them. So, network adapter manufacturers created their own proprietary drivers, typically including the protocol and device driver together in one monolithic chunk of code. Supporting a new protocol meant writing a whole new driver. Moreover, to support a new operating system, the manufacturer had to write a new set of drivers, one driver for each protocol and one set of protocols for each operating system. It was like having to develop a new type of fuel from scratch for each new car model sold.

What's more, this approach to device driver design supported only one protocol on a network adapter. If you wanted to run two different protocols on the same computer, you had to have two physical network adapters inside. However, even this approach worked only if the device drivers supported multiple adapters, and they typically didn't.

The NDIS Solution

To solve this problem, a standard, low-level device driver interface was needed that would decouple the transport protocols in the upper layers from the functions specific to the network adapter. Enter the *Network Driver Interface Specification,* or NDIS. Microsoft and 3Com jointly developed the original NDIS standard to solve these problems. Windows NT supports the NDIS 3.0 standard, which has been updated to portable, 32-bit C code that's enabled for SMP computers.

If a network adapter manufacturer writes its device driver to present the NDIS interface to the layers above it, any available NDIS-compatible protocol available for Windows NT can run through the adapter. This makes life much easier for the adapter manufacturers and for you. All you need is a single NDIS driver for your network adapter, and you're ready to go with whatever transport protocols you want to run on top of it. In addition, if a software developer writes a new transport protocol for Windows NT and uses the NDIS interface at its lowest level, the protocol can talk through any network adapter that has an NDIS driver.

The NDIS standard is only as powerful as its breadth of acceptance and support by the industry. Windows NT Server 4.0 includes NDIS drivers for many popular network adapters. Windows NT Workstation and Windows 95 include broad NDIS support as well. The same NDIS 3.0 drivers will play in any of these Microsoft 32-bit environments. If your adapter's driver isn't in the NT box, most manufactures of LAN and WAN cards are now shipping NDIS drivers along with their adapters. Some manufacturers even use NDIS on non-Microsoft platforms. For example, Digital Equipment Corporation uses NDIS drivers for their VMS and Ultrix networks. As standards go, NDIS has been quite successful at taming the proprietary chaos in the network driver world. Microsoft said, "N dis madness," and the industry listened.

The NDIS driver is responsible for managing the network adapter hardware and for transmitting and receiving data over the physical network connection. At the lowest level, the NDIS driver talks to the one or more physical adapters that it drives. It starts I/O operations and handles interrupts from the adapters. At the highest level, the NDIS driver is called by transport protocol drivers, which you'll learn about in the next section. The NDIS driver is responsible for notifying the transport drivers when data has been sent successfully and when it has been received from the network.

NDIS in OSI and NT

How do network adapter drivers and the NDIS interface relate to the OSI model you learned about in Chapter 3? The answer is that both exist in the data link layer. More specifically, they exist in the MAC sublayer of the data link layer. Figure 4-2 illustrates this.

How do network adapter drivers and the NDIS interface fit into the Windows NT architecture described in Chapter 2? As mentioned earlier in this chapter, these are device drivers that operate within the I/O manager, as shown in Figure 4-1. As we continue moving up the layers, you'll find that most of the upper layers live here as well, although they aren't strictly device drivers.

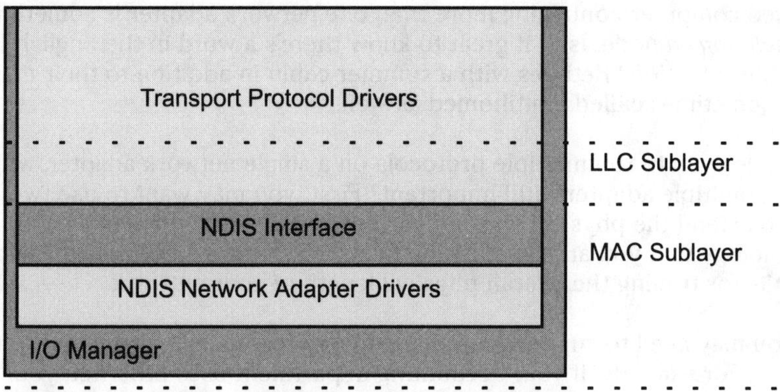

Figure 4-2: Network adapter drivers and the NDIS interface reside in the MAC sublayer of the data link layer.

NDIS Wrapper

To make the NDIS drivers independent of operating system details, they have access to a library of functions that handle requests to the operating system. This library is sometimes called the *NDIS wrapper,* because it effectively wraps around an NDIS driver to isolate it from the operating system.

NDIS isn't a layer itself. It's a well-defined interface between two adjacent layers, similar to the icing between layers of a cake. NDIS-compliant network adapter device drivers constitute the layer below this interface. NDIS-compliant transport protocol drivers make up the layer above this interface. Think of the NDIS wrapper as a utility library, and NDIS itself as the glue that binds adapter drivers below to protocol drivers above.

NDIS Benefits

Here's a summary of the advantages of the NDIS driver approach:

- ✦ NDIS supports multiple network adapters on a single computer. The number of adapters that you can place in a computer is limited only by the number of available card slots.
- ✦ NDIS supports multiple protocols on a single network adapter. For example, you can run protocols that talk to NT, NetWare, and UNIX servers simultaneously through the same adapter.
- ✦ NDIS provides a standard interface for network adapter drivers. You need only one NDIS driver regardless of how many types of protocols that you use.
- ✦ NDIS provides a standard interface for transport protocol drivers. Transport protocols can talk through any adapter that has an NDIS driver.

A networked computer containing more than one network adapter is sometimes called a *multihomed* node. Isn't it great to know there's a word in the English language for this situation? Retirees with a summer cabin in addition to their main house are sometimes called multihomed as well.

If NDIS enables you to run multiple protocols on a single network adapter, why is support for multiple adapters still important? First, you may want to use two adapters to extend the physical size of your network beyond the limits of the network technology that you are using. Using three adapters, for example, provides the potential for tripling the overall physical length of your network.

Second, you may need to support multiple network technologies attached to the same server. For example, if your accounting department uses Ethernet, your production department uses Token Ring, and your research and development group uses FDDI, you can hook them to a single server by installing an adapter of each flavor in the computer.

Finally, you may want to spread the network load over multiple adapters, to improve the performance of your server. If the network adapter is the performance bottleneck in your environment (and not the server itself), you can make some big performance gains this way.

If you're familiar with earlier versions of NDIS, used in OS/2 and Windows for Workgroups, you'll find that NDIS 3.0 makes your life a bit easier. Earlier versions of NDIS used the PROTMAN protocol manager to link networking layers together. The act of establishing communications between a network adapter driver and a transport protocol driver is called *binding*. With NDIS 3.0, Windows NT automatically handles bindings and stores them in the registry.

In earlier versions of Windows NT Server, NT wouldn't forward or route messages from one network to another, even if you had multiple network adapters in the system. You had to add a dedicated router to the network to accomplish this. Now with Windows NT Server 4.0, you can use a new feature called *MultiProtocol Routing*, or MPR, to connect LANs together or connect LANs to WANs.

If you've had experience with NetWare drivers, the NDIS approach may sound hauntingly familiar. NDIS provides virtually the same functionality as NetWare's *Open Datalink Interface*, or ODI, and their *Multiple Link Interface Driver*, or MLID.

Windows NT provides support for ODI drivers as well as NDIS. To use ODI network adapter drivers on NT, you need to enable ODI drivers to carry Microsoft network traffic by loading both NWLink and ODIHLP.

However, if you're going to access NetWare servers from Windows NT, I recommend you use NDIS drivers, Microsoft's NWLink IPX/SPX transport protocol, and Microsoft's NetWare requester for NT. These components are very stable and work well together. Use an ODI driver only if no NDIS driver is available for your network adapter.

Transport Protocols

The next layer above NDIS adapter drivers consists of transport protocol drivers. Like device drivers, they live in the NT I/O manager component and run in kernel mode. However, unlike device drivers, transport protocol drivers don't talk to hardware. They rely on the NDIS adapter drivers to do that.

At their lowest level, transport protocol drivers talk to NDIS drivers. Transport protocols carry on meaningful data transfers between nodes on the network. As their name suggests, they are responsible for transporting data across the network.

It's easy to get confused by terminology at this point. A transport protocol really stretches below the OSI model transport layer. It often includes part of the data link and network layers as well. In the NT world, just think in terms of the NDIS drivers handling the hardware, transport protocol drivers handling the data transmission, and the upper layers dealing with network applications and utilities.

Windows NT Server 4.0 provides five distinct transport protocols. They are

- ✦ NetBEUI
- ✦ IPX/SPX
- ✦ TCP/IP
- ✦ DLC
- ✦ AppleTalk

On the bottom of these transport protocols, the NDIS interface is used to communicate with the network adapter drivers. You've already learned about the role of the NDIS interface. Now I'll tell you a bit about the interface between transport protocols and the layers above them. Next, I'll take you on a tour through each of these protocols in turn. In Chapter 7, you'll use this background to select the right set of protocols for your Windows NT Server network.

The Transport Driver Interface

Just as NDIS provides an interface between network adapter drivers and the transport protocols above them, the *Transport Driver Interface,* or TDI, provides an interface between a transport protocol and the OSI session layer above it.

As long as a transport protocol driver is written to provide the TDI interface at its highest level and the NDIS interface at its lowest level, you can mix and match with any NDIS drivers below and any TDI-compliant session layer components above.

Now, here's a concept that should sound familiar. TDI isn't a layer itself. It's a well-defined interface between two adjacent layers. TDI-compliant transport protocols constitute the layer below this interface. TDI-compliant session layer components (such as redirectors and servers) make up the layer above this interface. Think of the TDI as the glue that binds transport protocols below to redirectors and servers above. The TDI plays a role similar to NDIS, but at a higher layer in the stack.

Transport Protocols in OSI and NT

How do transport protocol drivers and the TDI interface relate to the OSI model you learned about in Chapter 3? As you can see in Figure 4-3, TDI acts as the well-defined boundary layer between the OSI session and transport layers. Transport protocol drivers cover multiple OSI layers, including the transport layer, the network layer, and part of the data link layer. You'll see in the detailed protocol discussions that each transport protocol is positioned a bit differently relative to the OSI layers.

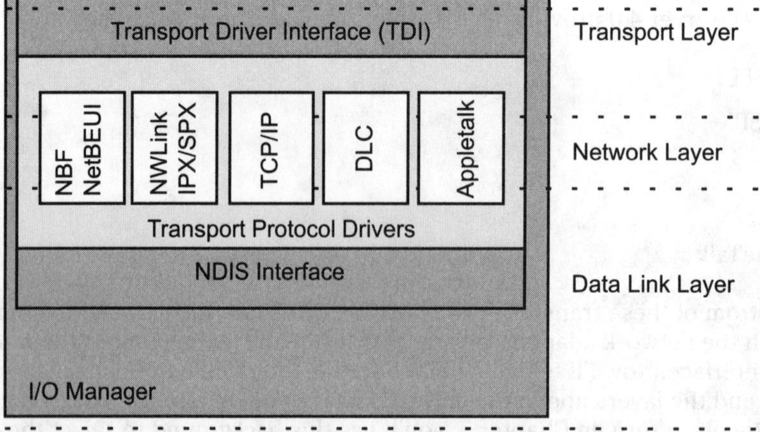

Figure 4-3: Transport protocol drivers and the TDI interface cover multiple layers of the OSI model.

How do transport protocol drivers and the TDI interface fit into the Windows NT architecture described in Chapter 2? As mentioned earlier in this chapter, transport protocols are NT drivers that operate within the I/O manager. You can see where the TDI and the transport protocol drivers fit in Figure 4-3.

NBF — The NetBEUI Protocol

The NBF transport protocol driver on Windows NT provides full network interoperability with all other Microsoft networking products including Windows 95, Windows for Workgroups, LAN Manager, MS-NET, and OS/2 1.x. It's also interoperable with IBM's OS/2 and LAN Server products.

NBF, which is really the name of the driver and not the protocol, stands for *NetBEUI Frame*. The *NetBEUI* protocol stands for *NetBIOS Extended User Interface,* first introduced in 1985. (NetBEUI is pronounced "netbooee," which sounds to me like a fisherman's knife.) It was originally intended for networks containing a few dozen computers, at most. NetBEUI included an application programming interface called *NetBIOS,* which stands for *Network Basic I/O System*. (You're probably already familiar with the BIOS that comes in ROM in your PC. The NetBIOS concept is similar, providing an interface to basic system services — in this case, network services. IBM even went so far as to implement NetBIOS in ROM at one point, so the concepts are parallel.) If we explode all of the acronyms, NBF is really the **N**etwork **B**asic I/O System Extended User Interface **F**rame. All you really need to remember, though, are these basic principles:

- NetBEUI is the transport protocol.
- NetBIOS is the application programming interface (API).
- NBF is the name of the driver that implements the transport protocol.

Figure 4-4 shows where all of this fits into the Windows NT network architecture and how it relates to the OSI model. Notice that NBF covers a portion of the data link layer, the network layer, and the transport layer. Also notice that, as with all good Windows NT transport protocol drivers, NBF communicates through the NDIS interface below and the TDI interface above.

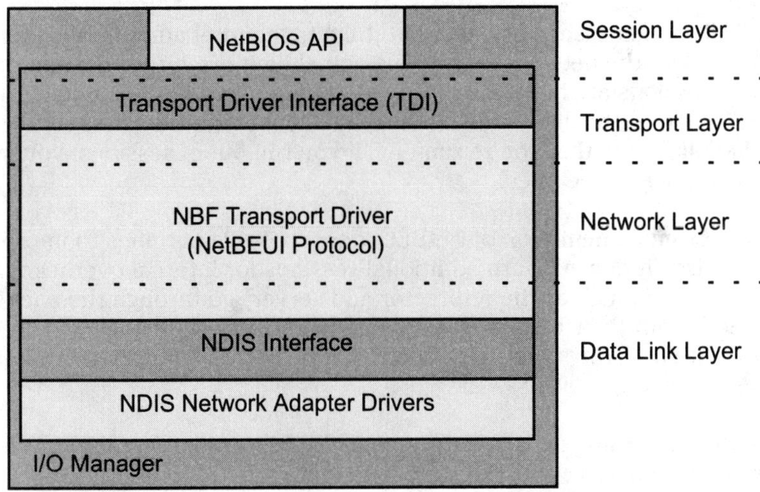

Figure 4-4: NetBEUI is the transport protocol implemented by the NBF transport protocol driver.

Think back for a moment to our discussion of NDIS. Recall that, prior to the advent of NDIS, a network adapter device driver included a transport protocol inside itself. Everything lived in one big chunk of monolithic code. NDIS decoupled transports from hardware drivers, enabling any transport protocol to run on top of any device driver.

Similarly, before the advent of Windows NT, DOS, and OS/2, NetBEUI drivers included the NetBIOS programming interface as part of the driver. This inextricably married programs using NetBIOS to the NetBEUI protocol, so they had to use it for data transmission. In fact, the NetBIOS interface and the NetBEUI protocol were so closely tied together that some people to this day incorrectly use the terms interchangeably. Windows NT has now decoupled the NetBIOS programming interface from the NetBEUI transport protocol. On NT, programs written to the NetBIOS interface can run on top of any transport protocol that you choose.

Windows NT supports applications that use the NetBIOS API in the DOS, Win16, and Win32 environments. So, existing 16-bit applications written to NetBIOS will run alongside newer Win32 NetBIOS applications.

NetBEUI's Character

The NetBEUI protocol features automatic flow control, very low protocol overhead in the data sent over the network, self-tuning capabilities, and error detection. It's quite fast, and client implementations (on DOS, for example) use relatively little system memory.

One of NetBEUI's weaknesses has been that it limits the total number of communication sessions over the network to 254. The actual limit is a bit lower than this, because some sessions are burned by internal system overhead. On a network with 100 to 200 nodes, this limitation can begin to cause problems, depending on the types of applications that you're running. If you run out of sessions, you must wait for some of them to be freed.

The Windows NT implementation of NetBEUI does a couple of things to improve this situation. First, it doesn't burn additional sessions for internal overhead. NT's internal components (such as the redirector and server) go through the back door and deal directly with the NBF driver via the TDI interface. They don't go through the NetBIOS API. This brings the session limit back up to 254, but that's still not a large number.

NBF helps ease the session limit more dramatically. In previous NetBEUI implementations, a node couldn't communicate with more than 254 other nodes. NBF enables each *process* on the Windows NT system to communicate with up to 254 nodes. There's no limit to the total number of sessions on the NT computer. The only practical limit is the number of processes that you can start and run comfortably on the system.

NetBEUI is efficient for small networks, particularly those that already use Windows 95, Windows for Workgroups, LAN Manager, MS-NET, or OS/2. In fact, for very small Microsoft networks. it's the fastest protocol available. However, NetBEUI can create problems on large networks.

Why? NetBEUI transmissions cannot be passed through a router. Although some functions of the OSI network layer are included in NetBEUI, no routing address information is added to the data transmitted. All nodes on the network are identified by unique names that you assign. Messages sent by a node looking for another node by name are broadcast across the entire network, even across bridges. Depending on the configuration and reliability of your network, these broadcasts may also occur multiple times for the same message, as the sending node attempts to retry. Thus, as your network grows, the overhead associated with NetBEUI can become a real performance issue.

If you have nodes on your Microsoft network that can speak only NetBEUI, and you want those nodes to talk to your Windows NT Server, install the NetBEUI transport protocol on your server. A common example of this situation is a DOS client running NetBEUI, because the protocol has the smallest memory footprint in DOS. On DOS computers with limited memory, NetBEUI may be your only practical protocol choice.

However, unless you are integrating with an existing LAN Manager network, you should consider converting all of your nodes to IPX/SPX or TCP/IP. For small and growing networks, IPX/SPX performs better than NetBEUI. TCP/IP provides great flexibility for larger networks and Internet access. For Windows NT Server, Microsoft actually recommends abandoning its NetBEUI baby in favor of these other two transport protocols.

NWLink – The IPX/SPX Protocol

The NWLink transport protocol driver, which stands for *NetWare Link,* is Microsoft's independent implementation of IPX/SPX. IPX/SPX stands for *Internetwork Packet Exchange/Sequenced Packet Exchange*. It's used as the transport protocol in Novell NetWare networks and is based on the Xerox Network Standard, known as XNS. Running the IPX/SPX transport protocol enables Windows NT to act as a server to NetWare clients. With a NetWare-compatible requester, NWLink can enable NT computers to access Novell servers.

IPX corresponds to the OSI network layer and is primarily responsible for getting data through routers. SPX corresponds to OSI's transport layer. You can see where IPX/SPX fits in to the OSI and NT models in Figure 4-5.

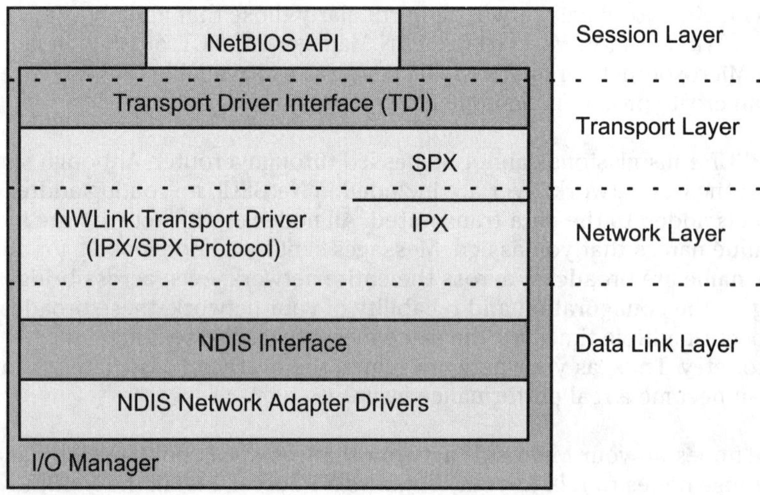

Figure 4-5: IPX/SPX is the transport protocol implemented by NWLink.

IPX/SPX Character

IPX/SPX is a routable protocol, which gives it a big advantage over NetBEUI, especially in larger networks. Many sites have replaced NetBEUI with IPX/SPX for just this reason.

Microsoft's IPX/SPX protocol enables Windows NT systems to play in existing NetWare installations. However, Microsoft has gone further in an attempt to unseat NetWare. They've done this by designing a relatively painless migration path to move from NetWare to Windows NT. Windows NT Server includes a migration utility that converts user account information from the NetWare account database (called the *bindery*) to NT's SAM database. This utility enables replacement of a NetWare server with Windows NT Server without requiring the user account database to be recreated from scratch. You'll find out more about this in Chapter 12.

Windows NT Server can't yet fully emulate and completely replace a NetWare server. (It can provide file and print services to NetWare clients, but NT Server doesn't emulate NetWare's NDS.) It can, however, easily connect NT client computers to a NetWare server. This is accomplished using the *Gateway Service for NetWare,* or GSNW, that ships with Windows NT Server.

In previous versions of Windows NT Server, the GSNW would only enable access to NetWare 3.x servers and earlier. You could access NetWare 4.x servers through Bindery Emulation Mode (which emulates NetWare 3.x). Now, using Windows NT Server 4.0, GSNW can fully access NetWare 4.x servers running NetWare Directory Services (NDS).

INSIDE STORY

The irate calls poured into Microsoft product support. There was a major problem. Blue Screens of Death were popping up on Windows NT, many times a day. "What's Microsoft going to do about it?" the customers demanded.

These NT customers had NetWare networks. They were using Novell's beta release of code that enabled NT to access their NetWare servers. The driver code was unstable, crashing the NT system frequently. Because the code ran in kernel mode, the operating system wasn't protected from its bugs. So, whenever the driver died, so did the operating system.

Product support engineers soon pieced together the cause of the customers' frustration. These people had called Novell, and Novell had referred them to Microsoft. After all, it must be an NT problem. Microsoft didn't control the Novell beta code, so they told the customers that Novell had to deal with the problem. These customers of both companies felt like Ping-Pong balls. Meanwhile, their computers were crashing around them.

Novell wasn't acknowledging the problem. They continued to claim NT was at fault. That is, until one day, when they suddenly called Microsoft to discuss cooperatively working on a solution to the problem. It was the day after a major industry publication had scolded Novell for its poor quality NT solution, labeling their attempt as "the first NT virus."

At the time, Microsoft didn't have a solution, but they were already working on one. An independent team of engineers was busily creating a set of compatible protocols. To avoid legal entanglements with their fierce competitor, the team had to take a *clean room* approach to the development project. They couldn't have any contact with the existing Novell beta product, nor with anyone who knew how it worked. They had to develop every stick of code from scratch, using only the product specifications as a guide.

The volume and intensity of the calls on this problem confirmed two things to Microsoft. First, Microsoft was on the right track in forging ahead to develop its own version of NetWare-compatible protocols for Windows NT. Clearly, robust interoperability with NetWare was critically important to NT customers. The very existence of NT depended on a solid solution, if Microsoft expected to keep NT systems installed at primarily NetWare sites. Second, it was now obvious that Novell was far away from shipping a working solution for NT. Microsoft had to fill the gap and fill it quickly. They did. Once released, Microsoft's solution was accepted by Windows NT customers as the way to go.

NT clients don't need to be running IPX/SPX to access the NetWare server through this gateway. The gateway running on NT Server translates whatever protocol the client is running to IPX/SPX before passing the traffic on to the NetWare server. An added benefit of using this gateway is that it uses up only one NetWare server connection. Many users can access the NetWare server through this single connection. This approach can save you big bucks on purchasing NetWare user licenses, a fact that Microsoft loves and Novell hates. I'll fill you in on the details of GSNW and integration of Windows NT Server with Novell networks in Chapter 12.

If you're adding Windows NT Server to an existing NetWare network, you should plan on running Microsoft's NWLink. This enables NetWare clients to access your NT server. NWLink is both NDIS-compliant and TDI-compliant, so you'll have no problem running other protocols such as NetBEUI or TCP/IP simultaneously on the same NT server.

The TCP/IP Protocol

It seems as though entire books, plays, and feature films have now been written about TCP/IP, which stands for *Transmission Control Protocol/Internet Protocol.* TCP/IP was originally developed by the U.S. Department of Defense back in the 1970s, for what now is known today as the Internet. TCP/IP provides communication among interconnected networks consisting of nodes based on a wide range of hardware and operating system architectures. In other words, it's good at connecting heterogeneous systems and networks. TCP/IP has become the most widely used protocol in the world today, enjoying support on virtually all available networking platforms. Even Microsoft now uses TCP/IP as the primary protocol on their internal corporate network.

In reality, TCP/IP actually refers to a large family or suite of standard protocols, tools, and diagnostics that offer a rich set of networking capabilities. Unfortunately, this richness yields more complexity than other protocols. To really understand all aspects of TCP/IP requires study and motivation, as there's a plethora of TCP/IP trivia out there. (If you've just decided that you want to memorize everything possible about TCP/IP, I recommend that you get a life instead.) In this book, I focus only on those aspects of TCP/IP that are relevant to your network administration efforts. You can use TCP/IP as the primary protocol on your network, as a means of connecting multiple networks, as a way of interoperating with UNIX systems, and as a link to the Internet. As with IPX/SPX, TCP/IP is a routable protocol, making it very suitable for large networks and WANs. Figure 4-6 illustrates how TCP/IP fits into the OSI and NT models.

IP lives at the network layer, and is responsible for breaking messages into packets and adding appropriate routing information to the transmission. TCP operates at the transport layer, providing reliable delivery of data in the proper sequence between processes running on different nodes.

TCP/IP Character

TCP/IP node addressing can be a complex proposition. Windows NT Server provides powerful features such as DHCP (Dynamic Host Configuration Protocol), DNS (Domain Name Service), and WINS (Windows Internet Name System), which automatically assign addresses and translate computer names to their respective addresses. You'll learn about these features in detail in Chapter 11.

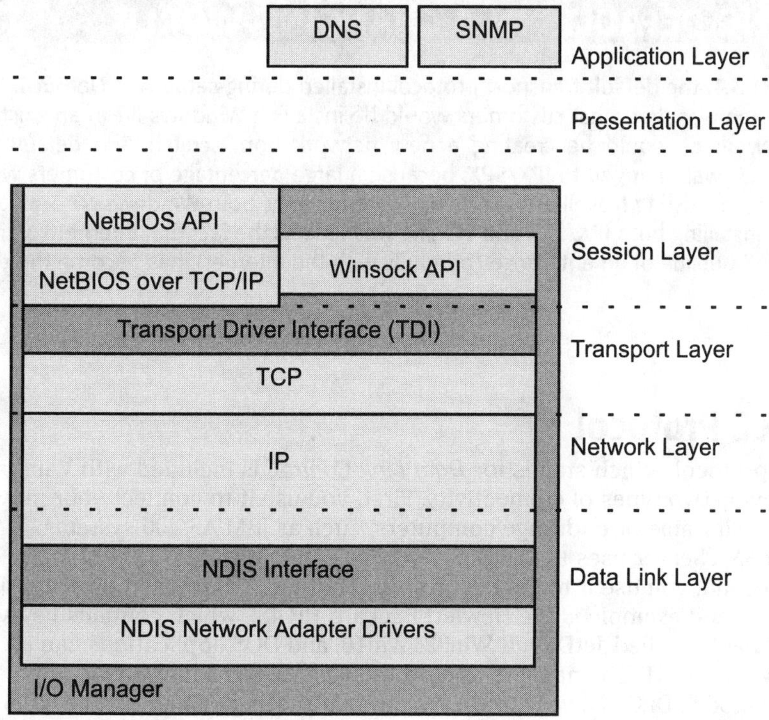

Figure 4-6: TCP/IP operates in the transport and network OSI layers, with higher-level services in the upper layers.

Several other members of the TCP/IP protocol suite haven't been discussed here. In Chapter 11, you'll read more about the TCP/IP protocol suite and how to get the most from it on your Windows NT Server network.

Software developers use two predominant APIs to write TCP/IP applications. One is our old friend NetBIOS, which I discussed earlier in this chapter. The other is the *Windows Sockets* API, commonly called *Winsock*. (No, I didn't leave out the *d*. It really is Winsock.) Winsock is an industry standard specifically designed for the Microsoft Windows product family. It enables the growing masses of Windows software developers to create Internet and TCP/IP programs more easily. If you've dealt with UNIX networks, the Winsock interface looks very similar to the Berkeley-socket interface, with some additions specifically geared to Windows programming. Winsock currently supports only TCP/IP and cannot make use of other protocols beneath it. A few tricks that these APIs do just don't make sense outside of the TCP/IP world. However, because it's becoming such a popular programming interface, efforts are now underway to see about running Winsock applications on top of other protocols.

CHANGING DEFAULTS IN A CHANGING WORLD

In Windows NT 3.1, the default transport protocol installed during setup was NetBEUI. The assumption then was that most customers would be installing Windows NT in an existing Microsoft network or would be creating a new network from scratch. The default for Windows NT 3.5 was changed to IPX/SPX, because a large percentage of customers were installing NT in an existing Novell environment. More recently, both Windows NT 3.51 and 4.0 default to installing both IPX/SPX and TCP/IP. This reflects the fact that internetworking, both within and outside of an enterprise (primarily with the Internet), has become the darling of the day.

The DLC Protocol

The DLC protocol, which stands for *Data Link Control,* is included with Windows NT to provide two types of connectivity. First, you use it to connect your network with IBM mainframe or midrange computers, such as IBM AS/400 systems. Microsoft SNA Server uses the DLC protocol to communicate with IBM mainframes. Second, you use it to connect to printers that are attached directly to the network. A good example is the Hewlett-Packard HP 4Si, which contains its own network adapter called JetDirect. Win32, Win16, and DOS applications can all use DLC on Windows NT. The name of this protocol gives you a hint about where it fits in the OSI model. DLC is a very low-level protocol, sitting just above the NDIS drivers inside the data link layer. DLC corresponds to the LLC sublayer of the data link layer. Figure 4-7 illustrates this.

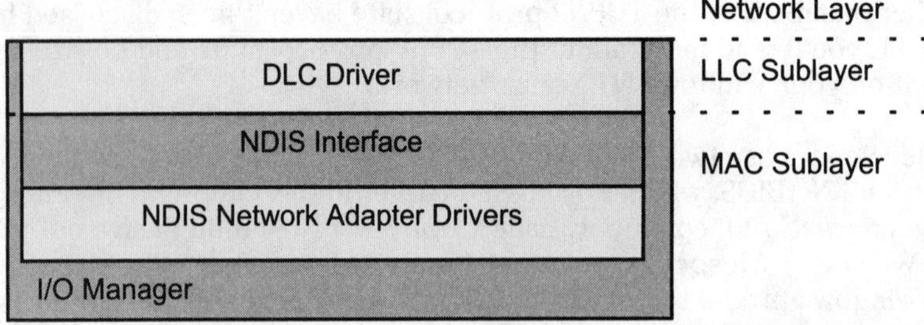

Figure 4-7: The DLC protocol operates within the OSI data link layer, just above the NDIS drivers.

The AppleTalk Protocol

In 1983, before releasing the first Macintosh computer to the rest of us, folks at Apple realized that office networking was becoming popular. When they decided to add networking to the Macintosh computer, they wanted to make it very simple, very inexpensive, and open. (Yes, Apple actually designed something that was open, rather than proprietary.) Their first attempt enabled sharing of the LaserWriter printer, and file-sharing soon followed. Thus, the AppleTalk transport protocol was born. As with TCP/IP, some other components exist at higher layers that I won't discuss at this point. AppleTalk can run over Apple's own network technology called LocalTalk, Ethernet (via Apple's EtherTalk), or Token Ring (via Apple's TokenTalk). The folks at Apple sure know how to "talk the Talk."

Windows NT Server provides AppleTalk protocol support through its *Services for Macintosh,* or SFM. It enables Apple Macintosh clients to share files and printers. In addition, Windows NT Server can act as an AppleTalk router. Other than an optional secure logon function, no additional software is required on the Macintosh client machines. Because the Macintosh uses a file system different from that used by PCs, Windows NT Server creates a special shared directory where the shared Macintosh files can be accessed. I discuss the details of how to install, configure, and use NT Server's SFM in Chapter 12.

Redirector

The redirector component provides your computer with the means to gain access to resources on another computer. It implements the client side of accessing files and printers on a remote server. The redirector operates at the session layer of the OSI model, as shown in Figure 4-1.

The Redirector Driver

The Windows NT redirector, which exists on both the Workstation and Server products, is implemented as an NT file system driver. Why a file system driver? The primary reason is that this approach enables applications to make the same I/O requests that they would make to any local file system. The application needn't know where the file is located. It just performs the appropriate operations on the file. In the eyes of the NT I/O manager, there's really no difference between accessing a file on a local disk and accessing a file on a remote system. The I/O manager simply uses two different device drivers to fulfill the requests — namely, the disk driver and the network adapter driver.

There's another advantage to having the redirector implemented as a file system driver. Because it's a driver, it operates within the I/O manager in kernel mode. This enables the redirector to call other drivers, the cache manager, and other kernel components directly, which reduces overhead and increases performance.

You'll sometimes see the redirector referred to as the workstation. The intent of this terminology is to distinguish more clearly the redirector's functionality from the server component. However, this terminology is confusing. I use the term *redirector* throughout this book to refer to the client-side session layer component that I'm discussing here.

The redirector communicates with the transport protocols below via the TDI interface. It's responsible for establishing connections to resources and reestablishing them when connections are broken.

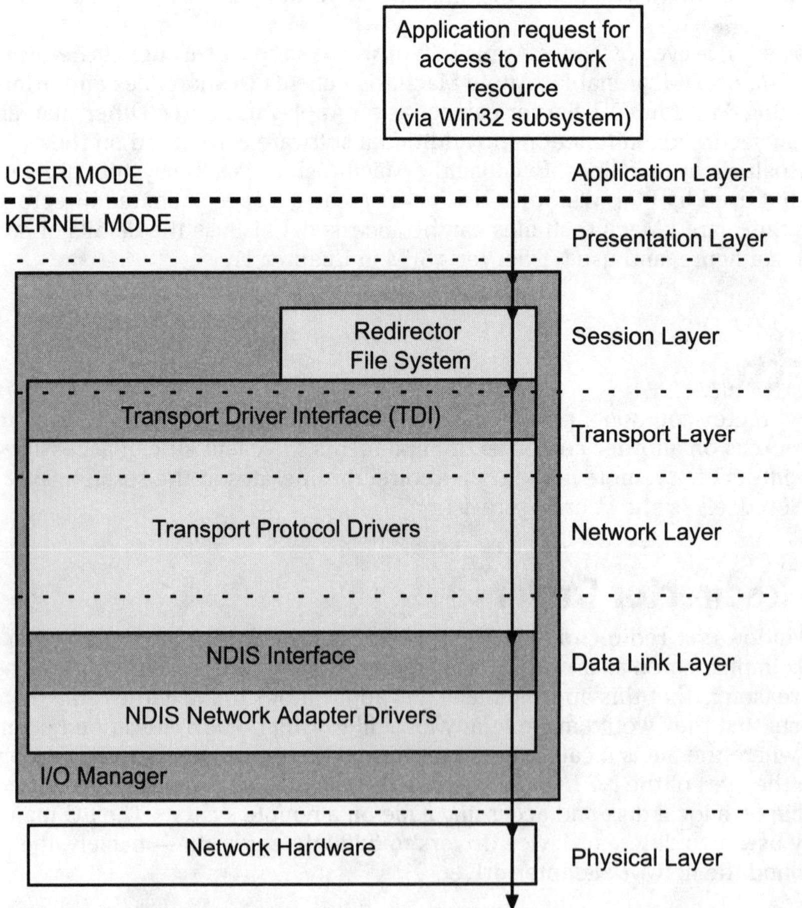

Figure 4-8: The I/O manager passes I/O requests destined for the network to the redirector component.

Sending a Client's Request

Let's follow the path of a file operation from the requesting application down to the network. A request for I/O, in this case a read of an already opened file, is passed to the I/O manager. The I/O manager recognizes this as a request for a resource on a remote system, so it passes the request to the redirector. The redirector passes the request down to the transport protocol, where it finds its way through the lower layers and out to the network. Figure 4-8 shows how this works. I'll pick up this example and continue with it in the next section, which covers the server component.

Server

The server component fields requests from client redirectors and provides them with access to the resources that they request. It implements the server side of sharing access to files and printers with remote clients. Like the redirector, the server operates at the session layer of the OSI model, as shown in Figure 4-1.

The Server Driver

The server component of Windows NT exists on both the Workstation and Server products. (On Windows NT Workstation, this component provides the server capabilities required for peer-to-peer networking.) The server component is implemented as an NT file system driver, just like the redirector. As you'll see in the next example, because most of the server component's interactions take place with other file system drivers, it makes performance sense for it to be a file system driver. The server component communicates with the transport protocols below it via the TDI interface.

Servicing a Client's Request

Let's follow through with the redirector example started in the previous section, and see what happens to the read request when it comes in from the network. The network adapter driver receives the request from the network and passes it up though the transport protocol driver. The server receives the request and passes it to the appropriate local file system driver (for example, FAT or NTFS). The local file system then calls the disk device driver, which reads the requested data from disk. The local file system passes the data back to the server, which in turn passes the data down through the protocol stack and out to the network. On the client computer, the data is passed back up through the protocol stack to the redirector. At that point, the redirector notifies the application that the read has been completed. Figure 4-9 illustrates this process.

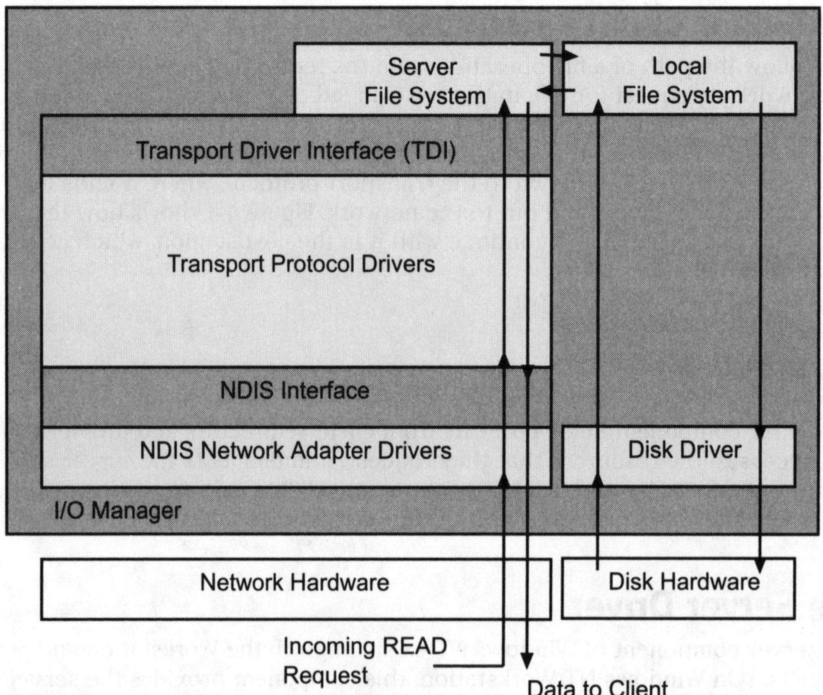

Figure 4-9: The server component cooperates with the local file system to get the data from disk and out to the network.

YET ANOTHER PROTOCOL?

The Microsoft server and redirector components in Windows NT use their own session layer protocol to communicate with each other. This protocol is called *Server Message Block,* or SMB. An actual message passed by this protocol is also called an SMB.

SMBs include commands that make and break connections between the redirector and shared resources, requests for access to resources, data destined for a remote print queue, requests for status of print jobs, and user messages sent between client computers. SMBs are independent of the underlying transport protocols. They define the content of the data conversation between the Microsoft redirector on the client side and the Microsoft server on the server end.

Multiple Providers

The redirector and server components that I've discussed are fine for Microsoft networks. They can speak SMBs to each other all day and get all sorts of work done for you. But what about getting Windows NT to make things happen with another type of network, such as Novell NetWare or Banyan VINES?

In the NetWare case, you saw that Windows NT can run IPX/SPX as a fully compatible transport protocol. However, above the transport protocol layer, NetWare speaks NCP, not SMB. NCP, which stands for *NetWare Core Protocol,* is the Novell equivalent of Microsoft's SMB. (In fact, the NetWare messages at this level are called NCPs.) Just running IPX/SPX gives you connectivity between an NT computer and a NetWare computer but doesn't give you interoperability. So, a NetWare requester that's NCP-literate is needed on NT to carry on a truly useful conversation with a NetWare server. This type of add-on client network component is known as a *provider.* The Microsoft redirector is a provider, as is Novell's client requester for NT. A provider establishes NT as a client of a remote server.

A Provider for Each Network Type

One of NT's strengths is its open support of third-party software components or additional components supplied by Microsoft. Each different type of network requires its own provider, and Windows NT supports multiple providers. This means you can load more than one provider and simultaneously access different types of networks. For example, you can have Microsoft's NT redirector and a NetWare requester loaded at the same time and access both NT servers and NetWare servers.

Microsoft includes providers for NetWare in both Windows NT products. NT Workstation includes Client Services for NetWare, whereas NT Server includes the Gateway Service for NetWare mentioned earlier. Other software developers, such as Banyan, market Windows NT providers for access to their networks.

UNC Names

Enabling the presence of multiple providers makes life a bit more complicated for Windows NT. At the application level, NT must sort out two types of network commands and hand them off to the appropriate provider. Many applications take actions on shared resources by specifying those shared resources using *Uniform Naming Convention,* or UNC, names. (I wanted to go to the last uniform-naming convention in Chicago, but my uniform, whose given name is Bob, was at the cleaners.) Applications call standard Win32 file I/O APIs, passing in UNC names to specify what resource they want to use. If you've ever used the NET command under DOS, you've used a UNC name to specify a server name and resource on that server. UNC names let you access server resources directly, without first establishing a connection. For example, you could use a UNC name in the DOS copy command to pull files from a server to your computer as follows:

```
copy \\myserver\public\clowns\*.* c:\bozos
```

In this example, myserver is the name of the server, public is the name of the shared resource (in this case, a disk directory) on that server, and clowns is a subdirectory within that resource. The command copies all of the files from the clowns directory on the server to the bozos directory on the local computer.

Multiple UNC Provider

UNC names are handled by a driver in NT called the *Multiple UNC Provider,* or MUP. This component, running in kernel mode, simultaneously shows the UNC name to all of the providers on the local system, until one of them claims that it recognizes and can deal with the name. The MUP then passes the entire command to that provider for execution, as shown in Figure 4-10. If it sees the same UNC name more than once, the MUP driver remembers this information for some period of time, uses it to skip the query step, and routes the command directly to the appropriate provider. (There's a rumor that work is progressing on a smaller version called a MUPpet, but Kermit and Miss Piggy have threatened to file suit if Microsoft uses this name.)

If multiple providers claim that they can handle the UNC name, the MUP must decide which one will do the work. In this case, the early bird gets the worm. The MUP uses the order in which the providers were loaded in the system. This order is driven by entries in Windows NT's registry database. I'll tell you all about managing the NT registry in Chapter 20.

WNet Calls

The second type of network command is issued by an application through Win32 WNet APIs. These APIs are designed to enable an application to connect to multiple networks seamlessly, browse through servers and resources, and transfer data among different network flavors. If you've ever used File Manager or Explorer, you've used this WNet API command interface without even knowing it.

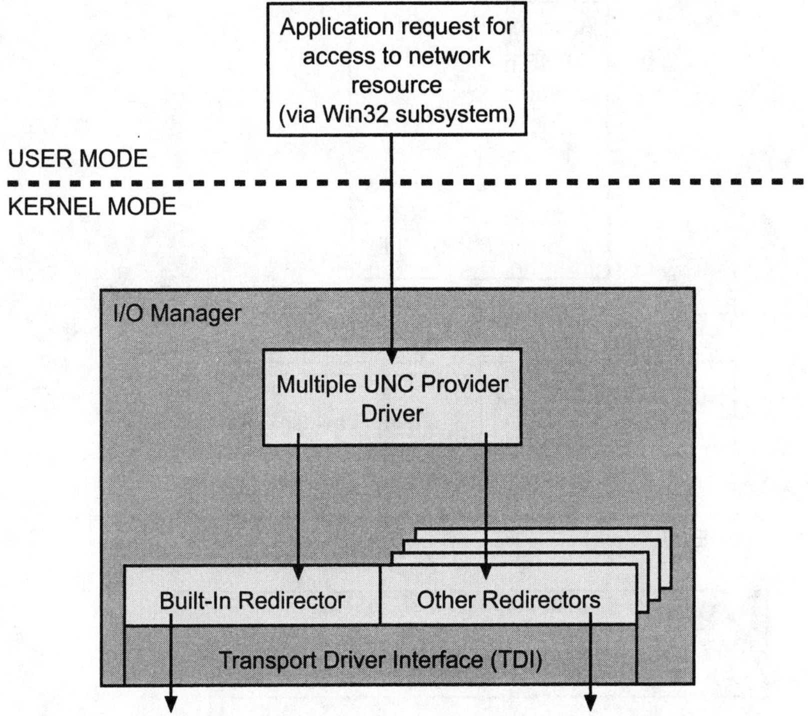

Figure 4-10: The Multiple UNC Provider (MUP) driver directs UNC name commands to the appropriate network provider.

Multiple Provider Router

Win32 WNet requests are handled by NT's *Multiple Provider Router,* or MPR. When a new provider is installed, two pieces are included. One is the equivalent of the redirector in kernel mode, and the other is a DLL that implements the WNet APIs for that redirector. The DLL presents a standard set of functions called the *provider interface.* Requests made by applications via the WNet APIs are sent immediately to the MPR. The MPR then polls each of the provider DLLs to determine which provider should deal with the WNet request. Like the MUP, the MPR prioritizes the providers based on their load order. Unlike the MUP, the MPR operates in user mode as a DLL, as shown in Figure 4-11. (Another example of a multiple provider router is the health insurance administrator who refers you from one HMO doctor to another.)

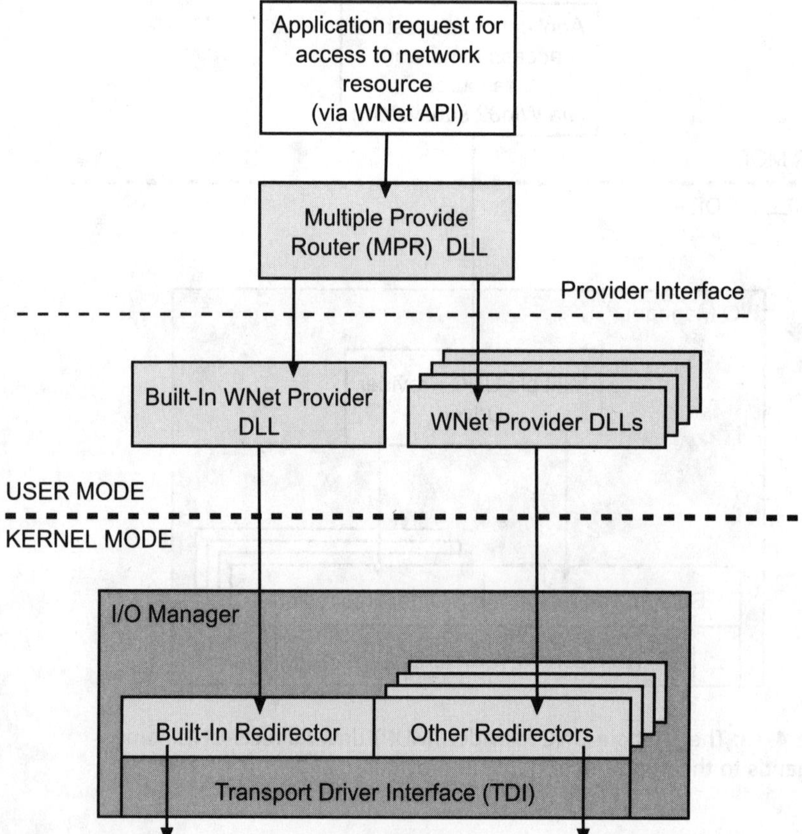

Figure 4-11: The Multiple Provider Router (MPR) DLL determines which provider should handle a WNet API request.

Windows NT Distributed Applications

Windows NT provides several ways for applications to access and communicate over the network. Whether or not you create Windows NT applications, you're likely going to run them. Thus, it's important for you to understand the different ways in which applications communicate over the network. Knowledge of what network facilities your applications use is an important weapon in your troubleshooting arsenal.

UNC and WNet

An application can access files and printers over the network without doing anything special. It can just use the appropriate UNC and call standard Win32 APIs. Command line utilities such as *copy* and *dir* are examples of this approach. If an application wants to browse and manage network resources, it can use the Win32 WNet APIs. The Windows NT Explorer is an excellent example of this. All of these application requests are handled by the appropriate provider, usually the redirector file system driver.

Truly distributed client/server applications, however, go beyond just accessing data on a remote computer. They share processing responsibilities between client and server processes on different computers. Windows NT offers a rich set of features that applications can employ to communicate directly with each other over the network, using the underlying networking facilities discussed so far.

NetBIOS and Winsock

The NetBIOS and Winsock APIs enable applications to make connections with each other and transmit data back and forth. Both NetBIOS and Winsock are implemented in Windows NT as combinations of user-mode DLLs and kernel-mode drivers. Applications call the APIs in the DLL, which in turn pass requests to the kernel-mode driver. These drivers operate at the same level as the redirector file system driver, at the OSI session layer. Use of these APIs enables an application to bypass the redirector and other providers. The application can then hold application-specific conversations between processes on different computers. Many of the TCP/IP utilities are examples of Winsock applications. Figure 4-6 shows where NetBIOS and Winsock fit.

Named Pipes and Mailslots

NT applications may also elect to communicate with each other using *named pipes* or *mailslots.* Named pipes enable applications to pass data easily back and forth between two processes, regardless of whether those processes are on the same computer. For example, Microsoft SQL Server makes heavy use of NT named pipes for communication between processes. Named pipes provide only a one-to-one conversation between two processes. The mailslot approach is very similar to named pipes but provides one-to-many and many-to-one communication. If you need to broadcast a message to several processes, mailslots can make this an easy task. On Windows NT, both of these features are implemented as file systems in kernel mode. The Named Pipe File System, or NPFS, handles named pipes; the Mailslot File System, or MSFS, deals with mailslots.

Remote Procedure Call

Probably the most flexible application communication facility on Windows NT is Remote Procedure Call (RPC), briefly discussed in Chapter 2. RPC is unique two ways. First, it enables a client application process to simply make a function call and have that function call execute automatically in a separate server process. The application needn't worry about where the server process is or how to establish communication with it. The application doesn't even need to know that the function is actually implemented in a different process.

The other unique aspect of RPC is that it uses other communication mechanisms to transmit data. For example, RPC may use named pipes, Winsock, or NetBIOS to converse between client and server processes. If both processes are on the same machine, RPC can use the fast LPC facility, discussed in Chapter 2. The RPC approach is illustrated in Figure 4-12.

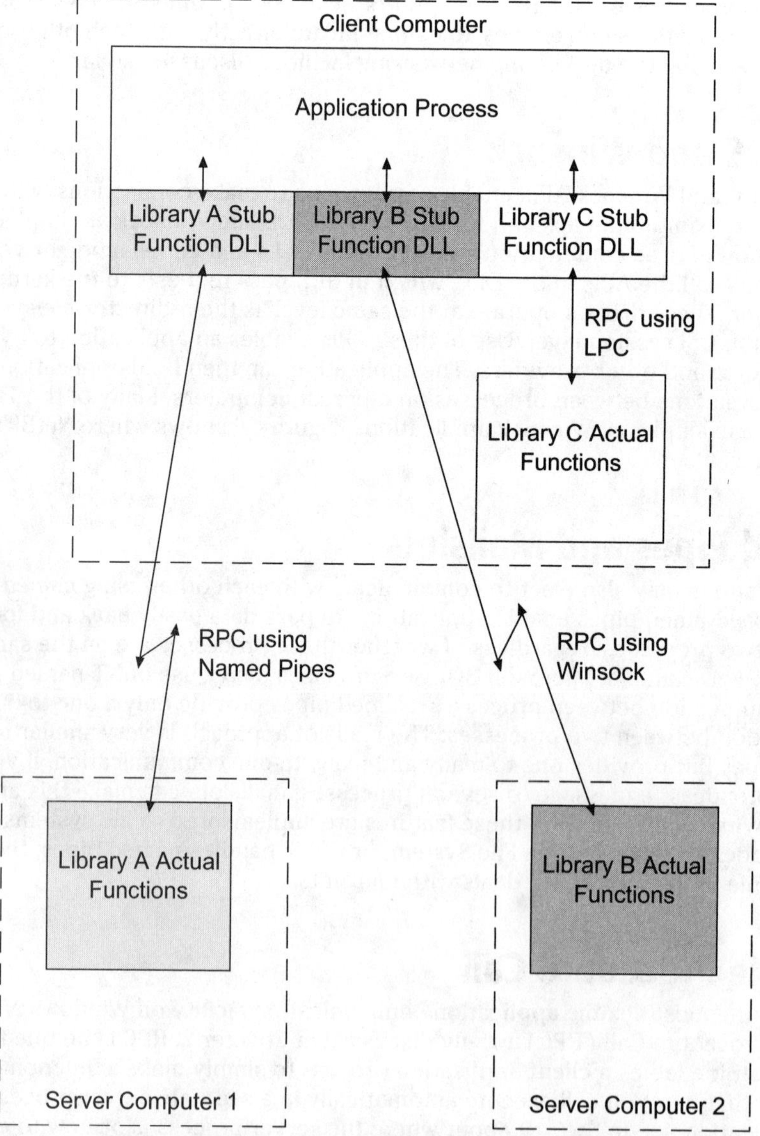

Figure 4-12: RPC enables applications to be oblivious to the communication process and can use the most efficient transmission path available.

Network OLE

One of the biggest revolutions in Windows computing has been the introduction of OLE, short for *Object Linking and Embedding*. This facility, present in Windows NT as well as in Windows 95 and Windows 3.x, enables software developers to create applications that are centered on your data. You don't have to focus on what application is needed for each component of a document. For example, with OLE, you can have a document that contains embedded text, spreadsheets, charts, and pictures. As you move through a component of your document, you automatically run the appropriate application that can edit that component. OLE provides many other capabilities, including generic object-oriented communication links between applications. Entire books have been written on the topic of OLE, because developers have traditionally had difficulty understanding and writing applications using OLE. I won't attempt to cover all the ins and outs of OLE in this book, but I bring it up in the context of network communication for an important reason.

Windows NT 4.0 provides, for the first time, what's being called by some *Network OLE*. It's officially called DCOM, for Distributed Component Object Model. DCOM enables all OLE communication to take place across the network, rather than just on the local computer. OLE capabilities are becoming very popular, partly because of their power and partly because Microsoft requires OLE support in Win32 applications to earn the Windows 95-compatible logo. Once an application has the appropriate OLE plumbing, it's a small step to support DCOM. Thus, it may well become a significant and common means of communication between client and server processes over the network.

Remote Access

Windows NT Server provides a powerful remote access server through its RAS facility. The server can handle up to 256 simultaneous incoming connections. RAS is really a multiprotocol router, in which the RAS server is dedicated to handling communications between multiple remote nodes and the local network. As mentioned in Chapter 1, RAS remote node is not the same as remote control, which dedicates the server to running an application controlled by a single remote computer.

RAS supports PPP, which stands for *Point-to-Point Protocol.* (I don't even have to try to make fun of this one. I've been in meetings where every mention of PPP elicits giggles from even the most seasoned and conservative managers.) PPP is an industry-standard set of protocols that negotiate various aspects of a remote node network connection. Because PPP is an existing standard, Windows NT clients can dial in to existing non-NT servers running PPP, and non-NT clients running PPP can dial in to Windows NT Server. You can run any combination of TCP/IP, IPX/SPX, or NetBEUI on PPP clients.

The most visible change to RAS in Windows NT 4.0 is support for automatic dialing in the RAS client. Whenever your application needs access to a remote resource, RAS automatically dials your modem or ISDN device to make the connection. You'll learn all about the RAS server and client in Chapter 11.

Windows NT Server Domains

I've mentioned several times that Windows NT Server eases your network administration burden by providing centralized management of user accounts and security. In this section, I describe NT Server's approach to making life easier for you and for your users.

The Trouble with Workgroups

Recall from Chapter 3 that a workgroup is an informal grouping of computers with peer-to-peer network capability. In this environment, user accounts are scattered across multiple servers. To get access to a resource offered by a server, you need a user account on that server, and you must log on to it before accessing the resource. If you ever need to change your password, you must manually change it on every server where you have an account. If you don't change your passwords everywhere, you end up having to remember different passwords on the different servers.

As a network administrator in a workgroup environment, you probably have the headache of deleting multiple user accounts when someone leaves the company or even changes departments. You likely have users who never change their passwords, because it's such a hassle to make the same change on multiple servers. This compromises the security of your network.

Workgroups are fine for a very small number of servers and users, but workgroups can quickly become administration nightmares for both you and your users.

Creating Order from Chaos

How does Windows NT Server address these issues? It organizes your network into a group of servers and clients with one administrative structure. This group of computers is called a *domain*. Within a domain, servers share a centralized user account database. You create user accounts for access to the domain rather than to individual servers. This approach lets you log on to the network with a single user account and password. Once you're on the domain, you can access any resource within the network regardless of what server it's on. Security privileges are assigned to each user account, again in the centralized database.

In a domain, you establish one Windows NT Server computer as the *primary domain controller,* or PDC. It has the responsibility of maintaining the centralized user account database. In addition, it validates user logon requests using this database and either grants or denies access to the user.

What happens when the PDC is down because of a hardware failure, scheduled maintenance, or software crash? Are all users suddenly unable to log on to the domain? Windows NT Server addresses this issue with *backup domain controllers,* or BDCs. In addition to the PDC, you establish one or more Windows NT Server computers in the domain as BDCs. Any updates to the central user account database on the PDC are transmitted to all of the BDCs, so that the BDCs are always up to date. This transmission of database updates to BDCs is called *replication.* A simple Windows NT Server domain is shown in Figure 4-13.

If a PDC computer goes down, BDCs can still authenticate user logon requests, using their own copy of the account database. In addition, if the PDC is going to be down for awhile, a BDC can be promoted to the role of PDC, taking on the responsibility of managing the central account database. Having one or more BDCs available in your network domain provides you with a high degree of fault tolerance.

Even when the PDC is alive and well, BDCs have the added benefit of distributing the responsibility of authenticating user logon requests. This lightens the processing load on the PDC, effectively balancing the effort of maintaining network security across multiple servers in the domain.

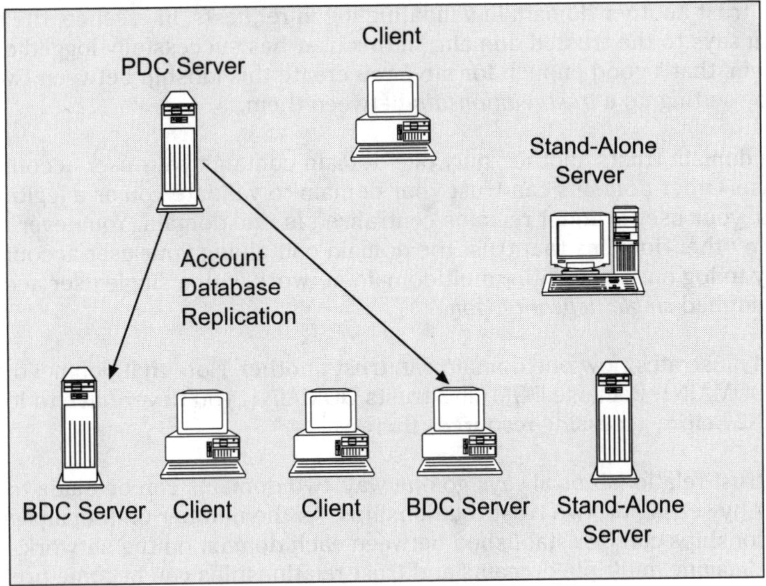

Figure 4-13: A Windows NT Server domain includes one PDC, one or more BDCs, and other computers.

An Out-of-Domain Experience

If you have several servers, you can certainly put them all in a single Windows NT Server domain and reap the benefits of easy administration. However, you might want to establish multiple domains for any combination of the following reasons:

- ✦ Some departments in your organization may prefer to manage their own resources. This is best accomplished by establishing their own network domain.
- ✦ Your organization may be geographically separated into multiple sites. Establishing a domain at each site avoids consuming precious bandwidth with replication over relatively slow WAN links.
- ✦ If you add too many servers to a single domain, performance can begin to suffer. Many BDCs must be updated with user account changes via replication. Breaking your network into multiple domains can alleviate this problem.

Once you establish more than one domain, there's potential for the benefits of centralized administration to go out the window. If you need to access resources on two different domains, don't you need an account on both domains? Doesn't this bring us back full circle to the drawbacks of workgroup networks? These are valid concerns.

Trusting Relationships

The good news is that Windows NT Server provides a feature that enables one domain to trust another domain in validating logon requests. In essence, the trusting domain says to the trusted domain, "If this user has successfully logged on to your domain, that's good enough for me." You create this kinship between two domains by setting up a *trust relationship* between them.

When one domain trusts another, only one domain contains your user account in its database. Other domains can trust your domain to validate you as a legitimate user. Thus, your user account remains centralized in one domain. You never need to log on to other domains that trust the domain containing your user account. The ability to log on to the entire multidomain network with a single user account has been dubbed *single network logon.*

Figure 4-14 illustrates how one domain can trust another. Note that you need only log on to DOMAIN1. Because DOMAIN2 trusts DOMAIN1, you never have to log on to DOMAIN2 before accessing resources there.

Although trust relationships always go one way, two domains can be made to trust each other by setting up two trust relationships. As the number of domains grows, trust relationships can be established between each domain on the network. As you might imagine, multiple domains and trust relationships can become pretty complex.

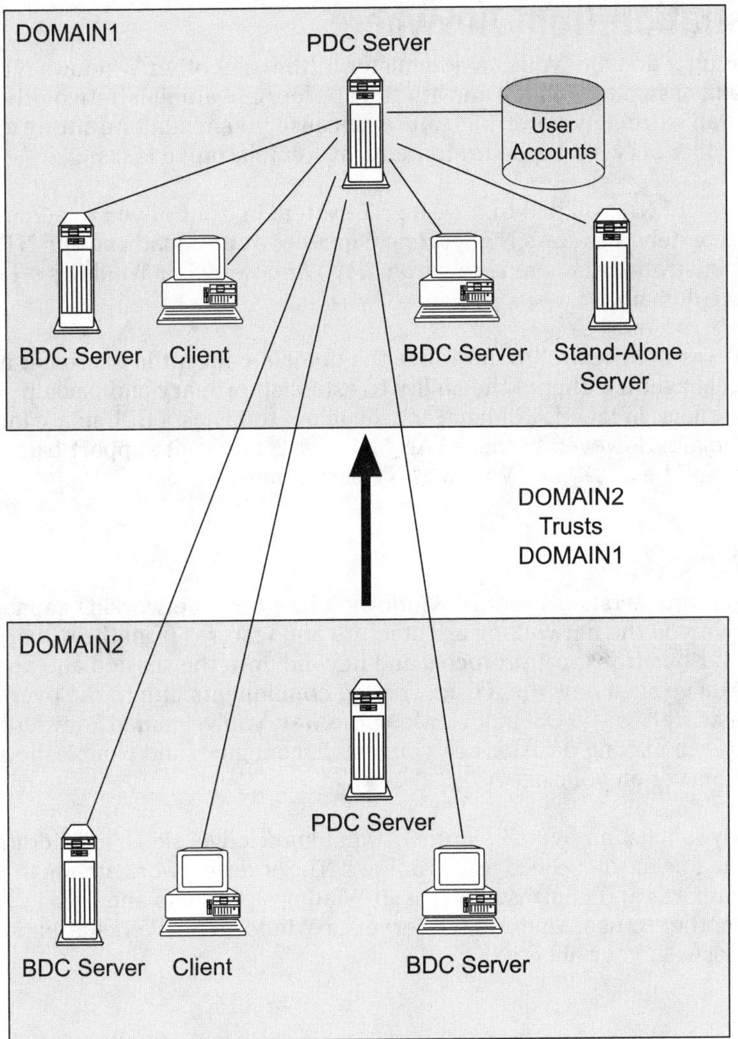

Figure 4-14: In a simple trust relationship, Domain2 trusts Domain1 to validate user logon requests.

In Chapter 10, I fill you in on several recommended approaches to setting up multiple domains to meet the requirements of your enterprise. There you'll get all of the information that you need to be master of many domains and to establish trust relationships. I also show you how Microsoft has implemented multiple Windows NT Server domains in their worldwide corporate network.

Administration from Anywhere

Once you set up a domain, you can administer it from any other Windows NT node on the domain, assuming you log on with the appropriate administrative privileges. This is an extremely powerful feature, because you needn't be sitting at the domain controller server's keyboard to perform administrative tasks.

In past versions of NT, you had to have an NT system in front of you to administer the domain remotely. Windows NT Server 4.0 enables you to load and run NT's network administration tools remotely from any Windows 95 or Windows NT system within the domain.

Windows NT was not the first to introduce the domain concept in Microsoft networks. LAN Manager 2.x offered the ability to establish primary and backup domain controllers. In fact, LAN Manager 2.x can act today as a BDC in a Windows NT Server domain. However, because LAN Manager 2.x doesn't support trust relationships, it can't be a PDC in a Windows NT Server network.

Summary

In this chapter you've taken a tour of Windows NT Server's networking capabilities. I've shown you the networking architecture and features from the driver level through the various transport protocols and beyond, into the session and application layers. You've seen how the NT networking components fit into the overall NT architecture, as well as the OSI model. Along the way, you've gained knowledge that is valuable in making decisions as you install, configure, and troubleshoot Windows NT Server on your network.

In Chapter 5, you'll get an overall picture of what knowledge, skills, and additional resources you'll need to succeed as a Windows NT Server network administrator. Chapter 6 compares and contrasts Microsoft Windows products and helps you determine whether to use Windows NT Server or Windows NT Workstation for specific purposes in your network.

Being a Successful NT Network Administrator

As a Windows NT Server 4.0 network administrator, you're involved in a career filled with both challenges and rewards. To do a great job, you need to understand the specific duties that you need to perform. You also must know where to find the information quickly that you require to solve problems, provide great support, and make informed decisions about your enterprise network.

In this chapter, I fill you in on what concepts and activities you'll need to understand and perform as an NT Server network administrator. I pass along some advice on what pitfalls to expect and how to handle them. Finally, I provide you with pointers to some key information resources that can help you succeed in your role. As you'll see in this and subsequent chapters, I emphasize planning and preparation, which makes dealing with the actual activities much easier.

Administering Your Network

In this discussion, I assume you're going to use the Windows NT Server domain model discussed in Chapter 4 to provide yourself with centralized administration capabilities. If you do, you or others in your organization need to understand and maintain a number of its components. They include domains, computer accounts, user accounts, user profiles, and group accounts. The sections that follow cover each one.

NT Domains

You'll need to understand the NT domain model, as described in Chapter 4 and further in Chapter 7. If your network covers more than one department or includes a large number of users or computers, read Chapter 10 to determine how many BDCs and domains you need in your enterprise. As network administrator, you need to keep tight control of new domains that are created to assure that they don't conflict with existing domains.

If you establish trust relationships between domains, you need to make sure that the administrators of each trusted domain implement the appropriate security policy of your organization. Likewise, you must keep track of which computers have been established as BDCs.

Computer and Domain Names

As discussed further in Chapter 7, you need to settle on naming conventions for your client computers, servers, and domains. Selecting and sticking with domain names are especially important. Changing your mind about the name of a domain creates lots of extra work and frustration for both you and your users.

If you're looking for suggestions on how to name your servers, consider selecting a theme. Pick something that your particular corporate culture can embrace. I've seen server naming schemes based on *Lord of the Rings* (Frodo, Bilbo, Gandalf), *Star Trek* (Spock, Kirk, Bones), planets, major cities, and even internal organs (spleen, liver, kidney). Whatever theme you choose, make sure that folks are comfortable with it, because it's a hassle to change server names once they're established.

Computer Accounts

Whenever you add an NT computer (a client workstation, a stand-alone server, or a BDC) to an existing domain on your network, you create a *computer account* for that computer. (The computer account is sometimes called a *machine account* in Microsoft's literature.) Either you or your users need to add accounts for each node added to the domain.

Computer accounts are sometimes confused with user accounts, but they're not the same things. In the NT world, multiple users can log on to a domain through the same computer, and one user can log on to the domain through multiple computers. If most of your users have more than one computer each, you'll have more computer accounts than user accounts. If many of your users share a single computer to do their work, you'll have fewer computer accounts and more user accounts.

User Accounts

You'll have to establish a user account for each user in the NT domain. User accounts grant specific privileges to users on local NT computers and on the network, much like keys grant access to specific rooms in your building. You certainly don't want everyone to have the master key, enabling them to access and change everything on the network. You'll encounter three broad classes of user accounts, as follows:

- **Users.** This is a standard type of account that you use to grant specific rights to a user. The bulk of your network users will have user accounts.
- **Guests.** Although you try to give your guests every courtesy when they visit, guests are nevertheless at the bottom of the NT privilege chain. Guests have limited rights to access the network.
- **Administrators.** In contrast, administrators are at the top of the privilege chain. They're able to add, delete, and alter accounts; change hardware configurations and just about anything else.

Windows NT Server provides built-in administrator and guest accounts that you can use immediately. You use the NT User Manager for Domains utility to add, delete, and maintain user accounts on your domain. Chapter 18 covers how to do this.

User Profiles

Most users want their own custom environment, where they can work comfortably and efficiently. User profiles contain desktop settings, logon information, and other data related to specific user accounts. By default, users accounts have different profiles on each computer that they use.

ACCOMMODATING ROVING USERS

If someone has a job that forces them to log on to the domain from many different computers during the course of a day, they may want a *roving profile* that enables their settings to follow them wherever they may go. You, as an administrator, will have to enable roaming profiles for your users at their request. You may also occasionally need to create and restore profiles for your users. Chapter 18 covers in detail user profile management using the System utility in Control Panel.

Group Accounts

Windows NT Server group accounts are similar in concept to group accounts on other multiuser operating systems. They provide a convenient way of assigning the same rights to a specific set of users. For example, rather than separately setting up each member of your team as an administrator, you can simply add their account to the Administrators group.

Windows NT Server contains several built-in groups that make your life as an administrator much easier. Table 5-1 lists these groups in alphabetical order.

Table 5-1
Windows NT Server 4.0 Built-In Group Accounts

Built-In Account	***Description***
Account Operators	Members can administer user and group accounts in the domain.
Administrators	Members can fully administer the computer or domain.
Backup Operators	Members can bypass normal file security to allow backup of files.
Domain Admins	Lists all designated administrators in the domain.
Domain Guests	Lists all guests in the domain.
Domain Users	Lists all users in the domain.
Guests	Members are granted guest access to the computer or domain.
Print Operators	Members can administer printers in the domain.
Replicator	Supports file replication within a domain.
Server Operators	Members can administer servers in the domain.
Users	Members are ordinary users of the domain.

Managing Security Policies

Although Windows NT Server offers the capability of tight security, it's only as secure as you make it. Virtually all of the security features are optional, so you need to determine what your organization's security policy should be. This is a sticky issue, which may cause a large portion of the grief that you receive from your users. Most of these folks are not used to security if they came from the DOS, MAC, OS/2, or Windows worlds. Software developers (bless their hearts) can be especially disdainful of tight security, if they've been used to a free-wheeling standalone or workgroup environment. (I was one of these folks a few years ago, and you can bet that I didn't like security.)

Your job may involve establishing security policies with your management. If so, you should start defining these policies early on, to avoid having to redo or undo your hard work. If you're inheriting a network with no established security policy, make it your business to create one. You may need to sell management and your users on the need for NT security. So, help them create the policy based on knowing what's possible with Windows NT Server. Most importantly, make sure that management stands behind security enforcement. I've seen some cases where all security was removed from above when one or two employees became vocal on the subject.

Documenting Your Network

Creating network documentation is a key aspect of network administration that's often overlooked in many organizations. I can't emphasize enough the critical importance of writing down information about your network and keeping it organized in a safe place. Many administrators keep this information in a notebook. Consider this notebook a physical component of your network.

Although you may be tempted to keep this information in a file on one of your computers, you should always keep a hard copy version. The information in this notebook is critical and may be required for you to restore your computer if it crashes. If the file is only online, you won't be able to view it.

Why is documenting everything so important? Experience reveals several reasons, some more obvious than others. What if you're sick or on vacation or have a sudden family emergency that takes you away from work for several days? Others in the team need to be able to understand how things are set up. You'll often be put under high pressure to fix network problems immediately. Under pressure, it's often easy to forget details. Having the network documentation up to date and close at hand allows you to recall details instantly.

I've seen cases where good network documentation has saved the day when a quick change was required while the network administrator was out of town. I've also seen critical problems languish until the resident guru returned from an extra-innings softball game, because no one else had a clue how the network was configured. In this case, the detailed documentation existed, but only in the form of neurons in the guru's head.

Inheriting a Network

If you're inheriting an existing network, find out if there's documentation. If so, get it, study it, and verify that it actually matches the existing infrastructure. If it does, great. If not, make it your business to update it now. If you're installing a network yourself, document every aspect of the network as you're building it. If you're having professionals install your network, be involved in the process and make sure that they provide you with full documentation of what they have done. If this is impossible, make it your job to document it as you go. You'll thank yourself later.

Installation Details

When you install Windows NT Server, include a list of all of the decisions that you made during installation. You can use a copy of the Windows NT Server Setup Worksheet included in Chapter 7. After installation, include a note for each major change that you make to the hardware or software of the network. Develop procedures for handling certain critical situations. This will serve as your team's handbook for handling known emergencies.

Inventories

Include software and hardware inventories. These questions come up more than you might think: "How many systems are connected to the network?" "How many 286 clients do we still have?" "Do we have the right number of licenses for the actual number of copies of Microsoft Word?" (You can use Microsoft's Systems Management Server to help gather inventory information from the computers on your network.)

Get It in Writing

Finally, don't worry about job security. Getting this information on paper allows you to appear more organized, to actually *be* more organized, and to show that you care about the company's operations. By championing documentation of your network, you'll be considered a team player, and you'll work more efficiently.

Managing Your Users

Probably the most important but least technical facet of your job as a network administrator is managing relationships with the users that you support. You're providing critical support to one or more departments in your organization, and the users in those departments are your customers. Your business is to keep them in business by providing reliable and available computing resources. Whatever exciting technical problems you have to solve in your job, never lose sight of the fact that your users are the center of your focus.

Building Your Relationships

Your users' perception of you and the network is critical to your success. I've worked with many MIS organizations in my career, and have learned a lot about what does and doesn't work, in terms of building relationships with users. If you're a seasoned administrator, you can probably skip this section. If not, and you're still learning your duties, here are a few tips on how to deal with your users:

✦ **Have integrity.** If you don't know something, don't make it up. Say you'll look into it and go ferret out the answer. This book is a great resource for answers. In Appendix C, I provide you with a list of other sources of information on Windows NT Server.

✦ **Follow through.** Follow through on your commitments. If you say you're going to have something done by a certain day and time, do it. If you can't, let the user know why and reset expectations. Keep them informed of what's going on so that they don't feel abandoned.

✦ **Pinpoint the problem.** You'll need good problem-solving skills and the ability to point out the trouble spot tactfully when everyone is pointing the finger at your network or at the change you made. Of course, if the problem is something that you caused, admit it and fix it.

✦ **Set expectations.** User and management expectations for network performance and availability will be high. Communicate what people should expect and keep them informed about scheduled downtime.

✦ **Be a calming influence.** Keep your cool in tough situations. Make it your goal to make people feel comfortable with you and with the technology that they're using.

✦ **Be flexible.** If possible, plan around key user needs and activities. For example, if a certain database needs to be available for reporting at a daily morning meeting, don't schedule that server's downtime in the early morning.

Some of this may sound like common sense. Much of it is. But it's very easy to get caught up in the technology and the problems of the moment, at the expense of building solid relationships and reputations with your users.

Listening to Your Users

Of course, planning around your users' needs means that you need to listen to and understand those needs. You need to know all you can about the capabilities of the server, network, NT, applications, users' systems, and what these folks are actually trying to accomplish.

When someone reports bizarre or unreproducible network behavior that doesn't have an obvious cause or solution, listen and make a note of it. It might be nothing, or it could be one small clue that, when connected with other clues, might uncover a problem that you can and should solve. Just as auto experts tell consumers to keep their ears open — that every new noise in a car is a symptom of something potentially disastrous — so should you listen to your network and your users for possible problems. Sometimes it's an offhand remark made by a user in the lunchroom that suddenly motivates you to find what's causing the strange behavior.

LEARNING THE BUSINESS

If you're in an MIS organization that serves the entire enterprise, you have a real opportunity to find out about how all of the different departments perform their business functions – and learning many aspects of the business never hurts anyone who wants rewards and career advancement. What's more, your users will appreciate your extra efforts to understand and meet their needs.

As soon as users attach their desktop computers to your network, you become at least partially responsible for their PCs. Make sure that you know what's out there and, especially, what network software people are loading on their machines. You should have a policy up front, for example, about loading and running beta software on machines attached to the network. At Microsoft, running an early Windows 95 beta caused some problems on our production network. Fortunately, only folks on certain segments were allowed to run it, so the trauma was limited to just one department.

Training Your Users

If there's one constant in network administration, it's that you always need to be explaining or reminding your users about something new. As a resident NT Server expert, you need to understand the needs of your users and get them the information that they need. Understand how these folks work, listen to the types of questions they ask, and keep their needs in mind as you learn about new NT features and capabilities.

Keep a record of the most frequently asked questions or the areas where users seem to need the most help. You may notice that your users have learned the minimum 10 to 20 percent of the applications and operating system that they need to do their jobs. However, typically, they're missing some great time-saving features that would really help them work smarter and faster. Because time is a precious commodity in today's corporate world, prioritize your training efforts according to payback in reduced support questions for you or higher productivity for your users.

For example, I've seen a few managers, who haven't had much exposure to NT security, send each other lengthy confidential files in e-mail rather than placing the files on a server where "anyone could look at the files." This can bog down the network and waste time for the recipients in downloading huge files. When these managers were exposed to the right information by the MIS department, they started placing the files on a server and setting permissions that allowed only specific managers to see them. This approach was just as secure, the folks involved worked more efficiently, and the network was less strained. You can create your own similar happy endings within your organization.

FEEDBACK NEVER HURTS

Solicit feedback from your users, on your performance, on their opinion of the network and server, and so forth. Never shy away from criticism. You're smart. You can separate the real issues from the simple whining or scapegoating. If you've developed a good rapport with your users, you'll be surprised at their goodwill toward you and their constructive suggestions. Ultimately, your users want you to succeed, too.

I've seen a couple of successful MIS departments survey their users through e-mail. When the departments applied what they learned from the feedback, they got even more useful input from the next survey. Because the users began to see that their feedback was important and would really make a difference, their next round of suggestions was more constructive.

You can use well-advertised FAQ (Frequently Asked Questions) sheets available on the network as one avenue for communicating this sort of information. Brown bag lunches and tech talks can also be effective methods, if you can find a way to grab people's attention enough to attend. Find creative ways to transfer knowledge to your users, and you'll be regarded as a hero.

Managing Your Management

Network user demand nearly always increases faster than predicted. Keep this in mind as you plan the hardware for your servers and your network. From your manager's perspective, one of your primary goals is to make the best use of your current assets, before asking for any more. It's your job to get the maximum from your existing equipment.

Don't overlook creative ways to increase server capacity without huge expenses — processor upgrades, more memory, faster net cards, and so forth. Always keep your ammunition handy for justifying appropriate upgrades. This implies doing your homework ahead of time. Not only will you appear more prepared, but you'll actually *be* prepared when the dollars become available to your department. Also, keep in mind that upgrades that you recommend must serve your organization for a reasonable time period. Few good managers enjoy seeing frequent upgrade requests cross their desks.

It's best to have short- and long-term plans. Know where your NT network is headed, and take short-term steps to hit the long-term goals. For example, wiring your enterprise with high-quality network cabling that can handle a much higher bandwidth than you'll need today is a good investment in support of your long-term plan. I talk more about this investment in Chapters 7 and 8.

INSIDE STORY

One drizzly afternoon in Redmond, a network adapter in one of my computers started chattering gibberish on the Microsoft network, bringing the entire segment to its knees. It happens. The adapter had simply gone nuts. After removing and replacing the demented board, I committed the cardinal sin of not labeling it as bad. Always a habitual pack rat, I also lacked the willpower and good sense to throw it away. Instead I tossed it into a box of used adapters that I kept in the corner of my office. One day, I got an additional desktop computer and inadvertently installed the bad network adapter into it. As you might expect, the same chattering incident happened again, and the network segment ground to a halt.

When I heard complaints about the problem, I immediately knew what I'd done. I got a good talking to from the MIS people, and frankly I deserved it. After I apologized profusely, we managed to part chums. Since then, I've thought twice before installing a used network adapter.

Have a small test network available to you, if at all possible. Use it to try out new hardware, new software, and new approaches to configuration. Keep it completely separate from the real production network. Remember, one of your main goals is to keep the production network running smoothly and efficiently. Testing new things offline is one way to protect your LAN. Of course, you'll encounter situations where something tests fine in the test network and causes big problems when it is put into a real-world environment. However, any negative effect on the real network is minimized by this approach. Work with your management to justify a small test network.

Installing and Managing Servers

Your Windows NT Server computers are typically more expensive and complex than other PCs in your organization. They represent a significant investment of your organization's capital. Thus, it's important that you know all of the gory details about these computers so that you can keep them up and running and available to your users at all times.

Unfortunately, you may not be able to rely on external support contracts for critical LAN and server functions. There's typically a lag time in getting a technician on site. The technician who comes may not understand the computer configuration as well as you do — and may even make things worse. (This is not true across the board but happens more often than anyone would like to admit. Of course, these situations surface at the most critical times, so they can be quite painful for everyone involved.)

All of this leads to the inescapable conclusion that, like it or not, you'll probably need to do general PC support as well as all of the other duties I've mentioned in this chapter. There's no getting around it. Your users and management will look to you as a PC expert, whether you are or not. So, become a PC expert and know your servers inside and out. If someone else set up your server, make it your business to know what they did.

Part of getting to know your servers and network includes looking at baseline statistics and observations during normal operations. Using the NT Performance Monitor utility and other tools, you can establish what normal behavior looks like. This enables you to do a couple of things. First, you can catch trends or changes in requirements over time, helping you plan for and justify upgrades to your equipment. Second, by comparing what good behavior looks like with the behavior that you see when there's a problem, you'll have pointers to where you can start looking for the source of the trouble. I discuss this further in Chapters 19 and 21.

Keep spares and fast suppliers handy, so that you can deal with equipment failures quickly. You need to be able to restore a failed server quickly. Keep all of the configuration materials (disks, documentation, and so on) in a protected but easily accessible place. For example, have at your fingertips your EISA configuration disks, PS/2 setup disks, Windows NT Emergency Repair disks (see Chapter 9), documentation on hardware configuration, and your network notebook.

Managing Network Change

If you're making big changes to your enterprise, such as a move to new facilities, over-plan everything. If possible, talk with each of the affected users (or at least their managers), understand their needs, and help set their expectations. Schedule everything, and share your schedule with your users. Keep them up to date on what's going on. If the schedule falls behind for some reason, let them know what's happening and what to expect. This assures a smooth transition and mutual understanding.

If you can, make changes gradually, one step at a time. This method makes it much easier to diagnose problems that new hardware or software might introduce. It's a nightmare to have to back off several changes just to get back in business, because you don't know which change caused the problem.

Once again, document everything so that you and your colleagues will be able to function efficiently as problems arise and additional changes are required.

Supporting Network Applications

Before you install new applications on your network, you need to check on their compatibility with NT, the server hardware, your network, and the client computers that you plan to use. Don't overlook verifying that your clients and servers have the capacity to handle the new application. Include any computer upgrade costs into the overall cost of the application. Chapter 7 provides you with some tools to assist in doing this sort of planning.

Some applications are designed for network installation, and others are quite difficult to install on a server. The latter might require lots of time, planning, and calls to the vendor. Sharing applications on the network can be complex. In some applications, such as Microsoft Office, many of the files live on the server, whereas some configuration files exist on the client.

Licensing is another issue to keep in mind. Some packages have built-in mechanisms that track and even enforce licensing. Others leave it up to your honesty. In any case, you want to operate a legal shop, so understand the licensing requirements of each package, and be sure that your license agreement covers how you intend to use the application.

Planning for Disaster

This is one area where grave pessimism can pay off big. Make sure that your organization has a comprehensive disaster recovery plan and that you stick to it. You can't possibly plan for every contingency in a disaster situation but having a plan enables you to deal creatively with any special circumstances. You won't have to invent the entire plan from scratch.

THEY'RE OUT TO GET YOUR DATA

It's a fact that hard disk failures occur more frequently on servers than on desktop computers. Many users pound on these disks over the network, generating a high volume of mechanical head travel. Moreover, these disks are probably spinning 24 hours a day, unlike most drives in desktop computers. The second most common failure is accidental erasure of a file by a user. Then come power surges, power outages, lightning strikes, floods, tornadoes, earthquakes, meltdowns, election years, and other disasters. The bottom line is that lots of forces are at work to cause data loss on your servers.

Creating daily backups of your server is probably the easiest and most important piece of the disaster plan. Beyond just making the backups, make sure that they run by checking the logs the following day. Periodically, perform a trial restore to make sure that data being written to tape can actually be restored. Don't wait for the need to restore a critical file only to find that the tape drive has been writing unreadable tapes for weeks.

Make and follow a backup schedule religiously, regardless of your denomination. This activity is critical to the operation of your business. The task is invisible and unglamorous, until a user has a disaster. Then, if you can restore what was lost, you're a hero. If not, you're villainously visible.

Be sure that your backup plan includes off-site storage of backups. Know how to get to the other site quickly to retrieve materials. Don't wait until a real disaster strikes before locating the storage facility on the map.

Another way to avert disaster is to take advantage of the fault tolerance options that Windows NT Server provides. It's best to plan fault tolerance into your server from the beginning, but with a little effort, you can add it later. In selecting RAID technologies (introduced in Chapter 1 and explained in Chapter 19), opt for NT Server's RAID 1 (mirroring) or RAID 5 (stripes with parity). These features provide on-the-fly recovery of data if a disk fails. RAID 0 (stripes without parity) doesn't provide you with any additional reliability. Chapter 19 discusses how to set up fault tolerance using the Disk Administrator utility.

Using Information Resources

From a technical viewpoint, the key to your success as a Windows NT network administrator is having the right information at the right time. The issues and concepts associated with Windows NT and networking in general can't all be carried around in your head, or even under your arm in this book. You'll need to know where to go for more information to meet the changing needs of your organization.

Expend some effort to develop research skills, to enable yourself to find quickly and retrieve NT information that isn't in your head. Get familiar with all of the resources listed here, so that you know firsthand the type of information available from each source. Then, if you don't know something off the top of your head, at least you know exactly where to look. These skills will help you be more successful on the job, and you'll become a valuable resource of information to your team and your enterprise.

FINDING THE RIGHT RESOURCES

Appendix C provides you with details on where to look for the additional information that you'll need in your arsenal. It covers technical support, training, the NT Resource Kit, Microsoft TechNet, and Microsoft Developer Network (MSDN). The appendix also provides a handy list of several NT Server-related Web sites, online newsletters, discussion groups, newsgroups, and CompuServe forums.

Summary

In this chapter, I've outlined the key areas for which you're likely going to be responsible as an NT network administrator. I've passed along some advice on what to expect when dealing with your users and management. Finally, I've pointed you to a list of resources in Appendix C that you can use to supplement your knowledge and help solve problems that you encounter in your role.

In Chapter 6, I help you select the right Windows products for specific needs in your organization. You'll see how NT compares with other Windows products and how Windows NT Server and Windows NT Workstation stack up against each other. Then, in Part II, we'll dive into the process of designing, preparing, and planning your server and network hardware in preparation for Windows NT Server 4.0 installation.

Choosing the Right Windows Products for Each Computer

With the proliferation of Windows operating systems across the PC marketplace, it's not always easy to understand the differences among these products. As a network administrator, you're probably involved in recommending or selecting the appropriate operating systems used on the various clients and servers on your network. Windows NT Server isn't the right product for every node. Therefore, you need to be armed with the knowledge of how Windows NT Server, Windows NT Workstation, Windows 95, Windows for Workgroups, and Windows 3.1 compare.

This chapter provides this knowledge. First, I present the similarities and differences in design and operation between Windows NT and other Microsoft Windows products. Then, I fill you in on how Windows NT Server and Workstation products compare. Along the way, I offer some practical advice on how best to apply each product in your network. By the end of this chapter, you'll know which operating systems to apply to the variety of requirements in your enterprise.

Windows NT vs. Windows

Although the operating systems in the Microsoft Windows family appear similar in many ways, they have very different underlying architectures. Wide differences separate Windows NT 4.0 from Windows 3.1. Although the gap narrows somewhat between Windows NT 4.0 and Windows 95, many significant contrasts remain.

In this section, you'll discover the major differences between the Windows NT operating system and other flavors of Windows. At this point, I won't include the superset features of Windows NT Server over Windows NT Workstation. You can safely assume that Windows 95 and Windows 3.1 don't include any of these additional NT Server features. I compare Windows NT Server with Windows NT Workstation later in this chapter.

Windows NT vs. Windows 3.x

Microsoft began working on a graphical extension to DOS, called Windows, in 1983. It released the first version, Windows 1.0, way back in 1985. It was replaced by an improved (but not very successful) 2.0 version in late 1987. However, it wasn't until Microsoft unleashed Windows 3.0 in 1990 that the industry sat up and really took notice. Great Microsoft marketing, public awareness of the benefits of a graphical operating system, a series of successive improvements to Windows, and the lower cost and larger capacities of PCs all seemed to align at the same time to usher in the Windows era. Windows 3.0 was wildly successful.

Who's Afraid of the UAE?

One of the most widely publicized problems with Windows 3.0 was the dreaded Unrecoverable Application Error, or UAE. Windows 3.0 would crash with this error whenever it detected that it was in an inconsistent state and couldn't continue. Windows 3.0 didn't validate any of the system requests made by applications. If an application had a bug that caused it to make an invalid request, Windows would obediently comply, often causing damage to the state of the operating system or other applications.

The main motivation for the development and release of Windows 3.1, in mid-1992, was to provide a more robust operating environment. Windows 3.1, although it fixed a number of 3.0 bugs and added a few new features, primarily added validity checking of application requests and a much more graceful error recovery mechanism.

Enter the Network

Windows for Workgroups, released in early 1993, was essentially Windows 3.1 with peer-to-peer networking and improved file and disk access performance. Otherwise, it was architecturally the same as Windows 3.1. Windows for Workgroups didn't make a big splash in the mass marketplace, because its primary incremental benefit over 3.1 was built-in network capabilities. However, because Windows for Workgroups eventually replaced Windows 3.1 on computers that shipped with Windows preinstalled, a large number found their way into customers' hands.

INSIDE STORY

The name Windows for Workgroups was not only cumbersome but also became a victim of ridicule due to perceived abysmal sales. Even Microsoft employees couldn't or wouldn't get the name right. In any given communication, it might be called *Workgroups for Windows, Workground for Windows, Windows for Working*, or *Windows for Windows*.

The popular name when sales looked grim became *Windows for Warehouses*, implying that unsold product boxes were stacking up in the warehouse. This particular vernacular found its way outside Microsoft, into the press, and into the minds of customers. In fact, I know that Microsoft took at least one call from a hapless customer wanting the "special version of Windows designed to run in warehouses." I'm sure they sold him something.

In the following discussions, I use Windows 3.x to refer collectively to Windows 3.1 and Windows for Workgroups. In Table 6-1, I use the term *WfW* in the Windows 3.x column to indicate that the feature is provided only in Windows for Workgroups.

The Case for 32 Bits

Windows 3.x is a 16-bit environment that requires application developers to master a nightmarish approach to memory management. To be fair, much of this method of dealing with memory is based on requirements of the early Intel x86 microprocessor architecture. Still, it drives developers up the wall and sometimes distracts them from developing new features in their applications.

Back in 1991, many application developers wanted to simplify their lives, and Microsoft wanted to get them to write applications to the Win32 interface. It seemed like a perfect alignment that would make the simpler Win32 API popular. However, no operating system products yet existed that supported Win32. The promise of a future Windows NT, and later Windows 95, couldn't overcome the existing and growing volume of Windows 3.x users.

To help assure a reasonable number of applications on its new 32-bit operating system platforms, Microsoft wanted to promote the Win32 interface before either Windows NT or Windows 95 were commercially available. At the same time, they wanted to whet developers' appetites with the benefits and simplicity of Win32. To meet these objectives, the NT group created Win32s, which provided libraries that offered a subset of the Win32 API on the Windows 3.x platform. If a 32-bit application stuck to this Win32s subset, it would run on Windows 3.x. Figure 6-1 illustrates the relationship of Win32s to the varieties of Win32 on Windows NT and Windows 95.

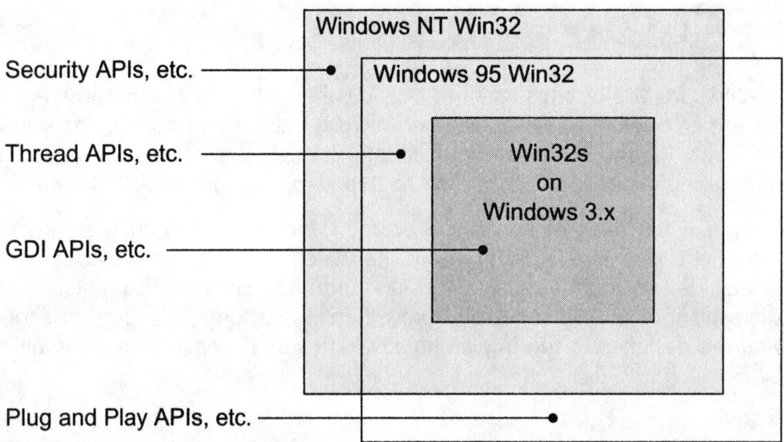

Figure 6-1: Win32s is a subset of the Win32 API, enabling 32-bit applications to run on Windows 3.x, Windows NT, and Windows 95.

Win32s is fundamentally a translation layer that enables an application to make Win32 API calls that are translated internally to their 16-bit equivalents on Windows 3.x. It's not fast, but it does enable some Win32 applications to run in this environment. In Table 6-1, the term *Win32s* is used in the Windows 3.x column to indicate that the feature is provided only by running Win32s on Windows 3.x.

How NT and Windows 3.x Compare

Table 6-1 highlights the differences between Windows 3.x and Windows NT. All Windows environments have literally thousands of features and functions in common, and I've stayed away from them. Don't treat the table as a complete feature list of the products. It's designed to highlight the differences only. In this section, I walk through the sections of Table 6-1 and discuss each area of comparison in turn.

As you study the table, keep in mind that third-party software developers often fill in the holes that Microsoft has left behind. Many of the features missing in the off-the-shelf Windows products represented here have already been supplied by third parties.

Table 6-1
A Comparison of Windows NT, Windows 95, and Windows 3.x

Feature	*Windows NT 4.0*	*Windows 95*	*Windows 3.x*
Architecture			
Pure 32-bit architecture	√		
Multithreading support	√	√	
Complete independence from DOS	√	Almost	
Extensible to support other operating system APIs	√		
OLE 2.x support	√	√	Limited
Win32 API application development support	√	√	Limited, with Win32s
Localization and internationalization	Unicode	Codepage/ Unicode	Codepage
Unicode support	√	Partial	
Scalability			
Disk volume maximum size	16EB	2GB	2GB
Takes full advantage of multiprocessor (SMP) platforms	√		
Portability			
Runs on Intel 386 CPUs	Dropped in 4.0	√	√
Runs on Intel 486, Pentium, Pentium Pro, and higher	√	√	√
Runs on RISC platforms (PowerPC, Alpha, MIPS)	√		
Reliability			
Cooperative multitasking of Win16 apps	√	√	√
Cooperative multitasking of Win32 apps			Win32s
Preemptive multitasking of Win16 apps	√		
Preemptive multitasking of Win32 apps	√	√	

(continued)

Table 6-1 *(continued)*

Feature	*Windows NT 4.0*	*Windows 95*	*Windows 3.x*
UPS support	√		
Automatic recovery from system crashes	√		
Manual recovery from application crashes	√	√	Limited
RAID disk fault tolerance and performance	√		
Operating system fully protected from errant apps	√		
Single input message queue (Win16)	√	√	√
Multiple input message queues	√	√	
Compatibility			
FAT (DOS) file system	√	√	√
VFAT (Windows 95) file system	√	√	
NTFS (Windows NT) file system	√		
HPFS (OS/2) file system	Dropped in 4.0		
Compression of FAT disk volumes		√	√
Compression of VFAT disk volumes		√	
Enhanced DriveSpace and Compression Agent		With Plus! pack	
Compression of individual files and folders (NTFS)	√		
Hardware compatibility	Great	Excellent	Good
Advanced Power Management support	Future release	√	
Overall 16-bit DOS and Windows compatibility	Good	Better	Best
Runs Windows 95 Win32 applications	Most	√	Limited to Win32s
Runs Windows for Workgroups Win16 apps	Most	√	WfW
Runs Windows NT Win32 apps	√	Most	Limited to Win32s
Runs DOS device drivers		√	√

Feature	*Windows NT 4.0*	*Windows 95*	*Windows 3.x*
Runs MS-DOS apps	Most	√	√
Runs OS/2 1.x character apps	√		
Runs OS/2 PM 1.x apps	With PM add-on		
Runs POSIX 1003.1 apps	√		
Runs Win16 real-mode apps		√	√
Runs Win16 device drivers		√	√
Runs Win32s applications	√	√	Win32s
Runs Win16 enhanced-mode apps	√	√	√
Runs Win16 standard-mode apps	Most	√	√
Maintainability			
System management standards support (SNMP, DMI)	√	√	
User profiles and system policies	√	√	
Remote performance monitoring	√	√	
Disk defragmentation		√	
Security			
C2 security	√		
Security on files and directories (NTFS)	√		
Usability			
Easier Windows 95 user interface	√	√	
Supports Windows 3.x user interface (optionally on Windows NT and Windows 95)	√	√	√
Full window drag	√	With Plus! pack	
Universal Inbox for e-mail and faxes	√	√	
Plug and Play support	Future release	√	
Automatic detection of hardware during install	√	√	Limited
Dynamic PCMCIA support	Future release	√	
Animated icons	√	With Plus! pack	
3D Pinball	√	With Plus! pack	

(continued)

Table 6-1 *(continued)*

Feature	*Windows NT 4.0*	*Windows 95*	*Windows 3.x*
Networking			
Peer-to-peer networking	√	√	WfW
Domain network model	√		
E-mail	√	√	WfW
Group scheduling	Dropped in 4.0		WfW
Remote access client	√	√	WfW, or with RAS add-on
Remote access server	Up to 256 users	With Plus! pack (1 user)	
NetWare-compatible requester	√	√	
Network OLE (DCOM)	√	Future release	
Network protocols: TCP/IP, IPX/SPX, NetBEUI, DLC	√	√	WfW: Net-BEUI IPX/SPX
Internet Explorer	√	With Plus! pack	
Microsoft Network (MSN) client (online service)	Future release	√	
Hardware Requirements			
Disk space footprint	115MB	40MB	16MB
Minimum recommended RAM for running multiple apps	16MB	8MB	4MB
Multimedia			
OpenGL 3D graphics	√	Future release	
Multimedia APIs: Direct Draw and Direct Sound	√	√	
Multimedia APIs: Direct Input and Reality Lab 3D graphics	Future release	√	
Support			
Periodic Service Pack patch releases	√	√	

Architectural Differences

In the architecture department, Windows NT and Windows 3.x are quite different. NT is 32-bit code throughout and is completely independent of DOS. Windows 3.x, on the other hand, is nearly all 16-bit code and requires the presence of DOS underneath it. In fact, Windows 3.x often isn't considered an operating system, rather just a graphical environment that enhances DOS.

Windows NT is much more scalable and portable than Windows 3.x. NT's scalability enables it to handle much larger disks and to take full advantage of multiprocessor systems. Running Windows 3.x on a multiprocessor system uses only one processor. Moreover, Windows 3.x isn't portable to other CPU architectures. Its design and source code are strongly tied to the Intel x86 architecture.

One advantage of Windows 3.x is its support of the Intel 386 processor. Support for the 386 was dropped in Windows NT 4.0. Thus, for computers based on the 386, you'll need to select either Windows 3.x or Windows 95.

NT Is More Reliable

In the area of reliability, Windows NT wins over Windows 3.x across the board. As discussed in Chapter 1, cooperative multitasking and a single message queue design are both sources of reliability problems. Although Windows NT simulates the Windows 3.x environment for Win16 applications by default, it enables you to transcend these problems by running each Win16 application within a separate WOW VDM. This eliminates both the cooperative multitasking and single message queue bottleneck issues.

Windows NT and Windows 3.x (via DOS 6.0 and later versions) take divergent approaches to providing disk compression. The DoubleSpace and DriveSpace compression schemes under DOS essentially compress an entire volume into a single large file. These methods aren't supported under Windows NT for three reasons. First, these schemes make the entire volume vulnerable to a single disk error. If only one sector within the huge file becomes damaged, the entire contents of the compressed file, and thus the entire volume, can be lost. Second, although the compressed file is typically hidden during normal use, it's too easy for a user to find the file and delete it, again destroying the volume. Finally, the DOS approach sacrifices performance to achieve smaller, compressed files.

Windows NT's NTFS file system provides data compression on a file-by-file basis and addresses the issues with DOS compression. First, if a disk sector becomes damaged, at most one file is lost. Using NT fault tolerance features, even this potential problem can be eliminated. Second, there's no vulnerable single file containing all of the data. Each file is individually compressed and appears as a normal file. Finally, the designers of NTFS compression opted to emphasize speed of compression and decompression, at the cost of slightly larger compressed files. Depending on the hardware configuration and data involved, the NT file system can provide very efficient compression with negligible performance overhead.

Compatibility

At its release, Windows 3.1 was lauded for its lengthy hardware compatibility list. Windows NT had a lot to live up to in assuring compatibility with a broad range of systems and hardware devices. Although the compatibility list accompanying the first release of NT wasn't as comprehensive as Windows 3.1, it soon met and even surpassed the 3.1 list in many categories. Now, the broad hardware compatibility of NT is a major selling point and a strong competitive advantage.

Here's a shocker. Windows 3.1 is 100 percent compatible with Windows 3.1 applications. This statement sounds silly — until you consider how difficult it is for other operating systems such as NT to achieve this level of compatibility. Windows 3.x application compatibility is defined by the application's behavior running on Windows 3.x. Thus, neither Windows NT nor Windows 95 can be any more compatible or even as compatible as Windows 3.x itself. Why? First, because NT imposes security restrictions on what an application can do, it prevents some applications from running as they would on Windows 3.x. Second, because no emulation of complex software and hardware is perfect, there'll always be some small quirk of Windows 3.x that isn't included in a simulated environment.

NT's Other Winning Categories

As Table 6-1 shows, Windows NT wins hands down over Windows 3.x in the categories of maintainability, usability, and security. In the networking area, Windows NT clearly provides more functionality, but Windows for Workgroups offers a reasonably good peer-to-peer networking environment. Hardware minimum requirements for both disk and memory are much higher for NT than for Windows 3.x. This has been one of the biggest objections to migration from Windows 3.x to the NT platform.

Microsoft's philosophy about supplying updates and patches to its customers in Windows 3.x can be summarized in the statement, "Let them wait for the next

INSIDE STORY

In the final days before shipping Windows NT 3.5, a bug was discovered that would cost several engineers a night's sleep and a large number of doughnuts. A very popular word processor program refused to print from NT. For some intuitive reason, we all felt that printing was important to word processor users, so we doggedly pursued the problem.

A top engineer named Bob (not the Microsoft Bob smiley face, a different Bob) ended up tracing though the application's assembly-language code to find out why it refused to print. After many hours of debugging and numerous phone calls, he discovered the reason. The application relied on the fact that a certain register contained the value 17 upon return from a Windows API call. If the value wasn't 17, the word processor wouldn't print. The value of this register was never documented anywhere, but Windows 3.x just happened to always set it to 17. Our simulation of Windows 3.x hadn't provided for this undocumented detail. After applauding Bob for his detective work, we changed NT to always set the register to 17 just to make this word processor print, and the printing problem was no more.

release of Windows." The Windows NT team took a different road. Approximately quarterly, Microsoft releases a *service pack* update to the NT system, containing fixes for any critical problems found by Microsoft or its customers. These patch releases are made available without charge via the Internet and other sources.

Where Does Windows 3.x Fit?

Since the advent of Windows 95, Windows 3.x is getting more difficult to find installed on new computers. However, it's still available and may be the right choice for some of your client computers. Of all of the Windows environments, Windows 3.x uses the least resources, so it's a good fit for older CPUs with less memory available. If you have DOS or Windows 3.x applications that use their own device drivers, they may not work as well under Windows 95 or Windows NT. This is a key reason for some folks to stick with Windows 3.x.

On the other hand, Windows 3.x is the least robust of the Windows platforms. Furthermore, it's almost entirely 16-bit code, Microsoft isn't going to update it, and few new applications are being written for it. Because of these factors, the reliability, performance, and support scores of Windows 3.x are low, relative to those for Windows NT and Windows 95. I don't recommend using Windows 3.x unless you're constrained by the hardware limitations of a client computer or you rely on applications that don't run on NT or Windows 95.

Windows NT vs. Windows 95

In 1991, Microsoft commenced work on a project code named Chicago, which would update and replace Windows 3.x and Windows for Workgroups. The primary objective of Chicago was to make Windows "easier." That's a broad objective, but virtually all of the changes made to this version of Windows supported the goal of greater simplicity.

Chicago was later named Windows 95, when the ship date was firmly set for 1995. Windows 95 became the most advertised, talked about, and hyped software product in history. Unless you were living in a cave in 1994 and 1995, you must have been inundated by the Windows 95 blitz. The product was so broadly and effectively publicized that some people who didn't even own computers marched to their local stores to purchase their copy of Windows 95. The mass hypnosis theory was never proven.

Windows 95 made Windows easier than Windows 3.x in the following ways:

- ✦ An improved, more intuitive user interface
- ✦ Automatic hardware detection and configuration
- ✦ Easier application development via the Win32 API
- ✦ Fewer limitations on resources and performance

With all of the industry hype associated with the new, improved Windows 95 user interface, it can become difficult to keep its pros and cons in perspective.

The new user interface is definitely a significant advance in ease of use, relative to the Windows 3.x interface. Microsoft has spent considerable time, effort, and dollars to research, develop, and deliver a vastly more usable graphical interface. They spent countless hours with existing and potential customers in their usability labs to find just the right combination of form and function.

Adjusting to Windows 95

Practically speaking, however, if you have users in your organization who are proficient with Windows 3.x or earlier versions of Windows NT, you'll likely encounter some hidden costs. You'll need to count on some investment in retraining people on the new model and probably some initial loss in productivity. Don't forget to include this factor in your budget. Oddly enough, this is one situation in which your inexperienced people are likely to get up to speed faster than the Windows diehards on your team.

If you have a few hold-out Windows 3.x users who flatly refuse to adjust to the new interface, both Windows 95 and NT 4.0 provide the familiar old File Manager and Program Manager. Just configure their systems to run these applications, and your hold-outs should feel right at home — that is, until they're converted to the new user interface through peer pressure. Of course, once they convert, they'll realize that the new interface is easier to use and more flexible than what they had been using, and they'll be hooked.

With appropriate hardware support, the Plug and Play feature of Windows 95 is a big step forward in reducing the frustration and pain of configuring hardware in PC systems. Microsoft worked closely with hardware manufacturers to enable the operating system and drivers to detect correctly and configure automatically hardware devices. Plug and Play is really catching on, but until hardware and drivers fully support it, the problem of hardware configuration won't disappear. Until then, we'll continue to "plug and pray."

Win32 and Windows 95

As mentioned in the Windows 3.x section earlier in this chapter, the Win32 API greatly simplifies application development. Developers needn't worry about complex memory management issues. Windows 95 offers a full implementation of Win32, unlike the relatively small subset provided by Win32s.

Windows 95 removed many of the resource restrictions present in Windows 3.x. Running multiple applications on the system no longer had to mean quickly running out of memory or slowing the system to a crawl, as was often the case on Windows 3.x.

THE THREE WIN32 API SETS

For a time, the Win32 API to be offered in Windows 95 was dubbed Win32c. The *C* stood for Chicago. The Win32c designation was dropped unofficially when confusion erupted (even within Microsoft) over why a universal 32-bit API had so many variations. The Win32c name was officially dropped when Microsoft determined the year in which Windows 95 would ship, and the Chicago code name became a part of Windows history. Until then, there were three official Win32 API sets – NT's Win32, Win32s, and Win32c. Talk about confused developers!

Microsoft offers an extension to Windows 95 called the Microsoft Plus! pack. It includes some visual enhancements such as desktop themes, enhanced disk compression, Internet Explorer, a one-user RAS server, and a few other goodies. It's available as a separate add-on product. I included Plus! pack features in Table 6-1, presented earlier in this chapter.

How NT and Windows 95 Compare

In this section, I walk through the comparison of Windows NT with Windows 95 in Table 6-1 (presented earlier in this chapter), discussing each area of comparison. Because Microsoft is still actively updating both operating systems, you'll see that each product is ahead in some areas and behind in others. In the table, both the Windows NT and the Windows 95 columns contain entries indicating that a feature will be provided in a future release. In Windows NT's case, this term refers to the next release after version 4.0. NT has now settled into an annual release cycle, so the next release after 4.0 will probably occur in 1997. At this writing, it's too early to tell how frequently Windows 95 will be released or even what name it will bear.

Microsoft has dubbed the Windows NT 4.0 release as the *Shell Update Release*, or SUR. This refers to the most visible change in NT 4.0 — namely, the adoption of the Windows 95 user interface. However, lots of other changes in NT 4.0 hide under the covers. For example, nearly all of the graphics subsystem functionality has been moved into kernel mode to enhance performance, as discussed in Chapter 2.

You'll notice that neither product is a superset of the other. Windows 95 has some features not found in Windows NT, and NT has many features not found in Windows 95. Because their development schedules aren't in sync, you'll see the products leapfrogging each other in some areas. For example, Plug and Play will be supported in the next release of NT after 4.0, whereas it's already supported in Windows 95. Likewise, as Windows 95 moves forward, it'll borrow some features from NT that make sense in its markets.

Architectural Differences

Although the Windows 95 programming interface and much of the system itself is 32-bit code, significant pieces of the operating system are still written in 16-bit code. Unlike Windows 3.x and Windows for Workgroups, which both run on top of MS-DOS, Windows 95 is independent of DOS — almost. A special version of MS-DOS is included with Windows 95 and is sometimes called upon to perform certain system functions. All of this contrasts with Windows NT, which is 32-bit code throughout and has no reliance on DOS.

Like Windows NT, Windows 95 provides preemptive multitasking and multiple message queues for Win32 applications. However, because Windows 95 doesn't supply an option to run Win16 applications in separate VDMs, it can perform only cooperative multitasking of Win16 applications. Windows 95 doesn't include any of the fault tolerance and recovery features of Windows NT and doesn't fully protect its operating system state from potential damage by errant applications.

In terms of scalability and portability, Windows 95 is on a par with Windows 3.x. Thus Windows NT wins in these categories by taking full advantage of SMP systems, large disks, and non-Intel CPU architectures. The only leg up that Windows 95 has in this area is support of the Intel 386 processor, but Windows 95 is so demanding on the CPU that Windows 3.x is really a better choice for these low-end systems.

Reliability

The Windows 95 approach to compression is compatible with the DOS approach discussed earlier. Windows 95 and the Microsoft Plus! pack for Windows 95 offer additional compression functionality. Windows 95 can perform compression at scheduled times and can compress selected files to even smaller sizes, at the cost of additional compression and decompression time. Still, Windows 95 retains all of the disadvantages of the DOS approach to compression that I discussed earlier in this chapter. The Windows NT method, using the NTFS file system, is much more robust.

THE RUMOR MILL

Rumors of secret projects in which Microsoft is porting Windows 95 to other CPU architectures are just that – rumors. The source code for Windows 95 is still very much tied to the Intel architecture. You won't see a port of Windows 95 to these other platforms. Windows NT, on the other hand, was designed with ease of portability in mind from day one. You'll eventually see it ported to new processors.

Compatibility

On the software front, Microsoft has included Windows NT compatibility as one of the requirements for obtaining the Designed for Windows 95 logo for Win32 applications. This forces developers to test their Win32 code on Windows NT, even if their primary target is Windows 95. Taking this approach only increases the availability of applications on Windows NT. Windows NT can run most Windows 95 32-bit applications, and Windows 95 can run many Windows NT 32-bit applications. Why not all? Although both use the Win32 API, each product has some number of unique Win32 APIs that the other product doesn't offer. For example, Windows NT provides a set of security APIs that make no sense on Windows 95. Windows 95 offers some new multimedia APIs that Windows NT doesn't yet have. Applications that stick to using APIs common to both products will run on both products.

Windows 95 hardware compatibility is excellent, because it can run DOS and Windows 3.x drivers and therefore inherits much of the Windows 3.x hardware compatibility list. In this area, Windows 95 is considered somewhat better than Windows NT.

The ability to manage and maintain Windows NT and Windows 95 systems are pretty much on a par. However, Windows NT's domain networking model, discussed in Chapter 4, brings a whole new level of maintainability to the enterprise network. Windows 95 doesn't have these features but can operate in the network as a good client. Usability between Windows 95 and Windows NT are almost equal, now that NT sports the Windows 95 user interface. NT lags a bit in hardware-related usability features such as Plug and Play and dynamic reconfiguration of PCMCIA cards. These features will show up in a future NT release.

NT vs. Win95 Networks

As Table 6-1 shows, networking features and hardware requirements of Windows 95 fall just about in the middle between Windows for Workgroups and Windows NT. Windows 95 offers approximately the same networking functionality as Windows for Workgroups, plus adding limited remote access and more network protocols.

Graphics – A Draw?

In the multimedia world, Windows 95 has tended to be ahead of Windows NT. This is no surprise, given the different markets in which these products are intended to play. Features that specifically cater to game development have typically appeared first on the home-oriented Windows 95 product. Windows NT isn't always behind in this area, though. For example, OpenGL, an API that offers fast, complex 3D graphics, has been available on Windows NT for two years but hasn't yet been offered on Windows 95. The level of multimedia sound support on the two platforms is almost identical.

Product Support

Like Windows NT, Windows 95 will have periodic releases of service pack updates to fix critical problems. It's too early to tell how frequently this will happen for Windows 95, but a six-month cycle is likely. The first update appeared in February 1996 and the second was released in the summer of 1996. (The Windows 95 service packs are made available to computer manufacturers to preinstall on the systems that they ship. They're also available for downloading at `http://www.microsoft.com/ windows/software`.) At the time of this writing, there's talk of Microsoft synchronizing the service pack release schedules for these two products.

Where Does Windows 95 Fit?

Windows 95 demands less hardware than Windows NT. This advantage alone is the basis for many buying decisions in Windows 95's favor. In addition, Windows 95 includes a few features that NT lacks, such as Plug and Play and power management. These features make it better suited to desktop and laptop computers. Although NT will have these features in the future, they're not there now.

Although both NT and Windows 95 support Win32 applications, some of these applications just aren't designed to run on NT. If you rely on applications that won't run on NT, then Windows 95 is the clear choice. Moreover, Windows 95 is more compatible with 16-bit applications than NT is, because NT has to prevent certain operations for security reasons. If you're reliant on 16-bit Windows applications, but you want the benefits that Windows 95 provides over Windows 3.x, once again Windows 95 may be the best choice. Of course, as mentioned earlier, Windows 95 is less robust than Windows NT, because Windows 95 allows applications to do whatever they wish, including harming each other. Even though it has networking capabilities equivalent to Windows for Workgroups, Windows 95 isn't the best choice for a file server, because it's less reliable than NT.

Although Windows 95 is considered by some to be the corporate client of choice, many MIS departments are skipping Windows 95 altogether and moving straight to Windows NT. With lower memory prices and faster CPUs becoming the norm, the incremental cost difference to meet NT's hardware requirements is becoming less significant. The hidden costs of installation, training, and support for each operating system upgrade have led folks to the conclusion that jumping straight into NT may be more cost effective in the long run. Finally, because the upgrade path between Windows 95 and NT isn't very smooth (as I discuss in Chapter 7), you can avoid these headaches by skipping Windows 95 entirely.

If you need high performance for streaming digital video or some other real-time application, you should choose Windows NT rather than Windows 95. Most of the high-end graphics and video editing packages are being ported to NT as their primary platform, because it provides the true 32-bit performance needed. Windows 95 still contains lots of slower 16-bit code. If you're targeting a Pentium Pro CPU, you're definitely better off with Windows NT, because the 16-bit code in Windows 95 bogs down this processor.

If your environment demands high security to control access to information and resources, Windows NT is the clear choice. Windows 95 lacks the C2 security and NTFS features built in to NT. However, as a client, Windows 95 can offer adequate security when it's accessing an NT server.

NT Server vs. NT Workstation

Because you're reading this book, you've already decided to run Windows NT Server 4.0 on one or more computers in your network. You may, however, still be faced with the decision of which NT product to use on other specific computers within your organization. There has been much confusion in the marketplace about exactly what the differences are between NT Server and NT Workstation products, and it's hard to pin even Microsoft down to a definitive list. Clearly, there's a price difference — NT Server typically costs more than twice as much as NT Workstation. In this section, I provide you with a list of key differences designed to help you decide which product to use in a given situation in your organization.

As mentioned in Chapter 1, the core NT operating system in the two products is identical. However, Windows NT Server is a significant superset, containing several additional features that set it apart for use in enterprise computing environments. Moreover, it's been tuned for better performance as a server and is less germane to interactive desktop applications than NT Workstation.

Table 6-2 summarizes the differences between the two products. Keep in mind that I haven't included all NT features in this table — only those that highlight key differences or that represent gray areas between the two products. Don't worry if you don't understand all of the features at this stage. I cover them in later chapters, and you can refer to the glossary in Appendix B, which defines many unfamiliar terms or acronyms.

Table 6-2
Feature Comparison between Windows NT Server and Workstation Products

Feature	*Windows NT Server*	*Windows NT Workstation*
Supports SMP computers (retail version)	1 to 4 CPUs	1 to 2 CPUs
Supports SMP computers (hardware-manufacturer-supplied version)	1 to 32 CPUs	1 to 32 CPUs
Acts as Macintosh file server	√	

(continued)

Table 6-2 *(continued)*

Feature	*Windows NT Server*	*Windows NT Workstation*
Acts as Macintosh print server	√	
Acts as AppleTalk router	√	
Supports volume sets (NTFS only)	√	√
Supports disk striping without parity (RAID 0)	√	√
Supports disk striping with parity (RAID 5)	√	
Supports disk mirroring and duplexing (RAID 1)	√	
Acts as primary domain controller	√	
Acts as backup domain controller	√	
Acts as stand-alone server	Unlimited clients	Up to 10 clients
Acts as Windows NT network client	√	√
Supports Remote Access Server (RAS) clients	Up to 256 clients	Only 1 client
Maintains trust relationships between NT Server domains	√	
Supports single network logon	√	
Provides directory replication	√	
Supports centralized user profiles	√	
Enables remote administration (including from Windows 95)	√	
Provides enhanced network cache	√	
Provides enhanced interactive responsiveness		√
Optimized for 32-bit server applications	√	
Recommended minimum memory	16MB	16MB
Requires minimum disk space (x86/RISC)	123MB/159MB	118MB/149MB
Includes DNS Name Server	√	
Includes DHCP Server	√	

Feature	Windows NT Server	Windows NT Workstation
Includes WINS Server	√	
Includes Microsoft Internet Information Server	√	
Includes Microsoft Peer Web Services		√
Includes MPR (MultiProtocol Routing)	√	
Supports remote booting of Windows 95 diskless computers	√	
DHCP Relay Agent	√	
DNS and WINS integration	√	
UNC support of DNS names	√	
User-defined Internet special groups	√	
DCOM (Distributed Component Object Model)	√	√
PPTP (Point-to-Point Tunneling Protocol)	√	
Administrative Wizards	√	
Runs BackOffice server applications	√	
Includes Gateway Service for NetWare	√	
Includes Migration Tool for NetWare	√	
Supports local desktop security per user	√	√
Provides computer lockout security	√	
Supports centralized account and security administration	√	

Selecting NT Server

From Table 6-2, it's clear that Windows NT Server offers significantly more than NT Workstation, especially in the areas of network functionality, administration, and fault tolerance. If you're setting up a file server or application server and you want the benefits of centralized network administration, I recommend Windows NT Server as the way to go. However, it's probably not the only flavor of Windows NT that you need in your network.

Selecting NT Workstation

If some of your users need high-performance CAD workstations for real-time 3D rendering, NT Workstation is the wiser choice. It's been tuned for better interactive responsiveness, and its CPU and memory resources are dedicated to the CAD tasks at hand. If a user needs to do digital video capture, in which consistently high disk performance is critical, he or she can use disk striping (without parity) on NT Workstation to gain high disk throughput.

Using the Domain Approach

As explained in Chapter 7, I strongly recommend that you base your server and network administration design around Windows NT Server's domain model. Even if your network is small, it makes administration easier now and in the future when your network grows. However, NT Server doesn't fit everywhere in your enterprise. Consider Windows NT Workstation for client computers that need the high performance features that it offers for interactive workstation computing.

Summary

Windows NT Server is not the ideal operating system for all of your networked computers. In this chapter, you've seen a comparison of Windows NT with other Windows operating systems. I've also presented a comparison of features in Windows NT Server and Workstation products to assist you in selecting products for specific needs in your organization. As the comparison of Windows NT 4.0 and Windows 95 shows, they have many similarities. Windows 95 borrowed heavily in several areas from Windows NT. In turn, Windows NT is now borrowing features from Windows 95 that make sense in its markets. The feature sets in these two products will leapfrog each other in the future.

In Chapters 7 and 8, you'll find out how to design, prepare, and plan your server and network in preparation for hands-on installation of Windows NT Server 4.0 in Chapter 9.

Getting Your NT Server Network Up and Running

✦ ✦ ✦ ✦

In This Part

✦ ✦ ✦ ✦

Designing and Preparing Your NT Server Computer

Making critical decisions is tough. Making critical decisions quickly during software installation can be asking for trouble. You often end up making wrong choices because you don't have all of the information you need and then you have to live with the consequences. Sometimes this means taking twice as much time by having to "do it right the second time."

The best way to approach Windows NT Server 4.0 installation is to gather and understand all of the information you need up front. This approach allows you to make the important decisions before even beginning the installation procedure. You'll avoid making mistakes that may require you to reinstall the software multiple times. Even if you're like me and just launch the install program and fly by the seat of your pants, this preplanning process can spare you from potential headaches when installing NT. You may grumble now, but you'll thank me later.

In this chapter, I'll walk you through several aspects of designing, upgrading, and preparing your server computer to allow smooth installation and operation of Windows NT Server 4.0. In addition, I'll walk you through most of the important decisions you'll be required to make before installing the operating system. At key milestones along the

way, you'll record those decisions on the worksheet at the end of this chapter. You'll need this completed worksheet in Chapter 9 when you perform the hands-on installation of Windows NT Server on your computer.

Once again, I can't emphasize enough the importance of this planning phase prior to Windows NT Server installation. Don't skip it. The time, frustration, and job you save may be your own. In addition, the Windows NT Server Setup Worksheet that you complete in this chapter will be a vital addition to your network notebook, which I discussed in Chapter 5.

Designing Your Server Hardware

If you have the luxury and challenge of starting from scratch to specify the requirements of your server hardware, you'll need to make a number of decisions before you start spending your company's money. In this section, I'll offer advice on the NT tradeoffs associated with each hardware component of the server. I'll also recommend what works best with Windows NT Server in the real world.

If you're inheriting existing server hardware and you're upgrading it to run Windows NT Server, read on. The information presented here will be valuable in arriving at your hardware upgrade strategy.

Setting Server Hardware Goals

As with any major purchasing decision, it's critical that you first understand and focus on the goals that you want to achieve with your Windows NT Server hardware. It also helps to prioritize those goals, in case you have to draw a line somewhere when you run out of hardware budget. Here's a list of typical server hardware goals:

- ✦ Maximize performance
- ✦ Maximize reliability
- ✦ Maximize expandability
- ✦ Obtain fast, reliable support
- ✦ Minimize cost (overall, or per user)

These are all excellent objectives. You probably have others specific to your own organization and situation.

Hardware Compatibility

The Windows NT hardware compatibility testing program was devised to assure that NT would run on a wide variety of hardware configurations and to confirm the quality of third-party NT device drivers. Microsoft provides hardware manufacturers with a compatibility test kit that allows them to test their own hardware and drivers running on Windows NT. In addition, Microsoft performs a large chunk of hardware compatibility testing in their own labs. The result of this broad testing effort is a lengthy hardware compatibility list, offering you a wide range of hardware choices. You can find an up-to-date copy by visiting `http://www.microsoft.com/BackOffice/ntserver/hcl` on the World Wide Web.

The NT Hardware Compatibility List isn't a comprehensive rundown of all hardware products that work with Windows NT. It's simply the list of all computers and devices that have been formally tested with NT. Some manufacturers choose not to test their products formally for compatibility with NT, but they work great with it, nonetheless. (Microsoft makes no distinction between NT Server and NT Workstation, when it comes to hardware compatibility.)

For example, the clone computer that I'm working on right now has never been on the NT compatibility list, but I've been successfully running various versions of NT on it since 1991. Likewise, the network adapter in this computer isn't on the compatibility list, but it's fully compatible with one that's listed. It operates without a hitch, using the network adapter driver that Microsoft tested with a different, but fully compatible, adapter.

Selecting Your Processor

In this section, I'll discuss the factors to consider when deciding which processor to use with Windows NT Server 4.0. This choice will have an effect on several other downstream decisions that you make about your server hardware.

Choosing Your CPU Architecture

Windows NT Server will run on Intel x86, DEC Alpha, MIPS R4x00, and PowerPC platforms. Performance benchmark tests show many of these systems to be great performers, and each platform offers a wide range of processor speeds and prices. In terms of reliability, the CPU architectures are pretty much equal.

Performance

Whether RISC processors will buy you much performance on a network server is debatable and highly dependent on your use of the server. If your server is only going to share files and printers (in addition to NT Server's logon validation responsibilities), the differences in performance between platforms is small. High-end Intel CPUs will do just as well as RISC processors.

Will you be running server applications, such as SQL server, SMS, SNA, or Microsoft Exchange server? If your server will be occupied with CPU-intensive activities by running the server side of a client/server application, some of the faster RISC processors can make a difference in the performance of your server.

However, since each manufacturer (including Intel) is continuously releasing new versions of its CPUs, the landscape will vary from month to month. Different CPU platforms have been leapfrogging each other to gain the performance lead.

My advice is to educate yourself on the latest CPU performance benchmark results. This knowledge will let you determine which processor is best for your particular requirements. Be sure to focus on benchmarks that best match how you intend to use your server. For example, if your NT computer is going to act as an application server, don't focus on interactive desktop-application benchmarks.

Software Compatibility

Many Win32 software developers are focusing primarily on the Intel platform, even though support of RISC platforms is just a recompile and testing cycle away. You may find that the important NT Server applications that you want to run are available only on Intel, and perhaps on a subset of the other NT-supported CPU platforms. Almost every vendor provides at least an Intel version of their Win32 applications, so this may be a factor in your processor decision.

If you're going to run 16-bit x86 applications regularly on your NT Server, you're better off with an Intel processor. Although RISC-based platforms will run most DOS and Win16 applications, they do so through software emulation. An Intel-based computer will execute these applications faster than RISC-based computers. Consider obtaining and running 32-bit versions of your applications, if they're available. Running 16-bit applications on your NT Server isn't the best use of its CPU power.

SITTING ON THE BENCHMARK

I've purposely steered clear of providing you with actual CPU performance benchmark results for several reasons. First, by the time you read this, a whole new set of CPU products will be available from most of these manufacturers. Second, each manufacturer tends to quote different industry benchmarks for their processors, making meaningful comparisons between architectures difficult. Some even use different benchmarks to rate processors within the same product line. Finally, different manufacturers' benchmark tests are performed on a wide variety of hardware configurations, making the results even more difficult to interpret and compare.

Your best bet is to look for the latest independent test results in PC periodicals. These tests are typically performed on virtually identical hardware configurations, using standard performance benchmarks in a controlled environment. Although benchmarks cannot fully emulate the real world of your enterprise network, they do provide a basis for comparison.

Platform Support

You can safely bet that Windows NT will support Intel x86-compatible processors far into the future. The worst thing that will happen in the Intel arena is dropped support for older CPUs, as the processing requirements of the operating system increase and the popularity of older CPUs decreases. You've already seen this happen with Microsoft's abandonment of the 386 in NT 4.0. Someday, when the child or grandchild of today's Pentium Pro becomes the standard desktop CPU, you may see diminished support for the 486 processor (and increased sales of Pentium OverDrive upgrades to breathe a few more months of life into these computers).

You can also bet that Windows NT will support other RISC processors in the future, as they prove themselves NT-worthy, both technologically and economically. Even though NT is portable, adding support for a new processor architecture represents a huge investment for both Microsoft and the CPU manufacturer. There's the initial investment of porting and testing NT on the new platform, requiring dozens of people and scores of computers based on the new CPU. Then there's the ongoing commitment to building and testing all future versions of the operating system and flavors of computers based on the new CPU architecture. So, the decision to move NT to a new platform isn't taken lightly at Microsoft. Likewise, if a platform just refuses to succeed in the marketplace, there's always the possibility that NT support might be dropped for that platform.

The Alpha CPU architecture appears to be around for the long haul. DEC is producing a continuous stream of increasingly faster Alpha CPUs and systems, including SMP computers. Several firms offer MIPS and PowerPC-based Windows NT computers, but neither platform has really taken off like gangbusters yet. Although these computers seem to be plentiful today running UNIX or Apple operating systems (in the case of PowerPC), systems running NT are slightly harder to come by. If you're taking the road to RISC, my recommendation is that you choose your hardware vendors carefully and include quality and timeliness of service and support in your purchasing decision.

In the following sections, I'll provide some additional information on each processor architecture, to aid in your CPU selection.

Intel Processor Roundup

Intel offers a wide range of x86-compatible CPUs, with more arriving every few months. Table 7-1 paints the current Intel processor landscape. I've focused on only those CPUs that Windows NT Server 4.0 supports.

I've listed both the internal CPU speed (the rate at which instructions are executed) and the system bus speed (the rate at which memory and peripherals are accessed). Both are important to the overall performance of the computer. Where they differ for a given processor, Intel has employed a clock multiplier to run the CPU internally at a higher rate than the rest of the computer. This approach improves performance significantly for CPU-bound applications (and for Windows NT itself), but the improvement becomes negligible if your application is memory- or I/O-intensive.

In Table 7-1, (I) refers to the instruction cache size, and (D) refers to the data cache. Both types of cache are discussed later in this section.

Table 7-1
The NT-Compatible Intel Processors

Intel CPU Family	*Internal Processor Speed*	*System Bus Speed*	*Level 1 Cache Size*	*Level 2 Cache on Chip*	*System Bus Width*
i486 DX	33MHz	33MHz	8K	none	32 bits
i486 DX	50MHz	50MHz	8K	none	32 bits
IntelDX2 (486)	50MHz	25MHz	8K	none	32 bits
IntelDX2 (486)	66MHz	33MHz	8K	none	32 bits
IntelDX4 (486)	75MHz	25MHz	16K	none	32 bits
IntelDX4 (486)	100MHz	33MHz	16K	none	32 bits
Pentium	60MHz	60MHz	8K(I)+8K(D)	none	64 bits
Pentium	66MHz	66MHz	8K(I)+8K(D)	none	64 bits
Pentium	75MHz	50MHz	8K(I)+8K(D)	none	64 bits
Pentium	90MHz	60MHz	8K(I)+8K(D)	none	64 bits
Pentium	100MHz	66MHz	8K(I)+8K(D)	none	64 bits
Pentium	120MHz	60MHz	8K(I)+8K(D)	none	64 bits
Pentium	133MHz	66MHz	8K(I)+8K(D)	none	64 bits
Pentium	150MHz	60MHz	8K(I)+8K(D)	none	64 bits
Pentium	166MHz	66MHz	8K(I)+8K(D)	none	64 bits
Pentium	200MHz	66MHz	8K(I)+8K(D)	none	64 bits
Pentium Pro	150MHz	66MHz	8K(I)+8K(D)	256K	64 bits
Pentium Pro	166MHz	66MHz	8K(I)+8K(D)	512K	64 bits
Pentium Pro	180MHz	66MHz	8K(I)+8K(D)	256K	64 bits
Pentium Pro	200MHz	66MHz	8K(I)+8K(D)	256K	64 bits
Pentium Pro	200MHz	66MHz	8K(I)+8K(D)	512K	64 bits

YE OLDE INTEL CPUs

The Intel 386 is dead, at least from Windows NT's perspective. Don't even attempt to install Windows NT Server 4.0 on a 386-based computer. Setup won't let you do it.

Older revisions of Intel processors have sometimes been the source of headaches under Windows NT. Some of the early 386 CPUs contained problems that were fixed in later revisions of the chip. The 386 B1-step revision wasn't supported at all by Windows NT. Now that the 386 isn't supported, this is no longer an issue.

The 486 C-step revision has a bug that affects Windows NT, but Setup recognizes this chip and installs a special HAL (hal486c.dll) to work around it. There's a slight performance cost when running in this configuration, but the tradeoff is reliable operation.

The 486 CPU

The minimum Intel processor for Windows NT 4.0 is a 486. Microsoft recommends a minimum of a 33MHz 486 CPU for Windows NT Server. Frankly, the 486/33 crawls when running NT, so I recommend at least a 486/66 (DX2) or 486/100 (DX4).

The 486 DX CPU is essentially a 386 processor combined with a 387 math coprocessor on a single chip. In addition, the 486 adds an on-chip (primary) cache, which significantly speeds memory access in many situations. The cache stores data and instructions used recently, as well as nearby data and instructions that are likely to be needed soon. Having this information in the cache minimizes the time that the 486 has to wait for slower memory-access cycles. Most, but not all, 486 motherboards also provide a larger external (secondary) cache, which increases the chances that the processor won't have to access slow memory.

Avoid the 486 SX, which is a 486 DX minus the math coprocessor. Since NT uses the floating point unit, and since your applications may also make use of it, you're better off starting with the DX version. If you start with an SX and decide later to add a coprocessor, you'll spend more in the long run.

Relative to the Pentium and Pentium Pro processors discussed in the next sections, the 486 is slow. I recommend that you strongly consider a Pentium-based server, if you have a choice. The cost difference between 486 and Pentium computers is getting pretty small, relative to the significant increases in performance of the Pentium. In fact, 486 computers are getting harder to find everyday.

The Pentium CPU

The PC industry expected the successor to the 486 to be called the 586, but when Intel discovered that it couldn't copyright numeric names for its processors, it dubbed the new product the Pentium. As Table 7-1 shows, the Pentium introduces a 64-bit data bus to the Intel processor line. The Pentium can execute up to two instructions per clock cycle, using two instruction pipelines (a feature traditionally found in RISC processors).

As shown by the (I) and (D) notations in Table 7-1, the Pentium splits its primary cache into two equal-size sections, allocated separately for instructions and data. Like the 486, most Pentium motherboards provide an external secondary cache to improve performance.

Pentiums are very powerful and much faster than 486 CPUs. Always opt for the highest motherboard bus speed available, currently 66MHz. This will minimize the time that your CPU will wait for memory accesses and will allow you to use the fast 133, 166, and 200MHz Pentium processors. Also, try to get the largest external cache possible on the Pentium motherboard.

YE OLDE PENTIUMS

Can there be such a thing as an *old* Pentium?

Shy away from the 60MHz and 66MHz Pentium processors, even at bargain basement prices. Because these CPUs used a higher voltage than more recent types, they had significant heat dissipation problems. Some computer manufacturers worked around the heat problem successfully; others didn't. The result is that some computers based on these chips behave erratically. This characteristic certainly won't meet your server reliability goal.

Early versions of the Pentium processor included, at no extra cost, the infamous Floating Point Division Error. This bug in the Pentium chip affects floating point division, remainders, and transcendental functions such as sine, cosine, and meditation (for those metaphysical calculations). If you rely on any of these functions, your results may be affected by this bug.

Windows NT provides a command line utility called PENTNT. (Type **PENTNT /?** at an NT command prompt for details.) It allows you to detect whether you have a Pentium CPU with the floating point problem. In addition, it provides you with the ability to bypass the chip's hardware floating point calculations and use a software emulator instead.

As you might expect, software emulation is significantly slower. Since NT itself uses some floating point functions, taking the software emulation road can slow down not only your applications but the operating system as well. A better approach to solving this problem is to contact your computer vendor or Intel for a replacement Pentium CPU (which they should give you at no cost). Use software emulation as a stop-gap measure only.

The Pentium Pro CPU

With the Pentium Pro CPU, Intel has gone out on a limb, at least from the perspective of many industry pundits. Back in 1991, when Intel began designing the Pro, they thought that we'd be living in a completely 32-bit world by now. The Pentium Pro is optimized to run 32-bit operating systems and applications. When fed 16-bit software, it actually performs more slowly than regular Pentium processors. Thus, Pentium Pro computers make lousy Windows 3.x and Windows 95 systems (since both contain lots of 16-bit code), but they make ideal Windows NT computers. At least, as long as you're running 32-bit applications.

The Pentium Pro can execute up to three instructions per clock cycle, as opposed to the Pentium's two per cycle. Unlike the Pentium, the Pro can actually reorder instructions, executing those that are ready while putting others on hold.

Like the Pentium, the Pro splits the cache into two 8K chunks, one for instructions and one for data. In addition, the Pentium Pro CPUs are the first Intel processors to include an on-chip secondary cache. If you look at Intel's standard picture of the Pro, you'll see two separate silicon chips in the large CPU package. One of those chips is the secondary cache.

Although the external data bus of the Pentium Pro is still 64 bits, some vendors are using DIMMs, or dual in-line memory modules, instead of SIMMs to achieve an effective data path that's 128 bits wide. The HP Vectra XU 6/150 was one of the first Pro-based computers to use this technique. Computers using this approach are blowing away the competition in performance benchmark tests. Look for this feature if you're on the market for screaming performance. Of course, it will cost you more. In this case, though, you do get what you pay for.

The Pentium Pro is a very new kid on the Intel block. At the time of this writing, nearly all existing Pro computers use the 150MHz chip, and 200MHz systems are just now starting to trickle into the market. One of Intel's Pentium Pro data sheets still says the CPU "may contain design defects or errors." We haven't yet seen what bugs in this processor might turn up after several months of use in the real world.

Intel Processor Upgrades

If all you're after is higher CPU speed, Intel offers several processor replacements that you can use to upgrade existing hardware today or future hardware tomorrow. If you have the appropriate socket available to accept the upgraded processor (Intel calls them OverDrive processors), you can increase the internal speed of your CPU with only minor surgery. Table 7-2 outlines the available upgrade paths using Intel products.

Table 7-2
Intel Processor Upgrade Paths

From Your Existing CPU	*Running at*	*Upgrade Your CPU to*	*Running at*	*System Bus Speed Remains*	*Socket Type Required*
i486 DX	25MHz	IntelDX2	50MHz	25MHz	1, 2, or 3
i486 DX	33MHz	IntelDX2	66MHz	33MHz	1, 2, or 3
i486 DX	25MHz	IntelDX4	75MHz	25MHz	1, 2, or 3
i486 DX	33MHz	IntelDX4	100MHz	33MHz	1, 2, or 3
i486 DX	66MHz	IntelDX4	100MHz	33MHz	1, 2, or 3
i486 DX	25MHz	Pentium	63MHz	25MHz	2 or 3
IntelDX2	50MHz	Pentium	63MHz	25MHz	2 or 3
i486 DX	33MHz	Pentium	83MHz	33MHz	2 or 3
IntelDX2	66MHz	Pentium	83MHz	33MHz	2 or 3
Pentium	60MHz	Pentium	120MHz	60MHz	4
Pentium	75MHz	Pentium	125MHz	50MHz	5 or 7
Pentium	66MHz	Pentium	133MHz	66MHz	4
Pentium	90MHz	Pentium	150MHz	60MHz	5 or 7
Pentium	100MHz	Pentium	166MHz	66MHz	5 or 7
Pentium	120MHz	Pentium	180MHz	60MHz	7
Pentium	150MHz	Pentium	180MHz	60MHz	7
Pentium	133MHz	Pentium	200MHz	66MHz	7
Pentium	166MHz	Pentium	200MHz	66MHz	7

Socket requirements are very strict. Each new processor technology has a different number and layout of pins, so your motherboard has to be equipped with the appropriate upgrade socket to handle the new processor. Check your computer documentation to determine what type of socket you have before you invest in one of these upgrades.

If you're thinking of upgrading a multiprocessor computer using an OverDrive processor, think again. Intel warns that Pentium OverDrive processors won't work properly in computers with more than one processor.

Intel currently has no plans to offer any OverDrive processor upgrades that will allow you to move from a Pentium to a Pentium Pro. Your only upgrade path from a Pentium is to a faster Pentium. Otherwise, you'll need a new motherboard to jump into the Pentium Pro world.

Several of Intel's competitors, such as AMD and Cyrix, have introduced x86-compatible processors that offer increased performance and, in some cases, lower cost. Some of these CPUs are designed as upgrades to existing computers; others are provided as standard equipment in off-the-shelf servers. I've seen many installations achieve excellent results with these third-party devices.

The NT software doesn't recognize some third-party upgrade processors as Intel counterparts. Make sure that your processor is recognized as at least a 486 by Windows NT, or you won't be able to install NT on it. Check the NT Hardware Compatibility List and the CPU manufacturer for compatibility information. Be sure to specify Windows NT 4.0 when you ask, since it won't install on anything that looks like less than a 486.

In general, I suggest steering clear of 386-to-486 CPU upgrades for NT computers. Although the processor itself runs dramatically faster than the 386 it replaces, the 386 computer likely has a slow bus speed, little or no external cache, and sometimes a BIOS that can't handle the higher-speed processor. Use these devices only as stop-gap measures until your new server hardware arrives.

MIPS Processor Roundup

Windows NT was ported to the MIPS CPU architecture just after the port to the Intel x86 was complete. A number of MIPS processors have emerged since then, and several others are in the works. Prior to NT, MIPS's big claim to fame has been its use as the core of powerful Silicon Graphics workstations. MIPS had a very strong start in the NT arena, but some of its recent offerings have been more expensive than and not as fast as Pentium Pros.

INSIDE STORY

Microsoft and DEC cooperated early on to port NT to the R3000, an earlier version of the MIPS RISC processor. It was used by the DECStation and a handful of other computers. Technology moves fast. By the time the port was nearly complete, MIPS technology had moved forward enough to make the R3000 version look sluggish. Thus, the R3000 variety of NT was never completed or released. (I took a few photos when Bill Gates met with our guest from DEC, who was working on the R3000 port. I've got the pictures to prove it. Of course, I can't prove that the pictures showed an R3000 running Windows NT. You'll just have to trust me on this.)

Table 7-3 shows the MIPS processor landscape as it stands at the time of this writing. A few of the faster processors are just about to be released. Like the Pentium and Pentium Pro, these processors have a 64-bit data path. System bus speeds vary up to 100MHz for some processors. Like the Pentium Pro, all MIPS processors include separate data and instruction on-chip primary caches, which are indicated in the table by (D) and (I). In most cases, the size of the primary cache is larger than that found on Intel's CPU offerings.

Table 7-3
The MIPS Processor Lineup

MIPS RISC CPU	*Internal Processor Speed*	*Level 1 Cache Size*	*Level 2 Cache Controller*
R4000	100MHz	8K(I)+8K(D)	external
R4200	80MHz	16K(I)+8K(D)	external
R4400	200MHz	16K(I)+16K(D)	up to 4MB
R4400	250MHz	16K(I)+16K(D)	up to 4MB
R4400	150MHz	16K(I)+16K(D)	up to 4MB
R4600	133MHz	16K(I)+16K(D)	up to 4MB
R4700	133MHz	16K(I)+16K(D)	up to 4MB
R4700	175MHz	16K(I)+16K(D)	up to 4MB
R5000	180MHz	32K(I)+32K(D)	up to 2MB
R8000	75MHz	16K(I)+16K(D)	up to 16MB
R8000	90MHz	16K(I)+16K(D)	up to 16MB
R10000	200MHz	32K(I)+32K(D)	up to 16MB

You may notice that MIPS processor clock speeds and cache sizes tend to be higher than those of Intel. This phenomena is due, in part, to RISC's requirement that the CPU execute more instructions to accomplish the same work. Also, because of the uniform size of RISC instructions, they tend to take up more space in memory than their Intel counterparts.

You must have a MIPS R4000 version 2.0 or later in order to run Windows NT Server. Check with your computer manufacturer to ensure that you have the appropriate version, and make sure to indicate that you're planning to run NT on it.

All but the R4000 and R4200 include an on-chip secondary cache controller. This isn't the same as having an on-chip secondary cache such as the Pentium Pro. The MIPS processors have the cache controller built into the chip, but the secondary cache memory still resides outside the chip, on the motherboard.

The MIPS R4x00 family includes PC, SC, and MC versions. The PC flavor is designed for low-cost desktop computers and supports no secondary cache. I recommend staying away from this version, for performance reasons. The SC is designed for high-performance, single-processor computers with lots of secondary cache on the motherboard, and MC is designed for multiprocessor computers with large secondary caches. (Because RISC instructions take more memory, the size of the secondary cache becomes increasingly important on MIPS and other RISC processors.) The SC and MC MIPS flavors, coupled with large secondary caches, are good choices for NT servers.

Depending on the processor model, MIPS CPUs can execute either three or four instructions per cycle. R10000 can execute up to four instructions per cycle. Like the Pentium Pro, it can shuffle the order of instruction execution.

The MIPS CPU is available from a handful of semiconductor vendors. MIPS-based computers that can run Windows NT Server are offered by a dozen or so system vendors including NEC, NeTpower, Siemens-Nixdorf, and Silicon Graphics. A few vendors recently announced that they're pulling out of the MIPS market in favor of manufacturing Intel SMP computers.

Alpha Processor Roundup

Once the MIPS port was completed, a team at DEC started working with Microsoft on a port of Windows NT to DEC's Alpha processor architecture. Alpha CPUs have become quite popular, especially in the high-end workstation market. DEC has successfully released an increasingly powerful series of products, including multiprocessor server computers. Of all the RISC platforms supported by NT, most application developers work on porting to the Alpha as soon as they complete their Intel version.

Table 7-4 shows the Alpha processor lineup as it stands at the time of this writing. Alpha CPUs can execute up to four instructions per clock cycle. They have a 64-bit data path, although some can optionally support a 128-bit bus. Like the MIPS and Pentium Pro, all Alpha processors include separate data and instruction on-chip primary caches, shown in Table 7-4 by (D) and (I). The clock rates are phenomenal, but keep in mind that, as a RISC processor, the Alpha must execute more instructions to accomplish the same work.

Like most MIPS CPUs, all Alpha processors include an on-chip secondary cache controller. The secondary cache memory either resides outside the chip, on the motherboard, or on-chip in the case of the 21164 Alpha processor.

Table 7-4
The Alpha Processor Line

Alpha AXP CPU	*Internal Processor Speed*	*Level 1 Cache Size*	*Level 2 Cache Controller*
21064A	200MHz	16K(I)+16K(D)	up to 16MB
21064A	233MHz	16K(I)+16K(D)	up to 16MB
21064A	275MHz	16K(I)+16K(D)	up to 16MB
21066A	100MHz	8K(I)+8K(D)	up to 16MB
21066A	166MHz	8K(I)+8K(D)	up to 16MB
21066A	233MHz	8K(I)+8K(D)	up to 16MB
21164	266MHz	8K(I)+8K(D)	96K on chip
21164	300MHz	8K(I)+8K(D)	96K on chip
21164	333MHz	8K(I)+8K(D)	96K on chip
21164	366MHz	8K(I)+8K(D)	96K on chip
21164	400MHz	8K(I)+8K(D)	96K on chip

PowerPC Processor Roundup

The PowerPC is the youngest of the NT-compatible CPU siblings. Official support for the PowerPC first emerged with Windows NT 3.51. Microsoft worked closely with both Motorola and IBM to make this happen. (Yes, cooperative efforts between Microsoft and IBM are still possible.) Except in the Apple arena, the PowerPC hasn't really taken off, primarily because it hasn't offered spectacular price/performance advantages over the other NT platforms. Table 7-5 presents the PowerPC processors available at the time of this writing.

Table 7-5
The PowerPC Processor World

PowerPC CPU	*Internal Processor Speed*	*Level 1 Cache Size*	*Level 2 Cache Controller*
601	66MHz	32K	external
603	66MHz	8K(I)+8K(D)	external
603	80MHz	8K(I)+8K(D)	external

PowerPC CPU	*Internal Processor Speed*	*Level 1 Cache Size*	*Level 2 Cache Controller*
603e	100MHz	16K(I)+16K(D)	external
603e	120MHz	16K(I)+16K(D)	external
603e	133MHz	16K(I)+16K(D)	external
603p	150MHz-200MHz	16K(I)+16K(D)	external
604	100MHz-200MHz	16K(I)+16K(D)	external
604e	150MHz-200MHz	16K(I)+16K(D)	external
620	133MHz	32K(I)+32K(D)	up to 128MB

The 601 and 603 series can execute up to three instructions per clock cycle. These chips can use a 32-bit or a 64-bit data bus. The 604 series can execute up to four instructions per clock cycle and have a 64-bit data bus. The 620 introduces an on-chip cache controller to handle up to 128MB of external secondary cache. In addition, the 620 increases the data bus width to 128 bits.

How Many Processors Do You Need?

Adding CPUs to multiprocessor computers is a great way to increase your server capacity. Contrary to what you might think, though, adding a second processor doesn't double your throughput. Coordination among CPUs requires some additional overhead. Results of increasing the number of processors vary from one model to the next. Some Intel computers show an 80 percent throughput increase with the installation of a second processor, with additional CPUs providing less incremental performance improvement. If your server is CPU-bound and is running multiple applications or multithreaded applications, you should consider selecting an SMP computer.

By the time you read this, SMP computer manufacturers should be using a new version of the Pentium Pro processor (called *A1 stepping*) that solves the so-called Wob Clobber bug. This bug delayed shipment of several four-processor Pentium Pro computers. Also, Intel is now building four-processor Pentium Pro motherboards for use by other computer manufacturers. This should yield lower-cost, more standardized SMP computers. Multiprocessor computers based on MIPS, Alpha, and PowerPC CPUs are available today, with more on the way. NT's Hardware Compatibility List provides examples of SMP computers based on each CPU platform.

The price of SMP computers is higher, even if you initially install only one CPU. However, the overall cost is typically much less expensive than purchasing separate server computers to achieve the same performance increase. Some of these products include redundant power supplies, hardware RAID drives, hot-swappable disk drives, and other components useful in a mission-critical environment. These features tend to increase their cost as well.

Selecting Your Motherboard

In this section, I'll discuss the issues to consider in choosing or upgrading your server's motherboard. Your decisions will drive and, in some ways, limit the choices that you make later.

Which Bus Should You Ride?

Several different PC bus architectures have been developed since the introduction of the first IBM PC in 1983. Newer technologies typically offer increased throughput. Some motherboards today combine these technologies to provide a cost-effective approach to building high-speed servers. In this section, I'll briefly discuss each of these bus technologies.

The ISA Bus

The standard 8-bit PC adapter slot provided in the original IBM PC, later expanded to 16 bits in the IBM PC/AT, has become known as the ISA (Industry Standard Architecture) bus. It's been widely adopted across the industry in PCs, so there are thousands of different adapters designed for it.

Relative to other PC bus architectures available today, the ISA is slow because of its limited speed and narrow data path. My recommendation is to steer clear of computers that have only ISA slots. Transferring data at an effective rate between 1.5MB and 5MB per second, your disk, network, and video performance will be abysmal in these machines. ISA is adequate for some client computers, but it definitely doesn't cut the mustard for servers, unless your network is very small.

The VESA Local Bus

The VESA Local Bus, or VLB, was developed as a high-speed supplement to the ISA bus. This type of bus was designed to give video adapters direct access to the CPU. Up to two 32-bit VLB slots are included on an otherwise ISA motherboard to provide data transfer rates up to a speedy 132MB per second. VLB is typically designed into 486-based motherboards, because of the difficulty of adapting it to the Pentium processor because of its higher speed and 64-bit data bus requirement.

VLB was developed originally for video acceleration. Although nonvideo adapters have been developed, there are few of them. Since a maximum of two VLB slots are available on an otherwise slow ISA motherboard, high-speed expansion options are limited. I don't recommend using a VLB/ISA motherboard in your server, unless your network is very small (say, ten nodes maximum) with low traffic.

A successor to VLB, called VESA II, has appeared in an attempt to provide a 64-bit solution for Pentium-based computers. However, it has gained little support in the industry because of the overwhelming popularity of PCI, discussed later in this chapter. I recommend avoiding VESA II motherboards, since they have very limited adapter choices and an uncertain future.

The MCA Bus

IBM introduced the Micro Channel Architecture (MCA) with the release of their PS/2 computer. It was a completely new bus design, allowing both 16-bit and 32-bit data paths to transfer information up to 40MB per second. In addition, MCA adapters have the ability to take control of the bus and perform their own data transfers without any CPU intervention. This technique, known as bus mastering, relieves the processor of significant I/O burdens. MCA is completely incompatible with existing ISA adapters. You can only put MCA adapters in an MCA computer.

Because of its respectable speed and bus mastering capability, MCA can be suitable as the basis for a server computer. Keep in mind, though, that choices of adapters are much more limited than for other architectures, since relatively few hardware vendors have jumped on the MCA bandwagon. (IBM decided to make the MCA design proprietary, and few manufacturers decided to pay IBM the requisite licensing fees to use it.) Also, many existing MCA motherboards have slow clock speeds and little or no cache. So, keep these factors in mind before deciding to run with MCA.

From an administrative viewpoint, MCA is a bit more difficult to configure and maintain, since it requires running a special configuration program for each adapter that you install. You must keep track of configuration floppy disks for each of your MCA computers and devices.

INSIDE STORY

"What the heck is that?" we asked, as the perspiring mover eased the beige behemoth into its place in the corner of the NT test lab. "It's the NCR PC you've been waiting on."

PC indeed! The size of a large refrigerator, this monster required its own tap into the Redmond power grid. With eight 486 CPUs, 128MB of RAM, and 15GB of disk storage, our new MCA-based SMP computer seemed to blur the line between a PC and a mainframe. It was the perfect desktop computer, if your desktop was the size of Rhode Island.

When we put this machine into service in the NT group, we appropriately and affectionately named it "Behemoth." After proving itself as a matchless download server for daily Windows NT builds, it became one of the family. Whenever Behemoth was down, many who relied on its high speed grieved. When it was healthy and happy, so were its users. Behemoth seemed to have power over the group that transcended its awesome CPU power.

The EISA Bus

Since most hardware manufacturers were unwilling to pay IBM for the rights to design MCA computers and adapters, several of them got together and defined the Extended Industry Standard Architecture, called EISA. Like MCA, this bus provides a 32-bit data path and bus mastering and requires running special configuration programs for each adapter. Unlike MCA, EISA offers full compatibility with ISA adapters and can even coexist with them in the same computer. Unfortunately, by maintaining ISA compatibility, EISA's speed is constrained to 32MB per second.

EISA is certainly preferable to ISA in terms of throughput, and the breadth of adapter choices is orders of magnitude greater than MCA. EISA's ability to support ISA adapters allows you to migrate from older, slower adapters to newer, faster ones as your network grows. If you have a choice between EISA and ISA, go with EISA. However, for high disk and network throughput in your server, look for PCI capability, which I'll discuss next.

The PCI Bus

At the time of this writing, Intel's Peripheral Computer Interface, or PCI, is the state-of-the-art in high-speed PC buses. It's designed with the Pentium in mind, providing a 64-bit data path. Like EISA, it supports bus mastering. However, PCI can operate at the speed of the system bus up to 66MHz, yielding a theoretical data transfer rate of up to 264MBps. In practice, today's PCI bus designs (version 2.0 and 2.1) peak at 132MBps. Several manufacturers are starting to support a faster design based on the PCI 3.0 specification, but you'll need both new motherboards and new PCI adapters to achieve the advertised speed of 264MBps. (Older PCI adapters will work in the new PCI 3.0 motherboards, but they'll run at the slower rate.)

Most available PCI motherboards contain three PCI slots, with the remainder being either ISA or EISA slots. A few motherboards are now emerging with four and six PCI slots, which makes them more relevant products for servers. Because of the high speed and relatively low cost (due to availability of a standard PCI interface chip set), a wide range of adapter choices are already available, with more appearing daily.

Choose established motherboard and adapter manufacturers for your PCI products and avoid older revisions of PCI equipment. It has taken time for the dust to settle on this standard. Many flawed hardware designs and driver bugs have wreaked compatibility havoc in the PCI world. Focus on the NT Hardware Compatibility List, and contact each adapter vendor to determine compatibility among their adapters, your motherboard, and NT.

For Windows NT Server, I recommend a PCI/EISA motherboard with as many PCI slots as possible. PCI/ISA motherboards are a second choice. You'll want to install disk adapters and network adapters in the PCI slots. If you plan on disk duplexing and network bridging, your need for PCI slots will quickly grow.

WORKSHEET ENTRY

In Worksheet 7-3 (Windows NT Server Setup) on line 6, record the make and model of your computer, along with the type of bus that the computer has (ISA, EISA, MCA, or PCI).

How Much Cache Do You Need?

The rule of thumb here is Bigger Is Better. The more primary and secondary cache that you have, the better your server's performance will be. Get a processor with as much internal cache as possible, and never choose a motherboard that doesn't provide room for an ample secondary cache.

Many vendors advertise internal CPU cache to make it sound like additional external cache. Don't be fooled. Make sure that you know both how much external cache is actually supplied on the motherboard and how much total cache the motherboard design will accept. Today Pentium motherboards typically accept a maximum of 512K, and a handful allow 1MB of cache.

There are many opinions about how much secondary cache is enough. Although there's no pat answer for all computer configurations, Table 7-6 provides some guidelines for Windows NT computers.

Table 7-6
Guidelines for Secondary Cache Sizes

System RAM Size	*Recommended Secondary Cache Size*
< 16MB	Doesn't apply to NT
16MB	256K
24MB	256K
32MB	512K
64MB	512K
> 64MB	512K–1MB

Because installation of secondary cache memory can be tricky, I recommend that you opt for as much external cache as you can afford up front. Today, most motherboards designed to be used as servers ship with 256KB or 512KB of external cache installed. Compaq was the first to offer a 1MB external cache in its server product line. (This is one of the perks of designing your own motherboards.)

Selecting Your Memory

The single most significant way to improve performance on a Windows NT server computer is to add more RAM. The more RAM that you have, the more that NT can keep cached in memory. Windows NT takes full advantage of all memory available to it. The more it has, the happier it is.

Don't put more than 16MB of memory on an ISA bus computer running Windows NT. Having more than 16MB can actually reduce performance dramatically, since NT has to perform special DMA buffering operations to memory above the 16MB line. If you're going to need more than 16MB of RAM on your server (and you will), opt for a system bus other than ISA.

How Much Memory Do You Need?

You can listen to Microsoft, who recommends a minimum of 12MB for Intel x86 computers and 16MB for RISC computers. You can listen to me when I tell you that the more RAM you have, the better off you are. But how much memory do you really need in your Windows NT server computer? Worksheet 7-1 will help you get to a ballpark figure. You can use this worksheet for estimating the memory for each of your NT Server installations. I've included RAM requirements for Microsoft's BackOffice applications, and you can add the memory requirements of other server applications that you plan to run.

Worksheet 7-1
Windows NT Server Memory Estimate

Line	*Memory Requirement*	*Minimum*	*Recommended*	*Estimate*
1	Number of concurrent users of this server			
2	Is line 1 under 25?	16MB	16–32MB	
3	Is line 1 between 25 and 250?	32MB	32–64MB	
4	Is line 1 over 250?	64MB	64–128MB	
5	Average size of open data files on the server, per user (in megabytes)			
6	Multiply line 1 by line 5			
7	Number of concurrent applications being run from the server			
8	Average size of application executables being run from the server (in megabytes)			

Line	*Memory Requirement*	*Minimum*	*Recommended*	*Estimate*
9	Multiply line 7 by line 8			
10	Running Microsoft Internet Information Server?	add 0MB	add 16–48MB	
11	Running Microsoft SNA Server?	add 0MB	add 8MB	
12	Running Microsoft Systems Management Server?	add 16MB	add 16–24MB	
13	Running Microsoft Exchange Server?	add 8MB	add 16MB	
14	Running Microsoft SQL Server?	add 0MB	add 8MB	
15	Subtotal (add lines 2–4, 6, and 9–14)			
16	Is server a RISC-based computer?	add 15% of line 15	add 15–25% of line 15	
TOTAL ESTIMATED RAM NEEDED (add lines 15 and 16)				

What Type of Memory Is Best?

Most computers today support standard DRAM (Dynamic RAM) in the form of SIMMs (single in-line memory modules) that plug into the motherboard. DRAM is typically fine for your NT server computer. Just be sure to use the appropriate speed recommended for your specific computer model.

EDO (Enhanced Data Output) RAM provides faster data throughput that some folks claim eliminates the need for a secondary cache. Indeed, in computers with no secondary cache, EDO RAM consistently outperforms DRAM. However, a cacheless EDO or DRAM computer is slower than a computer with a secondary cache. And a cacheless computer with EDO is typically slower than a computer using DRAM with a secondary cache (depending on the size of the cache). So take EDO's claim to bring about a "cacheless society" with a grain of salt.

As I mentioned earlier in this chapter, I strongly recommend having a secondary cache. In computers with a secondary cache, EDO RAM provides about a 5 percent performance improvement over DRAM. At the time of this writing, EDO RAM is significantly more expensive than DRAM. It's probably not worth the price premium to squeeze out that extra 5 percent. Once EDO costs come down and are more in line with DRAM, though, EDO will be certainly worth considering. However, keep in mind that some computers based on the Pentium Pro won't be able to use EDO RAM, since early versions of the Pentium Pro's PCI chip set don't support it.

ECC (Error Checking and Correcting) RAM can detect and correct single-bit errors in RAM. ECC RAM is starting to show up in high-end servers and workstations. Since a RAM parity error can bring Windows NT Server down, ECC provides an added level of robustness by catching and correcting single-bit errors before NT ever sees them. At the time of this writing, ECC RAM costs about 30 percent more than conventional DRAM.

Selecting Your Storage Devices

In this section, I'll discuss mass storage devices for your Windows NT server computer.

Floppy Drives

On an Intel-based computer, in order to install Windows NT Server 4.0, you'll need a high-density, 3.5-inch floppy drive. (There are ways to get around the floppy drive requirement, but you won't be able to create an Emergency Repair disk — which you'll need.) You'll also need to make sure the computer is configured to boot from this floppy drive. On RISC-based computers, there's no such thing as a boot floppy drive, but since these computers are ARC-compliant, they include a floppy drive anyway. (ARC stands for *Advanced RISC Computing,* a standard developed to ensure compatibility of new RISC-based computers with operating system software. The ARC standard specifies PC-like hardware and BIOS features required by RISC computers that are designed to run Windows NT.)

Hard Disks

In this section, I'll show you how to estimate the amount of disk space that you'll require on your NT Server computer, as well as your choices of disk hardware.

How Much Disk Space Do You Need?

I've provided you with another worksheet to complete, this time helping you to estimate how much free disk space you'll need on your server computer. Fill out Worksheet 7-2 for each of the NT servers that you're planning to install. I've included disk space requirements for Microsoft's BackOffice applications, and you can add the space requirements of other server applications that you plan to run.

Worksheet 7-2
Windows NT Server Disk Space Estimate

Line	*Disk Space Requirement*	*Minimum*	*Recommended*	*Estimate*
1	Default NT system space requirement	250MB		250MB
2	Server computer memory (in megabytes)			
3	Add line 2 and 162MB			

Line	*Disk Space Requirement*	*Minimum*	*Recommended*	*Estimate*
4	Copy line 1 or line 3, whichever is larger			
5	Average space required by an application installed on the server			
6	Number of applications being run from the server			
7	Multiply line 5 by line 6			
8	Average space allocated to each user on this server			
9	Number of users storing information on this server			
10	Margin for error/growth			1.15
11	Multiply lines 8, 9, and 10			
12	Running Microsoft Internet Information Server?	add 50MB	add 100MB	
13	Running Microsoft SNA Server?	add 30MB	add 30MB	
14	Running Microsoft Systems Management Server?	add 100MB	add 100MB	
15	Running Microsoft Exchange Server?	add 250MB	add 500MB	
16	Running Microsoft SQL Server?	add 45MB	add 100MB	
17	Subtotal (add lines 4, 7, and 11–16)			
18	Is server a RISC-based computer?	add 25% of line 17	add 25–30% of line 17	
TOTAL ESTIMATED DISK SPACE NEEDED (add lines 17 and 18)				

Of course, not all of this space needs to be on one disk drive or partition. Some network administrators choose to place the material on four separate partitions, using the following scheme:

- ✦ Operating system files
- ✦ User applications that are run over the network
- ✦ Server applications that run on the server
- ✦ User data

Have you looked at the list of NT-compatible hard disk drives and been shocked at the small number of devices there? Standard hard disk drives don't need their own device drivers. They typically work just fine on NT if they're attached to the computer via an NT-compatible adapter. Nonetheless, a handful of drive manufacturers have opted to certify their SCSI, IDE, and PCMCIA drives as NT-compatible. As a result, the number of hard disk drives on the compatibility list is frighteningly small. These few manufacturers saw marketing value in having their devices listed, even though there's no technical reason why these or any other hard disk drives shouldn't work on NT.

So, don't believe that the NT compatibility list is the definitive rundown of hard disks that you can use. As long as a hard disk drive meets the IDE, SCSI, or PCMCIA standard, it should have no problem running on Windows NT.

The Case Against IDE

IDE, which stands for Integrated Drive Electronics, is currently the most popular type of adapter/drive combination shipped in today's PCs. IDE owes its existence to predecessor PC hard disk drive technologies, including ST506 (used in the IBM XT) and ESDI (used in the IBM AT). Two drives, one acting as master and one acting as slave, can connect to one IDE adapter. Because of this relationship, only one of the two drives can be active at any given time. Moreover, if the master drive fails, both drives are down for the count. You can include up to four drives in a PC by using two IDE adapters. The four-drive limit can be a problem for servers that need to add more drives eventually.

EIDE, which stands for Enhanced Integrated Drive Electronics, is an extension of IDE that supports faster transfer rates, larger disk capacities, and storage devices other than hard disks. Unfortunately, it suffers from the same serialized drive access as IDE.

If you plan on using any of NT Server's fault-tolerance RAID options for data redundancy or improved performance, forget using IDE or EIDE drives. Writes to and reads from multiple drives are serialized, causing the performance of mirrors and stripes to go down the tubes rather quickly. Even if you're not using RAID features, using multiple IDE or EIDE drives can cause real server performance bottlenecks, as one drive locks the other out during disk accesses.

The Case for SCSI

The best high-performance disk solution for network servers is based on SCSI, the Small Computer Systems Interface. SCSI overcomes the serialization problem by allowing independent and concurrent access to each attached drive, and it allows more drives per adapter. You'll need SCSI drives if you want to implement the RAID features of Windows NT Server. (SCSI's ability to start an I/O operation, disconnect until the I/O is complete, and allow other devices to perform I/O during the disconnection make it ideal for RAID implementations.) Table 7-7 summarizes the characteristics of the SCSI technologies available at the time of this writing.

Table 7-7
Characteristics of Available SCSI Technologies

SCSI Technology	*Interface Data Path Width*	*Data Transfer Rate*	*Approach*	*Maximum Cable Length*
SCSI-1: SCSI	8-bit (narrow)	5MBps	Parallel data transfer	20 ft
SCSI-2: Fast SCSI	8-bit (narrow)	10MBps	Doubles bus clock rate of SCSI-1	20 ft
SCSI-2: Wide SCSI	16-bit (wide)	20MBps	Doubles data path width of Fast SCSI	20 ft
SCSI-2: Fast & Wide SCSI	16-bit (wide)	40MBps	Dual Wide 20MBps channels	10 ft
UltraSCSI Fast 20	8-bit (narrow)	20MBps	Doubles clock rate of Fast SCSI	5 ft
UltraSCSI Fast 40	16-bit (wide)	40MBps	Doubles data path of UltraSCSI Fast 20	5 ft
UltraSCSI Fast 80 (emerging)	16-bit (wide)	80MBps	Dual UltraSCSI Fast 40 channels	5 ft

You may see references to SCSI-3, sometimes erroneously equated with UltraSCSI. They aren't the same. UltraSCSI is probably the last step in parallel SCSI technology. SCSI-3 refers to a high-performance serial technology, which will likely be used primarily for digital video. FireWire is one implementation of SCSI-3. It's currently used by some digital camcorder manufacturers.

A SCSI bus can support as many devices as it has bits in its data path. In reality, one of these device addresses is automatically consumed by the SCSI adapter itself, since it's considered a SCSI device on the bus. So, an 8-bit SCSI bus can support up to seven devices attached to its adapter. A 16-bit wide SCSI bus can support up to 15 devices. Dual-channel SCSI adapters appear to the operating system as two separate adapters. Together, the two channels can support twice as many devices as single-channel adapters, consuming one device address for each channel on the adapter. For example, Fast and Wide SCSI adapters can support up to 30 devices attached to the bus.

Windows NT Server currently supports only eight SCSI addresses per adapter, including the adapter's address itself. So, 16-bit wide SCSI adapters on NT can only address 7 drives, not 15. Dual-channel adapters appear to NT as two distinct adapters, so if each channel supports up to 7 devices, a dual-channel adapter in NT can support up to 14 devices.

If you've had much experience with SCSI or IDE drives, you may have encountered an annoying behavior that seems to defy explanation. Occasionally, the drive disappears or goes to sleep for a few seconds, although it sounds as if the heads are seeking across the disk. This can happen when the drive is idle or just as the drive is being accessed. If the latter occurs, you notice a delay in responsiveness from the operating system or application that's trying to access the disk.

What's going on during this period when the drive seems to have a mind of its own? It's going through a thermal recalibration cycle, sometimes called *T-cal*. This is an internal housekeeping task in which the drive makes sure that all of its heads can still correctly read and write data, even though temperature changes have altered the mechanics of the drive. Some disk manufacturers now offer AV (audiovisual) drives, which have been tuned to minimize or completely eliminate this time-consuming operation. Although designed originally to prevent dropped video frames and sound samples in audiovisual applications, these drives provide excellent, consistent performance on servers.

Cabling SCSI Drives

Next to IRQ conflicts, the most common hardware configuration problems on PC servers stem from improper SCSI cabling and termination. If you're maintaining an NT Server, you should become an expert on these SCSI topics.

There are two types of wiring used in SCSI buses. The most common is called *single-ended,* which uses one wire for each signal on the bus. Single-ended SCSI is so widespread that it's often referred to as normal SCSI.

The less common approach is called *differential.* This approach uses two wires for each signal, sending the actual data on one wire and its logical inverse on the other. The receiving end uses the difference (or differential) between the two signals to determine and verify what was sent on the bus. Differential SCSI is less susceptible to external noise, allowing you to use longer cables for reliable data transfer. Although differential SCSI is a bit hard to find today, it's worth considering if you plan on placing a large number of devices on the SCSI bus, if you intend to push the SCSI cable length to its limits, or both.

Never mix single-ended SCSI peripherals or adapters with differential SCSI equipment on the same SCSI bus. Not only will you see strange behavior, but you could also lose valuable data on your disks.

SCSI bus termination is absolutely critical to your success, both in terms of performance and reliability. An improperly terminated SCSI bus will behave in ways that will make you lose lots of sleep. Sometimes, it will work just fine. Other times, you'll get high error rates and retries. In other instances, the computer won't even see some of the SCSI devices at boot time. Basically, both ends of the SCSI bus must be properly terminated. Figure 7-1 illustrates the three most common configurations and how they must be terminated.

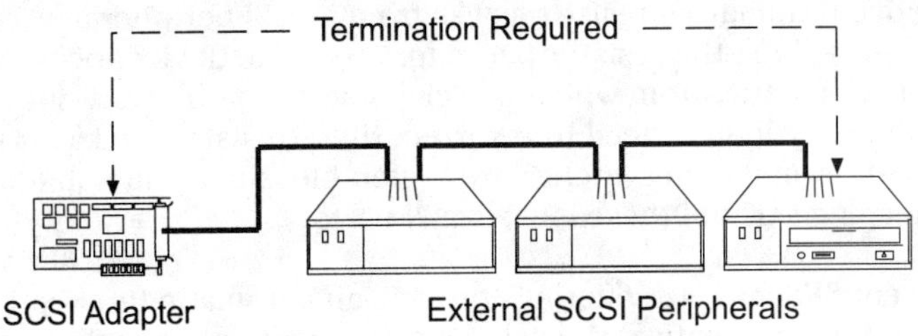

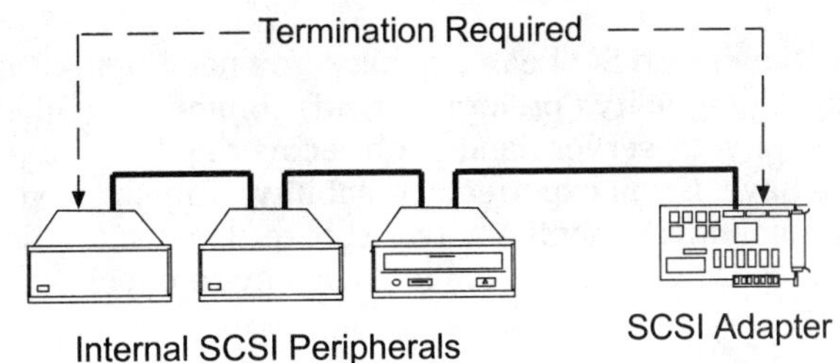

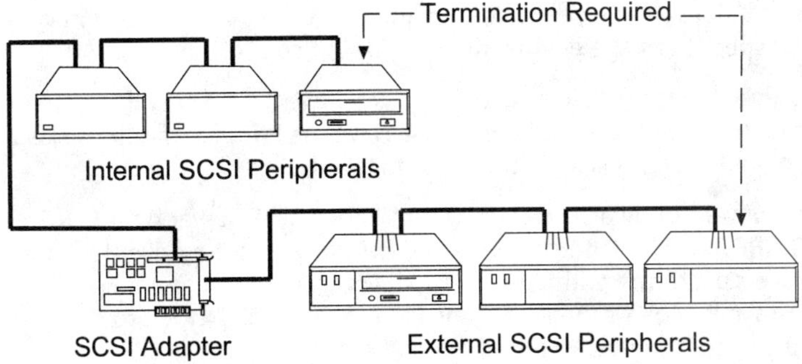

Figure 7-1: Proper termination is required at both ends of the SCSI bus.

The cabling and termination requirements become a bit more complicated when you're dealing with some of the new Wide SCSI adapters that include three connectors. A good example of this is the Adaptec AHA-2940W. Internally, the adapter includes both Fast SCSI-2 and Wide SCSI connectors. Externally, it provides a Wide SCSI connector. You can use any combination of two of the connectors, but not all three. So, the SCSI bus still has only two ends, and the devices at the far ends of the two cables that you use must be terminated. If you use only one connector, the SCSI adapter provides its own termination.

When you remove termination resistor packs from a SCSI peripheral or adapter, don't bend the pins. Tape the resistor packs for a specific device together, and label the bundle to identify from which device it came. If you ever want to reconfigure your SCSI bus, you may need to resurrect these resistor packs for reinsertion. Devices with termination switches are preferable, since you don't have to worry about keeping track of these loose small parts.

Some more recent SCSI adapter offerings provide an automatic termination feature. These adapters automatically sense the drives on the bus and establish their termination at boot time. If you can find these adapters, they do make SCSI life a bit easier for you.

Don't scrimp when it comes to SCSI cable quality. You need tight-fitting, well-shielded cables with high-quality (preferably gold) connectors. Otherwise, you'll invisibly waste some of your server bandwidth recovering from data errors that you don't know you have. If you experience reliability problems, even with good cabling, consider a small investment in active SCSI terminators, which provide higher reliability than passive terminators in some environments.

WORKSHEET ENTRY

In Worksheet 7-3 (Windows NT Server Setup) on line 3, list the SCSI adapters in your computer. Also, list any special storage devices that NT doesn't support directly.

If you're using storage devices (other than SCSI, IDE, or EIDE hard disks) that aren't on the NT Hardware Compatibility List, circle YES on line 4. Have the NT driver floppy disk supplied by the hardware manufacturer available during installation.

If you don't have a driver floppy disk, look on your Windows NT Server 4.0 CD-ROM in the \DRVLIB\STORAGE\RETIRED\<platform>\README.TXT file to see if a driver for your device is supplied. (Replace <platform> with I386, MIPS, ALPHA, or PPC, depending on what CPU platform you're installing.) Follow the instructions in the README.TXT file to create a driver floppy disk before you commence NT installation.

Selecting Your CD-ROM Drive

I strongly recommend that you attach an NT-compatible CD-ROM drive to the computer on which you plan to install Windows NT Server. Doing this will make the installation process in Chapter 9 much easier for you.

Unless you already have a non-SCSI CD-ROM drive attached to your server, I recommend that you use a SCSI CD-ROM drive. Having a SCSI drive will make it easier for you to install Windows NT and configure your system, since most such drives will work when attached to an NT-compatible SCSI adapter. Non-SCSI CD-ROM drives often require a special driver, either supplied with Windows NT or by the drive manufacturer. If your server is a RISC-based computer, Windows NT Server requires that you have a SCSI CD-ROM drive attached.

Stay away from portable CD-ROM drives that hang off the parallel port of your computer. Although they're quite convenient, driver support for NT is often lacking. Even with driver support, these drives are typically very slow. Likewise, if you're thinking about using a SCSI adapter that attaches to the parallel port, avoid this temptation for the same reasons.

A wide range of CD-ROM drive performance is available today. At the time of this writing, 2X drives are installed in low-end systems, and the drives themselves are down to commodity pricing. Many desktop computers ship today with 4X drives installed, 6X and 8X drives occupy the high end in powerful multimedia workstations and servers, and 10X drives are just now emerging on the market. (There are a few oddball 4.5X drives on the market. I think they were designed as a *Candid Camera* prank to confuse patrons of computer stores.) For your Windows NT Server, if you're just going to use the drive to install NT and application software, I recommend a minimum speed of 2X. If you're going to share the drive over the network with multiple users, opt for the 4X speed or faster.

CD-ROM changers, which shuffle three to six discs in a single drive, are great for keeping several CD-ROMs ready to run. However, don't use them to share CD-ROMs from your network server. The time required to change CD-ROMs mechanically is typically high, and two users accessing different CD-ROMs will drive each other (and your server) crazy as the discs are constantly swapped. If you need to share multiple CD-ROMs on the network, use separate drives attached to your server.

If you're planning to share your CD-ROM drive over the network, consider a drive with a large internal cache. CD-ROM drive caches range from 64KB to 1MB today. If all you're going to do is install NT and other CD-based software but aren't going to use the CD-ROM drive otherwise, a cache doesn't buy you much. If you're going to have multiple users accessing your drive, go for the biggest cache you can get.

WORKSHEET ENTRY

In Worksheet 7-3 (Windows NT Server Setup) on line 1, circle the type of CD-ROM drive that you're going to use for Windows NT Server installation. Circle SCSI, IDE, or Other. If you have non-SCSI CD-ROM drives, list them on line 3.

If you've circled SCSI, and you have more than one SCSI CD-ROM drive attached to your computer, determine the SCSI device address of each drive, and then identify which one has the lowest SCSI device address on line 2 of the worksheet.

Selecting Your Tape Drive

You'll need at least one NT-compatible tape drive to back up data on your Windows NT Servers and other computers on your network. Again, select a drive from the NT Hardware Compatibility List. Based on personal experience, I suggest that you shy away from tape drives that attach to the floppy controller. They're excruciatingly slow and often less reliable than SCSI tape drives.

I highly recommend SCSI tape drives for use with NT Server. If you can afford it, pick a 4mm DAT drive. These units are typically very fast, reliable, and capable of recording huge amounts of data on a single tape. If you need to perform unattended backup operations that span multiple tapes, there are a handful of SCSI robotic autoloader tape units available for NT. (NT's built-in NTBACKUP utility doesn't support autoloaders. You'll need third-party backup software, such as BackupExec, to take advantage of these high-end devices.

The NTBACKUP utility that comes with Windows NT Server doesn't perform software compression, so if you plan to use this program, expect to get about half the tape capacity advertised. You can either invest in a third-party backup utility that performs software compression or pick a tape drive that does its own compression in hardware. Either way, there's an extra cost that you need to consider.

Selecting Your System Unit

For a Windows NT server computer, a full-height tower case is best for maximum expandability and heat dissipation. Even if you don't need all of it right away, opt for at least a 300-watt power supply and as many open drive bays as possible. As your server needs grow, you'll be able to add disks and other devices easily. Also, make sure that your case can accommodate the largest motherboards (typically called standard AT size), in case you ever have to replace the motherboard.

Do You Really Need a UPS?

The answer to this question is a resounding "yes" for NT Server computers. Windows NT Server has full support for several UPS models. It allows you to connect the UPS to a serial port, take specific actions when the power fails, send notification messages to other nodes on the network, and perform an orderly shutdown of the server. When selecting a UPS, either pick one from the compatibility list, or make sure that the UPS manufacturer supplies the appropriate cables, software, and information to work with Windows NT Server.

Selecting Your Video Subsystem

The minimum requirement for video on Windows NT Server is VGA (640x480, 16 colors). This is perfectly fine for most servers out there, especially if you plan to perform your network and server administration tasks remotely from a different computer. In this situation, you'll only use the monitor attached to the server for infrequent maintenance and configuration tasks.

You may have been exposed to the concept of *headless servers,* which have no video monitor at all. Although some operating systems support this configuration, Windows NT Server doesn't. You need at least a VGA adapter and monitor installed on your NT computer. (You can use an electronic switch box to share your monitor between multiple computers, but that's the closest that NT comes to a headless server.)

If you plan to do your server administration at the server console, you'll probably want to consider higher-resolution video. You'll want to have the ability to run multiple administration and performance-monitoring applications and have them visible at the same time on the screen. In this situation, I recommend a minimum of a 17" monitor and an SVGA video adapter with 1024x768 resolution. You can certainly go up from there, but it might be difficult to justify. I advise against using a fancy graphics accelerator card that may burn one of your precious high-speed PCI slots. On a server, there are better uses for this slot, such as network and SCSI adapters.

I'm a firm believer in using screen savers to protect your investment in your video monitor. However, when selecting a screen saver to run on your Windows NT Server, think about its impact on your users.

Always select a screen saver that has very low CPU impact. Don't use OpenGL screen savers or third-party products that send kitchen appliances or bathroom fixtures careening across your server screen. Your server customers' needs come first. Be kind to them by using the simpler screen savers. The Blank Screen choice is always an excellent one.

WORKSHEET ENTRY

In Worksheet 7-3 (Windows NT Server Setup) on line 29, record the make and model of your video adapter. On line 30, record the video chip set that your adapter uses, if your adapter documentation includes this information. On line 31, indicate the number of colors that you want to use. Finally, on line 32, enter the screen resolution that you plan to use (for example, 640x480, 800x600, or 1024x768). You'll need all of this information toward the end of the NT installation process.

Regardless of what type of video adapter and monitor you select, Windows NT Server Setup will use VGA mode during the installation process. At the end of this process, you'll have an opportunity to select the appropriate resolution and color depth for your video adapter.

Selecting Your Input Devices

Keyboards are really a matter of personal preference. Most PC keyboards today are fully compatible with Windows NT, so the choice is pretty wide open. If you're going to spend significant time at the server performing network administration functions, you may want to opt for one of the ergonomic keyboards at an additional cost of $60 to $100. My fingers tend to slide off the slanted keys, but you may have better luck with them.

WORKSHEET ENTRY

In Worksheet 7-3 (Windows NT Server Setup) on lines 8 and 9, record the make and model of your keyboard and the special keyboard layout setting for your part of the world.

You need a mouse or some other NT-compatible pointing device on your server. In theory, you could do everything from the keyboard, using the command prompt for text and shortcut keys in windowed applications. However, you'll operate much faster and more efficiently if you use a mouse.

I recommend using an inport or PS/2 mouse that doesn't tie up one of your serial ports. Serial and inport mice work equally well, but if you take my earlier advice and attach your server to a UPS that requires a serial port, you'll only have one standard serial port left for a modem or serial printer. You don't want to waste that precious port on a serial mouse. Many motherboards today have mouse ports built into them in addition to two serial ports, so the decision has already been made for you on these computers.

In Windows NT Server 4.0, you'll definitely need two buttons on the mouse. The user interface consistently makes use of both buttons, unlike earlier versions of Windows and Windows NT. So, if you're considering using that one-button mouse that's hiding at the bottom of your hardware bin, don't.

WORKSHEET ENTRY

In Worksheet 7-3 (Windows NT Server Setup) on line 10, record the make and model of your pointing device.

Choosing Your File System

During Windows NT Server 4.0 installation, you'll need to specify which file system you want to use for the NT operating system files. If you have multiple hard disks and partitions, you'll be able to use a combination of file systems on your computer. However, during NT Setup, you'll need to select the file system on which NT itself will reside. Table 7-8 summarizes the pros and cons of the FAT/VFAT and NTFS file systems.

Table 7-8
Characteristics of Windows NT File Systems

File System Characteristic	*FAT/VFAT*	*NTFS*
Supports undelete (after rebooting to DOS and running UNDELETE)	Yes	No
Accessible by dual-booting to DOS, Windows 3.x, Windows 95, and OS/2	Yes	No
Allowed on system partition of RISC-based computer	Yes	No
Can be used on a floppy disk	Yes	No
Uses space efficiently on partitions under 200MB	Yes	No
Performance degrades as partition size increases	Yes	No
Supports long file names	Yes	Yes
Supports file security	No	Yes

(continued)

Table 7-8 *(continued)*

File System Characteristic	*FAT/VFAT*	*NTFS*
Offers file system recoverability	No	Yes
Supports hot-fixing when disk sectors fail	No	Yes
Supports large partitions	No	Yes
Supports large files	No	Yes
Uses space efficiently on partitions over 400MB	No	Yes
Supports POSIX applications	No	Yes
Supports Macintosh files	No	Yes
Supports file compression on Windows NT	No	Yes
Faster for small directories	Yes	No
Faster for large directories	No	Yes
Supports volume sets to expand existing partitions	No	Yes
Cluster sizes	512 bytes to 16KB	512 bytes to 4KB
Maximum partition size	2GB(DOS)/4GB(NT)	16 exabytes

Securing Your Data

If you're planning to dual-boot your server between Windows NT Server and other operating systems such as DOS or OS/2, and you want these other operating systems to have access to your files, select the FAT file system. Only NT can access files on partition formatted as NTFS. Other operating systems can't.

From a data security viewpoint, selecting NTFS is a better choice than FAT for two reasons. First, NTFS offers you file-by-file security, allowing you to restrict and grant individual users and groups different levels of access to files on the partition. Second, NTFS partitions can't be read directly if you run a different operating system on the computer.

However, don't assume that your data is secure from prying eyes if you use NTFS on your server and impose tight file security. If someone has physical access to your server computer, reboots it under DOS using a bootable floppy disk, has intimate knowledge of NTFS on-disk structures, and uses a low-level disk editing utility, they can read your NTFS files. NTFS doesn't encrypt your data.

It now requires even less knowledge of NTFS to access files from DOS. Students at the University of Oregon have developed a utility called NTFSDOS that can read NTFS files while booted under DOS, Windows 3.x, or Windows 95. They've made this program available on the Internet. So assume that data thieves have it in their toolbox, as you plan your security measures to thwart their efforts.

You can limit your exposure to this type of security breach. First, restrict physical access to your server by locking it in a room that only authorized people can enter. Second, configure the computer to boot only NT from hard disk, rather than presenting a dual-boot menu. In addition, on some computers, you can change the server's CMOS settings to prevent booting from a DOS floppy disk. Finally, you can use a RISC-based computer that can't boot to DOS at all.

Physical security of your server is critical. If a data marauder does get access to your server and can make off with your hard disk, they can attach it to another computer to access the data. To help thwart this plan, use internal hard disks rather than easily transportable external drives.

Converting FAT to NTFS

You can convert from FAT to NTFS either during the NT installation process or after installation using the CONVERT command line utility. You'll need about 100MB of free space on the partition to be converted, because NT needs this to write temporary information during the conversion process. Depending on the size and content of your FAT partition, conversion to NTFS can be a lengthy process. Conversion of a 1GB partition, for example, can take several hours. If and when you decide to convert a FAT partition to an NTFS partition, allow sufficient time to complete the process. Since the partition is inaccessible during the conversion, start the process in the evening and allow it to grind overnight.

Converting from FAT to NTFS is a one-way door. You can't go directly back to FAT. The only way back is to back up your data elsewhere, reformat the partition as FAT, and copy the data back to the partition.

Using Space Efficiently

On small disk partitions (say, less than 200MB), NTFS imposes more on-disk overhead than FAT does. Thus, NTFS burns a larger percentage of your disk space just to handle housekeeping chores. On disk partitions of this size, FAT uses space more efficiently. If your partition is between 200MB and 400MB, the two file systems are about on par in terms of on-disk overhead. As the partition size climbs above 400MB, NTFS becomes increasingly much more efficient since its on-disk overhead doesn't increase as the partition size grows. FAT, on the other hand, gobbles up more space for its own use as the partition size climbs.

NTFS supports compression on a file-by-file basis. Unlike DOS compression schemes that compress an entire disk partition into one huge file, you can select individual files and directories to be compressed automatically by NTFS. NTFS was designed to perform fast decompression of files, at the expense of having files that are slightly larger than those created by other compression schemes. You specify what you want to compress after you've installed Windows NT Server.

Comparing Performance

There are no easy answers to which file system is the faster one. The relative speeds observed are highly dependent on the operations being performed, the size of the directories, how badly fragmented the files are, and so on.

NTFS recoverability and security both add overhead to file access that FAT doesn't require. On the other hand, NTFS lays out its directories in a way that minimizes the number of disk accesses required to find a file. Moreover, NTFS handles small files much more efficiently than FAT.

On FAT, random access to a badly fragmented file typically takes longer than it does on NTFS. Creating new files and listing directories are quicker on FAT. Opening a file on FAT is sometimes faster than NTFS, unless the file is near the end of the directory. Then it's slower than NTFS.

In summary, performance differences between FAT and NTFS vary from one operation to the next and depend on the location of the file, size of the directory, and amount of fragmentation. Overall, the performance of the two file systems is on par, even though NTFS is more robust and secure than FAT.

Accounting for the RISC Factor

The boot partition on RISC-based computers must be formatted as FAT. This partition contains a few hardware-specific NT files. You can install Windows NT Server on this partition (if there's room), or on another one. I highly recommend installing NT on a separate partition, formatted with NTFS. This approach will give you maximum reliability and security of your NT system files.

Handling Unknown File Systems

Windows NT doesn't support DOS file compression, HPFS, or non-FAT file systems created by other operating systems. In addition, NT may not correctly recognize disks if they've never been partitioned or formatted. If you have any of these conditions on your computer, you'll need to do a bit of preparatory work before attempting to install Windows NT Server. In this section, I'll discuss what to do in each of these situations.

Compressed Partitions

Windows NT doesn't recognize or support DoubleSpace, DriveSpace, Stacker, or other disk compression schemes implemented for FAT under DOS. If you have compressed partitions, do the following on each one on your computers before commencing Windows NT installation:

1. Back up the data on the compressed partition.

   You'll need to back up either to tape or to another disk. Keep in mind that the data will occupy up to twice as much space on the backup, since it will be uncompressed.

2. Remove the compressed drive file(s) or reformat the partition as a normal FAT partition.

   If you choose to remove the compressed drive file(s), refer to your disk compression product documentation for details on what files to remove.

3. Restore the data from the backup.

   Again, keep in mind that the data will occupy up to twice as much space as it did on the original compressed partition.

HPFS Partitions

Support for the HPFS file system, originally designed for OS/2, has been phased out over the last few releases of Windows NT. Version 3.1 and 3.5 fully supported HPFS. Version 3.51 of NT supported it only to boot from an existing HPFS partition. Windows NT 4.0 has completely removed HPFS support. If you have one or more HPFS partitions and you want to use them under NT, do the following for each HPFS partition on your computer:

1. Back up the data on the HPFS partition.
2. Boot the computer to DOS and reformat the partition as a normal FAT partition.
3. Restore the data from the backup.

Unrecognized Partitions

If your computer's hard disks have never been formatted or they were formatted under another operating system such as UNIX or VMS, NT Setup may complain that it has detected a possible virus. Although it's possible that there really is a virus, Setup typically means that it found a nonstandard boot sector on one or more of your hard disks. (The boot sector is a common hiding place for viruses, so Setup concludes there might be a virus lurking in there. Since Setup doesn't want to take the chance of installing NT on an infected system, it stops. Disks formatted under DOS, OS/2, or NT won't generate this complaint, unless they actually do have a virus.)

If it's possible that your boot sector has a virus, use a virus scanner to detect it and remove it. You can avoid Setup's virtual virus complaint by doing a little extra work beforehand. If there's any data on the drives that you want to save, back it up. Boot to DOS and partition and format the potentially offending drives to FAT. If you're installing on a RISC platform, you can't boot to DOS. To succeed on a RISC-based computer, you may have to unplug all potentially offending drives except the system drive, install NT Server, and then plug the drives back in once NT is installed.

Making the File System Decision

I highly recommend that you use the NTFS file system on your server. Its excellent security, recoverability, and support of very large files and disks are critically important for your server now and as your system grows.

However, for the reasons I've discussed, you may decide to use FAT for some or all of the partitions on your server computer. If you do, I recommend using NTFS on the partition where you install the NT operating system itself, to protect your system files.

WORKSHEET ENTRY

In Worksheet 7-3 (Windows NT Server Setup) on line 13, circle your file system choice for the partition on which you plan to install the NT operating system.

Planning for Fault Tolerance

Although you don't establish fault-tolerance associations between disk partitions during installation, it's helpful to plan which, if any, of these features you'll be using. NT Setup allows you to review, delete, and create disk partitions in preparation for NT installation.

If you're planning on setting up a disk mirror (RAID 1), you'll need two equal-sized partitions on two different hard disk drives. A stripe set without parity (RAID 0) has the same requirement. If you're going to create a stripe set with parity (RAID 5), you'll need at least three equal-sized partitions on different drives.

If you don't deal with managing disk partitions during the installation process, you'll be able to manipulate them using Disk Administrator, which I'll describe in detail in Chapter 18. See Chapter 19 for details about fault tolerance.

WORKSHEET ENTRY

In Worksheet 7-3 (Windows NT Server Setup) on line 12, record your plans for deleting and creating disk partitions in preparation for NT installation. Also, indicate which partition you want to use for the NT operating system files.

Choosing Your Transport Protocols

Before you install Windows NT Server 4.0, you'll need to select the set of protocols that you want to run on the server. It's best to make an on-purpose decision up front, although you'll certainly be able to change your mind after installation. As with any major decision, you need to be armed with information. Table 7-9 summarizes the three main Windows NT Server protocols in terms of their general characteristics. You'll need to select at least one of them to run on your server. Refer to Chapter 4 for more details on each one.

Table 7-9
Characteristics of the Three Main NT Protocols

Protocol Characteristic	*NetBEUI*	*IPX/SPX*	*TCP/IP*
Best performer on small LANs	Yes	No	No
Best performer for file and print sharing	No	Yes	No
Best performer for application servers	No	No	Yes
Easy client configuration	Yes	Yes	No
Easy network administration	Yes	Yes	No
Breadth of use in the industry	Microsoft and IBM networks only	Most popular of all PC network protocols	Most popular network protocol across all networks
Open protocol specifications	No	No	Yes

(continued)

Table 7-9 *(continued)*

Protocol Characteristic	***NetBEUI***	***IPX/SPX***	***TCP/IP***
Network interoperability	Microsoft and IBM networks only	Available on several platforms	Available on almost all platforms
Ability to send packets across routers	No	Yes	Yes

Why not install all of the protocols for maximum flexibility? In theory, this is a fine idea, and it's supported by Windows NT Server. In practice, however, each transport protocol eats up resources on your server, both in terms of disk space and memory. Using multiple protocols on client computers is even more painful, since disk space and memory are even more limited there. Also, the more protocols you've loaded, the more difficult it is to troubleshoot the network when a problem occurs. So, select and install only the protocols that you need.

For example, if you need Internet access, you want to use NT Server as an application server; if you have several Macintosh clients and one HP JetDirect network printer, you should opt for TCP/IP, AppleTalk, and DLC. In this situation, stay away from NetBEUI and IPX/SPX, and use TCP/IP as the primary protocol between PC nodes on your network. As another example, if you are integrating NT Server into an existing NetWare network, you don't need Internet access; if your network is small, you could get away with IPX/SPX as your only transport protocol.

Table 7-10 shows the protocols that you'll need to install on Windows NT Server to satisfy a variety of network types and requirements. I can't tell you exactly what protocols to install, since networking needs differ. Moreover, your requirements will change over time. What I've done here is provide you with the kinds of criteria to consider when selecting a protocol.

Notice that TCP/IP appears to be the most flexible. However, as mentioned in the TCP/IP discussion in Chapter 4, the cost of that flexibility can mean added complexity for you. Remember that you'll need outside help to get your network addresses assigned. If you don't need Internet access right away and your network is fairly small, consider using IPX/SPX for now. When you need Internet access in the future, you can easily convert to TCP/IP.

Table 7-10
Protocol Selection Criteria

Network Type or Requirement	*NetBEUI (NBF)*	*IPX/SPX (NWLink)*	*TCP/IP*	*DLC*	*AppleTalk (SFM)*
Pure Microsoft [small] network	√				
Wide area network			√		
Large network			√		
Small network	√	√			
Integration with NetWare		√			
Integration with UNIX			√		
Integration with mainframe				√	
Integration with Apple Macintosh clients					√
Connection to the Internet			√		
Connection to network printers such as HP JetDirect				√	

WORKSHEET ENTRY

In Worksheet 7-3 (Windows NT Server Setup) on line 24, circle the protocol or protocols that you plan to install. If you want to install AppleTalk (SFM) or DLC, you'll be able to do so after you install Windows NT Server.

Naming Your NT Server

Each computer in your network needs a unique name, with a maximum of 15 characters. Windows NT Server computers are no exception. Once you assign a name to a server, it's difficult to change it.

Although you can include spaces in computer names, don't do it. First, if you have Windows for Workgroups computers in your network, they'll have trouble accessing servers with spaces in their names. Second, whenever you include the name of the computer in a command line, you'll have to remember to surround the name with quotes because of the spaces. So stay away from spaces.

It's important to give your servers names that won't have to change as your organization changes. Your network users need to be able to access server resources consistently. If you've changed a server name before, you're familiar with the downstream effect that it has on users who must change their batch files and other settings to point to the new server. Don't base server names on the names of people in your organization. As reorganizations occur and people leave, are promoted, or move from one department to another, server names shouldn't have to change. Likewise, you don't want to use a physical location as the computer name, since you may need to move the server to another office, building, or site.

If you've been using your server computer as a peer-to-peer server, and you're planning to install Windows NT Server on it, consider giving the computer the same name it had before. That way, other computers on the network will see this computer and be able to connect to it. They'll have no idea that you changed operating systems out from under their server.

WORKSHEET ENTRY

In Worksheet 7-3 (Windows NT Server Setup) on line 18, write the computer name for the NT Server that you're going to install.

Choosing NT Server's Role

You have two alternatives in designing the overall structure of your Windows NT Server network. You can set up a workgroup (or peer-to-peer) environment, much like what Windows for Workgroups offers, or you can establish one or more network domains. I discussed some of the pros and cons of workgroups and domains in Chapter 4, in the section entitled "Windows NT Server Domains." Table 7-11 summarizes the differences between these two approaches to establishing your network.

When you install Windows NT Server, you'll need to specify whether the computer is to act as a stand-alone server or as a domain controller. Even for small networks, I recommend taking the domain approach with Windows NT Server. Small networks have a way of growing into larger ones, usually more quickly than planned. If you start with a centralized approach to administration, you won't have a mess of user accounts and servers to clean up later. Moreover, you won't have to train yourself and your users twice if you begin with the domain model.

In the following sections, I'll cover the requirements for installing NT Server as a stand-alone (peer-to-peer) server, as a primary domain controller (PDC), and as a backup domain controller (BDC).

Table 7-11
Domains versus Workgroups

Characteristic	*Domain Model*	*Workgroup (Peer-to-Peer) Model*
Good for very small networks		√
Good for larger networks	√	
Easy to establish		√
Requires planning to establish	√	
Centralized user account management	√	
Centralized security management	√	
Single user has one account for the entire network (single network logon)	√	
Single user has separate accounts on each server accessed		√
User accounts scattered across multiple servers		√
Potential for different user passwords on different servers		√

Creating a Stand-Alone Server

If you elect to install Windows NT Server as a stand-alone server, it can participate in a domain or workgroup just like Windows NT Workstation or Windows for Workgroups computers. It will be able to share resources with other nodes on the network. It cannot act as either a PDC or BDC. A stand-alone server is preferable if it's going to be administered separately from the rest of the domain or if you plan to move it to another domain.

Make sure that you really don't want this Windows NT Server computer to be a PDC or BDC in your domain. If you change your mind later, you'll have to reinstall the operating system from scratch. There's no way to upgrade a stand-alone server to a BDC or PDC role.

Establishing a Domain — The PDC

A domain requires one and only one Windows NT Server computer playing the role of primary domain controller (PDC). You create the domain by installing Windows NT Server as a PDC on the network. The first Windows NT server computer in the domain must be the PDC. Once the domain is established, additional NT server computers can be added to the domain, to act as backup domain controllers (BDCs) or as stand-alone servers.

Before installing NT Server on your computer as a PDC, you need to make sure that it contains a working network adapter and is properly attached to the network. (You might not have any other computers on the network at this point, but that's OK.) During installation, the computer will check the network to assure that you aren't trying to duplicate an existing domain. If Setup can't scan the network, PDC installation will fail.

You'll need to select a name for your domain. Once you've established your domain, it's a nightmare to have to change its name. If you're setting up a domain for each department in your organization, you may want to use the department name as the domain name. However, if your department names change frequently, don't use this model. Changing a domain name is extremely painful, so pick a naming convention for your domains that will remain stable over time. See the previous section on "Naming Your NT Server" for more hints on naming strategies.

Creating BDCs in Your Domain

You'll need to plan on having at least one other Windows NT server computer on the network to play the role of BDC, in case your PDC computer becomes unavailable. When you install a BDC, you specify which existing domain it will join. (If you install more than one version of Windows NT Server 4.0 on your network, you'll need licenses to cover each of the copies that you install.)

How many BDCs does your domain need? If you have less than 2,000 users on your network, you can get by with one PDC and just one BDC. However, the more BDCs you add to your domain, the better responsiveness your users will see when they attempt to log on to the domain simultaneously. Extra BDCs spread the load of user authentication and provide an additional level of fault tolerance for your network, should the PDC or some of the BDCs go down. If you have more than 2,000 users or you're considering establishing multiple domains in your enterprise, take a look at Chapter 10 for the scoop on how to plan larger domain-based networks.

Before you install NT Server on your computer as a BDC, you'll need to make sure that several things are in place. First, your computer must be attached to a working network on which your existing PDC resides. Second, the PDC must already be up and running to allow the BDC to contact it during installation. Finally, you'll need to be armed with the domain administrator password in order to add the BDC to the domain.

WORKSHEET ENTRY

In Worksheet 7-3 (Windows NT Server Setup) on line 19, circle the role of this computer: PDC, BDC, or stand-alone server. Line 20 is there to remind you that you'll need the domain administrator password. For security reasons, don't write the password on the worksheet, but be sure to have it available during installation.

On line 27, write the new domain name that you've selected, if you're installing a PDC. If you're installing a BDC, write the name of the domain in which this computer will participate. If you're installing a stand-alone server, write the name of the domain or workgroup in which this computer will participate.

Choosing Your Licensing Option

Microsoft's license agreement for Windows NT Server and other BackOffice products requires a license for each server and each client on the network. For Windows NT Server, there are two licensing options from which to choose — namely, Per Seat licensing and Per Server licensing. Making the right choice requires some knowledge of how client computers will use your NT server computer.

Per Seat Licensing

Per Seat licensing is the easier to understand. You need a license for each server and a license for each client (seat) on the network. If you add a client, you pay only for one additional client license. If you add a server, you pay only for one additional server license. A Per Seat license is tied to the client computer and gives the client the right to access any number of NT server computers. The Per Seat license option is the more cost-effective approach if all of your network clients need to access your NT server at the same time or if your clients tend to connect to multiple NT server computers.

Per Server Licensing

Per Server licensing is a little more complicated. It's designed to save you money in certain situations. In this option, you license the server for the maximum number of clients connecting to your NT Server at the same time. Let's consider an example. Say you have 100 computers on your network, but you know that no more than 50 (any 50) of those computers need to access your NT server at any given time. With Per Seat licensing, you'd have to purchase 100 client licenses. With Per Server licensing, you'd save money by buying only 50 licenses. A Per Server license is tied to the NT Server computer and gives you the right to make a connection from any client on the network. The Per Server licensing option is the more cost-effective approach if only a subset of your client computers connect to your NT server at any given time, clients connect to only one server, or they connect infrequently.

If you're not sure which licensing option is best for you, select the Per Server option. If you decide later that Per Seat licensing is the way to go, you'll get a one-time free opportunity to convert to Per Seat licensing. However, you can't go the other direction for free.

If you have only one NT server on your network, opt for Per Server licensing. You can always change to Per Seat licensing later, if the number of servers in your network grows. If you have multiple NT servers, and the number of Per Server client licenses tied to these servers exceeds the total number of client computers in your network, you've reached the point where Per Seat licensing is cheaper.

WORKSHEET ENTRY

In Worksheet 7-3 (Windows NT Server Setup) on line 17, circle the licensing option you've chosen.

Upgrading to Windows NT Server 4.0

During NT Server installation, you'll have the opportunity to upgrade your existing operating system or install NT in a separate directory. If you choose the latter, you'll typically be able to dual-boot between your old and new operating systems. In this section, I'll fill you in on what to expect from each type of upgrade.

Upgrading from Previous NT Versions

If you decide not to upgrade an existing NT installation, NT Setup will create a new option in the system boot menu, allowing you to dual-boot between the old and new versions of NT.

If you elect to have Windows NT Server 4.0 upgrade an existing version of Windows NT Server on your computer, NT Setup will overwrite the old NT installation. You'll no longer be able to boot to the old version of NT that you upgraded, since system files will have changed. Setup will migrate your NT 3.x Program Manager settings into the NT 4.0 Start Menu and will bring forward just about everything else. It will retain your desktop settings, user account and security information, drive letters, fault-tolerance volume settings, and so forth.

If you decide to have Setup upgrade from Windows NT 3.1 or Windows NT Workstation 3.5x to Windows NT Server 4.0, the computer won't be able to act as either a PDC or BDC for your domain. If you want your Windows NT Server 4.0 computer to play the role of domain controller, you'll need to opt for a fresh installation of NT 4.0.

Upgrading from Windows 3.x and Windows for Workgroups

If you decide not to upgrade over 16-bit Windows, you'll probably have to reinstall your Win16 applications while running NT. Moreover, your desktop, Program Manager, and other settings won't appear in your NT 4.0 installation.

If you decide to install NT in your 16-bit Windows directory tree, NT Server will put most of its files into the SYSTEM32 directory under your Windows root directory. It will also put a few innocuous files (such as bitmap files) into the Windows root directory. Setup will migrate your Program Manager groups to the Start ⇨ Programs menu in NT 4.0. Setup will also migrate application .INI files.

If your Win16 applications are compatible with Windows NT, you'll be able to run them from the Start ⇨ Programs ⇨ . . . menu just as if you had clicked on icons in Program Manager. Some applications require OLE and DDE files that they installed in the Windows System directory. NT Setup might not migrate these files and thus may not find them when you run your Win16 application. To work around this, add the Windows directory to your NT search path. This will allow NT to find the missing files.

The first time that you log on to the newly installed NT, it will ask if you want to migrate your WIN.INI, CONTROL.INI, and Program Manager groups. Your Windows desktop settings will be brought forward.

WINFILE.INI won't get migrated, so if you're a diehard File Manager user, you'll need to tweak your File Manager settings when you use the program for the first time under NT.

Because of their complexity, there are a few other settings that NT Setup won't migrate for you:

- Any persistent net shares and net uses from Windows for Workgroups
- The default domain and user ID from Windows for Workgroups
- Any changes that you've made to the Main, Startup, Games, or Accessories Program Manager groups
- Font information for DOS character-mode command windows

Upgrading from Windows 95

If you're considering installing NT 4.0 as an upgrade over Windows 95, don't do it. At the time of this writing, Microsoft doesn't support installing Windows NT Server 4.0 on top of a Windows 95 installation. NT doesn't detect a Windows 95 installation on your computer, unless you installed Windows 95 in your Windows 3.x directory. Even if NT did detect it, though, NT's ability to migrate Windows 95 settings is extremely limited, because of a lack of standards in how Windows 95 applications install themselves. Microsoft is working with software developers to nail this down. But for now, I advise against installing NT 4.0 as an upgrade over a Windows 95 installation.

If you have Windows 95 on your computer, install a fresh copy of NT Server 4.0 in a separate directory, rather than attempting to upgrade. That way, you'll be able to dual-boot between Windows 95 and Windows NT Server 4.0. Note that you'll have to install your applications separately for each operating system — once while running Windows 95 and once while running NT. None of your Windows 95 application information will be brought forward into your Windows NT installation.

Although the bad news is that you'll have to reinstall all applications that you want to run under both Windows 95 and Windows NT, the good news is that you can probably install an application in the same directory both times. As long as the application's configuration information is limited to the registry and to .INI files that don't reside in the application's installation directory, you can install in the same place each time. However, if the application keeps configuration data in its installation directory, the second installation will overwrite the settings created by the first installation. Determine where your application's configuration files are kept, or consult your software manufacturer.

Upgrading from NetWare

Novell employees might argue that converting a NetWare server to a Windows NT server isn't an upgrade, but that's what a number of corporations are doing today. To make this process as smooth as possible, Microsoft provides a conversion utility that migrates NetWare account information to the Windows NT Server account database. The NWCONV utility supports upgrading from either NetWare 2.x or NetWare 3.x. It doesn't support conversion of NetWare 4.x servers to NT.

Upgrading from a NetWare server is a bit different from the other upgrades discussed so far. You'll need to have Windows NT Server installed on a computer that's different from your NetWare server. You'll then perform the migration over the network, between the two servers. Because there's no direct way to translate some of the account information from the NetWare world to the NT world, you should count on some manual efforts to complete the conversion. I'll cover the entire process in detail in Chapter 12.

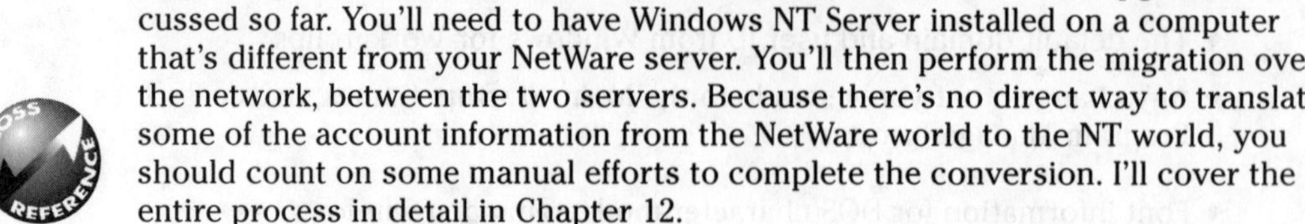

WORKSHEET ENTRY

In Worksheet 7-3 (Windows NT Server Setup) on line 5, circle YES if you're going to upgrade an older version of Windows NT. Otherwise, circle NO (because you want to dual-boot between the old and new versions). On line 11, circle YES if you're going to upgrade from a previous version of Windows. Circle NO if you aren't.

If you answered NO to both upgrade options, select a destination directory name where the NT system files should be installed. It must be an 8.3 file name, even if you're installing to NTFS. Write this name on line 14.

The Windows NT Server Setup Worksheet

If you've been making written entries at the points that I've suggested throughout this chapter, you're already quite familiar with the worksheet presented in this section. If you haven't, be sure to fill it out now. With the completed worksheet at your side during Windows NT Server installation, the process will go more smoothly for you — and you won't have to repeat it in order to correct bad decisions.

Worksheet 7-3
Windows NT Server Setup

Decision #		***Your Decision***
1	Circle your CD-ROM drive type.	**SCSI, IDE/EIDE,** or **OTHER**
2	If your CD-ROM drives are SCSI, which one has the lowest SCSI ID number (make/model)?	
3	List your SCSI adapters, non-SCSI CD-ROMs, and disk arrays.	
4	Do you have storage devices not compatible with NT (that require an NT driver disk)?	**YES** or **NO.** If YES, have the driver disk available.
5	Are you upgrading from an older version of Windows NT Server?	**YES** or **NO**
6	Enter your computer type (make, model, bus type).	
7	Display type (for Setup only).	**Auto Detect**
8	Enter your keyboard make and model.	
9	Enter your keyboard layout.	
10	Enter your pointing device (mouse) make and model.	

(continued)

Worksheet 7-3 *(continued)*

Decision #		***Your Decision***
11	Are you upgrading from Windows 3.x, Windows for Workgroups, or Windows 95?	**YES** or **NO**
12	List your plans to create/delete disk partitions. On which partition will you install NT system files?	
13	Which file system do you want on the partition where the NT operating system files reside?	**FAT** or **NTFS**
14	Under what directory name do you want the NT system files installed?	
15	Enter your name.	
16	Enter your organization name (optional).	
17	Circle the licensing option that you want to use.	**Per Server** or **Per Seat**
18	Enter the computer name for this server.	
19	Circle the role of this server on the network.	**PDC, BDC, Stand-Alone Server**
20	Have your domain administrator password available.	For security reasons, don't write the password here.
21	Choose to install optional components, unless you already have a non-Microsoft e-mail client.	**YES** or **NO**
22	Choose to install the Microsoft Exchange Client if you have or plan to install Exchange Server.	**YES** or **NO**
23	List your network adapters. See Chapter 8 for details.	
24	Circle the network protocols that you want to install on this server. See Chapter 11 for details on installing TCP/IP.	**NetBEUI, IPX/SPX, TCP/IP**
25	Do you want to install RAS? See Chapter 11 for details.	**YES** or **NO**
26	Enter your network adapter configuration information. See Chapter 8 for details.	
27	Enter the domain name.	
28	Enter your time zone.	
29	Enter your video adapter make and model.	
30	Enter your video adapter chip set information.	
31	Enter the number of screen colors.	
32	Enter your desired video resolution.	

Summary

In this chapter, I've given you advice about how to design your Windows NT server computer. In addition, you've made nearly all the decisions required prior to installation of the operating system. You've completed the Windows NT Server Setup Worksheet, which will help you successfully install NT. In Chapter 8, you'll learn the nuts and bolts of designing and installing your network hardware, including configuration of your network adapters. Then in Chapter 9, I'll walk you through the actual NT installation process.

Designing and Planning Your NT Network Hardware

✦ ✦ ✦ ✦

Chapter 3 gave you an overview of network hardware and software — the various nuts and bolts that interconnect computers. This chapter tells you how to plunge your hands into that pile of bolts and put them together into a state-of-the-art LAN based on Windows NT Server 4.0.

If you're going to use Windows NT Server as the basis of a new network, one of your first decisions will be what network hardware technology to employ. If you've already installed your network hardware or if someone else in your company is slated to do it, you can skip ahead to the section on setting up your network adapter and configuring Windows NT Server to work with it. You'll need to understand your network adapter configuration before you can proceed with NT installation in Chapter 9.

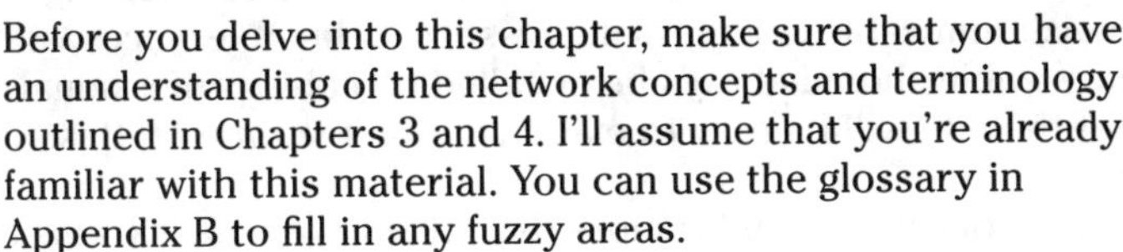

Before you delve into this chapter, make sure that you have an understanding of the network concepts and terminology outlined in Chapters 3 and 4. I'll assume that you're already familiar with this material. You can use the glossary in Appendix B to fill in any fuzzy areas.

INSIDE STORY

A manager in NT's network development team risked companywide humiliation when he agreed to a formidable wager. If the team didn't meet their midsummer deadline of getting NT network software in shape, he would have to swim across Lake Bill (the pond in the center of Microsoft's campus). And he'd have to wear a women's bikini to do it!

The team rallied around the cause, working extra hard to assure that their boss wouldn't have to drown in ignominy. The team ran into many tough problems. It seemed that fate was pushing the boss into the water. One nasty networking bug took over a month to chase, and it turned out to be caused by hardware. A SCSI adapter in the computer was interfering with the operation of the network adapter. Both manufacturers claimed, "It should work." The team was breaking its back to make progress and meet their goal, but there were just too many issues to solve.

Rather than don the bikini and wade in on the deadline, the boss renegotiated the terms of the agreement. The team would get another month to find and fix the trouble. If they failed to meet this new deadline, several of the engineers would have to join the boss in the infamous swim. In the end, after many long nights of debugging, dozens of phone calls, and even a few personal visits from the hardware manufacturers, the team discovered and solved the hardware problem. They met their revised goal, and the boss and his team canceled their embarrassing plans to go shopping for queen-sized bikinis.

Planning the Work

There are several considerations to mull over when deciding how much of your network you're going to install. Small networks are fairly easy to install, though putting cable through walls is hard to do. Stringing cables between offices through ceiling tiles is a risky business, and you need to comply with local fire codes. Making your own cables requires expensive tools, skill, patience, and luck. I recommend purchasing ready-made cable or having a professional create custom cable for you.

If you're going to do it yourself, make sure to know all of the rules: building wiring codes, fire codes, maximum cable lengths, safety issues, cable tolerances, and so on. High-performance cable should always be installed by cable professionals. Make sure that what they do will be easy to maintain. Don't scrimp on this.

If you're planning a network that includes more than 40 computers, it's wise to divide it into several segments connected by bridges or routers, discussed later in this chapter. Although you can learn the principles from books on enterprise networking, it's often best to have your large network designed by a professional who's made his or her mistakes on earlier clients.

If you do have a network cable professional do the job, watch, listen, learn, ask lots of questions, and take notes. In the future, you may have to crawl around and fix something quickly to support your company's payroll check run. You'll certainly also need to be able to handle small modifications to your network design, as well as deal intelligently with contractors to do major operations.

Regardless of who does the work, make sure to document all of the details of your network configuration in your network notebook, which is discussed in Chapter 5.

Network Technologies

In the past few years, two network technologies — Ethernet and Token Ring — have emerged as the most popular. Older systems such as ARCnet and StarLAN have lost favor due to their limited data-carrying capacity. Of course, new technologies are always emerging, with some looking more promising than others as we move into the next century of enterprise computing.

In reality, Ethernet and Token Ring have a lot in common. Both are widely supported by hardware and software vendors and have been set up as international standards by the 802 committee of the IEEE (Institute of Electrical and Electronic Engineers). Both share the bandwidth of the network cabling by allowing only one node to transmit at a time. Either technology can be used to build a versatile and reliable network based on Windows NT Server.

New multimedia applications such as video conferencing have begun to push Ethernet's 10Mbps capacity and Token Ring's 16Mbps capacity past their limits. In such cases, it's often the network cable component that restricts the speed of data throughput. Several new network technologies, including FDDI and Fast Ethernet schemes increase performance to 100Mbps. Ethernet switching technology and ATM give each pair of communicating nodes its own end-to-end connection to eliminate the data-flow restrictions caused by sharing the cable. Wireless network adapters (utilizing either radio or infrared communications links) have been entering the market. They can be useful for low-traffic situations where cabling is either impossible or impractical.

When you're choosing a LAN technology, as in any other endeavor, you need to balance cost, reliability, and performance. LAN technologies differ on the type of cable they use, how fast they run, how easily they allow you to troubleshoot the network, and how well they connect to larger computers.

In discussions of network hardware technologies, the access method is often a matter of heated debate. Actually, this is one of the least important technological differences, at least in comparing today's mainstream approaches. Most systems limit use of the network to one computer at a time. ATM is the exception to this rule.

In the following sections, I'll introduce the network cabling alternatives available to you and then discuss and compare the major network technologies from which you can choose. Once you've gone this far, I'll discuss selecting and configuring your network adapter hardware.

Network Media Types

No, this section isn't about television executives. Over the past 10 years, manufacturers have developed networks that can transmit data on just about any type of wiring, but generally they utilize one of five types of network media:

- ✦ Coaxial cable (coax)
- ✦ Shielded twisted-pair cable (STP)
- ✦ Unshielded twisted-pair cable (UTP)
- ✦ Fiber-optic cable (fiber)
- ✦ Wireless transmission

I'll present and compare each of these types of network media in the next sections.

Coaxial Cable

Before 1990, nearly all LANs used coaxial cable, or coax, that is similar to television cable. Coax consists of two conductors centered on a common axis (hence, the name *coaxial*). The center conductor is a thick copper wire. An insulation layer separates the two conductors and keeps the copper wire centered for peak performance. The outer shield conductor, typically made of foil or copper braid, prevents EMI from leaking into or radiating from the cable. The outer jacket is typically plastic or Teflon. Figure 8-1 illustrates the coax structure.

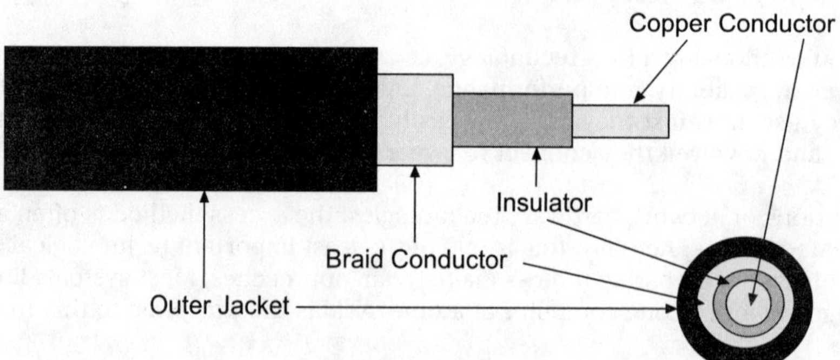

Figure 8-1: Coaxial cable (coax) uses two conductors to transmit data electrically.

There are several flavors of coax. One of the most common types in very small networks is called thin Ethernet, or thinnet. Many network starter kit products use this type of thin, black cable, sometimes referred to as RG-58. Thicker cables (known as thick Ethernet, thicknet, or "frozen yellow garden hose") are generally very expensive and inflexible but allow longer cable lengths and better performance. The industry trend has steadily been toward thinner coax.

Two kinds of coax are available for different types of office installations. *PVC coax* is flexible and can be routed in exposed office areas. PVC refers to the material (poly-vinyl chloride) used to construct the cable's insulation. *Plenum coax* can be routed above false ceilings (called the plenum area), because it uses insulation that is fire-resistant and produces less poisonous fumes if it does burn. Plenum cable is less flexible and more expensive than PVC.

Coax has been around for more than twenty years, so it's well-understood, reliable, and readily available. Installation is simple and cost-effective. The cable itself is inexpensive in its thinner forms, but thick versions can be quite expensive. Since it's used to implement a bus topology, any cable break along the way can bring down the network. If mice (the rodents, not the pointing devices) get hungry enough, they'll chew through coax cable. Although coax is highly resistant to EMI, it's not invulnerable, so avoid it in electrically noisy environments. Few modern network adapters support coaxial cable exclusively, and increasing numbers of adapters that don't support it at all are appearing on the market. Avoid coax-only support when selecting your network adapter.

Shielded Twisted-Pair Cable

Historically, the next type of cabling used after coax for network transmission was shielded twisted-pair, or STP. (No, this isn't a brand of motor oil.) STP cable contains a pair of insulated copper wires that are twisted around each other. The twists cause the wires to alternate positions, which has the effect of reducing absorption or radiation of EMI. In general, the more twists per unit of length (for example, 10 twists per foot), the better the cable's data transmission capabilities. A conducting shield, similar to that in coax cable, surrounds the twisted wires to further inhibit incoming or outgoing EMI. Most STP cables actually contain multiple twisted-pairs. In some cables, a common shield surrounds all pairs. In others, each pair has its own shield, to prevent interference between adjacent pairs. The outer jacket is typically made of plastic. Figure 8-2 illustrates the STP cable structure.

IBM Type 1 cable, used in Token Ring networks, is the only shielded twisted-pair cable in common use today. This flavor of STP contains two twisted-pairs surrounded by a common shield. A few versions of Ethernet adapters out there can use STP.

STP cable's size, cost, and bandwidth, as well as its installation costs are about on par with thin coax cable. EMI resistance and durability of STP are also close to that of coax. Because of its EMI resistance, STP is a good choice for Token Ring installations in electrically noisy environments such as factories and warehouses.

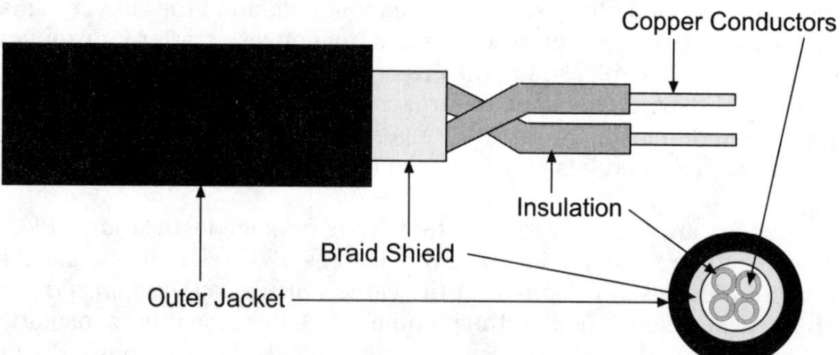

Figure 8-2: STP cable surrounds pairs of twisted wires with an outer shield conductor.

Like coax, STP has grown steadily less popular over time, especially since IBM endorsed the use of unshielded twisted-pair (UTP) cable for Token Ring installations. STP is more expensive and difficult to install than UTP cable, discussed next.

Unshielded Twisted-Pair Cable

Unshielded twisted-pair cable, or UTP, is very similar to the cable used by telephone companies, although of much higher quality. Like STP, UTP uses a pair of insulated wires twisted around each other to reduce incoming and outgoing EMI. Unlike STP, there's no shield conductor surrounding the wire pair. Lack of the shield reduces both the cost and physical bulk of the UTP cable but increases its susceptibility to EMI and its potential to radiate electrical noise. The bulk of the cable is reduced even further because UTP uses thinner wires than either coax or STP cables. Like STP, multiple pairs are often bundled together in a single cable. There are several types of connectors, but the most common is the RJ-45 connector, which looks similar to the modular plugs used in modern telephone connections. Figure 8-3 shows the UTP cable structure.

Although coax is used to wire physical bus topologies, UTP is typically used to wire physical star topologies. Thus, use of UTP requires wiring computers to hubs, as discussed in Chapter 3.

UTP cable varies greatly in quality and, therefore, in how well it can carry high-speed data. To avoid network nightmares, choose a more expensive, high-quality brand in the first place, and stay away from the temptation to mix your good cable with segments of unknown quality. In general, the rule is to never mix cable of different types or quality — even a single inferior segment can cause signal noise and data corruption.

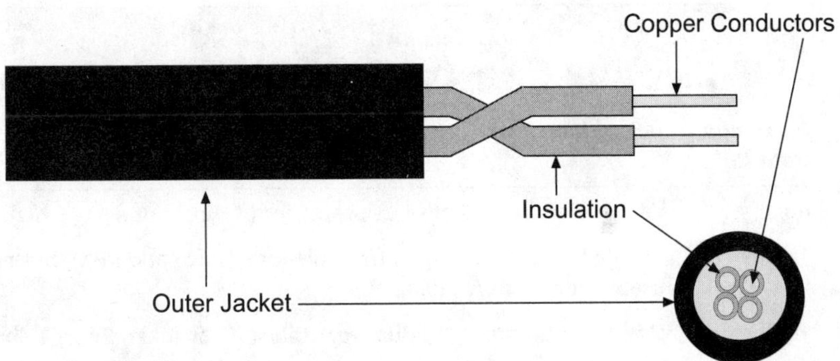

Figure 8-3: UTP cable consists of pairs of twisted wires with no outer shielding conductor.

Don't even think about using flat (untwisted) telephone cable, commonly know as "silver satin," to connect a computer network. Using just one six-foot length of this type of cable can prevent network data from passing through your entire network.

UTP is the least expensive of all types of cable, is relatively easy to install, is very flexible, and takes up very little space. Installation can be quite inexpensive, since many buildings in recent years have been prewired with high-quality UTP in anticipation of computer network and digital telephony needs. Because it's used to implement a star physical topology, a break in one cable won't bring down the net work, in contrast to coax. On the down side, UTP is more easily damaged and is more susceptible to EMI than any other cable type. Moreover, it requires the additional cost of hubs to connect nodes to the network, as explained in Chapter 3.

To help you determine if a certain type of UTP cable can effectively carry your network data, the EIA/TIA (Electronics Industries Association/Telecommunications Industry Association) has promulgated a UTP grading system. It categorizes UTP cable into five levels (sometimes called grades or categories).

Levels 1 and 2 should be used only for telephone voice and PBX applications, respectively. Most commercial telephone systems installed before 1990 use these lower-quality cables. Levels 3 and 4 can be used for either Token Ring or Ethernet LANs. Since 16Mbps Token Ring pushes the envelope of level 3 performance, you should use at least level 4 cable for 16Mbps Token Ring. Level 5 is the best grade of UTP cable. It can be used for Ethernet and 16Mbps Token Ring, as well as for the new Fast Ethernet running at a maximum rate of 100Mbps. Table 8-1 summarizes the maximum data rates of each of the UTP levels.

If you're installing a new network in your enterprise, opt for nothing less than level 5 UTP and install cable that contains extra pairs of wires. If you do, you'll pave the way for easily upgrading later to the full-duplex switching network technologies that are appearing on the horizon.

Table 8-1
UTP Cable Quality Levels

UTP Level	*Maximum Data Rate*	*Description*
1	none	Voice grade cable that's not usable for LAN data at all.
2	1Mbps	Usable for very low-speed transmissions (voice and PBX), but not usable at all for LAN data.
3	16Mbps	Usable for Ethernet (10Mbps, or 10Base-T) or Token Ring (4Mbps) LAN data.
4	20Mbps	Usable for Ethernet (10Mpbs, or 10Base-T) or Token Ring (4Mbps or 16Mbps).
5	100Mps	Usable for Ethernet or Token Ring, as well as Fast Ethernet at up to 100Mbps.

Because your network cable infrastructure should be designed to last ten years or more, you'll be much better off choosing level 5 UTP for any new network installation. The modest additional cost for the higher-quality cable will save you considerable time and labor later when you can confidently upgrade your network without installing new cable. Installing anything less than level 5 UTP today is a poor investment in the long run.

Some people think that level 5 UTP cable can't be used for 10Mbps Ethernet (called 10Base-T), which requires level 3 UTP. Actually, level 3 is only the minimum grade required — level 5 exceeds that minimum and works superbly with 10Base-T Ethernet systems. Keep in mind that level 5 can do anything levels 3 and 4 can do, and more.

Fiber-Optic Cable

Fiber-optic cable, or fiber, is the new kid on the network cable block, offering the best performance at the highest cost. It consists of a glass or plastic fiber core that transmits data using pulses of light. This nonelectrical approach makes fiber completely immune to EMI and corrosion. Surrounding the core, a glass coating (called *cladding*), is specifically designed to reflect signals back into the core to minimize signal loss. The outer jacket, typically made of Kevlar, can house one or more fibers. By bundling multiple fibers, you can fit many of them through the same space as a single copper cable. Many of today's fiber-optic cables contain two fibers, one for transmitting and one for receiving. Fiber cable technology uses a laser diode as its light source, which accounts for the bulk of the cost of this network media. Figure 8-4 shows the fiber cable structure.

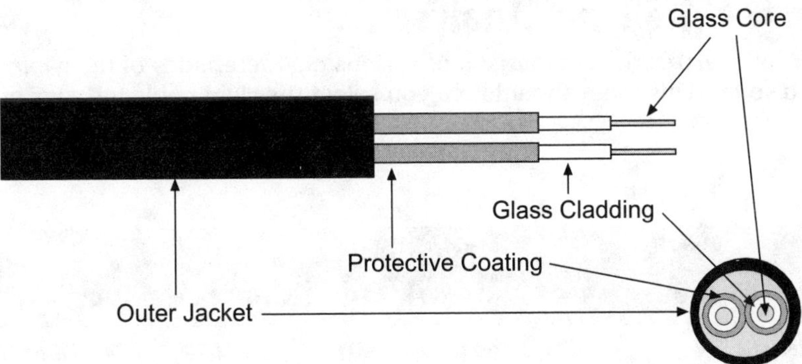

Figure 8-4: Fiber-optic cable uses light pulses to transmit data through a glass or plastic core.

Glass fiber cables can span miles without the need for repeaters, whereas plastic fiber is typically limited to the length of a football field. Data rates can potentially exceed one terabit per second, about 10,000 times faster than UTP cable. Installing fiber used to be very costly but can now be reasonably accomplished with the investment of a few hundred dollars in tools and a little training. The reduction in installation cost is primarily due to the recent development of simpler connectors. The cost of the cable itself is really no more expensive than thick coax. However, the real sticker shock hits for the transmission devices on each end. It can cost up to $1,000 to connect a node to a fiber network, although prices have been inching lower over time.

Because of fiber's high cost, organizations tend to use a mixture of fiber and copper cabling. For example, at Microsoft, we used a fiber-optic cable backbone to connect the several buildings on the Microsoft corporate campus. Within each building, we used less expensive, level 5, UTP copper cabling.

There are several advantages to using fiber in portions of a network. If you have or expect to have high traffic in a segment of your network, fiber can be a good investment that you won't outgrow for quite some time. Since fiber is completely immune to EMI from the environment, it's ideal for electrically noisy environments. Conversely, fiber radiates no electrical noise, so it's completely immune to electronic eavesdropping. Finally, fiber makes for good network connections between buildings. Since it isn't electrical, it doesn't attract lightning or cause data-corrupting ground loops, two problems often seen with copper cabling between buildings.

Cabling – The Final Analysis

Table 8-2 summarizes the comparison of various characteristics of the cable types discussed so far. This table should help you select the right cable for your organization.

Table 8-2
Comparison of Network Cable Characteristics

Characteristic	*Coax*	*STP*	*UTP*	*Fiber*
Data transmission bandwidth	High	Medium	Low to Medium	Highest
Sensitivity to EMI	Low	Low	High	None
Cable cost	Medium to High	Medium	Low	High
Installation cost	Medium	Medium	Low to Medium	Medium to High
Maintenance difficulty	Medium	Low	Low	High
Flexibility	Low to Medium	Medium	High	Low (no sharp turns)
Distance limitations	Medium to Long	Medium	Short	Very Long
Impact of damaged cable	High	Low	Low	Depends on topology
Security issues (eavesdropping)	Yes	Yes	Yes	No
Cost of support electronics	Low	Medium	Medium	High
Adapter choices	Broad but shrinking	Limited	Broad	Limited
Physical cable bulk	Medium to Thick	Medium	Thin	Very Thin
Attenuation of signal	Medium	Medium	High	Low
Functionality for network backbones	Thicknet only	No	No	Ideal
Component standardization	High	Medium	High	Low

The Wireless Alternative

Wireless technology currently comes in two flavors — namely, optical and radio frequency. Optical networks, which use the same type of infrared signals found in your television remote control, can be implemented as node-to-node transmissions or broadcast transmissions that fill a room. The former requires that the communicating computers be within sight of each other and that the placement of transmitters and receivers avoids interruption by people walking by. Broadcast transmissions typically go to one or more centralized hub-like devices and are rebroadcast to other nodes in the same room. This approach reduces the need for an unbroken line of sight between nodes but also reduces reliability, since signals are weaker and more susceptible to changes in ambient lighting. Optical networks can be used outside to cross streets between buildings and so on. However, since you need to maintain a clean line of sight between transmitter and receiver, performance and reliability suffer from such simple things as fog, rain, hail, and pigeons.

The radio frequency approach to wireless networks has the advantages of being able to penetrate walls and not requiring nodes to be within sight of each other. Two major network technologies are available in this realm. The first is called *spread spectrum,* which was developed by the U.S. military for transmitting secure information. This approach uses unlicensed radio frequencies (including those used in alarm systems, garage door openers, and radio-controlled model trains, planes, and automobiles). It spreads the signals across a spectrum of frequencies, picking whichever ones have the least interference and sometimes transmitting different parts of a message over different frequencies to add more security.

The second approach to radio frequency networks is based on cellular phone technology. This method uses a licensed radio frequency of 18GHz and is offered primarily by Motorola, who holds the frequency licenses in most major cities. Nodes in this type of network are organized into groups, called cells, covering a limited area. Typically, several network nodes are wired to a special user module via cables. The user modules communicate by radio frequency to a hub that's within the same room. Several hubs are often connected to each other via cables.

This approach sort of takes the "wireless" out of wireless networks. It's wireless only between the user modules (to which the nodes are wired) and the hubs (which are wired together). Since 18GHz can't penetrate walls, you're faced with wires between rooms (that is, between hubs) with this technology as well.

If you have special node mobility requirements, wireless can be a viable solution. A good example of a wireless network is the Avis rental car return area at many airports. Their system allows you to check in your returned car right there in the parking lot. Employees walk around with hand-held PCs that communicate over a wireless network. Imagine if they each needed a cable strung back to the office.

WHY WIRELESS?

Wireless is a very flexible solution for small physical areas with limited amounts of data communication. Because of the high cost and relatively low speeds associated with this technology, you should consider a wireless network only if there's some concrete reason why cabling is impractical or impossible. (In some environments, concrete *is* the reason that you can't string cables.) Otherwise, stick with cabling for now.

If you need to pick a wireless approach, I currently recommend using the spread spectrum technology. There's reasonable hardware and software support for this approach right now, you don't have to worry about line-of-sight issues (as you do with optical), it transmits through walls (unlike optical and 18GHz), and it actually is a wireless network (unlike the 18GHz approach).

Wireless technologies continue to improve in speed, reliability, and cost effectiveness. Although new standards are emerging in the wireless marketplace, some vendors are implementing higher-speed technologies at the expense of deviating from the new standards. Keep a lookout for breakthroughs in price and performance in this area.

In some buildings, you may be prohibited from installing cabling because of the age, historical, or religious significance of the structure. The need to pass your LAN across a public street may also bring wireless into the picture as a cost-effective alternative to leasing an expensive line from a telephone provider. Another factor to consider in deciding whether or not to go wireless is the real cost of moving computers in your organization. Wireless technology vendors tend to quote high costs for this activity, but you need to develop your own unbiased estimates for this cost.

Implementing Network Technologies

In this section, I'll discuss the most prevalent cabling options available for implementing specific network technologies. Here, you'll learn the details of setting up Ethernet, Token Ring, Fast Ethernet, FDDI, and ATM networks.

Ethernet Cabling

In Chapter 3, I introduced you to the Ethernet network technology. The IEEE 802.3 standard describes most modern Ethernet implementations. Ethernet II, developed by DEC, Intel, and Xerox (sometimes referred to as DIX), is older and differs from the 802.3 standard. Ethernet II is still in common use today in TCP/IP and DECnet environments. I won't differentiate between Ethernet and Ethernet II in this book, as the differences are minor. Regardless of the media or implementation, Ethernet's maximum bandwidth is 10Mbps. It's less than this with certain types of network media.

Of all the network technologies discussed in this chapter, Ethernet is the least expensive and most prevalent today. Many manufacturers build Ethernet ports into their computers, network adapters are available at commodity prices, and experienced technicians who understand Ethernet cabling and installation are easily available.

Thick Ethernet

Thick Ethernet is also known as thicknet, 10Base5, and my favorite — chunkynet. Thicknet was the original Ethernet cabling approach, consisting of half-inch diameter coaxial cable. To connect to the network bus, you need a transceiver (transmitter-receiver) tapped into the cable. The most common type of transceiver in the 10Base5 world is something out of a Brahm Stoker novel, called a *vampire tap.* It clamps onto the cable, sinking metal fangs through the insulation to make contact with the conductors inside. Less popular types of access units exist, but they're equally violent and less convenient — they require chopping the cable, forcing a special (N-series) connector onto the two ends, and connecting those ends to a special T-connector on the access unit. An AUI (attachment unit interface) or DIX (Digital-Intel-Xerox) connector is used to attach the node to the transceiver.

Thicknet is the most expensive and least convenient of the Ethernet cabling methods, but it does have a place in environments that require long segment lengths (for example, network backbone segments).

Thin Ethernet

Thin Ethernet, also known as thinnet, cheapernet, and 10Base2, was developed to reduce the cost of cabling and eliminate the need for separate transceivers. The transceiver function was moved to the network adapter. To connect to the network bus, you simply use a T-connector to tap into the main network cable. If you use preconfigured cable with preinstalled connectors, no cable cutting or vampire bites are required.

Always connect the T-connector directly to the node's network adapter. Although it may sometimes seem convenient to drop a short cable between the T-connector and the computer node, don't do it. This procedure may provide convenient network access to the node that you're cabling, but it can affect the main network cable enough to prevent other nodes from talking on the network.

Thinnet is much less expensive than thicknet, both in terms of cabling cost and support electronics. Its maximum segment lengths and the limit on the number of devices per segment is smaller. Since each node connection depends on three BNC connectors at the network adapter, any break in these connections can result in bringing the entire network segment down. Moreover, adding a node to a segment requires bringing down that segment during the connection process.

VIOLENCE ON THE NETWORK

There's some disagreement in the industry over what the BNC acronym really means. Scientist types say is stands for **biconic** (no, not bionic), based on its shape. Others say it stands for **b**ayo**n**et **c**onnector, based on the bayonet-like twisting action required to make the connection. The latter evokes a pretty gruesome image. Still other folks say BNC stands for **b**ayonet **n**ut **c**onnector. My advice? Never connect a nut with a sharp instrument like a bayonet. You never know what it might do.

Thinnet remains the low-cost leader, even against the more popular UTP alternative, since 10Base2 doesn't require a hub. If per-node cost control is crucial and ease of reconfiguring isn't important, I recommend 10Base2 only in very small networks (three to five nodes, at most) that coexist in one or two rooms. If you plan to grow the network beyond this (and most networks do grow), invest up front in UTP, discussed in the next section. Table 8-3 provides some details of 10Base2 characteristics and compares thinnet with other common Ethernet cabling alternatives.

Twisted-Pair Ethernet

Unlike 10Base2 or 10Base5, twisted-pair Ethernet, or 10Base-T, uses a physical star topology to connect nodes to hubs using level 3 UTP (or higher UTP grade) cable. Ethernet 10Base-T cables contain two twisted-pairs, one for transmitting and one for receiving. This allows the network to remain as a logical bus topology, just like 10Base2 and 10Base5. The cables often contain four pairs of wires, to allow for broken wires and future network expansion.

Hubs that handle between 4 and 128 nodes are available. They range in price and functionality from passive hubs to remotely manageable active hubs. As discussed earlier, the UTP hub approach is an extremely flexible alternative. You can add or remove nodes from the network without having to bring the network down. Reconfiguration and management of the physical star topology is infinitely simpler than the coax alternatives. Although 10Base-T cable is less expensive than coax, the cost of hubs can add from $20 to over $100 per node to the overall network cost. So, cost can't be the primary factor in selecting 10Base-T. If your network will grow and will need to be reconfigured and managed, opt for 10Base-T.

WHO'S ON BASE?

Where did the 10Base terms come from? These military-developed terms encode information about the cable medium. For example, 10Base5 refers to cable that uses baseband transmission to send data at 10Mbps with a maximum cable segment length of 500 meters. Can you guess what 10Base2 is? Did you say it's the same as 10Base5, except the maximum segment length is 200 meters? Well, you're close. The segment limit is 185 meters, but the standards folks rounded up. (10Base1.85 would have been too confusing, I suspect.) Of course, 10Base-T doesn't tell you anything about the maximum segment length. So much for encoded information in these names.

Table 8-3
Comparison of Common Ethernet Cabling Options

Characteristic	***10Base5***	***10Base2***	***10Base-T***
Cable type	Thick Coax	Thin Coax	Level 3 UTP or higher
Cable diameter	0.5 in.	0.2 in.	0.2 in.
Minimum cable bend radius (flexibility)	10 in.	1 in.	0.5 in.
Nicknames	Thick Ethernet, thicknet	Thin Ethernet, thinnet, cheapernet	Twisted-Pair Ethernet, UTP
Relative cable cost	High	Medium	Low
Maximum cable length from transceiver to node	164 ft (50 m)	N/A	N/A
Maximum cable length from hub to node	N/A	N/A	330 ft (100 m)
Maximum segment length	1640 ft (500 m)	600 ft (185 m)	N/A
Maximum number of transceivers on a segment	100	30	N/A
Termination	Each end of segment	Each end of segment	N/A
Maximum number of repeaters between most distant nodes	4	2	N/A

(continued)

Table 8-3 (continued)

Characteristic	***10Base5***	***10Base2***	***10Base-T***
Maximum network length	8200 ft (2500 m)	1800 ft (555 m)	N/A
Relative cost of support electronics	High	Medium	High
Optimal distance between node connections on the bus cable	Multiples of 8.2 ft (2.5 m)	Multiples of 1.64 ft (0.5 m)	N/A
Relative ease of reconfiguring	Low	Medium	High
Connector type	AUI or DIX	BNC	RJ-45

Token Ring

Back in Chapter 3, you were introduced to the Token Ring network technology. Originally developed by IBM, Token Ring is now defined by the IEEE 802.5 standard. Unlike 802.3, the 802.5 standard doesn't address cabling specifications. Thus, many in the industry have adopted IBM's cabling designs. Shielded or unshielded twisted-pair cabling is typically used, although some fiber and coax varieties exist. Token Ring's logical topology, a ring, is always implemented as a physical star topology. As explained in Chapter 3, nodes are connected to MAUs, and MAUs are connected to form an unbroken logical ring. The special connectors used to hook nodes to MAUs cause the ring to heal when the connector is removed, thus allowing the insertion and removal of nodes without disturbing the ring.

In general, you can hook up to 260 nodes and 33 MAUs to a single Token Ring. You can use repeaters to extend the physical size of a ring, although those repeaters also count as nodes. Token Ring capacity planning is a pretty involved process. IBM devotes a significant portion of their planning guides to calculating ring capacities and dimensions. Two speeds are available — 4Mbps and 16Mbps. Most MAUs and many network adapters today support both rates, so there's really no cost advantage to choosing the 4Mbps technology. Both are considered mature technologies.

Don't try to run a mixture of 4Mbps and 16Mbps nodes on the same Token Ring network. The network won't operate. Always choose and use a single speed for the entire ring. Mismatched speeds are the most common configuration problem on NT Token Ring networks today, especially with the availability of network adapters that can be configured through software to run at either rate.

Token Ring hasn't gained as much acceptance as Ethernet because it costs significantly more per node to implement, is still considered proprietary IBM technology by many, and is more complex, requiring more technical knowledge to maintain.

However, if you're tying your network to IBM mainframe equipment, or you need a very deterministic approach to providing network access to all of your nodes, Token Ring is well worth considering.

FDDI

Originally designed for WANs, FDDI is now used in many LANs that demand high speed. FDDI, which has a 100Mbps bandwidth, was initially intended for fiber-optic cable, but some copper wire implementations have appeared as well. FDDI functions very much like Token Ring. It uses a logical ring topology and token passing for access control.

FDDI is often configured to use two rings, each shooting data in opposite directions. Nodes attached to one of the rings are called *single-attached;* nodes attached to both are *dual-attached.* The dual rings can have a diameter up to 100 kilometers and are able to heal themselves in certain situations where a link fails in one of the rings. This is illustrated in Figure 8-5.

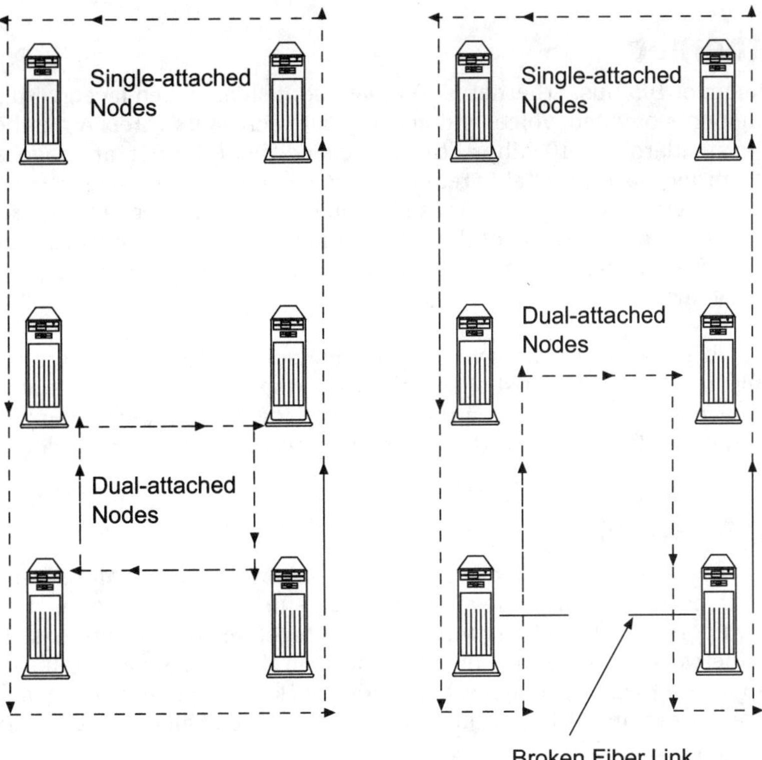

Figure 8-5: FDDI networks can heal themselves if a link breaks between dual-attached nodes.

HIGH FIBER, LOW CONSISTENCY

Pick up any four network hardware books, and you'll see four different definitions of FDDI. There's Fiber Distributed Data Interface, Fiber Data Distributed Interface, Fiber Digital Device Interface, and Fiber Data Distribution Interface. Note the common theme – they're all fiber interfaces. If you want a lower-fiber diet, you'll find implementations of FDDI over copper cabling (STP or level 5 UTP), sometimes called CDDI. CDDI has similar variations in definition, but you get the idea.

FDDI technology is ideal for high-speed network backbones and for connecting servers that stay up at all times. It isn't happy in a desktop workstation environment where devices are turned on and off frequently. FDDI hasn't gained as much support as Fast Ethernet (discussed next) because it costs significantly more per node to implement. Costs are drifting down, however. FDDI's fault tolerance when implemented as a dual ring, along with its Token Ring-like deterministic access method, make it worth the additional cost in some situations.

Fast Ethernet

At a maximum of 10Mbps, Ethernet is running out of steam when faced with pushing huge amounts of video, voice, and imaging data across its wires. A number of attempts to standardize a 100Mbps Ethernet, called Fast Ethernet, are ongoing. Most of the proposals on the table reduce the maximum network size, raise the minimum cable grade to level 5, increase the number of twisted-pairs required in the cable, or some combination of these. If you have an existing network infrastructure, some of these requirements may impose high costs in replacing and upgrading cabling.

Several Fast Ethernet products have emerged, including network adapters, hubs, and cabling. In general, they cost significantly less than FDDI. However, since the standards haven't been settled, you run the risk of investing in technology that might become obsolete once the standards are in place.

Switching Hubs

Several Ethernet hub products have emerged that provide a full 10Mbps bandwidth at each port, since they effectively make a temporary direct connection between two ports. By using two switching hubs together, you can increase the bandwidth between them by the number of ports in the hub. Some organizations use this approach to create a higher-bandwidth backbone between departments or buildings, for example. These hubs can extend the life of an existing Ethernet by increasing its bandwidth in critical paths within your network.

ATM

Put your credit card away. ATM is no cash machine. In fact, it will take your money. But you get what you pay for in high data bandwidth. Although very expensive now, many experts believe that ATM, or Asynchronous Transfer Mode, is the network technology of the twenty-first century. It's designed to be very scalable and to handle continuous large volumes of traffic (combinations of data, voice, and video) for extended periods.

As a network administrator, you should educate yourself about ATM and whether it's an alternative to consider. Since the ATM landscape is changing at a frenetic pace, I'll present the fundamentals here. By the time you read this, there will undoubtedly be some new developments in the ATM marketplace.

ATM is a switching technology, rather than a shared media technology such as Ethernet or Token Ring. In fact, ATM is really closer to a telephone network than a computer network in its design. Any node can directly connect to any other node, without sharing communication bandwidth with other nodes — similar to telephone calls with no party lines. It can transmit data between nodes from 1Mbps to more than 1Gbps and at various speeds in between. Connections that need high speed can get it. Connections that don't need high speed can transmit more slowly. Part of the connection negotiation process in ATM involves establishing end-to-end quality of service parameters — in other words, transmission speed and predictability of delays. This is quite different from other network technologies, which guarantee delivery of data, but never how fast or how predictably over time.

Transmitted data on ATM networks is performed using 53-byte packets called *cells.* The details of the physical layer aren't specified by ATM, so data can be transmitted on various types of network media including twisted-pair, fiber, and coax. Current ATM products entering the mainstream don't yet hit the 1Gbps mark. At the time of this writing, switches are typically offered for 25Mbps at the desktop, 155Mbps for workgroups, and up to 622Mbps for ATM backbones.

ATM is still an emerging technology, with standards for various aspects of it being set every few months. Thus, it's still plagued with incompatibilities among different vendor implementations. This problem is offset somewhat because many of the ATM products are completely software-upgradable to meet the new standards as they arrive. Thus, many network administrators are already becoming card-carrying ATM users. (I suspect that even after this technology dominates the network industry in the next century, folks will still be making double entendre comments about ATM cards.)

Lengthening Your Stride

As you've seen, each network technology is subject to physical limitations imposed by the hardware and the environment in which the network operates. As data travels through copper network cabling, the signal weakens because of resistance in the cable and can become distorted because of external interference from the environment. This fact of life is known as *attenuation.* It limits the amount of distance allowable between nodes on the network and varies with the type of cable used.

If you need to have longer distances between nodes on the network than allowed by the type of cable and network technology used, you need to employ a device called a *repeater.* A repeater does exactly what its name implies. On one end, it receives an incoming signal and retransmits (or repeats) it out the other end. In the process, it boosts and cleans up the signal, making it as fresh and clean as the original.

WANs typically use many repeaters along the way. If you need a down-to-earth example, consider a communication satellite orbiting the planet. Its primary function is to act as a repeater. The satellite receives a signal sent from one place on earth, amplifies and cleans it, and then retransmits it to another earth location.

Numerous network hub devices today include built-in repeaters, so connecting to these hubs has the effect of boosting and cleaning the signal. In most network installations, the use of active hubs containing repeaters completely eliminates the need to use separate repeaters in the network. On the other hand, coax LANs (that don't use hubs) typically require repeaters to extend the length of the bus cable.

Building Bridges

What if you have two networks that use different types of cabling? Build a bridge. What if you have a network that's overloaded with data traffic? Build a bridge. What if you want a more reliable and more secure network? Say it with me now. Build a bridge.

A *bridge* is a sort of smart repeater. At its most basic level, it performs the familiar function of a repeater by receiving, amplifying, and forwarding data on the network. However, a bridge does much more than this. It can link two network segments that use different types of cabling. This can be especially useful if different departments in your organization created independent networks, and you've inherited the task of hooking them together.

In addition, you can use a bridge to improve network performance. Insert a bridge in your network to break it into multiple segments. The bridge will isolate the segments from each other, except for data that must travel from a node on one segment to a node on the other segment. Local network traffic that used to be seen by the entire network is now only seen by the local segment.

For example, say, you use a bridge to separate your network into two equal-sized segments. Assuming the network traffic was evenly spread over the entire network, adding a bridge reduces the traffic on both segments by an average of 50 percent.

By segmenting your network this way and using bridges to link the segments, you also gain an additional measure of reliability and security. If one network segment goes down because of a broken cable or other equipment failure, the other segment is unaffected and can continue to operate. For larger networks, this can be extremely important. On the security front, you can design your network so that sensitive traffic is isolated to one segment. This limits your exposure to malicious folk with sniffers (the network analyzer kind, not the nose kind). Even if performance isn't a problem on the network, you may opt in some cases to segment your network, just to achieve the reliability and security benefits.

Selecting Your Network Adapter

Once you've selected the network technology and cabling (or lack of cabling) approach to take for implementing your network, the next step is to select network adapters for your servers and clients.

In the following sections, I'll cover the issues that you need to consider when selecting a network adapter for your Windows NT Server computers and other computers on your network.

Network Compatibility

Is the adapter compatible with both your network cable infrastructure and your chosen network technology? A few short years ago, thick Ethernet connectors started disappearing from many network adapters, and more recently thin coax connectors have become less prevalent. Be sure that you know what connectors are provided on the network adapter.

Is the adapter listed on the NT Hardware Compatibility List, or is it 100 percent compatible with another adapter that's listed? Although you may save a few dollars by purchasing unknown clone adapters, it's definitely worth the small premium to populate your servers with well-known, reliable brands (such as Intel, 3Com, or SMC for Ethernet; IBM, Proteon, SMC, or Madge for Token Ring). Remember, you're buying reliability for your server, a computer that must perform consistently for multiple users.

If you're using Token Ring, make sure that the adapter matches the speed of your ring. Better yet, use an adapter that will operate at either 4Mbps or 16Mbps. Most modern adapters support both.

NT Compatibility

Does the adapter have an NDIS 3.0 device driver available, either included in the NT installation, included in Microsoft's driver library, or provided by the adapter vendor? Check with the network adapter manufacturer and the NT Hardware Compatibility List for this information. (Visit `http://www.microsoft.com/BackOffice/ntserver/hcl` on the Web for an up-to-date list.)

Windows NT Server provides a number of certified network adapter drivers on the NT CD-ROM. Find them in \DRVLIB\NETCARD\X86 (or MIPS, ALPHA, or PPC, depending on what platform you're running). Under this directory, change to the subdirectory whose name matches your adapter. Many of these drivers include a readme file with specific installation instructions. If there's no readme file, just copy all of the files in the directory to the root directory of a floppy disk.

If you're planning to install multiple network adapters in your computer, check with the adapter manufacturer to assure that their NT driver supports multiple adapters. Most do, but occasionally they don't. It's best to check before purchasing, to avoid surprises.

Within the NT development group at Microsoft, the most widely used adapter has been the Intel EtherExpress 16. It's the adapter that Microsoft shipped with Windows for Workgroups, so they had lots of these available. Although this adapter is not inherently better than others, it's probably had more air time running NT than any other adapter on the market.

Server Compatibility

Does the adapter match your computer's bus (ISA, EISA, MCA, PCI, or VLB)? If you have PCI slots in your server, definitely use a PCI network adapter. If you have EISA slots in your server computer, opt for a network adapter that's EISA rather than ISA. You'll typically get better performance for a small incremental cost difference. Stay away from VLB network adapters. In theory they're fast, but they typically tap lots of CPU bandwidth and aren't transportable to more standard, non-VLB computers. In MCA computers, IBM adapters tend to be more reliable than others, in my experience.

If you're using a non-Intel platform, it's especially important to check ahead of time for driver availability, since some adapter manufacturers have chosen not to port their drivers to MIPS, Alpha, or PowerPC.

Will the adapter work in your computer without creating interrupt and memory conflicts? Be armed with the details of your computer's configuration before you purchase a network adapter. Know which interrupts and I/O addresses are available in your server. I've run into several situations where I can't use a network adapter because it provides very limited interrupt choices that all conflict with existing adapters.

Flexibility

Does the adapter allow for multiple types of cable, in case your approach to network cabling changes in the future? For example, if you're using coax today, but you're considering switching to UTP, check to see if the adapter provides both UTP and coax connections. This type of adapter is often called a *combo.* A few years ago, combos provided thicknet and thinnet on the same adapter. Later, combos more typically offered thinnet and UTP. Now, combos with 10Mbps UTP and 100Mbps UTP are available, and thinnet BNC connectors are beginning to disappear.

Since interrupts and I/O address ranges are precious commodities in the PC architecture, look for network adapters that support as many settings as possible. This level of flexibility will make installation of the adapter proceed more smoothly. Choosing an 8-bit ISA adapter isn't only a slow option for a server, but it's very inflexible because it only supports a small number of interrupts. If you need to use an ISA network adapter, opt for a 16-bit adapter that supports a wider range of IRQ settings.

NETWORKING – IT'S IN THERE

Several NT-compatible computers are now appearing with a network adapter built right into the computer's motherboard. Intel, DEC, AMD, and National Semiconductor are among the suppliers of these built-in network chips. You can recognize them in the Windows NT Hardware Compatibility List of network adapters by looking in the Bus Type column for the word "embedded." For example, a number of MIPS processor systems have the National Semiconductor SONIC network adapter sitting on the motherboard.

Building in network capabilities is cost-effective for both the computer manufacturer and you. The incremental price of a motherboard with an embedded network adapter is often much less than the cost of a separate adapter card. Moreover, if you need every precious expansion slot in the computer for other interface cards, these motherboards will save you a slot that you'd have burned for the network adapter card. As another plus, some of these chips may offer better performance than a comparable adapter card.

Like everything else, however, this approach has some disadvantages. For one thing, what you gain in cost savings, you lose in flexibility. Having a replaceable adapter card is preferable if you plan to upgrade your networking capabilities as prices fall, speed increases, and new networking technologies emerge. This is especially important for servers, which are constantly expected to offer high performance. Another issue to consider is network adapter failure. These devices do occasionally croak, and built-in adapters can't typically be replaced.

My advice is to stick with replaceable network adapter cards, if you can spare the motherboard slot. If you do get a computer with an adapter on the motherboard, though, be aware that you'll probably be using a slot sometime in the future when you need to upgrade or replace your network adapter.

Is the adapter easy to configure? Opt for a software-configurable adapter, if possible. You'll save time as well as wear and tear on your computer by not having to pop the adapter in and out to view or change jumper settings.

Installing Your Network Adapter

Since every network adapter is different, you can't substitute this section for your network adapter documentation. However, there are several common issues and points that should assist you in successful installation of your network adapter to work with Windows NT Server.

Avoiding Conflicts

Before installing and configuring your network adapter (or any other adapter, for that matter), you'll need to know what's in your computer and what resources are used. Make a list of all devices, their interrupts, I/O addresses, memory addresses, and DMA channels. You'll need this information to determine what resources are free for use by your network adapters. Most network adapters use one interrupt line, one to 16 I/O port addresses, and up to 64K of memory-mapped address space.

Here are some techniques to simplify gathering this information and avoiding conflicts:

- **Network adapter utility.** Some network adapters come with software that detects resource conflicts and helps determine what's safe for your network adapter to use.
- **BIOS configuration utility.** Your motherboard's built-in BIOS configuration utility can sometimes provide resource usage information on standard PC devices such as COM ports, parallel ports, and so on.
- **PCI 2.1 compliance.** If your motherboard and additional components comply with the PCI 2.1 voluntary standard, the hardware itself can help resolve interrupt conflicts, sometimes without your intervention. However, you'll still need to gather information on any ISA adapters using some of the other techniques listed here.
- **EISA configuration utility.** If your computer is an EISA machine, you can use the EISA configuration utility to gather resource information on all EISA adapters. Unfortunately, you'll need to resort to other techniques for gathering information on ISA adapters.
- **PS/2 reference disk.** If your computer is a PS/2 or other MCA-based computer, you can use the reference disk that came with your computer to gather the resource information for all adapters in the system. These computers will also tell you if you've created a resource conflict after installing a new adapter.

✦ **Configuration under DOS.** If all components are already installed and configured with their drivers to run under DOS, your chances are much higher that they'll run under Windows NT Server. This isn't a guarantee, as DOS only talks to one device at a time, so it's more forgiving of some conflicts.

✦ **Microsoft's MSD utility.** If you're running DOS 6.22 or higher or Windows for Workgroups on the computer, you can run the MSD utility that came with the operating system to scan your computer to determine what resources are in use.

✦ **Microsoft's WINMSD utility.** If you're already running NT version 3.5 or higher, you can run the WINMSD utility that came with NT to scan your computer for a list of resources in use.

✦ **Other utilities.** You can use one of several third-party software packages to scan your computer to determine what resources are in use. Checkit, Norton Utilities, QA Plus, Probe, and Manifest are examples of products designed to help in this area.

Don't take the results of MSD, WINMSD, or similar products as gospel. They may sometimes report that interrupts and I/O ports are free when they really aren't. This often happens if you've installed a device but haven't loaded the driver for it yet. The operating system sometimes has no way of detecting the device unless its driver is loaded.

Ultimately, you'll probably need to examine the jumpers physically or check the software configuration settings for each adapter in your computer. This is especially true of ISA adapters. Utilities won't tell you the whole story.

Selecting IRQs

Interrupt levels, or IRQs, are the most scarce device resource in your computer. There are only 16 of them, and all but three already have a standard assignment. You'll spend more time juggling IRQs to avoid conflicts than anything else. Table 8-4 outlines the IRQs used in a PC environment. This table provides typical interrupt assignments and some advice on whether to use a particular IRQ.

Table 8-4
Interrupt Assignments And Usage Advice

IRQ	*IRQ Assignment*	*Advice*
0	System clock (15ms timer tick)	IRQ 0 is hardwired and is never available to you. Don't use it.
1	Keyboard (8042 controller)	IRQ 1 is hardwired and is never available to you. Don't use it.

(continued)

Table 8-4 (continued)

IRQ	*IRQ Assignment*	*Advice*
2	8259 cascade from IRQ 9	IRQ 2, although apparently available to some adapters, actually isn't. It's triggered whenever IRQs 8 through 15 are triggered. Don't use it. (Some old VGA adapters use IRQ 2. Disable this usage under NT, if possible.)
3	COM2 and COM4 serial ports	IRQ 3 is occupied if you have two or more serial ports installed. If you have only one serial port, this IRQ may be available for assignment to another device.
4	COM1 and COM3 serial ports	IRQ 4 is occupied if you have one or more serial ports installed. If you have no serial ports (a rare condition), this IRQ may be available for assignment.
5	LPT2 parallel port	IRQ 5 is occupied if you have more than one parallel port installed. If you have only one parallel port, this IRQ may be available for assignment. (A virtual LPT2 port via a connection to a network printer doesn't consume this IRQ.)
6	Floppy disk controller	IRQ 6 is never available to you, unless your floppy controller allows setting the floppy disk IRQ to something other than 6.
7	LPT1 parallel port	IRQ 7 is occupied if you have one or more parallel ports installed. If you have no parallel ports (a rare condition), this IRQ may be available for assignment.
8	Real-time clock/calendar	IRQ 8 is hardwired and is never available to you. Don't use it.
9	8259 cascade to IRQ 2	IRQ 9, although apparently available to some adapters, actually isn't. It's triggered whenever IRQs 8 through 15 are triggered and is electrically tied to IRQ 2. Don't use it.
10	No typical assignment	IRQ 10 may be available for assignment.
11	No typical assignment	IRQ 11 may be available for assignment.
12	PS/2 mouse port or inport/bus mouse	IRQ 12 is typically occupied if you have a PS/2 mouse port installed. If you have a serial mouse instead, this IRQ may be available for assignment.
13	Math coprocessor error signal	IRQ 13 is never available in a Windows NT 4.0 computer, since 486 and higher processors all use it. Don't use it.

IRQ	IRQ Assignment	Advice
14	Disk controller	IRQ 14 is used by the standard primary IDE and EIDE (and older ESDI and ST506) hard disk drive controllers. If you have only SCSI drives in your computer, this IRQ may be available for assignment.
15	No typical assignment	IRQ 15 may be available for assignment.

Because of the arrangement of interrupt controllers in the PC design, IRQs 8 through 15 have higher priority than IRQs 3 through 7. Of the potentially available IRQs, it's most efficient to assign high-speed devices in the range 8 through 15, and lower-speed devices in the range 3 through 7. Network adapters and disk controllers belong in the high-priority range. However, if you're running out of IRQs, you may not have the luxury of assigning based on device throughput.

The amount of attention that you need to pay to PCI adapters depends on your motherboard and BIOS design. Some designs take interrupt and address assignments completely out of your hands, dynamically making assignments to adapters when the computer boots. For example, the HP Vectra XU series takes this approach, and it's sometimes difficult to determine which interrupt was assigned to which adapter. At the opposite end of the spectrum, some designs force you to assign specific interrupts to specific PCI slots statically using the BIOS configuration utility. Still other computers fall somewhere in the middle. They ask you to list interrupts available to PCI slots, and the BIOS makes dynamic assignments from this list at boot time. Although the first approach is the most automatic, I recommend the latter two approaches, as they provide you with more control over and knowledge of what resources are in use in your computer.

Many newer computers, especially PCI-based computers, contain secondary IDE or EIDE adapters built into the motherboard. These devices typically use up another interrupt resource beyond IRQ 14 used by the primary IDE. Be sure you know which interrupts are consumed by your built-in IDE/EIDE adapters.

Selecting I/O Addresses

Most network adapters require you to assign a range of I/O addresses to be used for I/O operations. Again, you need to assign a unique range to the adapter to avoid conflicting overlap with any other devices in the computer. Table 8-5 presents the typical I/O address ranges used in the PC, to assist in your quest for unused I/O address ranges.

Table 8-5
I/O Address Assignments in a PC

I/O Port Address Range	*Typical I/O Address Assignment*
170–17F	Secondary IDE/EIDE controller
1F0–1FF	Primary IDE/EIDE controller
200–20F	Joystick/game port
230–23F	Microsoft bus mouse or inport mouse
278–27F	LPT2 parallel port
2E8–2EF	COM4 serial port
2F8–2FF	COM2 serial port
280–29F	Used as default by some network adapters
300–31F	Used as default by some network adapters
320–32F	PC/XT hard disk controller (also used on some PS/2 models)
330–33F	Used as default by some common SCSI host adapters
378–37F	LPT1 parallel port
3C0–3CF	EGA video mode
3D0–3DF	CGA video mode
3E8–3EF	COM3 serial port
3F0–3F7	Floppy disk controller
3F8–3FF	COM1 serial port
A20–A2F	Used as default by some network adapters

It isn't always clear, even from the network adapter documentation, how many addresses an adapter actually consumes. If it isn't documented, assume that the adapter eats up 16 I/O addresses, and you'll be safe from overlap with other ranges.

Selecting Memory Addresses

Many network adapters use memory-mapped buffering, so they need a unique address range in memory to use for reading and writing data. Yet again, you have the task of assigning a unique address range to your adapter to avoid overlap with any other devices using memory address ranges. Table 8-6 shows you which address ranges are already consumed in a typical PC environment.

Table 8-6
Memory-Mapped Address Assignments in a PC

Memory Address Range	*Typical Memory Address Assignment*
A0000–BFFFF	EGA video memory
A0000–C4000	VGA video memory
B0000–B1000	Monochrome video memory
B8000–C0000	CGA video memory
C8000–CBFFF	Hard disk BIOS
CC000–CDFFF	Used as default by some network adapters
D8000–DBFFF	Used as default by some network adapters
E0000–EFFFF	System BIOS expansion: PS/2 extended BIOS or Plug and Play BIOS
F0000–FFFFF	System BIOS (in ROM)

Selecting DMA Channels

Some network adapters use DMA channels to bypass the CPU and communicate directly with system memory. DMA channels must be uniquely assigned in the computer as well. Standard PCs use only DMA 0 for DRAM refresh purposes and DMA 2 for the floppy disk drive. The remaining channels 1 and 3 through 7 are available for devices. You'll need to check the settings and documentation for each of your other installed devices to determine which DMA channels have been assigned.

Selecting the Connector

One of the most common errors in configuring combo network adapters is choosing the wrong connector. For example, one version of the Intel EtherExpress 16 adapter has both thicknet and thinnet (BNC) connectors. NT configuration of this adapter defaults to thicknet, so you'll need to explicitly change it to thinnet if you're using that type of cable. Before you install a combo adapter, know which type of connector you'll be using to hook to the network and configure the adapter appropriately.

Selecting the Speed

In the Token Ring world, the most common adapter configuration error is choosing a speed that doesn't match the speed of the ring. Attaching a node running at the wrong speed can bring down the entire ring, so make sure that you configure the adapter with the speed that matches your ring. As mentioned before, most modern Token Ring adapters support both speeds. This is both a blessing (in terms of flexibility) and a curse (in terms of providing an easy way to hose your network).

Once you have all of the configuration information about the network adapter and the existing components in your computer, write it all down and keep it in a handy location near or on the computer. Many folks keep the configuration information in a plastic or paper pouch attached to the side of the PC. I don't recommend putting this information in a file on the computer's hard drive, since you may need the configuration when you're unable to boot the computer.

Setting the Settings

If you have an older network adapter, you'll likely need to configure it using jumpers or DIP switches, according to the instructions accompanying your network adapter. I won't go into detail about how to accomplish this, except to advise you not to use a pencil to toggle DIP switches. The pencil lead not only makes a mess but also can fall into the switch, introducing a potential short circuit. Use a pen or paper clip end to set DIP switches. Most modern network adapters provide a software setup utility. A few have a combination of switches, jumpers, and software configuration.

Always use an antistatic wrist strap attached to a true ground when you're handling, inserting, or removing adapters. Even small amounts of static electricity can destroy both your adapters and your computer. Make sure that you're properly grounded before removing an adapter from its anti-static package.

If your computer is powered down but remains plugged in, you can attach the wrist strap to the metal PC case, since it's grounded as long as the computer is plugged in. (Unplugging the computer removes its connection to ground and invites static electricity.) If you use this approach for grounding, make absolutely sure that you've turned off the computer before you begin surgery.

If you're configuring an Intel x86 computer, install the adapter in your computer according to the manufacturer's instructions. (If your computer is RISC-based, you may first need to install the adapter in an Intel computer to run the DOS-based configuration utility. Check with your adapter manufacturer to determine if you need to do this.) Don't connect the adapter to your network at this stage.

If the adapter manufacturer provides a software configuration utility, it's probably a DOS-based program. (Most of these configuration utilities won't run properly under Windows NT, since they attempt to touch hardware directly. You'll need to run the utility under DOS, unless otherwise specified by your adapter manufacturer.) If your computer already has DOS installed, boot to DOS and run the utility provided. If you don't have DOS installed on the computer, use another computer to create a DOS boot floppy using the SYS command. Then, copy the network adapter configuration utility and all associated files to the DOS boot floppy, boot your computer using the floppy, and run the configuration utility.

WORKSHEET ENTRY

In Chapter 7, in Worksheet 7-3 (Windows NT Server Setup) on line 23, record the make and model of the network adapter installed in your computer. On line 26, record the configuration information for your network adapter, including IRQ, I/O address range, and any other network adapter configuration information. You'll need all of this information during Windows NT Server installation in Chapter 9.

After running the configuration utility, you may need to turn off your computer for a few moments before attempting to test the adapter. Follow the instructions provided by your adapter manufacturer.

Testing the Adapter

If you're going to install Windows NT Server as either a PDC or BDC, you'll need a completely functioning network adapter to succeed during installation. Thus, it's critical that you make sure your adapter is functioning before proceeding.

Some network adapters come with diagnostic utilities that you can use to test the adapter once you've installed it. The value of these utilities varies widely between manufacturers. Functionality ranges from simply reporting your configuration settings to actually sending data over the network to another computer.

If your diagnostic utility sends data over the network, it's best to connect it to another computer that's not on your production network, just in case the new network adapter isn't configured correctly or is malfunctioning. If you don't have this luxury, you can use another node on your production network. Just hang on tight to your rabbit's foot while you run the test.

If your network adapter doesn't come with a diagnostic utility, and you're installing on an Intel x86 computer, you can follow the adapter manufacturer's instructions to install DOS drivers to test the adapter. This may be a major task, so I recommend this last resort only if you're going to install NT as a PDC or BDC and your adapter doesn't come with it's own test utility.

Installing NT after the Adapter

Once the network adapter is physically installed in your computer, it's properly configured, and you've tested it to make sure it works, you're ready to install Windows NT Server. Chapter 9 will walk you through installation of the entire operating system, using the worksheet you completed in Chapters 7 and 8. In this section, I'll fill you in on what to expect during the portion of Windows NT Server installation that deals with your network adapter.

Assuming that you take my advice in Chapter 9 and allow NT to detect your network adapter, NT will present you with a dialog box requesting information on your network adapter settings. For example, if your network adapter is an Intel EtherExpress 16, you'll see a dialog box like the one shown in Figure 8-6. It asks for the IRQ, I/O address, channel ready setting, and cable type. Since different network adapters require different configuration parameters, your dialog box will probably vary from this example.

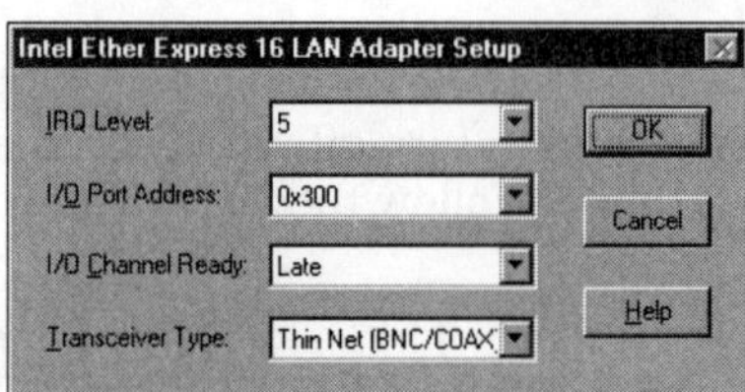

Figure 8-6: NT requests configuration information about your network adapter.

In each box, just type or select the information that you recorded on your worksheet, then click OK. A handful of network adapters ask for additional information. Type or select the additional settings requested and click OK to continue. Be sure that your settings exactly match how the adapter has been configured, or your network adapter won't operate correctly.

The list of available settings that NT presents during the configuration process doesn't always match the available settings for your adapter. For example, say you have a clone network adapter that's Novell NE2000 compatible. NT detects the adapter and recommends that you use the NE2000-compatible driver. When you do, you're presented with a long list of possible interrupt settings, but the adapter may only accept a small subset of these settings.

Moreover, don't assume that the default settings that NT shows you represent the current configuration of the adapter. If you elect to detect the adapter, NT detects the presence of the adapter but not necessarily its current configuration settings. Since NT doesn't yet support Plug and Play, what you see may be a good guess at the settings, but they don't necessarily reflect reality. Know what the settings should be ahead of time, and enter them as requested.

If NT doesn't detect your network adapter, or if you elect not to have NT scan for adapters, you'll need manually to choose from a list of adapters. Figure 8-7 illustrates this. Scroll through the list, highlight the appropriate network adapter using the mouse, and click OK.

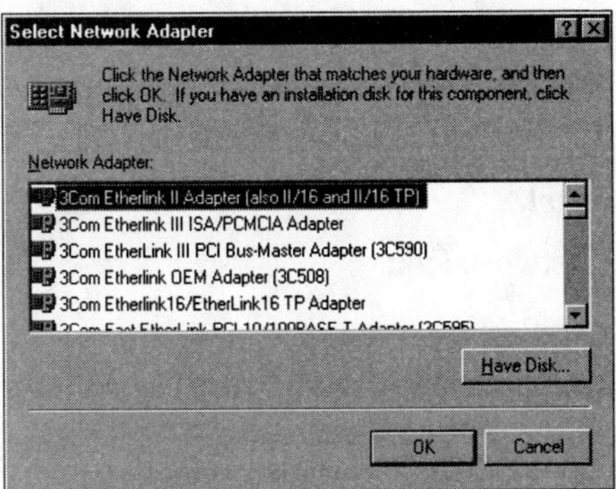

Figure 8-7: Pick the appropriate network adapter manually, if you elect not to autodetect.

If your adapter isn't on the list, you'll need to supply a network adapter driver floppy disk. Use the disk that came with your adapter or the one you created from the NT driver library earlier in this chapter, in the section called "NT Compatibility." Click Have Disk and follow the instructions displayed.

Once you configure your network adapter and other network components under Windows NT Server, NT will attempt to start the network on your computer. If it can't, you'll have the opportunity to review and correct your configuration settings.

That's really all there is to it. Keep what you've learned in this section in mind when you go through the complete Windows NT Server installation process in Chapter 9. Remember, record all of your adapter configuration settings on the worksheet before you begin NT installation.

Installing NT before the Adapter

Perhaps you're adding another network adapter to your existing Windows NT Server computer. Or you may have originally installed NT as a stand-alone server before you had a network adapter available. Or you may wish to replace the adapter with a more powerful one. In any of these situations, you can install a new network adapter after Windows NT Server is already installed on your computer.

To create a working Windows NT Server PDC, you must have a working network adapter in your computer *before* you install Windows NT Server on it. Before installing an NT BDC, you *must* have a working network adapter in the computer, and the existing PDC for the domain must already be up and running on the network. In these cases, you can't install your first network adapter after installing Windows NT Server.

Here are the steps for installing a new network adapter in a computer that's already running Windows NT Server:

1. Log on to the server as an administrator.
2. Click Start ➪ Settings ➪ Control Panel.
3. In Control Panel, double-click the Network icon.
4. Click the Adapters tab. Then click Add.

   NT will build and present a list of network adapters.
5. Choose one of the listed adapters or click Have Disk, if you have a driver disk for your adapter.
6. Follow the instructions on screen for configuration of the adapter.

   NT prompts you for a driver disk or to reinsert the CD-ROM from which you installed originally. It copies the appropriate driver to your NT installation, then asks you for configuration information. Use your worksheet to supply it.

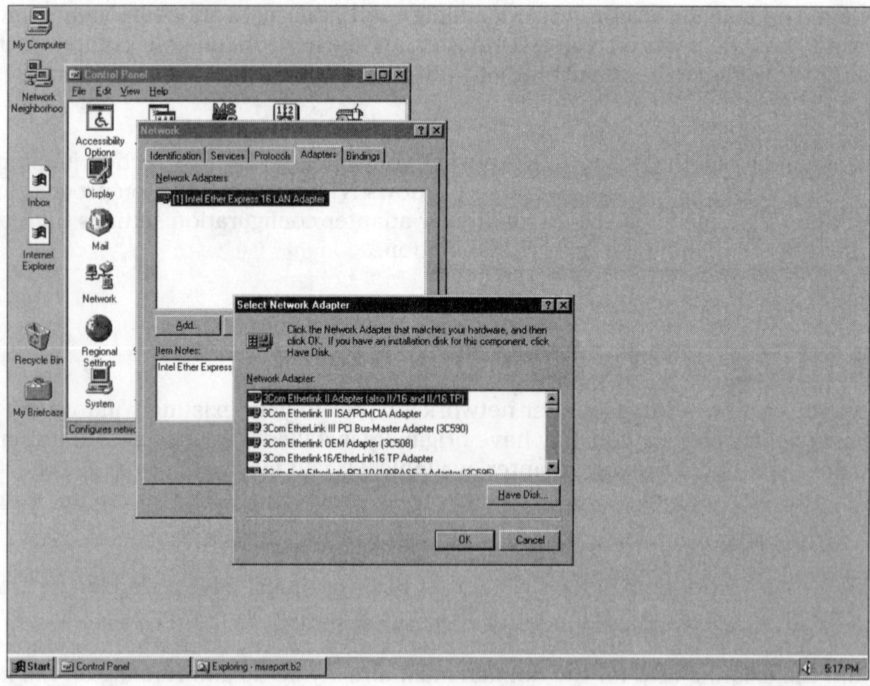

Figure 8-8: Using the Control Panel, you can install another network adapter after installing Windows NT Server.

Managing Network Bindings

As an NT network administrator, you need to be aware of network bindings and how they affect your networked computers. For example, if you want to run two different protocols on two different network adapters in your server, you'll need to manipulate network bindings. Moreover, to optimize network performance, you may want to change the order of bindings for the most efficient operation. In this section, I'll discuss what network bindings are and how you can manage them.

What Are Bindings?

Transport protocols are assigned to run on specific network adapters. When a protocol runs on a specific network adapter, the protocol and adapter are *bound* to each other. The act of creating this association between protocols and adapters is called *binding*.

The same terminology is also used to describe associations between higher-level network components (typically called *services*) and protocols. For example, on my Windows NT Server computer, the server component is bound to the NetBEUI protocol, which, in turn, is bound to the NE2000 network adapter. The chain of bindings linking the highest-level network component to the lowest is called the *binding path*.

Viewing Network Bindings

When you install Windows NT Server, Setup automatically creates an appropriate set of binding paths, linking the network components that you installed. By default, if you elected to install multiple protocols and multiple adapters, all of the installed protocols are bound to all of the network adapters in your computer. (If this configuration is what you intended, you need not worry about managing bindings.) Likewise, when you install a new protocol, it's automatically bound to your network adapters.

To view your current network bindings, perform the following steps:

1. Log on to the server as an administrator. Click Start ➪ Settings ➪ Control Panel.
2. In Control Panel, double-click the Network icon. Click the Bindings tab.
3. Under Show bindings for, select the level of the network component whose bindings you want to view. Click the plus (+) sign to expand portions of the binding path.

   Your options are all adapters, all protocols, and all services. Depending on which one you select, you'll be able to view the same information in three different ways.

If you select all adapters, you'll see all the network adapters, the protocols bound to those adapters, and the services bound to those protocols. I recommend using this view, since it provides a clear picture of the binding path for each adapter, as shown in Figure 8-9.

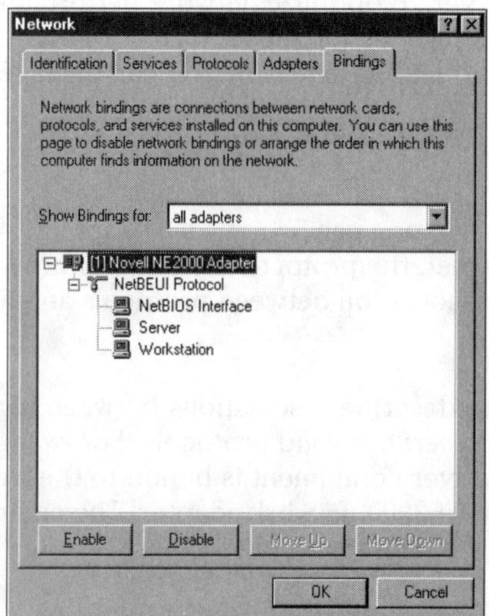

Figure 8-9: The adapters view shows the entire binding path for each network adapter.

If you select all services, you'll see the same information in reverse. For each service, you'll see the binding path to protocols and adapters, as illustrated by Figure 8-10. Selecting all protocols offers the least information, since it presents just the bindings between protocols and adapters. Services aren't included, as you can see in Figure 8-11.

Enabling and Disabling Bindings

Bindings can be enabled and disabled, based on your use of the network components installed on your computer. For example, you may want the TCP/IP protocol to run on only one of your network adapters.

To disable an existing binding, click the component that you want removed from the binding path, and click the Disable button. When you do, you'll see an icon next to the component indicating that it's disabled. Depending on the component that you selected, other components may be disabled as well.

For example, as shown in Figure 8-12, if you disable the NetBEUI protocol, all services bound to it are disabled. Since it's the only protocol bound to the network adapter, the adapter is no longer bound to anything and is disabled also. If you had another adapter in the computer, with its own set of bindings, those bindings would be unaffected.

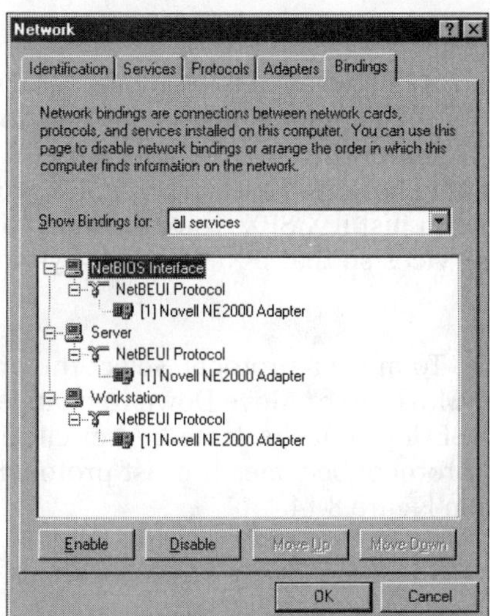

Figure 8-10: The services view shows the entire binding path for each service.

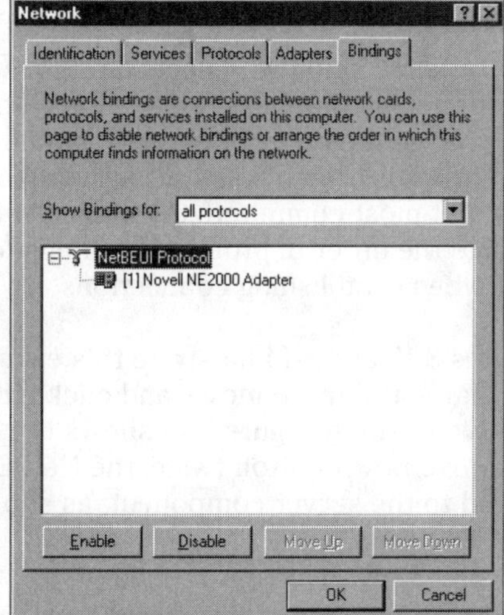

Figure 8-11: The protocols view shows the bindings between each protocol and adapter.

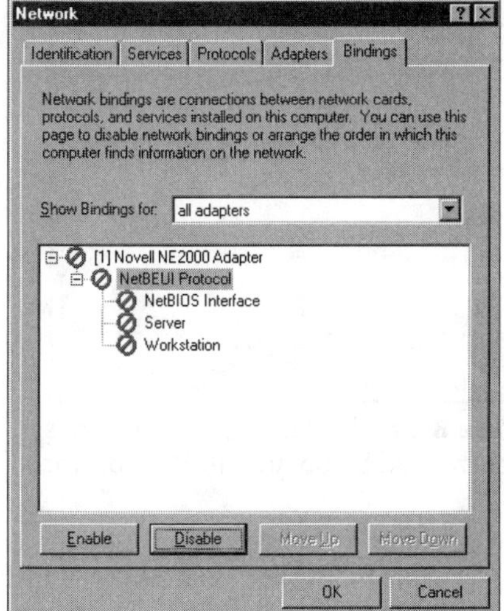

Figure 8-12: Disabling the only protocol binding on an adapter disables the entire binding path.

Enabling a binding is just as easy. Click the component you want enabled in the binding path, and click Enable. When you do so, the icons next to the affected components will change to reflect the enabled bindings.

Changing Binding Order

The order of bindings reflects a relative priority between network components. Components bound first have higher priority than components bound last. You can change the order of network bindings to optimize your computer's use of the network. For example, if your server is running both NetBEUI and IPX/SPX protocols, but most computers on your network run just IPX/SPX, you may want to change the order of protocol bindings to services so that IPX/SPX is always tried first when establishing connections.

Figures 8-13 and 8-14 illustrate this example. To move a protocol, select the protocol that you want to move, and click either Move Up or Move Down to change its relative position. Figure 8-13 shows the NetBEUI protocol selected. After clicking the Move Down button twice, the NetBEUI protocol becomes the last protocol bound to the server component, as shown in Figure 8-14.

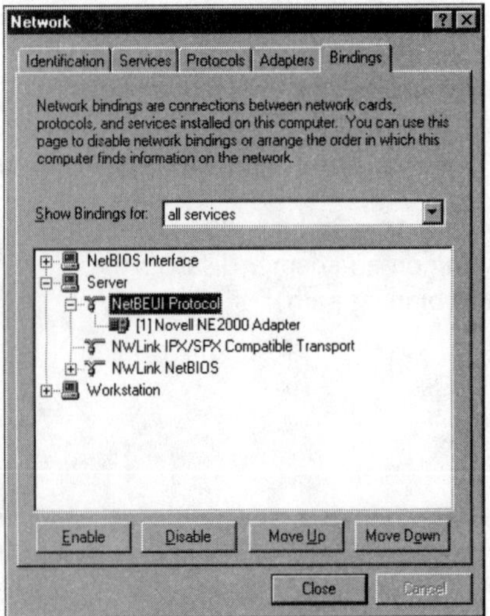

Figure 8-13: Select the protocol that you want to move.

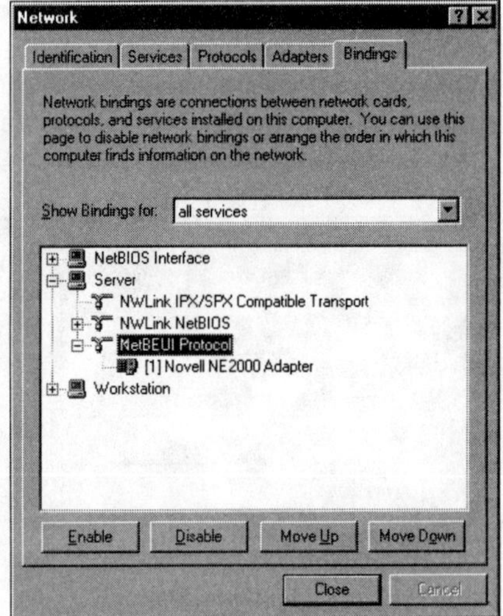

Figure 8-14: The NetBEUI protocol has been moved below the IPX/SPX protocol.

You can apply this same technique to other services. In this example, it's wise to change the protocol binding order under the workstation service (the redirector) in the same way. If you have Windows NT Workstation clients on your network, it's a good idea to optimize their protocol binding order as well.

INSIDE STORY

The NT product support folks crowded around one side of the long conference table. Test managers and project managers took their places on the other side. In the end, all would have to agree that NT was ready to ship, and at this point we were at a standoff on a major issue. It might mean slipping the schedule unless we could come to an understanding.

We had visited this topic many times before, but we covered the same ground again to bring any newcomers up to speed. During NT configuration of a certain network adapter on certain computer models, customers could select a set of parameters that would render the adapter useless. Recovery from this state involved removing the adapter from the computer, placing it in another computer, and running a special adapter setup utility. It was a nightmare scenario, if you happened to hit it.

"We have to prevent users from doing this," the product support folks collectively declared. "We'll have customers ringing the phone off the hook on this one, if we don't." The anxiety in everyone's voice gradually increased. "But this is a valid setting on most computers, and the adapter acts the same way under Windows for Workgroups," the test folks argued. "You have to have this specific card on this specific machine and use this specific combo of settings to make it happen. That's a pretty limited risk. Weigh that against the risk of adding a new screen to the product this close to shipping."

Several folks paused to weigh the risks, alternately shifting their right and left hands up and down, like a balance. "How many calls do you guys get from Windows for Workgroups customers on this issue?" Silence. No one had the numbers at hand. "Lots," whispered one support engineer under his breath. We tabled the issue until we could get more data on how big we expected this problem to be.

Later that day, the product support manager showed up in my office with a huge pile of network adapters, each of which had been rendered inoperable under NT. He solemnly entered my office, dumped the stack of dead adapters on my chair, and exited in silent protest. In our meeting the next morning, we again debated. That day, though, we finally agreed to make NT display a warning if the user attempted to set the killer configuration. Meanwhile, the pile of expired adapters on my desk awaited a decent burial.

Summary

In this chapter, you've learned the ins and outs of cabling, network technologies, and network adapters. Whether or not you're personally involved in designing and installing your network, you now have a better understanding of, and appreciation for, what's out there. Perhaps, I've presented some options and planning considerations that you haven't considered before.

Be sure to complete the network adapter information in the Chapter 7 worksheet before you proceed to Chapter 9. There, you'll use the worksheet to help perform an actual install of Windows NT Server on your computer. Because you've prepared well for installation, you'll have a lot less to worry about during the setup process.

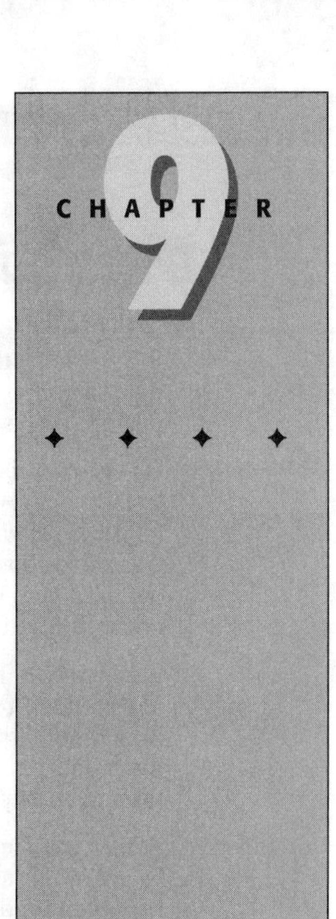

Installing and Repairing Windows NT Server

If you've had experience installing and configuring UNIX, NetWare, or other server operating systems, you'll find that installing Windows NT Server 4.0 is simpler. The product itself makes your life easier by providing lots of prompting and help along the way. Even so, quite a few steps are involved. In this chapter, I'll walk you through those steps to help you to complete successful installations on the first try.

You'll be less stressed during the installation process if you make several key decisions up front. If you haven't gone through Chapters 7 and 8 and recorded your installation decisions, now is a great time to do so. Have Worksheet 7-3 outlining your decisions close at hand before you begin NT installation.

You may have purchased your server hardware with Windows NT Server 4.0 preinstalled on the hard disk. If so, you may find that the term "preinstalled" is somewhat loosely defined. You'll probably have to complete most of the installation steps yourself. Refer to the documentation that came with your server computer to determine exactly where you need to start in the installation process.

Even if you're inheriting administration of a Windows NT Server network that has already been installed, there'll come a day when you'll need to build another NT server on your network. Or, you may be called upon to repair or reinstall NT on your current server. When those days arrive, turn to these pages for guidance.

INSIDE STORY

Steve pounded his clenched right fist on the podium. The microphone rattled, resonating the pounding throughout the meeting hall. Every employee in the Systems Division riveted their attention on Steve. The summer afternoon heat seemed suddenly to jump a few degrees, as he continued his tirade.

He screamed in his trademark booming, yet raspy voice, "Installation! Installation! Installation!" He excitedly related an allegory of installation trauma experienced with a range of software products on his home PC. As he shouted, his story reached frequent crescendos both in emotional intensity and volume. "There's not a single software company that's gotten it right! Pay attention to installation!" (Steve's volume has become legendary. He actually blew out a vocal chord at a similar event later that year.)

We squirmed. He was dead right. Software installation is one of the most critical features of a product. It has to be easy, and it has to be right. The user's first impression of the quality and simplicity of the product is formed during installation. And, after all, "If you can't get the product installed properly, it's gonna be kinda tough to use!" Steve's points were well taken, but they exposed the reality of the work ahead of us.

At that point in the life of NT, little attention had been paid to installation. (It's traditionally one of the last things to complete in a project, since it requires all of the other pieces to be there.) Inside Microsoft, installation of NT meant copying files over the network, editing a few text files, and going through a lengthy process that involved restarting the computer three times. Hardly what we wanted our customers to do.

Steve's ear-splitting comments marked the beginning of a long and challenging focus on installation. From that day on, if anyone spoke or acted as if installation were unimportant, many of us used Steve's mantra to pull them back in line. "Installation! Installation! Installation!" we'd scream, as we pounded our fists in our hands. It became a familiar and almost comforting sound in the halls of Building 2.

Later in this chapter, I'll also discuss how to handle installation on RISC-based computers. Finally, I'll deal with the grim tasks of repairing damaged installations or reinstalling the entire NT Server operating system. Along the way, I'll pass along some helpful hints and important caveats to remember.

Preparing to Install Windows NT Server

Regardless of how you choose to install Windows NT Server 4.0 on your computer, make sure to complete the following steps before proceeding with NT installation:

1. Ensure that your computer's hardware is compatible with Windows NT Server 4.0.

   Check the Windows NT Hardware Compatibility List to determine whether your computer and its peripheral devices are compatible with Windows NT Server.

Chapters 7 and 8 provide detailed guidelines on selecting and configuring hardware for your server computer.

Read the SETUP.TXT file on the floppy disk labeled "Setup Disk 2" for last-minute installation advice from Microsoft. This file may contain important installation tips for specific computer models or hardware devices.

2. If you need to supply drivers for some of your hardware devices, locate or create the driver disks.

See Chapter 7 for a discussion on how to create driver disks from the Windows Driver Library included on the Windows NT Server 4.0 CD-ROM.

3. Complete Worksheet 7-3 in preparation for installation on this computer.

   Making all of the installation decisions beforehand will save you time and aggravation during the installation process. Have the worksheet with you during the entire process.

4. Back up your hard disks.

   If the hard disks on your server computer contain any data that you want to retain, create a full backup of your hard disks before proceeding with installation.

   If you're upgrading from an old version of Windows NT Server to 4.0, make sure that your backup includes the old Windows NT directory tree, since NT 4.0 will overwrite it.

   If you're not upgrading, NT is designed to leave everything else on your system alone. However, since NT installation gives you the power to destroy and reformat disk partitions with a few keystrokes, minimize your risk by making a full backup now.

If your computer's hard disks have never been formatted, or if they were formatted under another operating system such as UNIX or VMS, Setup may tell you that it detected a possible virus and terminate installation. See the Chapter 7 section entitled "Handling Unknown File Systems" for information on how to avoid this problem.

5. Back up your Windows NT Server Setup floppy disks.

   Make copies of the three Setup floppy disks, store the originals in a safe place, and use the copies during the installation process.

6. If you have hardware devices that aren't supported by Windows NT, gather your hardware manuals, configuration information, and driver disks.

   Check the Windows NT Hardware Compatibility List to determine which hardware devices are supported by NT. Other devices may work with NT, but they often require NT device drivers supplied by the hardware manufacturer.

7. If you have a UPS device attached to the serial port of your computer, disconnect it before proceeding.

NT Setup automatically tries to detect serial devices, and this can cause trouble with your UPS.

8. On the Windows NT Server 4.0 CD-ROM, review the file \I386\SETUP.TXT. This file contains last-minute additions to information on known NT installation problems and workarounds.

   SETUP.TXT also contains information on how to diagnose and report NT installation problems to Microsoft.

9. If you're installing on an Intel x86-based computer, be sure that it's configured to boot from a 3.5-inch floppy disk.

   This may involve enabling floppy disk booting in the computer's CMOS configuration and perhaps swapping floppy disk cables to make your 3.5-inch drive the A drive. Refer to your hardware documentation, if your computer won't currently boot from a 3.5-inch floppy disk.

During the installation process, Setup will display the list of disk drives and partitions present on your computer. You can't count on the drive letters matching what you're used to seeing in DOS or even in earlier versions of Windows NT. So before starting Setup, make sure that the volume labels on your disk partitions are meaningful to you. That way, you can use the volume labels, and not the drive letters, to identify your partitions. You'll need to be able to identify them during the installation process.

Once you've completed these preliminary steps, you're ready to select your method of installation, which I'll describe in the next section.

Choosing Your Installation Method

Before you can even start to install Windows NT Server 4.0 on your computer, you'll need to select which method to use. Following are three distinct approaches:

✦ **Install from CD-ROM.** Use this method if you have a local CD-ROM drive attached to your computer and the drive is included in the NT Hardware Compatibility List.

✦ **Install over the network.** Use this method if you don't have a CD-ROM drive on your computer, but you do already have a working network with a server that can access a CD-ROM drive.

✦ **Install from an unsupported CD-ROM drive.** Use this method if you have a CD-ROM drive attached to your x86-based computer, but the drive isn't included in the NT Hardware Compatibility List.

Earlier versions of Windows NT Server provided the option of installing from a stack of more than 20 floppy disks, but Microsoft dropped support for floppy installation in NT version 4.0. Only CD-ROM and network installations are now supported.

Installation from a local Windows NT-compatible CD-ROM drive is the simplest and quickest approach to installing Windows NT Server 4.0. I heartily recommend using this method on your first NT Server installation. Incurring the cost of equipping your computer with an NT-compatible CD-ROM drive is worth the savings in additional complexity, time, and effort associated with the other methods. Use the Windows NT Hardware Compatibility List for recommended CD-ROM drives.

The network installation approach involves significant preparation. Moreover, it requires that you have a working network already up and running. However, if you have several computers on your existing network that need Windows NT Server installed, this approach can be more efficient in the long run. The existing network need not be a Microsoft network. It can be any network that allows you to copy files between computers. Because of its complexity, though, I don't recommend this approach for your very first NT Server installation.

The unsupported CD-ROM drive approach falls somewhere between the other two approaches, in terms of complexity. If your server computer has a CD-ROM drive that isn't compatible with NT, opt for this approach to perform the installation.

In the following sections, I'll outline the installation steps for each approach. Go directly to the section that presents the approach that you've selected, and begin there.

Steps to Install from CD-ROM on Intel

In this section, I'll show you how to install Windows NT Server 4.0 using a local CD-ROM drive on an Intel x86-based server computer. If your computer is based on a RISC processor, go to the section entitled "Steps to Install from CD-ROM on RISC," and follow the steps outlined there.

In this procedure, the CD-ROM drive must be included in the NT Hardware Compatibility List. This is the most straightforward approach to installation and requires the least amount of up-front preparation.

Gathering Your Materials

You'll need to assemble the following materials before you begin installation from your local CD-ROM drive:

- The installation worksheet that you completed in Chapter 7 (Worksheet 7-3)
- The Windows NT Server 4.0 CD-ROM

✦ One 1.44MB blank floppy disk, labeled "Emergency Repair"

✦ Three 1.44MB floppy disks included with Windows NT Server

Once you have all of this material close at hand, you are ready to install Windows NT Server 4.0.

You can boot from the Windows NT Server 4.0 CD-ROM if your Intel computer's BIOS supports the El Torito Bootable CD-ROM format. (Sounds as if it needs a side-order of cheese nachos.) Some Intel computers already provide this capability. Check the documentation that came with your computer to determine if your BIOS has this feature. If it does, you can perform the following steps without using the setup floppy disks.

Getting Setup Running

1. Insert the Windows NT Server 4.0 CD-ROM into your CD-ROM drive. Insert the "Setup Boot Disk" in drive A and restart the computer.

   If you have more than one CD-ROM drive, insert the NT CD-ROM into the drive with the *lowest* SCSI ID number. For example, if you have CD-ROM drives at ID 1 and ID 6, use the drive at SCSI ID 1 for Windows NT Server installation.

   You'll see several status messages as NT Setup examines your hardware and prepares for installation.

2. Setup asks for "Setup Disk 2." Remove the Setup Boot Disk from drive A, insert "Setup Disk 2," and press ENTER.

   Setup launches a minimal version of the Windows NT kernel on your computer. You've entered the first phase of Setup, called *text mode.* You'll see white text on a blue screen. The bottom line of the screen displays status information and lists your keyboard choices whenever you're asked for input.

   While in text mode, you can press F1 to display help information. Press F3 if you want to exit Setup. If you do exit, though, keep in mind that you'll have to start over again at step 1.

3. Setup asks if you want to set up Windows NT. Press ENTER to continue Setup.

   You also have the option of repairing a damaged NT installation. In a later step, you'll create an Emergency Repair disk. You'll use this disk with the repair option of Setup if your operating system files are ever damaged. If you need to repair an NT installation, refer to the section entitled "Repairing Windows NT Server," later in this chapter

Previous versions of Windows NT Server offered you a choice of Express or Custom Setup. Express Setup asked fewer questions but offered you less control over the operating system's installation. Windows NT Server 4.0 doesn't offer you this choice.

Detecting Storage Hardware

4. Setup asks if you want it to detect SCSI, CD-ROM, and other mass storage devices automatically or skip the detection process. Press ENTER to begin detection.

   Setup warns you that the probing it does during hardware detection may hang your computer. This rarely happens in practice. I recommend having Setup attempt to detect your hardware. It's easier than hunting through a list of adapters to find just the right one.

   In the unlikely event that your computer hangs, reboots, or exhibits unusual behavior during the detection process, go back to step 1. When you reach step 4 again, press *S* to skip the automatic detection process, then go to step 7.

5. Setup asks for Setup Disk 3. Remove "Setup Disk 2" from drive A, insert "Setup Disk 3," and press ENTER.

   Setup scans for several makes and models of SCSI adapters and other hardware. This process may take a few minutes. It tries all available drivers and continues even after it finds an adapter, since you might have more than one of them in your computer.

   Setup will scan for SCSI adapters, non-SCSI CD-ROM drives (such as IDE CD-ROMs), built-in IDE/PCI adapters, and special mass storage devices (such as disk arrays from Dell and Compaq). It won't look for non-SCSI hard disks or any device attached to a SCSI adapter. It will detect these devices later.

6. Setup lists the devices that it found and asks if you have additional devices to specify. If you have more SCSI host adapters in the computer that weren't automatically detected, press *S* and go to step 7. If the displayed list of devices is complete, press ENTER and go to step 8.

   Setup refers to the list of detected devices as "mass storage devices." However, the list doesn't include floppy disk drives, non-SCSI hard disk drives (IDE, EIDE, or ESDI), or devices attached to SCSI adapters. (Some integrated IDE/EIDE PCI adapters are included in the list.) Don't worry about these other devices. They're automatically detected by Setup later.

Adding Drivers Manually

7. Setup allows you to select drivers manually. Scroll through the driver list by pressing the UP and DOWN ARROW keys to select the driver that you need.

   If you change your mind and want to go back to step 6 at any time, press ESC.

   7a. If the required driver is in the list, select it and press ENTER. Then go to step 7d.

   7b. If the required driver isn't in the list, select the last choice in the list, called Other, and press ENTER.

You must have a driver disk supplied by the hardware manufacturer to continue with the next step. Setup refers to this disk as a "Manufacturer-supplied hardware support disk."

7c. Setup asks for a hardware support disk. Remove "Setup Disk 3" from drive A, insert the hardware support disk, and press ENTER.

7d. Setup adds the driver that you selected to its list of devices. If you have additional devices to add, go back to step 6. If not, press ENTER.

If you inserted a hardware support disk in step 7c, Setup asks you to reinsert Setup Disk 3. If Setup asks for this disk, remove the hardware support disk, insert "Setup Disk 3," and press ENTER.

Reviewing the License Agreement

8. Setup asks you to review the Microsoft End-User Licensing Agreement. Press PAGE DOWN to advance to the next page and PAGE UP to return to the previous page. You must proceed to the last page of the agreement. Press F8 if you agree to its terms or ESC if you don't agree.

   If you press ESC, indicating that you don't agree to the terms, Setup will terminate the installation process. If you later decide that you agree to the terms, you'll need to start again at step 1.

Unfortunately, you can't print the agreement at this point, since the operating system isn't installed yet. If you need to print the agreement later, you can find a copy of it in \I386\EULA.TXT on the Windows NT Server 4.0 CD-ROM.

Upgrading an Old Windows NT Server

9. If you already have one or more versions of Windows NT on your computer, Setup asks if you want to upgrade. If there's no version of NT already installed on your computer, go to step 10. If you want to install a fresh copy of NT Server, go to step 9a. If you want to upgrade an existing version of NT, go to step 9b.

See Chapter 7 for a discussion of what to expect when upgrading from a previous version of Windows NT Server.

9a. If you want to install a fresh copy of 4.0, separate from all other NT versions on your computer, press *N*. Then go to step 10.

This will allow you to dual-boot between the old and new versions of NT. It won't migrate any settings or applications from your old NT version to this one, however.

9b. If you want to install 4.0 as an upgrade to a previous NT installation, use the UP and DOWN ARROW keys to highlight the version of NT that you want to upgrade. Select it by pressing ENTER. Then go to step 15.

This will migrate settings and applications from your old NT version to the NT 4.0 installation. However, you'll no longer be able to boot your computer into the old version of NT. You won't be able to restore your old NT version either, unless you did a full backup before attempting to install NT 4.0.

Verifying Basic Hardware

10. Setup displays basic hardware information and asks you to confirm. If the items listed are correct, select the No changes option by pressing ENTER.

    Setup displays some rough details about your hardware configuration, including computer type, display, keyboard type, keyboard layout, and pointing device. It usually detects these details correctly. If any are incorrect, use the UP and DOWN ARROW keys to highlight the incorrect item. Press ENTER to select it and view a list of options.

    If you have a display adapter that offers higher resolution than VGA, don't bother changing the display driver at this stage. You'll have an opportunity later to configure the display adapter. Accept the default setting of Auto Detect for the display type. This will allow Setup to determine your display type automatically later on.

    If you're outside the United States, you'll likely want to change your keyboard layout to an appropriate setting that matches your particular keyboard.

Upgrading Windows 3.x to Windows NT Server

11. If Setup lists your hard disks and partitions, go to step 12. Otherwise, go to step 11a.

WINDOWS 95 AND NT

If you have Windows 95 on your computer, choose to install a fresh copy of NT 4.0 in a separate directory. That way, you'll be able to dual-boot between Windows 95 and Windows NT Server 4.0. None of your Windows 95 application information will be brought forward into your Windows NT Server installation. Go to step 11b to install a fresh copy of NT in a separate directory.

11a. If you have Windows 3.x on your computer, Setup asks if you want to upgrade it to Windows NT. If Windows 95 is installed on this computer, go to step 11b. If you don't want to upgrade a Windows 3.x installation, go to step 11b. If you want to upgrade a Windows 3.x installation, go to step 11c.

If you have Windows 95 installed on your computer, Setup will detect it only if you installed it in your Windows 3.x directory.

11b. If you want to install a fresh copy of NT 4.0, separate from other Windows products on your computer, press *N*. Then go to step 12.

Doing this will allow you to dual-boot between DOS/Windows and Windows NT. It won't migrate any settings or applications from your Windows 3.x installation to NT, however.

11c. If you want to install 4.0 as an upgrade to Windows 3.x, press ENTER. Then go to step 15.

This will migrate settings and applications from Windows 3.x to the NT 4.0 installation. You'll still be able to dual-boot between DOS/Windows and Windows NT 4.0.

See Chapter 7 for a discussion of what to expect when upgrading from Windows 3.x.

Managing Disk Partitions

Use extreme caution when navigating through this next portion of Setup. You can easily create, destroy, and reformat entire disk partitions with a couple of keystrokes. Keep in mind that you're running a cousin of the powerful and potentially destructive DOS FDISK utility.

12. Setup lists hard disks, partitions, and unpartitioned areas on your computer. It then asks you where to install NT 4.0. Use the UP and DOWN ARROW keys to scroll through the list and highlight a partition. Go to step 12a.

    You'll need to find a destination partition with at least 115MB of free space on which to install Windows NT Server.

    In the list, all non-SCSI drives are displayed as "IDE/ESDI Disk." A SCSI drive is displayed as "Disk # at id # on bus # on" followed by the name of the SCSI adapter driver. The ID number is the SCSI ID assigned to the drive.

    Areas of your disks that contain no partition are displayed as "Unpartitioned space." Partitions that have been created but not yet formatted are displayed as "New (Unformatted)" or as "Unformatted or Damaged." Don't worry about the latter. This is just NT's generic way of saying that it doesn't recognize a partition as formatted.

If you're installing Windows NT Server on a computer that contains a previous version of Windows NT and you were using disk stripes, mirrors, or volume sets, these partitions are shown as "Windows NT Fault Tolerance" partitions. Don't delete any of these partitions. See the section entitled "Migrating Fault Tolerance from Windows NT 3.x" in Chapter 19 for details on using existing fault-tolerance partitions.

If you don't see all of your partitions listed, you may just need to use the UP and DOWN ARROW keys to scroll and display them. Only hard disks are included in this list.

Don't panic if the drive letter assignments seem out of whack. They probably don't match the drive letters that you see under DOS or even under another version of NT. Once you've got NT up and running, you'll be able to change drive letter assignments very easily.

12a. If you're ready to select a partition on which NT 4.0 will be installed, highlight that partition, press ENTER, and go to step 13. If you're not, go to step 12b to delete an existing partition or step 12c to create a new partition.

You can select an unformatted partition or an existing formatted FAT or NTFS partition. Unpartitioned space isn't a valid destination for NT installation. You need to partition it first, in step 12c.

If the partition that you select isn't large enough, Setup will complain and send you back to step 12.

12b. If you need to delete an existing partition, highlight it and press *D*. CAREFUL! This will destroy all existing data on the partition. Setup will ask you to confirm your choice. Press *L* to confirm, and go back to step 12a.

If you change your mind before pressing *L*, press ESC to return to step 12. Be careful, though. When you get back to step 12, you'll be pointing at the C partition.

Setup won't let you delete the C partition. NT needs to install boot information there, even if you select a different destination partition for NT.

12c. If you need to create a partition from unpartitioned space, highlight the unpartitioned space and press *C*. Setup will display a valid range of sizes for the partition. Type the partition size that you want, press ENTER, and go back to step 12a.

If you change your mind before pressing ENTER, press ESC to return to step 12. Be careful, though. When you get back to step 12, you'll be pointing at the C partition.

Formatting the Destination Partition

13. Setup asks how you want the destination partition formatted. Use the UP and DOWN ARROW keys to highlight your choice.

 13a. If you selected an existing formatted partition and you want to preserve its current contents, highlight the Leave the current file system intact (no changes) option, press ENTER, and go to step 14.

 13b. If you selected an existing FAT partition and you want to convert it to NTFS, highlight the Convert the partition to NTFS option, press ENTER, and go to step 14.

 When NT Server boots for the first time after you've completed installation, NT will convert the FAT partition to NTFS. The contents of the original partition will be preserved.

 13c. If you selected an existing formatted partition and you want to completely reformat it before installing NT, highlight either FAT or NTFS. CAREFUL! This will destroy all existing data on the partition. Press ENTER and go to step 13e.

 13d. If you selected an unformatted partition, highlight either FAT or NTFS, and press ENTER.

 If you select FAT now, you can always convert it to NTFS later without losing any data.

 13e. Setup formats the destination partition using the file system that you selected.

 Setup initially formats NTFS partitions as FAT. When NT Server boots for the first time after you've completed installation, NT will convert the FAT partition to NTFS.

Specifying the Destination Directory

14. Setup asks for the destination directory in which to install Windows NT Server.

 Setup will create the destination directory that you specify. The directory will be created on the partition that you selected in step 12a.

 14a. The default directory is \WINNT. To accept this default, press ENTER, and go to step 15.

 14b. To change the destination directory name, use BACKSPACE to erase the existing name and type the destination directory name that you want. Then press ENTER.

 Even if you're installing to an NTFS partition, the directory name must follow the 8.3 DOS file-naming format. You can't use a long name or special characters in this directory name. If you do, Setup will complain and ask you to try again.

If you elected to install NT 4.0 into a fresh directory, don't type the directory name of an existing NT or Windows installation here. Setup will warn you that you could overwrite an existing installation that you meant to preserve.

Copying Files from CD-ROM

If you didn't insert your Windows NT Server 4.0 CD-ROM in step 1 or you inserted it in the wrong CD-ROM drive, Setup asks you for it now. See step 1 for details.

15. Setup asks if it should perform an exhaustive scan of your hard disks for errors. To begin the scan, press ENTER. When the scan is complete, Setup proceeds to step 16.

    Setup scans your C partition and whatever partition that you selected for NT installation. It doesn't scan the other partitions on your computer, since they won't be used by Setup.

    If you have large disks, this process can take several minutes to complete. If you're really pressed for time, you can skip the scan by pressing ESC. However, I strongly recommend performing the scan. It will save you from having to reinstall later if critical files aren't copied correctly because of bad spots on your hard disk.

    Setup is sometimes unable to scan your hard disks because of low memory or other problems. When this happens, it typically gives you a friendly warning. Unless it specifically says that you have errors on your disk, it's safe to proceed with installation.

If you're installing NT on an existing NTFS partition, you may notice that the scan takes a very short time relative to scanning FAT partitions. Don't worry. This is normal behavior.

16. Setup copies files from the NT CD-ROM to your hard disk. When it's done, proceed to step 17.

    This process can take several minutes. You can track its progress by watching the gas gauge.

    If Setup complains about not being able to copy a file, note the filename and the error message. Skip copying individual files at your own risk. If you do, you'll have a partial operating system that may not behave correctly. Seek your technical support resources to troubleshoot the problem.

17. Setup asks you to press ENTER to restart the computer. Remove the floppy disk from drive A. Remove the Windows NT Server 4.0 CD-ROM from your computer, if it's currently installed in a CD-ROM drive. Then press ENTER.

    Leaving the CD-ROM in the drive can cause booting problems on some computers that attempt to boot from CD-ROM.

    This concludes the text-mode phase of installation. Setup will now restart the system in NT's graphical mode. This will automatically launch you into the next phase of the installation process.

During the boot process, you'll see several messages about checking hardware, pressing SPACE for the Hardware Profile or Last Known Good configuration, choosing number of processors, selecting memory size, initializing, copying files, and so on. Don't worry about these messages. Proceed to step 18 and wait for the Setup Wizard window.

Entering Identification Information

18. Setup displays a graphical Setup Wizard window that outlines the remaining installation steps, as shown in Figure 9-1. Click Next to continue.

    Now that you're running Windows NT in graphical mode, you can use both the mouse and the keyboard. In most subsequent screens, you'll be able to navigate between Setup screens by clicking Back or Next.

    If you're installing a fresh copy of NT Server, Setup runs in VGA mode. If you're upgrading from a previous NT installation that used a higher display resolution, Setup uses that resolution. You'll have an opportunity later to change the display to another resolution.

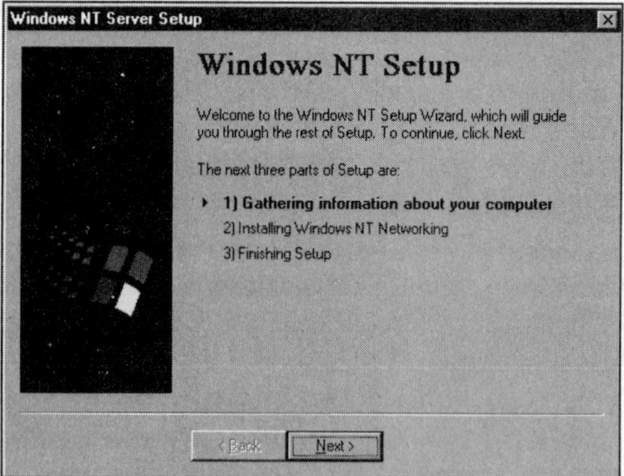

Figure 9-1: The Setup Wizard guides you through the remainder of the NT Server installation process.

19. If you're installing a fresh copy of NT Server, Setup asks for your name and organization, as shown in Figure 9-2. Type your name, press TAB, and optionally type your organization name. Then click Next.

Depending on how you obtained your copy of Windows NT Server 4.0, Setup may ask you to enter a product identification number or a 10-digit CD Key. If you have a product identification number, it's printed inside the back cover of the *Windows NT Server 4.0 Start Here* manual and on your NT registration card. If you have a CD Key, it's typically printed on a sticker on your NT CD-ROM cover. Keep this number handy, since Microsoft product support staff might ask for it if you ever have to call them.

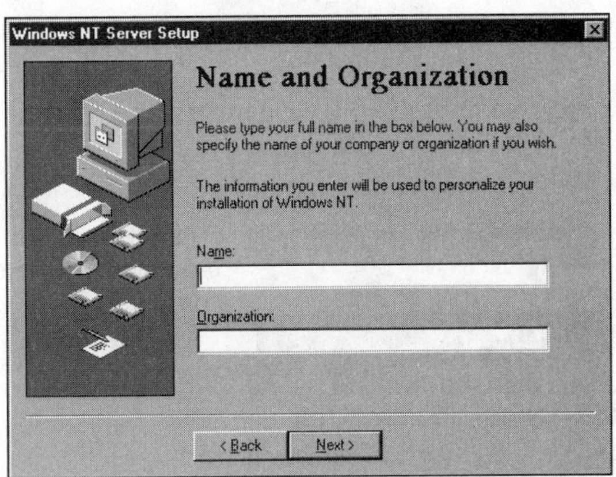

Figure 9-2: Setup asks you to enter your name and organization.

If you're upgrading from a previous version of NT Server, Setup doesn't ask for your name or organization, but it may ask for your product identification number or CD Key. After specifying it, go to step 24.

20. Setup asks you to indicate which licensing mode that you've chosen. Click Per Server or Per Seat, depending on the licensing mode that you want. If you selected Per Server, type the maximum number of concurrent network connections to this server. Figure 9-3 illustrates this. Click Next.

Per Server licensing requires a separate client access license for each concurrent connection to the server. Per Seat licensing requires a separate client license for each client node attached to the network. See Chapter 7 for a more detailed description of your NT Server licensing options.

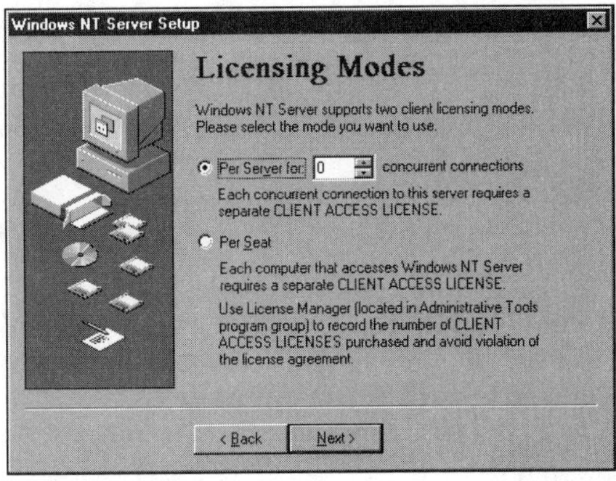

Figure 9-3: Setup asks you to choose between Per Server and Per Seat licensing modes.

21. Setup asks for the unique name that you want to assign to this computer, as shown in Figure 9-4. Type the computer name and click Next.

    The computer name must be unique on your network and must be no longer than 15 characters. Never include spaces in the computer name.

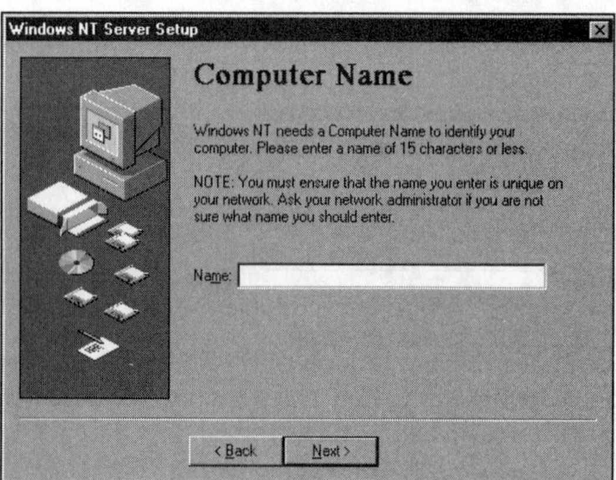

Figure 9-4: You must enter the unique name of this computer.

22. As shown in Figure 9-5, Setup asks you to select the type of server that you want to install: Primary Domain Controller, Backup Domain Controller, or Stand-Alone Server. Click the appropriate choice for this server. Then click Next.

    Each domain on your network can have only one PDC and one or more BDCs. The default selection is PDC. If this is the first Windows NT server in your domain, make it a PDC.

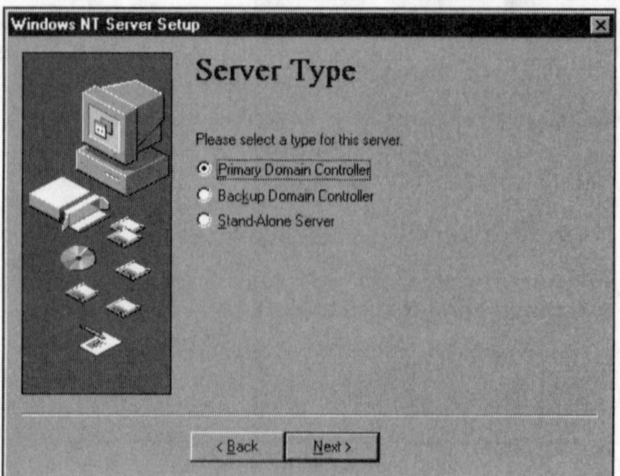

Figure 9-5: You select the role that you want this server to play: PDC, BDC, or stand-alone.

23. Setup asks for the password that you want to assign to the administrator account. Type the password that you want to assign, press TAB, and type the same password to confirm, as illustrated by Figure 9-6. Then click Next.

The administrator password must be 14 characters or less. Always assign an administrator password.

If you don't set an administrator password, you'll leave yourself open to unauthorized tampering. Unless you assign a password, anyone can log on as administration and delete or damage the files on your server. Always set an administrator password. Unlike previous NT versions, NT 4.0 won't warn you if you leave this password blank.

You must remember this password. If you forget it, you'll have to reinstall the operating system. Write down the password and lock it away in a safe place.

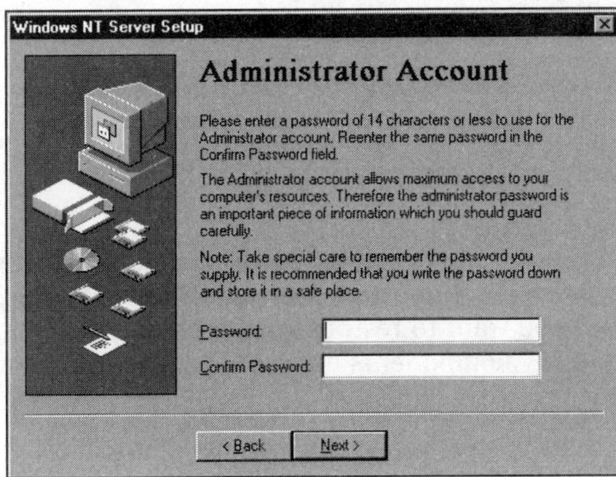

Figure 9-6: You should always specify and confirm the password for the administrator account.

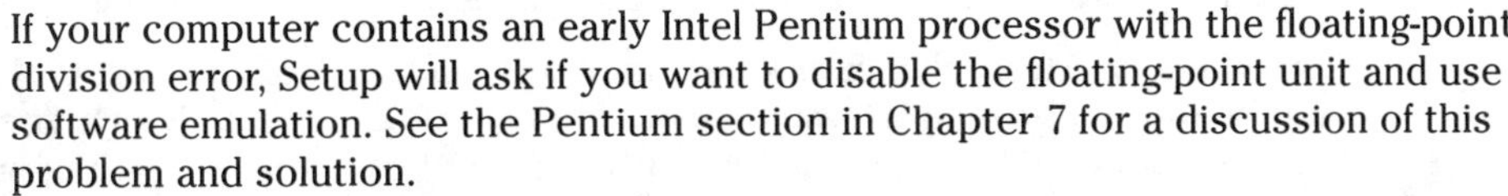

If your computer contains an early Intel Pentium processor with the floating-point division error, Setup will ask if you want to disable the floating-point unit and use software emulation. See the Pentium section in Chapter 7 for a discussion of this problem and solution.

24. Setup asks if you want to create an Emergency Repair disk, as illustrated in Figure 9-7. Click Yes, and then click Next.

    Always elect to create an Emergency Repair disk. In a later step, you'll actually create the disk. You'll use this disk to restore the system if your operating system files are ever damaged.

An Emergency Repair disk isn't interchangeable between computers. The repair disk contains very specific information about where you installed the operating system, the contents of your NT registry, details about device and disk partition configuration, the computer name, and so forth. You can't use a repair disk from one computer to recover another one. So, be sure to create a separate repair disk for each Windows NT installation that you perform.

If you're upgrading a previous version of NT Server, Setup informs you that it's about to upgrade network services. Click Next. It then informs you that it's about to upgrade network components. Again click Next. Then go to step 37.

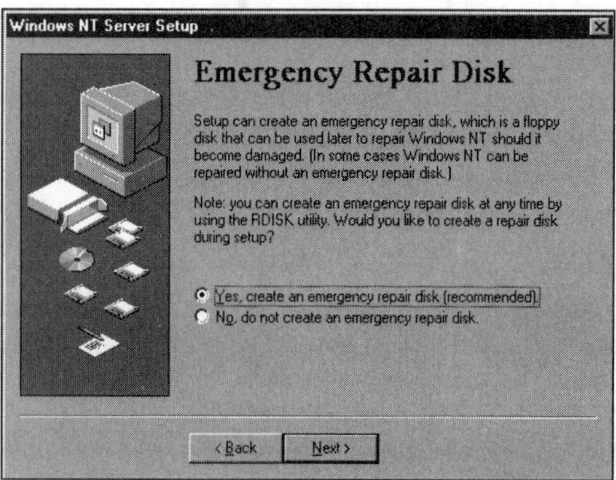

Figure 9-7: You should always choose to create an Emergency Repair floppy disk.

25. Setup asks you to select optional components to install. Review the optional components and select those that you want to install by clicking the appropriate check boxes, and then click Next.

    You'll see the Select Components dialog box. If you want to pick and choose from the available optional components, click Details to see a breakdown of each one. Click Reset if you want to restore your selections back to the defaults. If you exclude any components now, you can always install them later, if you need them.

    Some optional items take up disk space that you may not need or want to consume on a server. Accessories, games, animated mouse cursors, multimedia sound schemes, and wallpapers are good candidates for exclusion to save disk clutter. (OK, you can install the games. Just don't play them.)

The Windows Messaging component includes Internet Mail, Microsoft Mail, and Windows Messaging (essentially the Microsoft Exchange client). These mail components together consume about 6MB of disk space. If you're not going to use your server to send and receive e-mail, consider excluding these components. I'll discuss them in Chapter 16.

Configuring the Network

26. Setup displays a message indicating that it's about to install NT networking. Click Next.

    At this point, you can still click Back all the way back to step 18, if you want to make changes to any of your prior selections in the graphical phase of Setup.

27. Setup asks if this server is directly connected to your LAN or will dial into your network via RAS. Click to select the Wired to the network check box.

    Figure 9-8 illustrates the dialog box if you're installing a primary domain controller (PDC) or backup domain controller (BDC). Having a Windows NT Server PDC or BDC as a remote node connecting to your network via RAS is an unusual situation. Note that your selection here doesn't affect your server's ability to act as a RAS server to remote node clients.

If you elected to install Windows NT Server as a stand-alone server in step 22, you're given the option of installing network components during Setup, as shown in Figure 9-9. If you don't want to install network components, click to select the Do not connect this computer to a network at this time option, click Next, and go to step 37. If you want to install the network, click to select the This computer will participate on a network option and go to step 28. If you don't install networking components during Setup, you'll be able to install them later.

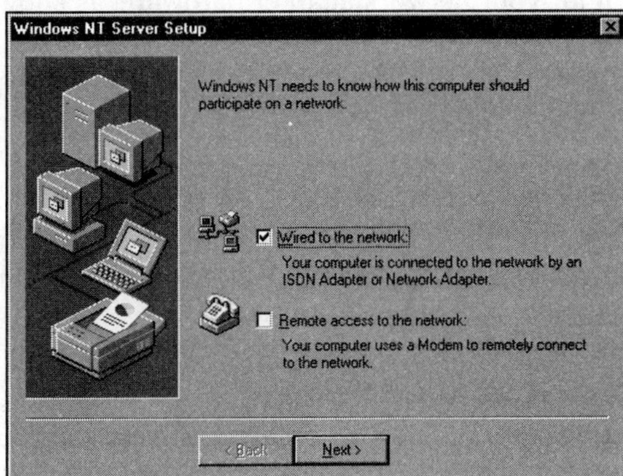

Figure 9-8: You can select between having your computer wired to the network or remotely connected when installing a PDC or BDC.

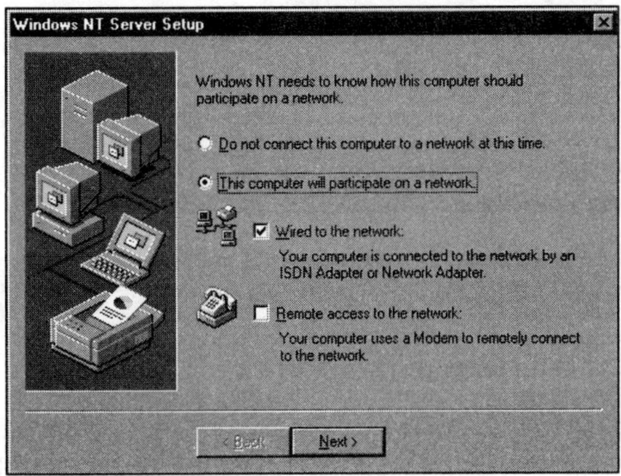

Figure 9-9: You can optionally skip network installation when installing a stand-alone server.

28. Click Next. Setup asks if you want to install the Internet Information Server. Click to clear the Install Microsoft Internet Information Server check box and click Next.

Although you're given the opportunity to install the Internet Information Server during NT installation, I recommend that you install it after you've got the operating system up and running.

In Part V, you'll learn how to set up your Windows NT Server computer as a Web server on the Internet. Chapter 22 covers the Microsoft Internet Information Server in detail.

If you elect to install the Internet Information Server during Windows NT Server installation, Setup will require that you also install the TCP/IP protocol in step 30. See Chapter 11 for details on installing and configuring TCP/IP.

29. Setup offers to search for your network adapter hardware, as shown in Figure 9-10. Click Start Search to begin the search.

    In previous versions of NT, Setup warned you that its network hardware probing at this step might hang your computer. It no longer warns you about this, but depending on your hardware configuration, there's still a remote possibility of this happening.

    If your system does hang at this point, restart your computer and begin again from step 18. When you reach step 29 again, opt to enter your adapter information manually by clicking Select from list.

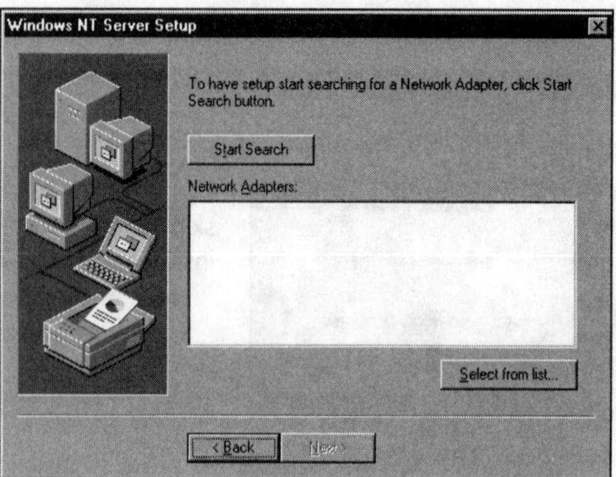

Figure 9-10: To begin the search for installed network adapters, click Start Search.

29a. If Setup finds a network adapter, it displays the first adapter that it detects, as shown in Figure 9-11. If Setup's list of network adapters is complete, click Next and go to step 30. Otherwise, go to step 29b.

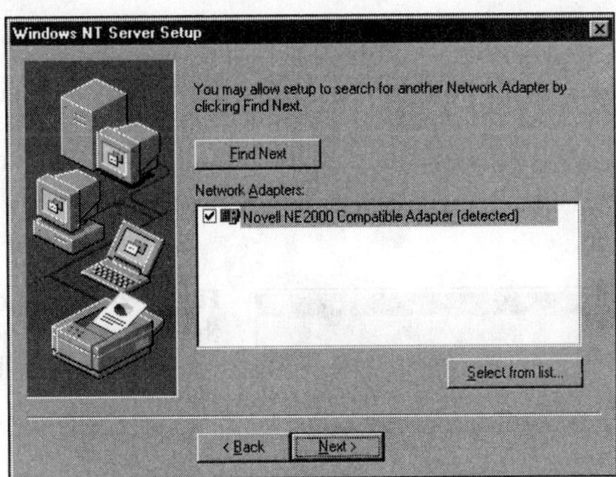

Figure 9-11: Setup lists the first network adapter that it finds and gives you the option of continuing the search.

29b. If you have additional network adapters in the computer, click Find Next to continue the search. See Figure 9-11.

If you have multiple network adapters in your computer, Windows NT Server will use any or all of them, depending on how you configure your system. You'll be able to bind specific protocols to specific network adapters selectively. Network binding is covered in Chapter 8.

29c. If you have a network adapter in the system that Setup doesn't detect and you have a driver disk provided by the adapter manufacturer, click Select from list. Then click the Have Disk button, insert the driver disk in drive A, and follow the instructions on the screen.

Some network adapters are supported by drivers in the Windows Driver Library. See Chapter 8 for details on how to create a driver disk for your adapter.

30. Setup asks you to select which protocols you want to install: TCP/IP, IPX/SPX, or NetBEUI. Click to select or clear desired protocol check boxes and click Next. See Figure 9-12.

By default, both TCP/IP and IPX/SPX are selected. You'll be able to add or delete protocols easily after you've installed the operating system. You can install any combination of these three protocols.

NetBEUI and IPX/SPX require no further configuration during installation. TCP/IP will ask for lots of additional information. If you choose to install TCP/IP at this point, see Chapter 11 for details on the decisions on DHCP and IP addressing that you'll be asked during TCP/IP installation.

Unless TCP/IP is the only protocol on your network, I recommend installing it after installing Windows NT Server. Installing TCP/IP can be a bit complex, and you need to understand several TCP/IP concepts and options in detail. Once you have experience installing TCP, you can include it during future NT operating system installations.

If you're going to use the Network Client Administrator to install network software on your DOS or Windows 3.x client computers over the network, as described in Chapter 13, install NetBEUI on your server now. The installation disk for DOS client software supports only the NetBEUI protocol. See Chapter 13 for more details on installing network clients.

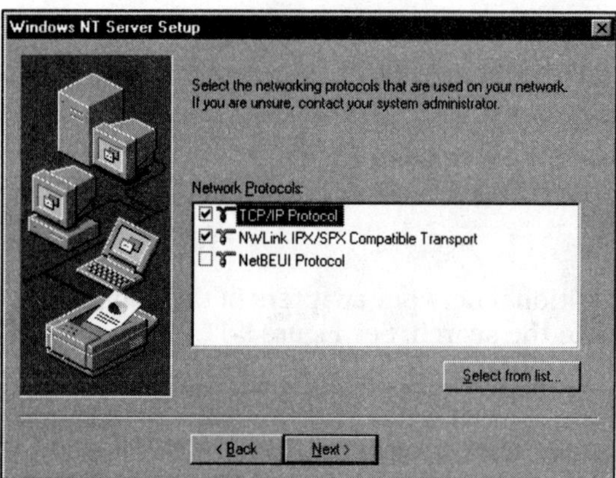

Figure 9-12: You can select the network protocols that you want to install.

31. Setup asks you to select which network services you want to install. Click Next.

    Doing this installs the workstation (that is, the redirector), server, NetBIOS interface, and RPC configuration services. These services, as shown in Figure 9-13, are required on Windows NT Server. If you want to select additional services, click the Select from list option.

    Unless you're sure that you want to install specific additional services, I recommend just clicking Next. You can always install additional services later, after the operating system is installed.

Of all the available additional services, I especially recommend that you don't install RAS at this time, especially if this is your first Windows NT Server installation. You're better off installing RAS after installing Windows NT Server, since it can be a bit complex and you need to understand the various RAS concepts and options in detail.

In Chapter 11, I'll show you the detailed steps to install RAS. Once you have background and experience installing RAS, you can include it during future NT operating system installations.

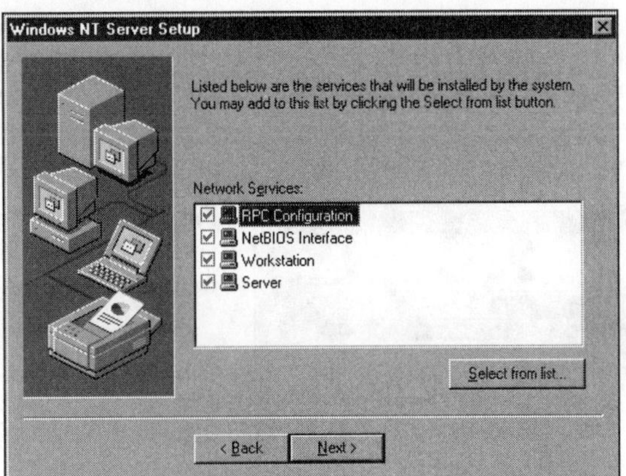

Figure 9-13: Setup enables you to view and specify additional network services.

32. Setup informs you that it's about to install network components. Click Next.

    At this point, you can still click Back to go all the way back to step 27, if you want to make changes to any of the network settings that you've specified thus far.

33. If your network adapter requires configuration, Setup asks you for adapter configuration information. When you've specified it, click OK. This step will be repeated for each network adapter that you're installing.

    The type of information required varies with each network adapter. Typically, you'll need to specify at least the adapter's IRQ and I/O port address. A simple example is shown in Figure 9-14. See Chapter 8 for details on configuring your network adapters and refer to Worksheet 7-3 for the information that you need to type here.

    Setup may display a warning dialog box indicating that it can't verify your network adapter settings. This is normal for some adapters. If you see this message, double-check that your entries are correct and click OK. If you want to change your network adapter settings, click Cancel and retype them.

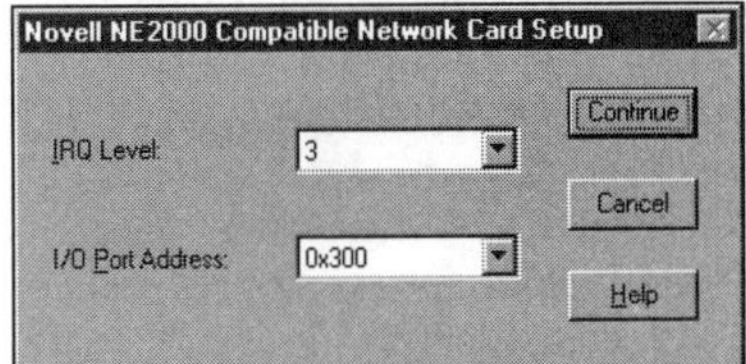

Figure 9-14: Network adapter configuration typically requires the IRQ and I/O address settings.

34. Setup allows you to review and change network bindings, as shown in Figure 9-15. Click Next.

Unless you're sure that you want to make specific changes to network bindings, click Next. You'll be able to make changes to bindings later, after you've installed the operating system. Chapter 8 covers when and how to change network bindings.

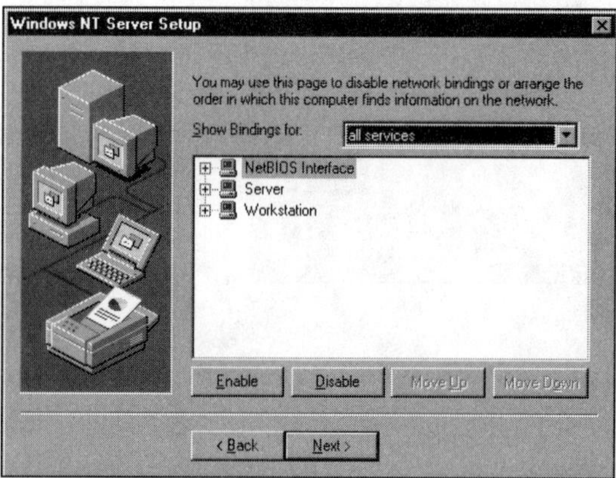

Figure 9-15: Setup allows you to review and alter network bindings.

35. Setup informs you that it's about to start the network. Click Next.
36. Setup asks for the name of the domain or workgroup in which this server will participate. Type the appropriate name and click Next.

    If you specified a PDC or BDC in step 22, you'll be asked for the domain name. In this case, press TAB, type the domain name, and click Next. Figure 9-16 illustrates this.

The default domain name is "DOMAIN." Be sure to change it to the name that you've chosen for your domain. Setup won't warn you if you just accept the default domain name. Once other computers have joined the domain, it's very difficult to change the domain name. Set it correctly now to avoid headaches later.

The domain name must be 15 characters or less. Setup displays the computer name that you entered earlier, but you can't change it on this screen.

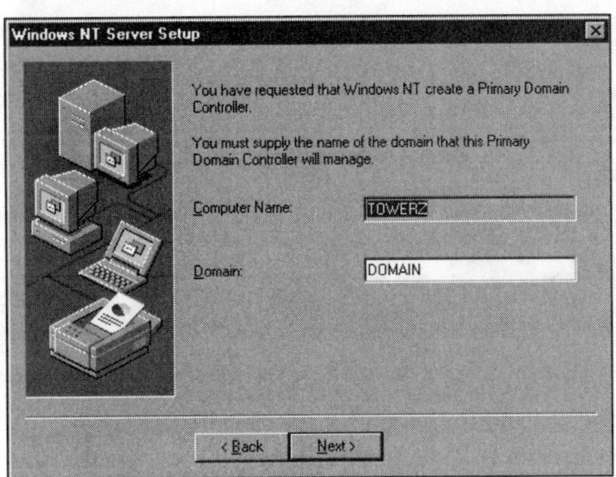

Figure 9-16: Enter the domain name when installing a PDC or BDC.

Figure 9-17 presents the dialog box that is displayed if you're installing a stand-alone server. You're asked for either a workgroup or domain name in which this server will participate. In this case, press TAB to reach the appropriate field and type the workgroup or domain name.

If you're specifying a domain, click the Create a Computer Account in the Domain option and click Next. Setup will ask for the user name and password that can create a computer account in the domain, as shown in Figure 9-18. Type them and click OK.

You can use the domain administrator account, if you know the password. However, I recommend creating a special domain account (with a password) for users to type when they're installing NT and adding computer accounts to the domain.

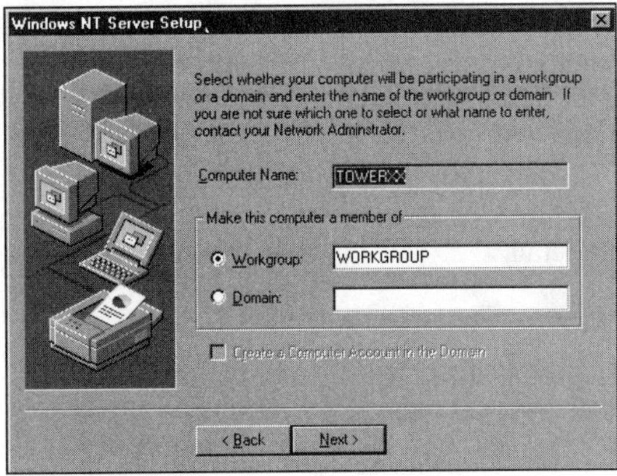

Figure 9-17: You should specify a workgroup or domain name when installing a stand-alone server.

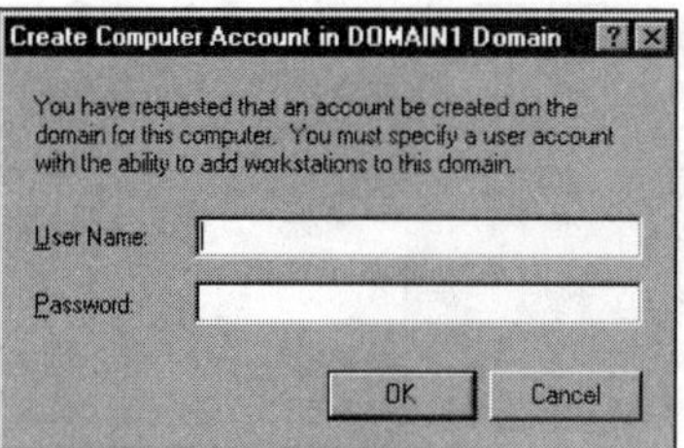
Create Computer Account in DOMAIN1 Domain

You have requested that an account be created on the domain for this computer. You must specify a user account with the ability to add workstations to this domain.

User Name:

Password:

OK Cancel

Figure 9-18: You specify the user name and password of a user account that has rights to create a computer account in the domain.

Once you click Next, it may take a minute or so before the next step begins.

If you're installing a BDC or stand-alone server and the PDC of the domain that you're trying to join is not available, Setup will display an error message. If you're installing a stand-alone server, you can opt to join a workgroup temporarily and continue with Setup. The server can join the domain later. If you're installing a BDC, you need to make the PDC available on the network to complete the BDC installation process.

Completing the Installation

37. Setup tells you that it's about to finish the installation process, as shown in Figure 9-19. Click Finish.

    If you're installing a fresh copy of NT Server, Setup lies. There are still several more steps to go. Once you click Next, you'll see lots of disk activity and status messages for a couple of minutes. At this stage, you've reached the point of no return. You can't click Back to change previous selections.

    If you're upgrading a previous version of NT Server, Setup asks if you want to install the Internet Information Server. Click to clear the Install Microsoft Internet Information Server check box and click OK. Then go to to step 43.

    Although you're given the opportunity to install the Internet Information Server during NT installation, I recommend that you install it after you've got the operating system up and running.

In Part V, you'll learn how to set up your Windows NT Server computer as a Web server on the Internet. Chapter 22 covers the Microsoft Internet Information Server in detail.

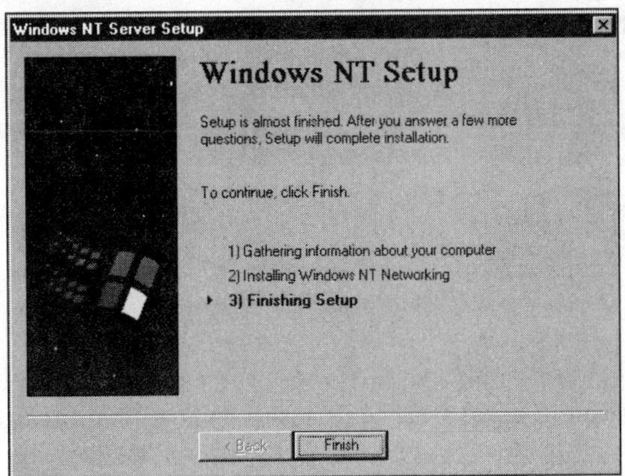

Figure 9-19: Setup teases you by claiming that it's finishing up the installation process.

38. Setup allows you to set the correct time zone for your area. In the time zone list, select your time zone and click Close, as shown in Figure 9-20.

    The actual date and time settings should be set correctly, since Setup reads this information from your computer's internal clock. If you want to verify it, click the Date & Time tab to see the date and time settings.

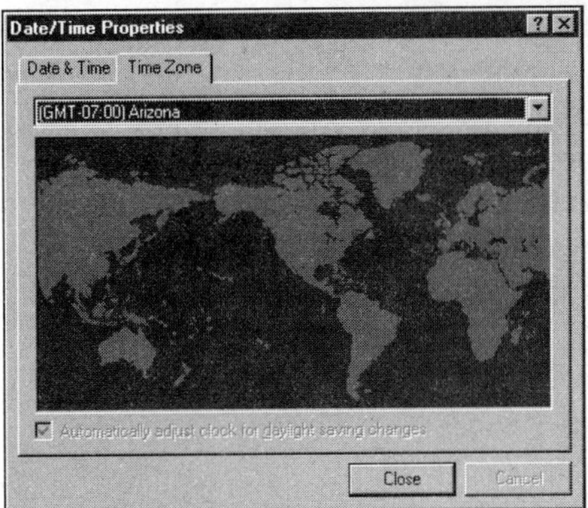

Figure 9-20: Select the time zone that matches your geographical location.

39. As shown in Figure 9-21, Setup detects your video hardware and selects a driver for your video display adapter. Click OK.

    Setup sometimes selects a generic video driver that handles the video chip set that your adapter uses. For example, Setup will select the S3 driver for almost all of the many video adapters that use the S3 chip set.

    Your video adapter documentation should indicate the chip set that your adapter uses. The Windows NT Hardware Compatibility List includes a list of NT-compatible video chip sets. Video adapters based on these chip sets are expected to work with Windows NT using the appropriate generic driver.

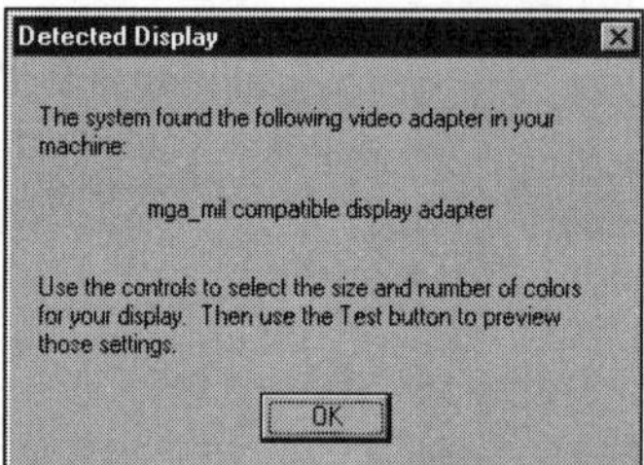

Figure 9-21: Setup detects your display adapter and selects a device driver – in this case, a Matrox Millennium adapter.

40. Setup shows your current video display settings, as shown in Figure 9-22. If you want to change them, go to step 40a. Otherwise, proceed to step 42.

    You can alter the settings and test your changes before committing to them.

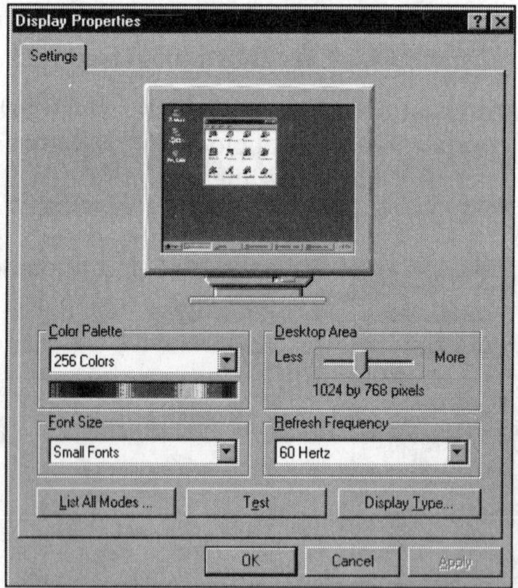

Figure 9-22: Setup gives you the opportunity to change and test your display adapter configuration.

40a. If you want to change the number of colors displayed, select the desired number of colors in the Color Palette box.

40b. If you want to change the display resolution, move the Desktop Area slider to the appropriate position.

The default position is 640x480, which is VGA resolution. Figure 9-22 shows the slider at 1024x768.

40c. If you prefer large fonts instead of small fonts, click Large Fonts in the Font Size box.

41. Test your new video settings by clicking Test.

41a. In the Testing Mode dialog box, click OK to see a five-second video test pattern.

The test pattern is self-explanatory, and varies depending on your video display settings. Make sure that the pattern displays what it says it's displaying.

41b. Setup asks if the pattern appeared correctly. If it did, click Yes and go to step 42. If not, click No, click OK, and go back to step 40.

If the pattern appeared incorrectly, check your video adapter and monitor documentation, go back to step 40, and try different video settings.

42. In the Display Settings dialog box, click OK. Then, in the Display Properties dialog box, click OK.

At this point, Setup displays configuration and file copying status messages. The file copy process may take several minutes.

43. Setup asks you for a blank floppy disk to be used as the Emergency Repair disk. Insert a disk in drive A and click OK.

The floppy disk should be 1.44MB; however, it doesn't have to be blank because Setup formats it for you. Make sure there's no important data on the disk, though, since it will all be erased.

Setup sometimes has trouble dealing with 2.88MB floppy disks. Even if you have a 2.88MB floppy disk drive, supply a blank Emergency Repair disk that's been formatted for 1.44MB, and you'll save potential headaches.

Don't skip this step. Always create an Emergency Repair disk. You need one for each Windows NT installation that you perform. Remember, the repair disks aren't interchangeable between different computers or between different installations on the same computer.

Setup formats the floppy disk and copies configuration files to it.

44. Setup tells you it's complete. Remove the Emergency Repair disk from drive A, remove the NT Server CD-ROM from the CD-ROM drive, and click Restart Computer.

This time, Setup doesn't lie. You're actually finished with the Windows NT Server 4.0 installation — you lucky devil.

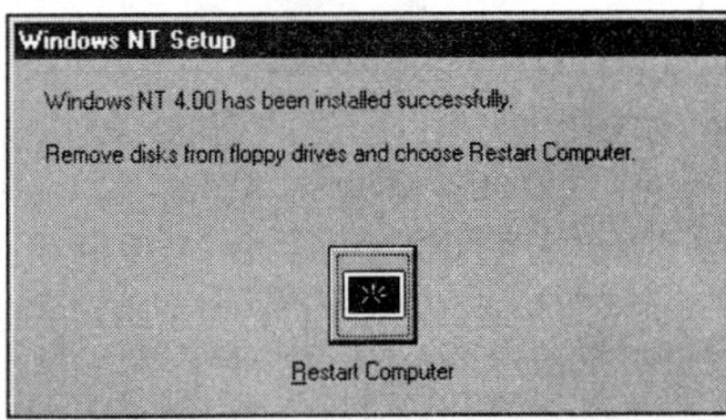

Figure 9-23: Good job! You've successfully installed Windows NT Server.

When you restart the computer, Windows NT Server will boot and run. See Chapter 14 for details on how to log on to the computer and get the most out of the new user interface.

Steps to Install over the Network

In this section, I'll show you how to install Windows NT Server 4.0 over the network. Using this approach, you don't need a local CD-ROM drive on the computer that you're setting up. You'll pull all of the required NT files over the network from a network server. This approach to installation requires some preparation. You'll need to have a network up and running before you begin.

The network that you have running need not be a Microsoft network, nor do you need any Windows NT Server computers to use this installation approach. For example, if you have an operational NetWare network, you can perform the network installation of Windows NT Server using the steps outlined in this section. Likewise, if you have a LANtastic or VINES network, you can use this procedure.

Since the computers on your existing network could be running any network operating system, I can't tell you specifically how to perform each action. For example, the action of a client logging on to a server to gain access to resources differs from one network operating system to the next. I'll outline the actions that you'll need to complete, and you'll then need to fill in the details of what to press, click, or type to accomplish those actions.

If you're planning to install Windows NT Server 4.0 over the network onto RISC-based computers, those computers must already be running a version of Windows NT. If they're not, you'll need to use the procedure outlined in "Steps to Install from CD-ROM on RISC."

Gathering Your Materials

You'll need the following materials close at hand before you begin installation over the network:

- ✦ The installation worksheet (Worksheet 7-3) that you completed in Chapter 7
- ✦ The Windows NT Server 4.0 CD-ROM
- ✦ One 1.44MB blank floppy disk for each computer on which you intend to install Windows NT Server. Label these disks "Emergency Repair."
- ✦ Three blank, formatted 1.44MB floppy disks. Label these disks "Setup Boot Disk," "Setup Disk 2," and "Setup Disk 3." You'll need one set of disks for each computer on which you intend to install Windows NT Server.

Be sure that the three blank disks are free of any viruses. This procedure won't reformat them, and you'll be booting the computer from one of these disks.

Preparing the Master File Server

Select an existing server on your network. You'll prepare this server to provide network access to the NT master files. I'll call this server the *master file server.* Other computers on your network will be able to install NT by accessing the master file server over the network.

I'll call the computers on which you want to install Windows NT Server 4.0 the *target computers.* You'll have other computers on your network as well, running as clients. These aren't target computers. Only the computers that need Windows NT Server 4.0 on them are target computers, including PDCs, BDCs, and perhaps stand-alone servers.

The master file server must have access to a CD-ROM drive, either locally or via the existing network. You'll need read and write access to the master file server, in order to write the NT files on its hard disk. Each target computer requires read access to the directories that you create on the master file server, to allow copying the NT files over the network.

On the master file server, you'll need enough free disk space to hold the master files that you copy from the NT CD-ROM. Here's a breakdown of the server master file disk space that you'll need for each NT platform you plan to install:

- Intel x86 master files require 45MB of disk space on the master file server.
- MIPS master files require 56MB of disk space.
- Alpha master files require 57MB of disk space.
- PowerPC master files require 52MB of disk space.

You only need the master files required by the target computers on which you plan to install NT. If you have all Intel x86-based target computers, you'll just need to copy the x86 master files to your master file server. However, if you have a mix of Alpha-based computers and x86 computers, you'll need both the x86 and Alpha master files on the master file server.

Don't be misled by the relatively small amount of disk space required for each platform. These files are compressed. They'll expand during actual NT installation on the target computers. Leaving them compressed for now saves disk space on your master file server and will make installation over the network a bit quicker.

If you're not sure what processors are in your target computers, you'll need to find out now, so that you can determine which sets of master files to copy to your master file server. Of course, computers running DOS, Windows 3.x, Windows for Workgroups, or Windows 95 are definitely Intel x86-based. If you're not sure of the processor that a target computer is using, check your hardware documentation.

If the target computer is already running a version of Windows NT, you can find out what processor it's using by peeking into its NT registry database. To do this, perform the following steps:

1. Run REGEDT32.

   You can launch it via the Program Manager File Î Run option or from the NT command prompt.
2. Click the HKEY_LOCAL_MACHINE window.
3. In the left side of the window, double-click the HARDWARE icon to expand it.
4. Double-click, in turn, on the DESCRIPTION, System, and CentralProcessor icons.

   As you do this, each icon will expand to show the next icon below it.
5. Double-click the 0 icon under the CentralProcessor icon.
6. In the right half of the window, the last line should begin with Identifier:REG_SZ:. To the right of this, you should see the processor type.

   For example, on an Intel 486, you'll see something like 80486-D0.

I'll cover the NT registry in detail in Chapter 20.

Use the following procedure to copy the required master files from the NT CD-ROM to the master file server:

1. Create a directory called \NTSFILES on the master file server.

   You can call this directory anything you wish, as long as it's a fresh directory on your master file server computer. For the purposes of this procedure, I'll assume \NTSFILES is the name of the directory.
2. Create a subdirectory for each platform that you plan to install.

   To keep life simple, use the same subdirectory names that appear on the NT CD-ROM. If you plan to install all platforms, you'll end up with I386, MIPS, ALPHA, and PPC subdirectories under \NTSFILES.

The name of the I386 directory on the CD-ROM may be confusing, since the 386 is no longer supported by NT 4.0. Microsoft continues to use this directory name to identify Intel x86 files for historical reasons.

3. Copy the master files from the NT CD-ROM to the appropriate subdirectories under \NTSFILES on your master file server.

   For example, say you're running Windows for Workgroups on your master file server, and you need to copy only the x86 master files. Use File Manager to copy the \I386 directory on your CD-ROM to the \NTSFILES\I386 directory on your master file server.

Don't forget to include all subdirectories when you copy the files. Each of the four platform directories contains subdirectories that you'll need on the master file server. If you don't include them, you'll experience problems when you install NT.

4. Share the \NTSFILES directory on your network.

   For example, if the master file server is running Windows for Workgroups, you'd use File Manager to share the directory on the network.

Preparing the Target Computers

You'll install NT Server on each target computer by pulling the required files over the network from the master file server. A target computer can be based on an Intel x86, MIPS, Alpha, or PowerPC processor.

RISC-based target computers must already be running a version of Windows NT for this procedure to work. Otherwise, they must use the local CD-ROM installation procedure outlined in the section called "Steps to Install from CD-ROM on RISC."

Each target computer must be attached to your network and must be able to connect to and access the master file server \NTSFILES directory that you shared in the previous section. Each target computer needs a total of approximately 115MB of free disk space before installation begins. RISC-based target computers require 147MB of free space.

An Intel-based target computer must be running DOS, Windows 3.x, Windows for Workgroups, Windows 95, or Windows NT. Be sure that your network software is running on the target computer. In the following section, you'll execute either a 16-bit DOS utility or a Win32 utility that pulls the appropriate files over the network from the master file server.

Copying Master Files to the Target Computer

1. Go to the target computer's command prompt and log on to the master file server.

   Some network operating systems don't require this step. Just do whatever you need to do on the target computer to connect to resources on the master file server.

2. Connect local drive letter X on the target computer to the shared directory \NTSFILES on the master file server.

   For example, if the target computer is running DOS with the Microsoft network client, you'd run the NET USE command to connect to the shared resource.

   You can use whatever drive letter you choose. For this procedure, I'll assume you're using drive X.

3. Make drive X the current drive on the target computer.

If you're running DOS, for example, simply type **X:** at the command prompt and press ENTER.

4. Change to the appropriate platform subdirectory (I386, MIPS, ALPHA, or PPC) that matches the target computer.

   If you're running DOS, for example, type **CD \NTSFILES\I386** at the command prompt and press ENTER.

5. At this point, you'll execute a utility that pulls the NT Server files across the network and creates customized Setup floppy disks.

In this procedure, I've included creation of the three Setup floppy disks. I strongly recommend that you create them, use them for installation, and keep them in a safe place along with your Emergency Repair disk. If you have problems later with your NT installation, you may need all of these disks to repair the operating system.

Nonetheless, some NT administrators prefer to take the risk of not having these disks available. You can save time, effort, and disks by adding a /B option to the WINNT command in steps 5a and 5b. The /B option tells Setup to skip the creation and use of the floppy disks altogether. This approach will allow you to skip steps 7a through 10. Setup won't ask for any Setup floppies during the remainder of the installation process.

5a. If the target computer is running Windows 95 or Windows NT, type **WINNT32** and press ENTER.

5b. If the target computer is running DOS, Windows 3.x, or Windows for Workgroups, type **WINNT** and press ENTER.

From here on, I'll call this utility WINNT, regardless of whether you invoked WINNT32 or WINNT.

6. WINNT asks for the drive letter and path to the master NT files. Type the full path to the master file server platform subdirectory and select Continue.

   For example, if you're installing on an Intel x86 target computer, type **X:\NTSFILES\I386.**

7. WINNT copies files across the network from the master file server to the target computer.

WINNT won't clean up after itself, if you cancel the installation process before it's complete. It stores its temporary files in a directory named WIN_NT.~LS and leaves them there if you quit WINNT. If, for any reason, you need to cancel WINNT between step 7 and step 11, you can free the disk space consumed by these temporary files by deleting the WIN_NT.~LS directory.

Creating WINNT Floppy Disks

7a. While copying files from the server, WINNT asks you to insert the disk labeled "Setup Disk 3." Insert this disk in drive A and select OK.

WINNT needs to create three floppy disks that are designed specifically for this installation. You can't use the floppy disks that came in the Windows NT Server 4.0 package.

WINNT writes the contents of Setup Disk 3 to the floppy disk. The order in which WINNT requests these disks might be confusing. WINNT wants you to end up with the Setup Boot Disk in drive A by the time you reach step 10.

8. WINNT asks you to insert the disk labeled "Setup Disk 2." Remove Setup Disk 3 and insert the disk labeled "Setup Disk 2" in drive A. Select OK.

   WINNT writes the contents of Setup Disk 2 to the floppy.

9. WINNT asks you to insert the disk labeled "Setup Boot Disk." Remove Setup Disk 2 and insert the disk labeled "Setup Boot Disk" in drive A. Select OK.

   WINNT writes the contents of the Setup Boot Disk to the floppy. When it's complete, leave the Setup Boot Disk in drive A.

Getting Setup Running

10. WINNT asks you to restart the target computer. With the newly created Setup Boot Disk still in drive A, restart the computer by selecting Restart Computer.

11. Go to step 2 under "Steps to Install from CD-ROM on Intel, Getting Setup Running" to guide you through the remainder of the installation process.

In the remaining steps, use the floppy disks that you created in this procedure, not the disks that came in the Windows NT Server 4.0 package. The disks that you just created are the only ones that will work to complete the NT Server installation on this computer successfully.

Ignore any references to the NT CD-ROM in the remaining steps under "Steps to Install from CD-ROM on Intel." Your target computer already has copies of all of the required NT files on its local hard disk.

Do you need to install Windows NT Server 4.0 on several different target computers? Assuming your target computers are connected to the network and ready for installation, and assuming your master file server is reasonably fast, you can start the WINNT (or WINNT32) process on all of your target computers and have them pull the files from the server at the same time. If your master file server has a large cache, it'll go even faster.

Steps to Install from an Unsupported CD-ROM Drive

In this section, I'll show you how to install Windows NT Server 4.0 on a computer with a CD-ROM drive that's not supported by Windows NT. Although NT supports many CD-ROM drives available today, its support is limited for non-SCSI and non-IDE proprietary drives that attach to sound cards, for example. Some CDR (CD-Recordable) drives also won't work on NT today.

If you have an NT device driver floppy disk supplied by your CD-ROM manufacturer, you can use the instructions in "Steps to Install from CD-ROM on Intel." You can add your CD-ROM driver in steps 7b through 7d and use the CD-ROM drive to install NT as if the drive were supported.

The procedure outlined in this section will work only for Intel x86-based computers. If you want to install Windows NT Server 4.0 on a RISC-based computer, it must have an NT-compatible CD-ROM drive or have a previous version of NT installed on it to allow installation over the network. You'll need to use the procedures outlined in "Steps to Install from CD-ROM on RISC" or "Steps to Install over the Network" to install Windows NT Server on your RISC-based computer.

If you have a CD-ROM drive that you can access while running DOS, but it isn't supported by NT, this section describes how to install NT on your computer using the unsupported drive. Keep in mind that, because your CD-ROM drive isn't supported by NT, you won't be able to use this drive once NT is installed and running. Dual-booting back to DOS will be your only means of accessing this CD-ROM drive. If you don't configure the system to dual-boot, and you run only Windows NT Server on the computer, you won't have access to the CD-ROM drive after installing NT.

I view this installation method as a temporary measure to use while you wait for the NT-compatible CD-ROM drive that you've ordered to arrive. I strongly recommend adding a supported CD-ROM drive to your NT server. Since many NT applications and NT Server itself are delivered on CD-ROM, it's important to have a drive that you can access while NT is running.

In this situation, you can install Windows NT Server over the network, as described in the previous section. However, the method described here doesn't require that you have a network up and running, and you'll have significantly less preparation to do.

Gathering Your Materials

You'll need the following materials close at hand before you begin installation from a local unsupported CD-ROM drive:

✦ The installation worksheet (Worksheet 7-3) that you completed in Chapter 7

✦ The Windows NT Server 4.0 CD-ROM

✦ One 1.44MB blank floppy disk, labeled "Emergency Repair"

✦ Three blank, formatted 1.44MB floppy disks. Label these disks "Setup Boot Disk," "Setup Disk 2," and "Setup Disk 3."

Be sure that the three disks are free of any viruses. This procedure won't reformat them, and you'll be booting the computer from one of these disks.

You'll install NT Server on the computer by pulling the required files from the local CD-ROM drive (unsupported by NT) to your local hard disk. In this situation, your computer *must* have an Intel x86 processor and *must* be able to run DOS. Moreover, you need to have all of the appropriate drivers loaded to allow access to the CD-ROM drive.

You'll need a total of approximately 165MB of free disk space before installation begins. In the following section, you'll execute a 16-bit DOS utility that pulls the appropriate NT files from the local CD-ROM drive.

Copying the NT Files

1. Insert the Windows NT Server 4.0 CD-ROM into your CD-ROM drive.

   From here on, when I refer to the CD-ROM drive, I'm referring to the local CD-ROM drive that Windows NT doesn't support.

   If you have multiple CD-ROM drives, you can use any of them, as long as you can access the drive from DOS.

2. At the command prompt, make the CD-ROM drive the current drive. Type the drive letter of your CD-ROM drive followed by a colon (:) and press ENTER.

   On my computer, the CD-ROM drive is G:.

3. Change to the Intel x86 platform subdirectory by typing **CD \I386** and press ENTER.

In this procedure, I've included creation of the three Setup floppy disks. I strongly recommend that you create them, use them for installation, and keep them in a safe place along with your Emergency Repair disk. If you have problems later with your NT installation, you may need all of these disks to repair the operating system.

Nonetheless, some NT administrators prefer to take the risk of not having these disks available. You can save time, effort, and disks by adding a /B option to the WINNT command in step 4. The /B option tells Setup to skip the creation and use of the floppy disks altogether. This approach will allow you to skip steps 7 through 10. Setup won't ask for any Setup floppies during the remainder of the installation process.

4. At this point, you'll execute a utility that pulls the NT Server files from the CD-ROM and creates customized Setup floppy disks. Type **WINNT** and press ENTER.
5. WINNT asks for the drive letter and path to the master NT files. Type **G:\I386** and select Continue.
6. WINNT copies files from the CD-ROM to the hard disk.

WINNT won't clean up after itself if you cancel the installation process before it's complete. It stores its temporary files in a directory named WIN_NT.~LS and leaves them there if you quit WINNT. If, for any reason, you need to cancel WINNT between step 6 and step 11, you can free the disk space consumed by these temporary files by deleting the WIN_NT.~LS directory.

Creating WINNT Floppy Disks

7. WINNT asks you to insert the disk labeled "Setup Disk 3." Insert this disk in drive A and select OK.

   WINNT needs to create three floppy disks that are designed specifically for this installation. You can't use the floppy disks that came in the Windows NT Server 4.0 package.

   WINNT writes the contents of Setup Disk 3 to the floppy disk. The order in which WINNT requests these disks might be confusing. WINNT wants you to end up with the Setup Boot Disk in drive A by the time you reach step 10.
8. WINNT asks you to insert the disk labeled Setup Disk 2. Remove Setup Disk 3 and insert the disk labeled "Setup Disk 2" in drive A. Select OK.

   WINNT writes the contents of Setup Disk 2 to the floppy.
9. WINNT asks you to insert the disk labeled Setup Boot Disk. Remove Setup Disk 2 and insert the disk labeled "Setup Boot Disk" in drive A. Select OK.

   WINNT writes the contents of the Setup Boot Disk to the floppy. When it's complete, leave the Setup Boot Disk in drive A.

Getting Setup Running

10. WINNT asks you to restart the computer. With the newly created Setup Boot Disk still in drive A, restart the computer by selecting Restart Computer.
11. Go to step 2 under "Steps to Install from CD-ROM on Intel, Getting Setup Running" to guide you through the remainder of the installation process.

In the remaining steps, use the floppy disks that you created in this procedure, not the disks that came in the Windows NT Server 4.0 package. The disks that you just created are the only ones that will work to complete the NT Server installation successfully.

Ignore any references to the NT CD-ROM in the remaining steps. Your computer already has copies of all of the required NT files on its local hard disk.

Steps to Install from CD-ROM on RISC

Installation on a RISC computer, based on a MIPS, Alpha, or PowerPC CPU, is similar to the Intel x86 CD-ROM installation, except for the initial steps. Windows NT requires that RISC-based computers comply with the ARC (Advanced RISC Computing) standard. This standard specifies a RISC-based computer that has many similarities to standard Intel x86 PCs. Although Windows NT-compatible RISC platforms are ARC-compliant under the covers, each manufacturer has implemented these systems differently.

For this reason, this book (and every other book on Windows NT, including Microsoft's *Windows NT Server Installation Guide)* refers you to the RISC computer manufacturer's instructions for starting installation. You should be familiar with this documentation before beginning an NT Server installation on your RISC computer.

Gathering Your Materials

You'll need to assemble the following materials before you begin installation from your local CD-ROM drive:

- The installation worksheet that you completed in Chapter 7 (Worksheet 7-3)
- The Windows NT Server 4.0 CD-ROM
- One 1.44MB blank floppy disk, labeled "Emergency Repair"
- The RISC computer manufacturer's instructions that came with the computer

Once you have all of this material close at hand, you're ready to prepare your RISC-based computer for NT installation.

You can boot from the Windows NT Server 4.0 CD-ROM if your RISC computer's BIOS supports the El Torito Bootable CD-ROM format. Several RISC-based computers already provide this capability. Check the documentation that came with your computer to determine if it has this capability and to find out which initial installation steps you can skip.

Preparing the Computer

The RISC computer must have a FAT-formatted system partition no smaller than 2MB. This partition contains the hardware-specific files required to load Windows NT Server. If the system partition is over 150MB, you can opt to install NT Server on this partition. If you do this, however, you can't take advantage of NTFS security to protect system files, since the system partition must be formatted as FAT forever.

To protect your operating system files from malicious or accidental damage, put the bare minimum required on the system partition and install the NT operating system on a separate partition running NTFS. This approach protects your operating system installation from everyone but those with administrator privileges.

If your computer's disk isn't initialized at all or doesn't have a system partition, refer to your manufacturer's instructions for help in setting up the disk. Some manufacturers offer a menu choice at boot time that provides utilities in ROM to initialize and even format your system partition. Once your system partition is in place and formatted, you're ready to start the installation.

Starting a Typical RISC Installation

In this section, I'll describe the steps required in a typical RISC-based installation of Windows NT Server 4.0. Keep in mind that, since each RISC manufacturer takes a slightly different approach, you should consult the computer's documentation for additional details and differences from this procedure.

1. Insert the Windows NT Server 4.0 CD-ROM into your CD-ROM drive.

   If you have multiple CD-ROM drives, check your computer hardware documentation to determine which CD-ROM drive to use.

   Usually, if you have more than one CD-ROM drive, you should insert the NT CD-ROM into the drive with the *lowest* SCSI ID number. For example, if you have CD-ROM drives at ID 1 and ID 6, use the ID 1 drive for Windows NT Server installation. However, your computer documentation is the final authority on which drive to use.

2. Restart the computer.

   If you're already running a version of Windows NT on this computer, be sure to shut down the system properly.

3. The computer displays the initial ARC menu screen. From the menu, select Run a Program.

   Some systems may use different wording, but all ARC-compliant systems must provide an initial option to run a program.

4. The computer asks for the path of the program that you want to run. You need to run SETUPLDR.EXE from the CD-ROM directory appropriate to your RISC platform.

   4a. If you're installing on a MIPS-based computer, type **CD:\MIPS\SETUPLDR** and press ENTER.

   4b. If you're installing on an Alpha-based computer, type **CD:\ALPHA\SETUPLDR** and press ENTER.

   4c. If you're installing on a PowerPC-based computer, type **CD:\PPC\SETUPLDR** and press ENTER.

Some RISC computers don't recognize the CD-ROM device prefix "CD:." You may have to enter a long ARC device name, which very specifically identifies the hardware adapter, device, device id, and so forth. For example, to specify a particular CD-ROM drive, you may be required to type something like
scsi(0)cdrom(4)fdisk(0)\MIPS\SETUPLDR

Check your computer hardware documentation for details on how to specify your CD-ROM device. (ARC device names are covered in more detail in Chapter 21.)

5. Follow the instructions on the screen provided by SETUPLDR. Go to step 3 under "Steps to Install from CD-ROM on Intel, Getting Setup Running" to guide you through the remainder of the installation process.

   Ignore any references to the Setup floppy disks in the remaining steps. RISC installation uses only the NT CD-ROM.

Repairing Windows NT Server

If your Windows NT Server operating system ever reaches the point where it's unable to start, there's hope for recovering it. NT can get into an unbootable state if key operating system files are damaged or deleted or if your boot sector becomes corrupt. A more common cause of trouble is erroneous configuration. Loading a new driver that's unstable or not correctly configured to match the hardware can get you into this situation as well. As you saw within the first three steps of Setup, Windows NT provides a mechanism to handle such emergencies. In this section, I'll walk you through all of the various repair options that NT offers.

There are four lines of defense that you can use to make repairs to a damaged Windows NT Server system. They are

- ✦ Boot to VGA mode to recover from an invalid video adapter configuration (x86 computers only).
- ✦ Use the last known good configuration to recover from an invalid system configuration change.
- ✦ Use an NT boot floppy disk to jump-start the system using key boot files (x86 computers only).
- ✦ Use the Emergency Repair disk to restore the original system files, configuration, boot information, and the hard disk boot sector.

Some of these recovery approaches are geared to very specific situations. In the following sections, I'll cover each of the alternatives in turn.

Booting to VGA Mode

Perhaps you've just installed a new video driver or reconfigured your old one. You restart your computer only to discover that your video display is now so garbled that you can't see a thing. This typically occurs when you attempt to drive your video monitor at a frequency or resolution that it can't handle. How are you going to log on if you can't see the screen? Don't panic. There's hope.

The designers of Windows NT anticipated this common problem and provided an easy way out. If you've installed Windows NT Server on an Intel-based computer, you probably noticed that Setup inserted two options in the system boot menu. The second option is identical to the first, except that it starts the system in VGA video mode regardless of the video adapter settings that you've established. If the last configuration change that you made involved your video adapter settings, start with this approach to recovery.

To recover from an invalid video adapter configuration, perform the following steps:

1. Turn off your video monitor.

   You want to avoid potential damage caused by driving it at the wrong frequency.

2. Restart your computer and turn your video monitor back on.

   To restart your computer, you'll have to use the computer's reset button or turn the system off and then on again. Pressing CTRL+ALT+DELETE won't work in this situation.

3. From the system boot menu, select the VGA mode flavor of your NT installation and press ENTER.

Your computer will start using VGA video mode. You'll then be able to work on configuring your video adapter properly. Even if you mess up the video settings again, you'll always have VGA mode as a fallback position.

Using the Last Known Good Configuration

The VGA mode approach just discussed is specifically designed for recovery from a poorly configured video adapter. NT always allows you to revert to VGA mode, which is a known bootable video configuration by definition.

However, what if you've added a new buggy driver or configured some other device incorrectly through the Control Panel or Registry Editor? (In Chapter 20, I'll explain how you can really mess up your configuration using the Registry Editor.) Now the system won't boot. Hang in there. All's not lost.

Once again, the folks who brought you NT anticipated your trauma. When you start the NT operating system (after selecting from the system boot menu), you're given the option of using the last known good configuration. NT stores away the last bootable configuration that you used. It assumes that if you could log on successfully, the system must have booted completely, you were able to read what was on the screen, and you could type the appropriate information.

To recover the last known good configuration, perform these steps:

1. Restart your computer.

   You'll have to use the computer's reset button or turn the system off and then on again. Since NT hasn't booted, pressing CTRL+ALT+DELETE won't work in this situation.

2. From the system boot menu, select the appropriate version of NT and press ENTER.

3. As soon as the words "OS Loader" appear in the upper left corner of the screen, press the SPACEBAR.

   Be quick! You only have a few seconds to do this.

4. NT displays a menu of choices. Select the Use Last Known Good Configuration option and press ENTER.

   All configuration changes that you made to the system since the last time Windows NT Server successfully booted will be lost. You are, in fact, overwriting the entire system configuration with the one that last allowed you to start NT.

Your computer will boot using the old configuration. You'll then be able to work on determining which change caused the configuration problem. Even if you create an invalid configuration again, you'll have the last known good configuration available as a fallback position.

The *last known good* concept isn't new. For many years, terrain-following aircraft have used on-board computers and radar automatically to fly the aircraft as close to the ground as possible, avoiding enemy radar detection. If the stream of terrain data stops flowing into the computer for some reason, the computer starts using its *last known good data* to control the flight path. The success of this approach depends on how high those mountains in front of you really are.

Using an NT Boot Floppy

If you've supported DOS-based computers in the past, you know the value of a DOS boot floppy disk to start an unbootable DOS system. Although there's no hope of fitting all of Windows NT Server onto a boot floppy disk, you can create a special disk that will help you to jump-start a dead NT computer under certain conditions.

On an Intel x86 computer, a few critical files required for starting the system reside in the root directory. If one or more of these files is corrupted, deleted, or renamed, NT refuses to boot. It complains that it can't open or find a particular file.

To succeed with this approach to recovery, you'll need to create the special boot floppy disk *before* disaster strikes, when everything is still working. Here's how to create the disk:

1. Label a blank floppy disk NT 4.0 Boot Disk. While running Windows NT, insert this disk in drive A.
2. Format the floppy disk under Windows NT. At the Command Prompt, type **FORMAT A:** and press ENTER.

For this procedure to work, it's imperative that you format the floppy disk under Windows NT. If you format the disk under DOS or Windows 3.x, the boot sector written to the disk will point to DOS boot files. The boot sector that NT writes to the floppy disk will point to the NT boot files. You'll need the NT boot sector on the floppy disk for this procedure to work.

3. Start Windows NT Explorer. On the View menu, click Options, then click the View tab. Under the Hidden files option, click Show all files. Then click OK.

The files that you're about to copy to the NT floppy disk are hidden system files. You need to see them in Explorer before you can copy them. (See Chapter 14 for details about using NT Explorer.)

4. Use Explorer to copy the following files from your boot drive root directory (typically C:\) to the floppy disk in drive A.

   NTLDR

   NTDETECT.COM

   BOOT.INI

   NTBOOTDD.SYS

   If you don't find NTBOOTDD.SYS in your root directory, you don't need it. This file exists only if your Windows NT Server installation resides on a SCSI hard disk drive.

If Windows NT ever refuses to start because it's unable to find or open NTLDR, NTDETECT.COM, BOOT.INI, or NTBOOTDD.SYS, you can recover by booting from this floppy. NT will use these files from the floppy and then start the rest of NT from your hard disk.

Using the Emergency Repair Disk

The recovery mechanisms presented so far will help you to deal with some very common, specific problems. However, if the NT repairs that you need go beyond these narrow conditions, your next line of defense is the Emergency Repair disk. If you took my advice and created a repair disk to go with your NT installation, you have key information needed to recover a damaged system. Although not all repairs require this disk, having it available prepares you for recovering from a wider range of problems.

An Emergency Repair disk isn't interchangeable between computers. The repair disk contains very specific information about where you installed the operating system, the contents of your NT registry, details about device and disk partition configuration, the computer name, and so forth. You can't use a repair disk from one computer to recover another one. So, be sure to create a separate repair disk for each NT installation that you perform.

Just as periodic backups of your server data files are vital to protecting your valuable business information, it's critical that you keep your Emergency Repair disk up to date. Each time that you make a configuration change to the system (or at least periodically), use the RDISK utility to update the configuration information on your repair disk.

For example, I generally update my repair disk when I add devices and their drivers to the system, change disk partitions, add or remove significant networking components, or change the name of my computer. This isn't an exhaustive list, but it provides you with a general idea of the type of changes that should trigger thoughts about updating the repair disk. Changing wallpaper or color schemes on the server desktop don't qualify for repair disk update, in my view. Any configuration change that isn't critical to the reliable behavior and operation of the server can wait until the next critical update to the repair disk. In Chapter 17, I'll cover in detail how to use RDISK to keep your repair disk up to date.

Don't update your Emergency Repair disk until you're sure the changes that you made are valid ones. Be sure to restart your computer and test your configuration changes, and only then update the repair disk using the RDISK utility. If you update the repair disk right away, before you've tested the configuration changes, you just might destroy your best means of recovering from a bad configuration change.

Gathering Your Materials

You'll need to assemble the following materials before you begin the repair process:

- The installation worksheet (Worksheet 7-3) that you completed in Chapter 7 for this computer
- The Windows NT Server 4.0 CD-ROM
- Your up-to-date Emergency Repair disk created for this computer
- If you're repairing an Intel computer, the three Setup floppy disks used or created to install NT on this computer
- Any records of system configuration changes, drivers that you've installed, and so forth

The following two sections provide the preparatory steps to perform on the Intel or RISC computers that you're trying to repair.

Preparing for Repair on Intel

1. Locate the Setup Boot Disk, insert it in drive A, and restart the computer.

   This disk is either the one that came in the Windows NT Server 4.0 package or the one you created during a network or unsupported CD-ROM install. Use the Setup Boot Disk that you used when you installed NT Server on this computer.

   If you opted not to create floppy disks during a network or unsupported CD-ROM install, use the disk that came in the Windows NT Server 4.0 package and cross your fingers.

2. If you installed from CD-ROM, insert the Windows NT Server 4.0 CD-ROM into the same CD-ROM drive used to install NT originally.
3. Restart the computer.
4. Setup asks for Setup Disk 2. Remove the Setup Boot Disk from drive A, insert Setup Disk 2, and press ENTER.

   From here on, you can press F1 to display help information or press F3 if you want to exit the repair procedure.

5. Go to step 1 in the section called "Starting the Repair Procedure" and follow the steps there.

Preparing for Repair on RISC

1. Insert the Windows NT Server 4.0 CD-ROM into your CD-ROM drive.
2. Restart the computer.
3. The computer displays the initial ARC menu screen. From the menu, select Run a Program.

   Some systems may use different wording, but all ARC-compliant systems must provide an initial option to run a program.

4. The computer asks for the path of the program that you want to run. You need to run SETUPLDR.EXE from the CD-ROM directory appropriate to your RISC platform.

   4a. If you're installing on a MIPS-based computer, type **CD:\MIPS\SETUPLDR** and press ENTER.

   4b. If you're installing on an Alpha-based computer, type **CD:\ALPHA\SETUPLDR** and press ENTER.

   4c. If you're installing on a PowerPC-based computer, type **CD:\PPC\SETUPLDR** and press ENTER.

   Some RISC computers don't recognize the CD-ROM device prefix "CD:." You may have to enter a long ARC device name, which very specifically identifies the hardware adapter, device, device id, and so forth. Check your computer hardware documentation for details on how to specify your CD-ROM device.

5. Go to step 1 in the next section and follow the steps there.

Starting the Repair Procedure

1. Setup asks if you want to set up Windows NT now or repair a damaged installation. Press *R* to initiate the repair procedure.

2. Setup displays a list of the areas of the system that it can examine. By default, all options are selected. Press ENTER.

   If this is your first repair procedure, I recommend selecting and exploring all of the options. This will take longer to complete, but it will familiarize you with the various pieces.

   If you prefer to select specific options, use the UP and DOWN ARROW keys to highlight the option that you wish to change and then press ENTER to change the option. Once you've selected all of the areas that you want to cover, select Continue and press ENTER.

   If you opt to check registry files, Setup will examine registry files for corruption. If any are found to be corrupt, you'll have the option of restoring them from your repair disk.

   If you choose to restore the startup environment, Setup will inspect the startup environment for a specific NT installation on your computer. If necessary, Setup will use information from your repair disk to reconstruct it.

   If you elect to verify system files, Setup examines all of the NT files that you originally installed to determine if they're missing or corrupt. If it needs to restore any files, it will ask you for the NT CD-ROM. On an NTFS partition, Setup will also remove security from all system files and directories, just in case you accidentally set permissions on them that prevent Windows NT from accessing them.

Make sure to go back after recovery and set appropriate permissions on these files and directories. Since Setup removes security from them, they're vulnerable to unauthorized alteration or deletion until you set their permissions again. See Chapter 18 for a discussion of how to manage security on files and directories.

   If you want the boot sector restored, Setup will inspect and, if necessary, rewrite the boot sector on your hard disk with a valid Windows NT boot sector.

3. Setup asks if you want it to detect SCSI and CD-ROM devices or skip the detection process. Press ENTER to begin detection.

4. If you're repairing an Intel x86 computer, Setup may ask for Setup Disk 3. If so, remove Setup Disk 2 from drive A, insert Setup Disk 3, and press ENTER.

5. Setup lists the devices that it found. Verify that this list matches the configuration of the computer. Press ENTER.

6. Setup asks if you have an Emergency Repair disk. If you do, press ENTER and go to step 7. If you don't, press ESC and go to step 8.

   If you took my advice during installation, you created an Emergency Repair disk when you installed Windows NT Server, either on your Intel or RISC computer.

   If you don't have a repair disk for this installation of NT, you can cross your fingers and press ESC. Setup will do its level best to figure out how to find and repair your system. Don't count on success. Use a repair disk.

7. Setup asks for the repair disk. Remove any floppy disk present in drive A and insert the Emergency Repair disk. Then press ENTER.

The next step involves restoring the NT registry from the repair disk. Note that any configuration changes that you've made to the system since your last update to the repair disk will be lost when you perform this restoration. This is another argument for keeping your repair disk updated.

8. Setup asks which portions of the NT registry you want to restore. Select any or all of SYSTEM, SOFTWARE, DEFAULT, and SECURITY/SAM. By default, none of the options is selected. Use the UP and DOWN ARROW keys to highlight the option that you wish to change and press ENTER to change the option.

   Press F1 for a complete description of each option and the implications of restoring each portion of the configuration registry. Then, determine which portions you want to restore.

   For example, if the problem was caused by a bad or poorly configured driver, you should definitely restore SYSTEM. Likewise, if you have a damaged user accounts database, restore SECURITY/SAM.

If you ask Setup to restore the SECURITY/SAM database that you originally installed NT as a PDC on this computer and you've since demoted the PDC to act as a BDC, you need to take special care when restoring the registry.

When you restore the SECURITY/SAM database, Setup will restore this computer to its original role of PDC. Before rebooting the computer after you complete the repair process, make sure to disconnect this server from the network to avoid having multiple PDCs in the domain. Then, manually demote this server to the BDC role and reconnect it to the network. See Chapter 18 for information on promoting and demoting domain controllers.

9. Once you've selected all of the options that you want, select Continue and press ENTER

10. If you asked Setup to verify system files in step 2, it scans the files and tells you if it's found a problem.

    10a. If you want Setup to restore the file to its original version, press ENTER.

    10b. If you've manually added the file to the system since installation and you want to retain it, press ESC. Setup will leave the file alone.

10c. If you want Setup to restore this file and all subsequent files to their original versions, and potentially back out any manual changes that you've made, press *A*.

I prefer examining each file about which Setup complains rather than performing a wholesale, invisible change. You may not recall a manual change that you made, and the *A* option backs out changes without telling you.

11. Setup asks you to remove the repair disk from drive A and restart the server. Remove the disk and press ENTER.

Rather than waiting for trouble and driving through this procedure for the first time under intense pressure to fix a problem, I recommend that you schedule an NT repair training session for yourself. Since you have to bring down the server to do this, you'll probably want to include this time as part of your next scheduled maintenance slot. Doing this will familiarize you with the process and allow you to operate much more efficiently and calmly when the inevitable disaster strikes.

Reinstalling Windows NT Server

Having to completely reinstall Windows NT Server from scratch may seem like a last resort approach to disaster recovery, especially now that you've seen what it takes to install the system. Although it's true that reinstallation is the next logical step if you can't recover a damaged system any other way, there are other reasons that you may need to reinstall, including:

- ✦ Upgrading the operating system to a new version
- ✦ Moving a PDC or BDC server to a new domain
- ✦ Changing the server's role from a stand-alone server to a PDC or BDC

All of these activities require you to reinstall the Windows NT Server software completely. Upgrades from one version of NT to another are the most innocuous. Just follow the instructions provided with the upgrade. Your configuration will just migrate from the old NT version to the new one.

If you need to reinstall Windows NT Server on a computer that doesn't play the role of a PDC or BDC and it isn't a member of an existing domain, you can use the standard installation procedures described earlier in this chapter.

If you need to reinstall to move a server from one domain to another, to change the role of the server from stand-alone to BDC or PDC, or to restore the health of a PDC, life gets a bit more complicated. Before you make the decision to reinstall Windows NT Server, you need to understand the implications for your network. I'll outline them here and then tell you how to proceed.

What's in a Computer Name?

When you assign a computer name to an NT computer (either NT Workstation or NT Server), there's more to that computer name than meets the eye. NT internally and automatically assigns a special password-like value to the computer itself, called a security ID, or SID. The SID is passed along with the computer name whenever the computer attempts to log on to the domain. Why isn't the name alone good enough?

NT was designed to verify that a computer actually is who it claims to be. It says, in effect, "I recognize your name, but how do I know that's *really* you?" By asking this question, NT prevents one form of unauthorized access to network resources. You can't install NT on a computer, use the same name as another computer in the domain, and automatically gain access to the domain. The domain will refuse to recognize the new computer. The domain will act like a hospital refusing service to your computer because it doesn't have a Blue Cross number.

This authentication activity takes place only between NT computers. Computer names of down-level computers running DOS, Windows 3.x, Windows for Workgroups, or any other non-NT operating system are taken at face value. These computers don't have SIDs, so the computer name is all that the domain can use.

SIDs are also assigned to domain names. If you reinstall your domain controller using the same domain name as the previous installation, your domain controller won't be recognized by other NT computers in the domain or by any other domains that trust it. Because it has a brand-new SID, it will be treated like a brand new domain.

The procedures for overcoming these security obstacles differ depending on whether you're reinstalling a PDC or non-PDC NT Server. I'll present both procedures in the next sections. In the following steps, I'll call the computer on which you want to reinstall Windows NT Server the *target computer.*

Steps to Reinstall a BDC or Stand-Alone Server

To avoid the SID problem discussed earlier, you'll need to remove all traces of the target computer's old NT installation from the domain and then add the new NT installation back into the domain. Here's how:

1. Shut down the Windows NT Server target computer.
2. Log on with administrator privileges to the domain in which the target computer resides.
3. Run Server Manager by clicking the Start ➪ Programs ➪ Administrative Tools ➪ Server Manager option.
4. Delete the target computer from the domain by selecting the target computer from the list of computers. On the Computer menu, click Remove from Domain. Confirm your decision as prompted.

5. Reinstall NT Server on the target computer by going to step 1 under "Steps to Install from CD-ROM on Intel, Getting Setup Running."

   Be sure that you elect to install a fresh version of NT. Don't upgrade the existing installation. During installation, take the opportunity to create a new computer account in the domain.

   If you don't create a new computer account during reinstallation of NT on the target computer, you can do so as an administrator after the fact using Server Manager. On the Computer menu, click Add to Domain. Follow the prompts to complete the operation.

Steps to Reinstall a PDC

You need to take different approaches to reinstalling a PDC, depending on whether you already have a BDC in your domain. I've outlined both procedures here.

Reinstalling with a BDC

If you have a BDC in the domain, the procedure is relatively simple. If at all possible, arrange to have at least one Windows NT server acting as a BDC in your domain before attempting to reinstall the PDC. Here's how to reinstall a PDC, if you have a BDC in its domain:

1. Select a BDC computer in the domain to act temporarily as PDC. Use Server Manager to force synchronization of the SAM database to this BDC. Then use Server Manager to promote this BDC to PDC.

   You want to make sure that the BDC you've chosen to act as PDC is fully synchronized with all of the latest updates to the account database. Promoting the BDC automatically demotes the PDC target computer to BDC status. See Chapter 18 for details on how to synchronize the account database and promote domain controllers.

2. Shut down the target computer.
3. Reinstall NT Server on the target computer as a BDC by going to step 1 under "Steps to Install from CD-ROM on Intel, Getting Setup Running."

   Be sure that you elect to install a fresh version of Windows NT Server. Don't upgrade the existing installation. Select BDC as the role of the target computer. You'll change its role to PDC in a later step.

4. Restart the target computer, which is now acting as a BDC.
5. Use Server Manager to promote the freshly installed target computer to act as PDC.

   This action automatically demotes the PDC created in step 1 back to BDC status. See Chapter 18 for details on how to promote domain controllers.

Reinstalling without a BDC

If you don't have a BDC, the amount of leg work and network downtime required is much greater. No BDC will be available to validate requests to log on to the domain, and you'll have to visit every NT computer in the network, forcing each to recognize the new PDC. This procedure is extremely disruptive to you, your network, and your users.

1. Shut down the Windows NT Server PDC target computer.

   During this period, no server will be able to validate logon requests.

2. Reinstall NT Server as a PDC by going to step 1 under "Steps to Install from CD-ROM on Intel, Getting Setup Running."

   Be sure that you elect to install a fresh version of Windows NT Server and select PDC as the role of this computer. Don't upgrade the existing installation.

3. On each Windows NT computer (NT Workstation and NT Server) in the domain, perform steps 4 through 9.

4. Run Control Panel by clicking the Start ➪ Settings ➪ Control Panel option. In Control Panel, double-click the Network icon.

5. Click the Identification tab and indicate that the computer is now a member of a workgroup, rather than a domain. Then click OK.

6. Restart the computer.

7. Repeat step 4.

8. Click the Identification tab, and indicate that the computer is now a member of the domain, rather than a workgroup. Then click OK.

   Be sure to specify the domain name of your PDC.

You can see that it's important and worthwhile to have at least one Windows NT Server BDC, so you can avoid the nightmare of performing this operation on every NT computer in the domain.

Summary

In this chapter, you've gained familiarity with the various methods of installing Windows NT Server 4.0. You've learned how to deal with Intel and RISC computers, repair damaged installations, reinstall NT Server, and avoid common problems during installation. I've also alerted you to some pitfalls about which Setup doesn't warn you.

In Chapter 10, you'll learn how Windows NT Server 4.0 fits into larger networks and how to plan and organize your network for growth. I'll even share with you how Microsoft has implemented its worldwide network based on multiple domains using Windows NT Server.

INSIDE STORY

I read the digital clock on my computer monitor: "9:00 p.m., October 19." Our first victory lay just within our grasp. In only 12 short hours, we'd bless the Windows NT Pre-Release Development Kit (PDK) and ship it to software developers. This would be the very first external release of the Windows NT code outside Microsoft.

NT was more stable and complete than it had ever been. Software developers waited anxiously for the operating system and tools that would allow them to create applications for this 32-bit marvel. Encouraged by the current quality of the product, I nevertheless continued to monitor e-mail and the database of bug reports, scanning for any new surprises that might halt shipment. All was quiet . . . too quiet.

My office door was suddenly flung open by a frenzied engineer, the knob making a small dent in the resisting wall. "Have you heard about the DOS problem?" he asked breathlessly. No. "If you try to install NT over any DOS earlier than DOS 5, that's all she wrote. Your system hangs!" I couldn't believe it. There were certainly customers, even among software developers, who would attempt to install NT on computers running DOS 3.1. This was bad.

Most folks had headed home for the day, but we needed someone to investigate this catastrophe, so I quickly dialed the phone number of one of the NT developers. "John, we've got trouble. Can you come in right now? We're going to hold the release until we can figure out what's going on with this."

Around 10:00 p.m., John showed up. As he slaved away on the problem, I met with my manager next door. Even if we found the trouble, we reasoned, dare we make any risky changes at this late stage? How much retesting would we have to do? Should we just ship a copy of DOS 5 with the product and ask people to upgrade?

After two hours of debugging, John discovered the cause of the trouble. NT's loader was misinterpreting the older DOS 3.x boot sector. Fixing it would involve a one-byte change to the loader code. My manager and I looked at each other, thinking the same thought. "We'll take the fix," we said in unison. We woke up some test engineers and pounded on the slightly modified NT loader code into the wee hours of the morning. At 9:00 a.m. the next day, we declared victory and shipped the PDK to an excited crowd of software developers.

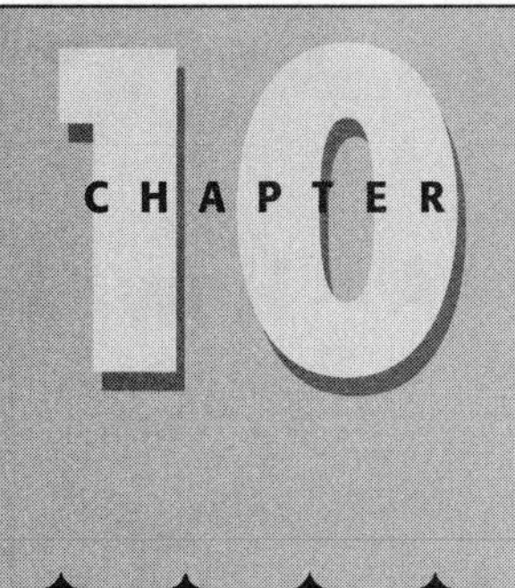

Growing Your NT Server Network

As your network grows in number of users, number of computers, overall network traffic, and number of geographical sites, you need to maintain an acceptable level of network performance. Unfortunately, as some of these factors increase, performance will decrease unless you do some careful planning.

In this chapter, I'll fill you in on how to plan single domain and multiple domain networks to handle large numbers of computers and users. I'll show you how to analyze your network requirements and design a network containing multiple domains. Finally, you'll get a glimpse of how Microsoft has used Windows NT Server domains as the basis for its huge worldwide network.

How Many BDCs Do You Need?

In planning large domains, you need to consider the number of BDCs required in each of them. As I said in Chapter 7, you should always have at least one BDC in each domain, even if your domain is small. This allows users to log on to the domain when your PDC is down.

How many additional BDCs are needed? The answer depends on the number of user accounts in your domain. The rule of thumb is that each BDC can support up to 2,000 users. So, if your domain contains 4,000 users, you need at least two BDCs. Likewise, if you have 10,000 users, you need five BDCs. If you use this formula, you'll do an effective job of spreading the user validation load across your domain controller computers.

How Many Domains Do You Need?

Many organizations, especially those that are small- or medium-sized, do just fine with a single Windows NT Server domain to centralize security and administration for the entire enterprise. Indeed, this is the simplest approach for organizing and administering an NT Server-based network. There are, however, a few reasons why you might want to divide your enterprise network into multiple domains. These include

- ✦ Administering by autonomous departments
- ✦ Administering multiple sites connected by WANs
- ✦ Offering increased security between departments
- ✦ Enhancing performance
- ✦ Increasing the number of computers
- ✦ Increasing the number of users

All of these are excellent reasons for designing an NT network based on multiple domains. Some of them are based on your organizational structure. For example, if you have two departments, each with local network administration responsibility, you'll want to consider giving each department its own domain. Moreover, you may want to prevent users in one department from having access to certain information or resources in another department. Or, perhaps your organization is divided into multiple sites, each with local administration responsibility. The remaining reasons for using multiple domains are based primarily on the size of your network, in terms of network traffic, number of computers, and number of users.

If you're familiar with NetWare, NT domain design is similar to NDS in NetWare 4. NDS is considered somewhat more flexible, but also a lot more complex. As you'll see later in this chapter, NT's multiple domain approach uses trust relationships to design multiple levels of network hierarchy. By using NT domains as basic building blocks for directory services, you can create just about any network structure.

One of the key reasons why folks use multiple NT domains is to improve performance. First, you can lighten the load on the PDC and BDCs and thus lessen overall network traffic within a domain. PDCs, especially in large networks, can spend all of their time replicating account database updates over the network. What's more, they can generate lots of network traffic to keep all of those BDCs in sync. The problem is exacerbated if the database updates are being done over a slower WAN link to another site. Once all this database updating becomes a performance bottleneck, your real applications (and your users) begin to suffer.

What about Central Administration?

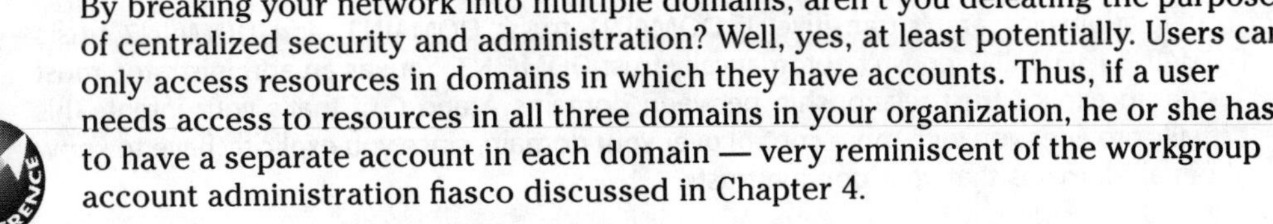

By breaking your network into multiple domains, aren't you defeating the purpose of centralized security and administration? Well, yes, at least potentially. Users can only access resources in domains in which they have accounts. Thus, if a user needs access to resources in all three domains in your organization, he or she has to have a separate account in each domain — very reminiscent of the workgroup account administration fiasco discussed in Chapter 4.

You can set up your accounts this way, but you'd defeat the whole purpose of Windows NT Server domains. As I mentioned in Chapter 4, NT Server provides a solution to this problem — namely, trust relationships.

Developing a Trust Relationship

By setting up trust relationships between domains, a user needs only one account in one domain. If that user's domain is trusted by another domain, the other domain will accept his or her initial logon as valid. There's only one user account to maintain, but the user has access to resources in multiple domains. This approach, called single network logon, makes your life as an administrator much easier. Just log on to your own domain, and all domains that trust your domain will grant you access. Trust relationships move the benefits of centralized administration from the domain level to the network level. As an administrator, you need only create one account for each user on the network.

It's easy to lose sight of who is really being trusted here. When you allow your domain to trust another domain, you're actually saying that you fully trust the administrator of the other domain to provide adequate security and prevent unauthorized access to the network. You're essentially putting access to your domain in the other administrator's hands. Of course, if you administer both domains, you're just saying that you trust yourself, and I hope you do.

Trust relationships always go one way (that is, one domain trusts another domain). However, you can set up two separate trust relationships between two domains, so that they trust each other. One domain can trust many other domains, and many domains can trust one domain. This allows you to build up all sorts of combinations of relationships.

You may hear or read about two-way trust relationships. This really implies two separate one-way trust relationships. Each domain must be explicitly told to trust the other domain.

TRUST ONLY GOES SO FAR

Trust relationships aren't transitive. If DOMAIN1 trusts DOMAIN2, and DOMAIN2 trusts DOMAIN3, DOMAIN1 doesn't automatically trust DOMAIN3. You, as an administrator, must set up an explicit trust relationship between domains A and C, if that's your intent. This actually provides you with more control over your domain, since you explicitly have to know about all domains that your domain trusts.

For example, say you have a domain established for each department in your organization. The accounting department might need access to resources in all other departments to continuously gather budget and invoice information. However, you don't want other departments to have access to all of the accounting department's resources, such as the payroll database, for example. So, you set up trust relationships wherein each departmental domain trusts the accounting domain. Thus, users in the accounting domain can access resources using their accounting domain user accounts. However, folks in other departments can't access the accounting domain, unless they have a separate account in that domain.

Now, say you have a product development department and a customer support department, each with its own domain. You want to allow these departments to access each other's resources, so you establish two trust relationships, one in each direction, between the domains. Users in the product development domain can use their accounts to access resources in the support domain, and vice versa. In this situation, the network appears to users as one large domain, although the two groups log on to different domains.

Establishing a Trust

There are two tasks you need to perform to establish a trust relationship between two domains. Let's say you want DOMAIN2, the *trusting* domain, to trust DOMAIN1, the *trusted* domain. First, you must warn DOMAIN1 that DOMAIN2 is about to trust it. At this point, you establish a password for the trust relationship that will be required to complete the arrangement. Then, you need to tell DOMAIN2 to trust DOMAIN1.

If the two domains are administered by two different people, a quick way to complete this task is for one administrator to perform steps 2 through 8 in the following steps. The other administrator can then perform steps 9 through 15. The two of you can talk on the phone as you walk through the steps. You'll need to agree on a password for the trust relationship anyway, and you can communicate any error conditions to each other immediately.

If you have administrative access to both domains, you can create both sides of the trust relationship from a single computer. When you need to administer a different domain, just use User Manager for Domains, click Select Domain on the User menu, and select the domain you need to alter.

Here are the steps to create a trust relationship between two domains:

1. Make sure that the PDCs for both domains are running on the network.
2. Log on as an administrator to the PDC of the domain to be trusted and perform steps 3 through 8 there.
3. Start User Manager for Domains by clicking Start ➪ Programs ➪ Administrative Tools ➪ User Manager for Domains.

You'll find out more about User Manager for Domains in Chapter 18.

4. On the Policies menu, click Trust Relationships.
5. Click Add next to the Trusting Domains box, as shown in Figure 10-1.

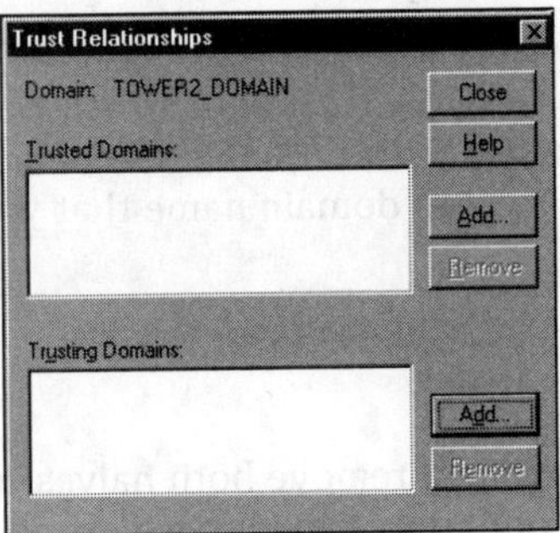

Figure 10-1: You click Add to add to the list of trusting domains.

6. In the Trusting Domain box, type the name of the trusting domain, as shown in Figure 10-2.
7. In the Initial Password box, type the password for this trust relationship. Then, type the same password in the Confirm Password box, as shown in Figure 10-2.

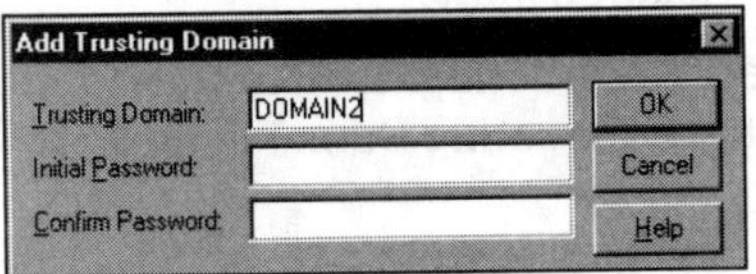

Figure 10-2: You add a trusting domain by typing its name and assigning a password to the trust relationship.

8. Click OK.

   The trusting domain that you typed is now added to the Trusting Domains list.
9. Log on as an administrator to the PDC of the trusting domain and perform steps 10 through 15 there.
10. Start User Manager for Domains by clicking Start ➪ Programs ➪ Administrative Tools ➪ User Manager for Domains.

11. On the Policies menu, click Trust Relationships.
12. Click Add next to the Trusted Domains box.
13. In the Domain box, type the name of the trusted domain, as shown in Figure 10-3.

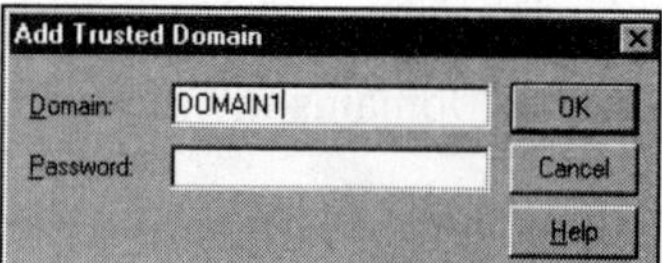

Figure 10-3: You add a trusted domain by typing its name and specifying the trust relationship password.

14. In the Password box, type the password for this trust relationship. This is the same password entered in step 7. See Figure 10-3.
15. Click OK.

    If the password is correct and the trusted domain is able to confirm, the trust relationship is established. The trusted domain name that you typed is now added to the Trusted Domains list.

Breaking a Trust

To break a trust relationship completely, you must remove both halves of the trust. Again, this requires administration tasks in both domains involved in the trust relationship. Here are the steps to break an existing trust between two domains:

1. Make sure that the PDCs for both domains are running on the network.
2. Log on as an administrator to the PDC of the trusted domain and perform steps 3 through 6 there.
3. Start User Manager for Domains by clicking Start ➪ Programs ➪ Administrative Tools ➪ User Manager for Domains.
4. On the Policies menu, click Trust Relationships.
5. In the Trusting Domains box, select the trusting domain to be removed from the list. Then click Remove next to the Trusting Domains box.
6. Click OK.

   The trusting domain name that you selected is now removed from the Trusting Domains list.

7. Log on as an administrator to the PDC of the Trusting Domain and perform steps 8 through 11 there.
8. Start User Manager for Domains by clicking Start ➪ Programs ➪ Administrative Tools ➪ User Manager for Domains.

9. On the Policies menu, click Trust Relationships.
10. In the Trusted Domains box, select the trusted domain to be removed from the list. Then, click Remove next to the Trusted Domains box.
11. Click OK.

    The trusted domain name that you typed is now removed from the Trusted Domains list. The trust relationship has now been broken.

The password used to establish a trust relationship is immediately changed internally by the operating system, once the trust relationship is created. Thus, you can't use this same password again to reestablish a trust relationship that's been half torn down. Each trust relationship must be completely broken and started from scratch with a fresh password.

Sizing Up Your Domain

Beyond purely organizational and location issues, a key reason for creating multiple domains as a network grows larger is to improve network and server performance. In this section, I'll help you to analyze your network size parameters to determine if and when you should use multiple domains. The primary consideration for domain size is the size of the SAM database required to manage it. Its size has implications on both server hardware requirements and network traffic.

The Size of SAM

Your NT domain's SAM database consists of computer accounts, user accounts, and groups. Each of these consumes space in the SAM database. Computer accounts take up about 512 bytes each. User accounts occupy 1KB each, and every group eats up 4KB. (Your group mileage may vary depending on the average number of members in each group, but use 4KB as a rule of thumb.) Built-in local groups (such as Administrators, Guests, and Server Operators) consume 44KB right off the top. Since the SAM database consists of all of these elements, you can't just look at the number of computers or the number of users in a vacuum and determine the total size of the database. You need to look at a combination of factors in your particular network environment.

How large should you allow your domain's SAM database to grow? Faster processors and more memory on your PDC and BDC computers translate to the ability to handle larger SAM databases. Table 10-1 shows what minimum processors and memory sizes are recommended in PDCs and BDCs within a domain to handle various sizes of SAM databases. Remember that since BDCs can act as PDCs, all BDCs must be just as well-equipped to deal with a large SAM database as the PDC.

Table 10-1
PDC and BDC Hardware Recommendations for SAM Databases

SAM Database Size	*Minimum CPU Recommended*	*Minimum RAM Recommended*
5MB	486/33	32MB
10MB	486/66	32MB
15MB	Pentium or RISC	48MB
20MB	Pentium or RISC	64MB
25MB	Pentium or RISC	96MB
30MB	Pentium or RISC	128MB
35MB	Pentium Pro or RISC	144MB
40MB	Pentium Pro or RISC	160MB
> 40MB	Not recommended in a single domain	Not recommended in a single domain

Microsoft recommends that you don't grow your SAM database larger than 40MB. This is the upper limit of what they've successfully tested in the lab. If you exceed this limit, you'll probably experience degraded performance, both in terms of database replication from the PDC to BDCs and lengthy waits while the database loads into memory for administration tasks. If the analysis that you do in this section leaves you with a database approaching this limit, it's definitely time to establish multiple domains.

As you proceed through this size analysis, think in terms of your immediate plans as well as your plans 6 to 12 months down the road. You may want to move to multiple domains now, in anticipation of later network growth or changes in your organizational structure.

What's in a SAM?

As mentioned earlier, the SAM contains several elements. Whenever you add a computer running Windows NT (client workstation, stand-alone server, or BDC) to an existing domain, you create a computer account for that computer. Although you may have multiple users making use of the same computer during a given day, you only have one computer account per NT node in your network. Thus, you can calculate how the number of computers in your network will affect SAM's size.

Computer accounts are created in the SAM database only for computers running Windows NT Workstation or Windows NT Server. Other operating systems (such as Windows 95 or Windows for Workgroups) don't participate in computer account validation.

You need an account for each user in your domain. Some users may utilize multiple computers, whereas some may share a single computer. Still others may require multiple user accounts for specific purposes. When calculating the volume of the SAM database required to handle your user accounts, keep all of these situations in mind.

There are two flavors of groups in the SAM database: local groups and global groups. If you've dealt with groups in a single domain model, you're already familiar with local groups.

Local Groups

A local group describes access permissions to resources that are local to the domain. The scope of a local group is limited to the domain in which it was created. It can't describe access permissions to resources outside of this domain. Moreover, you can't see or use a local group outside of its home domain. However, you can include a user account from another domain within a local group, as long as the other domain is trusted by the local domain. This capability allows you to grant resource access to users in other domains. (You can also include global groups within local groups, but I'll discuss global groups later in this chapter.)

The Guests group is an example of a predefined local group provided by NT. You can grant permission to access resources in the local domain to members of the Guests, but you can't specify access permissions to resources in other domains.

Global Groups

A global group, on the other hand, is simply a list of users from a specific domain. A global group includes user accounts only from within the domain in which the global group was created. A global group can't contain any other groups (global or local), and you can't assign access permissions to it.

The Domain Users group is an example of a predefined global group provided by Windows NT Server. You can't assign any access permissions to this group, but you can include it in a local group in any trusting domain, thus granting access permissions in that domain to the users in the Domain Users group.

Global vs. Local Groups

So what good are global groups if you can't use them to define access permissions? If local groups can include user accounts from other trusted domains, why not just include them directly in local groups as needed and skip the global group idea completely? Doing so can become unwieldy, especially when there's a large number of user accounts from another domain that you want to include in multiple local groups.

Think of a global group as a building block that can be used in other domains to build local groups. Global groups provide a handy means of exporting a group of users in a domain to other domains on the network. When you define a local group within a domain, you can include a global group of users within that local group. The resource access permissions that you assign to the local group are granted to the users in the global group, even though those users exist in a different domain.

As long as the domain that defines a local group trusts the domain that defines the global group, the global group can be added to the local group and users within the global group have the same access permissions as other members of the local group. Table 10-2 summarizes the characteristics of local and global groups. Figure 10-4 illustrates the relationship among local groups, global groups, and user accounts.

Table 10-2
A Comparison of Local and Global Groups

Group Characteristic	*Local Group*	*Global Group*
Group can contain individual user accounts defined in the domain in which the group was created.	√	√
Group can contain individual user accounts defined in a different (trusted) domain.	√	
Group can contain global groups defined in the local domain.	√	
Group can contain global groups defined in a different (trusted) domain.	√	
Group can contain local groups.		
Group can be assigned privileges in the domain in which the group was created.	√	
Group can be assigned privileges in other domains.		Only through membership in a local group

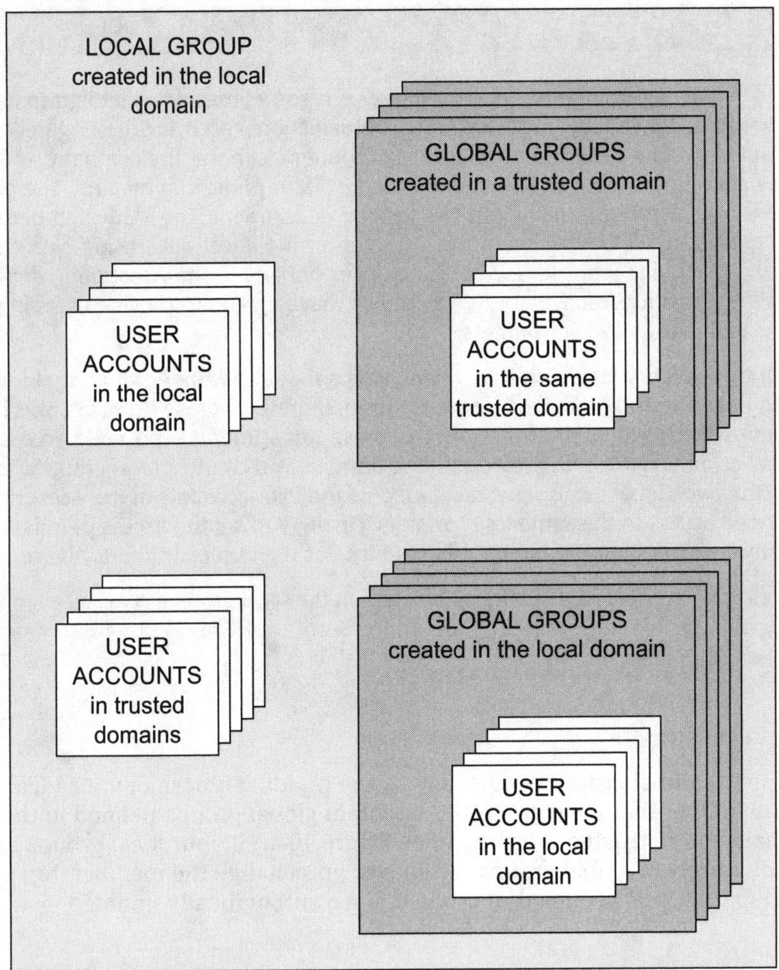

Figure 10-4: Local groups can contain both individual user accounts and global groups, defined in either the local domain or a trusted domain.

TIME TO REGROUP?

The distinction between global groups and local groups is sometimes difficult to grasp. Let's look at a practical example. Say you have three domains, one each for the Engineering, Accounting, and Marketing departments. Because Accounting controls the company's purse strings, they've somehow managed to get all of the best laser printers in the firm. The poor engineers have only clunky dot-matrix printers in their department. The Marketing department has no printers at all, having spent their budget on the latest advertising blitz. Both Engineering and Marketing want to use the fancy laser printers in the Accounting department. You, as the domain administrator in Accounting, have agreed to provide users in the other domains with access to your printers.

To accomplish this, you first establish trust relationships that allow the Accounting domain to trust the Engineering and Marketing domains. Then, in both of those domains, you create global groups that include all of the users in these departments who need access to the printers in Accounting. Next, in the Accounting domain, you create a local group whose members are the two global groups just created, plus the user accounts in the Accounting domain that need access to the same laser printers. Finally, you set the access permissions on these printer resources so that the members of the local group can print to them.

At this point, all local user accounts that you included in the local group as well as all members of both global groups have access to the printer resources. Figure 10-5 illustrates the group relationships in this example.

Consider using global groups exclusively as the building blocks of your local groups. Remember that local groups can contain global groups defined in the local domain and in trusted domains. (See Figure 10-4.) If your local groups are composed entirely of global groups, whenever you change the membership of a global group, the local groups that contain it are automatically updated — a real time-saver.

Built-In Groups

Windows NT Server includes several built-in groups, as mentioned in Chapter 5. Table 10-3 presents a list of these built-in accounts, indicating which are local groups and which are global. Groups that are local only on PDC or BDC computers are created when you install Windows NT Server as a domain controller (either primary or backup). Note that the Power Users group exists only when NT Server is installed as a stand-alone server.

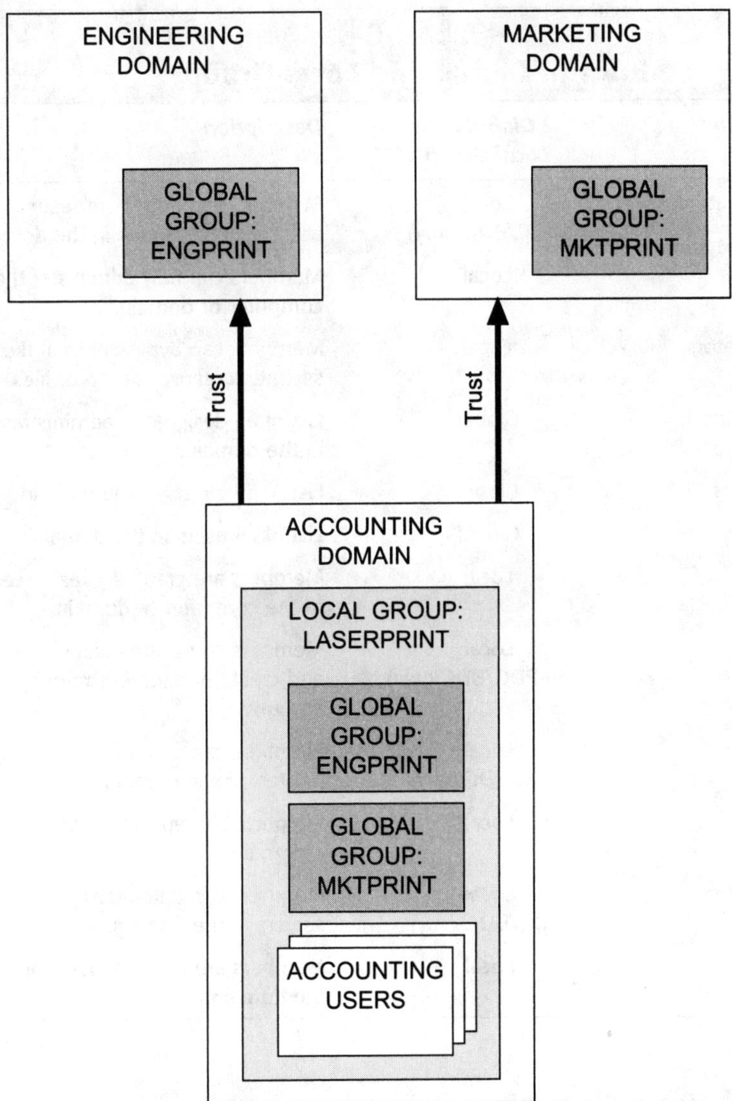

Figure 10-5: A local group in the Accounting domain provides access to members of global groups in two trusted domains.

Table 10-3
Built-In Global and Local Groups

Built-In Group	***Global or Local Group***	***Description***
Account Operators	Local (PDC/BDC only)	Members can administer user accounts and groups in the domain.
Administrators	Local	Members can fully administer the computer or domain.
Backup Operators	Local	Members can bypass normal file security to allow backup of files.
Domain Admins	Global	List of all designated administrators in the domain.
Domain Guests	Global	List of all guests in the domain.
Domain Users	Global	List of all users in the domain.
Guests	Local	Members are granted guest access to the computer or domain.
Power Users	Local (non-PDC/BDC only)	Members can share resources and create nonadministrator accounts.
Print Operators	Local (PDC/BDC only)	Members can administer printers in the domain.
Replicator	Local	Supports file replication within a domain.
Server Operators	Local (PDC/BDC only)	Members can administer servers in the domain.
Users	Local	Members are ordinary users of the domain.

SAM and Your Domain

Once you've estimated the number of users, number of groups, and number of nodes in your network, estimating the size of your domain's SAM database is straightforward. Worksheet 10-1 provides guidelines for calculating the SAM size and number of domains that you'll need. Again, be sure to plan for the future in your calculations, so that you can live with your decisions for a reasonable period of time.

Worksheet 10-1
Calculating the Number of Domains That You Need Based on Network Size

Line	SAM Database Elements	Requirements
1	Number of computers running Windows NT on your network	
2	Number of network users	
3	Number of groups that you define	
4	Multiply line 1 by 0.5KB	
5	Multiply line 2 by 1KB	
6	Multiply line 3 by 4KB	
7	Size of built-in NT groups	44KB
8	Total SAM size in KB (Add lines 4 through 7)	
9	Total SAM size in MB (Multiply line 8 by 0.001024)	
10	Divide line 9 by 40	
11	Number of domains needed (Round up line 10 to the nearest whole number)	

For example, if your network has 10,000 computers, 5,000 users, and you define 50 groups, your SAM database requires 10.5MB and can be handled within one NT domain. As another example, say you have 40,000 users. You know you're already over the limit of one domain. If you have 30,000 computers and 1,000 groups, you'll need about 60MB for the SAM database, and you'll have to split it across two domains. If these calculations lead you to the conclusion that you need multiple domains, you'll probably need to start with a multiple master domain model, described later in this chapter.

Understanding Windows NT Domain Models

A grouping of one or more NT domains along with the trust relationships established between them is collectively referred to as a *domain model*. In this section, I'll present several common and recommended NT domain models, along with their pros and cons. The models are

- ✦ Single domain
- ✦ Single master domain
- ✦ Multiple master domain
- ✦ Complete trust domain

If you determined that the size of your SAM database warrants multiple domains, you can skip directly to the section on the multiple master domain model. As with any other modeling approach, your particular situation might warrant deviation from these models. However, it's important to understand the characteristics of each model as a starting point for your own multiple domain planning.

The Single Domain Model

The single domain model is the one with which you're already familiar — a single PDC with one or more BDCs, some number of stand-alone servers, and client workstations. Using this model, all network administrators can administer all servers in the network, since they're all in the same domain. This is, by far, the simplest model. As I mentioned before, it enables you to accommodate a SAM database of up to 40MB.

As your single domain network grows, you and your users must deal with increasingly longer lists of users, groups, and resources. Network browsing takes longer, and changes to the SAM database take longer to replicate to BDCs. In this model, the PDC can become a bottleneck to network performance.

If trust between departments isn't an issue, and everyone is happy with centralized control of the network, the single domain model is a good choice. However, if you have or plan to have a SAM database larger than 40MB, you'll need to consider the multiple master domain model described later in this chapter.

HINT FOR BRANCH OFFICES

If your network is organized across branch offices linked via WAN connections and you plan to use the single domain model, place at least one BDC at each branch office to handle logon validation locally. This approach allows local users to log on even if the WAN link to the PDC is down. Adding more BDCs provides additional local fault tolerance if your BDC goes down. Figure 10-6 illustrates this approach.

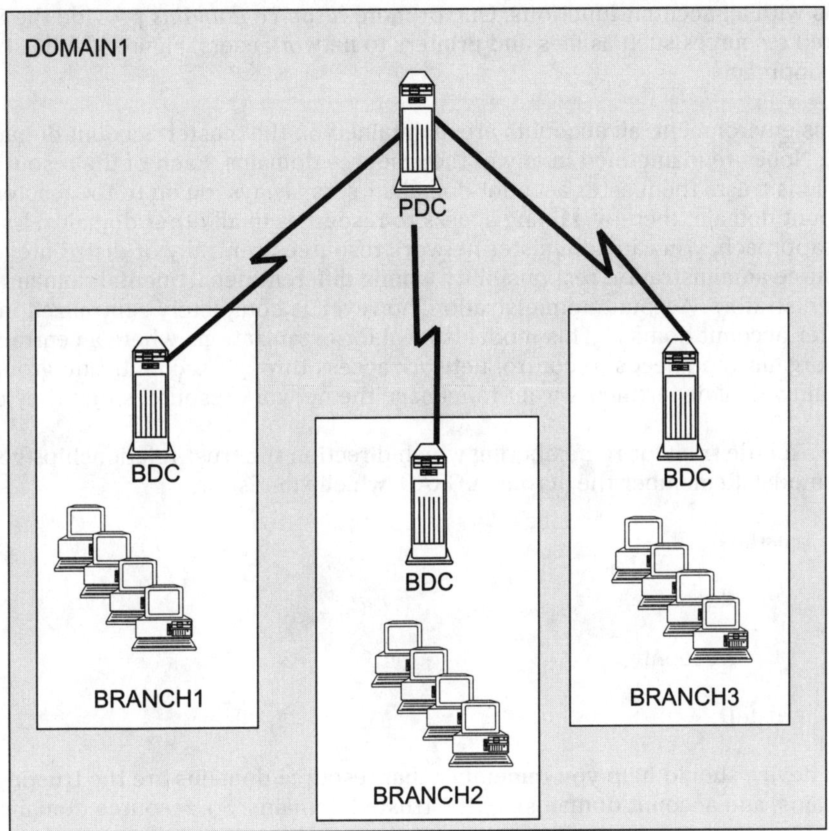

Figure 10-6: You should place a BDC at each branch office, if you're linked by a WAN to the PDC.

The Single Master Domain Model

If you need to split your network into multiple domains for organizational reasons, but your network is still small enough to be handled by a single PDC, the single master domain model is a good choice. In this model, you break the network into two or more domains, assigning one as the *master account domain* that deals with all account functions. One or more *resource domains* provide the actual shared resources such as files and printers to network users. Figure 10-7 illustrates this approach.

In this environment, all accounts are maintained on the master account domain PDC. None are maintained in any of the resource domains. Each of the resource domains trusts the master account domain. Users always log on to the master account domain, thereby gaining access to resources in all other domains. Using this approach, you can administer network resources centrally or distribute the resource administration responsibility among different departmental domain administrators. Account administration, however, is completely centralized in the master account domain. This model is ideal for organizations where a centralized MIS organization needs to control network access through accounts and groups, but individual departments want to manage the network resources that they offer

Here's a little trick for remembering which direction the trust relationships go in this model. Remember the acronym GRAD, which stands for:

trustin**G**

Resource

Account

truste**D**

This device should help you remember that resource domains are the trusting domains, and account domains are the trusted domains. So, resource domains trust the account domain.

As shown in Figure 10-7, the single master domain model imposes a sort of hierarchy of domains on the network. Because of this, the master account domain is sometimes called the *first-tier domain,* and all of the resource domains are called *second-tier domains.*

As your single master domain network grows, you and your users must deal with increasingly longer lists of users and groups, but resources are grouped by the resource domains in which they reside. So, resource browsing time increases only to the extent that the number of resources in individual resource domains increases. Administration changes and replication of updates to the SAM database take longer, just as they do in the single domain model. However, the individual resource domains may not see any slowdown, if the master account domain is on a separate LAN from the resource domains. In the single master domain model, the solitary master account domain PDC can still become a bottleneck to network performance.

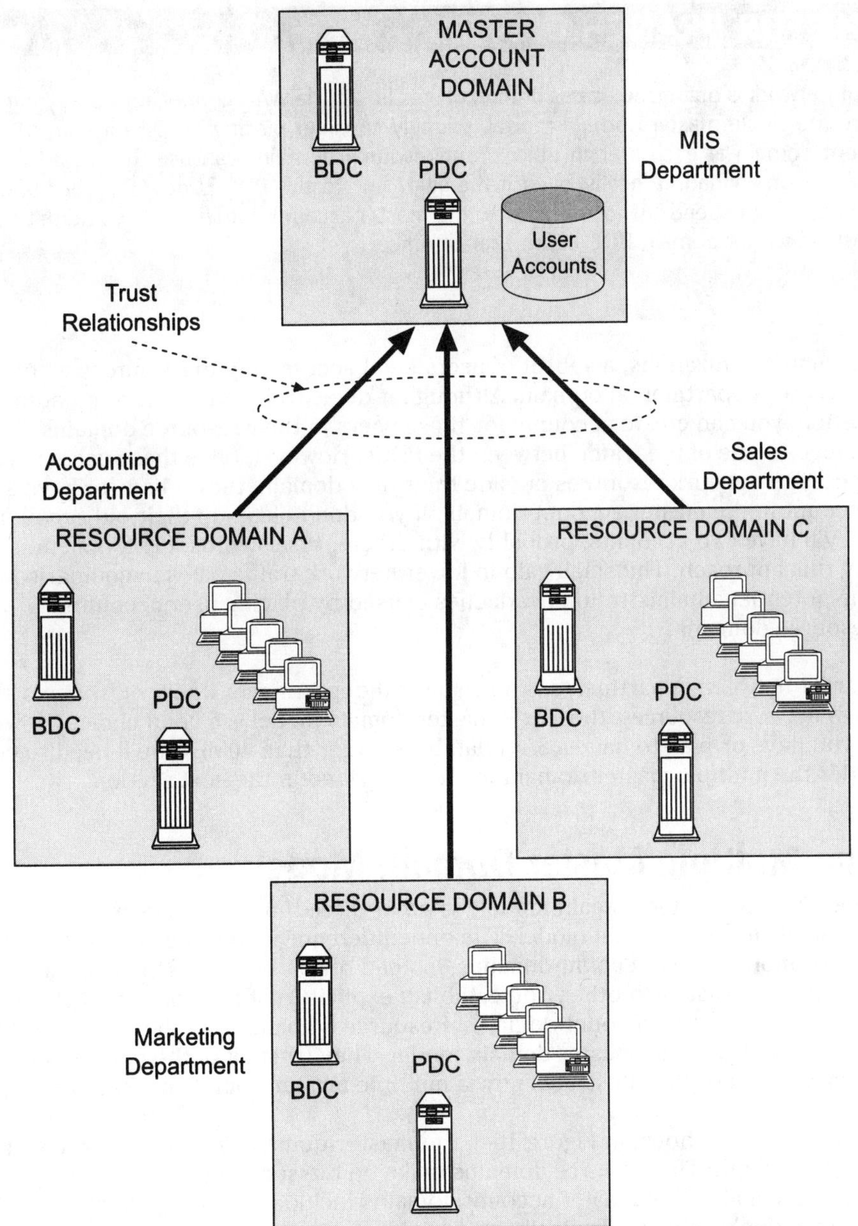

Figure 10-7: The single master domain model centralizes accounts and administration into a single domain and uses resource domains for sharing files and printers.

HINT FOR BRANCH OFFICES

If your network is organized across branch offices linked via WAN connections and you plan to use the single master domain model, strongly consider placing a BDC for your master account domain at each branch office. Your resource domains can use this local BDC to handle logon validation locally, even if the WAN link to the PDC is down. If your branch office has a high-speed LAN connection to the master account domain PDC, you don't need a master account domain BDC at the branch office.

In some organizations, a subset of users need access only to resources within their own departmental domain. Although it decentralizes user account administration, you can create accounts for these users in their resource domains. This reduces some of the traffic between the PDCs. However, once these users need access to network resources outside their own domain, they'll have to have an account in the master account domain. If you don't clean up their old account, they'll have two accounts, probably with different passwords. I recommend avoiding this approach. The small gain in lower network traffic pales in comparison to the potential administration headaches caused by placing user accounts in resource domains.

If trust between departments is an issue and departments want control over their own network resources, the single master domain model is a good choice. However, if you have or plan to have a SAM database larger than 40MB, you'll need to consider the multiple master domain model described in the next section.

The Multiple Master Domain Model

The multiple master domain model (say *that* three times fast) is very similar to the single master domain model. The only difference is that the network includes two or more master account domains, instead of just one. These master account domains all trust each other. You establish explicit trust relationships between each pair of master account domains. Resource domains play the same role as they did in the single master domain model. They trust all of the master account domains. Figure 10-8 illustrates how a multiple master domain is organized.

Once again, as shown in Figure 10-8, the master domains comprise the first-tier of the network. The resource domains make up the second-tier. Collectively, the accounts in all of the master account domains include all user accounts on the organization's network. Typically, an individual user has an account on only one master domain. How do you decide which accounts go in which domains? Some organizations break the accounts up by business function, whereas others divide the accounts geographically.

For example, if you have operations in North America, Europe, and Asia, you can create a master account domain in each of these locations. Accounts for users in North America live in the North America domain, European user accounts go in the Europe domain, and so on. Since each of the master domains trusts the others, any user with an account in one of the master domains can log on to his or her own master domain and access resources on the entire worldwide network.

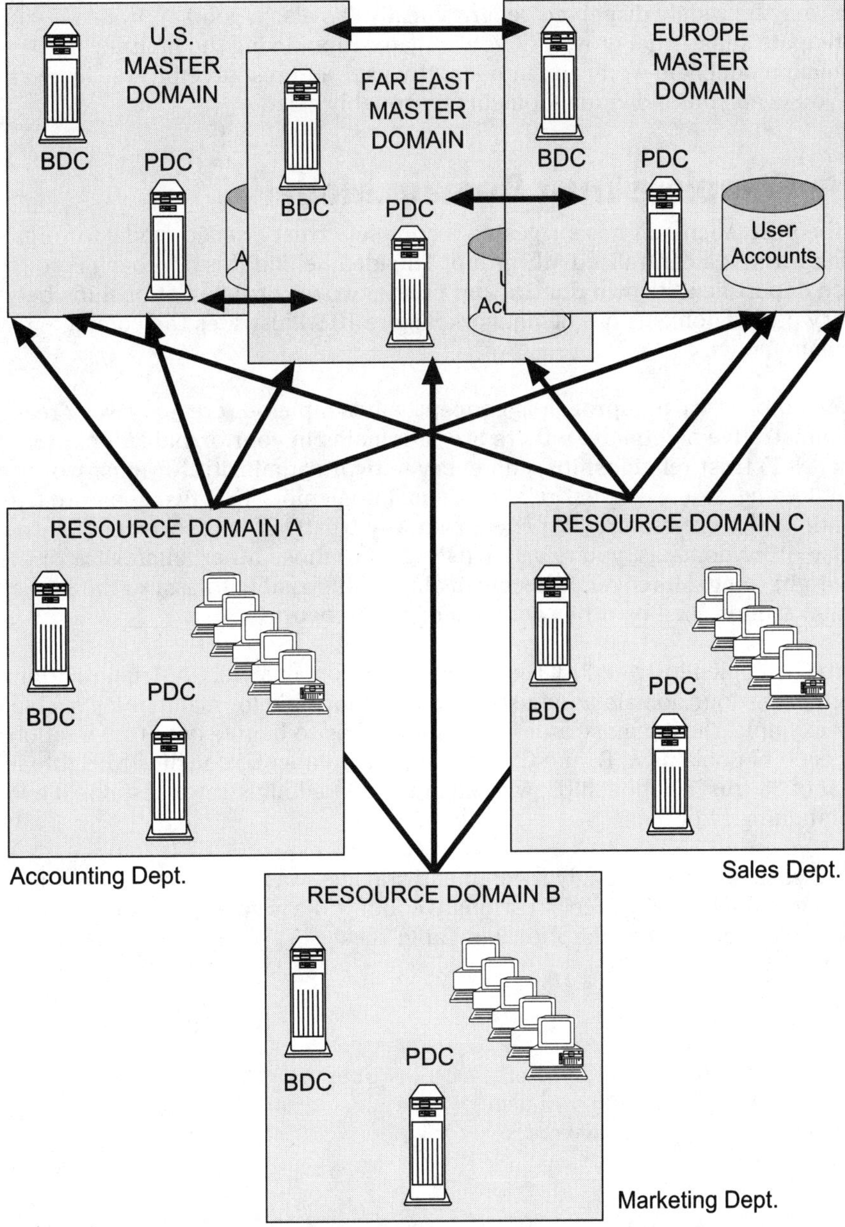

Figure 10-8: The multiple master domain model uses multiple domains for account administration.

Avoid grouping user accounts in master account domains based on their last names or other random approaches. Dividing folks up geographically or by business function will make it easier to create groups and manage the user accounts.

As you can see, the multiple master domain model is best for large organizations that may be widely dispersed geographically. It's also a good approach if you anticipate substantial growth of your organization. Using the multiple master domain model, you won't run into lengthy user and resource browse lists, as long as you keep your individual domains reasonably sized.

The Complete Trust Domain Model

In the past, Microsoft has suggested a complete trust domain model for organizations without a centralized MIS group. The idea behind this approach is to give each department its own domain and create two-way trust relationships between every pair of domains on the network. Figure 10-9 illustrates the complete trust domain model.

The complete trust approach is conceptually simple but creates a very real administrative nightmare. If there are N domains in your organization, there are N × (N–1) trust relationships, and every network administrator must worry about maintaining 2 × (N–1) trust relationships. (Remember that two separate trust relationships are required for every two-way trust.) Of course, when you trust all those other domains, you're also trusting all of those other administrators to do the right thing. Moreover, it becomes almost impossible to assure the integrity of global groups used by other domains on the network.

In the example illustrated by Figure 10-9, four domains yield 12 trust relationships. Each of the four domain administrators is responsible for maintaining six trusts. For example, the administrator for domain D has to handle two trust relationships for each of domains A, B, and C. Doubling the number of domains to eight yields a total of 56 trust relationships, with each domain administrator responsible for maintaining 14 of them.

For these reasons, I strongly recommend staying away from a complete trust domain model. In fact, I feel so strongly about it that I've left it out of the comparison of domain models, shown in Table 10-4.

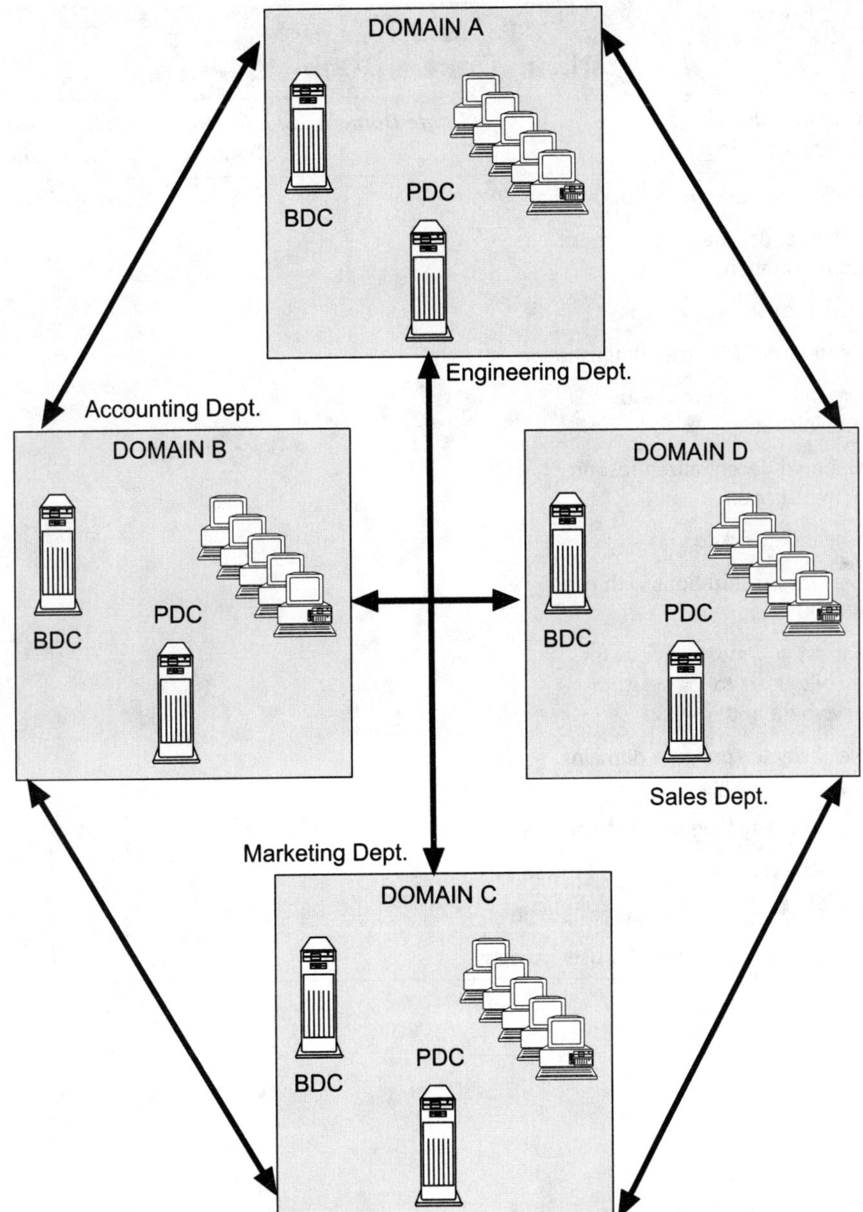

Figure 10-9: The complete trust model uses two-way trust relationships between every pair of domains on the network.

Table 10-4
Comparison of the NT Domain Models

Domain Model Characteristic	*Single Domain*	*Single Master Domain*	*Multiple Master Domain*
Centralized account administration	√	√	√
Optional decentralized account administration			√
Use of trust relationships		√	√
Centralized resource administration	√		
Optional centralized resource administration		√	√
Optional decentralized resource administration		√	√
Single network logon	√	√	√
Best for organizations with over 40,000 users			√
Easiest and most efficient for mobile users to log on from anywhere in the world			√
Flexibility to configure domains organizationally		√	√
Possible very long user browse lists	√	√	
Possible very long resource browse lists	√		
Logical grouping of resources possible		√	√
Multiple domains used for user accounts			√

Inside Microsoft's Corporate Network

One of the most interesting case studies of Windows NT Server networks is Microsoft's worldwide corporate network. They started planning and implementing the conversion from OS/2 to NT Server domains long before NT 3.1 was released. By reading the weekly update in the company's weekly *MicroNews* publication, employees could watch the bar chart decline of OS/2 servers and the increase in NT servers across the corporation.

With over 20,000 users and 40,000 nodes spread over 150 different sites, the Microsoft corporate network presented NT Server with an acid test for use in a real-world enterprise network. Since every user requires access to e-mail and other shared corporate resources, Microsoft opted to base its network design on the multiple master domain model, discussed earlier in this chapter. As you might expect, they encountered a few situations in which they had to deviate from this model, for security reasons. You'll see how in the following sections.

Microsoft's Information Technology Group, or ITG, is in charge of the MIS function at the company. They were responsible for rolling out NT Server to the corporate network, working closely with the NT development and test teams to assure a smooth transition.

Multiple Master Domain Model Organization

Figure 10-10 illustrates the general organization of the domain structure that ITG implemented on the corporate network. The first tier consists of master account domains, in which all user accounts are maintained. These domains are broken up by geographic location. ITG wanted to keep the number of master account domains as small as possible, as it's easier to break up a large domain than it is to combine several small domains.

In classical multiple master domain fashion, all second-tier resource domains trust all master account domains in the first tier. User logons are validated by one of the trusted master account domains.

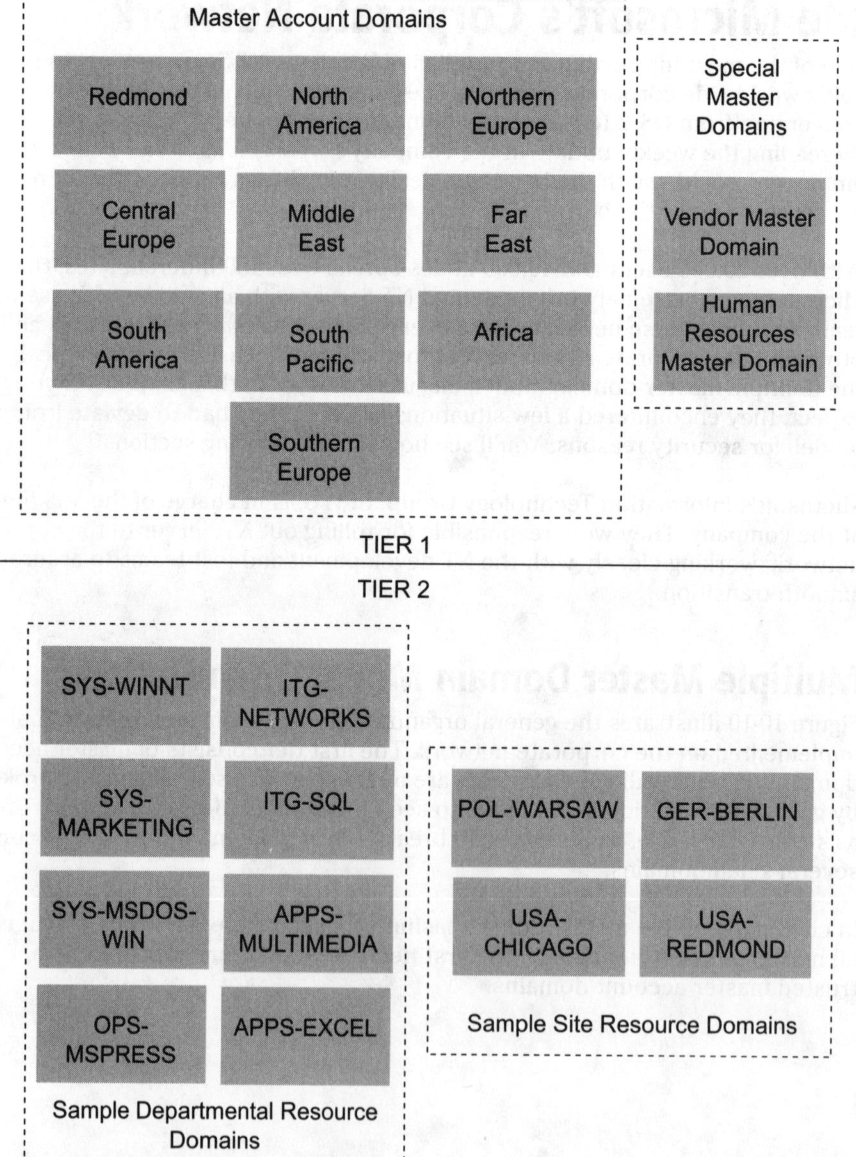

Figure 10-10: Microsoft's corporate network uses a multiple master domain model.

The First Tier

Even though there's a North America master domain, Redmond rates its own master domain since over half of the company's employees hang their umbrellas there. Redmond is the home for the Redmond, North America, and South America domain controllers. Others are distributed close to their user communities around the world. All European master domain PDCs are physically located in England.

ITG has implemented a couple of special master domains to deal with specific security issues. First, it has provided a special master domain for third-party hardware and software vendors, allowing them to transfer files electronically to and from Microsoft. Employees can access this domain through a trust relationship, but the third-party vendors can't access anything but the special vendor domain. Vendors such as Compaq, for example, use this domain to provide updated drivers and other files used for testing at Microsoft.

Second, because of the sensitive nature of its data within the corporation, the Microsoft Human Resources department has been given its own isolated master domain in the first tier. This prevents unauthorized access to confidential employee data.

The Second Tier

In general, each department and each site gets its own second-tier resource domain. Every product development organization is allowed one second-tier domain that trusts all master account domains. The naming convention used for departmental domains appends the department name to the division name. For example, Sys-WinNT is the second-tier domain for the Windows NT product group within the Systems division. Every site outside of the Redmond corporate campus is allowed to create one resource domain that trusts the master account domains. The naming convention used for sites includes the country and city names. For example, the Chicago site has a domain called USA-Chicago.

ITG has full administrative access to every domain in the corporation. This enables them to back up and restore every PDC and to load new NT builds and patches onto these computers. ITG maintains global groups and works with the Human Resources department to add, delete, and move users between groups as individuals change organizations.

If a group requests it, ITG will supply administration services to second-tier resource domains. Typically, a resource domain is administered jointly by the group that set it up and by ITG.

BDC Placement

Sites are connected via WAN links, and some of the links are quite slow. In some countries, these links can't be upgraded yet, so ITG must place BDCs strategically to maximize network availability and performance. At each remote site, ITG has placed a BDC for the master account domain serving that region. For example, although the PDCs for all European master account domains live in England, ITG has placed BDCs for each European domain at the appropriate European sites.

Summary

In this chapter, you've learned about designing single and multiple domain networks to handle large numbers of computers, users, and groups. You've analyzed your network to determine the number of domains that you need and the number of BDCs within each domain. I showed you four domain models, which you can use as starting points for designing your large, multiple domain network. You also peeked into the inner sanctum of the ITG group at Microsoft to see how they've successfully implemented a Windows NT Server-based worldwide network.

INSIDE STORY

One team in the test group, called Network User Test and Support, was particularly instrumental in the successful rollout of Windows NT Server to the corporate network. They shook out the latest builds of NT on real-world servers within the NT group and passed along advice and critical information to ITG, the folks in charge of Microsoft MIS.

With new builds of NT arriving daily, they had the impossible and thankless task of keeping all of our departmental servers updated with the latest and (hopefully) greatest code. Other groups would often ask me about these unsung heroes of getting NT Server into the real world. "What's that team's name again?" they asked. "Network User Test and Support. That's NUTS, to you." This team acronym became one of our favorites in the NT group.

Linking Nodes and Networks – RAS and TCP/IP

✦ ✦ ✦ ✦

These days, no computer or network is an island. As enterprises become more geographically dispersed, as users become more mobile, and as the Internet becomes a more compelling force in the computing world, the need to access remotely and interconnect networks steadily increases. Windows NT Server 4.0 addresses these needs with two powerful features — namely, Remote Access Service and the TCP/IP protocol.

In this chapter, I'll fill you in on how to plan and configure a RAS server. Then, I'll get into the important aspects of TCP/IP and walk you through its installation. Finally, I'll show you how to use RAS and TCP/IP together. There are lots of acronyms defined in this chapter. If you forget the meaning of an acronym, you'll find it defined in the glossary in Appendix B.

Understanding the World of RAS

Microsoft's Remote Access Service, or RAS, which I briefly introduced in Chapter 4, allows a variety of clients to become nodes on your LAN via modem, ISDN, or X.25 connections. Once connected, they operate as equal citizens with all other nodes attached to the network and are able to access any and all resources allowed by their user account. For a refresher on the differences between remote node, as offered by NT Server, and remote control products, see Chapter 1.

RAS Clients

Windows NT Server 4.0 RAS supports a variety of RAS clients, including non-Microsoft clients that conform to certain standards. In NT 4.0 and Windows 95, clients support a new feature called AutoDial, which makes connecting automatic. It remembers the connections that you've made over RAS and automatically reconnects you the next time you attempt to access that resource. (It can be a little jarring to click a drive letter in Explorer and suddenly hear the modem dialing, but it beats having to manually reconnect each time.) Table 11-1 presents the clients that can connect to a Windows NT 4.0 RAS server, along with the software required on the client. Recall from Chapter 4 that PPP stands for Point-to-Point Protocol, which is used by RAS to communicate between RAS clients and servers.

Table 11-1
Clients Supported by NT Server's RAS

Clients	*Using RAS*
Windows NT 4.0	Built-in Microsoft RAS or PPP
Windows NT 3.51	Built-in Microsoft RAS or PPP
Windows NT 3.5	Built-in Microsoft RAS or PPP
Windows NT 3.1	Built-in Microsoft RAS (no PPP support)
Windows 95	Built-in Dial-Up Networking
Windows for Workgroups	Microsoft Network Client 3.0 (included with NT Server 4.0)
DOS 3.1 (or later)	RAS version 1.1a
Microsoft OS/2 1.3	RAS version 1.1
Non-Microsoft PPP client	PPP using TCP/IP, IPX/SPX, or NetBEUI

MODEM COMPATIBILITY

Most of the hundreds of NT-compatible modems comply with industry standards and should interoperate with each other without a hitch. However, I've seen some difficult-to-diagnose problems arise from using a different modem on each end of the connection. The manufacturers have sometimes interpreted the "standards" in slightly different ways.

Thus, if you have the luxury of selecting modems for your RAS computers, use the same type of modem on clients and servers. Doing this will remove one potential trouble spot.

RAS Server

RAS Server supports TCP/IP, IPX/SPX, and NetBEUI protocols. Any combination of protocols can be handled across the maximum 256 RAS clients, as long as the RAS server computer is running those protocols. As I'll show you later in this chapter, each protocol can be individually configured to access either just the RAS server or the entire network.

On the security front, RAS server includes password encryption during the authentication process, along with encryption, to maintain security of your data in case someone is eavesdropping. In addition, you can configure RAS to call back specific users at a predetermined phone number before allowing them access to the network.

On top of all this, NT 4.0 RAS offers an exciting new feature called Point-to-Point Tunneling Protocol, or PPTP, which allows you to use the Internet as a secure WAN connection between your LANs. I'll show you how to set this up later in this chapter.

Preparing to Install RAS Server

Before you install RAS on your Windows NT Server computer, make sure that the computer already meets all of the following RAS communications hardware requirements. Check the Windows NT Hardware Compatibility List to determine whether these devices are compatible with Windows NT Server:

- The computer must contain a Windows NT-compatible network adapter card with an NDIS driver. See Chapter 8 for details on selecting and installing network adapters.
- If your RAS clients are using phone lines to connect, the computer must have one or more NT-compatible modems attached to an available serial port. You'll also need a separate phone line for each modem. (Over 1,000 modems are listed as compatible.)

If you want acceptable performance from multiple modems attached to your RAS server, install an NT-compatible multiport serial card. Products like those offered from DigiBoard offer high-performance serial ports. Just over 15 cards have been certified compatible, and most of them are DigiBoards.

- If your RAS clients are using ISDN lines to connect, the computer must include one or more NT-compatible ISDN adapters. You'll also need a separate ISDN line installed for each ISDN adapter. (Just over a dozen ISDN adapters are listed as compatible.)
- If your RAS clients are using X.25 connections, the computer must be equipped with an NT-compatible X.25 smart card. (There's a handful of compatible X.25 cards.)

The default COM2 device interrupt (IRQ 3) has slightly higher priority than the COM1 (IRQ 4) interrupt. If you have two serial ports, use COM2 for your higher-speed serial device (such as a high-speed modem).

All of the RAS communications hardware just listed must be installed, configured, connected, and powered up before you install RAS. This will make installation proceed smoothly and prevent wasted effort. RAS sometimes leads you along until it suddenly discovers that you don't have all of the required hardware installed properly.

Some modems not on the Windows NT Hardware Compatibility List may work with RAS. How-ever, this is one area where I highly recommend that you stick with what's on the list. Differences in modems are subtle, and the resulting problems are very difficult to solve. So, adhere to the NT Hardware Compatibility List as gospel in the modem area. (If you do, you'll also avoid having to deal with the painful process of understanding and modifying RAS's MODEMS.INF file, which is covered in the NT RAS online documentation.)

Installing RAS after NT Installation

I recommend performing your RAS server installation after you have Windows NT Server up and running. Here are the steps you need to follow if you're installing RAS after installing Windows NT Server on your computer:

1. While logged on with administrator privileges, click the Start ➪ Settings ➪ Control Panel option. Double-click the Modems choice.
2. Follow the Modem Wizard through the modem detection process. When you've completed modem installation, you should see a Modem Properties dialog box, similar to the one in Figure 11-1.
3. While still logged on with administrator privileges, select the Start ➪ Settings ➪ Control Panel option. Double-click the Network entry to start the Network Control Panel Application (NCPA).
4. In the Network dialog box, click the Services tab. Then click Add.
5. Under Network Services, select the Remote Access Service option and click OK, as shown in Figure 11-2.
6. NCPA asks for the path to the system files on your Windows NT Server 4.0 CD-ROM. Insert the NT CD-ROM in your CD-ROM drive. Type the path and click Continue, as Figure 11-3 illustrates.

   On my computer, the path is F:\I386. Type the drive letter of your CD-ROM and the subdirectory corresponding to your CPU platform.

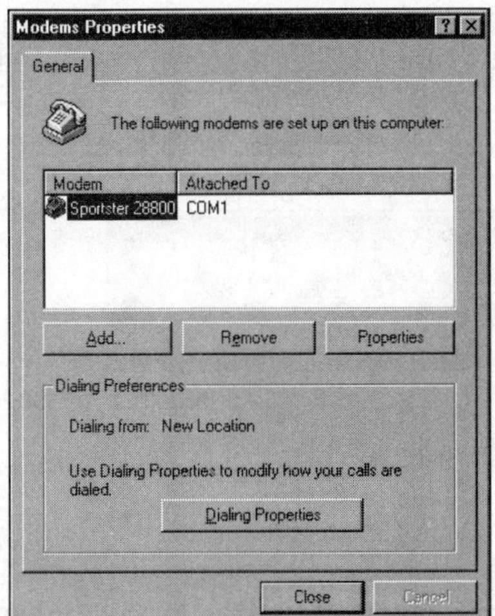

Figure 11-1: Modem properties result from the modem detection and installation process.

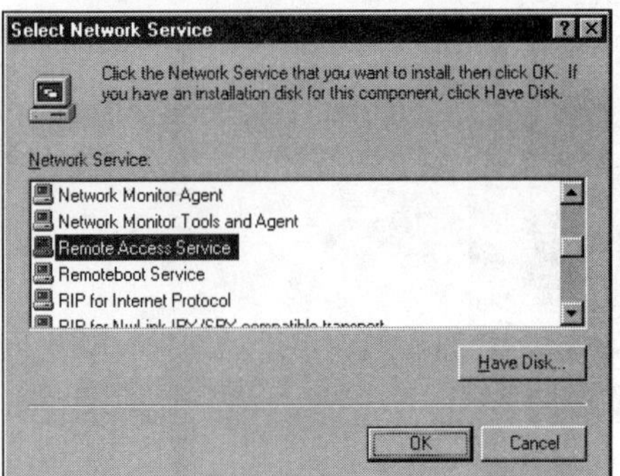

Figure 11-2: Select Remote Access Service for installation.

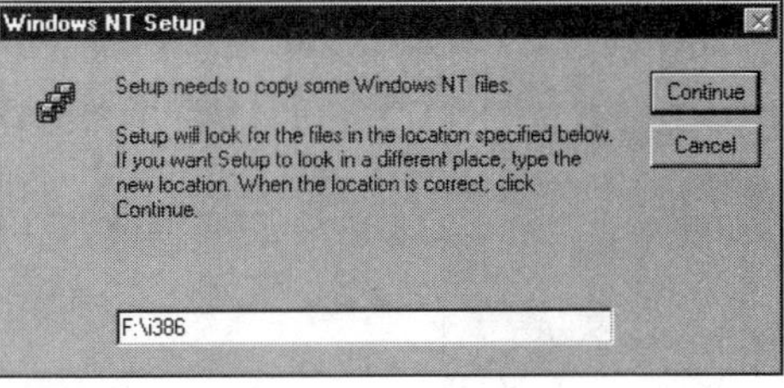

Figure 11-3: Type the path of your Windows NT Server CD-ROM files.

7. If RAS couldn't detect your serial port, modem, or other RAS device, you'll see the error message shown in Figure 11-4. If you see this message, click OK, then recheck the configuration and connection of your serial ports, modems, ISDN adapters, and so on. Then go back to step 1. If you don't see this message, go to step 8.

The most common reason for this error is a modem that's not turned on. Another typical problem is an interrupt conflict that has prevented the serial driver from loading.

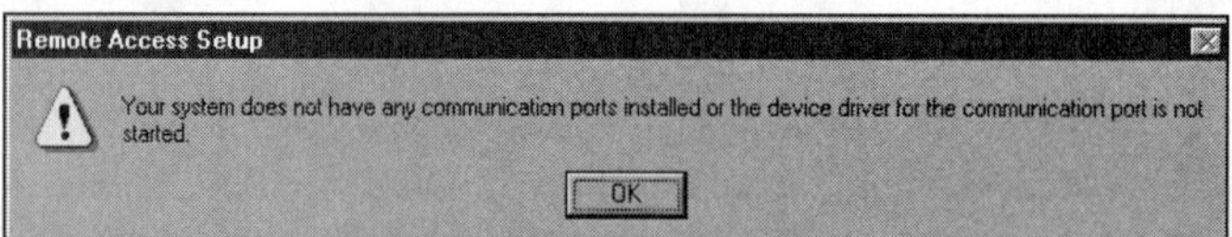

Figure 11-4: If RAS can't find your RAS hardware, you'll see this message.

8. In the Add RAS Device dialog box, verify that your serial ports, modems, and other RAS devices are listed correctly. Then click OK, as shown in Figure 11-5.

   If you need to install an additional modem, select the Install Modem option and follow the prompts. If you need to install an X.25 device, click the Install X.25 Pad entry and follow the prompts.

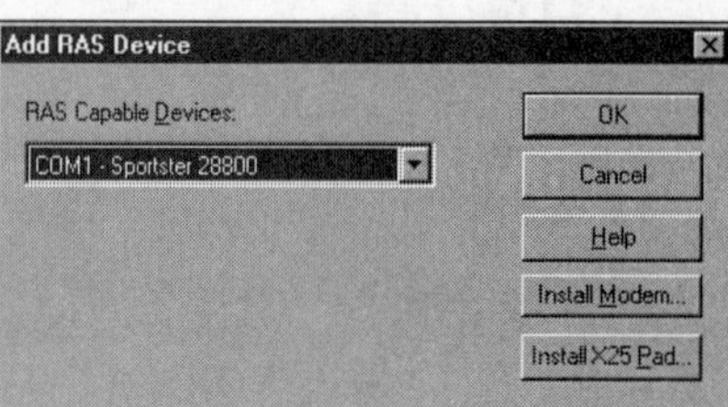

Figure 11-5: Verify that your RAS devices have been correctly detected.

9. In the Remote Access Setup dialog box, select the Configure option to establish how the device will be used by RAS. See Figure 11-6.

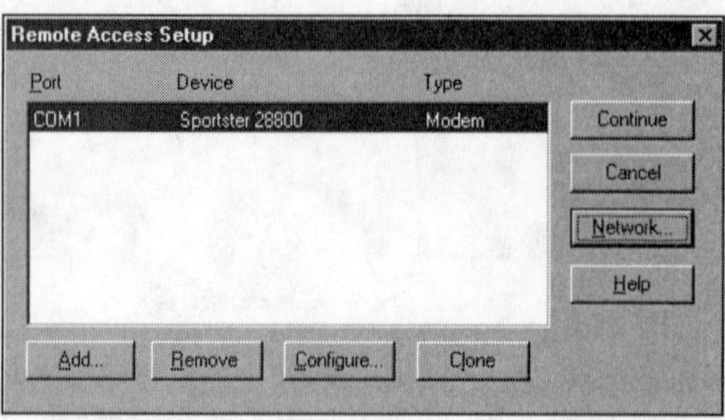

Figure 11-6: Remote Access Setup allows you to configure the RAS device and network parameters.

10. In the Configure Port Usage dialog box under Port Usage, choose either the Dial out only, Receive calls only, or Dial out and Receive calls options. Then click OK, as shown in Figure 11-7.

    The default entry is Receive calls only. This is the correct setting for a typical RAS server. If you're going to enable security callback of clients, you should select the Dial out and Receive calls option. Also, if you're going to act as a RAS client from the RAS server computer, you can enable dial-out capability.

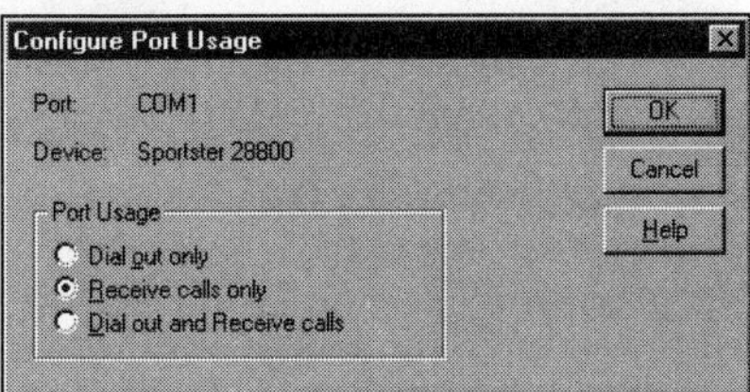

Figure 11-7: Select the Remote Access Service port usage.

11. In the Remote Access Setup dialog box, select the Network option to configure network protocols used by RAS. See Figure 11-6.
12. In the Network Configuration dialog box, under Server Settings, click to set or clear the check boxes associated with the network protocols that you're planning to run on RAS clients. See Figure 11-8.

    You can choose any or all of NetBEUI, IPX/SPX, or TCP/IP. Just be sure that you're already running these protocols on the NT Server computer where you're installing the RAS server.

    I recommend using the default of Microsoft encrypted authentication. See online Help for an explanation of the differences between the encryption settings.

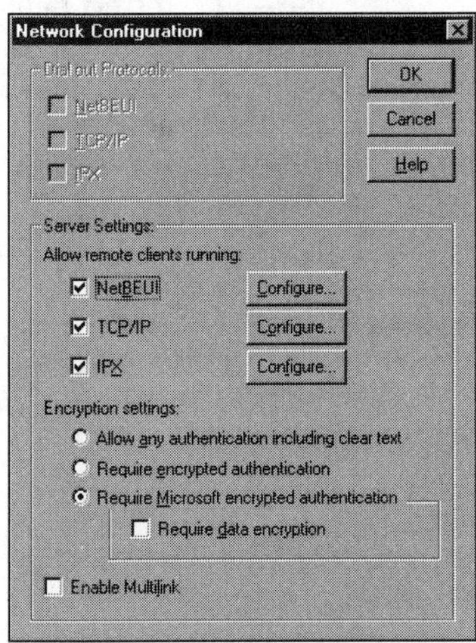

Figure 11-8: Select and configure the protocols that your RAS clients will be running.

12a. If you've selected NetBEUI, click the Configure entry next to NetBEUI. If you want to grant NetBEUI clients access to the RAS server only, and not to the entire network, select the This computer only option. Then click OK. Figure 11-9 illustrates this.

Otherwise, RAS clients running NetBEUI will have access to nodes on the network running the NetBEUI protocol. Grant access to the entire network, unless you have a specific reason for limiting access of these clients to just the RAS server.

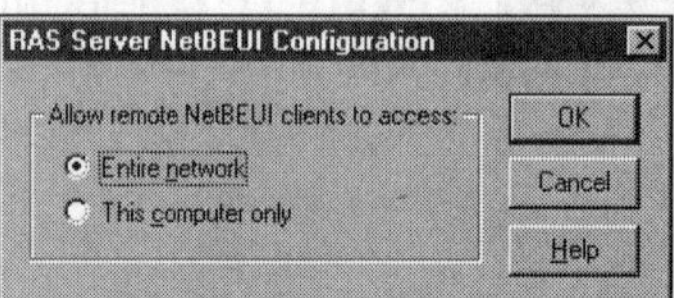

Figure 11-9: Grant or restrict network access to NetBEUI clients.

12b. If you've selected TCP/IP, select the Configure entry next to TCP/IP. If you want to grant TCP/IP clients access to the RAS server only, and not to the entire network, click the option for This computer only.

If you want to control the range of IP addresses assigned to RAS clients, select the Use static address pool option. Then type the range of IP addresses that the RAS server can assign and any IP address ranges to exclude from automatic assignment. Click OK. Figure 11-10 illustrates this.

For a detailed explanation of IP addresses and Dynamic Host Configuration Protocol (DHCP), which automatically assigns them, see the appropriate sections later in this chapter.

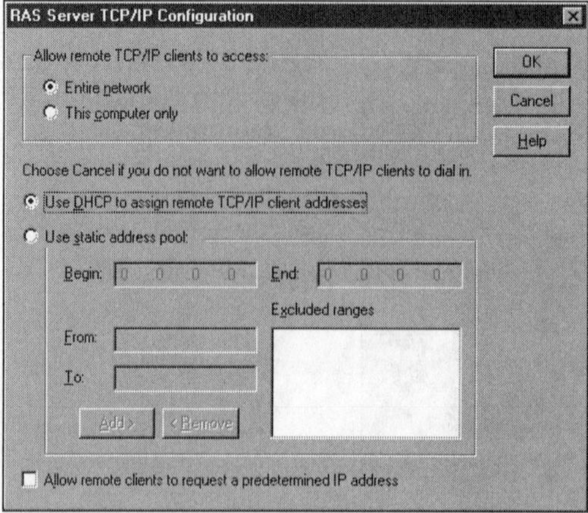

Figure 11-10: Grant or restrict network access to TCP/IP clients and configure TCP/IP addressing.

If you're using the Dynamic Host Configuration Protocol (DHCP) to assign IP addresses automatically, and you're using a static IP address pool for RAS clients, you must be sure that DHCP won't assign any addresses in the range that you specify for the RAS server. If they overlap, you'll have duplicate IP addresses on your network. See the DHCP section later in this chapter for more details.

12c. If you've selected IPX, click the Configure entry next to IPX. If you want to grant IPX clients access to the RAS server only, and not to the entire network, select the This computer only option, as shown in Figure 11-11. Then click OK.

This dialog box also allows you to configure how network numbers are assigned. You can keep the default settings for now. See Chapter 12 for details on how to integrate the NT RAS server into a NetWare environment.

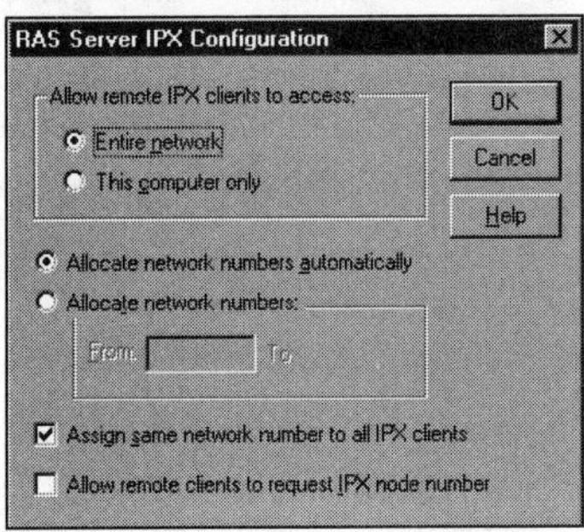

Figure 11-11: Grant or restrict network access to IPX/SPX clients.

13. In the Network Configuration dialog box, click OK. In the Remote Access Setup dialog box, click Continue.
14. NCPA again asks for the path to the system files on your Windows NT Server 4.0 CD-ROM. Verify that the NT CD-ROM is in your CD-ROM drive. Type the path and click Continue.
15. Click Close. After configuration completes, restart your computer as prompted.
16. Start the Remote Access Admin utility by selecting the Start ➪ Programs ➪ Administrative Tools ➪ Remote Access Admin entry. See Figure 11-12.

You may see a message indicating that the RAS server isn't running on this computer. If you wait about two minutes, this message will disappear, and you'll be able to continue. If the message doesn't go away, use Event Viewer to determine if RAS had a problem loading. See Chapter 21 for additional RAS troubleshooting tips and details about using Event Viewer.

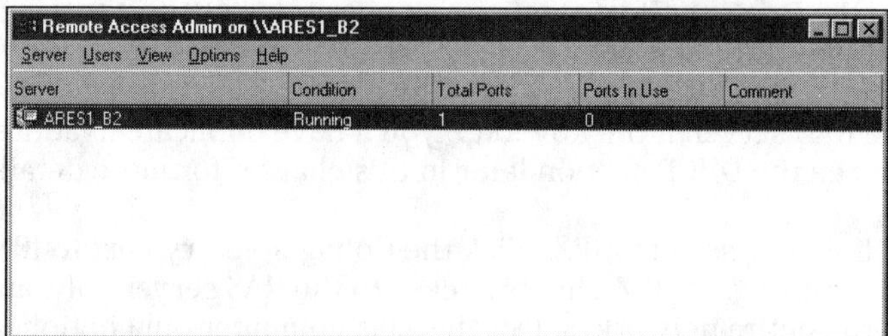

Figure 11-12: Use Remote Access Admin utility to complete configuration of your RAS server.

17. On the Users menu, click the Permissions check box. In the Remote Access Permissions dialog box, select individual user accounts that will be used on RAS clients and configure their dial-in and callback permissions, as shown in Figure 11-13. When you're done, click OK.

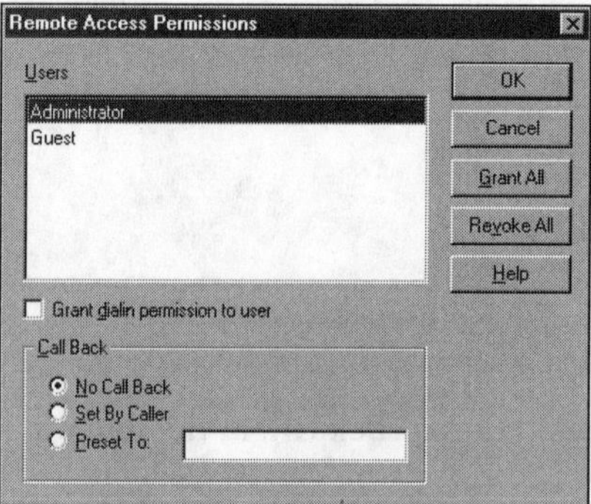

Figure 11-13: Set RAS permissions for each user account that will participate as a RAS client.

You've now completed configuration of the RAS server. You can use the Remote Access Admin utility in the future to manage RAS permissions. This utility has some additional features that you can learn about through the online Help. In Chapter 13, I'll discuss how to configure various types of client computers, including RAS clients.

Enabling PPTP

PPTP (Point-to-Point Tunneling Protocol) is a new feature in Windows NT Server 4.0 that allows you to create virtual private networks (VPNs) over the Internet. You can create a completely secure connection between remote client computers and your corporate network, running NetBEUI, TCP/IP, IPX, or any combination of these protocols. PPTP encapsulates and encrypts packets before sending them on the Internet. As a result, you can shift the burden of supporting modems or ISDN adapters to Internet Service Providers (ISPs) and can save money that you'd have spent on long-distance dial-in charges.

To use PPTP, you must enable it for each network adapter that will participate in PPTP connections. For a PPTP connection to succeed, both the RAS server and the client must have PPTP installed. Once you've installed PPTP on a specific network adapter, only PPTP packets will get through this network adapter to your computer. Other packets will be ignored. Thus, you'd typically want to have multiple network adapters in your server with the one dedicated to PPTP connected to the Internet. The remaining adapters should be connected to your corporate network. Client computers running PPTP can then gain access to your corporate network through the dedicated adapter in your server.

Before enabling PPTP, you need to have the TCP/IP protocol already installed. You can find detailed instructions for doing this later in this chapter. Once you have TCP/IP installed, here are the steps you must complete to enable PPTP on your server:

1. While logged on with administrator privileges, select the Start ⇨ Settings ⇨ Control Panel option. Double-click the Network entry to start the Network Control Panel Application (NCPA).
2. In the Network dialog box, click the Protocols tab. Select TCP/IP Protocol and click Properties.
3. In the Microsoft TCP/IP Properties dialog box, click the IP Address tab. Then click Advanced.
4. Select the adapter that you want to participate in PPTP connections and click the Enable PPTP Filtering check box. When you're done, click OK.

   If you want more than one of your adapters to filter for PPTP packets, repeat this step for each of them.
5. In the Microsoft TCP/IP Properties dialog box, click OK.
6. Click Close and restart the computer as prompted.

Understanding the World of TCP/IP

If you've worked before with UNIX running the TCP/IP protocol suite, you know that TCP/IP has a world of concepts and terminology all its own. If you haven't worked with it before, you'll soon see that this is true. As mentioned in Chapter 4, if you want to know everything there is to know about TCP/IP, you'd better start now and hope you live to a ripe old age. I won't burden you with every detail — just the salient points that you need to install and administer TCP/IP in an NT or mixed network environment.

If you're really interested in the detailed meanings of TCP/IP components, you'll find them defined in a series of RFC (Request for Comments) documents. On the Web, visit `http://www.internic.net` and follow the trail to the RFCs, which you can download via FTP.

In the TCP/IP world, all nodes connected to the network are called *hosts*, whether they're servers, clients, or even network-connected printers. The original definition of host assumed only one network interface per computer, but computers today can contain multiple network adapters. So, each adapter is really considered a separate host. Thus, if your computer running Windows NT Server contains two network adapters, it's really considered two hosts by TCP/IP.

Addressing Your Host

I'm about to dig into the nitty-gritty details of how hosts are addressed in TCP/IP. Do we really *have* to? Yes, and here's why. First, you'll be expected to shoulder the burden of responsibility for managing the TCP/IP addresses within your network. Second, Windows NT Server 4.0 provides some key features that make this whole addressing effort easier for you to manage. You'll first need to understand TCP/IP addressing to make effective use of these features.

Every host on a TCP/IP network must have a unique 32-bit address, known as its *IP address*. The addressing scheme uniquely identifies a specific network adapter in a specific computer on a specific network. Can it *be* more specific? In theory, if each computer contained only one network adapter, the IP addressing scheme would allow unique identification of nearly four billion computers. If you think that's plenty, you might be surprised to learn that folks are already working on ways to expand the addressing scheme to handle even more computers. (If you have anywhere near four billion computers within your own corporate network, your needs and problems are somewhat beyond the scope of this book.)

Since TCP/IP is the protocol of the Internet, if you hook your LAN to the Internet, every one of your hosts must have a unique address that differentiates it from all other hosts in the world. So, who is responsible for assigning these addresses and assuring they're unique, and who in their right mind would want to do this? Well, this responsibility is shared. An organization called the Internet Network Information Center, or InterNIC, assigns unique network addresses. You, as network administrator, are then responsible for further assigning addresses to individual hosts within your own network.

Dissecting an IP Address

IP addresses are typically expressed as four decimal numbers separated by periods, representing the four bytes of the 32-bit address (for example, 129.37.15.6). This is called *dotted-decimal notation*. The IP address contains two pieces of information — namely the network address and the host address. The network address, which is the part assigned by InterNIC, uniquely identifies your network. The host address, which you assign, uniquely identifies a node within that network.

GET YOUR OWN ADDRESS

If you know that you'll never connect your network to the Internet or to any other TCP/IP network, you can get away with assigning your own network address without any involvement from InterNIC. However, I strongly advise against doing this. Few organizations today want to isolate themselves from the Internet. If you decide in the future to connect your network to it, you'll have to reassign IP addresses to your network.

You're much better off getting a legitimate network address from InterNIC up front and using it from the start. InterNIC can be reached via e-mail at hostmaster@internic.net, by phone in the U.S. at 1-800-862-0677, or by phone outside the U.S. at 703-742-4777. InterNIC also maintains a very informative Web site at `http://rs.internic.net/rs.internic.html`. InterNIC may refer you to an ISP (Internet Service Provider) to obtain your new network address from them. You may have to pay a fee for obtaining a network address, depending on your ISP.

If you pick up literature on TCP/IP, you'll probably run across the term octet in the context of IP addresses. Just mentally translate this to mean "byte." The term octet was used earlier, before computers standardized on an 8-bit byte. For some reason, the term has attached itself like a leech to IP address discussions and won't let go. I won't use the octet term again in this book.

There are three ways that the bytes of the IP address are sliced to create the network and host addresses. The Internet community has created different classes of IP addresses, designed to accommodate different network sizes. Table 11-2 presents these classes. In the table, I've used the notation *a.b.c.d* to represent the dotted-decimal notation for the four bytes of an IP address.

Table 11-2
Classes of IP Addresses

Class	*Network Address*	*Host Address*	*Total Number of Networks*	*Total Number of Hosts per Network*
A	a (1 byte)	b.c.d (3 bytes)	126	16,777,214
B	a.b (2 bytes)	c.d (2 bytes)	16,384	65,534
C	a.b.c (3 bytes)	d (1 byte)	2,097,151	254

As Table 11-2 shows, relatively few Class A addresses are available, but each Class A network can accommodate over 16 million nodes. Class B and C addresses are much more common, with fewer nodes per network available in each class. When requesting a network address, make sure that the class you request will accommodate your network now and in the future.

Never assign the values 0, 1, or 255 to any byte of an IP address. These values are reserved internally for broadcast and other purposes. If you use them in IP addresses, you'll run into communication problems on your LAN. Some NT utilities prevent you from doing this, but others don't.

Also, IP address 127.0.0.1 is reserved as a loopback address. If you send a packet to this address, it should get back to you unless there's a network problem.

Looking Behind the Subnet Mask

Let's say you've been assigned a Class B network address. However, your network is actually a WAN made up of several LANs scattered across the country, and each LAN has under 50 nodes. The number of LANs in your network will grow, but you know the number of nodes per LAN won't ever go above 60. Rather than applying for a different network address for each of your LANs, you can break your block of IP addresses into smaller chunks, called *subnets*, one for each of your LANs.

In a Class B address, 16 bits are consumed by your assigned network address. The remaining 16 bits are meant for uniquely identifying hosts on your network. Since your individual LANs are never going to have more than 60 nodes each, you can allocate six bits for your individual host addresses and the remaining ten bits for your individual LAN network addresses (subnet addresses). In a sense, you're further subdividing the block of IP addresses that you've been assigned to meet the specific needs of your network. You're using the portion of the IP address intended for host identification to identify your LANs and nodes within those LANs.

Now, what's the subnet mask, and how do you use it to accomplish this subdivision? A subnet mask looks almost like a four-byte IP address. For example, the standard subnet mask for a Class B network address is 255.255.0.0. The mask tells your nodes which part of the IP address is used for the network address and which part is the host address. The bits set to 1 in the subnet mask indicate which bits of the IP address make up the network address. The bits set to 0 in the mask indicate which bits of the IP address constitute the host address. Figure 11-14 illustrates this approach, using our example.

You can't get away with an empty subnet mask. The default subnet mask for a Class B address is 255.255.0.0, since the first 16 bits are used for the network addresses, and the remaining 16 bits are used for the host address. So, a Class B address of 129.37.15.6 with a subnet mask of 255.255.0.0 tells you that 129.37 is the network address and 15.6 is the host address on that network. Likewise, the default subnet mask for a Class A address is 255.0.0.0 and the Class C default mask is 255.255.255.0.

In our example, only the last six bits of the subnet mask are set to zero, since you're only using six bits for the host address. All of the remaining bits in the subnet mask are set to one. Thus, the subnet mask in this situation is 255.255.255.192, as shown in Figure 11-14.

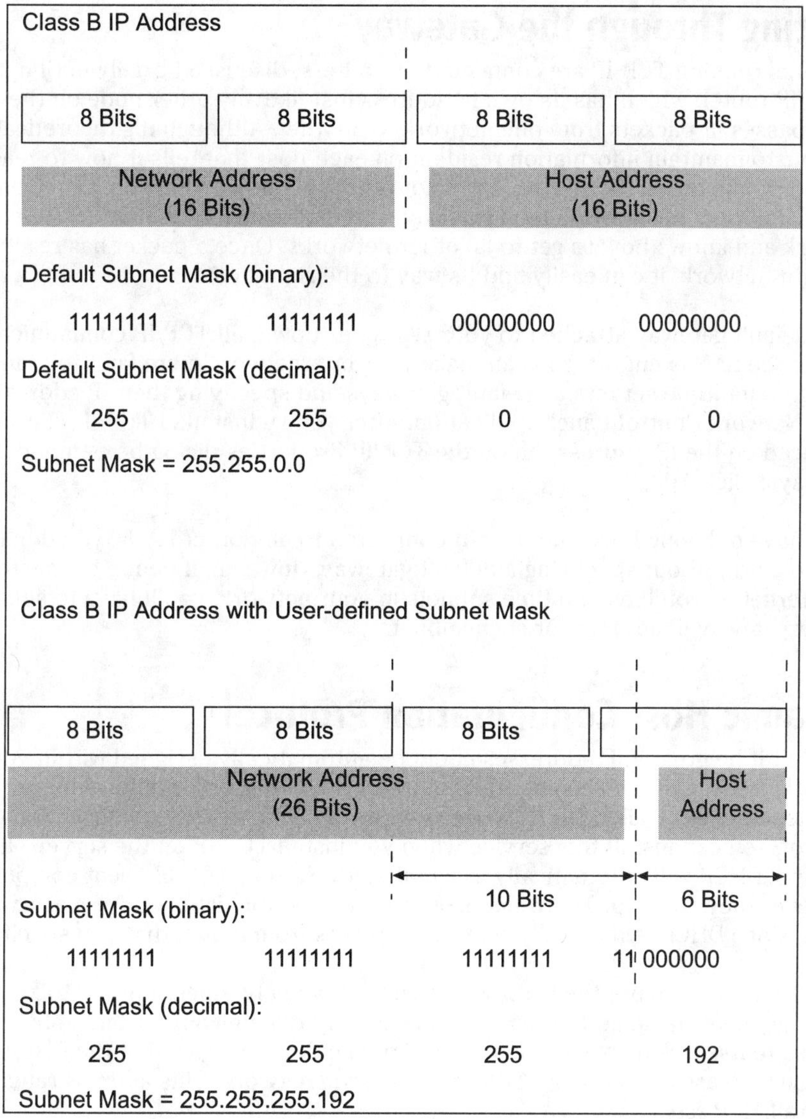

Class B IP Address

8 Bits | 8 Bits | 8 Bits | 8 Bits

Network Address (16 Bits) | Host Address (16 Bits)

Default Subnet Mask (binary):

11111111 11111111 00000000 00000000

Default Subnet Mask (decimal):

255 255 0 0

Subnet Mask = 255.255.0.0

Class B IP Address with User-defined Subnet Mask

8 Bits | 8 Bits | 8 Bits |

Network Address (26 Bits) | Host Address

10 Bits | 6 Bits

Subnet Mask (binary):

11111111 11111111 11111111 11 000000

Subnet Mask (decimal):

255 255 255 192

Subnet Mask = 255.255.255.192

Figure 11-14: A subnet mask further subdivides the block of IP addresses that you've been assigned.

All nodes on your subnet *must* use the same subnet mask, the same network address, and a unique host address. Otherwise, you'll definitely run into problems communicating among computers running TCP/IP on your network.

Routing Through the Gateway

Networks running TCP/IP are connected by routers, discussed briefly in Chapter 3. A TCP/IP router, which has its own IP address just like any other node on the network, passes IP packets from one network to another. Although it's theoretically possible to maintain information resident on each host that tells it how to reach all other hosts on earth, this is clearly not practical. Instead, one host is given the responsibility of being the *default gateway*. A default gateway is attached to each network and knows how to get to all other networks. Once a packet has reached the right network, it can easily find its way to the right host.

If the default gateway attached to your LAN goes down, all TCP/IP communication outside the LAN is cut off. You can make your internetwork more fault tolerant by setting up multiple servers as default gateways and specifying their IP addresses in the Network Control Panel Application. After you've installed TCP/IP, click Advanced on the IP Address tab on the TCP/IP Properties dialog box. Under Gateways, click Add.

If you have only one LAN, and it's not connected to any other LANs, you don't have to worry about specifying a default gateway. However, if you're connected to the Internet or you have multiple subnets in your network, you'll have to specify a default gateway IP address for each subnet.

Dynamic Host Configuration Protocol

Wouldn't it be great if IP addresses could be automatically assigned within your network, freeing you of keeping track of every host address? Windows NT Server provides a service called DHCP, which stands for *Dynamic Host Configuration Protocol*. You can install this service when you install TCP/IP on the server. Once installed, DHCP will automatically assign IP addresses to TCP/IP client computers whenever they start up. There's no need to keep a static list of address assignments, since DHCP dynamically selects addresses from a pool that you specify.

You'll have to configure the DHCP server itself manually, since it needs to know the range of available addresses and since it can't dynamically assign an IP address to itself. You specify the range or pool of IP addresses that the DHCP server can use to assign to other TCP/IP nodes in the network. This address range is called a DHCP *scope*.

Use the DHCP approach on your NT server, unless you really enjoy manually updating files with a text editor and paying a visit to every computer on your network to set its IP address correctly. I know there are some people who really enjoy this sort of thing, so the manual approach is still there for those two people.

Windows NT Server includes a version of the TCP/IP protocol stack for Windows for Workgroups that can be dynamically configured by a Windows NT server running

DHCP. I'll show you how to install and configure network clients in Chapter 13. The NT DHCP server service is compatible with other products that comply with the RFCs defining the DHCP protocol.

If you use DHCP, I recommend that you use the WINS feature of Windows NT Server to perform dynamic translation of computer names to IP addresses. WINS works closely with DHCP to keep these translations up to date at all times. I'll discuss setting up a WINS server later in this chapter.

The routers in your network must support RFCs 1532, 1533, 1541, and 1542. They specify how to handle forwarding DHCP packets across the router. If your routers don't support these RFCs, the DHCP packets will be dropped by the router. On some routers, routing of these packets is a configuration option. Contact your router vendor for information on how to configure or upgrade your router software to handle these packets.

What if you have TCP/IP nodes on your network that don't know how to work with DHCP? And what if you have nodes, like TCP/IP routers, that require fixed IP addresses? Using NT's DHCP Manager utility, you can handle all of these situations by telling DHCP which addresses are static, which addresses not to dole out to other nodes, and so forth. Although dealing with these exception cases does take some effort on your part, DHCP can handle assignment of IP addresses automatically for the majority of TCP/IP nodes in your network.

You can avoid annoying pop-up error messages and network communication problems by installing the DHCP server before you install TCP/IP on any other computers that are running Windows for Workgroups or Windows NT. That way, all of the remaining computers can ask the DHCP server for an IP address while you're installing NT on them.

Leasing an Address

The DHCP server actually leases IP addresses to nodes for a fixed period of time, similar to how auto dealers lease cars. The lease must be renewed on a set schedule. If it isn't renewed, DHCP repossesses the IP address for use on some other network node. For example, if a computer that was assigned an IP address by DHCP is shut down for a week and the lease expires during that time, DHCP may reuse that address for a different computer. When the first computer is powered back up, DHCP will assign it a new IP address.

You can control the length of the DHCP server's lease period using DHCP Manager. Here are a few guidelines for picking the right lease length:

- ✦ If you make frequent and drastic changes to your network structure (such as moving computers from one subnet to another), consider setting the lease period to less than a week.

✦ If you have many portable laptop computers on your network, and they're removed from the network frequently or are moved from one part of your network to another, opt for a shorter lease period (for example, under a week).

✦ If the demand for IP addresses is high on your network (or the supply of available addresses is low), opt for a short lease period. For example, if you have only 254 available IP addresses and you have nearly as many users, the demand for IP addresses is high.

✦ If the structure of your network is fairly stable and moving computers around is rare, consider setting the lease period to a month.

A Host by Any Other Name

If you're like most humans, you probably prefer to address computers by name rather than by IP address. Your users probably feel the same way. If you're running DHCP to assign IP addresses dynamically, the computer name becomes the only consistent way of referring to a particular node on your network.

The activity of translating between computer names and IP addresses is called *name resolution*. Several methods have been implemented over the years to perform this translation automatically. The earliest solution involves the use of simple text files. Each computer has a copy of a file containing a one-line translation for each host address on the network. This approach can work for very small networks but breaks down quickly in large networks that change frequently. Keeping all of the copies of the text file up to date on every computer can become a nightmare. Windows NT Server supports two text file approaches, discussed later in this chapter.

More modern approaches to name resolution centralize the required mapping information on one or more servers, removing the need for a mapping file on every computer. These server methods predominate today, but the text file methods still exist to support older TCP/IP implementations and to act as a backup mechanism if the name resolution servers fail.

An Internet address consists of two components — namely, a *host name* and a *domain name*. (Unfortunately, this domain name isn't the same as an NT Server domain name. Yet another overloaded term.) The host name is the name of your computer, which is typically the computer name that you assigned when you installed the operating system. The domain name is typically the name of an organization followed by the type of organization. The organization type is called a domain extension, which is similar to a file extension. Table 11-3 presents the domain extensions in use today on the Internet. Microsoft's domain name is microsoft.com, where microsoft is the organization name and .com is the domain extension — in this case, a commercial organization.

The domain name structure of the Internet is really organized as a hierarchical tree. The root of the tree is unnamed. The top-level domain names consist of

Table 11-3
Domain Extensions and Their Organization Types

Domain Extension	*Organization Type*
.com	Commercial enterprises
.edu	Educational institutions
.gov	Government organizations
.mil	Military organizations
.net	Network support organizations
.org	Organizations that don't fall into the above categories

organization types (as shown in Table 11-3) and geographical country codes. Although a U.S. country domain exists, most domains in the U.S. are organized under the organizational types. The second-level domain names are those assigned to specific organizations such as Microsoft, Adobe, or CMU. Figure 11-15 illustrates this tree structure.

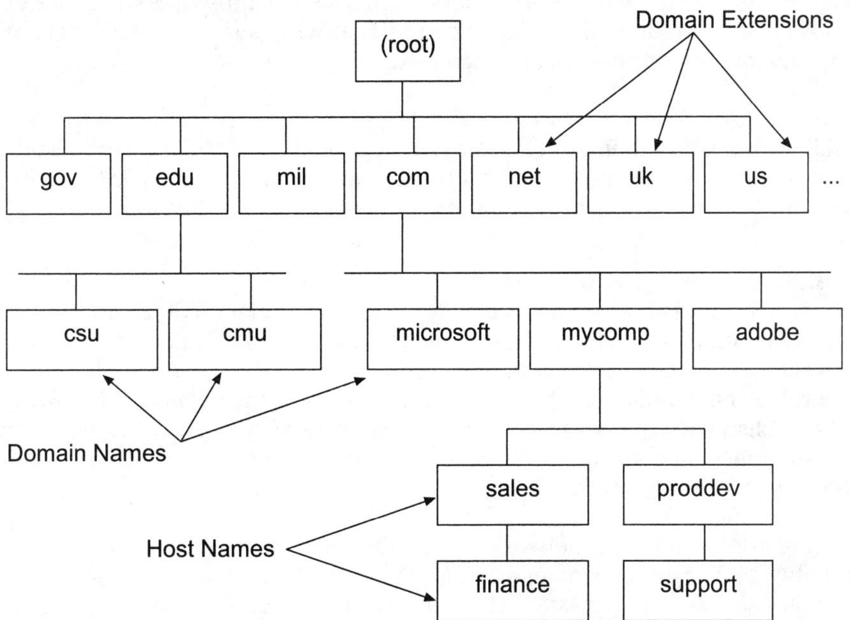

Figure 11-15: Domain names are organized into a hierarchical tree structure.

The domain name and the host name combine to generate a Fully Qualified Domain Name, or FQDN, for the computer. (You just don't see many Qs in acronyms anymore, do you?) Using the tree illustrated in Figure 11-15, the FQDN of the sales computer is sales.mycomp.com.

Microsoft WINS

No, this isn't a prediction about how Microsoft will do in the operating system race. WINS stands for Windows Internet Name Service. WINS automatically performs name resolution by translating between computer names and their associated IP addresses. It's the easiest, most recommended method for name resolution on a Windows NT server network. In most configurations, WINS is faster and more reliable than other approaches.

You establish a WINS server by running the WINS service on any Windows NT Server computer that's running TCP/IP. To assure availability of the service, you can establish backup WINS servers. WINS dynamically maintains a database of TCP/IP addresses and their associated computer names. It works hand-in-hand with DHCP to keep this database current. In fact, handling name resolution on a network using DHCP is almost impossible without a WINS server in the picture to sort everything out. Whatever other name resolution methods that you install, I recommend that you include WINS servers in your TCP/IP network.

At a minimum, establish one WINS server and one backup WINS server for every 10,000 client computers. Establishing additional WINS servers in your network will provide more fault tolerance and load balancing.

Servers running WINS need to have fixed IP addresses. They shouldn't look to DHCP for obtaining their addresses dynamically. Since DHCP servers have the same requirement, I recommend that you install your primary WINS server on the same Windows NT Server computer that's running the DHCP server.

Domain Name System

DNS, which stands for Domain Name System, is a standard TCP/IP utility used for name resolution on the Internet. It implements a distributed database of mappings between host names and IP addresses. Unlike WINS, DNS is a static database that requires manual updating when changes are made to the network. Like WINS, you can establish backup DNS servers to balance the load and provide a degree of fault tolerance. In contrast to WINS, which maps computer names to IP addresses, DNS translates between FQDNs and IP addresses.

If you're connecting your network to the Internet, and your network is small, you'll probably get the address of an existing DNS server from your ISP. If your network is large, you may want to establish your own DNS servers. However, be prepared for significant manual configuration in setting up a DNS server.

I recommend using DNS if you're operating in a network with computers running UNIX or if you're attached to the Internet (which implies communicating with UNIX computers). DNS will provide the additional name resolution that you need for Internet domain and host names.

Putting DNS and WINS Together

DNS doesn't dynamically update its database as WINS does. By using DNS and WINS together, you can get the best of both worlds. A Windows NT Server computer that's set up to serve as both a DNS and a WINS server must not be configured to use DNS for Windows name resolution. When you configure TCP/IP, make sure the Enable DNS for Windows Resolution check box is clear on the WINS Address tab in the Microsoft TCP/IP Properties dialog box.

HOSTS and LMHOSTS

Computers located on LANs that don't use WINS need to use static text files for name resolution. As mentioned earlier, these methods were developed before DNS and WINS were developed and represent the fallback position for subnets that don't support WINS or that don't have a working WINS server.

Since it's so easy for these files to get out of date, I recommend that you identify one computer that holds the master text files, make all changes on that computer, and then propagate copies of the master files to all other nodes on the network. If you start editing independent copies of these files on various network nodes, the situation will quickly get out-of-hand, especially on a large network.

The most primitive form of this mapping text file is called HOSTS. It's equivalent to having a local DNS. The HOSTS file simply contains a list of IP addresses and their associated host names. Once you've installed TCP/IP, you can find a sample HOSTS file in \SystemRoot\SYSTEM32\DRIVERS\ETC\HOSTS. Use a text editor (such as Notepad) to add a host address and name for each TCP/IP computer with which you need to communicate.

If you're familiar with BSD UNIX 4.3, the Windows NT Server HOSTS file format is identical to the /etc/hosts file. The file serves the same function, but it must reside in the \SystemRoot\SYSTEM32\DRIVERS\ETC directory on Windows NT computers.

Translations between computer names and IP addresses can be accomplished using the LMHOSTS file. It's equivalent to having a local WINS server. The LMHOSTS file contains a list of IP addresses and their associated host names. Unlike the HOSTS file, LMHOSTS also allows several special directives. Once you've installed TCP/IP, you can find a sample LMHOSTS file in \SystemRoot\SYSTEM32\DRIVERS\ETC\LMHOSTS.SAM. Copy the LHMOSTS.SAM file to LMHOSTS before editing it to add host names and addresses.

If you're familiar with the LAN Manager 2.x TCP/IP LMHOSTS file, the Windows NT Server LMHOSTS file format is fully compatible with it. The file serves the same function and uses exactly the same syntax. On NT, it must reside in the \System-Root\SYSTEM32\DRIVERS\ETC directory.

Installing TCP/IP during NT Installation

If you want to install the TCP/IP protocol while you're installing Windows NT Server, follow the steps outlined here. If you've already installed NT Server and you want to add the TCP/IP protocol to it, go to the next section for step-by-step instructions.

1. Setup asks if you're going to use a DHCP server for IP addressing, as shown in Figure 11-16. If you want an existing DHCP server automatically to assign IP addresses to this computer, click Yes. If you want to manually configure this computer's IP address, click No.

   If this is your first Windows NT Server TCP/IP installation, you'll want to configure this computer's IP address manually and then make it a DHCP server. I'll show you how to set up a DHCP server later in this chapter.

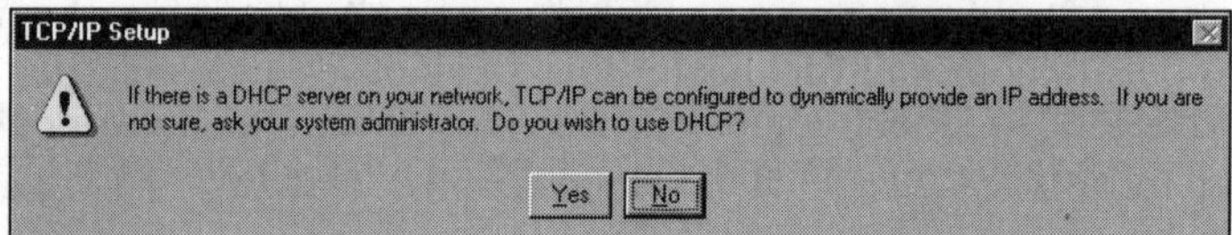

Figure 11-16: Select either automatic DHCP IP address assignment or manual configuration of this computer.

2. In the Microsoft TCP/IP Properties dialog box, click the IP Address tab.
3. Type the IP address and subnet mask in the appropriate fields. If you need to specify a default gateway, type its IP address in the appropriate field. Then click OK. See Figure 11-17.

   If you need to specify IP addresses for multiple adapters or you have multiple default gateways, click Advanced to enter this information. Then click OK. Figure 11-18 illustrates the advanced options.

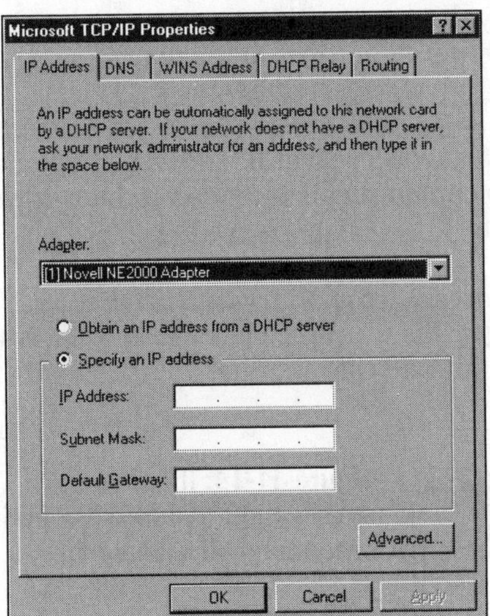

Figure 11-17: Set the node IP address, subnet mask, and default gateway.

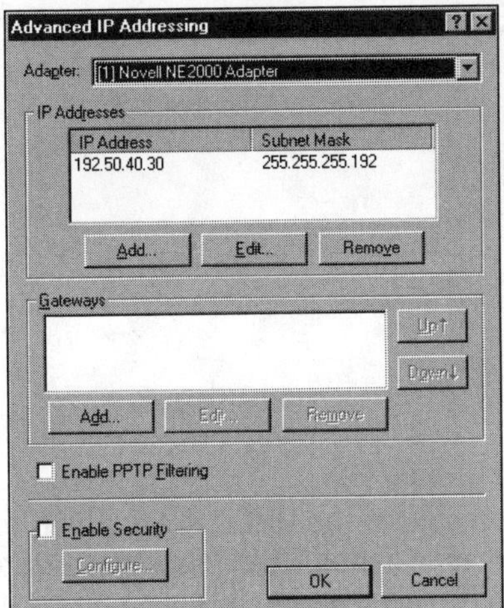

Figure 11-18: Use Advanced IP Addressing to specify addresses for multiple adapters and multiple default gateways.

4. If you know the IP address of your primary WINS server, click the WINS Address tab. Type the WINS server IP address and click OK, as shown in Figure 11-19.

   You can also specify a secondary WINS server IP address, if you have one. If the computer you're currently configuring is intended to be a WINS server, you can skip this step completely.

   If you don't specify a WINS address, Setup will warn you that no WINS address was specified. If you get this warning, click Yes to specify a WINS address or No if you want to continue without one.

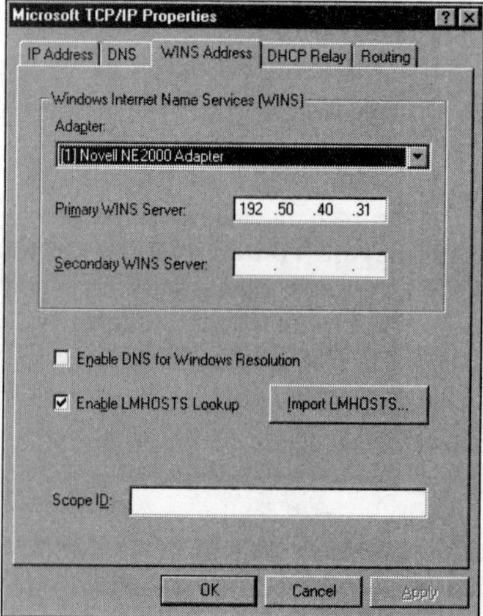

Figure 11-19: If you're using WINS, specify the IP addresses of primary and secondary WINS servers.

Specifying TCP/IP during NT installation causes the DHCP Relay Agent to be installed by default. If you don't specify an existing DHCP server IP address, Setup will warn you and won't install the DHCP relay service. If there's an existing DHCP server on your network and you know its address, you can specify it when prompted by Setup.

Installing TCP/IP after NT Installation

Here are the steps you need to follow if you're installing the TCP/IP protocol suite after installing Windows NT Server on your computer:

1. While logged on with administrator privileges, select the Start ➪ Settings ➪ Control Panel option. Double-click the Network entry to start the Network Control Panel Application (NCPA).

2. In the Network dialog box, click the Protocols tab. Then click Add.
3. Under Network Protocol, choose TCP/IP Protocol and click OK, as shown in Figure 11-20.

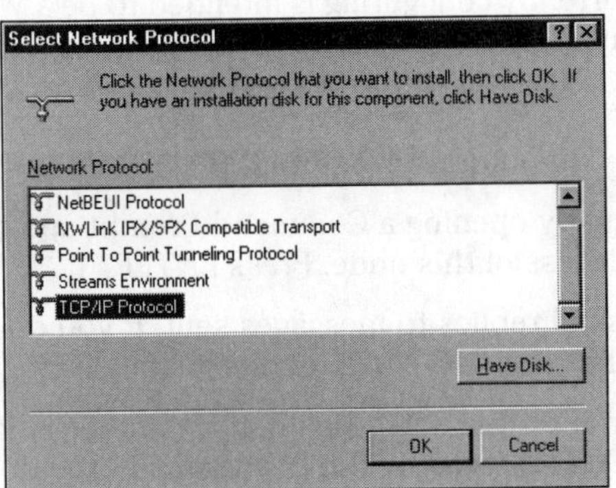

Figure 11-20: Select the TCP/IP protocol for installation.

4. NCPA asks if you're going to use a DHCP server for IP addressing, as shown in Figure 11-16. If you want an existing DHCP server to assign IP addresses to this computer automatically, click Yes. If you want to configure this computer's IP address manually, click No.

   If this is your first Windows NT Server TCP/IP installation, you'll want to configure this computer's IP address manually and then make it a DHCP server. I'll show you how to set up a DHCP server later in this chapter.

5. NCPA asks for the path to the system files on your Windows NT Server 4.0 CD-ROM. Insert the NT CD-ROM in your CD-ROM drive. Type the path and click Continue.

   On my computer, the path is F:\I386. Type the drive letter of your CD-ROM and the subdirectory corresponding to your CPU platform.

6. In the Network dialog box, click Close. After a few moments, NCPA displays the Microsoft TCP/IP Properties dialog box.

   If you ever want to change your TCP/IP configuration, you'll be able to bring up this dialog box by clicking the Protocols tab, selecting TCP/IP Protocol, and clicking Properties.

7. In the Microsoft TCP/IP Properties dialog box, click the IP Address tab.
8. Type the IP address and subnet mask in the appropriate fields. If you need to specify a default gateway, type its IP address in the appropriate field. Figure 11-17 illustrates this procedure.

   If you need to specify IP addresses for multiple adapters or you have multiple default gateways, click Advanced to enter this information. Then click OK. Figure 11-18 illustrates the advanced options.

9. If you know the IP address of your primary WINS server, click the WINS Address tab. Type the WINS server IP address and click OK, as shown in Figure 11-19.

   You can also specify a secondary WINS server IP address, if you have one. If the computer that you're currently configuring is intended to be a WINS server, you can skip this step completely.

10. In the Microsoft TCP/IP Properties dialog box, click OK.

11. Click Close and restart the computer as prompted.

12. Verify that TCP/IP is running by opening a Command Prompt and typing **PING** followed by the IP address of this node. Press ENTER.

    You should see four successful replies to messages sent. If you don't, go back into NCPA and make sure that the TCP/IP protocol is installed.

13. If you have another computer on the network already running TCP/IP, go to that computer and type **PING** followed by the IP address of the node that you just configured. Press ENTER.

    You should see four successful replies to messages sent. If you see an error message such as "destination host unreachable," verify that the subnet masks are identical and that the IP address is correct.

Establishing a DHCP Server

Once you've installed Windows NT Server, you can set it up as a DHCP server. I highly recommend installing the DHCP server on your first Windows NT server that uses TCP/IP. Doing this will make subsequent TCP/IP installations go more smoothly. The DHCP server will be able to assign IP addresses to the new computers when they come up.

Here are the steps required to establish the DHCP server on a computer running Windows NT Server:

1. While logged on with administrator privileges, choose the Start ➪ Settings ➪ Control Panel option. Double-click the Network entry to start the Network Control Panel Application (NCPA).

2. In the Network dialog box, click the Services tab. Then click Add.

3. Under Network Service, select Microsoft DHCP Server and click OK, as shown in Figure 11-21.

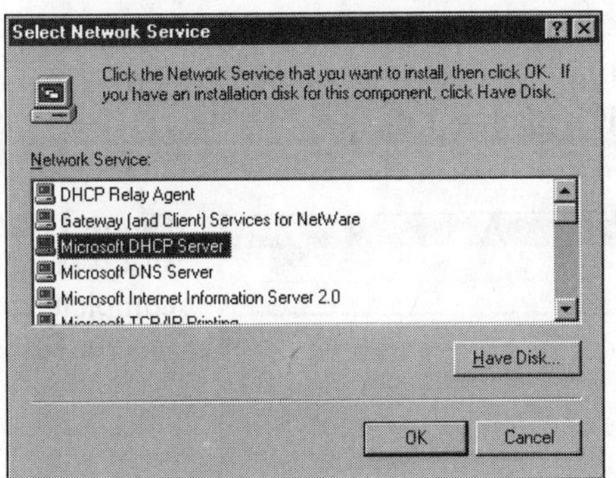

Figure 11-21: Select the DHCP server for installation.

4. NCPA asks for the path to the system files on your Windows NT Server 4.0 CD-ROM. Insert the NT CD-ROM in your CD-ROM drive. Type the path and click Continue.

   On my computer, the path is F:\I386. Substitute the drive letter of your CD-ROM and the subdirectory corresponding to your CPU platform.

5. NCPA warns that you need to configure all network adapters in this computer with fixed IP addresses, as shown in Figure 11-22. Click OK.

   In other words, the DHCP server can't automatically assign an IP address to itself. You'll have to assign one to each network adapter in the DHCP server computer. If you configured TCP/IP on this server to use DHCP for IP addressing, you'll be forced to specify fixed IP addresses for your adapters in step 6.

Figure 11-22: You'll have to configure the IP addresses manually for the DHCP server.

6. Microsoft DHCP Server appears in the list of network services. Click Close.

   If you configured TCP/IP on this computer to use fixed IP addresses, NCPA will close. If you've configured TCP/IP to use DHCP for its IP addresses, NCPA displays the Microsoft TCP/IP Properties dialog box. You must specify fixed IP addresses for each network adapter in this server. For details, see step 3 in the section entitled "Installing TCP/IP during NT Installation" earlier in this chapter.

7. Restart the computer as prompted.
8. Start the DHCP Manager utility by selecting the Start ➪ Programs ➪ Administrative Tools ➪ DHCP Manager option. See Figure 11-23.

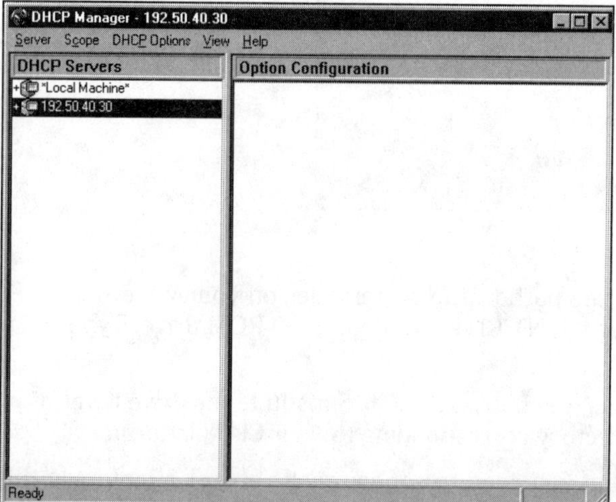

Figure 11-23: Use the DHCP Manager to complete configuration of your DHCP server.

9. On the Server menu, click Add. Type the IP address of the DHCP server that you're configuring and click OK, as shown in Figure 11-24.

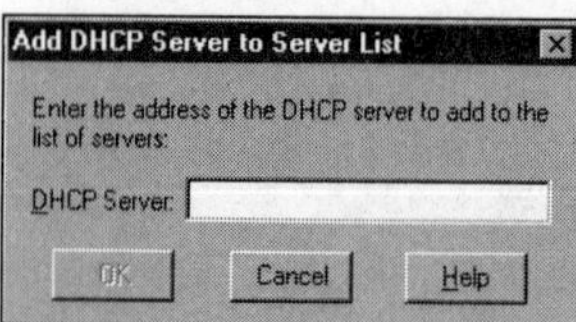

Figure 11-24: Add the IP address of your DHCP server.

10. On the Scope menu, click Create. Under IP Address Pool, specify the range of IP addresses that this server can assign, the subnet mask for your network, and any IP address ranges to exclude from automatic assignment. Figure 11-25 shows this.

Be sure that your DHCP server's own IP address doesn't fall within the range of addresses it can hand out to other computers. If the range that you specify includes the DHCP server's address, you must explicitly exclude it in the list of excluded addresses. This rule applies to all DHCP servers on your network. DHCP Manager won't warn you if you include the server's address in the pool of assignable addresses.

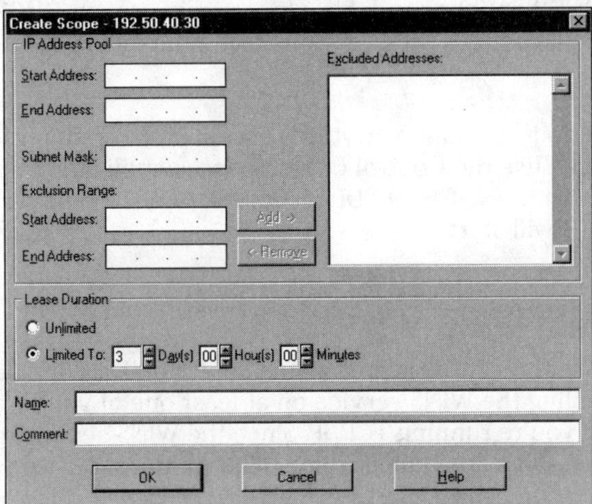

Figure 11-25: Create a scope for your DHCP server to manage.

11. Under Lease Duration, specify how long an address remains valid for a node. The default is three days.

    As discussed earlier in this chapter, the lease duration depends on various aspects of your network. You can stick with the default for now and adjust it later.

Even though NT gives you the option of setting an unlimited lease period, don't do it. As changes occur on your network or while computers are shut down for long periods, the DHCP server will eventually run out of IP addresses to dole out. Unlimited leases make sense only if your computers remain up continuously and you don't make any changes to your network configuration over time. Even then, you should opt for a long lease period (such as six months) rather than an unlimited lease.

12. You can type an optional Name and Comment to describe the scope that you're creating. Then click OK.
13. If the information that you've entered appears to be valid, DHCP Manager will ask if you want to activate the scope that you've created. Click Yes. If there are errors in the address information, you'll be prompted to correct them. After you do so, click OK.

    Common mistakes include typing a range of addresses where the start of the range is higher than the end of the range, typing an invalid subnet mask, or specifying an excluded address that doesn't fall within the IP address range.

If you ever want to alter the configuration of a DHCP scope, go to the Scope menu in DHCP Manager and click Properties. You'll then be able to edit all of the information that you entered when you created the scope.

There are many other DHCP options available. Once you have your DHCP server up and running, you can explore these other options using the online Help provided in DHCP Manager.

DHCP Manager lets you do just about everything except start or stop the DHCP server. To do this, you can use the Control Panel Services application or type commands at a Command Prompt. NET STOP DHCPSERVER will stop the service, and NET START DHCPSERVER will start it.

Establishing a WINS Server

Once you've installed Windows NT server, you can set it up as a WINS server. I highly recommend installing the WINS service on at least one of your Windows NT Server computers, if you're running TCP/IP. Since the WINS server must be assigned a fixed IP address, it's convenient to install it on the same server that's running DHCP.

Here are the steps to follow to establish the WINS server on a computer running Windows NT Server:

1. While logged on with administrator privileges, select the Start ➪ Settings ➪ Control Panel option. Double-click the Network entry to start the Network Control Panel Application (NCPA).
2. In the Network dialog box, click the Services tab. Then click Add.
3. Under Network Service, select the Windows Internet Name Service option and click OK, as shown in Figure 11-26.

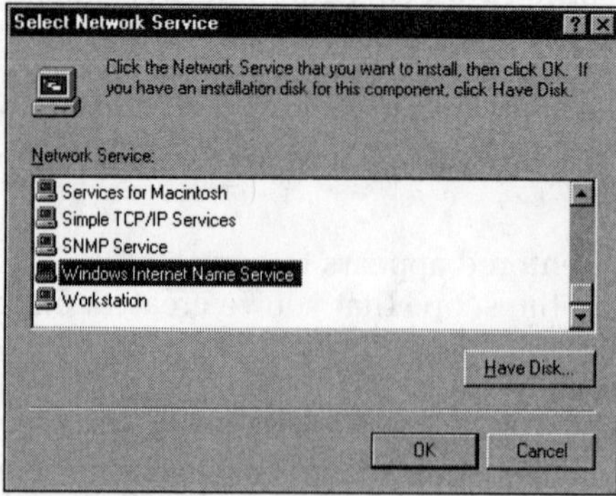

Figure 11-26: Select the WINS service for installation.

4. NCPA asks for the path to the system files on your Windows NT Server 4.0 CD-ROM. Insert the NT CD-ROM in your CD-ROM drive. Type the path and click Continue.

On my computer, the path is F:\I386. Type the drive letter of your CD-ROM and the subdirectory corresponding to your CPU platform.

5. Windows Internet Name Service appears in the list of network services. Click Close.
6. Restart the computer as prompted.
7. Start the WINS Manager utility by selecting the Start ➪ Programs ➪ Administrative Tools ➪ WINS Manager option. See Figure 11-27.

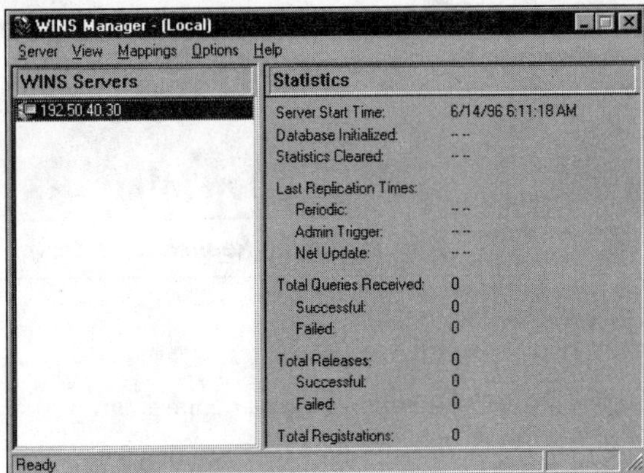

Figure 11-27: Use the WINS Manager to complete configuration of your WINS server.

8. If you have other WINS servers on your network, click Replication Partners on the Server menu. Add other WINS servers to the list of partners, and specify both Push Partner and Pull Partner under Replication Options. See Figure 11-28.

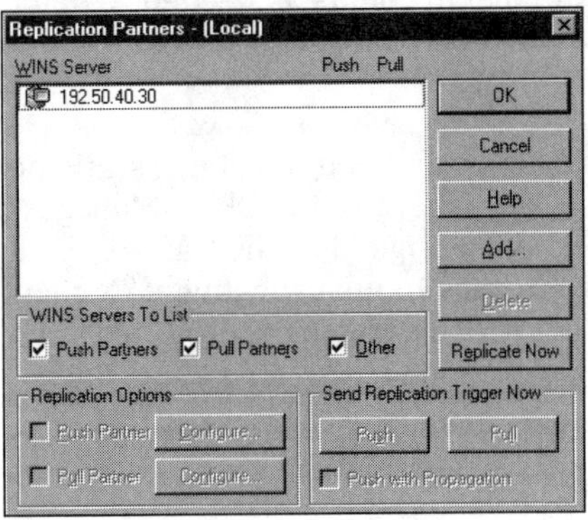

Figure 11-28: Establish push/pull replication partnerships with other WINS servers.

For each pull partner, click Configure and specify the replication time interval, as shown in Figure 11-29. To optimize the amount of replication traffic, use the replication interval guidelines in Table 11-4 to select appropriate values.

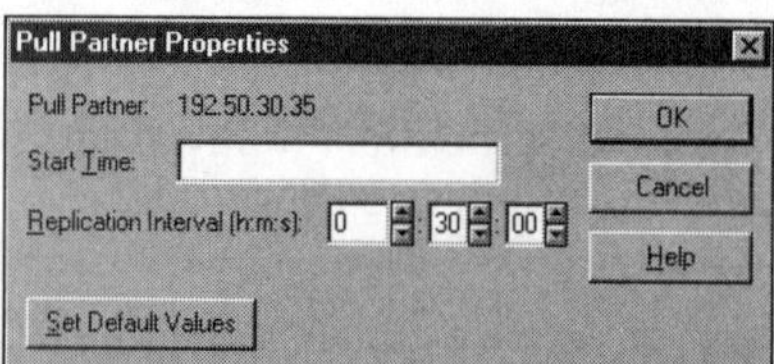

Figure 11-29: Specify the replication time interval between replication partners.

Table 11-4
Recommended WINS Replication Intervals

Link between WINS Servers	***Recommended Replication Interval***
LAN connection	15 minutes
Local WAN connection	60 minutes
Long, domestic WAN connection	90 minutes (at a nonpeak time)
International WAN connection	8 to 12 hours (at a nonpeak time)

Using TCP/IP and RAS Together

Since RAS supports multiple protocols, including TCP/IP, you can transparently use a RAS client to dial in to your network and communicate with your LAN nodes running TCP/IP. The RAS server can reserve a pool of IP addresses (much like DHCP does) and dole them out to RAS dial-in clients as needed. When this happens, the RAS server creates an IP address for the client using its own network address and a unique host address.

If you're using DHCP to assign IP addresses and you're using a static pool of IP addresses for RAS clients, be careful. You must use the DHCP Manager utility to exclude the pool of addresses that you've assigned to the RAS server. If you don't, DHCP will happily hand out those addresses to unsuspecting LAN clients, and before you know it, you'll have duplicate IP addresses on your network.

You can think of the RAS server's role in TCP/IP as that of a mini-DHCP server. The RAS server dynamically assigns IP addresses to each RAS client that's running TCP/IP. The lease duration of the address is the length of time that the RAS client remains remotely connected to the RAS server. The next time that the client dials in, it's assigned a different IP address from the pool available to the RAS server.

Once an IP address has been assigned to a RAS client, the RAS client node participates in the network just as if it were directly connected to the LAN. It uses WINS and other mechanisms discussed in this chapter to deal with name resolution. Since it has its own IP address, the RAS client can use any TCP/IP resource that it could access if it were physically attached to the LAN.

Summary

In this chapter, you've discovered how to connect remote nodes and LANs together. I've shown you how to establish a RAS server to allow remote clients to act as nodes on your network. You've also learned the gory details of installing and configuring the TCP/IP protocol on your Windows NT server. You've seen that DHCP and WINS servers can make administration of the IP addresses on your network much easier. Although there's more to the topics and utilities than I've covered in this chapter, I've focused on the key areas that will get your network up and running.

In Chapter 12, I'll discuss how to integrate your Windows NT Server network with existing networks such as NetWare, UNIX, and Apple. In Chapter 13, you'll learn how to install and configure network clients to talk to your NT servers.

INSIDE STORY

"NO!" shouted the software build engineer, his voice echoing off the walls in the cramped lab. "We can't take any more fixes. The next build is already on its way! Folks have been waiting on it since 2:00 a.m."

"But this bug is an approved show-stopper," the RAS developer pleaded. "The RAS server is broken, and I have a fix. Don't you want to make the build better?"

The build engineer stood firm. "If I took your fix now, I'd have to take the other 60 posted on the board over there. You'd never see a build."

Every day of every week, the tiny build team would crank out another version of Windows NT. Their build lab was the closest thing that the NT group had to an "engine room." Tucked away in the bowels of Building 2, the build lab was crowded with the latest powerful SMP computers, RAID disk arrays, and huge monitors displaying streams of status information on the health of the build. The equipment would churn away for 6 to 18 hours for each build, depending on how much of the NT product had to be reconstructed. The team members sometimes wore yellow hard hats to protect themselves from insistent developers and impatient testers. (Yes, they literally wore hard hats in the lab!) If the flow of daily builds stopped for any reason, the entire NT project seemed to grind to a halt. Fixing build problems was not unlike dealing with plumbing leaks. It was a dirty, thankless, but extremely vital job.

The insistent developer didn't have to wait long. The build was dead on arrival because of another problem. So, the RAS server fix was folded in a few hours later. No one in the group ever saw or knew about the problem. Except the build engineer, the RAS developer, and you, of course.

Integrating Windows NT Server with Other Networks

When you were a kid, did you ever try to mix oil and water, even when your folks told you that it couldn't be done? If you were like me, you stirred, shook, and poured the concoction to see how much or how long you could get them to mix. At best, they'd appear to blend for a few fleeting seconds, only to separate again into their own parts of the jelly glass. Getting dissimilar networks to mix well together can be as frustrating and fascinating as trying to blend oil and water, but at least you won't be fighting the laws of physics that make cohesive integration impossible.

Perhaps you already have a heterogeneous system, and you're familiar with the trials and triumphs of combining dissimilar networks. Or maybe your corporate network is purely homogenous, and the introduction of Windows NT Server 4.0 heralds the first departure from the existing consistency that you know and love. In either case, you'll need to know how to get Windows NT Server to work effectively with other types of networks.

For example, as Windows NT gains inroads into existing NetWare installations, most enterprises are opting to phase NT into their operation rather than performing a wholesale swap. As another example, many enterprises want to tie existing PC and Macintosh networks into a single corporate network. So, it's critically important to understand how to incorporate Windows NT server into your existing network environment.

In this chapter, I'll cover NT server integration with existing AppleTalk, NetWare, UNIX, and other networks. I'll present the steps for installing the various NT components, migrating existing data and account information, and avoiding traps associated with each form of integration.

In discussing NT server integration, I'll assume that you're already familiar with your existing network. So, I won't provide a tutorial on NetWare, AppleTalk, or other environments. Instead, I'll focus entirely on how to integrate Windows NT server into your existing environment. The rest will be up to you.

Integrating with AppleTalk Networks

Many enterprises today have both PC-based networks and AppleTalk networks made up of Apple Macintosh computers. You typically see Macintosh networks in creative departments that deal with desktop publishing of books, newsletters, and creative marketing materials. The hardware and software solutions offered by the Macintosh platform have traditionally been superior to PC solutions in this area of computing. As a result, it's often difficult to centralize shared files, expensive storage and printer resources, and administration under the PC-centric corporate network umbrella.

Services for Macintosh

To address the need to integrate Macintosh computers with PCs, Windows NT Server 4.0 provides a powerful feature called Services for Macintosh, or SFM. In a nutshell, SFM provides server functionality for Macintosh client computers. Here's what SFM lets you do:

- **Share files.** You can use Windows NT server disk resources as repositories for files created and processed by Macintosh computers. What's more, applications written for both PC and Macintosh platforms (for example, Excel for Windows and Excel for Macintosh) can work on shared files stored on an NT Server's disk.
- **Share printers.** PCs and Macintosh computers can share the same printer resource (for example, an expensive, high-speed PostScript color printer). If you have multiple printers attached to your Windows NT Server computer,

both Macintosh and PC clients can print to any of them. They can also print to any PostScript printer that registers itself as a LaserWriter on the AppleTalk network. NT Server spools print jobs to disk, allowing the Macintosh clients to get on with their tasks without waiting for print jobs to complete.

✦ **Centralize network administration.** NT server provides file sharing and security for Macintosh clients and eliminates the need for a separate Macintosh server. There's only one set of user accounts to maintain, instead of two separate sets. SFM provides consistent security by translating between Macintosh access privileges and NT file permissions. Moreover, you can control all shared printer queues from a central location.

✦ **Keep passwords secure.** SFM provides a more secure logon mechanism that avoids sending readable passwords over the network, where prying sniffers can see them. In addition, each Macintosh volume can be assigned its own password for use by Macintosh clients.

✦ **Connect AppleTalk networks.** If you want to form an internet of AppleTalk networks, you can connect them using the routing capabilities of SFM. (SFM supports AppleTalk Phase II but doesn't route AppleTalk Phase I.) NT server can also act as a seed router to establish AppleTalk network address information.

In the following sections, I'll discuss specific issues to consider when connecting a PC network to a Macintosh network using Windows NT Server SFM. This information will help you in planning how to get the most from SFM.

Macintosh Volumes

You can share Windows NT Server files on an NTFS partition (or on a CD-ROM) with Macintosh clients. To share files with Macintosh clients, you place them in a directory that you've designated as accessible by Macintosh computers. This directory is called a Macintosh *volume.* I'll show you how to do this later in this chapter.

You'll see the term *volume* used elsewhere synonymously with hard disk partition. As mentioned in Chapter 1, the term *volume* set refers to a collection of disk partitions. In the SFM world, however, the meaning of volume isn't the same. A Macintosh volume refers to an NT server directory that's been explicitly designated as accessible by Macintosh clients.

Normally, when you share a directory on Windows NT server, you can share the same directory more than once using different names. You can share a subdirectory of an already shared directory. You can also share a directory that contains a subdirectory that's already been shared. However, when you designate a directory as a Macintosh volume, you can't do any of these. You can have only one Macintosh volume in a directory tree. No other directories above or below it can be designated as Macintosh volumes.

MACINTOSH SPEAKS VOLUMES

Each Macintosh volume must have a name, which can contain up to 27 characters. There's a limit to the number of volumes that a Macintosh client can see. An internal buffer 4624 bytes long must be able to hold all of the volume names. In addition to the name itself, each volume name requires an additional two bytes of overhead. Thus, the maximum number of Macintosh volume names that you can have depends on the length of the names and can be expressed by

```
M = 4624 / (L + 2)
```

where M is the maximum number of volume names and L is the average length of a volume name. For example, if the average length of your volume names is 8 characters, you can have up to 462 volume names. The maximum number drops to 159, if you increase the average name length to its maximum of 27. If you plan to have many Macintosh volumes, you'll need to strike a balance between meaningful volume names and the maximum number of volume names on your network.

When you establish a Macintosh volume on NT server, you can optionally assign a password to it. Macintosh users are required to supply this password before gaining access to the volume, whereas PC users don't need to supply this password.

Macintosh Filenames

When using SFM, NT server needs to deal with three different sets of file naming rules — namely, those of the Macintosh, NTFS, and FAT file systems. Macintosh users can create legal Macintosh filenames that are too long for DOS or that contain characters that are illegal in NTFS (smiley faces, for example). SFM maintains these names within NTFS, so Macintosh users never see any translation of Macintosh-created filenames. However, NT must translate them for access by other clients.

Table 12-1 summarizes how Macintosh filenames are translated when viewed by various types of clients. The shaded areas in the table pinpoint where translation occurs. The white areas maintain the filename as originally created. You can use this table to find out what to expect when you share files between PCs and Macintosh computers. You can also use it to help develop naming conventions for these shared files.

Filename truncation can be annoying and confusing to users who share files with each other. Probably the worst example of truncation occurs when an NTFS file

Table 12-1
How Filenames Are Seen by Network Clients

Filename Created	*Macintosh Client Sees*	*Windows NT Client Sees*	*DOS (FAT) Client Sees*
FAT (DOS) 8.3 convention	Original 8.3 name	Original 8.3 name	Original 8.3 name
Macintosh 31-character limit (all legal NTFS characters)	Original Macintosh or NTFS name	Original Macintosh or NTFS name	Truncated 8.3 name
Macintosh 31-character limit (with illegal NTFS characters)	Original Macintosh name	Macintosh name with illegal NTFS characters replaced	Truncated 8.3 name after NTFS illegal character replacement
NTFS 256-character limit	Truncated 8.3 name	Original NTFS name	Truncated 8.3 name

name exceeds the 31-character Macintosh limit, resulting in Macintosh clients seeing the measly 8.3 short version of the filename. Although this same translation occurs when the file is accessed from DOS, DOS users are used to this sort of limitation. Macintosh users aren't. For this reason, if you're going to use long names, I recommend keeping them under 31 characters to keep your Macintosh users happy and sane.

Files shared between Macintosh and NT can freely use long filenames up to 31 characters without fear of shortening. However, if you have DOS or Windows 3.x computers that need to access files shared with Macintosh computers, you may want to consider using 8.3 filenames for these files. If you do, DOS and Windows 3.x users won't have the disadvantage of having to figure out what the NT-generated short filenames really mean. To accomplish this, you need to ask your Macintosh users to implement the 8.3 naming convention for all files to be shared with non-NT PC clients. In practice, getting Macintosh users into this habit will take time.

Macintosh File Security

SFM translates between NTFS file permissions and Macintosh access privileges. Table 12-2 summarizes the relationship between NTFS and Macintosh permissions. When permissions are set for a specific user account on one platform, you can use the same user account to access files from the other platform. The table illustrates what a user would see if they set permissions on one platform and accessed the file or folder from the other.

Table 12-2
Mapping between NTFS and Macintosh File Security

Security Action	*Result*
Macintosh user sets Make Changes permission on a folder.	PC user has Write and Delete permission.
Macintosh user sets See Files permission on a folder.	PC user has Read permission.
Macintosh user sets See Folders permission on a folder.	PC user has Read permission.
Macintosh user sets See Files and See Folders permissions on a folder.	PC user has Read permission.
PC user sets Read permission on a directory or file.	Macintosh user has both See Files and See Folders permission.
PC user sets both Write and Delete permissions on a directory or file.	Macintosh user has Make Changes permission.

In the Macintosh world, privileges can be set only on folders (that is, directories), not on individual files. A file within a folder effectively inherits the privileges of its containing folder. Since NTFS allows you to set separate permissions on each file, more restrictive permissions on individual files override permissions set on folders. For example, if a Macintosh user has Make Changes permission to a folder but only has Read permission to a specific file within that folder, the user can only read the file.

On the Macintosh, permissions can be set at three levels — owner, group, and everyone. The *owner* is the user who created the file. The *group* is the user's NT primary group, assigned to the user account via the User Manager for Domains utility. *Everyone* literally includes all users of the server, including users with only guest access.

The NT primary group, which can be set in the Group Memberships dialog box inside User Manager for Domains, applies only to SFM. It has no other meaning or use besides defining a Macintosh group. You should place Macintosh users in primary groups with other users who have similar network resource needs. I'll cover the User Manager for Domains utility in depth in Chapter 18.

Macintosh Printing

Macintosh clients can send jobs to any printer directly connected to the Windows NT Server computer, whether it's a PostScript printer or not. (PC clients can't send PostScript jobs to non-PostScript printers. The translation only occurs for Macintosh clients.) All printers attached to the NT server look like Apple LaserWriter printers to the Macintosh clients. SFM performs any necessary translation for non-PostScript printers to yield the correct printed output.

In addition, PC clients can send jobs to printers connected to the AppleTalk network. You can opt to give SFM complete control of these printers (called *capturing* the printers). Doing this centralizes their control to NT server administrators, even though the printers aren't directly connected to the NT Server computer.

Capturing an AppleTalk printer has a few advantages beyond just centralized control. First, it prevents users from directly accessing the printer and resetting it, which can wreak havoc with the spooling process. Second, it prevents what's known as "LaserPrep Wars." This phenomena occurs when different Macintosh versions keep telling the printer to load or unload different versions of a PostScript preparation file (called the LaserPrep file). Each time this happens, the printer has to spit out a startup page. This not only takes time to perform but also can actually reduce the life of the printer. Having NT server capture the printer eliminates this issue.

You don't want NT server to capture an AppleTalk printer that's meant to receive jobs from other sources such as minicomputer users attached to the AppleTalk network. In this situation, you should leave the printer uncaptured and live without the capturing advantages discussed earlier.

Account Passwords

No additional software is required on the Macintosh client computer to access Windows NT server's SFM. AppleShare client software and System 7 File Sharing is already present on Macintosh computers.

Unfortunately, from a security perspective, the supplied Macintosh software sends password text verbatim over the network. This approach makes the network vulnerable to sniffers looking for user passwords. Moreover, these passwords are limited to eight characters, making them relatively easy to guess.

Although SFM supports this approach, it offers a much more secure alternative: By installing an optional user authentication module (UAM) on your Macintosh clients, you can achieve password encryption across the network and use passwords that contain up to 14 characters.

Planning AppleTalk Connectivity

On the network technology front, you have several choices. SFM supports LocalTalk, Ethernet, Token Ring, and FDDI. Apple products that correspond to the latter three are EtherTalk, TokenTalk, and FDDITalk. (Talk, talk, talk.) I discussed all but LocalTalk in Chapters 3 and 8. LocalTalk is the slowest at 230Kbps, over 40 times slower than Ethernet. You'll need to decide which network technology or combination of technologies to use on your network.

Since Macintosh computers include built-in LocalTalk hardware, the cheapest way to connect Windows NT Server to an existing LocalTalk network is to add a LocalTalk network adapter to your NT Server computer. In addition, if you opt to use LocalTalk, you don't need to incur the labor cost of performing surgery on your Macintosh computers to add a network adapter. On the other hand, given the slow speed of this technology, you get what you pay for.

If you're going to use one of the other network technologies, you need to install the appropriate type of network adapter in each Macintosh computer (for example, an EtherTalk adapter to connect to Ethernet). This approach is definitely more expensive but provides much better network performance. If you can afford the additional hardware cost and installation time, I recommend going with Ethernet or Token Ring, if you want reasonable performance.

As a compromise in both price and performance, you can install a LocalTalk router to translate between an existing LocalTalk network and your PC network. For example, several manufacturers offer LocalTalk/Ethernet router products. Taking this approach (dare I say *route?*) is much cheaper than equipping each Macintosh with an EtherTalk network adapter, but you still end up living with the low speed on the LocalTalk portion of your network.

Windows NT server itself can act as a LocalTalk router, converting between LocalTalk technology and the network technology used for the rest of your network. To do this, you need both a LocalTalk network adapter and a network adapter that matches your PC network technology (for example, Ethernet) installed in the NT Server computer. By connecting your LocalTalk network to this one NT computer, the Macintosh clients can access other servers on the PC network in addition to the NT computer to which they're connected.

Windows NT server running SFM can also act as a seed router. However, it must be the first server you start, so that it can initialize other routers with network information. If it's not a seed router, it can't be started until another seed router has been started. If your Windows NT Server computer is up and running at all times, it's a good choice to set it up to act as a seed router.

Dedicated hardware routers are also supported. For improved network reliability, I recommend having at least two routers established as seed routers on your network.

Determining placement of seed routers and assigning network numbers, network ranges, and zones to your AppleTalk network are beyond the scope of this book.

Refer to your AppleTalk network documentation for details on the best way to design these aspects of your network. You'll need this information when you install SFM on your NT Server computer.

The LocalTalk zone concept is similar to the NT server domain concept. Like a domain, a zone logically groups a set of computers, so you're limited in what you see when you browse for network resources. Unlike domains, however, zones don't define user accounts or centralize network administration.

Preparing to Install SFM

Before installing SFM on your Windows NT Server computer and connecting to your Macintosh network, you need to make sure that each of your Macintosh client computers meets the following criteria:

- ✦ The computer must be able to use AppleShare, Apple's networking software. All Macintosh computers, except for the XL and 128K models, meet this requirement.
- ✦ The computer must be running version 6.0.7 or later of the Macintosh operating system. Version 7.1 or above is preferred. I recommend version 7.5.
- ✦ If you're using Ethernet, Token Ring, or FDDI to connect your Macintosh computers, they must contain an appropriate network adapter. If you're using LocalTalk to connect your Macintosh computers, no additional network hardware is needed in the Macintosh clients.
- ✦ The computer must support AppleTalk Phase II, which provides routing capability and relaxes several restrictions that were present in AppleTalk Phase I. SFM requires that you use Phase II.
- ✦ The computer needs to support AppleTalk Filing Protocol (AFP) Version 2.0 or 2.1. Version 2.1 is recommended.

In addition, SFM supports the Apple LaserWriter printer version 6.x or later. Make sure that the printers you plan to use with SFM are up to this revision level.

Before installing SFM, you need to prepare the Windows NT Server computer as follows:

1. Have Windows NT Server 4.0 up and running on the computer where you intend to install SFM. Be sure that the server has at least 2MB of free disk space, required by the SFM software itself.
2. Prepare at least one partition formatted with the NTFS file system, on which files visible to both Macintosh and PC clients will be stored. Be sure that this partition contains enough room for these shared files.
3. Install the network adapters on which you plan to run AppleTalk. The adapters must be installed before you can fully configure SFM.
4. Attach your NT server to the network.

Installing SFM on NT Server

Once you've verified that your Windows NT Server computer is ready for SFM installation, you need to follow these steps:

1. While logged on to your Windows NT Server computer with administrator privileges, click on Start ➪ Settings ➪ Control Panel. Double-click Network to start the Network Control Panel Application (NCPA).

2. In the Network dialog box, click the Services tab. Then click Add.

3. Under Network Services, select Services for Macintosh and click OK, as shown in Figure 12-1.

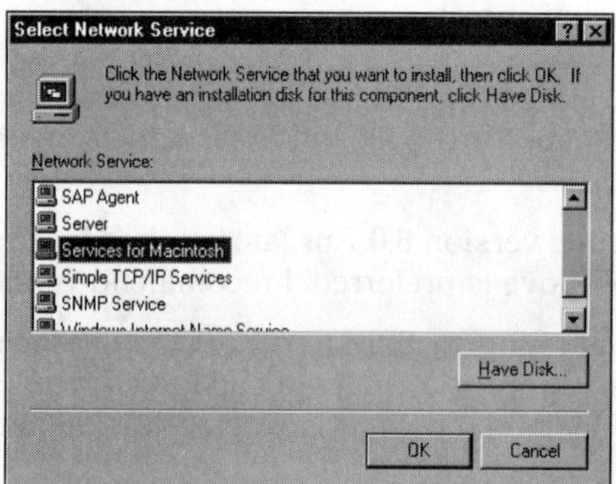

Figure 12-1: Select Services for Macintosh for installation.

4. NCPA asks for the path to the system files on your Windows NT Server 4.0 CD-ROM. Insert the NT CD-ROM in your CD-ROM drive. Type the path and click Continue, as Figure 12-2 illustrates.

   On my computer, the path is F:\I386. Type the drive letter of your CD-ROM and the subdirectory corresponding to your CPU platform.

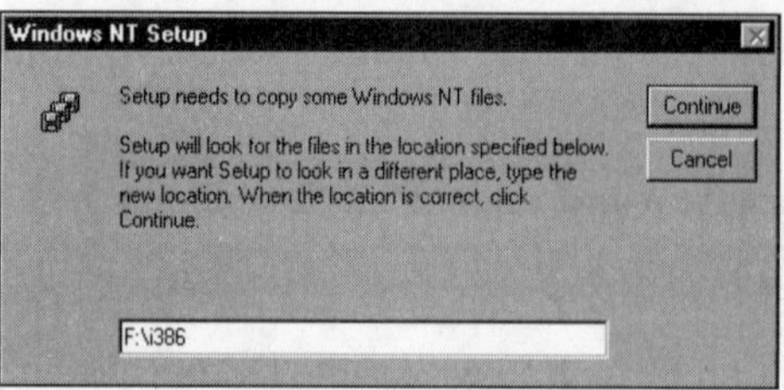

Figure 12-2: Type the path of your Windows NT Server CD-ROM files.

5. The Services for Macintosh option appears in the Network Services list. Click Close, as shown in Figure 12-3.

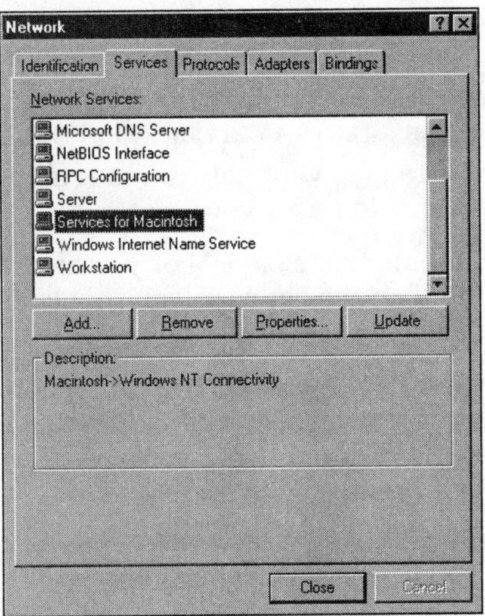

Figure 12-3: SFM appears in the list of installed services.

6. In the AppleTalk Protocol Properties dialog box, click the General tab. Select the default network adapter on which you want to run the AppleTalk protocol. See Figure 12-4.

   If you already have a device on your network that provides AppleTalk routing information, you'll see a list of zones under the Default Zone option. If so, you may click the zone where you want AppleTalk services to appear. This is the zone in which the File Server for Macintosh and printers connected to Windows NT Server will appear whenever Macintosh users select them in the Chooser application.

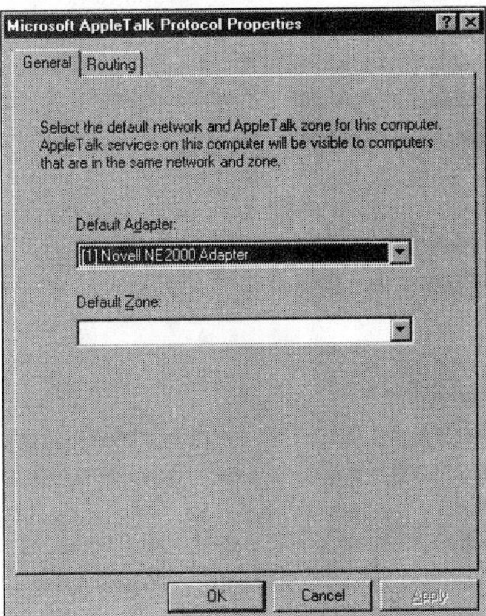

Figure 12-4: Select the network adapter and zone in which SFM services will appear to Macintosh users.

7. If you want this NT server to act as an AppleTalk router, click the Routing tab. Otherwise, go to step 8. If you want NT to act as a seed router, click the check box labeled Use this router to seed the network. See Figure 12-5.

   Refer to previous sections in this chapter and to your AppleTalk network documentation for details on how to plan your network to establish what the network range and default zones should be for your router.

   If this is your only NT Server computer running SFM or you have no other devices acting as AppleTalk routers on the network, you should enable seed routing.

Enabling routing makes sense only if you bind the AppleTalk protocol to more than one network adapter in your server. If you do, Macintosh computers on all bound networks will see your Windows NT Server computer. See Chapter 8 for a discussion of how to configure network bindings.

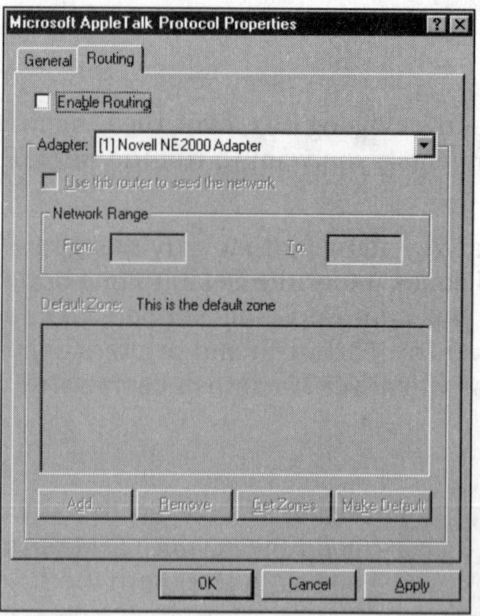

Figure 12-5: Enable or disable AppleTalk router and seed router functionality.

8. Click OK.
9. Restart your computer as prompted.

Configuring Macintosh Clients

Once you have SFM installed and running on your NT server, you're ready to configure the Macintosh clients to communicate with it. The steps required to configure these clients vary slightly, depending on the version of the Macintosh model and Apple operating system version that you're running. In this section, I'll assume you're running System 7.5. I'll also assume you're familiar with the Macintosh user interface. Perform all of the following steps on your Macintosh client computer:

Connecting to the Authentication Files

1. Connect your Macintosh computer to the network, using a transceiver for LocalTalk or a network adapter for other network technologies. Complete this step according to the documentation that came with your Macintosh computer or your Macintosh network adapter.
2. On the Apple menu, click Control Panel ➪ Network. Then select LocalTalk or EtherTalk (or other Talk), depending on how this computer is connected to the network.
3. On the Apple menu, click the Chooser icon. Click the AppleShare icon. Then select the AppleTalk zone in which your Windows NT server running SFM resides.
4. From the list of file servers, select the name of the Windows NT Server computer. Then click OK.
5. If you're asked to choose a logon method, select the Microsoft Authentication option. Then click OK.

You can use Apple's built-in user authentication method instead of the Microsoft UAM. If you do, however, you'll be sending password text over the network when users log on. This may be an unacceptable security risk in your network environment. I recommend using the Microsoft UAM, which encrypts passwords, to avoid this risk.

6. Click the box for Registered User. Type your user account name and password. Then click OK.
7. Under the option Select the items you want to use, select Microsoft UAM Volume and click OK. Close the Chooser dialog box.

Installing the Authentication Files

8. Double-click the Microsoft UAM Volume folder to open it.
9. In the Microsoft UAM Volume window, select the AppleShare Folder and drag it to your System Folder.

If you're told that you already have an AppleShare Folder in your System Folder, don't overwrite it. You should maintain the files in your existing AppleShare Folder. Double-click the AppleShare Folder in the Microsoft UAM Volume to open it. Then, drag the MS UAM file and drop it into your existing AppleShare Folder within your System Folder. Doing this will maintain any other UAMs installed previously (for example, the NetWare UAM).

10. Restart your Macintosh client computer.

Once this procedure is complete, when the Macintosh user connects to the Windows NT server running SFM, he or she will be asked for a user name and password, which will be encrypted using the Microsoft UAM.

If the Macintosh client is running System 7.1 or later, the user will be given only one choice — Microsoft Authentication. If it's running an earlier version, the user will have a choice of either the standard Apple UAM or Microsoft's UAM. This choice will appear even if the Apple UAM has been disabled. Instruct your affected Macintosh users always to select the Microsoft UAM.

Configuring Macintosh Volumes on NT Server

Once you've installed SFM on your Windows NT Server computer and you've got your Macintosh clients configured, you can set up a Macintosh volume on your NT Server computer. How do you do this?

When you installed SFM, a new application called MacFile was added to Control Panel. This utility is accessible through the Start ➪ Settings ➪ Control Panel ➪ MacFile option. You can also reach it through Server Manager (Start ➪ Programs ➪ Administrative Tools ➪ Server Manager). If you go through Server Manager, you'll be able to create and configure Macintosh volumes. In the following procedures, I'll assume you're going to access the MacFile utility through Server Manager.

Let's say you want to create a volume called BIGMAC that's accessible by Macintosh clients. You want BIGMAC to reside on your TOWER3 computer, which is running Windows NT Server with SFM installed. Here's what you need to do:

1. Using NT Explorer or a Command Prompt, create a directory called BIGMAC on an NTFS partition on your server.
2. While logged on with administrator privileges, click the option Start ➪ Programs ➪ Administrative Tools ➪ Server Manager. Select the TOWER3 server, as shown in Figure 12-6.

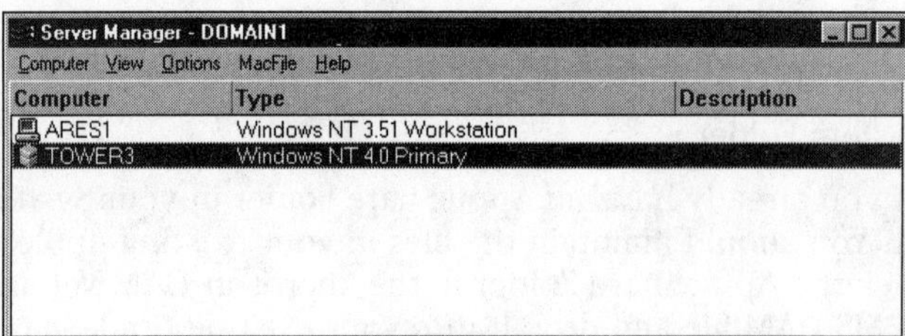

Figure 12-6: Start Server Manager to create a Macintosh volume.

3. On the MacFile menu, click the check box for Volumes. Under Volumes, you'll see the Microsoft UAM Volume used in the previous section. Click the Create Volume option, as illustrated in Figure 12-7.

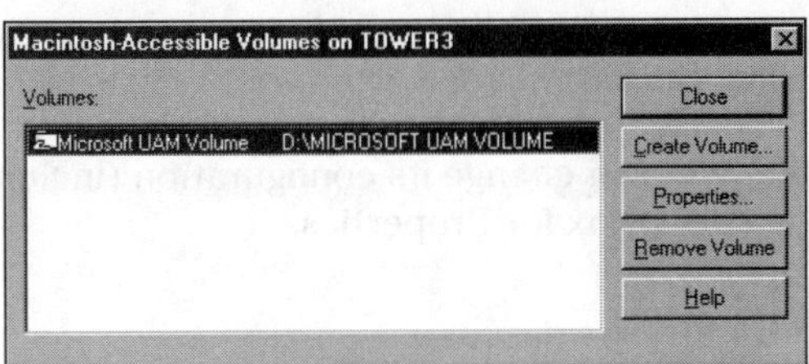

Figure 12-7: List the existing volumes and create a new one.

4. In the Create Macintosh-Accessible Volume dialog box, type the volume name (up to 27 characters). Type the path to its subdirectory and an optional volume password (up to eight characters). If you specify a password, confirm it. Then, set the volume security and user limits as appropriate, as shown in Figure 12-8.

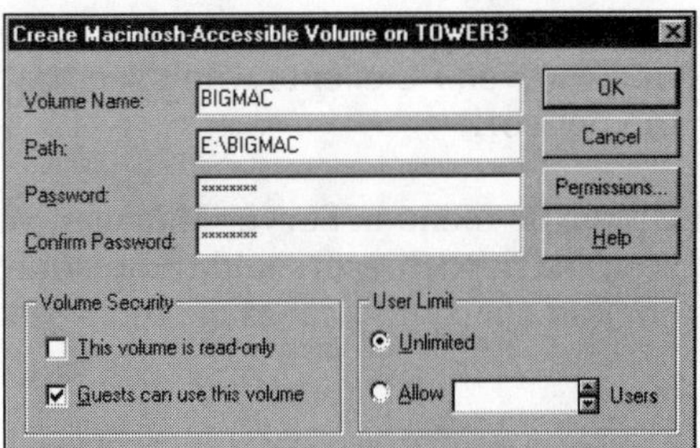

Figure 12-8: Provide information on the new volume that you're creating.

5. Click the Permissions check box. In the Directory Permissions dialog box, set the permissions on this volume for each user as appropriate. When you're done, click OK. See Figure 12-9.

The Directory Permissions dialog box is very similar to what Macintosh users see when they set access privileges on a folder. Macintosh users will see slightly different dialog boxes, depending on the version of operating system that they're running.

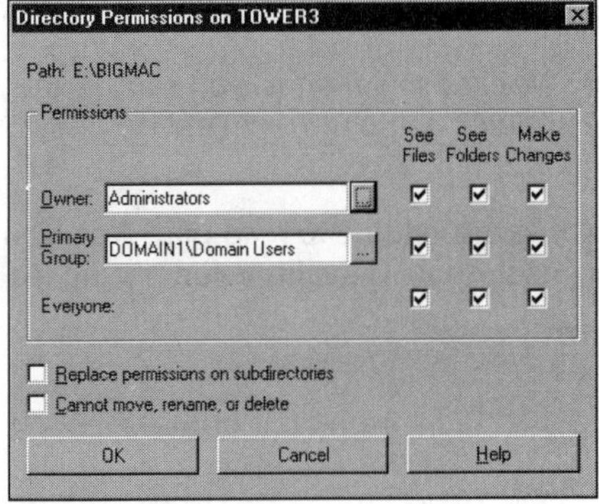

Figure 12-9: Set permissions on this volume using Macintosh access privileges.

6. Click OK. The new volume is added to the list of Macintosh volumes, as shown in Figure 12-10. Click Close.

   After creating the volume, you can change its configuration (including its password). Just click the check box for Properties.

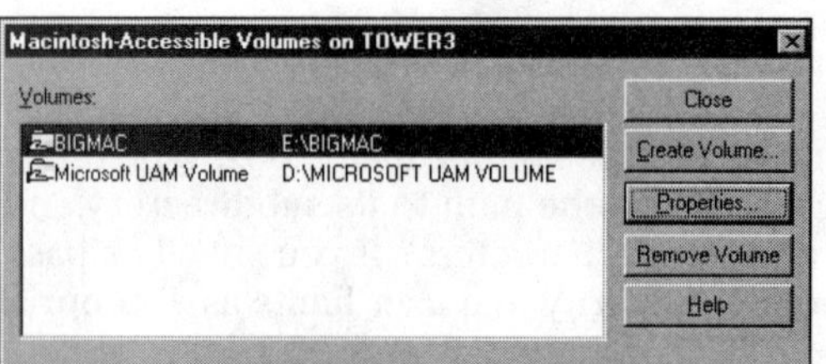

Figure 12-10: The new Macintosh volume is added to the list.

Once you've successfully configured a Macintosh volume, Macintosh users can access it from their client computers. However, PC clients won't see the directory unless you explicitly share it over the network.

Using the Properties options on the MacFile menu in Server Manager, you can gather all sorts of statistics about your Macintosh users and the resources they're using. With the Send Message option, you can send a message to all Macintosh users connected to the server.

SFM Batch Processing

If you're a dyed-in-the-wool command-line administrator, SFM provides a command line utility that can perform all of the volume and server administration functions offered by the graphical tools you've just seen. Just type **MACFILE** at any NT Command Prompt, and you'll see a description of its syntax. This tool is useful for automating SFM administrative tasks in batch files.

CD-ROM SPEAKS VOLUMES, TOO!

In addition to turning NTFS directories into Macintosh volumes, you can do the same for CD-ROM directories. Just follow steps 2 through 4 to turn a CD-ROM directory into a Macintosh volume. Then finish the job by performing step 6.

Notice that you don't have the choice of setting the volume to read-only. Also, you can't set permissions on a CD-ROM volume. All Macintosh users view this volume with See Files and See Folders permissions.

INSIDE STORY

"Ken, come over to Building 1. You need to see something now." I instantly recognized the high-strung voice of a key SFM developer on the phone. I quickly made my way across the breezeway between the buildings, wishing for a mid-July breeze to make the trek more pleasant. It was a late Thursday afternoon, and the team was performing the final tests on Windows NT 3.1 before its planned release to manufacturing on Friday. It appeared that we would ship on time – that is, until this phone call.

A test engineer visiting from Aldus had discovered that PageMaker 5 wouldn't print the correct fonts to a PostScript printer using SFM. Regardless of the fonts used in the document, all of them looked the same on the printed output. The results weren't only wrong, but ugly. We had to fix this, or die trying.

Discovery of this bug marked the beginning of a three-day weekend of sleepless days and nights for a handful of development and test engineers. As one solution was found, a new and even more devastating bug was discovered – one in the graphics subsystem, another in the printing module, one that ate up huge amounts of disk space, and so on. The cycle ground on hour after hour. Engineers debugged, fixed, tested, retested, and consumed pizza, candy, and donuts to stay awake. One engineer's wife came in to sleep on his office floor, so she could drive him home when he was done. She had a good long sleep.

One of the nasty bugs was in the Aldus code. We all wanted PageMaker to run well on NT. So we worked together to get around the problem by changing the NT code. In the end, we got PageMaker and NT to work together like old pals. Aldus was happy. Microsoft was happy. But we engineers and managers could barely keep our eyes open for the shipment celebration on Monday afternoon. It was a bitter-sweet ending to a four-year Herculean effort. And what a way to spend a weekend!

Integrating with NetWare Networks

Windows NT Server 4.0 provides a number of key features that allow you to integrate it into existing NetWare installations.

If your clients need access to both Windows NT servers and NetWare servers, you have two choices. First, you can simply load both protocol stacks on the clients. This consumes more memory on the client computers and slightly increases the complexity of configuring them. On the other hand, this approach offers better performance when communicating with NetWare servers and offers the full feature set of the native protocols. Second, you can load a single protocol stack on the clients and allow them to access NetWare servers through an NT server acting as a gateway. This method requires fewer memory resources on the clients, makes client configuration less complex, but introduces a performance penalty when accessing NetWare servers. In this situation, the gateway translation process may reduce the number of features available to clients.

In the following sections, I'll cover the configuration options associated with establishing communication with existing Novell NetWare networks, version 4.1 and earlier.

Installing the IPX/SPX Protocol

IPX doesn't require you to make configuration decisions during its installation. If you opted to install IPX when you installed the NT Server operating system, then it's already up and running. In most cases, no further configuration is necessary.

NWLink, Microsoft's implementation of IPX/SPX, supports several frame types. If you prefer a specific frame type, you can specify it, but using the default setting of auto detection will work as well. You can also specify an internal network number. If you select any value other than the default of zero, be sure the number that you choose doesn't conflict with other internal NetWare network numbers on your network. Refer to your NetWare documentation for information on the appropriate settings for these items.

Here are the steps for installing and configuring NWLink:

1. While logged on with administrator privileges, click the Start ➪ Settings ➪ Control Panel option. Double-click the Network entry to start the Network Control Panel Application (NCPA). If you've already installed NWLink and you just want to configure it, go to step 4.
2. In the Network dialog box, click the Protocols tab. Click Add. Under Network Protocol, select the NWLink IPX/SPX Compatible Transport option and click OK.
3. NCPA asks for the path to the system files on your Windows NT Server 4.0 CD-ROM. Insert the NT CD-ROM in your CD-ROM drive. Type the path and click Continue.

   On my computer, the path is F:\I386. Type the drive letter of your CD-ROM and the subdirectory corresponding to your CPU platform.

   Once files are copied, if you want to accept the default configuration, go to step 8. Otherwise, go to step 4 and continue configuration.
4. In the Network dialog box, click the Protocols tab. Under Network Protocols, select the NWLink IPX/SPX Compatible Transport option. Then click Properties, as shown in Figure 12-11.

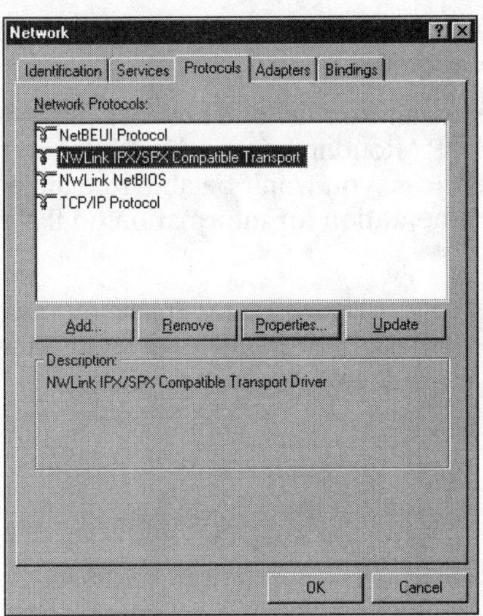

Figure 12-11: Change the configuration of the NWLink protocol driver.

5. Click the General tab. Set the network number and frame type as appropriate. See Figure 12-12.

   Refer to your NetWare documentation for information on the appropriate settings for these items.

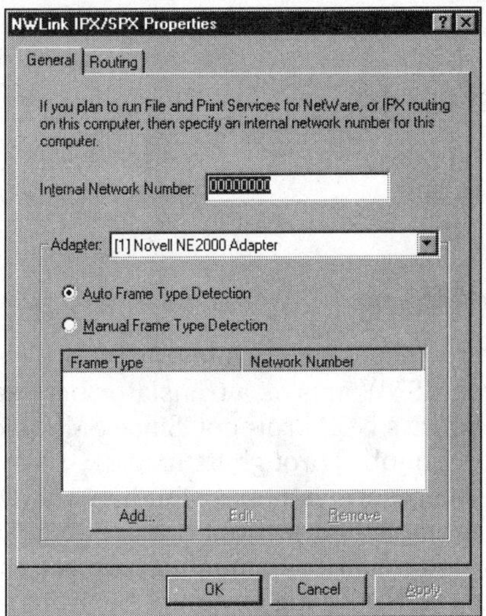

Figure 12-12: The General tab allows you to specify the network number and frame type for IPX/SPX.

6. Click the Routing tab. If you want this server to act as an IPX router, click to select the Enable RIP Routing check box.

   This option requires that you have more than one network adapter running IPX/SPX. Also, if you don't have RIP (Routing Information Protocol) for NWLink IPX installed under Network Services, you won't be able to enable RIP routing. Refer to your NetWare documentation for information on IPX routing.

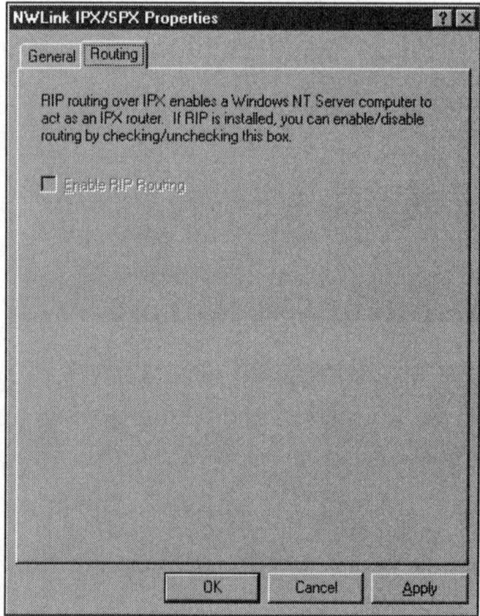

Figure 12-13: Enable RIP routing if you want NT Server to act as an IPX router.

7. In the NWLink IPX/SPX Properties dialog box, click OK.
8. In the Network dialog box, click Close.
9. Restart your computer as prompted.

Gateway Service for NetWare

As mentioned in Chapter 4, NT Server's GSNW facility allows network clients to access resources on a NetWare server. GSNW acts as a translator between Windows NT's SMB protocol and NetWare's NCP protocol. Since SMB and NCP are dramatically different, GSNW has a tough job. Through its magic, GSNW makes NetWare server resources appear to Microsoft clients as standard shared resources on an NT server. This is accomplished without the need for NetWare user accounts for each person. Only one NetWare account is required to allow the Windows NT Server computer running GSNW to log on to the NetWare server.

If your client computers are so short on memory that they can't run multiple protocols, but they need to access resources on both NT servers and NetWare servers, GSNW is an excellent solution. It allows the client to run only one protocol and still access both types of servers.

You can share up to 22 NetWare resources through the gateway. I'll show you how to do this in detail in the following sections, but in a nutshell, you associate a NetWare shared resource with an NT resource name. Your users then access the resource using the NT server and resource name. For example, if your gateway NT Server computer is TOWER3, and you associate the NT resource name NWDATA with the actual NetWare resource \\nw4\sys\data, your users access this NetWare resource through the gateway by establishing a connection to \\TOWER3\NWDATA.

File Attribute Considerations

NetWare and NT file attributes are quite different from each other. The gateway handles translation of some of the NetWare attributes, but others that don't make sense to NT server are ignored. Table 12-3 shows how each NetWare file attribute is treated by the gateway. The attribute translation, if any, takes place when a NetWare file is opened through GSNW.

Table 12-3
GSNW Treatment of Netware File Attributes

NetWare File Attribute	*Gateway Translation*	*Preserved on Copy to NetWare Server*
Ro (Read only)	R (Read only)	√
Di (Delete inhibit)	R (Read only)	
Ri (Rename inhibit)	R (Read only)	
A (Archive)	A (Archive)	√
Sy (System)	S (System)	√
H (Hidden)	H (Hidden)	√
RW (Read Write)	No translation	
S (Shareable)	No translation	
T (Transactional)	No translation	
P (Purge)	No translation	
Ra (Read audit)	No translation	
Wa (Write audit)	No translation	
Ci (Copy inhibit)	No translation	

If you want to set NetWare attributes that aren't supported by GSNW, you can use the NetWare filer and rights utilities to set them. The Microsoft clients accessing these files won't see these additional attributes, but NetWare clients will.

Running NetWare Utilities

You can use many of the DOS-based utilities supplied with NetWare to manage the NetWare network from a Windows NT computer. The following NetWare utilities are supported under Windows NT:

chkvol	help	rconsole	settts
colorpal	listdir	remove	slist
dspace	map	revoke	syscon
fconsole	ncopy	rights	tlist
filer	ndir	security	userlist
flag	pconsole	send	volinfo
flagdir	psc	session	whoami
grant	pstat	setpass	

The NT command NET USE can be used to perform the same functions as the NetWare utilities ATTACH, LOGIN, LOGOUT, and CAPTURE. You can use NT's net view command to do the same thing as NetWare's slist command.

Preparing the NetWare Server

On the NetWare server, it's wise to establish two accounts to allow the NT Server computer to log on to it. You want to be able to access the NetWare server from the NT Server computer in two ways: as an administrator to perform supervisory operations, and as a user of the gateway to access NetWare server resources. You certainly don't want to give administrative privileges to all users of the gateway, so I recommend establishing two separate NetWare accounts for these two purposes.

On the NetWare server, perform the following steps using the NetWare syscon utility:

1. Create a group called NTGATEWAY. Assign rights to this group that will be available to all users who access this server through the NT gateway.

   These rights must grant appropriate access to all NetWare server resources your users will need to access.

2. Create a user account for use by the NT gateway. Make this account a member of the NTGATEWAY group.

   You can name this user account whatever you wish. Three popular names for this account are GATEWAY, GATEUSER, and GSNWUSER.

   If you have more than one NT gateway that's going to access this NetWare server, create one unique user account for each gateway and add them all to the NTGATEWAY group. In this situation, you'll probably want to name your user accounts with numbers or letters differentiating them. For example, you might use GATEWAY1, GATEWAY2, and so on.

3. Create a NetWare supervisor account with appropriate rights to perform administrative functions. (This is optional, but highly recommended.)

   You probably either log on to the network using the NT administrator account, or you use an account that you've created with administrator privileges. To simplify your life, name the account on the NetWare server the same as the account you use to log on to the NT network. Configure the passwords to be the same on both the NT and NetWare servers.

   If more than one network administrator will be logging on to the network through this NT server computer to perform administrative functions on the NetWare server, you'll need to create a separate account for each administrator.

Once these steps are complete, the NetWare server is ready, and you can turn your attention to configuring your NT server to act as a gateway.

Preparing NT Server for GSNW

Before installing GSNW on your Windows NT server computer, you must remove any existing NetWare redirectors from the system. A typical example is Novell's NetWare Services for Windows NT. (If you don't have a NetWare redirector already installed on your Windows NT server computer, you can skip directly to the next section, where you'll install GSNW.)

Here's how to remove an existing NetWare redirector from NT:

1. While logged on with administrator privileges, click the Start ➪ Settings ➪ Control Panel option. Double-click the Network entry to start the Network Control Panel Application (NCPA).
2. Under Network Services, select the existing NetWare redirector and click Remove.
3. The NetWare redirector is removed from the Network Services list. Click Close.
4. Restart your computer as prompted.

If you don't already have NWLink (IPX/SPX) installed on your Windows NT server computer, follow the instructions in the earlier section entitled "Installing the IPX/SPX Protocol." Once you've done this, proceed with GSNW installation as outlined in the next section.

Installing the Gateway

Be sure to complete the steps in the previous two sections ("Preparing the NetWare Server" and "Preparing the NT Server for GSNW") before installing GSNW on your NT server computer. Here are the steps required to complete the installation:

1. While logged on with administrator privileges, click the Start ➪ Settings ➪ Control Panel option. Double-click the Network entry to start the Network Control Panel Application (NCPA).

2. In the Network dialog box, click the Services tab. Then click Add.
3. Under Network Services, select the option for Gateway (and Client) Services for NetWare and click OK, as shown in Figure 12-14.

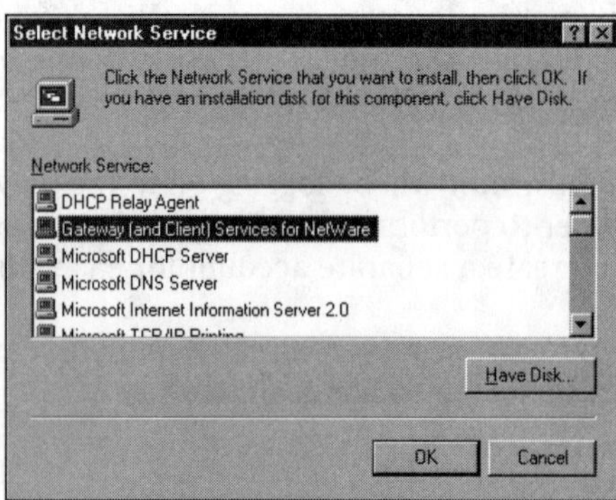

Figure 12-14: Select Gateway Services for NetWare for installation.

4. NCPA asks for the path to the system files on your Windows NT Server 4.0 CD-ROM. Insert the NT CD-ROM in your CD-ROM drive. Type the path and click Continue.

   On my computer, the path is F:\I386. Type the drive letter of your CD-ROM and the subdirectory corresponding to your CPU platform.
5. The selection Gateway Service for NetWare appears in the Network Services list. Click Close, as shown in Figure 12-15.

   Unlike other network services, you configure GSNW using an application that's added to Control Panel. The application is called, appropriately, GSNW. Its icon shows a network cable with a Novell-red end — even more appropriate.
6. If IPX/SPX (NWLink) protocol wasn't previously installed, it will be installed automatically. Click OK.

   In most cases, no additional configuration will be necessary. See the section in this chapter entitled "Installing the IPX/SPX Protocol."
7. Restart your computer as prompted.
8. While logged on with administrator privileges, click Start ➪ Settings ➪ Control Panel. Double-click GSNW.
9. In the Gateway Service for NetWare dialog box, configure the NetWare environment for the user whose name appears under Username.

   If your NetWare server is using NDS (Novell Directory Services), click the Default Tree and Context option and specify these items. If your NetWare server isn't using NDS, click the entry for Preferred Server and specify it. Set the Print Options and Login Script Options as appropriate for this user.

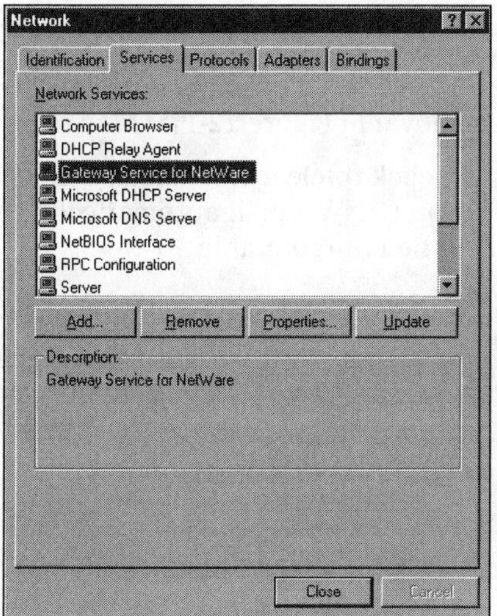

Figure 12-15: GSNW appears in the list of installed services.

The name that appears in this dialog box is the name of the user who's currently logged on to the NT server. The changes that you make in this dialog box apply only to that user account. Figure 12-16 illustrates this. The changes will take effect the next time you log on.

For a description of preferred servers, default trees, and contexts, see your NetWare documentation.

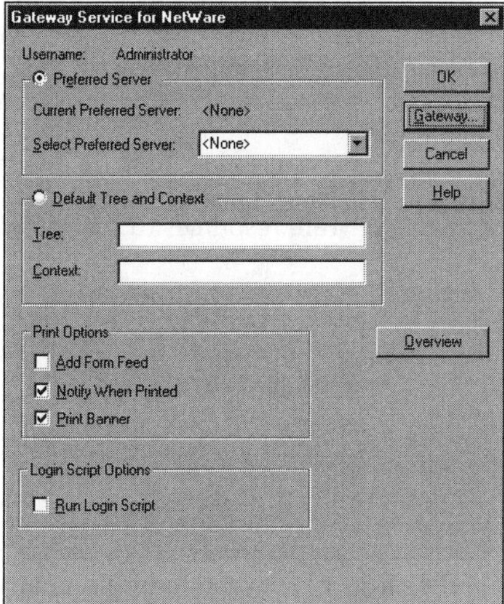

Figure 12-16: Configure the NetWare environment for this user account.

10. Click the Gateway option. In the Configure Gateway dialog box, click Enable Gateway. Type the gateway user account that you created in step 2 under "Preparing the NetWare Server." Type the account password in the Password and Confirm Password fields, as shown in Figure 12-17.

If you ever need to disable the gateway, click to clear this check box. If you use the Control Panel Services application to stop GSNW, you'll automatically stop other important services, and the results may be unpredictable.

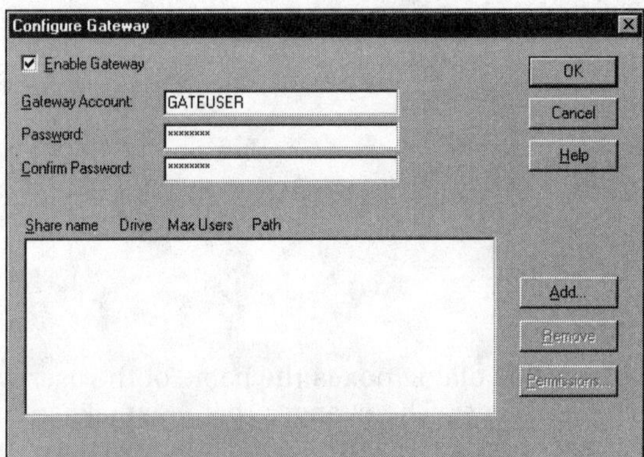

Figure 12-17: Enable and configure the gateway with shared NetWare resources.

11. Click Add. Create a shared NetWare resource through the gateway by typing the NT share name, the path to the NetWare resource, and an optional comment describing the resource, as shown in Figure 12-18. Then click OK.

    In the example in Figure 12-18, if the name of the NT server is TOWER3, Microsoft clients will see the resource as \\TOWER3\NWDATA. The actual NetWare resource that they'll access is \\nw4\sys\data on the NetWare server.

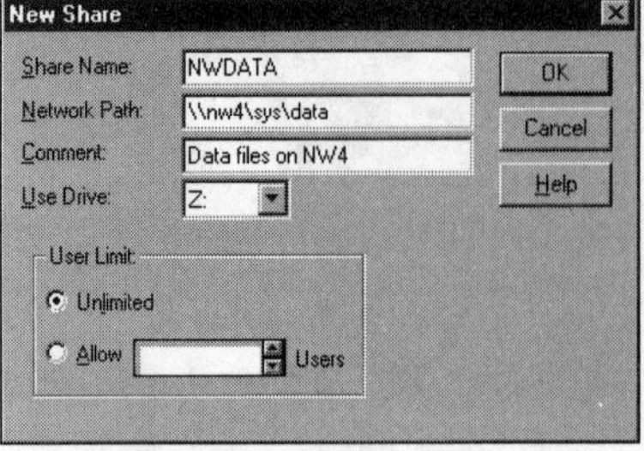

Figure 12-18: Add new shared NetWare resources to the gateway.

If you specified a NetWare bindery-style gateway user account, you can only establish shares for non-NDS resources. If you want to share NDS resources through the gateway, always use the bindery-style \\server\share name format to specify each resource that you share through the gateway. Use the bindery-style name format even if the NetWare resources actually reside on the NDS tree.

When you click OK, NT immediately attempts to connect to the NetWare resource. If it fails, you'll get an error message within a few seconds.

12. Repeat step 11 for all shared resources that you want to make visible through the gateway. When you're done, click OK.

    You can specify up to 22 shared resources through the gateway.

13. If you want to set permissions on the share you've created, select the share and click Permissions.

    By default, Everyone is granted Full Control over the share. To change this, select the option for Add and Remove to select user accounts and change the permissions as appropriate. I'll discuss permissions in detail in Chapter 18.

14. In the Gateway Service for NetWare dialog box, click OK.

If the account passwords aren't in sync between the NT server and the NetWare server, you'll be asked for a password each time you establish a connection to the NetWare server. To avoid this annoyance, use the NetWare setpass command to change your account's password on the NetWare server to match the password on NT. Once you do this, you can enter your password just once, when you log on to the network.

Migration Tool for NetWare

Windows NT server comes with a migration tool that allows you to pull account information from an existing NetWare server to a Windows NT server. The two environments are different enough to prevent a complete translation of all information. However, if you're migrating from NetWare to Windows NT server, this tool can save you significant time. Here's what the migration tool, called NWCONV, lets you do:

- ✦ Transfer and preserve most user account information to your NT PDC, and create new passwords for all user accounts
- ✦ Control the transfer of user and group names, disposition of duplicate accounts, account restrictions, and administrative rights
- ✦ Select and control the transfer of files and folders, preserving effective rights

In addition, NWCONV lets you perform a trial-run migration, to see the results of the translation before actually committing yourself to do it. When you do perform the migration, this tool provides comprehensive logs containing details of the translation process.

I strongly recommend that you take advantage of the trial migration before performing an actual migration. This process will allow you to see how much work the tool will perform automatically, what information is retained and lost, and how much manual effort you'll have to expend in completing the process.

Preparing for Migration

Before proceeding with the migration process, you need to be sure that you've addressed the following prerequisites:

- ✦ Your NetWare server needs to already have all the accounts that you want to migrate to Windows NT server.
- ✦ You can migrate only to a Windows NT server acting as either the PDC or a BDC in your network.
- ✦ The NT server to which you're going to migrate must have the IPX/SPX (NWLink) protocol installed. The steps for doing this were presented earlier in this chapter.
- ✦ The NT server must have Gateway Services for NetWare installed, enabled, and properly configured. See the previous section for step-by-step instructions. (The account that you use to log on to Windows NT server must have supervisor privileges on the NetWare server to be migrated.)
- ✦ If you want to preserve permissions on files and folders migrated from the NetWare server, your NT server must have an NTFS partition to receive these files and folders. (Migrating to a FAT partition will cause this information to be lost.)

Although NTFS isn't strictly a requirement for file system migration, I consider it essential. Otherwise, you'll lose file system security information during the migration process.

For the existing NetWare clients, you need to decide how you want to provide services to them. One option is to upgrade the clients to run Microsoft networking. This approach allows the clients to take full advantage of features offered by Windows NT server. Another approach is to purchase and install File and Print Services for NetWare (FPNW), available from Microsoft. Taking this approach means you don't have to make any changes to existing clients.

If you plan on migrating multiple NetWare servers to multiple NT servers, you'll need to decide where each set of NetWare users fits in your Windows NT server domain structure. (See Chapters 7 and 10 for help in deciding how to organize your NT domains.) If you want to consolidate user accounts and data from several NetWare servers to a single Windows NT Server computer, you'll need to specify a list of the NetWare source servers. If you want to distribute accounts and data from a single NetWare server to multiple Windows NT server domains, you'll need a list of destination NT servers and domains.

It's a good idea to plan carefully the order of migration, if you're migrating several NetWare servers to NT. Since you may have duplicate user accounts on different NetWare servers, it's usually best to migrate the server with the largest number of user and group accounts first. Then you can use the migration tool to control disposition of duplicate accounts. Doing the biggest job first also makes the remaining smaller ones a relative piece of cake.

Account and File Considerations

Before performing a migration, you'll need to decide what you want to migrate from each NetWare server — user accounts, files (including volumes and folders), or both. You'll also need to understand how accounts and files are migrated, which I'll outline in this section.

NetWare user account passwords aren't preserved during the migration process. Why? For security reasons, NetWare provides no mechanism (even via system APIs) to obtain an existing account password. Although this is appropriate in a secure operating system, it makes your job of transferring accounts a bit more difficult. The migration tool offers you some options for assigning initial passwords, so the new NT accounts don't have to be totally exposed.

If you're using a master domain model in which the master domain contains user accounts and other domains are used for network resources, you'll need to decide if you want the migrated NetWare user and group accounts to be created on the master account domain or on the NT server that will receive the NetWare files and folders. If you're using this domain model, I recommend transferring the migrated accounts to the master PDC. See Chapter 10 for a discussion of master account domains.

NetWare default account restrictions are set using Supervisor Options and can be overridden by changing restrictions on individual accounts. NT server sets account restrictions on individual accounts and uses account policies to set restrictions on all accounts within an NT domain. (You'll see how account restrictions work in Chapter 18.) Table 12-4 illustrates how NetWare account restrictions are translated during the migration process. Restrictions with no check marks in the two columns on the right aren't transferred during migration.

Table 12-4
NetWare Account Restriction Migration

NetWare Account Restriction	*Windows NT Server Translation*	*By User Account*	*As NT Policy*
Account Disabled	Same	√	
Allow User to Change Password	User Cannot Change Password	√	
Days Between Forced Changes	Maximum Password Age		√
Expiration Date	Same	√	
Force Periodic Password Changes	Password Never Expires	√	
Grace Logins	None (without FPNW) Same (with FPNW)	√ (FPNW)	
Intruder Detection and Lockout	Account Lockout		√

(continued)

Table 12-4 *(continued)*

NetWare Account Restriction	*Windows NT Server Translation*	*By User Account*	*As NT Policy*
Limit Concurrent Connections	None (without FPNW) Same (with FPNW)	√ (FPNW)	
Login Scripts	None (without FPNW) Same (with FPNW)	√ (FPNW)	
Minimum Password Length	Same		√
Require Password	Permit Blank Password		√
Require Unique Passwords	Password Uniqueness		√
Station Restrictions	None		
Time Restrictions	Logon Hours	√	
User Disk Volume Restrictions	None		

When transferring files and folders, file attributes are migrated according to Table 12-3, presented earlier in this chapter. NetWare file and folder rights are migrated according to Table 12-5.

Table 12-5
Translation of NetWare File and Folder Rights to Windows NT Server

NetWare File and Folder Right	*Windows NT Server File Permission*	*Windows NT Server Folder Permission*
A (Access Control)	P (Change Permissions)	P
C (Create)	Not applicable	WX (Write and Execute)
E (Erase)	RWXD (Read, Write, Execute, and Delete)	RWXD
F (File Scan)	Not applicable	RX (Read and Execute)
M (Modify)	RWXD	RWXD
R (Read)	RX	RX
S (Supervisory)	All	All
W (Write)	RWXD	RWXD

Performing a Migration

Before migrating from NetWare to Windows NT Server, be sure to cover the preparatory material under "Migration Tool for NetWare." You'll need to understand the issues covered in that section to efficiently complete the migration process efficiently. When you're ready, complete the following steps:

Selecting Your Servers

1. While logged on to Windows NT Server with administrator privileges, click the Start ➪ Run option. In the Open box, type **NWCONV** and click OK.
2. In the Select Servers for Migration dialog box, under the From NetWare Server option, choose Browse. Select a NetWare source server and click OK. Under the option for To Windows NT Server, click Browse. Click a domain name and a server name and click OK, as shown in Figure 12-19. Click OK.

   You'll see this dialog box only if this is the first time that you're running NWCONV. It allows you to specify the first source and destination servers. You'll be able to specify more sources and destinations in a later step.

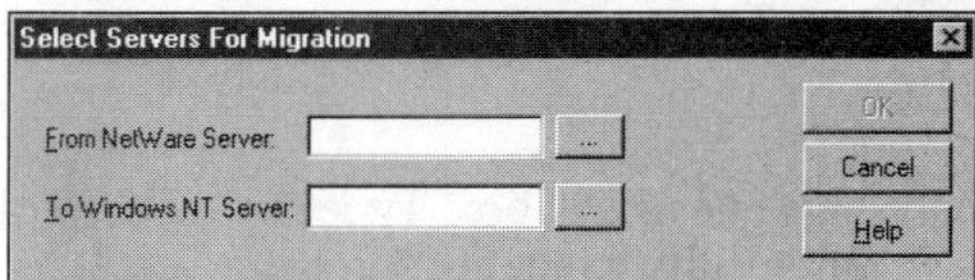

Figure 12-19: Specify the NetWare source and NT destination of the migration.

3. Choose the Logging option. Click to select the Verbose User/Group Logging and Verbose File Logging check boxes. Then click OK. If you have no more source or destination servers to specify, go to step 5. Otherwise, go to step 4.

   If you want error conditions to pop up a message and halt the migration process, click to select the Popup On Errors check box. If you just want to review the logs after the trial or actual migration, make sure that this option is cleared.
4. Click Add. Under the From NetWare Server option, choose Browse. Select a NetWare source server and click OK. Under the option for To Windows NT Server, click Browse. Click a domain name and a server name. Then click OK. Repeat this step for each additional server.

   The account that you use to log on to Windows NT Server must have supervisor privileges on each NetWare server that you select. Likewise, you must have administrator privileges on each NT server before migration can commence.

   If you change your mind and want to remove a pair of servers, select the pair and click Delete.

Selecting Account Transfer Options

5. Select a pair of source (NetWare) and destination (NT) servers. Click User Options.

   The Transfer Users and Groups check box should be set by default, indicating that accounts will be transferred from this NetWare server. Don't clear this check box unless you want to ignore all user and group accounts on this NetWare server.

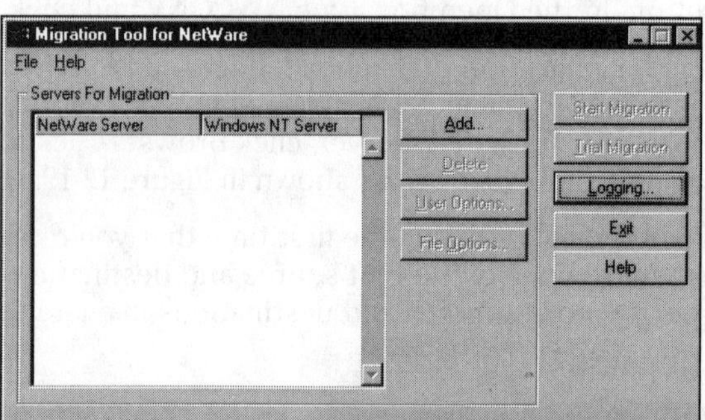

Figure 12-20: Control the migration process using the Migration Tool for NetWare.

6. Click to select the Use Mappings File check box. Type the name of the editable mappings file that you want the utility to create for you.

   You need to type a unique filename for each NetWare server that you're going to migrate. The mappings file gives you full control over how you want each account transferred. It associates a NetWare account name with a new Windows NT account name and lets you control the initial account password on NT. I strongly suggest that you use this option.

7. Click the Passwords tab. Click the appropriate options to control how you want initial passwords assigned to the migrated accounts.

   The old NetWare passwords can't be migrated. You can specify that the new NT accounts will have no password, a password the same as the user account name, or a standard password that you assign to all migrated accounts. If you select the latter, type the standard password that you want to assign. NT server passwords can be up to 14 characters and are case sensitive.

   You can also specify whether the user will be forced to change his or her password when first logging on to NT. This option is selected by default, and I recommend leaving it alone.

Pick the password option that will apply to the majority of user accounts that you're migrating. Since you're creating an editable mappings file, you'll be able to override these choices manually on specific accounts. Letting the majority rule your decision at this stage will save you manual effort later on. If you want to specify a unique password for each migrated account, select the No Password option. This will save you from having to delete text when you edit the mappings file.

8. Click the Usernames tab. Click the appropriate options to control how you want duplicate user account names to be handled.

   A user account name that you're attempting to migrate may already exist on the Windows NT server or domain. You can log the conflicting account names and ignore them, ignore the conflicts without logging them, or overwrite the NT account with the migrated NetWare account. Alternatively, you can add a prefix to the conflicting account name and then migrate it. If you choose the latter, type the prefix that you want to add to all conflicting account names.

   Log Error, which logs the conflict and ignores the account, is the default choice.

Keep the account name prefix as short as possible. Windows NT Server account names are limited to 20 characters, and you don't want to generate even more errors by exceeding this limit. The same limitation applies to group names in step 9.

9. Click the Group Names tab. Click the appropriate options to control how you want duplicate group names to be handled.

   A group name that you're attempting to migrate may already exist on the Windows NT server or domain. You can log the conflicting names and ignore them, ignore the conflicts without logging them, or add a prefix to the conflicting group name and then migrate it. If you choose the latter, type the prefix that you want to add to all conflicting group names.

   Ignore, which ignores the group name conflict without logging it, is the default choice.

10. Click the Defaults tab. Click to clear the Use Supervisor Defaults check box if you want to use the NT server's account policy restrictions. If you want to use the NetWare supervisor account policy restrictions, click to select this check box.

    The affected policy settings are listed in Table 12-4 with a check mark in the "As NT Policy" column.

11. If you don't want to grant NT administrative rights to NetWare accounts that have supervisor rights, click to clear the Add Supervisors to the Administrators Group check box. If you want all NetWare supervisor accounts to have full administrative rights on NT, click to select this check box.

    This check box affects both user accounts and groups. If you decide not to grant administrative rights on NT now, you can later do so manually with the User Manager for Domains utility.

If you decide to migrate NetWare supervisor rights to NT administrative rights, be absolutely sure to know which accounts (and the people who use them) have these rights. By selecting this option, you're giving these folks carte blanche on your NT network.

12. If you're using a master domain model and you want the migrated user accounts to be created on the master domain controller, click Advanced, click to select Transfer Users to Trusted Domain, and select the name of the master domain.

If you're using the master account domain model, I strongly recommend sending the migrated user and group accounts to the master domain.

Migrated groups are transferred as global groups in the master domain and are created as local groups on the NT server to which you're migrating. The local group contains the master domain global group.

13. Click OK. When asked if you want to edit the mappings file (see step 6), click Yes. Using Notepad, make all necessary changes to the file, save the changes, and close Notepad.

    You can now edit the mappings file using Notepad. The file contains a section for each user and group account. For user accounts, the format of the entry is

    ```
    [OldNetWareUser]
    NewName = WindowsNTName
    Password = NewPassword
    ```

    where OldNetWareUser is the name of the existing NetWare user account, WindowsNTName is the name that you assign to the new NT account, and NewPassword is the password that you assign to the new NT account. Group account entries are similar, except that they don't have a password field.

    Remember, account names can be up to 20 characters, and passwords can be up to 14 characters.

14. Repeat steps 5 through 13 for each pair of source and destination servers.

Selecting File Transfer Options

15. In the Migration Tool for NetWare dialog box, select a pair of source (NetWare) and destination (NT) servers. Click File Options.

    The Transfer Files check box should be set by default, indicating that files and folders will be transferred from this NetWare server. Don't clear the check box unless you want to ignore all files on this NetWare server.

    By default, all NetWare files will be copied to the NT server. Hidden and system files are excluded, as are files in \SYSTEM, \MAIL, \LOGIN, and \ETC. The migration tool will attempt to copy files to an NT share point with a name that matches the NetWare volume name. If a matching share point doesn't exist, a destination share point is created automatically on NT.

16. If you want to exclude a volume from the file transfer process, click the volume name under the Source Files option and click Delete. Repeat this step for each volume you want to remove from the list.

    By default, all volumes on the NetWare server are listed and will be transferred to the NT server.

17. If you want to add a volume (that isn't already listed) to the file transfer process, click Add. Type the volume name and the destination share point and folder. Then click OK. Repeat this step for each volume you want to add to the list.

If you inadvertently deleted a volume name in step 16, you can use this option to restore it. You must also use this option if you created a new volume on the NetWare server after starting the migration tool and you want that volume to participate in the file transfer to NT.

18. If you want to specify a different NT destination share point or directory, click Modify. In the Modify Destination dialog box, click the share point name or click New Share to create a new one. Click OK.

    Type a subdirectory name, if you want the files transferred to a subdirectory under the shared directory.

19. If you want to specify which files and folders you want to migrate, click the Files option. Click individual folders for an expanded view of their contents. Next to individual files and folders, click to clear the check box if you want to exclude the item from migration. Click to select the check box if you want the item to be migrated. When you're finished, click OK.

    Hidden and system files aren't migrated by default. If you want to transfer hidden or system files, on the Transfer menu, select the Hidden Files and/or System Files options as appropriate.

If any files or folders are created on the NetWare volume after you've completed step 19, they'll automatically be migrated if any other files in their folder are tagged for migration.

Running a Trial Migration

20. In the Migration Tool for NetWare dialog box, select Trial Migration. When you see the Transfer Completed dialog box, click the View Log Files option. When you're done reviewing the logs, close the LogView window.

    The three log files generated are stored in the same directory as NWCONV.EXE. ERROR.LOG lists all failures during the migration process. LOGFILE.LOG contains information on migrated users and groups. SUMMARY.LOG includes a list of all source and destination servers, along with statistics on the migration process.

    Review the log files and correct any conditions that caused unwanted errors or unexpected behavior. Common errors include running out of disk space on a destination server, inability to access a server due to lack of privileges, or a server going down.

If you run a migration more than once, the log files will be renamed automatically by changing their .LOG extensions to numeric extensions. Each generation of log files is saved separately by incrementing the numeric extension.

Running a Real Migration

21. In the Migration Tool for NetWare dialog box, select the Start Migration option. When you see the Transfer Completed dialog box, choose View Log Files. When you're done reviewing the logs, close the LogView window. Then click Exit.

    Review the new log files to make sure the migration completed as expected.

Client Service for NetWare

Windows NT Workstation 4.0 includes a feature called Client Service for NetWare. It allows NT workstation computers to access file and print resources directly on NetWare servers that are running NetWare 2.x or later. It supports connection to NetWare 4.x servers that are running NDS or bindery emulation. In addition, Client Service for NetWare fully supports NetWare login scripts.

Windows NT Server includes Gateway Services for NetWare, which, in turn, includes Client Services for NetWare. GSNW is discussed earlier in this chapter. To learn more about how to install and configure this NT Workstation feature, consult your Windows NT Workstation online Help.

Integrating with UNIX Networks

The bulk of issues dealing with integration of NT with UNIX revolve around correct installation and configuration of TCP/IP. In Chapter 11, I covered TCP/IP on Windows NT Server in sometimes painful detail. Configuring TCP/IP on your Windows NT Server computer is 90 percent of the battle for UNIX connectivity. I'll discuss the other 10 percent here.

File Transfers

Both client and server versions of FTP are included with Windows NT Server, allowing simple file transfers among your NT and UNIX computers. FTP is installed automatically when you install the TCP/IP protocol. Simply invoke it from an NT Command Prompt.

If you need more advanced data-sharing capabilities, including access to remotely mountable file systems such as Sun's NFS (Network File System), you need to install Microsoft LAN Manager for UNIX on the UNIX computer. This product uses the SMB protocol to allow you to connect to shared UNIX resources just as with Windows NT resources. If you want a UNIX computer to access shared resources on your Windows NT server, several software manufacturers offer Windows NT versions of NFS.

TCP/IP Printing

Perhaps you want to send print jobs from a computer on your Windows NT network to a printer attached to a UNIX computer. On one Windows NT computer (workstation or server), just install and configure the TCP/IP protocol (as described in Chapter 11) and then install the Microsoft TCP/IP Printing service using the following steps:

1. While logged on to your Windows NT Server computer with administrator privileges, select the Start ⇨ Settings ⇨ Control Panel option. Double-click the Network entry.
2. In the Network dialog box, click the Services tab. Then click Add.
3. Under Network Services, select Microsoft TCP/IP Printing and click OK.
4. You're asked for the path to the system files on your Windows NT Server 4.0 CD-ROM. Insert the NT CD-ROM in your CD-ROM drive. Type the path and click Continue.

   On my computer, the path is F:\I386. Type the drive letter of your CD-ROM and the subdirectory corresponding to your CPU platform.
5. Microsoft TCP/IP Printing appears in the Network Services list. Click Close.

This NT computer will act as a gateway between your clients and the UNIX printer. Now, create and share the printer as you would any other networked printer, as described in Chapter 18.

If the only reason that you're using TCP/IP on your NT network is to connect to printers on UNIX computers, you need to install and run TCP/IP only on the NT computer that's acting as a gateway (as described in this section). Your clients can run any protocol. As long as they can communicate with this NT computer, they can print to the UNIX printer.

Integrating with Other Networks

Several software manufacturers offer solutions to connectivity with other networks that I haven't mentioned. For example, Banyan provides a requester to allow you to access resources on VINES servers from a Windows NT computer.

In planning connectivity with other networks, you need to deal with integration at three levels. First, you must have a compatible underlying transport protocol. For example, connectivity with UNIX typically requires both computers to run TCP/IP. Second, you need a compatible higher-level protocol for management of connections and shared resources. For example, Microsoft networks require SMB, and

NetWare networks require NCP. Connectivity to UNIX at this level typically requires either running SMB on the UNIX side or NFS on the NT side. Third, you need to understand how your applications use the network, to determine if those applications are compatible with the underlying protocols that you're using to connect NT to the other environment. For this, you need to consult your application vendors or the manufacturers of the protocols, if they have application compatibility lists.

Installation of each product varies, but most require that you install protocols and services using the Network Control Panel Application. There are several examples of how to accomplish this in this chapter and Chapter 11. With this knowledge, an understanding of your existing network, and instructions provided by the software manufacturer, you should have the tools to complete a successful network integration.

Summary

In this chapter, you've learned about integrating Windows NT Server 4.0 with existing AppleTalk, NetWare, UNIX, and other networks. I've presented the steps to prepare, install, and configure the various Windows NT components and included some hints and warnings along the way. In Chapter 13, I'll show you how to install and configure network software on your client computers running DOS, Windows 3.x, Windows for Workgroups, Windows NT Workstation, and Windows 95.

Installing Your Network Clients

If you've ever had a sales job, do you remember wishing that a certain client would just go away? Even if you liked people in general, occasionally a guy would just get in your face and on your nerves. Perhaps you were annoyed by his high-pitched, whiny voice, his wimpy inability to make a buying decision, his petty haggling over price, or his incessant chatter about nothing. Didn't you sometimes wish that you could pick and choose your clients?

In computer networks, as in sales, picking and choosing your clients is usually just wishful thinking. Most cost-conscious organizations won't allow you to discard or replace your legacy computers purely to reduce your stress level. As a result, all of your clients won't have the latest and greatest hardware with a state-of-the-art operating system. Invariably, some of them will be old, slow systems in need of constant attention and patience. They might even have disk drives with a familiar high-pitched whine, making you wince as you remember your days behind the sales counter.

As an NT network administrator, you can't focus solely on designing, planning, and installing NT Server 4.0 and its server components. Whether you like it or not, you'll probably be responsible for getting your network clients up and running, whether they're NT clients or not.

In this chapter, I'll walk you through installing and configuring the network client software on each type of Microsoft client, including Windows NT Workstation, Windows 95, Windows for Workgroups, Windows 3.x, and DOS. (I covered configuring Macintosh clients in Chapter 12.) Windows NT Workstation and Windows 95 have the required client network software built in. Software for the remaining platforms is provided on the Windows NT Server CD-ROM. In addition, I'll fill you in on how to establish RAS clients to be used with the RAS server that you set up in Chapter 11.

Preparing to Install Network Clients

Regardless of how you choose to install your network clients, make sure to complete the following steps before proceeding with the installation process for each client computer:

1. Ensure that the operating system is installed and running on your client computer. Have your original operating system installation media (floppy disks or CD-ROM) close at hand.

   In some cases, you may be asked to insert original disks from your operating system disk set to install files that support network operation. For example, Windows 95 client installation will require files from the original media, and Windows 3.1 client installation may ask for Disk 6 from the original floppy disk set.

2. Install the network adapter hardware in your client computer. Configure the appropriate switches, jumpers, or software settings.

   Installing network adapters in client computers is much the same as installing the hardware in your server. Follow the instructions provided by your network adapter manufacturer and gather the resource information of other devices in your computer to avoid conflicts. Then, install and configure the adapter. If you're installing RAS on the client, make sure that your RAS devices (modem, ISDN adapter, or X.25 card) are properly installed and configured.

   For general information on network adapter selection and configuration, see Chapter 8. Don't worry about Windows NT hardware compatibility (unless your client computer is going to be running Windows NT Workstation). Just make sure that your network adapter is compatible with your client computer's hardware and with that computer's operating system software.

   Make note of the adapter's configuration information for later use when you install the network software. A good place to record this information is in your network documentation notebook, which I discussed in Chapter 5.

Although client computer hardware and software configurations will differ, you may want to consider standardizing on one or a small number of network adapters in your client computers. Doing this will minimize the number of different configurations with which you need to deal as you or your team members visit each client computer to prepare it for network communication. Of course, if you already have your client computers and network hardware in place, you'll need to deal with what you have.

3. Have your original Windows NT Server 4.0 CD-ROM close at hand. You'll need it if you're going to install network client software on DOS, Windows 3.x, Windows for Workgroups (TCP/IP only), or OS/2 1.3.

   If you're planning to install the client-based network administration tools, you'll need the NT Server CD-ROM, regardless of what operating system is running on your client.

4. Back up your configuration files.

   Make backup copies of your existing client computer configuration files such as AUTOEXEC.BAT, CONFIG.SYS, and so on. In some cases, the network client installation process will modify these files. Although the process will save the old versions, it's sometimes easy to forget where these copies have been placed. Make your own backup copies and record where they are kept in case you need to restore them.

5. Have a supply of blank, formatted floppy disks available for network client software.

   You'll need blank floppy disks to create the various network client disk sets required for your network. Use Table 13-1 to determine the number of disks that you'll need for each type of client.

6. If you have network adapters that aren't directly supported by the client operating system, gather together your hardware manuals, configuration information, and driver disks supplied by the adapter manufacturer.

7. Be sure that your client computer has a 3.5" or 5.25" high-density floppy disk drive attached.

   The network client installation process supports only high-density floppy disks. Low-density installation disks aren't supported.

8. Know the name of the domain or workgroup to which this client will belong and the unique computer name that you want to assign to your client computer.

Table 13-1
Blank Floppy Disks Required for Network Client Installation Sets

Network Client Software	*Number of Floppy Disks Required*
Network Installation Startup Disk for installing DOS and Windows 3.x network software	1
Network Installation Startup Disk for installing Windows 95	1
Network Client 3.0 for DOS and Windows 3.x	2
LAN Manager 2.2c for DOS	4
LAN Manager 2.2c for OS/2 1.3	4
TCP/IP 32 for Windows for Workgroups	1
RAS 1.1a for DOS	1

Although the Windows NT Server 4.0 CD-ROM includes network client software (and even the Windows 95 operating system) at no extra charge, you still must purchase client licenses according to the licensing options outlined in Chapter 7. If you don't purchase the appropriate number of client licenses, you'll be in violation of your Windows NT Server license agreement.

Introducing the Network Client Administrator

Windows NT Server 4.0 makes it fairly easy to create network software installation media for your client computers. NT Server includes several client components on its CD-ROM. In addition, it provides a handy utility called the Network Client Administrator for creating installation floppy disks for each of these clients. This utility enables you to

- **Create a network installation startup disk for installing DOS and Windows 3.x network software.** You can use this floppy disk to start a DOS or Windows 3.x client computer, attach to your NT Server, and install network client software over the network.
- **Create a network installation startup disk for installing the Windows 95 operating system.** You can use this floppy disk to start a client computer, attach to your NT Server, and install Windows 95 over the network.
- **Create installation floppy disk sets for the clients listed in Table 13-1.** You can then use these disk sets to install network client software on a number of client computers.
- **Copy client-based NT network administration tools to client nodes.** You can use these tools to administer your network from non-NT nodes.

All of the client software is contained within the CLIENTS directory on the NT Server CD-ROM. If you know exactly what you need, you can pull the required files directly from the appropriate subdirectories. However, I highly recommend using the Network Client Administrator utility to sort everything out for you. It will save you time and effort.

To start the Network Client Administrator utility, log on to your Windows NT Server computer with administrator privileges. Click Start ➪ Programs ➪ Administrative Tools ➪ Network Client Administrator. You'll see the dialog box shown in Figure 13-1.

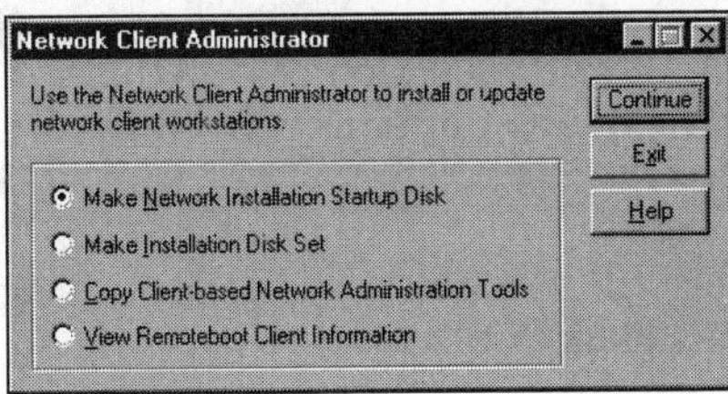

Figure 13-1: The Network Client Administrator utility enables you to manage client installation and tools.

In the following sections, I'll show you how to take advantage of the features that this utility offers.

As Microsoft adds new capabilities to the Network Client Administrator, they provide updated instructions on the CD-ROM in \CLIENTS\SUPPORT\README.TXT. View this file for additional information on managing network client installation.

Working with Installation Startup Disks

Network Client Administrator allows you to create a bootable floppy disk that contains just enough software to connect your DOS or Windows 3.x client computer to Windows NT Server and install network client software over the network. You can also create a startup disk that will enable you to install the entire Windows 95 operating system over the network. You share the required files either directly from the NT CD-ROM or from a hard disk directory on the server. It's a convenient way to install and minimizes the number of floppy disks that you have to use.

Because the installation startup disk will use NetBEUI during the client network software installation process, be sure that the NetBEUI protocol is installed on your computer running Windows NT Server. If you verify this now, you'll save time in later steps.

Creating an Installation Startup Disk

Here are the steps to follow to create a network installation startup disk:

1. Prepare a single high-density floppy disk by formatting it under DOS. Make it bootable using the SYS command under DOS. Label the floppy disk "Network Installation Startup Disk."

   Use either a 3.5" or 5.25" high-density floppy disk. The size needs to match drive A in your client computer. On the floppy disk label, indicate whether this is going to be a DOS/Windows startup disk or a Windows 95 startup disk (they are different).

You must format this floppy disk under DOS, not under Windows NT or any other operating system. You want this floppy to boot to the version of DOS that's installed on the floppy. You need to create the floppy under DOS to end up with a DOS boot sector.

2. Start the Network Client Administrator utility as discussed earlier. Click Make Network Installation Startup Disk. Then click Continue.
3. In the Share Network Client Installation Files dialog box, select whether you want to share files over the network directly from the NT CD-ROM or copy the files to the hard disk and share them from there. Click your choice and then click OK. See Figure 13-2 for an illustration.

   The default choice of sharing directly from the CD-ROM is fine, but be sure to leave the CD-ROM in the drive as long as the clients need it for installation.

   If you plan on removing or replacing the CD-ROM, then opt to copy the files to your hard disk and share them there. This approach requires about 64MB of free disk space on the server.

   Depending on the speed of your network and the amount of memory on your server, your client installations may go faster if you put the files on hard disk rather than sharing the CD-ROM directly.

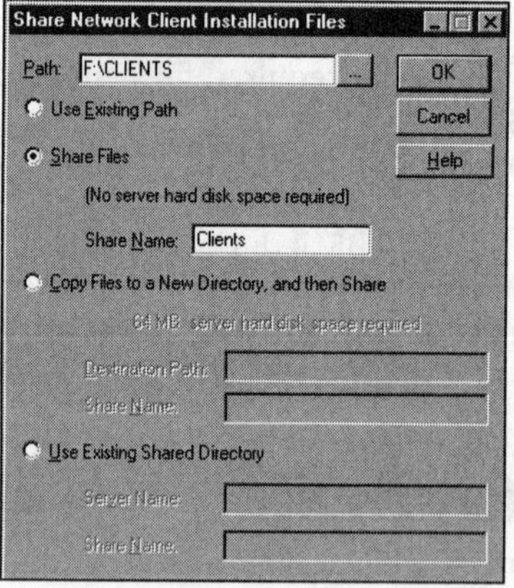

Figure 13-2: You must determine how you want to share the installation files for client installation over the network.

4. In the Target Workstation Configuration dialog box, under Floppy Drive, click the size of the client computer's drive A. See Figure 13-3.

   The floppy drive size that you specify here must match the floppy disk size you chose in step 1.
5. Under Network Client, click either Windows 95 or Network Client v3.0 for MS-DOS and Windows, depending on which type of network installation startup disk you're creating. See Figure 13-3.

The Windows 95 startup disk is designed to install the entire Windows 95 operating system over the network. The DOS/Windows startup disk is designed to install network client software over the network.

6. Under Network Adapter Card, select the network adapter that matches the adapter in your client computer. Click OK, as shown in Figure 13-3.

   If your client computer's network adapter doesn't appear in the list, you'll have to configure the boot disk manually. It must be set up so that the appropriate network adapter driver supplied by your network adapter manufacturer is loaded.

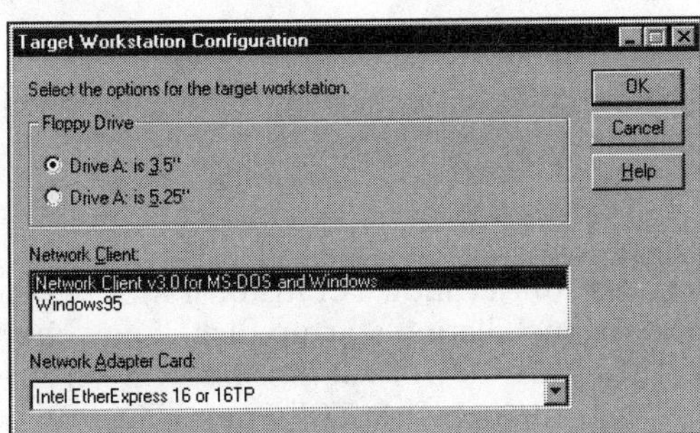

Figure 13-3: Select the client floppy drive size, network client, and network adapter type.

7. In the Network Startup Disk Configuration dialog box, type the client computer name that you want to use temporarily during installation using the floppy disk you're creating. See Figure 13-4.

The computer name that you select here will not affect the computer name of the client after network software installation. The computer name that you're specifying at this point is used by the client only during installation over the network, while booted from the startup floppy disk that you're creating in this procedure.

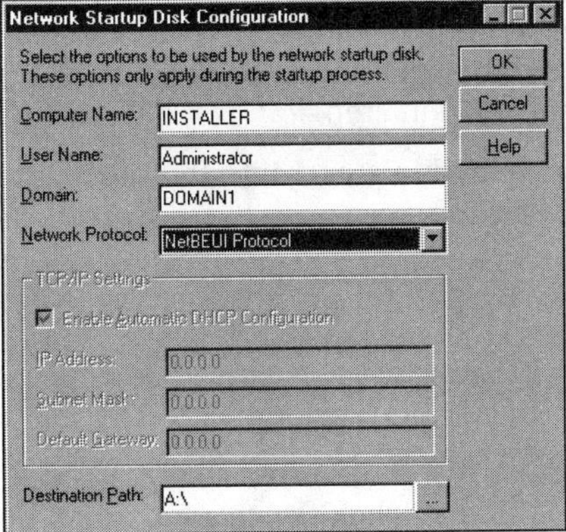

Figure 13-4: You configure the temporary computer name, user name, domain name, and network protocol to be used during network client installation.

8. Type the user account name that you want the installation disk to use when logging on to the domain during the install process. Type the name of the domain where you want the installation disk to log on. See Figure 13-4.

   The domain name defaults to the domain name of the Windows NT Server where you're creating the floppy disk. You can change it to any domain name in your network. Just make sure that the user account exists in that domain.

If you're logged on as Administrator, the user name will default to this account. To avoid giving the client full administrator access to your server during network installation, create a user account in the domain that allows read access to the directory that you shared in step 3.

9. From the Network Protocol list, select NetBEUI Protocol. See Figure 13-4.

   Don't worry. The NetBEUI protocol that you select at this stage will be in effect only during the client installation process. It has no influence on what combination of protocols you can run once the network client software is actually installed.

Even though you're given the choice of NetBEUI, TCP/IP, or IPX/SPX, you *must* choose NetBEUI to create a working installation startup disk. If you choose either of the other protocols, things will appear to work at first but will fail later, when it comes time to actually connect over the network. TCP/IP and IPX/SPX protocols will only run on top of NDIS 3.0 drivers (the kind used by NT), but DOS requires NDIS 2.0 drivers. NetBEUI is the only protocol of these three that you can successfully run on top of DOS NDIS 2.0 drivers.

Because you'll be running NetBEUI during installation, make sure that your client node is on the same network as the Windows NT Server node containing the shared installation files. Since the NetBEUI protocol isn't routable, these two computers must not be separated by a router. Otherwise, they won't see each other, and you won't be able to install the client software over the network.

10. If you want to create the installation floppy disk in a drive other than drive A, type the appropriate path in the Destination Path field. Then click OK.

    Remember, you want to create an installation floppy that matches drive A of your client computer. The size of the destination drive must match the size that you chose in step 1 and specified in step 4.

11. Insert the floppy disk that you created in step 1 into the destination drive that you specified in step 10. Click OK.

    If the same dialog box returns, asking you to insert the floppy disk, make sure that you're inserting it in the correct drive and that it's a bootable DOS floppy disk.

12. In the Confirm Network Disk Configuration dialog box, verify that the settings are correct and then click OK. See Figure 13-5.

    If the settings aren't what you intended, click Cancel, and you'll be returned to step 7.

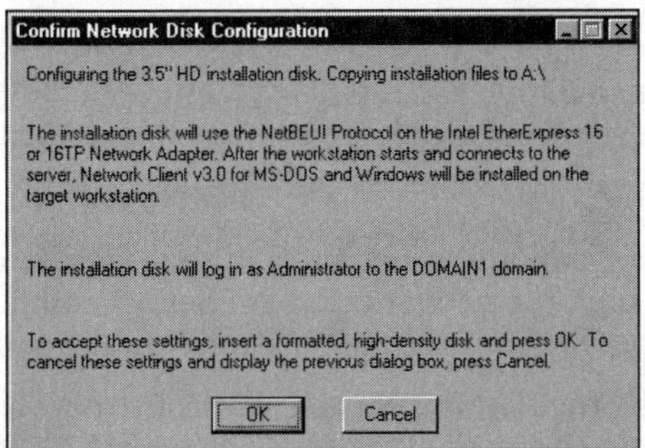

Figure 13-5: You can confirm the configuration before creating the network installation startup disk.

13. Files are copied from the CD-ROM to the floppy disk. When the operation is complete, click OK.

Configuring Your Startup Disk

The floppy disk that you created in the previous section allows you to install the Windows 95 operating system or DOS/Windows network client software over the network on a client computer. The Network Client Administrator creates this floppy disk using the default settings for the client network adapter that you selected. Therefore, its configuration may not (and probably won't) match your client's actual network adapter configuration.

For example, when I selected the Intel EtherExpress 16 adapter, the network installation startup disk was configured to use the default IRQ3. However, since I have a COM2 port in my client computer, IRQ3 is already in use. The network adapter is actually configured to use IRQ5. To make the startup disk work correctly, I had to edit manually A:\NET\PROTOCOL.INI to change the IRQ setting for the adapter. You'll have to use your knowledge of the actual adapter settings and information supplied by the network adapter manufacturer to determine which files need to change.

Even if you use the default settings on some client nodes, they probably won't all have the same network configuration. If you want to install their network software over the network, you'll need to create different flavors of network installation startup disks, using the steps outlined in the previous section. I recommend using this procedure to create one floppy disk for each type of network adapter. Then, duplicate the disks and modify the individual adapter settings as appropriate. Clearly label every disk as you create and modify them.

Once you have a network installation startup disk that matches your client computer configuration, you can proceed with the steps in the following sections.

Using a Startup Disk for DOS and Windows 3.x

During creation of the network installation startup disk, if you selected Network Client v3.0 for MS-DOS and Windows, perform the following steps to install the client software over the network:

1. Ensure that your NT Server computer is running and that the client software directory is properly shared on the network. The NT Server computer containing the client installation files must be running the NetBEUI protocol.

   The steps performed in the previous section automatically took care of sharing the client software directory. If you opted to share the NT CD-ROM directly, make sure that the CD-ROM is in the drive before proceeding.

2. Insert the DOS/Windows network installation startup disk, which you created in the previous section, into drive A on your client computer. Restart the computer to boot from this floppy disk.

3. After a few moments, you'll see the screen shown in Figure 13-6. Press ENTER to install the network client software.

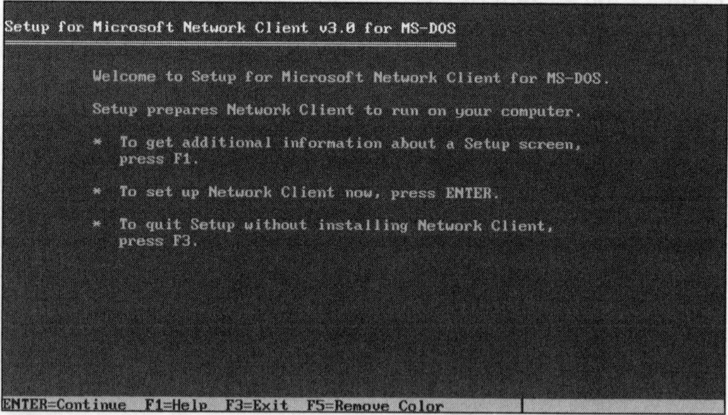

Figure 13-6: You should find out about Network Client Setup or start the client installation process.

4. As shown in Figure 13-7, you're asked for the destination directory where the network client software will be stored. Type the destination path and press ENTER.

   The default path is no help at all in this situation. It directs the files to A:\NET, but you want to install the network software on your client's hard disk. Specify an appropriate hard disk directory, such as C:\NETWORK, for example.

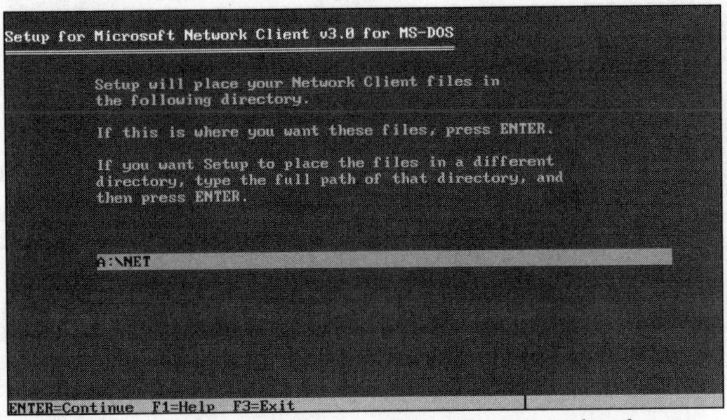

Setup for Microsoft Network Client v3.0 for MS-DOS
Setup will place your Network Client files in the following directory.
If this is where you want these files, press ENTER.
If you want Setup to place the files in a different directory, type the full path of that directory, and then press ENTER.
A:\NET
ENTER=Continue F1=Help F3=Exit

Figure 13-7: You specify where you want the network software installed.

5. Review the network configuration and make changes to the configuration of this client. Use the arrow keys to select an item to change, and press ENTER to change it. See steps 5a, 5b, and 5c for details. When you've completed all changes, select The listed options are correct. Then press ENTER. Figure 13-8 illustrates.

Setup for Microsoft Network Client v3.0 for MS-DOS
Names:
Your User Name is Administrator
Setup Options:
Use the Full Redirector.
Run Network Client.
Network Configuration:
Modify your adapter and protocols with this option.
Change Names
Change Setup Options
Change Network Configuration
The listed options are correct.
ENTER=Continue F1=Help F3=Exit

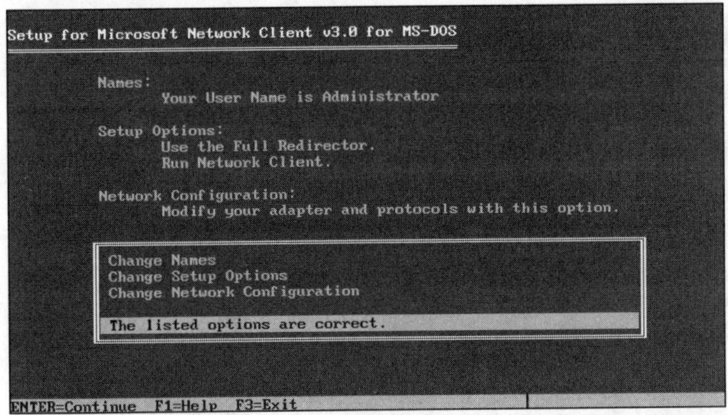

Figure 13-8: You can make network configuration changes unique to this client computer.

5a. Select Change Names to change the user name, computer name, workgroup name, and domain name. When you're done, select The listed names are correct. Then press ENTER, as shown in Figure 13-9.

You need to select a unique name for this computer and change it here. Likewise, you probably need to change the default user name to something other than the default.

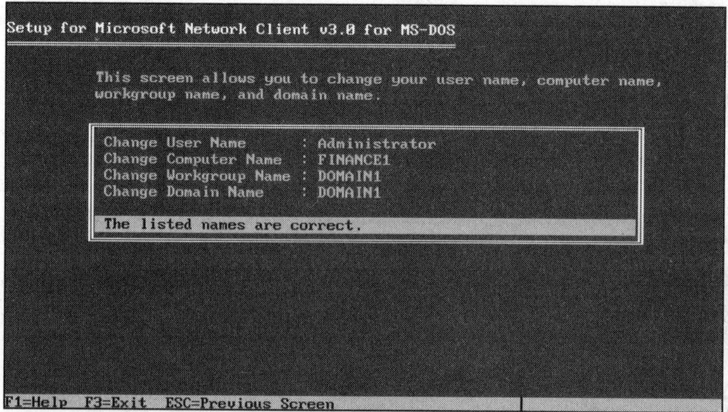

Figure 13-9: You can change the computer name, default user name, domain name, and workgroup name.

5b. Select Change Setup Options to change various network client options, as shown in Figure 13-10. Make any necessary changes. When you're done, select The listed options are correct. Then press ENTER.

I recommend leaving all of the settings at their default values, except for Change Logon Validation. Change this setting to Logon to Domain.

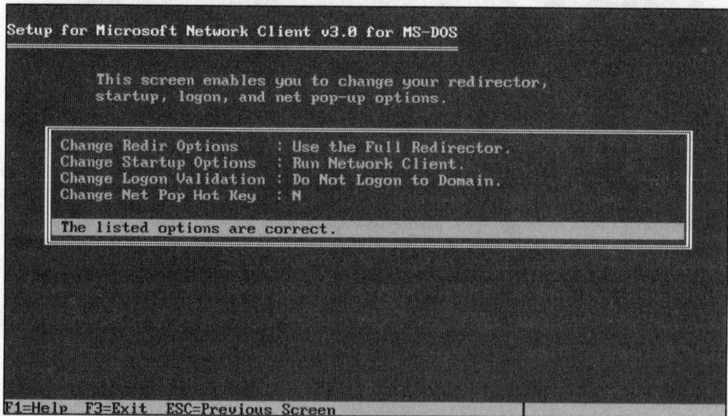

Figure 13-10: You can change redirector, startup, logon and other settings for the client computer.

5c. Select Change Network Configuration to add or remove adapters and protocols and to change network adapter hardware settings (such as IRQ, I/O address, and so on). Make the necessary changes and then select Network configuration is correct. Then press ENTER, as shown in Figure 13-11.

The network adapter and protocol settings are picked up from the network installation startup disk. Therefore, the adapter settings should be correct. If you want the client to run additional protocols, now is the time to add them. Likewise, if the client contains multiple network adapters, select them now.

If you have a network adapter that isn't recognized or directly supported by the client software, select Add Adapter, press ENTER, select Not shown in the list below, and press ENTER. You'll be asked for the path to the driver files provided by your network adapter manufacturer. Follow the prompts and the instructions provided by your adapter manufacturer.

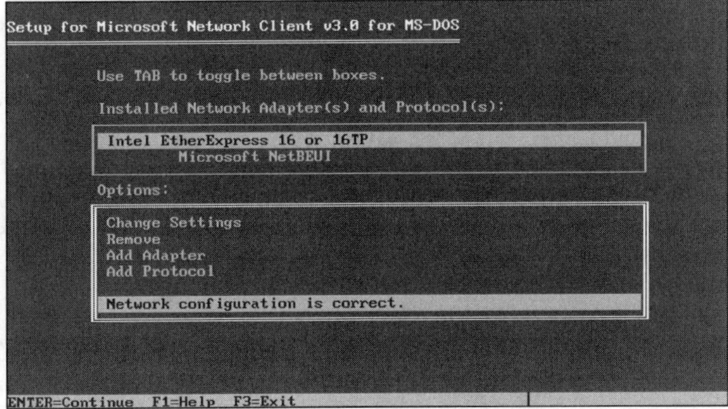

Figure 13-11: You can change network adapter settings and protocols.

6. Files are copied over the network from the server to your client computer. As shown in Figure 13-12, Setup modifies your AUTOEXEC.BAT and CONFIG.SYS files and makes backup copies in the root directory of drive C. Remove the floppy from drive A and press ENTER to restart the computer.

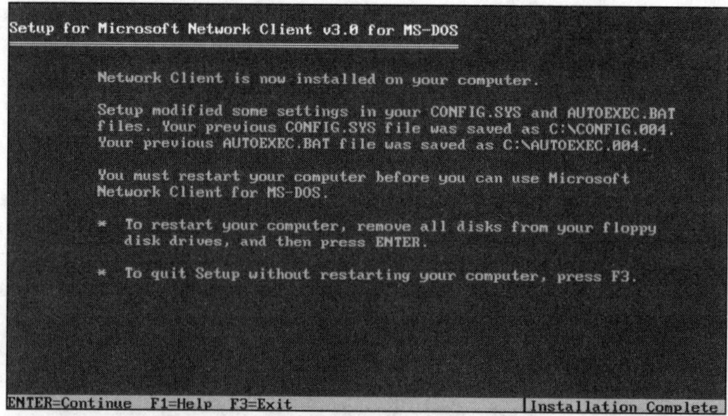

Figure 13-12: Setup automatically modifies your configuration files.

Using a Startup Disk for Windows 95

During creation of the network installation startup disk, if you selected Windows 95, perform the following steps to install Windows 95 operating system software on the client computer over the network:

1. Ensure that your NT Server computer is running and that the client software directory is properly shared on the network. The NT Server computer containing the client installation files must be running the NetBEUI protocol.

   The steps performed during floppy disk creation automatically took care of sharing the client software directory. If you opted to share the NT CD-ROM directly, make sure that the CD-ROM is in the drive before proceeding.

2. Insert the Windows 95 network installation startup disk into drive A on your client computer. Restart the computer to boot from this floppy disk.
3. Your hard disks are scanned for errors. When this operation is complete, Windows 95 Setup runs. Follow the installation prompts to complete the installation.

   Refer to the section entitled "Installing Windows 95 Client Software" for details on installing and configuring Windows 95 network components.

Creating Installation Disk Sets

The Network Client Administrator utility enables you to create installation floppy disk sets for a variety of clients. Table 13-1 lists the disk sets that you can create, along with the number of floppy disks required for each set.

Creating Client Network Disk Sets

Here are the steps to follow to create installation disk sets:

1. Prepare the number of blank, formatted floppy disks required by the disk set that you're planning to create and label them appropriately.

   Use either 3.5" or 5.25" high-density floppy disks. The size needs to match drive A in your client computer.
2. Start the Network Client Administrator utility as discussed earlier. Click Make Installation Disk Set. Then click Continue.
3. In the Share Network Client Installation Files dialog box, click OK.
4. In the Make Installation Disk Set dialog box, under Network Client or Service, select the type of installation disk set that you want to create, as shown in Figure 13-13. If you're creating the disks in a floppy drive other than drive A, change the Destination Drive. Check Format Disks, if you want the floppy disks formatted before creation. Finally, click OK.

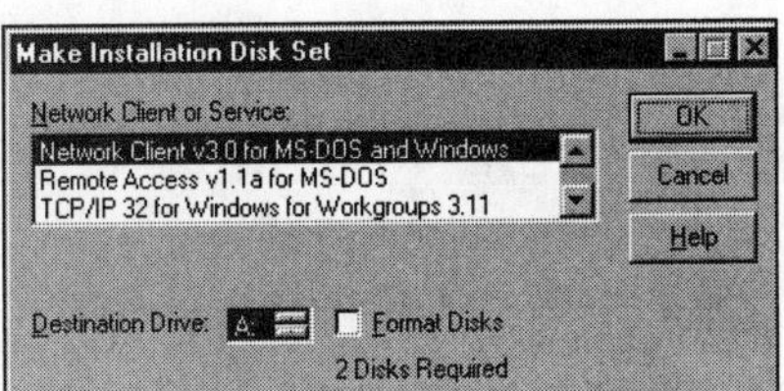

Figure 13-13: You can select the type of installation disk set that you want to create.

5. Insert and remove floppy disks as instructed by the prompts. When the disks have been created, click OK on the summary of files and directories created.

Sharing Client-Based Network Administration Tools

The Network Client Administrator utility enables you to share the client administration tools from the NT CD-ROM and, optionally, to copy them to hard disk for sharing over the network. You can use these tools to administer a Windows NT server or domain from any client computer running Windows 95, Windows NT Workstation, or Windows NT Server. Here are the steps to follow to create installation disk sets:

1. Start the Network Client Administrator utility as discussed earlier. Click Copy Client-based Network Administration Tools. Then click Continue.
2. In the Share Client-based Administration Tools dialog box, select whether you want to share files over the network directly from the NT CD-ROM or copy the files to the hard disk and share them from there. Click your choice and then click OK. See Figure 13-14.

The default choice of sharing directly from the CD-ROM is fine, but be sure to leave the CD-ROM in the drive as long as the clients need it.

If you plan on removing or replacing the CD-ROM, then opt to copy the files to hard disk and share them there. This approach requires about 15MB of free disk space on the server.

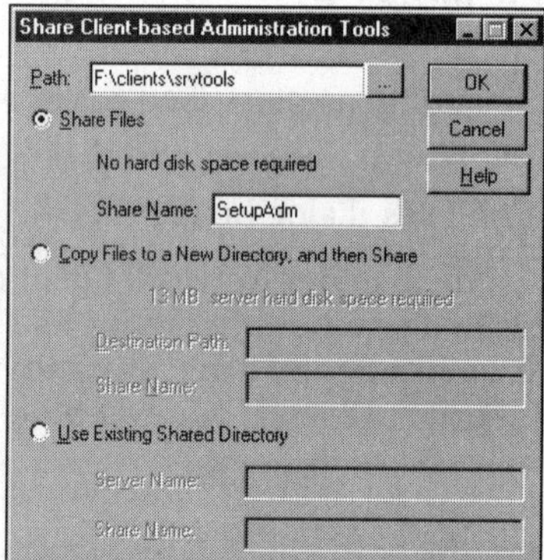

Figure 13-14: You can determine how you want to share the client-based administration tools over the network.

3. Click OK.

Installing DOS and Windows 3.x Clients

If you decided not to install network client software over the network, as I discussed earlier in this chapter, you can install from a floppy disk set. Once you've created a set of Microsoft Network Client 3.0 disks, you can proceed with the following steps to install the network client software locally:

1. Insert Disk 1 of the disk set in drive A. At the A: prompt, type **SETUP** and press ENTER.
2. Perform steps 3 through 5c in the section entitled "Using a Network Startup Disk for DOS and Windows 3.x," earlier in this chapter.
3. When you've completed those steps, files are copied from floppy to your hard disk. Remove and insert disks as prompted.

   Setup modifies your AUTOEXEC.BAT and CONFIG.SYS files and makes backup copies in the root directory of drive C. (See Figure 13-12.) Remove the floppy from drive A and press ENTER to restart the computer.

Installing Windows 95 Clients

Here are the steps to follow for configuring a Windows 95 client to communicate with a Windows NT Server computer:

1. While running Windows 95, click Start ➪ Settings ➪ Control Panel. Double-click Network to start the Network Control Panel Application (NCPA).
2. Click the Configuration tab and click Add, as shown in Figure 13-15.

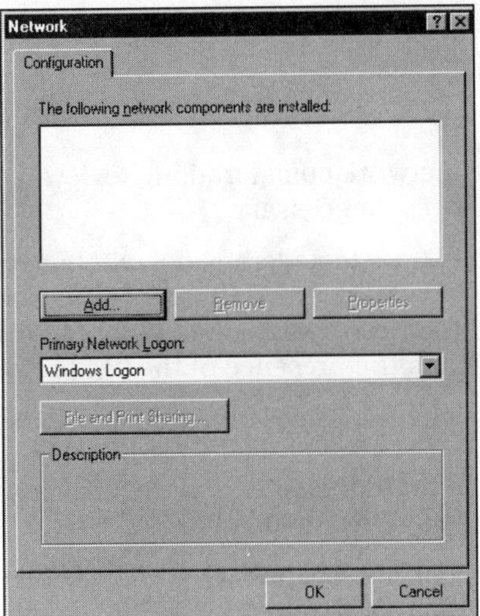

Figure 13-15: You can add networking to Windows 95 through the Network Control Panel Application.

3. In the Select Network Component Type dialog box, select Adapter and click Add, as illustrated in Figure 13-16.

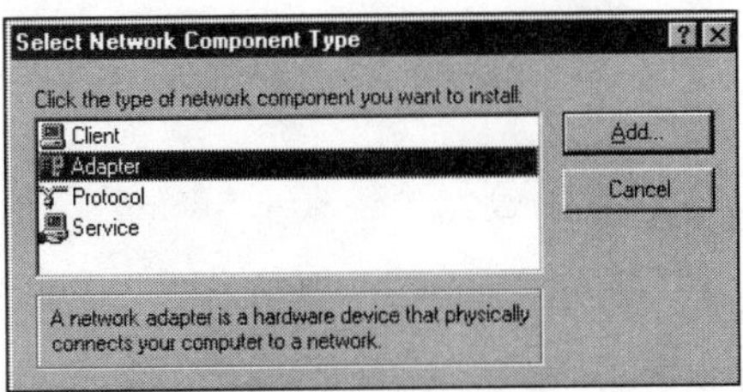

Figure 13-16: You begin by adding the network adapter.

4. In the Select Network adapters dialog box, select the manufacturer of your network adapter. Then, select the specific network adapter model. Click OK. See Figure 13-17.

   If your manufacturer or network adapter model doesn't appear on the list and you have a driver disk supplied by the manufacturer, click Have Disk and follow the prompts to install the driver.

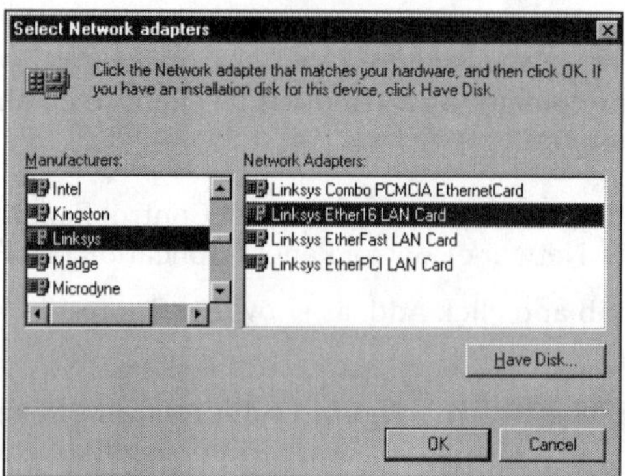

Figure 13-17: You can select the make and model of your network adapter.

5. Figure 13-18 shows the resulting network configuration. Review the Configuration tab and make changes if necessary.

   For example, both NetBEUI and IPX are installed by default, but you may only want to run NetBEUI. Select IPX/SPX-compatible Protocol and click Remove to remove the IPX protocol and the NetWare client. (They both disappear because the NetWare client requires the presence of the IPX protocol.)

   If you want to add a protocol, click Add, select Protocol, and click Add again. Select the protocol manufacturer, then the specific protocol that you want to install. Click OK. Double-click the protocol name to make changes to the protocol configuration through the Properties dialog box.

   If you're adding the TCP/IP protocol, see Chapter 11 for details on assigning IP addresses, DHCP, and other information required for TCP/IP communication.

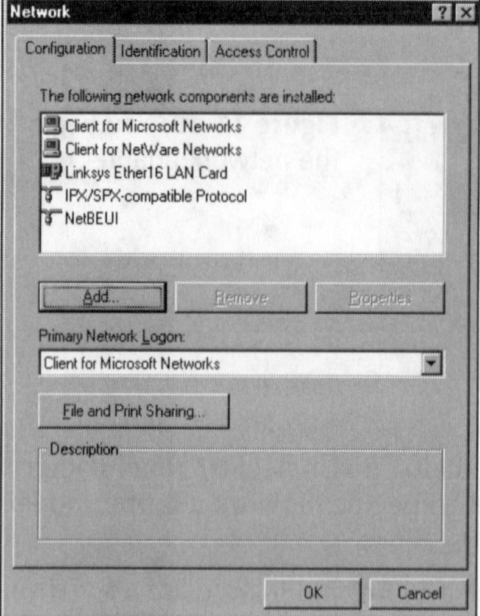

Figure 13-18: Protocols and clients are added automatically when you install a network adapter.

6. Double-click the name of the network adapter. In the Properties dialog box, click the Driver Type tab and make sure that the driver is set to Enhanced mode, as shown in Figure 13-19.

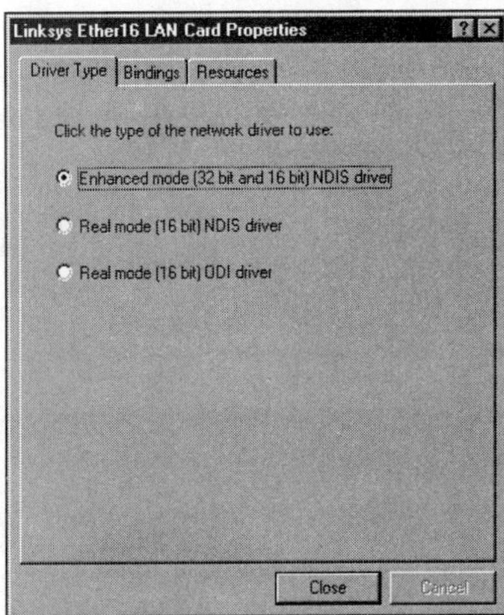

Figure 13-19: Double-clicking the adapter name displays the network adapter properties.

7. While still in the Properties dialog box, click the Resources tab. Correct the displayed settings to make them match the actual configuration of your network adapter, as shown in Figure 13-20. When you're done, click Close.

An asterisk in front of a setting indicates that Windows 95 sees a resource conflict with another device in the computer. Once you've changed the settings to match your adapter, make sure that you don't have any conflicts remaining.

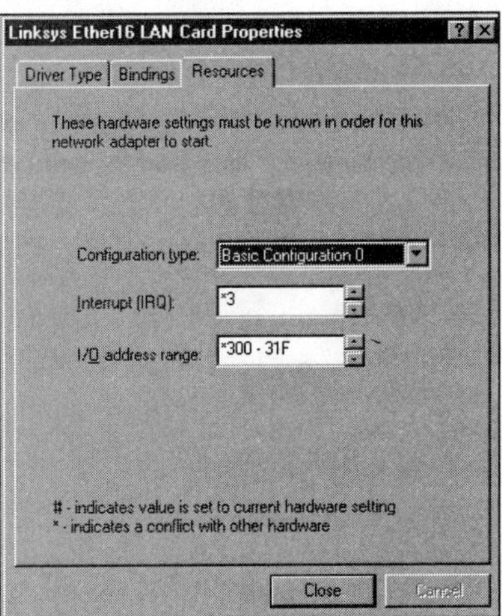

Figure 13-20: You use the Resources tab to change your network adapter configuration.

8. As shown in Figure 13-21, in the Network dialog box, click the Identification tab. Type the unique computer name that you've chosen for this client computer.

   If you're not using Windows NT Server domain model, type the name of the workgroup in which this client computer will participate.

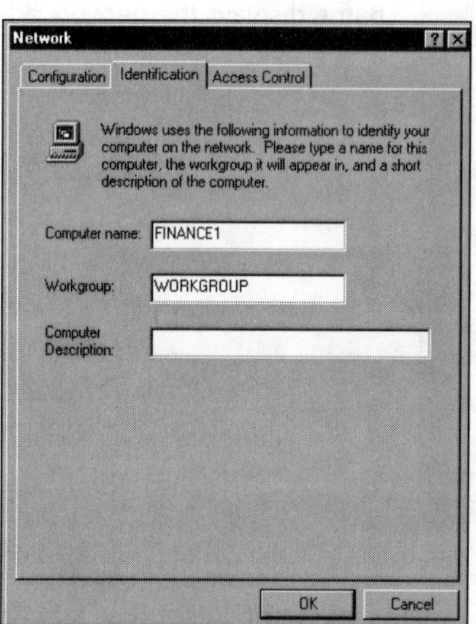

Figure 13-21: You use the Identification tab to set your computer name and workgroup.

9. Click the Configuration tab and click File and Print Sharing. Click the appropriate check boxes if you want to share files or printers over the network (that is, if you want this computer to act as a peer-to-peer server). Then click OK. See Figure 13-22.

   If you don't select either type of sharing, the Windows 95 computer will act only as a client on the network.

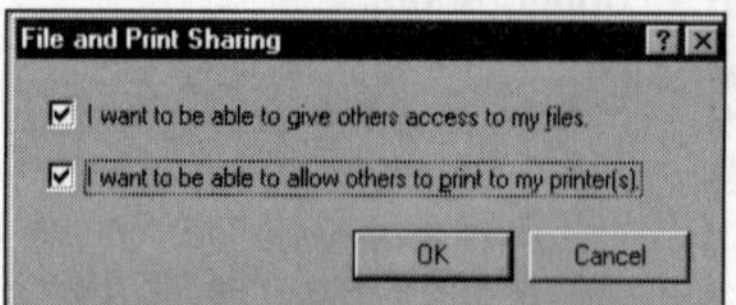

Figure 13-22: You can specify whether you want to share files and/or printers.

10. If you're using the Windows NT Server domain model, double-click Client for Microsoft Networks. On the General tab, under Logon validation, click Log on to Windows NT domain. Then, type the name of the NT domain and click OK. See Figure 13-23.

    If you're not using the NT Server domain model, you can skip this step.

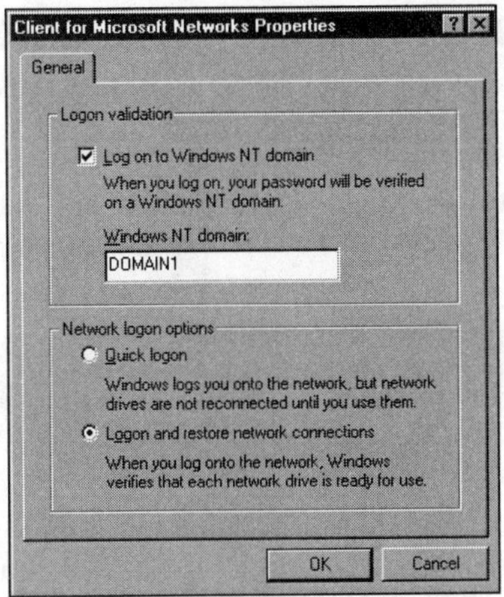

Figure 13-23: You can specify which domain should validate this client's logon.

11. Click OK. If the Windows 95 CD-ROM isn't in the drive, you'll be asked to insert it. Do so. Files will be copied from the CD-ROM to your hard disk.
12. Restart your computer as prompted.

Installing Windows NT Workstation Clients

The steps required to configure a Windows NT Workstation 4.0 computer to act as a client in a Windows NT Server network are different, depending on whether you've already installed networking features on the computer. I'll outline both approaches in the following sections.

WINDOWS NT COMPUTER ACCOUNTS

Each NT Workstation or NT Server that's a member of your domain will need its own computer account. If you're going to be adding several Windows NT Workstation or Server computers to your network, or if your users will be adding them, create a user account on your PDC that has rights to add workstations to the domain. Assign a password to this account and provide both the user name and password to those involved in adding NT workstations to the network. Don't give this account full administrator privileges.

Configuring a Client before Network Installation

Here are the steps to follow to configure a Windows NT Workstation 4.0 client, if networking isn't yet installed on the NT Workstation computer:

1. While logged on with administrator privileges, click Start ➪ Settings ➪ Control Panel. Double-click Network to start the Network Control Panel Application (NCPA).
2. Click Yes to indicate that you want networking installed.
3. Follow the prompts provided by the Network Setup Wizard, including selecting protocols. When you're asked for the name of a workgroup or domain, go to step 4.

See Chapter 8 for details on how to configure your network adapter on Windows NT Server. The same rules apply to Windows NT Workstation. Likewise, refer to Chapters 9 and 12 for information on configuring your network protocols.

4. If you're using the Windows NT Server domain model, under Make this computer a member of, click Domain and type the name of the domain that you want this client to join. Click Create a Computer Account in the Domain. Then click Next. See Figure 13-24.

   If you're not using the Windows NT Server domain model, click Workgroup and type the name of the workgroup that you want this client computer to join. Then click Next.

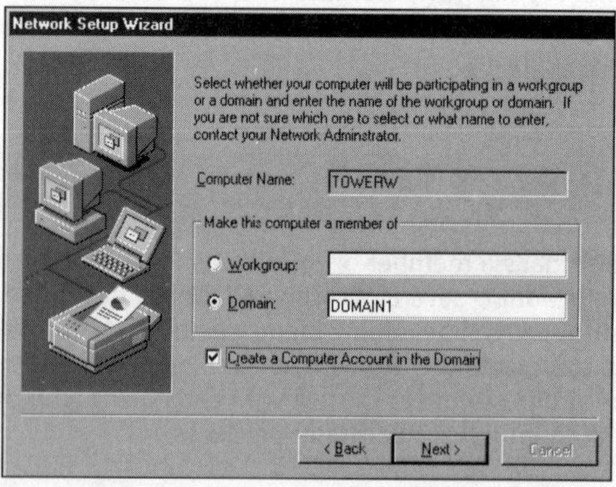

Figure 13-24: You can specify which domain or workgroup this client will join.

5. If you're joining a domain, you're prompted for a user name and password. Type a user name and password that allows you to add a computer account to the domain, as shown in Figure 13-25.

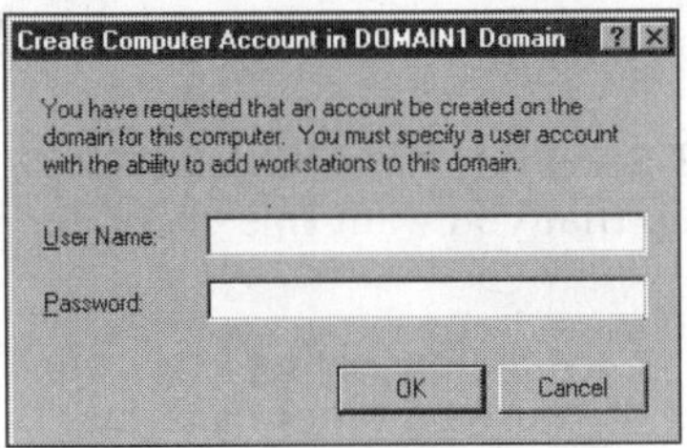

Figure 13-25: You can specify an account that allows adding computers to the network.

6. Restart your computer as prompted.

Configuring a Client after Network Installation

If you already have networking installed on your Windows NT Workstation computer, it's likely that the computer is participating in a workgroup. Here are the steps to follow for configuring a Windows NT Workstation 4.0 client, if networking is already installed on the NT Workstation computer:

1. While logged on with administrator privileges, click Start ➪ Settings ➪ Control Panel. Double-click Network to start the Network Control Panel Application (NCPA).
2. Click the Identification tab. Then click Change, as illustrated in Figure 13-26.

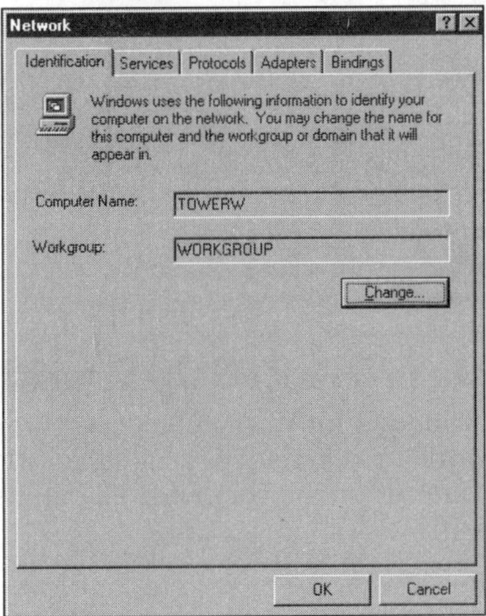

Figure 13-26: You can change the membership of this computer via the Identification tab.

3. If you're using the Windows NT Server domain model, under Member of, click Domain and type the name of the domain that you want this client to join. Click Create a Computer Account in the Domain. Type a user name and

password that allows you to add a computer account to the domain. Then click OK, as shown in Figure 13-27.

If you're not using the Windows NT Server domain model, click Workgroup and type the name of the workgroup that you want this client computer to join. Then click OK.

After a few moments, you should see a welcome dialog box from the workgroup or domain that you're joining. If your computer can't find the domain controller, make sure that the PDC is up and running. Then, verify that you're using the correct domain name, that your computer is physically connected to the network, and that it's running the same protocol(s) as the PDC server.

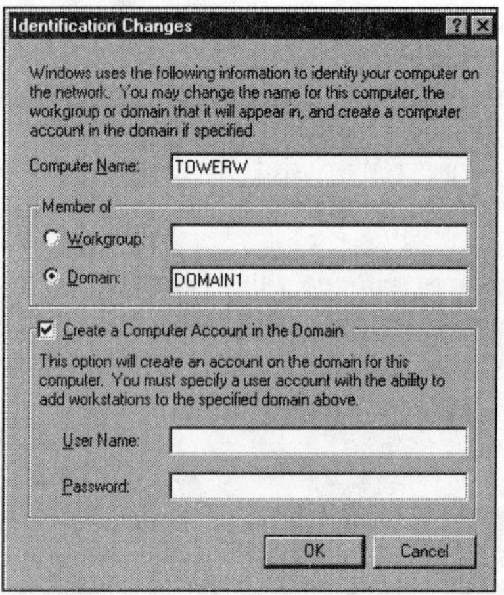

Figure 13-27: You can specify the workgroup or domain that this client computer will join.

4. Click Close.
5. Restart your computer as prompted.

Installing Windows for Workgroups Clients

The steps required for configuring a Windows for Workgroups computer to act as a client in a Windows NT Server network are different, depending on whether you've already installed networking features on the computer. I'll outline both approaches in the following sections.

Configuring a Client before Network Installation

Here are the steps to follow to configure a Windows for Workgroups client, if networking isn't yet installed on the Windows for Workgroups computer:

1. In Program Manager, in the Main group, double-click Windows Setup. The Network entry should say, "No Network Installed," as shown in Figure 13-28. If a network is installed, go to the next section and start at step 1.

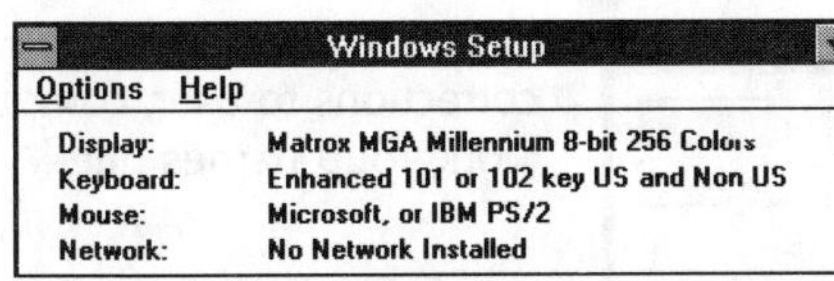

Figure 13-28: You prepare to install Windows for Workgroups networking.

2. On the Options menu, click Change Network Settings. Under Network Settings, click Networks. Click Install Microsoft Windows Network. Then click OK.
3. Click Sharing. Click the appropriate check boxes if you want to share files or printers over the network (that is, if you want this computer to act as a peer-to-peer server). Then click OK.

   If you don't select either type of sharing, the Windows for Workgroups computer will act only as a client on the network. I recommend enabling sharing of both files and printers.
4. Click Drivers. Click Add Adapter. Select the name of your network adapter from the list. Click OK.
5. You'll be presented with network adapter configuration prompts, asking for IRQ, I/O base address, and so on. Type the values that match your adapter's settings and click OK. In the Network Drivers dialog box, click Close. See Figure 13-29.

   Both NetBEUI and IPX protocols are installed by default.

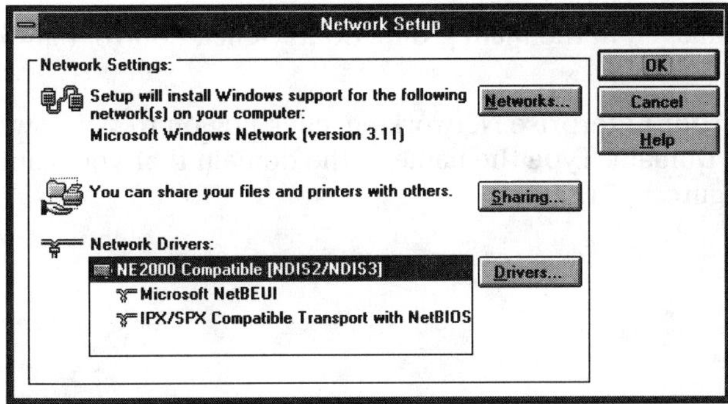

Figure 13-29: The Network Setup dialog box shows the state of network installation.

6. In the Network Setup dialog box, click OK. In the Microsoft Windows Network Names dialog box, type any corrections to the user name, workgroup name, or computer name. Then click OK, as shown in Figure 13-30.

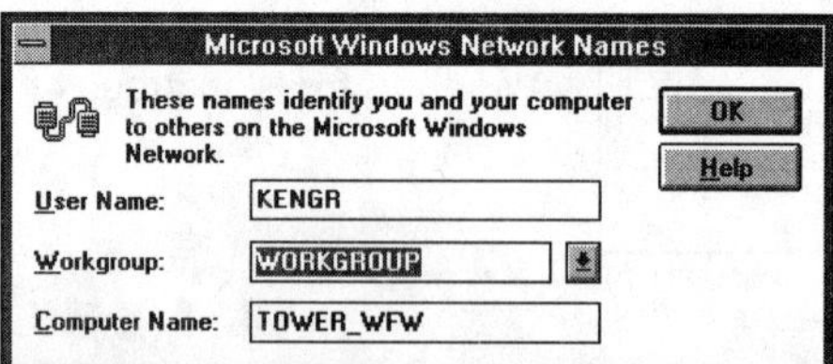

Figure 13-30: You can make any corrections to user, computer, or workgroup names here.

7. Files are copied from your installation media to your hard disk. Setup modifies some of your configuration files and lets you know where the backup copies have been placed. Click OK.
8. Restart your computer as prompted.
9. If you're using the Windows NT Server domain model, go to step 1 in the next section to join your Windows NT Server domain.

Configuring a Client after Network Installation

If you already have networking installed on your Windows for Workgroups computer, it's likely that the computer is participating in a workgroup. If you're not using the NT Server domain model, you're done configuring Windows for Workgroups networking. If you're using the Windows NT Server domain model, here are the steps to follow for configuring a Windows for Workgroups client, if networking is already installed on it:

1. In Program Manager, in the Main group, double-click Control Panel. Double-click Startup.
2. Under Options for Enterprise Networking, click Log on to Windows NT or LAN Manager Domain. Type the name of the domain that you want this client to join. See Figure 13-31.

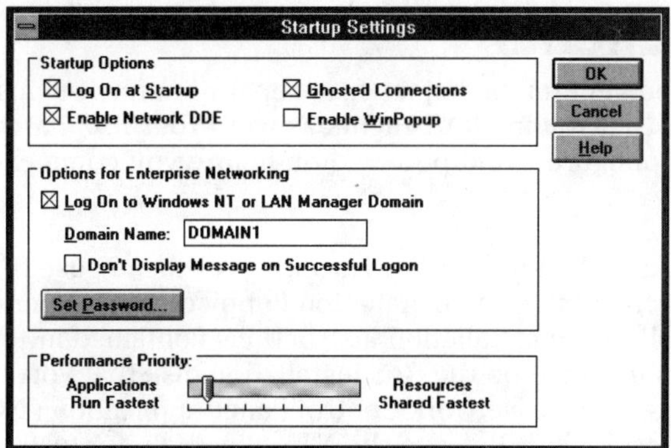

Figure 13-31: You can specify which domain that you want your client to join.

3. Click OK. Click OK again.
4. Restart your computer as prompted.

To speed up network responsiveness on your Windows for Workgroups client computer, Microsoft has included a handful of updated system files. On the Windows NT Server 4.0 CD-ROM in the CLIENTS\UPDATE.WFW directory, copy *.386 and *.DLL to your Windows for Workgroups SYSTEM directory (typically \WINDOWS\SYSTEM). Then, copy NET.EXE and NET.MSG to your Windows for Workgroups root directory (typically \WINDOWS).

Installing Windows for Workgroups TCP/IP-32 Clients

If you're running TCP/IP on your network and you have Windows for Workgroups clients, consider installing the 32-bit TCP/IP protocol provided with Windows NT Server 4.0. It includes the TCP/IP transport protocol plus several useful TCP/IP utilities including FTP, PING, NETSTAT, and TELNET.

Use the Network Client Administrator to create the TCP/IP-32 installation floppy disk, as described earlier in this chapter. Then, follow the installation instructions contained in MTCPIP32.HLP, which is included on the installation disk. See Chapter 11 for information on using TCP/IP with Windows NT Server.

If you're already running a TCP/IP product on your Windows for Workgroups computer, you must remove it before installing TCP/IP-32. Otherwise, you'll run into problems communicating on the network.

Installing RAS Clients

In Chapter 11, I provided general guidelines for preparation for RAS installation. These guidelines apply to installing RAS clients as well. Your RAS hardware needs to be installed, configured, and powered on before you commence RAS software installation.

For DOS, Windows 3.x, and Windows for Workgroups RAS clients, use the Network Client Administrator to create the RAS installation floppy disk, as described earlier in this chapter. Then, follow the installation instructions contained in USER_REF.TXT, which is included on the RAS installation disk that you created. For Windows NT RAS clients, use the Network Control Panel Application (NCPA) to install the Remote Access Service. Refer to the NT online Help for further details. For Windows 95 RAS clients, use the Add/Remove Programs application in Control Panel to install Dial-Up Networking.

Summary

In this chapter, I've presented a step-by-step guide to installing various types of Microsoft network clients, including DOS, Windows 3.x, Windows 95, Windows for Workgroups, and Windows NT. You've seen how NT's Network Client Administrator can streamline installation, especially for DOS, Windows 3.x, and Windows 95 clients.

In Part II, I've focused on installation and configuration of your network, server, and clients. In Parts III and IV, you'll learn the ins and outs of using and administering your Windows NT Server-based network.

INSIDE STORY

It was probably the most obscure problem that we'd found. No one could believe it. Ten people looked at each other around the long conference table. Some smiled and shook their heads. Others stared in disbelief.

"Just so everyone's clear," the support engineer explained, "here's what the customer did." Some of us leaned forward, hoping to catch some additional clue about what was going on. "He set the locale on his Windows for Workgroups client to Turkish. Problem doesn't happen unless he does this. Then, he accesses an NT file on FAT with a certain Turkish vowel in the file name. It has to be FAT, and the file name has to have this Turkish vowel in it. And the client hangs the server. Simple as that."

The root cause and the solution to this bug have long since been forgotten, but the name we coined for the problem lives on in the hearts and minds of the NT team to this day – "The FAT Turkey Fiasco."

Using Windows NT Server

✦ ✦ ✦ ✦

In This Part

✦ ✦ ✦ ✦

Navigating and Managing Your NT Server Desktop

The Windows NT 3.x user interface was modeled after Windows 3.1. The new Windows NT 4.0 user interface, which is nearly identical to that of Windows 95, was designed to be easier to use and more flexible than its predecessors. In general, it actually is easier, especially for folks who aren't used to the Windows 3.1 way of doing things. Users starting from scratch or those already familiar with Windows 95 will have the easiest time adjusting. Users who know the Windows 3.x interface inside and out may need a little time to adjust to the new world.

In this chapter, I'll cover the key areas of the NT 4.0 user interface, or *shell,* to give you a start toward understanding, navigating, and customizing it. I'll also cover the basics of logging on and off the computer and accessing online Help, since you'll need to do both right out of the gate. The skills that you acquire in this chapter will allow you to function efficiently with the new user interface. They'll also be invaluable as you bring other NT users in your organization up to speed.

When I talk about the old, Program Manager-based user interface, I'll refer to it as the Windows 3.x interface, even though it was also present on Windows NT 3.x. I'll assume, as mentioned in Chapter 1, that you're already familiar with using a version of Windows, so I won't discuss the basics of mouse clicking and other fundamentals. If you're already familiar with both Windows NT 3.x and Windows 95, you can skim this chapter. Much of it will be old hat to you. However, don't skip the section entitled "Managing Multiple Users."

Learning the Essentials

In this section, I'll present the basic concepts for logging on to the computer, recognizing and using some essential elements of the shell, and logging off and shutting down the computer. (As a child, I had nightmares that I had a television I couldn't turn off. So at several levels, it's important for me to tell you how to shut down the system right away.) Later on in this chapter, I'll delve more deeply into other important aspects of navigating and managing the NT shell.

Throughout this chapter, you'll find that many common actions can be performed in several different ways. For example, there are at least seven ways to start an application. If you're like me, you'll tend to find a few methods that are most intuitive for you and stick with them. I'll expose you to the available alternatives, and you can settle in to what's most comfortable for you.

Logging on to NT

Before you can experience the user interface and actually use the operating system, Windows NT requires that you log on. When you start your computer, you're presented with the Begin Logon dialog box shown in Figure 14-1. Here's how to log on:

1. Press CTRL+ALT+DEL to log on to Windows NT Server.

   I find it physically painful to think about trying to press these three keys with one hand, as the icon implies.

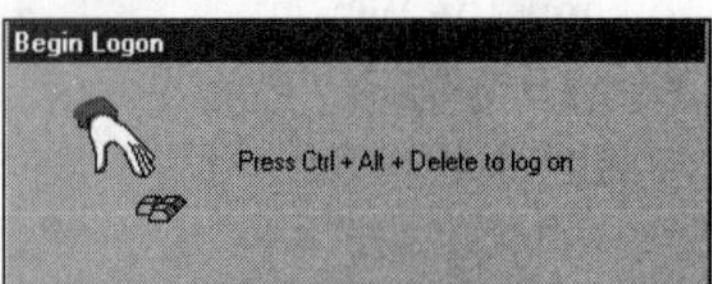

Figure 14-1: Press CTRL+ALT+DEL to start the NT logon sequence.

2. You're presented with the Logon Information dialog box. Type your user name and password. If you're logging on to a domain, select the appropriate domain name from the list. Then click OK.

As an NT administrator, you can use the built-in account called administrator, whose password you set during installation of the operating system. See Chapter 18 for details on how to create additional user accounts.

GETTING NT'S ATTENTION

Why was CTRL+ALT+DEL selected as the keyboard combination to initiate an NT logon operation? Isn't this what you use to restart DOS or recover from a hung application in Windows 3.1? Absolutely. For security reasons, the NT designers needed to establish a known key combination, called a *secure attention sequence*, that they were sure no legitimate application would ever need to use. Because CTRL+ALT+DEL was reserved for system use in DOS and Windows, it became an ideal secure attention sequence. Applications don't use it.

How does this help NT security? Let's say I wanted to steal your user name and password. If I wrote a program that presented you with dialog boxes just like those displayed during the logon process, you might be fooled into typing your user name and password. My Trojan horse program could file away that information, to be used later to access your computer (perhaps with administrator privileges). Since CTRL+ALT+DEL is always intercepted by the NT operating system and is never passed on to an application, I can't write a program to mimic the logon sequence. The secure attention sequence guarantees that you're interacting with the operating system when you log on.

Likewise, changing your password while you're logged on requires that you press CTRL+ALT+DEL to get NT's attention. You wouldn't want a password-stealing program impersonating the Change Password dialog, would you? Again, secure attention sequence to the rescue.

If this is the first time that you're logging on immediately after restarting the computer, you may experience a delay of several seconds before your NT desktop appears. During this time, NT is starting internal network services. The delay is sometimes longer when you're logging on to the domain PDC right after a reboot.

Using the Shell

The first time that you log on to Windows NT Server, you're presented with a desktop display similar to the one shown in Figure 14-2. The Welcome dialog box in the middle of your screen is displayed only the first time that you log on after installing the operating system. Click Close to dismiss it. In subsequent sessions, NT will display usage tips, which you'll be able to read and dismiss or disable in future sessions. (Frankly, I find these tips a bit annoying and turn them off the first chance I get. But some folks really like them.)

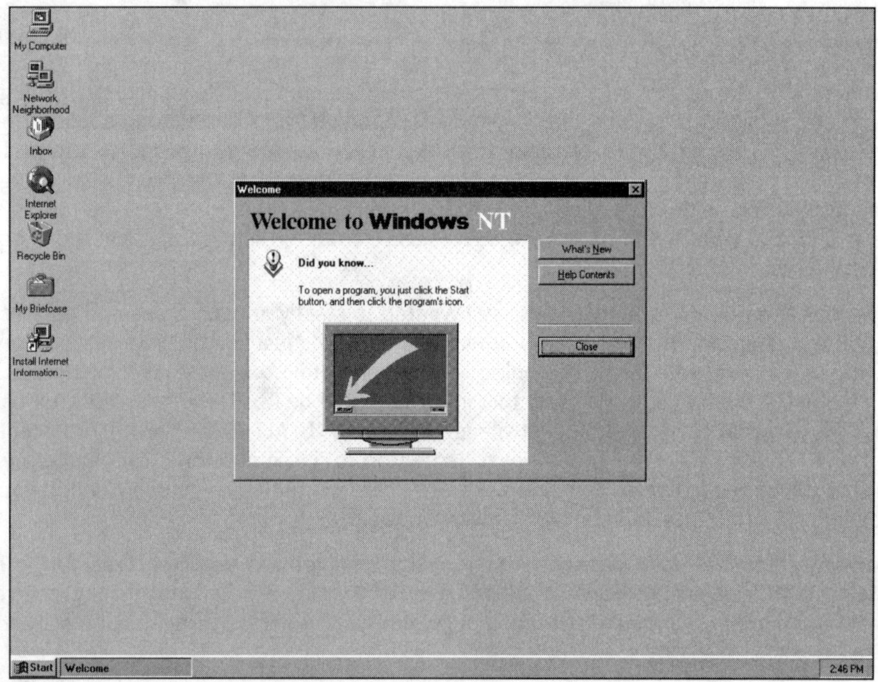

Figure 14-2: After logon, the Windows NT Server desktop is displayed.

The Taskbar

The taskbar is the long gray area that appears at the bottom of your display, as shown in Figure 14-2. When you first start Windows NT Server, the taskbar contains a Start button at the extreme left and displays the time of day at the extreme right. Each application you start will add a button to the taskbar. Clicking these buttons is one way of switching between applications. (There are other ways to do this, which I'll discuss later in this chapter.) When an application is terminated, its button disappears.

For example, there's a button in the Figure 14-2 taskbar representing the Welcome application. When you close the Welcome dialog box, the Welcome button disappears from the taskbar. (The taskbar was originally called "the tray," since it acts as a sort of a work-in-progress basket for your active applications.)

The Start Button

The Start button is the center of the NT user interface universe, even though it's off to the left. Just about everything that you do interactively begins with the Start button. By clicking it, you can run applications, access online Help, search for files, change operating system settings, shut down the computer, and start a wide range of administration tools.

If you prefer to use your keyboard instead of your mouse, you can bring up the Start menu any time by pressing CTRL+ESC. This has the same effect as clicking the Start button. You can then use the arrow keys to move through the menu and press ENTER to select an item.

The Start Menu Hierarchy

The Start button allows you to access a set of menus that play the same role in NT 4.0 as Program Manager did in Windows 3.x. Like Program Manager, you can group together program icons and start them by pointing and clicking. When you install an application that would have created a program group in Windows 3.x, it creates a menu in NT 4.0.

The Start menu approach is much more flexible than the old Program Manager groups, because these menus can be organized into a hierarchy of groups. (Recall that Program Manager only allowed one level of groups. If you had lots of groups, you had to search for them through a linear list.) In NT 4.0, using the Start menu, you can create groups within groups, or rather menus within menus, as illustrated in Figure 14-3. In this figure, the Programs item on the Start menu contains another menu consisting of programs and other menus. The Administrative Tools item in turn contains a menu of all of the NT administrative applications.

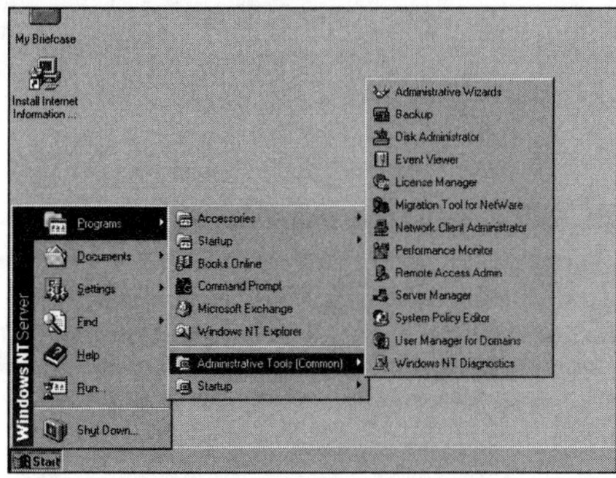

Figure 14-3: Organize and start applications from a hierarchy of menus.

Notice in Figure 14-3 that these program menus have the potential of getting fairly long. Therefore, it's best to take advantage of the hierarchy approach to keep individual menus short. Menus within menus are called *submenus*. You can always tell if an item has a submenu by the little arrow to the right of the item name. For example, in the Start menu, the first four items have submenus. As you point to one of these items (without clicking), its submenu appears.

Starting Your Applications

As mentioned before, there are many ways to start an application on Windows NT Server. I'll describe the most common approaches here, to give you an idea of the breadth of choices available. Notice that many of these techniques begin with the Start button. Don't worry if you don't understand all of the approaches listed here. By the end of this chapter, you will.

- ✦ Click Start. Point to successive submenus until you're pointing to the application that you want. Then click the name of the application. (See Figure 14-3.)
- ✦ Click Start ➪ Run. Type the name of the application that you want to start and click OK. See Figure 14-4.

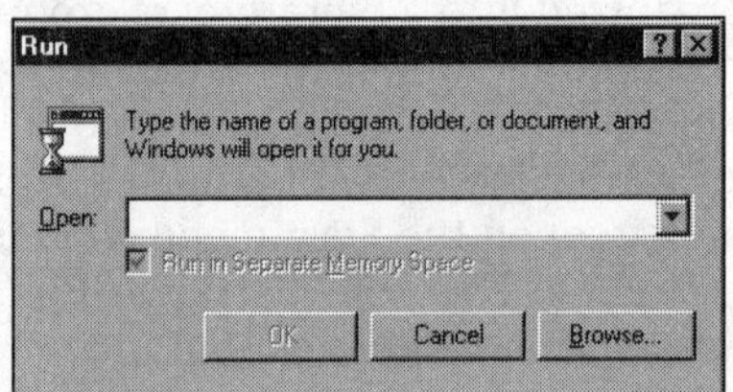

Figure 14-4: Start an application using the Run command on the Start menu.

- ✦ Click Start ➪ Programs ➪ Windows NT Explorer. Navigate to the application that you want to run and double-click its name, as shown in Figure 14-5. (You'll find out more about Explorer later in this chapter.)

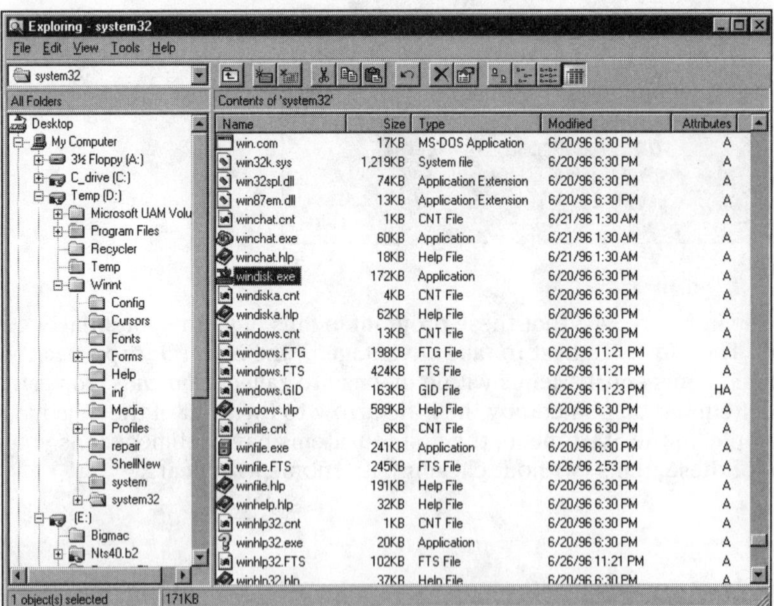

Figure 14-5: Start an application using the Windows NT Explorer.

- ✦ Click Start ➪ Programs ➪ Command Prompt. At the prompt, type the name of the application that you want to start and press ENTER.
- ✦ Click Start ➪ Programs ➪ Command Prompt entry. At the prompt, type **START** followed by the name of the application and press ENTER. This action starts the application in a separate window from the Command Prompt.
- ✦ Right-click the taskbar and click Task Manager. Then, click the Applications tab and click New Task. In the Create New Task dialog box, type the name of the application that you want to start and click OK. See Figure 14-6. (I'll cover Task Manager later in this chapter.)

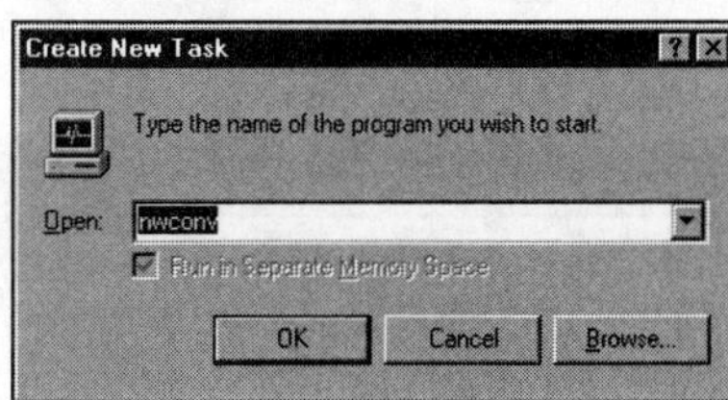

Figure 14-6: Start an application using the Task Manager.

- ✦ On your desktop, double-click the My Computer icon. Navigate to the application that you want to run by double-clicking a drive, folders, and, finally, the application's name. See Figure 14-7. (You'll read more about using My Computer later in this chapter.)
- ✦ On your desktop, double-click the icon representing the application that you want to start. (I'll show you how to add commonly used application icons to your desktop later in this chapter.)

FOLDERS VS. DIRECTORIES

In the NT 4.0 shell, the term folder is typically used to refer to what you already know as a directory. The two terms are synonymous. However, since the shell itself uses the term folder almost exclusively, I'll do the same in this chapter. I'll use the term directory only in the context of the NT Command Prompt.

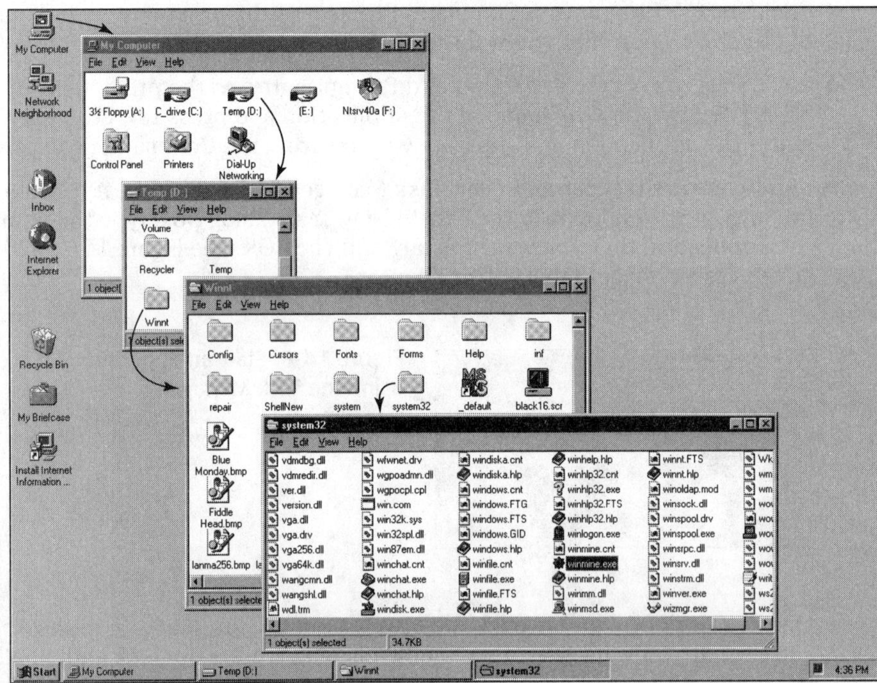

Figure 14-7: Start an application by navigating through drives and folders under My Computer.

Controlling Your Applications

Windows in the NT 4.0 shell include buttons that give you control over your application. In the Windows 3.x user interface, each window had a Control-menu box in the upper left corner (affectionately called the "coin slot" in the halls of Microsoft) and two buttons in the upper right corner to control window size and minimization. The NT 4.0 shell provides similar control with a slightly different look. (If you've already used Windows 95, you'll find most of this to be familiar territory.) Figure 14-8 illustrates the new buttons. Here's what they do:

✦ Click the Close button to terminate the application. This action removes its button from the taskbar. (In Windows 3.x, you had to double-click the control menu to close the window.)

If you're used to double-clicking in the upper left corner of your windows to close the application, this technique still works in the new shell. Just double-click the program icon in the window's upper left corner, and the window will close. Although it's one less mouse click to use the Close button in the upper right corner, if you're having trouble breaking the coin-slot habit, double-clicking might be more efficient for you.

GIVING A WIN16 APPLICATION ITS OWN SPACE

I mentioned in Chapter 2 that, by default, 16-bit Windows applications run together in a single, shared address space to simulate the way that Windows 3.x runs applications. I also mentioned that you can opt to run an individual Win16 application in its own separate address space, to isolate and protect it from all other Win16 applications. In Chapter 2, I showed you one way of doing this. You're about to discover more ways to give a Win16 application its own space.

As you saw in Figures 14-4 and 14-6, starting an application from Start ➪ Run or from New Task in Task Manager gives you the option of running the program in a separate address space. In these figures, this option is disabled, since all 32-bit applications already run in their own address spaces. However, if you type the name of a 16-bit application, this option is enabled, allowing you to choose how you want to run the application. Click the Run in Separate Memory Space check box if you want the application to have its own space separate from all other Win16 applications.

If you're starting a Win16 application using the START command from within a Command Prompt window, you can put the application in its own space by using the /SEPARATE option. For example, to start IMGMGR.EXE in its own address space, the command line would be

```
START /SEPARATE IMGMGR
```

- ✦ Click the Minimize button to make the window disappear from the desktop but leave its button on the taskbar, indicating that the application is still running. (In Windows 3.x, minimizing reduced the window to an icon on the desktop.)
- ✦ Click the Maximize button to make the window expand to fill the entire display. The Maximize button then changes to a Restore button. (This behavior is identical to Windows 3.x.)
- ✦ Click the Restore button to cause the window to revert to its previous size, before it was maximized. (Again, Windows 3.x behaves the same way.)
- ✦ Click the program icon to display the window menu. See Figure 14-8 for a list of window menu options, which may vary from one application to the next.

You can get to the same window menu by right-clicking the application's button on the taskbar. This handy feature lets you control the application even if the window isn't displayed on the desktop. (If the application isn't minimized, right-clicking its button on the taskbar will still bring up the window menu, and it will also bring the application to the top of the stack of windows on the desktop.)

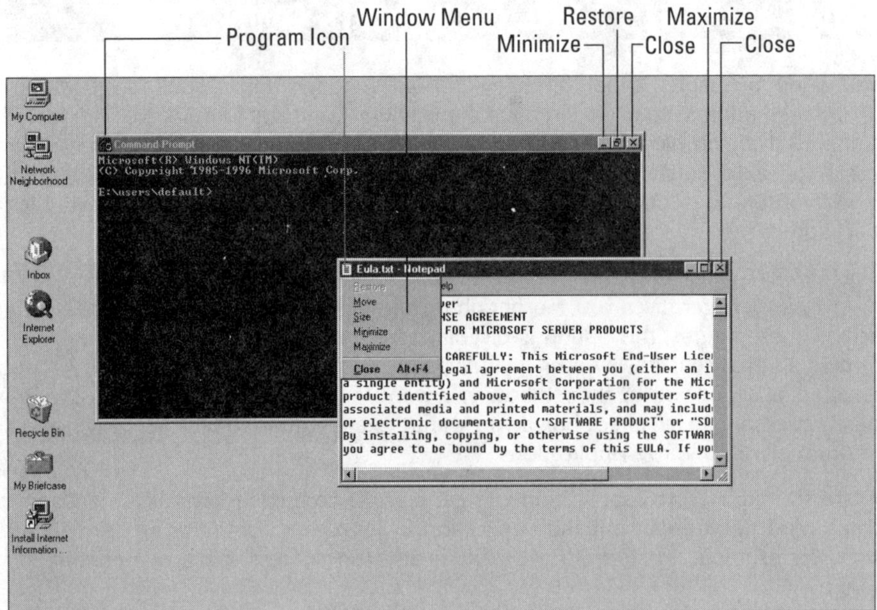

Figure 14-8: Use the window buttons to control the size, visibility, and termination of your application.

Although you can terminate all of your running applications by logging off or shutting down the computer (explained later in this chapter), I recommend explicitly closing your applications yourself. Some applications don't always do the right things when they're forced to terminate by the operating system during a logoff or shutdown operation. I've seen a couple of applications lose data during a shutdown because they neglected to ask the user whether unsaved data should be saved to disk.

Switching between Your Applications

Once you've got more than one application running, you need to be able to switch between them as you work. As you might expect at this point, there's more than one way to do this on Windows NT Server.

- ✦ If the window that you want is visible on the desktop, click in the window.
- ✦ Click the button on the taskbar that represents the window that you want.
- ✦ Press ALT+TAB and repeatedly press TAB while holding down the ALT key, until the icon for the application you want is highlighted. (This technique works similarly in Windows 3.x.)

✦ Right-click the taskbar and click Task Manager. Then, click the Applications tab, select the application that you want, and click Switch To, as shown in Figure 14-9.

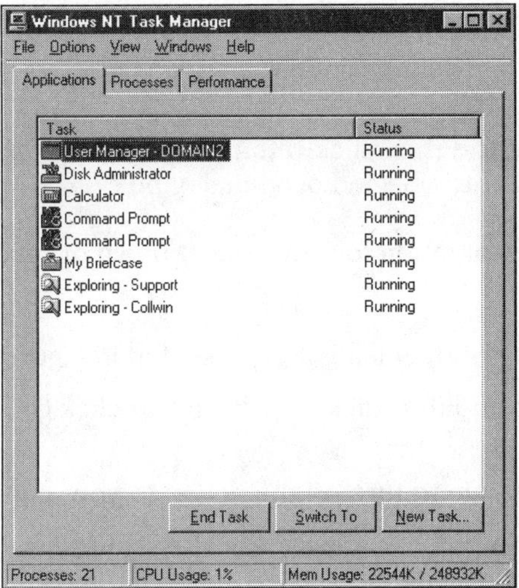

Figure 14-9: You can switch to an application by selecting it in Task Manager's list of applications.

Logging Off and Shutting Down

Logging off terminates all running applications and takes the computer back to the Begin Logon dialog box, shown in Figure 14-1. At this point, it's ready for you or another user to log on. If you opt to shut down the computer, NT performs an orderly shutdown of the operating system, including flushing cached information to disk.

Never power down or reset your NT computer until you've properly shut it down using one of these methods. If you do power it down, you'll very likely lose data. There's a lot of critical information cached in memory while Windows NT Server is running. Proper shutdown flushes this cached data to disk. Simply logging off isn't enough. You must do a full shutdown before turning off the power to your computer or pressing its reset button. Always wait for the message indicating it's safe to turn off your computer.

Using CTRL+ALT+DEL to Stop

There are a couple of ways to log off or shut down your computer. One way is to press CTRL+ALT+DEL while you're logged on. You'll see the Windows NT Security dialog box, as shown in Figure 14-10. This dialog box offers several useful options in addition to logging off and shutting down.

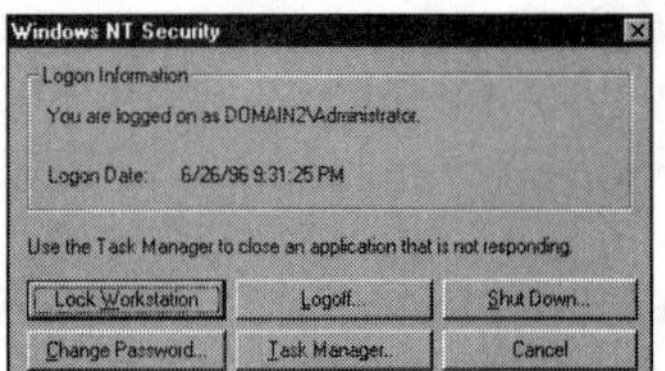

Figure 14-10: Pressing CTRL+ALT+DEL while you're logged on allows you to log off or shut down the computer.

If you want to log off, click Logoff and then click OK. After disconnecting your network connections, you'll be back at the Begin Logon dialog box.

To shut down the computer, in preparation for powering it down or resetting it, perform the following steps:

1. Click Shut Down, and you'll see the dialog box presented in Figure 14-11.
2. If you want to turn off the computer, click Shutdown and click OK. If not, go to step 3.

   You'll be informed when it's safe to turn off the power to your computer.
3. If you want to restart the computer automatically after shutdown, click Shutdown and Restart and click OK.

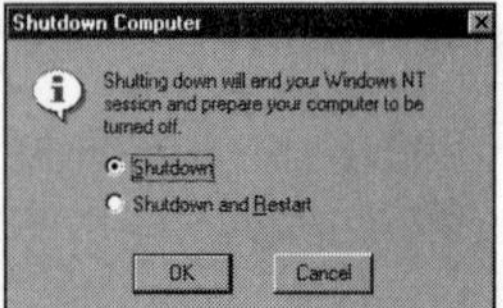

Figure 14-11: You can either shut down before turning off your computer or automatically restart it.

Using Start to Stop

Another approach to logging off and shutting down involves the ever-popular Start button. Click Start ➪ Shut Down, and you'll see the dialog box shown in Figure 14-12. As you can see, you can elect to shut down the computer, automatically restart it, or log off to get back to the Begin Logon dialog box. See Figure 14-1.

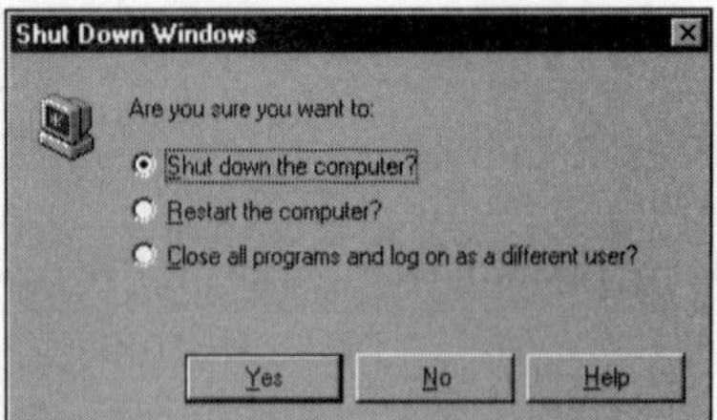

Figure 14-12: You can log off or shut down using the Start menu's Shut Down command.

Helping Yourself

Windows NT Server provides online Help in several ways. First, it offers a searchable Help system that covers the key NT topics. Next, it provides the Windows NT Server manuals in electronic form. Finally, it provides you with context-sensitive Help accessible from many areas of the user interface. I'll cover how to reach each of these features in the following sections.

Windows NT Help

Windows NT Server provides a searchable online Help system, which you can reach in one of the following ways:

✦ Click Start ➪ Help.

✦ On the desktop, double-click the My Computer icon. On the Help menu, click Help Topics.

✦ Click Start ➪ Programs ➪ Windows NT Explorer. On the Help menu, click Help Topics.

However you arrive at Windows NT Help, the first time that you run it and attempt to perform a search, you'll see the Find Setup Wizard as shown in Figure 14-13.

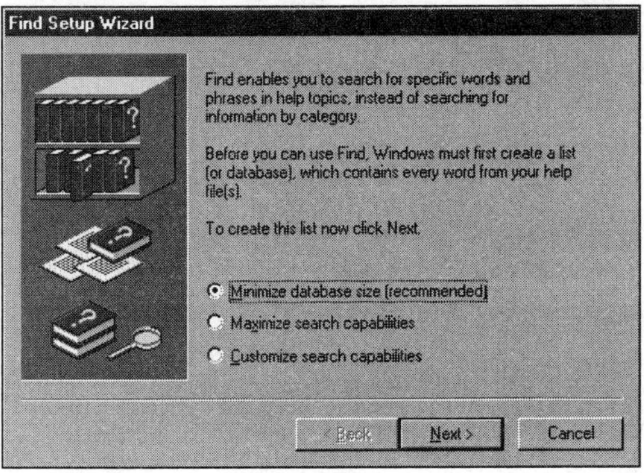

Figure 14-13: The Find Setup Wizard lets you control the configuration of search capabilities.

If you have plenty of disk space and you're new to Windows NT Server, I recommend selecting Maximize search capabilities. This option takes the most disk space but increases the chances that you'll find what you want. Moreover, I suggest staying away from Customize search capabilities, since you need to be very familiar with the contents of each Help file to make meaningful choices. If you ever change your mind and want to save disk space or increase your search capabilities, just click the Find tab and click Rebuild to get back to the Find Setup Wizard.

Click the appropriate database choice and click Next, then click Finish. Depending on the speed of your computer, creating the search database can take from a few seconds to several minutes. When it's done, you're able to search for any word or combination of words.

There are three ways to use Windows NT Help. Click the Contents tab, and you can dig into specific topics by double-clicking successively detailed topics, as shown in Figure 14-14. On this tab, topics are grouped together by subject, just as in a book.

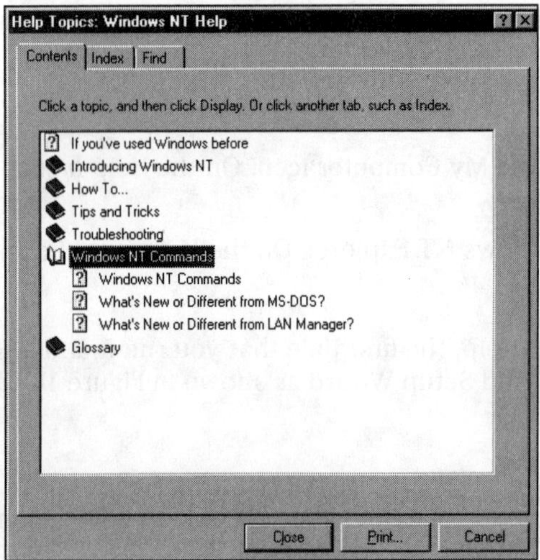

Figure 14-14: Search for help by double-clicking topics.

If you click the Index tab, you can search for help in an alphabetical index of topics, similar to the index in the back of a book. Figure 14-15 illustrates this.

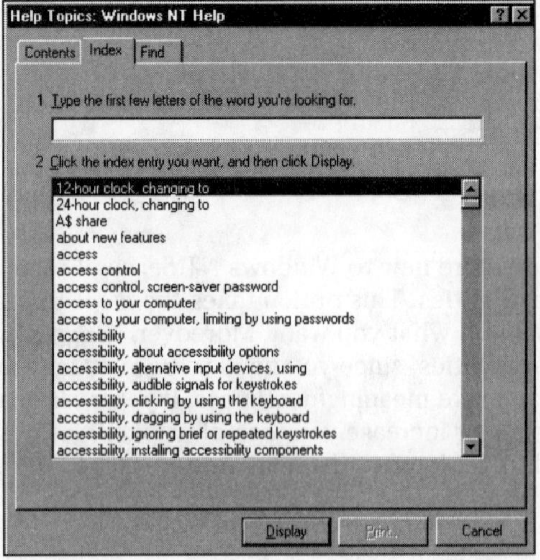

Figure 14-15: Search for help in the Help index by typing or selecting the topic that you want.

Click the Find tab to perform a search of the entire online Help system for specific words you type, as shown in Figure 14-16. This is the most flexible area of Windows NT Help, but common words can yield a ton of resulting topics that you need to sift through. Click the Options button to get more detailed control over your search.

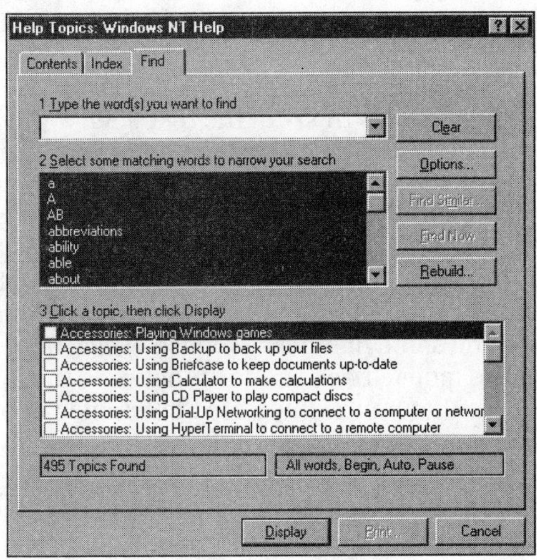

Figure 14-16: Perform a full text search of Help topics based on the words that you type.

Books Online

All of the Windows NT Server manuals are shipped on the NT CD-ROM. They're located in the \SUPPORT\BOOKS directory. You can access these manuals to read, search, and print them by clicking Start ➪ Programs ➪ Books Online. You'll be asked for the path to the Books Online files on your CD-ROM. Type it and click OK, as shown in Figure 14-17. Then follow the instructions presented.

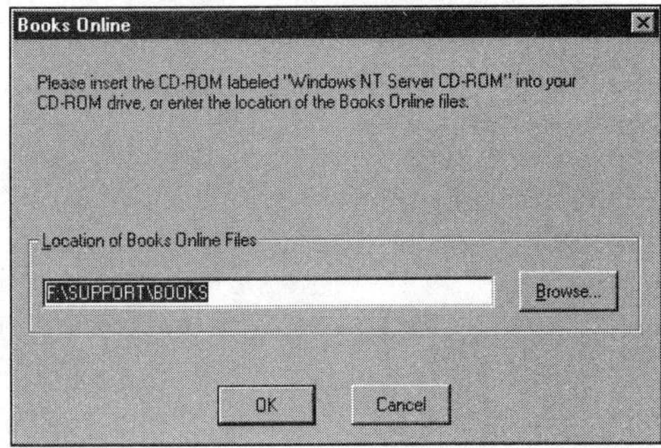

Figure 14-17: Point to the Books Online area of your NT CD-ROM to access the Windows NT Server manuals.

The "What's This?" Button

Many dialog boxes presented by the shell contain a button in the upper right corner that bears a question mark. This button is called "What's this?" To use it, click it and then click an item in the dialog box that you want to know more about. The mouse cursor changes to include a question mark, indicating that you can click buttons and other controls without actually activating them. (You may have seen this feature referred to as *balloon Help* in other books and on other operating systems.)

Figure 14-18 shows an example of asking "What's this?" in the text field of the Windows NT Help Find tab. In this instance, you're getting help on how to use Help. (I've always wondered about the phrase, "help on Help." How much help can Help be if you need help on how to use Help? Need any help understanding that?)

In some windows that have this feature, you can simply right-click the dialog box item to display a What's this? button. Click it to see the context-sensitive Help text. Although this approach requires the same number of mouse clicks, it's sometimes more convenient than moving the mouse back and forth between the upper right corner of the window and the item that you're interested in learning about.

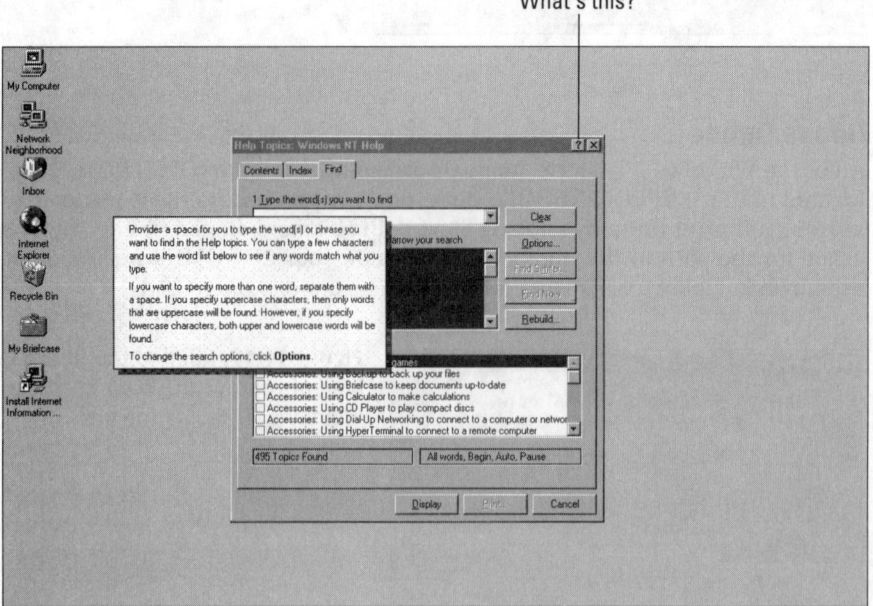

Figure 14-18: Use the What's this? button to get context-sensitive help on any dialog box item.

Managing Your Desktop

In this section, I'll present several ways to manage and customize your desktop. Although some of these changes are purely a matter of personal preference, others can streamline your work and help you get the most out of the NT operating system.

The changes that you make to customize your desktop will, in general, apply only to the user account that you used to log on to the computer. So if you're logged on as administrator, the changes will apply only to the administrator account. See the section later in this chapter called "Managing Multiple Users" to learn about how to handle multiple user accounts.

Changing the Desktop Look

Just as in Windows 3.x, NT 4.0 gives you control over how your desktop looks. Most of these attributes are managed by the Display application in Control Panel. To start the Display application, click Start ➪ Settings ➪ Control Panel and double-click the Display icon. The Display Properties dialog box provides several tabs from which to choose, as shown in Figure 14-19. Select the appropriate tab to change the attributes of your display. The tabs are self-explanatory, except for the Plus! tab, which lets you change default icons and set several miscellaneous attributes.

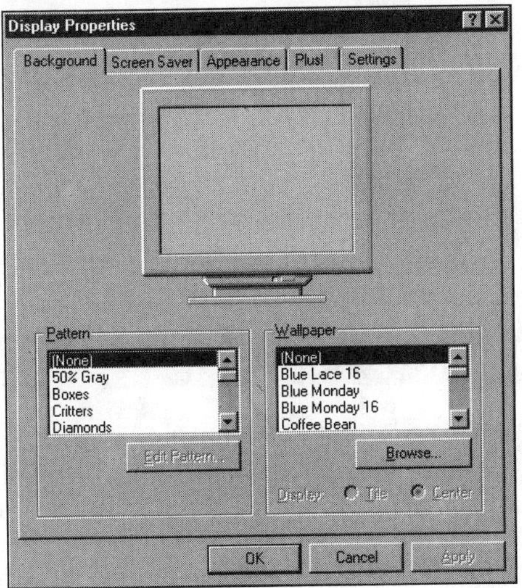

Figure 14-19: The Display application in Control Panel gives you full control over the attributes of your video display.

You were already exposed to the Settings tab during NT installation. Unlike Windows 95, changing your video display resolution in NT 4.0 requires restarting your computer. Be sure to use the Test button to verify that you've set the video parameters correctly before restarting to apply the change.

Customizing the Taskbar

You can control the location, size, and visibility of the taskbar, if you don't like how it behaves by default. In the following sections, I'll show you how to make these changes.

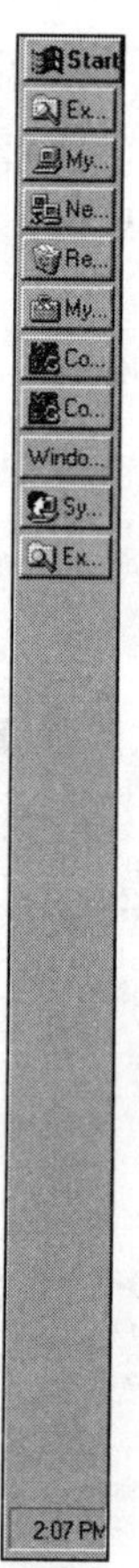

Figure 14-20: You can move the taskbar and dock it to any edge of the display.

Moving the Taskbar

If you don't like having the taskbar at the bottom of the display and would rather see it on some other edge, just drag it to that edge, and it will stick. For example, if you'd rather see the taskbar across the top of the display, point to an empty area on the task-bar and, while holding down the left mouse button, drag it to the top of the screen. You can move, or *dock,* the taskbar on any one of the four display edges. Figure 14-20 shows the taskbar docked on the right edge of the display.

As you can see, with the taskbar on the right display edge, the buttons aren't as wide, causing the text in them to be truncated. You can remedy this problem by making the taskbar wider, as discussed in the following section.

EDGING AROUND THE TASKBAR

Deciding which display edge to use for the taskbar may not be completely a question of personal preference. Your decision might be driven by the applications that you're running. For example, a particular application might require lots of detailed mouse activity near the bottom of the display. This might result in clicking the taskbar by mistake. You can eliminate some of this confusion by hiding the taskbar (described in a later section of this chapter), but even then you might accidentally bring up the taskbar. Experiment with the taskbar location that works best in your particular situation.

Changing the Taskbar Size

If you have several applications running at the same time, the taskbar can start to get crowded. Because NT assumes you want access to all applications, it shrinks the size of the application buttons to fit them all into the visible taskbar space. As the names of the windows are truncated on the smaller buttons with the addition of each new application, the taskbar can start to get confusing. Figure 14-21 illustrates this phenomenon.

Figure 14-21: A crowded taskbar can become confusing.

At the expense of consuming more space, you can increase the taskbar's size by positioning the mouse on the edge of the taskbar and dragging the edge (dragging the top edge upward, in this case). Notice in Figure 14-22 that, given enough room on the taskbar, the window buttons revert to their original default size.

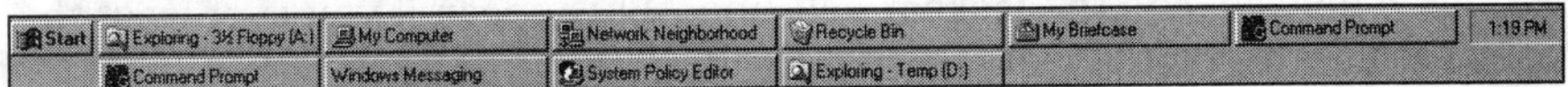

Figure 14-22: Relieve an overcrowded taskbar by changing its size.

Hiding the Taskbar

Let's say that you want to eliminate the taskbar completely from the display because you want the application that you're running to consume the entire screen. You want the taskbar to appear only when you need it and to make itself scarce when you don't. Fear not. There's an easy way accomplish this:

1. Click Start ➪ Settings ➪ Taskbar.
2. In the Taskbar Properties dialog box, click the Taskbar Options tab.
3. Click to select the Auto hide check box and then click OK, as shown in Figure 14-23.

   As soon as you do this, the taskbar will smoothly disappear from the bottom of the display (or from whichever edge it's docked).

You can also bring up the Taskbar Properties dialog box by right-clicking an empty area of the taskbar and clicking Properties. You'll find throughout this chapter that right-clicking just about any item will access its properties.

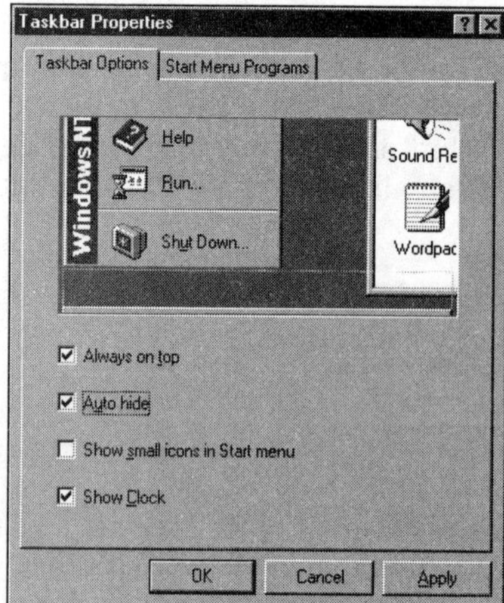

Figure 14-23: Hide the taskbar until you need it by setting its Auto hide property.

Now that the taskbar is gone, how do you call it back? Whenever you want the taskbar to show itself, just move the mouse to the edge of the screen where the taskbar is docked, and the taskbar will smoothly appear. If you ever want the taskbar to return permanently, just clear the Auto hide check box in the Taskbar Properties dialog box.

If you tend to run many applications at the same time but you don't want the taskbar to consume valuable screen real estate, try increasing its size (as described in the previous section) and hiding it. This approach lets you work without being disturbed by the taskbar but offers meaningful buttons when you bring it up.

Customizing the Start Menu

You can add applications and documents to the Start menu and to any of its submenus. (When you add a document to a menu and then click it, the application in which the document was created is started automatically.) Adding items to the menus can be much more efficient than searching for an application or document through My Computer or Explorer, which are both described later in this chapter.

Adding Menu Items

The simplest way to add an item to the Start menu is to drag the item to the Start button. This action adds the item to the top of the Start menu. Try it. And don't worry. You'll be able to remove it later.

Unfortunately, this approach doesn't allow you to control the name of the menu item in the Start menu. NT uses the filename as the name of the item in the menu. Another disadvantage of this technique is that it doesn't allow you to add an item to a submenu. You can only add items to the main Start menu. If you add very many items, the Start menu becomes unwieldy, and you lose the advantages provided by NT's hierarchy of menus.

If you want to add an item to one of the submenus or to the Start menu, perform the following steps:

1. Clcik Start ➪ Settings ➪ Taskbar (or right-click the taskbar and click Properties). In the Taskbar Properties dialog box, click the Start Menu Programs tab, as shown in Figure 14-24.

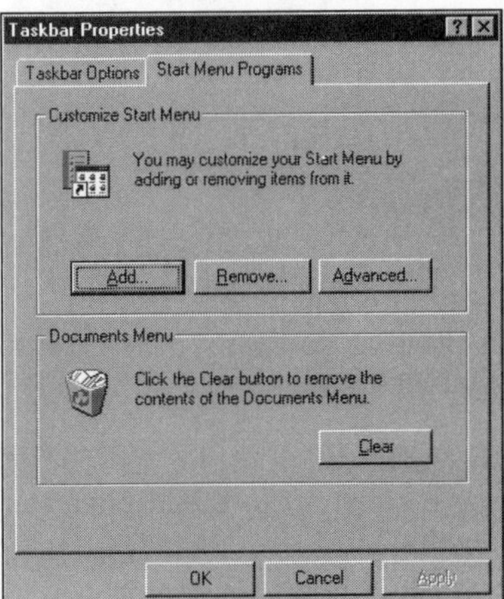

Figure 14-24: Use Taskbar Properties to manage the contents of the Start menu.

2. Click Add and type the name of the application, folder, or document that you want to add to a menu, as illustrated in Figure 14-25.

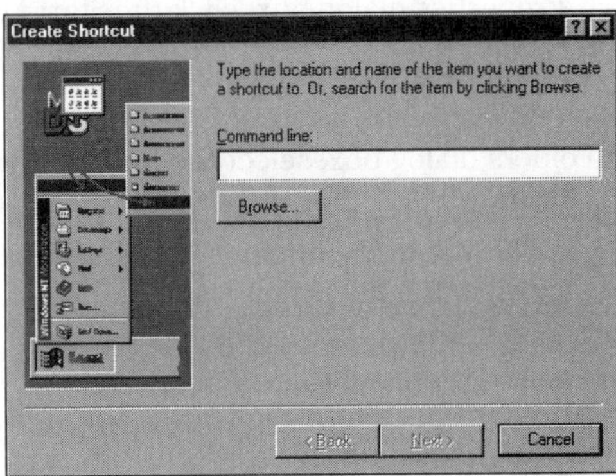

Figure 14-25: Add a new application to the Start menu or a submenu by specifying its name.

3. Click Next and select the menu to which you want to add the item.

   For example, if you want the item added to the Programs submenu, click Programs, as shown in Figure 14-26.

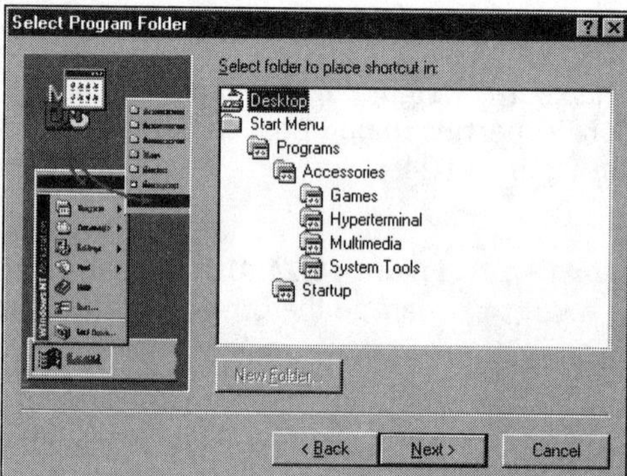

Figure 14-26: You can place the item anywhere in the submenu hierarchy.

4. Click Next and type the name of the item as you want it to appear in the menu. Click Finish and then click OK.

If you elect to add the item to the desktop rather than to the menu system, the item's icon will appear on your desktop as a shortcut to the application or document. I'll discuss shortcuts in the next section.

Removing Menu Items

If you want to remove an existing item from one of the submenus or from the Start menu, perform the following steps:

1. Click Start ➪ Settings ➪ Taskbar (or right-click the taskbar and click Properties). In the Taskbar Properties dialog box, click the Start Menu Programs tab, as shown in Figure 14-24.
2. Click Remove.
3. In the Remove Shortcuts/Folders dialog box, select the item that you want to remove and click Remove, as shown in Figure 14-27.

   A plus (+) sign indicates a folder that has something in it. Click the + sign to expand the folder and display all of the items contained in it. Click the minus (-) sign to collapse it.
4. Click Yes to confirm, click Close, and then click OK.

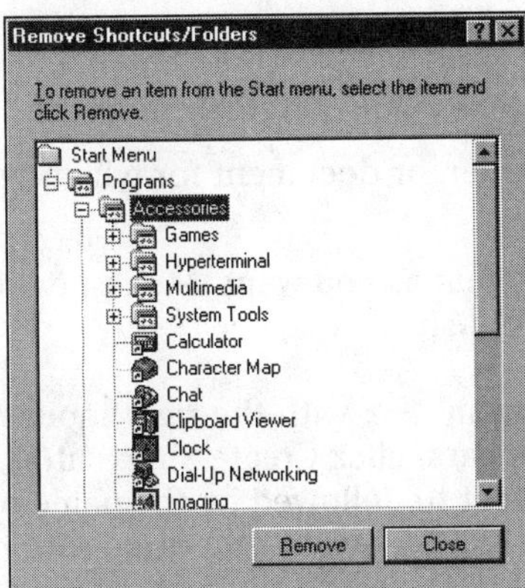

Figure 14-27: You can remove an item from the Start menu or a submenu.

Removing an item from the Start menu or from a submenu doesn't remove the item itself from the computer. The application, folder, or document remains where it was. It just doesn't appear on the menu any more.

Creating and Using Shortcuts

If you have applications, folders, or documents that you use frequently, you may want to consider placing icons for them on your desktop. That way, you don't have to deal with menus for these items at all — just double-click the icon, and you're there. For example, if you use a spreadsheet frequently, you may want to be able just to double-click a spreadsheet icon to fire it up.

You place an item on your desktop by creating a *shortcut* to it. A shortcut is really just a pointer to an item that can be located anywhere, on the local computer or on the network. When you double-click a shortcut icon, NT runs the application or opens the folder or file — just as if it were the item's original icon.

You can always tell the difference between a shortcut icon and a regular icon. The shortcut icon has a small, curved arrow in the lower left corner.

Why not use shortcuts for everything and forego putting anything in the Start menu and submenus? If you have lots of windows on the desktop, it's likely that most of your shortcuts will be obscured by them. Unless you want to use the taskbar to minimize all of the windows, it's best to have access to frequently used files through the Start menu and submenus as well. (Many people opt to put their frequently used files both in shortcuts on the desktop and in menu items accessible via the Start button.)

Here's how to create a shortcut on the desktop:

1. Right-click an exposed area of the desktop. Click New ➪ Shortcut.
2. Type the name of the application, folder, or document for which you want to create a shortcut. See Figure 14-25.
3. Click Next and type the name of the item as you want it to appear under the shortcut icon on the desktop. Click Finish.

You can also create a shortcut by dragging an item with the right mouse button to the desktop. On the pop-up menu that appears, click Create Shortcut(s) Here. The default name of the shortcut will be Shortcut to, followed by the name of the item. You can change the shortcut name after creation by clicking twice (not rapidly enough to be taken as a double-click) on the name and typing the new name.

Here's how to delete a shortcut from the desktop:

1. Right-click the shortcut you want to delete. Click Delete.

   Alternatively, you can select the shortcut and press the DELETE key. You can also drag the shortcut icon to the Recycle Bin. (I'll discuss the Recycle Bin later in this chapter.)
2. Click Yes to confirm.

   If you dragged the shortcut to the Recycle Bin, you won't be asked to confirm the delete.

Since a shortcut isn't the actual file, copying a shortcut to a floppy disk doesn't copy the file itself. Instead, it only copies the shortcut icon with nothing in it. Don't make the long trek home, with floppy disk in hand, to finish that last-minute project, only to discover all that you have is a shortcut, not the document that you expected.

Using My Computer

You can use My Computer to examine what's on your local disk drives. Figure 14-28 illustrates what the resulting window looks like when you double-click the My Computer desktop icon. Each drive on the computer (as well as each mapped network drive, described later in this chapter) is represented by an icon. You're also given an easy way to get to the Control Panel and the Printers folder. If you installed RAS, you're also given a shortcut to Dial-Up Networking.

Each hard disk partition on your computer appears in the My Computer window as a separate disk drive icon. In Figure 14-28, for example, both drives C and D are on the same physical hard disk drive.

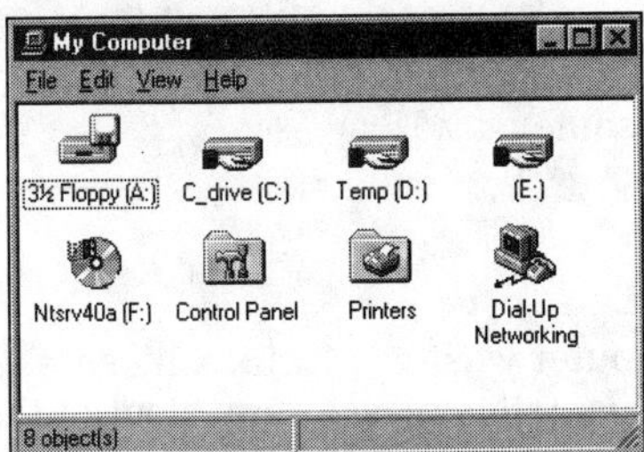

Figure 14-28: The My Computer icon lets you navigate through your local computer's folders and files.

Double-click a drive icon, and you'll open a new window showing the next level of detail on that drive. Double-click a folder, and you'll see the contents of the folder in a new window. Keep going deeper in the tree of folders until you reach individual files. In Figure 14-7, you saw an example of using My Computer to dig into the path D:\WINNT\SYSTEM32.

Now, navigation is great, but what's the goal? What can you do once you've found what you wanted? There are several things you can do. By double-clicking an application or document, you can start an application. You can also drag and drop files and folders to move or copy them from one folder to another or from a folder to the desktop. In addition, you can delete files and folders by dragging them to the Recycle Bin. By right-clicking a file or folder, you can view and adjust its properties (discussed later in this chapter).

Using Network Neighborhood

Whenever I see the Network Neighborhood introduced in books and articles about Windows 95 or NT, there's invariably a gratuitous reference to Mr. Rogers. Can you say "repetitious?" I knew you could. The Network Neighborhood is essentially the same as My Computer, except that it allows you to navigate resources shared by all computers on the network. You can view all of the computers in your workgroup or domain, double-click them, and view the resources that they each share. By double-clicking the Entire Network icon, you can even examine computers outside your domain or workgroup.

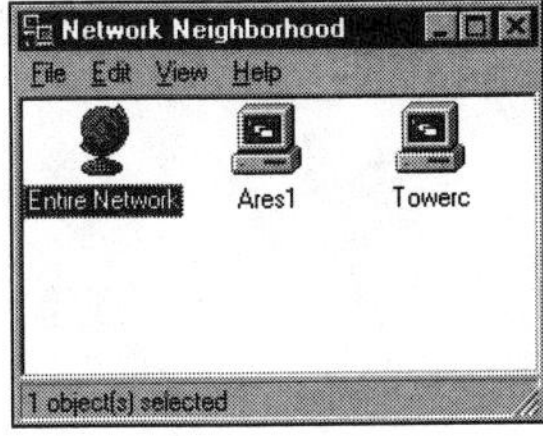

Figure 14-29: The Network Neighborhood icon lets you navigate through your network's shared resources.

Using Network Neighborhood, you can operate on individual files and folders much as you can with My Computer. Dragging and dropping, deleting, changing properties, and other operations all work the same way.

Recycle Bin

The Recycle Bin is a holding tank for your computer waste. (Macintosh users will recognize this concept as the modern, environmentally correct equivalent of the old trash can.) When you delete a file or folder using the graphical interface, it doesn't really go away. NT tosses it in the Recycle Bin, which acts as a sort of safety net in case you delete something that you really wanted to keep.

If you delete a file or directory from a Command Prompt or from File Manager, it doesn't go into the Recycle Bin. Likewise, deleting an item from a network drive or a floppy disk won't send it to the Recycle Bin either. It's actually deleted immediately, and there's no way to retrieve it if you deleted it in error. If you want the Recycle Bin safety net under you, use the NT 4.0 graphical interface whenever you delete files or folders. And be careful what you delete from network drives and floppy disks.

To avoid the need to get an industrial-sized dumpster (a larger hard disk) to contain an increasing amount of discarded material, empty the bin periodically. Remember, though, that once you empty it, you can't retrieve the material. To empty the Recycle Bin, right-click the Recycle Bin icon and click Empty Recycle Bin on the pop-up menu that appears. (Alternatively, you can double-click the Recycle Bin icon on the desktop. On the File menu, click Empty Recycle Bin.) You'll be asked if you're sure that you want to discard the contents forever. If you are, click Yes.

To fish something out of the trash that you accidentally deleted, double-click the Recycle Bin icon. The contents of the bin are displayed, as shown in Figure 14-30. Click the file that you want to retrieve. On the File menu, click Restore. Your discarded file will return to its original location. (If the folder that previously contained the file is no longer around, NT will recreate it at this point.)

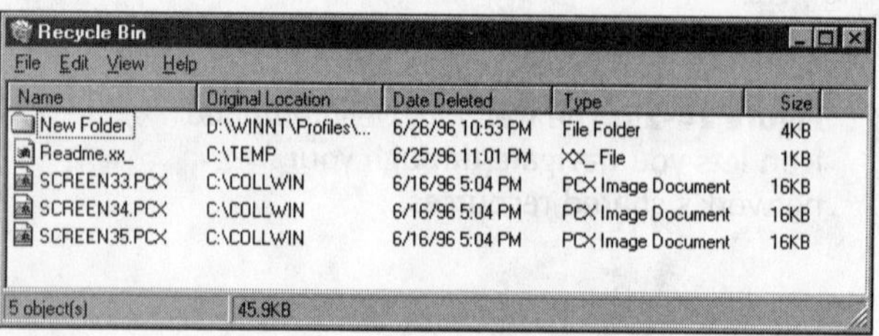

Figure 14-30: The Recycle Bin holds onto discarded objects until you empty it.

If you want to retrieve several items from the trash, hold down the CTRL key while clicking each item that you want to restore. Then, on the File menu, click Restore. All of the selected items will be restored and removed from the Recycle Bin.

My Briefcase

In my view, the briefcase feature isn't all that useful on Windows NT Server. It's better suited to laptop or desktop computers. In a nutshell, you can copy a set of files to your laptop or a floppy disk, work on the files off-line, and then quickly and automatically update the files on your network to reflect the changes that you made. Since this feature is primarily geared toward client computers, I won't delve into it here. If you want to find out more about using My Briefcase, check out online Help.

Other Desktop Icons

Depending on what optional components that you installed when you set up Windows NT Server, your desktop may contain additional icons. I'll briefly describe them in this section.

Inbox Icon

The Inbox icon is a universal repository for Microsoft Exchange, Microsoft Mail, and Internet Mail. If you elected not to include these optional components during NT installation, you'll still see the icon. If you double-click it, you're given the option to install the Microsoft Exchange client. I'll cover managing and using the various e-mail systems in Chapter 16.

Internet Explorer Icon

If you elected to install the Microsoft Internet Explorer as one of the optional components during NT Server installation, you'll see this icon on your desktop. Double-click the icon to start it. To use it to browse pages on your local intranet, just type the name of the local Web server.

If you want to use Internet Explorer to browse the Internet, you'll need to have installed both TCP/IP and RAS. You'll learn more about connecting to the Internet in Part V. TCP/IP and RAS are covered in Chapter 11.

Install Internet Information Server Icon

This shortcut icon is installed on your desktop if you opted not to install the Microsoft Internet Information Server during NT Setup. If you decide later to install IIS, double-clicking this shortcut is a convenient way to get it done. If you don't intend to install it and you view this shortcut as clutter, simply delete it by right-clicking the icon and clicking Delete. Installing and configuring the Internet Information Server is covered in detail in Chapter 22.

Using Windows NT Explorer

Windows NT Explorer is the most flexible way of dealing with files and folders on Windows NT Server 4.0. Although many of its functions can be accomplished using other features of the shell, I view Explorer as one-stop shopping for all of your file management needs. At a fundamental level, Explorer is a replacement for the old File Manager.

Navigating in Explorer

You invoke Explorer by clicking Start ➪ Programs ➪ Windows NT Explorer. As you can see in Figure 14-31, Explorer presents two views of related information. The left window contains the drive and folder structure. The right window shows the contents of whatever folder is open. Using Explorer, you can view and manipulate everything you could using My Computer or Network Neighborhood.

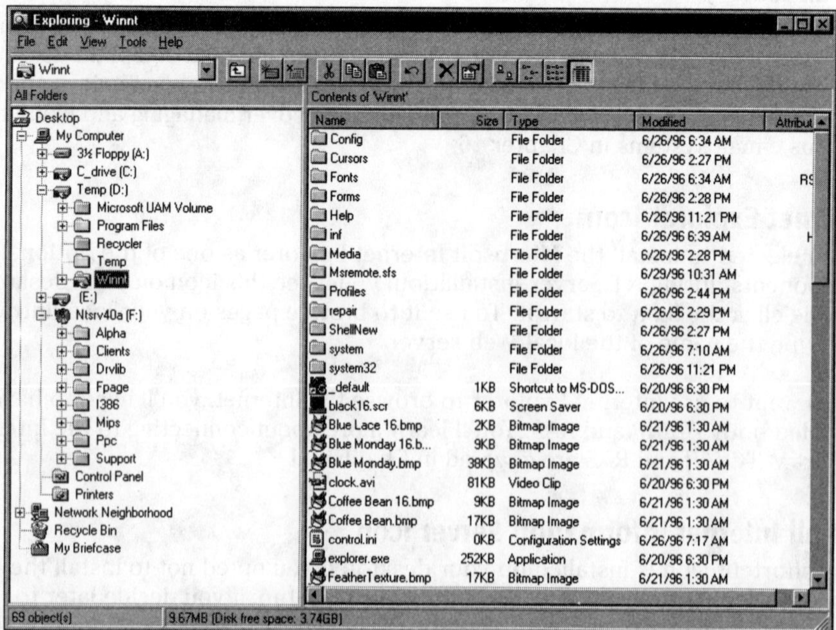

Figure 14-31: The Windows NT Explorer lets you perform all file and folder management in one utility.

By double-clicking items in the left window, you expand or collapse your view of the folder structure. A plus (+) sign indicates a folder that has subfolders in it.

Click the + sign to expand the folder and display all of its subfolders. Click the minus (-) sign to collapse it. For example, expanding Desktop shows you all of the icons on the desktop. Expanding My Computer displays all of the drives on your computer. Clicking a folder brings up a view of the contents of that folder. By clicking items in the left window, you change the contents displayed in the right window. Navigate in Explorer to get comfortable with it. You and your users will likely spend most of your file management time in this utility.

Creating New Folders

Creating a new folder is easy. Here's how:

1. Navigate through Explorer to the place where you want the new folder to go.
2. In the File menu, click New ➪ Folder.
3. At the bottom of the right window, you'll see a folder called New Folder. Type the name that you want to assign to the folder and press ENTER.

Renaming Files and Folders

To change the name of a file or folder, click the name once to select it, then click it once more. Notice that I didn't say double-click the name — you need to pause briefly between clicks. If you're not adept at this technique, right-click the name and click Rename. Then just type the new name over the old name and press ENTER.

Copying Files and Folders

The easiest way to copy involves dragging a file or folder in the right window to a destination folder in the left window. If you drag an item to a destination on a different drive, Explorer defaults to copying the item. However, if you drag a file or folder to a destination on the same drive, Explorer defaults to moving the item rather than copying it. You can force Explorer to copy the item on the same drive by holding down the CTRL key while dragging the item.

You can tell whether you're about to perform a copy operation if you see a plus (+) sign attached below the item that you're dragging when you're about to drop it in the left window. If there's no plus sign there, you're performing a move operation.

If you have several drives on your computer or you have many computers on your network, there's lots of potential for mistakes. To avoid any confusion between copy and move operations, I recommend that you (and your users) use the right mouse button to drag items to their destinations. When you release the button, you're given a choice of moving, copying, or creating a shortcut. This approach offers both precision and flexibility, and you don't have to remember when to hold down the CTRL key.

Moving Files and Folders

Moving files and folders is as easy as copying them. If you're moving items to destinations on the same drive, just drag and drop. If you're moving an item to another drive, you'll have to hold down the SHIFT key while dragging, to force a move instead of a copy. As I mentioned in the hint in the previous section, I recommend using the right mouse button for dragging, so there's no chance for confusion.

When dragging and dropping, be sure to aim carefully before you release the mouse button. If you drop an item too near another, it can end up inside the wrong object. For example, when rearranging folders, be sure that a nearby folder doesn't become highlighted. If this occurs, you know that the highlighted folder has become the target for the dragged item. If you release the mouse button, your item will drop inside the highlighted folder.

If you accidentally drag an item into the wrong place, simply double-click the target folder and drag the item out again. Alternatively, you can right-click the desktop and click Undo Move. Another trick is to press ESC before dropping the item, which cancels the process of dragging.

Managing Network Connections

You can connect drive letters to shared network resources just as you could in File Manager. To connect a drive letter to a shared resource on the network:

1. Click the Desktop icon in the left window. In the right window, double-click Network Neighborhood to open it. Double-click the server on which the resource resides.
2. In the right window, you'll see a list of shared resources. Click the resource to which you want to connect.
3. On the File menu, click the Map Network Drive. Select the drive letter that you want to assign and click OK, as shown in Figure 14-32.

   By default, the connection is made with the currently logged-on user account. If you want to connect using a different user account, type the account name in the Connect As field. If the account is in another domain, type the domain name, a backslash (\), and the user account name.

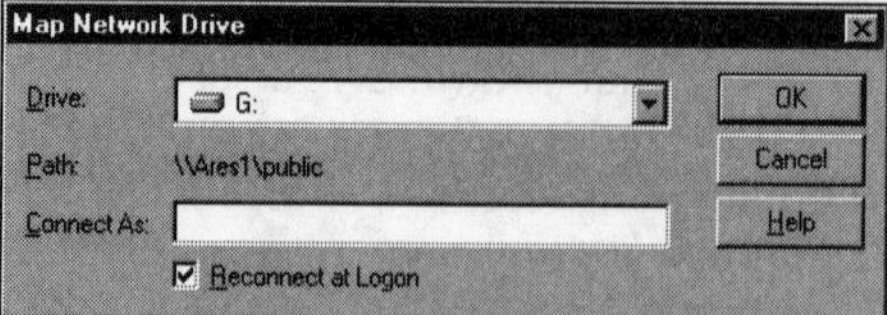

Figure 14-32: Map a drive letter to a shared network resource.

If you know the server and resource name and you don't want to navigate through Explorer, you can connect to the resource by clicking Map Network Drive on the Tools menu. You can then type the UNC path to the resource and click OK.

To disconnect from a network resource, perform the following steps:

1. On the Tools menu, click Disconnect Network Drive.
2. Select the resource from which you want to disconnect. Then click OK.

Managing Properties

No, I'm not talking about a "no money down" real estate course. Every file and folder has properties, including the familiar DOS attributes (such as read-only, hidden, and so on). Win32 applications and a few other file types (for example, font files) include detailed version information. Files stored on NTFS include compression, permission, auditing, and ownership properties. To view and modify these properties, right-click the item and click Properties. If you've selected a Win32 application residing on an NTFS partition, you'll see a dialog box similar to that in Figure 14-33.

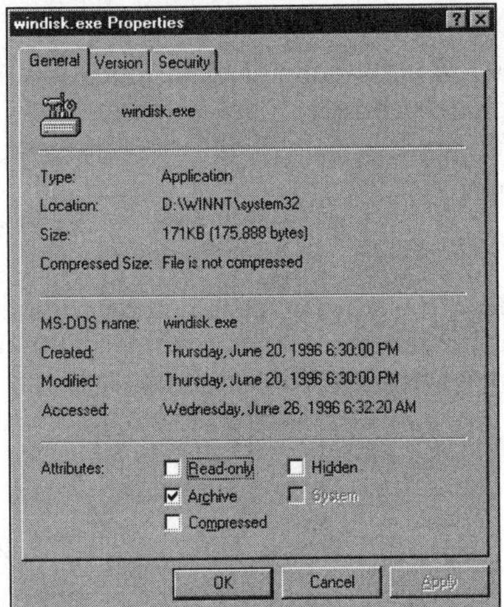

Figure 14-33: The Properties dialog box lets you view and modify attributes, version information, and security.

On the General tab, you can click the Attribute check boxes to select and clear the attributes of the file or folder. (Clicking to select Compressed will automatically compress the item on disk.) The Version tab lets you view (but not modify) version information attached to the file. The Security tab lets you view and change permissions, auditing, and ownership of the item. In Chapter 18, I'll cover security and auditing in detail. Chapter 19 will discuss NTFS compression.

Controlling What You See

You may have noticed in working with Explorer that, by default, it doesn't show you the file extensions that you're used to seeing in File Manager. You can control how much detail you see in the right window of Explorer. On the View menu, click Options and click the View tab. There you'll be able to display or hide files of specific types, display a different color for compressed items, and select other display options.

Changing File Associations

When you install an application, it often registers itself as being associated with a particular file type. When you double-click a file of this type, NT automatically starts the associated application. If you have more than one application that claims to be able to handle .DOC files, for example, you may want to control which application is associated with these files by default. You can explicitly change file type associations using the following steps:

1. On the View menu, click Options, then click the File Types tab.
2. Select the file type that you want to change. Then click Edit.
3. In the Actions list, click Open. Then click Edit.
4. To open all files of this type, type the full path name of the application that you want to start. Then click OK and click Close.

Start Menu Tools

The Start menu contains several handy tools to enable quick access to frequently used features, documents, and utilities. In this section, I'll cover some of the more useful ones. You'll be able to explore the rest on your own.

Dealing with Documents

You can access your most recently used documents quickly and easily through the Start menu. This technique saves you from having to hunt through directories or from starting your application to load a recent document using its File menu.

To access a recent document, just click Start ➪ Documents, then click the name of the document on the menu. NT will automatically start the correct application associated with this document.

If you start working on a new project, you may want to clear out the list of recently used documents and start fresh. To do this, right-click the taskbar, click Properties, and click the Start Menu Programs tab. Then click Clear and OK. This action removes all documents from the menu.

Using the Find Submenu

The Start menu offers a quick way of searching for files and folders. You can search for items based on filename, dates, age, size, file type, and included text strings. Just click Start ➪ Find ➪ Files or Folders. Once you've found what you want, you can drag and drop it directly from the Find dialog box.

Likewise, you can search for computers on the network based on computer name. Of course, you can use wildcards in your file, folder, and computer searches to help you if you're not sure exactly what you want. For example, you could specify AR* to find all items whose names begin with AR.

Using the Settings Submenu

The Start menu lets you quickly access and modify your computer's configuration settings. From this menu, you can access Control Panel, manage all aspects of printing, and configure both the taskbar and the Start menu.

Control Panel

The NT 4.0 Control Panel is very similar to the ones provided in Windows 3.x and Windows NT 3.x. However, this version contains much more, especially in the areas of hardware device configuration. I'll cover how to use the Control Panel applications in Chapter 18.

Printers

This menu item allows you quick access to the Printers folder, which lets you install new printers (either locally attached or remote printers on the network), control print server attributes, and manage individual print queues. I'll cover this area in detail in Chapter 18.

Taskbar

This menu item brings up the same dialog box as when you right-click the taskbar and click Properties. It lets you set taskbar and Start menu attributes. You've already seen how this works earlier in this chapter.

Managing Multiple Users

Because Windows NT is a multi-user operating system and because multiple users can log on to the same computer, it must keep track of different profiles for each user. If you're familiar with earlier versions of Windows NT, you know that individual user profile information was stored in the registry. In NT 4.0, all profile information (desktop icons, Start menu items, and so forth) is stored in a tree of folders. As an administrator, you can directly manipulate these folders on behalf of your users.

User Profile Folders

As you can see in Figure 14-34, all of the profile information is stored under SystemRoot\Profiles. Within this folder, NT creates three other folders — Administrator, All Users, and Default User. As you add user accounts to the computer, you'll find a new folder named after the new user account.

You can access and modify this information using Explorer, as shown in Figure 14-34. Alternatively, you can click Start ➪ Settings ➪ Taskbar option, click the Start Menu Programs tab, and click Advanced. This will bring up a copy of Explorer, pointing to the Profiles folder. I find it much easier to use Explorer directly to administer these folders.

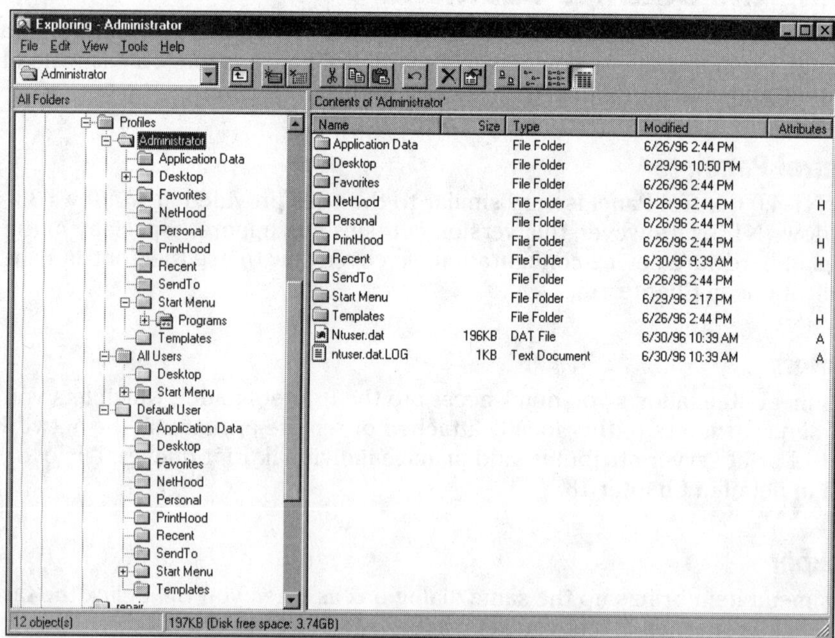

Figure 14-34: The Profiles folder contains folders with user profile information for all user accounts.

Assuming that you installed the operating system on an NTFS partition, only administrators can modify these three folders. Nonadministrators have read-only access to the All Users and Default User folders, but they can't modify them. I strongly recommend leaving these permissions as they are. If you grant write access to other users, they'll be able to make profile modifications that will affect all user accounts. (Of course, if you didn't install NT on NTFS, the users already have full power to do this sort of damage.)

The Administrator Folder

The Administrator folder is a good example of an individual user account profile. The information in this tree applies only to the administrator account, and any changes that you make while logged on as administrator will take effect in this part of the tree.

The All Users Folder

The All Users folder contains items that are added to every user's desktop. Let's say, for example, that you want all users to have a Start menu item pointing to a shared accounting program on a central server. To do this, you simply move a shortcut to the accounting program into the SystemRoot\Profiles\All Users\Start Menu folder.

The Default User Folder

The Default User folder contains a standard user profile that's copied whenever you create a new user account. When you first install Windows NT, the Administrator and Default User trees are identical. If you want to remove certain program menu items from all user profiles created for new user accounts, you'd remove the items from the SystemRoot\Profiles\Default User\Start Menu\Programs folder.

Summary

In this chapter, you've been introduced to the key components of the NT 4.0 shell. A recurring theme in the shell is that you can perform the same task in many different ways. I didn't present all the possibilities, leaving a few for you to discover on your own. I did focus some extra attention on the Windows NT Explorer, because I believe it's the most central and convenient way to manage your files, folders, and network connections. Once you master the skills covered in this chapter, you'll need to be prepared to share this knowledge and advice with your NT users.

In Chapter 15, I'll discuss several methods for sharing data between applications, documents, and users. In Chapter 16, you'll find out how to use the groupware applications that are included in NT. Then, in Part IV, I'll delve into the details of configuring, administering, and optimizing your Windows NT Server computer and network.

INSIDE STORY

The phone call was going well. The beta customer was happy. "Yes, I think NT 3.5 is ready to ship. All my problems have been fixed now." Music to my weary ears. Before releasing a version of NT, several key beta customers must agree that it's ready. This is just one of many criteria for release, but it's sometimes the most difficult to achieve. But this particular customer was happy, and so was I.

"Now, can you help me with the Windows 95 beta?" he asked. I said I'd do my best. "How do you install a printer on this thing? I know Windows 3.1 inside and out, but we've been struggling for three hours to find a way to install our printer under Windows 95."

At this early stage of Windows 95 shell development, little attention had been paid to printing. You had to know exactly what to run, since there were no shortcuts or menus that pointed to these features.

After admitting I didn't know either, the customer said, "So, you're really going to put this user interface on NT?" I shuddered. "Yes, but it'll be much easier to use than it is now. You'll be able to find the printing features quickly. Don't worry." As we ended the conversation, I was hoping the Windows 95 and NT teams would make an honest man out of me. Thankfully, they did.

Sharing and Distributing Data with NT Server

Wouldn't it be great if all of your applications spoke the same language using only one data file format? Wouldn't it be even better if you had a single application that could deal with all types of data? And wouldn't it save time if you could tell your data to distribute itself automatically across your network, without the need for messy batch files and scheduled updates?

Well, we haven't fully reached this digital Utopia, but you're about to discover how Windows NT Server takes you part of the way. The NT features covered in this chapter will save time and effort as you use and administer your network.

In Chapter 3, I introduced the concept of interoperability between nodes on a network to allow transmission of meaningful data. However, that kind of interoperability isn't enough, because you also want to perform useful work on a local computer or across a network. To do this, you need interoperability between applications.

Application interoperability — the ability of applications to communicate with each other in meaningful ways to share information — presents a couple of problems. The first challenge is finding a compatible means of communication between applications, in terms of the format, interpretation, and management of the data. The second problem involves how to share that data in a reliable, efficient way, whether the applications are running on a single computer or are distributed across a network.

✦ ✦ ✦ ✦

Although it's often possible for one application to read another application's data file, sometimes its difficult to correctly make sense of the translation. Witness the plethora of different file formats for databases, graphics files, word processors, and spreadsheets. One solution to this problem has been to include massive numbers of import/export file converters within the applications. Another approach has created a whole new class of software products, solely for the purpose of converting data into different file formats. All of this importing, exporting, and conversion of files can take its toll. These operations can be complex and inefficient and can lose information (because different manufacturers interpret data formats in different ways).

In this chapter, I'll cover Windows NT solutions to some of these problems. Although the application interoperability picture certainly isn't perfect yet, the situation has been greatly improved by technologies such as the Clipboard, ClipBook, DDE (Dynamic Data Exchange), OLE (Object Linking and Embedding), and directory replication. Some of these technologies already existed in Windows 3.x, but their implementation in Windows NT introduces some new considerations, especially in the security area.

The Windows NT Clipboard

Windows 3.x included the Clipboard for cutting and pasting data between applications. Similarly, Windows NT offers a single Clipboard, shared by all applications running on the operating system. There's no distinction between Clipboard data from Win16, Win32, DOS, OS/2, or POSIX applications, although the latter three have some limitations that I'll describe later in this chapter.

Data that's copied to the Clipboard is stored in memory and is retained until you replace it with something else, explicitly delete it (as described later in this chapter), log off, or shut down the computer. The data remains on the Clipboard even after you copy it somewhere else. This behavior allows you to copy Clipboard data to more than one destination. If you want to save the data for later use, you can use Clipboard Viewer to save it to disk and restore it when needed. Alternatively, using NT's ClipBook feature, you can share data with other applications across the network.

Using the Clipboard with Windows Applications

In Windows NT, the same Clipboard is used as a holding tank for data from all 16-bit and 32-bit applications. Almost every Win16 and Win32 application provides access to NT's Clipboard, typically through the application's Edit menu. Although applications differ slightly in their implementation of Clipboard functionality, most offer the operations outlined in Table 15-1. Note that the sources and destinations of Clipboard data can be documents, spreadsheets, bitmap graphics, text, and so on. The source and destination can be within the same application or can be different applications on the same computer.

Table 15-1
Typical Clipboard Features in Windows Applications

Clipboard Operation	*Typical Shortcut Key*	*Description*
Cut	CTRL+X	Move the selected data from the source to the Clipboard. The data is removed from the source. Any data resident on the Clipboard is replaced by the new data.
Copy	CTRL+C	Copy the selected data from the source to the Clipboard. The data isn't removed from the source. Any data resident on the Clipboard is replaced by the new data.
Paste	CTRL+V	Move the data from the Clipboard to the destination. The data isn't removed from the Clipboard and can be pasted to another destination.

The actions required to select data for cutting or copying vary according to the application. Consult your application's documentation for details on how to select data for Clipboard operations.

In some applications, you may also see Edit menu commands such as Copy Attributes or Paste Attributes. Although some of these functions may interact with the Clipboard, they usually implement application-specific interpretations of the data. Thus, they're not considered standard Clipboard operations.

Moreover, some applications maintain their own Clipboard and never use NT's Clipboard. In these applications, cut, copy, and paste operations take place only within the application, and the data can't be copied to or pasted from other applications. So, even standard commands on the Edit menu may not interact with the Clipboard at all.

Capturing Screens and Windows to the Clipboard

You may want to capture a full-screen image or window for use in software documentation, marketing materials, or product box illustrations. For example, if your MIS department develops a new order-entry system for use by the sales department, you may need to provide them with detailed documentation on the new software, including screen shots as illustrations. There are several powerful products available to help you capture and manage screen shots, including Collage Complete and HiJaak. However, the Clipboard can also handle the basics of this process.

Let's say that you want to capture the contents of an entire NT screen. After the screen appears exactly the way you want it, press the PRINT SCREEN key. (Some keyboards label this key PRT SCRN or something equally cryptic.) NT immediately creates a bitmap image of the entire contents of the screen and moves it to the Clipboard.

YE OLDE KEYBOARDS

If you have an older AT-style keyboard (prior to the enhanced keyboard design in common use today), pressing PRINT SCREEN may not copy anything to the Clipboard. If PRINT SCREEN fails, try ALT+PRINT SCREEN or SHIFT+PRINT SCREEN to copy the screen to the Clipboard. One of these should work. If ALT+PRINT SCREEN on your keyboard captures the entire screen, you may not be able to capture individual windows using this older keyboard.

If you want to capture only the active window, press ALT+PRINT SCREEN. NT immediately creates a bitmap image of the active window and moves it to the Clipboard. If a dialog box in the application is active, it's usually considered the active window. However, this can vary from one application to another. If you want to capture the main application window, close any subordinate dialog boxes before you perform the capture. When capturing individual windows, always visually verify what you've captured using the Clipboard Viewer, described later in this chapter.

Once you've got a captured image on the Clipboard, you can paste it directly to any application that can accept BMP bitmap files. NT's Paint and WordPad applications (under Start ⇨ Programs ⇨ Accessories menu) accept these pasted bitmaps without a hitch. Refer to your application documentation to determine if it can accept BMP files.

Using the Clipboard with Non-Windows Applications

On Windows NT, if an application can run inside an NT window (as opposed to running in full-screen mode), you can copy data displayed by it to the Clipboard. Thus, most DOS text- or graphics-mode applications and all POSIX and OS/2 text-mode applications can be the source of a copy to the Clipboard.

If you're running the Presentation Manager add-on for Windows NT 4.0, you can copy and paste text or bitmaps between OS/2 PM applications and the NT Clipboard.

I say *most* DOS applications can participate because some of them force themselves into full-screen mode. If you can't get to the window menu in the upper left corner of the Command Prompt window in which the application is running, you can't copy anything from the application to the Clipboard. If the application can run in an NT window, you can copy anything displayed within that window. (I'll discuss other aspects of the Command Prompt in detail in Chapter 17 and Appendix A.)

Some DOS applications operate as graphics-mode programs in text-mode clothing. DOS versions of Microsoft Word and WordPerfect can look as if they're running in text mode, but they're using graphics mode to be more WYSIWYG. If you copy text from these applications, you'll really be copying a bitmap image — probably not what you intended.

Most DOS applications that behave this way also have an option to run in actual text mode. If you run into this problem, force the application to run in text mode and then perform the copy operation. Check your DOS application's documentation to find out how to get it running in text mode.

Copying Data from a Non-Windows Application

Here's how to copy displayed data from a non-Windows application (running in a Command Prompt window) to the Clipboard:

1. If the source application from which you want to copy the data is a DOS application, and it's running in full-screen mode, press ALT+ENTER to revert to running it in a Command Prompt window.

   There's no such thing as full-screen mode on a RISC-based Windows NT computer. All applications run in a window on RISC. So you don't need to worry about switching modes in step 1 unless you're on an Intel platform.

2. Make the data you want to copy appear in the Command Prompt window.

   The only data that you can copy to the Clipboard is data that appears in the window. If all of your desired data won't fit in the window at once, you'll need to perform multiple copy operations.

3. Click the program icon in the upper left corner of the Command Prompt window. On the window menu, click Edit ➪ Mark. See Figure 15-1.

   At this point, the window changes to Select mode. The displayed contents are frozen while you perform steps 4 and 5.

If your application doesn't make use of the mouse, you can avoid step 3 completely by setting the Command Prompt window to QuickEdit mode. This will allow you to use the mouse to select the copy area (as described in step 4) without having to put the Command Prompt into Select mode. To set QuickEdit mode, click the program icon in the upper left corner to display the window menu. Click Properties and click the Options tab. Click to select the QuickEdit Mode check box.

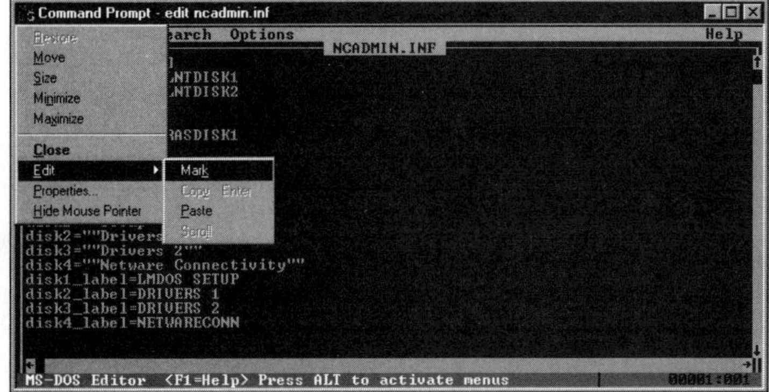

Figure 15-1: The Edit ➪ Mark command puts the Command Prompt window in Select mode, for selecting an area to be copied.

4. To select the area of the window that you want to copy, click the upper left corner of the area, hold down the mouse button, and drag it to the lower right corner. Then release the mouse button. See Figure 15-2.

   If you didn't select the area correctly, repeat this step until you're satisfied that the correct area has been selected.

Many folks who use the Command Prompt would prefer a mouseless society. If you're one of these people, you can select the area to be copied by using the keyboard. To do this, use the arrow keys to move to the upper left corner of the area that you want to copy. Then, while holding down the SHIFT key, use the arrow keys to move to the lower right corner of the area.

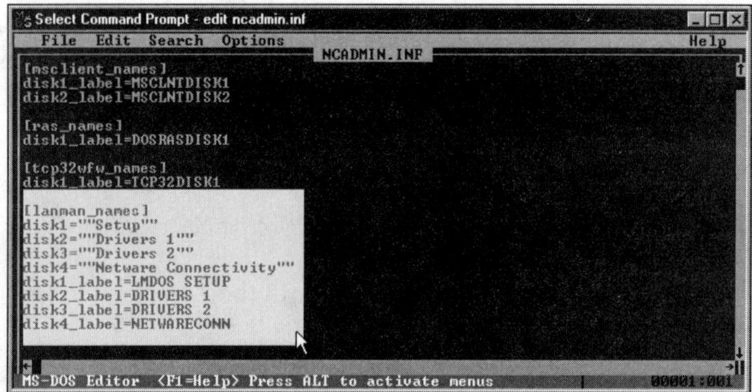

Figure 15-2: Select an area of the window to copy to the Clipboard.

You don't even need to be running an application to use this feature. You can copy text directly from a Command Prompt window using the same technique described here. Figure 15-3 illustrates copying the output of a directory listing to the Clipboard. When you want to copy just a portion of the text, you can select any rectangular area of the window.

```
Select Command Prompt

D:\clients>dir
 Volume in drive D is SCSI4GB
 Volume Serial Number is FC76-EA83

 Directory of D:\clients

07/01/96  10:01a        <DIR>          .
07/01/96  10:01a        <DIR>          ..
07/01/96  09:59a        <DIR>          lanman
07/01/96  10:00a        <DIR>          lanman.os2
07/01/96  09:58a        <DIR>          msclient
06/21/96  01:30a                 6,470 ncadmin.inf
07/01/96  09:58a        <DIR>          ras
07/01/96  09:58a        <DIR>          srvtools
07/01/96  09:58a        <DIR>          tcp32wfw
07/01/96  10:01a        <DIR>          win95
              10 File(s)          6,470 bytes
                          3,955,060,736 bytes free

D:\clients>
```

Figure 15-3: You can even select text from the Command Prompt window itself for copying to the Clipboard.

5. Press ENTER.

   Alternatively, you can click the program icon in the upper left corner of the Command Prompt window. Click Edit ➪ Copy on the window menu. I find pressing ENTER much quicker.

   The copied data is now on the Clipboard and can be pasted to other applications. The Command Prompt goes back to normal, and the application (if any) continues to execute.

Pasting Text to a Non-Windows Application

You can also paste text from the Clipboard to an application running in a Command Prompt window, or to the Command Prompt itself. The application must be in a position to accept a stream of text data, as if it were entered from the keyboard. (In fact, that's exactly how NT pastes data to the Command Prompt window. NT stuffs the data into the Command Prompt's keyboard input buffer.)

For example, if you're running the DOS EDIT application, you may want to paste text from the Clipboard into the file that you're editing. Perhaps you may want to try out a series of commands by pasting them directly to the Command Prompt for execution. Here's how to do it:

1. Position the cursor at the place within the Command Prompt window where you want the paste to begin.
2. Click the program icon in the upper left corner of the Command Prompt window. Click Edit ➪ Paste on the window menu. See Figure 15-4.

   If the Paste command isn't enabled, you probably don't have text on the Clipboard. Be sure that the Clipboard contains the text that you want to paste and repeat this step.

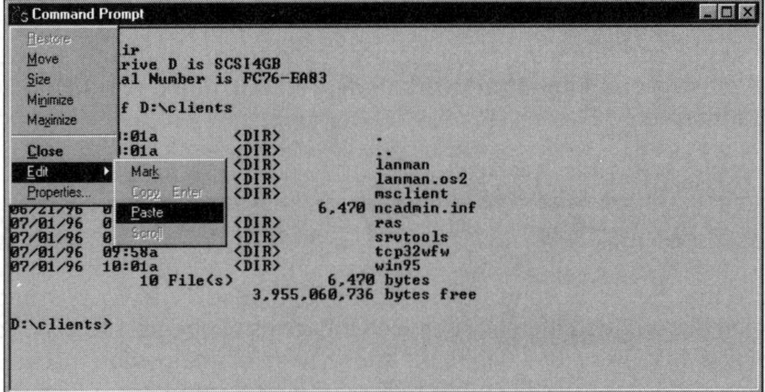

Figure 15-4: The Edit ➪ Paste command sends text stored on the Clipboard to the Command Prompt window.

3. The text from the Clipboard is sent to the Command Prompt window as if it had been typed on the keyboard.

   If you pasted the text directly to the Command Prompt, as in the example shown in Figure 15-4, the command processor will attempt to execute the text as commands.

If the text on the Clipboard includes any formatting information (for example, bold or italics), this information will be lost when you paste the text into a Command Prompt window. Only the plain text is pasted.

The Clipboard and OLE Objects

So far, I've primarily focused on using the Clipboard as a holding tank for text and bitmap graphics. The Clipboard also supports OLE objects. This means that you can use the Clipboard to hold documents, video clip files, wave files, and other objects. You'll be able to embed these objects into documents and, as long as your destination application supports the Paste Link operation (usually found under Paste Special in the Edit menu), you'll also be able to link these objects from the Clipboard. I'll discuss OLE later in this chapter.

The Clipboard Viewer

The Clipboard Viewer enables you to view, save, and erase the contents of the Clipboard. In addition, it provides you with the capability to create a *ClipBook* made up of pages from the Clipboard and to share those pages over the network with other nodes. Likewise, you can use Clipboard Viewer to connect to ClipBooks on other computers and access their shared pages.

Starting Clipboard Viewer

To start Clipboard Viewer, click Start ➪ Programs ➪ Accessories ➪ Clipboard Viewer. The first time that you do this after starting the computer, you may see a brief message displayed about starting NetDDE. NetDDE (short for Network DDE) is the interprocess communication mechanism used to communicate between Clipboard Viewers on different network nodes. I'll talk more about DDE and NetDDE later in this chapter.

CLIPBOARD VS. CLIPBOOK

You may notice that the application's window title is ClipBook Viewer, even though you started Clipboard Viewer. The difference between the terms *Clipboard* and *ClipBook* can be a little confusing at first. Think of a Clipboard as one page of information that you acquire, copy, then throw away. It lives its life exclusively on the local computer. A ClipBook, on the other hand, is a collection of many pages of Clipboard data that are stored for later use and can be shared across the network with other computers.

Viewing Clipboard Contents

It's often handy to be able to see what's on the Clipboard before you paste the data to another application. You can verify that you have the correct data on the Clipboard by using the Clipboard Viewer.

If you're doing lots of cutting and pasting, you may want to leave the Clipboard Viewer always active, displaying the current contents of the Clipboard. That way, you'll never have to worry about remembering what's on the Clipboard.

Here's how to view the Clipboard contents:

1. Click Start ➪ Programs ➪ Accessories ➪ Clipboard Viewer.

   If this is the first time that you're starting Clipboard Viewer after restarting your computer, you may have to wait a few moments for the NetDDE service to start.

2. Double-click the Clipboard button that's minimized at the bottom of the window. See Figure 15-5.

   This step may not be necessary if the Clipboard window is already displayed.

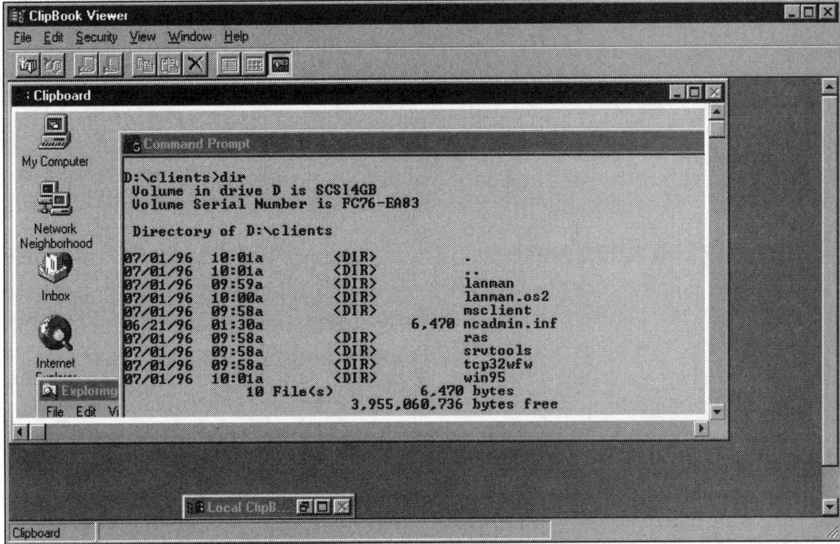

Figure 15-5: Use the Clipboard Viewer to view the current contents of the Clipboard.

INFORMATION HIDING

When you copy data to the Clipboard, it can include a lot of formatting information that you don't see. Depending on the applications that you're using, the default display of the Clipboard's contents may not look quite like what you expected. You can try to view the data in other formats by selecting options from the View menu. However, don't panic if the data doesn't look exactly right even then. As long as the application to which you're pasting the data can correctly interpret all of the formatting information, your data will probably be OK. Check your application documentation and perform a few tests to make sure that the formatting information is carried through to its final destination.

Saving and Restoring Clipboard Files

As I mentioned earlier, the contents of the Clipboard are volatile. The data is erased whenever you copy new data to the Clipboard, explicitly delete it, log off, or shut down the computer. You may want to save the current contents of the Clipboard for later use.

To save the Clipboard contents to a file, click Save As on the File menu. Type the filename that you want to assign, use the .CLP extension, and click OK. To pull a .CLP file back to the Clipboard, click Open on the File menu. Find the file that you want to restore and click OK.

The CLP file format is basically proprietary to Microsoft's Clipboard Viewer application. Few graphics applications can read and interpret these files, so don't count on using the CLP format as a standard way of distributing files to others (unless you want them to use Clipboard Viewer exclusively).

Clearing the Clipboard

Although memory resources aren't as much of an issue on the typical computer running Windows NT Server or Workstation, you can free memory for other uses by clearing out the contents of the Clipboard. Text and small bitmaps take up negligible space, but large, true-color bitmaps or OLE objects consisting of large video or audio files can eat up a good chunk of RAM. Although NT uses virtual memory, every chunk of free RAM helps if your computer is heavily loaded and is paging to disk.

To clear out the contents of the Clipboard, click the Clipboard window to make sure that it's the active one. Then click Delete on the Edit menu or click the button that looks like an *X*. Whatever data you had on the Clipboard will go to the big bit bucket in the sky.

Moving Data between Clipboard and ClipBook

Clipboard Viewer includes both the Clipboard, which we've been discussing so far, and the Local ClipBook. The latter is a repository for up to 127 pages of data that you want to save from the Clipboard and perhaps share with other computers over the network. I'll cover the sharing feature in the next section. For now, I'll focus on getting pages of data from the Clipboard into the Local ClipBook, and vice versa.

The Local ClipBook got its "Local" moniker because its contents are created and stored on the local computer. Later in this chapter, I'll show you how to connect to other ClipBooks shared on the network. Each of these other computers starts by pasting Clipboard pages to their Local ClipBook.

Creating a New ClipBook Page

Once you have data on the Clipboard that you want to make part of the Local ClipBook, switch to the Clipboard Viewer and perform the following steps:

1. Click the Local ClipBook window.
2. On the Edit menu, click Paste.
3. In the Paste dialog box, shown in Figure 15-6, type the name that you want to give the page and click OK.

   All pages must have a unique name. You've created a new page in the Local ClipBook, as shown in Figure 15-7.

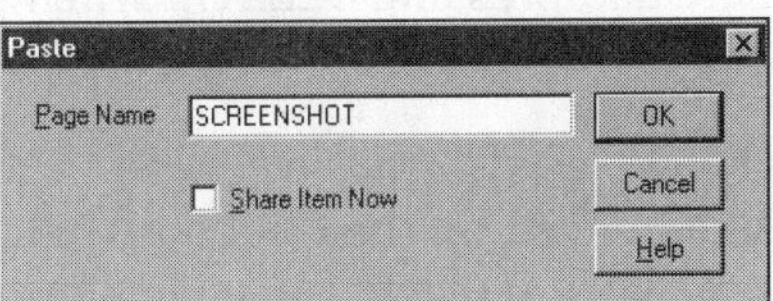

Figure 15-6: The Paste dialog box lets you type a name for your new ClipBook page.

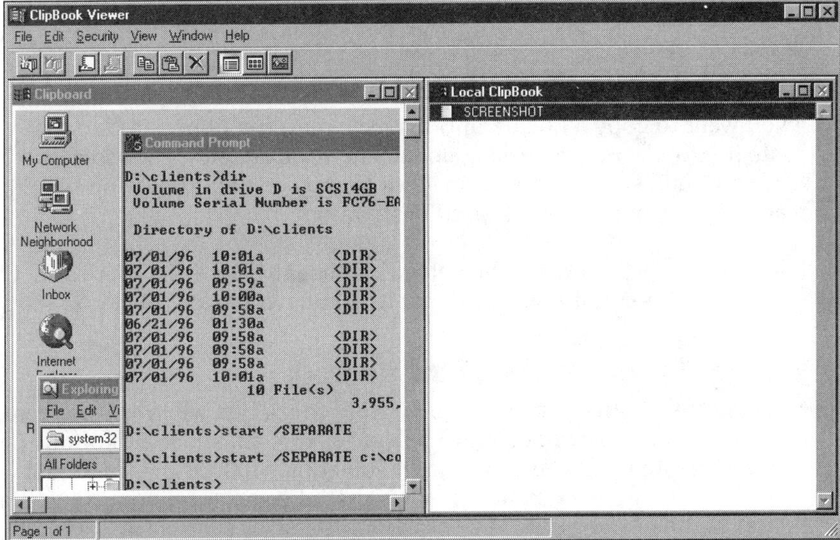

Figure 15-7: The new page appears in the Local ClipBook window.

There are a couple of ways to view the pages in ClipBooks. The View menu provides three options: Table of Contents, Thumbnails, and Full Page. The Table of Contents view produces a list view similar to Explorer or File Manager. Full Page displays the entire selected page within a ClipBook, obscuring all other pages. The Thumbnails view displays a miniature version of all the pages in the ClipBook. Although it's a great idea, so much detail is lost that I find the Thumbnails view virtually useless. I recommend using the Table of Contents view most of the time and using the Full Page view only when you want to see the detail of a particular page in a ClipBook.

Replacing an Existing ClipBook Page

If you want to replace an existing page in the Local ClipBook with what's currently on the Clipboard, click to select the page that you want to replace. Then click Paste to Page on the Edit menu. The contents of the Clipboard immediately replace the contents of the selected Local ClipBook page. Meanwhile, the page retains its name and all other attributes (including sharing status and security, covered later in this chapter).

Deleting an Existing ClipBook Page

The easiest way to delete an existing page in the Local ClipBook involves clicking to select the page that you want to delete and pressing DELETE. When you're asked to confirm, click OK. The page is then deleted from the Local ClipBook and is placed on the Clipboard.

Be sure that you don't have something important on the Clipboard before you delete a page from the Local ClipBook. When you delete the page, the contents of your Clipboard are erased and replaced by the contents of the deleted page. If you have something on the Clipboard that you want to save, save it to a .CLP file or paste it to a new page in the Local ClipBook before you delete any pages.

Using an Existing ClipBook Page

If you want to copy a Local ClipBook page onto the Clipboard (so that you can paste it into a word processing document, for example), click to select the page that you want. On the Edit menu, click Copy. The data is now on the Clipboard, ready to be pasted to the desired destination.

If you want other users on the network to use the pages in your Local ClipBook or you want to use ClipBook pages that others have shared, read on.

Sharing ClipBook Pages on the Network

You may have noticed the Share Item Now check box when you were specifying the name of your new Local ClipBook page. You can share a ClipBook page when you first create it, or you can share it sometime after you've created it. You'll see how other computers can access your shared pages (and how you can access theirs) in the next section.

If you've already created a page and you later want to share it, perform the following steps. (If you're creating a new page and you've selected the Share Item Now check box, start with step 3.)

1. In the Local ClipBook window, click to select the page that you want to share.
2. On the File menu, click the Share option.
3. If the page that you're sharing is unformatted text or a bitmap image, click OK. If the page that you're sharing is a file or OLE object, click to select the Start Application on Connect check box, as shown in Figure 15-8.

You must select the Start Application on Connect check box for any page that's more complex than simple text or a bitmap. Otherwise, the remote computer accessing the page won't know how to handle the data. If you don't want to intrude on the user's desktop when the application starts, click to select the Run Minimized check box before clicking OK.

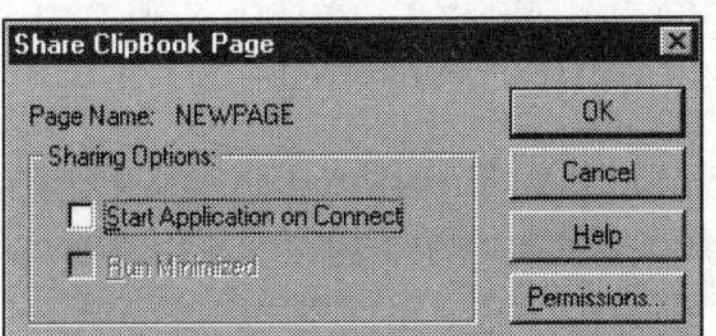

Figure 15-8: For pages more complex than text and bitmaps, automatically start the application when the shared page is accessed.

4. The page in the Local ClipBook is immediately shared on the network.

   Figure 15-9 shows a Local ClipBook containing four pages. SCREEN01 and SCREEN02 are shared, but NEWPAGE and SCREEN03 aren't.

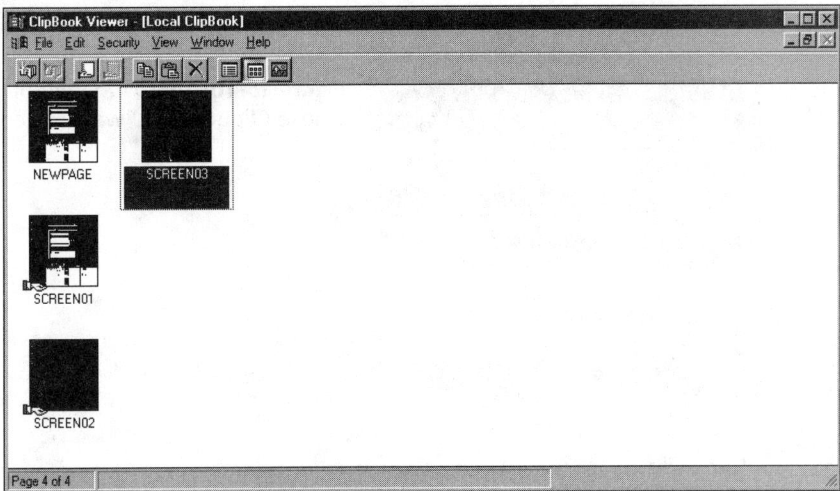

Figure 15-9: The Local ClipBook can share individual pages over the network.

It's easy to stop sharing a page in the Local ClipBook on the network. Click to select the page and click Stop Sharing on the File menu. That's all there is to it.

In theory, you should always be able to tell if a page in your Local ClipBook is shared on the network. But you can't always believe what you see. If a page is shared, the icon in the Table of Contents view includes a sharing hand. Likewise, if you're using the Thumbnails view, the mini-page is displayed with the sharing hand.

When you share a page, the hand shows up as expected. Unfortunately, when you stop sharing a page, the sharing hand isn't always erased. If you really want to know the sharing status of your pages after you've stopped sharing one of them, minimize the Clipboard Viewer window and restore it. Then you can trust that the sharing status displayed reflects reality.

Accessing Other ClipBooks on the Network

To use a shared page in a ClipBook on another computer, you need to connect to the other computer's Local ClipBook. Once you've connected, you can browse through the shared pages and copy a page to the Clipboard.

ClipBook was first introduced as a 16-bit utility in Windows for Workgroups and later as a 32-bit utility in Windows NT 3.1. You can share pages between computers running Windows for Workgroups, Windows 95, and Windows NT 3.1 or later.

Here's how to connect to a remote ClipBook:

1. On the File menu, click Connect.
2. Click the computer name (or type the computer name) to which you want to connect, as shown in Figure 15-10.

   If you have a large network, it may take a few moments to create the list of servers from which to choose.

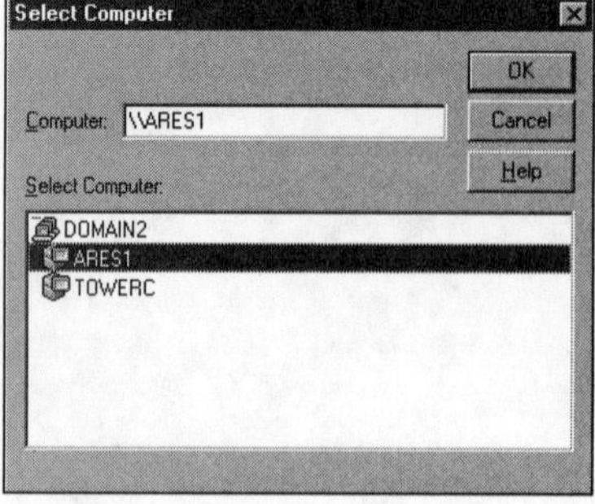

Figure 15-10: Specify the remote computer whose ClipBook you want to access.

3. Click OK.

A new window in Clipboard Viewer appears, providing a Table of Contents view of shared pages in the remote computer's Local ClipBook. The Clipboard Viewer in Figure 15-11 includes the view of the remote ClipBook on the \\ARES1 server.

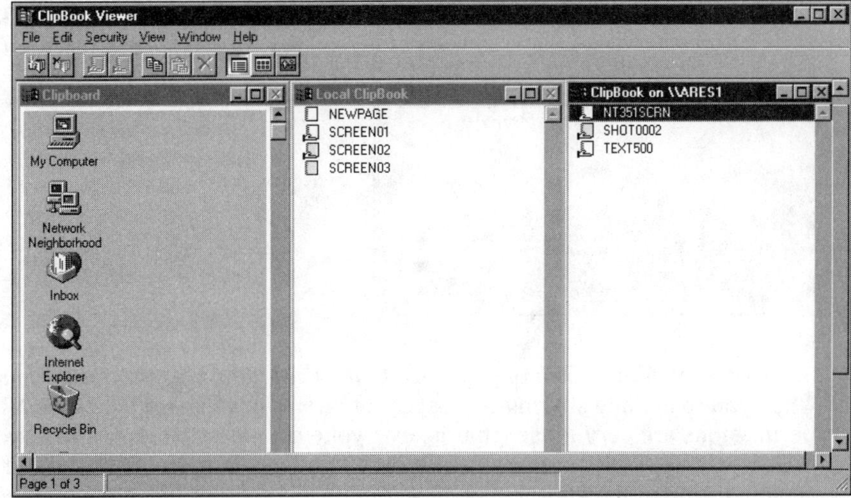

Figure 15-11: Clipboard Viewer presents views of the Clipboard, Local ClipBook, and remote ClipBooks.

Unfortunately, there's no support in Clipboard Viewer for dragging and dropping ClipBook pages. If you want to copy a shared page from a remote computer to your Local ClipBook, you must first copy the page from the remote ClipBook to your Clipboard and then paste the contents of the Clipboard into your Local ClipBook.

When you're done accessing a remote ClipBook, you can disconnect from it by clicking the remote ClipBook window that you're no longer interested in accessing. Then, on the File menu, click Disconnect. The connection is broken, and the window vanishes.

ClipBook Page Security

To keep things simple, I've ignored so far the question of security. Windows NT allows you to set separate access permissions on each shared page in your Local ClipBook. You may have noticed the Permissions button in Figure 15-8. You can set permissions on a page when you first share it (by clicking Permissions in the Share ClipBook Page dialog box) or later using the Permissions command on the Security menu.

By default when you share a page, NT grants administrators the right to change its contents (that is, administrators have Full Control permission) and lets everyone else read and link to the page. If this situation is OK, the default permissions are just fine, as shown in Figure 15-12.

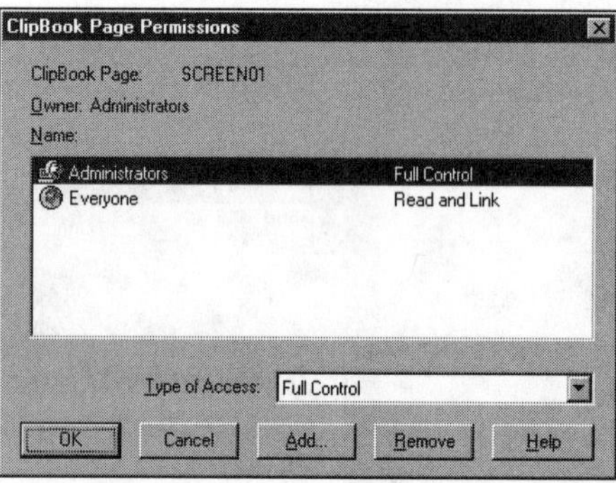

Figure 15-12: Default permissions on ClipBook pages allow everyone to read or link to them.

If you ever plan on restricting access to your shared page, set the permissions while you're initially sharing the page, not after you've shared it. Since NT's default permissions are very loose (that is, everyone on the network can read your page), the page is available to everyone until you change its permissions. If the data is sensitive, you don't want someone grabbing a copy of it between when you share it and when you set restrictive permissions.

Let's say, however, that you want to share a page in your Local ClipBook with a specific user (Fred) on the network, excluding all other users from seeing it. There are a couple of ways to implement this. One way is to remove access granted to Everyone by selecting Everyone and clicking Remove. Then use the Add feature to add specific access for Fred, as shown in Figure 15-13. Figure 15-14 shows the resulting permissions attached to the shared page called SCREEN01.

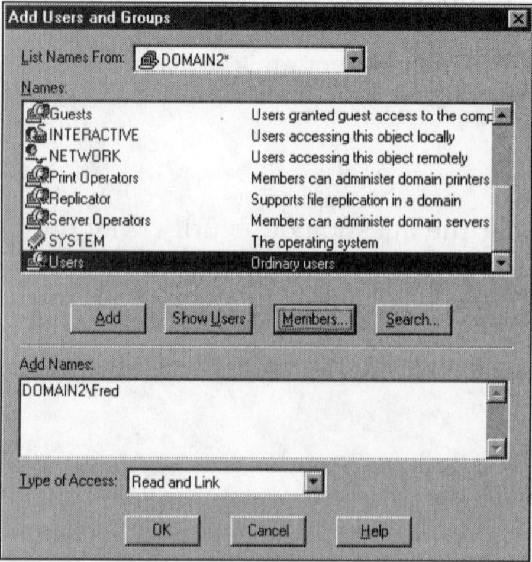

Figure 15-13: Add specific Read and Link permission for Fred, who is a member of the Users group.

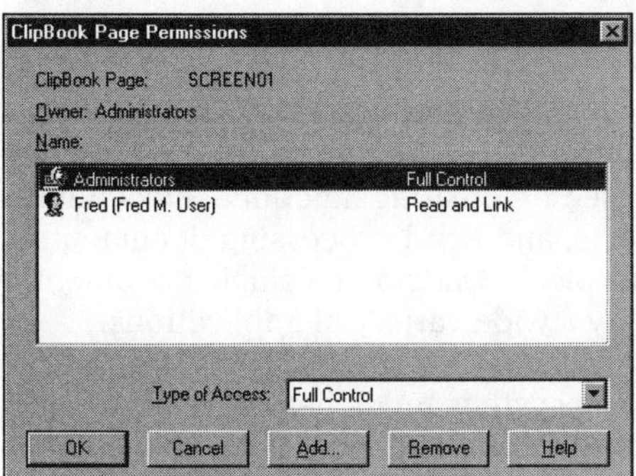

Figure 15-14: After you've edited the default permissions, Fred is the only nonadministrator account with access to the shared page.

In addition, using the Auditing command on the Security menu, you can track all accesses to your shared pages. For a more thorough discussion of managing security, including permissions and auditing, see Chapter 18.

Dynamic Data Exchange

Dynamic Data Exchange, more commonly called DDE, provides another approach to sharing data between applications. DDE has been around since the early days of 16-bit Windows. It's supported today in both Windows 95 and Windows NT, primarily for compatibility with existing applications that use it. DDE used to be the standard and most sophisticated way of passing data between applications, but it has been eclipsed in recent years by the advent of OLE, which I'll discuss later in this chapter.

The DDE mechanism allows two applications to carry on an invisible conversation with each other. One application acts as a server, offering data that might be useful to other applications. Client DDE applications request this useful data from the server application. (Here's that ubiquitous client/server concept again.) A network version of DDE, called NetDDE, allows the client and server applications to exist on two different computers. The ClipBook feature in Clipboard Viewer uses NetDDE to share and access ClipBook pages over the network. The Chat utility, discussed in Chapter 16, also uses NetDDE as its means of communication. NetDDE was first introduced in Windows for Workgroups and is available in all versions of Windows NT.

DDE and NetDDE are centered on sending and receiving data between applications, placing much of the burden of data-sharing details on the applications themselves. Since there's no standard way of implementing the user interface to DDE functions, each application takes a slightly different approach. So, you end up digging through the manuals of both applications to set up the conversation correctly. From a user's point of view, DDE isn't very intuitive to use.

Object Linking and Embedding

Windows NT supports Object Linking and Embedding, or OLE, to implement a model of data-sharing between documents. Unlike DDE, which is focused on transmitting data between applications, OLE is focused on creating functional links between documents (such as spreadsheets, charts, and word processing documents). For a user, OLE makes it easy to mix different pieces of data in a single document, even if those pieces are created and edited by a wide variety of applications.

Because OLE is now part of the operating system and is pervasive across so many applications, it's important to understand the basic concepts and capabilities of OLE on Windows NT Server (and Workstation). Both you and your users will need this foundation to make the most efficient use of this powerful feature.

If you don't fully understand OLE at first, you're in good company. Although it's designed to make life easier for users, the fact that the terms and concepts are so intertwined has made OLE one of the most difficult areas of Windows programming for software developers to master.

OLE CONVERGENCE

Microsoft originally considered OLE as an application technology, so the OLE development group was part of their Applications Division. As each new version of an application was developed, a new release of OLE was prepared. As a result, each version of every Microsoft application shipped with a slightly different version of OLE. For example, the OLE version that shipped with Word 6.0 was different from the one shipped with Excel 5.0. Because of this, customers reported incompatibilities between some versions and found that installing one application sometimes overwrote the OLE files that had been installed by an application already on their system. As a result, OLE got off to a slow start with both software developers and users.

OLE development and testing was finally brought under the operating system umbrella, in Microsoft's Systems Division. Microsoft made OLE an official part of both the Windows 95 and Windows NT operating systems, rather than an add-on that shipped with each application. Since then, OLE software releases and compatibility have become much more predictable, software developers have jumped on the bandwagon, and now most Windows document-centric applications support OLE. (The fact that Microsoft required OLE support as a prerequisite to earning the Windows 95 logo didn't hurt OLE's popularity either.)

Compound Documents

An OLE document is a *compound document*, containing any number of different types of data objects. A data object is a document or piece of a document that can be handled by a single application (for example, an Excel spreadsheet or a bitmap graphic image). Each data object is associated with an application that can edit and manipulate that object. Think of data objects as the building blocks of a compound document. Think of the applications as the tools used to modify those building blocks.

For example, you might have a Microsoft Word document that's really a compound document consisting of the Word document with several Excel spreadsheets, a few bar graphs, and a sound clip embedded in it. As you move through your compound document and attempt to edit a data object, you want the operating system to know which application you need to use for that object. You want it to start the right applications automatically so that you can edit each data object. You also want changes in the data underlying your bar graphs to be reflected in the graphs automatically. OLE makes all this possible.

The document in which a data object was originally created is known as a *source document.* In our example, source documents include spreadsheets, graphs, and sound clips. The document in which data objects are placed is called the *destination document.* Our example compound Word document is an instance of a destination document. Data objects from source documents can be embedded or linked into destination documents. (I'll describe the distinction between embedding and linking later in this chapter.) Figure 15-15 shows a simple example of a compound document.

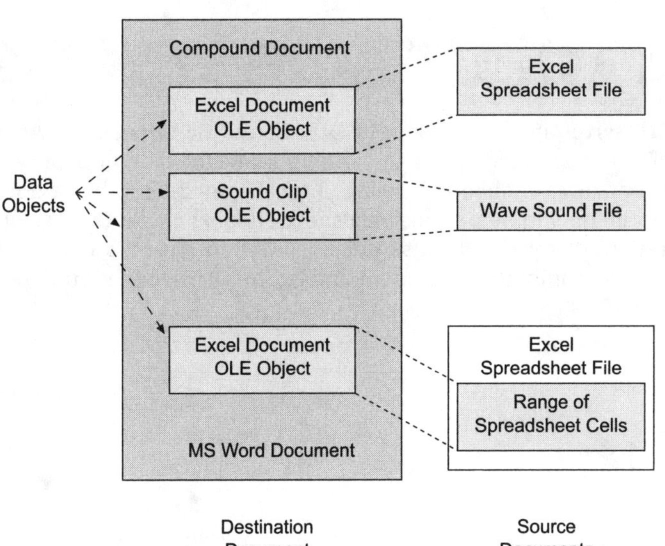

Figure 15-15: A compound document contains data objects of different types.

OLE Clients and Servers

Once again, another key component of Windows NT is implemented using a client/server approach. An *OLE server* application creates and edits an object that can be embedded or linked. An *OLE client* application accepts the object as part of a compound document.

In our example, Excel is one of the OLE servers (dealing with the embedded or linked spreadsheet object), and Word is the OLE client (accepting the spreadsheet as one of its compound document objects). An application can be both an OLE server and an OLE client. Microsoft Word is an example of both an OLE client and server, because you can also embed Word document objects in other types of documents.

Many applications and utilities can be only an OLE server or an OLE client, but not both. For example, since you can embed sound clips into documents, but you can't embed anything into a sound clip, the Sound Recorder utility is an OLE server but is never an OLE client. The Paint utility is in the same boat. Bitmaps can be embedded in other documents, but you can't embed other objects inside a bitmap. The Write application supplied in Windows NT 3.x acted only as an OLE client. It could deal with compound documents, but you couldn't embed a Write document into other documents.

Table 15-2 lists the built-in OLE objects in Windows NT Server 4.0. When you install other OLE-aware applications, the list grows. For example, installing Office 95 adds about 14 new OLE object types, depending on which optional components of Office you install.

HOW DOES AN OLE SERVER SERVE?

What service does an OLE server application offer to OLE clients? Good question. An OLE server provides the intelligence to create and operate on a particular type of data object. For example, Word can contain an embedded or linked Excel spreadsheet, but it doesn't have to know anything about how to deal with spreadsheets. It looks to the OLE server (in this case, Microsoft Excel) to worry about those details. All Word has to do is properly embed or link the object in its compound document and let the OLE server for that object do the rest.

Table 15-2
OLE Object Types and Their Associated OLE Server Applications

OLE Object Type	*OLE Server Application*
Bitmap Image	Paint
Image Document	Imaging
Media Clip	Media Player
MIDI Sequence	Media Player
Package	Object Packager
Paintbrush Picture	Paint
Video Clip	Media Player
Wave Sound	Sound Recorder
WordPad Document	WordPad

Of the OLE servers listed in Table 15-2, only WordPad can also act as an OLE client. You can insert any of the listed OLE objects into a WordPad document, including another WordPad document.

Embedded Objects

As its name implies, OLE can both link and embed objects in compound documents. It's important to understand the fundamental differences between linking and embedding.

An embedded object is the simpler of the two. When you embed an object, the object exists only within the compound document. The entire object is contained within the larger document file and doesn't exist elsewhere. In this case, OLE simply keeps track of the link to the application used to edit the object. Figure 15-16 illustrates this concept.

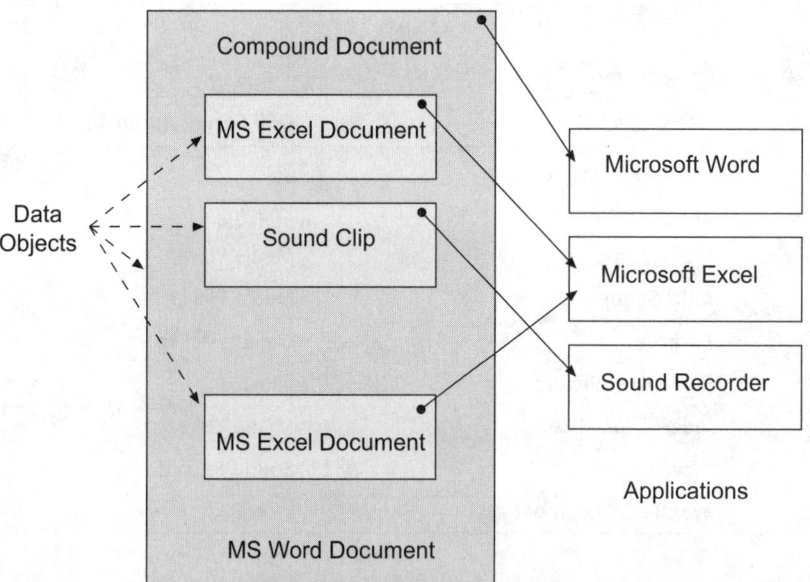

Figure 15-16: An embedded object is completely contained within the compound document, with a pointer to its associated application.

Let's say that your compound Word document contains an embedded Excel spreadsheet. OLE will let you edit the spreadsheet within the document, since it knows that Excel is associated with the embedded object. However, the spreadsheet doesn't exist as a separate .XLS file. It's completely contained within the compound Word document file.

Embedding an Object

To embed an object into a compound document, you typically perform the following steps:

1. Open the source document using the appropriate OLE server application.

   For example, open a spreadsheet file using Microsoft Excel.

   Refer to your application documentation to determine if it can function as an OLE server application. If it can't, you won't be able to embed documents created by the application.

2. Open the destination document using the appropriate OLE client application.

   For example, open a document file using Microsoft Word. The Word document will become a compound document as soon as you embed an object into it.

   Refer to your application documentation to determine if it can function as an OLE client (that is, it can deal with compound documents). If it can't, the object that you embed will be copied, and you won't be able to edit it.

3. In the source document, select the portion of the document that you want to embed. On the Edit menu, click Copy.

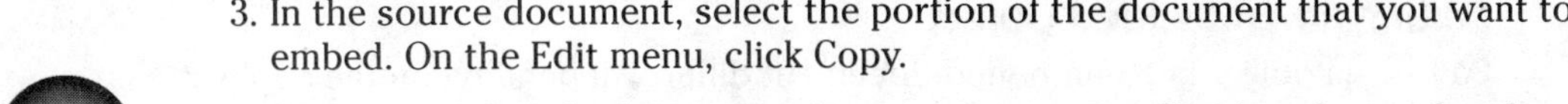

If you want to embed an entire document, many applications have a handy Select All command on the Edit menu.

4. In the destination document, position the cursor at the location where you want the object embedded.

5. On the Edit menu of the destination application, click Paste.

Some applications provide an alternative way of embedding objects. If the application has an Insert menu, check to see if there's an Object command on it. If there is, click it to see a list of all the data object types available on your computer. (The list will include the items shown in Table 15-2, as well as others registered by applications that you've installed since.) You can create a new object from scratch or pull in an object from a source document. When you exit, the object is inserted into the destination document. Look at the WordPad Insert menu for an example of this. (To start WordPad, click Start ➪ Programs ➪ Accessories ➪ WordPad.) Figures 15-17 and 15-18 illustrate the Insert Object dialog box in WordPad.

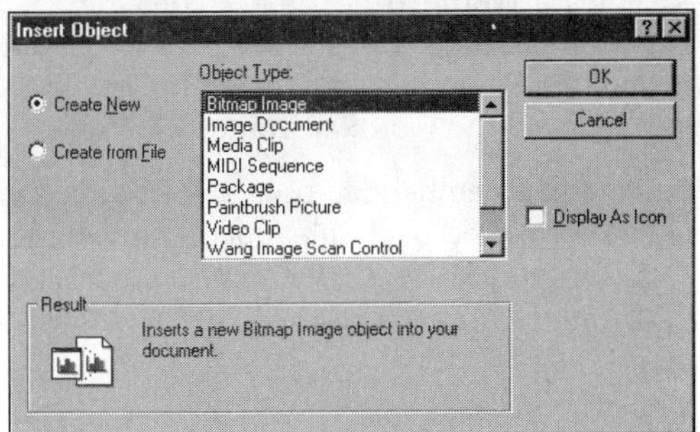

Figure 15-17: Insert ➪ Object enables you to create a new object of any OLE object type and embed it.

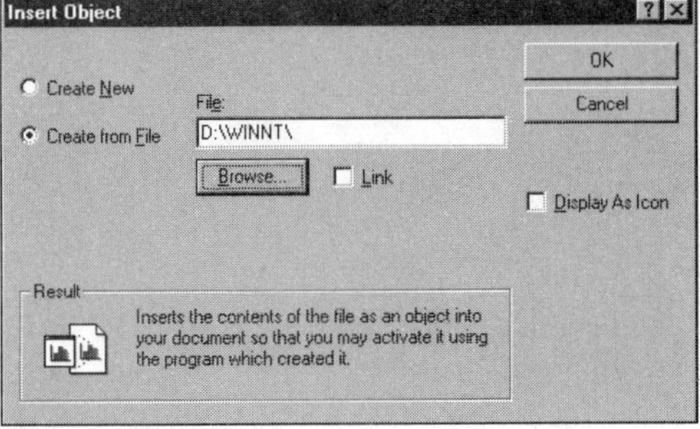

Figure 15-18: Insert ➪ Object also enables you to embed an existing object.

If you want to embed an entire file in your destination document and you're comfortable using Windows NT Explorer, you can drag file objects directly from Explorer and drop them into your destination document.

Editing an Embedded Object

Editing an object in a compound document differs, depending on the applications involved. In many cases, you can just double-click the embedded object, edit the object using the source application that's automatically started, and press ESC when you're done. Try this approach first. If it works, it's the easiest way to edit embedded objects.

In other applications, you may need to put the program into a special edit mode using a command on the Edit menu. Still others have a command on the Edit menu specifically for editing certain types of embedded objects. Refer to your application documentation for details on how to edit embedded objects.

MAGICAL MORPHS

If the applications with which you're working are compliant with the OLE 2.x specification, something almost magical occurs when NT starts the source application. Rather than seeing a new application window, the menus and tool bars of your current application "morph" (or change) into those of the source application. This behavior is known as *in-place editing*. For example, Figure 15-19 shows a WordPad document containing some embedded bitmaps. If you double-click one of the bitmaps, you still see the WordPad window, but the menus and tool bars are those of the Paint utility, as shown in Figure 15-20. When you're done editing the bitmap, press ESC and the WordPad controls reappear.

In the days of OLE 1.x, when you attempted to edit an embedded object, the source application started in a separate window. This behavior still occurs if the application with which you're working hasn't been updated to OLE 2.x compliance. Of the applications listed in Table 15-2, only Object Packager still acts like an OLE 1.x application. The rest have OLE 2.x behavior.

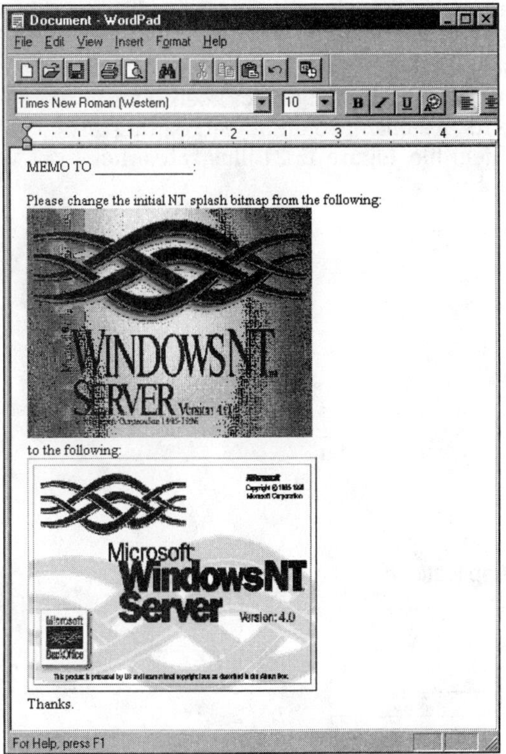

Figure 15-19: In WordPad, you can double-click an embedded object to edit it.

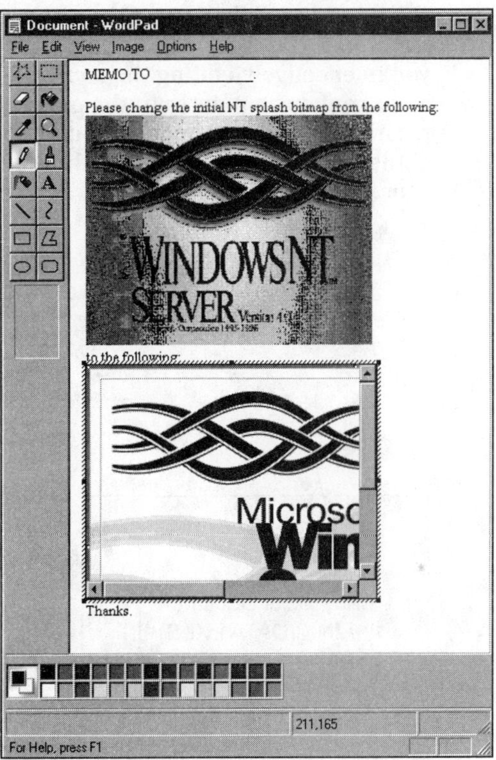

Figure 15-20: OLE 2.x in-place editing changes the menus and tool bars of WordPad to those of Paint, ready for bitmap editing.

Linking Objects

When you link an object into a compound document, the object appears to be the same as an embedded object. However, the object doesn't actually exist inside the compound document. It exists as a separate source document file. So, in this situation, there are two files instead of one — the compound document containing the link to the object and the separate data object (in the source document) to which the link points.

You can edit a linked object by either editing the source document or by editing the object (the link) within the compound document. When you do the latter, you're effectively editing the source document. Internally, the compound document contains a pointer to the object, rather than the actual object itself. Thus, regardless of how many compound documents are linked to an object, editing any of them is the same as editing the source object file. Figure 15-21 illustrates the concept of object linking.

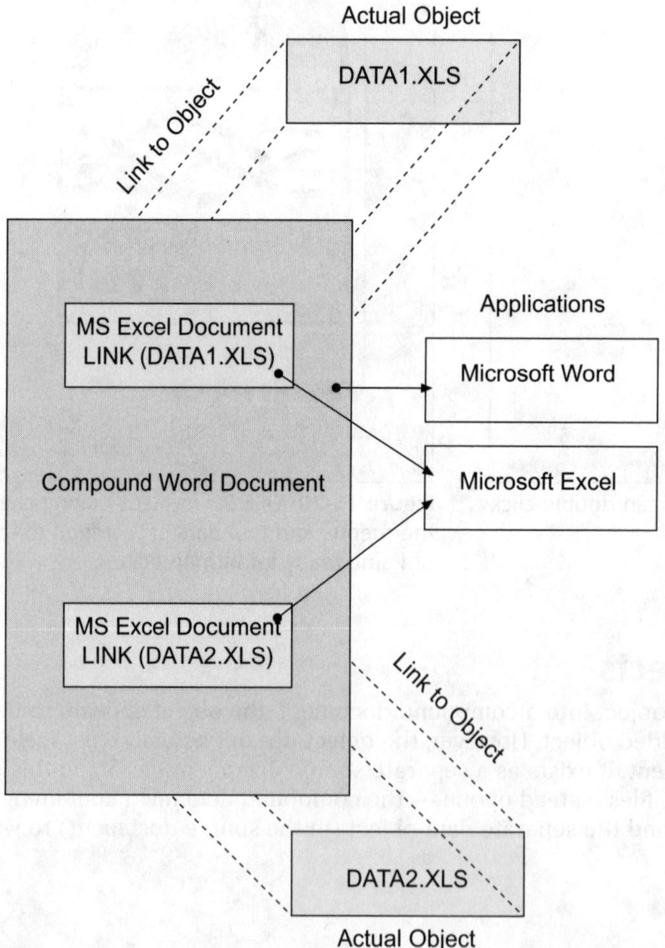

Figure 15-21: A linked data object is really just a pointer to the actual object, which exists as a separate file.

Let's say that your compound Word document contains a linked Excel spreadsheet. OLE will let you edit the spreadsheet within the document, since it knows that Excel is associated with the linked object. You can also use Excel to edit the separate .XLS file. Regardless of which one you edit, you're effectively changing the source document .XLS file. What's more, all other documents that have links to this spreadsheet file are automatically updated to reflect subsequent changes.

Because an OLE link points to an actual file, the source document must be saved to disk before you attempt to link it in a destination document. If you don't save the source document file first, the link operation won't work.

Linking an Object

To link an object into a compound document, you typically perform the following steps:

1. Open the source document using the appropriate OLE server application.

   For example, open a spreadsheet file using Microsoft Excel.

   Refer to your application documentation to determine if it can function as an OLE server. If it can't, you won't be able to link documents created by the application.

2. Open the destination document using the appropriate OLE client application.

   For example, open a document file using Microsoft Word. The Word document will become a compound document as soon as you link an object into it.

   Refer to your application documentation to determine if it can function as an OLE client (that is, it can deal with compound documents). If it can't, the object that you attempt to link will be copied, and you won't be able to edit it.

3. Select the portion of the document that you want to link. On the Edit menu, click Copy.

4. In the destination document, position the cursor at the location where you want the object linked.

5. On the Edit menu of the destination application, click Paste Special.

   If your destination application doesn't support OLE linking, you won't see a Paste Special command on the Edit menu.

6. Click to select Paste Link, then click the format that you want to use.

If your application has an Object command on its Insert menu, you can use it to link objects. In the Insert Object dialog box, click Create from File, type the name of the source document, and click to select the Link check box. Then click OK. See Figure 15-18.

Editing a Linked Object

Editing a linked object in a compound document is similar to editing an embedded object, although there are some key differences. The most important difference is that all destination documents with links to the source document being edited are affected by those changes. Perform the following steps to edit a linked object:

1. Double-click the linked object.

   NT starts the source application in a separate window.

   In other applications, you may need to put the program into a special edit mode using a command on the Edit menu. Still others have a command on the Edit menu specifically for editing certain types of linked objects. Refer to your application documentation for details on how to edit linked objects.

2. Edit the object as desired.

Remember that when you edit a linked object, you're effectively editing the actual source document file. All of the changes that you make will be immediately reflected in every destination document that has a link to the source document being edited. This is a powerful capability. Just be sure it's what you want to do. If you decide that you don't want to change the source document, exit the source application without saving.

3. On the File menu, click Save. Then, again on the File menu, click Exit.

   It's important that you save your changes before exiting the source application. Otherwise, the changes will be lost.

WHAT HAPPENED TO IN-PLACE EDITING?

When you edit a linked object, it may appear that you're seeing OLE 1.x behavior, because NT starts the source application in a separate window. However, this is how OLE 2.x behaves when dealing with linked objects. You're actually editing the source document itself, not the destination document that contains the link. So, it makes sense that you now have two different application windows going.

Controlling Link Updates

Many OLE applications enable you to manage linked objects within compound documents. If the application has a Links command on the Edit menu, you can access the Links dialog box, as shown in Figure 15-22.

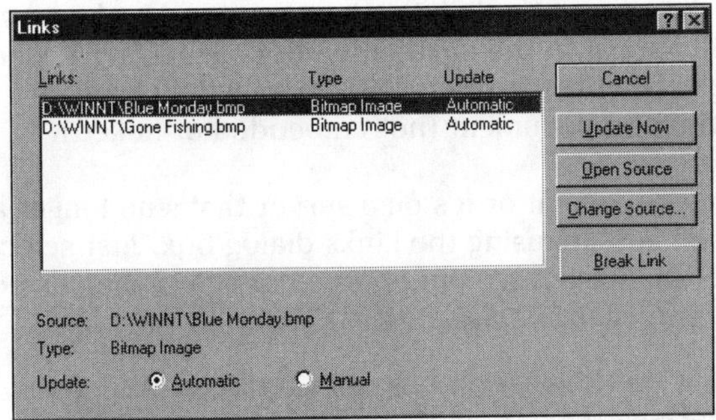

Figure 15-22: The Links dialog box enables you to manage linked objects within a compound document.

By default, all linked objects are updated automatically in destination documents. You may, however, want to control when changes actually show up in these documents. For example, if you're making a change to a source document over a period of several days, you may want to defer reflecting any updates in destination documents until you're done with all of the changes. To defer reflecting source document updates in a destination document, you need to complete the following steps:

1. Open the destination document. On the Edit menu, click Links.
2. In the Links dialog box, select the link that you want to control.

   You can select more than one link by holding down CTRL while you click to select each additional link.
3. Click to select Manual. Then click the Close button in the upper right corner of the window.

   No updates to the objects set to manual will be reflected in this destination document until you later click Update Now. You can restore automatic updating later by clicking to select the Automatic option.

If you don't want any destination documents to reflect the changes that you're making to your source document, you'll have to perform this procedure for every destination document that has a link to your source document.

Breaking and Repairing Object Links

In the previous section, you learned how to defer updates to a destination document when changes occurred in a source document. This approach is designed to disable automatic updates, but only temporarily.

If you no longer want to reflect object updates in a destination document, use the Links dialog box to break the link. Select the link that you want to break and click Break Link. The object will still appear in the destination document, but it won't be updated and you'll no longer be able to edit it. The object will behave as if it had been pasted into the destination document (not embedded or linked).

If you move or rename a source document or it's on a server that's no longer available, you can repair a broken object link using the Links dialog box. Just select the link in need of repair, click the Change Source option, type or select the correct path to the source document, and click OK. See Figure 15-22.

Linking and Embedding Packages

Let's say that you're creating a compound document that's primarily designed to be read online. You want to include some supplementary information in the document, which the readers can view at their option. Ideally, you want just an icon to appear in the document. If readers choose to double-click the icon, they'll see the additional information. Perhaps you want to insert an icon into a document which, when double-clicked, runs an application or batch file. You can use object packages to accomplish these goals.

Creating a Package from a File

To create a package containing a file (which could be a document, application, batch file, or other item), perform the following steps:

1. Click Start ➪ Programs ➪ Accessories ➪ Object Packager. In Object Packager, click the Content window. Figure 15-23 shows this.

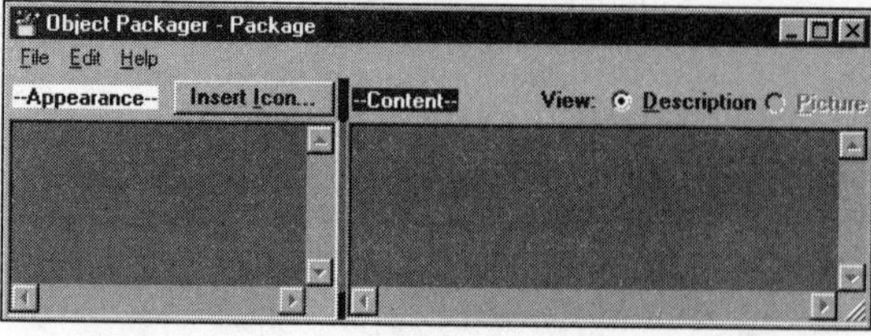

Figure 15-23: Object Packager enables you to create packages to be embedded in destination documents.

2. On the File menu, click Import. In the Import window, select the file that you want to package, then click Open.

The filename appears in the Content window, and the associated icon appears in the Appearance window, as shown in Figure 15-24. In this case, the package contains an application.

If you want, you can change the package's icon to something else by clicking Insert Icon, making the change, and clicking OK. You can also change the text under the icon. On the Edit menu, choose the Label option, type the new text, and click OK.

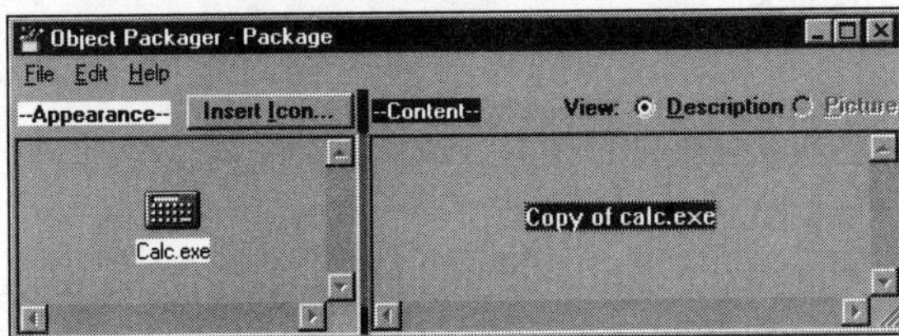

Figure 15-24: After you select a file to package, Object Packager shows the appearance and content of the package.

It's a good idea to change the text under the icon to something that will be meaningful to the reader of the destination document. Unless the icon is fully self-explanatory (rarely true) or the text in the destination document surrounding the icon will make it clear what's inside, a brief instructional statement is usually best. In the example in Figure 15-24, you might change the text from "Calc.exe" to "Click here to calculate."

3. On the Edit menu, click Copy Package.

   This action places the object package on the Clipboard. Use of the Clipboard was described earlier in this chapter.

4. Open the destination document using the appropriate OLE client application.

   Refer to your application documentation to determine if it can function as an OLE client (that is, it can deal with compound documents).

5. In the destination document, position the cursor at the location where you want the package embedded.

6. On the destination's Edit menu, click Paste.

   The package appears in the destination document as an icon. When you double-click the icon, the appropriate application will start.

When you double-click a package icon, different things occur, depending on the contents of the package. If it contains a sound or video file, the sound or video will play immediately. If the package contains a picture, text, spreadsheet, word processing document, or other object, the application associated with that object will start, allowing you to view and edit the document. For example, if the package contains a Word document, Word will start. Finally, if the package contains an executable file, that application will start immediately when the icon is double-clicked.

SAVE YOURSELF SOME LEGWORK

This can be a great way to make batch file changes on your users' computers or to send them patches and updates to overcome specific problems that they encounter. Assuming that your e-mail application understands OLE, you can send a batch file inside a package. When your users double-click the package icon, your batch file can connect to a central server, download files, update local standard batch files, and so forth. This can increase efficiency and accuracy. It sure beats sending out detailed instructions to everyone or visiting their computers to make the changes.

Creating a Packaged Command Line

You can create a package containing a command line that executes when the user double-clicks this icon. The command line can start a batch program or start another application. If you can type it in a Command Prompt window, you can package it and distribute it.

1. Click Start ➪ Programs ➪ Accessories ➪ Object Packager.
2. On the Edit menu, click Command Line. In the Command Line window, type a command line, including the full path, file extension, options, and parameters. When you're done, click OK.

   The command line appears in the Content window.
3. Click Insert Icon, select an icon to represent the command line, and click OK.

   You can also change the text under the icon. On the Edit menu, click Label, type the new text, and click OK.
4. On the Edit menu, click Copy Package.

   This action places the object package on the Clipboard. Use of the Clipboard was described earlier in this chapter.
5. Open the destination document using the appropriate OLE client application. In the destination document, position the cursor at the location where you want the command line package embedded.
6. On the destination's Edit menu, click Paste.

   The package appears in the destination document as an icon. In some applications, the package is automatically placed in the upper left corner of the document. When you double-click the icon, the appropriate command line will run.

As with any powerful feature, this one can also be dangerous. If your batch file deletes or replaces files, make sure that you know exactly how the program will behave in the wide variety of environments in which it might run. Be sure that you fully test the program in different environments before releasing it to all your users.

Creating a Package from a Document Fragment

If you want to create a package containing only part of a document (say, just a paragraph from a word processing file), you can do so using the following steps:

1. Open the source document using the appropriate OLE server application. Select the portion of the document that you want to link or embed. On the Edit menu, click Copy.

   Refer to your application documentation to determine if it can function as an OLE server application.

2. Click Start ➪ Programs ➪ Accessories ➪ Object Packager. Click the Content window.

3. On the Edit menu, click Paste (to embed the object) or Paste Link (to link to the object).

   For a description of the differences between embedding and linking, see sections earlier in this chapter.

   You can change the package's icon to something else by clicking Insert Icon, making the change, and clicking OK. You can also change the text under the icon. On the Edit menu, click Label, type the new text, and click OK.

4. On the Edit menu, click Copy Package.

   This action places the object package on the Clipboard. Use of the Clipboard is described earlier in this chapter.

5. Open the destination document using the appropriate OLE client application. Position the cursor at the location where you want the package to be linked or embedded.

6. On the destination's Edit menu, click Paste.

   The package appears in the destination document as an icon. In some applications, the package is automatically placed in the upper left corner of the document.

You can always right-click any embedded or linked object or package to find out about its properties. Right-click the object and then click Object Properties. In some cases, you can even change the view of the object within the document and convert the object to a different format. Figures 15-25 and 15-26 illustrate this.

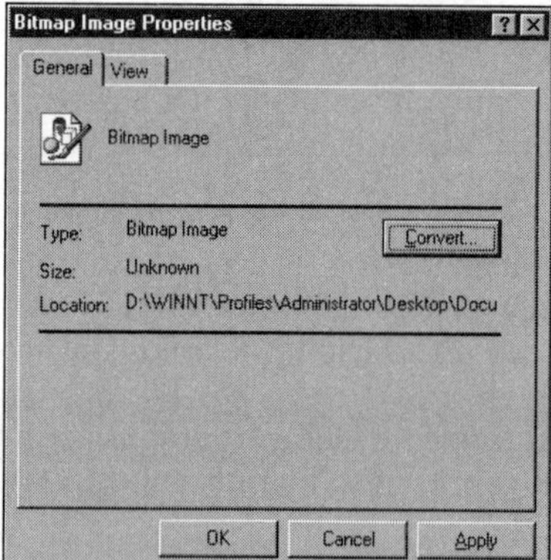

Figure 15-25: The General tab provides basic information about the object and enables you to change the format in some cases.

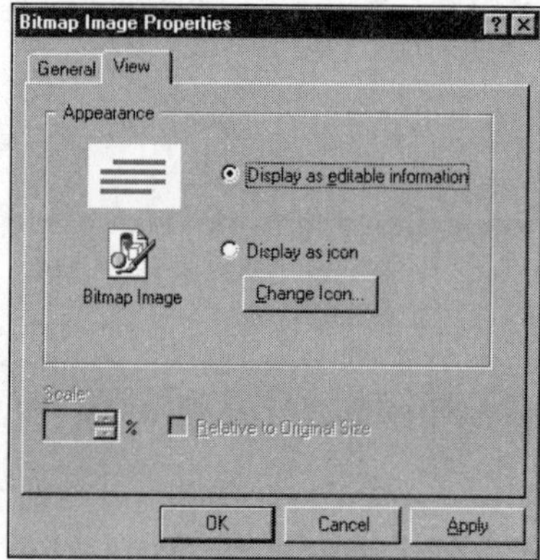

Figure 15-26: The View tab enables you to switch between icon and object views and to change the displayed size in some cases.

OLE and the Network

If you plan to use OLE links across the network, you need to be aware of a few issues, so that you know what to expect and can let your users know what to expect.

Creating ClipBook Links

As I discussed earlier, sharing ClipBook pages over the network is one way to share information with other users. Once you get a page on your local Clipboard, you can embed it or link it using the techniques covered in this chapter.

If you paste a link into your destination document, you're actually linking to the remote ClipBook page. If that shared page changes, so will your document. When attempting to edit an OLE object that you've linked this way, you'll need to make sure that the destination computer can run the appropriate OLE server application, either locally or over the network. Otherwise, you won't be able to edit the object.

BETTER NETWORK OLE

As mentioned in Chapter 4, Windows NT Server 4.0 includes DCOM (short for Distributed Component Object Model), formerly known as Network OLE. You won't really see anything different when using DCOM. Having it present, however, will enable software developers to create robust, distributed applications based on OLE. Under the covers, DCOM uses RPC, caching of objects, and other techniques to create a reliable approach to OLE over the network. Application developers will need to incorporate these features before you see the benefits of this technology. At the time of this writing, versions of DCOM for Windows 95 and the Macintosh are planned for release within six months to a year after Windows NT 4.0 is released.

Creating Remote File Links

You can create OLE links that point to drives on other computers. As long as the remote computer is running and you always assign its share point to the same drive letter, this approach will work. Again, the computer on which the destination document resides must be able to run the appropriate OLE server application, if you plan to edit the OLE object.

If the remote computer is down, the share point is no longer available, or the network itself is down, you'll get some nasty error messages when you attempt to access a linked object. Your options are to keep trying or to try again later. Neither is a good solution, if you're racing against the clock to complete a project.

OLE and NT Security

It's important to keep in mind, especially when distributing document components across the network, that Windows NT Server security is enforced on each file, directory, ClipBook page, and so on. When you begin to create complex documents with pieces living on different servers, you'll invariably run into access problems due to restrictive permissions on a critical piece of your document.

To implement a safe, practical security policy for each project, first carefully plan and communicate among the owners of the various components. Planning ahead will prevent panicked calls when someone doesn't have permission to access a document fragment that they need.

OLE and Down-Level Clients

To edit a compound document, you need enough memory resources to run not only the client OLE application, but also all the OLE server applications associated with objects in your document. This isn't a huge issue on Windows NT Server, since the computer typically has plenty of available RAM.

However, keep in mind that down-level clients such as Windows 3.x may not have the resources to work with a very complex compound document. You may end up creating documents that can't be edited or viewed on down-level computers on your network.

Directory Replication

Another powerful approach to sharing and distributing data uses a feature of Windows NT Server 4.0 called directory replication. You may recall replication from Chapters 7 and 10, mentioned in the context of PDCs keeping BDCs up to date by replicating their domain user account databases. Well, NT Server enables you to use this capability in a much more general way.

Data Duplication Drudgery

If you've had some experience as a network administrator, you know that duplicating data between servers is a common requirement. You may need to distribute the server load, because too many users are accessing a single server, or you may need to provide access to the same data across different domains. Regardless of the reason, you often end up writing specialized batch files or programs to accomplish the task. Even when your approach is designed to handle network errors, disk space problems, and other traps, the data is almost always out of sync unless your program runs constantly.

One important and common use for directory replication is distribution of logon scripts between domain controllers. I'll discuss this topic in Chapter 18.

NT Server's directory replication feature handles all of the details for you and keeps directories on different computers up to date whenever a change is made to the master directory. When computers or networks go down, NT knows how to get back in sync as soon as the systems are available again. It even removes deleted files and creates new subdirectories to match the master directory.

NT's directory replication doesn't remove subdirectories when they're deleted from the master directory being replicated. However, all deleted files within directories are removed automatically from the replicated directory trees.

The Export/Import Business of Replication

Establishing directory replication is a fairly straightforward process. First, you determine which directories on which servers contain data that you need to replicate to other computers. You then designate computers running Windows NT Server as *export servers,* from which data will be copied. Finally, you identify computers running either NT Server or NT Workstation as *import computers,* to which data will be copied. Figure 15-27 illustrates the replication possibilities.

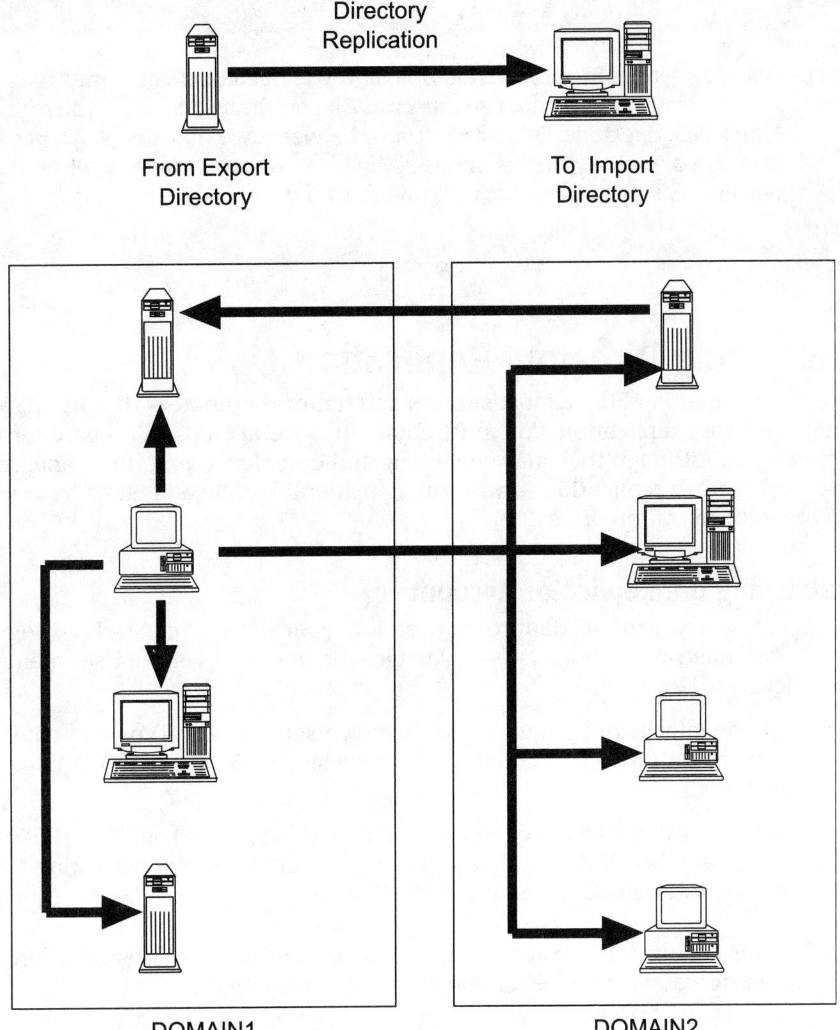

Figure 15-27: Directory replication can keep directories on multiple computers in sync.

The default export directory on export servers is SystemRoot\SYSTEM32\REPL\EXPORT. On import computers, the default import directory is SystemRoot\SYSTEM32\REPL\IMPORT. Both directories are created automatically when you install Windows NT Server, since a computer running NT Server can be both an exporter and importer of replicated data.

INTER-DOMAIN REPLICATION

To replicate between servers in two different domains, you need to create a trust relationship between them. The importing domain must trust the exporting domain. If you're going

to replicate directories in both directions between two domains, you'll need to establish a two-way trust relationship between them. It's best to set up these relationships before attempting to perform directory replication. See Chapter 10 for details.

Configuring Directory Replication

Once you've identified the export servers and import computers that will participate in directory replication, you must complete several steps to prepare for actual replication. Although they may seem long and complex at first, their final result — quick directory replication — will trim considerable time and effort from your network administration duties.

Establishing the Replicator Account

1. Create a new user account to be used for replication. Click Start ➪ Programs ➪ Administrative Tools ➪ User Manager for Domains. On the User menu, click New User.
2. Type the information required for the new user account. Type and confirm a password for the new account. Click to select the Password Never Expires check box.

Don't forget this password. You'll need it again in step 10. In Figure 15-28, the account is called DIRREPL. For more detailed information on creating user accounts, see Chapter 18.

A natural name for this account is Replicator, but you can't use this because NT has already used it as a built-in local group name.

Figure 15-28: Create a directory replicator user account in each domain that will perform replication.

3. Click Hours and enable the account to log on at any time on any day. Then click OK, as shown in Figure 15-29.

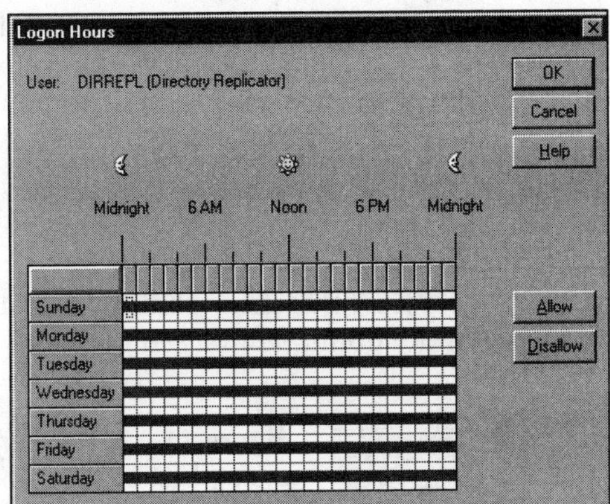

Figure 15-29: Assure that the directory replicator account can log on at any time.

4. Click Groups. Under Not member of, click Backup Operators. Click Add to add Backup Operators under Member of. Then click OK. See Figure 15-30.

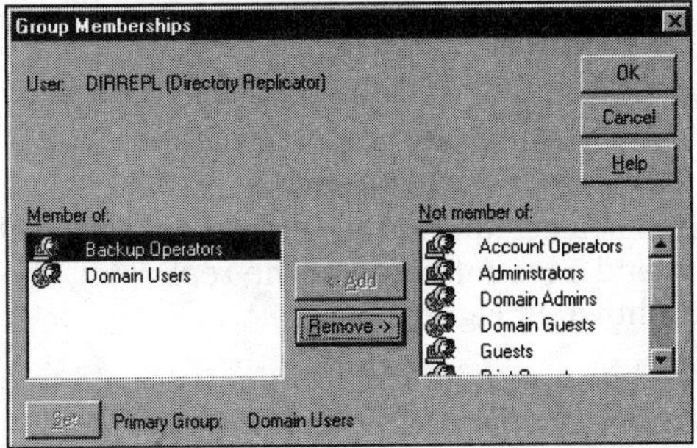

Figure 15-30: Make the directory replicator account a member of the Backup Operators group.

5. In the New User dialog box, click Add. Then click Close. See Figure 15-28.

   The new account that you created is listed in the upper half of the User Manager window.

6. Repeat steps 1 through 5 for each domain that will participate in directory replication.

Starting the Replicator Service

7. Click Start ➪ Programs ➪ Administrative Tools ➪ Server Manager.

8. Select the computer on which you want to start the replicator service. On the Computer menu, click Services.

The Services dialog box is covered in detail in Chapter 17.

You can also get to the Services dialog box through the Control Panel. Click Start ➪ Settings ➪ Control Panel and double-click the Services icon. I've taken you the Server Manager route because you'll likely need to start the replicator service on multiple computers. It's more convenient to do this from Server Manager.

9. In the Service list, select Directory Replicator and click Startup, as shown in Figure 15-31.

   Unless you've already started this service, the entry should have nothing in its Status column. The Startup column should be marked Manual.

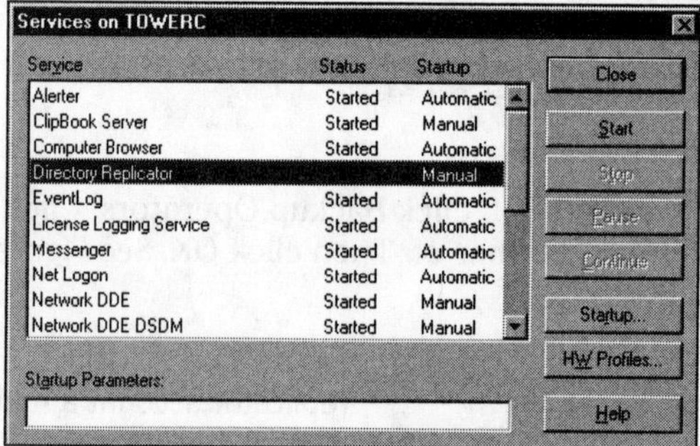

Figure 15-31: The Services dialog box enables you to start the replicator service.

10. Under Startup Type, click to select Automatic. Under Log On As, click This Account. Type the domain and account name of the replicator account that you specified in step 2, as shown in Figure 15-32.

To save typing, you can click the button to the right of the text field to browse through a list of accounts. Select the account name that you specified in step 2 and click Add.

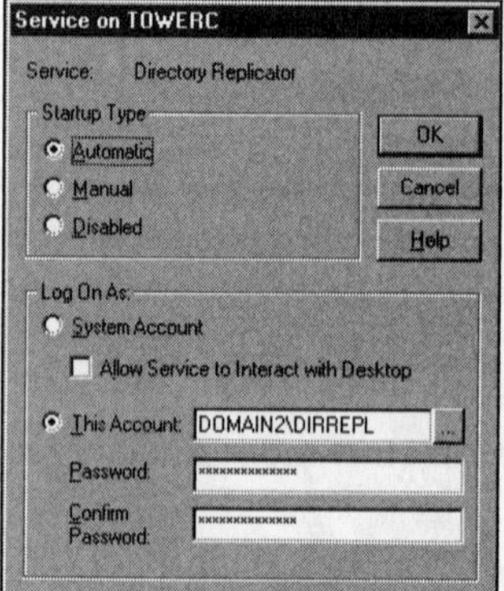

Figure 15-32: Set the replicator service to start automatically and to use the replicator account that you created.

11. Type and confirm the password that you specified in step 2. Click OK.

    You'll see either the message shown in Figure 15-33 or an error message. If you see an error complaining about an invalid or nonexistent account, verify that you typed the domain name, account name, and both passwords correctly.

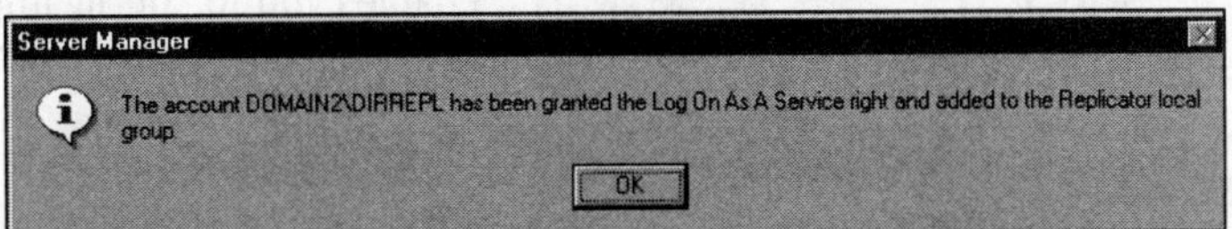

Figure 15-33: This message indicates that the replicator service started successfully.

12. Click OK. In the Services dialog box, select Directory Replicator again. Click the Start button in the Services dialog box.

    You'll see a message indicating that NT is attempting to start the service. When it's done, you'll be back at the Services dialog box. The Status column for the Directory Replicator service should now be changed to Started.

13. Click Close to return to the Server Manager window.

14. While still running Server Manager, repeat steps 8 through 13 for each computer that will be an export server or import computer participating in directory replication.

Establishing Export Servers

15. While still running Server Manager, double-click a computer that will act as an export server.

    This action displays the Properties dialog box, shown in Figure 15-34. Remember that all export servers must be running Windows NT Server.

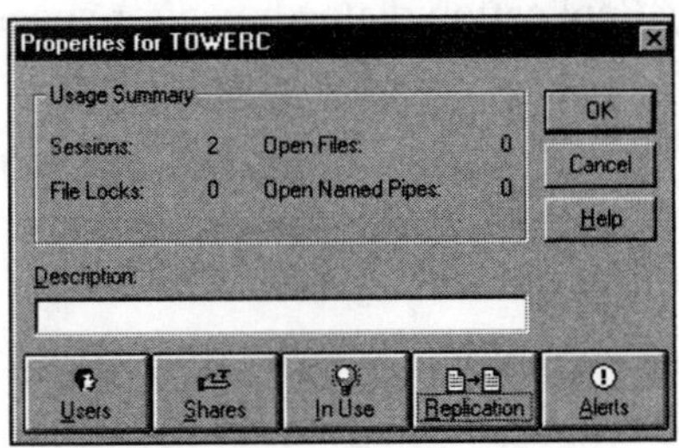

Figure 15-34: Use the Properties dialog box to configure several features, including replication.

16. In the Properties dialog box, click Replication. In the Directory Replication dialog box, click Export Directories. See Figure 15-35.

Although I recommend using the default export directory, you're given the opportunity to specify a different one here.

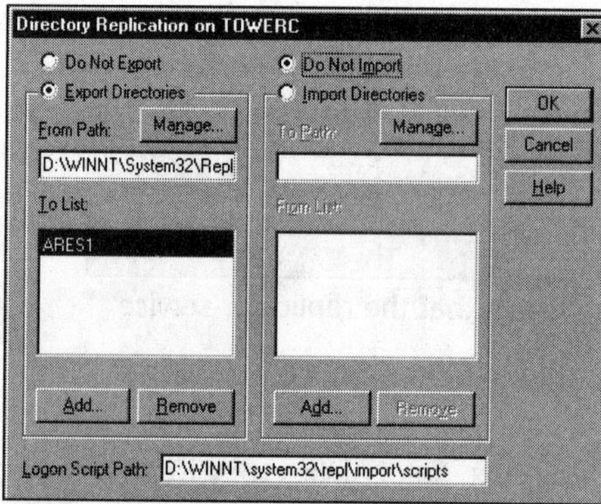

Figure 15-35: The Directory Replication dialog box for NT Server enables you to specify import computers and export servers.

17. Under Export Directories, click Add. In the Select Domain dialog box, type or select the domain name and computer name of an import computer that will accept replicated data from this export server. Click OK.

You can specify an entire domain, instead of individual computers, if you want every computer in the domain to act as an import server for replicated data from this export server. However, you'll have to configure each computer in the import domain as an import computer. See the next section in this chapter for details.

If your domains are connected via a WAN, replication to an entire domain may not work properly. To ensure that replication will work across the WAN, explicitly configure your export server to replicate to each import computer in the remote domain.

18. Repeat step 17 for each import computer that will receive replicated data from this export server. When you're done, click OK.

    Figure 15-35 shows the Directory Replication dialog box after specifying \\ARES1 as an import computer.

19. Repeat steps 15 through 18 for each export server participating in directory replication.

Establishing Import Computers

20. While still running Server Manager, double-click a computer that will act as an import computer.

    This action displays the Properties dialog box, shown in Figure 15-34. Import computers must be running either Windows NT Server or Windows NT Workstation.

21. In the Properties dialog box, click Replication. In the Directory Replication dialog box, click Import Directories.

    If you're configuring a Windows NT Workstation as an import computer, the Directory Replication dialog box will appear as shown in Figure 15-36. If you're configuring an NT Server computer, you'll see the dialog box in Figure 15-35.

    Although I recommend using the default import directory, you're given the opportunity to specify a different one here.

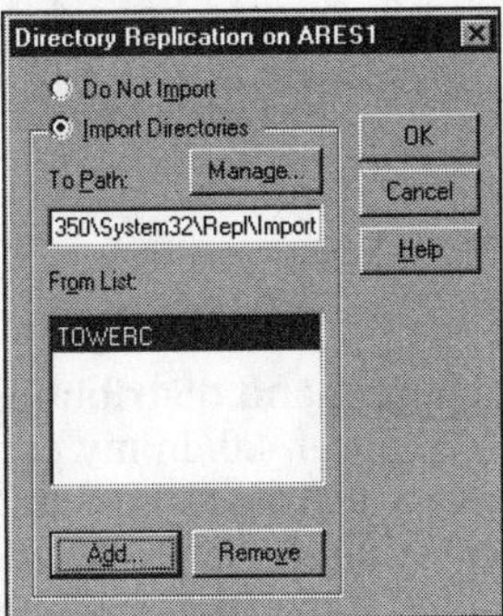

Figure 15-36: The Directory Replication dialog box for NT Workstation enables you to specify export servers.

22. Under Import Directories, click Add. In the Select Domain dialog box, type or select the domain name and computer name of an export server that will send replicated data to this import computer. Click OK.

23. Repeat step 22 for each export server that will send replicated data to this import computer. When you're done, click OK.

24. Repeat steps 20 through 23 for each import computer participating in directory replication.

Performing a Replication Test

25. Select an export server and import computer to participate in the replication test.

    You'll need to determine a policy governing who has access to the export directories on your export server. Set the directory permissions accordingly. See Chapter 18 for details on setting permissions.

26. Set up NT Explorer to view the contents of the import directory on the import computer.

27. Copy a few test files into the export directory on the export server.

Files are never replicated until they're closed. As long as a file is open, it will sit in the export directory and won't be copied. As soon as a file is closed, it's scheduled for replication.

28. Create a new subdirectory in the export directory.
29. Wait for a few minutes.

    After a short while, you should see the files and directories copied from the export server to the import computer's import directory. Once the initial replication is complete, updates will arrive on the import computers within minutes of their arrival in the export directory.

And now you're in the data replication business! You'll no longer need to write complex scripts and schedule them to run periodically, just to keep copies of files on various servers up to date or distribute data. Simply put the files in an export directory, sit back, and watch the data fly.

Summary

In this chapter, you've seen a few approaches to sharing and distributing data between applications and users using Windows NT Server 4.0. In my experience, many users are unaware of the capabilities offered by features like ClipBook and OLE. By learning these concepts and skills, you can share your knowledge with them to increase their productivity. As a network administrator, you need to be aware of the implications of using these technologies on your network.

In Chapter 16, I'll cover the groupware features provided with Windows NT 4.0, allowing users to communicate with each other in various ways over the network. The concepts that you've learned in the last two chapters will carry into Chapter 16, as we harness the user interface and data-sharing features to make user-to-user communication more effective.

INSIDE STORY

"Is it soup yet?" "Isn't it ready yet?" "Are we there yet?" The e-mail and phone calls poured in from Microsoft people in every corner of the NT project. They were champing at the bit for the latest NT build to use and test in their various areas of endeavor. In response to all this clamoring, the software build crew seemed to almost always answer "No" or "Just 1000 more files to go." With the huge number of people waiting for the daily NT build and constantly requesting status, it's a wonder that the build team ever got their real work done.

The NT software build team relied on directory replication to distribute the NT group's installation share points across many servers. If they had put only one copy of the files on a single server, the feeding frenzy of 600 people trying to copy every file would have been a network disaster. Each platform (Intel, MIPS, Alpha, and PowerPC) required more than 3,000 files to be copied. So, even with directory replication, it still took a few minutes to push all that data around the network.

Finally, after the latest build distribution was complete, a one-line e-mail would appear in over 600 mailboxes simultaneously. "It's soup."

Communicating and Collaborating with NT Server

I'm sure that you have your own opinion about electronic mail and chatting. Depending on whom you ask, you'll hear online communication described as either a great blessing or an odious scourge. Some folks change their opinions over time, as their use of e-mail evolves from dealing only with relevant information to wading through reams of trivia to get at the "good stuff." One supporter touts e-mail as the key to the paperless office, while his colleague down the hall prints a copy of every message he receives "for his files." Whatever your opinion of e-mail, you have to face the fact that it has been shown to increase productivity in offices with as few as 10 users. Electronic communication is an indisputable part of modern life, like it or not.

If used properly, e-mail and electronic chatting can improve communication, provide a very efficient and effective way to distribute information, and help solicit timely responses. Speaking with someone directly on the telephone is the most efficient way to get a response, but what if the line is busy, the person is out of the office, or just isn't answering due to higher-priority activities? Voice mail is a reasonable alternative, but it has been shown to be about half as effective as e-mail at soliciting a timely response. In addition, electronic chat programs can be effective in getting someone's direct attention when telephone tactics don't work. As a result, some businesses install a computer network just to reap the benefits of an e-mail system.

Many businesses today (perhaps including yours) use e-mail as their primary means of communication, and e-mail applications are the most commonly used tools on their networks. Microsoft Corporation is a prime example of this. Yes, they have meetings, occasional printed memos, a company newsletter, faxes, and voice mail. However, ask just about anyone in the company who has to communicate with others, and they'll point to e-mail as their primary tool. It's employed with equal frequency in international communication and collaboration within small workgroups.

In this chapter, you'll find out about the electronic communication tools provided with Windows NT Server 4.0 and how to implement them on your network. You'll learn about NT's e-mail options, including Microsoft Mail and Microsoft Exchange. You'll see that messaging capabilities reach beyond e-mail text to a world of electronic forms, group scheduling, and project management. You'll also discover the handy Chat utility included in the NT operating system. As you go along, you'll pick up some pointers on how to administer these components and assist your users in getting the most out of these powerful tools.

Windows NT Messaging

Starting with Windows 95 and Windows NT 4.0, Microsoft has chosen to call their communication technology *Windows Messaging*. Windows Messaging goes beyond sending text messages back and forth between users. You can embed, transmit, and receive documents, images, sounds, video clips, and so forth. (See Chapter 15 for details on embedding OLE objects.) With appropriate client software, you can perform efficient group scheduling, project management, and organization of your own busy schedule.

In the following sections, I'll zoom in on a few key messaging capabilities, focusing on what can be done, rather than on how it can be implemented. I'll then discuss the nuts and bolts of getting Microsoft Mail and Microsoft Exchange up and running on your network.

Understanding Mail Delivery

Microsoft Mail is included in Windows for Workgroups and Windows NT 3.x. Microsoft Exchange Server is a separate product that's part of the BackOffice Suite. Windows NT 4.0 and Windows 95 include a Microsoft Exchange client which you can use with either Microsoft Mail or Exchange Server.

Both Microsoft Mail and Microsoft Exchange use a *store and forward* approach to handling e-mail. Mail from the sender is stored in a central repository and is either forwarded directly to its final destination or to another repository on the way to its final destination. This approach is very similar to how a letter travels through

MAIL GATEWAYS TO THE WORLD

If you need to communicate outside of your organization or with other types of e-mail systems within your enterprise, you'll need a gateway. Several mail gateways are available for both Mail and Exchange. They include gateways to IBM PROFS, OfficeVision, X.400, SMTP, IBM SNADS, Fax Services, MHS, and AT&T Easylink Services.

the U.S. mail. In fact, Microsoft Mail's central repository for e-mail is called a *Postoffice.* (Yes, for some strange reason, Microsoft spells this as one word.)

A letter mailed to a local address goes to the local U.S. post office and is then delivered to the addressee in the same town. The local office knows that the recipient is in the same town. (Not all U.S. post offices out in the boonies have mail-sorting capabilities, so a letter that you mail to your friend down the street in Nowhere, Nebraska, may travel all the way to the main post office in Central City, where it's sorted and then sent back to Nowhere.)

If you mail a letter to a friend in a different state, the letter typically gets forwarded from your local post office to a regional post office covering your state. It then gets forwarded again to another regional post office, this time servicing your friend's state. Next, the letter is forwarded to your friend's local post office. Finally, it's delivered to your friend's home, a mere 38 days after you mailed it.

Although Mail and Exchange take different approaches to handling e-mail communication, these basic concepts are identical in the two products. You'll see both similarities and differences in their approaches to the same problems.

READ AND THEN DECIDE

In the following sections, I'll delve into several variations on solutions provided by both Mail and Exchange. I recommend that you read and understand the strengths and limitations of each approach before deciding which solution matches your organization's needs. In other words, read this chapter before you decide what to install.

If you have the budget and you want a flexible system that will grow with your enterprise, I recommend starting with or moving to Microsoft Exchange Server. However, Exchange may be more than you need, and Microsoft Mail-based approaches may be a better fit for your organization. I'll cover the various alternatives and let you decide. In making your decision, however, keep in mind that the Microsoft e-mail world is definitely going the way of Exchange. From a features, performance, and support standpoint, Microsoft Mail will be left behind.

Understanding Group Scheduling

Scheduling a good meeting time with several busy people can be frustrating and can consume hours of time. First, you must track them down to determine when they're available. Once you know everyone's availability, you have to find a workable time and inform everyone. By the time the process is completed, at least one of the people is probably no longer available at the meeting time that you've selected. So you have to start the process all over again.

Schedule+ provides a solution. If everyone keeps their schedule up to date in Schedule+, it's easy to find a meeting time that will work for everyone (assuming such a time actually exists). You can enter a list of attendees, view what times they're all available, instantly reserve a workable slot, update all of their schedules, and inform them of the meeting via e-mail. You can even get e-mail confirmations from each attendee. The time saved in your organization from this feature alone can be enormous.

You can also schedule the place of the meeting using Schedule+. If you have several meeting places such as conference rooms, just create an account for each location and schedule it along with the attendees. Training people to include rooms as meeting attendees takes a bit of mental conditioning, but they eventually get used to it. I've seen this approach work very effectively, especially when meeting room space is a scarce resource.

Since Schedule+ isn't included in Windows NT Server 4.0, I won't delve into the nuts and bolts here. However, keep in mind that Schedule+ is included in Windows for Workgroups and Windows NT 3.x. It's also available separately for Windows 95 and Windows NT 4.0, either alone or bundled with Microsoft Office and Exchange Server. Schedule+ works with both the Microsoft Mail and Microsoft Exchange products.

BEYOND GROUP SCHEDULING

Schedule+ goes beyond group scheduling by keeping track of your daily schedule, providing a handy contact manager, and tracking your prioritized "to do" lists. It can even be integrated with Microsoft Project, allowing a workgroup to maintain a project schedule electronically with only one copy of Microsoft Project.

Understanding Electronic Forms

Have you ever needed a series of approval signatures on forms you've filled out to make a small purchase, get tuition reimbursement, authorize an office move, and so on? Have you noticed that some folks with the magic "signature authority" let these forms pile up in their inboxes, waiting for the day when they get a few minutes to sign them? There's got to be a better way, right?

Microsoft offers an Electronic Forms Designer tool that enables you to create online forms. At the most fundamental level, you can use these forms simply to gather information in a structured way. However, you can go beyond this by creating forms that are automatically routed via e-mail through a chain of people to approve them. You can even create forms that track the workflow of a particular product or task.

If you need to customize the processing that takes place behind your electronic forms, you can use Microsoft Visual Basic to develop, test, and deploy your custom forms-based application. If you plan to use the electronic forms features, get to know Microsoft Visual Basic 4.0. Knowledge of this tool will help you to utilize all of the advanced features of e-forms and will prepare you to develop custom forms and applications for your organization.

Understanding Discussion and Collaboration

Using Microsoft Exchange, you can conduct organized discussions using public folders. These folders eliminate the irritation of wading through reams of e-mail messages to discover or recall who said what about opening a Cleveland office. (The debate might be quite lively on this topic.) Simply create a public folder called "Cleveland," and all of the topic's debate and history will be filed in one place.

You can also use public folders as central electronic libraries for items such as employee handbooks, product manuals, company reports, evolving product specifications, and so forth. Using a combination of forms and public folders, you can create a repository of information for sales or support staffs, giving them quick access to histories of customer contacts, problems, resolutions, or product orders.

Establishing Your Inbox

Windows NT Server (and Workstation) 4.0 includes a universal Inbox that's designed to allow Microsoft Exchange and Internet e-mail to commingle. The first time that you double-click the desktop Inbox icon (assuming that you installed it when you installed NT Server), you're greeted with an Inbox Wizard that guides you through the process of configuring your Inbox.

To enable your Inbox to include Internet Mail, you must have the TCP/IP protocol installed and running on the computer. It's best to install TCP/IP before you set up your Inbox. Chapter 11 covers TCP/IP installation and configuration in detail.

Here's how to configure your Inbox to operate as a Microsoft Exchange client:

1. Double-click the Inbox icon on your desktop. The Windows Messaging Setup Wizard dialog box appears.
2. Click Use the following information services, then click to select or clear the check boxes representing the available services. When you've selected the services that you want, click Next, as shown in Figure 16-1.

   The two available services are Microsoft Mail and Internet Mail. You can choose either one or both.

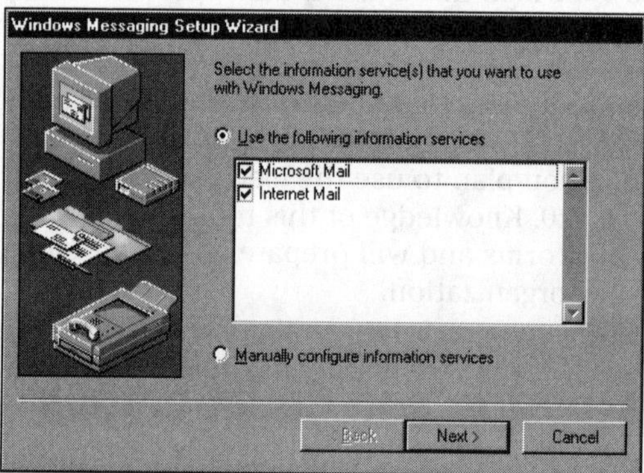

Figure 16-1: You can select Microsoft Mail, Internet Mail, or both services.

3. If you selected Microsoft Mail in step 2, type the path to the Postoffice and click Next. See Figure 16-2.

   I'll cover Microsoft Mail Postoffices later in this chapter.

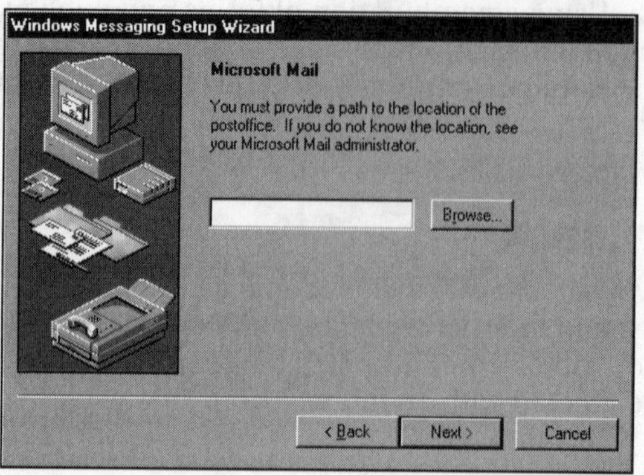

Figure 16-2: You point to the existing Microsoft Mail Postoffice on the network.

4. If you selected Microsoft Mail in step 2, type your existing e-mail account user name and password and click Next, as shown in Figure 16-3.

Figure 16-3: You specify your existing Microsoft Mail e-mail account information.

5. If you selected Internet Mail in step 2, click either Modem or Network, depending on how you intend to gain access to your Internet e-mail. Then click Next, as shown in Figure 16-4.

   If you selected Modem, you'll see the Phone Book Entry Wizard dialog box. Follow the on-screen instructions to define how you want to connect to the Internet using your modem.

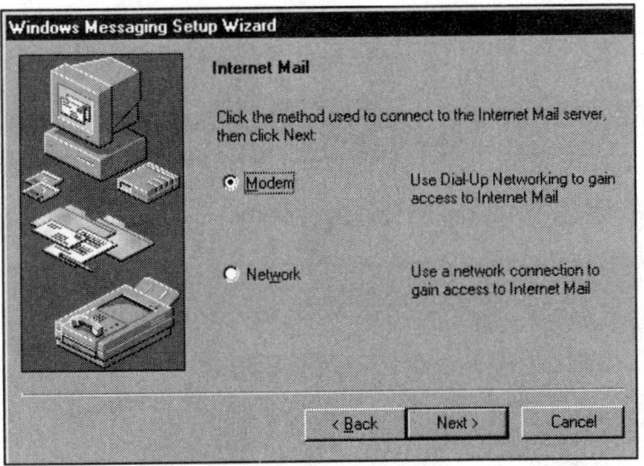

Figure 16-4: You can choose the means by which you'll gain access to your Internet e-mail.

6. If you selected Internet Mail in step 2, click either Specify the name or Specify the IP address and type the name or address of the server that you'll be using to receive e-mail. See Figure 16-5.

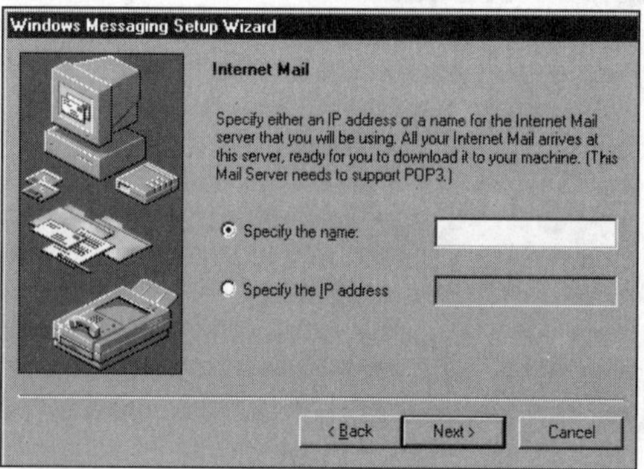

Figure 16-5: You can specify the server at which your Internet mail arrives.

7. If you selected Internet Mail in step 2 and you want to control manually when Internet e-mail will be sent and received, click Off-line. If you want the computer to receive or send Internet e-mail immediately whenever it's available, click Automatic. Then click Next. See Figure 16-6.

   I typically select Off-line, since I usually connect to the Internet at specific times of the day to send and receive Internet e-mail.

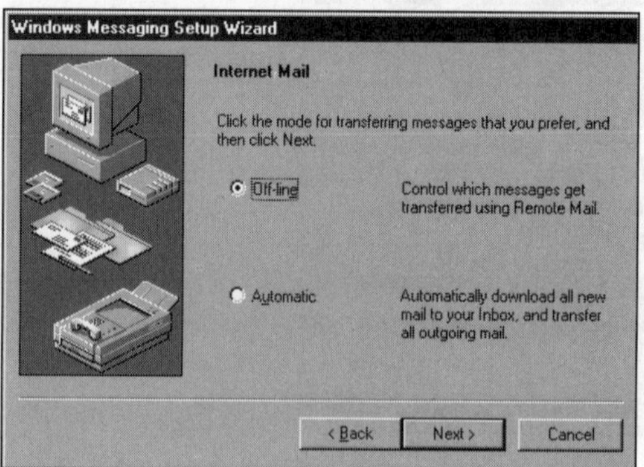

Figure 16-6: You can choose whether you want manual control of when your Internet e-mail is sent and received.

8. If you selected Internet Mail in step 2, type your Internet e-mail address and your full name. See Figure 16-7. Then click Next.

   This information is provided by your ISP (Internet Service Provider). If you have more than one Internet e-mail address, type the one that you're going to use for sending and receiving Internet e-mail in this Inbox.

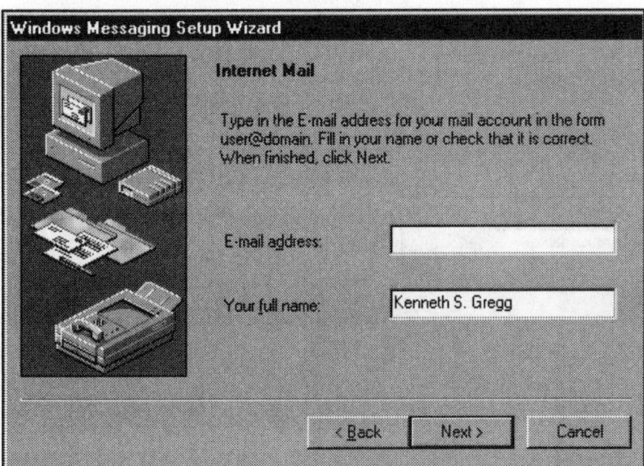

Figure 16-7: You specify your Internet e-mail address and your full name.

9. If you selected Internet Mail in step 2, type your Internet mailbox account name and password, as shown in Figure 16-8. Then click Next.

   This information is provided by your ISP. In most cases, your mailbox account name and password are case-sensitive.

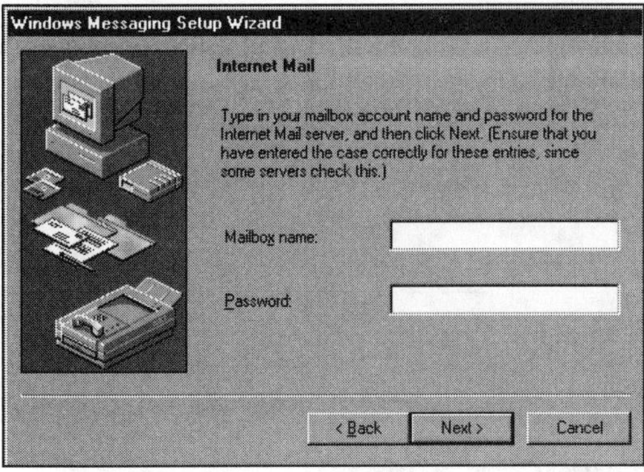

Figure 16-8: You specify your Internet mailbox account name and password, paying attention to case-sensitivity.

10. Type the path to your Personal Address Book file. If you're installing Windows Messaging for the first time on this computer, accept the default path, as presented in Figure 16-9. Then click Next.

    The Personal Address Book is a list of frequently used e-mail addresses maintained by the Windows Messaging client.

Figure 16-9: You accept the default path to your Personal Address Book file.

11. Type the path to your Personal Folder file. If you're installing Windows Messaging for the first time on this computer, accept the default path, as presented in Figure 16-10. Then click Next.

    The Personal Folder file houses the e-mail messages and folders on the local computer.

Figure 16-10: You accept the default path to your Personal Folder file.

12. Now that you've completed Windows Messaging client configuration, click Finish, as shown in Figure 16-11.

    If you selected Microsoft Mail in step 2, there's one more step to complete after this one.

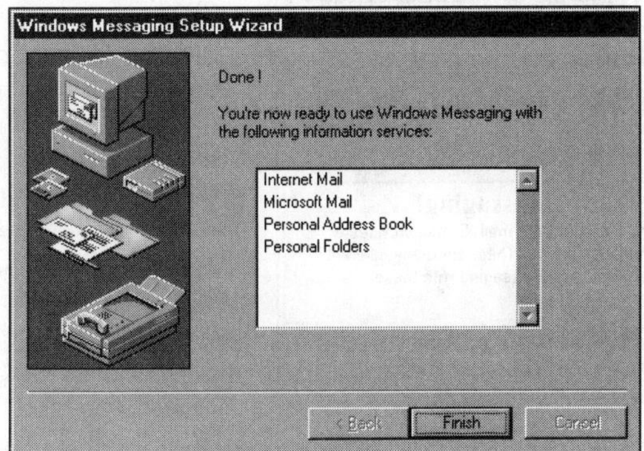

Figure 16-11: Exchange configuration is complete.

13. If you selected Microsoft Mail in step 2, you'll see the dialog box shown in Figure 16-12. In the Microsoft Mail dialog box, type the name of your Microsoft Mail Postoffice, your Mail account name, and your password. Then click OK.

    You can force Mail to remember your password between logons, so you don't have to type it each time. Click to select the Remember password check box. However, I don't recommend doing this, since it can present a security risk to your e-mail folder if someone accesses your computer and knows your user name.

If you click Offline, you can perform operations on your local mail folders without being connected to the Microsoft Mail Postoffice. Any messages that you send are stored locally and uploaded the next time that you connect to the Postoffice. While you're in this mode, you won't receive any messages either.

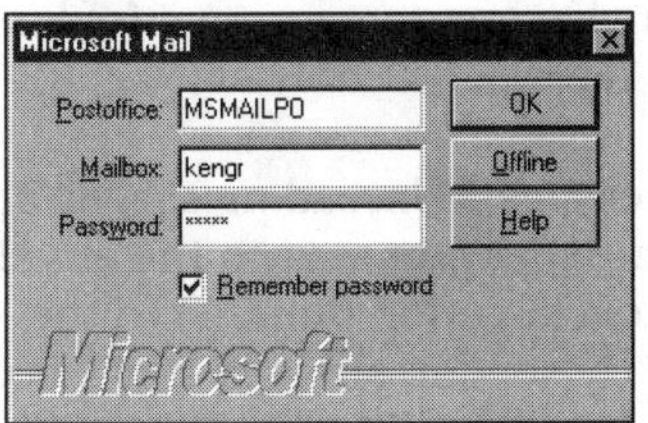

Figure 16-12: You log on to your Microsoft Mail account.

You'll see a message in your Inbox with the subject "Welcome!" Double-click the message to see its contents, as shown in Figure 16-13. It provides some helpful hints on how to get started using Windows Messaging.

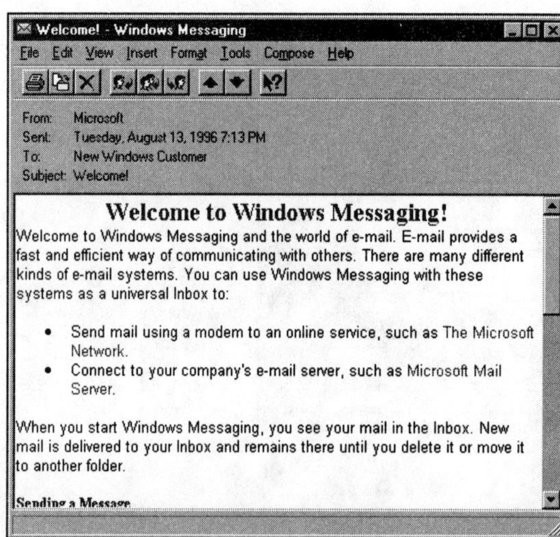

Figure 16-13: Your first e-mail message is a welcome from Microsoft.

Using Your Inbox

There are many rich features in the Exchange client provided with NT. In this section, I won't attempt to cover them all but will focus on the core set of features that will get you started sending, receiving, and organizing your e-mail.

After initial configuration of your Inbox, described in the previous section, you're presented with the e-mail viewer window, shown in Figure 16-14. On the View menu, click to select Folders. To the left, you can see the folders in which your e-mail is organized. You can expand or contract the view of a specific folder's contents by clicking on the plus (+) and minus (-) signs (just as you did in NT Explorer, described in Chapter 14). You can also create your own folders to organize your e-mail better.

On the right, you see a list of your e-mail messages. Unread messages are bold, messages with attachments are flagged by a paper clip next to the envelope icon, and urgent messages are highlighted by an exclamation point (!) to the left of the envelope icon. You can sort your messages by sender, subject, time received, and message size by clicking the appropriate column heading. In Figure 16-14, the messages in the Inbox are sorted by sender.

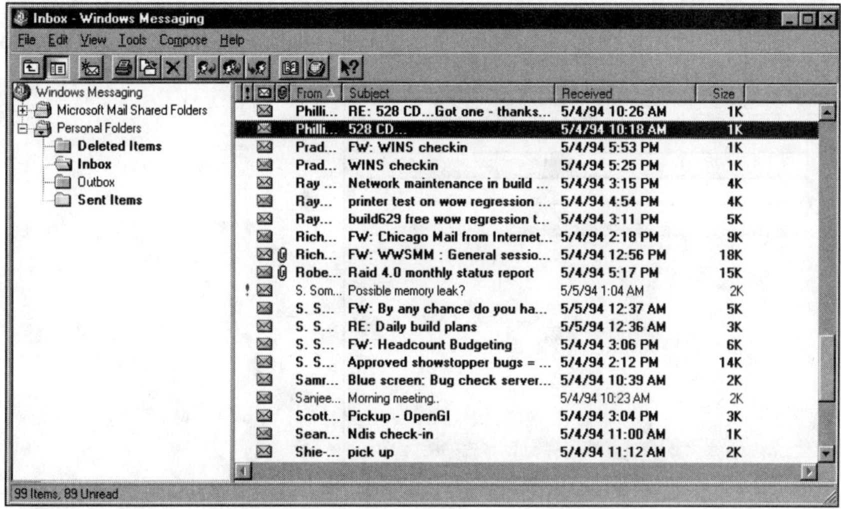

Figure 16-14: You view the mail in your Inbox, then can choose to leave it alone, delete it, or save it to another folder.

To read a message, double-click the line describing it. You can then move the message to another folder, delete it, reply to the sender, reply to all recipients, or forward the message to others. These functions can be accessed via the menus or toolbar. Slowly move your mouse over the buttons in the tool bar to learn what each button does.

The Deleted Items folder is similar to the Recycle Bin described in Chapter 14. Whenever you delete an e-mail message, the message is moved to the Deleted Items folder. To control the size of your message files, you periodically need to delete the items from your Deleted Items folder to remove them permanently.

To compose a new e-mail message, click New Message on the Compose menu. You'll see the New Message window shown in Figure 16-15. Composing a simple text message is pretty straightforward, but you'll want to explore the toolbar and menus to find additional features that will enhance your online communications.

The Bcc: line, which allows you to send blind copies of your message without other recipients knowing it, is new to Exchange. This feature wasn't available in Microsoft Mail, except through third-party add-on products. To enable this feature, click to select Bcc Box on the View menu in the New Message window.

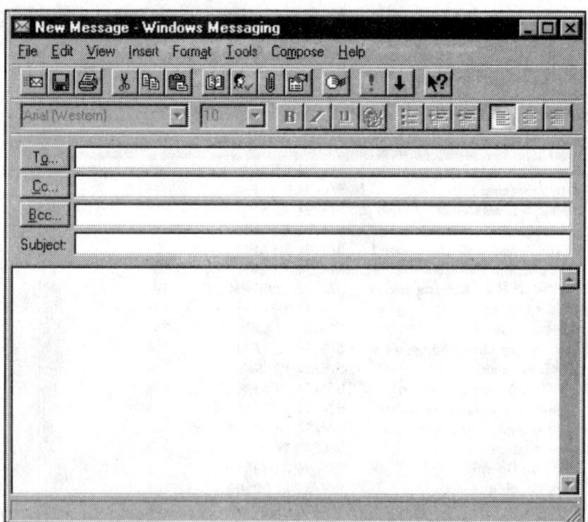

Figure 16-15: Use the New Message dialog box to compose a new e-mail message.

When you receive lots of e-mail, it's easy to find yourself searching for that one important message among a sea of other messages. The Exchange client provides a powerful search function that enables you to specify several criteria to find just the right message or set of messages that you want. Figure 16-16 illustrates the dialog box that appears when you click Tools ➪ Find in the main window.

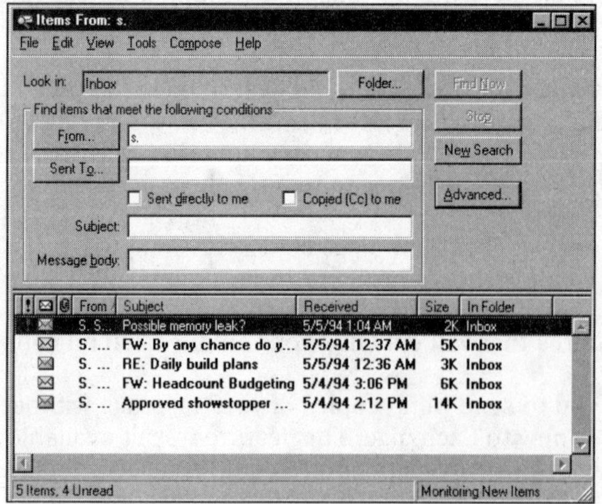

Figure 16-16: You can use the powerful search function to find e-mail messages quickly.

If you maintain a hefty Inbox or other large mail folders, you'll spend a lot of time using the search feature, so get to know it. Click Advanced to see how detailed your queries can get.

Repairing Your Inbox

If you've used or administered e-mail systems before, you know that, for various reasons, e-mail databases sometimes become inconsistent or corrupt. One of the key items in your fix-it kit is the Inbox Repair Tool, provided with Windows NT 4.0. To start it, click Start ⇨ Programs ⇨ Accessories ⇨ System Tools ⇨ Inbox Repair Tool. Figure 16-17 presents the initial dialog box, in which you must type the name of the personal folder file or off-line folder file that you want to scan and repair. When you click Start in the Inbox Repair Tool dialog box, the file that you specified is scanned for consistency. The entire process may take anywhere from a few minutes to a few hours, depending on the size and complexity of your folder file.

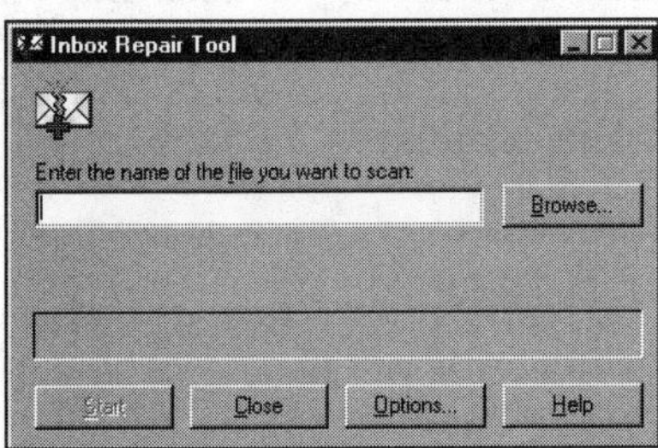

Figure 16-17: The Inbox Repair Tool enables you to scan and repair your Inbox.

Microsoft Mail

Microsoft Mail is included in Windows for Workgroups and Windows NT 3.x. In Windows NT 4.0, Microsoft Mail has been replaced by the Microsoft Exchange client, which I'll discuss later in this chapter. The Exchange client is compatible with the Mail Postoffice.

For additional capabilities and throughput, Microsoft offers Mail Server. This product used to be available as part of the BackOffice suite but is now offered as a separate product. In the following sections, I'll discuss several ways to configure Microsoft Mail and Mail Server, based on the needs of your organization.

The Workgroup Postoffice

In its simplest form, Microsoft Mail provides a single Postoffice for use by people in a workgroup. This is known as WGPO, or the workgroup Postoffice. In the WGPO world, all work is done on the client computers, and none is performed on the server. The server computer acts as a passive repository for the Postoffice, which is really just a collection of folders and files shared over the network.

The workgroup Postoffice provides the *store* part of the store and forward concept. No forwarding takes place in this arrangement, other than when the receiving client downloads e-mail from the Postoffice. As long as all of the users send and receive their e-mail through the same Postoffice, all is well.

Theoretically, a Postoffice can support up to 500 users. However, the practical limit is around 200, even with a relatively fast network and speedy disk drives. The slower your network and disk accesses, the fewer users the Postoffice can support. If the server on which you've placed your Postoffice also acts as a print server or a heavily used application server, the number of users that you can realistically support is reduced even further.

The WGPO arrangement is fine if your organization is small, you need only one Postoffice, and you don't have to route mail through gateways to other mail systems (such as the Internet). However, there's less room for growth or flexibility than with the other approaches discussed in this chapter.

Adding the Message Transfer Agent

What happens if you need more than one Postoffice, or you already have more than one Postoffice and you want your users attached to different Postoffices to communicate with each other? That's where the simple Mail workgroup Postoffice concept breaks down. It simply can't communicate between Postoffices.

In the U.S. mail analogy, someone at the post office has to make a conscious decision about whether a letter can be locally delivered or must be forwarded to another mail facility. In the simple workgroup Postoffice scenario, there's no active process running on the network to make this type of routing decision. The workgroup Postoffice is like a bird-brained carrier pigeon — it only knows one delivery route between source and destination.

A Message Transfer Agent, sometimes called MTA and other times called External, is required to exchange messages between Postoffices and to allow Postoffice access to remote Mail users. The MTA is a DOS process that runs on a network node. Its job is to act as the brains of the pigeon, deciding which messages need to be routed and then routing them to the right Postoffices.

MTA scans the outgoing messages in one Postoffice and forwards mail to the Inboxes of another one. At the same time, it scans the outgoing mail of the second Postoffice to see if it has any mail requiring forwarding to the first Postoffice. A single MTA can support delivery to up to 50 Postoffices, although it's typical to dedicate an MTA to no more than a handful of Postoffices, to distribute the load on the network better.

Due to the activity that it generates, an MTA reduces the number of supported users by about 10 on each Postoffice that it services. Keep this in mind as you assign users to Postoffices.

MTA is provided as part of Microsoft Mail Server 3.5. Although MTA solves the routing problem by allowing transmission of messages between Postoffices, it introduces some overhead into the process. Transfer of messages between users on the same Postoffice is much quicker than if the users are on different Postoffices and receiving messages routed by MTA.

Using the Multitasking MTA

One drawback of MTA is that it requires a dedicated computer, since it's a DOS-based program. This can become expensive and cumbersome to administer. You can't really skimp on the hardware, since you don't want the MTA to be painfully slow, but it's a shame to dedicate a powerful computer to running a single DOS program.

Since Windows NT can run DOS programs, you might consider running MTA on your Windows NT Server computer, alongside other server applications. This will work, but it's not the best solution. Microsoft offers a special version of MTA called Multitasking MTA, or MMTA. It's designed to run on Windows NT, provides greater throughput (especially in large network configurations), and removes the requirement for a dedicated computer. As an added bonus, it offers better support for Microsoft Mail Remote, a Mail-only remote access connection between remote computers and their Postoffices.

I haven't talked about Microsoft Mail Remote, since RAS is a much more powerful remote access solution. If you want to grant certain users remote access to their e-mail and to no other resources on your network, you may want to consider Microsoft Mail Remote. However, if you implement RAS, your users will be able to access all of the network resources that they normally access from their offices. See Chapter 11 for a discussion of RAS.

Planning Your Postoffice Structure

In this section, I'll present some tips for getting the best performance from your Microsoft Mail Postoffice.

If you have LANs connected by a WAN, you have Postoffices on each LAN, and you want to connect those Postoffices, put an MTA on each end of the WAN connection. Don't let an MTA communicate over a WAN directly with a Postoffice. Since MTAs communicate with each other by sending a single package of messages, you'll save WAN bandwidth by taking this approach. MTAs won't have to read and distribute individual messages across the WAN.

Where possible, put people who communicate with each other often on the same Postoffice. They'll get faster message service, and their traffic won't clog up your MTAs.

Keep the number of active users on any given Postoffice under 200. Even though the theoretical limit is 500, things start to slow down significantly if the number climbs above the 200 mark. There are a few files in the Postoffice that are accessed frequently, and the more users that you have, the longer the access delays will be.

On the other hand, don't create a bunch of very small Postoffices. If you do this, you'll end up having to run lots of inter-Postoffice traffic through MTAs, decreasing overall performance. Shoot for about 200 users per Postoffice.

Allocate 15MB of disk storage space for each Postoffice user. Although the average space used tends to be around 10MB per user, it's critical that you have enough space to handle high traffic periods or to account for some users who will require even more than 15MB. So, for 200 users, you'll need to arrange for about 3GB of disk space.

Strongly encourage your users to back up their MMF files and to keep them below 15MB. The tools used to restore corrupted MMF files are less successful when the files become larger than this.

Establishing a Workgroup Postoffice

What if you don't want to invest in Microsoft Exchange Server and you don't need the additional features of MTA? All you really want is basic e-mail capabilities on your network. An easy way to get e-mail is to create a Mail workgroup Postoffice and run both Mail and Exchange clients with it. (This is a bit like putting an old engine in a new car, but it can be a cost-effective approach for smaller installations. You'll save some money, but you'll lose some functionality. It may be a reasonable stop-gap measure, however, until you purchase Exchange Server.)

If you don't already have a Mail workgroup Postoffice on your network, you can create one using Windows NT 4.0 through the Microsoft Mail Postoffice application in Control Panel. Alternatively, you can create a new Postoffice using the Microsoft Mail client from either Windows NT 3.x or Windows for Workgroups.

Here's how to create a Microsoft Mail Postoffice from Windows NT Server 4.0:

1. On Windows NT 4.0 computer, click Start ➪ Settings ➪ Control Panel. Double-click the Microsoft Mail Postoffice icon.

You don't need to run this application on the same computer on which the Postoffice will reside. You'll be able to select a network drive in step 3 below, and install the Postoffice there.

2. You're given the choice of administering an existing Postoffice or creating a new one. Click to select Create a new Workgroup Postoffice and click Next.

After you've installed the Postoffice, you can run this Microsoft Mail Postoffice application again and click Administer an Existing Workgroup Postoffice. You'll be able to view Mail user account details, add new users, or delete existing users.

3. Type the drive and directory where you want the new Postoffice to reside and click Next. If you want to change the path, click Back. To confirm the path, click Next.
4. In the Enter Your Administrator Account Details dialog box, type the full name and mailbox ID that you want to use for the Postoffice administrator. Replace the default password with a new password for the Postoffice administrator account. When you're done, click OK.

   The remaining fields in this dialog box are optional.

It's critically important that you both safeguard and remember the Postoffice administrator password. You'll need it to administer user e-mail accounts (including resetting forgotten passwords). If you forget the Postoffice administrator password, you can't recover it, and you'll have to reinstall the Postoffice. Moreover, if your users forget their passwords, you won't be able to reset them without the administrator password, so they'll lose access to their existing e-mail folders.

Make sure to change the password to something other than the default. This will help keep disgruntled postal workers from destroying your Postoffice.

5. You'll get a message indicating that you need to share the new Postoffice directory. Click OK.

Be sure that all of your e-mail users have Change permission to this directory. They'll need this level of permission in the course of normal e-mail operations. Don't grant them Full Access, though, since you don't want them to be able to delete the directory or change its permissions.

Here's how to use either Windows NT 3.x or Windows for Workgroups to create a Mail Postoffice:

1. On Windows NT 3.x or Windows for Workgroups computer on which you've never started the Microsoft Mail program, double-click the Mail icon in the Main program group.

   If you've already run Microsoft Mail on this computer, you'll need to pick another computer or reinstall the operating system. You only have one shot at setting up a Postoffice. Once Mail has been set up as a client, you can't create a Postoffice from this computer.

You don't need to be running Mail on the same computer on which the Postoffice will reside. You can select a network drive in step 4 and install the Postoffice there.

2. As shown in Figure 16-18, you're given the choice of connecting to an existing Postoffice or creating a new one. Click Create a new Workgroup Postoffice and click OK.

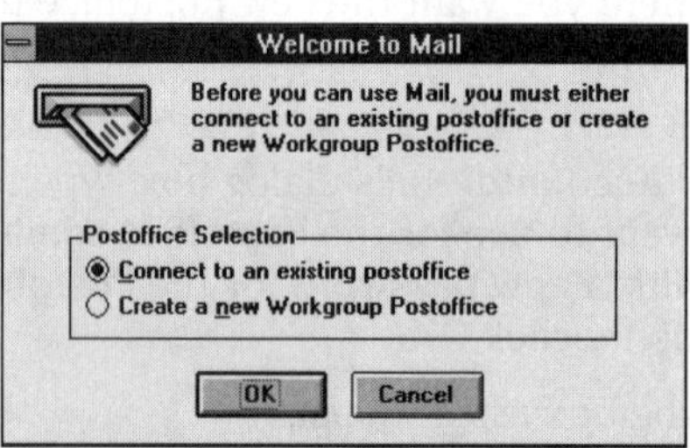

Figure 16-18: When you first start Mail, you choose between creating or connecting to a Postoffice.

3. You'll get a warning as shown in Figure 16-19. Read it and click Yes.

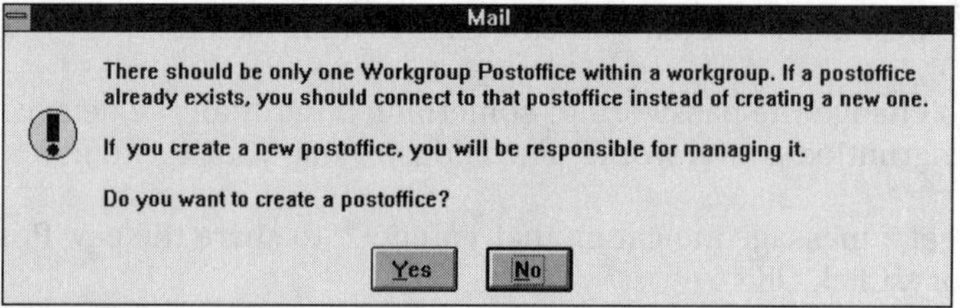

Figure 16-19: Heed the warning that you should have only one Postoffice.

4. In the Create Workgroup Postoffice dialog box, select the drive and directory where you want the Postoffice to reside. Click OK, as shown in Figure 16-20.

   It can be on a local or network drive. Mail will create a directory tree rooted at WGPO under the directory that you specify. See the section entitled "The Workgroup Postoffice" earlier in this chapter.

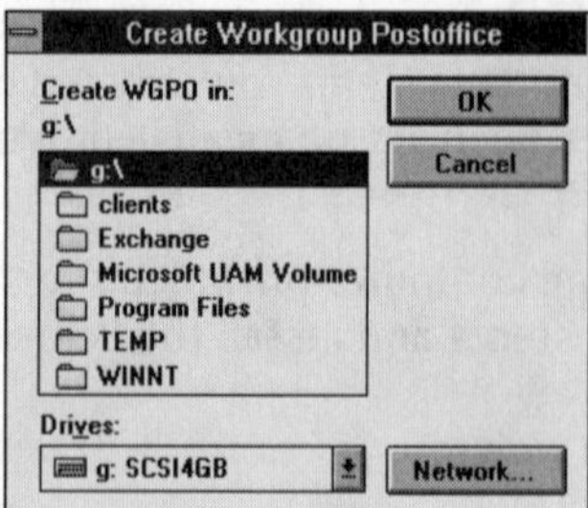

Figure 16-20: You select the location for the Mail Postoffice.

5. In the Enter Your Administrator Account Details dialog box, type the full name and mailbox ID that you want to use for the Postoffice administrator. Replace the default password with a new password for the Postoffice administrator account.

   The remaining fields in this dialog box are optional, as shown in Figure 16-21. Be sure that you safeguard and remember this password. Change it to something other than the default. When you're done, click OK.

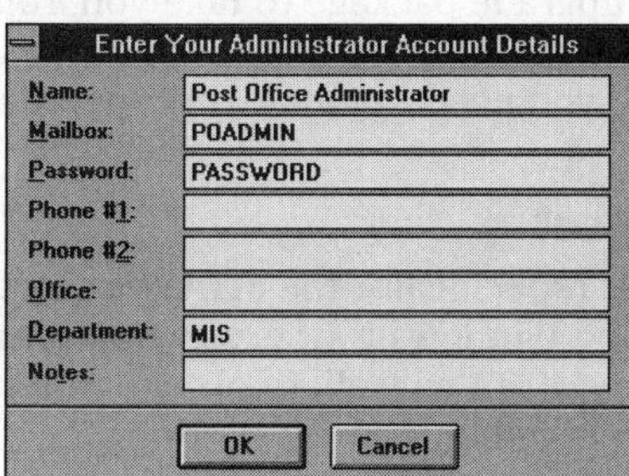

Figure 16-21: You enter information about the Mail Postoffice administrator account.

6. You'll get a message indicating that you need to share the new Postoffice directory, as illustrated by Figure 16-22. Click OK.

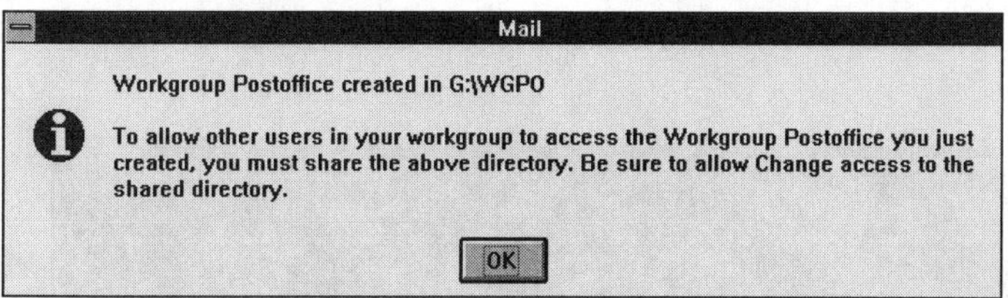

Figure 16-22: Follow the instructions about sharing your Mail Postoffice directory.

7. Click File ➪ Exit to close the Mail application.
8. Using Explorer, share the WGPO directory that you created in step 4.

   Be sure that all of your e-mail users have Change permission to this directory. Don't grant them Full Access.

Establishing a Mail Server Postoffice

If you need the additional capabilities that the Message Transfer Agent provides (Postoffice-to-Postoffice routing and remote Mail access), the following sections present the steps necessary to install either the DOS-based MTA or the Windows NT-based Multitasking MTA (MMTA).

If you're upgrading a workgroup Postoffice (WGPO) to the Mail Server, don't run the standard Mail Server installation. It won't allow you to complete the Mail Server installation. Microsoft offers a separate upgrade package to take you from WGPO to the Mail Server Postoffice. They used to include it on the BackOffice CD-ROM, but no more. Contact Microsoft for details, if you need to follow this upgrade path.

Installing the Message Transfer Agent

You can install the Microsoft Mail Server (specifically, the MTA) on any computer that can execute DOS programs, including Windows NT Server. However, if you're using Windows NT, plan on installing the MMTA as well, to obtain better performance. MMTA installation steps are presented in the next section.

Here are the steps required to install the Microsoft Mail Server MTA:

1. Connect drive M to the server that will contain your Microsoft Mail Postoffice.

   Some of the Mail utilities require that you use drive letter M.

2. On the first floppy disk of the Microsoft Mail 3.5 set, run SETUP.EXE.
3. In the Welcome window, shown in Figure 16-23, press ENTER.

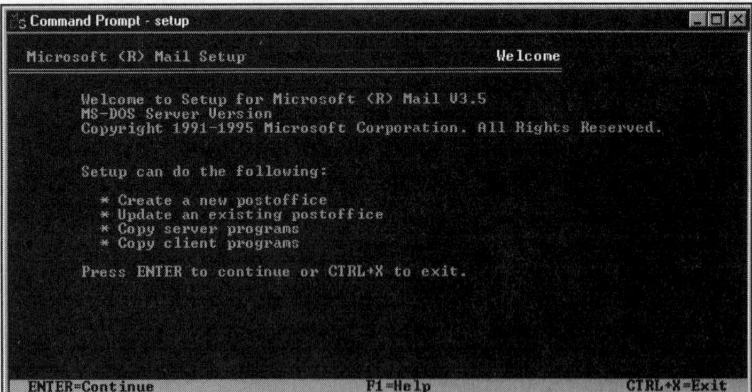

Figure 16-23: You establish a Mail Server Postoffice and install Mail server and client software with the Mail Server installation program.

4. Select Create a new postoffice. Then press ENTER, as shown in Figure 16-24.

The upgrade option on this screen doesn't allow you to upgrade an existing WGPO Postoffice. Instead it's designed to allow you to upgrade an existing older Mail Server Postoffice. Contact Microsoft for details on how to obtain a special version that enables you to upgrade a WGPO Postoffice.

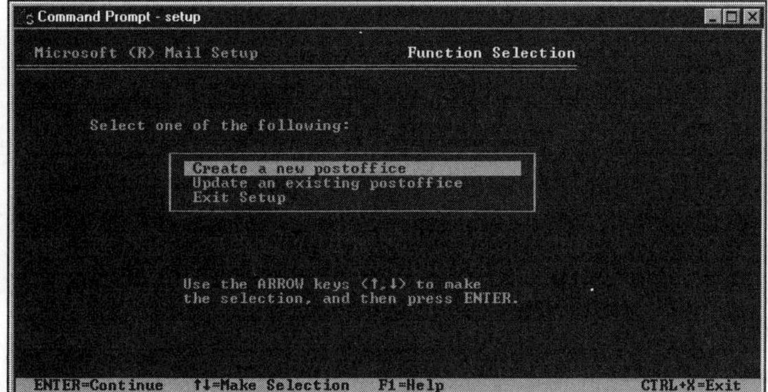

Figure 16-24: You can create a new Mail Server Postoffice or upgrade an existing one.

5. Type the path to your Microsoft Mail Postoffice data. This is typically M:\MAILDATA. Then press ENTER, as illustrated in Figure 16-25.

   The default is C:\MAILDATA. Change the C to M.

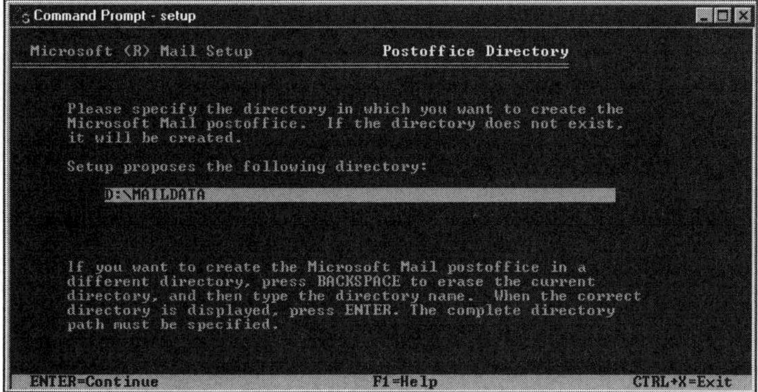

Figure 16-25: You specify where your Postoffice data will reside on the server.

6. Type the name of this Postoffice and press ENTER, as illustrated by Figure 16-26.

   Each Mail Server Postoffice needs a unique name. This allows MTA to route e-mail between Postoffices.

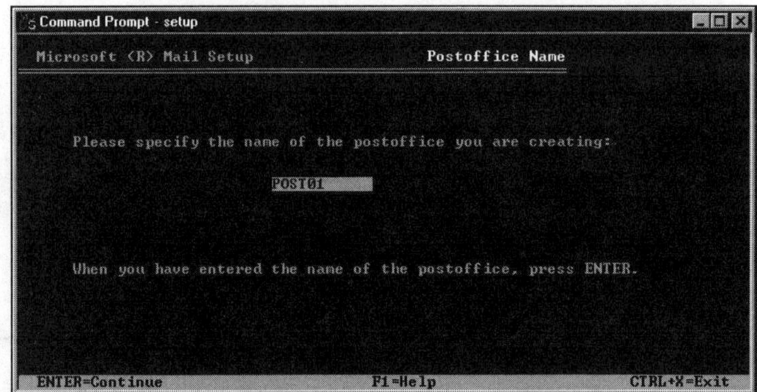

Figure 16-26: You enter a unique name for this Mail Server Postoffice.

7. Type the name of your organization or network and press ENTER, as shown in Figure 16-27.

   This can be any name up to 11 characters. Some organizations use their company site name, whereas others use their NT domain name.

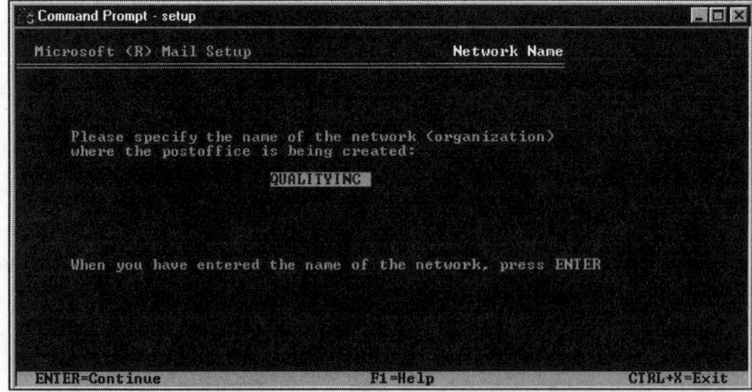

Figure 16-27: You enter the name of your organization or site.

8. Select Microsoft LAN Manager-compatible and press ENTER. See Figure 16-28.

   Refer to the Mail Server documentation if you're installing it in a NetWare environment.

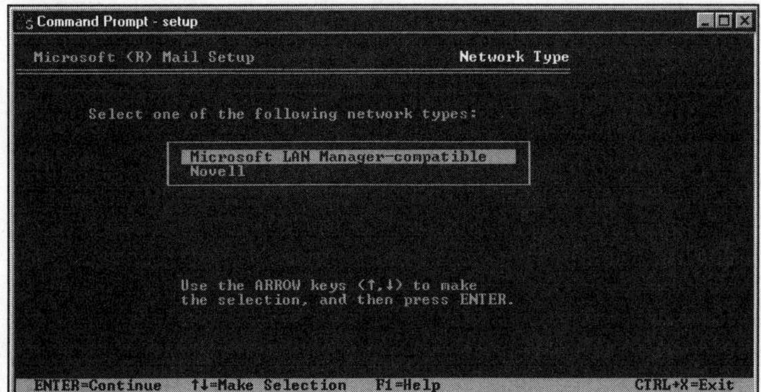

Figure 16-28: You select the Microsoft-compatible network for your Mail Server.

9. Highlight each of the three items (Administration and Utilities, Server Agents, and Modem script files) and press ENTER to select each one. Figure 16-29 shows this. Then highlight DONE and press ENTER.

   This will install all of the Mail Server software.

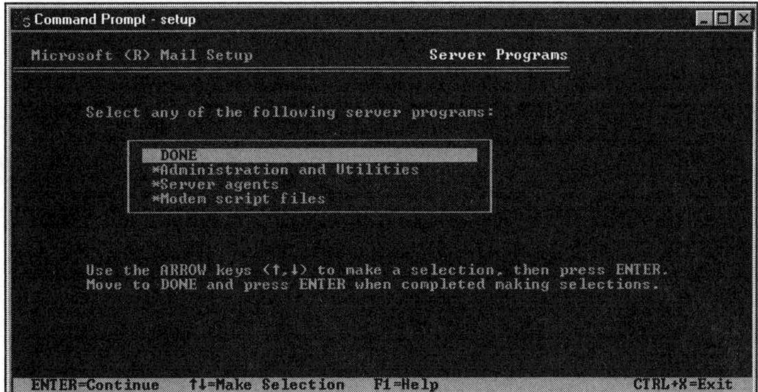

Figure 16-29: You can select all Mail Server options for installation.

10. Type the path to your Microsoft Mail executable programs. This is typically M:\MAILEXE. Then press ENTER, as shown in Figure 16-30.

    The default is C:\MAILEXE. Change the C to M.

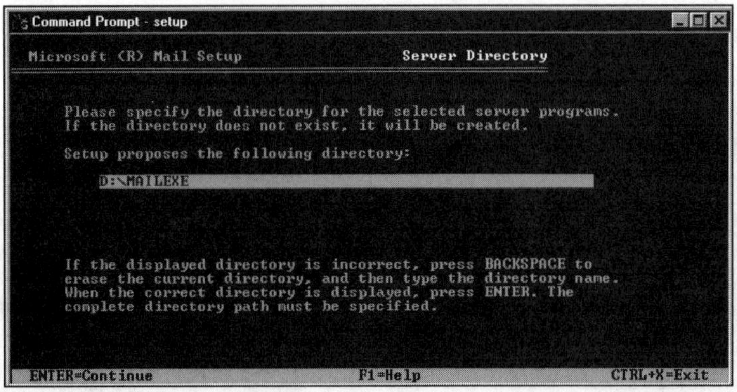

```
Command Prompt - setup
Microsoft (R) Mail Setup                      Server Directory

     Please specify the directory for the selected server programs.
     If the directory does not exist, it will be created.

     Setup proposes the following directory:

          D:\MAILEXE

     If the displayed directory is incorrect, press BACKSPACE to
     erase the current directory, and then type the directory name.
     When the correct directory is displayed, press ENTER. The
     complete directory path must be specified.

 ENTER=Continue                        F1=Help                  CTRL+X=Exit
```

Figure 16-30: You can specify where your Mail Server programs will reside on the server.

11. If you want to install the DOS Mail client over the network, highlight MS-DOS and press ENTER. If you want to install the Windows 3.x Mail client over the network, highlight Windows and Presentation Manager and press ENTER. (Note that you can select either option or both.) After you've made your selection(s), highlight DONE and press ENTER. See Figure 16-31.

    I recommend selecting both options, so that you have both types of clients available for installation over the network.

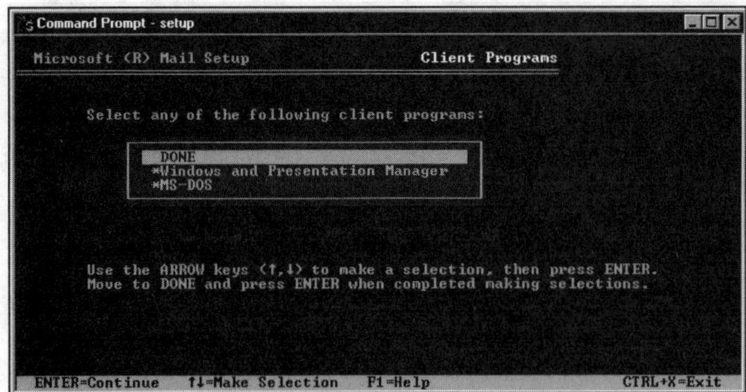

Figure 16-31: You can specify which Mail clients that you want to be able to install over the network.

12. Type the path where you want the Mail client programs stored on the server, as shown in Figure 16-32. Then press ENTER.

Although the default directory is \MAILEXE, I recommend that you choose another directory for the client software. You don't want to give all of your clients access to the directory containing the Mail Server administration software. It's wisest to keep the client software in a separate directory. I usually call it \MAILCLI.

The default is C:\MAILEXE. Change the C to M and select a different directory name.

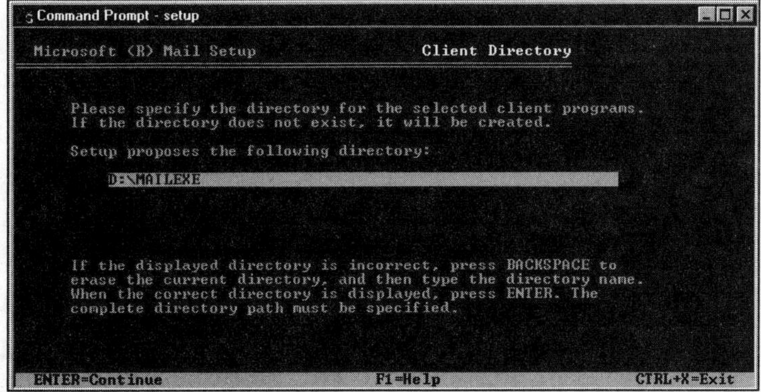

Figure 16-32: You can specify where your Mail client files will go.

13. As shown in Figure 16-33, you're given the opportunity to review your choices and make changes, if necessary. If you want to make changes, follow the on-screen instructions. When you're done, select NO CHANGE and press ENTER.

    At this point, files are copied from the installation media to your hard disk. If you're installing from floppy disks, you'll be asked to insert new disks along the way.

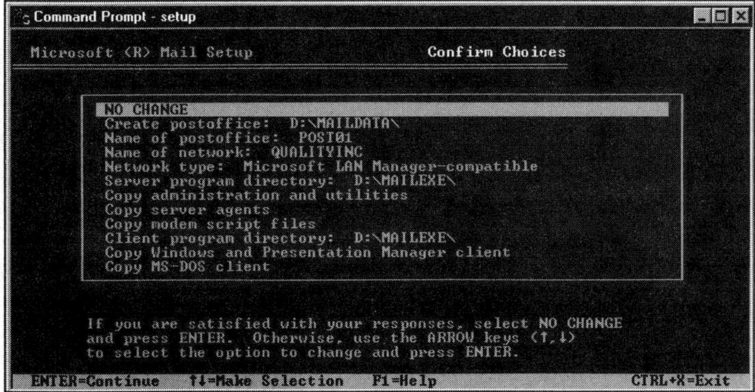

Figure 16-33: You can review and modify your Mail Server selections.

14. On the Installation Complete screen, press ENTER.

Installing the Multitasking MTA

If you're running MTA on Windows NT, you can take advantage of the better performance offered by MMTA, as discussed earlier in this chapter. Before proceeding with these steps, you must have completed the steps in the previous section entitled "Installing the Message Transfer Agent."

1. Connect drive M to the server containing your existing Microsoft Mail Postoffice.

   In this situation, you can use another drive letter, but drive M keeps you in the habit of using it for Postoffice connections. Other utilities sometimes require that you use drive letter M.

2. On the CD-ROM or first floppy disk of the MMTA set, run SETUP.EXE.
3. In the Welcome window, click Continue.
4. Type the path to your Microsoft Mail Postoffice data. This is typically M:\MAILDATA. Click Continue.
5. Type your Postoffice administrator name and password. Click Continue.

   If you haven't changed them, the default administrator name is "admin" and the default password is "password."

6. Type the path to your Microsoft Mail administration utilities (agent programs). This is typically M:\MAILEXE. Click Continue.
7. Setup asks if you want to overwrite the EXTERNAL.INI file. If you want to retain its contents, click Do not overwrite. Otherwise click Overwrite. Then click Continue.

   The EXTERNAL.INI file contains the global settings for Postoffice administration. If you've changed the settings from the original defaults and you're happy with them, opt to leave the existing file alone. If you prefer to return to the defaults, ask Setup to overwrite the file.

   At this point, Setup copies several files to your Postoffice directory structure.

8. Setup asks which program group (meaning menu item, in NT 4.0) that it should use to install its icon (meaning submenu item, in NT 4.0). Click the appropriate one and click Continue.

MMTA was developed before Windows NT 4.0 was released, so it doesn't know anything about the new user interface. Thus, it refers to program groups and icons instead of menus and submenu items. You'll have to perform the mental translation during MMTA installation.

9. Setup informs you that installation is complete. Click Continue to close Setup.

Installing Microsoft Mail Clients

Your Microsoft Mail client computers can be running DOS, Windows 3.1, Windows for Workgroups, or Windows NT 3.x. In addition, you can use the Exchange clients included in Windows 95 and Windows NT 4.0 as clients to Microsoft Mail Postoffices. Even OS/2 and Macintosh client computers can communicate with Microsoft Mail.

If you have network users who run DOS, they can participate in e-mail exchanges using the DOS version of Microsoft Mail. It provides only limited functionality and has a pretty clunky interface, but it does the job. If you accepted the defaults during your Microsoft Mail Server installation, you'll find MAIL.EXE in the \MAILEXE folder. Just copy this file to the DOS client computer, connect drive M to the shared Postoffice network resource, and run it. If you use the Windows version of Microsoft Mail on the same computer, you'll be able to access your messages using either DOS or Windows.

Mail features that are available in the Windows client but not in the DOS client include attaching multiple files within the text of your message, spell-checking messages, and filtering messages by various criteria. DOS clients don't get a chance to use these features.

The Windows 3.x version of Microsoft Mail is also available in the \MAILEXE directory. Run Setup in that directory to install the Windows version of Mail — MSMAIL.EXE — on your Windows client computer. (Don't just copy the program to your Windows computer. You need to run Setup to install it properly.) Connect drive M to the shared Postoffice network resource and run MSMAIL by double-clicking the Mail icon after installation. Windows for Workgroups already includes MSMAIL.EXE. Double-click the Mail icon in the Main program group and indicate that you want to join an existing Postoffice, as shown in Figure 16-18.

If any of your clients are running Windows NT 3.x, a 32-bit version of Mail, called MSMAIL32.EXE, is already installed. Double-click the Mail icon in the Main program group and indicate that you want to join an existing Postoffice. See Figure 16-18.

Windows 95 and Windows NT 4.0 include the Microsoft Exchange client, which I'll discuss later in this chapter. You can use this client software to connect to existing Microsoft Mail WGPO and Mail Server Postoffices.

You can also install Microsoft Mail clients on Macintosh and OS/2 computers. See the *Microsoft Mail User's Guide* for details on incorporating these clients into your Microsoft Mail installation.

Table 16-1 summarizes the requirements for the various Microsoft Mail components.

Table 16-1
Requirements for Microsoft Mail Components

Mail Component Recommended	*Minimum Processor*	*Minimum Operating System*	*Minimum Memory*
Message Transfer Agent (MTA)	DOS-capable PC	DOS 3.3	1MB
Multitasking MTA	486 PC	Windows NT Server 3.51	16MB
DOS Client	DOS-capable PC	DOS 3.1	512K
Windows 3.x Client	386 PC	Windows 3.1	4MB
Macintosh Client	Macintosh Plus	System 6.0.3	
OS/2 Client	386 PC	OS/2 1.2	8MB
Electronic Forms Designer 1.0	386 PC	Windows 3.1	6MB

Microsoft Exchange

Unlike Microsoft Mail, Microsoft Exchange is truly a client/server application. The workload is shared between client applications and a central server application running on Windows NT Server. Exchange defines and manages enterprise messaging by breaking the organization into objects called *sites* (typically, physical locations) and *servers* (individual server computers). An organization can contain several sites, and a site can contain several servers.

If you've done much reading about Exchange Server, you've probably found that the term *Microsoft Exchange* can, unfortunately, have several meanings these days. It can refer to the Exchange Server product, which includes a server component and various client components. It can also refer to just the server component of the software or to the physical server computer on which it runs. The term is sometimes used to refer to clients as well.

Understanding Exchange Connectors

Connectors, which can be thought of as mail gateways, play a pivotal role in the Exchange world. They enable Exchange to communicate with other messaging systems. These systems include Microsoft Mail on PC and AppleTalk networks, Schedule+, Internet mail, and third-party mail systems such as PROFS. Several connectors are included with Exchange Server, and many others are offered by other software vendors.

Planning Your Exchange Server

One of the key decisions to make first is whether you plan to have one centralized Exchange Server or multiple servers. Plan your organization, site, and server naming conventions accordingly.

Next, you need to determine your hardware requirements, especially in the area of available disk storage space. For a full installation, plan on using up 150MB of disk space for the software (including multiple connectors and online documentation). In terms of per-user storage, a good rule of thumb is to use the same formula that you used in Microsoft Mail — allow 15MB per user.

Exchange Server runs several NT services. Those services need an NT account that they can use to log on and gain access to system resources. (Before setting up directory replication in Chapter 15, you created a special account for the Directory Replicator service. The concept is the same.) Here's how to create a new account that will be used internally by Exchange services:

1. Click Start ➪ Programs ➪ Administrative Tools ➪ User Manager for Domains option. On the User menu, click New User.
2. Type the information required for the new user account. Type and confirm a password for the new account. Click to select the Password Never Expires check box.

I typically call the account EXCGSVCS, unless there's already an account by that name. Don't forget the password. You'll need it again in the next section. For more detailed information on creating user accounts, see Chapter 18.

3. Click Hours and enable the account to log on at any time on any day. Then click OK.
4. Click Groups. Under Not member of, click Backup Operators. Click Add to add Backup Operators under Member of. Then click OK.
5. In the New User dialog box, click Add. Then click Close.

   The new account that you created is listed in the upper half of the User Manager window.

STORAGE EFFICIENCY IN EXCHANGE

A bit of good news about Exchange is that it uses what's known as *single-instance storage.* Let's say that you send a copy of a large object such as a video clip file to 20 users. If all of those users utilize the same Exchange server, Exchange stores the file in its database only once. All of the e-mail recipients get pointers to the file, but only one copy ever exists. (The last one to delete the e-mail causes Exchange to remove the centralized copy of the item.)

Installing Exchange Server

Here are the steps to follow when installing Microsoft Exchange Server on your Windows NT Server computer:

1. While logged on to Windows NT server as an administrator, run BackOffice Setup, select installation of Microsoft Exchange Server and click OK.

   Refer to the instructions that came with your BackOffice CD-ROM to find out how to start BackOffice Setup.

2. In the Exchange Server welcome dialog box, click OK. See Figure 16-34.

Figure 16-34: Exchange Server Setup enables you to install Exchange on your Windows NT Server computer.

3. Review the destination directory and click Change Directory if you want to change it. Then click Complete/Custom, as shown in Figure 16-35.

   The destination defaults to \EXCHSRVR on the drive where you installed Windows NT Server. I strongly recommend selecting custom installation, since it gives you more control over the process and more knowledge about what you're installing.

4. Review the Exchange components that you want to install. Click to clear any check boxes that you don't want to install and click to set any check boxes that you do want to install.

   If you want to view and select individual subcomponents for installation, click the check box about which you want to see details and click Change Option, as shown in Figure 16-36.

Don't use the disk space consumption shown in Figure 16-36 as a guide to your installation decisions. Your version of Microsoft Exchange may require different amounts of disk space, depending on when you purchased it.

I recommend installing all of the Exchange Server and Exchange Administrator components. If you're low on disk space, you can skip installation of Books Online.

Figure 16-35: You can select the type of installation and where you want the files to go.

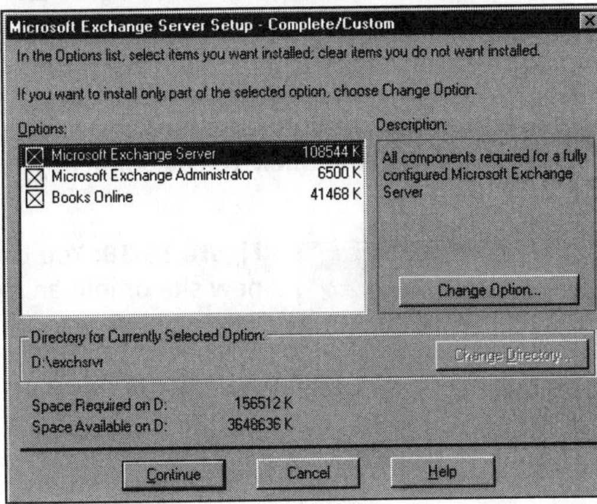

Figure 16-36: You can select which components of Exchange Server you want to install.

5. Click Continue. In the Choose Licensing Mode dialog box shown in Figure 16-37, click Per Server or Per Seat, depending on the Exchange Server licensing mode that you want to use. Then click Continue.

   Click Help for details on Exchange Server licensing options.

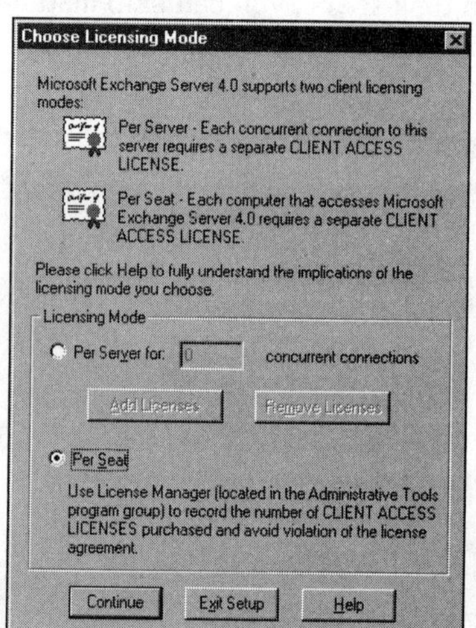

Figure 16-37: You can select the Exchange Server licensing mode that you want to use.

6. Read the licensing warning message. If you agree, click I agree and click OK.

   You must agree to purchase the appropriate client licenses, or Setup won't proceed.

7. Click Create a new site. Type the name of your organization and the name of your site. Then click OK. See Figure 16-38. Click Yes to confirm your choice.

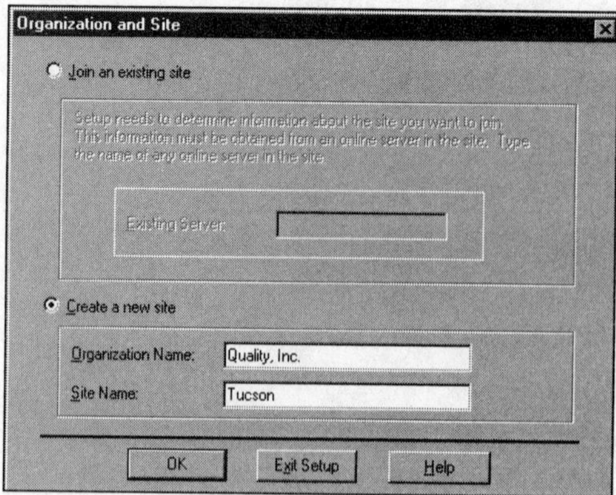

Figure 16-38: You can create a new site or join an existing site.

8. In the Site Services Account dialog box shown in Figure 16-39, click Browse and select the special NT account that you created in the previous section. Type the password of the account and click OK.

The default account that appears in the Account Name field is the account that's currently logged on. Don't accept the default. Change it to the account that you created in the previous section.

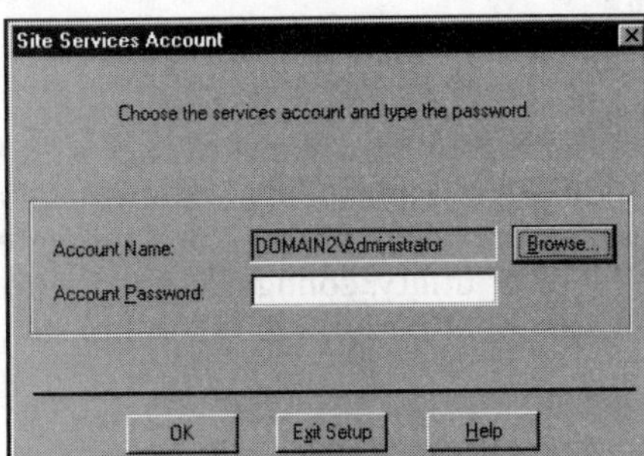

Figure 16-39: You can specify the NT account and password used by Exchange services.

9. You'll see a message indicating rights granted to the account, as shown in Figure 16-40. Click OK.

   At this point, files are copied to your hard disk, and Exchange configuration is completed in several minutes.

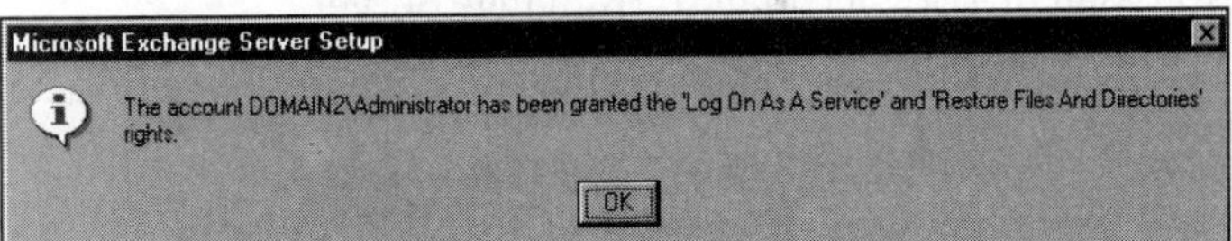

Figure 16-40: This message indicates that appropriate rights have been granted to the administrator account.

10. As shown in Figure 16-41, you're given the choice of running the optimizer or exiting Setup. Exchange installation is now complete, and optimization is optional.

    I'll briefly discuss the optimization process in the next section. If you opt to skip optimization now, you can always run it later.

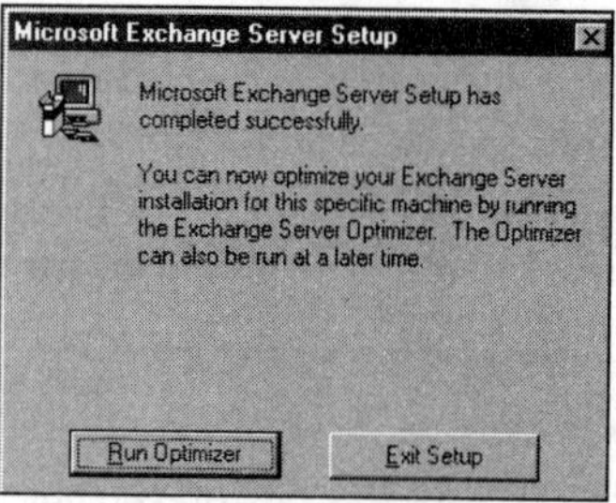

Figure 16-41: You can either run the Exchange Optimizer or complete installation of Exchange Server.

The number of menu items added under Start ➪ Programs ➪ Microsoft Exchange can be a little intimidating. (I got 10 different items, based on my installation choices. Your mileage may vary.) Don't worry. Five of these are templates for use with the Windows NT Performance Monitor utility, configured to monitor different aspects of Exchange Server. (You'll learn about Performance Monitor in Chapter 19.) The rest of the items are

- **Administrator.** This utility enables you to administer centrally all of the objects associated with an Exchange Server installation.
- **Optimizer.** This utility finds the right place for your Exchange Server files and fine-tunes Exchange's configuration to optimize performance.
- **Setup Editor.** This utility enables you to specify customized Setup options for Exchange clients.
- **Migration Wizard.** This utility gives you the option of migrating from Microsoft Mail or Lotus cc:Mail to Exchange Server.
- **Books Online.** This menu choice points to Exchange Server documentation in online Help format.

Optimizing Exchange Server

Exchange Server includes an optimizer that asks you several questions about how your Exchange Server will be used, examines the performance of your available disk hardware, and determines the optimal location for its files as well as some other low-level configuration options. To start the optimization process, click Start ➪ Programs ➪ Microsoft Exchange ➪ Microsoft Exchange Optimizer. A wizard guides you through the optimization steps. Once it determines where to place various files, it will actually move them for you.

During the optimization process, you'll be required to shut down any Exchange services that are running on your Windows NT Server computer. If you don't want to do this because people are actively using Exchange Server, plan to perform this optimization procedure at a time when it's OK to shut down Exchange.

For example, I ran an Exchange optimization on a computer with a couple of relatively slow IDE drives and a high-performance Fast and Wide SCSI drive. The optimizer put all of the frequently accessed files on the SCSI drive and the less-often accessed log files on one of the IDE drives. Once you get Exchange Server installed, I recommend running the optimizer to assure the best performance.

Migrating to Exchange Server

If you're already running Microsoft Mail or Lotus cc:Mail, you can migrate these Postoffices to Microsoft Exchange Server. The wizard that guides you through this process will even create Windows NT accounts for each e-mail user account, if you want. To migrate from an existing mail system, click Start ⇨ Programs ⇨ Microsoft Exchange ⇨ Microsoft Exchange Migration and follow the on-screen instructions.

If you're migrating from Microsoft Mail to Exchange Server, a good approach involves installing the Exchange client on all client computers. Until Exchange Server is installed on the server, the clients continue to use the Mail Postoffice on it without a hitch. Next, use the Migration Tool to convert e-mail users, inboxes, folders, and address books. (If you have both a PC and AppleTalk network, Microsoft Mail Connector enables AppleTalk Microsoft Mail users to communicate with PC users.)

Installing Microsoft Exchange Clients

Your Microsoft Exchange client computers can be running DOS, Windows 3.1, Windows for Workgroups, or Windows NT 3.x. Of course, Exchange clients are included in Windows 95 and Windows NT 4.0, but upgraded clients for these platforms are included with Exchange Server and should be used instead to communicate with Exchange Server. (Macintosh client computers can communicate with Exchange Server via the Microsoft Mail Connector, mentioned earlier in this chapter. In addition, the most recent update of Exchange Server includes a Macintosh Exchange client.)

If you have network users who run DOS, they can install and use the Microsoft Exchange client for DOS. This client is provided with Exchange Server. It has less functionality than its Windows-based counterparts but can fill the bill for clients that just aren't up to running Windows. Find the DOS Exchange client software on the BackOffice CD-ROM. (The English version is in \EXCHANGE\CLIENTS\ENG\DOS.) On the DOS client computer, run Setup and follow the on-screen instructions.

Other clients have similar installation procedures. The BackOffice CD-ROM includes folders for Windows 3.x (Windows 3.1 and Windows for Workgroups), Windows 95, and Windows NT 3.x Exchange clients. In each case, run Setup from the appropriate Exchange client folder on the client computer.

EXCHANGE FOR WINDOWS 95

You may have noticed a Windows 95 client included in both Windows 95 and the Exchange Server product. They're different. The version included in Windows 95 is a "lite" version, whereas the Exchange Server version is a complete Exchange client. Always opt to install the full version on your Windows 95 computers.

Windows NT Chat

No, this isn't the title of a late-night cable talk show featuring the titillating fantasies of NT users. Chat is a very simple messaging system that enables you to "dial" another computer on the network and carry on a real-time text conversation. Whereas e-mail is analogous to calling someone and leaving a voice message, using Chat is similar to calling someone and reaching them to converse (or at least ringing their phone and annoying them).

Let's say you're urgently trying to reach a colleague, and he's on the telephone. What are your options? You can leave him a voice mail message and hope he checks it and responds to you soon. Alternatively, you can send him an e-mail message, again with the hope that you'll get a timely response. Or you can use Chat to make his computer ring (literally) and then hold a text conversation with him.

Chat is one of those utilities that people either love or hate. Many folks think it's a great tool for immediately reaching someone who's already on the phone. Others are annoyed by the interruptions caused by Chat. If it's used frequently for communication that's better suited to e-mail or voice mail, Chat can indeed be a bothersome time-waster. On the other hand, if you're walking one or more users through resolving a problem, and the time required for each step varies, Chat offers an effective approach to communication. You don't need the phone pressed to your ear, you don't need to switch between phone lines, and you can continue with other work on your computer until the person at the other end is ready for you to intervene again.

The Chat utility is included in Windows for Workgroups and in all versions of Windows NT, but it isn't included in Windows 95. You can only hold Chat conversations between computers that have the Chat utility.

Placing a Call through Chat

To start Chat, click Start ➪ Programs ➪ Accessories ➪ Chat. The first time that you do this after starting the computer, you may see a brief message displayed about starting NetDDE. NetDDE (short for Network Dynamic Data Exchange) is the interprocess communication mechanism used to communicate between Chat applications on different network computers. (It's also used by Clipboard Viewer, which I discussed in Chapter 15.)

The Chat utility contains two text windows. The upper window is used for typing your text, and the lower window displays the text typed on the other computer. Figure 16-42 illustrates a brief conversation using the Chat utility.

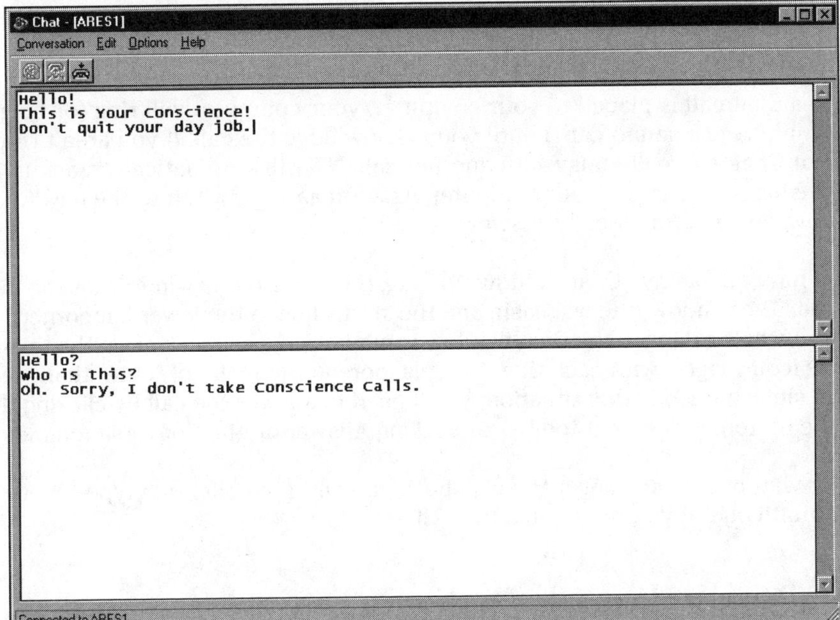

Figure 16-42: Using Chat, you type text into the upper window and view responses in the lower window.

Unlike e-mail, the text in a Chat conversation is transferred in real-time. Each character typed is immediately displayed on the other computer. (You can even see the other user backspacing over their mistakes.)

Here's how to place a call using the Chat utility:

1. Click Start ➪ Programs ➪ Accessories ➪ Chat.
2. On the Conversation menu, click Dial.

   Alternatively, you can click the leftmost button on the Chat toolbar, which does the same thing.
3. In the Select Computer dialog box, type or select the name of the computer that you want to contact. Then click OK.
4. In the lower left corner of the Chat window, a status line indicates that the remote computer is being dialed.

At this point, your computer will beep every five seconds. Each beep corresponds to a ringing sound on the computer that you're trying to contact. (The remote computer will literally ring if it contains a properly configured sound card.) The beeping and ringing will continue until the person at the other computer picks up the call or until you hang up.

Answering a Chat Call

When a Chat call is placed to your computer, your computer will ring (or beep, if you don't have a sound card) until you acknowledge the call. If you aren't running Chat or Chat is already busy with another call, NT will automatically start up a new instance of Chat on your computer. As soon as you switch to the new Chat window, you'll automatically answer the call.

If you have an inactive Chat window running, NT will use this window for the incoming call. The window title will flash, and the status line in the lower left corner will tell you who's calling. If the Chat window is minimized, the receiver on the telephone icon wiggles with each ring. (This is more in the realm of "cute" than "real-world simulation.") In this situation, you'll need to answer the call by clicking the middle button on the Chat toolbar or clicking Answer on the Conversation menu.

Either way, once you answer the call, both you and the caller can type text to each other until one of you terminates the call.

Conversing through Chat

Communication through the Chat utility is full-duplex — both parties can type text simultaneously without waiting for each other.

The Edit menu enables you to cut or copy text from a Chat window and put it on the Clipboard. You can even paste text from the Clipboard to your Chat window, and the person on the other end will think you're an amazingly fast typist. In the Options menu, you can change the text font, background color, and text window orientation. You can also use it to turn off the sound and avoid that incessant ringing in your ears. (If you hear ringing, voices, or other sounds when Chat isn't running, the Options menu can't help you; try your friendly therapist.)

The Preferences command on the Options menu allows you to display your own font or your conversation partner's font. Although some folks like to use larger fonts for more dramatic statements, using different fonts can become disorienting. It's more difficult to match up responses in the conversation.

If a group within your organization uses Chat frequently, you may want to have them agree to use a standard font. If everyone uses the same font, conversations will look the same to everyone, regardless of whose font you're displaying.

You can change Chat to display side-by-side windows. Some people prefer this, since it can help to relate the responses to each other. To do this, click Preferences on the Options menu, click to select Side by Side, and click OK.

Conducting Multiple Conversations

Although Chat doesn't allow party lines or conference calls, it does let you carry on multiple conversations simultaneously. Let's say you're assisting one of your users over the phone and using Chat to walk another user though solving another problem. Yet another user gets a busy signal on your phone, so he or she attempts to get your attention via Chat.

That user won't get a busy signal. NT will open another Chat window and ring your computer. If you answer (as described earlier in this chapter), you'll be able to chat with two different users using two separate Chat windows. The telephone analogy is a multiline phone, where you switch between lines as you switch between Chat windows.

If you get confused about which conversation you're having, check the bottom left corner of each Chat window to see the name of the computer to which you're connected. Unfortunately, Chat doesn't show you the user name, so you'll have to keep a mental note of who is on the other end. Of course, if your computer names are derivatives of user names, you'll have an easier time of it.

Hanging Up

Just as in a phone conversation, either party can terminate the call. You can simply exit the Chat utility, click the Hang Up button, or click Hang Up on the Conversation menu. When one party hangs up, the other party is notified with a message on the status bar at the bottom of the Chat window. At this point, either party can initiate a new conversation.

Disabling Chat

If you don't want to be bothered by Chat calls, you can effectively disable it on your computer in one of two ways. One way involves renaming the SystemRoot\SYSTEM32\WINCHAT.EXE file to something else. (If you installed NT on an NTFS volume, you'll need administrative privileges to do this.) When a Chat call is placed to your computer, it won't find the Chat utility and will fail to connect. This is the approach that I recommend. Alternatively, as an administrator, you can use the Services application in Control Panel to disable the Network DDE service. This prevents Chat connections but also has the side effect of disabling ClipBook connections and any other applications that might use NetDDE. Chapter 17 provides details on using Control Panel to manage services.

In either case, the calling computer will be told that your computer isn't responding. This is as close as Chat gets to a busy signal but is more analogous to "The number you have reached is no longer in service."

Summary

In this chapter, you've learned about the communication and collaboration capabilities of Windows NT Server. Although Microsoft Mail is no longer included in NT 4.0 per se, you can still create and administer a Postoffice using the Microsoft Mail Postoffice application in Control Panel. You can also access new or existing Microsoft Mail Postoffices with the built-in Exchange client in NT. Microsoft's Windows Messaging technology is clearly moving toward a communications environment based on Microsoft Exchange Server. Although this product isn't included in Windows NT Server, I covered the basics of installing this BackOffice component to take full advantage of the included Exchange client software. Finally, you learned about the Chat utility that enables you to have text conversations in real-time.

If you set up and maintain these communication tools in your organization, your users will look to you as an expert. Therefore, it's important to learn as much as you can about e-mail and Chat, so you can pass along this knowledge to your users.

Now that you know how to use Windows NT Server 4.0, you're ready to delve into the details of configuring and administering your servers and network in Part IV.

INSIDE STORY

In the NT group at Microsoft, we used e-mail for absolutely everything — and I mean everything. If a restroom was going to be shut down for maintenance, there was an e-mail about it. When we'd buy dinner for the engineers working late, we found it convenient to send e-mail to the entire group announcing the room location and type of cuisine for the evening (for example, pizza, subs, donuts, cake, spring rolls, and so on).

Sometimes, we'd take a head count of people interested in food by polling them via e-mail. People would respond with one-line messages "I would like some pizza," "Save me a slice," "Gimme some," or just "Me, me, me!"

We sometimes ignored the scope and power of this type of e-mail. Folks forgot that the e-mail alias to which they were sending these messages included over 850 people scattered across the planet. Occasionally, we'd be jarred into remembering this when a Microsoft employee from Australia would ask us to save a slice for her, or someone at Microsoft Canada would ask us to mail a slice. Occasionally, the recipient thought the mail was local and would ask for directions to room 2/2142, even though they were in Paris and the room was in Redmond. This type of exchange really gave those nightly dinners an international flavor.

Configuring and Administering Your NT Server Network

✦ ✦ ✦ ✦

In This Part

✦ ✦ ✦ ✦

Configuring and Customizing Windows NT Server

Since you've chosen to work with computers, it's likely that you used to spend lots of time with Tinker Toys, LEGOs, or Erector sets when you were a child. (Perhaps you still do.) What's the fascination with this genre of toys and what's the parallel with computers? Configuration and customization. Regardless of what you create, you can determine the shape and style. Even if you work from a set of plans, you can add in, leave out, or modify specific pieces. Almost everything in Windows NT Server can be customized in some way, making it a virtual Erector set of operating system software.

Knowing how to configure your Windows NT Server computers (and, indeed, all Windows NT computers) will provide you with a powerful set of skills that you can use and share in your organization. This knowledge will give you the power to shape your NT configuration to match your needs and preferences and those of your organization, enabling you and your users to work more comfortably and efficiently.

In this chapter, you'll learn how to use Windows NT Server's Control Panel applications to configure and customize your computer. I've also provided additional detail in the more difficult areas — device drivers, services, hardware, and recovery issues. In addition, you'll find out how to configure environments for DOS, Windows 3.x, and OS/2 1.x applications on NT.

Using Windows NT Control Panel

Windows NT Control Panel provides access to most system configuration options in Windows NT Server. As shown in Figure 17-1, it offers a wide variety of functions, from changing the look of your desktop to installing and configuring hardware devices.

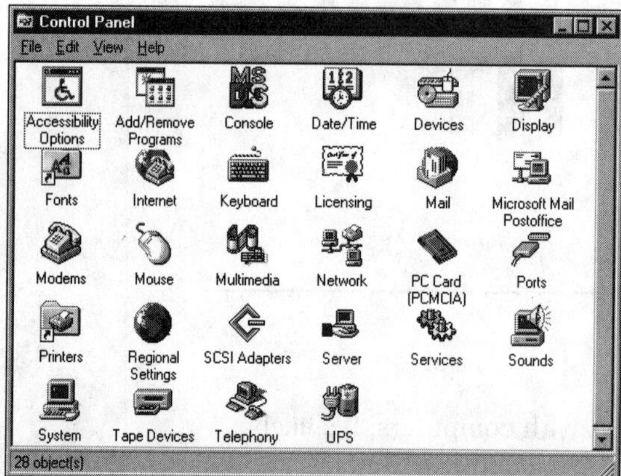

Figure 17-1: Windows NT Control Panel provides access to most configuration options.

You may find the applications in Control Panel referred to in the literature as *applets,* for mini-applications. Many of these programs are quite complex, so I'll call them applications.

The following sections discuss each of the Control Panel applications in the order in which they appear in the Control Panel window — alphabetically. If you didn't install each of the optional components during Windows NT Server operating system installation, your Control Panel window won't display all of the applications covered in this chapter.

Not every detail of each application is covered; some are more self-explanatory than others. Therefore, I'll focus on the key aspects that will be most valuable in your role as NT administrator.

Accessibility Options Application

The Accessibility Options application is used to change the behavior of the keyboard, sound card, and mouse to accommodate users with hearing or motor control disabilities.

A wide variety of third-party applications, utilities, and specialized hardware devices are available to make Windows NT easier for people with disabilities. To find out more, click Start ➪ Help, click the Find tab, and search for "Products and Services for People with Disabilities." Then double-click "Getting More Information."

Add/Remove Programs Application

Remember back in Chapter 9 when you installed Windows NT Server and had to make all of those painful decisions about installing optional components? The Add/Remove Programs application enables you to pick up anything that you may have left behind during NT installation. If you installed everything, there's nothing to add, but you can also use this application to remove items that you regret having installed. In the Add/Remove Programs Properties dialog box, click the Windows NT Setup tab and follow the on-screen instructions.

You can also use this tool to install and uninstall other applications. Click the Install/Uninstall tab, as shown in Figure 17-2. Just click the Install button and follow the on-screen instructions of your application's installation program. Applications that register themselves to be uninstalled by Windows NT are listed in the bottom half of the Install/Uninstall tab. Any application that shows up in this list can be later uninstalled using this dialog box. When it's time to remove one of these applications, click its name on the list and click Add/Remove.

Not all applications register themselves to be uninstalled by NT. If the application that you want to remove from the computer isn't in the list on the Install/Uninstall tab, refer to the application's documentation for details on how to uninstall it.

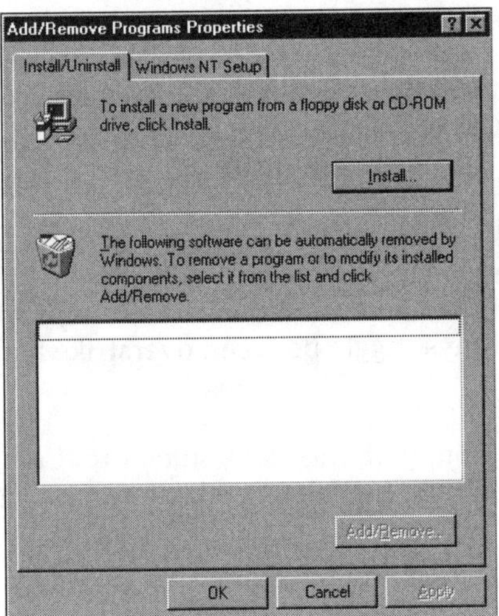

Figure 17-2: The Install/Uninstall tab is used to install and remove applications.

AUTOPLAY CAN DO THIS, TOO

Most CD-ROM applications arriving on the market as Windows 95 compatible include a feature called *autoplay,* present on Windows 95 and NT 4.0. As soon as you insert the CD-ROM into the drive, a program on the CD-ROM is automatically run that enables you to install or uninstall the application. This feature minimizes the need for the Add/Remove Programs application, but it will be some time before all of your applications behave this way. Until then, you can use Add/Remove Programs to manage installation.

Console Application

The Console application provides a rich set of controls for customizing the look and behavior of NT Command Prompt windows. If you spend much time at a Command Prompt, you'll really appreciate these features.

The changes that you make using the Console application apply to all Command Prompt windows subsequently created by the user who's currently logged on. You can tweak the same parameters for an individual Command Prompt window by clicking the upper left corner of the window and clicking Properties. In this case, you will be asked whether the changes that you make should apply only to the individual Command Prompt window or to the shortcut that started that instance of the Command Prompt window.

As shown in Figure 17-3, the Options tab controls cursor size, windowed versus full-screen display, command history retention, and editing modes. The command history feature is similar to the DOSKEY command under DOS. You can specify the number of commands to retain and then call up the list by pressing F7 or simply press the UP and DOWN ARROW keys to scroll through the list.

If you often repeat the same command several times while in a Command Prompt, I recommend that you select the Discard Old Duplicates check box, to eliminate the clutter of duplicate command lines in the command history.

QuickEdit Mode, mentioned in Chapter 14, lets you select and copy a chunk of the window to the Clipboard, without using any menu commands. Selecting the Insert Mode check box changes the default typing mode in the Command Prompt window from overstrike to insert. (You can always toggle between overstrike and insert modes by pressing INSERT.)

The Font and Colors tabs need no explanation. (OK, they let you control Command Prompt fonts and colors, respectively.) However, the Layout tab, shown in Figure 17-4, does require some clarification.

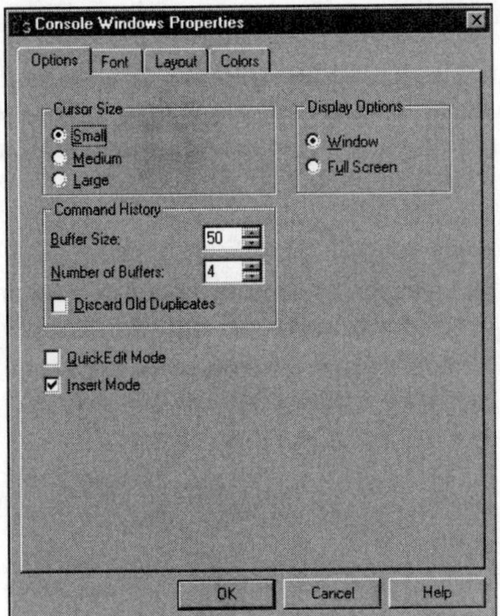

Figure 17-3: The Options tab controls basic Command Prompt behavior.

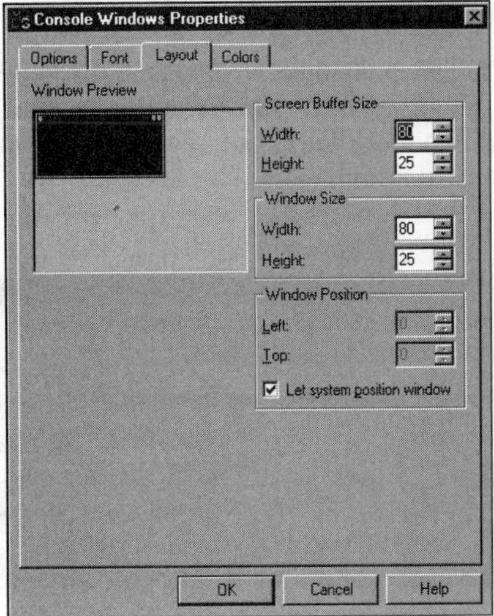

Figure 17-4: The Layout tab gives you control over screen buffer and window sizes.

You can control the dimensions of the displayed Command Prompt window. The default size is 80 characters by 25 lines. I prefer 50 visible lines when I'm working in a Command Prompt window, so this is one of the first settings that I change.

When you use ALT+ENTER to switch a Command Prompt window to full-screen mode on an Intel computer, NT will do its best to pick the right number of lines to display. Most displays can handle 25, 43, or 50 lines of text, so if you do much switching to full-screen mode, you may want to pick one of these heights. Click the Layout tab and select the appropriate number of lines in the Height field under Window Size.

In addition, you can create a screen buffer larger than the displayed window size and scroll (or perhaps a better word is "pan") through the buffer. This feature is useful when you need to refer to the details of an interaction, rather than just a list of commands that you've issued.

Date/Time Application

You were introduced to the Date/Time application in Chapter 9, during the Windows NT Server installation process. This application is used for setting the date and time in your computer's clock, as well as the correct time zone for your geographical location. Click the appropriate tab, make the required changes, and click OK. Changes made to the time and date using this application will be reflected in the CMOS system clock in your computer.

Devices Application

The Devices application provides you with the capability to start, stop, and configure the startup behavior of Windows NT device drivers. Figure 17-5 shows the Devices dialog box that appears when you double-click the Devices icon in Control Panel.

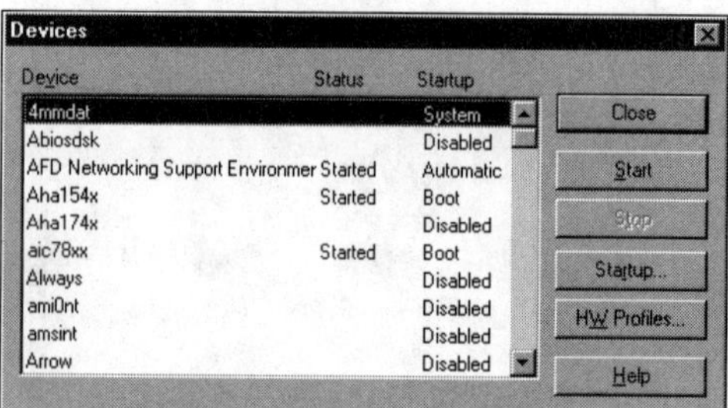

Figure 17-5: You can start, stop, and configure NT device drivers using the Devices application.

An installed device driver can be in one of two states: started or stopped. The state of the driver is displayed in the Status column of the Devices dialog box. (A blank entry in this column means the driver isn't running.)

There are five startup types for drivers: Boot, System, Automatic, Manual, and Disabled. Boot, System, and Automatic are almost identical, since they all start the driver automatically when the operating system starts. The distinction among them involves when they come to life during the boot process. Drivers set to Boot (such as hard disk controller drivers) are started earliest, since the operating system might need to boot from them. Drivers set to System (such as keyboard, mouse, and CD-ROM drivers) are started after the kernel is loaded, but before the operating system is completely up. Automatic drivers (such as network adapter and parallel port drivers) are started after NT has completed its initialization. (See the section entitled "Understanding the Boot Sequence" in Chapter 21 for details about the steps involved in the Windows NT boot process.)

If you scan through the drivers, you may be surprised to find the startup type of some of the file system drivers set to Disabled, even though the drivers are started. NTFS, FAT (called Fastfat), and CDFS fall into this category. Don't panic. This is normal. Since the I/O subsystem loads these drivers, they aren't loaded in the Boot, System, or Automatic phases of the operating system initialization process. The NT designers didn't have a startup type to cover this situation. They didn't want to set the drivers to Manual, or users might inadvertently try to stop or start them. So they decided to mark the file system drivers Disabled.

If you set a driver to Manual, it won't start unless you explicitly start it, either from the Devices application or by running an application or other service that tries to start it. Setting a driver to Disabled is self-explanatory. You can't start a Disabled driver until you change it to one of the other startup types.

Installing and Removing Drivers

It's best to install drivers using the other interfaces or installation applications available to you. Starting and stopping drivers with the Devices application should be used only as a last resort or as a troubleshooting technique. Installation and removal of drivers vary from one device to another. Some drivers are installed and configured automatically when you install applications that use them and are removed when you uninstall the applications. Others are explicitly installed and removed through applications such as the Network application in Control Panel.

(See Chapter 8 for an example of installing a network adapter driver using the Network application.)

Controlling a Driver

It's easy to start a stopped driver or stop a running driver. (One way to stop a running driver is to give him his car back.) Just click the driver that you want to control and click the appropriate button to start or stop it. If you try to stop a driver that's being used for a critical function (such as a boot device), NT will prevent you from stopping it.

When you start or stop a device driver, you'll typically see a message indicating that NT is attempting to carry out your request. If it's successful, the status of the service displayed in the Devices dialog box will reflect the change.

Configuring a Driver

To change a device driver's startup behavior, click the driver that you want to configure and click Startup. To change its startup type, click Boot, System, Automatic, Manual, or Disabled under Startup Type. Then click OK.

Display Application

I've already covered several of the features included in the Display application, to control the look and behavior of your Windows NT desktop. See the section entitled "Changing the Desktop Look" in Chapter 14.

Fonts Shortcut

The Fonts folder shortcut enables you to view a list of installed fonts and manage their installation, removal, and properties. When you double-click the Fonts icon in Control Panel, you get an Explorer-like window displaying a list of installed fonts. When you click a font file, you can use the File menu to view it, delete it, or see its properties. As in Explorer, you can use the View menu to craft the window so that it displays just the information that you need.

If you use TrueType fonts exclusively, you can instruct NT to display only those fonts within your applications. To do this, click Options on the View menu, click the TrueType Fonts tab, and click to select the Show only TrueType fonts check box.

Installing a new font is simple. On the File menu, click the Install New Font option. Select the directory containing the font files that you want to install, select your font, and click OK.

At this point, you may miss the little font preview window provided by Windows NT 3.x and Windows 3.x. You can still preview fonts by clicking the font and clicking Open on the File menu.

Internet Application

The Internet application in Control Panel enables you to configure access from this computer to the Internet over the LAN via a proxy server. (If you're connecting this computer directly to the Internet, you don't need to use this application.) Figure 17-6 presents the Internet Properties dialog box.

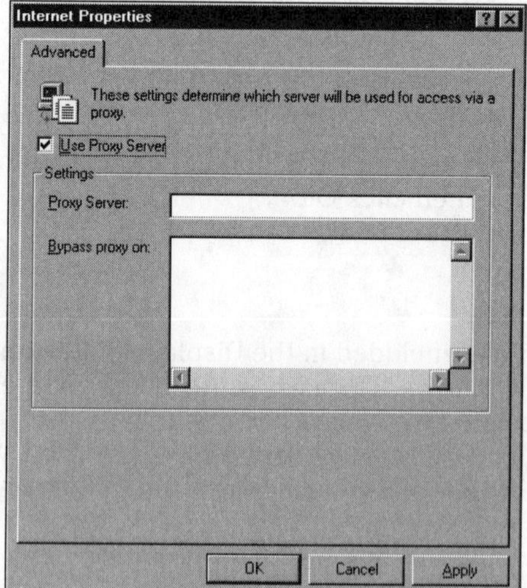

Figure 17-6: You can filter all Internet requests through a proxy server.

If you click to select the Use Proxy Server check box and specify a proxy server address and port number, all requests to and from the Internet are filtered through the proxy server. The proxy server acts as a firewall barrier between the Internet and your internal LAN, keeping users on the Internet from accessing information on your LAN.

You can also list specific Internet server addresses that you want to access directly, bypassing the proxy server completely. List them under Bypass proxy on, separating the addresses by commas. See Chapter 24 for more details about Internet server security.

Keyboard Application

The Keyboard application is used to control keyboard repeat, input cursor blink rate, and the layout of your keyboard based on locale. In addition, you can install or change keyboard device drivers. Here's how to install or change a keyboard driver:

1. In the Keyboard Properties dialog box, click the General tab and click Change.
2. In the Select Device dialog box, click Show all devices. Click the specific model of your keyboard, as shown in Figure 17-7.

   If your keyboard manufacturer or model isn't listed, and you have an NT driver disk supplied by the manufacturer, click Have Disk and follow the on-screen instructions to install the keyboard driver.

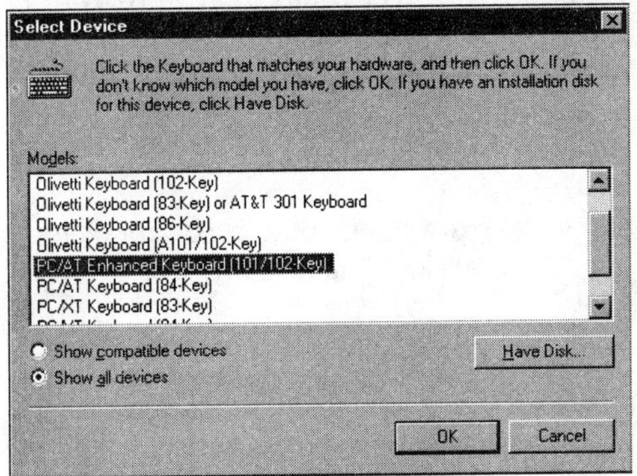

Figure 17-7: You can change keyboard drivers using the General tab.

3. Click OK and restart the computer if prompted to do so.

The Input Locales tab in the Keyboard Properties dialog box is identical to the Input Locales tab in the Regional Settings application discussed later in this chapter. NT won't allow you to have both tabs open simultaneously. Changes in one application will be reflected in the other.

Licensing Application

The Licensing application enables you to manage client licensing on your Windows NT Server network. You can use it to change between Per Server and Per Seat licensing, add and remove client licenses assigned to NT Server, and control replication of licensing information. (For a comparison of Per Server and Per Seat licensing, see Chapter 7.) Figure 17-8 presents the Choose Licensing Mode dialog box.

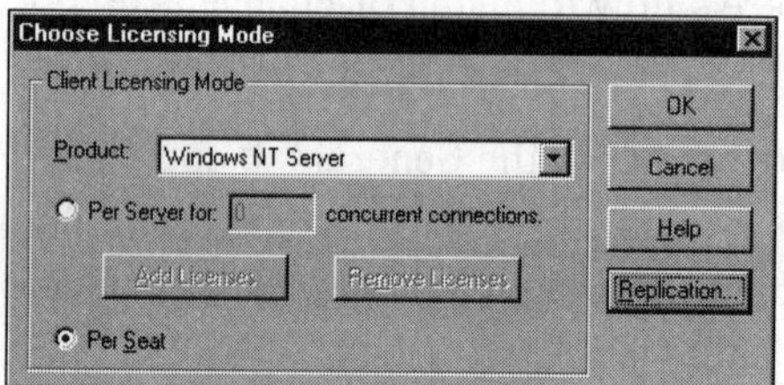

Figure 17-8: The Licensing application enables you to choose and manage your Windows NT Server licensing mode.

By default, the domain's primary domain controller (PDC) is used as the central repository for all licensing data. Every 24 hours, the data is replicated automatically to the PDC. If you want to use another server that's central to your entire enterprise to act as the licensing data repository or you want to control the replication frequency, click Replication. Figure 17-9 shows the Replication Configuration dialog box.

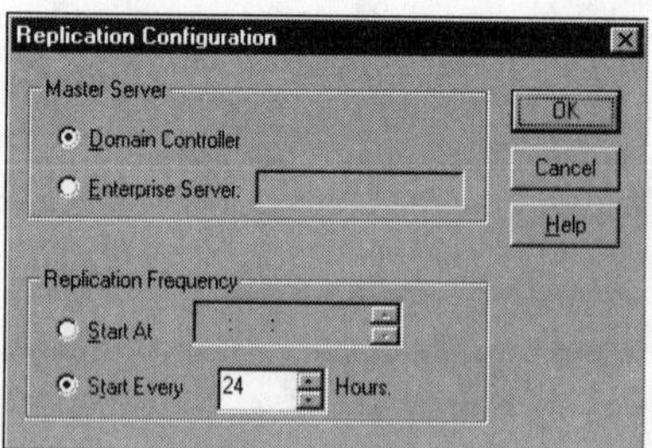

Figure 17-9: You can control where and when licensing data is replicated.

Under Replication Frequency, you can elect to replicate the licensing data from this computer at a specific time every day (using Start At), or you can replicate at specific intervals using Start Every. The default replication frequency is every 24 hours.

I strongly recommend that you stay away from Start At and always select a Replication Frequency that's based on a Start Every interval. If you use Start At, unless you manually set different start times on each server, all of the replication will happen at the same time and degrade network performance. By selecting Start Every, NT will automatically stagger the replication start times, minimizing the impact on your network.

Mail Application

Once you've started using the Microsoft Exchange client, you can view and display various properties of your Exchange client installation using the Mail application in Control Panel. See Chapter 16 for details on installing and using the Microsoft Exchange client software included with Windows NT Server 4.0.

Microsoft Mail Postoffice Application

You use this application to create and administer a Microsoft Mail Postoffice. For detailed information about this application, see Chapter 16.

Modems Application

When you start the Modems application for the first time, it will attempt to install a new modem.

1. If you don't want NT to detect your modem automatically, click to select the Don't detect my modem check box, shown in Figure 17-10.

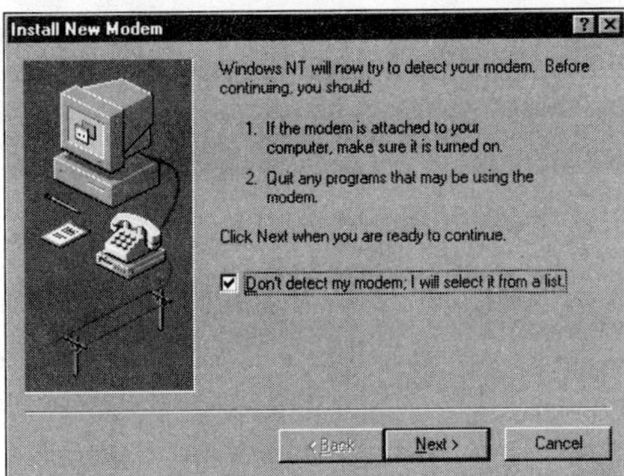

Figure 17-10: Decide whether you want NT to detect your modem automatically.

2. Click Next. If you elected to select your modem manually, click the manufacturer and model and click Next, as shown in Figure 17-11.

   If your modem manufacturer or model isn't listed and you have an NT driver disk supplied by the manufacturer, click Have Disk and follow the on-screen instructions to install the driver.

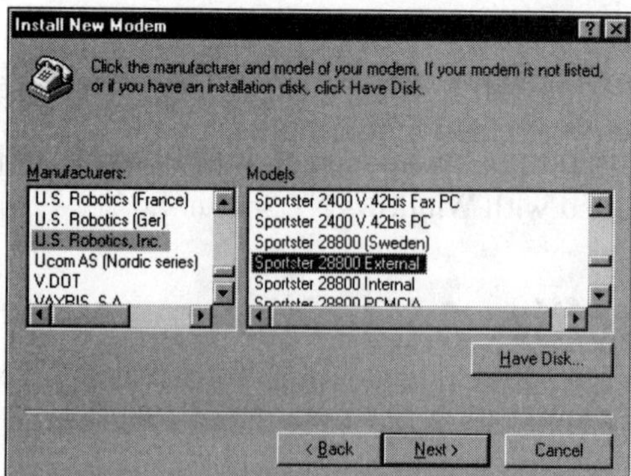

Figure 17-11: Select your modem manufacturer and model.

3. Click the serial port on which you've installed the modem and click Selected Ports. Then click Next.
4. Configure the modem as prompted by the on-screen instructions.

Mouse Application

The Mouse application in Control Panel controls the various aspects of mouse operation, including right- or left-handed operation, double-click speed, mouse pointer appearance, mouse pointer motion, and installation of mouse device drivers.

Here's how to install or change a mouse device driver:

1. In the Mouse Properties dialog box, click the General tab and click Change.
2. In the Select Device dialog box, shown in Figure 17-12, click the Show all devices. Click the manufacturer, then the specific model of your mouse.

   If your mouse manufacturer or model isn't listed and you have an NT driver disk supplied by the manufacturer, click Have Disk and follow the on-screen instructions to install the driver.
3. Click OK, and follow the on-screen instructions.

   Configuration of each driver is different. If you're installing an inport (or bus) mouse, you'll need to know its IRQ, I/O address, and so on. If you're installing a serial mouse, you'll need to know which COM port it uses.
4. Restart the computer if prompted to do so.

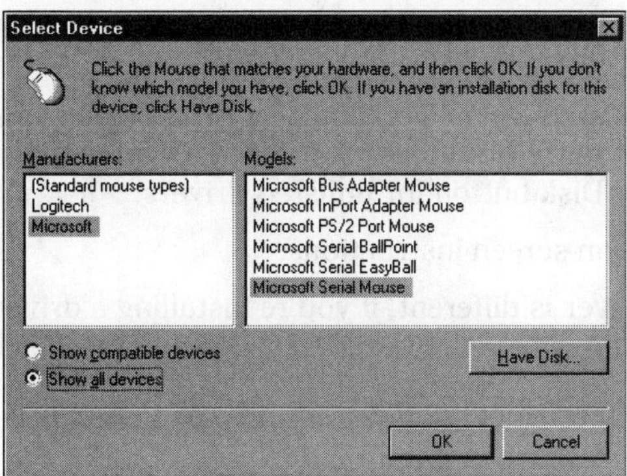

Figure 17-12: You can change mouse drivers using the General tab.

Multimedia Application

The Multimedia application in Windows NT 4.0 controls the recording and playback volume of WAV files, the size of AVI video file playback, MIDI output, audio CD volume, and installation of multimedia device drivers.

Here's how to install a multimedia device driver:

1. In the Multimedia Properties dialog box, click the Devices tab and click Add, as shown in Figure 17-13.

   You'll see the same complete list of available drivers regardless of what you've selected under Multimedia Devices.

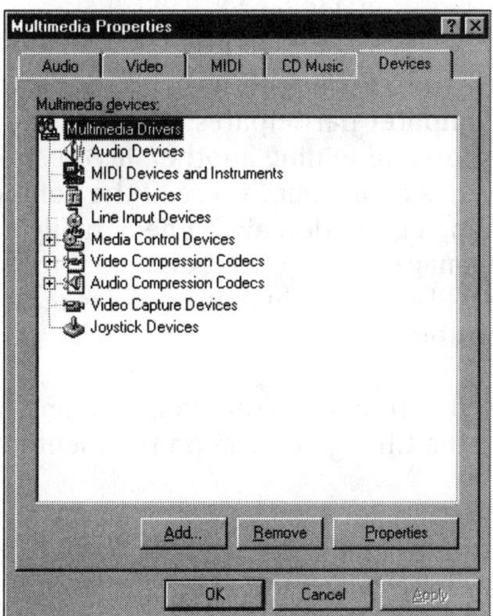

Figure 17-13: Install multimedia drivers using the Devices tab.

2. Click the driver that you want to install, or click Unlisted or Updated Driver, if you don't see your driver in the list.

   If you're installing an unlisted driver, you'll need a driver disk from the multimedia hardware manufacturer. Note that most other driver installation applications in NT use a Have Disk button for unlisted drivers.

3. Click OK, and follow the on-screen instructions.

   Configuration of each driver is different. If you're installing a driver for an adapter, you'll need to know its IRQ, I/O address, DMA channels, and so on.

4. Restart the computer if prompted to do so.

I've left exploring the rest of this application on Windows NT Server as an exercise for you.

If you're familiar with Windows 3.x or Windows NT 3.x, you may recognize that parts of this application were called Drivers and Joystick in Control Panel.

If you have an audio card installed and configured, by default you'll see a speaker icon on the taskbar, next to the time of day. Double-clicking this speaker gives you quick access to the audio volume control.

Network Application

If you've already read previous chapters, you're familiar with the Network application in Control Panel. You've used it to install and configure services, protocols, network adapter drivers, and network bindings. The one area not yet covered is using the Identification tab, shown in Figure 17-14, to change the computer name or domain name of the computer. To do so, click Change.

If the computer is a stand-alone server (or NT Workstation), you can change the domain or workgroup in which this computer participates. This has the effect of leaving the current domain or workgroup and joining another. If you specify a new domain, make sure that the computer has an account there. If the computer is a PDC (primary domain controller), changing the domain name actually changes the name of the domain that the PDC is managing. (You can't change it to point to a different, existing domain.) Changing a PDC's domain name has far-reaching implications. Avoid changing it, if at all possible.

I can't emphasize enough how painful it is to change the domain name of a PDC. It seems easy to change the name using the Change button on the Identification tab, but there's a lot more to it.

Every Windows NT (Server or Workstation) computer must leave the old domain and join the new one. Windows NT Server on each BDC (backup domain controller) must be reinstalled from scratch to move them to the new domain. You must reconfigure all trust relationships in which the old domain participated. Changing a domain name leaves behind a real mess. Don't do it.

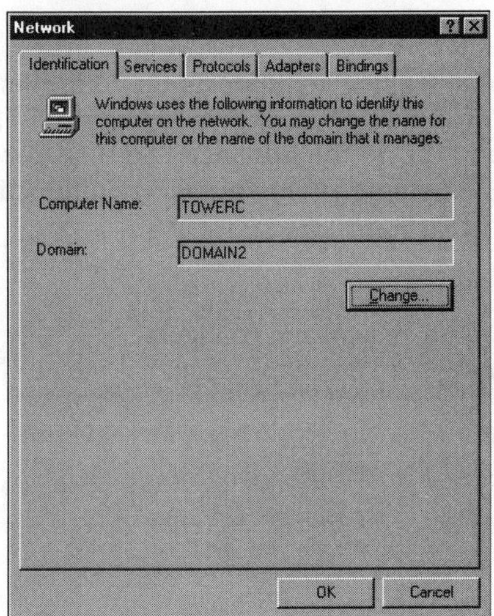

Figure 17-14: Use the Identification tab to change the computer name and workgroup or domain information.

Chapter 8 covered installation and configuration of network adapters and management of network bindings. Chapters 9, 11, and 12 covered installation and configuration of protocols, and Chapters 11 and 15 provided examples of installing network services.

PC Card (PCMCIA) Application

The PC Card application manages PCMCIA devices installed in your computer. (PC Card is the new name for the unpronounceable technology formerly known as PCMCIA.) Although few computers running Windows NT Server contain PC Card adapters, some may exist.

To add, remove, or configure a PC Card driver, click a PC Card in the list of installed cards, click Properties, and click the Driver tab. Then click Add, Remove, or Configure, depending on what you want to do. In some cases, a Resources tab is provided. If it is, click it, then click to clear the Use Automatic Settings check box. Then change the settings as you wish.

If a red *X* appears next to the PC Card device, Microsoft doesn't offer a driver for it, and Windows NT may not support it. Contact the card manufacturer to determine NT driver availability.

Ports Application

The Ports application provides a means of managing serial ports on your computer. To add a serial port, click Add in the Ports dialog box shown in Figure 17-15. Type the port number, I/O port address, and IRQ in the Advanced Settings for New Port dialog box, as shown in Figure 17-16. To enable an on-chip FIFO buffer, click to select the FIFO Enabled check box.

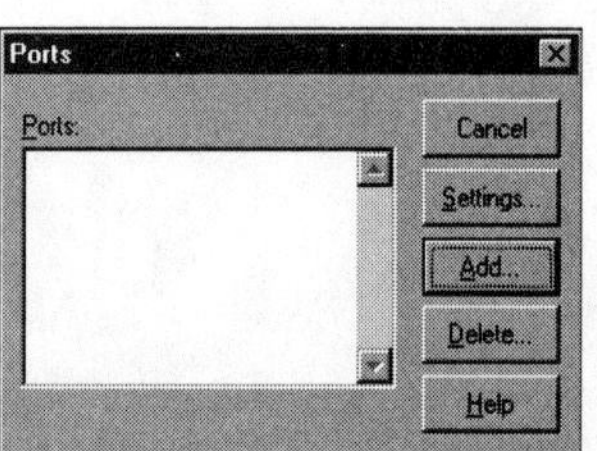

Figure 17-15: Add, delete, and configure serial ports using the Ports application.

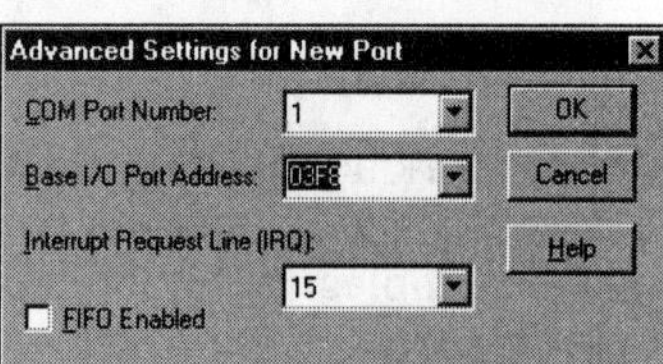

Figure 17-16: You can set the COM port number, I/O port address, IRQ, and FIFO settings in the Advanced Settings for New Port dialog box.

To delete a serial port, in the Ports dialog box click the port that you want to delete and click Delete. To change the baud rate, data bits, parity, stop bits, and flow control of an existing port, click the port and click Settings. Figure 17-17 illustrates this. If you want to change the hardware configuration of the port itself, click Advanced. You'll see a dialog box similar to the one shown in Figure 17-16.

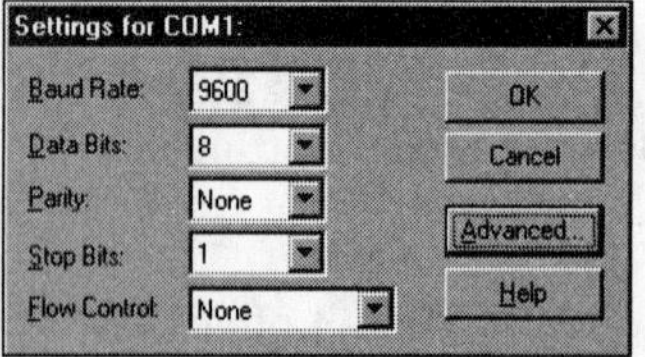

Figure 17-17: Change the basic serial communication parameters using the Settings dialog box.

Printers Shortcut

For convenience, Control Panel includes a shortcut to the Printers folder, where you can add, delete, and manage printers. I'll cover printer management in Chapter 18.

TO FIFO OR NOT TO FIFO

It's usually best to enable the FIFO on your serial port chip, to get better performance. However, some older versions (circa 1990) of the 16550 UART serial port chip contain a bug that may cause data loss when the FIFO is enabled. I recommend enabling the FIFO, then disabling it if you experience transmission problems.

Regional Settings Application

The Regional Settings application enables you to configure the computer's locale and how numbers, currency, time, and date are displayed. Applications that support international settings will pick up these settings and use them to display and interpret data correctly. Figure 17-18 illustrates the Regional Settings Properties dialog box.

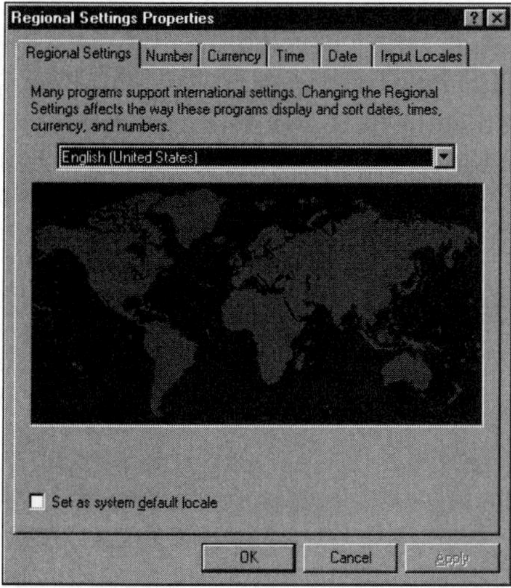

Figure 17-18: The Regional Settings application enables you to control international settings for use by applications in displaying and interpreting data.

The Input Locales tab in the Regional Settings Properties dialog box is identical to the Input Locales tab in the Keyboard application discussed earlier in this chapter. NT won't permit you to have both tabs open simultaneously. Changes in one application will be reflected in the other.

SCSI Adapters Application

The SCSI Adapters application lets you manage installation of SCSI host adapters. You can also use the SCSI Adapters application to delete a SCSI adapter from the computer by deleting its device driver.

If you're familiar with Windows NT 3.x, installation of SCSI drivers took place in the Windows NT Setup application in the Main program group. SCSI host adapter device driver management has now been moved under the Control Panel umbrella.

Installing a SCSI Adapter

Here are the steps required to install a new SCSI host adapter driver:

1. Install the SCSI host adapter hardware on your computer. Then start Windows NT Server.

   Be sure that the SCSI device ID of the adapter itself doesn't conflict with other SCSI devices attached to it. Make sure that the SCSI bus is properly terminated and that any attached devices are powered on when you start the operating system.

   It's a good idea to attach at least one SCSI device to the adapter, so that you can test its operation after installing the driver.

2. Click Start ➪ Settings ➪ Control Panel, and double-click the SCSI Adapters icon.
3. Click the Drivers tab and click Add, as shown in Figure 17-19.

If your computer has a PCI bus or has any IDE CD-ROM drives attached, you may see some or all of your IDE devices listed in the SCSI Adapters application. Although this seems a little weird, take it from me, it's normal. Figure 17-19 shows an example of a built-in IDE PCI interface showing up in the list of SCSI drivers.

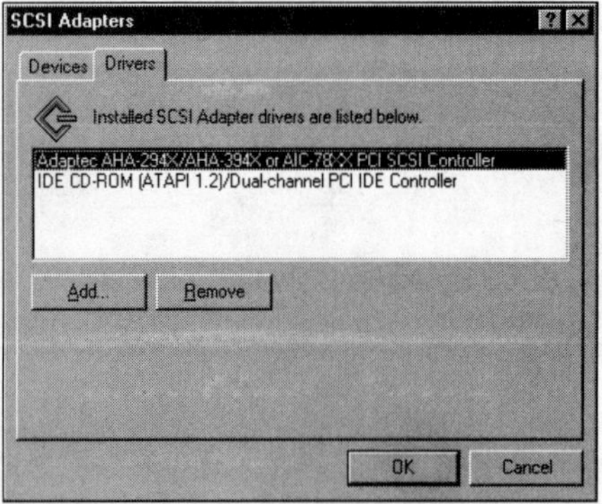

Figure 17-19: Add a new SCSI host adapter driver to the drivers list.

4. In the Install Driver dialog box, shown in Figure 17-20, click the SCSI adapter manufacturer under Manufacturers, then click the specific type of adapter under SCSI Adapter. Click OK.

If your SCSI adapter manufacturer or host adapter type doesn't appear in the list and you have a Windows NT driver disk supplied by the adapter manufacturer, click Have Disk and follow the on-screen instructions for installing the new device driver.

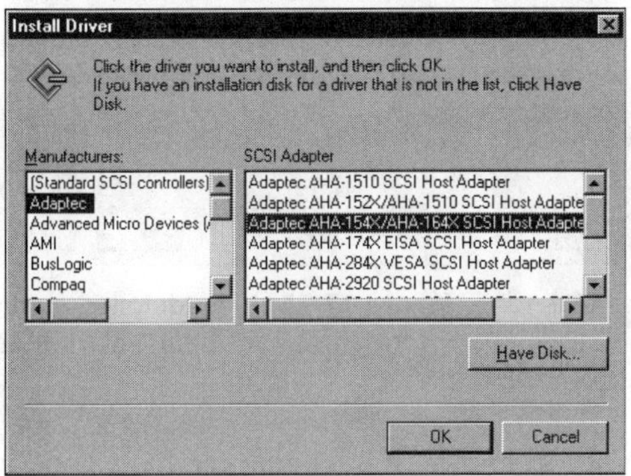

Figure 17-20: Select the manufacturer and SCSI host adapter type.

5. As prompted, insert your Windows NT Server 4.0 CD-ROM and enter the path to the NT files for your CPU platform. Then click OK.

   On my computer, the CD-ROM is drive F, and the path is F:\I386, as shown in Figure 17-21. Once you click OK, the driver is copied to your hard disk and is started.

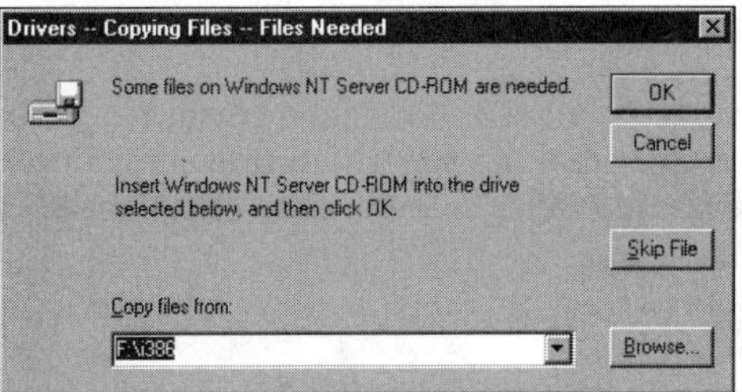

Figure 17-21: You specify where the SCSI Adapters application can find the required SCSI device driver files.

6. Restart your computer as prompted.

Testing a SCSI Adapter

You can view a SCSI adapter's properties any time using the SCSI Adapters application. Just click the Devices tab and double-click the SCSI adapter that you want. You'll see a list of attached SCSI devices, shown in Figure 17-22. Click Properties to see detailed information on the adapter that you've selected, as illustrated in Figure 17-23. You can even view details on each attached SCSI device by clicking the device on the Devices tab and clicking Properties.

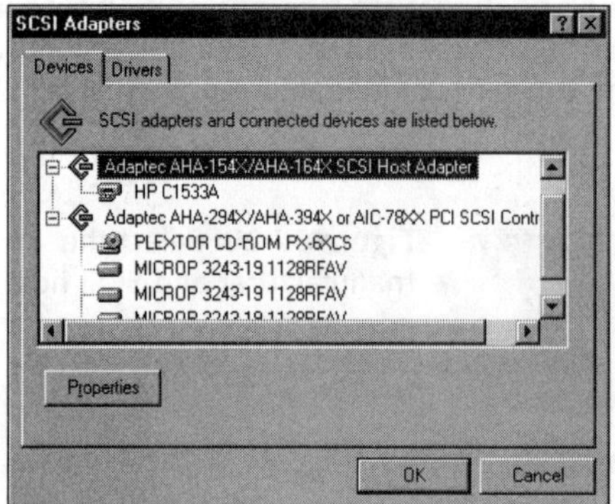

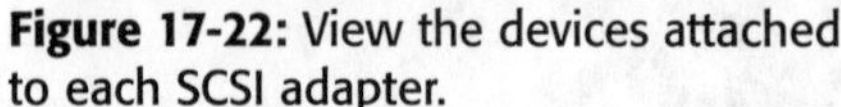
Figure 17-22: View the devices attached to each SCSI adapter.

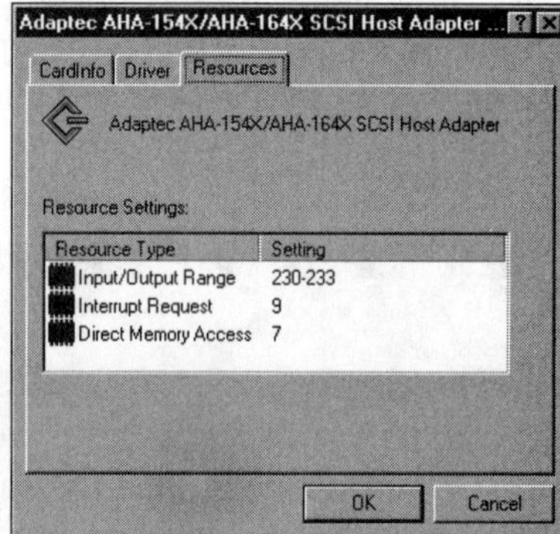

Figure 17-23: View detailed configuration information about each SCSI adapter.

Once you've installed the driver for your SCSI host adapter, it's a good idea to test the adapter with at least one attached SCSI device to verify that it works.

Removing a SCSI Adapter

Removing a SCSI host adapter driver is straightforward. In the SCSI Adapters dialog box, click the Drivers tab. Click the driver that you want to delete and click Remove. Click Yes to confirm, and the driver will be shut down and removed from the list. You'll need to restart your computer to complete the process.

Server Application

The Server application enables you to view and manage certain aspects of your server. Figure 17-24 shows the Server dialog box, which presents server statistics and provides options for viewing and managing user sessions, shared resources, directory replication, and alerts.

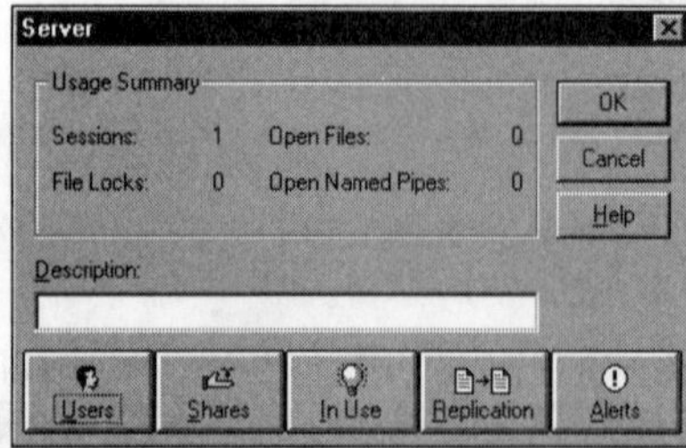

Figure 17-24: The Server application enables you to view and manage several aspects of your server.

Managing Users and Resources

Clicking Users presents the User Sessions dialog box, shown in Figure 17-25. You can view the list of user sessions, disconnect a particular user, or disconnect all users from the server by clicking the appropriate buttons.

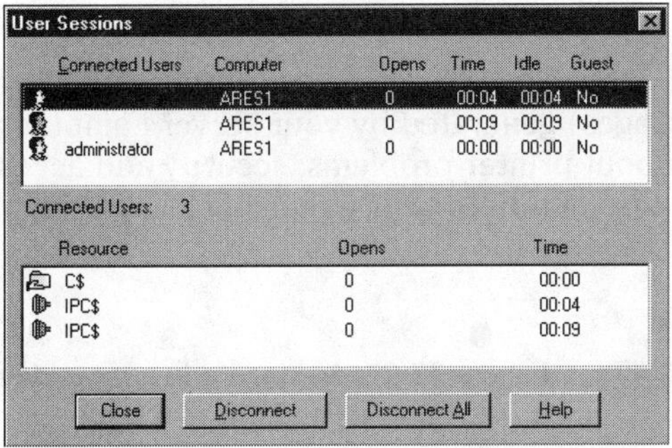

Figure 17-25: The User Sessions dialog box lists all users connected to your server and is where you can disconnect users.

Clicking Shares presents the Shared Resources dialog box, shown in Figure 17-26. You can view the list of shared resources, disconnect a particular user from a specific share, or disconnect all users from a specific share by clicking the share, clicking the user, then clicking the appropriate button.

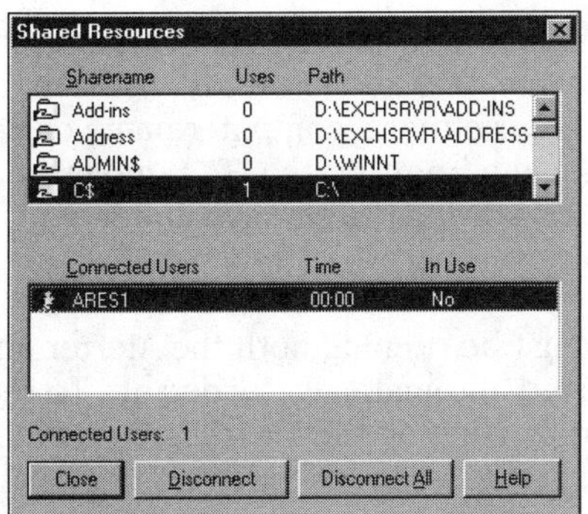

Figure 17-26: The Shared Resources dialog box lists all shared resources and users connected to those shares.

If you click In Use, you'll see a list of all open resources on the server. From the Open Resources dialog box, you can selectively close individual resources or close them all.

Managing Directory Replication

If you click Replication in the Server dialog box, you'll be able to control directory replication. You can get to the same dialog box through the Server Manager utility by double-clicking the server and clicking Replication in the Properties dialog box. (See Chapter 15 for a detailed explanation on how to manage directory replication.)

Managing Administrative Alerts

Click the Alerts button to view and control which computers and users will see administrative alerts (warning messages) generated by your server computer. These messages include warnings about printer problems, security and access problems, server shutdown due to loss of power (if you're using a UPS with a serial port), and so forth. Figure 17-27 presents the Alerts dialog box.

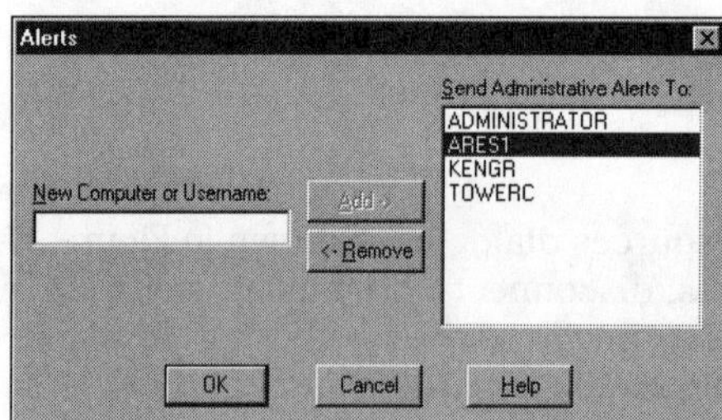

Figure 17-27: Manage a list of recipients of alert messages from this server using the Alerts dialog box.

To add a recipient of administrative alerts from this server, type a computer name or user name in the New Computer or Username field and click Add. Unfortunately, there's no browse capability, since you can enter either a computer name or user name in the same field. You must type each name from scratch. To remove a name from the list of recipients, click the name that you want to remove under Send Administrative Alerts To, then click Remove.

To send administrative alerts, your server must be running both the Alerter and Messenger services. These services are started automatically by default. To receive administrative alerts, other computers must be running the Messenger service. For a description of configuring and starting NT services, see the next section.

Services Application

The Services application is where you can start, stop, pause, continue, and configure the startup behavior of Windows NT services. Figure 17-28 shows the Services dialog box that appears when you double-click the Services icon in Control Panel. Notice the striking resemblance between the Devices application, discussed earlier in this chapter, and the Services application.

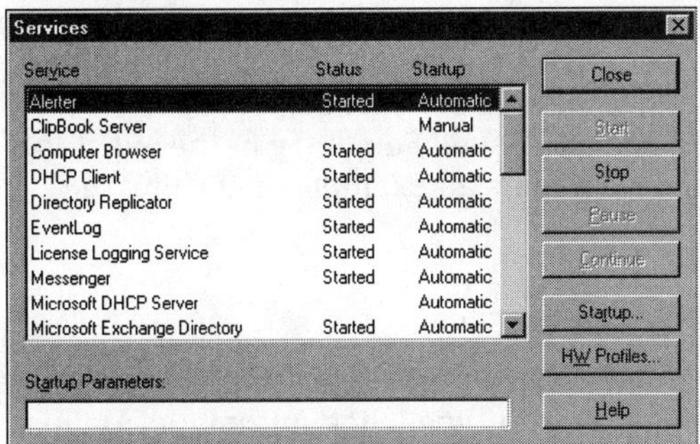

Figure 17-28: You can start, stop, pause, continue, and configure NT services using the Services application.

An installed service can have one of three statuses: started, paused, or stopped. The status of a service is displayed in the Status column of the Services dialog box. (A status of stopped is represented by a blank entry in the Status column.)

There are three startup types: Automatic, Manual, and Disabled. If you set a service to start automatically, it will load and run when you start the computer, without the need for intervention. If you set a service to Manual, it won't start unless you explicitly start it, either from the Services application, from a Command Prompt using the NET START command, or by running an application or other service that tries to start it. A good example of this is the service called ClipBook Server. It's set to Manual by default and is started when you first run the Clipboard Viewer application. Setting a service to Disabled is pretty self-explanatory. You can't start a Disabled service until you change it to either Manual or Automatic startup.

Installing and Removing Services

Installation and removal of services vary from one service to another. Some services are installed and configured automatically when you install applications that use them and are removed when you uninstall the applications. Others are explicitly installed and removed through applications such as the Network application in Control Panel.

(See Chapter 11 for examples of installing the WINS and DHCP services using the Network application.)

If a service requires command line parameters passed to it at startup time, you can specify them under Startup Parameters in the Services dialog box. Note that the backslash (\) character is used as an escape character, so type two backslashes for each literal backslash that you want to include in the command line.

Controlling a Service

It's easy to start a stopped service, pause or stop a running service, or continue a paused service. Just click the service that you want to control and click the appropriate button.

When you start or stop a service, you'll typically see a message indicating that NT is attempting to carry out your request. If it's successful, the status of the service displayed in the Services dialog box will reflect the change. If the action can't be carried out, you'll get an error message and usually an entry in the event log (described in Chapter 21). Chapter 15 contains an example of starting the Directory Replicator service.

Configuring a Service

To configure a service's startup behavior, click the service that you want to configure and click Startup. To change its startup type, click Automatic, Manual, or Disabled under Startup Type as appropriate. Then click OK. Figure 17-29 illustrates this.

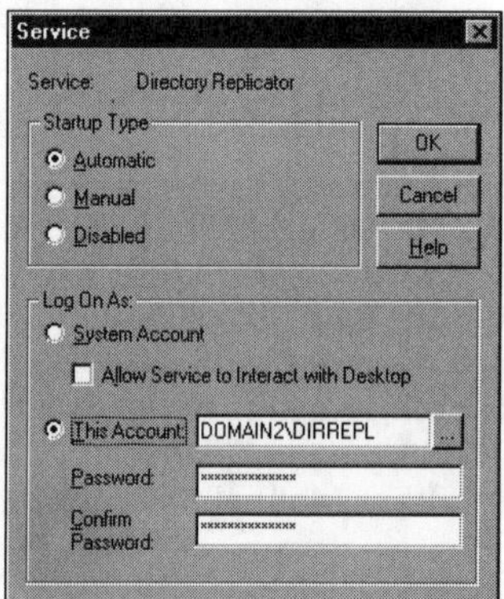

Figure 17-29: For each service, you can configure how it's started and how it logs on to the computer.

A service typically starts before you log on to your computer and usually continues running after you've logged off. For security reasons, a service needs to log itself on using a valid account, so that it can be granted permission to perform its task on the computer.

As shown in Figure 17-29, you can specify the account and its password or use the System account (which is the account used by the operating system itself). If the service uses the System account, you can control whether it's allowed to communicate with logged-on users through a user interface on the desktop.

Sounds Application

The Sounds application assigns sounds to specific system events, if your computer is equipped with a sound card that's Windows NT compatible. You instruct NT to play selected WAV files when an event occurs (such as closing an application). To do this, click an item under Events and select a WAV file under Sound, as shown in Figure 17-30.

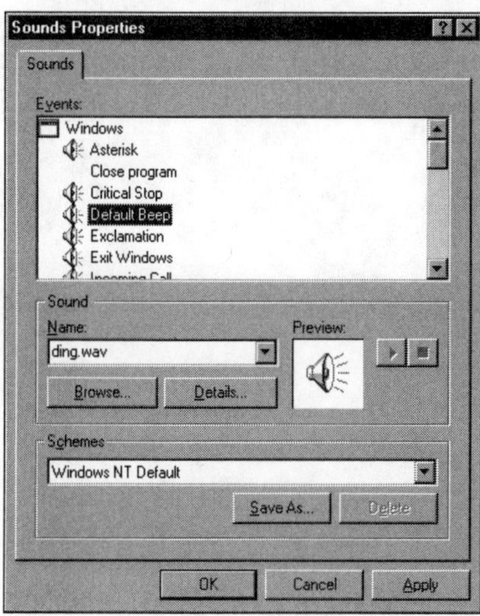

Figure 17-30: The Sounds application is where you can assign sounds to system events.

You can also pick a sound scheme, which assigns a batch of related sounds to various system events all at once. You can even save your own customized sound schemes. This is done under Schemes in the Sounds Properties dialog box.

Although the Sounds application falls closer to the realm of play than to the realm of production servers, I have seen system sounds used effectively to alert an administrator to a problem or trend on a server when he or she is across the room working on another problem. It can be useful to flag the need for administrator attention in a room containing multiple servers.

System Application

The System application is a catch-all for several key configuration capabilities. (Since there are so many juicy functions in this application, you can reach it quickly by right-clicking the My Computer icon on the desktop and clicking Properties.) Following is an explanation of these tabs.

Viewing General Information

The General tab displays information about your computer's processor, memory size, the version of Windows NT that's running, and product registration data. Figure 17-31 provides an example of what you'll see on the General tab.

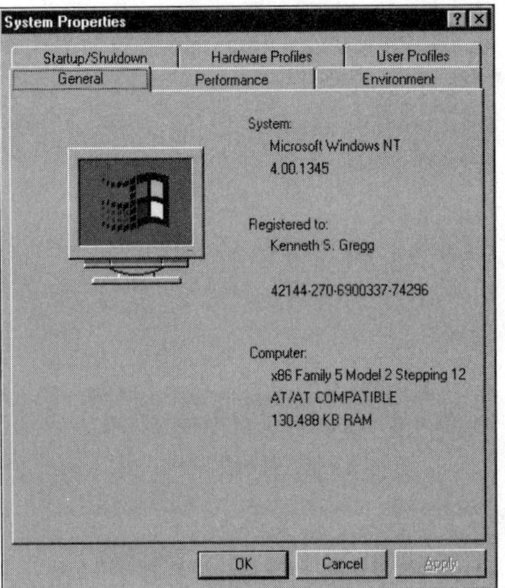

Figure 17-31: The General tab provides information about your computer and the version of Windows NT running on it.

Controlling Responsiveness

The Performance tab enables you to adjust the responsiveness of foreground applications and manage the size, number, and location of paging files, as shown in Figure 17-32.

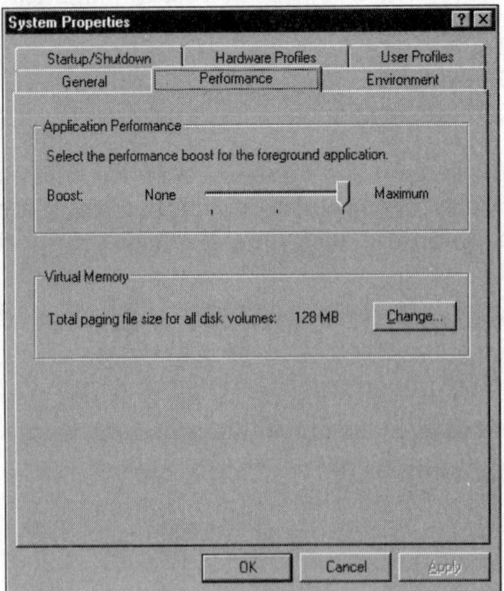

Figure 17-32: The Performance tab enables you to tune interactive responsiveness and control paging file size and placement.

By moving the Application Performance slider all the way to the right, the foreground application (the one whose window has the focus) is given highest priority, maximizing responsiveness of the computer. Moving the slider to the extreme left treats foreground and background processes as equal citizens. If you move the slider to the left, depending on what you're running, you may see some delay when you try to get an application's attention with the mouse or keyboard. (If you're familiar with Windows NT 3.x, you reached this same feature by clicking the Tasking button in the System application.)

Even though you're running a Windows NT Server computer, whose primary function is probably to act as a network server rather than an interactive workstation, I recommend leaving the slider in its default rightmost position. When you do use the computer interactively, you don't want delays in response to your mouse and keyboard actions.

Managing Virtual Memory

To view and modify the size and location of paging files, click Change under Virtual Memory. This action displays the Virtual Memory dialog box, shown in Figure 17-33. (If you're familiar with Windows NT 3.x, you reached this same feature by clicking the Virtual Memory button in the System application.)

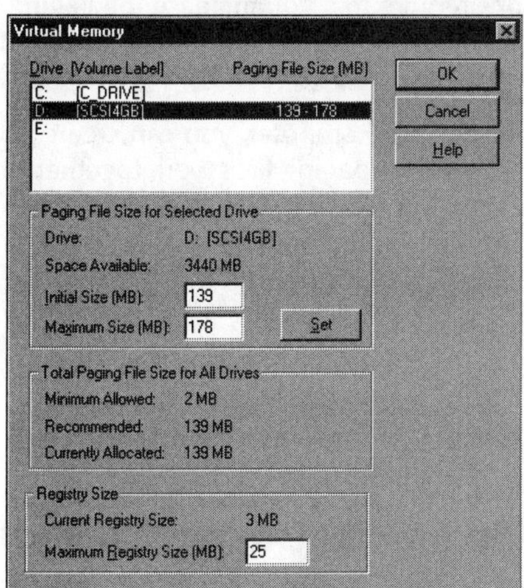

Figure 17-33: You can control the size, location, and number of paging files, as well as the size of the NT registry.

WHAT IS PAGEFILE.SYS?

Windows NT implements its virtual memory architecture (discussed in Chapter 2) using one or more paging files called PAGEFILE.SYS. As physical RAM is consumed, 4KB pages are swapped out to paging files and are read again when needed. (If you're experienced with Windows 3.1, the approach is similar to its swap file.) One paging file is automatically created during NT installation in the root directory of the partition where you installed the operating system. The size of this initial paging file is equal to the size of physical memory, if you have enough disk space available for a file of this size. NT automatically grows and shrinks paging files as needed. The absolute minimum paging file size recommended is summarized in Table 17-1. The minimum paging file size is calculated as

S = MAX((32MB–M), 2MB)

where S is the minimum paging file size, and M is the amount of physical memory in the computer. Notice that S is never less than 2MB, even for very large physical RAM sizes.

If you're actually going to run applications on the computer (and I suspect that you are), you need to have a paging file that's larger than the minimum. The Virtual Memory dialog box recommends a size (typically 11MB higher than the physical memory size), and it's best to use this recommended size rather than the minimum. In Figure 17-33, the physical RAM size is 128MB, the minimum paging file size is 2MB (according to the formula above), and the recommended size is 139MB. For convenience, Table 17-1 includes the paging file sizes recommended by Windows NT. Some applications require that you increase the paging file size even more, for optimal performance. Refer to your application documentation to determine if it has special paging file size requirements.

If you have multiple physical hard disks attached to your computer, you can create up to one paging file in the root directory of each disk. Multiple paging files work together to make up the total paging file space. Thus, you could break up the recommended 139MB into three paging files across three different disks. The files could be 50MB, 50MB, and 39MB, for example. You'll learn more about paging file strategies in Chapter 19.

Table 17-1
Minimum and Recommended Paging File Sizes as a Function of Physical RAM Size

Physical RAM Size	*Bare Minimum Paging File Size*	*Recommended Paging File Size*
16MB	16MB	27MB
24MB	8MB	35MB
32MB	2MB	43MB
40MB	2MB	51MB
64MB	2MB	75MB

Physical RAM Size	Bare Minimum Paging File Size	Recommended Paging File Size
96MB	2MB	107MB
128MB	2MB	139MB
256MB	2MB	267MB
512MB	2MB	523MB

Here's how to add a paging file or change its size:

1. In the Virtual Memory dialog box, click the drive letter on which you want to add a paging file.
2. Click the Initial Size field and type the desired initial paging file size.

   Use the recommended paging file size from Table 17-1.
3. Click the Maximum Size field and type the desired maximum paging file size.

   NT will automatically grow the paging file as needed, but it will stop growing when it reaches the maximum size that you specify in the Maximum Size field. A good rule of thumb is to specify a size that is 50MB larger than the recommended size specified in step 2.
4. Click Set, then click OK. In the System Properties dialog box, click Close.
5. Restart your computer as prompted.

In addition to managing your paging files, you can use the Virtual Memory dialog box to set an upper limit on the size of the NT registry on this computer. NT automatically grows the registry database as needed but won't exceed the limit specified in the Virtual Memory dialog box. I'll tell you more about the NT registry in Chapter 20.

Managing Environment Variables

You can examine, modify, add, and delete environment variables using the Environment tab. System variables are common to all users on the local computer, and user variables apply only to the current logged-on user account. Figure 17-34 illustrates this tab.

To delete a variable, click the variable name and click Delete. To change the value of a variable, click the variable, type the new value, and click Set. To create a new user variable, type the new variable name in the Variable field, type its value, and click Set.

It's possible to have conflicting environment variables in several places. To resolve this problem in an orderly fashion, Windows NT always sets system environment variables first, then sets variables defined in AUTOEXEC.BAT, and finally sets user environment variables. Subsequent settings of the same environment variables always override previous settings.

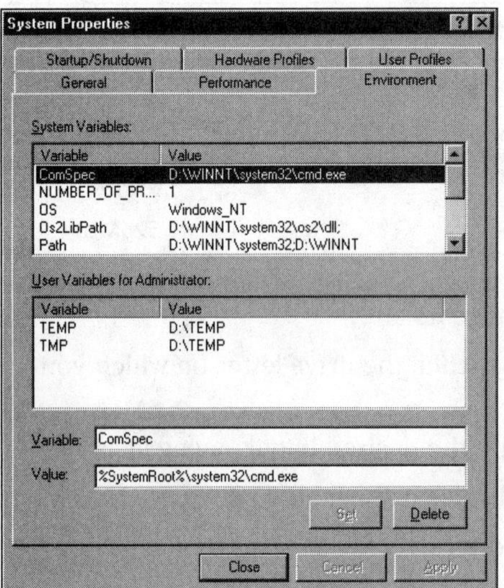

Figure 17-34: The Environment tab is where you can view, modify, and add system-wide and per-user environment variables.

Managing the Boot Menu

The Startup/Shutdown tab, shown in Figure 17-35, controls which operating system is started by default and the amount of time that you have to choose from the boot menu before the default operating system starts. Under System Startup, select the operating system that you want to boot by default from the list of operating systems. Then type the number of seconds that you want the menu to appear before the default operating system starts. During this time, users will have the opportunity to select an alternative operating system from the boot menu. (In Chapter 21, I'll show you how to modify your boot menu manually by editing the BOOT.INI file. You are actually editing portions of the BOOT.INI file when you make changes using the System application.)

Managing Crash Recovery

Under Recovery, several options control the behavior of the operating system when it crashes. By default, all of these options are selected, causing the following actions to take place when the system crashes:

- ✦ A description of the crash is written to the system event log (described in Chapter 21).
- ✦ An alert message is sent to administrators on the network, informing them of the problem.
- ✦ A copy of physical memory is dumped to a file on disk, for later analysis.
- ✦ The computer is automatically restarted.

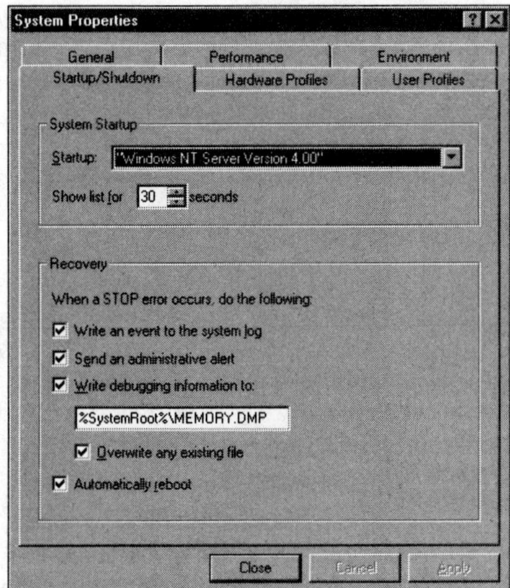

Figure 17-35: The Startup/Shutdown tab gives you control over how the computer boots and how it behaves if the system crashes.

For production servers running the Windows NT Server operating system, I believe these default settings are completely appropriate. You want to minimize downtime of the server, but you also want to gather enough information to diagnose the problem later.

The System Startup settings and the Recovery settings work hand-in-hand when the system crashes. If you've set the computer to restart automatically under Recovery, you need to be sure that the System Startup setting points to the operating system version that you actually want to start. Make sure that the default operating system started is the production system that you want to launch automatically after a system crash.

Managing Hardware Profiles

You can create and manage a list of *hardware profiles* using the Hardware Profiles tab. (Oh great, that was helpful.) What's a hardware profile? It's a new feature of NT 4.0 that will create a snapshot of your computer's hardware configuration to meet a specific need. Say you have a laptop computer with NT 4.0 installed on it. If the laptop has a docking station, you probably need to have a different hardware configuration if the computer is docked or undocked. For example, if your docking station contains a network adapter, you want the operating system to recognize and configure these devices when the computer is docked. When the computer is undocked, you don't want NT to touch these devices and generate error messages, since the devices aren't attached.

At first glance, you may think that the hardware profiles feature isn't useful for a Windows NT Server computer. After all, much of this feature is geared to supporting dockable laptops, and it's frankly quite unusual to install Windows NT Server on a laptop computer. However, the hardware profiles feature can be used for other purposes. For example, if you need to perform scheduled maintenance on your Windows NT Server computer and you want to completely (and easily) disable all of its network adapters while you perform the work, you can define a hardware profile that has the network disabled and start the operating system using this profile while you perform local maintenance.

Creating different hardware profiles for different configurations allows you to select from among them when you start the operating system, thus customizing the set of active devices during the boot process. Figure 17-36 shows the Hardware Profiles tab. Windows NT creates a profile called Original Configuration by default when you install the operating system.

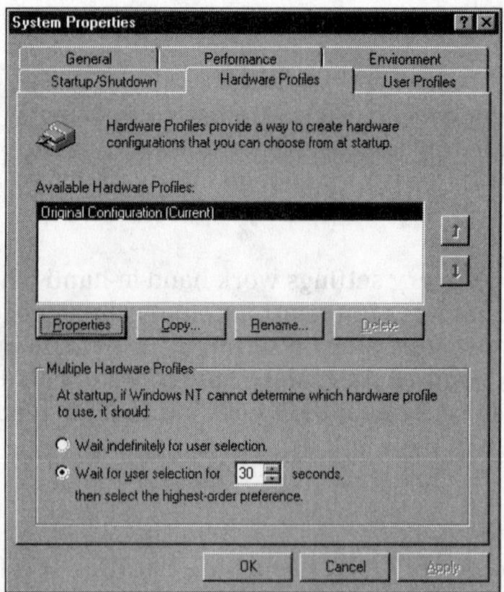

Figure 17-36: You can manage a list of hardware profiles that you'll be able to select at boot time by using the Hardware Profiles tab.

Here's how to create a new hardware profile from the Hardware Profiles tab:

1. Click an existing hardware profile that you want to use as a basis for the new hardware profile that you're creating.

   A good choice is Original Configuration.

2. Click Copy and type the name that you want to use for the new hardware profile, as shown in Figure 17-37. Then click OK.

Never make changes to or delete the Original Configuration hardware profile. This is your safety net if you misconfigure other hardware profiles and need to revert to a known state. Unfortunately, NT won't prevent you from destroying this default profile.

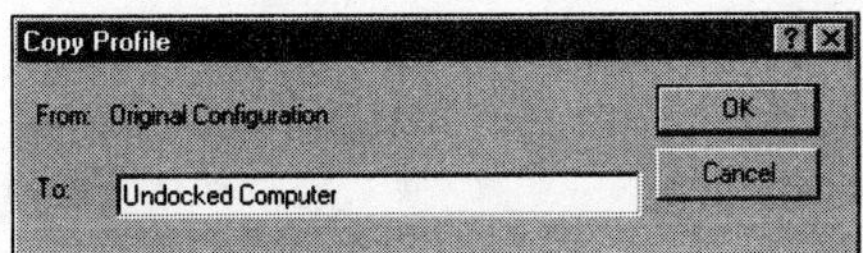

Figure 17-37: You can create a new hardware profile by first copying an existing profile.

3. Click the new hardware profile name and click Properties. If the computer is a dockable laptop computer, click the General tab, click to select the This is a portable computer check box, and click the appropriate docking state associated with this profile. Figure 17-38 illustrates this.

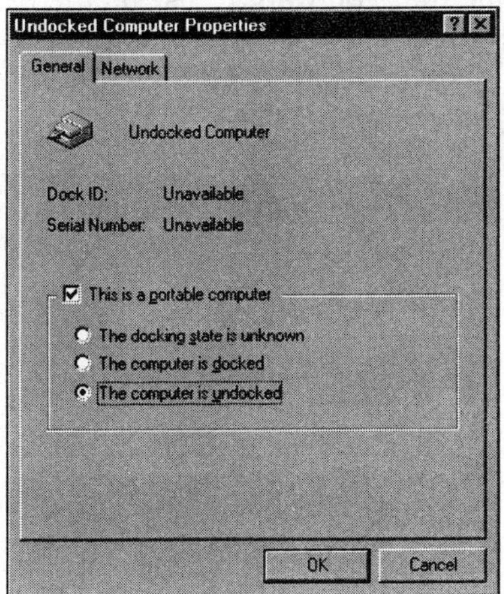

Figure 17-38: You can set a laptop computer docking state using this hardware profile.

4. Click the Network tab. If you want to disable all network adapters in this hardware profile, click to select the Network-disabled hardware profile check box, as shown in Figure 17-39.

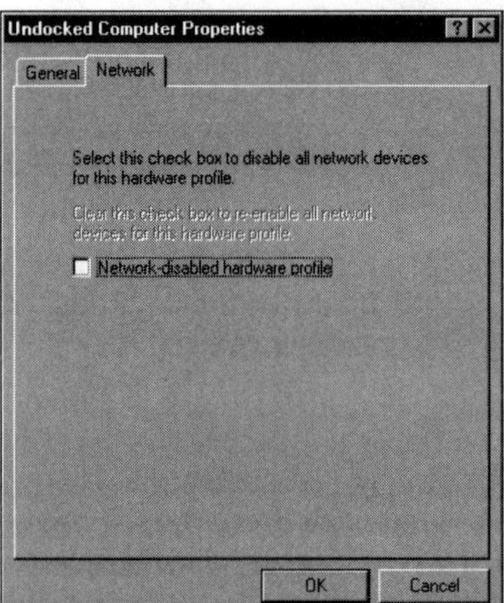

Figure 17-39: You can completely disable all network devices in the hardware profile by selecting this check box.

5. Click OK. Click the hardware profile that you want to use as the default when you start the computer. Click the arrow buttons to the right of the profile list to move this profile to the top of the list.

The order of this list is important. The hardware profile at the top of the list will be used by default when you start the computer, so be sure to put the profile that you'll use most often in the top position. The order of the remaining items will dictate the order of menu items displayed in the hardware profiles menu, described later in this section.

6. Under Multiple Hardware Profiles, click to select how long the menu of hardware profiles is displayed before selecting the default profile at boot time. See Figure 17-36.

   If you select Wait indefinitely for user selection, the computer will display the list of profiles and wait for you to pick one. If you select Wait for user selection for X seconds, type the number of seconds that the computer will delay before booting with the default (first) profile.

If you don't want the hardware profiles menu displayed at all, and you want the computer to select the default hardware profile automatically, type zero seconds as the menu time-out. If you want to select a different hardware profile, you can press the SPACEBAR during system startup (when the words "OS Loader" appear in the upper left corner of the screen). This action will display the hardware profiles menu.

7. In the System Properties dialog box, click OK.

While you're booted from a hardware configuration, any changes that you make to hardware devices (installing or deleting drivers, changing driver configuration, and so on) will be reflected in the current hardware profile. For example, if you want a hardware profile that disables one of your SCSI adapters, start the computer using that profile, disable the SCSI adapter by removing the driver (as described earlier in this chapter), and restart the computer.

You can enable or disable individual services and device drivers in specific hardware profiles using the Services and Devices applications in Control Panel, described earlier in this chapter. You don't need to have started the computer using the hardware profile that you want to modify. For example, in the Services application, click the service whose status you want to change, click Hardware Profiles, click the hardware profile that you want to modify, and click Enable or Disable to toggle the state of the service within this profile. Figure 17-40 illustrates this. The same technique works in the Devices application, when you want to enable or disable device drivers in a particular hardware profile.

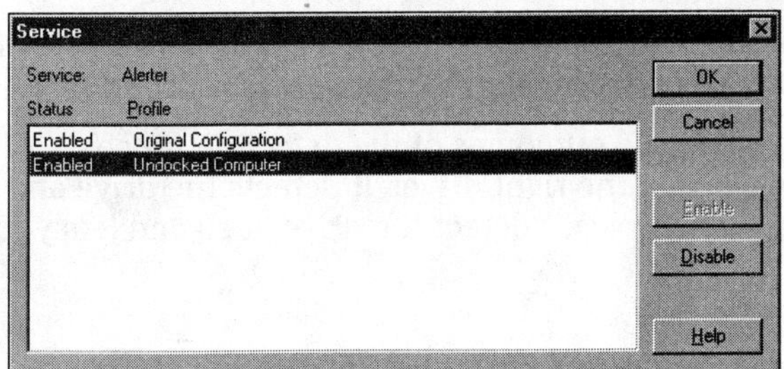

Figure 17-40: You can enable or disable services within hardware profiles using the Services application.

Deleting a hardware profile is straightforward. On the Hardware Profiles tab, click the hardware profile that you want to delete and click Delete. NT prevents you from deleting the current hardware profile in use by the operating system.

Managing User Profiles

The User Profiles tab in the System application is where you can create and control profiles that contain user desktop settings and other information related to a user's logon environment. For each user, you can create a different *user profile* on each computer that the user accesses or create a *roaming profile* that follows the user to whatever NT computer he or she accesses. I'll discuss user profiles in more detail in Chapter 18.

Tape Devices Application

The Tape Devices application manages installation of tape device drivers. Windows NT automatically detects some SCSI tape drives and streamlines installation of the driver. Other types of drives require that you select from a list of drivers before installation. You can also use the Tape Devices application to delete a tape drive from the computer by deleting its device driver.

If you're familiar with Windows NT 3.x, installation of tape device drivers took place in the Windows NT Setup application in the Main program group. Tape device driver management has now been moved under the Control Panel umbrella.

Installing a Tape Device

Here are the steps required to install a new tape device driver:

1. Install the tape drive hardware on your computer. Then start Windows NT Server.

   If the tape drive is a SCSI device, be sure that its device ID doesn't conflict with others on the SCSI bus, the SCSI bus is properly terminated, and the drive is powered on when you start the operating system.

2. Click Start ➪ Settings ➪ Control Panel, and double-click Tape Devices.
3. If your tape drive is automatically detected, you'll see a dialog box similar to Figure 17-41. If so, click OK and go to step 6. Otherwise, proceed to step 4.

   There are actually three possible outcomes of the detection process. NT detects the drive and picks just the right driver, it detects the drive and lets you pick the right driver, or it doesn't detect the drive at all and lets you specify everything.

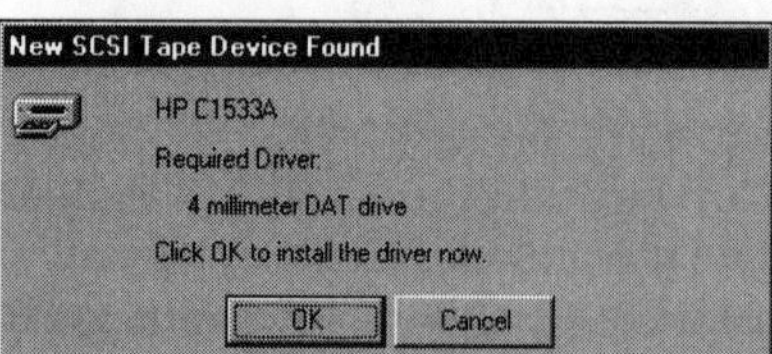

Figure 17-41: NT automatically detects some SCSI tape drives and offers to install the device driver.

4. If a new tape drive appears on the Devices tab, as shown in Figure 17-42, click it. Otherwise, click Detect. Then click the Drivers tab and click Add.

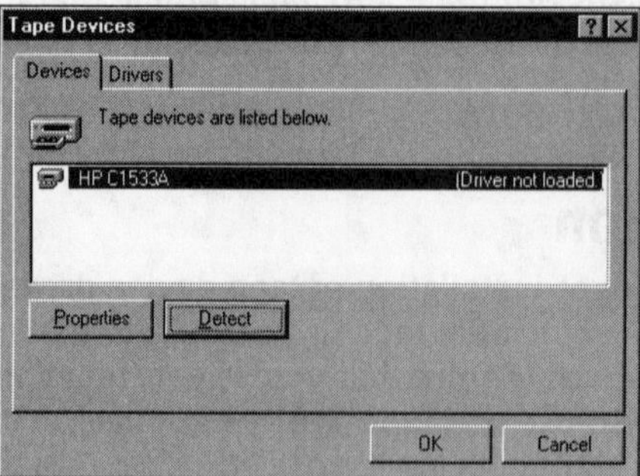

Figure 17-42: A tape device may already appear on the Devices tab.

5. In the Install Driver dialog box, shown in Figure 17-43, click the tape drive manufacturer under Manufacturers and click the specific type of drive under Tape Devices. Then click OK.

   If your tape drive manufacturer or drive type doesn't appear in the list and you have a Windows NT driver disk supplied by the drive manufacturer, click Have Disk and follow the on-screen instructions for installing the new device driver.

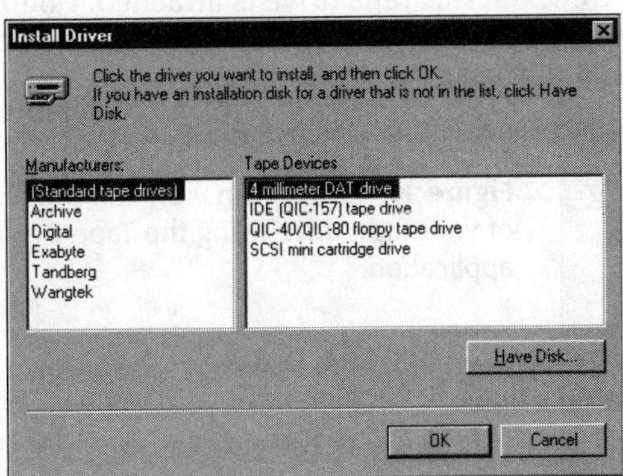

Figure 17-43: Select the manufacturer and tape drive type.

6. As prompted, insert your Windows NT Server 4.0 CD-ROM and enter the path to the NT files for your CPU platform. Then click OK.

   On my computer, the CD-ROM is drive F, and the path is F:\I386. Once you click OK, the driver is copied to your hard disk and is started. You should see the driver added to the list on the Drivers tab, as shown in Figure 17-44.

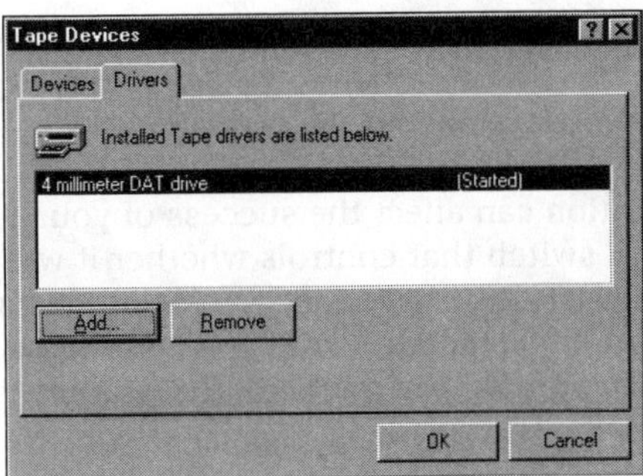

Figure 17-44: The newly installed and loaded tape driver appears on the list.

Testing a Tape Device

You can see the tape drive's properties any time using the Tape Devices application. Just click the Devices tab, click the tape drive that you want, and click Properties. A typical result is shown in Figure 17-45.

If your tape drive is a SCSI device, you can reach this same Properties dialog box from the SCSI Adapters application in Control Panel. Click Start ➪ Settings ➪ Control Panel and double-click the SCSI Adapters icon. Click the Devices tab and double-click the SCSI adapter to which this tape drive is attached. Double-click the tape drive, and you're there. This is a handy approach if you want to view information about several attached SCSI devices.

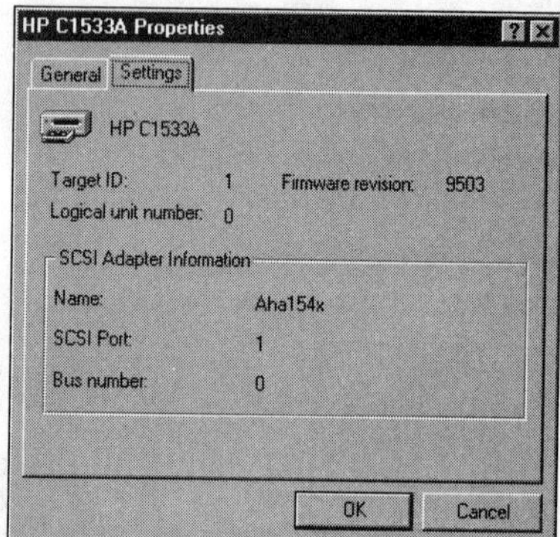

Figure 17-45: You can view the properties of your tape drive using the Tape Devices application.

Once you've installed the driver for your tape device, you'll be able to use it with Windows NT Backup or third-party backup applications. I'll discuss Windows NT Backup in Chapter 18.

Run a test using NT Backup or some other backup application to ensure that you can both back up *and* restore data. Do this now, before you start relying on your backup process to protect your data.

Sometimes physical drive configuration can affect the success of your backup. For example, the HP C1533A drive has a switch that controls whether it will write data to standard 4mm audio DAT tapes (that don't have the DDS Media Recognition System). If you attempt to write data to a standard DAT tape with this switch set, the write will fail. The point is, make sure to iron out all of these issues when you install the tape drive device driver.

Removing a Tape Device

Removing a tape device driver is straightforward. In the Tape Devices dialog box, click the Drivers tab. Click the driver that you want to delete and click Remove. Click Yes to confirm, and the driver will be shut down and removed from the list.

Telephony Application

"Can you tele-phony from the real thing?" The Telephony application in Control Panel lets you supply basic information about your telephone system and how to dial phone numbers. The information that you specify is used by other applications and services that make use of NT's telephony features.

Specifying Dialing Information

Figure 17-46 presents the Location Information dialog box that appears when you first double-click the Telephony icon.

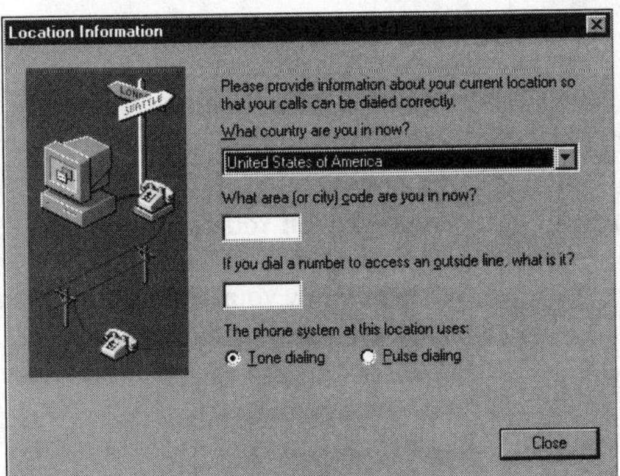

Figure 17-46: You can specify basic information about your telephone system in the Telephony application.

If an application that uses NT's telephony features senses that you've never run the Telephony application, it may start it for you to ensure that you've specified how you want phone calls handled.

When you click Close, you see the Dialing Properties dialog box, as shown in Figure 17-47. On the My Locations tab, you can define multiple dialing locations, each with a different set of dialing parameters, including calling card numbers, disabling of call waiting, pulse or tone dialing, and so on.

If you're going to use your telephone line for data communication, always disable call waiting, or you'll lose data or connections as soon as someone attempts to call you.

Managing Telephony Drivers

If your telephony applications require drivers other than TAPI (the Win32 API interface used by many third-party telephony applications) and Unimodem (which deals with all modems that understand the AT modem command set), you can install and configure other telephony drivers using the Telephony Drivers tab in the Dialing Properties dialog box. Figure 17-48 illustrates this.

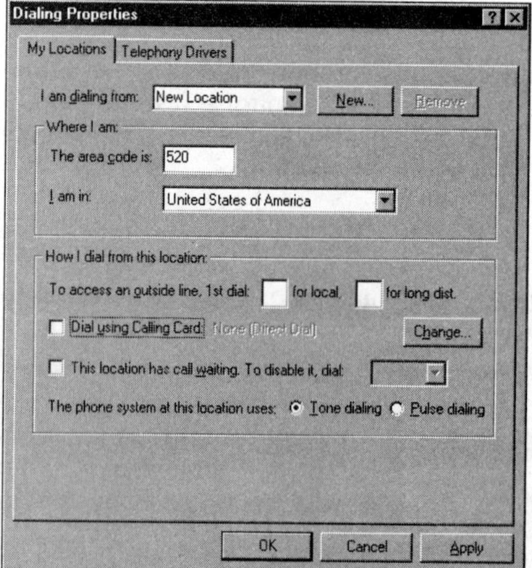

Figure 17-47: In the Dialing Properties dialog box, you can define different telephone dialing locations with unique dialing parameters.

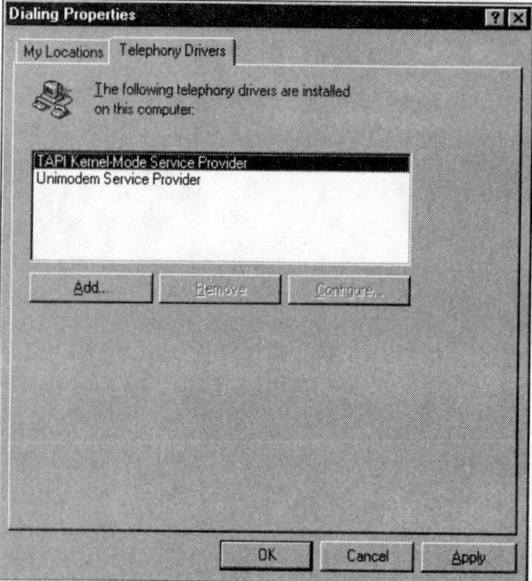

Figure 17-48: You can install and configure additional telephony drivers, as needed by your application, in the Dialing Properties dialog box.

You can use this same tab to delete telephony drivers that you've installed.

Don't delete either the Unimodem or TAPI drivers. Some applications and operating system features, including RAS, rely on the presence of these drivers. (RAS is covered in Chapter 11.)

UPS Application

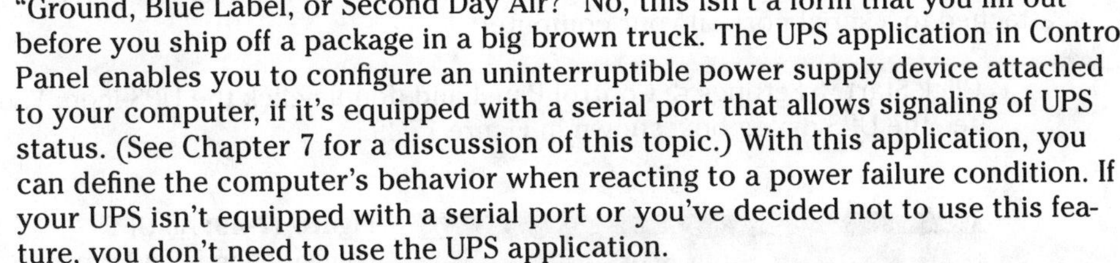

"Ground, Blue Label, or Second Day Air?" No, this isn't a form that you fill out before you ship off a package in a big brown truck. The UPS application in Control Panel enables you to configure an uninterruptible power supply device attached to your computer, if it's equipped with a serial port that allows signaling of UPS status. (See Chapter 7 for a discussion of this topic.) With this application, you can define the computer's behavior when reacting to a power failure condition. If your UPS isn't equipped with a serial port or you've decided not to use this feature, you don't need to use the UPS application.

Preparing for UPS Configuration

To properly configure your serial-connected UPS, you'll need to have the UPS manufacturer's documentation and the correct serial cable attached between your UPS and your Windows NT Server computer.

A standard RS-232 serial cable won't properly connect your computer to a UPS device. To use the UPS service supplied with Windows NT, you need a special cable that meets the requirements outlined in Table 17-2. (Note that some UPS devices don't support remotely turning off the UPS.) Your best bet is to obtain the proper cable from your UPS manufacturer.

The cable configuration is highly dependent on the UPS software that you plan to use. For example, if you're going to use APC's PowerChute Plus UPS software, you need a cable with a pinout different from one that you'd use with NT's built-in UPS service.

Table 17-2
UPS Signals on a Serial Cable Required by NT's Built-In UPS Service

Serial Port Pin Number	*UPS Signal*	*Standard RS-232 Signal*
1	Low battery	DCD
4	Turn off UPS	DTR
8	Power failure	CTS

Configuring Your UPS

Here are the steps required to configure a UPS device that's been properly attached to a serial port on your computer:

1. Click Start ➪ Settings ➪ Control Panel and double-click the UPS icon. You'll see the UPS dialog box, shown in Figure 17-49.

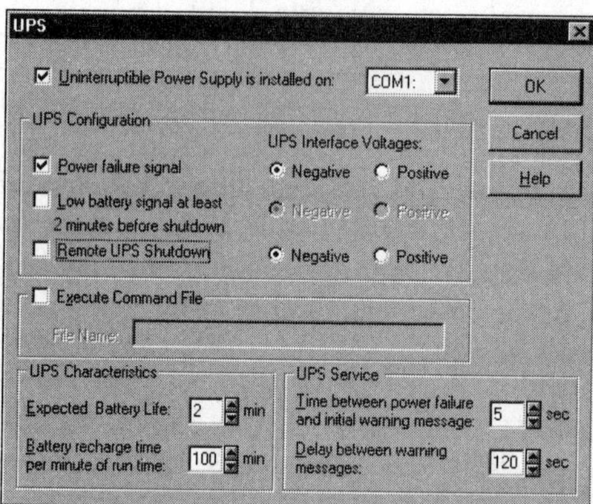

Figure 17-49: All UPS configuration is performed in the UPS dialog box.

2. Click to select the Uninterruptible Power Supply is installed on check box. Then select the serial port to which the UPS is connected (COM1, 2, 3, or 4). See Figure 17-49.

3. Under UPS Configuration, if the UPS can signal that AC power has failed, click to select the Power failure signal check box. Then click the appropriate voltage level for this signal.

   Refer to your UPS documentation to determine if this feature is supported and to find the appropriate voltage level for this signal.

4. Under UPS Configuration, if the UPS can signal a two-minute low battery warning, click to select the Low battery signal check box. Then click the appropriate voltage level for this signal.

   Again, refer to your UPS documentation to determine if this feature is supported and to find the appropriate voltage level for this signal.

5. Under UPS Configuration, if the UPS supports remote shutdown, click to select the Remote UPS Shutdown check box. Then click the appropriate voltage level for this signal.

   Refer to your UPS documentation to determine if this feature is supported and to find the appropriate voltage level for this signal.

6. If you want the computer to execute a command file prior to shutdown, click to select the Execute Command File check box and type the full path to the command file (.BAT or .CMD) that you want to run.

Don't try to do too much in this command file. To ensure that it runs to completion, you need to be certain that it will complete its work within 30 seconds. Otherwise, the computer may shut down before the command file has finished running.

7. If your UPS doesn't support the low battery signal, specify appropriate estimates under UPS Characteristics.

   Under Expected Battery Life, specify the worst-case estimate of how long the UPS can run after power failure, supporting the load of all attached devices. Under Battery Recharge Time, indicate how long it takes to charge the UPS for one minute of power failure run time, again accounting for the load of all attached devices.

   Refer to your UPS manufacturer's documentation and load information about attached equipment to help provide these estimates.

8. Under UPS Service, specify the delay before the first warning message and between subsequent messages once a power failure has occurred.

   This feature operates only on UPS devices that support the power failure signal. See step 3.

   When a power failure occurs, the UPS service sends out a warning message to all attached users, after the initial delay that you specify. The default delay is five seconds. Another warning message is then sent according to the delay between messages that you specify, which defaults to two minutes.

To minimize users running panicked into the streets, you should set the delay before the initial message high enough to avoid warning messages on quick outages that might occur in your area. For example, my office loses power for about eight seconds (or less) at least twice a week, so I've set my server UPS's initial message delay to nine seconds. The power failure is logged, but the users are never informed of these short outages.

9. When you've completed configuring your UPS, click OK.

The UPS service runs at high priority to allow it to act quickly in the event of a power failure condition. However, it doesn't degrade the performance of your computer, since it remains dormant until your UPS signals a power failure.

Configuring Other Application Environments

So far, I've focused on configuring the environment in which Windows NT applications run. However, because each type of application supported by Windows NT hails from a different operating system environment, a few tweaks are sometimes required to make these other types of applications work well on NT. In the following sections, I'll cover some special configuration considerations for running DOS, Windows 3.x, and OS/2 applications.

Configuring the DOS Environment

As discussed in Chapter 2, Windows NT provides the capability of running most DOS applications. In addition to limiting direct access to hardware resources for security and robustness reasons, there are a few additional issues to consider if you're going to be running DOS applications on NT. The following sections discuss these issues.

Managing AUTOEXEC and CONFIG

When Windows NT starts, it appends all path and environment variables found in C:\AUTOEXEC.BAT to its existing list and ignores the remainder of this file. C:\CONFIG.SYS is completely ignored by NT (unless it's an OS/2 CONFIG.SYS, discussed later in this chapter).

When you install Windows NT, it creates AUTOEXEC.NT and CONFIG.NT in the SystemRoot\SYSTEM32 directory. In the NT world, these files take the place of AUTOEXEC.BAT and CONFIG.SYS. The locations and filenames are different, but the purpose is the same. Each time that you start a DOS application, both CONFIG.NT and AUTOEXEC.NT are read to initialize the environment of the DOS VDM. You can change the contents of these files with any text editor and just rerun the DOS program for the changes to take effect. There's no need to restart the computer after making changes to CONFIG.NT or AUTOEXEC.NT.

Not all commands in these files are interpreted by Windows NT. The following list of commands is accepted by NT in the CONFIG.NT file, and the rest are ignored:

country	device	dos	dosonly	echoconfig
fcbs	files	install	loadhigh	ntcmdprompt
rem	shell	stacks		

Setting Properties vs. PIFs

If you've run many DOS applications on Windows 3.x or Windows NT 3.x, you're probably familiar with the concept of Program Information Files, or PIFs. A PIF provides environmental information on how best to run a DOS application. These settings override the configuration files discussed in the previous section. In Windows NT 4.0, defining a PIF is no longer necessary. You now provide this environmental information using the Properties dialog box associated with a DOS application. You can use this dialog box instead of the PIF Editor utility.

PIFs haven't actually disappeared. They've just been hidden by one level of abstraction. Whenever you make a change to an element in the Properties dialog box for a DOS application, a new PIF is generated automatically. However, you no longer need to edit the PIF itself.

Most of the settings are straightforward. Use the What's this? button to find out more about specific options on each of the tabs in the Properties dialog box. I've discussed this Help technique in Chapter 14.

If you set EMS (Expanded Memory) or XMS (Extended Memory) to Auto, no limit is imposed on your DOS application. However, some DOS applications expect limits and behave erratically without them (just as people sometimes behave strangely if no limits are imposed). If your DOS application needs limits, set these values to 8192.

Running Bound Applications

If you have a bound program, designed to run on both DOS and OS/2, NT will attempt to run it as an OS/2 application by default. If you want the program to run as a DOS application and bypass the OS/2 subsystem entirely, you must use the FORCEDOS command to run it. From a Command Prompt, type **FORCEDOS** followed by the entire command line of the application that you want to start, including any required command line switches. This will force the application to start as a DOS program. For example, to run the bound application MYAPP in the \BNDAPPS directory, with /D and /F command line switches, type the command:

```
FORCEDOS \BNDAPPS\MYAPP /D /F
```

Configuring the Windows 3.x Environment

If you upgrade from Windows 3.x to Windows NT in the original Windows 3.x directory, configuration is taken care of during the NT installation process. When you log on to Windows NT for the first time after installation, NT migrates program groups and other information. (See Chapter 7 for a discussion of what to expect during an upgrade.)

If you didn't upgrade and you want your Windows 3.x applications installed under Windows NT, you must reinstall them while running NT. If you dual-boot between Windows 3.x and NT, any new applications that you install under Windows 3.x won't be migrated to NT.

If you're running Windows NT only, but you run Windows 3.x applications on it, NT maintains WIN.INI and SYSTEM.INI files for the 16-bit applications that require them. However, unlike Windows 3.x, no Windows system information is kept in these INI files. All of this information is maintained in NT's registry. The INI files on NT are used only for application-specific information.

Configuring the OS/2 Environment

As mentioned in previous chapters, the Intel version of Windows NT will run OS/2 1.x 16-bit character-based applications (and 16-bit Presentation Manager applications using an add-on). Bound applications, designed to run on both OS/2 and

DOS, will run on Intel NT platforms via the OS/2 subsystem and on RISC NT platforms as DOS programs. (You can force bound applications to run as DOS programs on Intel using the FORCEDOS command, described in the "Running Bound Applications" section earlier in this chapter.)

Migrating OS/2 Settings

If you install Windows NT on a computer that was previously running OS/2 1.x, NT picks up the OS/2 settings that it finds in the OS/2 CONFIG.SYS file and migrates them into the NT registry. In the process, it appends appropriate paths to point to the NT installation tree where key OS/2 subsystem files are stored (for instance, in SystemRoot\SYSTEM32\OS2\DLL).

NT supports the OS/2 configuration commands CODEPAGE, COUNTRY, DEVICENAME, DEVINFO=KBD, LIBPATH, PROTSHELL, and SET. All other commands are ignored. SET commands for COMSPEC, PROMPT, VIDEO_DEVICES, VIO_IBMVGA, and VIO_VGA are also disregarded.

If NT can't find CONFIG.SYS or the file isn't an OS/2 configuration file, NT makes up some default information and puts it in the registry. You can view and edit these settings using the Registry Editor utility (covered in Chapter 20), or you can use the technique discussed in the next section.

NT creates a system environment variable called OS2LIBPATH, which consists of SystemRoot\SYSTEM32\OS2\DLL followed by the list of directories extracted from the LIBPATH line in CONFIG.SYS. To change the OS/2 library path within a Command Prompt, use the SET command to alter the value of OS2LIBPATH. If you want to change the value of OS2LIBPATH for all Command Prompt windows on the computer, you'll need to use the System application (described earlier in this chapter) in Control Panel to alter this system environment variable.

STARTUP.CMD is treated as a standard batch file and is not run automatically by Windows NT. If you want this batch file to run automatically when you log on, you'll have to add it to the Startup menu.

WHICH FILES MAKE UP THE OS/2 SUBSYSTEM?

Four key files are used to implement the OS/2 subsystem. OS2SRV.EXE is the OS/2 subsystem server process. It's started automatically when you first attempt to start an OS/2 application. OS2.EXE is the client side of the subsystem for each OS/2 application. DOSCALLS.DLL implements the OS/2 DOS APIs. NETAPI.DLL implements the LAN Manager OS/2 APIs.

Changing the OS/2 CONFIG.SYS

As mentioned earlier, all OS/2 configuration information is stored in the NT registry. The designers of the OS/2 subsystem provided a relatively painless way of editing this information without having to resort to the Registry Editor utility. To use this simpler method, you must have an OS/2 text editor (that is, a text editor application that's in OS/2-executable format). You also must be logged on to NT with administrator privileges.

When you attempt to open a file called C:\CONFIG.SYS with an OS/2 text editor, the OS/2 subsystem figures out what you're trying to do, copies the registry information to a temporary file, and hands that file to the text editor. After you've made your changes, save them and exit the editor. The OS/2 subsystem uses the temporary file to update the registry data. It's actually pretty amazing, although you do feel a little deceived when you do it for the first time.

Updating Your Emergency Repair Disk

In this chapter, I've shown you how to make many changes to your Windows NT Server configuration. As I mentioned in Chapter 9, it's important to keep your Emergency Repair Disk up to date to reflect any configuration changes that you've made to the operating system since you installed NT or last updated the repair disk. You can create an updated repair disk using the RDISK utility, shown in Figure 17-50.

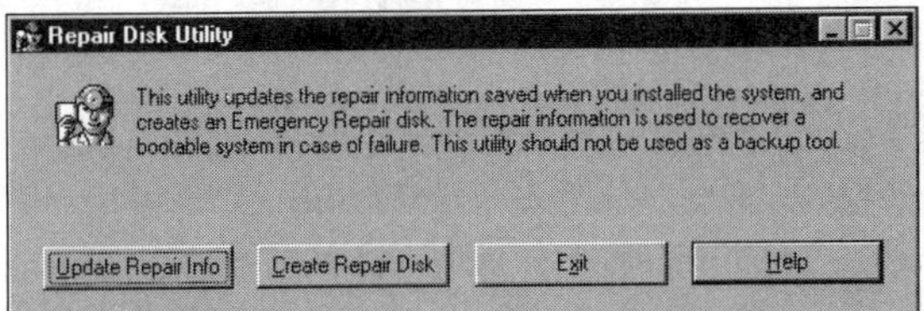

Figure 17-50: You can use the RDISK utility to update or create an Emergency Repair Disk.

Each time that you run RDISK, it generates a new Emergency Repair Disk from scratch. The prudent thing to do is use a fresh floppy disk for the updated version and retain your previous version. That way, if anything goes wrong with the new disk during the format or copy process, you'll still have your old (albeit, out-of-date) disk to use. Don't keep more than two repair disk generations around, though, as things will start to get confusing. Also, be sure to label the disks appropriately, so you always know which one has the latest configuration data.

To create an updated repair disk, click Update Repair Info and click Yes to confirm. Click Yes to create a new repair disk. Insert an appropriately labeled floppy in drive A and click OK. RDISK will format the floppy and write the new repair information to it.

Summary

In this chapter, you've learned about several ways of customizing your Windows NT server computer to meet your needs and those of your organization. You've walked through step-by-step instructions for installing and configuring many areas of the NT operating system.

Few of the configuration instructions in this chapter went beyond the bounds of the server computer that you were configuring. In Chapter 18, we'll venture out onto the network and deal with administration tasks that have more far-reaching effects. Then, in Chapter 19, you'll see how to tune your computer and network to squeeze out as much performance as possible.

INSIDE STORY

As the dawn of a new day began to turn the Redmond sky into a somewhat lighter shade of dingy gray, two bleary-eyed NT test managers organized themselves for the hunt. "Got your supply of sticky notes?" Yes. "Pen and pad?" Uh huh. "Comfortable shoes?" Of course. "You take Building 1, and I'll take Building 2. We'll rendezvous in my office at 7:00 a.m." Got it. "OK, let's move out and gather those stress test results!"

The war was against bugs in the NT operating system, specifically the non-network components. The weapon was the desktop stress test suite. This set of merciless tests was designed to beat the life out of all local device drivers and interactive desktop software components such as graphics and window management. If you saw a computer running this set of tests, you'd likely step back a little to avoid the explosion that seemed sure to happen. And the noise generated by the floppy and hard disk test grated on the nerves of anyone sharing the same room with one of these computers under siege. (When everyone on the team ran the test and left their office doors open, the sound and fury bellowing through the hallway made some folks call it the Microsoft Psych Ward.) Talk about stress!

And stress was on the minds of the two reconnaissance scouts as they made their early-morning rounds to collect test results and tag computers for engineers to debug later. They prudently knocked on each office door before entering. They never knew who might have stayed all night writing, debugging, or testing new code. Some office denizens were heavier sleepers than others. Occasionally, they would push open a door only to be thwarted by a sleeping body blocking the way. (These folks literally took their lumps for the cause of winning the war against bugs.) Each morning, one of the stress test scouts could count on stepping over a particular developer, whose powerful snores provided entertainment as he copied down the screen contents of a failed test computer and left a sticky note that read "Do Not Reboot until 10 a.m." As he stepped back over the exhausted body and gently closed the door, his ears were still ringing with those shuddering snores — a common refrain in the stress anthem that accompanied the development of Windows NT.

Administering Your Windows NT Server Network

Whenever I get a new job, I look up all of the words in my title in the dictionary just to make sure that I understand what I'm supposed to do. A coworker of mine once joked that after he did this, his software engineering manager got angry with him when he took one of the definitions literally and showed up wearing a railroad hat. Perhaps you've done this, too (looked up your job title in the dictionary, that is, not worn a funny hat). If you have, you know that being an administrator involves managing (your network and your users), dispensing (resources, knowledge, and perhaps your own form of justice), and applying (repairs to malfunctioning servers and networks).

In this chapter, you'll learn important skills that will allow you to become a successful administrator in every sense of the word. You'll discover how to organize and manage your disk storage, how to implement an effective backup strategy, how to create and maintain user accounts, how to apply NT's security model to your network users and resources, and how to audit access to your network resources.

Administering Your Disk Storage

Aside from your data, disk storage space is probably the most important asset on your Windows NT Server network, and you need to make the most of it. As a server administrator, you'll need to organize your disks into partitions and volumes, select appropriate labels and file systems for each volume, accommodate access to your volumes by other operating systems, and make the most efficient use of the free space available on your disks. As your servers and your network grow, you'll run into these issues whenever you add more disk storage.

By wisely deploying your available disk space, making the most efficient use of it for the various roles that your servers play, and knowing how to change disk organization quickly based on changing needs, you'll be well on your way to being a disk administration hero.

Introducing Disk Administrator

Disk Administrator is a graphical utility that lets you administer disk resources on your NT computer. Although you can think of Disk Administrator as a replacement for the DOS FDISK utility (and a few others such as FORMAT and CHKDSK), it goes far beyond these capabilities. With Disk Administrator, you can:

- ✦ Graphically display the status of all disks attached to the computer
- ✦ Create and delete disk partitions (and logical drives within extended partitions)
- ✦ Format, label, and assign drive letters to partitions
- ✦ Scan disks and recover from errors
- ✦ Migrate disk configurations from one installation of NT to another
- ✦ Create or extend volume sets by combining existing regions of free space
- ✦ Create and delete fault tolerance volumes

In the following sections, I'll focus on the fundamental features of Disk Administrator. Once you're familiar with its basics, you'll be prepared to understand its fault tolerance capabilities, which I discuss in Chapter 19, along with other performance-tuning strategies. However, fault tolerance isn't purely a performance optimization feature. It can also dramatically increase the robustness of your servers. So, even if you're not ready to begin performance-tuning your servers, plan to read the Chapter 19 sections on fault tolerance.

INSIDE STORY

In very early versions of Windows NT, the Disk Administrator utility was called Disk Manager. As you might imagine, there were a few bugs in the early, untested code that caused data loss. For awhile, a few test engineers dubbed the tool "Disk Mangler." (Ten years earlier, I was working at Texas Instruments with an engineer who developed a utility called Disk Manager 3, which others in the group called "Disk Mangler 3." Seems as though *some* naming conventions are universal.

Navigating in Disk Administrator

To start Disk Administrator, log on with administrator privileges and click Start ➪ Programs ➪ Administrative Tools ➪ Disk Administrator option. When you start Disk Administrator for the first time after installing Windows NT Server, you'll see the dialog box shown in Figure 18-1, indicating that a new disk configuration has been detected. Click OK.

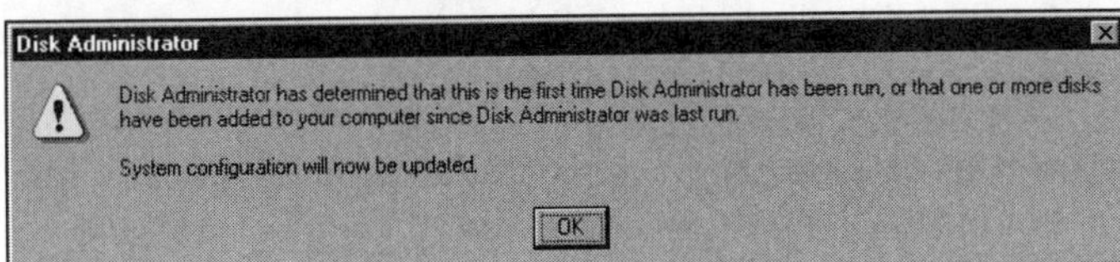

Figure 18-1: Disk Administrator warns that it's dealing with a new disk configuration.

Actually, you'll see this dialog box at other times, too. Whenever you add a new hard drive to the computer, change its configuration under another operating system, remove a hard drive, eat pizza, or breathe air, you'll probably see this message. Not to worry. This is normal.

Once you dismiss the warning, you'll see the Disk Configuration view, an example of which is shown in Figure 18-2. This view graphically shows you the layout of physical disk regions, the drive letter assigned to each partition or logical drive, the file system used to format each volume, and the size of each region.

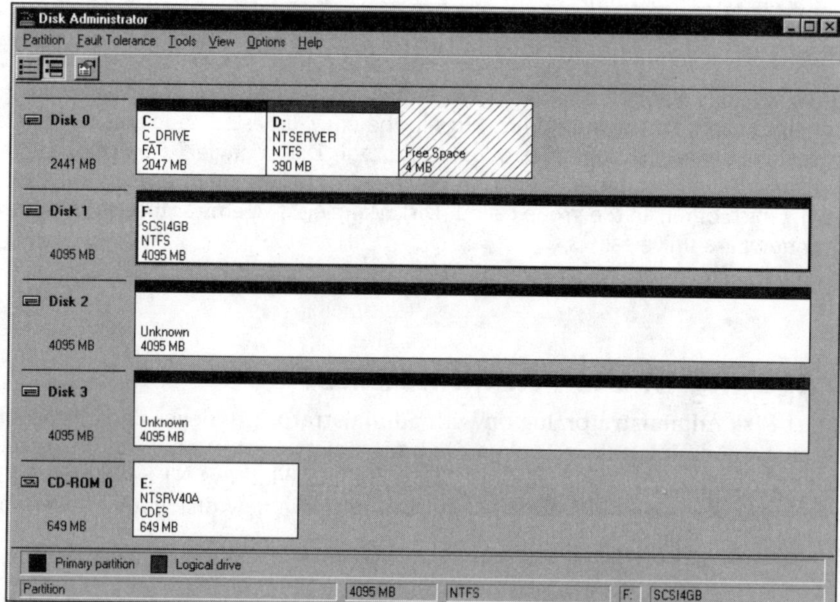

Figure 18-2: The Disk Configuration view shows all drives and regions on those drives.

Notice that each type of partition is color-coded, and the color-code legend appears near the bottom of the Disk Administrator window. You can change the displayed colors by clicking Colors and Patterns on the Options menu.

Changing Your Views

You can change the view to see additional details about each volume by clicking Volumes on the View menu. Figure 18-3 shows an example of the Volumes view corresponding to the Disk Configuration view shown in Figure 18-2. To get back to the default graphical display of regions, click Disk Configuration on the View menu.

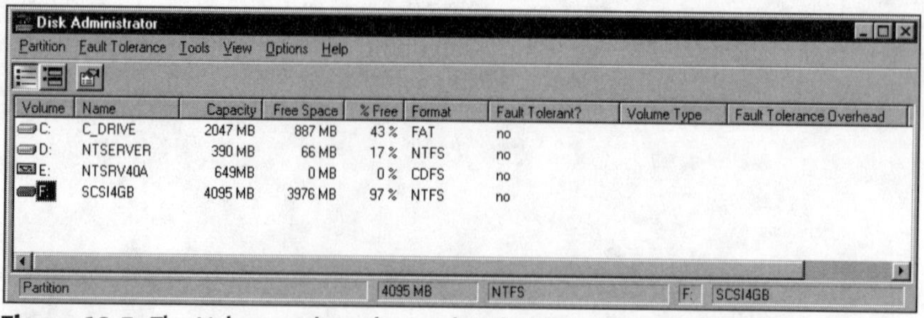

Disk Administrator

Partition Fault Tolerance Tools View Options Help

Volume	Name	Capacity	Free Space	% Free	Format	Fault Tolerant?	Volume Type	Fault Tolerance Overhead
C:	C_DRIVE	2047 MB	887 MB	43 %	FAT	no		
D:	NTSERVER	390 MB	66 MB	17 %	NTFS	no		
E:	NTSRV40A	649MB	0 MB	0 %	CDFS	no		
F:	SCSI4GB	4095 MB	3976 MB	97 %	NTFS	no		

Partition 4095 MB NTFS F: SCSI4GB

Figure 18-3: The Volumes view shows detailed information on each volume on your computer.

I prefer to work in the Disk Configuration view, since it lays out very clearly all of the regions of each disk, including free space. I only use the Volumes view when I need the additional information that it provides. However, it can be difficult to work in the Disk Configuration view if you have both very large and very small regions. For example, Figure 18-4 shows the view of Disk 0 after telling Disk Administrator to size the displayed regions based on their actual size. Notice that the 4MB of free space at the end has completely disappeared from the display. Compare this with the Disk 0 layout shown in Figure 18-2, where I told Disk Administrator to display all regions equally, regardless of their actual size.

To control the region display size, click Region Display on the Options menu. As shown in Figure 18-5, click to select either Size regions based on actual size or Size all regions equally. Then click OK. I don't recommend having Disk Administrator decide since it sometimes uses different rules for different disks, and this can lead to confusion. You can specify the display setting for all disks at once (which I recommend), or individual disks (which I think creates confusion).

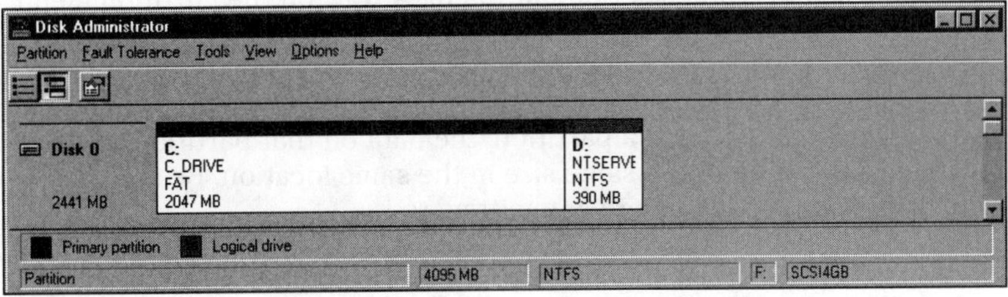

Figure 18-4: Displaying regions based on their actual size can cause relatively small regions to disappear, overwhelmed by larger ones.

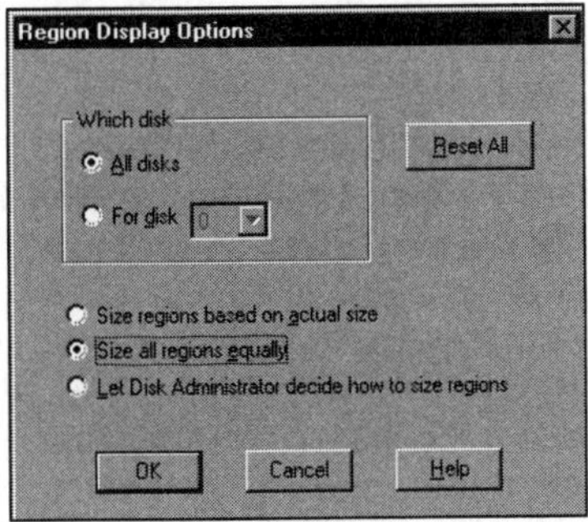

Figure 18-5: You can control how regions are sized in the disk configuration display using the Region Display Options dialog box.

Selecting Regions

When you want to perform an action on a particular region in either view, select it by clicking it, then use the menus to do what you need to do. The most common confusion about the Disk Administrator user interface occurs when people forget to click the region in which they're interested and then find the menus that they want to use are disabled because no region has been selected.

When you select a region, it's displayed with a slightly wider black border. This isn't always easy to see on some display configurations. Experiment by clicking different regions so you can learn how to tell when a region has been selected. The status line at the bottom of the window provides an additional indicator of which region you've selected.

Making Commitments

The second most confusing part of Disk Administrator's behavior is that some changes (such as creating and deleting partitions) don't actually take place until you *commit* the changes to disk. For example, if you create a new partition from a free region, the display of that region reflects the change, but nothing is actually changed on disk until you click Commit Changes Now on the Partition menu. Until you do this, you can't format the new partition or do anything else with it.

Once you commit a destructive change to disk, there's no way to undo it. If the change that you made deletes a partition, the data on that partition is lost, even if you recreate a partition of the same size in the same location. Be sure that you're satisfied with your change before committing to it.

This behavior is actually a safety net. Since your Disk Administrator changes have such dramatic effects (potentially wiping out large blocks of data with a few mouse clicks), the tool gives you the opportunity to study the changes that you've made before committing to them. For example, let's say that you delete a small partition containing data because you want to create a larger one. You suddenly remember that you can extend an existing partition using a volume set (described later in this chapter) without losing your existing data. As long as you don't commit the change, you can back out of deleting the partition.

If you decide to revert to your last committed version, simply close Disk Administrator and click No when you're asked if you want to save the changes that you've made.

When you do commit changes, you're given a reminder to update your Emergency Repair Disk, as shown in Figure 18-6. The procedure for creating an up-to-date repair disk is provided in Chapter 17. If you're going to make several changes to your disk configuration in one sitting, I recommend making all of the changes and then using RDISK to update your repair disk to reflect the entire batch of alterations.

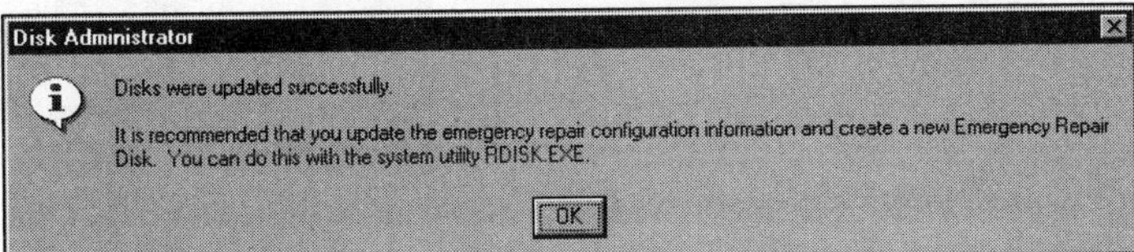

Figure 18-6: Heed the reminder to update your Emergency Repair Disk after making changes to your disk configuration.

If you're familiar with Windows NT 3.x, you'll be pleased to discover that many Disk Administrator operations no longer require you to restart your computer before they take effect. In most cases, just committing the changes to disk is enough to complete the disk configuration change. This is a real timesaver in Windows NT 4.0.

Understanding Partitions and Volumes

I often encounter even seasoned administrators who are confused about the various types of partitions and the differences between partitions and volumes. So far, I've used the term *region* to describe an area of the disk that could be either free space, a partition, or a volume. I'll now nail down exactly what partitions and volumes are, starting with the fundamental building block — the partition.

Just as in DOS and other operating systems, you need to organize the drive into one or more partitions before you can put anything on a hard disk. A *partition* is a portion of the physical hard disk that functions as if it were a physically separate drive.

Primary vs. Extended Partitions

Each physical hard disk drive can contain between one and four partitions. Two types of partitions are available: primary and extended. A *primary partition* is a disk partition from which an operating system can boot. Once you create a primary partition, the entire partition can be formatted and accessed as a single drive letter.

An *extended partition*, on the other hand, is not directly usable for storage. It must be further subdivided into *logical drives* that need to be individually formatted. Why have extended partitions? Recall that you can't have more than four partitions on a single physical drive. If you need more than four logical drives on a single physical hard disk, an extended partition is the only way to get there. An extended partition can be organized into one or more logical drives, each with its own drive letter.

DOS can only recognize a single primary partition — the partition from which DOS is booted. If you need to dual-boot your computer to DOS, and you want your drives visible while booted under DOS, place only one primary partition on each drive and create additional logical drives using an extended partition. Of course, you need to format all partitions using FAT, if you want DOS to see the files and folders. (Note that dual-booting your Windows NT Server computer to DOS and having your partitions and files visible there represents a security risk.)

Types of Free Space

You'll encounter two different types of *free space* when dealing with Disk Administrator. Free space is most often used to describe a region of the disk that's not yet partitioned. If your entire disk is one block of free space, that space can be divided into as many as four partitions, as I mentioned earlier. Free space is also used to describe a region within an extended partition that hasn't yet been organized into a logical drive within that partition.

The distinction is subtle but important. Both types of free space are graphically labeled as such in Disk Administrator. However, you need to pay attention to the direction of the shading lines and the status line in the lower left corner of the window. Figure 18-7 shows the two different types of free space.

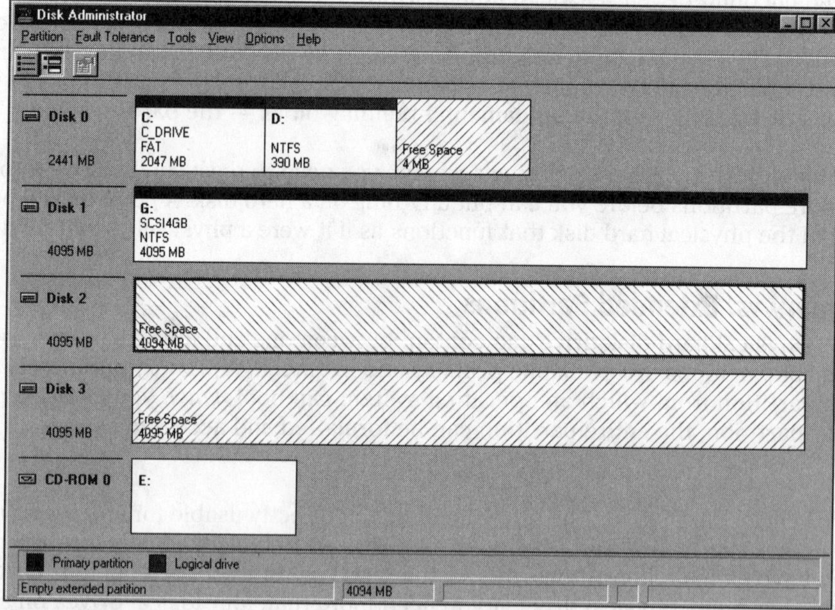

Figure 18-7: Disk free space looks similar, whether it represents unpartitioned space or empty space within an extended partition.

Disk 2 is an extended partition containing no logical drives. Disk 3 is a completely unpartitioned drive. Disk 0 contains an unpartitioned chunk of free space, too. When Disk 2 is selected, as in Figure 18-7, notice the shading lines going in different directions and the words "Empty extended partition" in the status bar. When Disk 3 is selected, the status bar simply reads "Free space."

System vs. Boot Partitions

The terms *system partition* and *boot partition* refer to the location of operating system files on disk. The system partition contains hardware-specific files required to load the operating system (for example, NTLDR, BOOT.INI, and so on). On Intel computers, the system partition must be a primary partition that's accessed during the computer's boot process. This is typically the drive C partition and is also known as the *active partition*. The system partition can never be part of a RAID stripe set (covered in Chapter 19) or a volume set (covered later in this chapter). On RISC computers, the system partition must be formatted with the FAT file system.

The *boot partition*, which may or may not be the same partition as the system partition, contains the Windows NT operating system files. In other words, it contains the directory tree (SystemRoot) created during Windows NT operating system installation. It can be formatted as either FAT or NTFS and can participate in stripe sets, mirrors, and volume sets.

If the system partition and boot partition are on different physical disk drives and the disk containing the system partition becomes inaccessible (for example, it dies), you can still boot NT using the special NT boot floppy, covered in Chapter 9. This floppy plays the role of a system partition to boot the rest of the operating system from a working boot partition.

Partitions vs. Volumes

You may sometimes see the terms *partition* and *volume* used interchangeably. Although the concepts are similar, there's a subtle distinction. Once formatted with a file system, a primary partition or a logical drive within an extended partition becomes known as a *volume*. A volume is assigned a unique drive letter and is used by the operating system and applications to store directories and files.

You can think of partitions as the raw material and volumes as the finished product. Partitions without file system formatting and drive letter assignments are useless. Volumes, on the other hand, can actually be used by the operating system and applications. Volume sets, which I'll describe in detail later in this chapter, provide a good illustration of the distinction. They combine free space on multiple partitions into a single logical volume. The multiple partitions are the raw material, and the volume set is a usable logical disk.

Using Disk Administrator, you can view all of the partitions and regions of free space by clicking Disk Configuration on the View menu. You saw an example of this view in Figure 18-2. Click Volumes on the View menu to see detailed information on each volume, as shown in Figure 18-3.

Managing Partitions

In the following sections, I'll show you how to create primary and extended partitions using the Disk Administrator utility. You create partitions only from existing regions of free space on the hard disk.

Once you've completed the appropriate steps, commit the created partition or logical drive to disk. To do this, either click Commit Changes Now on the Partition menu or exit Disk Administrator and confirm the change by clicking Yes.

Creating a Primary Partition

You can create up to four primary partitions on each physical hard disk drive. The limit reduces to three primary partitions, if you need an extended partition on the drive. A primary partition can range in size from 1MB (not a very useful size) to the length of the entire physical drive.

Here's how to create a primary partition:

1. Click to select the region of free space that you want to convert to a primary partition.
2. On the Partition menu, click Create.
3. If there's already a primary partition on this physical drive, you'll see a warning message as shown in Figure 18-8. If you see this warning, click Yes to confirm.

   Remember that if you reboot the computer under DOS, DOS can only see one primary partition per physical disk drive.

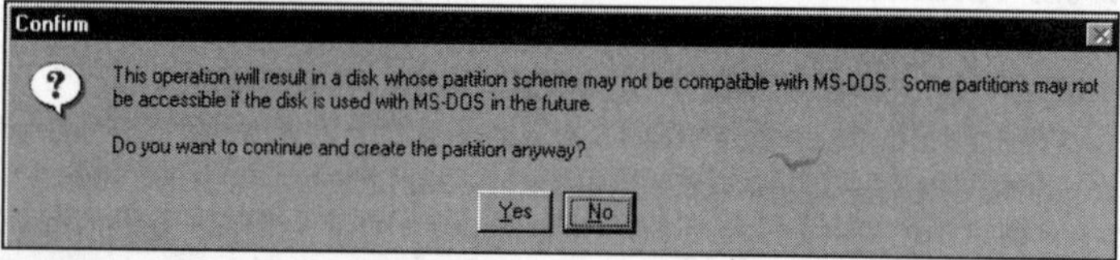

Figure 18-8: Disk Administrator warns you that you're creating a partition that DOS won't be able to see.

4. In the Create Primary Partition dialog box, type the size of the primary partition that you want to create, as shown in Figure 18-9. Click OK.

   The dialog box provides you with the minimum and maximum sizes of the primary partition. It can be as large as the entire region of free space that you selected in step 1.

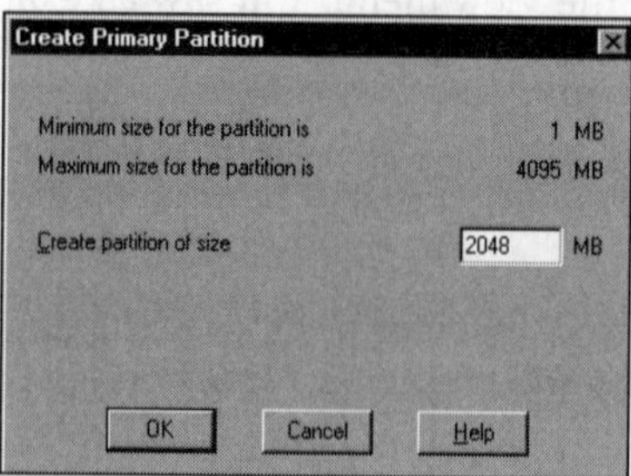

Figure 18-9: In the Create Primary Partition dialog box, you specify the size of the primary partition that you're creating.

5. If you create a primary partition that's either too large for DOS to handle or it's starting and ending points on the drive are too large for DOS, you'll get a warning message shown in Figure 18-10. Click Yes to confirm.

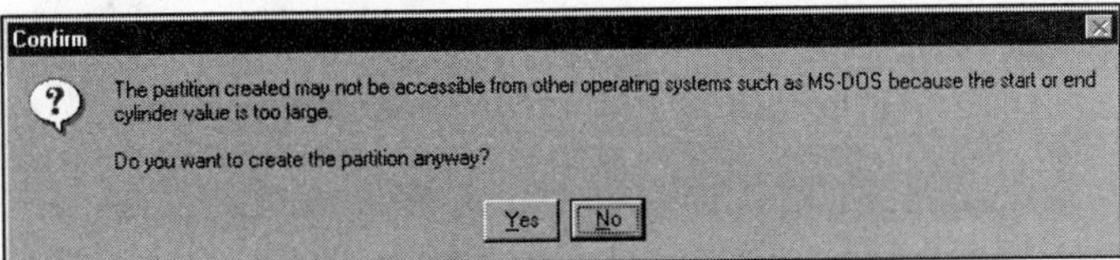

Figure 18-10: Disk Administrator warns you if the starting or ending points of the partition are too large for DOS.

Figure 18-11 shows the resulting disk configuration display. Disk Administrator automatically assigned drive letter H to the new partition, which is tagged as Unformatted. The new partition is now ready to be formatted, as described later in this chapter. Notice that the remaining region not included in the partition is still tagged as free space.

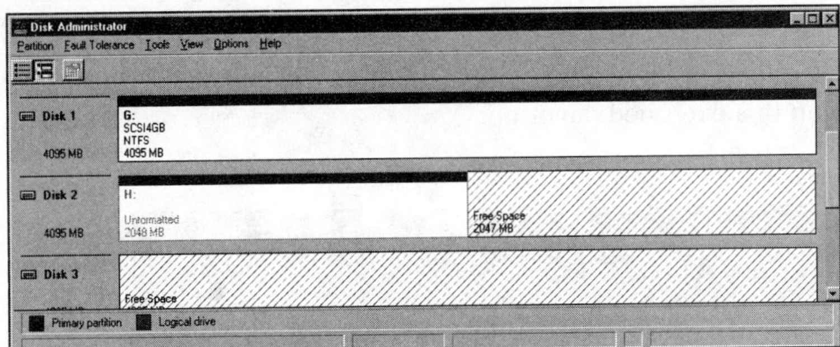

Figure 18-11: The new partition is automatically assigned a drive letter and is ready for formatting.

Creating an Extended Partition

You can create one extended partition on each physical hard disk drive. If you do, you can create up to three additional primary partitions on each drive that contains an extended partition. An extended partition can range in size from 1MB to the size of the entire physical drive.

Here's how to create an extended partition:

1. Click to select the region of free space that you want to convert to an extended partition.

2. On the Partition menu, click Create Extended.
3. In the Create Extended Partition dialog box, type the size of the extended partition that you want to create, as shown in Figure 18-12. Click OK.

   The dialog box provides you with the minimum and maximum sizes of the extended partition. It can be as large as the entire region of free space that you selected in step 1.

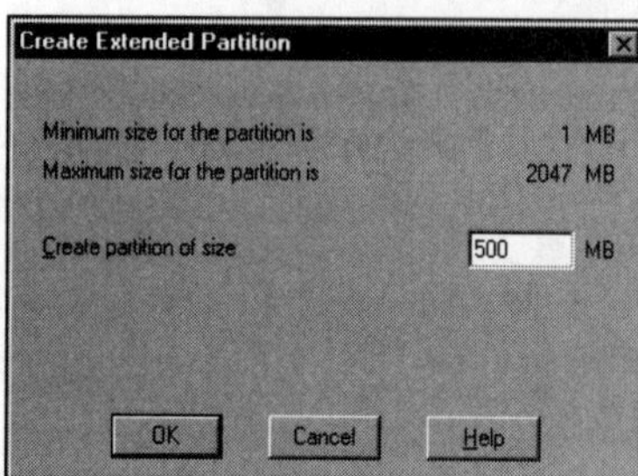

Figure 18-12: In the Create Extended Partition dialog box, you specify the size of the extended partition that you're creating.

4. If you create an extended partition that's either too large for DOS to handle or its starting and ending points on the drive are too large for DOS, you'll get a warning message shown in Figure 18-13. Click Yes to confirm.

   In this situation, DOS won't be able to access the logical drives that you create on this extended partition.

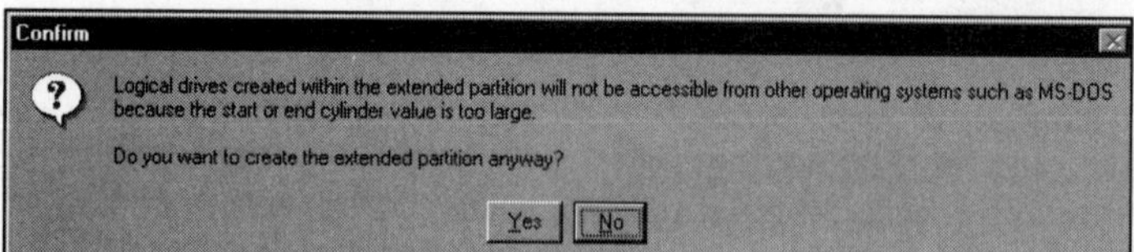

Figure 18-13: Disk Administrator warns you if the starting or ending points of the partition are too large for DOS.

Figure 18-14 shows the resulting Disk Configuration view. Disk Administrator changed the direction of shading in the second region on Disk 2 to indicate that it represents free space on an extended partition. No drive letter is assigned, since no logical drives have yet been created on the extended partition. (You'll assign logical drives in the next section.) Notice that the status line at the bottom of the window indicates that this region represents an empty extended partition.

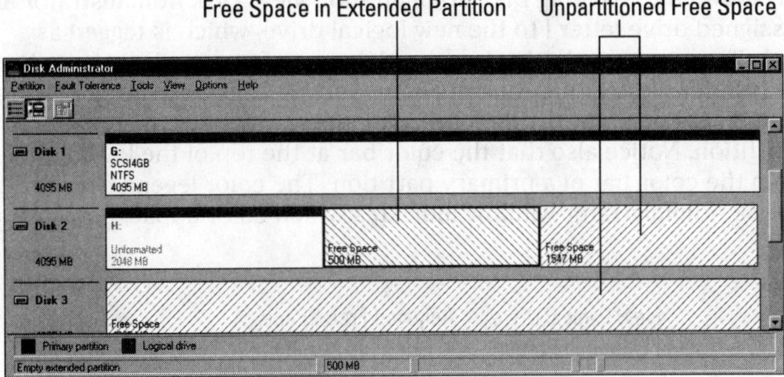

Figure 18-14: The new extended partition is still shown as free space, but with different shading.

Creating a Logical Drive

Once you've created an extended partition, you need to create logical drives within that partition. Here's how:

1. Click to select a region of free space within an extended partition in which you want to create a logical drive.
2. On the Partition menu, click Create.

   Because you've selected a free space region that belongs to an extended partition, Disk Administrator knows that you want to create a logical drive.
3. In the Create Logical Drive dialog box, type the size of the logical drive that you want to create, as shown in Figure 18-15. Click OK.

   The dialog box provides you with the minimum and maximum sizes of the extended partition. It can be as large as the entire region of free space that you selected in step 1.

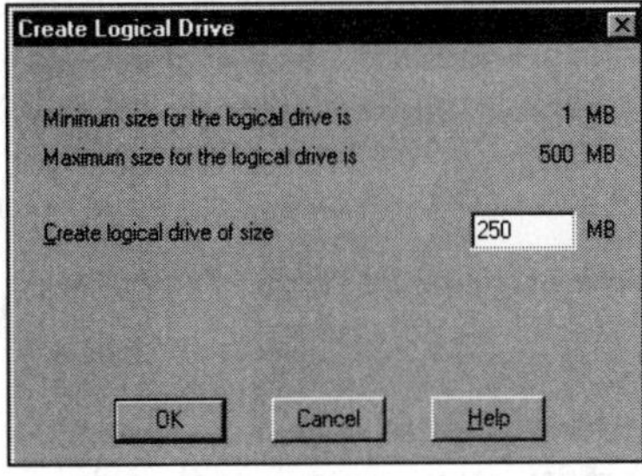

Figure 18-15: In the Create Logical Drive dialog box, you specify the size of the logical drive that you're creating within the extended partition.

Figure 18-16 shows the resulting Disk Configuration view. Disk Administrator automatically assigned drive letter I to the new logical drive, which is tagged as Unformatted. The new logical drive is now ready to be formatted, as described later in this chapter. Notice that the remaining portion of the extended partition is still tagged as free space, but the direction of shading indicates that it's part of the extended partition. Notice also that the color bar at the top of the logical drive is different from the color bar of a primary partition. The color legend near the bottom of the Disk Administrator window indicates which color applies to which type.

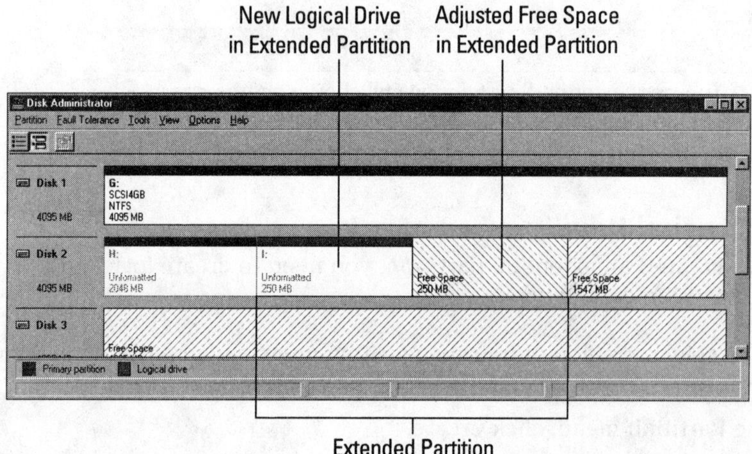

Figure 18-16: The new logical drive is automatically assigned a drive letter.

Deleting Partitions and Logical Drives

Occasionally, you may need to reorganize and delete some of your disk partitions or logical drives. The following sections tell you how to accomplish this.

When you delete a logical drive or partition, all data in that region will be lost forever once you commit the deletion using the Partition menu or by confirming when you exit Disk Administrator. Be very careful to delete the correct partitions and logical drives, and be sure to have a backup copy of any data that you want to salvage.

Here's how to delete a partition or a logical drive within an extended partition:

1. Click to select an existing primary partition, empty extended partition, or logical drive.

To delete an existing extended partition, you must first delete each logical drive from it. When the extended partition is empty, you can select it and delete it.

2. On the Partition menu, click Delete.

To commit the deleted partition to disk, click Commit Changes Now on the Partition menu, or exit Disk Administrator and confirm the change by clicking Yes.

Creating a Volume

Once you've created a primary partition or a logical drive in an extended partition, you must turn it into a volume by formatting it. This allows access to the drive by the operating system and applications. In the following sections, I'll show you how to format and label a partition or logical drive, change the drive letter assignment, and convert a FAT volume into an NTFS volume.

Formatting a Partition

Before formatting a new partition or logical drive, you must commit the changes to disk, as described earlier. Once the changes are committed, you can proceed with the formatting procedure.

1. Click to select an existing primary partition or logical drive.
2. On the Tools menu, click Format.

   Alternatively, you can format volumes from the Command Prompt, using the FORMAT command.
3. In the Format dialog box, in the File System list, click FAT or NTFS, depending on which format you want to use. See Figure 18-17.

See Chapter 7 for a discussion of file system selection criteria.

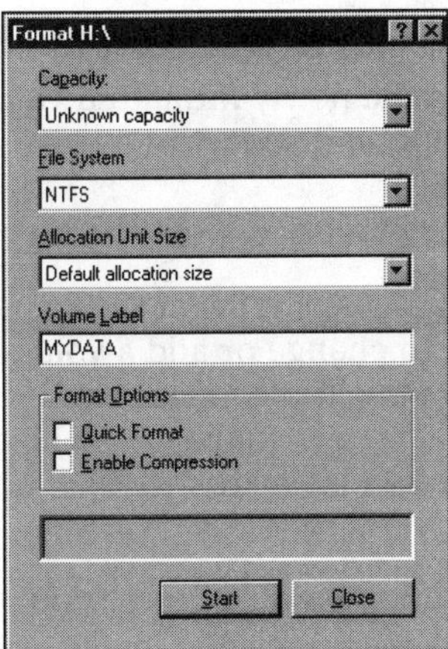

Figure 18-17: In the Format dialog box, select your file system, allocation unit size, volume label, and options.

4. In the Format dialog box, in the Allocation Unit Size list, click Default allocation size. See Figure 18-17.

   If you're formatting using the FAT file system, this is your only choice. If you're formatting with the NTFS file system, you can select a fixed allocation size, but it's best to go with the default, which varies depending on the size of the volume.

5. In the Volume Label field, type the name that you want to assign to the volume.

   The volume label can be up to 11 characters.

6. If you're formatting with NTFS and you want the entire contents of the volume compressed, click to select the Enable Compression check box.

   If you select compression, files and folders written to this volume will be automatically compressed. They'll be automatically decompressed when read. This option is available only on volumes formatted with NTFS.

   (See the section entitled "Deciding on NTFS Compression" in Chapter 19 for a detailed discussion of compression on Windows NT.)

7. If you want to *quick format* the volume, click to select the Quick Format check box.

   Quick formatting writes the file system data structures but doesn't take the time to check the disk area for bad sectors.

8. In the Format dialog box, click Start. You'll get a final warning that all data will be deleted from this partition or logical drive. Click OK to confirm that you want to proceed with the formatting operation.

9. When you see a dialog box indicating that formatting is complete, click OK. In the Format dialog box, click Close.

The display of the partition or logical drive will now be updated with the file system and volume label. You can begin to access the newly formatted volume from NT Explorer, applications, the Command Prompt, and so forth.

Assigning a Volume Label

When you format a volume, you can assign it a volume label at the same time, as described in the previous section. If you want to change or add a volume label after a volume is formatted, click Properties on the Tools menu. Click the General tab, type the new volume label, and click OK. The new volume label immediately appears in the Disk Configuration view in Disk Administrator.

Assigning a Drive Letter

Disk Administrator assigns drive letters to new partitions and logical drives automatically. However, you may want to change these drive letters to suit your needs and preferences. For example, some applications prefer to use specific drive letters for specific purposes.

DRIVE LETTERING MAYHEM

When NT automatically assigns drive letters, it uses DOS drive lettering rules. As physical drives, primary partitions, or logical drives on extended partitions are added or deleted, drive letters can dynamically move around to match the DOS drive lettering conventions. The changes may seem somewhat random, and they can play havoc with applications that expect certain drive letters. To avoid this, opt for the drive lettering alternative discussed in this section.

Unlike DOS, Windows NT lets you assign drive letters to each volume in Windows NT. This capability is sometimes called *static assignment* of drive letters. Some folks call it *sticky drive lettering.* (Drive letters are the only sticky things that you should ever let near your drives.) Here's how to assign a sticky drive letter to a volume:

1. Click to select a volume, whether or not it already has a drive letter assigned to it.

You can use this same procedure to assign drive letters to CD-ROM drives. Click to select a CD-ROM drive and proceed with the remaining steps outlined here.

2. On the Tools menu, click Assign Drive Letter.
3. In the Assign Drive Letter dialog box, click the drive letter that you want to assign to this volume, as shown in Figure 18-18. If you don't want to assign a drive letter, click Do not assign a drive letter.

   Disk Administrator presents a list of all available drive letters. Any drive letters in use, including those used for network connections, aren't included in the list.

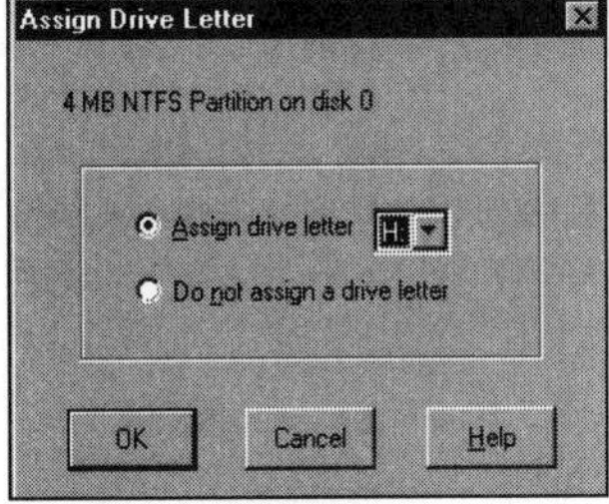

Figure 18-18: You can assign specific sticky drive letters to disk volumes.

4. Click OK. Click Yes to confirm.

   The new drive letter (or no drive letter, if you elected not to assign one) will immediately appear in the disk configuration display of the volume that you selected in step 1.

If you want to swap drive letter assignments between two volumes, you can do this by removing the drive letters from both volumes. Then assign the correct drive letters to the volumes using the sticky drive lettering technique discussed in this section.

Converting a Volume from FAT to NTFS

If you have a volume that's already formatted as FAT and contains data, you can convert it to NTFS while leaving your data intact. (This technique is often called *in-place file system conversion.*) To do this, you need to use the CONVERT command from a Command Prompt. For example, to convert drive K to NTFS, you type the following command:

```
CONVERT K: /FS:NTFS
```

Just substitute the drive letter that you want to convert in this command. The conversion requires some free space on the volume to perform the conversion, so if your volume is almost completely full of files and folders, the conversion may not succeed. The CONVERT utility will tell you how much free space it needs for the conversion, so you can clear this amount of space on the volume and try again.

CONVERTING THE BOOT PARTITION

The Windows NT boot partition can't be converted while the operating system is running, since many of the files on this volume are in use. If you start the conversion process on the boot partition, you'll be told that CONVERT can't perform the conversion now. (You'll get the same message if the drive you're attempting to convert is in use by any applications or Command Prompt windows.)

You'll then be asked if you want to schedule conversion when the computer restarts the next time. Respond by pressing Y (for yes), followed by ENTER. Then shut down and restart the computer as described in Chapter 14. The conversion process will take place early in the boot cycle and may cause the computer to restart several times. This is normal behavior. After the conversion process is complete, you'll be able to log on and access your converted NTFS volume

Managing Volume Sets

Have you ever been faced with running out of space on a volume, and you'd like to be able to increase its size without backing up and completely reformatting the disk? Have you ever been in the situation of having several small chunks of free space on your hard disks, none of which is large enough to be useful, and you'd like to combine them into one logical disk? The volume set feature of NT may be the answer to your prayers.

A Windows NT volume set assembles a series of smaller regions of free space into one large logical volume. The volume set can span more than one physical disk (which is why it's sometimes called *volume spanning*) and can include multiple free space regions from a single disk.

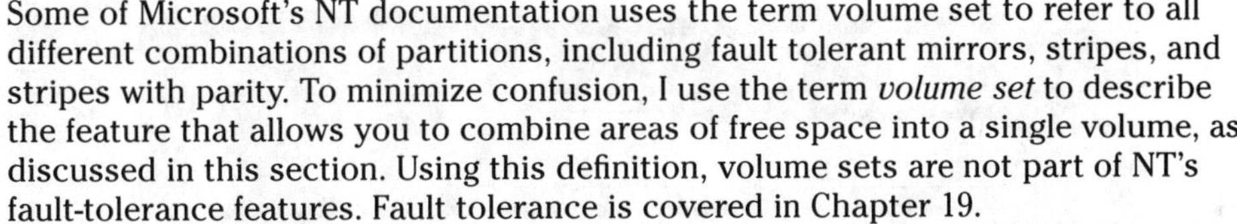

Some of Microsoft's NT documentation uses the term volume set to refer to all different combinations of partitions, including fault tolerant mirrors, stripes, and stripes with parity. To minimize confusion, I use the term *volume set* to describe the feature that allows you to combine areas of free space into a single volume, as discussed in this section. Using this definition, volume sets are not part of NT's fault-tolerance features. Fault tolerance is covered in Chapter 19.

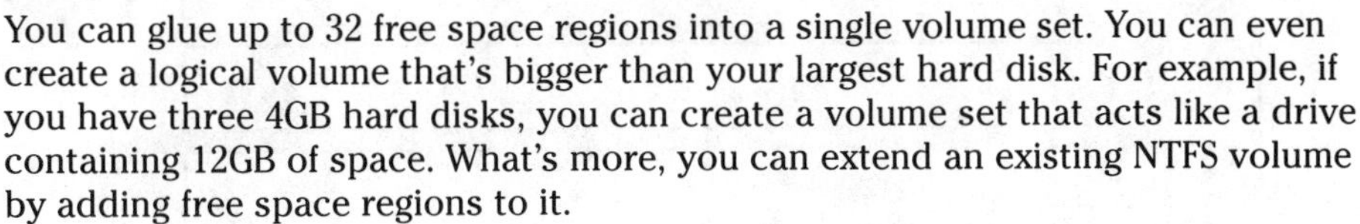

You can glue up to 32 free space regions into a single volume set. You can even create a logical volume that's bigger than your largest hard disk. For example, if you have three 4GB hard disks, you can create a volume set that acts like a drive containing 12GB of space. What's more, you can extend an existing NTFS volume by adding free space regions to it.

VOLUME SET RELIABILITY

Although the volume set feature is often listed under NT's fault-tolerance capabilities, there's nothing fault tolerant about it. This is purely a convenience feature. If any one of the hard disks participating in a volume set dies, you'll lose the entire logical volume. There's no redundancy of data and no way to recover the contents of any portion of the volume, other than to bring the data back from a backup copy. To minimize your risk, you need to make frequent backups of the contents of your volume set.

Reliability of a volume set decreases with each additional physical hard disk added to the set. The mean time between failure, or MTBF, measures the average number of hours that a hard disk is expected to operate without failure. Assuming that the advertised MTBF for each participating drive is identical, the MTBF of a volume set is equal to the MTBF for the individual hard disks divided by the number of hard disks participating in the volume set. For example, if the MTBF of each of your drives is 100,000 hours (about 11 years), and 8 drives are involved in a volume set, the MTBF of the volume set is 12,500 hours (about 1.5 years).

If the MTBF of the participating hard drives differ, things get a bit more complicated. Just know that the MTBF of your volume set is always worse than the least reliable drive in the set.

Creating a Volume Set

You can create a volume set out of several regions of free space. Here are the steps required to create a volume set:

1. Click to select the first region of free space that you want to include in the volume set.
2. While holding down the CTRL key, click to select another region of free space that you want to include in the volume set.

   If you want to include more regions, continue holding down CTRL while you click to select additional regions of free space. Figure 18-19 shows three regions selected.

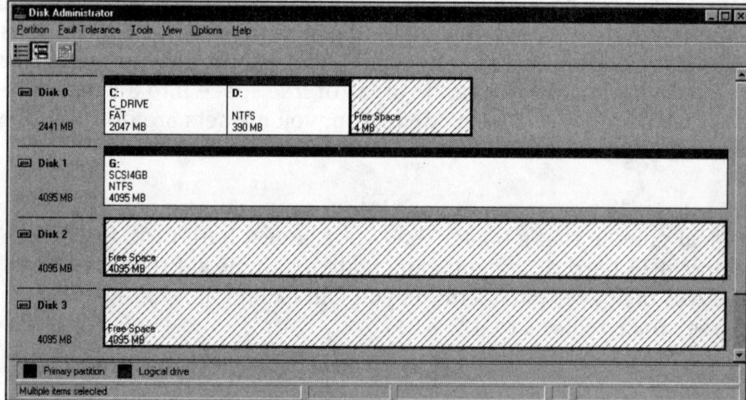

Figure 18-19: You can select which regions of free space will participate in the volume set.

3. On the Partition menu, click Create Volume Set. In the Create Volume Set dialog box, type the total size of the volume set that you want to create. Then click OK.

   The dialog box provides you with the minimum and maximum sizes of the volume set. It can be as small as the smallest region, and as large as all of the selected regions combined.

The Disk Configuration view is immediately updated with the volume set information. As shown in Figure 18-20, a volume set of 8194KB has been created from a 4MB region and two 4GB drives. To applications, the three regions appear as a single large volume.

Once you've successfully created a volume set, and you've committed the changes to disk, you can easily format it and assign a volume label and drive letter to it. Just click to select any region participating in the volume set and follow the instructions presented earlier, under the section "Creating a Volume."

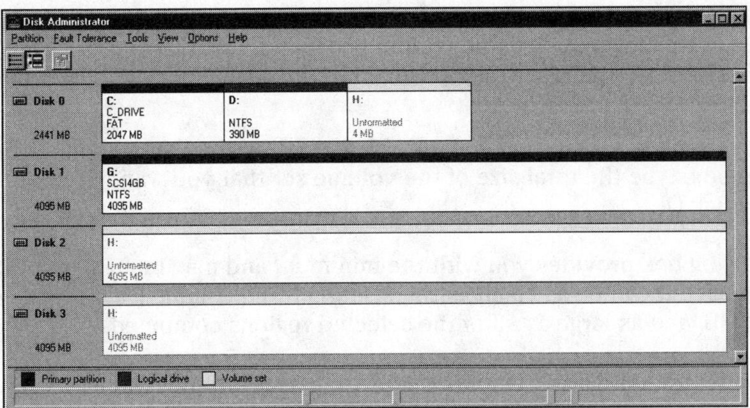

Figure 18-20: The volume set consists of three regions on three different drives.

Extending an Existing Volume

You can extend the size of an existing NTFS volume or volume set by adding one or more regions of free space to it. Here's how:

1. Click to select the NTFS volume that you want to extend, as shown in Figure 18-21. If you're extending an existing NTFS volume set, see Figure 18-22.

   You can't extend existing FAT volumes or volume sets, stripe sets, or mirror sets.

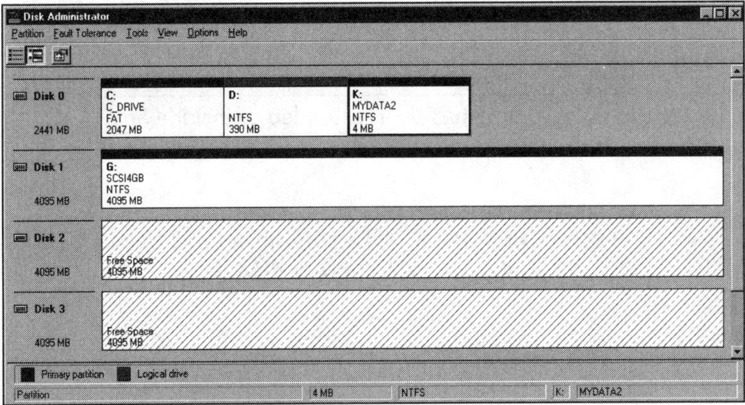

Figure 18-21: You can select an NTFS volume to be extended – in this case, drive K.

2. While holding down the CTRL key, click to select a region of free space that you want to add to the existing volume or volume set. To add more regions of free space, continue holding down CTRL while you click to select additional regions.

3. On the Partition menu, click Extend Volume Set. In the Extend Volume Set dialog box, type the total size of the volume set that you want to create. Then click OK.

   The dialog box provides you with the minimum and maximum sizes of the volume set. It can be as small as the existing NTFS volume (or volume set) plus 1MB, and as large as all of the selected regions combined.

The disk configuration display is immediately updated with the extended volume set information. Figure 18-22 shows that the NTFS volume, drive K, has been extended from its original 4MB to 4099MB, making use of a new 4GB drive. To applications, the two regions appear as a single large volume.

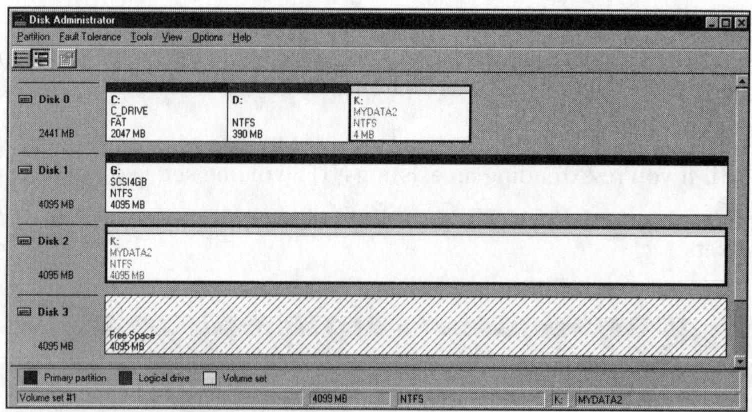

Figure 18-22: The NTFS volume has been extended to include an additional 4GB.

Figure 18-23 shows that the drive K NTFS volume set has been extended from 4099MB to 8194MB, making use of yet another 4GB drive.

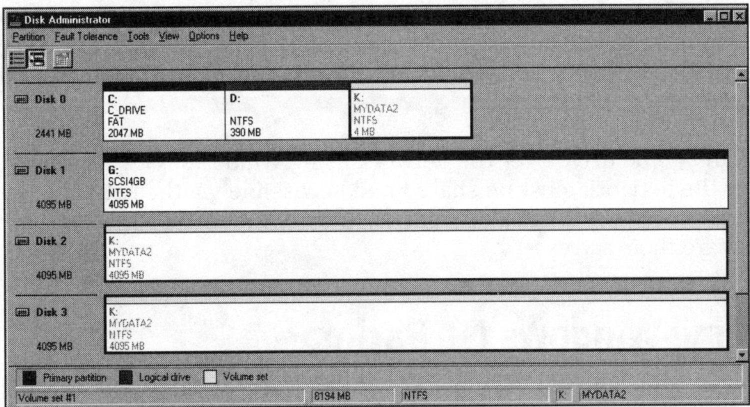

Figure 18-23: The NTFS volume set has been extended to include an additional 4GB.

Deleting a Volume Set

To delete a volume set, click to select any region participating in the set. On the Partition menu, click Delete. Click Yes to confirm. The disk configuration display is immediately updated to reflect the deleted volume set. All participating regions are tagged as free space.

Even if you created your volume set by extending an existing volume with additional free space regions, deleting the volume set will delete all participating regions. You'll lose the contents of the original volume that you extended, too. So, if you have any data that you want to retain, back it up before deleting the volume set.

Backing Up Your Network Data

Probably your most vital function as a network administrator is ensuring that frequent and reliable backups of your network data are done consistently. You may rarely need to actually restore lost data. However, when that day comes (and it will), you'll be the famous hero of the hour riding in on your white horse with backup tapes in hand. (If you don't have the backups, you'll be infamous.) Creating frequent backups of your network servers is the easiest but most important piece of your overall disaster plan.

In the following sections, I'll give you some practical advice on the different types of backups available to you and how they might match your particular needs and backup schedule. You'll then see specifically how to back up and restore data using the Windows NT Backup utility.

You can't share a tape drive over the network using Windows NT. Files that you back up over the network must be shared and accessible via the network. So, all computers that you want to back up over the network must be able to act as servers, to share their drives.

Introducing Windows NT Backup

Windows NT Backup is a graphical utility that enables you to back up and restore data. You can back up the contents of your hard disks, CD-ROMs, or connected network drives to tape and restore the data from tape to the original or different locations. You can opt to back up data on servers across the network, or you can place a tape drive at each server and back up the data locally.

NT Backup stores the data on tape in Microsoft Tape Format, or MTF. Each time that you perform a backup operation, a new *backup set* is created on tape. In fact, each disk volume that you back up creates its own backup set. For example, if you specify that you want drive C and part of drive L backed up, you'll get two backup sets on tape: one for drive C and one for the files backed up from drive L. The backup set is just the collection of backed-up files, along with information on when the backup was performed, who can restore it, and so on. You can put multiple backup sets on a single tape, and a single long backup set can span multiple tapes.

THE BACKUP NAME GAME

The NT Backup utility was developed by folks who have been in the tape backup business for years. Since the beginning of the NT project, their name has changed a few times, due to acquisitions and mergers. When the project started, they were called Maynard, then Archive, then Conner, then Arcada, and now Seagate (at the time of this writing, anyway).

Seagate offers a more feature-rich version of the NT Backup software, called BackupExec. You may want to study its current feature list to determine if it better suits your needs. Of course, other third-party software developers have high-end backup products as well. Remember from Chapter 7 that NT Backup doesn't support autoloader tape units, so if you're planning to use one of these, you'll need a third-party backup solution.

Navigating in NT Backup

To start NT Backup, click Start ➪ Programs ➪ Administrative Tools ➪ Backup. If you haven't installed a tape device driver, you'll get a warning message from NT Backup. See the section entitled "Tape Devices Application" in Chapter 17 for step-by-step instructions on tape device driver installation.

When you start NT Backup, you'll typically see two windows. The Tapes window displays the contents of your tape, if there's one in the drive. The Drives window displays a list of your disks (including hard drives and CD-ROM drives). You can switch between these windows by clicking them, or by using the Window menu to select the window that you want to bring forward. Figure 18-24 shows an example of the Tapes window. Notice that there's a tape in the drive, but it's currently blank.

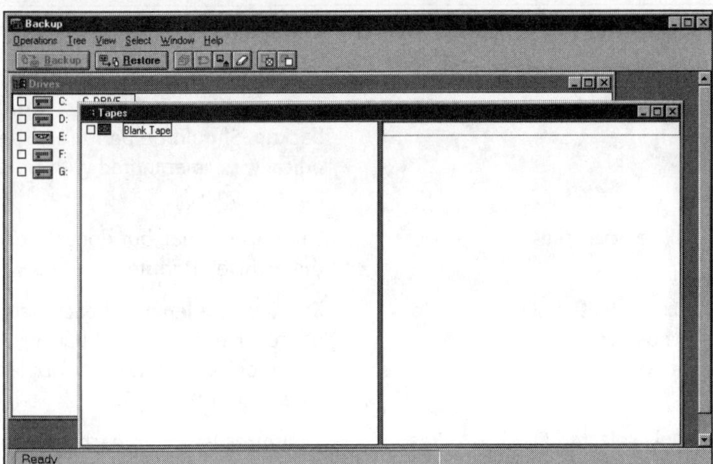

Figure 18-24: Windows NT Backup presents views of your disks and the contents of your tape drive.

When you're viewing the Tapes window, notice that the Restore button is enabled. Likewise, when you're viewing the Drives window, the Backup button is enabled.

In both windows, you double-click a drive (disk or tape) to see more details about its contents. Click the plus (+) sign to expand a folder and the minus (-) sign to collapse it. This behavior is similar to Windows NT Explorer, discussed in Chapter 14. But unlike Explorer, NT Backup includes check boxes next to each object so that you can select which drives, folders, and files to include in a backup or restore operation.

Understanding Backup Types

Windows NT Backup enables you to choose from five types of backup operations. Some simply copy files from disk to tape. Others make use of the archive file attribute both to decide if a file should be included and to signal that a file has been backed up. The five types of backup are Normal, Copy, Differential, Incremental, and Daily. It's important to understand how each one works, and how they can work together to complement each other. I'll cover each backup type in the following sections. Table 18-1 summarizes the characteristics of each of the five backup types.

Table 18-1
Summary of Types of Backups

Backup Type	*Backs Up*	*Clears Archive Attribute*	*Comments*
Normal	All selected files	Yes	Most thorough and longest form of backup. Should be performed periodically, supplemented with other backup types.
Copy	All selected files	No	Same as normal, but doesn't reset the archive attribute.
Differential	Only selected files whose archive attribute is set	No	Shortens the length of each backup, relative to a normal backup. Good for daily backup to supplement weekly normal backup.
Incremental	Only selected files whose archive attribute is set	Yes	Minimizes length of each backup, but may require multiple tapes to restore data. Good for creating checkpoint backups during the day.
Daily	Only selected files modified on the day of backup	No	Good for creating checkpoint backups during and at the end of the day.

Normal Backup

As shown in Table 18-1, the most thorough type of backup is called *normal* (sometimes also referred to as a *full* backup). A normal backup copies all of the files that you specify to tape, then clears the archive attribute to signal that the files have been archived. The advantage of this approach is simple restoration of the data, since you have to deal with only one tape (or set of tapes) to perform a restore operation when the time comes. The disadvantage of this type of backup is that all selected files are copied, whether or not they've changed since the last backup was performed.

There's no substitute for a periodic normal backup. Typically, you'll want to combine another type of backup to supplement your periodic normal backups to minimize the amount of time required for each backup operation. You'll learn about approaches to combining backup types in the sections that follow.

Copy Backup

The *copy* backup is just like a normal backup, but it doesn't clear the archive attribute on the files that it copies to tape. In effect, the copy backup acts as if you were performing a DOS XCOPY command to transfer files from disk to tape. This approach is typically used only in back up schemes that don't rely on the state of the archive attributes. It is rarely combined with other types of backup, so it always retains the disadvantage of copying all files whether they need to be copied or not.

The copy backup can also be used if you need to make a quick backup of a disk and you don't want to interrupt your regular backup schedule by changing archive attributes on files. For example, say, you're doing a weekly normal backup with daily incremental backups and you want to back up a drive to give the tape to a customer. You can use a copy backup to create the customer tape, and your next incremental backup will work as if nothing happened.

Differential Backup

A *differential* backup copies only those files whose archive attribute is set, indicating that the file has changed since the last normal backup. Differential backups are typically used in combination with normal backups, to reduce the time required for each individual backup operation. For example, you may want to perform a normal backup on Sunday evening when you have the largest window of opportunity for the backup operation. Each day of the workweek, you can perform a differential backup to copy all of the files that have changed since the normal backup was done on Sunday.

Since differential backups don't clear the archive attribute, each successive differential backup becomes progressively longer, accumulating all files that have changed since the last normal backup. So, if you perform differential backups each day of the week, the time and tape length required for each backup will increase until the next normal backup is performed.

The restore process is slightly more complex than a simple normal backup. Restoration of data requires that you first restore the normal backup and then the latest differential backup. For example, if your normal backup was done on Sunday and you need to restore data due to a disk crash on Thursday afternoon, you'd have to restore the Sunday normal backup and then the Wednesday differential backup.

Incremental Backup

Incremental backups are very similar to the differential type. In an *incremental* backup, only files whose archive attribute is set are copied. However, unlike a differential backup, an incremental backup clears the archive attribute on each file that it copies. So, each successive incremental backup copies only those files that have changed since the previous incremental backup.

This approach is typically used in conjunction with a periodic normal backup (for example, the Sunday night weekly backup discussed in the previous section). The big advantage of the incremental approach is that each day's backup deals only with the files that have changed since the previous day, so the time and tape length required are minimized.

The price, however, is a more complex restore process. To restore a disk to its latest state, you must first restore the most recent normal backup, followed by each successive incremental backup. For example, a disk crash on Thursday would require restoration of the Sunday normal backup, followed by the Monday, Tuesday, and Wednesday incremental backups.

Daily Backup

During a *daily* backup operation, only files that have been modified on the current calendar date are included in the backup. The archive attribute is neither read nor written. Only the file modification date is examined.

If you want to make checkpoint backups during the day, use either the incremental or daily backup type. If you opt for incremental, each successive checkpoint backup will include only those files updated since the previous one. Each successive daily backup will contain all files modified that day, so the length of the backup will increase over the course of the day.

Maintaining a Backup Schedule

The success of your backup activities stands or falls on developing and maintaining an effective backup schedule. Several factors contribute to this schedule, including the speed and capacity of your tape hardware, the frequency and volume of file modification on your network, and the amount of data that you're willing to lose between backup operations. However you define your backup schedule to meet the needs of your organization, create it and follow it without fail. Make sure that everyone involved in performing backups knows the schedule, which tapes to use when, and how to restore data from tape when necessary.

Most organizations want to minimize or even eliminate the possibility of lost information between backups. On the other hand, you also want to minimize the disruption caused by the backup process itself and assure that what's captured on tape is consistent, useful, and recoverable data. Here are a few things to do to minimize lost data and the impact of the backup process:

- ✦ Use a combination of normal and incremental or differential backups to minimize the length of each backup. For example, you might perform a normal backup on the weekend supplemented by incremental backups on each weekday.
- ✦ Create frequent incremental or daily backups during the day to capture altered files between periodic backups. You have to keep track of many tapes using this approach, but it can minimize lost data in environments where files are frequently updated.
- ✦ Perform each backup using a blank tape, to eliminate the time required to search across multiple backup sets.
- ✦ Schedule backups during periods of the lowest file activity. If you have a night shift during which backups are performed, the hours between 3 a.m. and 5 a.m. are best in most organizations.
- ✦ Perform as many local server backups as possible, minimizing network traffic caused by backup data, and potentially reducing the actual backup time by about a third. This implies investing in tape drives directly attached to each server.
- ✦ Use the fastest tape drives possible. The latest 4mm DAT drives can transfer data at up to 60MB per minute. If money is no object and speed is critical, invest in the latest DLT tape drives. A DLT drive can back up 100MB per minute for about three times the cost of a DAT drive
- ✦ Copy data destined to be backed up to a separate hard drive first, then locally back up the hard drive to tape at your leisure.
- ✦ Rotate tapes through your backup schedule, to even out wear and tear across multiple tapes.
- ✦ Develop a plan that creates long-term archival storage of tapes, preferably at an off-site storage facility.

Don't count on tapes lasting for more than three years. Like anything else, they physically deteriorate over time, even in the best of storage conditions. Plan to copy each tape after three years or plan on losing the data.

Handling Open Files

Many backup utilities don't attempt to copy files that are held open by other applications, since what they copy may be in a changing state. NT Backup waits to see if the file will be closed, then attempts to copy it. If the file doesn't close after 30 seconds, NT Backup reports an error and moves on to the next file.

Some software packages, such as e-mail systems, keep their files open constantly. If you have software that behaves this way, you need to schedule a periodic shutdown of the software to allow backup.

BACKING UP THE NT REGISTRY

The NT registry, which contains virtually all operating system and application configuration data, is held open by the operating system while it's running. The NT designers realized that backing up the registry is an important requirement, so they included special APIs to accomplish this feat. NT Backup and third-party backup solutions use these APIs when they need to back up or restore registry files.

You can back up the local registry using NT Backup, but you can't back up the registry on a remote computer. I'll show you how to include the local registry in your backups later in this chapter. In Chapter 20, you'll learn more about the NT registry itself.

If you're running Exchange Server, discussed in Chapter 16, it provides an extension to NT Backup. The extension gives you a new window where you can select Exchange sites and servers to include in your backup. You can choose to back up the Directory Database and Information Store Database as individual objects on each server. The Exchange backup, which can be done over the network, is completed without interrupting service for Exchange users.

Many database applications hold their files open as long as the database engine is running, even if no applications are accessing the database. To compensate for this, most of these programs provide a built-in mechanism to create a backup copy of the database. If so, take advantage of this by periodically generating a backup database and then back it up to tape using the techniques described in this chapter.

Preparing for Backup

To back up or restore files, you must log on with administrator privileges, or you must be a member of the Backup Operators group. (Specifically, you need the Back up files and directories and/or the Restore files and directories rights on your account to perform backups and restores, respectively). If you plan on backing up files over the network, use NT Explorer or a Command Prompt to attach drive letters to the network resources that you want to back up. Do this before you start the NT Backup utility, or you won't see the network drives.

Most tapes today don't require much preparation before use, but some do. Here are your tape preparation options, offered on the Operations menu:

✦ **Erase Tape.** Click this command to erase previous backup data from the tape. You'll have a choice of Quick Erase (deletes tape header information only) or Secure Erase (wipes out all data present on the tape).

Always use a new or erased tape when performing unattended backup operations. If NT Backup has to skip over existing data on the tape and has trouble reading it, the backup operation will fail. If no one is present to correct the problem, you'll skip a night of backups. So, if you're going to insert a previously used tape for an unattended backup, erase it first.

✦ **Retension Tape.** DC-6000 and DC-2000 tape cartridges require periodic *retensioning*, which fast-forwards and rewinds the entire tape to equalize the tape tension. Retension these tapes before you use them for the first time and then after every 20 backup operations.

✦ **Format Tape.** Some tapes contain formatting information that can be rewritten to the tape. Most of these tapes are sold preformatted. If a tape starts generating errors, you can try reformatting it, although you'll lose all data on the tape (just as you do when reformatting a disk).

Performing a Backup

Here are the steps for performing a backup to tape:

1. Insert a tape in the tape drive and start NT Backup by clicking Start ➪ Programs ➪ Administrative Tools ➪ Backup.

   If you intend to either append a new backup set or overwrite existing data on the tape, your tape doesn't need to be blank.

2. Click the Drives window. Click to select the check box next to each drive, folder, or file that you want to include in the backup, as shown in Figure 18-25.

   Double-click a drive to see more detail. Click the plus (+) sign to expand a folder and the minus (-) sign to collapse it. In Figure 18-25, I've elected to back up all of drive C and most of drive G (everything except the G:\TEMP directory).

If you back up material from more than one drive, a separate backup set is written to tape for each drive that you're backing up. You'd get the same effect by performing two separate backups for the two different drives.

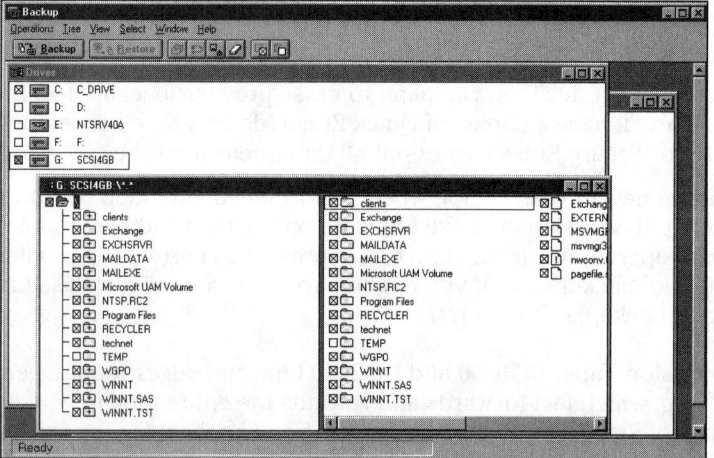

Figure 18-25: You can select which drives, folders, and files to include in the backup.

3. When you're done specifying what you want to include in the backup, click the Backup button. You'll see the Backup Information dialog box, as shown in Figure 18-26.

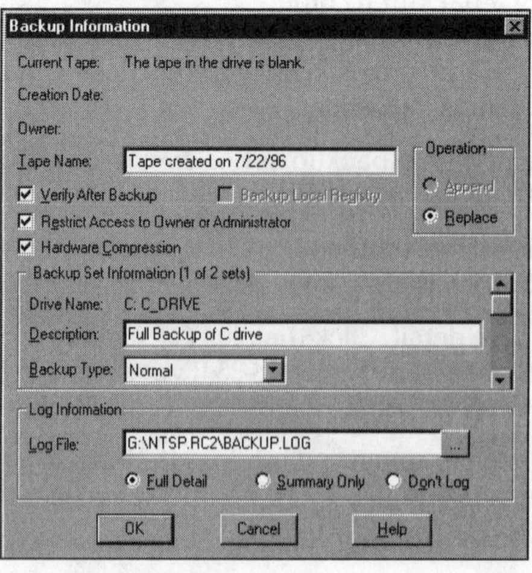

Figure 18-26: You must supply the options for this particular backup operation.

4. In the Backup Information dialog box, under Operation, click Replace if you want to overwrite all data on the tape with this new backup. Otherwise, click Append to add this backup to the other backup sets already on the tape.

   If the tape is blank, Replace is your only choice. When Replace is selected, you can optionally change the Tape Name to something other than the default shown in Figure 18-26. The tape name applies to the contents of the entire tape.

5. Click to select the check boxes labeled Verify After Backup, Restrict Access to Owner or Administrator, Hardware Compression, and Backup Local Registry, if they are available.

   Always select the Verify After Backup check box. This causes NT Backup to read all of the data that it has written to tape, comparing it with the original on disk. Although this may add some extra time to the backup process, it's vital to have the assurance that the tape you've created can actually be restored later.

   The Restrict Access to Owner or Administrator option essentially puts a lock on the tape so that only its creator or an administrator can access files on it. Thus, if your tape falls into the wrong hands, that person will have a tough time accessing the data. I recommend selecting this option for added security, especially if the data that you're backing up is e-mail or personnel files.

   The Hardware Compression option may or may not be available, depending on your tape drive hardware capabilities. If it isn't available, the check box will be disabled. If it's available, I always select it to squeeze as much data as possible on a tape.

Unlike most commercial backup software products, NT Backup doesn't perform any software compression on the data that it writes to tape. So the DC-2120 tapes that advertise a 250MB capacity hold only about 125MB when used with NT Backup. The advertised tape capacity assumes that the software compresses the data before writing it to tape. Drives that support hardware compression can achieve the advertised tape capacity because they perform the compression themselves. The down side to using hardware compression is that it limits the portability of your tape to other drives that might not support compression in hardware.

   If you've included the boot volume in your backup, you can opt to back up the local NT registry. I recommend including the registry in all of your backups.

6. Under Backup Type, click the type of backup that you want to perform for this drive: Normal, Copy, Differential, Incremental, or Daily.

   The backup types are discussed in detail earlier in this chapter, in the section called "Understanding Backup Types."

7. In the Description field, type a brief description of the backup set that you're creating.

8. Repeat steps 5 through 7 for each drive that you're backing up.

It's easy to miss the scroll bar to the right of Backup Set Information. Under Backup Set Information, click the arrows to scroll through the volumes that you're backing up, and specify the appropriate Description and Backup Type for each one. Each volume included in the backup has its own description and its own backup type.

Recall that each drive that you specify is written to tape as a separate backup set. Each backup set can be individually configured. Figure 18-27 shows the Backup Information dialog box after scrolling down to drive G. Notice that the Backup Local Registry option is available, since drive G is the boot volume.

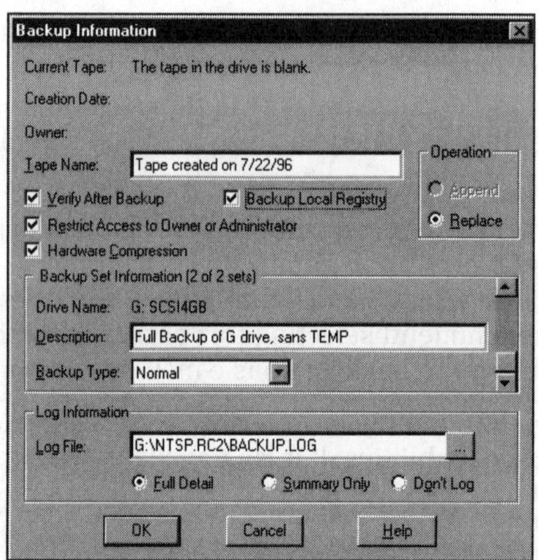

Figure 18-27: You can specify a different set of options for each drive that you're backing up.

9. Under Log Information, click Full Detail.

   The log file is your only means of determining the success of your backup, after you've dismissed the status dialog box, described in step 11.

10. Click OK to start the backup. You'll see the Backup Status dialog box during the backup process, as shown in Figure 18-28.

    Pay particular attention to the count of corrupt files (which may indicate a tape or disk hardware problem) and skipped files (which may indicate that files that you wanted to back up are open).

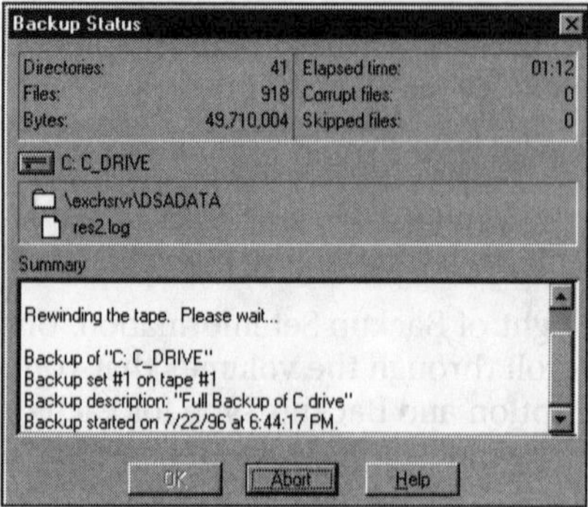

Figure 18-28: NT Backup provides status information throughout the backup process.

11. If you opted to verify the tape contents, you'll see the Verify Status dialog box, as shown in Figure 18-29. When both the backup and verification are complete, click OK. Check the backup log to review any problems that may have occurred.

    In Figure 18-29, one error was encountered during the verification process. A file on disk changed between when the file was backed up and when it was verified. This is typical of a harmless verify error.

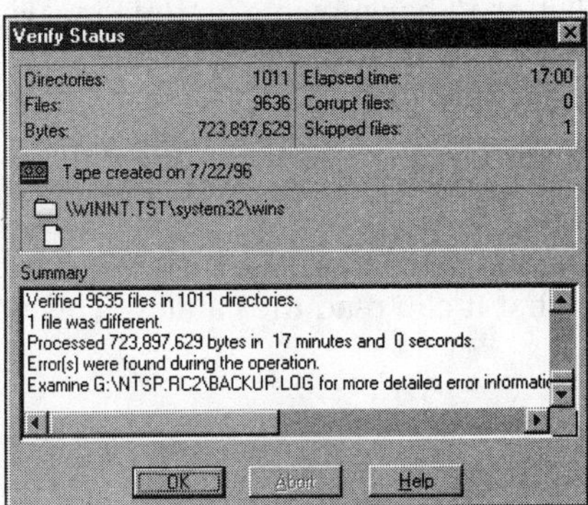

Figure 18-29: The Verify Status dialog box keeps you informed of any problems found during verification.

Preparing for Restore

Your server's main disk drive suddenly starts emanating a grating, high-pitched banshee's scream, a warning of impending data doom. Before you have time to think, you hear the disheartening sound of the disk drive spinning down to its last revolution in this life. After saying a few last words at its passing (I won't repeat them here), you know what you have to do. Time to break out the backup tapes and a new disk drive and resurrect that server. As your boss strides over to learn about the problem, little beads of sweat pop out on your forehead. Fortunately, you already have your backup tapes in hand.

NT Backup enables you to restore the contents of an entire tape, specific backup sets on the tape, or individual files and folders within a backup set. You can also opt to restore just the local registry from tape.

Prior to starting the restore process, you need to identify the tapes containing the files you need to restore. You also need to decide where you want the restored files to go — either to their original drives and folders or to new locations.

If you're restoring data from multiple tapes, make absolutely sure that you restore the backup sets in the same order in which they were created, so that you end up with the latest copies of all files. If you restore the tapes out of order, you could easily overwrite a file with an older version.

Performing a Restore

Here are the steps to follow to restore data from a tape backup:

1. Click Start ➪ Programs ➪ Administrative Tools ➪ Backup. Click the Tapes window.
2. Insert the first tape that you want to restore in the tape drive. NT Backup reads the catalog of backup sets from the tape and displays them as shown in Figure 18-30.

   The catalog, which contains a list of all backup sets on the tape, is located after all backup sets. On some tape drives, the search for the catalog can take several minutes. The cataloging process on a DAT drive takes a few seconds.

   If NT Backup doesn't search for the catalog, you can force it to by clicking Catalog on the Operations menu.

If you're restoring a backup set that spans more than one tape, NT Backup will ask you to insert the appropriate tape so that it can read the catalog. This will typically be the last tape of the backup set.

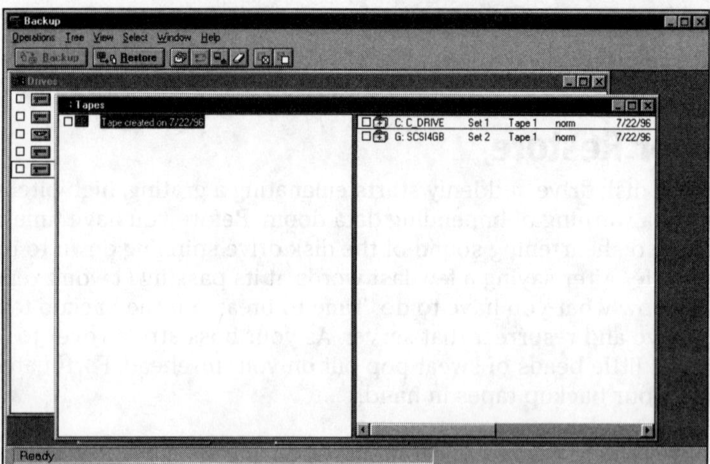

Figure 18-30: The Tapes window displays the catalog of backup sets on the tape.

3. Click to select the check box next to each backup set, drive, folder, or file that you want to restore, as shown in Figure 18-31.

   Double-click a backup set or drive to see more detail. Click the plus (+) sign to expand a folder and the minus (-) sign to collapse it. In Figure 18-31, I've elected to restore just the WGPO and technet folders on drive G.

If you want to restore just the registry, you need to select at least one file in the appropriate backup set to restore, in order to properly activate the Restore button. (If you don't select a file, clicking Restore will result in an error pop-up.) You'll be able to specify registry restoration in a later step.

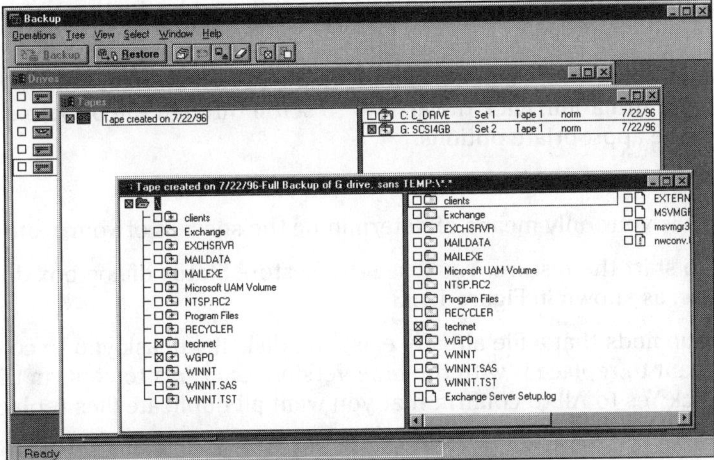

Figure 18-31: You must select which backup sets, drives, folders, and files that you want to restore.

4. When you're done specifying what you want to restore, click the Restore button. You'll see the Restore Information dialog box, as shown in Figure 18-32. Click to select the Verify After Restore check box.

   I recommend selecting the verify option. This causes NT Backup to read all of the data that it has restored to disk, comparing it with the original data on tape.

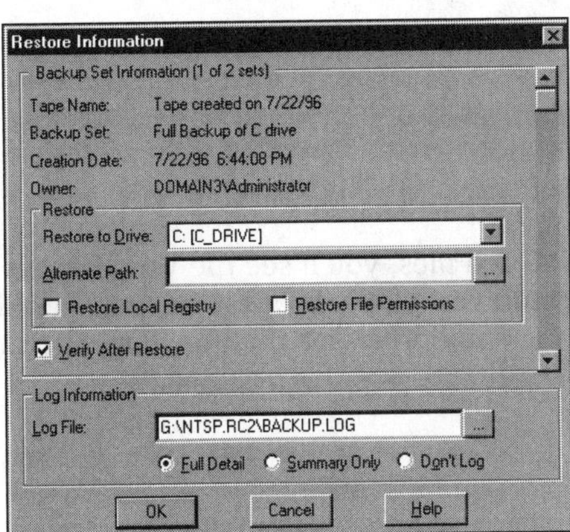

Figure 18-32: You can supply the options for the restore operation.

5. Click to select the Restore File Permissions check box. If you want to restore registry files, click to select the Restore Local Registry check box.

   You can only restore file permissions to an NTFS volume. If you're restoring to a FAT volume, the check box will be automatically cleared.

6. If you want to restore to a disk location other than the original source, click the drive in the Restore to Drive list and type the new destination directory in the Alternate Path field.

7. Repeat steps 5 and 6 for each backup set that you're restoring. Under Backup Set Information, click the arrows to scroll through the backup sets, and select the appropriate options.

8. Under Log Information, click Full Detail.

   The log file is your only means of determining the success of your restore.

9. Click OK to start the restore. You'll see the Restore Status dialog box during the process, as shown in Figure 18-33.

   If NT Backup finds that a file already exists on disk, it will ask you to confirm that you want to replace it with the tape version. Click Yes to confirm the single file. Click Yes to All to confirm that you want all duplicate files replaced during the restore process.

   Pay particular attention to the count of corrupt files (which may indicate a tape or disk hardware problem) and skipped files (which may indicate that files you wanted to restore are open).

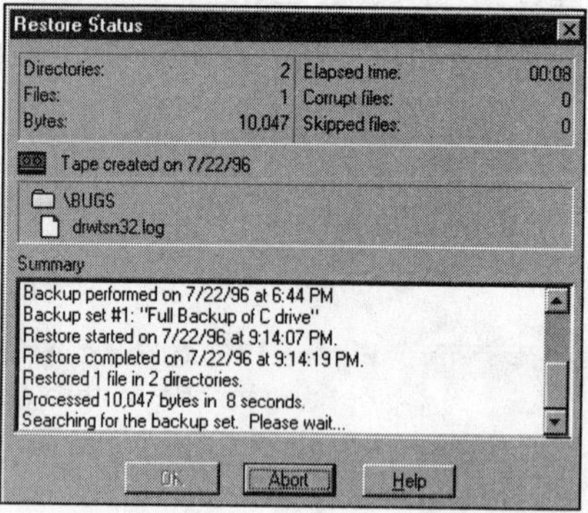

Figure 18-33: NT Backup provides status information throughout the restore process.

10. If you opted to verify the restored files, you'll see the Verify Status dialog box. When both the restore and verify operations are complete, click OK. Check the backup log to review any problems that may have occurred.

Using NT Backup in Batch Mode

The graphical NT Backup utility doesn't support macros, so if you need to create complex backup procedures for repeated execution, you'll need to use the command line version of NT Backup. With it, you can back up contents of folders, but you can't specify individual files. Table 18-2 lists the NTBACKUP command line parameters and their equivalent actions in the graphical NT Backup utility.

Table 18-2
NTBACKUP Command Line Parameters and Their Equivalent Functions

Command Line Parameter	*Equivalent Action in Graphical NT Backup*
/A	Select Append to existing backup set(s).
/B	Select the Backup Local Registry check box.
/D "text"	Type the "text" in the Description field.
/E	Click Summary Only under Log Information.
/HC:OFF	Clear the Hardware Compression check box.
/HC:ON	Select the Hardware Compression check box.
/L "filename"	Type the "filename" in the Log File field.
/R	Select Restrict Access to Owner or Administrator check box.
/T COPY	Select a Backup Type of Copy.
/T DAILY	Select a Backup Type of Daily.
/T DIFFERENTIAL	Select a Backup Type of Differential.
/T INCREMENTAL	Select a Backup Type of Incremental.
/T NORMAL	Select a Backup Type of Normal.
/TAPE:number	Click the destination tape drive. Specifies the tape drive number on which the backup or eject operation will be performed.
/V	Select the Verify After Backup check box.
BACKUP	Click the Backup button.
EJECT	Click Operations ➪ Eject Tape. Use the /TAPE command line parameter to specify which tape you want to eject.
Path	Click the source drives and folders that you want to include in the backup.

For example, to perform a normal backup of drive C, drive G, and the F:\MYDATA folder, with restricted access, full verification, hardware compression, and a detailed log, you'd type the following command in a Command Prompt window:

```
NTBACKUP BACKUP C: G: F:\MYDATA /V /R /HC:ON /T NORMAL
```

When you use the command line version of NT Backup, you'll notice that it starts the normal graphical version of the utility and runs it automatically. You can view progress of the backup operation by watching the Backup Status window. If things are going wrong and you want to shut down the backup, you can click the Abort button in this window to stop the backup operation.

See Chapter 21 for tips on using the NTBACKUP command line to recover bad tapes and salvage data from backup sets with missing or damaged tapes.

Administering Windows NT Accounts

Years ago, I did some research on software maintenance, asking software development managers what they felt was the primary cause of maintenance nightmares. Over half put "users" at the top of their list. "If users wouldn't use this stuff, we wouldn't have to constantly change it." And so it is with networks. Without users, you could perfectly configure your servers and your network, fine-tune them for optimal performance — and then run out of things to do. The moment you add your first user account to the network, your real challenges begin. There's no getting around it. Networks were designed for users, and your job is designed to support them.

In the following sections, you'll see how to create and manage user and group accounts. Accounts don't just provide basic security by requiring users to identify themselves before logging on with a user name and password. They also provide the basis for securing access to just about everything on the network, including files, printers, and other shared resources. (I'll discuss more security concepts and strategies in the section called "Administering Windows NT Security," later in this chapter.) The central tool for performing account management tasks is the User Manager for Domains utility. You'll come to know this tool well as you deal with user accounts on your NT Server network.

Introducing User Manager for Domains

User Manager for Domains is a graphical utility used to view, create, modify, and delete user accounts, local groups, and global groups. (See Chapter 10 for a discussion of the differences between local and global groups.) In addition, you can administer system-wide policies dealing with how accounts behave, what events are audited, and what rights each user and group has. Think of User Manager for Domains as your interface to the SAM database (discussed in Chapter 2) of your domain and other domains on your network.

Windows NT Workstation includes a similar utility called User Manager. It enables you to manage user and group accounts on a single workstation. User Manager for Domains has some significant differences, but if you're already familiar with User Manager, you should be comfortable with much of the NT Server version.

Navigating in User Manager for Domains

To start User Manager for Domains, log on with administrator privileges and click Start ➪ Programs ➪ Administrative Tools ➪ User Manager for Domains. (Members of the Account Operators group can also administer accounts, but they can't manage administrator accounts or domain policies.) You'll see the window shown in Figure 18-34. The upper half displays a list of user accounts. NT Server automatically creates the two accounts Administrator and Guest. The lower half presents a list of local and global groups.

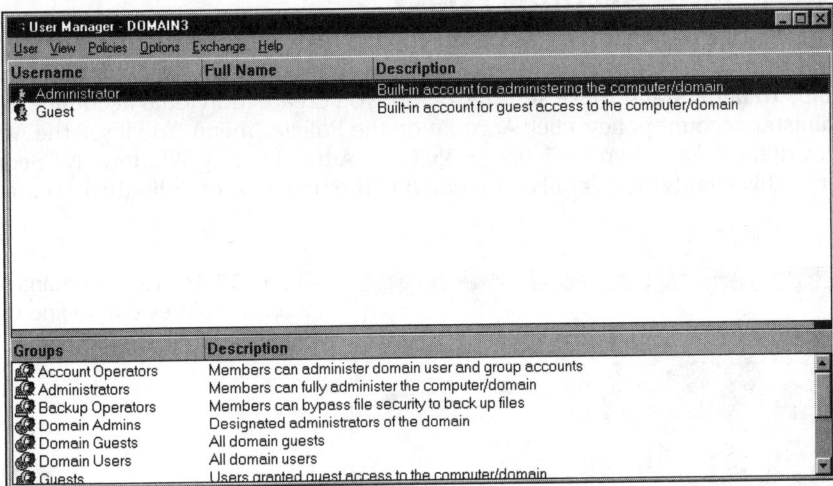

Figure 18-34: User Manager for Domains provides you with a window on the SAM database in your domain and in other domains.

The Guest account, automatically created by NT during installation, allows users with no formal account or password to access resources on the network. Users in untrusted domains can gain access to your domain. This can be a big security hole. The good news is that by default, the Guest account is disabled. I recommend leaving it that way. Unfortunately, you can't delete the Guest account.

By default, you're looking at the accounts in your own domain. User Manager for Domains can administer accounts in other domains as well. To attach this utility to another domain, click Select Domain on the User menu. In the Select Domain dialog box, type or click the domain that you want to administer and click OK.

If you're responsible for administering several domains, you may want to start multiple copies of User Manager for Domains, each pointing to a different domain. This approach can be a real time-saver, allowing you to switch your attention quickly between domains to handle account maintenance tasks.

If you're the only administrator in the network making changes to the account database, what you see in the User Manager for Domains windows reflects the actual state of the SAM database. However, if there are multiple administrators performing account maintenance on the network at the same time, you won't see each others' changes displayed immediately. This utility periodically polls for changes made by other administrators on the network. If you want to be sure that what you're seeing is absolutely up to date, click Refresh on the View menu. This will force the utility to gather the latest information. (This synchronization activity isn't performed continuously because it can lead to added network traffic.)

Establishing Account Policy

Before creating any new user accounts, it's a good idea to establish overall policies regarding how accounts should behave. You can modify this behavior any time, but it helps to understand these settings before you create individual accounts. To administer account policy, click Account on the Policies menu. You'll see the Account Policy dialog box shown in Figure 18-35. (See "Administering Windows NT Security" later in this chapter for details on modifying the behavior of individual accounts.)

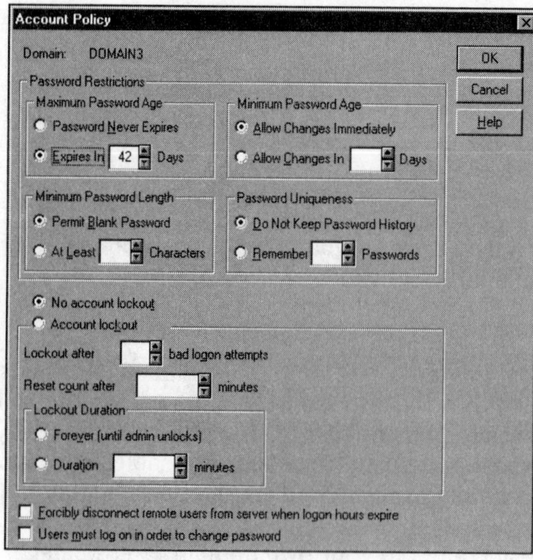

Figure 18-35: You can manage account policies that define the behavior of all user accounts.

The following sections outline what you can control with this powerful dialog box.

Password Restrictions

The Account Policy dialog box enables you to establish specific restrictions on passwords, and apply these restrictions to all accounts. The password parameters are:

- ✦ **Password Expiration.** You can make passwords live forever, or expire after a certain number of days. The default is a 42-day expiration on all passwords. I recommend expiring all user passwords every 30 to 60 days.
- ✦ **Password Length.** You can either allow blank passwords (which is the default), or specify a minimum length. I recommend setting a minimum length of at least eight characters.

Don't allow blank passwords. It's far too easy for unauthorized folks to guess user account names, since they're often some combination of employees' first and last names or initials. If you allow accounts with no passwords, you're leaving your network doors open. Require passwords for every account.

- ✦ **Password Uniqueness.** Some users swap between two standard passwords whenever their password expires. Although this is easy for them, it provides little password security. You can direct NT to save a history of previous passwords, then use this information to force a user into changing his or her password to something brand new. The default keeps no history. I recommend keeping a history of at least four passwords.
- ✦ **Password Aging.** You can allow passwords to change any time, or prevent changes for a certain number of days. The default allows changes immediately, with no minimum waiting period. I recommend setting the minimum waiting period to seven days.

You need to consider how password uniqueness and password aging interact with each other. For password uniqueness to be effective, you must not allow immediate changes to passwords. If you allow immediate changes, users who like to cycle between two standard passwords can immediately change passwords several times to get back to their old standard ones.

By default, NT allows a user to log on once after his or her password has expired. It then forces the user to change the password. If you click to select the Users must log on in order to change password check box at the bottom of the dialog box, NT won't extend this courtesy. If a user's password expires, an administrator (probably you) will have to intervene.

Account Lockout Restrictions

Unauthorized users often attempt to gain access to a computer or network with a valid user account name (which is easy to guess in many organizations). All they have to do is guess the password. Some of these folks write programs to perform many repeated logon attempts over a short period of time. I'm a firm believer in implementing an account lockout policy for failed logon attempts as a key element in any security policy.

With the Account Policy dialog box, shown in Figure 18-35, you can disable the abused account after the number of failed logon attempts that you specify under Lockout After. I recommend setting this to four attempts. Under Reset Counter After, you can specify the maximum number of minutes between any two failed logon attempts for lockout to occur. Set this field to its maximum value.

Under Lockout Duration, you can specify whether an administrator needs to intervene to re-enable the account after lockout by clicking Forever. You can also click Duration and type the number of minutes that the account should remain disabled. I highly recommend selecting Forever, so that you hear about every account lockout that occurs on your network. It's less convenient for you, but knowing about each lockout is well worth the hassle — you may discover a security breach.

Pay attention to the units used for numeric values in this dialog box. Some are expressed in minutes, others in days. It's easy to get confused if you're not paying attention to the units.

Logon Time Restrictions

As I'll discuss later in this chapter, you can specify a maximum number of logon hours for each account. Normally when this time limit expires, the user's existing server connections remain active, but he or she can't connect to additional servers.

If you want to force all users to disconnect from all servers when the logon time limit is reached, click to select Forcibly disconnect remote users from server when logon hours expire, as shown in Figure 18-35. This will cause NT to cut immediately all connections that the user has to servers in the domain when the logon hours expire.

Preparing for User Account Creation

NT provides only the Administrator and Guest accounts by default. You'll need to add all individual user accounts yourself. Before creating accounts, you need to decide on a naming convention for them. In addition, you'll need to decide how you want to manage user profiles, which control how users' environments are configured.

Preparing User Account Names

Each user account must have a unique name. User names can be up to 20 characters long. I recommend limiting their length to eight characters, so that you can use the names for users' home directories for DOS and Windows 3.x clients on your network. If you use names longer than eight characters, you'll have to find an alternative approach to naming home directories, if you have non-NT network clients.

Many naming conventions for user accounts are employed today. In practice, I've seen two work well. The first approach concatenates the user's first name with the first letter of their last name. To avoid duplication, additional letters from the last name are added. For example, when creating an account for Bozo Clown, if a BOZOC account already exists, use BOZOCL.

The second approach that seems to work well involves concatenating the first letter of the first name with the last name (for example, BCLOWN). In either approach, you can resolve duplicates by adding numbers to the end of the user name.

Preparing a User Profile Strategy

Perhaps you have individual users who log on to the network from various computers during the day. Of course, each person has their environment of desktop and menus set just how they like them, and you'd like that environment to follow the user around from one computer to the next. Every time a person logs on, he or she is greeted with his or her familiar desktop environment. Perhaps you want to present the same environment to all your users and control it centrally, to avoid problems caused by users tweaking their environments in nonstandard ways. Windows NT Server enables you to centralize and download these environments, called *user profiles.*

User Profiles

There are three flavors of user profiles: local, roaming, and mandatory. Local profiles are local to the computer on which they're created and don't follow you if you log on to another computer. Roaming profiles act like your shadow, following you from one computer to the next as you log on to the network. Mandatory profiles are similar to roaming profiles, but they're created and controlled by the network administrator. Both roaming and mandatory profiles live on a server and are downloaded to your computer when you log on to the network.

You may remember that in Windows NT Server 3.x, profiles were stored in a single file. On Windows NT Server 4.0, the same information is stored in multiple files within a folder.

You create a user profile with the System application in Control Panel. Click the User Profiles tab, select an existing profile that you want to copy, click Copy To, and provide a destination on the network. To change the user or group that's allowed to use the profile, click Change.

During user account creation, you'll need to specify a location where user profiles are centrally stored. Select a computer that is running Windows NT Server. The profiles are generally stored in the SystemRoot\PROFILES directory, under a separate subdirectory for each user. For example, the profile for KENGR on my NT server would be stored in G:\WINNT\PROFILES\KENGR. Within each profile directory, there's a file called NTUSER.DAT. To convert this to a mandatory profile, change the name to NTUSER.MAN.

Logon Scripts

A logon script is simply a batch file that's automatically run when you log on to the Windows NT Server network from an NT, DOS, Windows for Workgroups, or OS/2 computer. Logon scripts aren't as powerful as profiles, but they're the only way to go if you're logging on to the network from a non-NT computer. So, if a user will be logging on from computers running different operating systems, you may want to assign both a user profile and a logon script to his or her user account.

Logon scripts are stored in the directory SystemRoot\SYSTEM32\REPL\IMPORT\SCRIPTS. Typically, one master set of logon scripts is stored on the primary domain controller (PDC). You then use directory replication to keep up-to-date copies on other domain controllers. By taking this approach, you're assured that users will have access to their logon scripts, regardless of which domain controller accepted their logon. (See Chapter 15 for details on how to set up directory replication between NT computers.)

When you create a user account, you can specify the name of its logon script. You can specify a unique batch filename for each user, or use a common batch file for several users. If you take the latter approach, you can be sure that users are working in a consistent environment, as they would be if you used mandatory profiles.

Home Directories

Each user account has a home directory associated with it, to be used for storing personal files. (This is similar to the UNIX home directory concept.) You can configure the user account to place the home directory on the user's local computer, or you can opt to store home directories on the network. The latter approach is more flexible, since users can then access their home directories regardless of which computer they use to log on to the network.

If you place home directories on the network, you'll need to identify a server and directory where you want them to be located. When you create the account, specify a UNC path name to the user's home directory (for example, \\TOWER3\HOMEDIRS\KENGR). NT automatically creates this directory and sets permissions on it to allow access only by the user account that you're creating. (I'll talk more about permissions later in this chapter.)

Preparing Account Restrictions

For each user account that you create, you'll need to decide in which groups you want the user to be a member, whether to restrict the user's logon hours, whether to restrict logons to certain workstations, and whether the account itself should expire.

Adding a User Account

Here's how to add and configure a new NT user account:

1. On the User menu, click New User. Type the appropriate values in the Username, Full Name, Description, Password, and Confirm Password fields, as shown in Figure 18-36.

   The Description field is optional. You can use it for department names, job titles, office locations, and so forth.

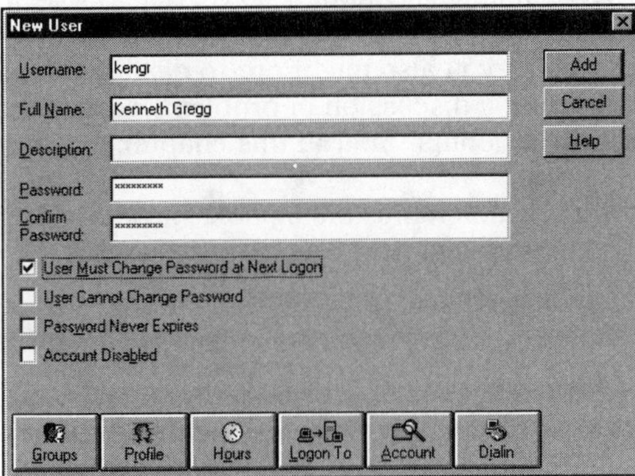

Figure 18-36: In the New User dialog box, you can add a new user account by specifying its name, password, and other information.

2. Click to select the User Must Change Password at Next Logon check box.

   This check box is selected by default. Forcing your users to change their passwords to something unknown to administrators provides maximum security.

3. If you don't want the user to be able to change the account password, click to select the User Cannot Change Password check box.

   If more than one user will share this account, you may want to prevent the users from changing passwords on each other. However, I advise against letting users share accounts.

   In some enterprises, passwords are managed centrally by the MIS group, to ensure that they're not easily guessed passwords. In this situation, you'd want to prevent users from changing their own passwords.

   If neither situation applies to you, I recommend leaving the option cleared and allowing users to change their own passwords.

4. If you want to prevent this particular account password from expiring, click to select the Password Never Expire check box.

   Doing this overrides the account policy that you set earlier in this chapter. There may be rare specific instances when you want a password to live forever, but for maximum security, you should avoid this.

5. If you want this account temporarily disabled so that no one can use it, click to select the Account Disabled check box.

If the new employee for whom this account is created hasn't yet arrived, disable the account until his or her first day on the job. Likewise, temporarily disable the account of employees who go on a long vacation or leave. (Of course, if they'll be using RAS to access the network while they're away, don't disable their account.) If an employee leaves the company, you also might opt to disable the account quickly rather than deleting it. (For a discussion of problems associated with deleting accounts, see "Deleting Accounts" later in this chapter.)

6. Click Groups. In the Group Memberships dialog box, shown in Figure 18-37, under Not member of, click to select the groups that you want this account to join. Then click Add. When you're done adding groups, click OK.

   You can also withdraw the account from group memberships by clicking the groups under Member of and clicking Remove. By default, all accounts are members of the Domain Users group.

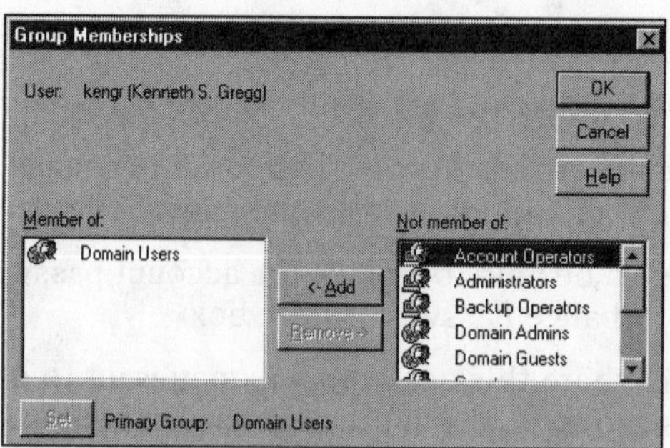

Figure 18-37: In the Group Memberships dialog box, you can make this account a member of existing groups.

7. Click Profile. As shown in Figure 18-38, if this account has a centralized user profile, type the UNC path to it in the User Profile Path field. If this account has a logon script, type its filename in the Logon Script Name field.

   Under Home Directory, if the home directory of this user will exist on the local computer, click Local Path and type the path on the user's local computer. If the home directory is on the network, click Connect, select a drive letter, and type the UNC path to the user's home directory. When you're done, click OK.

   See the section earlier in this chapter called "User Profiles."

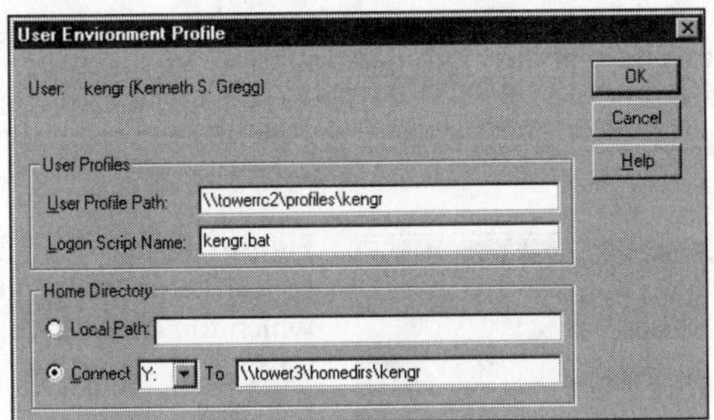

Figure 18-38: In this dialog box, you can manage the account's user profile, logon script, and home directory.

8. Click Hours. You'll see the Logon Hours dialog box, as shown in Figure 18-39. If you want to restrict the hours during which the user can log on, select the hours that you want to restrict and click Disallow. When you're done, click OK.

   Hours marked with a dark blue bar are the hours during which the user is allowed to log on. The default setting allows the user to log on at any time.

If you want to select an entire day, click the button labeled with the day of the week. To select an hour slot across all days of the week, click the appropriate button at the top of the hour column.

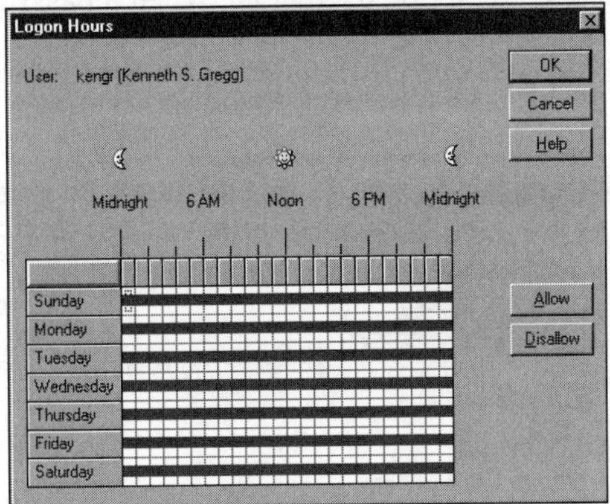

Figure 18-39: You can restrict the hours during which the user can log on.

9. Click the Logon To option. In the Logon Workstations dialog box, shown in Figure 18-40, if you don't want to restrict the locations from which the user logs on, click User May Log On To All Workstations. If you want to restrict logons to a subset of computers, click User May Log On To These Workstations and type the computer names from which the user can log on. Then click OK.

You can specify up to eight computer names from which the user can log on. Depending on your choices during NT installation, you may have additional options in this dialog box. If so, click Help to learn about these additional options.

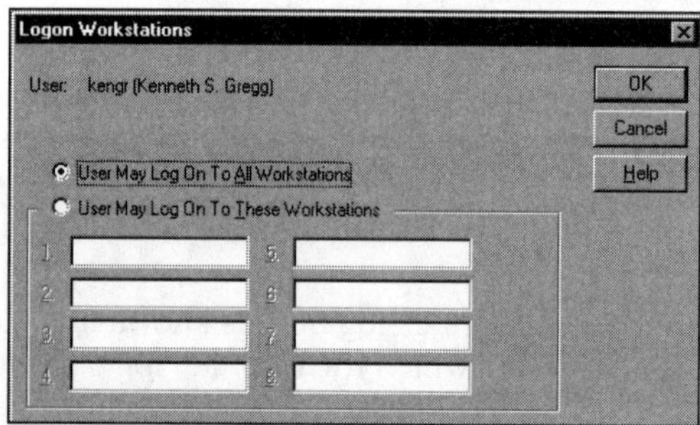

Figure 18-40: NT enables you to restrict the computers from which the user can log on.

10. Click Account. In the Account Information dialog box, shown in Figure 18-41, click Never under Account Expires if you want the account to live forever. If you want it to expire, click End of and type the date on which you want it to expire. Then click OK.

Account expiration is different from password expiration, discussed earlier in this chapter. When an account expires, it can't be used at all. When a password expires, the account remains active. Depending on the options selected, the user may be able to change an expired password without administrator intervention.

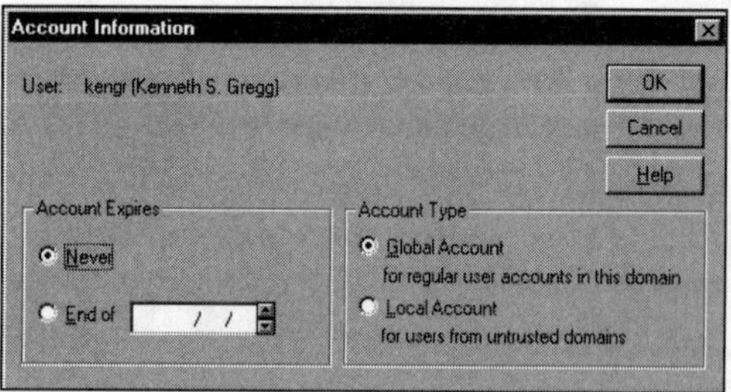

Figure 18-41: This dialog box is where you can control account expiration.

11. Click Dialin. In the Dialin Information dialog box, shown in Figure 18-42, click to select the Grant dialin permission to user check box if you want the user to be able to dial in to the network using RAS. When you're done, click OK.

    You can also set the RAS callback behavior for this account by clicking the appropriate choice under Call Back. If you want the server to call back the user at a fixed telephone number, click Preset To and type the phone number. See Chapter 11 for a discussion of RAS.

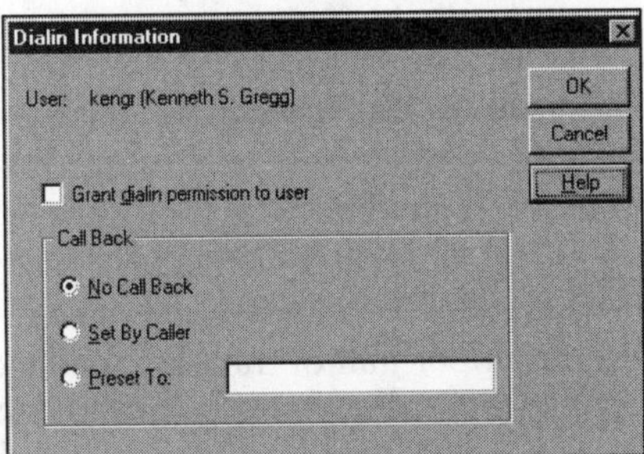

Figure 18-42: You can control the user account's dial-in capabilities.

12. When you're done modifying the account, click Add in the New User dialog box to add it to the account to the database.

If you're adding numerous new accounts with similar characteristics, see the section called "Using Account Templates" in Chapter 21.

Managing a User Account

If you've added a user account, you already know almost everything about managing it. In the User Manager for Domains window, double-click the account that you want to modify. You're presented with a dialog box that's strikingly similar to the New User dialog box. Figure 18-43 shows the User Properties dialog box.

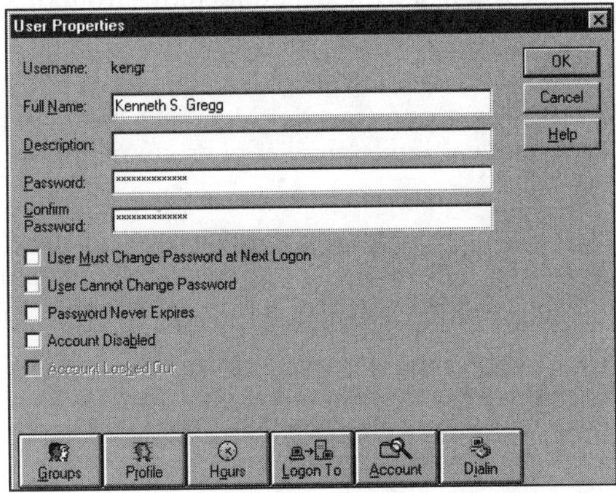

Figure 18-43: The User Properties dialog box is nearly identical to the New User dialog box.

Notice that you can't change the Username field, but all of the remaining options are accessible and identical to what you encountered when adding the account originally.

One additional check box, called Account Locked Out, is normally inaccessible. However, if the account is locked out due to failed logon attempts (described earlier in this chapter), the check box is accessible, and you can unlock the account by clearing the check box.

Adding a Group Account

Now that you've become an expert on the upper half of the User Manager for Domains window, let's take a look at the lower half, where the group accounts live. Several group accounts are created for you automatically when you install Windows NT Server. See Table 10-3 in Chapter 10 for a description of these built-in groups.

You can easily tell the difference between local and global groups just by looking at the group icon. Figure 18-34 shows that local group icons have a workstation in the background and global group icons have a globe in the background.

Creating a Global Group

Here's how to create a global group with User Manager for Domains:

1. On the User menu, click New Global Group. Type the name of the group in the Group Name field. Type a description of the group in the Description field.

   The group name is required and can be up to 20 characters long. Descriptions are optional but are very useful when viewing a long list of groups.

2. Under Not Members, select the user accounts that you want to include in this global group, and click Add. You'll see the accounts move from the Not Members list to the Members list.

   This can be a little confusing. You're selecting accounts from a list of users that aren't currently members of the group (the Not Members list). Then you're using the Add button to move them to the list of group members (the Members list).

   Deleting user accounts from the group is just the opposite. Select the user accounts under Members that you want to remove and click Remove. The accounts are removed from the Members list and moved to the Not Members list.

3. Click OK to add the global group.

Creating a Local Group

Here's how to create a local group using User Manager for Domains:

1. On the User menu, click New Local Group. Type the name of the group in the Group Name field. Type a description of the group in the optional Description field. Then click Add.

2. In the Add Users and Group dialog box, select a user account or group that you want to add to the local group that you're creating. Click Add.
3. Repeat step 2 for each user or group that you want to add. When you're done, click OK.
4. If you want to delete user accounts or groups from the new local group, select the user accounts under Members that you want to remove and click Remove.
5. Click OK to add the local group.

Managing a Group

If you've added groups, you already know everything you need to know about modifying groups. In User Manager for Domains, double-click the group that you want to modify. Other than the fact that you can't change the group name, all of your other options are identical to those presented when you created the group.

Deleting Accounts and Groups

You can delete any user accounts and groups that you create, but you can't delete built-in user accounts or groups. Deleting an account has some important consequences that you need to consider. Since each account has a unique SID (security ID) associated with it, deleting and recreating an account with the same name yields a different internal SID. So the new account won't have any of the permissions that the old account had. The bottom line is that once you delete an account, you can't bring it back.

Having said that, there are certainly situations in which you may want to delete accounts. For example, if someone leaves the organization permanently and you've taken ownership of all of their files, you may want to get rid of their user account completely. Likewise, if a group disbands, it makes sense to delete its associated group. To do so, click the user account or group that you want to delete. On the User menu, click Delete. Click OK in response to the warning and click Yes to confirm the delete.

Administering NT Print Servers

Although printer prices have fallen and capabilities have increased dramatically over the past few years, sharing printers remains a key motivation for network installation. It's likely that your network will include several shared printers of different makes and models.

Both Windows NT Server and Workstation provide *print spoolers,* which store the print jobs on disk until the printer is ready to accept them. The NT spooler maintains a prioritized list of jobs, called a *print queue,* destined for the printer. (Microsoft sometimes calls the print queue a *logical printer,* since from the client's viewpoint, the queue acts like a printer.)

In the simplest and most common case, one print queue is associated with each physical printer. However, you can associate one queue with a *pool* of identical printers. In this situation, the print spooler sends the next job in the queue to the first available printer. You can also have more than one queue associated with a single printer. For example, jobs sent to one queue might be printed immediately, whereas jobs sent to another might be printed overnight on the same physical printer.

Preparing for Printer Installation

You can connect your NT computer to an existing printer that's already shared on the network, install a printer on your NT computer for local use, or share that local printer with other computers over the network. In the following sections, I'll discuss some preliminary considerations that you need to address in each of these scenarios before proceeding with printer configuration on NT.

Preparing to Connect to a Printer

If you're going to connect your NT computer to an existing printer that's shared by another computer on the network, make sure that the remote printer hardware and software are already installed and running before proceeding to install any printer software on your NT computer. Also, be sure that the printer is already shared and visible to other network computers. In this scenario, your computer will act as a client to a remote print server.

Preparing to Install a Local Printer

If you're installing a printer locally, be sure to attach the printer to the appropriate port on your computer and properly configure the port before proceeding with NT printer software installation. If you're planning on sharing the printer over the network, this computer will act as a print server. Make sure that your network software is installed and running before proceeding.

Preparing to Share a Local Printer

If you're creating a print server, make a list of the operating system, version, and CPU platform of all computers that will act as clients to this print server. You'll need this information to install appropriate printer drivers on your print server.

Preparing to Install a Network-Attached Printer

For a successful installation of a printer attached directly to the network, such as Hewlett-Packard's JetDirect series, you need to make sure that the correct network protocol is installed and configured before proceeding with NT printer configuration. Refer to your printer documentation to determine what network protocol you need.

The HP network-attached printers require the DLC protocol. To install DLC, click Start ➪ Settings ➪ Control Panel and double-click the Network icon. Click the Protocols tab, then click Add. Click DLC Protocol and click OK. Type the path to your Windows NT Server CD-ROM and click OK. Click Close and restart your computer as prompted.

Some network-attached printers use TCP/IP as their network communication protocol. See Chapter 11 for details on installing and configuring TCP/IP.

Installing a Printer

Here's how to install a printer driver and configure your printer on NT:

1. Click Start ➪ Settings ➪ Printers to display the Printers folder, as shown in Figure 18-44.

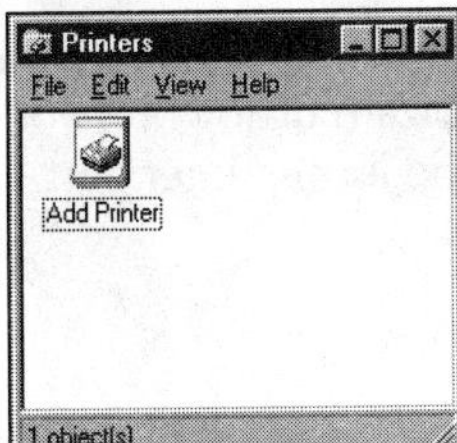

Figure 18-44: The Printers folder is where you add and configure printers.

2. Double-click the Add Printer icon. You'll see the Add Printer Wizard dialog box, as shown in Figure 18-45.

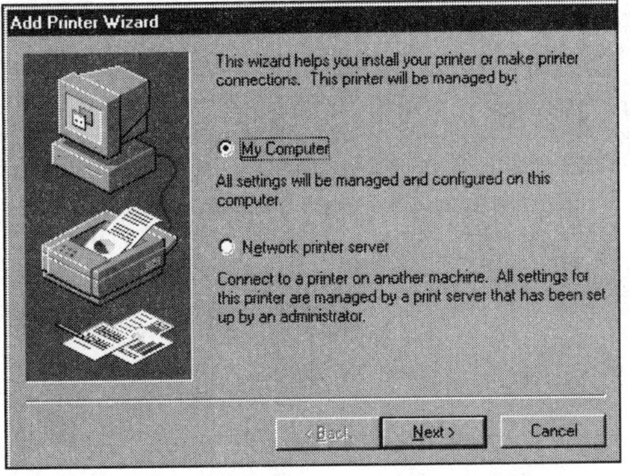

Figure 18-45: You can specify whether the printer is attached locally or out on the network.

3. If you're installing a printer attached locally to the computer, click My Computer in the Add Printer Wizard dialog box, click Next, and go to step 5. If you're connecting to a printer shared on the network, click Network printer server, click Next, and go to step 4.
4. In the Connect to Printer dialog box, type or select the shared printer to which you want to connect. If you already have a printer installed, click Yes or No, depending on whether you want this printer to be the default printer for your Windows-based applications. Click Next and click Finish. Then go to step 11.
5. Click to select the port to which this printer is attached, as shown in Figure 18-46. Then click Next.

If you want to create a *printer pool,* which is a collection of several identical (and I do mean *completely* identical in every way) physical printers associated with one logical printer, click to select the Enable printer pooling check box. This feature will typically increase printing throughput by sending queued print jobs to the first available printer in the pool. See the section entitled "Configuring a Print Queue" later in this chapter.

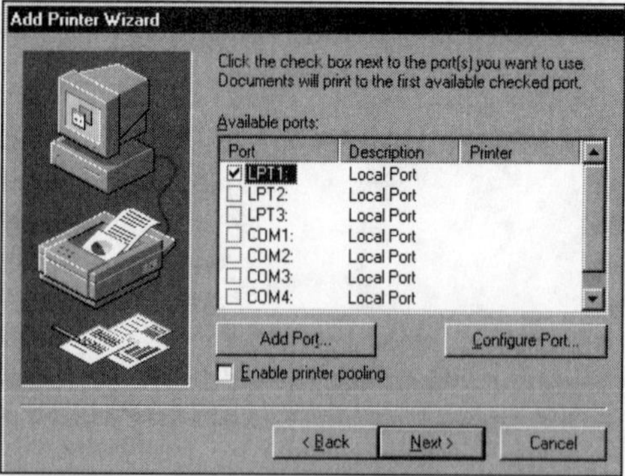

Figure 18-46: In the Add Printer Wizard dialog box, you can select the local printer port.

6. In the Add Printer Wizard dialog box, shown in Figure 18-47, click the manufacturer, then the specific printer model. Click Next.

   If your printer manufacturer or model isn't listed and you have an NT driver disk supplied by the manufacturer, click Have Disk and follow the on-screen instructions to install the driver.

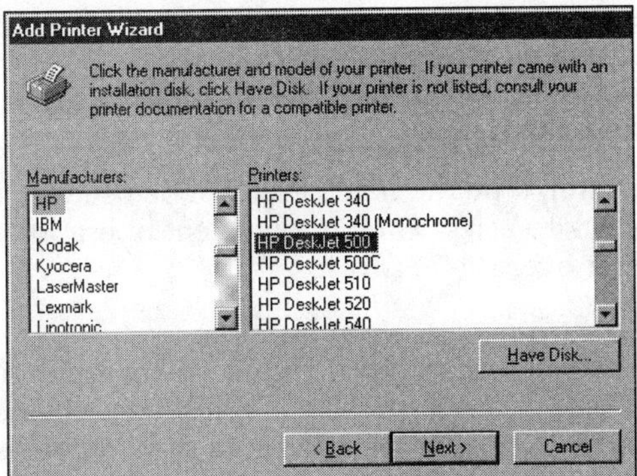

Figure 18-47: In the Add Printer Wizard dialog box, you select the manufacturer and model of your printer.

7. Under Printer name, type the name that you want to assign to this printer and click Next.

   This name is used as the name of the icon representing this printer.

A PRINTER DRIVER SMORGASBORD

Windows NT and Windows 95 computers that will use your shared printer don't keep their own copies of printer driver files in order to print to an NT print server. When they connect to your printer, they automatically download the required printer driver from the print server.

Different drivers are required for Windows 95, various versions of Windows NT (4.0, 3.5x, and 3.1), and different NT CPU platforms (Intel, MIPS, Alpha, and PowerPC). You need to make sure that all of the required printer drivers are available on your print server to support each of the operating systems running on computers that will use your printer.

It's safest to select all of the operating systems in the list so that you have all versions of the drivers available on the print server. However, you can save disk space if you know, for example, that no Windows NT 3.1 computers and no PowerPC computers will access this printer. The same printer drivers are used on NT Workstation and NT Server.

In the example shown in Figure 18-48, I've selected Windows 95, all Windows NT 4.0 CPU platforms, and Windows NT 3.51 on Intel. The Windows NT 4.0 Intel platform is implied, since that's where the printer is installed, and the Intel driver is already in place.

8. If you want to share this printer on the network (that is, you want this computer to be a print server and offer this printer resource to other computers), click Shared, as shown in Figure 18-48. If you only want to use the printer on the local computer, click Not shared.

   If you opt to share the printer, type the name that will be used for the network share point. Then click to select each of the client operating systems that will access this printer over the network.

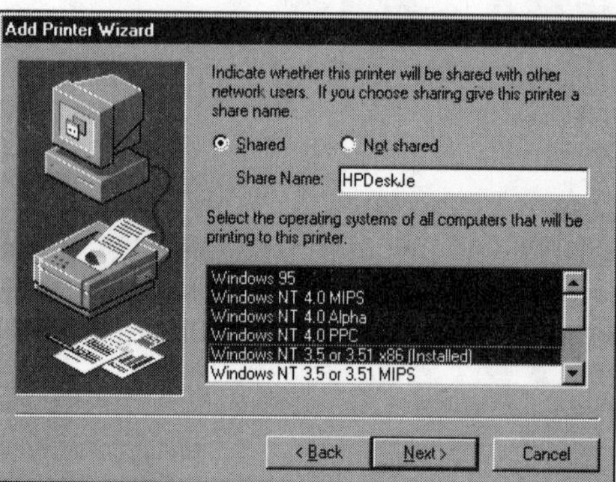

Figure 18-48: In the dialog box, you can specify whether you want to share the printer on the network.

9. Click Next. Click Yes to print a test page and ensure that the printer and driver are working properly. Then click Finish.
10. As prompted, insert your Windows NT Server 4.0 CD-ROM and enter the path to the NT files for your CPU platform. Then click OK.

    On my computer, the path is F:\I386. Once you click OK, the driver is copied to your hard disk and is started.

    If you selected Windows 95 as one of the client operating systems in step 7, you'll be asked for the Windows 95 CD-ROM. Insert it, type the appropriate path, and click OK. If you selected other NT CPU platforms, you'll be asked to provide the appropriate paths to these drivers as well.
11. A new printer icon appears in the Printers folder. Double-click it to view and manage the printer, as described later in this chapter.

Deleting a Printer

Deleting an installed printer or connection to a printer on the network is straightforward. Here's how:

1. In the Printers folder, click the icon of the printer that you want to delete.
2. On the File menu, click Delete.

3. Click Yes to confirm that you want to delete the printer or connection to a network printer.
4. If you've deleted the last printer or printer connection on your computer, click OK when warned that no printers remain installed.

Configuring a Print Queue

Once you've installed a logical printer, you can configure it using the Printers folder. Click Start ➪ Settings ➪ Printers and double-click the icon of the printer that you want to configure. On the Printer menu, click Properties, and click the Scheduling tab, as shown in Figure 18-49.

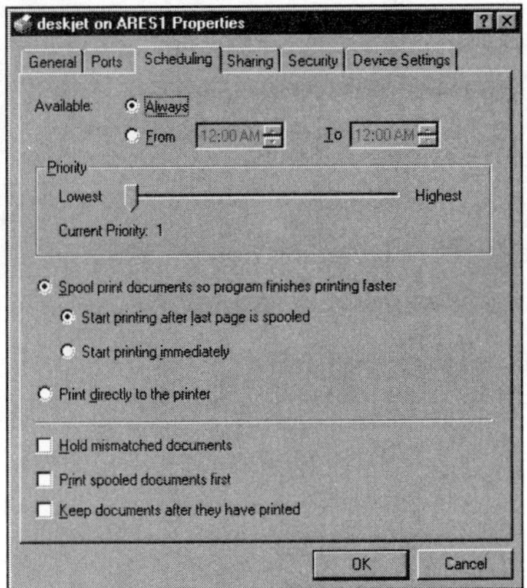

Figure 18-49: You can configure the installed printer using the Properties dialog box.

You can use this dialog box to configure several aspects of printer behavior. First, under Available, you can restrict the hours that jobs are sent to the printer. During off hours, jobs are held in the print queue. During the printer's available time, jobs held in the queue are sent to the printer. This feature is useful for delaying print jobs for overnight printing, for example.

Under Priority, you can use the slider to specify the default priority of documents entering this print queue. Higher-priority documents are printed before lower-priority ones. This setting is used only when more than one print queue is assigned to the physical printer. By setting one queue to a higher priority, jobs sent to that queue will always be printed first.

There are several spooling options. If you click Print directly to the printer, your jobs will bypass the spooler completely. This can tie up your application the longest, since the application may have to wait for actual printing to complete. It's best to select Spool print documents so program finishes printing faster. If you elect to spool, you can opt to begin printing immediately, even before the document is done spooling, or you can wait until the entire document is spooled. The latter approach frees up your application more quickly but takes longer to start printing the first page of output.

The Print spooled documents first check box causes the spooler to give higher priority to documents that have been completely spooled versus documents that are still in the process of spooling. If all jobs are still spooling, the spooler gives preference to larger jobs. I recommend selecting this option since it maximizes printer efficiency.

If you click to select the Keep documents after they have printed check box, the spooler will hang onto the spooled files after printing, allowing you to resubmit the same job directly from the spooler, without involving the originating application. This is handy if you plan on printing multiple copies of documents, but you're not sure how many when you begin the print job. However, it can quickly consume large amounts of disk space.

Other tabs in the Properties dialog box allow you to configure specific printer device settings, printer sharing, security, hardware port configuration, and other miscellaneous settings. I'll cover NT security — including printer security — later in this chapter.

Controlling Print Jobs

Figure 18-50 shows the window that appears when you click Start ➪ Settings ➪ Printers and double-click a printer icon in the act of printing.

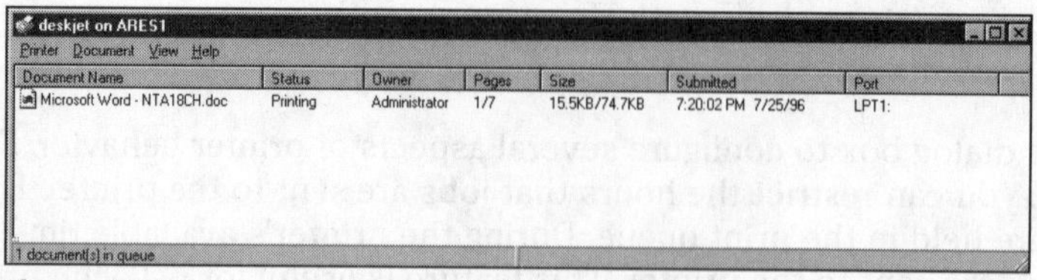

deskjet on ARES1

Printer Document View Help

Document Name	Status	Owner	Pages	Size	Submitted	Port
Microsoft Word - NTA18CH.doc	Printing	Administrator	1/7	15.5KB/74.7KB	7:20:02 PM 7/25/96	LPT1:

1 document(s) in queue

Figure 18-50: You can view print jobs and manipulate them via the Printers folder.

All of the displayed columns are pretty self-explanatory, with the exception of Status. The Status column communicates the current state of the print job. It's typically Spooling, Printing, Paused, or Deleting. If it's blank, the document is simply waiting to be printed.

Commands on the Printer menu enable you to control the behavior of the entire print queue. You can pause or resume all printing activities by clicking Pause Printing, or delete all documents in the queue by clicking Purge Print Documents.

The Document menu, on the other hand, gives you control over individual documents in the print queue. You can select a printing document and pause or resume printing. You can restart printing a document from the beginning by clicking Restart. (This feature is handy if your printer has jammed and damaged pages of output.) As long as the document is still in the queue, you can restart it. If you want to remove a document from the queue, click the document and click Cancel on the Document menu.

Canceling a printing document is a somewhat messy business. Since most of today's printers buffer several pages of output, the document may not quit printing as quickly as you'd like. If the document is removed in the middle of printing a page, the printer may not get the form feed that it needs to eject the current page, and your next job might start printing in mid-page. A manual form feed is usually the best solution to this. In addition, depending on what you're printing and the state of your printer, you may need to reset the printer before printing the next document, since the canceled document may have put the printer into an unknown state.

Administering Windows NT Security

Windows NT Server security may be the one thing that most challenges your relationships with both users and management. Implementing a solid security policy is vital to protect your valuable data resources, but many will view it as intrusive and cumbersome — something that prevents them from getting their jobs done.

Educating yourself and then educating both users and management are the keys to success in this area. Your plan of attack is simple. First, learn all about Windows NT Server security in the following sections. Then, develop a plan of how you want to protect your servers from unauthorized use, how you want to protect users from each other, and how much control that you need over server resources. Come to an agreement with management on your security plan, explain it to your users, and implement it. The process may seem daunting at first, but it's done every day by network administrators just like you. (According to Microsoft's NT sales figures, security implementation is steadily increasing.)

Attaching your network to the Internet introduces another dimension to basic NT security issues. After you read the following sections in this chapter, plan to continue your security education. See Chapter 24 for more information on NT security and to find out how to design the most secure NT network possible.

Understanding NT Security

Security is pervasive through Windows NT Server. In the following sections, I'll provide some fundamental definitions and explanations that will be crucial to your understanding of the NT security model and how you can put it to work for you. User accounts and passwords control fundamental access to the network. They also provide the platform for a rich set of security features that apply to almost every resource on the network. Before proceeding with the following sections, read "Administering Windows NT Accounts" earlier in this chapter.

SHACKLES MADE OF ACLs

Internally, when you grant a specific set of permissions allowing a user account to access a particular file or other object, NT adds that information to a list of permissions assigned to that object. That list is called the Access Control List, or ACL. The ACL contains one or more Access Control Entries, or ACEs, that contain the permission and user account information that you specify. ACLs and ACEs are handled internally, but you may run into the terms in Microsoft documentation and other sources.

Understanding Your Rights

You have the right to remain silent, as you read this section. A *right* (often called a *privilege)* authorizes a user to perform specific actions on the Windows NT computer. When you log on to the computer using an account that's been granted the rights to carry out an action (either directly or by membership in a group that has the appropriate rights), NT will let you proceed. If the account doesn't have rights to do what you're trying to do, NT will prevent you from doing it.

For example, to perform a backup, you need the rights associated with either the Backup Operators group or the Administrators group. As you'll see later in this section, NT automatically assigns rights to some of its built-in groups (discussed in Chapter 10).

Rights apply to actions on the computer, whereas permissions (discussed later in this chapter) apply to specific objects such as files, folders, and shared resources. You assign rights to users and groups via the User Manager for Domains utility. Rights granted to a user can exceed the permissions granted to access specific objects. For example, if your user account is a member of the Backup Operators group, you have the ability to read every file on the computer, even if permissions on those files explicitly prevent you from accessing them. Rights to perform actions *always* take precedence over permissions on files and folders.

Because some rights override file and folder access permissions, you must safeguard any user accounts or groups that have these rights granted to them. For example, the Backup Operators group can read every file regardless of its permissions. So be careful which accounts you add to this group, and make sure that the computers logged on to perform backups are physically secured in a locked room.

Table 18-3 presents a list of all of the Windows NT rights available, the corresponding actions allowed by these rights, and the built-in groups to which NT Setup grants these rights by default. (For a description of built-in group accounts, see Table 10-3 in Chapter 10.) There are two categories of rights: basic and advanced. Although all of the basic rights are important to you as a network administrator, only a couple of the advanced rights will be of use. The remaining advanced rights are helpful only to software developers. I've included them all in Table 18-3, in case you or others on your MIS staff will be developing in-house applications for Windows NT Server.

Table 18-3
Windows NT Basic and Advanced Rights

Windows NT Server Rights	*Corresponding Actions Allowed*	*Granted to Built-in Groups*
Basic Rights	**The User Can**	
Access this computer from network.	Connect to resources on this computer over the network.	Administrators Everyone
Add workstations to domain.	Create new computer accounts within the domain.	
Back up files and directories.	Back up files and folders to tape, overriding all file and folder permissions.	Administrators Backup Operators Server Operators
Change the system time.	Change the date and time of day using the Date/Time application in Control Panel or the DATE and TIME commands from a Command Prompt.	Administrators Server Operators
Force shutdown from a remote system.	This right will be implemented in a future version of Windows NT.	Administrators Server Operators
Load and unload device drivers.	Install and remove device drivers, typically using Control Panel applications.	Administrators
Log on locally.	Log on to the computer directly using the attached keyboard (as opposed to logging on over the network).	Administrators Account Operators Print Operators Server Operators
Manage auditing and security log.	Specify resource accesses to audit, view the security log, and clear it. (This right doesn't include managing system auditing, which only Administrators can do.)	Administrators

(continued)

Table 18-3 *(continued)*

Windows NT Server Rights	*Corresponding Actions Allowed*	*Granted to Built-in Groups*
Basic Rights	**The User Can**	
Restore files and directories.	Restore files and folders from tape, overriding all file and folder permissions.	Administrators Backup Operators Server Operators
Shut down the system.	Shut down the local computer using Start ➪ Shut Down or CTRL+ALT+DEL.	Administrators Account Operators Backup Operators Print Operators Server Operators
Take ownership of files or other objects.	Take ownership of folders and files owned by other user accounts.	Administrators
Advanced Rights (useful to network administrators)	**The User Can**	
Bypass traverse checking.	Navigate through a tree of folders and subfolders, even if permissions on those folders prevent access. (This right doesn't override access to files.)	Everyone
Log on as a service.	Log on to the computer and register a process as a service. (The Replicator service does this.)	
Advanced Rights (useful to programmers)	**The Application Can**	
Act as part of the operating system.	Operate as a trusted component of the operating system. (This right is used by most NT environment subsystems.)	
Create a pagefile.	This right will be implemented in a future version of Windows NT.	Administrators
Create a token object.	Create access tokens. (This is used by the Local Security Authority, described in Chapter 2.)	
Create permanent shared objects.	Create special objects that are used internally by Windows NT.	
Debug programs.	Debug threads and other objects.	Administrators

Windows NT Server Rights	*Corresponding Actions Allowed*	*Granted to Built-in Groups*
Generate security audits.	Send new entries to the security audit log.	
Increase quotas.	This right will be implemented in a future version of Windows NT.	Administrators
Increase scheduling priority.	Boost the priority of a process.	Administrators
Lock pages in memory.	Force pages to remain in memory and never be paged out to a paging file.	
Log on as a batch job.	This right will be implemented in a future version of Windows NT.	
Modify firmware environment values.	Add, delete, or change system environment variables. (Users can change user environment variables without this right.)	Administrators
Profile single process.	Use internal NT performance profiling features on a single process.	Administrators
Profile system performance.	Use internal NT performance profiling features on the entire system, including the operating system. (Doing this can dramatically degrade system performance.)	Administrators
Replace a process level token.	Modify a process's security access token. (This right is used only by the operating system itself.)	

If you also run Windows NT Workstation on your network, you'll find that some of the Windows NT Server basic rights are listed as advanced rights on NT Workstation. The list of basic rights on NT Server is longer than it is on NT Workstation.

Notice that the "Bypass traverse checking" right is granted to the Everyone group. This means that all users on your network can view and navigate through all folders and subfolders, even if the permissions on those folder are designed to prevent access. (They can't see the files themselves, just the folders.)

Although this may be harmless, I've seen cases in which users have deduced sensitive company information (upcoming layoffs, poor corporate earnings, personnel problems, and so on) by spelunking through an executive's folder structure and drawing conclusions based on folder names. The problem is exacerbated by the use of long, meaningful names for folders. Be sure that your users understand that everyone can see their directory structure or opt to take away this right from the Everyone group.

In addition to the copious rights listed in Table 18-3, the built-in groups (discussed in Chapter 10) have abilities that are inherent in the groups and can't be changed. Even though you have no control over them, it's useful to know what special abilities these groups have. Table 18-4 summarizes these abilities, which you can think of as inalienable rights.

Table 18-4
Windows NT Abilities Inherent in Built-In Groups

Windows NT Built-In Abilities	*Granted to Built-In Groups*
Create and manage user accounts.	Administrators
Create and manage local groups.	Administrators Users
Assign rights to user and group accounts.	Administrators
Manage auditing of system events.	Administrators
Lock the computer while logged on.	Administrators Everyone
Override a lock to access a locked computer.	Administrators
Format a hard disk drive.	Administrators
Create common submenus.	Administrators
Share and stop sharing folders.	Administrators
Share and stop sharing printers.	Administrators

MIGHTY MORPHIN' POWER USERS

Get the feeling that the Administrators group has all of the power? If you have Windows NT Workstation on your network, you've probably run into the built-in Power Users group. On NT Workstation, members of the Power Users group have most of the special abilities that the Administrators group has, as detailed in Table 18-4. Exceptions are assigning user rights, managing system event auditing, overriding a locked computer, and formatting a hard disk. Otherwise Power Users can do whatever Administrators can do. NT Server has no built-in Power Users group.

Understanding Special Groups

If you referred to Table 10-3 to refresh your memory about NT's built-in groups, you may have noticed that the Everyone group isn't listed there. That's because it's one of NT's five *special groups* (sometimes called *special identities).* These aren't groups in the normal sense, since you can't add or remove users from them. Their membership is predefined and automatically updated. Special groups play an important role in NT security, since they provide a convenient way to describe sets of users that might change dynamically over time. For example, the Everyone group always includes all users in the domain, regardless of which user accounts you add or delete. Table 18-5 defines the special groups provided by Windows NT Server.

Table 18-5
Windows NT Special Groups

Special Group	*Definition*
Everyone	Automatically contains all users in the domain, including guests and users from trusted domains. Use Everyone to assign rights that all users have in common.
INTERACTIVE	Automatically includes users who interactively log on to the computer from the local keyboard (as opposed to over the network). Rights assigned to INTERACTIVE are in force only while the user is logged on locally.
NETWORK	Automatically includes all users who access the computer's resources over the network. Rights assigned to NETWORK are in force only while the user is logged on over the network.
SYSTEM	Represents the NT operating system itself. You can't change the default rights NT grants to SYSTEM, nor would you want to.
CREATOR OWNER	Represents the user who created or took ownership of an object (file, folder, or shared resource).

You can change the rights assigned to Everyone, INTERACTIVE, or NETWORK. You can't change rights assigned to SYSTEM or CREATOR OWNER (defined in the next section), but you can use any of the five special groups in assigning permissions to resources.

Understanding Ownership

Every folder and file on Windows NT has an owner. The owner is typically the user who created the folder or file, but not always. Ownership can be transferred from one user to another. You can't give away ownership to another user, but you can grant them permission to take ownership from you. (This prevents you from creating a file, then making it appear to belong to another user. The other user has to know about it before ownership can be transferred.) If you're the current owner of a folder or file, you have a new title called *CREATOR OWNER*.

To manage permissions (discussed in detail in the next section), you typically need administrator privileges. However, if you own a folder or file, you can manage its permissions. In fact, you can restrict access to prevent even administrators from accessing your data, affording you complete privacy when you need it. The ability to assign permissions at the discretion of the owner is called *discretionary access control*.

Your privacy isn't quite complete. Administrators must have the ability to take ownership of any file on the network, since they often need to access files of departed employees. However, since an administrator can't return ownership of a file to its original owner, his or her access to your file leaves a trail behind. So, administrators can't access your private files on a whim without someone knowing about it.

Understanding Permissions

Now that we've covered the concepts of rights, special groups, and ownership, let's delve into another fundamental element of NT security — permissions. A permission is a rule that governs which users have access to an object and how they can access it. Permissions can be assigned to folders, files, network share points, printers, and shared ClipBook pages (as discussed in Chapter 15). Table 18-6 summarizes the basic Windows NT permissions.

When you assign permissions to an object, you typically don't assign the permissions outlined in Table 18-6 directly. NT defines several standard combinations of permissions that cover the most common permission requirements. Table 18-7 presents a list of these *standard permissions,* defining how they correspond to basic permissions when applied to folders and directories. Some of these standard permissions can be applied only to folders. Others can be applied also to files or share points according to the "Apply to" columns in Table 18-7.

File and folder permissions can be assigned only to objects on NTFS volumes. If you're using FAT, you won't get the benefits of file and folder security. Shared FAT folders benefit from permissions assigned to share points, but you can't assign permissions to individual files and folders within the shared folder.

Table 18-6
Basic Windows NT Permissions

Permission	*Abbreviation*	*Permission Granted When Applied to File*	*Permission Granted When Applied to Folder*
Read	R	Read the file's data.	View file and subfolder names in the folder.
Write	W	Change the file's data.	Add files and subfolders to the folder.
Execute	X	Run the file, if it's an executable.	Change to subfolders within. the folder.
Delete	D	Delete the file.	Delete the folder.
Change Permissions	P	Change the file's permissions.	Change the folder's permissions.
Take Ownership	O	Take ownership of the file.	Take ownership of the folder.

Table 18-7
Standard NT Folder and File Permissions

Standard Permission for Folder	*Permissions Granted for Files*	*Permissions Granted Directly*	*Apply to Files Directly*	*Apply to Share Points*	*Description*
No Access	None	None	Yes	Yes	Prevents any access to folders or files.
List	RX	Access not specified	No	No	View folder contents and change to subfolders.
Read	RX	RX	Yes	Yes	View folder contents, change to subfolders, read files, and run executable files.

(continued)

Table 18-7 (continued)

Standard Permission	*Permissions Granted for Folder*	*Permissions Granted for Files*	*Apply to Files Directly*	*Apply to Share Points Directly*	*Description*
Add	WX	Access not specified	No	No	Create sub-folders and files.
Add and Read	RWX	RX	No	No	View folder contents, create subfolders and files, change to subfolders, read files, and run executable files.
Change	RWXD	RWXD	Yes	Yes	View folder contents, create or delete sub-folders and files, change to subfolders, read and change files, and run executable files.
Full Control (all)	RWXDPO	RWXDPO	Yes	Yes	All operations allowed on files and folders.
Special Directory Access	Choose from Full Control or any combination of RWXDPO.	Access not specified	No	No	Assigns customized permissions to folders.

Standard Permission	*Permissions Granted for Folder*	*Permissions Granted for Files*	*Apply to Files Directly*	*Apply to Share Points Directly*	*Description*
Special File Access		Choose from Access not specified, Full Control, or any combin-ation of RWXDPO.	No	No	Assigns customized permissions to files within a folder.
Special Access		Choose from Full Control or any combination of RWXDPO.	Yes	No	Assigns customized permissions directly to files.

Standard printer permissions are different from file and folder permissions. Table 18-8 summarizes the permissions that you can assign to a printer.

Table 18-8
Standard NT Printer Permissions

Printer Permission	*Description*
No Access	Prevent any access to the printer.
Print	Send a print job to the printer.
Manage Documents	Pause, resume, restart, and delete documents. Control document settings.
Full Control	In addition to the Manage Documents permission, change printer properties and permissions, and delete printers. Control document printing order. Pause, resume, and purge print queues.

MUCH ADO ABOUT NO ACCESS

If you assign the No Access permission to a folder or file for any group to which a user belongs, the user loses all access to that object. This happens even if the user account is granted explicit permission to access it. Why? No Access permission *always* overrides permissions granted to other groups or individual user accounts.

(continued)

MUCH ADO ABOUT NO ACCESS *(continued)*

Since the No Access permission will even lock out administrators (unless they actually take ownership of the object, as discussed earlier in this chapter), you need to use No Access with care. Use it only when you want to be absolutely sure that no one needs access to the object. It's a good idea to revoke permissions from specific groups or accounts, instead of using No Access, to avoid the side effects that No Access may have on other group accounts.

Managing Permissions on Folders

Here are the steps to follow to change permissions on a folder:

1. In Explorer, right-click the folder that you want to manage and click Properties. Click the Security tab and click Permissions.
2. In the Directory Permissions dialog box, as shown in Figure 18-51, click the account whose permissions you want to change for this folder, and select the appropriate permission under Type of Access.

   Refer to Table 18-7 for a complete list of permissions that you can apply to folders. Notice in Figure 18-51 that the basic permissions for both the folder and the files within the folder are listed in parentheses after the standard permission name. For example, the Everyone group has the standard permission Change, which translates to the basic permissions RWXD for the folder and RWXD for the files within the folder.

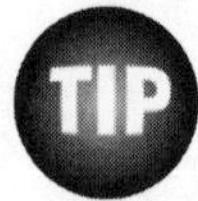

If the standard permissions aren't exactly what you need, you can customize a set of basic permissions by selecting Special Directory Access under Type of Access. When you do, you can specify individual basic permissions assigned to the folder, as shown in Figure 18-52. Likewise, you can select Special File Access to specify a customized set of basic permissions assigned to the files within the folder, as shown in Figure 18-53.

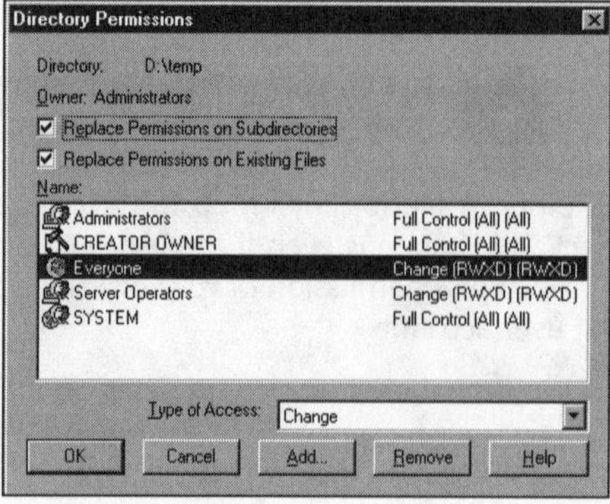

Figure 18-51: You use the Directory Permissions dialog box to manage folder permissions.

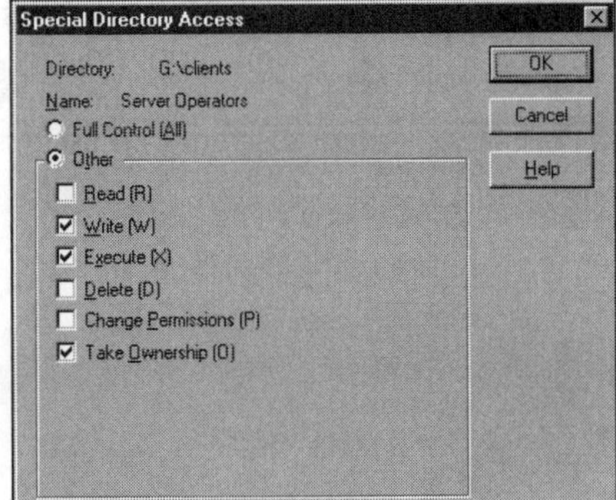

Figure 18-52: You can customize a set of basic permissions for the folder.

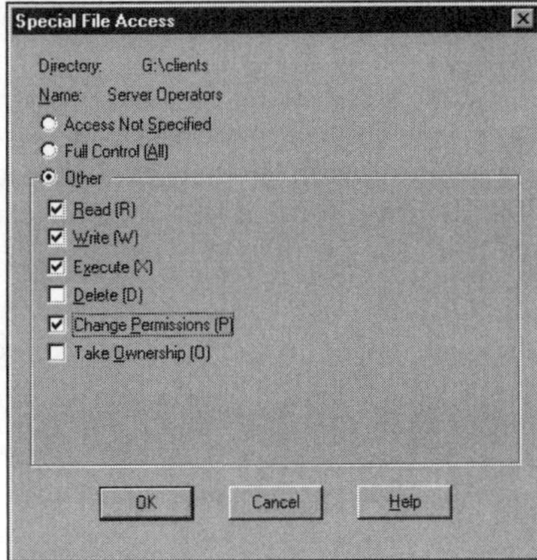

Figure 18-53: You can customize a set of basic permissions for the files within the folder.

3. If you want to add more accounts to the list, click Add in the Directory Permissions dialog box. In the Add Users and Groups dialog box, shown in Figure 18-54, click the user or group that you want to add to the list, click Add, and click the appropriate permission under Type of Access. Then click OK.

   Repeat this step for each additional user account or group that you want to add to the permissions list for this folder.

You can add multiple accounts within the Add Users and Groups dialog box, but you must grant the same type of access to all of the accounts. Once they're added to the Directory Permissions dialog box, you can adjust their types of access individually.

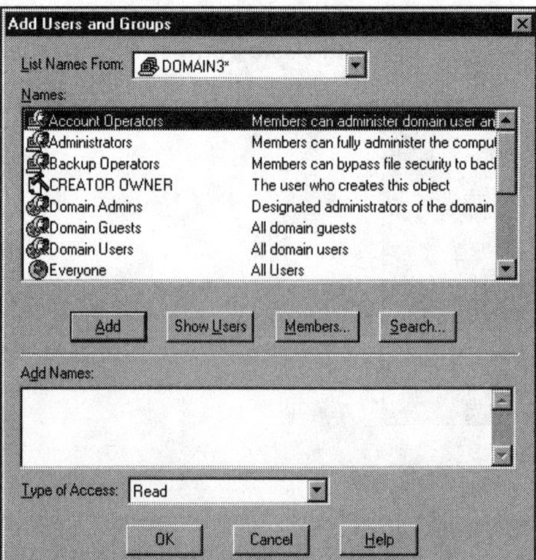

Figure 18-54: You can use the Add Users and Groups dialog box to add to the list of accounts to which you want to grant permissions.

4. If you want to remove an existing account from the list, click the account that you want to remove and click Remove. Repeat this step for each account that you want to remove from the permissions list.
5. When you're satisfied with the permissions list, click OK in the Directory Permissions dialog box. Then click OK in the Properties dialog box.

Managing Permissions on Files

Here's how to change permissions on a file:

1. In Explorer, right-click the file that you want to manage and click Properties. Click the Security tab and click Permissions.
2. In the File Permissions dialog box, click the account whose permissions you want to change for this folder, and select the appropriate permission under Type of Access.

   Refer to Table 18-7 for a list of permissions that you can apply directly to files. As in folder permissions, you can create a customized set of basic permissions. Click Special Access under Type of Access, and specify the custom permissions, as shown in Figure 18-55.
3. If you want to add more accounts to the list, click Add and proceed as described earlier in this chapter. If you want to remove an existing account from the list, click the account that you want to remove and click Remove.
4. When you're satisfied with the permissions list, click OK in the File Permissions dialog box. Then click OK in the Properties dialog box.

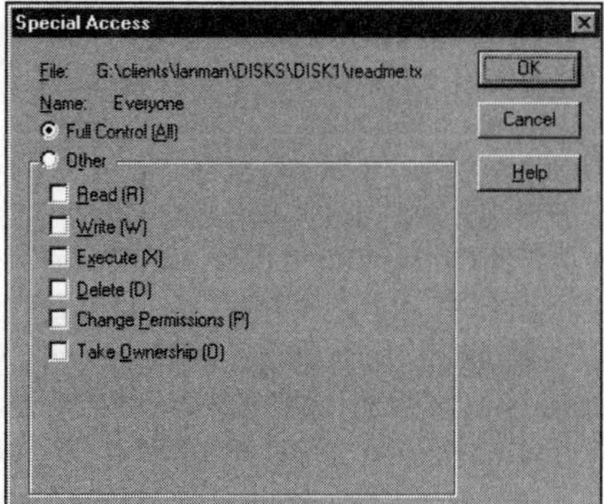

Figure 18-55: In the Type of Access dialog box, you can customize a set of basic permissions for the file.

Managing Permissions on Share Points

Here's how to manage permissions on an existing network share point:

1. In Explorer, right-click the shared folder that you want to manage and click Properties. Click the Sharing tab, click Shared As, and click Permissions.
2. In the Access Through Share Permissions dialog box, shown in Figure 18-56, click the account that you want to change, and select the appropriate permission under Type of Access.

   Refer to Table 18-7 for a list of permissions that you can apply to share points.

   If you want to add other accounts to the list, click Add and proceed as described earlier in this chapter. If you want to remove an existing account from the list, click the account that you want to remove and click Remove.

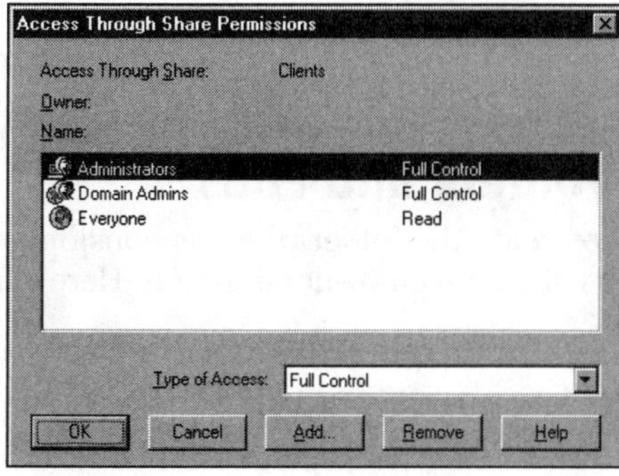

Figure 18-56: You can manage share point permissions using the Access Through Share Permissions dialog box.

3. When you're satisfied with the permissions list, click OK in the Access Through Share Permissions dialog box. Then click OK in the Properties dialog box.

Managing Permissions on Printers

Any user with Full Control permission to the printer can manage its permissions. Here's how:

1. In the Printers folder, double-click the icon of the printer that you want to manage. On the Printers menu, click Properties. Click the Security tab. Then click Permissions.

2. In the Printer Permissions dialog box, shown in Figure 18-57, click the account that you want to change, and select the appropriate permission under Type of Access. Refer to Table 18-8 for a list of printer permissions.

   If you want to add other accounts to the list, click Add and proceed as described earlier in this chapter. If you want to remove an existing account from the list, click the account that you want to remove and click Remove.

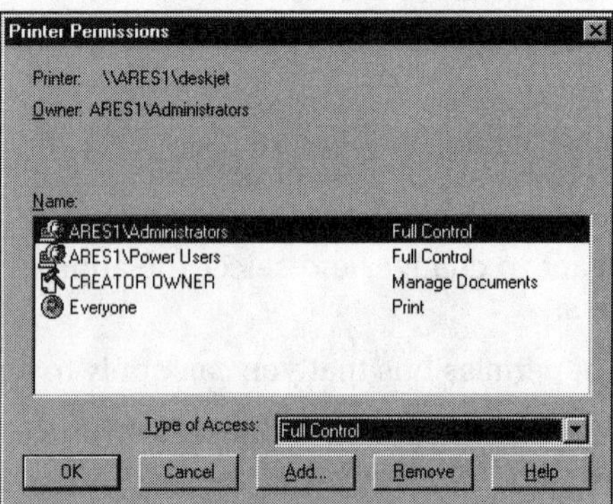

Figure 18-57: You can manage printer permissions using the Printer Permissions dialog box.

3. When you're satisfied with the permissions list, click OK in the Printer Permissions dialog box. Then click OK in the Properties dialog box.

Taking Ownership of Folders and Files

The user account that was used to create the folder or file is considered its owner, unless another account has since taken ownership of it. Here's how to take ownership:

1. In NT Explorer, right-click the folder or file of which you want to take ownership. Click Properties.

2. Click the Security tab, then click Ownership.

3. In the Owner dialog box, click Take Ownership. In the Properties dialog box, click OK.

Taking Ownership of Printers

The user account that was used to create a printer is considered its owner. Any user with Full Control permission to the printer can take ownership of the printer, using the following steps:

1. Click Start ➪ Settings ➪ Printers and double-click the icon of the printer of which you want to take ownership.
2. On the Printers menu, click Properties. Click the Security tab. Then click Ownership.
3. In the Owner dialog box, click Take Ownership. In the Properties dialog box, click OK.

Auditing Events

Windows NT Server's auditing capabilities are very useful when you're trying to understand how resources are being used or misused on your network. You can audit activities related to domains, folders, files, and printers and collect all of the information in one central log.

If you decide to audit lots of different events, and any of them occur at a very high frequency, you can easily bog down your server with the activity of writing the logs generated by the auditing activity itself. This can hurt overall server performance. Pick and choose what you want to audit, to avoid undue stress on your server.

Auditing Domain Events

No, not "D'Main Events," domain events. To audit domain events, start User Manager for Domains as described earlier in this chapter. On the User menu, click Select Domain and pick the domain that you want to configure for auditing. On the Policies menu, click Audit. Figure 18-58 shows the Audit Policy dialog box.

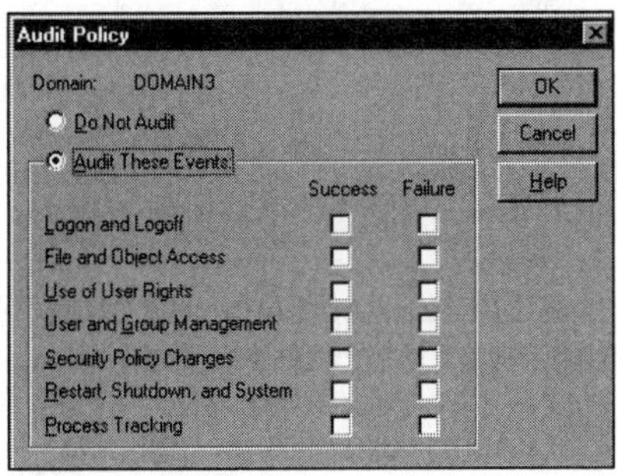

Figure 18-58: You can audit events related to domains.

To audit events, click Audit These Events and click to select the check boxes of the events that you want to monitor. For each event, you can log successes, failures, both, or neither.

The File and Object Access check box acts as the master switch for the auditing of all file, folder, and printer events. If this check box is cleared, no file or object accesses are monitored, even if individual auditing of these objects is enabled.

When you're done selecting events to audit, click OK. From that moment on, the events that you've selected will be recorded in the security event log, which I'll introduce later in this chapter.

Auditing Folders and Files

To configure auditing of folders and files, right-click the file or folder in NT Explorer and click Properties. Click the Security tab and click Auditing. Figure 18-59 shows the Directory Auditing dialog box that you see when you configure auditing on a folder.

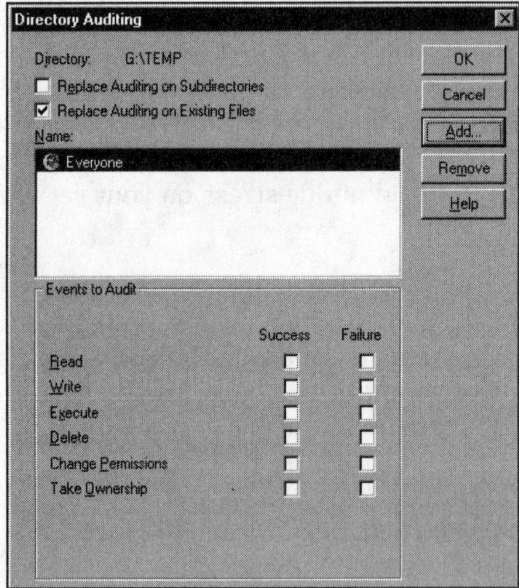

Figure 18-59: You can audit events related to folders and files.

If you click to select the Replace Auditing on Subdirectories check box, the auditing changes that you make will propagate to all subfolders of the folder you're working on. Likewise, if you click to select the Replace Auditing on Existing Files check box, you can change the auditing settings on all files within the folder.

To audit events, you must first add the user accounts and groups that you want to monitor to the Name list by clicking Add. Use of the Add Users and Groups dialog box is described in the section earlier in this chapter entitled "Managing Permissions on Folders." Once the desired user accounts and groups are listed, click to select the check boxes of the events that you want to monitor. For each event, you can log successes, failures, both, or neither. When you're done selecting events to audit, click OK.

The File Auditing dialog box is virtually identical to the Directory Auditing dialog box. It's missing the two check boxes at the top but is otherwise the same.

Auditing Printers

Printer auditing is particularly useful in determining who is using or abusing tangible goods such as toner and paper. To configure auditing printers, click Start ➪ Settings ➪ Printers, right-click the icon of the printer that you want to configure for auditing, and click Properties. Click the Security tab and click Auditing. Figure 18-60 shows the Printer Auditing dialog box that you see when you configure auditing on a printer.

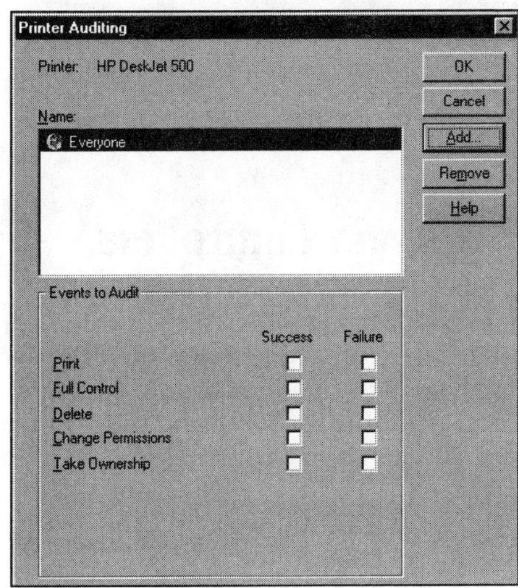

Figure 18-60: You can audit events related to printers.

To audit printer events, you must first add the user accounts and groups that you want to monitor to the Name list by clicking Add. Use of the Add Users and Groups dialog box is described in the section earlier in this chapter entitled "Managing Permissions on Folders." Once the desired user accounts and groups are listed, click to select the check boxes of the events that you want to monitor. For each event, you can log successes, failures, both, or neither. When you're done selecting events to audit, click OK.

Examining the Audit Log

To review the logged events, you need to use the Event Viewer utility. Start it by clicking Start ➪ Programs ➪ Administrative Tools ➪ Event Viewer. On the Log menu, click Security. You'll see a window similar to that shown in Figure 18-61. Each line represents one audited event. To see more detail on a particular event, double-click it. Each event with a key icon indicates a successful event, and each one with a lock represents a failure event.

Event Viewer - Security Log on \\TOWERRC2

Log View Options Help

Date	Time	Source	Category	Event	User	Computer
7/25/96	10:39:41 PM	Security	Object Access	560	Administrator	TOWERRC2
7/25/96	10:39:41 PM	Security	Object Access	562	Administrator	TOWERRC2
7/25/96	10:39:41 PM	Security	Object Access	560	Administrator	TOWERRC2
7/25/96	10:39:41 PM	Security	Object Access	562	Administrator	TOWERRC2
7/25/96	10:39:41 PM	Security	Object Access	560	Administrator	TOWERRC2
7/25/96	10:39:41 PM	Security	Object Access	562	Administrator	TOWERRC2
7/25/96	10:39:41 PM	Security	Object Access	560	Administrator	TOWERRC2
7/25/96	10:39:41 PM	Security	Object Access	562	Administrator	TOWERRC2
7/25/96	10:39:41 PM	Security	Object Access	560	Administrator	TOWERRC2
7/25/96	10:39:41 PM	Security	Object Access	562	Administrator	TOWERRC2
7/25/96	10:39:41 PM	Security	Object Access	560	Administrator	TOWERRC2

Figure 18-61: You can view security audit information using Event Viewer.

I'll cover Event Viewer in more depth in Chapter 21.

Promoting and Demoting Domain Controllers

If you need to perform maintenance on your primary domain controller (PDC) computer, or your PDC becomes unavailable for some other reason, you need to promote one of your backup domain controllers (BDCs) to act in the PDC role. When you do this, users can continue logging on to the domain, and administrators can continue to update the accounts database. Only resources on the PDC computer are inaccessible; otherwise, the domain continues to function normally.

Even though the process of promoting a BDC is straightforward, don't take it lightly. Any network connections that client computers have to the BDC or PDC will be terminated during this process. Your best bet is to perform the promotion during a time when your users aren't connected to resources on these two servers. If users are connected, warn them beforehand that their connections will be terminated.

Promoting a BDC with the PDC Active

It's best to promote a BDC while the PDC is still running. Otherwise, the state of the PDC when it returns to active duty isn't well defined. You'll have the luxury of taking this approach when you're going to perform scheduled maintenance on your PDC computer.

If you're connected to the network via RAS, and one of the two computers — either the BDC that you want to promote or the PDC that you want to demote — is the RAS server being used for the connection, you won't be able to complete the operation. Your RAS connection will be severed before the role reversal is complete. You must either connect to a different RAS server or perform the operation from a computer that's directly connected to the network.

Here's how to promote a BDC to the role of PDC:

1. Click Start ➪ Programs ➪ Administrative Tools ➪ Server Manager. On the View menu, click Servers.
2. On the list of computers, click to select the BDC that you want to promote to PDC status.
3. On the Computer menu, click Promote to Primary Domain Controller.
4. You'll see a warning that the promotion will take a few minutes and that client connections will be closed on both servers. Click Yes to continue.

   Again, either perform this operation during off hours or warn your users that they'll lose their connections to resources on these two computers.

The role reversal will take a few minutes to complete. You can use Server Manager to monitor the status of both servers. The original PDC is automatically demoted to the role of BDC when the promoted BDC takes on its PDC role.

Promoting a BDC with the PDC Unavailable

When the PDC computer is unavailable because of a hardware or software crash, you promote a BDC to PDC status using the same steps outlined in the previous section. However, since the dead PDC doesn't know what you've done, there's some potential confusion when it comes back to life. Server Manager warns you that the PDC is unavailable and that you'll likely see errors when you restart the old PDC.

When the old PDC comes back up, you'll probably see an error dialog box on the Begin Logon screen, indicating a failure during system startup. If you log on and examine the event log (described in Chapter 21), you'll find an event recorded by the NETLOGON component that indicates another PDC is already running the domain.

In Server Manager, the old PDC's icon appears dimmed, indicating that it thinks it's supposed to be the PDC but is inactive because another PDC was found operating in the domain. Here's how to demote the inactive PDC:

1. Click Start ➪ Programs ➪ Administrative Tools ➪ Server Manager. On the View menu, click Servers.
2. On the list of computers, click to select the inactive (old) primary domain controller that you want to demote to BDC status.
3. On the Computer menu, click Demote to Backup Domain Controller.

   This menu command is available only if you've selected the duplicate PDC.

Demotion of the inactive PDC to BDC status takes a few minutes to complete. You can use Server Manager to monitor the status of the server.

Summary

In this chapter, you've picked up skills that are critical to your success as an NT network administrator. You've learned about the key areas of disk management and tape backup. You've also gained insight into administering user accounts and groups, setting up NT print servers, managing NT security, and auditing security events on your network.

In Chapter 19, you'll go a step further and learn how to optimize and tune your servers and network to get the best possible performance for your users. You'll also delve deeper into Disk Administrator, as you learn how to apply its fault-tolerance features to your servers, increasing both performance and reliability.

INSIDE STORY

"Should we do it? Should we really do this thing?" The controversy raged. Should the NT team build a new file system (NTFS) or just convert the old standbys of DOS's FAT and OS/2's HPFS to run on NT? Developing a new file system had many implications. It was a huge development and testing project. The code would be responsible for maintaining the integrity of the users' data, so it had to work right out of the chute. But would customers accept yet another file system? The marketers were worried about this. The OS/2 team, still working with IBM on OS/2 2.0, fought vehemently against the creation of yet another file system. They reasoned that they could improve HPFS's shortcomings.

Neither the FAT nor HPFS design could currently achieve NT's stated goals. Their weaknesses included limited or no file security, almost no recoverability, many potential points of failure, and severe limits on the sizes of disks and files. All of these flaws contributed to concern that NT with these file systems couldn't be the backbone of an enterprise computing environment. Although many factors contributed to the final decision, security was one of the most critical in winning support. Without file system security, much of the Windows NT security model is of little value.

And so, with the security banner waving on high, the NTFS battle was won one step at a time. "OK, go ahead and write a specification for it, but don't write any code yet." "OK, you've got the code and you've tested it, but let's put a disclaimer on the beta about using it." "OK, so it passes the grueling overnight stress tests with flying colors, but let's give it more air time." Today, NTFS is the file system of choice for Windows NT. Achieving its high level of reliability and performance not only pushed the team's development and test engineering skills to the limit, but it helped lots of folks at Microsoft polish up their debating skills along the way.

Optimizing Your Windows NT Server Network

Plumbing problems can be frustrating. Basically, they fall into two categories: reliability and performance. Reliability problems happen when the plumbing components don't do what you expect them to do, resulting in trauma ranging from small leaks to flooded living rooms. Performance problems occur when, although the system is operating correctly, the water just isn't moving fast enough. Partially clogged drains and low water pressure exemplify plumbing performance problems. Some performance problems, if not addressed, can lead to reliability problems. A slow drain, for example, can lead to a clogged drain, which can lead to an overflowing sink and a real mess. Likewise, reliability problems can cause poor performance or lost time. Therefore, you need to give equal consideration to reliability and performance when you're trying to optimize the draining capacity of your kitchen sink.

And so it is with software. When most people think of optimization, they identify it with improving the speed of a system. However, optimization involves more than just tuning for speed and throughput. It also implies tuning for the highest level of reliability. If you think of your time and the time of your users as valuable (as most organizations do), server and network downtime results in wasting valuable "people time." The time needed to restore data from backup tapes, replace hard drives while users wait for the server to come up, and other recovery activities all reduce the performance of your organization.

In this chapter, I'll show you how to maximize both performance and reliability. You'll learn how to identify performance bottlenecks, take steps to fix them, and find the right mix of configuration changes for your Windows NT Server network. Some of the techniques that I'll discuss can help you achieve improvements in both performance and reliability. NT Server's fault-tolerance features, for example, allow you to improve reliability, minimize server downtime, and even push data to and from your hard disks faster. What's more, you'll learn how to make the most of the powerful performance analysis tools of the trade included in Windows NT Server 4.0.

Implementing NT Fault Tolerance

As a network administrator, you want to tune your servers to be as fast and as reliable as possible. Windows NT Server fault tolerance offers both capabilities. When coupled with a solid backup plan (as described in Chapter 18), NTFS for file system recoverability and security, and appropriate use of UPS technology, NT fault tolerance will give you solid peace of mind. You'll need to worry less about lost data and can devote more time to serving your users' computing needs.

In the sections that follow, I'll fill you in on the specifics of NT Server's fault-tolerance features and show you how to make the best use of them on your servers.

Disk Administrator is your primary tool for managing fault tolerance. For basic information on starting and navigating in Disk Administrator, see the section entitled "Administering Your Disk Storage" in Chapter 18.

Understanding RAID

I briefly introduced you to RAID (redundant array of inexpensive disks) technology in Chapter 1. Recall that the two goals of RAID are improved disk performance and increased reliability of data storage. The six levels of RAID, numbered 0 through 5, meet these goals to varying degrees. Since no two environments are alike, you'll need to weigh the tradeoffs in performance, reliability, and cost that best meet the needs of your organization.

In the following sections, I'll discuss each of the RAID levels that Windows NT Server 4.0 supports: RAID 0, 1, and 5. Because RAID 0 and RAID 5 are so closely related and because RAID 1 is the most straightforward, I'll cover RAID 1 first.

RAID 1 – Mirroring and Duplexing

Disk mirroring involves configuring two disk drives to maintain identical copies of all data written to disk. Mirroring provides redundancy of data, but no performance improvement. You use Disk Administrator to establish a *mirror set,* whose members are identical partitions on two separate disk drives. One of the partitions is designated as the *primary member* and the other is the *shadow member.* Think of the primary member as the partition being mirrored and the shadow member as its mirror image.

The overloaded term *primary partition* is sometimes used in Microsoft documentation and other sources to describe the primary member of a mirror set. To minimize confusion, I'll always use the term *primary member* to refer to the member of a mirror set and *primary partition* to refer to a bootable partition, as described in Chapter 18.

A mirror set looks to applications such as a single volume that's the size of the primary member. The shadow member is essentially invisible. Whenever data is written to a mirror set, the same write operation is performed on both members. When you read data from a mirror set, the data is read from the primary. If the primary disk dies, data is read automatically from the shadow. If the shadow disk dies, then all reads and writes are performed only on the primary. When operating with one of the member disks disabled, data redundancy is lost, but you don't see any performance degradation. Figure 19-1 illustrates disk mirroring.

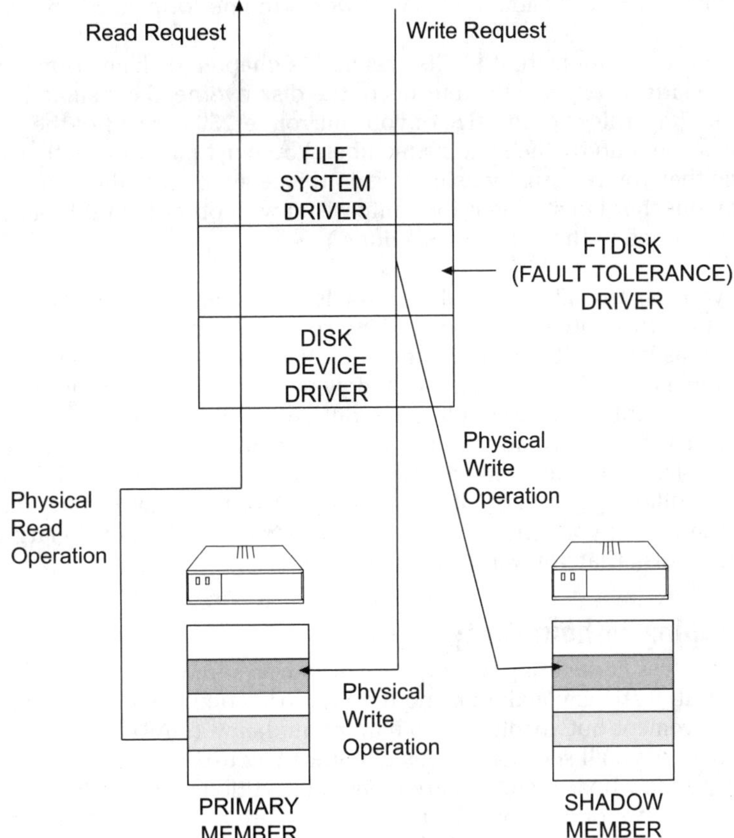

Figure 19-1: All writes are performed to both the primary and shadow members of the mirror set.

By funneling all writes through a single disk controller, the requirement of writing everything twice can slow performance. The magnitude of the slowdown depends on the capabilities of the controller and its NT driver. Even in the best case, there's some overhead added. To buy back the lost performance and increase redundancy a bit, you can opt for disk duplexing. To do this, put the two disk drives on separate disk controllers. Then, use Disk Administrator to establish a mirror relationship between them.

Windows NT Server doesn't distinguish between mirroring and duplexing. Disk Administrator doesn't keep track of the controllers to which you've attached your disks. The FTDISK driver doesn't either, except to route the redundant write requests to the correct devices. Duplexing is purely a matter of hardware configuration.

Even if your main goal is data redundancy, you certainly don't want to decrease disk access performance on your server. So, if disk mirroring meets your needs, I highly recommend duplexing. The added cost of an additional disk controller (under $300 for a PCI Fast/Wide SCSI adapter) is well worth the performance benefit.

Of the fault-tolerance options that I'll discuss in this chapter, disk mirroring and duplexing are relatively expensive, in terms of the disk overhead consumed by redundant data. Regardless of the size of your mirror set, 50 percent of the disk space is always taken up by the shadow member. You must pay for exactly twice the disk space that you're actually using to gain this level of redundancy. (This may seem obvious, but I'm stating it for comparison with other fault-tolerance approaches discussed in the following sections.)

Even though you can mix different makes, models, and sizes of drives in a mirror set, you may run into some frustration in doing so. The shadow member partition must be at least as large as the primary member of the set. However, differences in disk geometry can cause NT to require a shadow member that's slightly larger than the primary member. For example, such differences in drives might require that a shadow member be 103MB versus a primary member of 101MB. Unfortunately, even disks from the same manufacturer with the same model number can sometimes have differing geometry. If you're putting together a mirror set, the safe bet is to make sure that your shadow member disk is one that's actually larger than the primary disk that you want to mirror.

RAID 0 – Striping without Parity

Disk striping involves configuring two or more disk drives to distribute data evenly across them. RAID 0 striping maintains no parity information, so it achieves performance improvement but absolutely no data redundancy. (RAID 5 striping adds data redundancy, as you'll see later in this chapter.) You use Disk Administrator to establish a *stripe set*, whose members are identical partitions on from 2 to 32 separate disk drives. Blocks of data, which are 64KB long, are assigned to the member disks in a round-robin fashion. The first block is stored on the first disk, the second block on the second disk, and so on. If three disks are participating in a stripe set, the third data block goes on the third disk, and the fourth block is written to the first disk. Likewise, if 32 disks make up a stripe set, the 33rd data block wraps around to the first disk drive.

A stripe set looks to applications like a single volume that's the size of the sum of all member partitions. For example, if three 2GB drives are members of a stripe set, the stripe set appears to be a single 6GB drive. Whenever data is written to or read from a stripe set, the operation is performed on the appropriate drive, depending on where the block has been assigned. Figure 19-2 illustrates these concepts.

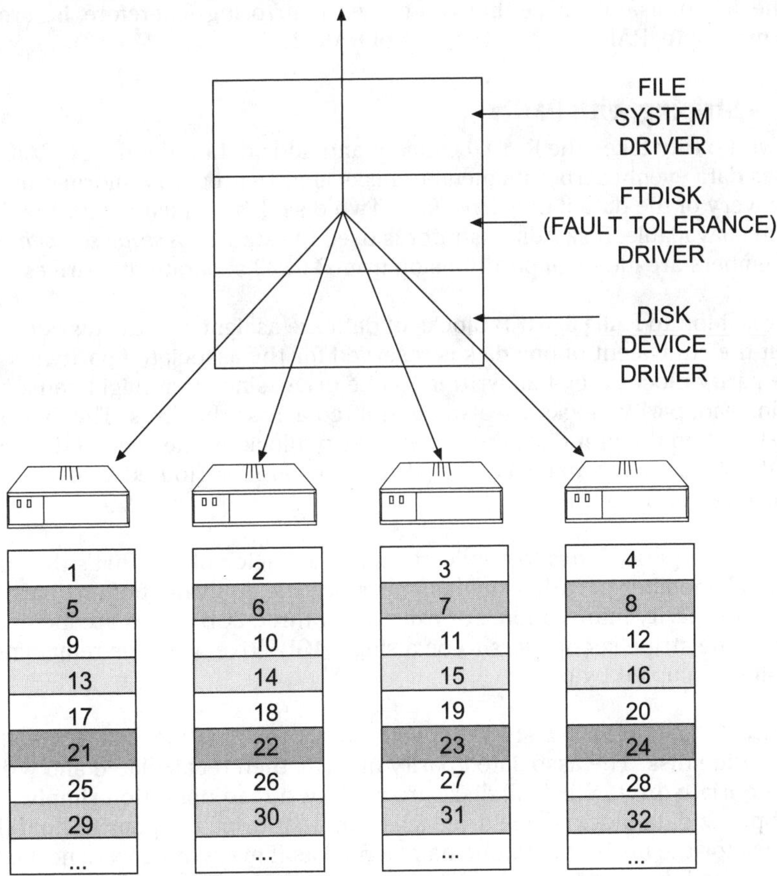

Figure 19-2: In a RAID 0 stripe set, data blocks are distributed evenly across multiple disks.

If one of the member drives fails, the entire stripe set is unreadable, and all of the data is lost. In this respect, RAID 0 stripe sets are similar to the volume sets described in Chapter 18 — one drive fails, and all is lost.

The performance improvement gained by disk striping depends on several factors, including the speed and capabilities of your disk controller(s), the number of disks participating in the stripe set, the speed of those disks, and the pattern of usage. As long as your disk controller allows multiple I/O operations in parallel (which implies that it's a reasonably recent SCSI adapter), you should see a performance improvement over operating with a single disk.

Of all of the RAID levels supported by NT, the RAID 0 stripes without parity level has a minimum hardware cost equal to that of RAID 1 mirroring. However, with RAID 0, you get to use all of the disk space for data, since there's no redundant data storage. A stripe set with two 4GB drives yields total usable storage of 8GB versus the 4GB of usable space that you get with mirroring. Therefore, in terms of cost per megabyte, RAID 0 is half the cost of RAID 1.

RAID 5 – Striping with Parity

Striping with parity takes the RAID 0 concept and adds data redundancy. RAID 5 distributes data evenly across its member disks along with parity information, to allow recovery of the data if one drive fails. Two disk drives must fail for the data to become unavailable. Disk Administrator is used to establish a *stripe set with parity*, whose members are identical partitions on from 3 to 32 separate disk drives.

In similar fashion to RAID 0, 64KB blocks of data are assigned to the disks round-robin, but the equivalent of one disk is reserved for the associated parity information. The parity blocks aren't all written to one drive, since that might cause a bottleneck. Instead, parity blocks are also distributed across the disks. The first parity block is stored on the first disk, the second parity block on the second disk, and so on. Data blocks associated with the parity block are distributed across the remaining disks of the set.

A stripe set with parity looks to applications like a single volume that's the size of the sum of all member partitions minus one, since the equivalent of one partition is reserved for parity information. For example, if three 2GB drives are members of a stripe set, the stripe set appears to be a single 4GB drive, with the remaining 2GB invisibly occupied by parity.

Whenever data is written to a stripe set with parity, the data block is written to the appropriate disk. The associated parity block is then recalculated and written to its appropriate drive. When all disks are healthy, a read operation simply reads the appropriate data block. If one drive fails, and that drive happens to hold the parity block for the desired data, the data is read as if everything were normal. If, however, the bad drive contains the data that you're trying to read, NT reconstructs the data block using the existing data and the parity block. As you might imagine, the reconstruction process can significantly degrade performance, since it involves multiple reads and some additional calculations. However, the data is delivered without any interruption in service. Figure 19-3 illustrates a RAID 5 configuration.

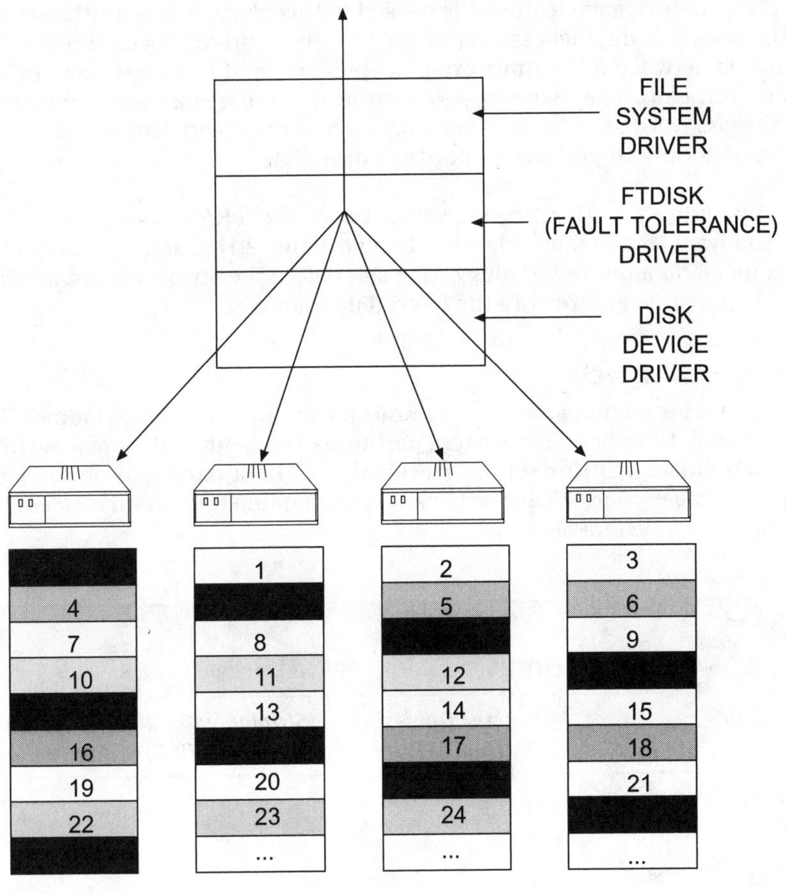

Figure 19-3: In a RAID 5 stripe set, data and parity blocks are distributed evenly across multiple disks.

The performance improvement offered by RAID 5 is slightly less than RAID 0, because of the additional processing and writing of the parity information. Moreover, when a disk fails and NT has to reconstruct missing data blocks on the fly, there's a severe performance degradation when those blocks are read. The fact that parity and data blocks are distributed across the disks tempers this performance impact, however. For example, in a five-disk set, a failed drive means that, on average, 20 percent of all of the blocks will have to be reconstructed when read.

Of all of the fault-tolerance features discussed in this chapter, the RAID 5 stripes with parity level has the highest cost of entry — three drives. Its data redundancy overhead falls between RAID 1 mirroring (50 percent) and RAID 0 stripes without parity (no overhead). The percentage of overhead decreases as you add more disks to the set. A 3-disk set has about a 33 percent overhead, whereas a 10-disk set uses only 10 percent for parity information.

You can't upgrade a RAID 0 stripe set without parity to a RAID 5 stripe set with parity. If you want to add fault tolerance to an existing stripe set, your only option is to back up all data on the existing stripe set, delete the stripe set, create a new stripe set with parity, and restore the backed-up data.

Comparing RAID Levels

Table 19-1 provides a comparison of the RAID levels supported by Windows NT Server. Notice that the boot and system partitions can be members of a mirror set but can't participate in stripe sets. Mirroring the NT boot partition can reduce the time required to get your NT Server back up and running if the hard disk containing your operating system files dies.

Table 19-1
Comparison of NT Server RAID Features

Characteristic	*Mirroring/ Duplexing (RAID 1)*	*Striping without Parity (RAID 0)*	*Striping with Parity (RAID 5)*
Available on Windows NT Workstation		√	
Available on Windows NT Server	√	√	√
Provides data redundancy and recovery	√		√
System partition can participate as a member	√		
Boot partition can participate as a member	√		
One disk failure destroys all data on the set		√	
Recovers automatically from one disk failure	√		√
Performance degrades when one disk is disabled		N/A	√
Minimum participating disk drives required	2	2	3

Characteristic	*Mirroring/ Duplexing (RAID 1)*	*Striping without Parity (RAID 0)*	*Striping with Parity (RAID 5)*
Maximum participating disk drives possible	2	32	32
Maximum data redundancy space overhead (using the minimum number of drives)	50 percent	N/A	<34 percent (3 drives)
Minimum data redundancy space overhead (using the maximum number of drives)	50 percent	N/A	<4 percent (32 drives)
Performance degrades relative to single disk configuration	√ (Duplexing helps)		
Performance improves relative to single disk configuration		√	√

Disk striping makes more efficient use of available disk space than does disk mirroring, and the advantages increase with the number of drives that you use. For example, a four-disk stripe set uses only 25 percent for parity information, and a five-disk set uses only 20 percent. The percentage of nondata disk usage decreases as you add more disks to the stripe set.

LIFE BEYOND RAID 5

You may have already seen products claiming to be RAID 6, RAID 7, and RAID followed by two-digit numbers. Although there's no set standard for how these later technologies are numbered, here's a quick guide to help you interpret them.

RAID 6 goes beyond RAID 5 by adding more parity information, allowing recovery of data even if two drives fail. It requires additional drives for parity (adding to the expense) and can have slower performance than RAID 5 (due to the additional parity writes).

RAID 7 and above tend to be either proprietary hardware solutions or combinations of other RAID technologies. Since any level RAID can be configured to look like a single large disk drive, it's possible to build systems that use a RAID array in place of a disk drive and combine these arrays into an array of virtual drives. For example, the term *RAID 10* typically means RAID 0 (stripes without parity) that uses RAID 1 (mirrors) instead of individual disk drives. In this case, the stripes provide improved performance but no redundancy, whereas the mirrors provide redundancy but no improvement in performance. By their very definition, these solutions require at least part of the RAID technology to be implemented in hardware. In the example, the RAID 1 component is implemented in hardware, and the RAID 0 component is implemented with either hardware or software.

Software vs. Hardware RAID

Windows NT Server supports both software and hardware approaches to RAID. The software approach is implemented in a low-level driver called FTDISK. It operates just below the file system drivers, allowing both FAT and NTFS to use it. Because it adds a thin layer of driver software between the application and disk, the FTDISK solution does introduce a small amount of overhead. However, this overhead is negligible compared to the performance benefits gained by using stripes without parity (RAID 0) or stripes with parity (RAID 5).

RAID hardware solutions off-load all of the logic for generating redundant data and on-the-fly data recovery to the RAID controller. These devices appear as a single physical drive to the operating system, even if they contain 20 or more actual disk drives. All you need to use a hardware RAID device is an NT device driver for it. Beyond low-level I/O, all of the RAID capabilities are handled in hardware.

Here are a few issues to consider when deciding whether a hardware RAID solution is right for you:

- **Speed.** Hardware fault tolerance is generally faster, due to lack of processing requirements on the computer and specialized hardware and firmware optimized for the integrated drives. If you need the absolute maximum speed possible, consider a hardware approach.
- **Cost.** Software fault tolerance is less expensive than hardware solutions, since the software is built into the operating system and you can assemble the array of drives using widely available drives and controllers.
- **Openness.** Because many hardware solutions are based on proprietary hardware, software, or firmware, selecting this approach may lock you into a single vendor when it comes time for service or upgrades.
- **Flexibility.** The software approach is generally more flexible, in terms of the number of drives, drive sizes, and disk controllers that you can use. Hardware approaches may have limitations imposed by the physical dimensions of the product. For example, a hardware RAID cabinet may allow only 21 drives, whereas the software approach enables you to have up to 32.

  On the other hand, hardware solutions can sometimes be more flexible. You can sometimes combine levels of RAID, as in the RAID 10 example discussed earlier in this chapter.
- **Additional reliability features.** Some hardware solutions include features that increase reliability and minimize downtime of your server. For example, some offer redundant power supplies that can be replaced without powering down the RAID subsystem. Others offer "hot swapping" capability, so that you can replace dead drives without powering down the RAID subsystem or your server.

✦ **NT Server compatibility.** The software approach is guaranteed to be NT compatible, if the off-the-shelf hardware that you use is on the NT Hardware Compatibility List. When selecting a hardware RAID solution, make sure that the equipment is listed as well, and be sure it comes with monitoring software to feed RAID status information to NT's event log.

Installation, operation, and recovery procedures vary with each hardware RAID solution. Consult your manufacturer's instructions for details. You can find additional background on RAID technology in *The RAIDbook — A Source Book for Disk Array Technology*, published by the RAID Advisory Board, St. Peter, Minnesota.

Preparing for Fault Tolerance

In general, setting up a fault-tolerance disk set requires multiple partitions of equal size on each participating disk drive. RAID 1 mirror sets require exactly two partitions. RAID 0 stripe sets require 2 to 32 partitions, and RAID 5 stripe sets require 3 to 32 partitions.

Partitions that participate as members of fault-tolerance sets needn't occupy entire physical disk drives. For example, if you have a 4GB drive, 3GB of the drive can be a member of a set, and the remaining 1GB can be used for something else. However, keep in mind that you can degrade performance significantly by placing a frequently used volume on the same drive with a member of a fault-tolerance set. Every time the other volume is accessed, the disk will have to move the heads away from the fault-tolerance member and then return when the next I/O operation is performed on the member.

Use of fault tolerance without the knowledge of how to recover from bad disks can be worse than not using fault tolerance at all. It doesn't help to have a redundant copy of your data if you don't know how to get to it. Familiarize yourself with the recovery procedures of RAID 1 and RAID 5 sets, so that you can act quickly if disaster strikes one of your disks. Even run a test to make sure that you can successfully recover your data. Having the knowledge, tools, and experience close at hand will help you recover more quickly and provide a better safety net for your organization.

Don't be lulled into a false sense of security when using fault-tolerance features. Fault tolerance isn't a wonder drug vaccine that prevents data loss. Although the most common occurrence is the loss of a single drive, more catastrophic disasters happen every day. Two disks can die at the same time. (I once had car batteries in two different cars die on the very same morning, with no logical explanation.) Power problems, earthquakes, and broken pipes can take out your entire server or bank of servers in one shot. Failures in memory, cabling, or disk controllers can put corrupt data on your disks. There's nothing that substitutes for a good plan for performing backups. See Chapter 18 for a discussion of backups.

Establishing a Mirror Set

A mirror set requires an existing partition that may or may not be formatted or contain data. This is the primary member partition that you want to mirror. You also need an area of free space, on another physical drive, that's equal to or greater in length than the primary member. This region of free space will become the shadow member. Once you've chosen the participants, follow these steps to create a mirror set:

1. In the Disk Administrator window, click the existing partition that you want to use as the primary member. Then, while holding down the CTRL key, click the area of free space that you want to use as the shadow member.

   Figure 19-4 shows two regions selected. Disk 1 (drive M) is the NTFS volume that will act as the primary member of the mirror set. Disk 2 is the region of free space that will act as the shadow member.

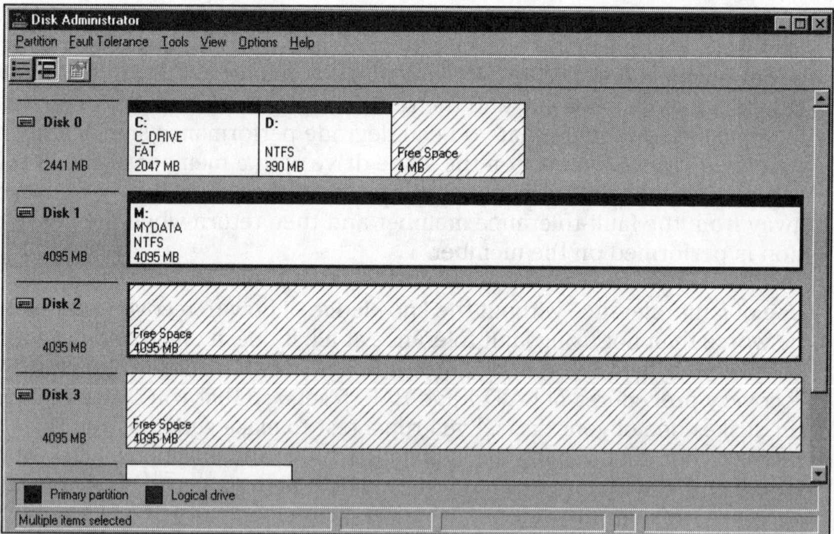

Figure 19-4: Select the partition that you want to mirror (primary member) and the free space region to be used as the mirror image (shadow member).

2. On the Fault Tolerance menu, click Establish Mirror. Both partitions now appear to be identical.

   If your primary member is your system partition, you're reminded to create a fault-tolerance boot floppy disk.

3. On the Partition menu, click Commit Changes Now. Click Yes to confirm, then click OK.

   If you're within sight of the member disk drives, you'll see both access lights glow almost continuously. NT is creating the mirror image by copying everything from the primary member to the shadow.

In most cases, you won't need to restart the computer before using the mirror. However, Disk Administrator sometimes requires a restart. If it does, restart your computer as prompted and proceed to step 4 after the restart.

4. Click either member partition. In the status line at the bottom of the window, you'll see the status of the mirror set, as shown in Figure 19-5.

   Depending on the size of the partitions and the speed of your disks, controller, and computer, the status line will display the word "initializing" for anywhere from a few seconds to several minutes. When the mirror has been completely generated, the status becomes "healthy."

   Just as a frame of reference, it took 25 minutes to complete initialization of the 4GB mirror in the example shown in Figure 19-5, using a Pentium 166MHz computer with a Wide SCSI adapter and Wide SCSI AV-tuned drives.

   Unfortunately, the status of the mirror set isn't automatically updated in Disk Administrator. You can update it manually either by clicking one of the mirror set members or by clicking Refresh on the View menu.

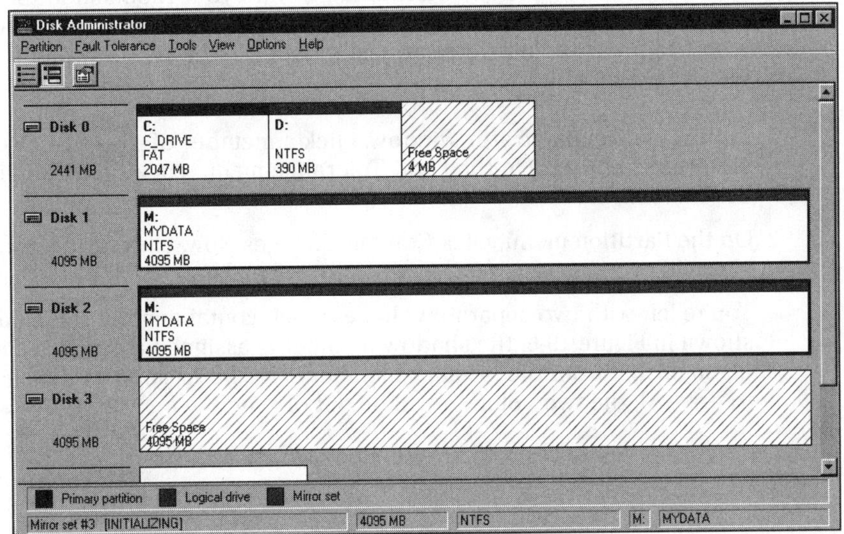

Figure 19-5: The status is reported as "initializing" while the mirror image is being generated.

You can also determine when the initialization is complete by using Event Viewer to check the system log. Click Start ➪ Programs ➪ Administrative Tools ➪ Event Viewer. On the Log menu, click System. You're looking for entries with a source of FTDISK. Double-click each individual event to read it. When the mirror initialization is complete, you should find an FTDISK event that says, "Mirror initialization or synchronization is complete." (I'll cover Event Viewer in

more detail in Chapter 21.)

5. If you're mirroring the system partition, click Mark Active on the Partition menu. Then click OK.

   This step is required if you want to boot from the shadow member when the primary member fails.

6. Update your Emergency Repair Disk using the RDISK utility, as described in Chapter 17.
7. You can now use the mirror set just like any other disk volume.

If you want to remove a mirroring relationship that you've created, never delete the mirror set. If you do, you'll lose all of the data on both members, including the original data on the primary member. Instead, break the mirror set, as described in the next section. This approach will retain the data on both members.

Breaking a Mirror Set

If you're superstitious, you may want to hang on to your rabbit's foot before you start breaking mirrors in this section. Before deleting any mirror set partitions, it's always best to break the mirror relationship first. That way, you won't lose any data. Here's how to do it:

1. In the Disk Administrator window, click a member of the mirror set that you want to break. On the Fault Tolerance menu, click Break Mirror. Click Yes to confirm.
2. On the Partition menu, click Commit Changes Now, click Yes to confirm, and click OK.

   You're left with two separate volumes, each containing the same data. As shown in Figure 19-6, the shadow member is assigned a new drive letter F, to distinguish it from the primary member drive M. As soon as data is written to drive M, the two volumes will be out of sync.

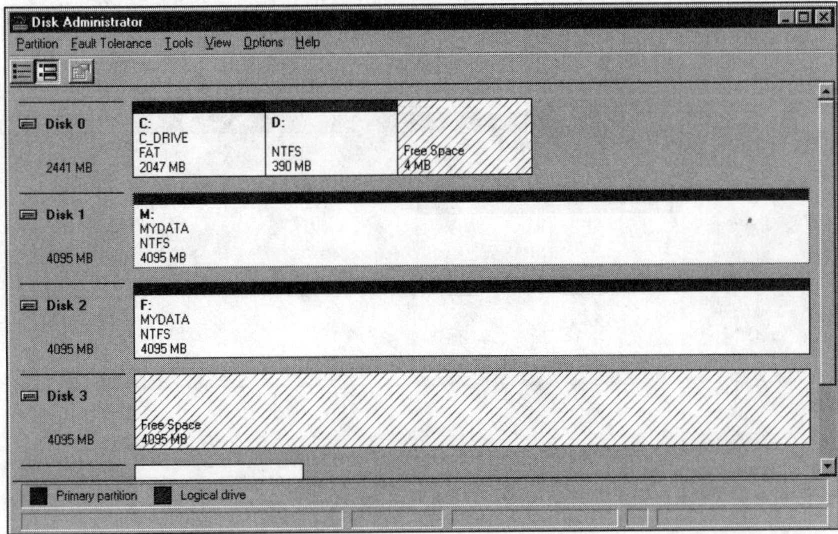

Figure 19-6: Breaking a mirror results in two separate volumes with data intact (and perhaps seven years of bad luck).

3. If you want to free the former shadow member for other uses, click it, click Delete on the Partition menu, and click Yes to confirm.

4. Update your Emergency Repair Disk using the RDISK utility, as described in Chapter 17.

Establishing a Stripe Set

In this section, I'll present the steps required to establish either a RAID 0 or RAID 5 stripe set. A RAID 5 stripe set with parity requires at least three equal-sized regions of free space. A RAID 0 stripe set without parity requires at least two free space regions. When you've decided which regions will participate in the stripe set, follow these steps to create it:

1. In the Disk Administrator window, while holding down the CTRL key, click each of the existing regions of free space that you want to include in the stripe set.

Figure 19-7 shows three regions selected. All of Disks 1, 2, and 3 will participate in the stripe set.

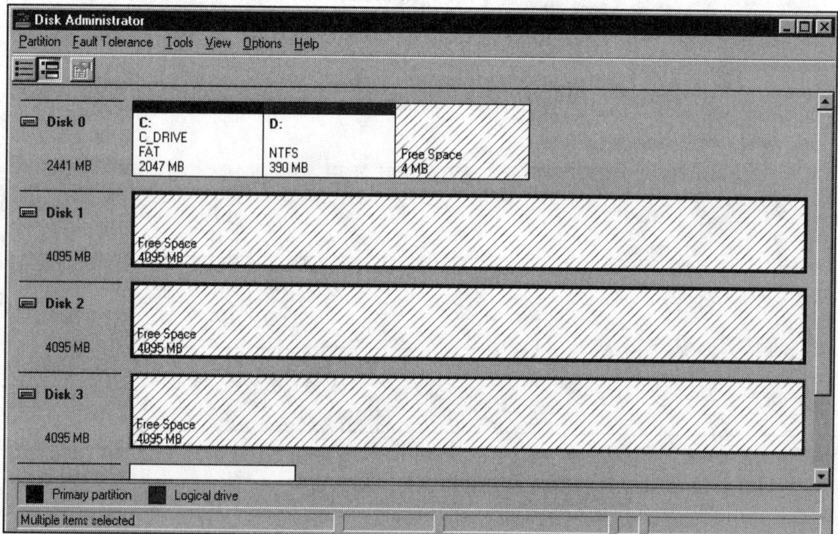

Figure 19-7: Select the free space regions that you want to participate in the stripe set.

2. If you're creating a stripe set with parity (RAID 5), click Create Stripe Set with Parity on the Fault Tolerance menu. If you're creating a stripe set without parity (RAID 0), click Create Stripe Set on the Partition menu.

   The location of the two options on different menus acts as a reminder that a RAID 5 set is fault tolerant and that a RAID 0 set is simply a large partition similar to a volume set.

3. In the Create stripe set of total size field, type the number of megabytes that you want the stripe set to include. Then click OK.

   By default, the stripe set is equal to the size of the smallest participating free space region multiplied by the number of regions that you selected in step 1. If you specify a smaller total size, the unused space on each participating region remains free space.

If you're creating a RAID 5 stripe set with parity, the total size can be a little misleading. It includes the space used for parity information, so the total size available for data storage will be less than the total size that you specify in this dialog box. The total size of a RAID 0 stripe set, on the other hand, represents the actual available data storage area. In the example shown in Figure 19-7, RAID 0 and RAID 5 sets each yield a total size of 12GB. The total size available for data storage under RAID 0 is 12GB, whereas the total size for data storage under RAID 5 is only 8GB.

4. On the Partition menu, click Commit Changes Now. Click Yes to confirm, then click OK.

If you're within sight of the member disk drives and you're creating a RAID 5 stripe set, you'll see all of the drive lights flicker in succession. NT is creating the stripe set by calculating parity stripes across the member partitions.

5. Click any of the member partitions. In the status line at the bottom of the window, you'll see the status of the stripe set. Figure 19-8 illustrates a RAID 5 status line.

   RAID 0 stripe sets are generated almost immediately, since there's no parity information to calculate.

   RAID 5 is a different story. Depending on the size of the partitions, the speed of your drives, and the speed of your computer, the status line displays the word "initializing" for anywhere from a few seconds to several minutes. When the stripe set has been completely generated, the status becomes "healthy."

   Just as a frame of reference, it took 60 minutes to complete initialization of the 12GB RAID 5 stripe set in the example shown in Figure 19-8, using a Pentium 166MHz computer with a Wide SCSI adapter and Wide SCSI AV-tuned drives.

   The status of the RAID 5 stripe set isn't automatically updated. Update it manually either by clicking one of the stripe set members or by clicking Refresh on the View menu.

You can also determine when initialization is complete using Event Viewer, as discussed under "Establishing a Mirror Set" earlier in this chapter. When RAID 5 stripe set initialization is complete, you should find an FTDISK event that says, "Synchronization of a stripe with parity set is complete." No event log messages are generated for RAID 0 stripe sets.

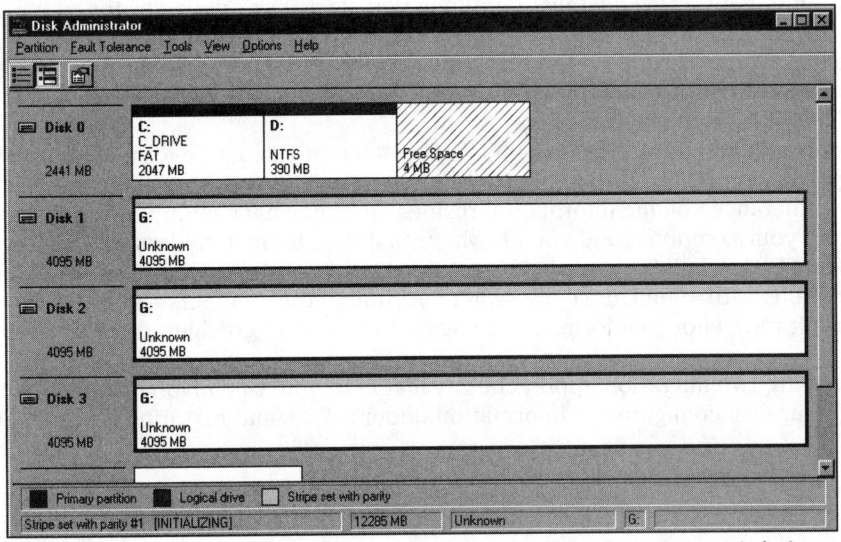

Figure 19-8: The status is reported as "initializing" while the stripe set is being generated.

6. Once the status changes to "healthy," you can format the stripe set and use it as you would any other disk volume.

7. Update your Emergency Repair Disk using the RDISK utility, as described in Chapter 17.

Deleting a Stripe Set

Deleting a stripe set is a destructive process. When you do it, all data on all member partitions is lost. If you want to retain any of the data on the stripe set, back it up to another disk drive or to tape. (See Chapter 18 for details on performing tape backups.) Once you've salvaged any data that you want keep, here's how you can delete the stripe set:

1. In the Disk Administrator window, click any member of the stripe set that you want to delete. On the Partition menu, click Delete. Click Yes to confirm.
2. On the Partition menu, click Commit Changes Now, click Yes to confirm, and click OK.

   You're left with free space regions in place of all of the partitions that participated in the stripe set. All data on the stripe set is gone.

3. Update your Emergency Repair Disk using the RDISK utility, as described in Chapter 17.

Migrating Fault Tolerance from Windows NT 3.x

If you install Windows NT Server 4.0 as an upgrade over an existing version of Windows NT Server, Setup automatically migrates all of the fault-tolerance information to your NT 4.0 installation. When you start Disk Administrator, you'll see all of your fault-tolerance volumes, drive letters, and so forth, just the way you left them in Windows NT 3.x. Since much of this information resides in the NT registry, it's migrated during the upgrade.

However, if you install Windows NT Server 4.0 into a separate folder and don't upgrade your NT 3.x installation, Setup has no way of knowing where the existing fault-tolerance volume information resides. You may have multiple copies of NT 3.x on your computer, and you may have installed them in folders with unusual names. Disk Administrator shows fault-tolerance members as primary or extended partitions with an unknown file system. Although the members are intact, NT 4.0 doesn't have enough information to figure how they're configured.

There are two migration approaches available to you. One involves explicitly saving your disk configuration information under NT 3.x and restoring it under 4.0.

This approach requires starting NT 3.x to save the configuration to a floppy disk and then starting NT 4.0 to restore it. The other method involves letting Disk Administrator search for the information and attempt to restore it directly. This latter approach doesn't require a floppy or a restart to a different version of the operating system.

Either way, when you perform these operations, all existing drive letters and volume types could change as a result. Don't proceed unless you're absolutely sure that you want to completely replace your current disk configuration.

Restoring an Old Disk Configuration

If you explicitly want to save your fault-tolerance disk configuration under Windows NT Server 3.x and then restore it under NT Server 4.0, here's how:

1. Start your computer under Windows NT Server 3.x. Log on with administrator privileges. In Program Manager, double-click the Administrative Tools program group and double-click the Disk Administrator icon.
2. On the Partition menu, click Configuration ➪ Save.
3. As shown in Figure 19-9, you're asked to insert a formatted floppy disk into drive A. Do so and click OK. When the copy is complete, click OK.

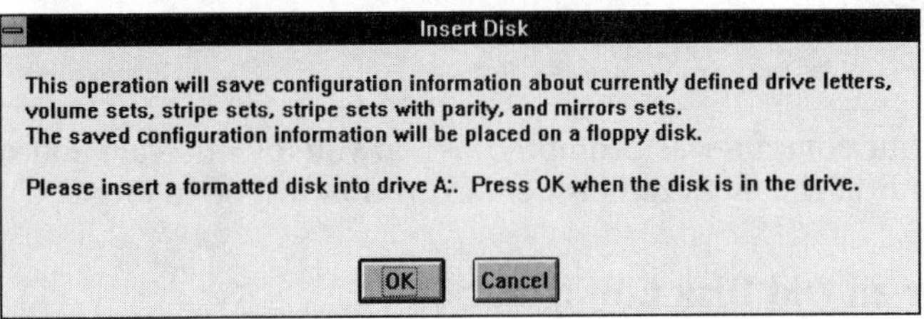

Insert Disk
This operation will save configuration information about currently defined drive letters, volume sets, stripe sets, stripe sets with parity, and mirrors sets.
The saved configuration information will be placed on a floppy disk.
Please insert a formatted disk into drive A:. Press OK when the disk is in the drive.
OK
Cancel

Figure 19-9: Insert a floppy disk to store disk configuration information.

4. Start your computer under Windows NT Server 4.0. Log on with administrator privileges. Start Disk Administrator.
5. On the Partition menu, click Configuration ➪ Restore. You're given a warning that your current configuration will be overwritten, as shown in Figure 19-10. Click Yes to confirm.

At this point, your existing disk configuration hasn't changed. You can still back out by clicking No.

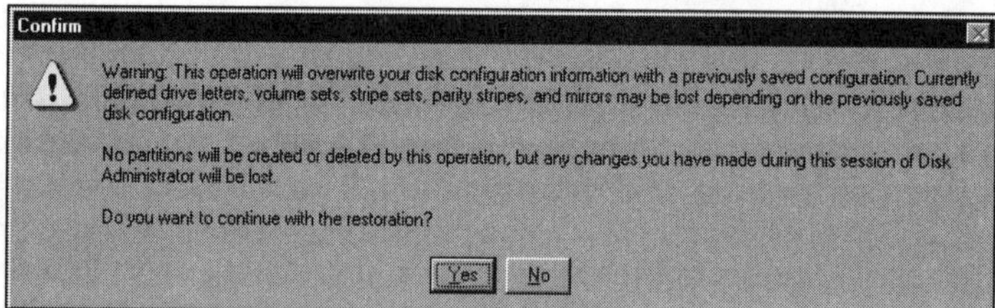

Figure 19-10: You're warned about restoring disk configuration information and overwriting your current configuration.

6. As shown in Figure 19-11, you're asked to insert the floppy disk containing the configuration in drive A. Do so and click OK.

   This is the floppy disk that you created back in step 3.

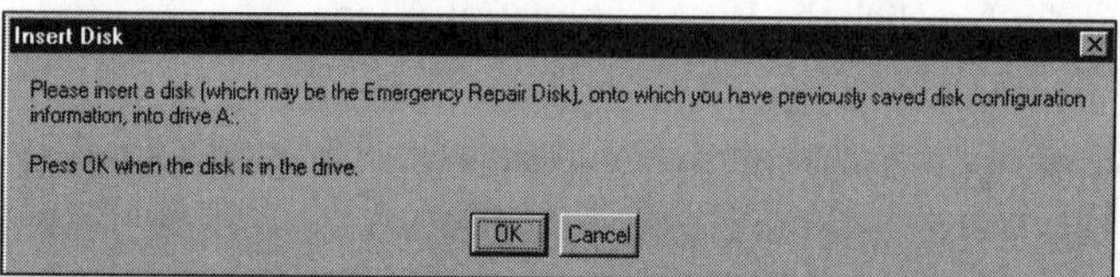

Figure 19-11: You're asked for the floppy disk containing the configuration that you saved.

7. Restart your computer as prompted. When you log on again and run Disk Administrator, the migrated disk configuration will be in force.

Searching for an Old Disk Configuration

If you want Disk Administrator in NT Server 4.0 to search for your old NT 3.x fault-tolerance disk configuration, here are the steps:

1. Start Disk Administrator. On the Partition menu, click Configuration ➪ Search.
2. You'll see a warning about overwriting your disk configuration with an old one, as shown in Figure 19-12. Click Yes to confirm.

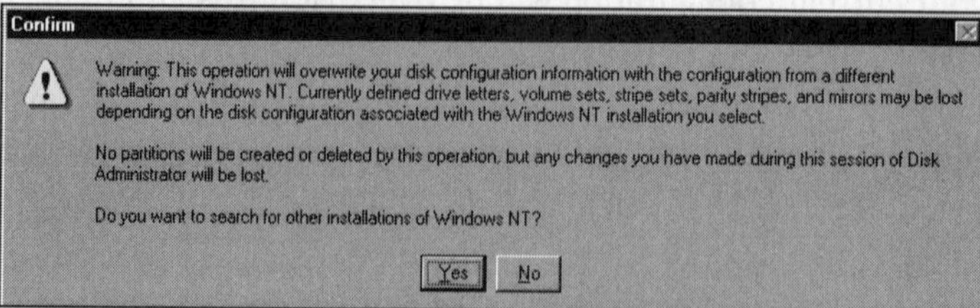

Figure 19-12: You're warned about restoring disk configuration information from an older version of NT.

3. Disk Administrator searches your entire computer for any other NT installations and lists them for you, as shown in Figure 19-13. In the Get Previous Disk Configuration dialog box, click the SystemRoot that contains the disk configuration that you want and click OK.

At this point, nothing has been done to your current disk configuration, but when you perform step 4, you'll completely overwrite it with a configuration from an older version of NT.

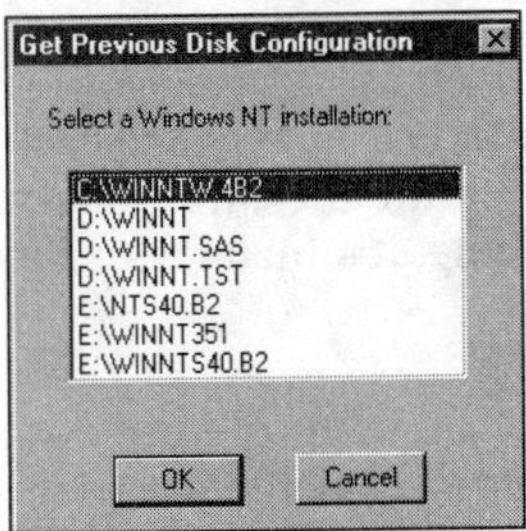

Figure 19-13: Pick the old NT installation that you want to use to migrate your disk configuration.

4. You're again warned about overwriting your current disk configuration, as shown in Figure 19-14. This is the point of no return. Click Yes to confirm.

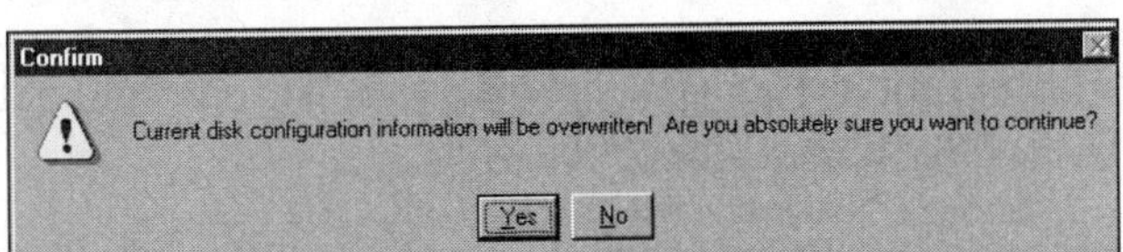

Figure 19-14: You're given a final warning about overwriting your current disk configuration.

5. Restart your computer as prompted. When you log on again and run Disk Administrator, the migrated disk configuration will be in force.

Recognizing a Broken Set

When a single drive that's a member of a fault-tolerance set (either a mirror set or a stripe set with parity) fails, it becomes an *orphan*. This may seem like a poor human analogy, since the dead disk is really a deceased sibling drive. However, if you think of the FTDISK driver as the mother of all fault-tolerance set disks, the idea of orphaning begins to make sense. When the maternal FTDISK recognizes that one of its poor little drives has passed away, it immediately routes all I/O requests to the other drives in the set and abandons the orphan drive.

FTDISK orphans a bad drive only during write operations, when the data written can be affected. The initial error message that you see on the screen or in the event log will vary, depending on what operation is being performed when the failure occurs and the type of failure. If the failure happens during normal system operations, FTDISK will report an error to the screen and to the event log, indicating that a fault-tolerance member is no longer accessible. If the failure occurs during system initialization, you'll see an error in the event log as the member is automatically orphaned.

Preparing to Recover from a Broken Set

After a single disk failure in either a RAID 1 or RAID 5 set, users are able to access the data without interruption, since NT uses the redundant data (mirror image or parity stripes) to reconstruct it. So for the time being, it's business as usual for your users. But not for you.

You need to consider this a temporary condition. The fault-tolerance set is no longer fault tolerant, so one more disk failure could take out all data on the entire set. What's more, performance of RAID 5 sets can be severely degraded because of the need to regenerate the data on the fly. Your goal must be to get back to a fault-tolerant state as quickly as possible.

There are two classes of disk failures that break fault-tolerance sets. The first is a severe problem in which the drive becomes completely unusable. This class of failure is typically due to a head crash, fried drive electronics, inability to spin up, or power problems within the drive. In this case, you must replace the drive before you can rebuild the fault-tolerance set.

The second class of failure is caused by a temporary condition that doesn't physically damage the drive. Loss of drive power or signal due to cabling problems is an example of this less severe class. In this situation, after correcting whatever caused the trouble, you can use the same drive to reconstruct the mirror or stripe set.

When either type of disk failure occurs, immediately make a backup of all critical data on the set. Then schedule time on the server to perform drive replacement (if necessary) and regeneration of the fault-tolerance set as soon as possible after the failure. The following sections outline the steps required to get back to a fault-tolerant state after a disk failure.

If the surviving drives are in use by a paging file, Microsoft SQL Server, Systems Management Server, or some other system service, NT will display an error message when you attempt recovery of the set. It will refuse to perform the recovery operation because the drives are locked by these services. You'll need to relocate the paging file or shut down these services temporarily before you perform the steps in the following sections.

Recovering a Mirror Set

Here's how to recover from the failure of a mirror set member drive:

1. In the Disk Administrator window, break the mirror relationship between the failed drive and the surviving drive, as described in "Breaking a Mirror Set" earlier in this chapter.

   The surviving volume is assigned the drive letter that was originally assigned to the mirror set.

2. Shut down the computer and replace the failed drive (or correct the problem that caused the failure). Restart the computer.

   When you add a new drive to the computer, NT may ask permission to write a disk signature on the drive. If you're prompted for this, confirm by clicking Yes.

It's wisest to replace the bad drive with a drive that's as similar as possible to the surviving member. However, if the two drives in your original mirror set were dissimilar, pick a replacement drive that most closely matches the original primary member of the set. Microsoft recommends that you try to match number of heads, cylinders, and sectors per track when selecting a replacement drive.

3. If the failed volume contains the NT system or boot partition, go to step 5. Otherwise, proceed to step 4. If the failed drive contains the shadow member, even if it contains a mirror of the boot partition, go to step 4.

4. Restart the computer. Reestablish the mirror relationship by following the steps under "Establishing a Mirror Set" earlier in this chapter. Then go to step 12.

5. Use an NT boot floppy disk to restart the system, as described in the Chapter 9 section called "Using an NT Boot Floppy."

6. Using Disk Administrator, reestablish the mirror between the boot partition and the surviving mirror partition by following the steps in the section called "Establishing a Mirror Set" earlier in this chapter. Close Disk Administrator.

7. Restart the computer again using the NT boot floppy disk.

   At this point, NT will recreate the original boot partition based on the contents of the surviving shadow member. Notice that, unlike the original configuration, the shadow is now acting as the primary member. The replacement drive is acting as the new shadow member. This is a temporary configuration, to get Disk 0 reconstructed.

8. Wait for the reconstruction operation to complete by checking the status line in Disk Administrator or monitoring the event log, as described earlier in this chapter.

9. Using Disk Administrator, break the mirror relationship again, as described in "Breaking a Mirror Set" earlier in this chapter.
10. Change the drive letters to ensure that Drive 0 is drive C and that the other original member of the mirror set is assigned another drive letter.

    See the section called "Assigning a Drive Letter" in Chapter 18 for details on how to change drive letters.
11. Restart the computer.

Disk 0 has now been restored but isn't mirrored. If you want to reestablish a mirror, follow the instructions in "Establishing a Mirror Set" to create a new mirror relationship. The volume will now be accessible for normal operations.

Recovering a Stripe Set

Here's how to recover from the failure of a stripe set member drive:

1. Shut down the computer and replace the failed drive (or correct the problem that caused the failure). Restart the computer.
2. In the Disk Administrator window, click any surviving member of the stripe set that you want to reconstruct.
3. While holding down the CTRL key, click a region of free space on the new drive that's large enough to act as a replacement member of the stripe set.
4. On the Fault Tolerance menu, click Regenerate. Close Disk Administrator and restart your computer.

   When the computer restarts, NT regenerates the missing data and parity information on the new member that you specified in step 3. This process occurs in the background and will take anywhere from a few seconds to many minutes, depending on several factors. For more details, see step 5 in the section earlier in this chapter called "Establishing a Stripe Set."

When the state of the stripe set changes to "healthy" in the status line of the Disk Administrator window, you're back in business.

In some cases, Disk Administrator may not assign any drive letter or may not assign the drive letter that you expect to the reconstructed stripe set. You may need to assign or change a drive letter to the volume. See the section called "Assigning a Drive Letter" in Chapter 18 for details on how to do this.

Measuring Performance on Windows NT

As an NT network administrator, you're expected to know not only the anatomy of your network and servers but also the state of their health. Just as you're much better off if you have periodic medical and dental checkups to catch small problems before they become big problems, your servers and network should get the same sort of attention. Recognizing trends and fixing small problems is certainly preferable to frantically mopping up after major network crises. Actively monitoring your servers and network to predict, prevent, and diagnose major problems will not only make you a hero and a resident guru but may also even lower your stress levels and help you live longer.

Windows NT Server 4.0 provides some powerful and not-so-powerful tools for monitoring the health of your enterprise computing environment. By using these tools to examine healthy computers and networks, you'll be better able to recognize when and how things are going awry.

Examining Performance with Task Manager

If you're interested only in a very basic snapshot of performance information, Windows NT Server 4.0 includes a little performance viewing tool inside Task Manager. To use it, right-click the taskbar, click Task Manager, and click the Performance tab. As shown in Figure 19-15, you can watch moving graphs of CPU and memory usage. Task Manager also provides counts of handles (the number of objects in the system), threads, and processes, as well as information on current and peak memory usage.

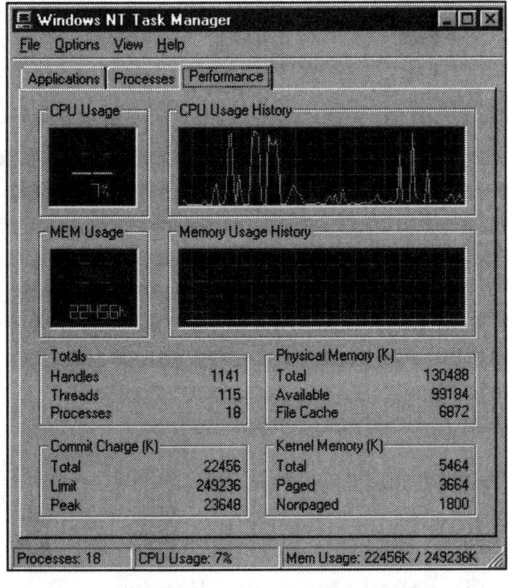

Figure 19-15: Task Manager offers a simple way to view basic system performance information.

If you want to know where your CPU time and memory are going, you can click the Processes tab to see a breakdown of all processes running on the computer, along with the CPU time that they've consumed and the amount of memory that they're currently occupying, as shown in Figure 19-16.

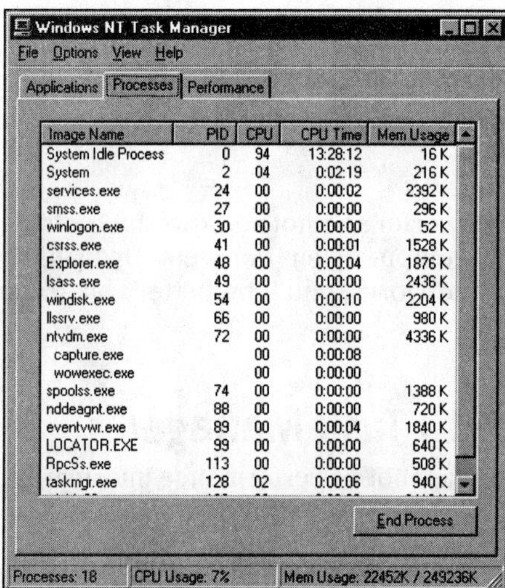

Figure 19-16: You can see where the CPU time and memory are going by viewing the list of processes.

You can delve into the details of what each displayed statistic means by checking out Task Manager's online Help. I recommend using the Task Manager for quick checks of your computer's temperature and pulse, but for serious performance analysis, you need to get familiar with Performance Monitor.

Introducing Performance Monitor

Performance Monitor is a graphical utility for examining the performance of local or networked computers in great (sometimes excruciating) detail. It monitors an almost overwhelming number of system parameters, including CPU usage, memory usage, hard disk performance, and network hardware and software statistics. Applications can install their own performance measurement counters in the system, and you can include these custom counters in Performance Monitor. You can create graphs, generate reports and baseline log files, and even cause the computer to send you messages when certain performance thresholds are reached.

NT's Performance Monitor is an extremely powerful tool that offers features supporting both the science and art of system performance monitoring. In this chapter, I'll introduce you to its key features and how to use them. However, if you really want to immerse yourself in performance monitoring, I recommend reading Volume 4 of the Windows NT Resource Kit, called *Optimizing Windows NT*. See Appendix C for additional information on the NT Resource Kit.

Using Performance Monitor

To start Performance Monitor, log on with administrator privileges and click the Start ➪ Programs ➪ Administrative Tools ➪ Performance Monitor option. (Administrator privileges are required to enable a few of the more invasive performance measurements, but most monitoring can be performed in a normal user account.) Figure 19-17 shows the Performance Monitor window that appears when you first start it.

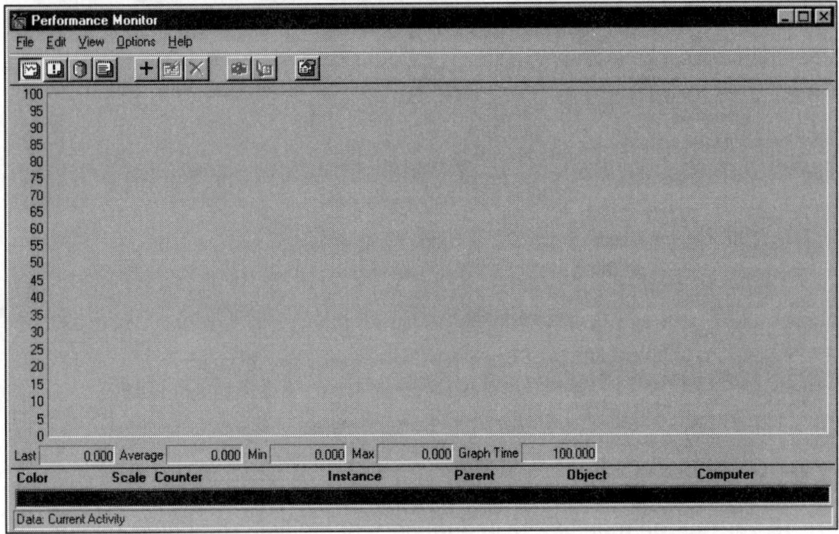

Figure 19-17: You can create a performance chart in the initial Performance Monitor window.

Of course nothing is being monitored, so the window is meaningless at this point. (I've seen several folks react to this initial screen with "OK, now what?" It's as if Microsoft is silently asking, "What do you want to measure today?") The first order of business is to create a performance chart.

As you explore the Performance Monitor menus, you may discover that it lacks any printing commands. You're not missing something. The utility doesn't provide a way to print directly. The only way to print charts or other information from Performance Monitor is to copy the screen to the Clipboard, then use Paint or another application to print its contents. See "Capturing Screens and Windows to the Clipboard" in Chapter 15 for details.

Creating a Performance Chart

Performance charting is probably the coolest, most visible feature of the Performance Monitor utility. Figure 19-18 shows a chart that's continuously monitoring CPU usage on two computers: ARES1 and TOWERRC2. The two lines at the bottom of the window provide a color-coded legend of the statistics displayed in the chart. As you add more measurements to a chart, new entries appear in the legend. Several summary statistics for the selected counter are presented between the legend and the chart itself, in an area called the *value bar.* The Last field contains the most recent sample, Average contains the average of all samples taken since you created the chart, Max and Min contain the highest and lowest samples taken, and Graph Time indicates the number of seconds displayed in the chart.

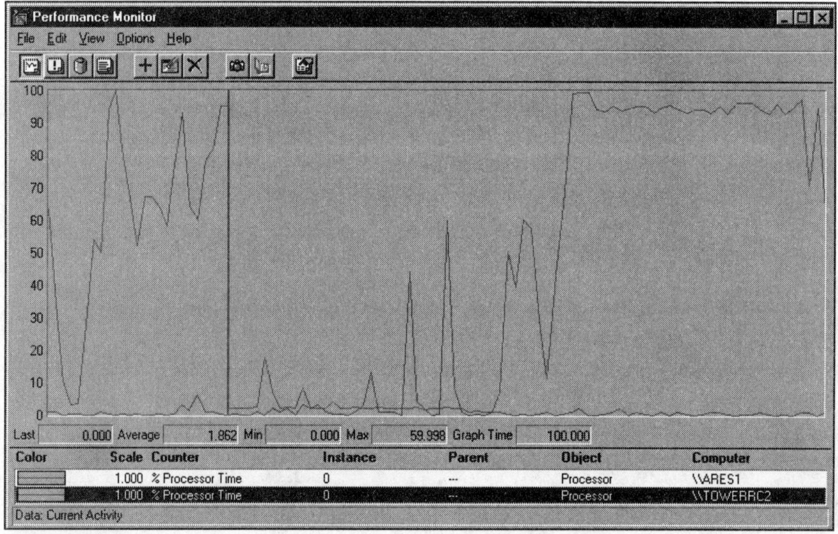

Figure 19-18: You can monitor the performance of multiple computers on the same chart – in this case, CPU usage.

It's not evident on the printed page, but Performance Monitor dynamically updates the chart every second. (You can change this sampling frequency, as you'll see later in this chapter.) When the chart reaches the right side of the window, it wraps around to the left. The thick vertical line you see in the left half of the chart represents "now" on the timeline. The most recent sample is charted just to the left of this line, and the oldest displayed sample is immediately to its right.

In Figure 19-18, the erratic higher chart line is a 486/66 NT Workstation computer with a small RAM size running several applications. Notice that the CPU percentage hits 100 a couple of times during the sampling period. The lower, more stable chart line is a Pentium 166 running almost no applications.

Here's how the Figure 19-18 chart was created. These steps depict in general how you can create a chart using Performance Monitor:

1. On the Edit menu, click Add to Chart. You'll see the Add to Chart dialog box. Click Explain. Figure 19-19 illustrates the resulting dialog box.

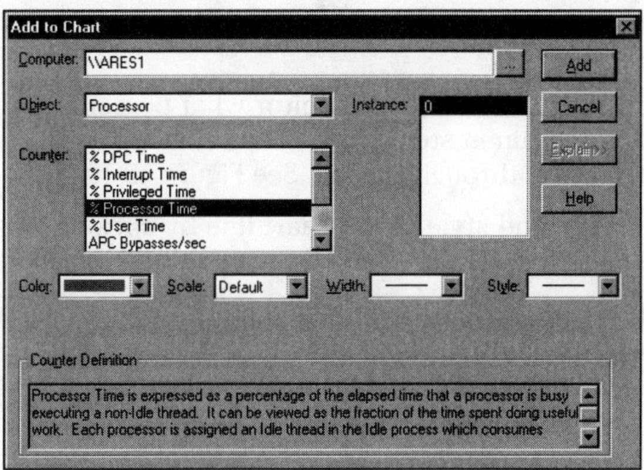

Figure 19-19: You can add a wide variety of statistics to a performance chart.

2. In the Computer field, type the UNC name of the computer that you want to sample.

   In the example, the first computer specified is \\ARES1, a remote computer on the network. You can monitor several computers within the same chart.

3. In the Object list, click the type of object that you want to monitor.

   In this case, click Processor to monitor statistics on the computer's CPU. Performance Monitor provides a wide range of both hardware and software objects to monitor. The length of the list depends on your installation options and any applications that you may have installed. In the example, the list contains 17 different objects to monitor.

   The Instance list presents all instances of the object that you select in this step. For example, if you select Processor and you have one CPU, the Instance list contains only one entry. (Processors are numbered starting with zero, as shown in Figure 19-19.) If you had an SMP computer with four processors, there'd be four items in the Instance list from which to select by clicking the desired instance. By default, the first instance is always selected.

   Notice that each object (and, in fact, each instance of each object) has its own set of counters. As you scroll through the Object list, you can view the Counter list for each object.

If all this talk about monitoring computers, objects, instances, and counters is a little confusing, think of these items in terms of a hierarchy:

Computers on the network

Objects on the computer

Instances of an object

Counters for each instance

4. In the Counter list, click the object counter that you want to monitor in the chart.

   In this case, click % Processor Time to monitor what percentage of time the CPU is busy. Clicking Explain in step 1 provides a detailed explanation of each counter as you scroll through the list. See Figure 19-19.

5. Change the color, width, and style of the chart line by clicking your selection in the appropriate list.

   By default, each new chart line is assigned a different color. To multiply each sample value by a scaling factor, click a factor in the Scale list. I recommend leaving this set at Default in most circumstances. It's easy to generate a confusing chart if you significantly change scaling factors.

6. Click Add. The chart will then be updated every second with the value of the object counter that you've selected.

7. Repeat steps 1 through 6 for each object counter that you want to monitor in the chart. When you're finished adding items to the chart, click Done.

8. Save your chart settings by clicking Save Chart Settings As on the File menu. Specify the folder and filename that you want to use and click Save.

   Performance Monitor charts have a .PMC file extension. Note that only the chart settings are saved, not the performance data itself. To record performance data in a file, see the section called "Creating a Performance Log File" later in this chapter.

Modifying a Performance Chart

If you want to change the basic parameters and behavior of the chart, click Chart on the Options menu to see the dialog box shown in Figure 19-20. With it, you can turn on and off the display of various chart elements, toggle between graph and histogram format, and change the frequency of sampling from the one-second default.

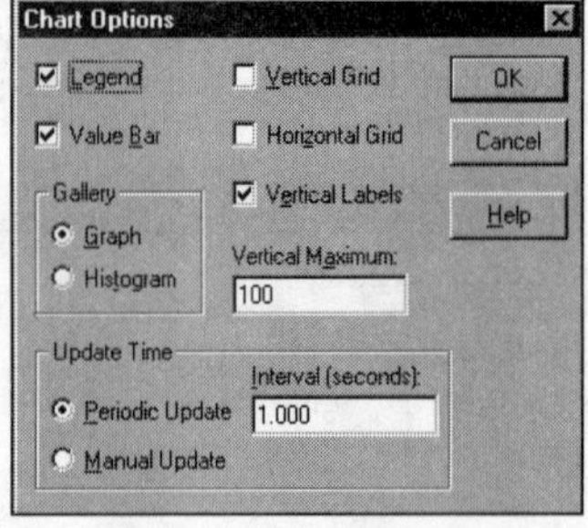

Figure 19-20: You can control how a chart is displayed using the Chart Options dialog box.

If you want to determine manually when to take a sample of the counters that you've selected, click Manual Update under Update Time in the Chart Options dialog box. Whenever you want to take a sample, click Update Now on the Options menu. (Think of automatic updating as shooting a movie at a default rate of one frame per second, and manual updating as taking a single snapshot at your discretion.)

It's easy to edit the color, width, style, and scale characteristics of a specific item in an existing chart. Just double-click the item that you want to edit in the legend at the bottom of the chart. Then make the changes in the Edit Chart Line dialog box and click OK.

If you want to monitor a different computer, object, instance, or counter, you must add a new item to the chart, as described in "Creating a Performance Chart" earlier in this chapter. If you want to delete an existing item, click it in the legend and press DELETE or click Delete From Chart on the Edit menu. After you've modified your chart, don't forget to save your chart settings, as described in step 8 in the previous section.

Creating a Performance Log File

As I mentioned earlier, it's important for you to know how your network and servers are behaving under normal conditions, so you can recognize and diagnose trends and problems as they emerge. It's wisest to collect logs periodically and keep them for comparison when you're analyzing a problem. Some installations create weekly log files, whereas others collect this data less frequently.

What's in a performance log file? Recall that when you created a performance chart, you selected the computer to monitor, objects on that computer, instances of those objects, and specific counters to sample and display on the chart. When you create a performance log, you specify the computer to monitor and the objects on that computer. Performance Monitor then collects data on all instances and counters associated with those objects.

Here's how to create a performance log:

1. On the View menu, click Log. On the File menu, click New Log Settings.

   These actions put Performance Monitor in log file mode and clear out any old log information.

2. On the Edit menu, click Add to Log. You'll see the Add to Log dialog box, as shown in Figure 19-21.

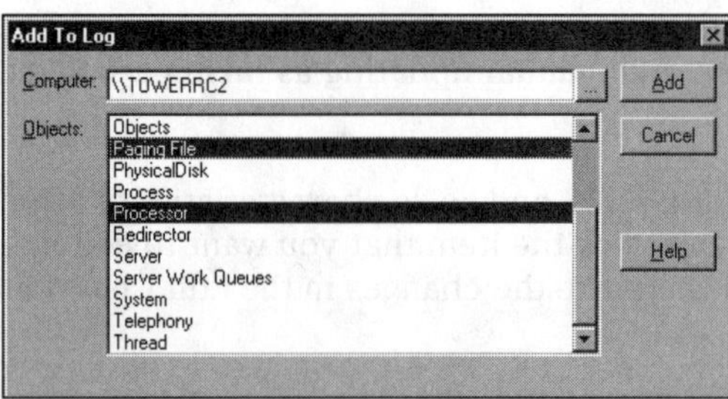

Figure 19-21: You can select a computer and add objects to monitor in the Add to Log dialog box.

3. In the Computer field, type the UNC name of the computer that you want to sample.

   You'll be able to monitor several computers within the same log file.

4. In the Object list, click the type of object that you want to monitor. You can select multiple objects. When you're done, click Add.

   In the Figure 19-21 example, Processor and Paging File are selected. You can select multiple items and ranges using the CTRL and SHIFT keys, as in any standard list.

   The variety of objects in the list depends on your installation options and any applications that you may have installed.

5. Repeat steps 3 and 4 for each computer that you want to monitor in this log file. When you're finished selecting computers and objects, click Done.

6. On the Options menu, click Log. In the Log Options dialog box, as shown in Figure 19-22, select the folder and type the filename in which you want to store the log information.

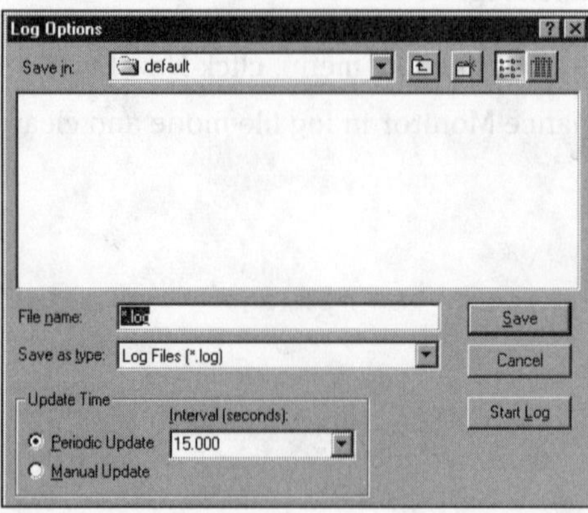

Figure 19-22: Select the log filename, sampling interval, and start the logging process.

7. Under Update Time, click Periodic Update and type the sampling interval, if you want something other than the default interval of 15 seconds. If you want to select samples manually using Options ➪ Update Now, click Manual Update.

There's a reason why the default sampling rate for log files is 15 times slower than the default chart sampling rate. If sampling occurs too frequently, your log files can quickly become very large. What's more, the amount of data to sift through can become huge. Don't select a sampling rate that's more frequent than you need. The 15-second interval is fine for most situations.

8. In the Log Options dialog box, click Start Log.

   This starts the sampling activity. Figure 19-23 shows logging in progress, gathering processor and paging file data on two computers. All data is stored in SAMPLE01.LOG. Check the File Size field for the current length of the log file.

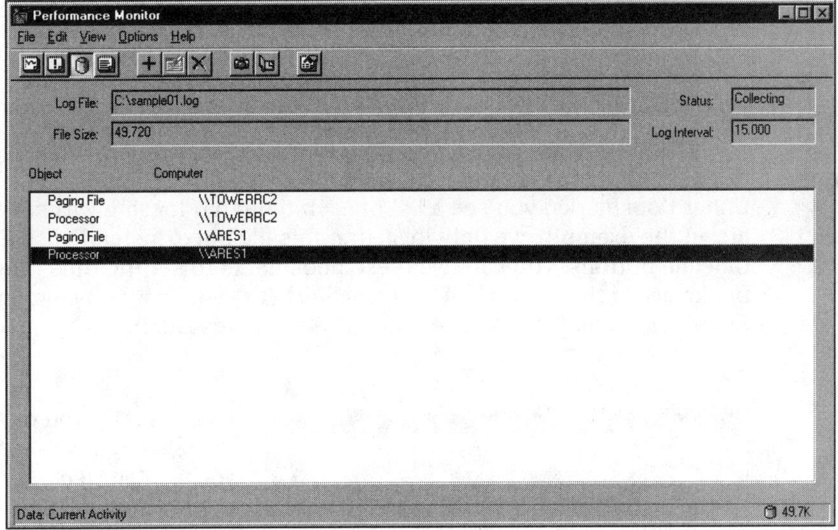

Figure 19-23: Performance Monitor displays the status of the log file that you're creating.

9. When you've collected the amount of data you want, click Options ➪ Log ➪ Stop Log.

10. Save your log settings by clicking Save Log Settings As on the File menu. Specify the folder and filename that you want to use and click Save.

    Performance Monitor log settings files have a .PML file extension. Note that only the log settings are saved, not the performance data itself. The data is recorded in the log that you just created.

Viewing a Performance Log File

Once you've created a performance log file, you'll probably be curious to see the data you've collected. To view an existing log file, you must stop logging to it, and the file must be closed. Make sure that you've stopped logging to the file before proceeding. Here's how to view the contents of a log file:

1. On the Options menu, click Data From. In the Data From dialog box, as shown in Figure 19-24, click Log File. Type the name of the log file that you want to view and click OK.

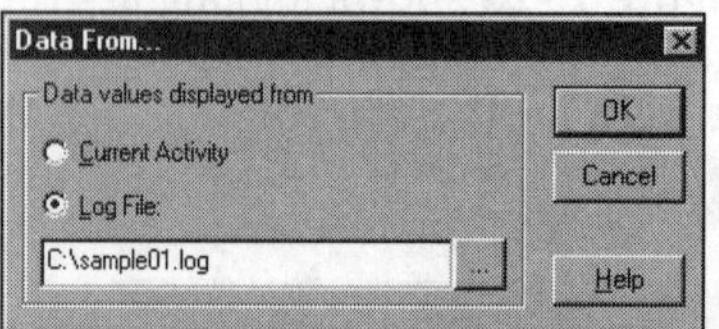

Figure 19-24: You can view current data or data stored in a log file.

2. On the Edit menu, click Time Window. In the Input Log File Timeframe dialog box, slide the buttons at either end of the timeline to specify the beginning and end of the range that you're interested in viewing. Figure 19-25 illustrates this.

   Under Bookmarks, you see a list of each time that logging was started to this file. In the example, we only logged to this file once. Instead of sliding the timeline buttons, you can use these bookmarks to set the time range. Click a bookmark in the list and click Set as Start (to use it as the beginning of the range) or Set as Stop (to use it as the end of the range).

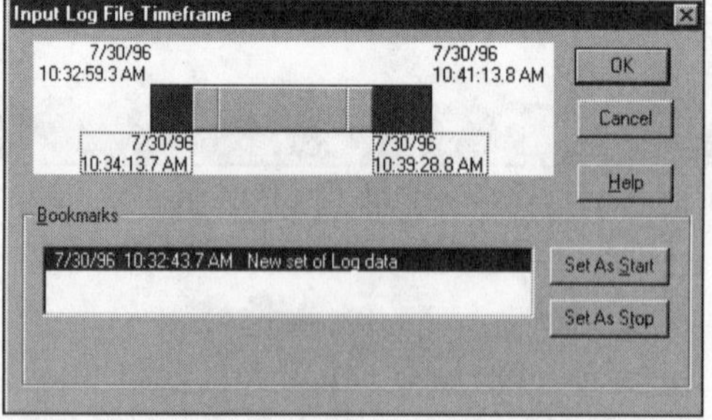

Figure 19-25: You can specify the range of times in which you're interested.

3. When you're done specifying the range of times, click OK. Then click Chart on the View menu.
4. To turn the collected data into a chart, manually add computers, objects, instances, and counters to the chart, as described in "Creating a Performance Chart" earlier in this chapter.

Adding items to a chart works exactly the same as before, but you're limited to selecting only those computers and objects that you selected when you created the log file. All instances and counters for the logged objects are available to you.

In Figure 19-26, I've selected one counter for each of the four objects monitored in the log file. Notice that one of the CPU usage graphs is relatively choppy, due to the 15-second sampling rate.

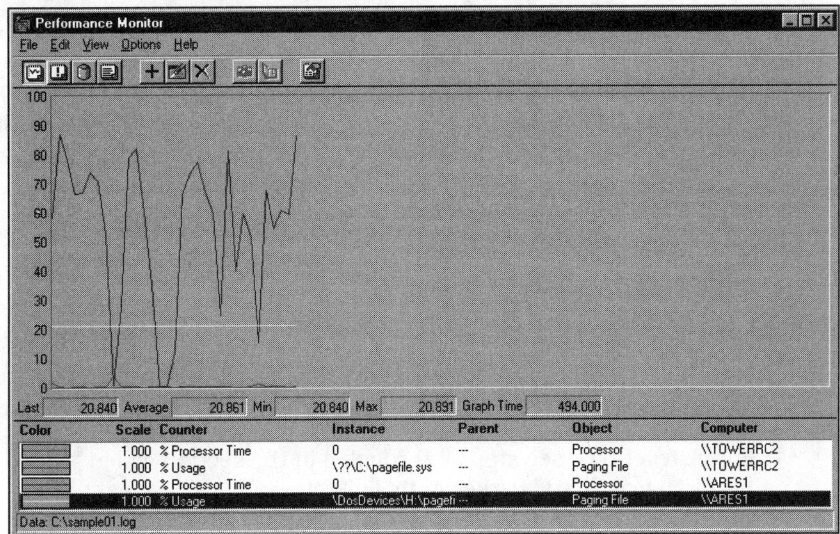

Figure 19-26: You can later view selected counters from the computers and objects that you specified in the log file.

5. Save your chart settings, as described earlier.

After viewing log file data, it's easy to forget to go back to viewing current performance data. When you're done looking at log files, don't forget to click the Options ➪ Data From ➪ Current Activity ➪ OK option.

Creating a Performance Report

Charts aren't always the best way to analyze performance data. Sometimes it's more useful to study the numeric data behind the charts. Performance Monitor enables you to generate reports that present detailed data collected from current system activity or from a previously created log file. (Performance reports are typically used to display data from performance log files but can also be used to take a real-time snapshot of current performance statistics.)

Here's how to create a performance report:

1. On the View menu, click Report. On the File menu, click New Report Settings.

   These actions put Performance Monitor in report mode and clear out any old report information.

2. On the Edit menu, click Add to Report. You'll see the Add to Report dialog box, as shown in Figure 19-27.

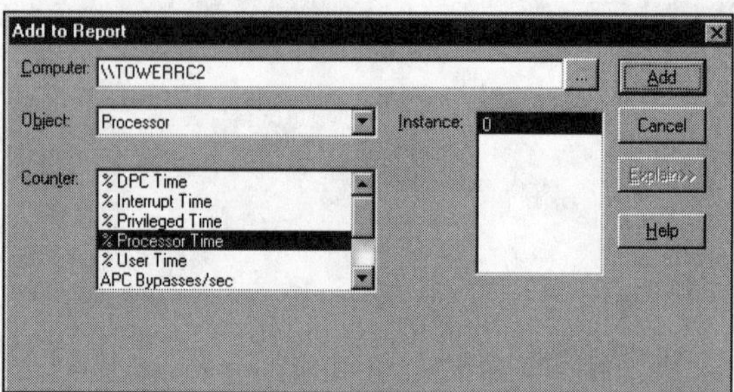

Figure 19-27: You can select computers, objects, instances, and counters to add to your report.

3. Specify the computer, object, instance, and counter that you want to include in the report. When you're done, click Add.

   For instructions, see steps 2 through 4 in the section called "Creating a Performance Chart" earlier in this chapter.

   If you're creating a report from a log file, your choices will be limited to the information that you included in the file.

4. Repeat step 3 for each counter that you want to add to the report. When you're finished, click Done.

   Figure 19-28 shows the resulting report. Notice that the computer/object/instance/counter hierarchy shows up in the format of the report.

5. Save your report settings by clicking Save Report Settings As on the File menu. Specify the folder and filename that you want to use and click Save.

   Performance Monitor report settings files have a .PMR file extension. Note that only the report settings are saved, not the data itself. To record performance data in a file, see the section called "Creating a Performance Log File" earlier in this chapter.

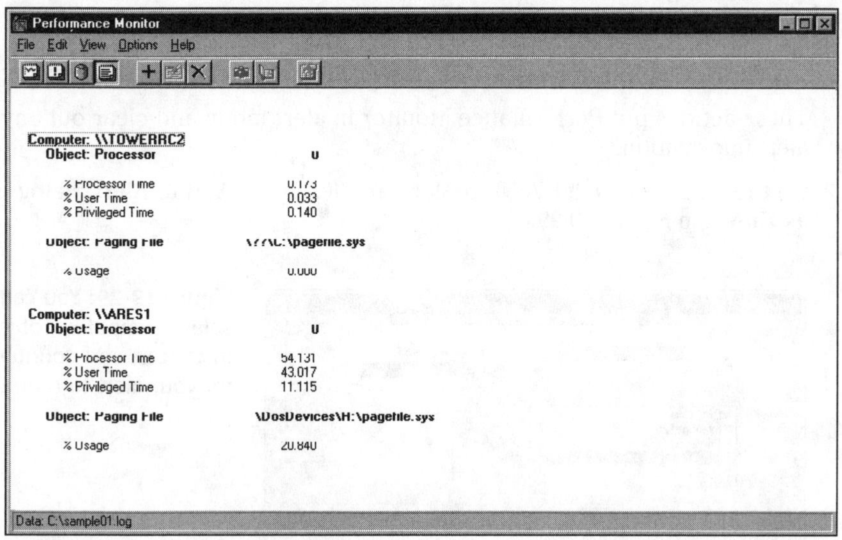

Figure 19-28: You can create a report from data in a log file, as shown here, or from current performance data.

If you're creating a report using current performance data instead of a log file, you can specify the frequency with which the report is updated. On the Options menu, click Report. To specify automatic updating, click Periodic Update and type the number of seconds between samples. If you want to update the report manually, click Manual Update. When you want to update the report contents, click Options ➪ Update Now.

You can export a report as tab-delimited or comma-delimited text for use in a spreadsheet, word processor, or other application. To do this, click Export Report on the File menu. Under Save as type, click either TSV (tab-delimited) or CSV (comma delimited). Specify the folder and filename and click Save.

Managing Performance Alerts

Performance Monitor can give you a wake-up call when one of the counters that you specify crosses a certain threshold. Using alerts in this way is a proactive approach to what I call "looking for trouble." By instructing Performance Monitor to send you a message and log an event when a counter starts creeping into an unacceptable range, you can catch problems before they occur. For example, you could set an alert to monitor a particular server and let you know whenever its CPU usage climbs over 90 percent or its free disk space dips below 10 percent.

Here's how to set up a Performance Monitor alert:

1. On the View menu, click Alert. On the File menu, click New Alert Settings.

   These actions put Performance Monitor in alert mode and clear out any old alert information.

2. On the Edit menu, click Add to Alert. You'll see the Add to Alert dialog box, as shown in Figure 19-29.

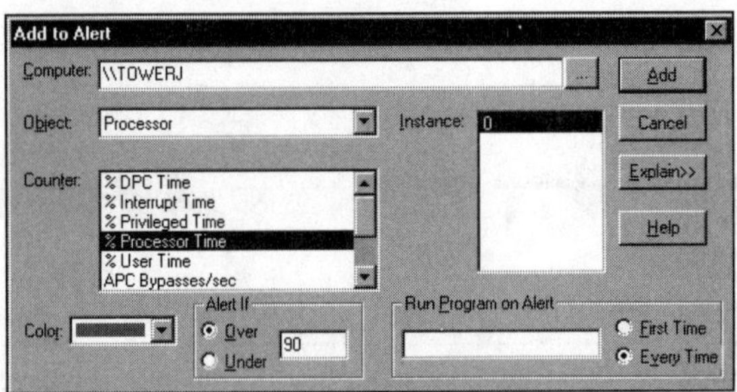

Figure 19-29: You can select computers, objects, instances, and counters for your alert to monitor.

3. Specify the computer, object, instance, and counter that you want to include in the list of alerts. When you're done, click Add.

   For instructions, see steps 2 through 4 in the section called "Creating a Performance Chart" earlier in this chapter.

4. Under Alert If, click Over or Under, depending on which condition you want to signal, and type the threshold value.

   For example, if you selected % Processor Time in step 3, click Over and type 90 to indicate that an alert should be sent when the CPU usage creeps over 90 percent.

5. If you want to run a program whenever the alert is triggered, under Run Program on Alert, type the name of the program. If you want the program to run whenever the alert is triggered, click Every Time. If you want it to run only on the first alert, click First Time.

6. Repeat steps 3 through 5 for each counter that you want to add to the list of alerts. When you're finished, click Done.

   Figure 19-30 shows the resulting alert list and alert log. The lower half of the window contains the list of conditions being monitored. The upper half contains the log of triggered alerts. It looks as if the \\ARES1 computer has very little space on drive C and is occasionally using more than 80 percent of its CPU.

7. Save your alert settings by clicking Save Alert Settings As on the File menu. Specify the folder and filename that you want to use and click Save.

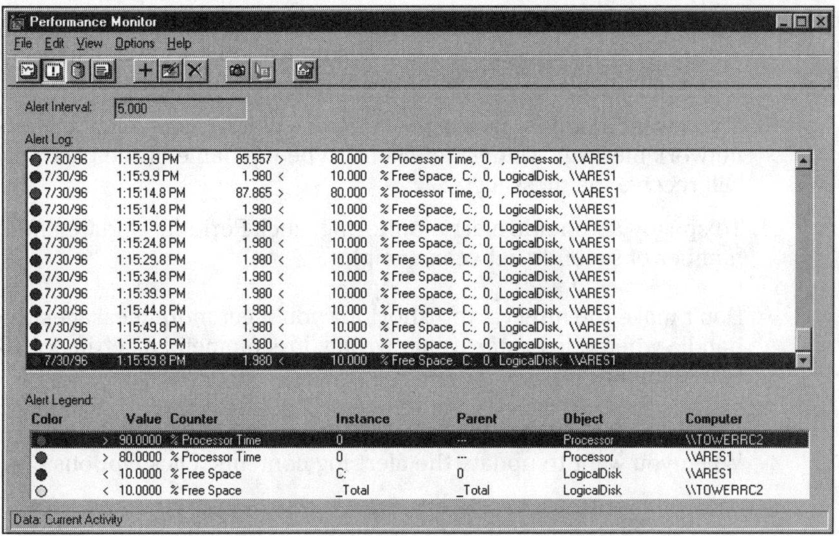

Figure 19-30: You can set and monitor alerts for multiple conditions on multiple computers.

Performance Monitor alert settings files have a .PMA file extension. Note that only the alert settings are saved, not the data itself. To record performance data in a file, see the section called "Creating a Performance Log File" earlier in this chapter.

If you're working on a combination of alerts, charts, logs, and reports in Performance Monitor, you can save your settings from all four areas at once. On the File menu, click Save Workspace and specify the PMW filename that you want to use to save your settings.

8. On the Options menu, click Alert. In the Alert Options dialog box, as shown in Figure 19-31, select the options describing the behavior of all alerts in the alerts list.

   If you want Performance Monitor to immediately switch to alert mode when an alert is triggered, click to select Switch to Alert View. I find this behavior annoying, so I leave it cleared.

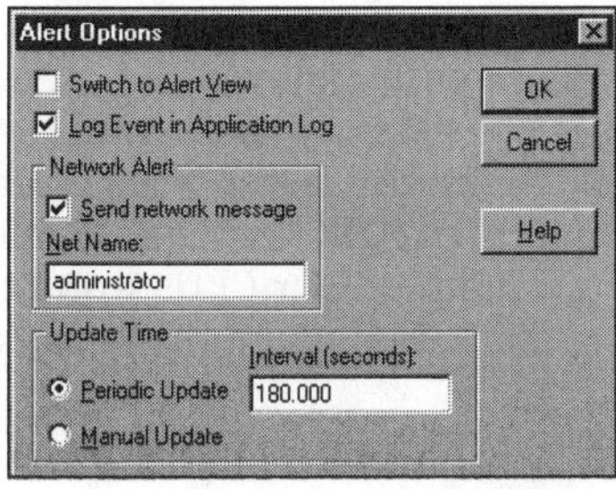

Figure 19-31: You can control the behavior of all alerts using the Alert Options dialog box.

9. If you want alert events logged so that you can later review them using Event Viewer, click to select Log Event in Application Log. (I'll discuss Event Viewer in Chapter 21.) I recommend logging these events.
10. If you want a pop-up message sent when alerts occur, click to select Send network message. Under Net Name, type the name of the user account that will receive the message.
11. To specify automatic alert monitoring, click Periodic Update and type the number of seconds between samples.

    Don't make the interval too short, or you'll get more messages than you can handle when things start to go wrong. I recommend a setting of 180 seconds (three minutes).

    If you want to monitor for these conditions manually, click Manual Update. When you want to update the alert log contents, click Options ➪ Update Now.

Improving Server and Network Performance

Now that you know how to use the tools of the trade, specifically the tools in Performance Monitor, it's time to look at how to detect and react to performance problems on your server. I'll begin by focusing on key areas within your server computer that affect overall performance. Later in this chapter, I'll focus on network-specific performance issues.

As I mentioned earlier, the number of measurements that Performance Monitor provides can be a bit daunting. In the sections that follow, I'll point out various areas of focus from which you can branch out to handle the specific behavior of your servers.

As you use Performance Monitor to measure the performance of your computers, make sure you do so under a typical load. Numbers that you gather on an idle computer aren't worth gathering. The goal is to determine how your system performs under its intended load of disk accesses, network traffic, user interaction, and so forth.

It's easy to improve the performance of your servers and network by investing more money in faster, bigger hardware. I offered several server hardware recommendations in Chapter 7. However, before you spend your precious budgetary dollars, it's best to understand where that money will buy you the biggest performance benefit. For example, if your server is consistently waiting for disk I/O operations to complete, it's wiser to funnel your bucks into faster disks or controllers, not into a faster CPU. Likewise, if you're running an SMP (symmetric multiprocessing) computer with two processors, making a jump to four CPUs won't do you much good if your second processor isn't getting used much these days.

By understanding and reporting on actual performance, you'll be able to prioritize and justify the most cost-effective plan for improving performance. This is the sort of research (sometimes called homework, legwork, staff work, and night work) that management loves to see.

Your Windows NT Server computers are probably used as file servers, application servers, or some combination of the two. Fast disk subsystems are critical to file server performance, as are high-performance network adapters. Physical memory size is important, to allow adequate caching of data on the server. Application servers, in which the server portions of client/server applications run, are best served (pun intended) by increases in both CPU speed and memory. Of course, disk-intensive client/server applications can benefit greatly from faster disk performance, too. Memory size and disk performance go hand-in-hand. As soon as you start running into the upper bounds of your RAM, extra demands are placed on the disk subsystem to provide virtual memory. Before you start to think that I've already spent all of your money, read on.

Managing Disk Performance

Before measuring disk performance, you need to enable Performance Monitor disk counters on each computer that you plan to monitor. By default, these counters are disabled because maintaining the counters themselves can significantly hurt system performance. While logged on with administrator privileges, type **DISKPERF -Y** at a Command Prompt and restart the computer. (When you're finished analyzing disk performance, don't forget to turn off disk counters by typing **DISKPERF -N** and restarting the computer.)

Measuring Disk Performance

Using Performance Monitor, under the Logical Disk object, examine % Disk Time for each of your server's drives. This counter tells you what percentage of time the drive is busy performing I/O. If the percentage climbs above 90 percent, monitor the Avg. Disk Queue Length counter for each logical drive. If the queue length typically averages two or above, consider spreading your disk access load to other drives or servers.

QUEUE LENGTHS ON STRIPE SETS

If your logical drive is consists of multiple physical drives (that is, a stripe set or stripe set with parity), then the average queue length for the logical disk can be longer. It's too long if the average queue length exceeds twice the number of physical drives involved in the stripe set. So, on a stripe set containing four disk drives, the average queue length should be below eight. If it's higher, consider increasing the number of drives in the stripe set, to spread the load across more disks. This rule of thumb applies both to RAID 0 and RAID 5 stripe sets.

It's important to know whether your computer suffers from a disk or a memory bottleneck. If you have too little physical memory, you'll see increased disk activity as the disks are deluged by virtual memory requests. Use Worksheet 19-1 to determine the percentage of disk time used for paging. Consider any result higher than 10 percent of the total disk activity to be excessive paging, and think about increasing the computer's physical RAM size.

Worksheet 19-1
Percentage of Disk Activity Due to Paging

Line	*Performance Measurement*	*Result*
1	Measure the Pages/sec counter in the Memory object	
2	Measure the Avg. Disk sec/Transfer counter in the Logical Disk object	
3	Multiply line 1 by line 2	
4	Percentage of disk time used for paging (multiply line 3 by 100)	

Resolving Disk Bottlenecks

If you encounter disk bottlenecks, here are some approaches that can relieve them:

✦ If investing in faster hardware isn't an option, consider spreading the current load over more drives, disk controllers, or servers, as mentioned earlier.

✦ Use disks with the fastest available seek times. Spend the extra money to get average seek times of 9ms or less. (The ratio of time spent seeking versus the time for actual data transfer is typically more than 10 to 1.) Consider paying a premium for AV-tuned drives to avoid thermal recalibration delays, as discussed in Chapter 7.

✦ Use 32-bit PCI SCSI host adapters, if you have a PCI-based motherboard. If your computer is MCA, EISA, or PCI, opt for a bus mastering host adapter. They're faster than DMA or PIO adapters, because they off-load more work from the CPU. See Chapter 7 and Appendix C for more details on these adapter architectures.

✦ Don't use IDE or EIDE drives if you're interested in performance. The performance difference between IDE and SCSI can be dramatic.

✦ Use SCSI host adapters that support asynchronous I/O, allowing multiple attached drives to seek in parallel. This is particularly important when using multiple paging files and when employing stripe sets.

✦ Create a stripe set (RAID 0 or RAID 5) to distribute the load over multiple drives, as described earlier in this chapter. If you already have a stripe set, consider adding more drives to the set.

✦ Think about adding more physical memory to the computer. This typically increases file cache size, resulting in better overall disk throughput. If line 4 in Worksheet 19-1 is 10 percent or higher, definitely add more RAM.

✦ Consider investing in a hardware RAID solution. Hardware-based RAID is more expensive than software solutions but is typically faster and occupies less memory than NT's RAID 5 approach.

Implementing a Paging File Strategy

Recall from Chapter 17 that paging files are used to implement virtual memory paging, described in Chapter 2. When your physical memory fills up with applications, data, and large caches, PAGEFILE.SYS can be accessed frequently by the operating system as pages are pulled in and out of memory. So it's important to make sure that access to this file (or these files, if you have more than one) is as efficient as possible.

If you have a single hard disk drive in your computer, your only tuning option is to adjust the size of your single paging file. Chapter 17 presents guidelines to help establish the correct size of PAGEFILE.SYS. You can use Performance Monitor to determine if your paging file is large enough. Monitor the Paging File object's % Usage Peak counter. If it nears 100 percent under a typical load, increase the size of the file.

If you have multiple hard disks, more options are available to you. If you have more than one paging file, you can determine if your overall paging file size is appropriate. Monitor the % Usage Peak of the _Total instance of the Paging File object in Performance Monitor. Just as in the single paging file case, if it nears 100 percent, it's time to increase the overall paging file size on your computer.

Splitting up the overall paging file space into multiple PAGEFILE.SYS files on different drives can improve performance. However, the success of this technique is highly dependent on your disk hardware. For example, placing paging files on two IDE drives that share a disk controller does nothing to improve performance and can sometimes degrade it because the two IDE drives can't be accessed simultaneously.

AVOIDING PAGING FILE GROWTH

Whenever NT has to extend the size of a paging file, time is lost. If you set the paging file size large enough, you can avoid automatic paging file growth. Examine the Memory object's Commit Limit and Committed Bytes. Whenever the Committed Bytes value exceeds Commit Limit, NT has to grow the paging file. Consider monitoring Committed Bytes over a period of time to determine its peak value. Then, set the total paging file size to that maximum amount plus 10 percent, for good measure.

Simultaneous access to the disks is the key to better performance using multiple paging files. Therefore, modern SCSI adapters and drives are your best bet. Even so, if two drives differ in speed, you may see better performance by placing one paging file on the faster drive instead of splitting it across two drives.

Never split paging files across multiple volumes on the same disk drive. Doing this will almost certainly degrade performance (and increase drive wear and tear) as the disk head travels back and forth between the two volumes. NT won't stop you from doing this, but don't be tempted.

Use the System application in Control Panel to change the number and size of your paging files. See the section called "Managing Virtual Memory" in Chapter 17 for details.

Deciding on NTFS Compression

As mentioned in earlier chapters, NTFS supports folder and file compression to save disk space. As with any compression scheme, there's a trade-off between file size and speed of compression and decompression. The designers of NTFS compression opted for speed over reduced file size.

Having said that, there is, in fact, a performance penalty for compression. Every time that a compressed file is written and closed, NTFS must compress it before it's written to disk. Whenever a compressed file is read, NTFS has to decompress it before presenting it to the application. The additional time required to perform these operations is offset somewhat because smaller and fewer disk I/O operations are required to transmit the data between disk and memory.

In an NT Workstation environment, NTFS compression doesn't seem to introduce significant overhead. However, when used on an NT Server computer, the impact varies dramatically, depending on the traffic pattern of the server. For servers that primarily provide access to files but have few or infrequent updates to them (that is, data is primarily read from the server), the impact of NTFS compression is small. Servers that have much read and write activity, however, show significant performance degradation when the accessed files are stored in compressed form on NTFS.

My bottom-line advice on NTFS compression is to avoid it on frequently accessed files on production servers. For example, don't compress databases, shared documents, application executable files that are run over the network, and so on. Compression is fine for saving disk space on files and folders that aren't accessed frequently. Even though disk space is getting cheaper these days, every little bit helps. Just use compression judiciously and avoid creating a performance problem on your servers.

Never compress the files in your system partition's root directory (including paging files) or the executable files in SystemRoot where you installed Windows NT Server. You can render your computer unbootable at worst, and slower at best. It's certainly OK selectively to compress bitmaps and other nonexecutable files within the SystemRoot tree.

Compression is treated as an attribute of files and folders on NTFS, just as the read-only, archive, and system attributes. You can use NT Explorer to control the compression attribute, by bringing up the Properties dialog box associated with a file or folder, clicking the General tab, and clicking to select or clear the Compress check box. See Chapter 14 for more information on NT Explorer.

Once you start using NT Explorer to compress files and folders on your NTFS volumes, it's cumbersome to dig into the object's properties to determine whether it's compressed. Instead, on the NT Explorer View menu, click Options, then click the View tab. Click to select the Display compressed files and folders with alternate color check box and click OK. That way, you'll be able to tell at a glance which objects are compressed. Compressed objects are displayed in blue, so don't set your background or text color to blue.

If you attempt to compress a folder, Explorer asks you whether you want to compress just the files in the folder or its subfolders also. If you opt not to compress subfolders, the subfolders and their contents will retain whatever compression attributes they had before.

If you want to compress, decompress, or view compression status from a Command Prompt, you can use the COMPACT command. Unlike Explorer, COMPACT won't ask you if you want to compress subfolders. It will just do it automatically. Type **COMPACT /?** for details of its syntax.

If the system happens to crash while performing a compression or decompression operation, the compress attribute might not match the actual state of the file. You can correct this situation by using the force (/F) option of the COMPACT utility to force the compression or decompression to complete.

When copying or moving compressed and uncompressed files between NTFS folders, here are three basic rules:

- ✦ When you move a file from one folder to another, the moved file retains its original compress attribute, regardless of the destination folder attributes.
- ✦ When you copy a file to a new destination, the new file inherits the compress attribute of the destination directory.
- ✦ When you copy a file to replace an existing file, the new file retains the compress attribute of the file that you replaced.

Since FAT doesn't support file and folder compression, whenever you copy or move a file from NTFS to FAT, the compress attribute of the file is lost, and the file is automatically decompressed. If you copy or move a FAT file to an NTFS folder, the file inherits the compress attribute of the destination folder. Copy a file from FAT to replace a file on NTFS, and the file will inherit the compress attribute of the NTFS file that you're replacing.

The rules of behavior of NTFS compressed file moves, copies, and replacements can be a bit confusing, until you get accustomed to them. Table 19-2 presents the compression behavior to expect when using the applications and utilities supplied with Windows NT. Third-party applications may act differently.

Table 19-2
NTFS Compression Behavior When Moving, Copying, or Replacing Files

File Action	***Source File Compressed (Before)***	***Resulting File Compressed (After)***
MOVE		
Move a compressed file to a compressed folder	√	√
Move a compressed file to an uncompressed NTFS folder	√	√
Move an uncompressed file to a compressed folder		
Move an uncompressed file to an uncompressed NTFS folder		
Move a compressed file to a FAT folder	√	
Move an uncompressed file to a FAT folder		
Move a FAT file to a compressed NTFS folder		√
Move a FAT file to an uncompressed NTFS folder		

File Action	*Source File Compressed (Before)*	*Resulting File Compressed (After)*
COPY – To new file destination		
Copy a compressed file to a compressed folder	√	√
Copy a compressed file to an uncompressed NTFS folder	√	
Copy an uncompressed file to a compressed folder		√
Copy an uncompressed file to an uncompressed NTFS folder		
Copy a compressed file to a FAT folder	√	
Copy an uncompressed file to a FAT folder		
Copy a FAT file to a compressed NTFS folder		√
Copy a FAT file to an uncompressed NTFS folder		
COPY – To replace existing file		
Copy a compressed file to replace a compressed file	√	√
Copy a compressed file to replace an uncompressed NTFS file	√	
Copy an uncompressed file to replace a compressed file		√
Copy an uncompressed file to replace an uncompressed NTFS file		
Copy a compressed file to replace a FAT file	√	
Copy an uncompressed file to replace a FAT file		
Copy a FAT file to replace a compressed NTFS file		√
Copy a FAT file to replace an uncompressed NTFS file		

Managing Processor Load

Installing a faster CPU or faster motherboard may seem like an obvious choice when attempting to improve server performance. Likewise, adding more processors to a multiprocessor computer sounds like a reasonable way to increase speed. However, even if overall server performance is unacceptable, these relatively expensive upgrades may have little or no effect if the performance bottleneck lies elsewhere. In the following section, I'll focus on detecting whether a CPU bottleneck exists.

Measuring Processor Load

The key to detecting CPU bottlenecks is to keep track of the Processor object's % Processor Time counter. This tells you what percentage of time a processor is performing nonidle work. (Processors that are waiting for work aren't actually idle. During these periods, they spend their time executing an idle thread. The % Processor Time counter doesn't include this so-called idle time.)

If the percentage of processor time measurement consistently climbs near 100 percent, there are a couple of possibilities. Either the processor is truly a bottleneck, or you have applications on your computer that are so CPU-intensive that they need to be moved to another computer or scheduled during off-hours. (I'll discuss how to schedule tasks for off-hours in Chapter 21.)

Resolving Processor Bottlenecks

If you determine that you truly have a processor bottleneck, here are some possible solutions:

- As mentioned in Chapter 7, don't run complex screen savers on your server. When they kick in, they can absorb a large percentage of your processor's time, at the expense of real work. Choose a blank screen saver.
- If investing in faster hardware isn't an option, consider spreading the CPU load of multiple server applications across different servers.
- Consider upgrading the processor to a faster CPU speed. In Chapter 7, I discussed several upgrade alternatives.
- If the motherboard is running at 33MHz or slower, consider replacing it with a faster one. 66MHz motherboards are standard in Pentium-based servers, at the time of this writing. Even faster motherboards are on the way.
- If you don't have an SMP (symmetric multiprocessing) computer, consider investing in one. Make sure that your server applications can take full advantage of the added CPUs.
- If you have an SMP computer that's upgradable to additional CPUs, you can opt to add more processors to your computer.

Before you add more processors to an SMP computer, make sure that all existing processors are being used in your environment. By measuring each Processor object instance individually, you may find that some CPUs are fully loaded, whereas others remain idle. This can happen when you run single CPU-intensive applications that aren't designed to be multi-threaded. In this situation, adding more processors costs you money and buys you nothing.

Managing Memory Performance

So far, all roads seem to lead to adding more physical memory to your NT Server computer. Adding more memory is always a good thing, since it can also help disk and network throughput. However, before you invest in additional RAM, it's important to understand whether you already have the right amount.

Monitoring Memory Usage

One of the key indicators of memory performance is the Memory object's Pages/sec counter. This value tells you how many pages per second are written to or read from disk to satisfy references to pages that aren't in memory. If the number consistently averages above five pages per second, you probably have a memory bottleneck in your system. If the average is consistently above 10, your disks will grind so wildly that you'll be lucky to gather the performance results.

Another way to examine memory performance involves monitoring the cache. Watch the Memory object's Cache Faults/sec counter to determine how frequently the system can't find data in the cache and must find it on disk. If you see an increasing trend in this counter, it's a signal that you may be heading for a condition called *thrashing,* in which almost every access to data requires a disk I/O operation.

Applications sometimes have bugs called *memory leaks,* which cause them to consume memory resources and never return them to the system after use. Often, just closing the application and restarting it will free the memory resources.

So how do you find out what process is consuming memory resources with reckless abandon? It's pretty time-consuming to use Performance Monitor to view the memory resources of every process in the computer. A quick way to see who's gobbling memory is to use Task Manager's Processes tab. This gives you a quick snapshot of all of the processes in the system and how much memory is being used by each. Look for relatively large numbers that grow over time.

Resolving Memory Bottlenecks

If you determine that you have a memory bottleneck, and not just a memory-hogging or memory-leaking application, here are a few straightforward alternatives to consider:

- ✦ The most obvious solution is to add more physical memory to the computer. This approach can improve other aspects of performance, including disk throughput (due to larger caches and less paging activity) and network throughput (due to larger network caches and improved disk throughput). If line 4 in Worksheet 19-1 is 10 percent or higher, definitely add more RAM to your computer.
- ✦ In addition to RAM expansion, consider faster disk drives and drive controllers, as discussed earlier. This will improve virtual memory performance.
- ✦ Split your paging file space across several of your fastest disks, as discussed earlier in this chapter.
- ✦ If possible, reduce memory requirements on your server. Uninstall features that you don't need in order to save memory. RAID 5, TCP/IP, and RAS all require lots of memory. NT runs many services in your behalf, some of which you may not need. For example, Spooler isn't necessary if you don't have a printer attached. You can use the Services application in Control Panel to shut it down.

Managing Network Performance

Network counters in Performance Monitor are organized according to their transport protocols. To get the biggest benefit from your analysis, start by examining the protocols that are used most frequently on your network. Each protocol has a slightly different set of counters, but the bulk of them are the same from one protocol to the next.

To use TCP/IP counters in Performance Monitor, you must first install the SNMP service. This will enable the communication of TCP/IP counters over the network. Use the Network application in Control Panel to install the SNMP service after you install the TCP/IP protocol. You must install SNMP on all computers from which you need to gather TCP/IP performance counters.

Monitoring Network Performance

Errors are always present on a network, even on a healthy one. Many of the counters that you find under each transport protocol measure or accumulate error counts. In general, don't think of the errors themselves as problems to be addressed. Pay more attention to the changes in error rates — these are the more accurate signs of trouble.

As a result, it's critically important, especially in the networking area, to log important error counters periodically and save the log files for later comparison. Make sure to gather this data when the network appears to be performing well, so that you have a basis for comparison. When the network slows down, you'll then be able to identify where the problems may lie.

Start by checking the Failures Adapter counter, which is actually an accumulated total of dropped connections due to failure in the network adapter. High and increasing numbers here are both a performance concern and a reliability consideration. The network adapter hardware may be heading for total failure, so consider swapping it out for an adapter that you know is working and test the suspect adapter off-line.

Another error counter to examine is Frame Bytes Re-Sent/sec, which measures the rate at which actual data bytes must be resent by the computer due to errors. Again, the value itself isn't as big a concern as an increasing trend.

Improving Network Performance

On Windows NT Server, the server component is probably the most significant in terms of resource usage. You can tune the server to trade speed for memory. To do this, start the Network application in Control Panel, click the Services tab, click Server, and click Properties. Figure 19-32 shows the resulting dialog box.

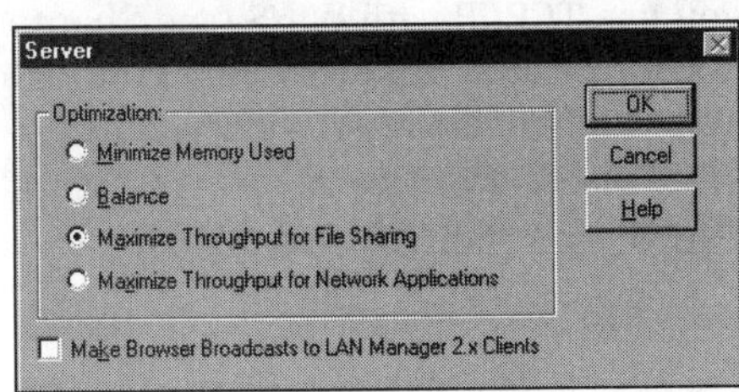

Figure 19-32: You can tune the amount of resources used by the server component.

Table 19-3 presents the trade-off between memory usage settings and the number of network users that the server can comfortably support. Note that the limit on the number of users isn't actually enforced. Servicing more users will work, but users will see significant performance degradation.

Table 19-3
The Trade-off between Server Resources and Number of Users

Server Resource Setting	*Number of Users*
Minimize Memory Used	Up to 10
Balance	10 to 64
Maximize Throughput for File Sharing	64 or more (file server)
Maximize Throughput for Network Applications	64 or more (application server)

Many books actively encourage you to dig into the NT registry and make changes there to optimize your network. I'll discuss in detail how to make registry changes in Chapter 20, but in general I recommend keeping your hands off the registry as much as possible. In tweaking the registry, it's easy to create an unbalanced system, in terms of both performance and reliability. So I recommend using the features that NT provides in its supplied utilities and changing the registry only as a last resort.

Beyond making registry changes — directly or through the utilities — here are some other ways to optimize your NT server's network performance:

- Use 32-bit, bus mastering network adapters. Don't skimp on the network adapters that you install in your servers. Use the fastest NT-compatible that you can afford.
- Consider adding more physical memory to the computer. This approach can improve network throughput (due to larger network caches and improved disk throughput).
- Install only the network protocols that you use. Don't leave unused protocols loaded, since they not only consume memory but can also steal time away from other protocols.

- Adjust network bindings to match your network usage pattern. Bind most frequently used protocols first. If you use TCP/IP with WINS (see Chapter 11), binding NetBIOS to TCP/IP first will cut down on broadcasts on your network. See Chapter 8 for details on managing network bindings.
- Consider upgrading network adapters. Mixing fast and slow adapters on the same network can impede performance, especially when a fast adapter sends data to a slow one.

Summary

In your kitchen, the sink is draining faster than ever. At your office, all of your NT servers are running like greased lightening — with little or no downtime for maintenance or repairs. But should you run into trouble — a disk bottleneck, for example — you have all of the tools you need to fix the problem. No need to wait for the landlord or plumber. You can do it yourself.

In this chapter, you've learned how to maximize both performance and reliability of your Windows NT Server computers and your network. You've gained the know-how to set up and administer robust fault-tolerance volumes and to squeeze extra performance out of your disks. I've also shown you how to use NT's powerful Performance Monitor utility, to help you diagnose and pursue performance problems.

In Chapter 20, I'll show you how to understand and maintain the Windows NT Server registry, which contains virtually all of the computer's configuration information. Then in Chapter 21, I'll share some tricks and troubleshooting techniques that will help you stand out as a stellar NT Server administrator.

INSIDE STORY

The computer manufacturer executives glared at me over the long conference room table, barking out their pointed questions: "How do you test software that only runs when a disk sector goes bad or a disk drive dies? Gather up as many hard drives as you can find that are on their last legs? Do you unplug disk drives while they're running? Well, what's the story?"

These executives were earnestly trying to evaluate the robustness of Windows NT Server, hoping to put together something to convince their customers of the reliability of NT fault tolerance. I could tell that they were trying to make me squirm, but the squirming never happened.

"Well, finding a bunch of dying hard drives is certainly part of the plan," I calmly explained, "but a very small part. Here's how we test for fault tolerance." I then proceeded to explain how the layered driver model in NT lets a test engineer place a special driver between the FTDISK driver and the physical disk device driver. This special driver is called SIMBAD, which stands loosely for SIMulated BAD sectors. Install it, and you can make specific or randomly selected disk sectors appear to go bad at any time. It's like pulling a rug (or magic carpet?) out from under the file system, and it works effectively to exercise every aspect of NT's fault-tolerance functions.

As I told them the tale of SIMBAD, my computer executive audience acted as if they'd seen a genie. There were "Ohhs" and "Ahhs" throughout the room when one of them aptly observed, "So the design of NT itself makes it possible for you to test its most critical functions? That's amazing. In fact, it's magic!"

Understanding and Using the NT Registry

Did you ever try to build a house of cards? If so, I'll bet you paid lots of attention to creating the most solid foundation possible to support the upper levels. Each card on the lower deck essentially became a load-bearing wall of your 52-card masterpiece. By making these cards lean and depend on each other, you created a structure that might even withstand a curious poke from the paw of your cat.

Now, imagine removing just one of the cards on the lowest level. With a combination of luck and skill, you can get away with it, perhaps only causing the structure to lean a bit. However, dislodge or take away another card, and you'll probably play "52-Pickup." Because all of the cards that make up the foundation play critical roles in supporting the overall structure, and because many of them depend on each other to function properly, the whole house comes tumbling down.

Windows NT Server is a very stable, robust operating system. Just as any other structure, it has a foundation — called the *registry* (or more formally, the *registry database* or *registration database*). If you start pulling individual parts out of that foundation or replacing pieces with inferior elements, you can make NT lose its balance and even come crashing down. Parts of the registry depend on each other. If you remove one value, it can have a cascading, ill effect on many others. For example, a seemingly innocent change or deletion in your network adapter configuration can cause the transport protocols, server, redirector, and numerous other services to fall over dead.

Most of the configuration changes that you'll make to the operating system will be through Control Panel, described in Chapter 17, and other administrative tools. These applications offer a relatively safe way to make changes to the registry. However, there will be times when you must change the registry in order to modify settings that aren't handled by the standard user interface, alter configurations of remote computers, or fix a problem under the direction of a product support specialist. Doing so without totally destroying your computer's configuration requires a combination of knowledge, practice, and contingency planning.

In this chapter, you'll learn about the Windows NT Server registry, where virtually all of the operating system and application configuration data is stored. I'll show you how to examine and modify it using the Registry Editor utility. You'll read so many warnings about the risks of editing your registry that you'll begin to believe it's as bad as a combination of tobacco, alcohol, fatty foods, caffeine, tornadoes, and swimming right after eating.

Whenever possible, use tools such as Control Panel and User Manager for Domains, rather than the Registry Editor, to change your computer's configuration. Even the most experienced Windows NT Server administrator sometimes renders his or her computer completely unbootable by editing the NT registry directly. The key to success is planning to allow for quick recovery from a registry misstep. Make frequent backups of the registry (as discussed in Chapter 18), update your Emergency Repair Disk (as discussed in Chapter 17), and know how to recover quickly a computer that won't boot (as discussed in Chapter 9).

I can't adequately emphasize the point that *making changes to the registry can render your computer unbootable.* In the worst case, you'll have to completely reinstall Windows NT Server to recover. If you plan properly, you won't need to take this drastic step. Perform all registry editing at your own risk.

You'll find that working with the registry is a necessary evil if you want to be an expert NT administrator. Microsoft's own online Help files, product support personnel, and technical notes for sidestepping common problems all point you to specific locations in the registry. Without registry skills, you won't be able to take advantage of these important resources. So take a few deep breaths, and let's get started.

Introducing the Windows NT Registry

So what exactly is this registry? It's a hierarchical database containing virtually all of the configuration information that used to be CONFIG.SYS, AUTOEXEC.BAT, WIN.INI, SYSTEM.INI, CONTROL.INI, PROTOCOL.INI, LANMAN.INI, and other configuration files. Microsoft has rolled all of this information under one roof and has provided a single database editor to deal with it. (I'll show you how to use the Registry Editor utility later in this chapter.)

As with many other parts of NT 4.0, the registry approach has evolved over time. It was first introduced with Windows 3.1, in which some information was stored in INI files and some in the registry. Today, NT stores everything in the registry but provides physical manifestations of a few INI files for those older Windows applications that need them to run. Writing to these INI files automatically changes the registry.

Both Windows NT and Windows 95 use registry databases to store most of their configuration information. Although the underlying format of the two databases is the same, the contents differ.

Since NT 4.0 can't be installed as an upgrade from Windows 95, you may be tempted to copy the Windows 95 registry database to NT. Don't do it. It won't work. Even though there are similarities between the two registries, there are plenty of critical differences. If you want your Windows 95 applications to show up when running NT, reinstall them while running NT.

The registry database has some fault tolerance built into it. If the computer loses power or crashes while the registry is being edited, log files are maintained that allow NT to recover it to a good state by fixing any damage. (Of course, it doesn't recover itself from an invalid change that you might make to the registry. That's up to you to avoid.)

The structure of the registry is probably most closely related to what you've seen in Windows INI files. It contains sections that describe all of the details of your hardware configuration, desktop settings, application settings, your user account, and a bunch of other things. The registry goes beyond the INI file concept by allowing a hierarchical structure, similar to folders and files on disk. In fact, you refer to paths to the elements in the registry just like folders and files, as you'll see later in this chapter. What's more, the registry itself contains multiple versions of this information, allowing you to recover a previous version if you make a wrong move and render your computer unbootable.

If you've worked with DOS and Windows before, you've probably often wished that you had an easy way of saving copies of all your configuration files before installing new drivers or applications. Perhaps you've created an elaborate scheme to do this, only to find that you didn't include all of the configuration files that you needed. The NT registry simplifies your life, at least in this respect.

Introducing the Registry Editor

The Registry Editor is a graphical utility that enables you to view, search, modify, and save the NT registry database. You can think of Registry Editor as playing the same role for the registry as Notepad plays for text files. Notepad is an objective facilitator; it allows you to view, search, modify, and save text files but never examines or makes judgments about the content of the text that you're editing. With

Registry Editor, you can do the same for the registry database. In addition, just as Notepad can open and edit a file on a remote computer over the network, Registry Editor can open and edit a registry database on a remote computer.

This point is very simple but vitally important. Registry Editor doesn't understand, recognize, or enforce rules on the values that you type. It blindly does exactly what you ask it to do, as long as you have the privileges to make the change. Be extremely careful about what you change, since you won't be warned when you make a mistake. And be prepared to restore the old registry in case you render your computer unbootable.

To start Registry Editor, log on with administrator privileges and click Start ⇨ Run. Type **REGEDT32** and click OK. In the Registry Editor window, on the Options menu, click to select Read Only Mode. Figure 20-1 shows the resulting window.

Get into the habit of placing Registry Editor into read-only mode whenever you run it. Doing this will ensure that you (or someone else who walks by and uses your computer) won't inadvertently make a catastrophic change to the registry. Take it out of read-only mode only when you are sure that you're ready to make a correct modification. To do this, click to clear Read Only Mode on the Options menu, then make your change.

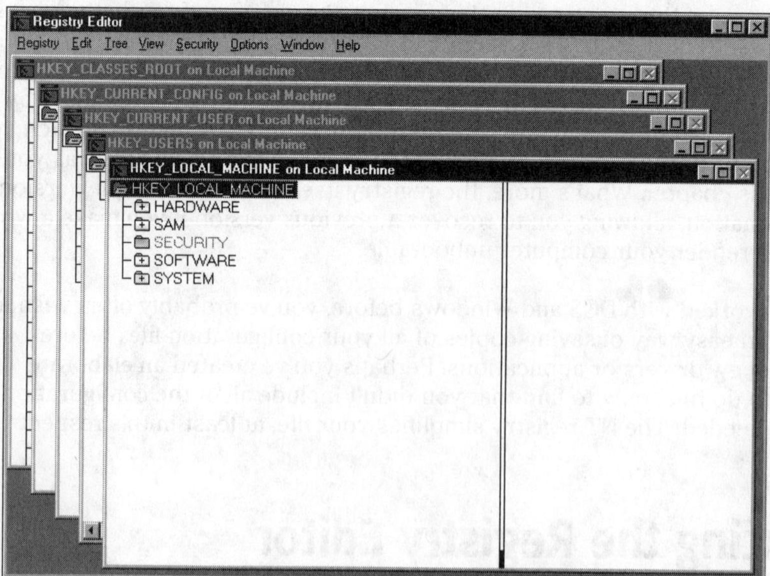

Figure 20-1: Registry Editor presents five subtrees of the registry database.

As added protection, make sure the Confirm on Delete command is always checked on the Options menu. Since it's easy to delete certain items from the registry simply by pressing the DELETE key, requiring this confirmation avoids accidental deletions.

If you've used Windows 3.x, you may be tempted to start REGEDIT instead of REGEDT32. NT includes the 16-bit REGEDIT application purely for compatibility purposes. It allows you to edit the REG.DAT file used by WOW (Win16 on Win32 support) and Win16 applications. However, REGEDIT won't let you edit the NT registry. REGEDT32 is required for this. You can tell if you've inadvertently started the 16-bit version if you see the window shown in Figure 20-2.

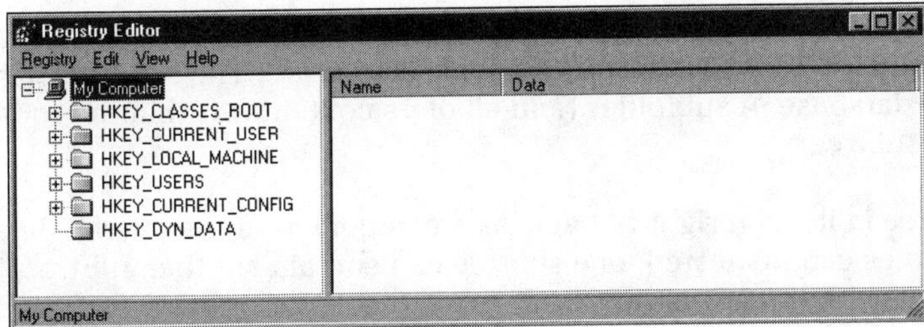

Figure 20-2: You know you've started the wrong Registry Editor if you see this window.

When you first start Registry Editor, you'll see the five windows shown in Figure 20-1, the significance of which I'll explain later in this chapter. Each window represents a view of a different part of the registry database. Switch between the different windows by clicking them. You can also minimize and maximize the windows within the main Registry Editor window.

The windows are split down the middle. The left half displays the hierarchical structure of the database including subtrees and keys (I'll define these later in this chapter) and enables you to navigate easily through it. The right half provides a view of entries containing actual data values. You'll see examples of this split later in this chapter.

Folder icons are used throughout this chapter and in the Registry Editor interface itself to express the hierarchy within the registry database. Although the registry itself is actually stored in files on disk (which I'll discuss later), the folder icons represent a hierarchy organization within the registry files. It's helpful to think of this database hierarchy in terms of folders, but keep in mind that these folder icons don't represent actual folders on disk.

You expand and collapse folder icons in Registry Editor the same as you do in NT Explorer. The only real difference is that the plus and minus signs in Registry Editor appear on the folder icons, as shown in Figure 20-1. A plus (+) sign indicates that there are more items inside the folder. Double-click the + sign to expand it, and double-click the minus (–) sign to collapse it.

Understanding NT Registry Structure

Much of the terminology in the NT registry world describes the hierarchical structure of the registry database. The entire database is considered a tree, whose root is at the top. The database tree is divided into several *subtrees,* which I'll discuss in detail in the next section.

Think of the registry database in terms of a folder structure. The root folder represents the entire database. A subfolder (and all of its contents) within the root folder represents a subtree.

A subtree is a tree in its own right but acts as a component of the overall database tree. Since subtrees can be nested, one subtree can contain another subtree, just as one folder can contain another folder. Because this is a database, each node (or folder) in the tree is also called a *key.* Keys can have *subkeys,* and subkeys can have their own subkeys. Typically, the root of a subtree is called a key, and the nodes below it are called subkeys.

Again, if it's easier for you to think in terms of a folder structure, think of keys as the folder names. Since you can have subfolders within folders, keys can have subkeys. Think of the subkey as a subfolder name. Just as a subfolder is also called a folder, subkeys are also called keys.

To make it easier to refer to specific items within the registry database, Microsoft has adopted a naming convention that is similar to a folder (or directory) structure. As you traverse down the registry tree, keys are separated by backslashes (\). Figure 20-3 illustrates the concepts of subtrees, keys, and subkeys and how they relate to the registry naming convention.

THE CASE OF THE DISAPPEARING KEYS

Most of the registry database is stored in files on disk and survives from one operating system boot to the next. Some portions of the registry, however, are regenerated each time you restart the computer. They're never stored in a disk file and live only while the operating system is running. These disappearing keys are known as *volatile keys.* Information on detected system hardware, for example, is stored in volatile keys, as you'll see later in this chapter.

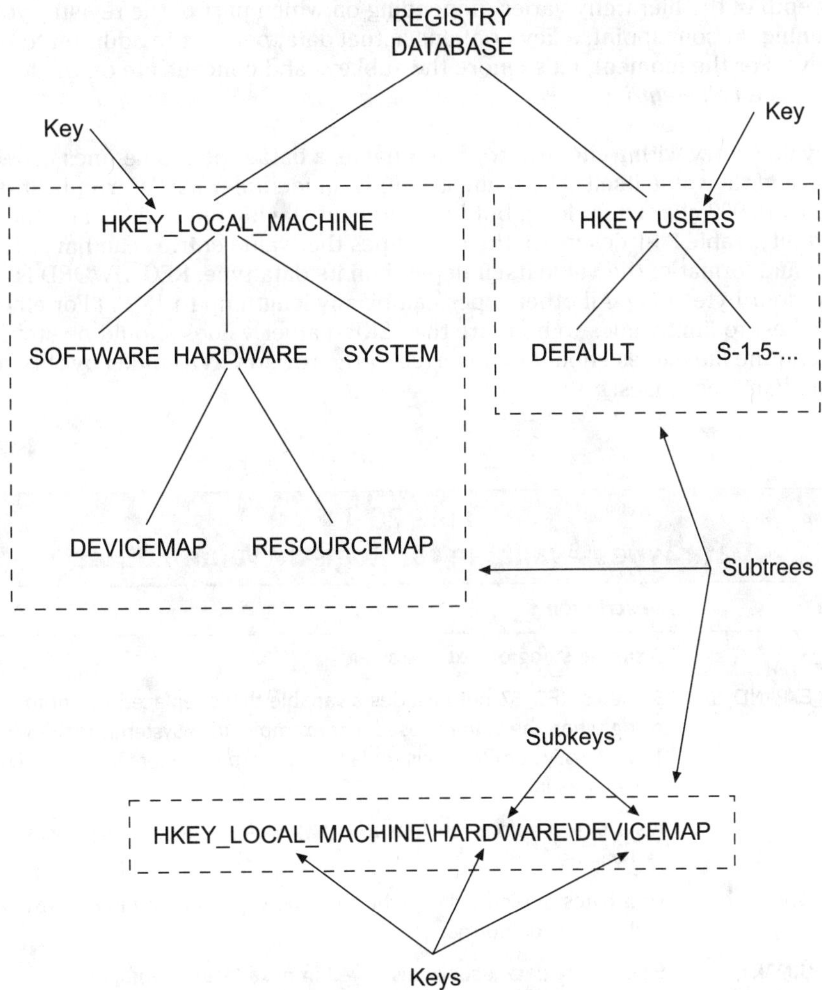

Figure 20-3: You can relate the registry database structure to a folder structure on disk.

Understanding Value Entries

So far, all I've talked about is the organization of the database into subtrees made up of keys and their subkeys. So is there any data in this database, or is it just a big empty tree structure? Yes, Virginia, there's data in the database. When you drill down as far as you can go into the registry hierarchy, you'll run into the actual data. In fact, along the way, you may encounter some of the actual data, before you get to the lowest levels.

The depth of the hierarchy varies, depending on which part of the registry you're examining. At some point, a key contains actual data, perhaps in addition to other subkeys. For the moment, let's ignore the subkeys and concentrate on the actual data, called *value entries.*

Each value entry within the registry has a name, a data type (sometimes called a class), and the value itself. The name is simply an identifier like "Current." It can be up to 16,000 characters long, but I recommend staying under 20 characters for readability. Table 20-1 describes the data types that value entries can have. The length and format of the value itself depend on its data type. REG_DWORD is always four bytes long. All other types can be any length up to 1MB. (For efficiency, it's best to limit values to no more than 2KB. Larger values should be stored in files, and the file names should be inserted in the registry. NT abides by this rule of thumb in most cases.)

Table 20-1
Data Types Available for Registry Value Entries

Type	*Description*
REG_SZ	A simple string of text characters.
REG_EXPAND_SZ	Same as REG_SZ but includes a variable that's replaced by another string when the value is used. For example, in %SystemRoot%\SYSTEM32, %SystemRoot% is replaced by the path where Windows NT Server was installed.
REG_MULTI_SZ	A set of text strings (such as REG_SZ), typically used to express a list of text values.
REG_DWORD	Four bytes of binary data, which can be expressed in binary, hexadecimal, or decimal format.
REG_BINARY	Raw binary data, usually displayed in hexadecimal notation.

As an example, let's look at the key HKEY_LOCAL_MACHINE\SYSTEM\Select. It contains four value entries, including this one:

```
Current:REG_DWORD:0x1
```

where Current is the value entry name, REG_DWORD indicates that the value is a four-byte number, and 0x1 is the actual value expressed in hexadecimal.

You may encounter other data types in your exploration of the registry. For example, there's a type somewhere in there called REG_FULL_RESOURCE_DESCRIPTOR. New data types can be defined by programs and are often used internally by the application or operating system. Registry Editor exclusively supports managing the types listed in Table 20-1, so you need only concern yourself with these types.

Understanding Registry Subtrees

The Windows NT registry is typically depicted as five major subtrees in a hierarchical tree structure. As you'll see in the following sections, these subtrees aren't all rooted at the same place in the database. Only two of the five are actually in the database root — HKEY_LOCAL_MACHINE and HKEY_USERS. All other subtrees live below one of these two and are depicted separately only for convenience in editing the registry.

The HKEY_LOCAL_MACHINE Subtree

The HKEY_LOCAL_MACHINE subtree, which exists at the root of the database, contains all of the information about the hardware configuration of your computer, as well as applications and services running on it. Some of the hardware information is updated automatically each time you restart the operating system, as new hardware configurations are detected. The data stored in this part of the registry is common to all users of this computer.

Of all the hours that you spend working directly with the registry, you'll likely spend most of them inside this subtree. I'll cover portions of it in more detail later in this chapter.

HKEY_LOCAL_MACHINE contains its own set of subtrees. Table 20-2 presents these five subtrees. All subtrees except the HARDWARE subtree are stored in separate files in the SystemRoot\SYSTEM32\CONFIG folder of your NT Server installation tree.

Table 20-2
Subtrees of HKEY_LOCAL_MACHINE

Subtree	*Database File Names*	*Description and Advice*
HARDWARE	None (This is a volatile key that's never stored on disk.)	Contains hardware configuration information, regenerated by NTDETECT and the NT kernel each time that the computer is restarted. This subtree contains mostly binary information that you shouldn't attempt to edit directly. Use Control Panel to make any changes, or you may render your computer unbootable.

(continued)

Table 20-2 (continued)

Subtree	*Database File Names*	*Description and Advice*
SAM	SAM SAM.LOG	Contains the Security Account Manager (SAM) database, including user accounts, group accounts, and domain security information. Utilize User Manager for Domains to make changes, or you might prevent users from logging on.
SECURITY	SECURITY SECURITY.LOG	Contains local computer security information, including rights, account policies, and local group memberships. This subtree is used only by the NT security subsystem and can't be edited using the Registry Editor.
SOFTWARE	SOFTWARE SOFTWARE.LOG	Contains information on the local computer's software configuration, including applications, file associations, and OLE information. Use applications themselves to change application configuration and OLE information. Use Explorer to change file associations.
SYSTEM	SYSTEM SYSTEM.ALT	Contains the configuration information required to start the operating system, beyond what is recognized and stored in the HARDWARE subtree. This is where most of your manual changes are likely to occur.

If you want to find out quickly which database files go with which registry subtrees, look in the HKEY_LOCAL_MACHINE\SYSTEM\CurrentControlSet\Control\hivelist key. You'll find the list of subtrees and files, similar to what's presented in Table 20-2. (You'll find out why this key is named "hivelist," later in this chapter.)

The HARDWARE subtree isn't stored in a file, since NT automatically regenerates it at boot time by running NTDETECT.COM (the hardware recognizer utility) and the NT kernel itself. Both of these programs feed the registry with hardware information during the boot process. (NTDETECT runs on Intel platforms only. On RISC platforms, NT extracts this information from the firmware.)

The remaining subtrees are stored in two files each. The files without a file extension (SAM, SECURITY, SOFTWARE, and SYSTEM) are the actual registry database files. The files with extensions are used for fault tolerance and backup purposes. Each .LOG file is actually a journal of registry modifications, used to reconstruct the registry file if a power failure or other crash leaves it in an inconsistent state while it's being changed. Because the SYSTEM registry file is vital to the boot process, SYSTEM.ALT is a complete backup copy of the SYSTEM file and is used to boot the computer if the SYSTEM file becomes corrupt. I'll talk more about how the registry participates in the boot process later in this chapter.

The HKEY_CLASSES_ROOT Subtree

No, this isn't some sort of registry pep rally. The HKEY_CLASSES_ROOT subtree contains file association information and the OLE registration database (REG.DAT, if you're a Windows 3.x guru) to keep track of which applications to launch when you double-click on files, objects, and icons. For example, it maps video files ending in .AVI to the action of starting MPLAY32.EXE (NT's Media Player utility) whenever you double-click the .AVI file.

This subtree is actually a pointer into the HKEY_LOCAL_MACHINE subtree — specifically, HKEY_LOCAL_MACHINE\SOFTWARE\Classes. Figure 20-4 shows the relationship between HKEY_CLASSES_ROOT and HKEY_LOCAL_MACHINE. Changes made in HKEY_CLASSES_ROOT are immediately reflected in HKEY_LOCAL_MACHINE, since they occupy the same space.

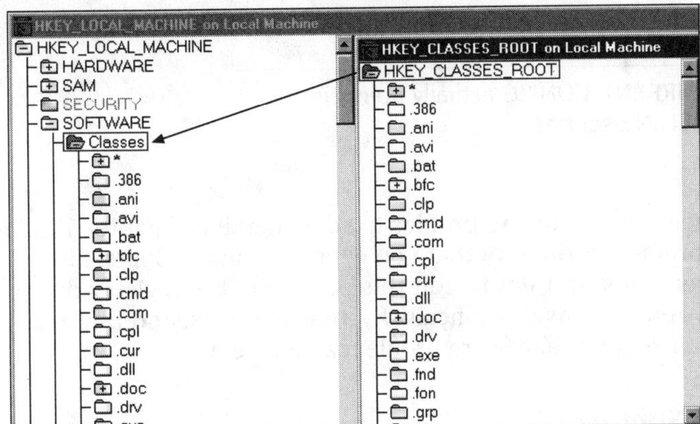

Figure 20-4: HKEY_CLASSES_ROOT actually points inside the HKEY_LOCAL_MACHINE subtree.

I discussed how to change file associations using Windows NT Explorer in Chapter 14.

The HKEY_CURRENT_CONFIG Subtree

The HKEY_CURRENT_CONFIG subtree has been introduced for the first time in Windows NT 4.0. It contains information about the specific hardware profile used to start the computer. This subtree is actually a pointer into the HKEY_LOCAL_MACHINE subtree — specifically, HKEY_LOCAL_MACHINE\System\CurrentControlSet\Hardware Profiles\Current. Figure 20-5 shows the relationship between HKEY_CURRENT_CONFIG and HKEY_LOCAL_MACHINE. Changes made in HKEY_CURRENT_CONFIG are immediately reflected in HKEY_LOCAL_MACHINE, since they occupy the same space.

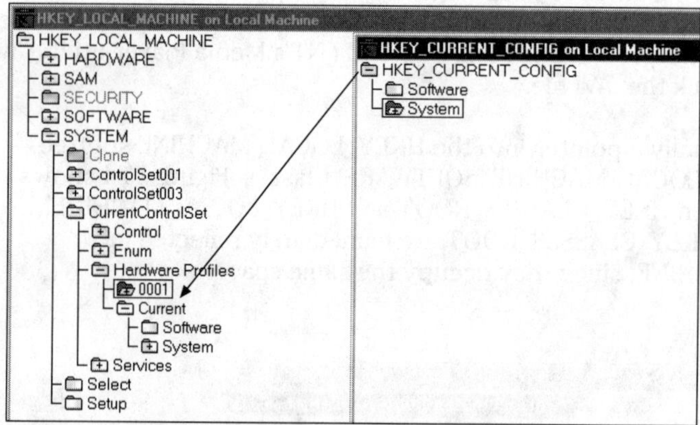

Figure 20-5: HKEY_CURRENT_CONFIG actually points inside the HKEY_LOCAL_MACHINE subtree.

I discussed management of hardware profiles in some detail in Chapter 17. This subtree stores the profile information that you generated using Control Panel applications. In general, it's best not to edit this portion of the registry directly, since Control Panel applications (specifically System, Services, and Devices) provide you with full control over hardware profile management.

The HKEY_USERS Subtree

The HKEY_USERS subtree, which exists at the database root, contains user profiles for all user accounts on the computer. Recall from Chapter 17 that user profiles contain environment information (such as desktop settings) specific to an individual user account.

This subtree also contains a default user profile (appropriately called ".DEFAULT") that's summoned when a new user logs on for the first time. Then, when the first-time user logs off, his or her profile information is saved in HKEY_USERS under the SID (security ID) assigned to that user account.

The HKEY_CURRENT_USER Subtree

The HKEY_CURRENT_USER subtree contains the user profile information associated with the user who's currently logged on to the local computer. The contents of this subtree change, depending on which account is used to log on to the computer.

This subtree is actually a pointer into the HKEY_USERS subtree. As you can see in Figure 20-6, each user profile on the computer is stored under its own unique SID within the HKEY_USERS subtree. HKEY_CURRENT_USER points to the SID associated with the user who's currently logged on. Notice that the SIDs under HKEY_USERS always start with an *S* and are very long, unique numbers. Since there are two SIDs listed, you can tell that only two accounts have logged on to this computer, so they're the only ones with established profiles. Changes made in HKEY_CURRENT_USER are immediately reflected in HKEY_USERS, since they occupy the same space.

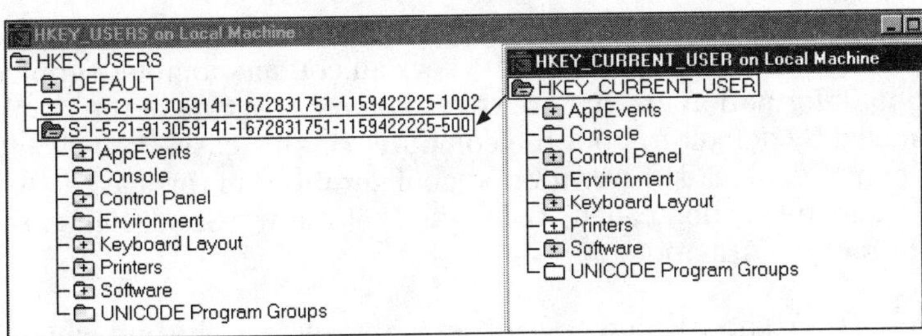

Figure 20-6: HKEY_CURRENT_USER actually points inside the HKEY_USERS subtree.

Understanding Control Sets

The HKEY_LOCAL_MACHINE\SYSTEM subtree is intimately involved in the NT boot process. It contains all of the information required to start the operating system (other than the basic hardware data that's provided automatically in the HKEY_LOCAL_MACHINE\HARDWARE subtree). Thus, most of the modifications that you make to troubleshoot the boot process will be made in the SYSTEM registry database file. Figure 20-7 shows what's stored under SYSTEM.

The Setup and DISK keys are used exclusively by the operating system, so I won't discuss their contents. I'll discuss the roles of the Select, CurrentControlSet, ControlSet001, ControlSet002, and Clone keys in the boot process.

You may see a different combination of numbered control sets. Typically, only two control sets are stored in the SYSTEM subtree, but there can be up to four. The numbers may or may not be sequential. For example, on another computer in my office, the SYSTEM subtree contains ControlSet001 and ControlSet003. For the sake of discussion, I'll use ControlSet001 and ControlSet002 in the examples.

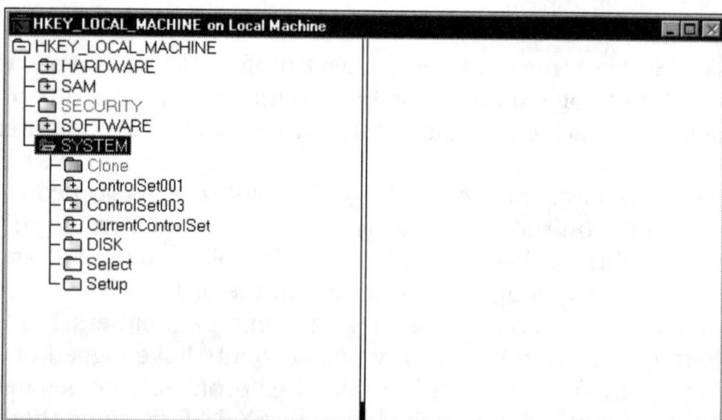

Figure 20-7: The SYSTEM subtree stores information required for booting the operating system.

The ControlSet001, ControlSet002, and Clone keys all contain complete copies of the required boot information in what are called *control sets.* One of the numbered control sets is used by default to boot the computer (in this case, ControlSet001), and the other contains the Last Known Good configuration (in this case, ControlSet002). See the section called "Using the Last Known Good Configuration" in Chapter 9 for more information.

How does Windows NT know which control set is the current one and which is the Last Known Good configuration? The Select key keeps track of this information, as shown in Figure 20-8. The Current value (0x1) indicates that ControlSet001 was used to boot the computer this time and that CurrentControlSet points to it. The Default value (0x1) indicates that ControlSet001 is used by default to start the computer. The Failed value indicates which control set last failed to boot, requiring use of the Last Known Good configuration. A value of zero indicates that none of the configurations have failed. The LastKnownGood value (0x2) indicates that ControlSet002 contains the Last Known Good configuration, which you can select during the boot process.

For administrative convenience, CurrentControlSet is a pointer to whichever control set was used to boot the computer. In this case, CurrentControlSet points to ControlSet001, as shown in Figure 20-8. So, by editing CurrentControlSet, you're assured that the changes are made to whichever control set is currently in force. There's no need to look under the Select key to figure out which control set is the current one.

What about the Clone key, and why is it grayed out? Each time that the computer starts, the control set used to boot the system is copied to the Clone key. If the startup is successful, the Clone contents are copied to another control set key, which is used as the Last Known Good configuration during the next boot process. The previous Last Known Good configuration is discarded.

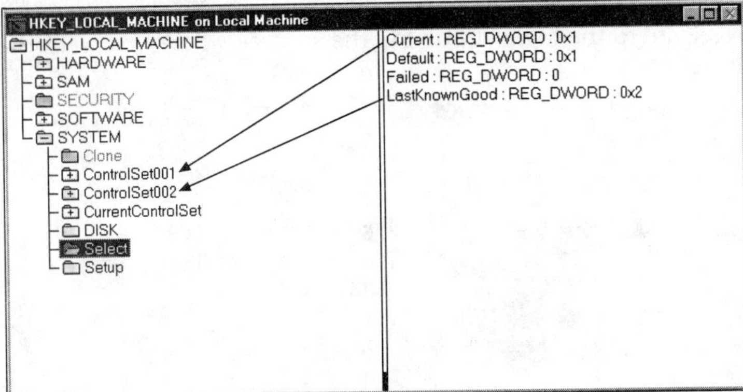

Figure 20-8: The Select key keeps track of which control set was used to boot the computer and which one is the Last Known Good configuration.

Conceptually, this is similar to saving multiple copies of CONFIG.SYS under DOS, including a backup copy that's known to boot the computer correctly. The good news is that NT takes care of saving the latest working configuration and allows you to revert to it during the boot process.

Managing the Windows NT Registry

Most of the work that you do on the registry will be through Control Panel applications, User Manager for Domains, or other graphical interfaces provided with NT Server. You'll also see instructions in various places (including Chapter 21) that require editing the registry directly with Registry Editor.

The goal of the following sections is to provide you with the skills needed to carry out those instructions and to avoid registry problems. I can't provide you with the details of the contents of the registry. Microsoft's *Windows NT Resource Guide,* which is part of the Windows NT Resource Kit, devotes over 220 pages to describing all of the registry keys and their values. The kit also includes REGENTRY.HLP, an online Help version of the registry key descriptions. See Appendix C for details on the NT Resource Kit.

Finding Registry Keys

One of the biggest headaches in working with the registry is remembering where a particular key is stored so that you can view or modify its value entries. Fortunately, Registry Editor supplies a simple search function. Here's how to find a needle in a haystack — er, a key within the registry.

1. Click the Registry Editor window containing the subtree that you want to search. Navigate to the highest point in the subtree where you want the search to begin.
2. On the View menu, click Find Key. You'll see the Find dialog box, as shown in Figure 20-9.

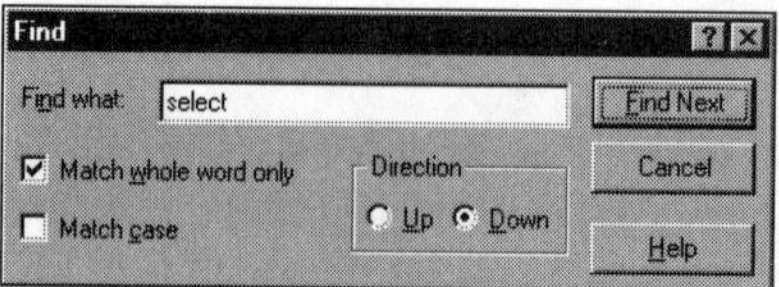

Figure 20-9: You can search for a particular key within the registry database.

3. Type the name of the key that you want to find. If you're sure of its capitalization, click to select the Match case check box. If you've specified the entire key name, click to select the Match whole word only check box.

   You can search for the partial name of a key by clicking to clear the Match whole word only check box.

   In this example, Direction is set to Down, since we're searching from the highest point in the subtree. You can search up the tree as well by clicking Up.

4. Click Find Next. If it finds a match to the key for which you're looking, Registry Editor positions you to that key in the database. If it finds the key that you want, click Cancel. If you want to continue the search, repeat step 4 until you've found the key that you want.

Unfortunately, you can't search for a value entry name, so get into the habit of thinking (and remembering) the names of keys, so that you'll be able to search for them easily if you forget where a key is located.

Fortunately, some enterprising software developers have created third-party tools that can simplify your search in the registry. For example, the Somarsoft DumpReg utility dumps the NT registry as text, making it easy to find keys and values matching a particular string. Entries can be sorted according to the time that they were last modified, letting you see changes made by recently installed software. You can download an evaluation copy, which has printing and Clipboard functions disabled, from `http://www.somarsoft.com`. A fully functional version costs $10. The Opalis Grep_Reg utility recursively searches for a string in the registry. It's available free from `http://www.opalis.com/goodies.html`.

Editing Registry Value Entries

Once you've found the key whose value(s) you want to edit, here's what to do:

1. On the Options menu, click to clear Read Only Mode, so that you can alter a value in the registry.
2. In the left-hand window, navigate to the key whose value(s) you want to edit. Make sure that the value entry that you want to edit is visible in the right-hand window.
3. Double-click the value entry that you want to edit.
4. An Editor dialog box appears, appropriate to the data type that you're editing. Type your new value.

This is the moment of truth. Once you click OK in this dialog box, you've changed the registry. Before you click OK, you can still change your mind by clicking Cancel. Remember that Registry Editor won't check the validity of your data, so if you make an error, you won't know until later when something doesn't work or the computer doesn't boot. Be careful!

Figure 20-10 shows an example of the String Editor dialog box, which is used for editing REG_SZ and REG_EXPAND_SZ data types. REG_MULTI_SZ strings are edited with the Multi-String Editor dialog box, as shown in Figure 20-11. In this case, type or edit each string, pressing ENTER after each one.

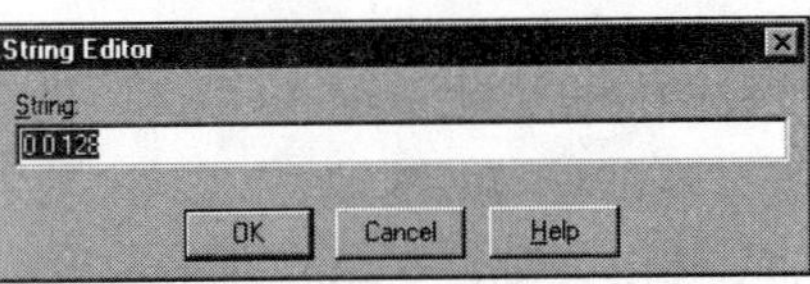

Figure 20-10: You can edit REG_SZ and REG_EXPAND_SZ string values using the String Editor dialog box.

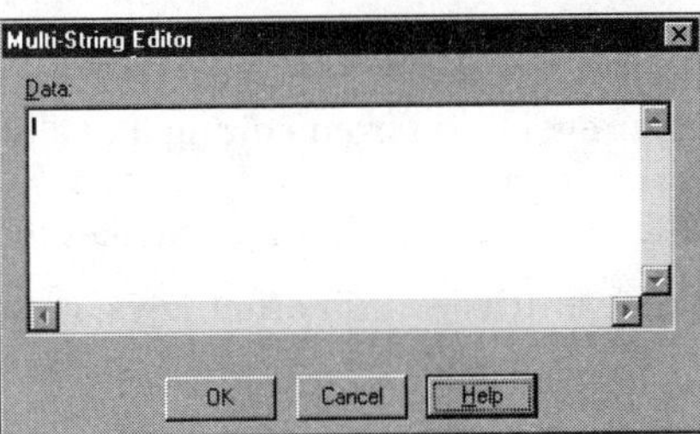

Figure 20-11: You can edit REG_MULTI_SZ values using the Multi-String Editor dialog box.

Figure 20-12 shows an example of the DWORD Editor dialog box. Under Radix, you can click Binary, Decimal, or Hex, depending on how you want to enter the value. This doesn't affect how the value will be displayed after you've edited it — it will still show up in hexadecimal.

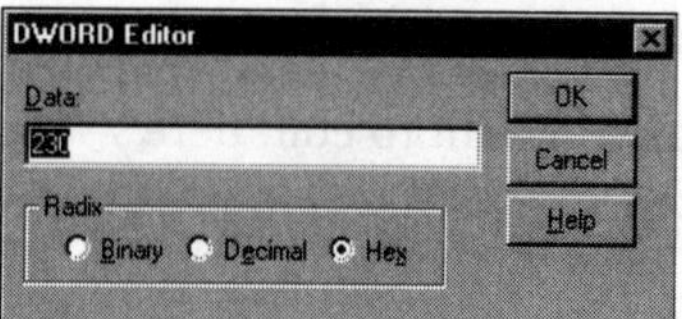

Figure 20-12: You can select decimal, hexadecimal, or binary format when editing REG_DWORDs.

Figure 20-13 shows an example of the Binary Editor dialog box. Under Data Format, you can click Binary or Hex, depending on how you want to enter the data. This doesn't affect how the data will be displayed after you've edited it — it will still be in hexadecimal.

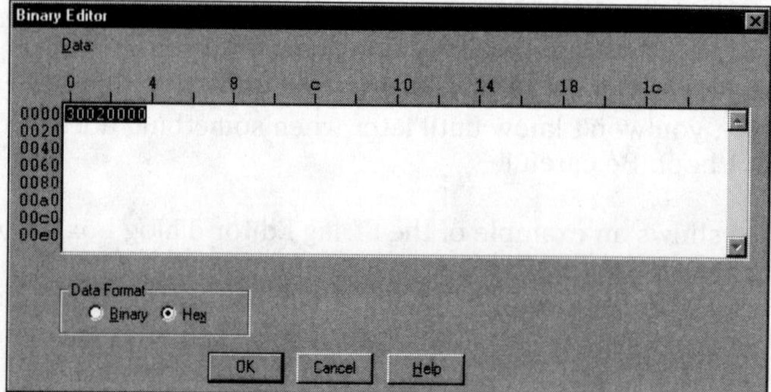

Figure 20-13: You can edit binary data using the Binary Editor dialog box.

5. Click OK. The value entry displayed by Registry Editor immediately reflects your change.

If the key that you're editing is a volatile key (not stored in a registry database file), Registry Editor may tell you and prevent you from editing its value entry.

6. If you want to edit additional value entries within the same key, go to step 3.
7. If you want to edit additional value entries within other keys, go to step 2.
8. When you're done editing value entries, click to select Read Only Mode on the Options menu.

Adding Registry Keys

In rare cases, you might need to add a key to the registry. For example, if you must install a device driver that doesn't have its own installation program (ouch!), the manufacturer may instruct you to add a registry key in a specific location within the registry hierarchy, then add value entries that the driver expects. (If this happens to you, complain loudly to the device manufacturer, request that they write an installation program, and then read on.)

Here's how to add a key to the registry:

1. On the Options menu, click to clear Read Only Mode, which allows you to add a key to the registry.
2. Navigate to the key under which you want to add the new key. Select it and click Add Key on the Edit menu.

   Alternatively, you can press the INSERT key to quickly bring up the Add Key dialog box.
3. In the Key Name field, type the name of the new key. Leave the Class field blank, as shown in Figure 20-14.

The name that you assign to the new key can't contain any backslash (\) characters and must be unique, relative to other key names at the same level in the hierarchy. You can't create two keys at the same level with the same name.

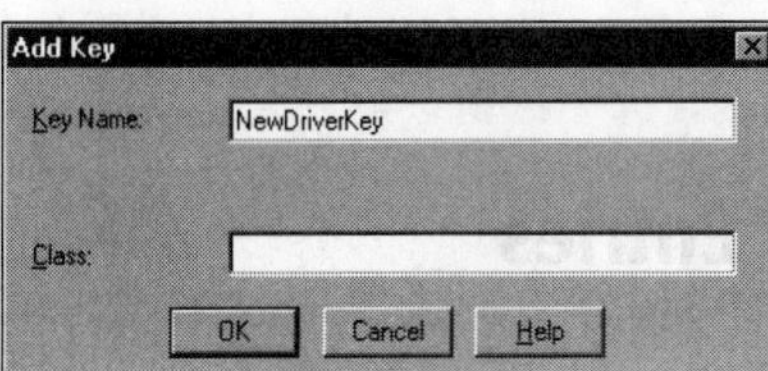

Figure 20-14: You can add a new key by specifying its unique name.

4. Click OK. The new key is now visible in the left-hand window. If you need to add more new keys, go to step 2.
5. When you're done adding keys, click to select Read Only Mode on the Options menu.

The key that you've successfully added to the registry is empty. You can now add additional subkeys within it by following the same instructions that you just completed in this section. You can also add value entries within the key by completing the steps in the next section.

Adding Value Entries

If you've added a new key to the registry, or you need to follow instructions that require adding a value to an existing registry key, here's how to do it:

1. On the Options menu, click to clear Read Only Mode, which allows you to add a value to the registry.

2. Navigate to the key to which you want to add a value entry. Select it and click Add Value on the Edit menu.
3. Figure 20-15 shows the Add Value dialog box. In the Value Name field, type the name of the value entry. In the Data Type list, select the data type that you want to use for this value entry.

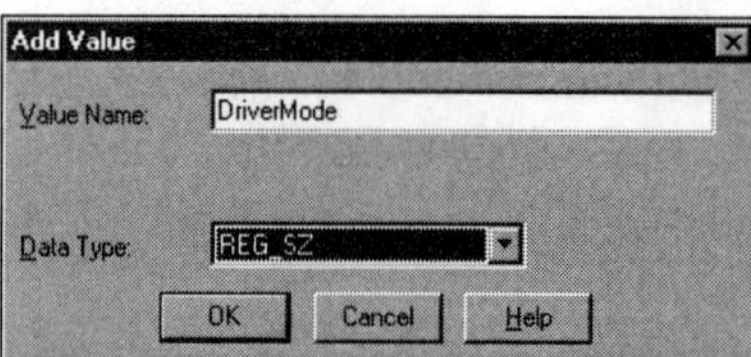

Figure 20-15: You can add a value entry to a key by specifying its name and data type.

4. Click OK. Depending on the data type that you selected, you'll see an appropriate Editor dialog box. Follow the instructions in steps 4 and 5 of the section called "Editing Registry Value Entries," earlier in this chapter.
5. If you want to add more value entries, go to step 2.
6. When you're done adding value entries, click to select Read Only Mode on the Options menu.

Deleting Keys and Value Entries

Deleting items from the registry is very risky business. Once you delete a key or a value entry, there's no "undo" function to get it back. The only way to retrieve it is by rebooting the computer using the Last Known Good configuration (assuming the key or value that you need to restore wasn't created since the computer was last started). See Chapter 9 for details.

If you must resort to this approach, you'll lose all of the configuration changes made since you last started the computer. So, make sure to pay attention to what you're deleting and make sure that you have the Confirm on Delete command checked on the Options menu before proceeding.

Here's how to delete an existing key or value entry from the registry:

1. On the Options menu, click to clear Read Only Mode, which allows you to delete a key or value from the registry.
2. Navigate to the key or value that you want to delete and select it.

If you want to delete only a value, be sure that you've selected the value in the right half of the window. Otherwise, you'll delete the entire key that contains the value.

If you elect to delete a key, you'll also delete all subkeys and value entries under that key. In other words, if the key that you select represents a subtree of the registry, you're deleting that entire subtree.

3. Press DELETE.
4. If you are 110 percent sure that you've selected the correct key or value entry for deletion, click Yes to confirm.

   Unfortunately, the confirmation dialog box doesn't show you what you're deleting. If there's any doubt in your mind, click No and go back to verify that you've selected what you want to delete.
5. When you're done deleting keys or value entries, click to select Read Only Mode on the Options menu.

Managing the Registry of a Remote Computer

One of the very cool (and extremely dangerous) features of Registry Editor is its ability to reach into registry databases on other NT computers and view or modify their configurations remotely. This can be handy if a user has rendered a computer unusable in some way, but the operating system is still running. For example, I may accidentally change all of my screen colors to bright green, and now I can't see anything at all. You can come to the rescue by reaching into my registry and readjusting my screen colors to something usable. (Don't relate this example to your users. They might try it, and then you'll have lots of extra work to do cleaning up after them.)

Here's how to use Registry Editor to edit another NT computer's registry:

1. On the Registry menu, click Select Computer. In the Select Computer dialog box, type or select the name of the computer that you want to manage. Then click OK.
2. You may see a warning indicating that the AutoRefresh feature isn't available remotely and will be disabled. Click OK.

   This means that changes made to the registry won't automatically be reflected on the display. Refreshing is disabled to avoid unnecessary network traffic. If you want to refresh the contents of the Registry Editor windows, you must manually click Refresh All on the View menu.
3. You'll see new windows in the Registry Editor for the HKEY_LOCAL_MACHINE and HKEY_USERS subtrees of the remote computer, as shown in Figure 20-16.

   If you have the appropriate access rights, you can view and modify keys and value entries in the remote registry using the instructions presented earlier in this chapter. If you have administrator privileges on the remote computer, you'll be able to perform these operations.

You see only two subtree views of a remote computer compared to the five subtrees that you see when editing the local registry. Recall from earlier in this chapter that the remaining three subtrees are really just pointers to locations within the HKEY_LOCAL_MACHINE and HKEY_USERS subtrees. So, with a little mental translation, you can still get to everything in the remote registry. See the section called "Understanding Registry Subtrees" earlier in this chapter.

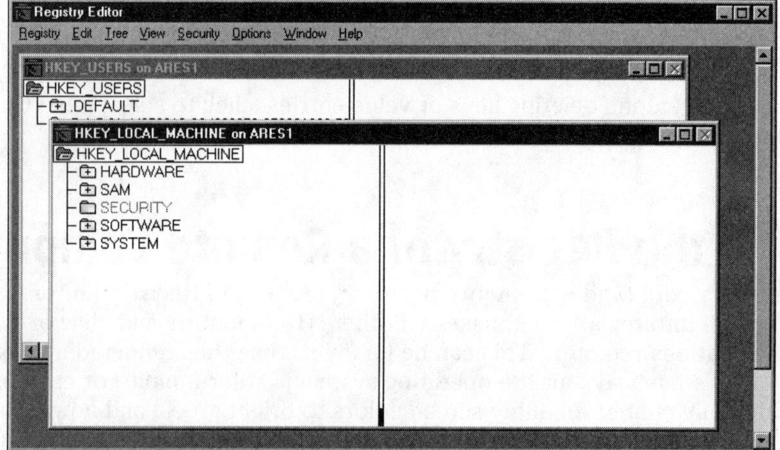

Figure 20-16: You can view and edit the HKEY_LOCAL_MACHINE and HKEY_USERS subtrees on a remote computer.

Managing Registry Security

As I've stressed in this chapter, monkeying around with the Windows NT registry can be dangerous business. In inexperienced or malicious hands, Registry Editor can wreak havoc on your NT computers, if you don't take some security precautions. Here are some guidelines to add to your security plan, if you haven't already included them:

✦ Never add users to the Administrators group unless they're responsible for administering the network. Even granting temporary access opens up a window on all NT computers' registries.

✦ Never leave Registry Editor running on your computer unattended.

✦ Use Registry Editor to restrict permissions to specific user accounts, as described later in this section.

✦ Use Registry Editor to audit changes made to registry databases, as described later in this section. Review the audit logs periodically so you know who's doing what to registries.

✦ Consider removing REGEDT32.EXE from all NT computers that don't need to manage registry databases. You may want to designate one or two physically secured server computers as central points for all registry administration.

Removing the REGEDT32 utility won't thwart the malicious user, who'll find a way to get his or her hands on the Registry Editor program. It will, however, eliminate the problem of curious users running all the programs on their computers just to "see what they do."

✦ Use NTFS for your boot partition (where the NT SystemRoot tree is stored, including the registry database files). If you don't use NTFS, you won't be able to secure the individual database files.

Loaded registry database files are held open by the operating system while it's running, so they can't be deleted. However, database files that aren't loaded (user profiles, for example) aren't held open and can be deleted by users if they're not protected by NTFS file permissions.

You can assign permissions to an individual key within a registry database, audit events that involve a specific key or subtree below a key, and take ownership of a key. These functions work just as they do for files, as described in detail in Chapter 18. Figure 20-17 shows the Registry Key Permissions dialog box that appears when you select a key and click Security ➪ Permissions. Figure 20-18 shows the Registry Key Auditing dialog box that appears sure when you click Auditing on the Security menu. See Chapter 18 for details on how to work with permissions and auditing objects.

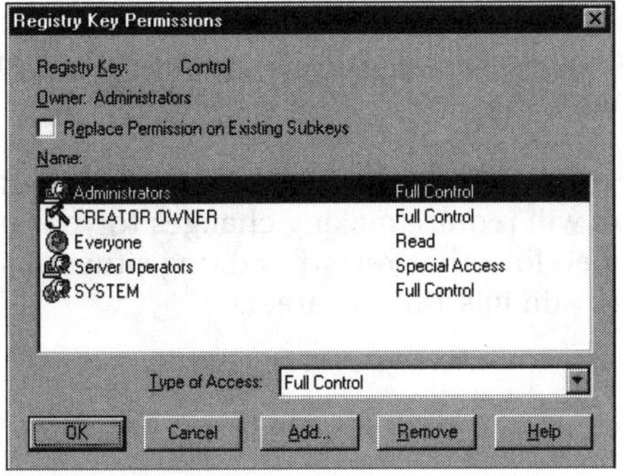

Figure 20-17: You can set permissions on individual registry keys.

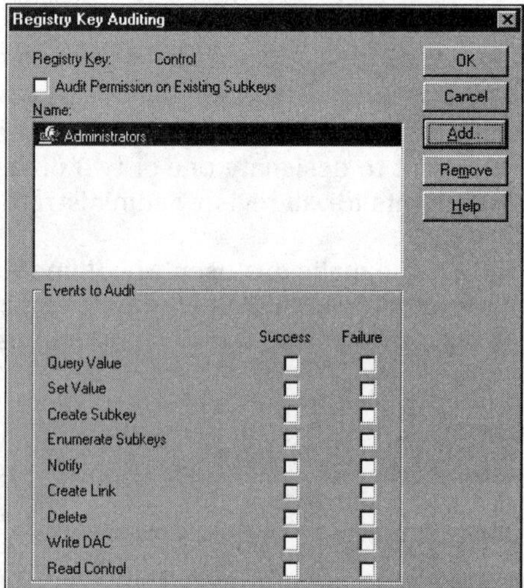

Figure 20-18: You can audit security events involving specific registry keys.

Restricting permissions on registry keys can cause components of the operating system that manipulate those keys to fail. Always be sure to provide full access for the Administrators group and System. This will allow the computer to boot and enable administrators to change the permissions, if they're too restrictive.

Summary

Well, did I warn you enough about the perils of registry editing? I hope that you'll treat registry editing at least as gingerly as building your house of cards. As I mentioned earlier, there's no getting around the need to know how to do it. In this chapter, you've picked up the basic knowledge and skills that will allow you to perform these tasks when necessary. You've learned how to examine and modify the registry using NT's powerful and dangerous Registry Editor. Hopefully, you've been warned enough that it really is hazardous.

In Chapter 21, you'll have a chance to exercise your registry-editing skills. Some of the tips and tricks that you'll find there will require making changes to your NT Server's registry. This will get you primed for other registry-editing situations that you may encounter in your NT network administration career.

INSIDE STORY

"A hive! . . . Yeah, what you need is a new hive . . . Don't ask me from where!" I could almost make out the desperate queries on the other end of the phone, as I listened to the one-sided conversation in my office. When the development engineer finally banged down the receiver, he whirled around in his chair and sneered, "What a bozo! He was using an obsolete hive. When I told him what he needed, he didn't even know what I was talking about. Maybe I should have called it a registry. Umph!"

"Hive" was the original term used within Microsoft to describe the registry, since it's the place where all the "honey" (critical configuration data) is stored in a compartmentalized way (similar to a bee hive, although I've never actually been inside one). In NT's manuals, online Help, and other NT literature, you'll often find the term hive used to describe the actual individual files that make up the registry database.

Early on in the NT project, when engineers tried to modify their own registries and then couldn't boot their computers, their systems were said to have "a case of the hives." As new revisions of registry databases were made available by the software build team on a centralized server, the e-mail announcement sometimes read, "Get the hives from the server." Anxious engineers were typically just itching to get at these new files.

NT Server Tips, Tricks, and Troubleshooting

✦ ✦ ✦ ✦

Have you ever tried to perform magic tricks such as pulling an endless string of scarves from your sleeve or extracting a quarter out of your niece's ear? You know that what looks like magic to some is really just a secret technique that's typically quite simple. If you know the trick and give it lots of practice, you can make amazing, seemingly magical things happen.

So it is with NT network administration. If you know what nooks and crannies to visit, and you know the mechanics of what to do when you get there, you can perform amazing feats. In this chapter, you'll pick up a wide range of tips, tricks, and troubleshooting techniques that will help you get the most out of your NT Server network and occasionally raise you to heroic status in the eyes of your users. I'll introduce you to the available troubleshooting tools and provide specific guidance on how to tweak your servers to match your specific environment. By the end of this chapter, you'll have a bag of tricks at your side that will serve you well in your network administration adventures.

Many of the techniques presented in this chapter involve editing the NT registry. Before proceeding with any registry changes, be sure to read Chapter 20, which strongly emphasizes the risks involved. Editing the registry can be hazardous to the health of your NT computer!

Windows NT Troubleshooting Tools

Windows NT Server provides several troubleshooting tools that help you gather information to diagnose and resolve problems. In the following sections, I'll introduce you to these tools.

Using Windows NT Diagnostics

NT includes a handy tool called Windows NT Diagnostics, with which you can examine detailed configuration information stored in the registry. It's better suited for viewing this information than the Registry Editor since it presents the information in a meaningful way and doesn't give you the chance to change it. Although much of this information is available through other applications (in Control Panel, for example), Windows NT Diagnostics provides a convenient way to examine several aspects of the system in one package.

To start NT Diagnostics, click Start ➪ Programs ➪ Administrative Tools ➪ Windows NT Diagnostics. You're presented with nine tabs, which give you access to the following data:

- ✦ **Version** displays operating system version information.
- ✦ **System** shows you the status of the computer's bus, BIOS, and CPUs. It also indicates which HAL is being used.
- ✦ **Display** provides detailed data on the video adapter and its driver.
- ✦ **Drives** presents a list of local and network-connected drives. Double-click an icon to expand the list of drives and to see additional detail. You can display drives by letter or by drive type.
- ✦ **Memory** provides information on memory usage, including the details shown by Task Manager on the Performance tab. It also gives you details about usage of each paging file on your computer.

- ✦ **Services** lets you view the state of all installed services and drivers on the computer. This is essentially the same information that you see in the Devices and Services applications in Control Panel, discussed in Chapter 17.
- ✦ **Resources** contains detailed information on which drivers are using which IRQs, I/O port address ranges, DMA channels, and memory mapped address ranges. This is probably the most valuable part of the utility. See Figures 21-1, 21-2, and 21-3 for three of the five available resource views.

Windows NT Diagnostics is the first place to look if you've made hardware configuration changes and you want to verify that you don't have conflicts and that NT sees the configuration that you expect it to see. The registry contains the same information, but it's very difficult to pull it all together in one place, the way that Windows NT Diagnostics has managed to do.

✦ **Environment** lets you view the list of all system and user environment variables. This is the same information that you can find in Control Panel's System application on the Environment tab.

✦ **Network** provides details on current network settings and status, including several network performance counters. This is a handy way to see the general status of your network components at a glance.

Windows NT Diagnostics has no Help file, so you'll have to use your judgment in interpreting the displayed network statistics. It's not always clear how they map to the counters available in Performance Monitor, described in Chapter 19.

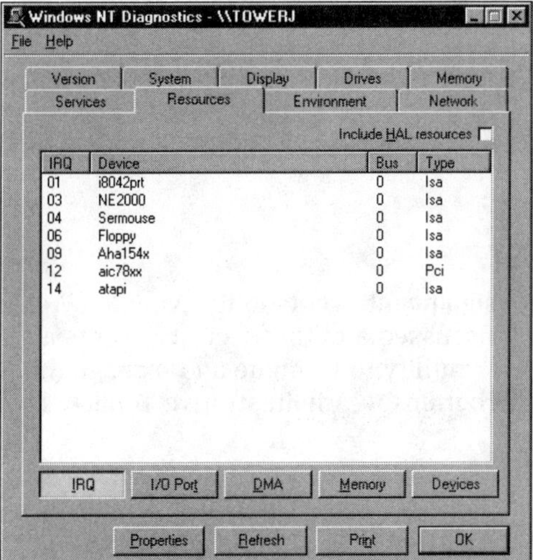

Figure 21-1: You can see which devices are using which IRQs.

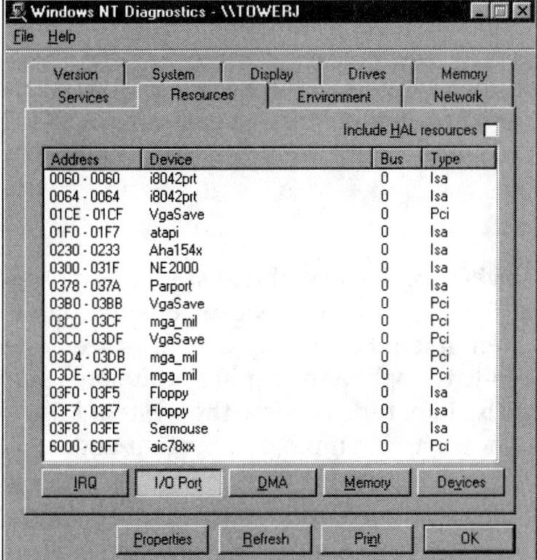

Figure 21-2: You can examine the I/O port address ranges assigned to each device.

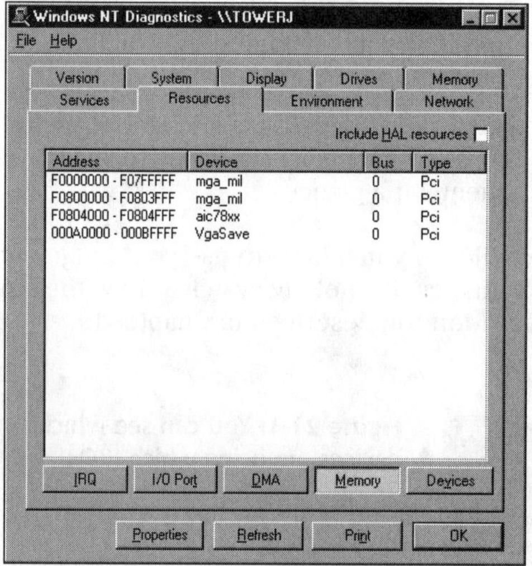

Figure 21-3: You can also see the memory address ranges assigned to each device.

Introducing Event Viewer

Windows NT Server keeps a record of significant events in its event log. You saw a glimpse of this in Chapter 18, where I discussed auditing security events and viewing the results. You use the Event Viewer utility to examine and manage the NT event log. Start it by clicking Start ➪ Programs ➪ Administrative Tools ➪ Event Viewer.

As with other NT administrative tools, you can use Event Viewer to reach into another computer's event log. Just click Log ➪ Select Computer, type or select the computer whose log you want to view, and click OK. This enables you to administer the logs of several computers from a central location. You can even clear logs remotely.

Event Viewer only displays the events that were logged before you started the utility. It doesn't automatically update the display when new events are logged. To update the display manually at any time, click Refresh on the View menu.

Rolling off Three Logs

NT actually maintains three different event log flavors: the System Log, the Security Log, and the Application Log. The System Log records events that are of significance to components of the system itself. For example, events are added to the System Log when a device driver fails to load, a mirror set completes synchronization, or a hardware device conflict is detected. To view the System Log, click System on the Log menu. Figure 21-4 shows an example of a System Log.

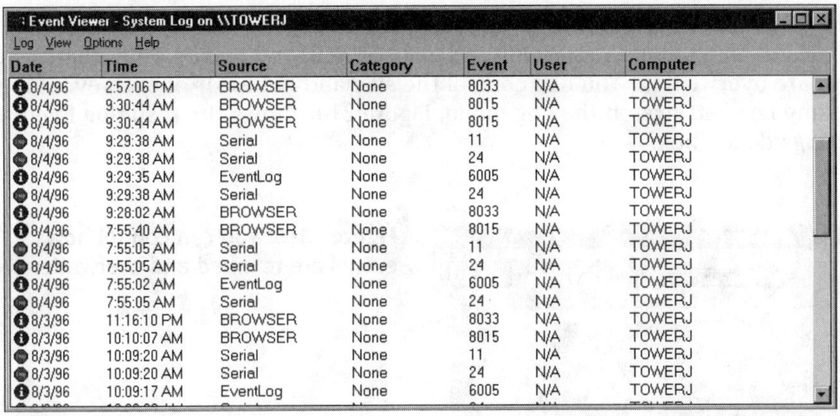

Event Viewer - System Log on \\TOWERJ

Log View Options Help

Date	Time	Source	Category	Event	User	Computer
8/4/96	2:57:06 PM	BROWSER	None	8033	N/A	TOWERJ
8/4/96	9:30:44 AM	BROWSER	None	8015	N/A	TOWERJ
8/4/96	9:30:44 AM	BROWSER	None	8015	N/A	TOWERJ
8/4/96	9:29:38 AM	Serial	None	11	N/A	TOWERJ
8/4/96	9:29:38 AM	Serial	None	24	N/A	TOWERJ
8/4/96	9:29:35 AM	EventLog	None	6005	N/A	TOWERJ
8/4/96	9:29:38 AM	Serial	None	24	N/A	TOWERJ
8/4/96	9:28:02 AM	BROWSER	None	8033	N/A	TOWERJ
8/4/96	7:55:40 AM	BROWSER	None	8015	N/A	TOWERJ
8/4/96	7:55:05 AM	Serial	None	11	N/A	TOWERJ
8/4/96	7:55:05 AM	Serial	None	24	N/A	TOWERJ
8/4/96	7:55:02 AM	EventLog	None	6005	N/A	TOWERJ
8/4/96	7:55:05 AM	Serial	None	24	N/A	TOWERJ
8/3/96	11:16:10 PM	BROWSER	None	8033	N/A	TOWERJ
8/3/96	10:10:07 AM	BROWSER	None	8015	N/A	TOWERJ
8/3/96	10:09:20 AM	Serial	None	11	N/A	TOWERJ
8/3/96	10:09:20 AM	Serial	None	24	N/A	TOWERJ
8/3/96	10:09:17 AM	EventLog	None	6005	N/A	TOWERJ

Figure 21-4: The System Log contains events generated by NT system components.

The Security Log houses security auditing events based on the auditing settings that you specify in User Manager for Domains, as discussed in Chapter 18. Only administrators have access to the Security Log. To view it, click Security on the Log menu. Figure 18-61 in Chapter 18 provides an example of a Security Log.

The Application Log keeps track of events logged by applications. For example, NT Backup (discussed in Chapter 18) adds events to the Application Log when it begins and ends various phases of the backup process. Performance Monitor (covered in Chapter 19) puts events in the Application Log when an alert condition that you specified is triggered. If NT has to repair inconsistencies on disk during the boot process, the AUTOCHK program logs events to record what it fixed. To view the Application Log, click Application on the Log menu. Figure 21-5 shows an example of an Application Log from a computer that's mainly used to run backups.

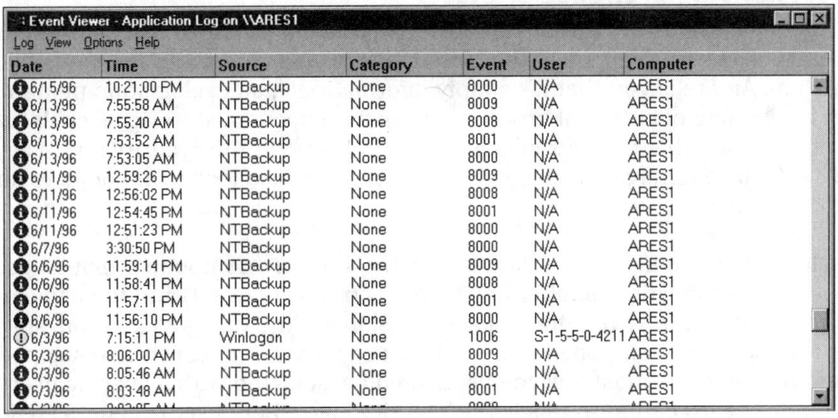

Event Viewer - Application Log on \\ARES1

Log View Options Help

Date	Time	Source	Category	Event	User	Computer
6/15/96	10:21:00 PM	NTBackup	None	8000	N/A	ARES1
6/13/96	7:55:58 AM	NTBackup	None	8009	N/A	ARES1
6/13/96	7:55:40 AM	NTBackup	None	8008	N/A	ARES1
6/13/96	7:53:52 AM	NTBackup	None	8001	N/A	ARES1
6/13/96	7:53:05 AM	NTBackup	None	8000	N/A	ARES1
6/11/96	12:59:26 PM	NTBackup	None	8009	N/A	ARES1
6/11/96	12:56:02 PM	NTBackup	None	8008	N/A	ARES1
6/11/96	12:54:45 PM	NTBackup	None	8001	N/A	ARES1
6/11/96	12:51:23 PM	NTBackup	None	8000	N/A	ARES1
6/7/96	3:30:50 PM	NTBackup	None	8000	N/A	ARES1
6/6/96	11:59:14 PM	NTBackup	None	8009	N/A	ARES1
6/6/96	11:58:41 PM	NTBackup	None	8008	N/A	ARES1
6/6/96	11:57:11 PM	NTBackup	None	8001	N/A	ARES1
6/6/96	11:56:10 PM	NTBackup	None	8000	N/A	ARES1
6/3/96	7:15:11 PM	Winlogon	None	1006	S-1-5-5-0-4211	ARES1
6/3/96	8:06:00 AM	NTBackup	None	8009	N/A	ARES1
6/3/96	8:05:46 AM	NTBackup	None	8008	N/A	ARES1
6/3/96	8:03:48 AM	NTBackup	None	8001	N/A	ARES1

Figure 21-5: The Application Log contains events generated by applications.

Controlling Event Logs

By default, each log has a maximum size of 512KB, and events older than seven days are overwritten. You can control the size and behavior of each event log by clicking Log Settings on the Log menu. Figure 21-6 shows the resulting Event Log Settings dialog box.

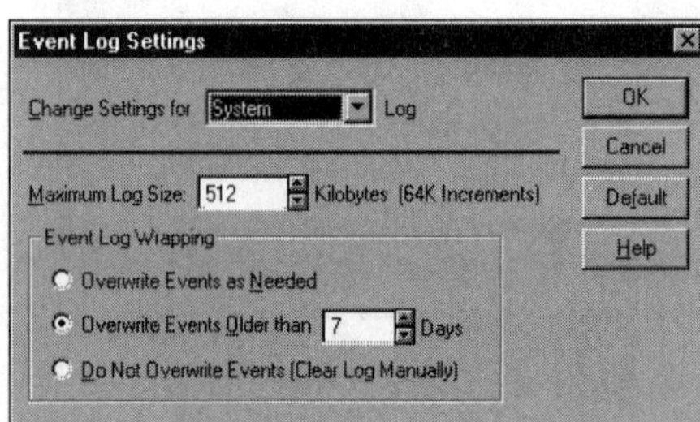

Figure 21-6: You can control how events are retained and overwritten.

To change settings, click the log that you want to change in the Change Settings for list. Type the new maximum log size in the Maximum Log Size field and click the desired retention behavior under Event Log Wrapping. Then click OK.

If you select the Do Not Overwrite Events (Clear Log Manually) option, keep two things in mind. First, you'll need to schedule a periodic visit to the Event Viewer to clear the log by hand (by clicking Log ➪ Clear All Events). Second, when the event log fills up, no more events are logged until the log is cleared. You'll get a pop-up message indicating that the log is full, but if you're not there to see it, all new events will be lost until the log is cleared. (It seems as if NT should log an event indicating that the event log is full, but that becomes sort of a Catch-22. In some cases, though, NT actually does log an event that the log is full. Go figure.)

Understanding Event Log Entries

The one-line event descriptions displayed by default provide basic information about each event. The icon at the far left gives you a clue about the severity of the situation. An *i* tells you that it's simply informational, an exclamation point indicates a warning of potential problems downstream, and a stop sign signals an error condition that has caused something to break. In the Security Log, a key icon indicates the auditing of a successful access, whereas a lock icon points to an audit of a failed access.

The log entry also includes a time stamp, the software component that logged the event, an identification number unique to each type of event, and the name of the computer where the event took place. I've skipped the Category column, since most NT software components these days don't specify one. I've also skipped the User column, since most logged events aren't associated with a specific user account. The exception to this is the Security Log, where user accounts are logged and are indeed important.

Viewing Event Details

You can get more detailed information on any event by double-clicking it. Figure 21-7 shows an example of an Event Detail dialog box reporting detection of an IRQ conflict between a serial port and a network adapter. Click Previous or Next if you want to see details of adjacent events in the log. (By default, events are listed from newest to oldest, so clicking Next has the nonintuitive behavior of moving to the next oldest event.)

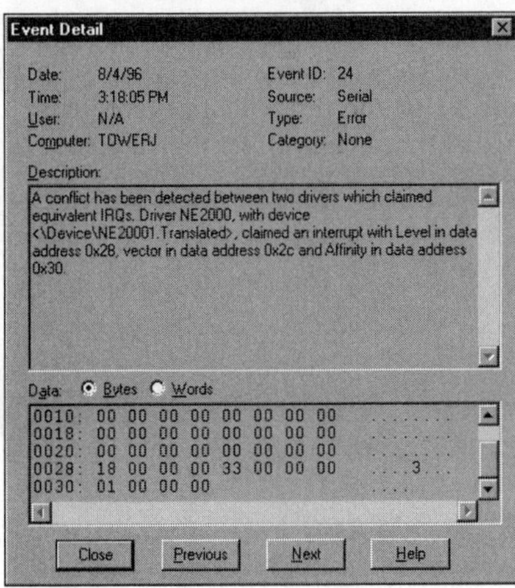

Figure 21-7: You can see more detail on an event by double-clicking its one-line description.

The additional detail on each event consists of a text message under Description and some associated raw binary data under Data. The text often refers to specific locations in the data block, as in the example in Figure 21-7. The byte at address 0x2C within the data block indicates that IRQ 3 is the offending interrupt.

Finding and Filtering Events

You can search for a specific event based on any of the fields displayed in the one-line event description. Just click Find on the View menu. Figure 21-8 shows the resulting Find dialog box. Enter your search criteria and click Find Next to begin the search.

In addition to finding specific events, you can narrow the list of events by applying a filter. This feature can be particularly useful when you need to study what happened during a particular portion of the afternoon when the network slowed down to a crawl. Being able to narrow your focus using a filter can help you pinpoint causes of server and network behavior, without having to wade through reams of superfluous logged events. On the View menu, click Filter Events, specify your filter criteria, and click OK. When you want to go back to viewing all events, click View ➪ All Events. Figure 21-9 illustrates this.

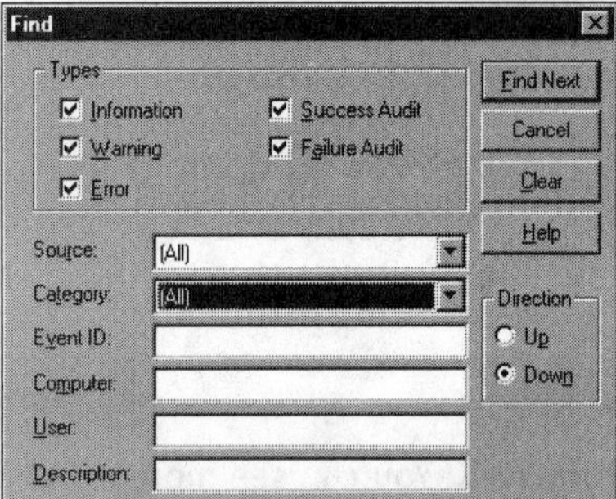

Figure 21-8: You can search for events based on any of the displayed fields.

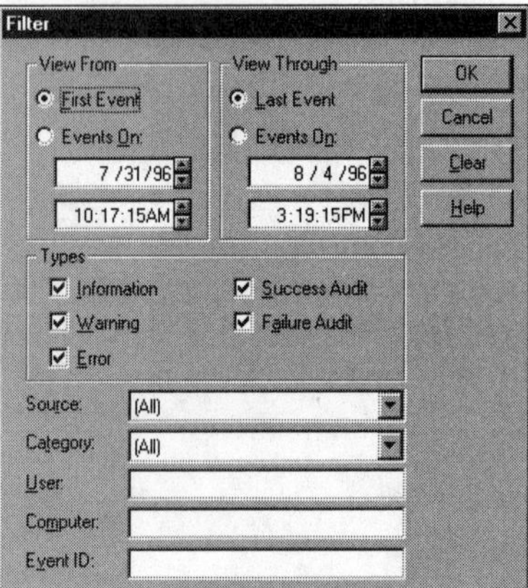

Figure 21-9: You can filter an event log to view just those events that match your criteria.

You can use Event Viewer to look at an event log on a LAN Manager 2.x server as well as on an NT server. You can even filter it, as described in this section. However, since the information contained in a LAN Manager 2.x event log is different from that on NT, you can only filter the information based on the time stamp in the event log entry. View From and View Through are the only filters that you can use for these servers; the rest are ignored.

Saving and Viewing Event Log Files

The act of clearing events from a log is a destructive process. Once you clear them, you can't retrieve them. Likewise, when old events are overwritten as new ones are added to the log, the old events are lost forever. So, you may want to save event logs to disk. Here's how:

1. Select the log that you want to save by clicking either System, Security, or Application on the Log menu.
2. If you simply want to save the current event log without deleting existing events, click Save As on the Log menu and go to step 5.

3. On the Log menu, click Clear All Events.
4. Click Yes to confirm that you want to save the log before clearing it.
5. In the Save as type list, select Event Log Files (which can be viewed later with Event Viewer), Text Files, or Comma-Delim. Text. Type or select the filename that you want to use and click Save.
   Note that binary event log data is dropped from text files.

If you want a printed copy of a log file for future reference, save it as comma-delimited text and then print that file. If you plan on viewing a log later with Event Viewer, save it in event log format. You can always save it again as text if you want to print it.

To view a saved event log file, click Open on the Log menu, specify the file and click Open. In the Open File Type dialog box, click the type of log that the file represents: System, Security, or Application. The saved file doesn't include the type of the original log. If you select the wrong type, the detailed descriptions of the events will probably be incorrect.

Employing Dr. Watson

Dr. Watson has been unemployed ever since Sherlock Holmes stopped solving cases. It's time to put him back to work. Dr. Watson is NT's post-mortem debugger for Win32 applications. (If you're familiar with Windows 3.1, its Dr. Watson utility performed a similar function for Win16 applications.) It can be a valuable troubleshooting tool if you're getting exception conditions in applications supplied with NT, third-party applications, or applications that you're developing in-house. In the first two cases, it provides valuable information that you can share with product support personnel over the phone or electronically.

Unless you're proficient with assembly language and Win32 programming, the information supplied by Dr. Watson won't make much sense to you. It's valuable, however, to whoever developed the offending Win32 application.

If a Win32 application generates an exception, Dr. Watson will catch it, generate a detailed log file, and log an event in the NT event log. The detailed file, which is stored by default in SystemRoot\DRWTSN32.LOG, includes system configuration information, a list of applications that were running at the time of the exception, details of the exception, and the state of each thread.

Dr. Watson is enabled by default when you install Windows NT, even though it doesn't appear as an icon on the Task Manager list of processes. It operates completely invisibly until a Win32 application error occurs.

Here's how to configure Dr. Watson's diagnostic behavior:

1. Click Start ➪ Run. Type **DRWTSN32** and click OK.

   You'll see the Dr. Watson for Windows NT dialog box as shown in Figure 21-10.

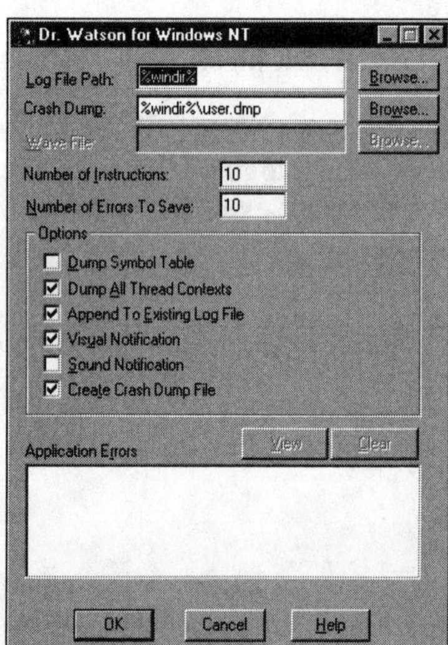

Figure 21-10: Dr. Watson enables you to log Win32 application errors.

2. In the Log File Path field, type the path of the folder where you want the DRWTSN32.LOG file written.

The folder into which Dr. Watson writes his logs must be accessible for read and write by all users of the computer. Rather than giving write permissions to the SystemRoot folder to all of your user accounts, I recommend creating a separate folder somewhere for these log files. You can grant read and write permissions to the special Everyone group and configure Dr. Watson to write his log files in the new location. That way, you can protect your SystemRoot directory.

   Dr. Watson can optionally create a crash dump file that contains a snapshot of the failed process. This file can be examined by a software engineer using the NT debugger to determine what went wrong with the application. If you want to create a dump file, click to select the Create Crash Dump File check box. In the Crash Dump field, type the full path name of the dump file that you want to create. I recommend using the same folder as you did for Log File Path.

If you have a sound card installed and configured in the computer and you click to select the Sound Notification check box, you can type the name of a .WAV file in the Wave File field. Every time that Dr. Watson catches a Win32 application error, the wave file will play. I've seen administrators assign screams, trumpets, and the ever- popular "Uh-Oh" sounds to these grim events.

3. In the Number of Instructions field, type the number of assembly language instructions that you want Dr. Watson to disassemble before and after the place in the code where the exception occurred.
4. In the Number of Errors To Save field, type the number of Win32 application errors that you want saved in the log file.

   If the number of errors exceeds this threshold, the oldest error in the log will be discarded.
5. If you want Dr. Watson to include the symbol table in the log file, click to select the Dump Symbol Table check box.

   A symbol table dump can make your log file huge. I recommend avoiding this option, unless the application vendor requests that you include it in the log.
6. Click to select the Dump All Thread Contexts, Append to Existing Log File, and Visual Notification check boxes.

   I recommend selecting each of these options. The log file needs to contain information about what each thread was doing when the exception occurred. It's always best to append to your existing log file, so that you don't lose the previous error information. You need to be notified visually, or the offending Win32 application will just quietly disappear.

Under Application Errors in the Dr. Watson for Windows NT dialog box, you can scan though the existing errors in the log. Click View to view the details of individual errors. Click Clear to clear all of the errors from the log.

Dumping Registry Subkeys

There may be times when you need to study the contents of a registry subtree (a key and everything stored under it). You can dump a registry subtree to a text file or to the printer. In Registry Editor (described in Chapter 20), select the key that you want to save or print as text. If you want to save the subtree to a text file, click Save Subtree As on the Registry menu, specify the filename, and click Save. If you want to print the subtree, click Print Subtree on the Registry menu.

Managing Memory Dump Files

As discussed in the Chapter 17 section called "Managing Crash Recovery," you can cause Windows NT to dump an image of memory to a file when it crashes. The memory dump file can then be analyzed off-line by support personnel to determine what caused the problem. (In Microsoft documentation and other sources, you'll see many terms used to describe a crash: kernel STOP error, blue screen, Blue Screen of Death, kernel error, and trap.)

If you take the approach of automatically dumping and immediately restarting the server, be sure to rename the MEMORY.DMP file after each system crash. Otherwise, the next crash will overwrite the existing MEMORY.DMP file, and you'll lose the information from the previous crash.

The size of a memory dump file is equal to the size of your computer's physical memory. A 64MB RAM size will produce a 64MB dump file. Transmitting a file of this size can sometimes pose a logistical problem. On the Windows NT Server CD-ROM in the \SUPPORT\DEBUG folder, Microsoft has included some utilities to help manage these huge files. Look in the subfolder that matches your CPU platform for the actual utility files. For example, \SUPPORT\DEBUG\I386 contains the Intel executables.

Before you go to the trouble of analyzing or transmitting a huge dump file, it's wise to verify that a valid dump file was, in fact, created. You can do this using the DUMPCHK utility. DUMPCHK analyzes all of the addresses in the dump file to make sure that they're valid. At a Command Prompt, type **DUMPCHK /?** for its command-line syntax.

Microsoft supplies DUMPEXAM to allow you to analyze memory dump files, generating a summary into a text file that can be used by support personnel to determine the cause of the system crash. (DUMPEXAM sounds to me like a test that you have to pass before you can manage a landfill.) Usually the output of DUMPEXAM provides all of the information that's needed to diagnose the problem, saving you the hassle of shipping the entire dump file for analysis. It's easiest to run DUMPEXAM right from the NT Server CD-ROM. At a Command Prompt, type **DUMPEXAM /?** for command line syntax. This utility collects debug symbol information (API names and global variable names) from symbol files in the SYMBOLS subfolder on the CD-ROM. It uses these symbols to make the dump analysis more meaningful.

If DUMPEXAM's output doesn't provide enough information to diagnose the computer's problems, you may need to ship the entire dump file to support personnel on floppy disks. Believe me, I don't envy you this tedious procedure. But if you have to do it, at least Microsoft has made the job easier by providing you with the DUMPFLOP utility. It compresses the data as it writes to each floppy, using about half as many disks as would be required for the uncompressed dump file. (That's a small comfort if you have to create 23 disks for a 64MB computer.) At a Command Prompt, type **DUMPFLOP /?** for command-line syntax.

THE CRASHDUMP AFTERMATH

When you first boot after a dump is taken, a process called SAVEDUMP will execute. Its job is to save the dump in a file so that, if another crash occurs, the first dump won't be lost. If your server has lots of RAM, this copy process can take awhile. During this period, the process can eat up huge amounts of memory, and you may get warnings that you're running low on that commodity. It's wisest just to let the copy complete before trying to do anything useful on the computer.

Sniffing for Trouble with Network Monitor

Windows NT Server 4.0 is the first version to include a copy of the Network Monitor utility that enables your computer to act as a network sniffer. (See the section called "Legitimate Eavesdropping" in Chapter 3 for a brief discussion of network sniffing.) Network Monitor used to be available only as part Microsoft's Systems Management Server (SMS).

Teaching you how to interpret the contents of network packets as they fly by on the wire is beyond the scope of this book. If you're already experienced with network sniffers, you'll be productive with Network Monitor right away. Even if you don't have this expertise, though, you can use some of the statistical features of Network Monitor for general troubleshooting.

Here's how to install Network Monitor from your Windows NT Server 4.0 CD-ROM:

1. While logged on with administrator privileges, click Start ➪ Settings ➪ Control Panel. Double-click Network to start the Network Control Panel Application (NCPA).
2. In the Network dialog box, click the Services tab. Then click Add.
3. Under Network Service, click Network Monitor Tools and Agent. Then click OK.
4. NCPA asks for the path to the system files on your Windows NT Server 4.0 CD-ROM. Insert the NT CD-ROM in your CD-ROM drive. Type the path and click Continue.

   On my computer, the path is F:\I386. Type the drive letter of your CD-ROM and the subdirectory corresponding to your CPU platform.
5. In the Network dialog box, click Close.
6. Restart your computer as prompted.

After your computer has restarted, you can run Network Monitor by clicking Start ➪ Programs ➪ Administrative Tools ➪ Network Monitor. To see it in action, on the Capture menu, click Start. If there's much network activity, you'll see the bar graphs and statistics dynamically change to reflect it, as shown in Figure 21-11.

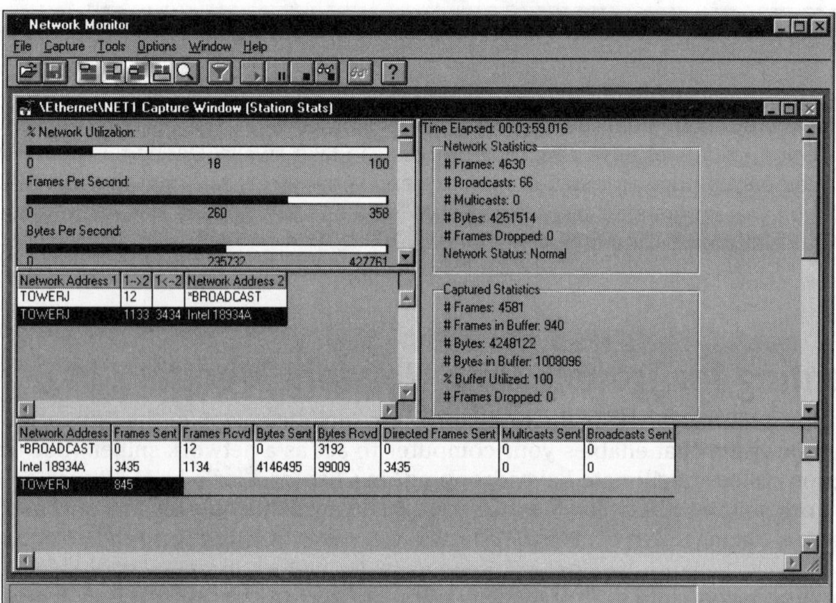

Figure 21-11: Network Monitor enables your computer to act as a network sniffer, capturing packets as they travel by.

Network Monitor is a feature-rich tool. You can capture data from the network, save it to a file for later analysis, define a trigger condition to start a capture, and filter both the captured and displayed data. You can even detect other Network Monitor installations on the network.

Like other network sniffers, the tool interprets (or *parses*) the packets for you, so you don't necessarily have to translate the individual bytes of the packet. However, you do need to have in-depth knowledge of the information transmitted in each protocol to interpret what you're seeing successfully, even after it's been translated. Microsoft includes parsers for a slew of network protocols. You can see a list of them by clicking Options ➪ Default Parsers ➪ Yes and scrolling through the Enabled Protocol Parsers list. When you're done looking at the list, click Cancel.

Don't disable any of the protocol parsers listed in the Protocol Parsers dialog box, unless you're absolutely sure what you're doing. Disabling a parser can have downstream effects on other parsers.

Network Monitor's online Help is comprehensive, but it doesn't teach you about the contents of packets on the network. Instead it refers you to several excellent books on the topic. To see the list, click Help ➪ Contents. Double-click Reference and double-click Reference Guide to Books on Networking.

Managing the Boot Process

It seems as though all roads lead to the NT boot process. If you can't get the operating system booted, it's not much fun for anyone. In this section, I'll provide you with some important background to help you to understand, diagnose, and gain control over the process of getting NT up and running.

Understanding ARC Path Names

If you were paying attention during the text-mode phase of NT installation or if you've ventured into the BOOT.INI file, you've probably noticed some extremely arcane notations that refer to the disk drives on your computer. These device path names are called ARC path names (or sometimes just *arcnames*). Recall that ARC stands for Advance RISC Computing, a standard designed to allow NT to run on a wide variety of RISC-based computers. Well, for better or worse, ARC path names are used on the Intel CPU platform as well, so understanding how they work is essential to management of the NT boot process.

Multis vs. SCSIs

ARC path names generally appear in one of the following forms:

multi(a)disk(b)rdisk(c)partition(d)\...

scsi(a)disk(b)rdisk(c)partition(d)\...

where the letters within parentheses are replaced by decimal numbers. The *multi* element refers to IDE, EIDE, and ESDI disk controllers. So multi(0) refers to the first such disk controller installed in the computer, and multi(1) points to a secondary disk controller. Drives on the same controller (up to a maximum of two per controller) are identified by either rdisk(0) or rdisk(1). In ARC path names that start with multi, the second element of the name is always disk(0).

For example, if you have two IDE controllers installed, and each has two drives attached, the ARC path names for the four drives are:

multi(0)disk(0)rdisk(0)	1st drive on 1st controller
multi(0)disk(0)rdisk(1)	2nd drive on 1st controller
multi(1)disk(0)rdisk(0)	1st drive on 2nd controller
multi(1)disk(0)rdisk(1)	2nd drive on 2nd controller

The *scsi* element refers, as you might have guessed, to SCSI host adapters. The element scsi(0) refers to the first SCSI adapter in the computer, scsi(1) to the second, and so on. Multiple SCSI hard disks on the same adapter are identified using the *disk* element with the SCSI ID number of the drive. For example, scsi(0)disk(6) refers to the drive with SCSI ID 6 on the first SCSI adapter. In ARC path names that start with scsi, the *rdisk* element is typically rdisk(0). If you have more than one SCSI logical unit number, or LUN, per SCSI ID, rdisk refers to the LUN. Most configurations these days have just one LUN per SCSI ID, so the rdisk number is typically zero.

Partition Numbers

So far, I've been showing you incomplete ARC paths. (Shame on me.) Let's turn our attention to the *partition* element of the ARC path name, to complete the picture. Before proceeding, you may want to review the section called "Primary versus Extended Partitions" in Chapter 18.

The partition element identifies the specific partition or logical drive on the physical hard disk. Partitions are numbered starting from one, according to the following rules:

- Primary partitions are numbered first, in order of their appearance on the physical drive.
- Logical drives within extended partitions are numbered next, in order of appearance of the extended partitions and in order of appearance of the logical drives within the extended partition.
- DOS extended partitions, unused partitions, and EISA configuration partitions aren't recognized by NT and aren't assigned a partition number.

The element partition(0) has a special meaning. It's reserved to refer to the entire physical disk, ignoring all partition boundaries and logical drives. Don't use it in your ARC path names, or you'll run into trouble.

MULTIPLE PATHS TO THE SAME DRIVE

In some cases, you'll see multi used to refer to a SCSI adapter. The scsi element is used only when you have a bootable drive on a SCSI adapter with its BIOS disabled, a dual channel SCSI adapter, or multiple SCSI adapters. The real difference between multi and scsi is that multi relies on the BIOS to access the disks, whereas scsi relies on an NT device driver, NTBOOTDD.SYS, loaded during the boot sequence.

So, it's possible to refer to the same SCSI drive in two different ways, if the SCSI adapter's BIOS is enabled and the NT device driver is present. To refer to the second physical drive, with a SCSI ID of 6, you could use either of the following ARC path names:

```
multi(0)disk(0)rdisk(1)
scsi(0)disk(6)rdisk(0)
```

Now that you've identified the partition or logical drive on a specific hard disk on a particular adapter, you can venture into more familiar territory. The remainder of the ARC path name uses normal disk directory (or folder) notation. For example, if NT is installed on the second IDE disk attached to a single IDE controller and the drive has one primary partition, the ARC path name of the SystemRoot directory is expressed as:

```
multi(0)disk(0)rdisk(1)partition(1)\WINNT
```

Understanding the NT Boot Sequence

Understanding the NT boot sequence on both Intel and RISC platforms can help you to pinpoint problems if NT ever refuses to start. In the following sections, I'll present an overview of the steps that NT goes through to get itself up and running.

Starting NT on Intel Platforms

When you install Windows NT Server on an Intel-based computer, the Setup program alters the system partition's boot sector to look for and run a program called NTLDR, which lives in the root of the system partition. (NT Setup saves the old DOS boot sector, which looks for IO.SYS and MSDOS.SYS, in a file called BOOTSECT.DOS.) Setup also creates a file called BOOT.INI in the root of the system partition or modifies it if it already exists. If DOS is found on the computer, a DOS boot choice is inserted in the BOOT.INI menu of operating system choices. Likewise, if Setup finds OS/2, the alternate operating system boot choice is OS/2. With this in mind, you can understand the following steps of the Intel boot sequence:

1. When you restart the Intel computer, the system BIOS reads the MBR (master boot record) from the first sector of the system partition. The boot sector code then loads and starts NTLDR (which is short for NT Loader).

DEALING WITH DUAL CHANNELS

Many modern SCSI adapters have more than one channel on a single adapter, allowing attachment of up to 14 SCSI devices. Manufacturers have implemented these dual-channel adapters in different ways. In most cases, the following approach works:

Dual SCSI channels are typically labeled A and B or 0 and 1 by the manufacturer. Assign 0 to the first channel and 1 to the second. Calculate the disk element of the ARC path name by multiplying the channel number by 32, then add the drive's SCSI ID. For example, a drive with SCSI ID 4 on channel 0 would be:

```
scsi(0)disk(4)rdisk(0)
```

But a drive with SCSI ID 5 on channel 1 would be

```
scsi(0)disk(37)rdisk(0)
```

2. NTLDR starts running and immediately switches the Intel CPU from DOS real mode to 32-bit mode.

You can tell when NTLDR starts running — the screen clears and an "OS Loader" message is displayed in the upper left corner of the display.

3. NTLDR reads and interprets the BOOT.INI file, which contains a list of bootable operating systems. Based on information in BOOT.INI, NTLDR presents a menu of operating system choices.
4. You either select an operating system from the menu or let the default operating system boot after the timer counts down to zero.

If the default operating system starts immediately without presenting a boot menu, the time-out in the BOOT.INI file has been set to zero. I'll cover the contents of BOOT.INI in detail later in this chapter.

5. If step 4 resulted in selecting a version of NT, go to step 6. Otherwise, BOOTSECT.DOS (the old DOS boot sector) is loaded and run. Whatever operating system was the default before installing NT is then booted, and the boot sequence is complete. (In other words, the computer doesn't proceed to step 6 if you selected a non-NT operating system in step 4.)
6. NTLDR starts NTDETECT.COM (the hardware recognizer), which collects hardware configuration information, passes it back to NTLDR, and terminates.

At this point, the Intel-specific portion of the boot process is complete. The boot sequence continues with step 1 in the section entitled "Continuing the Boot Process" later in this chapter.

Starting NT on RISC Platforms

On RISC-based NT platforms, the boot selection menu is built into the ARC firmware. In addition, NTDETECT.COM isn't needed because all of the information that it gathers is already stored in the ARC firmware. Here's how the RISC boot process starts:

1. When you restart the RISC computer, the self-test gathers hardware configuration information and places it in the ARC firmware for later use.
2. The ARC firmware determines where its boot drive is. It reads the MBR (master boot record) from the first sector of the system partition to determine if it's formatted with the FAT file system.

   If the system partition's file system isn't FAT, the computer won't be able to boot NT.
3. The ARC firmware looks for and loads OSLOADER.EXE. OSLOADER.EXE picks up relevant hardware configuration information from the ARC firmware.

4. The ARC firmware then displays a menu of boot choices, the format of which varies between RISC manufacturers.
5. You select an operating system from the firmware menu.

At this point, the RISC-specific portion of the boot process is complete. The boot sequence continues with step 1 in the next section.

Continuing the Boot Process

After the platform-specific portions of the boot process are complete, as described in the previous two sections, the boot sequence continues with the following steps. I'll use the generic term *loader* to refer to both NTLDR on Intel and OSLOADER.EXE on RISC.

1. At this stage, NTOSKRNL.EXE (the NT kernel) and HAL.DLL (the hardware abstraction layer) are loaded into memory. The loader then pulls the registry subtree HKEY_LOCAL_MACHINE\SYSTEM into memory from the SYSTEM registry database file.
2. Based on information in the registry, the loader brings low-level device drivers into memory. It then passes control to NTOSKRNL.EXE.

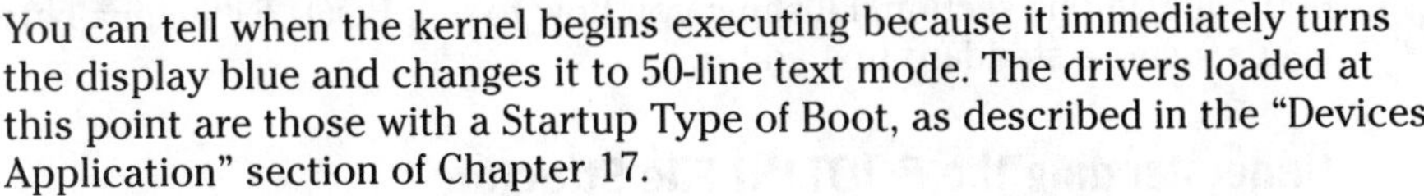

   You can tell when the kernel begins executing because it immediately turns the display blue and changes it to 50-line text mode. The drivers loaded at this point are those with a Startup Type of Boot, as described in the "Devices Application" section of Chapter 17.

3. The kernel initializes the drivers loaded in step 2 and uses them to load any additional drivers. The additional drivers loaded at this stage are those marked with a Startup Type of System, as described in Chapter 17.

   The HKEY_LOCAL_MACHINE\HARDWARE registry subtree, described in Chapter 20, is populated with configuration data gathered by the loader. At this point, the kernel also initializes the registry control sets.

4. The kernel starts a process called Session Manager (SMSS.EXE), which manages the next phase of the boot sequence. It typically starts AUTOCHK.EXE (a special version of CHKDSK designed to run before the operating system is completely booted) to make sure that the disk data structures are healthy.

   If you scheduled a file system conversion from FAT to NTFS to run at the next restart, Session Manager performs the conversion at this step.

5. If all is well on the disks, Session Manager creates the NT paging files, according to information in the registry. It then starts the Win32 Subsystem (CSRSS.EXE).
6. The Win32 subsystem immediately runs Winlogon, which in turn starts the service controller (SERVICES.EXE), the local security authority (LSASS.EXE), and the print spooler (SPOOLSS.EXE).

If you use the Task Manager Processes tab to peek at the running processes, you can see the order in which things were started. The kernel shows up as System. It's followed by SMSS.EXE, CSRSS.EXE, WINLOGON.EXE, SERVICES.EXE, LSASS.EXE, and SPOOLSS.EXE. (SERVICES.EXE used to be called SCREG.EXE in the Windows NT 3.x products.)

7. Drivers and services marked with a Startup Type of Automatic are loaded at this stage. See the sections called "Devices Application" and "Services Application" in Chapter 17 for details on driver and service startup types.
8. The remaining high-level components of Windows NT Server are loaded, and the computer displays the Begin Logon dialog box.

Managing the Boot Menu on Intel

If you're running NT on an Intel CPU platform, the BOOT.INI file, in the root directory of your system partition, controls the display of the initial boot menu that you see when you restart the computer. (If you're running NT on a RISC platform, this is all handled in the computer's firmware.) You can use the System application in Control Panel to alter the menu time-out and default operating system choice, as described in Chapter 17, but you can't add, remove, or edit any other portions of the file. In this section, I'll show you how to edit BOOT.INI manually to suit your needs, using a standard text editor.

Understanding the BOOT.INI File Structure

The BOOT.INI file consists of two sections. The first section, named *[boot loader]*, contains the menu time-out value (in seconds) and a pointer to the default operating system to boot.

The time-out value specifies the number of seconds that the boot menu is displayed before the default operating system is automatically selected and booted. If the time-out is set to zero, the boot menu isn't displayed at all, and the default OS loads automatically. By default, NT sets this time-out to 30 seconds. You can change it either by editing the BOOT.INI file or through the System application in Control Panel.

The default value is simply the ARC path name of the operating system that will boot by default. (See the section "Understanding ARC Path Names" earlier in this chapter for details.) The boot menu item corresponding to this path is highlighted during the time-out countdown. You can change the default value by manually editing it, or you can change it to another existing menu entry using the System application in Control Panel.

If the default value is DOS or some other non-NT operating system, the value of default isn't an ARC path name. In the case of DOS, for example, the default value is typically the C:\ directory.

The second section of the BOOT.INI file is named *[operating systems]*. It's simply a list of ARC path names associated with menu items to be displayed on the boot menu. If you've retained the ability to dual-boot to DOS, the last entry equates the root directory of drive C to "MS-DOS."

Each time you install a version of Windows NT Server (or NT Workstation, for that matter), two additional entries are added to the top of this section of BOOT.INI. In addition, Setup changes the default value in the [boot loader] section to point to the first entry in the [operating systems] section.

Editing BOOT.INI

Although you can have any number of entries in this file, only the first 10 choices are displayed. This usually isn't a problem, unless you have several versions of operating systems installed on the same computer or you've had to reinstall NT several times. Each NT installation adds another two options to this menu: a standard boot option and an option that boots using VGA video mode. (See the section in Chapter 9 called "Booting to VGA Mode" for details.)

You can edit BOOT.INI with any standard text editor. The DOS EDIT and Windows Notepad applications work just fine. However, before you edit the file, you must change its file attributes. When NT Server is installed, the BOOT.INI file has the read-only and system file attributes set. You need to remove these attributes, edit the file, and then restore the attributes. (NT expects these attributes to be intact during the boot process.) Here's a batch file that you can run from a Command Prompt whenever you need to edit BOOT.INI:

```
c:
cd \
attrib -r -s boot.ini
edit boot.ini
attrib +r +s boot.ini
```

You can substitute your favorite text editor for the DOS EDIT command in the batch file.

You may be tempted to remove the VGA-mode menu item, thinking that you'll never need it. Don't give in to this temptation. It's an important escape hatch. Even if you're not changing your video mode, you may need this option to deal with hardware failures and driver upgrades. For example, an SVGA video adapter with RAM that's going bad may be unusable at high resolutions but can sometimes operate just fine in VGA mode. I've also run into one case where a vendor supplied an updated video driver and required customers to boot to VGA mode before the new driver could be installed. So keep your mitts off the VGA-mode menu item.

To illustrate, here's an example of a BOOT.INI file on a Windows NT Server 4.0 computer. Notice that it retains the ability to boot to the previous version of NT, which is NT Workstation 3.51. Notice also that the old version of NT lives on drive C (an IDE drive), and NT Server 4.0 is installed on a SCSI drive with SCSI ID 2.

```
[boot loader]
timeout=15
default=scsi(0)disk(2)rdisk(0)partition(1)\WINNT
[operating systems]
scsi(0)disk(2)rdisk(0)partition(1)\WINNT="Windows NT Server 4.00"
scsi(0)disk(2)rdisk(0)partition(1)\WINNT="Windows NT Server 4.00
      [VGA mode]" /basevideo /sos
multi(0)disk(0)rdisk(0)partition(1)\WINNT.351="Windows NT
      Workstation 3.51"
multi(0)disk(0)rdisk(0)partition(1)\WINNT.351="Windows NT
      Workstation 3.51 [VGA mode]" /basevideo /sos
c:\="Windows 95 (Press F4 for MS-DOS)"
```

Since this computer also has both DOS and Windows 95 on it, notice that the administrator has changed the menu text on the last line from "MS-DOS" to "Windows 95 (Press F4 for MS-DOS)," since this menu item causes Windows 95 to boot, instead of DOS.

Watching Drivers as They Load

If you're having trouble booting the operating system and you suspect that a driver is at fault, you can get NT to list each driver as it loads during the boot process. That way, you can determine which driver is causing the problem. Just add the /SOS switch to the end of the menu line in BOOT.INI corresponding to the version of the operating system you're booting. For example,

```
scsi(0)disk(0)rdisk(0)partition(2)\WINNT="NT Server 4.0" /SOS
```

NT Setup automatically adds the /SOS switch to the VGA-mode version of the boot menu entry. Since you're booting using VGA mode, Setup assumes that you need some extra information during the boot process. This is helpful if you expect it but can be disconcerting if you don't.

Keeping the UPS Alive during Boot

During the boot process, NT briefly chats with each serial port to determine what sort of device is attached. Unfortunately, some UPS devices interpret this as a signal to shut themselves down. This results in the computer powering down during the boot process — certainly not what you had in mind.

If your UPS has this problem, you can work around it by disabling NT's serial device detection on the port to which the UPS is attached. On the menu line in the BOOT.INI file, add the switch

```
/NoSerialMice=COMx
```

where *x* is the number of the serial port to which the UPS is attached. When you add this switch, your UPS won't shut itself down at this inopportune moment.

Dealing with Missing Memory at 1MB

If you see the following error during operating system initialization:

```
OS LOADER: Image can't be relocated, no fixup information.
The system did not load because it cannot find the following file:
<winnt root>\system32\ntoskrnl.exe
Please re-install a copy of the above file.
Boot failed
```

it probably means that your computer doesn't appear to have memory in the 1MB address range. The Intel version of the NT kernel must always be loaded at a fixed address and can't be relocated somewhere else. The loader attempts to place the kernel at 1MB.

Some computers on the market, including the Compaq SystemPro XL, have no memory in this range by default. In most cases, you can remedy this by changing the EISA or BIOS configuration to make the memory at this location visible. On the SystemPro XL, for example, change the EISA memory parameter from "640K Linear" to "640K Compaq Compatible." See your computer manufacturer's instructions for details.

Customizing the Logon Process

Certain aspects of the logon sequence, as described in Chapter 14, can be customized to fit the needs of your organization. Unfortunately, since Microsoft doesn't provide an application to do this, you must edit the registry to customize the logon process. The following sections describe the logon tricks that you can play.

Displaying a Custom Bitmap before Logon

If your organization wants its own company logo displayed on NT computers that aren't logged on, rather than the standard NT bitmap, you can edit the registry to make this happen. Under the HKEY_USERS\.DEFAULT\Control Panel\Desktop key, change the value of Wallpaper to the full path name of the custom bitmap that you want to display. Log off to see the new bitmap, which will be displayed behind the Begin Logon dialog box.

Displaying a Custom Logon Message

For legal or security reasons, your organization may require that a notice or warning message be displayed before users log on to their computers. For example, you may need to display a notice warning of the implications of unauthorized access to the network.

You can insert a customized dialog box between the Begin Logon and the Logon Information dialog boxes. When you press CTRL+ALT+DEL at the Begin Logon dialog box, NT can display the custom dialog box that you define. You must click OK to acknowledge it. NT then displays the Logon Information dialog box to gather your user name and password as usual.

Under the HKEY_LOCAL_MACHINE\SOFTWARE\Microsoft\Windows NT\CurrentVersion\Winlogon key, change the value of LegalNoticeCaption to the text that you want to appear as the dialog box title. Change the value of LegalNoticeText to the text message that you want to appear within the dialog box. Log off and press CTRL+ALT+DEL to see the new dialog box. Click OK and proceed to the Logon Information dialog box.

Logging On Automatically

In some special cases, you may want to provide access to a computer without asking for a user name or password. For example, you may have an NT print server in the printer room down the hall, and all users must be able to access the print queue. You can set up the computer to log on automatically, completely bypassing the logon sequence.

Here's how to configure an NT computer to log on automatically:

1. Select the HKEY_LOCAL_MACHINE\SOFTWARE\Microsoft\Windows NT\CurrentVersion\Winlogon key.
2. Determine which user account to use for the automatic logon, then change the value of DefaultUserName to this user account name.

From a security viewpoint, bypassing the logon process can be extremely dangerous. Make sure that the account being used for automatic logon (the one specified as the value of DefaultUserName) has reasonable access restrictions to prevent people from using this computer for unauthorized access or damage to the network. Under no circumstances should the default user have administrative privileges.

3. Add a new value entry called AutoAdminLogon. Set its data type to REG_SZ and its value to 1.
4. Add another new value entry called DefaultPassword. Set its data type to REG_SZ and its value to the password of the account specified in step 2.

When you log off, NT will automatically log on the user that you specified in step 2. Whenever anyone logs off this computer, NT logs the default user on again. If you want to revert to requiring a normal logon, change the AutoAdminLogon value entry that you created in step 3 to a value of 0.

Enabling Shutdown without Logon

By default, Windows NT Server doesn't allow you to shut down the computer without first logging on. You certainly don't want to allow some unauthorized person to shut down your server with a simple click of the mouse. The Logon Information window includes a Shut Down button, but it's disabled. (NT Workstation has the same button enabled, since it's much less detrimental to shut down a workstation computer.)

You can enable the Shut Down button in the Logon Information window by editing the registry. Under the HKEY_LOCAL_MACHINE\SOFTWARE\Microsoft\WindowsNT\CurrentVersion\Winlogon key, change the ShutdownWithoutLogon value to 1. If you ever want to disable the button again, simply change its value back to 0.

The button is disabled by default to prevent unauthorized server shutdowns. If you enable it, be sure that your server is physically secured so that unauthorized users can't shut down your server on a whim.

Customizing Network Behavior

You'll do most of your NT network customization through the Network application in Control Panel, as described in previous chapters. However, there are a few less common tweaks that require changes to the NT registry. I'll present some of the more useful ones in the sections that follow.

Raising File Server Priority

By default, the print server has higher priority than the file server. The print server is set by default to priority 2, whereas file server has priority 1. (Higher numbers equal higher priority.) This can cause printing activity to impede file server performance. You can raise file server priority to 2, at the expense of some loss of printing performance. Under the HKEY_LOCAL_MACHINE\SYSTEM\CurrentControlSet\Services\LanmanServer\Parameters key, add a new value entry called ThreadPriority. Set the data type to REG_DWORD and the value to 2.

Controlling BDC Database Update Frequency

The accounts database replication process that takes place between the primary domain controller (PDC) and all backup domain controllers (BDCs) in the domain soaks up both CPU time and network bandwidth. (See Chapter 7 for a discussion of PDCs and BDCs.) By default, NT attempts to select an update frequency (called a *pulse*) that's appropriate to the current load on the PDC. The default pulse is 300 seconds (five minutes). All changes to the database made during this interval are collected and sent to the BDCs that need to be updated.

You may want to force this pulse update to occur at specific intervals, so that you always know exactly how far out of date your BDCs are. If you want to have control over this frequency, there are several values that you can add and modify in the registry.

Under the HKEY_LOCAL_MACHINE\SYSTEM\CurrentControlSet\Services\ Netlogon key, you can add a new value entry called Pulse. Set its data type to REG_DWORD and its value to the number of seconds that you want to elapse between pulses. I recommend selecting a value between 300 seconds (5 minutes) and 3600 seconds (60 minutes).

When the PDC sends out notification to the BDCs that it has database updates, it typically releases up to 20 notifications at one time. The BDCs respond with requests to send these updates. This barrage of requests from BDCs can bog down your PDC, depending on the available CPU cycles on this server and the number of BDCs in your domain.

You can set the maximum number of outstanding pulses under the same key where you added the Pulse value entry. This time, add a new value entry called PulseConcurrency, set its data type to REG_DWORD, and set its value between 1 and 500. Higher numbers will increase the load on the PDC but will complete replication to all BDCs more quickly. Lower numbers will decrease the load on the PDC but can drag out the time needed to get all of the BDCs in the domain updated. I recommend setting this value to the number of BDCs in the domain. You can then experiment with lower values if you see PDC performance suffer when the pulse occurs.

Rigging Browser Elections

In your work with Windows NT Server so far, you've probably run into quite a few Browse buttons that allow you to view available servers and resources both inside and outside your domain. You may have noticed that creating these resource lists is sometimes painfully slow. Perhaps you've also noticed that deleted servers and their resources seem to take forever to leave the browse lists. You may have even seen entries in NT event logs about lost and won "browse master elections."

NT network browsing behaves according to the following rules:

- One computer on the network plays the role of *master browser* (or *browse master*). It designates one or more computers as *backup browsers.* Backup browsers ask the master for updates every 15 minutes. Both master and backup browsers can satisfy requests for browse information.
- Each transport protocol on your network needs its own set of browsers, if you want all resources to appear in the browse lists.
- Servers offering network resources announce themselves after 1, 4, 8, and 12 minutes. From then on, they announce themselves on the network every 12 minutes.

✦ If a server is removed, the master browser keeps it in the browse list for 36 minutes (three 12-minute announcement periods) and then removes it from the list. (It does this just in case the server returns.)

✦ Since backup browsers ask for updates every 15 minutes, a backup browser may not see a server disappear until up to 51 minutes (36 + 15 minutes) after the server actually went away.

Elections on the network, as in politics, consume lots of time and resources. It's best to take proactive steps to minimize the number of elections and the number of candidates for master browser.

If you have Windows for Workgroups computers on your network, you don't want them acting as master or backup browsers. Not only can this generate performance bottlenecks, but it can also result in empty browse lists. On your Windows for Workgroups computers, add a line that says

```
MaintainServerList=No
```

to the [network] section of the SYSTEM.INI file.

If you don't want Windows 95 computers to act as browse masters or backups, you can prevent them from participating in elections as well. On the Windows 95 computer, click that Start ➪ Settings ➪ Control Panel option and double-click the Network icon. Click the Configuration tab and click File and Printer Sharing. Click Properties and set the value of Browse Master to Disabled.

IF THE ELECTION WERE HELD TODAY

The role of master browser is an elected office. Elections are held whenever a server that's acting as a master browser is shut down. (In this case, an election is held immediately. However, if the master browser is simply turned off, no election is held until a computer requests browse information and doesn't get it.) Elections aren't entirely democratic – family name, experience, and how you rig your network all enter into the decision. (I guess it *is* like human politics, after all.)

In selecting a new master browser, NT Server computers are given preference over computers running NT Workstation. NT Workstation computers are given preference over any remaining computers, including Windows for Workgroups, LAN Manager servers, and so forth. In case of a tie between NT Server computers, PDCs are given preference. You can take steps to control which computers do and don't become master browsers, as you'll see later in this section.

If you're running only the TCP/IP protocol, you can essentially rig the election and appoint a permanent master browser. (I call this the *dictator browser,* who has the job for life.) By assigning this role to one server, you take the risk of being without a master browser when the server goes down. However, some administrators argue that their NT Server computer is typically running 24 hours a day, and the rare inconvenience caused by the server being down is minor compared to the network hubbub caused by incessant browser elections. Under the HKEY_LOCAL_MACHINE\SYSTEM\CurrentControlSet\Services\Browser\Parameters key, change the value of IsDomainMaster from FALSE to TRUE. This approach works only for TCP/IP and won't work for other transport protocols.

If you're running TCP/IP and its resources don't appear on your browse lists, this problem could be caused by NetBEUI and IPX/SPX protocols soaking up all of the CPU's attention. If you don't need the other protocols loaded, remove them to improve TCP/IP browsing. (In fact, getting rid of unneeded protocols almost always results in better overall performance.) If you need the other protocols, change the network bindings so that TCP/IP is bound first, as described in Chapter 8.

Performing Administrator Tricks

In the following sections, I'll present some useful tips and tricks to help you get your job done more efficiently and impress your coworkers.

Creating Invisible Share Points

You can create invisible share points on your server by making the last character of the share name a dollar sign ($). When users browse for shared resources on your server, they won't see this share point. However, if they know its name, they can connect to it by explicitly typing it.

When you install Windows NT Server, Setup invisibly shares the root directory of each drive on your computer over the network. These share points are named C$, D$, and so forth. NT also shares the SystemRoot directory as ADMIN$. Access is restricted to members of the Administrators group. You can see these share points by using the Server application in Control Panel. Click Shares to see a list of all share points on your server, including the invisible ones.

Don't use invisible share points as a replacement for security; use them in addition to NT security. It's easy for hackers to guess share point names and add dollar signs to the ends of them. If you're sharing confidential information over the network, apply NT security to the share point or, better yet, to the individual folders and files on the server.

Scheduling Automated Batch Jobs

NT Server includes a Schedule service that enables you to set up tasks to run unattended after hours, over the weekend, and periodically. You establish an account for the Schedule service so that it can log itself on and perform the assigned tasks at any time of the day or night.

You can also configure NT's Schedule service to work only when someone is logged on to the computer, but that sort of defeats the purpose of off-hours scheduling of tasks.

Here's how to set up the schedule service:

1. Establish an account that the Schedule service will use to log itself on to perform the work that you assign.

   If you're going to have it perform unattended backups, make sure to add the user account that you create to the Backup Operators group. (See Chapter 18 for details on creating accounts and managing groups.)

2. Log on with the account that you created in step 1. Make sure that you can actually perform the tasks that you're planning to schedule.

   If you find that you don't have rights to perform certain necessary operations, add the account to the appropriate groups to grant these rights.

If you can possibly avoid it, don't add the Schedule service's account to the Administrators group. There's nothing more disconcerting and dangerous than having an account with God-like privileges logging itself on to perform some unsupervised task. Also, don't forget to assign a password to this account.

3. Click Start ➪ Settings ➪ Control Panel. Double-click the Services icon. In the Services dialog box, double-click the Schedule service.
4. Under Startup Type, click Automatic. Under Log On As, click This Account. Type the user account name that you created in step 1, along with the password. Confirm the password and click OK, as shown in Figure 21-12.
5. If the Schedule service is running, click Stop.

   This step is required to allow the service to pick up the changes that you made in step 4.

6. Click Start to start the Schedule service. Then click Close.

Now that the Schedule service is properly configured and running, you can schedule jobs using the AT command. At a Command Prompt, you can type **AT /?** to see its syntax. When you schedule a job, it's given a unique ID and is added to a list of all scheduled jobs.

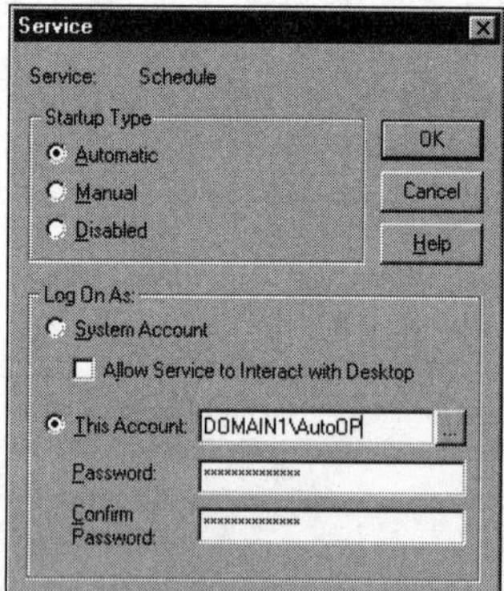

Figure 21-12: Set the Schedule service to start automatically and log on with its own account.

For example, if you want to schedule a batch file called NITETASK to run at 2:00 a.m. every Monday, Wednesday, and Friday, the AT command is:

AT 02:00 /EVERY:MONDAY,WEDNESDAY,FRIDAY "NITETASK"

To run the same batch file at midnight on the 15th of every month, the AT command is:

AT 00:00 /NEXT:15 "NITETASK"

To see a list of all scheduled jobs (including their ID numbers), just type **AT** with no command line parameters. To delete a job from the schedule, use the /DELETE switch. For example, to delete the job with an ID of 5, the command is:

AT 5 /DELETE

For unattended tasks that run when there's no one logged on to the computer, don't use the /INTERACTIVE switch on your AT command line. If you do, the task will attempt to attach itself to a desktop that doesn't exist, and this may cause the whole task to fail.

Protecting Administrators from Themselves

For each person with administrator responsibilities, assign them two accounts: one with administrator privileges and one with normal user privileges. Encourage them to utilize their normal user account for normal business such as e-mail and other activities. Tell them to reserve their administrative account only for performing operations that require this privilege level. Although logging on and off will incur some overhead, this practice will help to protect your network from damage due to viruses or accidents.

Using Account Templates

If you need to create a bunch of user accounts that are nearly identical, create a single account to be used as a standard template for the rest. Disable the account so that it can't be used. Once you've done this, it's easy to use the template to create other accounts:

1. In the User Manager for Domains window, select the account that you want to copy.
2. On the User menu, click Copy.
3. In the Copy of dialog box, fill in the details of the new account that you're creating. When you're done, click Add.

See Chapter 18 for details on creating user accounts with User Manager for Domains.

Speeding Up NTFS at a Price

As mentioned in earlier chapters, NTFS translates all of its long names for folders and files into equivalent 8.3 names that are acceptable to DOS, Windows 3.x, and other clients. If you have applications or users that perform many directory enumerations on an NTFS volume, you can disable 8.3 name generation to increase directory enumeration performance. This is especially effective for directories that contain many long names. To do this, under the HKEY_LOCAL_MACHINE\SYSTEM\CurrentControlSet\Control\FileSystem key, change the value of NtfsDisable8dot3NameCreation from 0 to 1.

If you have DOS and Windows 3.x clients on your network, don't make this change on an NTFS volume that may be shared over the network. These clients won't be able to see folders and files with long filenames at all. No 8.3 translation will be provided.

Controlling CD-ROM AutoPlay

On both Windows 95 and Windows NT, when you insert a CD-ROM, the operating system automatically "plays" it, attempting to run a program called AUTORUN on the CD-ROM. If it's equipped with this program, the CD-ROM typically enables you to install or explore it. (Inserting an audio CD in the drive causes the operating system to run the CD Player multimedia application.) This feature is called AutoPlay, which was originally introduced in Windows 95.

This feature is called both AutoPlay and AutoRun in the software and Microsoft's documentation. Both terms interchangeably refer to the same feature.

If you do much CD-ROM swapping and you don't want NT to run the AUTORUN program every time you insert a disc, you can disable the feature completely by editing the registry. Under the HKEY_LOCAL_MACHINE\SYSTEM\CurrentControlSet\Services\Cdrom key, change the value of Autorun from 1 to 0. If you ever want to enable this feature again, change the value of Autorun back to 1.

Troubleshooting Your NT Server

Some of the NT troubles that you encounter will involve your server computer itself. Even before it's connected to a network, you'll need to worry about the health of its hardware and how to ensure that it has the latest and greatest operating system files installed. The following sections will help you through these rough spots.

Dealing with NMI Errors

Occasionally, you may have a computer running NT that gets intermittent or consistent NMI (Non-Maskable Interrupt) errors. These high-priority signals are typically generated by memory parity errors, although some devices and motherboard components can cause them as well. If you get an NMI error, the first thing to do is check your RAM.

Here are some guidelines you can follow to minimize problems in this area:

- Don't use memory that has no parity checking. This is one way to eliminate the NMI parity error, but if you have memory problems, NT won't be able to catch that you have bad data floating around your computer until it's too late.
- Use SIMMs that are the same brand and speed and avoid mixing and matching. Even if the speed of all of the SIMMs is fast enough for the motherboard, differences of 10ns can wreak havoc when running NT.
- Use high-quality memory to get more uniformity in speed between SIMMs. In other words, don't buy your memory off the street from a guy in a trench coat. You get what you pay for, and sometimes less.
- Adjacent chips within a SIMM can also vary in speed. You can overcome this by increasing memory wait states in the BIOS, at the cost of degraded system performance.
- Some SIMMs operate at their specified access speed until they warm up and slow down. If you encounter consistent NMI errors after the computer has reached its operating temperature, this may be the cause.

The same memory can fail on one computer and work on another due to differences in how the BIOS handles memory access timing. If you have multiple computers and lots of time, you can experiment with moving memory to other computers or changing BIOS memory wait state timing.

Even if your computer runs just fine under DOS and Windows 3.x, Windows NT has a knack for uncovering hardware problems that you never knew you had. NT makes full use of system resources and may touch parts of memory or devices that DOS and Windows 3.x have never gone near. One computer manufacturer once observed to me, "Just running NT is the best overall memory hardware diagnostic I've ever seen."

Replacing System Files

There may be occasions when a problem is traced to a missing or corrupted system file or you need to replace a system file with a newer version to fix a problem. An NT message might explicitly tell you what file needs replacement, or you may be directed by support personnel to replace a file that's causing trouble.

One of the most common problems on Intel platforms is the "Couldn't find NTLDR" error message. This often happens if your system partition is formatted as FAT and the NTLDR file is inadvertently deleted. To resolve this quickly, copy the file \I386\NTLDR from your Windows NT Server CD-ROM to the root directory of drive C.

If a file is missing (perhaps due to accidental or malicious erasure), you can easily replace it from the Windows NT Server CD-ROM. Change to the appropriate platform folder on the CD-ROM (I386, ALPHA, MIPS, or PPC) and find the file that you need. Because most files on the CD-ROM are compressed, the last character of the filename will be an underscore (_). Use the EXPAND command-line utility to decompress the file and change its name to the correct one. Then, copy the expanded file to the appropriate location.

If you need to replace or update a specific file (say, a device driver) and that file is currently in use by the operating system, here's how:

1. Retrieve the new system file in uncompressed form. (Use the EXPAND command, if the file is compressed on the CD-ROM.)
2. Rename the system file that you need to replace.

   You'd think this would cause problems, but it doesn't. As long as the file remains in use, you can change its name all day long.
3. Copy the replacement file into the location of the file that you're replacing. Make sure that it has the correct filename.
4. Restart the computer. The new file is now in effect, and the old file (the one that you renamed) can be discarded or archived.

Determining if a Service Pack Is Installed

As you install successive Windows NT Service Pack updates on your NT computers, it's handy to know how to tell whether a particular service pack has been installed on a specific computer. There are actually several places you can look, but the two easiest detection methods are

- ✦ At a Command Prompt, type **WINVER.**
- ✦ In Windows NT Explorer, click Help ⇨ About Windows NT.

In either case, you'll see a dialog box that contains version information. The service pack number, if any, is included to the right of the NT version number. Service packs are cumulative — if you have Service Pack 4 installed, it includes all changes from the previous three service packs.

If you need to check the service pack status on several NT computers remotely, your only option is to use the Registry Editor. Look in the HKEY_LOCAL_MACHINE\SOFTWARE\Microsoft\Windows NT\CurrentVersion key. On computers running Windows NT 3.5 and later, if a service pack is installed, you'll see a value entry named CSDVersion. Its value is set to the words "Service Pack" followed by the service pack number. On computers running Windows NT 3.1, CSDVersion will have a hexadecimal value indicating which service pack is installed.

You may occasionally see an NT service pack referred to as a *CSD,* as in this registry entry. CSD stands for customer service disk, a term used by IBM back in the early OS/2 days to describe their patch releases. These days, both IBM and Microsoft refer to a patch release as a *service pack.*

Troubleshooting the Network

Network components can be the most challenging to troubleshoot. You've already been exposed to some network troubleshooting techniques in previous chapters. Here are some additional techniques to add to your bag of tricks.

Dealing with Slow Early Morning Performance

Lots of folks feel sluggish in the early morning. A similar disposition may seem to affect your NT domain controller. If most of the people in your organization arrive at the same time each day, your PDC can be flooded with logon requests. If the PDC is overloaded, your users will see a noticeable delay between the time they click OK in the Logon Information window and the time their desktop appears. This is actually one of the most common complaints users make, especially when they're used to instantaneous access at other times of the day.

This behavior is a clear sign that you need to establish more BDCs to help lighten the load on your domain's PDC. Chapter 10 provides some guidelines on planning for multiple BDCs in a single domain.

Dealing with Slow Browsing Performance

Another frequent complaint among users, especially in growing networks, is the sluggishness of network resource browsing. If you follow the advice in the section called "Rigging Browser Elections" earlier in this chapter, you can improve the situation significantly.

However, as your domain grows and the list of servers and resources continues to increase, the length of the lists alone will begin to slow down browsing. In this situation, you can consider splitting your network into multiple domains, as discussed in detail in Chapter 10.

Troubleshooting TCP/IP

As you discovered in Chapter 11, TCP/IP is the most complex of all of the protocols provided with NT. Since there are many ways to misconfigure TCP/IP, there are also many error conditions. The best advice is to follow the suggestions made in the error messages.

If problems persist, the best way to isolate them is to use the PING command, as described in Chapter 11. This allows you to verify that you have a connection between two computers and allows you to isolate which nodes are having trouble communicating. If PING is unsuccessful, ensure that the TCP/IP protocol is installed on both computers. You also need to make certain that both computers have been restarted since TCP/IP installation and that both have valid and unique IP addresses.

If PING gets a response from an IP address but gets no response from its host name, you probably have a name resolution problem. Check that the correct host names and IP addresses are present in the HOSTS file or other name resolution files, as described in Chapter 11. If PING works fine but you're having trouble connecting by using server and share point names, ensure that the computer is enabled for WINS, the WINS server addresses are specified correctly, and your WINS servers are up and running.

Troubleshooting RAS

The biggest headaches that you'll encounter with RAS will involve incorrect configurations on clients, servers, or both. (This is really not unique to NT RAS but is generally true of any hardware/software combination that involves modems.) Your best bet is to begin with the simplest configuration between a RAS client and server and then enable additional features only when you know that your current configuration is working. (This is pretty good advice for networking in general but is especially useful in the RAS context.) Keep detailed records of the RAS problems that you encounter and their solutions — it will save you lots of time trying to remember how you solved a particularly complex RAS issue.

Incompatible modems will also be a source of trouble, unless you opt to take my advice from Chapter 11 and use identical modems for all RAS participants. I recommend that you set up a test bed with two identical modems. When you get these working with RAS, insert one of the other modem types that you want to use. If you encounter trouble, this approach will help you nail down whether you have a configuration or compatibility problem.

You can use the Dial-Up Networking Monitor application, which is installed in Control Panel when you install RAS, to view RAS traffic and monitor transmission error rates. Click the Status tab to see this information, as shown in Figure 21-13. High error rates are a sign of either a noisy connection or potentially misconfigured hardware.

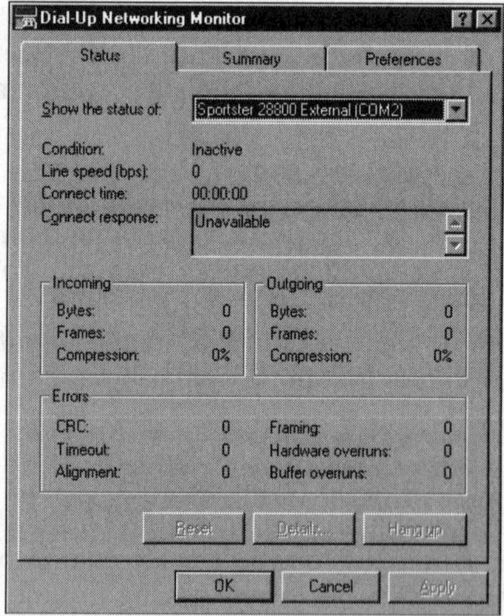

Figure 21-13: You can monitor error rates using the Dial-Up Networking Monitor application.

RAS contains some built-in logging features, but they're so built-in that you can only get to them through the registry. Once you enable logging in the registry, the RAS logs will be written as text files into the SystemRoot\SYSTEM32\RAS folder. You can generate a log of PPP information called PPP.LOG that will help you debug PPP connections. Under the HKEY_LOCAL_MACHINE\SYSTEM\CurrentControlSet\Services\RasMan\PPP key, change the value of Logging from 0 to 1. To generate a log of modem commands called DEVICE.LOG, change the value of Logging from 0 to 1 under the HKEY_LOCAL_MACHINE\SYSTEM\CurrentControlSet\Services\RasMan\Parameters key.

Troubleshooting SFM

Because Windows NT and Macintosh come from two different worlds, compatibility among the names of their files and paths can be a problem. I discussed the main issues in Chapter 12, but there are a few other gotchas.

NT can't handle path lengths longer than 260 characters, but Macintosh can. From Macintosh clients, you'll be able to create huge paths, but when it's time to back up the Macintosh volume on the NT Server computer, NT won't be able to access those files. Keep your Macintosh paths shorter than 260 characters, and you won't run into this problem.

Macintosh filenames can include a trailing space. When you attempt to access the file from NT, it will complain that it can't find the file. The only workaround is to rename the file from the Macintosh client to exclude the trailing space. NT will then be able to access it.

Troubleshooting Backup Problems

If your backup tapes are damaged, you can't recover the data from them. However, you can often salvage bad tapes for later use or recover at least some data from sets of tapes that are partially missing or damaged. In the following sections, I'll tell you how.

Dealing with Incomplete Backup Sets

If any tapes from a backup set that spans multiple tapes are damaged or missing, you may need to ask NT Backup to rebuild the catalog by reading through each tape. To do this, type the following command at a Command Prompt:

```
NTBACKUP /MISSINGTAPE
```

This will start the lengthy process of Backup reading through each surviving tape to rebuild the catalog as best it can. Of course, it can't recover the data from your missing or damaged tapes, but it can recover the data stored on the surviving ones. Whatever data you salvage is probably worth the lengthy catalog rebuild process.

Dealing with Bad Tapes

If NT Backup displays an error message indicating either a tape drive error or a bad tape in the drive, you can often recover from the problem by simply erasing and reformatting the tape that generated the error. However, because Backup attempts to read the tape when it first starts, you may not be able to erase it by simply clicking Operations ➪ Erase Tape. If Backup won't let you erase the bad tape, from a Command Prompt, type:

NTBACKUP /NOPOLL

On the Operations menu, click Erase Tape. When the erasure is complete, click Operations ➪ Format Tape. When the formatting is complete, close the Backup application and restart it normally, without the /NOPOLL option.

Don't include any other parameters on the command line with /NOPOLL. And don't attempt to perform any normal backup, restore, or catalog operations while the /NOPOLL parameter is in effect. You're guaranteed to run into problems if you do. Always restart Backup without the /NOPOLL parameter before attempting any normal operations.

INSIDE STORY

It was a challenging climb, especially after a sleepless marathon in the test lab the night before. As I crawled up onto the four-foot reception desk counter, steadying myself against the wall, I looked down on scores of tired but eager faces. I also looked up at some faces hanging over the railing of the second-floor gallery, occasionally pelting the masses below with bits of popcorn and chips.

We'd had this sort of get-together many times before – our Weekly Integration Meeting (WIM) in the lobby of Microsoft Building Two. Every Friday afternoon, the entire NT team would flock to the WIM to partake of munchies and standing-room-only camaraderie. Sometimes there were pep talks, sometimes award ceremonies. Managers would stand on the reception desk and hurl "NT Bug Finder" T-shirts to the development and test engineers who had found or fixed the most bugs during that week. Occasionally, a hero would step up to receive the coveted "NT Guerrilla Testing Award," which consisted of a toy military tank with a pile of dead bugs in front of it.

But despite the usual stress-busting silliness, the atmosphere at today's WIM was different. The room buzzed with an excited energy that you could almost touch. Its source was collective anticipation – we were just days from shipping Windows NT, and everyone could taste victory. So, although the various managers stood on the counter and boomed forth inspiring words, their speeches weren't really necessary. As people mingled in the lobby, they re-energized each other to make the last-minute push toward the ship date.

For many, there was also a tinge of regret at seeing the project draw to a close. We were about to achieve what the team had focused on exclusively for over four years. However hard the tasks had been, and whatever trials the next few days would bring, the extraordinary experience of working on the development of Windows NT would never be equaled in our lifetimes.

Summary

In this chapter, you've been exposed to a variety of ideas that will help you become an NT magician within your organization. You've learned about several troubleshooting tools, picked up some time-saving tips, and seen how a few small changes can customize the behavior and performance of your servers. You're now ready to go forth and collect your own set of techniques that will bring you even greater success as a Windows NT Server network administrator.

Windows NT Server on the Internet

✦ ✦ ✦ ✦

In This Part

✦ ✦ ✦ ✦

Inside the Microsoft Internet Information Server

✦ ✦ ✦ ✦

Microsoft's Internet Information Server, or IIS, is included free on the Windows NT Server 4.0 CD-ROM. You can use IIS to establish a fully functional World Wide Web site, complete with full search and database access capabilities. In addition to being a cost-free solution, IIS is a high-performance Web server that's well integrated with Windows NT Server. This chapter focuses on how to install, configure, and use IIS. You'll also learn how to connect Web pages to a database and how to make your Web site fully searchable.

You must have the TCP/IP protocol already installed and configured on your Windows NT Server computer before proceeding with IIS installation. If you haven't already installed TCP/IP, see Chapter 11 for details.

If you're already familiar with the World Wide Web, Web servers, and the terminology and acronyms associated with them, you can skip directly to the section entitled "Installing Internet Information Server." Otherwise, the following section provides some background that you'll need before you install IIS.

Establishing Web Servers

Before setting up your Web server and using it to publish Web pages to the Internet (or internally to your intranet), it's important to understand what makes Web servers tick. HyperText Transfer Protocol (HTTP) is the primary language of the Web, used by Web servers and browsers to communicate with each other. When a user running a Web browser types the address of a Uniform Resource Locator (URL) such as `http://www.microsoft.com/default.html`, the browser first locates the server called www.microsoft.com and requests the file default.html from the Web server. The Web server then transmits the requested file to the browser and terminates the connection. After retrieving the file, the Web browser formats and displays it for the user.

To establish a Web server on your local intranet, all you need is a LAN on which the nodes are running the TCP/IP protocol, a server computer running Windows NT Server, and Web Server software (such as Microsoft Internet Information Server or Netscape Enterprise Server). In addition, your client computers must have appropriate Web browser software (such as Microsoft Internet Explorer or Netscape Navigator).

If you want to create content for your Web server, and I suspect that you probably do, you'll want to have Microsoft FrontPage (included with Windows NT Server 4.0) and Microsoft Office on hand. In Chapter 23, I'll discuss how to use these tools to simplify creation of your own Web pages. If you want to publish a database or feed user-supplied information into a database, you'll need appropriate database management software. Candidates include Microsoft Access and Microsoft SQL Server.

To venture into the outside world and establish your Web server on the Internet, you'll need to have a connection to it. A 28.8 Kbps modem link is the absolute minimum. Although this is the least expensive approach, it is also the slowest. A Plain Old Telephone Service (POTS) modem link to the Internet will cause your Web server to become excruciatingly slow to navigate as soon as several users begin accessing your Web site simultaneously.

If you can't afford a high-bandwidth connection to the Internet, such as Frame Relay or ISDN (Integrated Services Digital Network), you can use a Web space provider to remedy the problem of limited bandwidth. Most Internet Service Providers (ISPs) offer Web server space, typically charging a monthly fee proportional to the amount of disk space that your data occupies. In this arrangement, they run your Web server, and you provide the content.

For practical reasons, many organizations today implement their Web servers in two phases — an intranet phase followed by an Internet phase. If you opt for a high-bandwidth connection to the Internet, you typically won't get it budgeted, approved, arranged, installed, paid for, and running overnight. Likewise, obtaining your IP network address and domain name may take some time. While you wait for your connection to the outside world, you can establish your Web server on your local intranet, create and publish Web pages to the employees in your organization, and effectively use your LAN as a test bed for your Web site. Then, when your Internet connection is ready to go, your Web site will have already benefited from live air time and feedback from the folks in your organization.

Installing Internet Information Server

If you've already installed Microsoft Internet Information Server (IIS), you can skip directly to the section called "Configuring Internet Information Server," later in this chapter. IIS can be installed and configured in just a few minutes. Here's how to install it on your Windows NT Server computer:

1. Insert the Windows NT Server 4.0 CD-ROM in your CD-ROM drive.
2. While logged on with administrator privileges to your Windows NT Server computer, click Start ➪ Settings ➪ Control Panel and double-click the Network icon.
3. The Network dialog box appears. Click the Services tab. A list of installed network services is displayed, as shown in Figure 22-1.

   If you see Microsoft Internet Information Server 2.0 as one of the installed services, skip to the section called "Configuring Internet Information Server," later in this chapter.

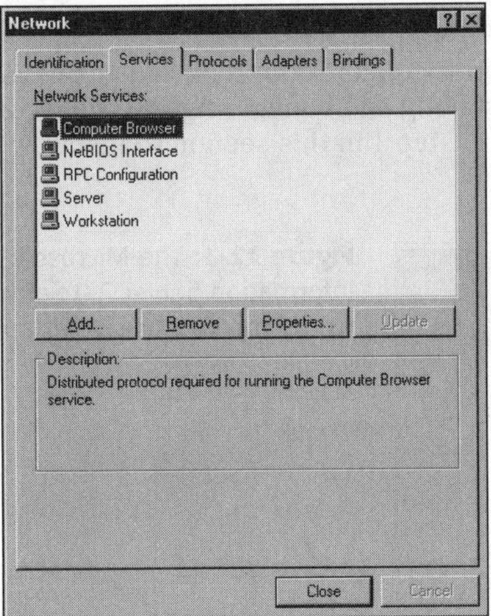

Figure 22-1: You can install IIS using the Network application in Control Panel.

4. Click Add. In the Select Network Service dialog box, click Microsoft Internet Information Server 2.0 as shown in Figure 22-2. Then click OK.

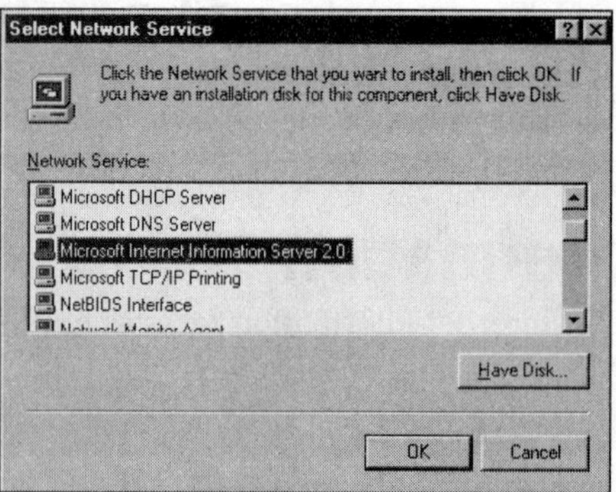

Figure 22-2: You can select IIS from the list of available network services.

5. The IIS Setup application asks for the path to the system files on your Windows NT Server 4.0 CD-ROM. Type the path and click OK.

   On my computer, the path is F:\I386. Type the drive letter of your CD-ROM and the subdirectory corresponding to your CPU platform.

6. The Microsoft Internet Information Server 2.0 Setup dialog box, shown in Figure 22-3, warns you to close all Windows applications before continuing. When you're done closing other applications, click OK.

   IIS Setup needs to copy several DLL files to NT's SYSTEM32 directory. If these files are in use by other applications, Setup may fail or result in an unstable IIS installation.

If you haven't installed the TCP/IP protocol, IIS Setup tells you at this point and terminates the installation. After installing and configuring TCP/IP according to the instructions in Chapter 11, go back to step 1 in this section to install IIS.

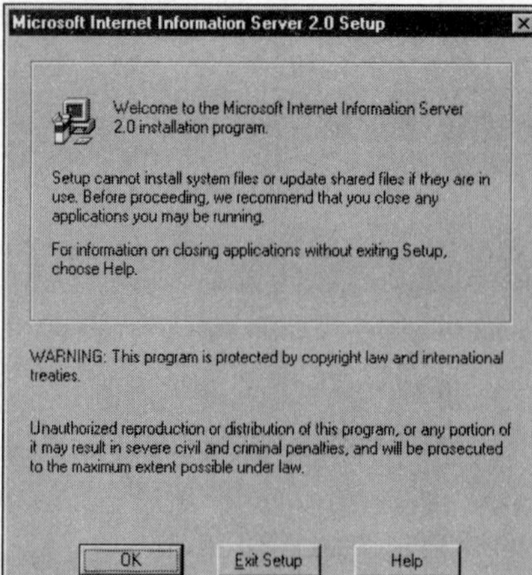

Figure 22-3: The Microsoft Internet Information Server 2.0 Setup dialog box warns you to close other applications.

7. You're given the option of installing various IIS components, as shown in Figure 22-4. Choose the ones that you want to install by clicking to select or clear the appropriate check boxes. If you want to change the IIS destination directory, click Change Directory and make the change. When you're done selecting the options and the IIS destination directory that you prefer, click OK.

   If you don't plan to use the Gopher Service, click to clear its check box. I recommend that you install all other IIS options. If the destination directory that you specify doesn't exist, you'll be asked to confirm that you want to create it.

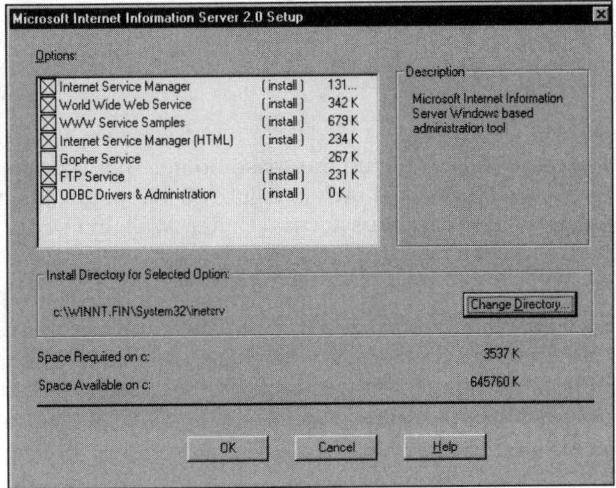

Figure 22-4: You can select the IIS options that you want to install.

8. Specify where your published files will reside on your NT Server computer in the Publishing Directories dialog box, as shown in Figure 22-5.

I strongly urge you to establish your publishing directories on an NTFS volume for security reasons. If you use a FAT volume, you won't be able to set file and directory permissions to prevent unauthorized users from accessing your published material.

See Chapter 18 for a discussion of file and directory permissions on NTFS. See Chapter 24 for more information about Internet server security.

   When you're done specifying the information publishing directories, click OK. If any of the specified directories don't exist, you'll need to confirm that you want Setup to create them.

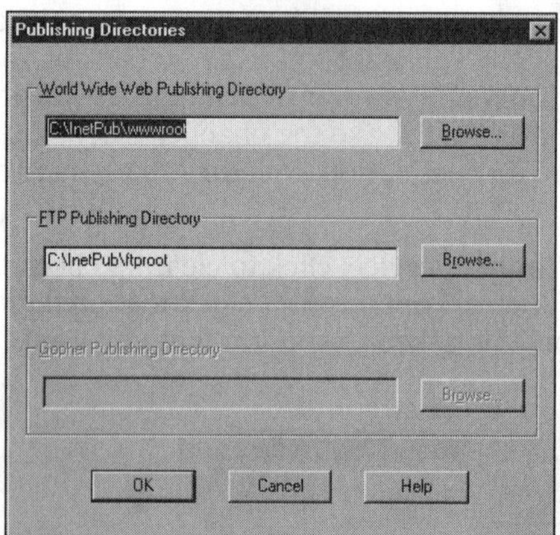

Figure 22-5: You can specify where you want your published WWW, FTP, and Gopher files to reside.

9. If you elected to install ODBC (Open Database Connectivity) drivers in step 7, the Install Drivers dialog box shown in Figure 22-6 appears. It's used to install an ODBC driver for database access. Under Available ODBC Drivers, click SQL Server, and click OK.

Once IIS is installed, you'll be able to experiment with its included sample ODBC database applications. However, you'll need to have Microsoft SQL Server installed on your NT Server computer to experiment with them. Later in this chapter, in the "Using the Internet Database Connector" section, I'll show you how to create a Web interface to a Microsoft Access database using ODBC and the Internet Database Connector (IDC).

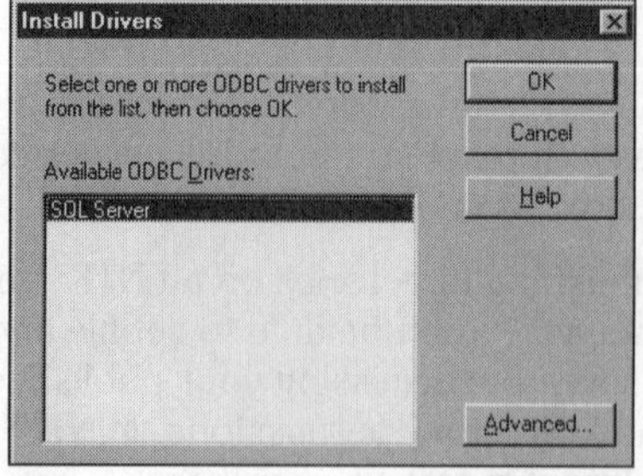

Figure 22-6: You must install the SQL Server ODBC driver to allow access to your databases.

10. Click OK when IIS Setup tells you that it's complete, as shown in Figure 22-7.

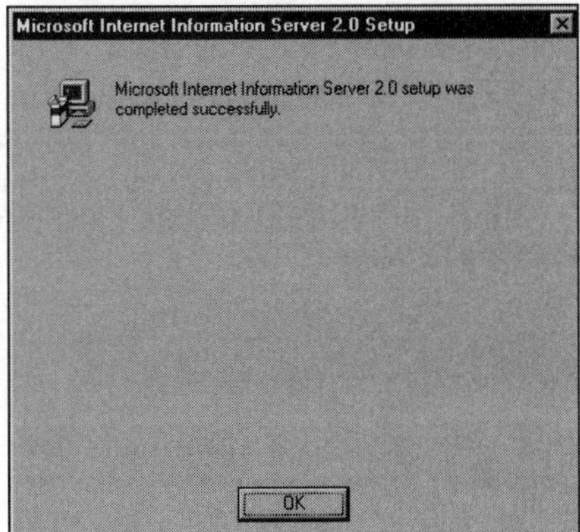

Figure 22-7: IIS has been installed successfully.

IIS is now installed and ready for use. You can verify that IIS is properly installed by clicking the Services tab in the Network application in Control Panel. If IIS is properly installed, it's listed among the other installed network services, as shown in Figure 22-8.

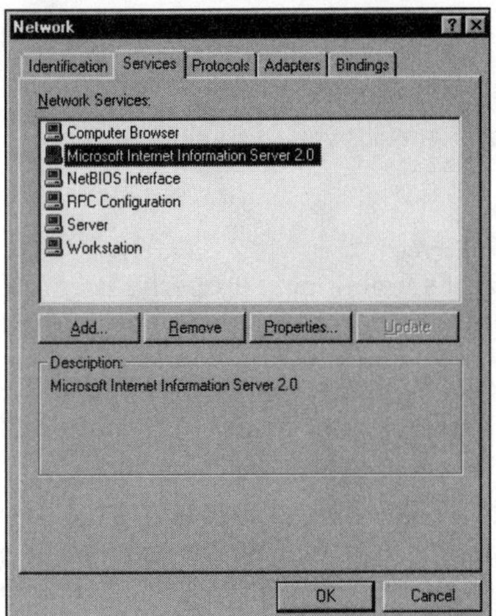

Figure 22-8: IIS appears in the list of installed network services.

If you ever need to add or remove IIS components, update your IIS installation, or remove the IIS installation completely, you can use the IIS Setup program to perform these tasks. Click Start ⇨ Programs ⇨ Microsoft Internet Server ⇨ Internet Information Server Setup and follow the on-screen instructions.

Configuring Internet Information Server

The Internet Service Manager utility is used to administer all aspects of IIS. In addition to enabling you to configure IIS, it's used to stop and start IIS components installed on your network. With this feature, you can centralize administration of all IIS installations on your network. After you've successfully installed IIS, here's how to use the Internet Service Manager to test your IIS installation:

1. Click Start ➪ Programs ➪ Microsoft Internet Server ➪ Internet Service Manager.
2. Ensure that the WWW and FTP services are running, as shown in Figure 22-9. If either of these services isn't running, right-click the service that's stopped, and click Start on the pop-up menu that appears.

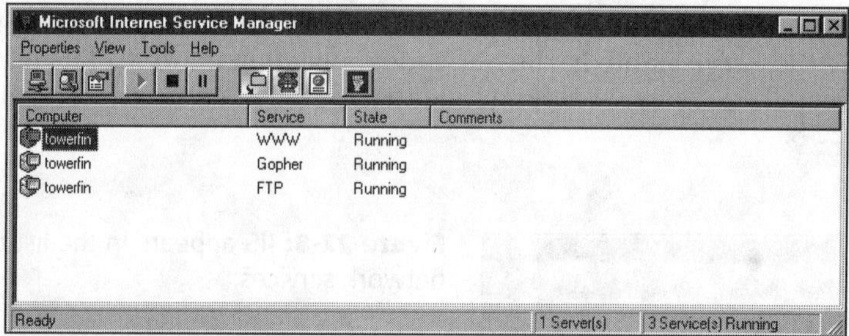

Figure 22-9: The Internet Service Manager enables you to administer your IIS components.

3. Before configuring IIS, make sure that it's functioning properly. Start Internet Explorer by double-clicking the Internet Explorer icon on the desktop. In the Address field, type the DNS address of your server (for example, www.server.com). If the server is on your intranet, you can type http:// followed by the server's WINS address (for example, its computer name) or IP address. If IIS is installed properly, the Web page shown in Figure 22-10 appears.

   Browse the IIS default Web page to explore various features of IIS and how they're implemented. Remember that Microsoft SQL Server is required to try out the database examples. If you don't have SQL Server, you can still use IIS's Internet Database Connector (IDC) as demonstrated later in this chapter in the "Using the Internet Database Connector" section.

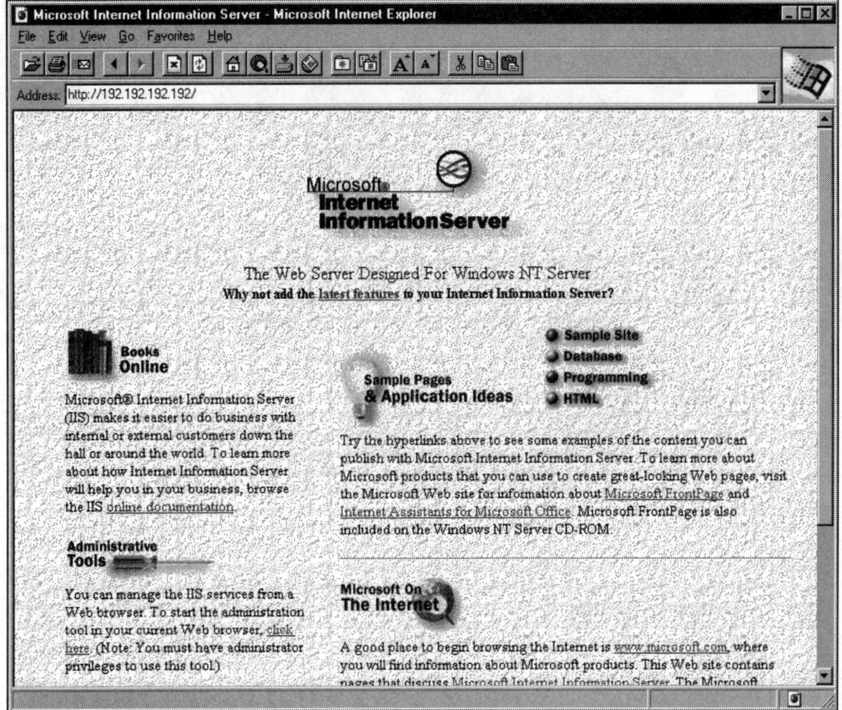

Figure 22-10: You can test your Web installation by accessing the IIS default Web page using Internet Explorer.

Since HTTP (HyperText Transfer Protocol) and FTP (File Transfer Protocol) are two of the most widely used Internet protocols for distributing information, this chapter focuses on how to configure them in IIS. Refer to the Microsoft IIS documentation for information about using Gopher.

Configuring the WWW Publishing Server

Once you've verified that the WWW service is operating correctly, here's how to configure it using the Internet Service Manager:

1. In the Internet Service Manager window, right-click the WWW publishing service that you want to configure, as shown in Figure 22-9. On the pop-up menu, click Service Properties. The dialog box in Figure 22-11 appears.

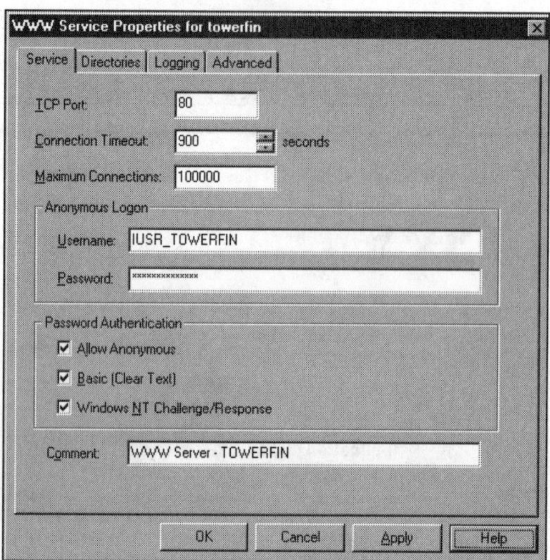

Figure 22-11: Use the Service tab of the WWW Service Properties dialog box to configure your WWW service.

2. Leave the default TCP/IP port set to 80, unless you're already running an Internet application that uses that port. If you need to change it to avoid a port conflict, select an unused port greater than 1024.

   For example, if you're already running the Netscape Enterprise Server, it's probably already occupying TCP/IP port 80. In this case, you'll need to specify a different port for IIS.

3. If you have a limited-bandwidth Internet connection, you'll need to reduce the Maximum Connections field to a smaller value.

4. The Password Authentication settings are used by IIS to enforce security on your Web server. Click to select the Allow Anonymous check box if you want to allow users to navigate your Web site without providing a user name and password.

   You can use Windows NT NTFS security to restrict access to selected parts of your Web site. For example, NTFS file permissions can be used to allow only certain users to access files in a directory. When an anonymous user attempts to access information in this directory, IIS will authenticate the connection by asking for a user name and password. See Chapter 18 for details on file and directory permissions.

   IIS supports two password authentication mechanisms: Basic (Clear Text) and Windows NT Challenge/Response. Each mechanism has its own pros and cons. Basic (Clear Text) authentication offers very little security because user names and passwords aren't encrypted before they're transmitted over the network.

   On the other hand, Windows NT Challenge/Response authentication offers a higher level of security because user authentication information is always encrypted before it's transmitted over the network. Unfortunately, only Microsoft's Internet Explorer 2.0 (and above) supports it. Therefore, use Windows NT Challenge/Response authentication only if you're certain that your users will only be using Internet Explorer to access restricted areas of your Web site.

Click to select or clear the appropriate check boxes under Password Authentication.

5. Use the Directories tab of the WWW Service Properties dialog box, shown in Figure 22-12, to configure how IIS handles directories. If you want to create a new file directory alias, click Add.

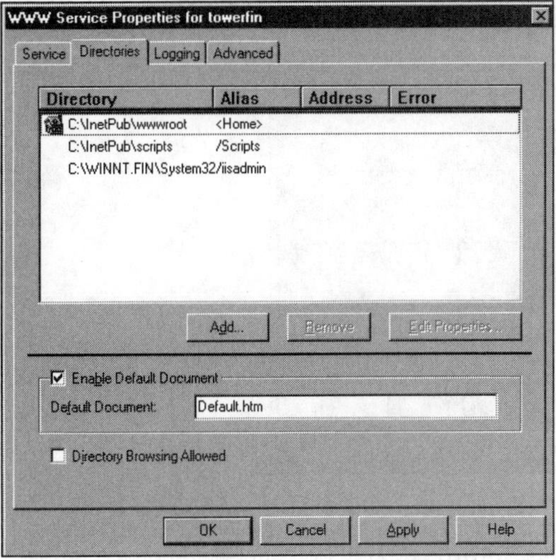

Figure 22-12: You can use the Directories tab of the WWW Service Properties dialog box to control the behavior of your WWW directories.

6. If you want to send a default document whenever a user specifies a URL without a filename at the end (for example, http://www.server.com/directory/ or http://www.server.com/), click to select the Enable Default Document check box. Then, in the Default Document field, type the filename of the document that you want to send.

7. Click to select the Directory Browsing Allowed check box, if you want to permit Web browsers to view contents of all directories.

I recommend that you refrain from selecting this check box for security reasons. It's dangerous to have users roam all over your Web server directory structure, as they might stumble onto something that you don't want them to see.

8. Web server access logging is key to determining who accessed what on your Web server. The Logging tab of the WWW Service Properties dialog box, shown in Figure 22-13, is used to configure how IIS logs Web server accesses.

IIS allows accesses to be logged to an ODBC data source or to a plain text file. If you've invested in an application that analyzes Web server log files, you should log to a plain text file by clicking Log to File. I recommend automatically opening a new log file once a week.

On the other hand, if you're comfortable with ODBC/Visual Basic programming, you may want to write a small Visual Basic application to analyze Web server access statistics and generate a customized statistics report. In this case, click Log to SQL/ODBC Database.

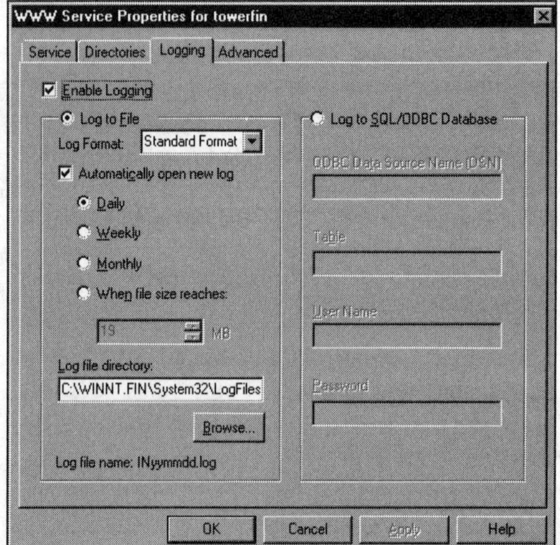

Figure 22-13: You use the Logging tab of the WWW Service Properties dialog box to control how Web site accesses are logged.

9. The Advanced tab of the WWW Service Properties dialog box, shown in Figure 22-14, is used to configure various IIS network access settings.

   This dialog box can be used to deny access to certain computers based on their IP addresses. The Advanced tab can also be used to limit network bandwidth used by IIS, if this becomes an issue.

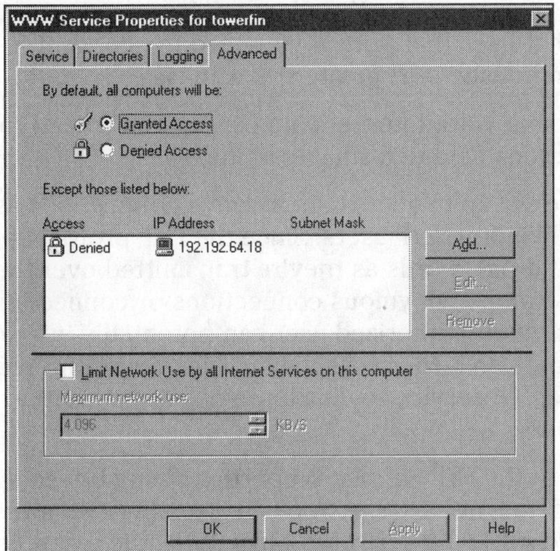

Figure 22-14: You use the Advanced tab to limit access from specified computers and limit the network bandwidth used by the service.

Configuring the FTP Publishing Server

Here's how to configure the FTP service using the Internet Service Manager:

1. In the Internet Service Manager window, right-click the FTP publishing service that you want to configure, as shown in Figure 22-9. On the pop-up menu, click Service Properties. The dialog box in Figure 22-15 appears.

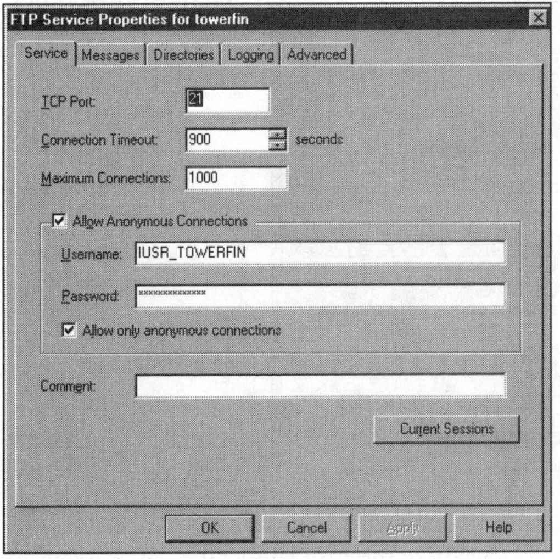

Figure 22-15: You use the Service tab of the FTP Service Properties dialog box to configure your FTP service.

2. Leave the default TCP/IP port set to 21, unless you're already running an Internet application that uses that port. If you need to change it to avoid a port conflict, select an unused port greater than 1024.
3. If you have a limited bandwidth Internet connection, you'll need to reduce the Maximum Connections field to a smaller value.
4. IIS's FTP server can be set up to access anonymous connections as well as connections made by Windows NT users. Since the FTP protocol doesn't encrypt user names and passwords as they're transmitted over the network, I don't recommend allowing anonymous connections or connections made by Windows NT users. An unauthorized user can potentially intercept a user name and password and use it to access your NT Server computer. I recommend that you use the FTP service to distribute only nonsensitive information to anonymous users.
5. Use the Messages tab in the FTP Service Properties dialog box to specify a Welcome message and an Exit message. You can also specify a message that's displayed whenever your FTP server is too busy to handle a new connection.

   You might want to establish messages similar to the ones that appear in Figure 22-16. It's always a good idea to provide the name, e-mail address, and phone number of a person to contact if a user encounters a problem with your FTP server. You can use the messages in Figure 22-16 as a template for your own personalized messages.

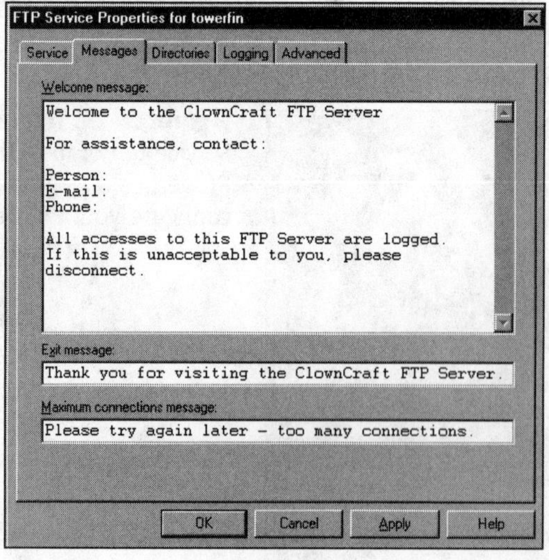

Figure 22-16: You use the Messages tab of the FTP Service Properties dialog box to specify welcome, exit, and busy messages.

6. Use the Directories tab to create various directory mappings and control how directory information is displayed by the FTP server, as shown in Figure 22-17. If you want to create a new file directory alias, click Add.

I recommend that you select the UNIX directory listing style on the Directories tab since some older Web browsers don't understand MS-DOS style directory listings.

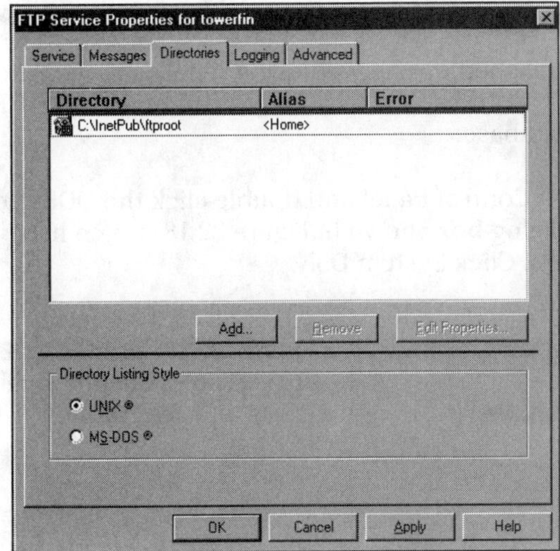

Figure 22-17: You use the Directories tab of the FTP Service Properties dialog box to control how your FTP directories behave.

7. The functionality of the Logging and Advanced tabs of the FTP Service Properties dialog box are identical in functionality to their counterparts in the WWW Service Properties dialog box. For details, see steps 8 and 9 in the section called "Configuring the WWW Publishing Server," earlier in this chapter.

Using the Internet Database Connector

The Internet Database Connector (IDC), which is included with IIS, can be used to publish ODBC data sources on the Web. Perform the following steps to create a Web interface to an ODBC data source:

1. Install an ODBC driver for your database application, if one isn't installed already.
2. Set up the data source as an ODBC data source.
3. Create the HTML form used to enter the data.
4. Create the Internet Database Connector (IDC) file that will process the data.
5. Create the IDC HTML template file that formats data returned to the user.

I'll show you an example of how to create a Guest Book using the IDC. Refer to the documentation of your database application or ODBC driver for information about installing an ODBC driver and creating a System Data Source Name (System DSN) for a database that will be published on the Web. The following section assumes that you've already created a Microsoft Access database that will contain the Guest Book entries.

Creating a System Data Source Name for a Database

Before a database can be published on the Web using the IDC, it needs to be set up as a System DSN. Here's how to use the ODBC application in Control Panel to create a System DSN for a database:

1. Click Start ➪ Settings ➪ Control Panel and double-click the ODBC icon. You'll see the Data Sources dialog box shown in Figure 22-18, which lists various user data source drivers. Click System DSN.

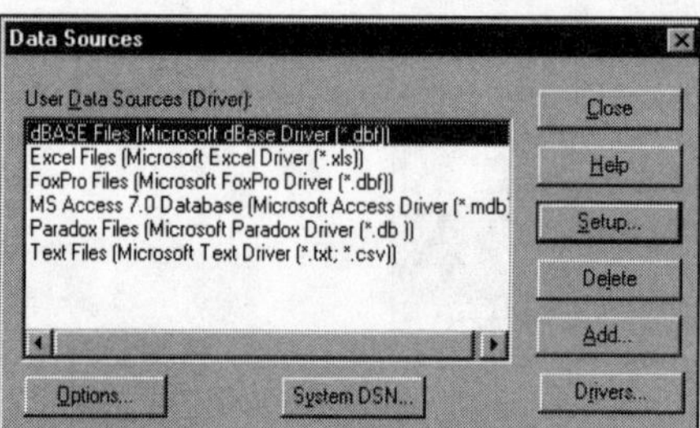

Figure 22-18: Use the ODBC application in Control Panel to create a System DSN.

2. The System Data Sources dialog box appears, listing various System DSNs installed on your system. Click Add to set up the Guest Book database as a System DSN, as shown in Figure 22-19.

At the end of this section, after your database is set up as a System DSN, I recommend that you bring up this dialog box again to verify that it has been properly set up as a System DSN.

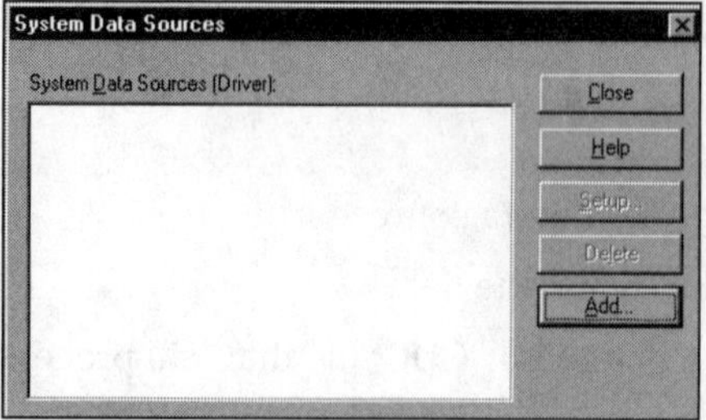

Figure 22-19: The System Data Sources dialog box is used to create a System DSN for a database with an ODBC driver.

3. Use the Add Data Source dialog box in Figure 22-20 to select an ODBC driver for the database that will be set up as a System DSN. For example, if the database that you intend to publish on the Web is a Microsoft Access database,

select the Microsoft Access driver. Click the appropriate database driver, then click OK.

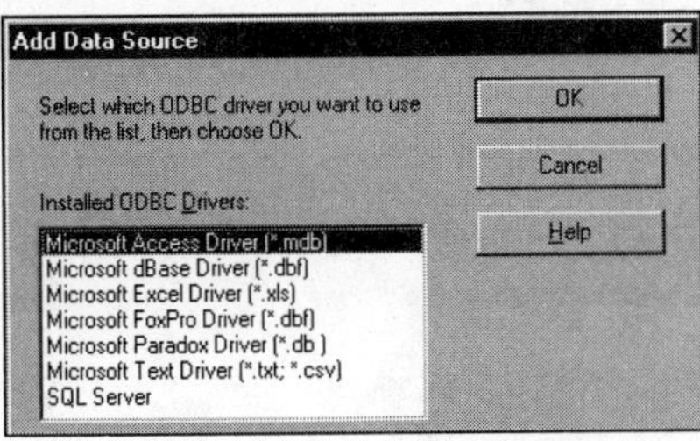

Figure 22-20: The Add Data Source dialog box is used to select an ODBC driver for the database that will be set up as a System DSN.

4. Use the ODBC Microsoft Access 7.0 Setup dialog box, shown in Figure 22-21, to specify various settings of the System DSN. Type the name of the System DSN in the Data Source Name field. I recommend that you give it a descriptive name that's easy to remember. You'll need to refer to the name of the System DSN when you create the IDC file for it. Type the System DSN description in the Description field. Then click Select, select a database, and click OK.

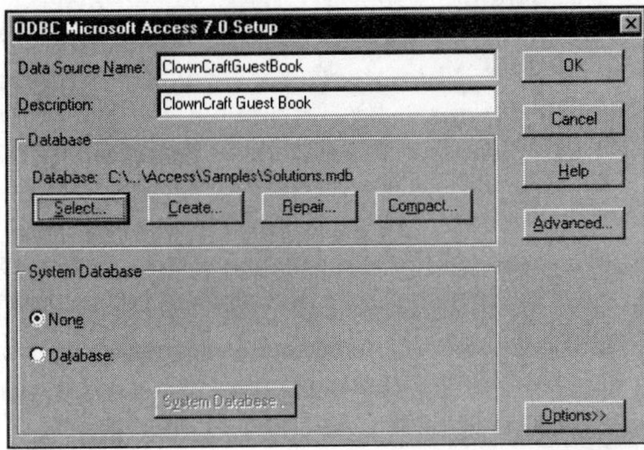

Figure 22-21: You use the ODBC Microsoft Access 7.0 Setup dialog box to specify the name, description, and database of the System DSN.

The database that you intend to publish on the Web is now set up as a System DSN. All that's left to do is create the HTML form that's used to interface with the database and create the IDC files that will process the data submitted by the HTML form.

Creating the HTML Form

An HTML form has to be created to interface with the Guest Book database that will be published on the Web. The source code of the HTML form in Figure 22-22 follows. One of the biggest advantages of using an HTML form for data entry is that you can use selection lists, radio buttons, and check boxes to ensure that users only enter valid data.

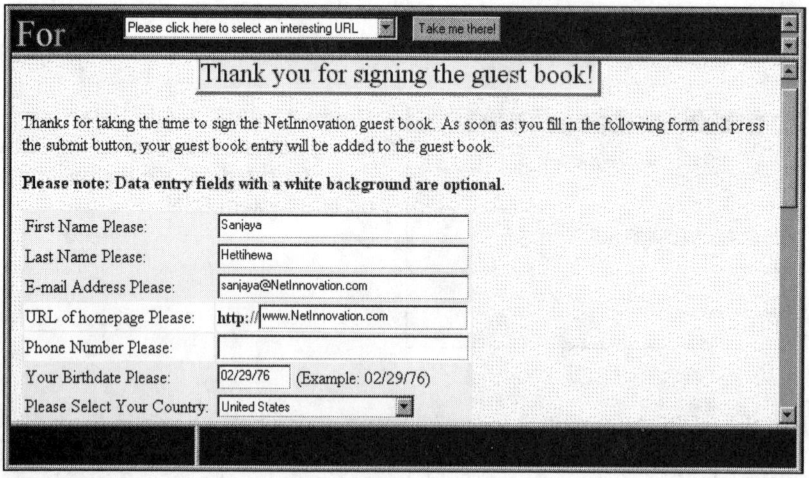

Figure 22-22: The source code listed in the text generates the HTML form of the Guest Book.

For example, the <SELECT NAME="Country" SIZE=1> data entry field is used to ensure that users can't enter the name of a country that doesn't exist. Notice the ACTION tag (<form action="/cgi-bin/GuestBookSubmit.IDC" method="POST">) of the HTML form listed in the following. When the Guest Book data is submitted, it's processed by the IDC file "GuestBookSubmit.IDC." The next section discusses how the IDC file inserts the HTML form data into the database that you selected in Figure 22-21.

Here's the HTML source code that generates the form shown in Figure 22-22. I've removed some of the country options in the list of countries. Normally, you'd include every possible valid entry.

```
<HTML>
<HEAD><TITLE>Submit Guest Book Entry</TITLE>
</HEAD>
<BODY BGCOLOR="#F7FFF4">

<CENTER><TABLE BORDER=3 BGCOLOR=FFFFCC>
<TR><TD><FONT  SIZE=+2>Thank you for signing the guest
     book!</FONT></TD></TR>
</TABLE></CENTER>

<p>Thanks for taking the time to sign the NetInnovation guest
       book. As soon as you fill in the following form and press
       the submit button, your guest book entry will be added
       to the guest book.</p>
```

```
<P><B>Please note: Data entry fields with a white background are
      optional.</B></P>
<form action="/cgi-bin/GuestBookSubmit.IDC" method="POST">
<TABLE BGCOLOR=FFFFCC>
<TR>
<TD>First Name Please: </TD><TD><INPUT NAME="FirstName"
      TYPE="TEXT" COLS=50 SIZE="43" ALIGN=left></TD>
</TR>
<TR>
<TD>Last Name Please: </TD><TD><INPUT NAME="LastName"
      TYPE="TEXT" COLS=50 SIZE="43" ALIGN=left></TD>
</TR>
<TR>
<TD>E-mail Address Please: </TD><TD><INPUT NAME="EMailAddress"
      TYPE="TEXT" COLS=50 SIZE="43" ALIGN=left></TD>
</TR>
<TR BGCOLOR=FFFFFF>
<TD>URL of homepage Please: </TD><TD><B>http://</B><INPUT
      NAME="UserURL" TYPE="TEXT" COLS=50 SIZE="35"
      ALIGN=left></TD>
</TR>
<TR BGCOLOR=FFFFFF>
<TD>Phone Number Please: </TD><TD><INPUT NAME="Phone"
      TYPE="TEXT" COLS=50 SIZE="43" ALIGN=left></TD>
</TR>
<TR>
<TD>Your Birthdate Please: </TD><TD><INPUT NAME="Birthdate"
      TYPE="TEXT" COLS=10 SIZE="10" ALIGN=left> (Example:
      02/29/76)</TD>
</TR>
<TR>
<TD >Please Select Your Country: </TD><TD>
<SELECT NAME="Country" SIZE=1>
<OPTION>United States </OPTION>
<OPTION>Afghanistan   </OPTION>
…and other countries from Albania to Zambia…
<OPTION>Zimbabwe      </OPTION>
</SELECT>
</TD>
</TR>
<TR>
<TD>City / State / Province </TD><TD><INPUT NAME="City"
      TYPE="TEXT" COLS=50 SIZE="43" ALIGN=left></TD>
</TR>
</TABLE>

<TABLE BGCOLOR=FFFFFF>
How did you discover WWW.NetInnovation.com?<BR>
<TEXTAREA NAME="Source" WRAP=VIRTUAL ROWS=2 COLS=82 SIZE="82"
      ALIGN=left></TEXTAREA><BR>
Please type your comments below. (Feel free to use HTML!)<BR>
<TEXTAREA NAME="Comments" WRAP=VIRTUAL ROWS=10 COLS=82
```

```
      SIZE="82" ALIGN=left></TEXTAREA><BR>
</TABLE>

<TABLE BGCOLOR=000000>
<input type="submit" value="Submit Comments">
<input type="reset" value="Clear Form">
</TABLE>

</form>

<HR>
In case you are curious, after you press the
submit button, your guest book entry is inserted to a
Microsoft Access database.</strong>
<HR>
<h5>Copyright &#169; 1995 Sanjaya Hettihewa. All rights
      reserved.<br>
Revised: June 29, 1996.</h5>
<p> </p>
</body>
</html>
```

Creating the Internet Database Connector Files

The IDC file, GuestBookSubmit.IDC, which actually processes the information submitted by the HTML form follows. It inserts the data to the data source named NetInnovationGuestBook. The Template file (Template: GuestBookSubmit.htx) formats the results of the data entry. The RequiredParameters statement refers to various data entry fields of the HTML form that must be completed for the data entry to be accepted. Finally, the statement, SQLStatement:, inserts various data entry fields of the HTML form to corresponding data entry fields in a table of the Guest Book database, which you selected in Figure 22-21.

```
Datasource: NetInnovationGuestBook
Username: sa
Template: GuestBookSubmit.htx
RequiredParameters: FirstName, LastName, EMailAddress,
      Birthdate, City
SQLStatement:
+  INSERT INTO GuestBookEntries
+  (FirstName, LastName, EMailAddress, UserURL, Phone,
      Birthdate, City, Country, Source, Comments)
+  VALUES('%FirstName%', '%LastName%', '%EMailAddress%',
      '%UserURL%', '%Phone%' ,
+   '%Birthdate%', '%City%', '%Country%', '%Source%',
      '%Comments%' );
```

When a user submits information using the IDC, it's wise to inform the user that the data was successfully submitted. You might also want to take the opportunity to thank the user for submitting the data and offer several URLs to make it easy to continue browsing your Web site. The Guest Book registration confirmation Web page in Figure 22-23 is generated by the Template file (GuestBookSubmit.htx) and is listed here.

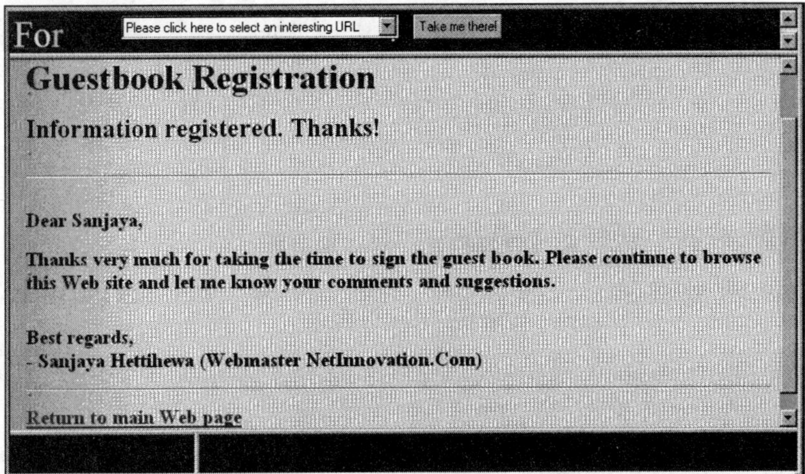

Figure 22-23: The source code listed in the text generates this result of a successful Guest Book submission.

```
<html>
<title>Guestbook Registration</title>
<BODY BACKGROUND="/samples/images/backgrnd.gif">
<BODY BGCOLOR="FFFFFF">
<TABLE>
<tr>
<TD></TD>
<TD>
<hr>
<h1>Guestbook Registration</h1>
<h2>Information registered. Thanks!</h2>
<hr>
<BR>
<H3>
Dear <%idc.FirstName%>,<P>
Thanks very much for taking the time to sign the guest book.
       Please continue to browse this Web site and let me know
       your comments and suggestions.<P>
<BR>
```

```
Best regards,<BR>
- Sanjaya Hettihewa (Webmaster NetInnovation.Com)
<HR>
<A TARGET="_TOP" HREF="/index.html">Return to main Web page</A>
</H3>
</td>
</tr>
</table>
</body>
</html>
```

The Template file used by the IDC is just a regular HTML file. Information entered by a user can be echoed back using the syntax <%idc.[Data Field Name]%> as in the case of <%idc.FirstName%>.

Using Microsoft's Index Server

The Microsoft Index Server, code-named Tripoli, can be used to make a Web site fully searchable in a matter of minutes. Here's how:

1. Download a free copy of the Microsoft Index Server from `http://www.microsoft.com/ntserver/search/`.

   Follow the instructions for registration and download provided on this and subsequent Web pages.

2. Copy the downloaded Index Server file SRCHENU.EXE to a temporary directory to execute it. When asked if you want to install Tripoli, click Yes.

3. The Tripoli End User License Agreement (EULA) appears as shown in Figure 22-24. Read it and, if you agree to its terms, click Yes.

   If you click No, you won't be permitted to install Tripoli.

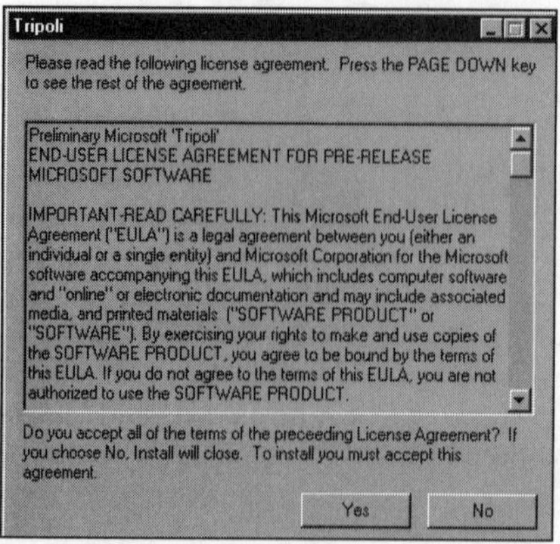

Figure 22-24: You must read the Tripoli license agreement and indicate your acceptance.

4. The dialog box in Figure 22-25 asks you to confirm that you want to install Tripoli, which is an ISAPI (Internet Server Application Programming Interface) extension for Microsoft's IIS. Click Continue.

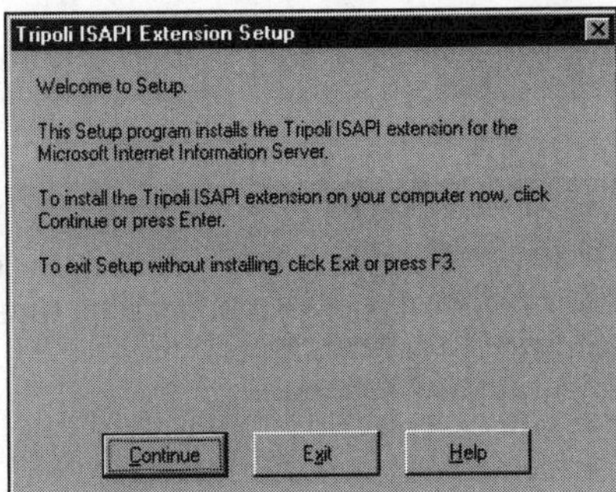

Figure 22-25: You must confirm that you want to install the Tripoli ISAPI extension to IIS.

5. The Tripoli ISAPI Extension Setup dialog box appears, as shown in Figure 22-26. Type the full path name of IIS's CGI (Common Gateway Interface) directory. Click Continue.

   Tripoli will copy its sample scripts into the specified directory. Refer to the IIS configuration settings to determine the name of IIS's CGI directory if you're not familiar with it.

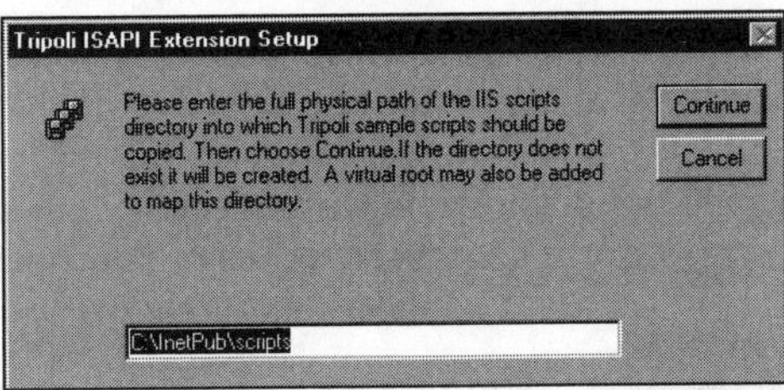

Figure 22-26: You specify the CGI directory where the Tripoli sample scripts will go.

6. The Tripoli ISAPI Extension Setup dialog box appears, as shown in Figure 22-27. Type the full path name where you want the HTML sample pages stored. Then click Continue.

   Tripoli will copy its sample pages into the specified directory. This directory is usually the document root directory of your Web server.

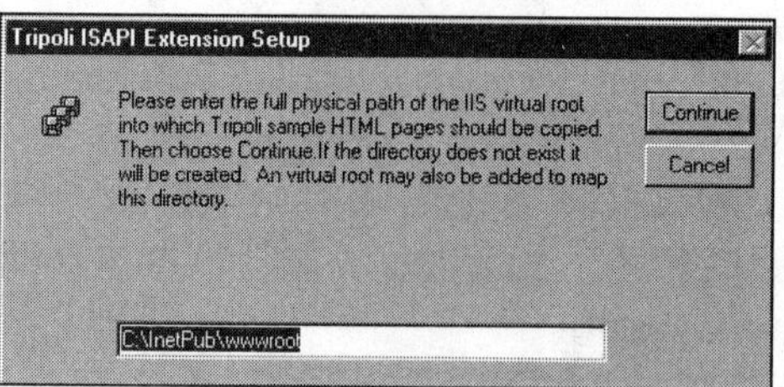

Figure 22-27: Specify the document root directory where the Tripoli sample HTML pages will go.

7. You need to specify where Tripoli will store the various search indexes that it creates. Type the full path name of the Tripoli server's index directory, as shown in Figure 22-28. Click Continue.

   The path that you specify must already exist. Unfortunately, Tripoli Setup can't create it for you.

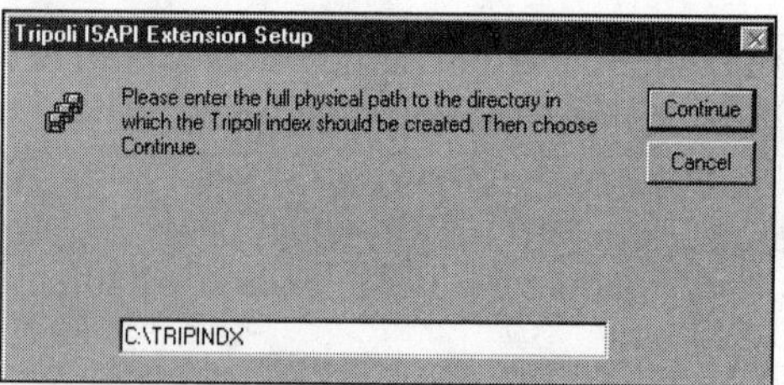

Figure 22-28: You specify the path name of the Tripoli Server's index directory.

8. Click Exit to Windows. The Microsoft Index Server is now installed and ready for use.

   Note the sample search page location shown in the dialog box in Figure 22-29. You'll be able to use it later to perform generic searches of your Web site.

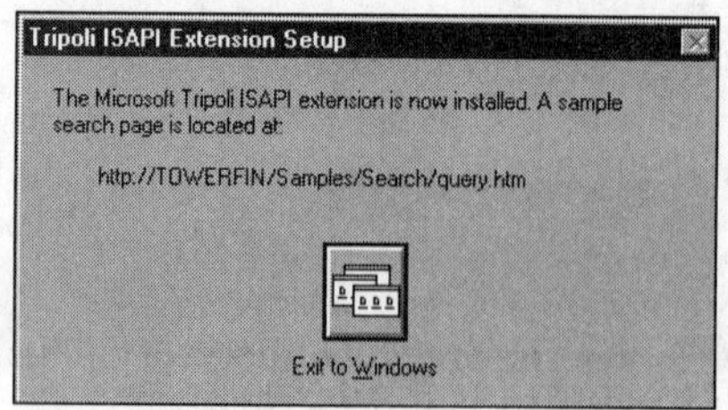

Figure 22-29: The Microsoft Index Server has been successfully installed.

9. Before users can search your Web site using the Tripoli server, you must create a search index.

   Using Internet Explorer, browse the URL `http://www.server.com/samples/Search/Admin.htm` to access the Tripoli server's administration menu. (Replace www.server.com with the DNS, WINS, or IP address of your

IIS computer.) The Tripoli Administration Web page is shown in Figure 22-30. Click Start to the right of Force scan virtual roots to create a search index for your Web site.

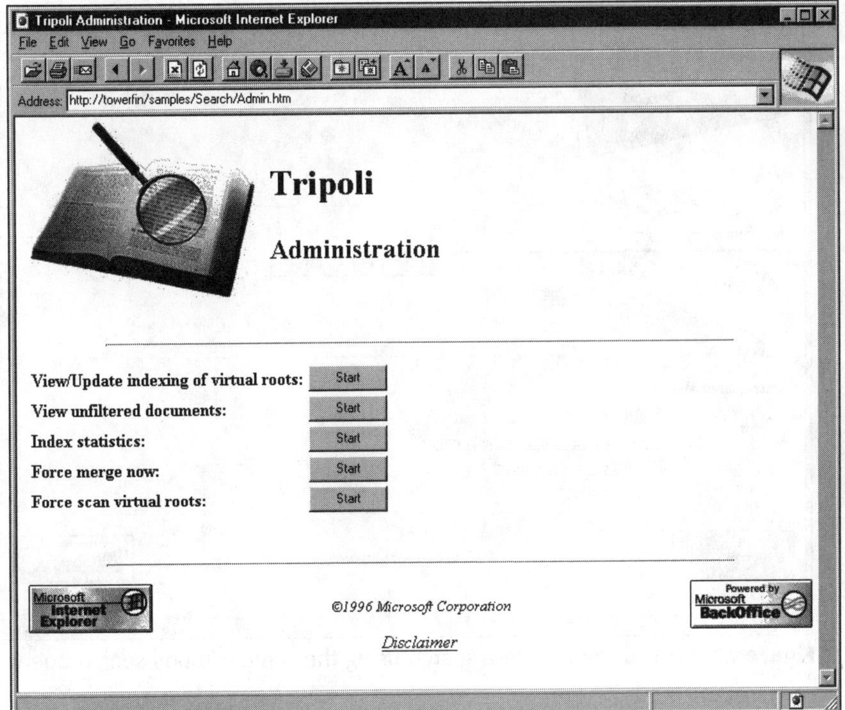

Figure 22-30: The Tripoli Index Server administration menu is used to create a search index.

Once a search index is created, use the URL `http://www.server.com/samples/Search/query.htm` to execute search queries as shown in Figure 22-31. The URLs listed under Other query pages can be used to initiate more sophisticated queries, such as locating all files modified after a certain date.

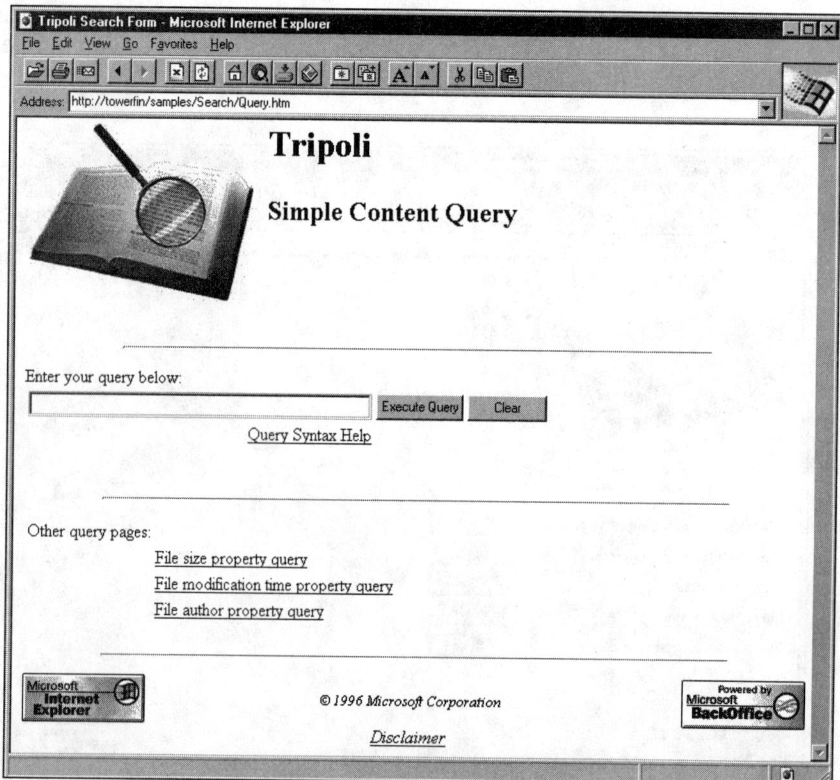

Figure 22-31: You can initiate a search using the sample Tripoli search query.

Summary

The Microsoft Internet Information Server is a powerful Web server that can be used to build a fully functional Web site based on Windows NT Server. Compared with other Windows NT Web servers, IIS is a very attractive Web server solution because it:

- ✦ Is well-integrated with Windows NT, yielding high performance, robustness, security, and scalability
- ✦ Uses NTFS security. NT Explorer can be used to restrict access to selected parts of your Web site by requiring a user name and password
- ✦ Includes database connectivity via the Internet Database Connector and ODBC
- ✦ Supports an optional Index Server to make your Web site fully searchable
- ✦ Costs little (included free with Windows NT Server)

In this chapter, you've learned how to install the Microsoft Internet Information Server, how to configure WWW and FTP services, and how to handle forms and data using the Internet Database Connector (IDC). You've also seen how to install and use the Microsoft Index Server (Tripoli), to simplify searching for information on your Web site.

In Chapter 23, you'll learn how to create content for your Web site using Microsoft's Office and FrontPage products. Then, in Chapter 24, you'll discover how to make your Internet server and your LAN as secure as possible from external prying eyes.

Creating Web Pages on Windows NT

✦ ✦ ✦ ✦

If you've completed installation and configuration of the Microsoft Internet Information Server (IIS), described in Chapter 22, your Web server is now ready for publishing information to the Internet (or to your intranet). Dozens of Web page development tools are currently available for Windows NT. In this chapter, I'll focus on using Microsoft Excel, Word, and FrontPage to create content for your Web site. By the end of this chapter, you'll have the skills to

✦ Install Internet Assistants for both Microsoft Excel and Microsoft Word

✦ Create Web pages from Microsoft Word documents

✦ Publish a Microsoft Excel spreadsheet on your Web site

✦ Install and use Microsoft FrontPage, a powerful set of Web site creation and management tools

You'll need to download Internet Assistants for Office from Microsoft's Web site in order to "Web-enable" Office applications. All Internet Assistants discussed in this chapter are available free of charge.

The Excel and Word information in this chapter is based on the Microsoft Office 95 suite. Future versions of Office will include Web publishing features, so you won't have to download and install Internet Assistants.

Creating Web Content with Microsoft Office

You can easily publish Microsoft Office files on your Web site either in their original *native* format or as HTML Web pages using an Internet Assistant. I'll cover the benefits and drawbacks associated with both approaches in the following sections.

Publishing Office Files in Native Format

You can publish Office files in their native format whenever you have full control over the client operating system, the Web browser, and installed application software. For example, in an intranet environment, if Office is the standard productivity suite on virtually all of your desktop computers, it makes sense to use the native format. Users who have Office installed on their computers can then use it to view and manipulate these files. Users who don't have Office installed can download and use a stand-alone viewer from Microsoft's Web site to view the documents in read-only mode. Following are several benefits to publishing native Office documents:

- **Saves you time.** You waste no time converting files from one format to the other.
- **Supports richly formatted content.** The contents of a Web page can be richly formatted, using all of the features provided by the Office application.
- **Supports interactive content.** For example, a published Excel spreadsheet can be both viewed and manipulated by users browsing your Web site. Users can also edit a Word document from within their Web browser.
- **Presents a familiar user interface.** Since Office files are viewed as Active Documents inside Internet Explorer, the user's experience is familiar. For example, when an Excel spreadsheet is published to the Web, the pop-up menu that users see when they right-click a spreadsheet cell is identical to the menu presented in Microsoft Excel.

Publishing Office Files in HTML Format

If you don't have full control over the client operating system, the Web browser, and installed application software, you'll want to publish your files in HTML format. With the aid of Internet Assistants, you can convert Microsoft Office files into HTML Web pages. Although some layout and formatting attributes may be lost in the process, the final product is portable across many platforms and Web browsers. This is especially important when you publish Office files on the Internet because the Web browser software used in the Internet community is extremely diverse.

THE BEST OF BOTH WORLDS

Depending on the target audience of your Web site, you'll have to decide on the best approach for your organization. You can have the best of both worlds by publishing Office files both as HTML Web pages and in their native format. Users of Microsoft's Internet Explorer can then view Office documents natively, while users of other browsers can see the converted HTML Web pages.

Creating Web Content with Internet Assistants

The following sections demonstrate how Internet Assistants for Microsoft Word and Excel can be used to develop content for the Web. (Visit the Microsoft Office Web site `http://www.microsoft.com/msoffice/default.htm` for the latest updates on Office Internet Assistants and how to use them.)

Although I won't cover creating Web content from Microsoft PowerPoint or Schedule+ files in this chapter, Internet Assistants are available for these products as well. You can download the Internet Assistant for Microsoft PowerPoint from `http://www.microsoft.com/mspowerpoint/fs_ppt.htm`. If you need the Internet Assistant for Schedule+, you'll find it on the `http://www.microsoft.com/msscheduleplus/fs_sch.htm page.`

Developing Web Content with Microsoft Word

You can use Internet Assistant for Microsoft Word to develop Web pages and convert existing Word documents to HTML format. It provides a quick and easy way to turn your formatted text into professional-looking Web pages.

Installing Internet Assistant for Microsoft Word

Here's how to obtain and install Internet Assistant for Word:

1. Download a free copy of the Internet Assistant for Microsoft Word from the `http://www.microsoft.com/msword/fs_wd.htm` page.

   You'll need to follow the links from this page to the appropriate download page, read and agree to the license agreement, and select the appropriate language version that matches your Office applications.

2. If Microsoft Word is currently running on your computer, close it before proceeding to step 3. Doing this will avoid problems in subsequent installation steps.

   If you have multiple copies of Word running on your computer, close them all before proceeding.

3. Create a new directory and copy the downloaded executable file into it.

   The executable file name starts with WRDIA followed by its version number (for example, WRDIA20Z.EXE).

4. Execute the file. Click Yes to install Internet Assistant for Microsoft Word. Then click Continue, as shown in Figure 23-1.

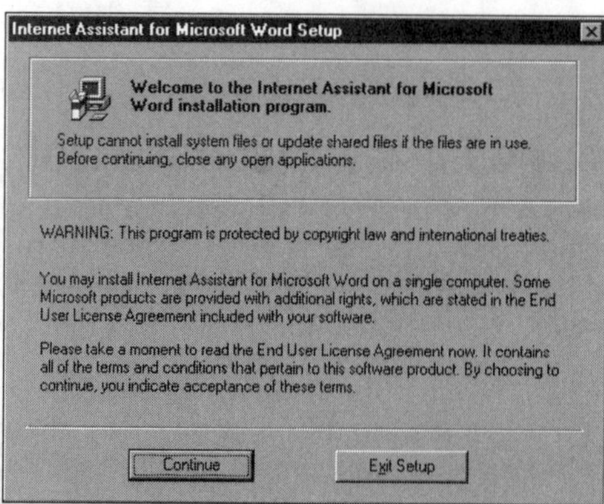

Figure 23-1: You install Internet Assistant for Microsoft Word by running the downloaded executable file.

5. Read the license agreement and click Accept if you agree to its terms.

   If you don't agree, click Exit Setup. You won't be able to install Internet Assistant unless you accept the terms of the license agreement.

6. You can change the installation folder by clicking Change Folder and specifying a new folder. When you're ready to continue, click Complete, as shown in Figure 23-2.

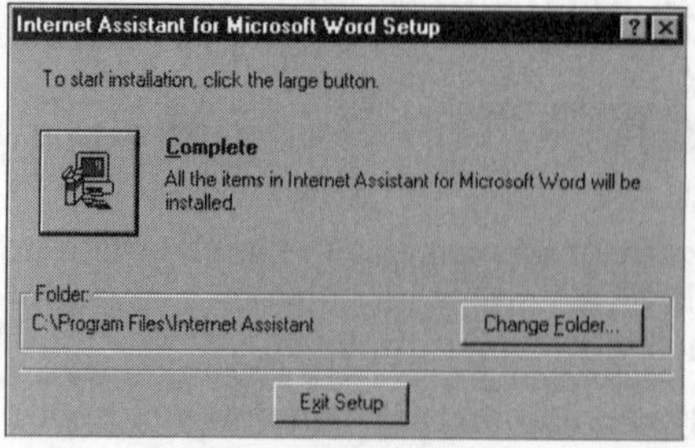

Figure 23-2: You can specify the installation destination folder.

7. Click Exit Setup, then click OK.

8. Start Microsoft Word. On the File menu, verify that the Browse Web command has been added, as shown in Figure 23-3.

This indicates that the Internet Assistant for Microsoft Word has been installed successfully.

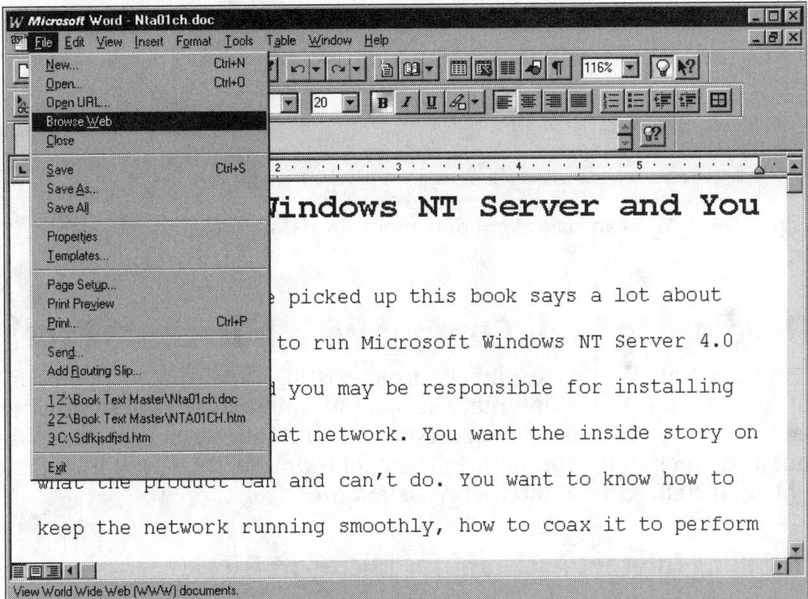

Figure 23-3: The Internet Assistant adds a Browse Web command to Microsoft Word's File menu.

Using Internet Assistant for Microsoft Word

Now that you've installed Internet Assistant for Microsoft Word, you can save any Word document in HTML format by loading it into Word, and clicking Save As on the File menu. In the Save as type list, select HTML Document (*.htm). Then click Save, as shown in Figure 23-4. That's all there is to it!

You can find useful tips and answers to commonly asked questions about Internet Assistant for Microsoft Word, HTML, and Web page development in general by clicking Browse Web on the File menu.

Internet Assistant does its best to translate Word formatting attributes to HTML statements. However, due to incompatibilities between the formats, some settings may be lost in the translation process. After saving a Word file in HTML format, view it using a Web browser to verify that the file was successfully translated.

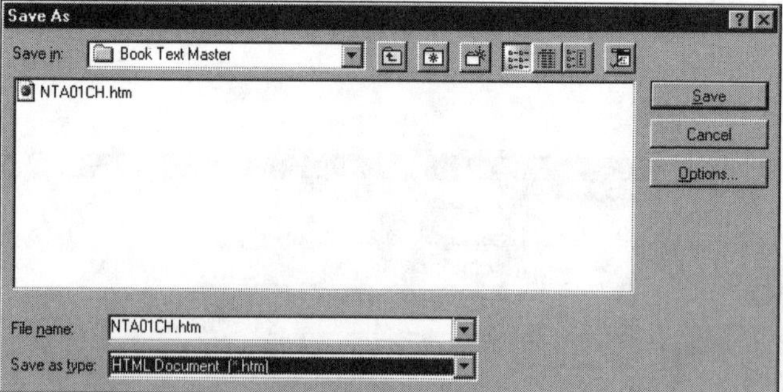

Figure 23-4: You can save Word documents in HTML format.

Developing Web Content with Microsoft Excel

You can create Web pages directly from existing Excel spreadsheets (or portions of spreadsheets) using Internet Assistant for Microsoft Excel. It provides you with an easy way to convert your spreadsheets to HTML, preserving not only the data, but also much of the formatting. In the following sections, you'll learn how to obtain, install, and use Internet Assistant for Excel.

Installing Internet Assistant for Microsoft Excel

Here's how to obtain and install Internet Assistant for Microsoft Excel:

1. Download a free copy of the Internet Assistant for Microsoft Excel from `http://www.microsoft.com/msexcel/fs_xl.htm`.

   You'll need to follow the links from this page to the appropriate download page, read and agree to the license agreement, and select the appropriate language version that matches your Office applications.

   This Internet Assistant is an Excel add-in macro file called HTML.XLA.

2. Copy HTML.XLA to your Microsoft Excel Library directory.

   This directory is typically C:\EXCEL\LIBRARY (for stand-alone Excel) or C:\MSOFFICE\EXCEL\LIBRARY (for Microsoft Office Excel).

3. Start Microsoft Excel. On the Tools menu, click Add-Ins.

4. In the Add-Ins dialog box, shown in Figure 23-5, click to select the Internet Assistant Wizard check box. Then click OK.

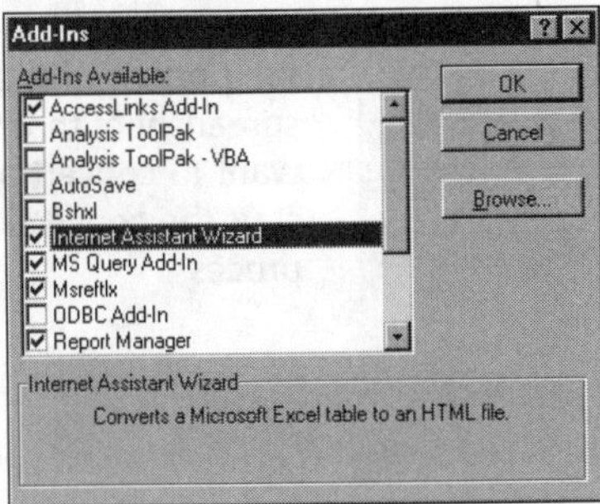

Figure 23-5: You can select the Internet Assistant Wizard add-in.

Using Internet Assistant for Microsoft Excel

Once you have Internet Assistant for Microsoft Excel installed, it's easy to turn Microsoft Excel spreadsheets into HTML Web pages. Here's how to convert the spreadsheet shown in Figure 23-6 (the sample spreadsheet shipped with Excel) to HTML format:

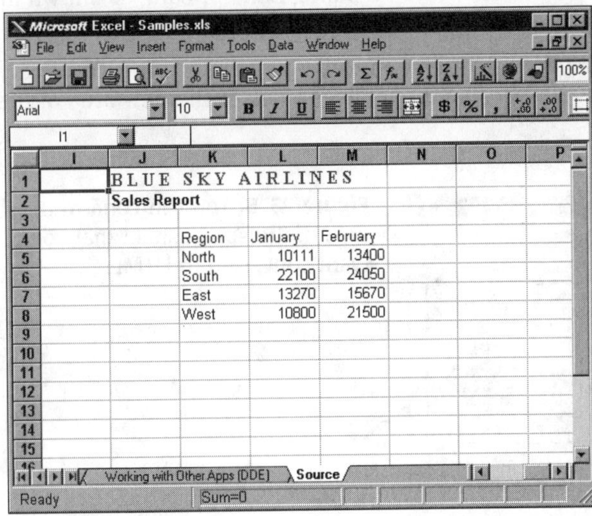

Figure 23-6: You'll convert this sample Excel spreadsheet to HTML format.

1. With your spreadsheet loaded in Microsoft Excel, select the area of the spreadsheet that you want to convert to HTML. On the Tools menu, click Internet Assistant Wizard, as shown in Figure 23-7.

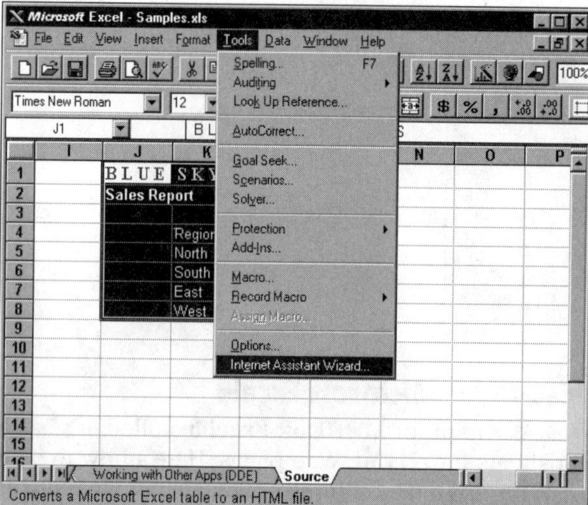

Figure 23-7: You select the portion of the spreadsheet that you want to convert and start the conversion process.

2. The Internet Assistant Wizard — Step 1 dialog box appears, as shown in Figure 23-8. Confirm the area that you selected by clicking Next.

   If you want to change the selected area to be converted, type the range of cells in the field provided or use the mouse to select the new area of the spreadsheet.

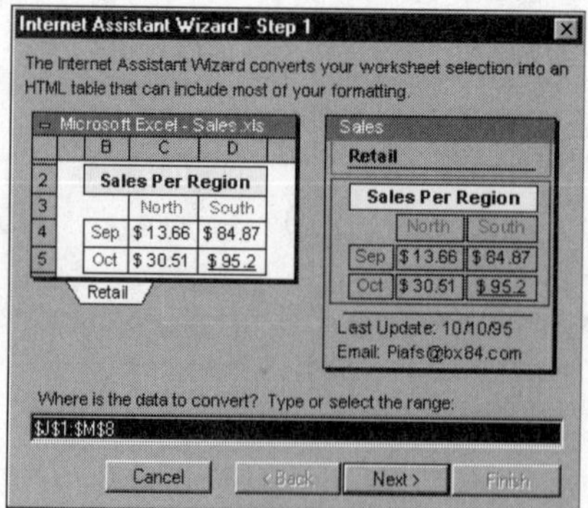

Figure 23-8: You can confirm the area of the spreadsheet that you want converted to HTML.

3. You can create an independent HTML document that's complete and ready to view (including headers and footers). You can also insert the spreadsheet into an existing HTML document. These two choices are presented in the Internet Assistant Wizard — Step 2 dialog box, shown in Figure 23-9. Click to select your choice, then click Next.

   In this example, the selected spreadsheet data will be used to create a new Web page.

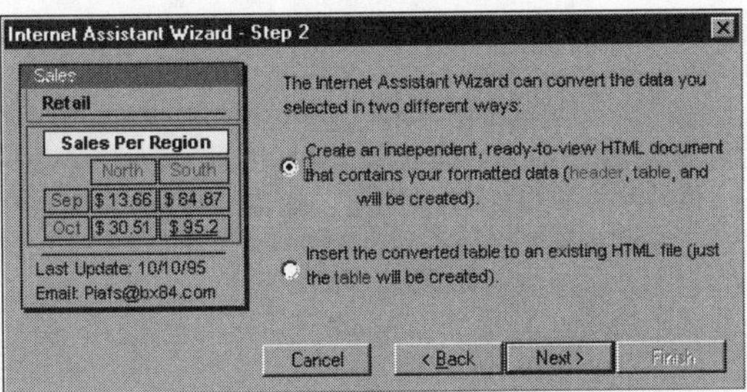

Figure 23-9: You can create a whole new Web page, or insert the spreadsheet into an existing one.

4. You can specify the Web page's header and footer using the Internet Assistant Wizard — Step 3 dialog box, as shown in Figure 23-10. When you're done, click Next.

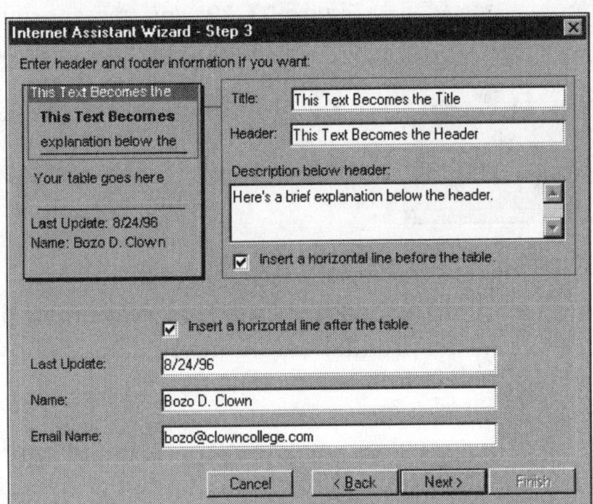

Figure 23-10: You can specify the Web page's header and footer information.

5. In the Internet Assistant Wizard — Step 4 dialog box, select whether you want the spreadsheet data and all its formatting converted or just the data itself converted. Click to select your choice, then click Next.

   Excel spreadsheets can be richly formatted using various fonts, colors, borders, shading, and other attributes. Unfortunately, most of these attributes aren't supported by HTML 2.0, so they're meaningless to older Web browsers. However, HTML 3.0 and 3.2 support many text formatting attributes that can be used to create attractive Web pages. I recommend that you click to select Convert as much of the formatting as possible, as shown in Figure 23-11.

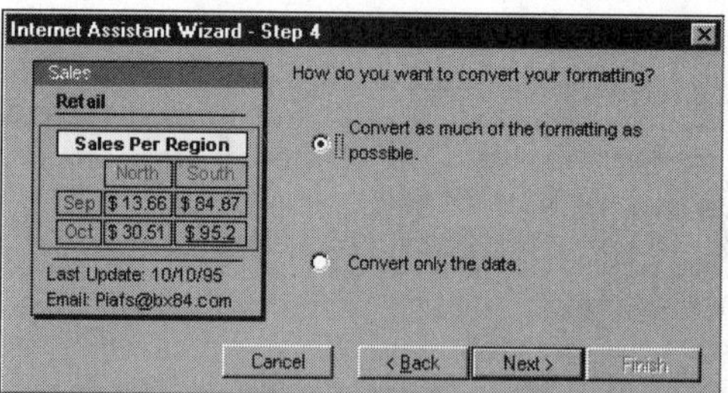

Figure 23-11: You can specify how much of the formatting you want to convert to HTML.

6. In the Internet Assistant Wizard — Step 5 dialog box, shown in Figure 23-12, type the full path name that you want to use for your new Web page file. Click Finish to create the new file.

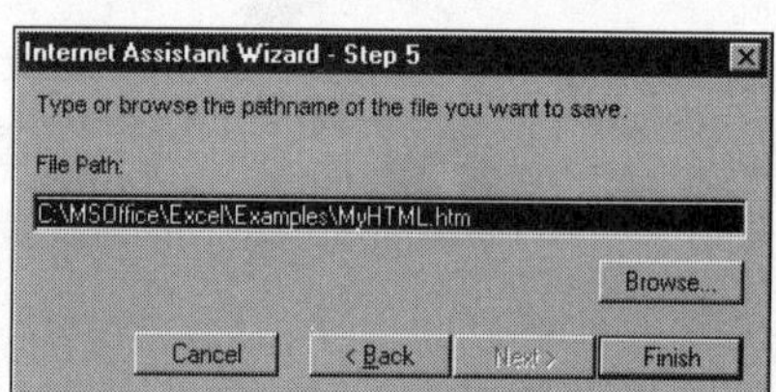

Figure 23-12: You can specify the destination of your new Web page file.

7. Start Internet Explorer and point to the HTML file that you created in step 6. The HTML version of the sample spreadsheet in Figure 23-6 is shown in Figure 23-13.

   Notice how the fonts and other attributes used in the original spreadsheet are preserved by the Internet Assistant Wizard during the conversion process. Notice also that the header and footer information that you specified in step 4 is included and appropriately formatted. (Some folks think that the HTML document is better-looking than the original Excel spreadsheet.)

If you'll be publishing spreadsheets in an intranet environment, you don't have to use the Internet Assistant for Microsoft Excel. If your users run Internet Explorer and have either Microsoft Excel or the Excel viewer installed, they can view Excel spreadsheets directly in their native format — no conversion is necessary.

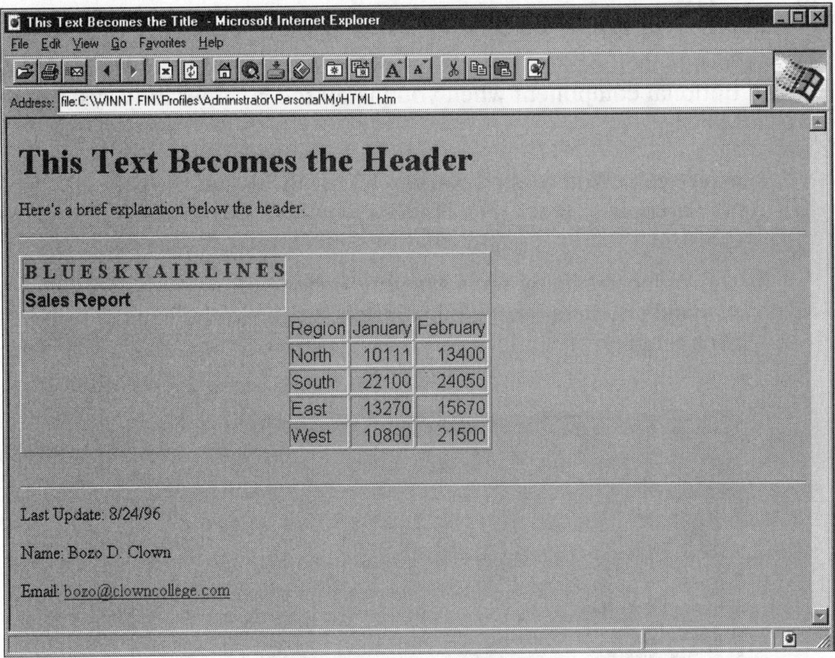

Figure 23-13: You can view the newly created Web page using Internet Explorer.

Introducing Microsoft FrontPage

Microsoft FrontPage is a feature-rich set of tools that simplifies the task of creating Web site content, creating customized Web pages, and managing your Web site. With FrontPage you can:

- ✦ View and manage your Web site graphically using FrontPage Explorer.
- ✦ Create and modify Web pages graphically using FrontPage Editor.
- ✦ Maintain a To Do List of tasks that need to be completed on your Web site development project.
- ✦ Use a rich set of templates and wizards to create professional-looking content — from individual Web pages to entire corporate Web sites.

In the following sections, you'll learn how to install FrontPage and use it to create a corporate Web site.

Installing Microsoft FrontPage

FrontPage is included on the Windows NT Server 4.0 CD-ROM, but it isn't included as an optional component when you install the NT operating system. Here's how to install it:

1. Insert your Windows NT Server 4.0 CD-ROM into the CD-ROM drive. Use NT Explorer to start \FRONTPG\FRONTPG\SETUP.EXE directly from the CD-ROM.
2. The Welcome dialog box asks you to close other running Windows programs to avoid conflicts during installation, as shown in Figure 23-14. Do so and click Next.

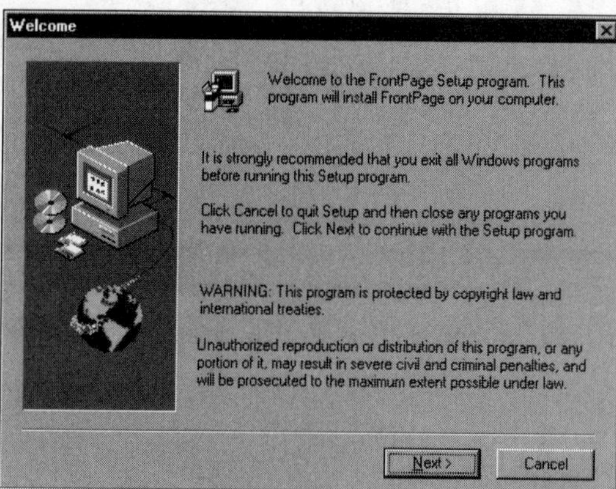

Figure 23-14: You should close other Windows applications before proceeding with FrontPage installation.

3. The Destination Path dialog box appears, as shown in Figure 23-15. If you want to change the destination directory from the default, click Browse and select the new directory. When you're done, click Next.

   In Figure 23-15, I've changed the destination to C:\FRONTPG. You need to specify a drive with at least 8.5MB of free space available.
4. In the Setup Type dialog box, click Custom and click Next, as shown in Figure 23-16.

   Although Typical installation is recommended for most users, I recommend that you, as a network administrator, always select Custom. You'll gain more knowledge about what and where components are installed on your computer.

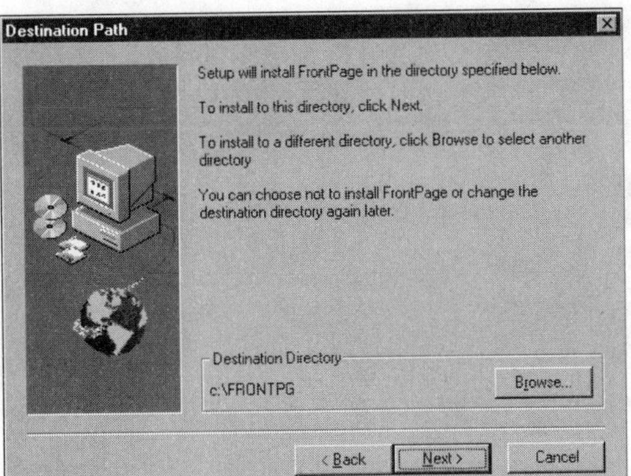

Figure 23-15: Specify the destination directory for FrontPage installation.

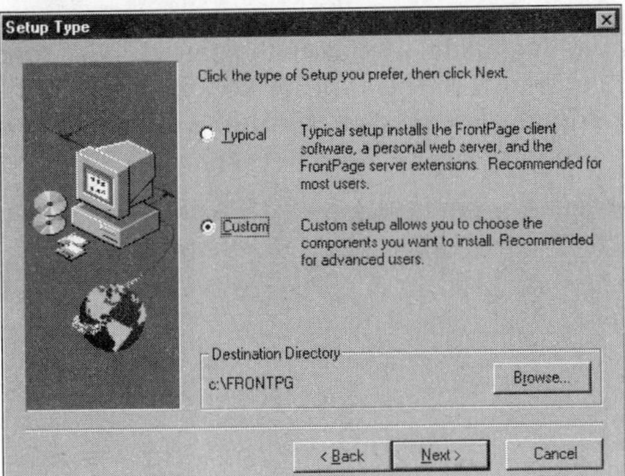

Figure 23-16: You should always select custom installation.

5. In the Select Components dialog box, shown in Figure 23-17, click to select the Client Software and Server Extensions check boxes. Then click Next.

   I don't recommend installing the Personal Web Server, since you already installed the Internet Information Server in Chapter 22.

If you don't have enough free disk space on the destination drive, you can click Disk Space to find out how much space is available on each drive. If you need to alter the destination path, you can still click Browse to change it.

6. In the Select Program Folder dialog box, click Next to create a new Microsoft FrontPage program folder.

   When you've completed FrontPage installation, you'll see a Microsoft FrontPage item on the Start ➪ Programs menu.

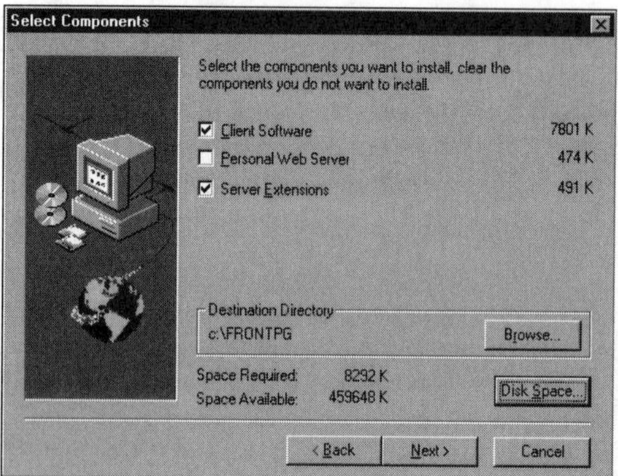

Figure 23-17: You select the individual components to install.

7. Review the decisions you've made, as shown in Figure 23-18. If you change your mind, click Back to return to the appropriate dialog box and make your changes. When you're done, click Next in the Start Copying Files dialog box.

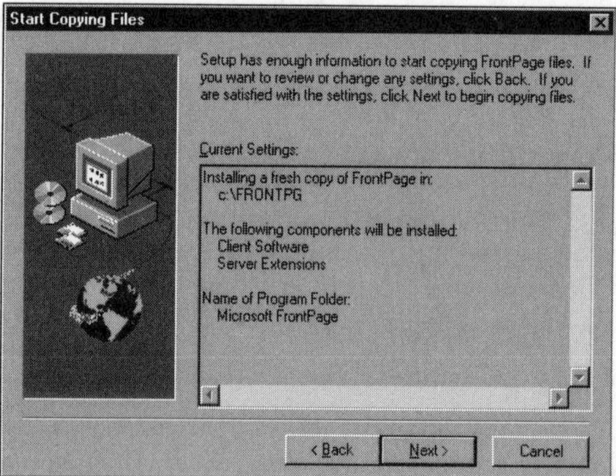

Figure 23-18: You can review your selections and make changes if necessary.

8. In the Setup Complete dialog box, click Finish.

Installing the FrontPage IIS Extensions

Before you can make full use of FrontPage, you need to install the FrontPage extensions to the Microsoft Internet Information Server. Here's how:

1. Insert your Windows NT Server 4.0 CD-ROM into the CD-ROM drive. Use NT Explorer to start \FRONTPG\IISEXT\IISEXT.EXE directly from the CD-ROM.

2. The Welcome dialog box asks you to close other running Windows programs to avoid conflicts during installation. Do so and click Next.
3. In the Ready to transfer files dialog box, click Next.
4. In the Setup Complete dialog box, click to select the Run the Server Administrator now check box. Then click Finish.
5. In the FrontPage Server Administrator dialog box, click Install. In the Configure Server Type dialog box, under Server type, select MS Internet Information Server. Then click OK.
6. In the Server Configuration dialog box, type the Server Port number, which is typically 80 for IIS. Click OK. Review your choices and click OK.

You may be asked for a user name and password, for use later in accessing the content authoring functions of FrontPage. Type the user name, password, confirm the password, and click OK. If you don't want to password-protect FrontPage's authoring features, click Cancel.

7. Click OK and click Close.

Creating a Web Site with FrontPage

The FrontPage tools are very powerful, and I can only introduce you to the basics in this chapter. This information will jump-start your use of FrontPage. You can then use its comprehensive online Help to expand your knowledge and skills. In the next section, I'll step you through the process of creating a Web site using one of FrontPage's supplied wizards. This example will acquaint you with several important concepts and leave you with the skeleton for a professional-looking corporate Web site.

Once you've completed this example, I recommend going through the online tutorial supplied with FrontPage. To run it, click Start ➪ Programs ➪ Microsoft FrontPage ➪ FrontPage Editor. On the Help menu, click Microsoft FrontPage Help Topics. Click the Contents tab and double-click the Learning FrontPage icon. Then, take the five tutorial lessons to learn the skills that you'll need to be successful with FrontPage.

Creating a Corporate Presence

FrontPage includes several templates and wizards for creating different types of Web sites. In this section, I'll show you how to establish the most common type of organizational Web site — the "corporate presence." For most organizations, this is their first step out onto the Web.

The number of steps may seem daunting at first, but believe me, creating your site this way is orders of magnitude faster than writing the HTML code from scratch. Here's how to create your corporate presence on the Web:

1. Click Start ➪ Programs ➪ Microsoft FrontPage ➪ FrontPage Explorer. On the File menu, click New Web.
2. In the New Web dialog box, under Template or Wizard, click Corporate Presence Wizard. Click to select the Add to the current web check box, as shown in Figure 23-19.

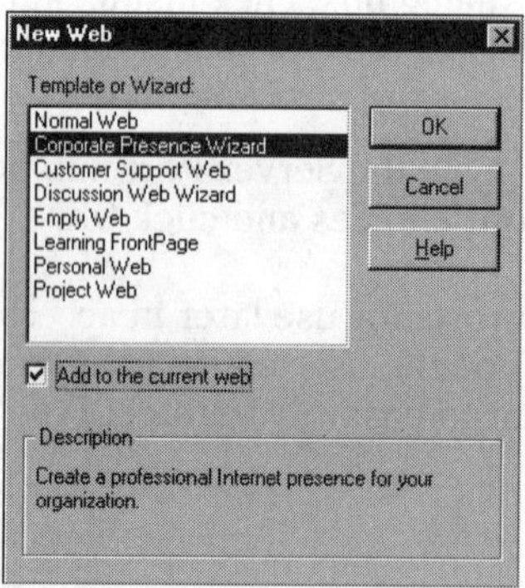

Figure 23-19: FrontPage provides a wizard that helps you to create a corporate presence on the Web.

3. In the Corporate Presence Web Wizard dialog box, click Next.

   As you proceed though the steps, remember that you can always click Back to return to previous dialog boxes, if you change your mind about decisions you've made.
4. As shown in Figure 23-20, click to select the check boxes corresponding to the pages that you want to include in your corporate Web site. The Home page is required. When you're done, click Next.

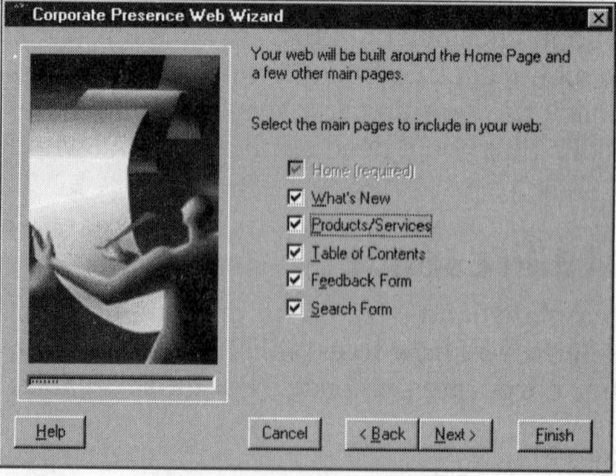

Figure 23-20: You specify the initial set of standard pages that you want.

In this example, I've selected all of the optional pages. The order and content of subsequent steps depend on selections made in previous steps. If you select other options, you'll see a different set of dialog boxes.

5. As shown in Figure 23-21, click to select the topics that you want to include on your Home page. When you're done, click Next.

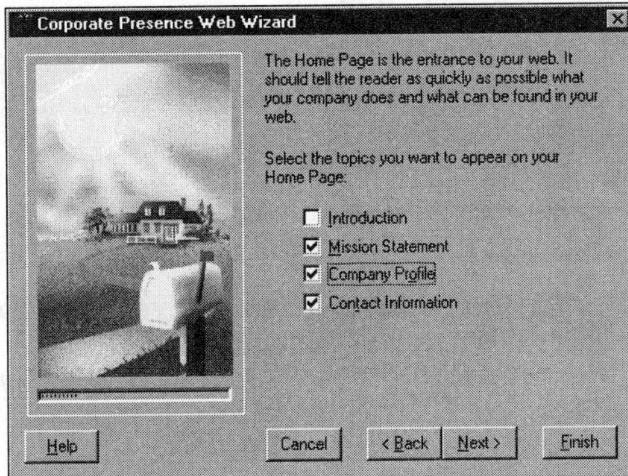

Figure 23-21: You can specify the contents of your corporate Home page.

6. As shown in Figure 23-22, click to select the sections that you want to include on your What's New page. When you're done, click Next.

   Frequent visitors to your Home page will look at this page to get an update on the latest news about your organization and your Web site.

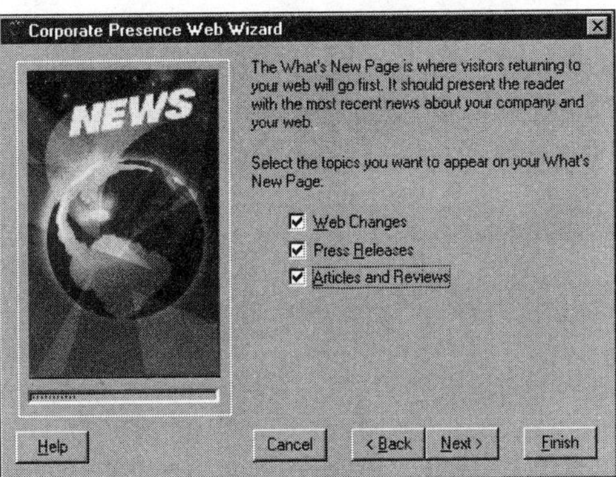

Figure 23-22: You can specify what you want to include on your What's New page.

7. Each product and service that you offer will have an associated link to its own page. In the Products box, type the number of product links that you want to include. In the Services box, type the number of services links. Then click Next, as shown in Figure 23-23.

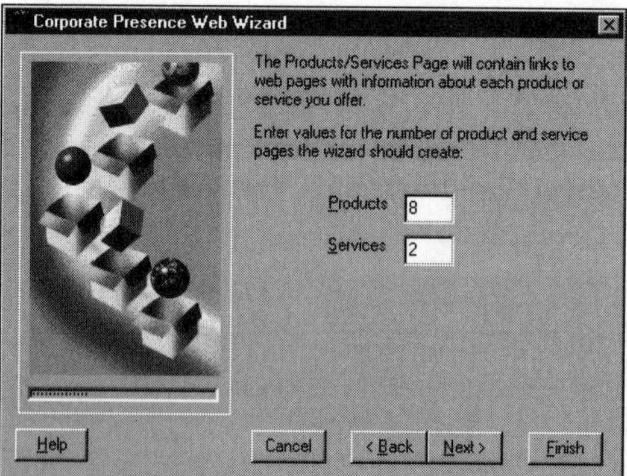

Figure 23-23: You can specify how many product and service pages you plan to create.

8. As shown in Figure 23-24, click to select the items that you want to display for your products and services. When you're done, click Next.

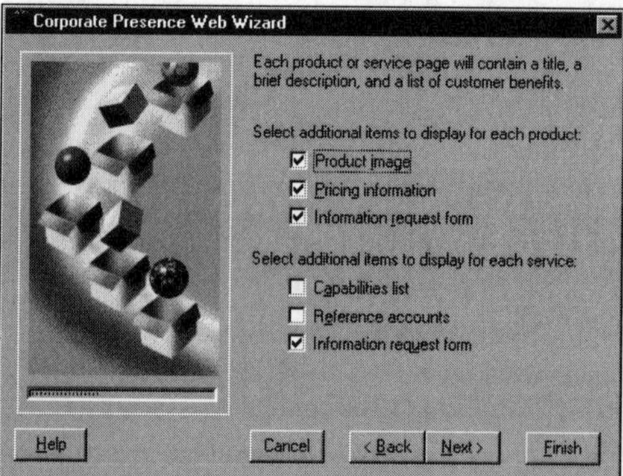

Figure 23-24: You can specify the information that you want to display about your products and services.

9. As shown in Figure 23-25, click to select the information that you want to collect from customers who give you feedback through your Web site. When you're done, click Next.

I highly recommend including a means for customer feedback and suggest gathering as much contact information as possible. You can get valuable feedback on your organization, its products and services, and your Web site. The contact information can lead to sales, company growth, and career advancement for you — all resulting from the Web site that you're building now!

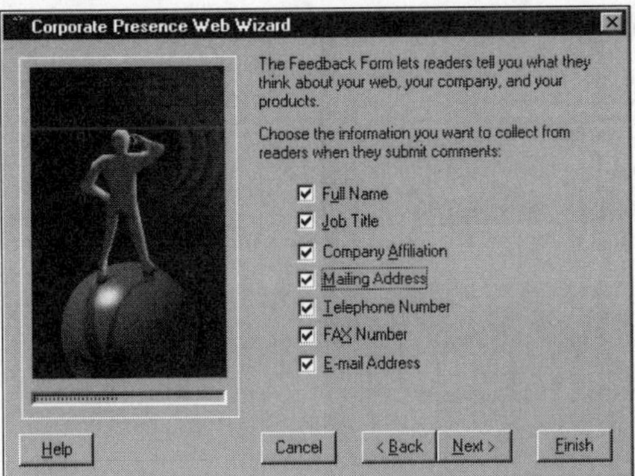

Figure 23-25: You can choose what information to gather from customers who send you feedback.

10. Click to select whether you want customer feedback to be stored as text files or in Web page format. Then, click Next. Click to select the display options for your Table of Contents page and click Next.
11. As shown in Figure 23-26, click to select the items that you want to appear in the header and footer of each page on your Web site. When you're done, click Next.

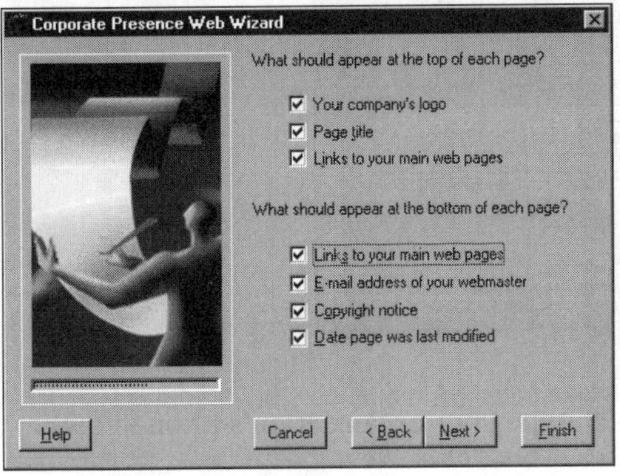

Figure 23-26: You can specify header and footer information for each page.

12. Click to select your style of Home page: Plain, Conservative, Flashy, or Cool. Then click Next.

    In the left portion of the dialog box, you can see a preview of each style by clicking each style.
13. Select your Home page background and text colors, as shown in Figure 23-27. When you're done, click Next.

    Again, you can see a preview of your settings in the left portion of the dialog box.

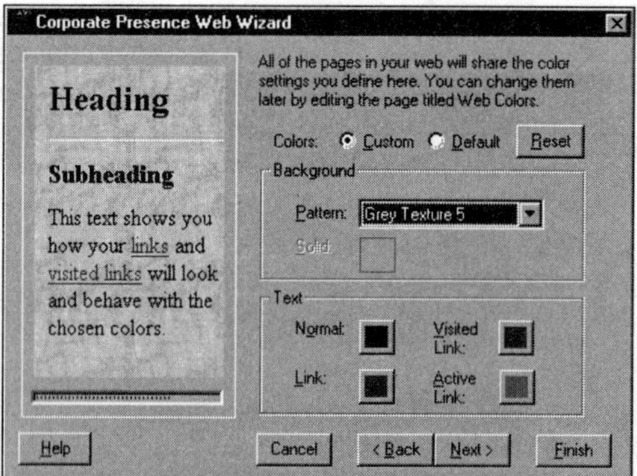

Figure 23-27: You can select your Home page background and color scheme.

14. If you want to mark unfinished Web pages with the "under construction" sign, click Yes. Otherwise, click No. Then click Next. As shown in Figure 23-28, type your organization's name and address, then click Next.

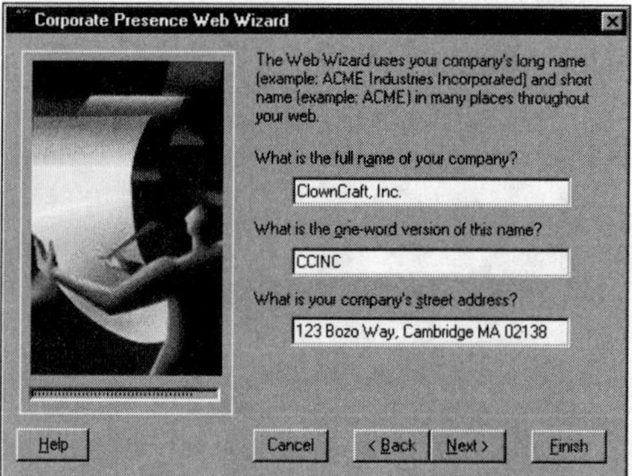

Figure 23-28: You can specify your organization's name and address.

15. As shown in Figure 23-29, type your organization's phone number, fax number, and e-mail addresses. Then, click Next.

16. As shown in Figure 23-30, click to select the Show To Do List after web is uploaded check box. Then, click Finish.

    The skeleton of your Web site is now complete. However, you're not done yet.

You can view and manage your Web site's To Do List at any time by clicking Show To Do List on the Tools menu of either FrontPage Explorer or FrontPage Editor.

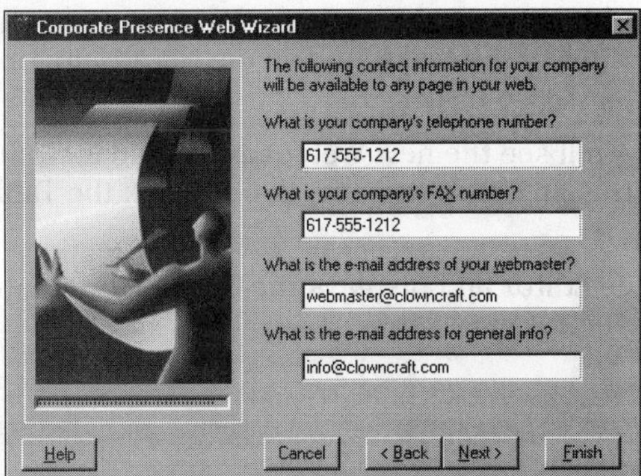

Figure 23-29: You can provide contact information for your organization.

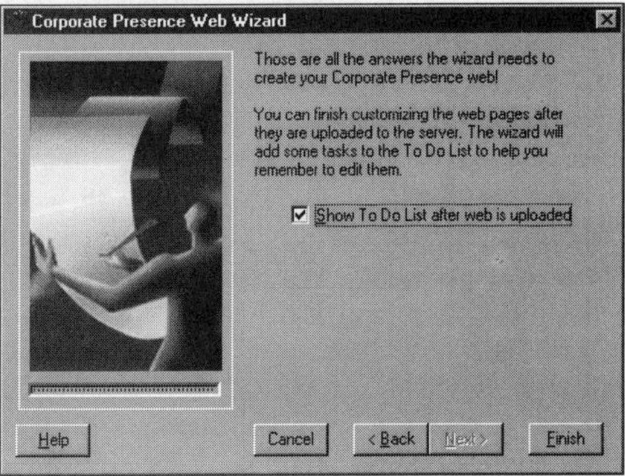

Figure 23-30: You're done with the Corporate Presence Wizard.

17. FrontPage presents a FrontPage To Do List window, to remind you of what work remains to be done to complete your corporate presence Web site. Figure 23-31 illustrates this. When you're done viewing and adjusting the list, click Close.

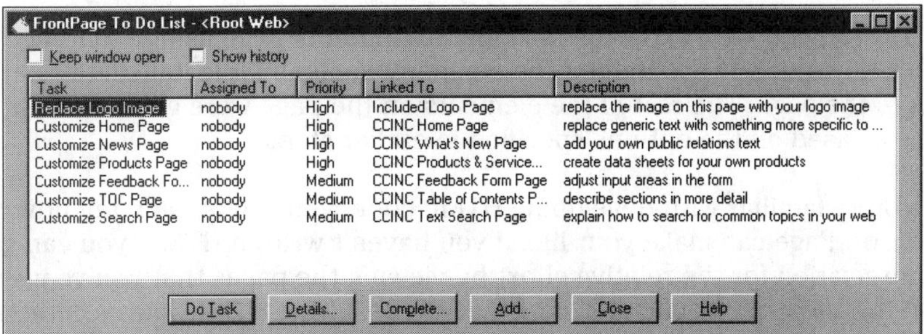

Figure 23-31: You can view and manage a list of outstanding work items required to complete your Web site.

This is one of the handiest features of FrontPage. You can assign tasks to individuals, adjust priorities of the tasks, and so on. Click Help for details on how to manage FrontPage To Do Lists.

18. In FrontPage Explorer, you'll see the new Web pages added to your Web site. Figure 23-32 illustrates this. In the right pane, double-click the Table of Contents Page icon.

    This starts the FrontPage Editor and displays the Table of Contents page generated by the previous steps.

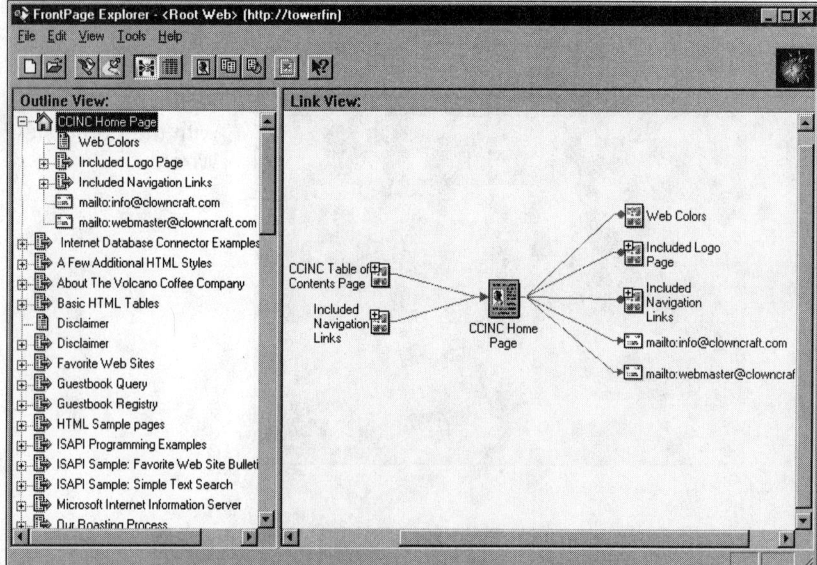

Figure 23-32: You can view and manage your new Web site graphically using FrontPage Explorer.

19. You can view and edit the Table of Contents page using FrontPage Editor. In Figure 23-33, I've added the company name in large italic letters at the top of the page. The rest of the elements on the page were generated automatically, based on the options specified in earlier steps.

If you're familiar with developing HTML code, you can already tell how much easier FrontPage can make your life. If you haven't written HTML, you can gain an appreciation for the relative effort by viewing the pages that you've just created. On the View menu, click HTML to see the resulting HTML source code, as shown in Figure 23-34.

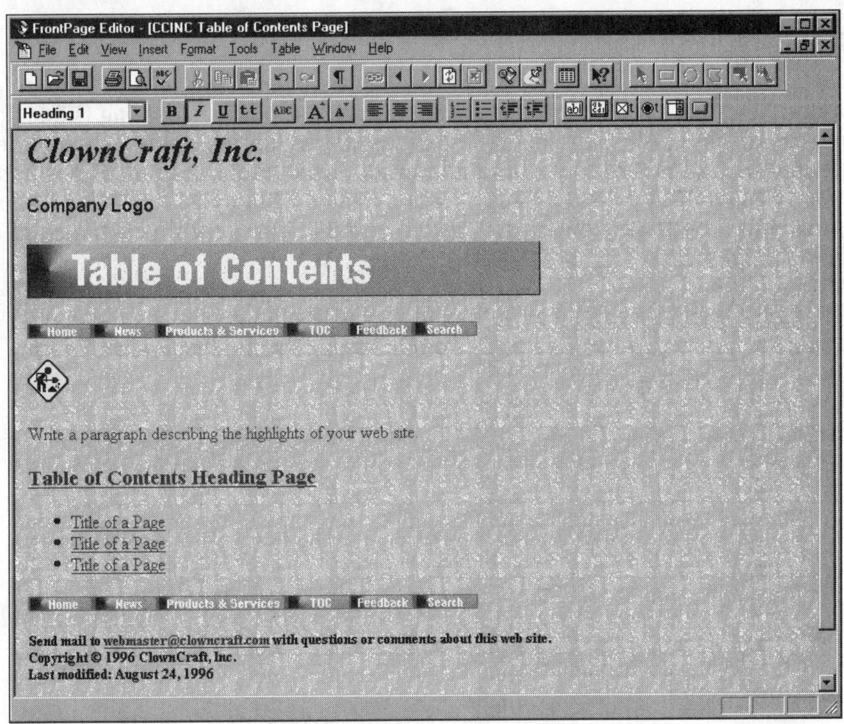

Figure 23-33: You can view and edit the resulting pages using FrontPage Editor.

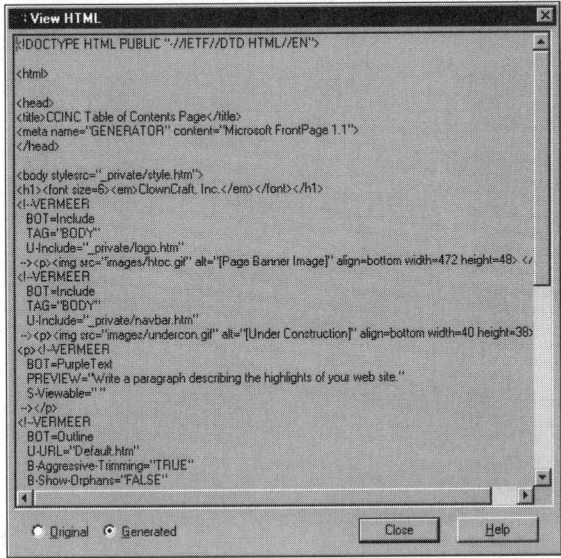

Figure 23-34: You can see the HTML code associated with the page that you're editing.

Summary

In this chapter, you've learned how to use Microsoft Office applications such as Word and Excel to create Web pages effortlessly and publish existing Office documents on the Web. Although Microsoft Office 95 has limited built-in capabilities for creating Web content, you can obtain Internet Assistants free from Microsoft's Web site to "Web-enable" your Office applications. In addition, you've been introduced to Microsoft FrontPage, which provides powerful features for developing and managing your Web site.

In Chapter 24, you'll learn all about how to establish tight security for your Internet server, to protect your LAN from hackers and the disasters they can cause.

Establishing Internet Server Security

You've finally gotten your Web site installed, configured, and connected to the Internet. You're so excited that you call a friend in London, and sure enough, she can view your beautiful new Web page. Amazing as it seems, it's true — tens of millions of people worldwide have access to the very computer sitting in front of you. You fantasize about all of the new customers who are going to find out about your company's products and services. And then you consider that some of these Internet visitors are going to be your competitors. Perhaps tens of thousands of them are high school hackers on summer vacation with nothing better to do than . . . Yikes! A cold sweat breaks out on your forehead, and you want to yank the ISDN line right out of the wall. Maybe you should! How can you be sure that your network is going to be safe?

The very thing that makes the Internet so powerful — worldwide access to the information on your computers — makes it a huge risk to the integrity and security of that same information. In this chapter, I'll show you the types of risks that a connection to the Internet brings, as well as some techniques to minimize those risks. Much of this discussion is relevant even to networks *not* connected to the Internet (for example, for sensitive servers on a corporate intranet). Many computer attacks come from *inside* companies, not from outside. So, whether your network is connected to the Internet or you're operating an intranet within your organization, read on.

Understanding the Consequences

Before we talk about *how* these security risks come about, let's look at the bottom line. What's the worst that can happen if you don't pay attention to Internet security? It's not a pretty picture. Failure to pay attention to Internet security leaves you open to

- Exposure of sensitive information
  - Proprietary information — source code, business plans, client lists
  - Customer information — credit card numbers, names, confidential information
  - Security information — passwords and account names that can be used to propagate attacks on other computers and sites
- Denial of service
  - Disks filled to capacity and unable to receive more information (mail, orders, and so on)
  - Internet bandwidth consumed by inappropriate use
  - Processor cycles consumed by inappropriate use
  - Loss or damage inflicted to information in files
- Misrepresentation
  - Malicious or inaccurate information displayed and propagated in your name
  - Security credentials or credit information stolen and used in your name or your clients' name
  - Hacking other sites via your site, making you look like the perpetrator

Is your forehead sweating yet?

Understanding the Types of Network Attack

Hackers, and even buggy programs, can wreak havoc on your servers and network in quite a few ways. The following sections discuss several types of attack.

Attacking with Brute Force

Armed with a tireless program, a list of actual or likely account names (Guest and Administrator come to mind as prime targets) for your servers, and a standard dictionary, a hacker is ready to strike. His or her program can try thousands of user name and password combinations an hour to try to break into your system.

Services that hackers may try include file sharing, Web servers, mail servers, and FTP servers, just for starters. They may then gain access to shared volumes, mail folders, Web pages, or anything else stored on your server. They may even be lucky enough to download or alter NT registry information, or even steal account names and passwords for other computers or networks.

Spoofing

A hacker can send packets into your network from the outside, making such packets look as if they came from a trusted computer on the inside. Although your network's routing protocols probably won't send results of these transactions back out through the Internet, a clever hacker may still be able to send in commands that result in a security breach, simply by sending in his or her part of the network conversation and assuming that the operation is working as planned.

For example, a private mailing list server may be configured to accept only connections from inside your corporate network. However, hackers can send in their half of a network conversation that instructs your list server to e-mail them a list of all members of your mailing lists. These hackers won't see the server's replies on your network, but they will get the resulting e-mail. Now they have a list of valid account names to use in a brute force attack, described earlier in this chapter.

Eavesdropping

Anyone with physical access to your network cabling, to your Internet provider's cabling, or to a computer at any intermediate site can monitor the Internet traffic going across the network at the point of access. Simple network monitoring software (such as Microsoft's Network Monitor, discussed in Chapter 21) or a hardware sniffer will easily reveal any unencrypted information passing by.

For example, a network monitoring program can be set to monitor all POP mail or FTP data packets containing the words "USER" or "PASS." Hackers know that these packets contain unencrypted user names and passwords. If one of yours goes by, the listening hacker knows your user name and password on your server and can, at the very least, read your e-mail and gain your FTP transfer rights. Most NT e-mail servers use NT's user names and passwords for access control. If you've bound TCP/IP to the file-sharing services on your NT machines and haven't blocked this from outside access, the hacker can also access your shared volumes.

What's more, even encrypted passwords can be captured and replayed, if the encryption method isn't time-sensitive or based on an ever-changing challenge-response technique.

Using Trap Doors and Open Doors

Buggy, insecure, or misconfigured software on your server can be exploited to suit a hacker's ends. Bugs and debugging "features" (trap doors) in server programs are quickly publicized in the hacker community and exploited. If they can query your server and find out that it's running version X of program so-and-so, and there's a juicy security hole in that program, believe me, they'll find out about it before you do.

There was a legendary bug in many UNIX mail systems about 15 years ago which allowed *anyone* to mail in a replacement password file for the entire system. That one was fixed eventually, but how many such bugs lurk in the 200 megabytes or so of software on your server?

Even correct operation of improperly installed software may leave you vulnerable; if trap doors are dangerous, open doors are even worse! NT file-sharing over TCP/IP is an easy access route if it's not restricted from outside access. Plus, most TCP/IP services are typically run as NT services with generous file access permissions. Mail servers, Web servers, and so on potentially have access to your entire file system. If they're accidentally allowed to grant access to sensitive directories, they will.

For example, NT's built-in FTP server relies on NT's file permission system to restrict access to various directories, but FAT-formatted volumes don't have this protection. If the FTP server is allowed to share a FAT format volume, the *entire* volume will be accessible by FTP.

If hackers gain write access to your CGI directory, they can send in their own programs and then use their Web browsers to run the programs at the security level of your Web server.

Some programs are nothing short of security disasters. For example, the Windows NT 3.51 Resource Kit includes a remote command server REMOTE.EXE. It accepts and executes command lines from anyone, with no security whatsoever! Even the more secure RSHSVC.EXE sends unencrypted (clear text) passwords across the Internet. Installing this service allows any eavesdropper to execute arbitrary commands on your server. Even if you do install this type of service for internal use, block it from use across your firewall (which I'll discuss later in this chapter).

Using Trojan Horses and Viruses

A clever hacker can trick one of your users into running software on his or her behalf. The malicious software can then

- Gather secured information and secretly pass it back to the hacker.
- Alter or delete information on your computer.

✦ "Tunnel" Internet traffic from the hacker's computer right past your security firewalls to your computer. Once it's attached to your computer, it can probe your servers at will or even pass back out through the Internet to attack another site, making you look like the perpetrator.

It's not unheard-of for a disgruntled internal user, or one frustrated by the security measures that you've implemented for his or her own protection, willingly to run one of these programs.

Using Social Engineering

The best lock isn't much use if you give away the keys. A hacker can simply convince someone in your organization to supply the information that he or she wants. Larger organizations are especially vulnerable to this kind of attack. The scheme depends on the hacker representing himself as a legitimate user who's forgotten his password. The cry for help usually comes through e-mail or a phone call. If anyone on your MIS staff can be talked into giving out or changing a password, what good is a firewall?

Causing Denial of Service

Some attacks don't involve access at all. They simply make it impossible for you to use your own computer or network. For example, some simple utilities found on nearly every computer connected to the Internet can be pointed at your NT server and can completely consume all of the bandwidth of your Internet connection with meaningless network traffic, effectively shutting you out. A small program can deluge your servers with meaningless requests, completely tying up the processor. Similarly, your computers and routers can be attacked, causing them to crash, shut down, or misroute network traffic.

Finally, a disgruntled hacker or even a berserk mail server could send you thousands of multi-megabyte e-mail messages, filling up your hard disk and preventing you from receiving legitimate e-mail.

Whether a security breach is due to a malicious attack, an inadvertent mistake, a hacker, or a buggy program, it doesn't make much difference. In any case, you've been compromised. So I'll refer to these sources of risk as "attacks" since the effect on you is the same.

Well, I don't know about you, but *my* forehead is definitely sweating now. Fortunately, with a relatively small investment in time, software, and equipment, you can wipe your brow and minimize your exposure to Internet attacks. Most measures involve just time, thought, and planning on your part. Although it's impossible to make your server and network completely impervious to attack, in the following sections I'll point out several specific things that you can do.

Protecting Your Network from Attack

It's important to start planning for security *before* you start building your network, since you'll have to consider security as you make choices about software, hardware, and Internet connectivity. (From that standpoint, perhaps this should have been Chapter 1 instead of 24.)

In the most general sense, there are two ways to approach security of *any* sort. They are:

✦ Allow everything, but block access as dictated by safety

or

✦ Block everything by default and grant access as dictated by need.

Think about this for a moment. The first strategy requires that you know beforehand everything that you need to block. How will you find out if you've made a mistake or when someone gains access that they shouldn't have? The second strategy requires only that you know in advance everything that you'll need to allow. And if you make a mistake, someone won't get the access they need. Now, which mistake do you think you'll hear about first, and which is going to be easier to fix? Right — the second.

Now I'll apply the approach of blocking everything by default to the four main lines of computer defense:

1. **Passive resistance.** Eliminate unnecessary risks before they can be attacked.
2. **Active resistance.** Actively resist known methods of attack.
3. **Logging and monitoring.** Test your defenses and detect breaches.
4. **Disaster planning.** Prepare for recovery after an attack.

Passive Resistance includes the following:

✦ Investing time in planning and policies

✦ Structuring your network to restrict outside access

✦ Installing only needed services

✦ Using software known to be secure and bug free

✦ Properly configuring your servers, file systems, software, and user accounts to maintain appropriate access control

✦ Hiding from the outside world as much information about your network as possible

Active Resistance includes the following:

- ✦ Installing firewalls to block dangerous or inappropriate Internet traffic as it passes between your network and the Internet at large
- ✦ Using proxies and gateways to expose only some of your servers and their services to the Internet
- ✦ Using encryption and authentication to limit access based on credentials (such as a password)
- ✦ Keeping up to date on security and risks, especially with respect to Windows NT Server

Logging and Monitoring include the following:

- ✦ Testing your defenses before you connect to the Internet
- ✦ Monitoring Internet traffic on your network and on the connection to your Internet service provider or other networks
- ✦ Detecting and recording suspicious activity on the network and in application software

Disaster Planning includes the following:

- ✦ Making permanent, archived baseline backups of exposed servers *before* they're connected to the Internet and any time that system software is changed
- ✦ Making frequent backups once you're online

- ✦ Writing and *maintaining* documentation of your software and network configuration (see Chapter 5 for details)

- ✦ Maintaining written, thorough, and *tested* server restore procedures (see Chapters 5 and 18 for details)
- ✦ Having a Security Incident Plan

Implementing Passive Resistance

Passive resistance — eliminating unnecessary risks before they can be attacked — is the easiest and cheapest form of defense. Simply remove the object of attack. No object, no attack. Although this may sound like a no-brainer, the problem is that a network installation using all of the default settings will probably allow much more access than you want to provide.

Planning and Creating Security Policies

Before plugging in an Internet connection, you'll need to come up with a plan for the types of Internet access that you're going to permit. The best approach is to define clearly an access policy, then implement the rest of these protective strategies. At every step, you can then ask, "Does what I'm doing leave enough room for desired access, and does it permit things that I've decided not to allow?"

If you make your security policies too restrictive (for example, no browsing of the World Wide Web from inside your network), your users may become frustrated enough to try to breach your security measures. That could be as disastrous as having a completely wide-open site.

Here are some questions to consider while planning your security policy:

- ✦ What services do you want to make available to users on the network inside your organization?
- ✦ Which of these inside services do you want to make available to your users when they're off-site or at home?
- ✦ Which of these inside services do you want to make available to other outside Internet users?
- ✦ What outside services do you want to offer to your inside users?

By *services,* I mean software services and protocols accessible over the Internet. These can include

- ✦ Windows NT file and printer sharing
- ✦ NetWare file and print services
- ✦ Windows NT BackOffice services, such as SQL Server
- ✦ Web services
- ✦ FTP services
- ✦ Mail delivery (SMTP)
- ✦ Mail reading (POP3)
- ✦ News (NNTP)

Later on in this chapter, I'll discuss some of the risks associated with these services. You already know the benefits. Before you set up your Internet connection, you'll need to weigh the risks and benefits of each service and then decide whether to allow them to be used across the Internet connection.

It's a good idea to create management and personnel policies regarding network security and appropriate use of computer resources, if you haven't already. When you do, educate your users about them. Your security measures won't work if your users try to circumvent them, even if they mean well.

Here are a few ideas for official policies:

✦ Require that all accounts be protected by a good password. Consider deleting Guest accounts and any accounts that haven't been used recently.

✦ Require that all passwords be kept personal and confidential. In particular, they must never be stored in files or sent by e-mail under any circumstances. They should never be given to someone over the phone, unless the caller *knows for sure* who's on the other end of the line. Even MIS support staff needs to follow these rules.

✦ Don't permit users to run unapproved or unofficial software, especially software obtained from BBSs, downloaded over the Internet, or carried in on floppy disk. Make virus-scanning software available and run it frequently. Always scan files obtained via FTP.

✦ Create and communicate a policy on the confidentiality of e-mail, receipt of personal e-mail on corporate computers, personal use of Web browsers, and storage or viewing of potentially offensive material. You may decide to be very hard-nosed or you may permit your users to operate at their own discretion, but you should consider this and let your users know in advance.

It's much easier to start with strict policies and loosen them over time to match the needs of your organization. If you start with a loose set of policies and later try to tighten them, you'll meet with lots of resistance. Connecting your network to the Internet for the first time is an opportune time to tighten security. The change will meet with less resistance if you make your users aware of the added risks that connection to the outside world brings.

✦ Consider and communicate the disciplinary consequences of failing to comply with security policies.

Structuring Your Network to Restrict Access

When you've decided on the set of services to allow inside your network and across the Internet, you'll need to design a system to enforce that policy rigidly. Based on the type of access that you want to allow, you can connect your network to the Internet in several ways. Figure 24-1 shows several methods, from the most to the least secure.

In Model A, sometimes called the physical isolation model, there's no connection between your network and the Internet. It's perfectly appropriate when your security policy dictates that no inbound or outbound Internet access is to be permitted. For example, you can bet the CIA's internal servers aren't anywhere *near* an Internet connection. They're probably behind lead walls three feet thick.

Model B, the gateway model, puts only a sacrificial server on the Internet itself. The gateway host receives e-mail and provides all services that are accessible to the outside world — HTTP, FTP, and so forth.

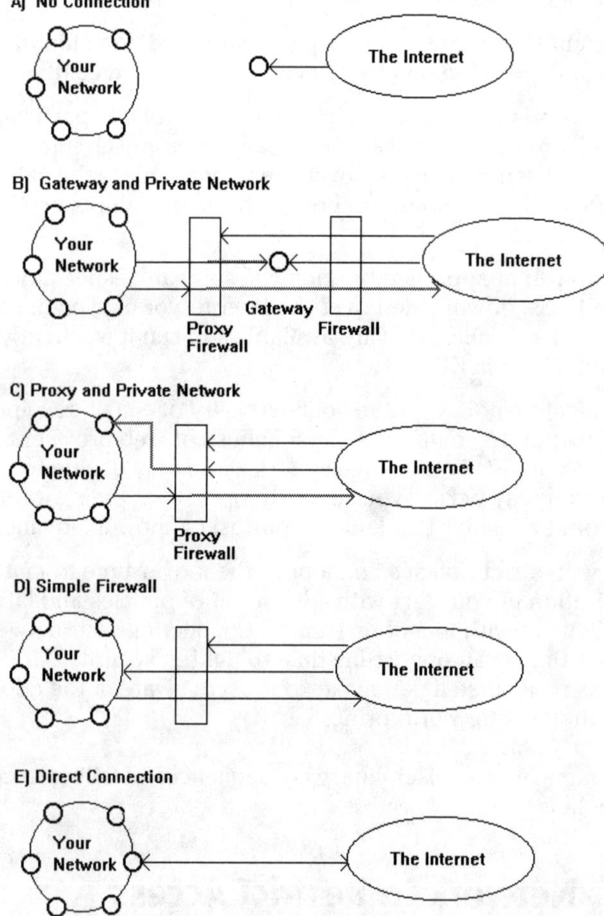

Figure 24-1: There are five basic models for connecting your network to the Internet.

The gateway computer and the internal network are protected by firewalls. A *firewall* is hardware or software in the data path between the Internet and your internal computers which examines packets coming in one side and decides what to pass along to the other side. In this model, the outside firewall protects the gateway computer, and the internal firewall prevents outside users from reaching the inside network at all.

Model C, the proxy model, makes your internal network invisible on the Internet, but the router forwards requests in and out based on rules in its configuration tables. The proxy software makes all Internet requests on behalf of internal users and directs incoming connections for specified services to specific servers. This does keep outside users from probing your network. However, requests from the outside are still processed on internal computers, and you're vulnerable to trap doors.

It's best to use a proxy as used with Model B as well, as shown in Figure 24-1. This prevents any direct communication between the inside network and the Internet. It may seem a bit extreme, but this is the configuration used by almost all medium- and large-sized corporations.

Model D, the simple firewall, uses an external router to provide an Internet connection along with firewall protection. It can block undesired services but still leaves your network open to probing from the outside.

Model E, the direct connection model, uses one of your internal computers to make the connection to an Internet Service Provider (ISP) via modem, ISDN, or some other method. Some third-party firewalls are available for NT for this type of connection, but in general, you have very little protection from direct attacks from the outside. I'll describe what little you can do later on, but for now, just remember that an external firewall gives you one place to concentrate your security measures. A direct connection requires that *each and every* computer on your network be secured independently.

You may also consider providing two ways in to your network: one for your own employees and one for the rest of the world as shown in Figure 24-2. A RAS connection with required-CHAP security gives you a way of allowing trusted users to gain access not otherwise permitted through your corporate firewall. (See Chapter 11 for details on installing and configuring RAS.)

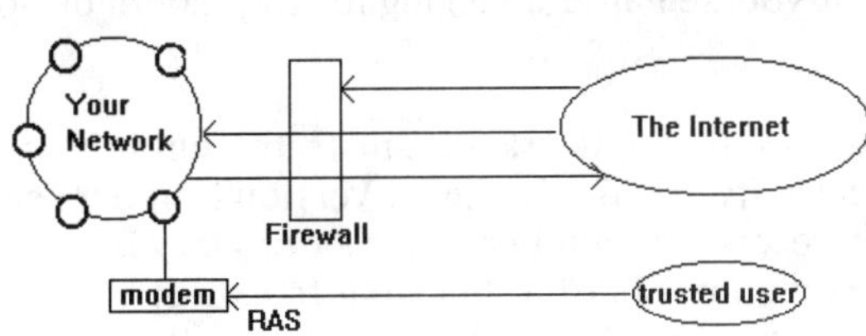

Figure 24-2: You can provide private paths to your network for trusted users.

The type of Internet connection that you need to use also depends on the type of services that you'll make available to the outside world. If you're not providing *any* servers for outside use, you can consider using a "dial-on-demand" connection. It's established only when an inside user attempts to send data out to the Internet and is dropped after a time of disuse. However, if you're going to make your servers available to the Internet at large, then you either need a dedicated, 24-hour connection or an arrangement with your ISP for demand-dialing from their site to yours. (Few ISPs will do this, however, due to the likelihood of toll charges.) Dedicated connections can use a standard modem, ISDN, Frame Relay, dedicated data service lines, or other services provided by your ISP and telecommunications companies.

Installing Just the Services That You Need

A service that isn't installed on your servers can't be attacked. For example, before you install the FTP server, consider whether it's really needed. You can always transfer files via e-mail. Likewise, before you install a Web or e-mail server, consider whether your ISP can host your Web site or hold your e-mail for you. It's safer to allow someone else to run risky software.

Also, if you don't plan on allowing outside Internet users access to your NT file and print services, and you don't need to use TCP/IP as an internal protocol on your LAN, don't bind your Workstation and Server services to TCP/IP on *any* computer on your network. This prevents Internet users from accessing your shared volumes, with or without a password. See Chapter 8 for details about binding.

Using Known Good Software

Software that's accessible from the Internet and that has access to your computer may not be as careful at what it does as you might want, think, or hope. My philosophy here is to use the simplest program possible to accomplish a given job — the smaller and simpler the program, the greater the chance that it's been completely tested, and the lower the chance that it has undesirable "features" that you haven't yet discovered.

Use software from a reputable source. If you use noncommercial software, try to get its source code and compile it yourself after checking for trap doors or other unexpected features.

This is not a new concept to the seasoned network administrator, but it bears repeating. For any mission-critical software, Bob's Law of Version Numbers says, "Avoid Versions 1.*x* and *x*.0," where *x* is any number. Brian's Corollary is, "Wait for Service Pack 2." (Of course, it's sometimes hard to tell what to expect based on the version number. The first version of Windows NT was 3.1, even though it was both a 1.x and x.0 release of the new operating system.)

Configuring Your Network and Software

Probably the most important task, and the messiest, is being sure that every computer on your network is safe from unauthorized and unexpected use. If you manage more than a few computers, or more than a few users, you already know how difficult this is even before throwing in the added dimension of risk from the outside world.

You can use the guidelines in Table 24-1 to organize a security review of every computer on your network.

Table 24-1
Security Guidelines for Several Areas of Risk

Security Risk Area	*Security Recommendations*
File-sharing	Unless you have a private network (Models A, B, or C previously discussed), need to use TCP/IP as an internal protocol, or truly want to allow outside users to use your shared volumes, never bind TCP/IP to Workstation or Server services. This eliminates the risk of any undesired outside access, except via standard Internet services (such as FTP). This is especially important if you have a direct Internet connection to one of your NT computers, because you won't be able to protect yourself with a firewall. See Chapter 8 for details on binding.
Passwords	Require every account to have a fairly long password (eight or more characters) and require that passwords be changed frequently. Be sure to set up initial passwords using random letters and numbers. Disable Guest accounts. See Chapter 18 for details on password and account administration.
Volumes	Use NTFS on all volumes used for Internet server software and data. If possible, create separate volumes for FTP files and mail files, so that one service can't fill up a volume and stop the others.
Services	For services such as HTTP, FTP, mail, and so on, create separate user accounts for each service that you install. Give each account the minimum access privileges to the fewest directories necessary for it to operate. Using the Services application in Control Panel, use the Startup button to specify the Log On As, This Account, and Password for each of these services.
Access Control	Restrict the number of users with administrator privileges. Set the minimum permissions possible on all shared volumes. Be sure that the Internet server accounts have Write permission to only those directories that they require.
FTP	If you've installed an FTP server, be sure to specify directories on NTFS volumes. Never allow FTP access to floppy disk drives or any non-NTFS volumes. (You specify FTP directories individually using Internet Service Manager, discussed in Chapter 22. Double-click the FTP service and click the Directories tab in the FTP Service Properties dialog box.) Never allow Write access to an outgoing FTP directory. If you're going to allow incoming FTP, I strongly recommend that you create a separate NTFS volume just for FTP Write access. If you allow incoming FTP, check every file with a virus-scanning program before executing it.

(continued)

Table 24-1 *(continued)*	
Security Risk Area	***Security Recommendations***
FTP *(continued)*	If you've enabled anonymous FTP (on the Service tab of the FTP Service Properties dialog box in Internet Service Manager), create a special account for anonymous FTP users (never use Guest) with minimal permissions. Grant the account only List and Read access on exactly one subdirectory of one FTP-visible volume. If you must give the anonymous FTP account write permission on a directory, deny Delete, Change, Read and List access to it. (Otherwise, you may find that your server has become a repository for someone's pornographic images or illegally obtained information). However, I strongly urge you not to allow any Write permission to the anonymous FTP account. If your customers or clients need to send files to you, you can create a special account and password for them with minimal privileges, just enough to write into a directory accessible by FTP.
Mail	Consider storing incoming mail on a separate volume. If your mail server software allows incoming mail to be stored automatically in files, be sure that the mail server's logon account doesn't have access to any directories except ones that you select for mail storage and logging.
HTTP	Be absolutely certain that your Web server is set up to retrieve files only in or below a specific subdirectory. Consider putting the log files on a separate volume to avoid running out of disk space from a barrage of requests. Consider disabling "directory browse" and similar features unless they're absolutely necessary. Use password access control for all confidential information. Be certain that no outside user, using FTP or any other means, has Write access your CGI directory. This avoids Trojan horses. (I allow only the Administrator account to install CGI programs.)
Logging	Enable security logging for all NT and Internet services. You should even log successful logons. If there's a security breach, it will be helpful to know when it happened.
IP Routing	If an NT workstation or server has two network cards or a network card and a RAS connection, you have the option of disabling IP routing. This effectively prevents TCP/IP traffic from crossing from one network interface to the other. With a direct connection to the Internet, this can be a means of protecting computers on one network from attacks coming from the other. With IP routing disabled, only the computer with the direct connection to the Internet will be vulnerable to Internet attack. You control IP routing via the Network application in Control Panel, as shown in Figure 24-3.

Security Risk Area	Security Recommendations
Physical Security	Be sure that your servers and network cabling inside your firewall are physically secure from unauthorized access.

NT file-sharing and FTP or POP Mail are a bad combination to allow through your firewall. NT's file-sharing encrypts its passwords, but FTP and POP don't. FTP and POP will reveal your user's NT passwords to any eavesdropping hacker.

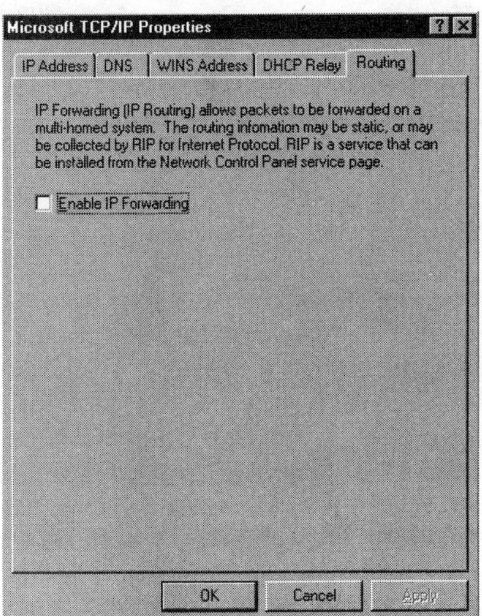

Figure 24-3: The Windows NT router isolation model relies on leaving IP routing disabled.

The FTP Service Properties dialog box allows you to specify an initial home directory. If a subdirectory of this home directory exists with the same name as an FTP user's logon name, the FTP server will automatically change to that directory when that user connects. You can create subdirectories in advance for each of your FTP user accounts and give them read and write permissions in these subdirectories. But *don't* give them any access to the home directory or higher. This will keep the other directories completely hidden from them. Users can still move above the home directory, if they have access. Make sure they can't.

Since Windows NT has no utilities to print out these configuration choices, I recommend printing screen shots of each configuration setting that you make. You can use these hard copies to help you detect inadvertent changes later on or to reconstruct your servers after a crash.

Hiding Information from the Outside World

Hide from the outside world as much information about your network as possible. The more that a potential hacker knows about your network, the more vulnerable your system is. Here are some practical approaches to hiding your network information using the strategy, "Block everything, permit what's needed":

- ✦ Consider using a private network, as shown in Models B and C of Figure 24-1. Because private networks have no routing path from the outside world, no one on the outside can address packets to the computers on your network. Your computers don't exist to the outside world.
- ✦ If you do use a connected network, be sure to disable RIP (Routing Information Protocol) on the router interface connected to your ISP. There is no need to advertise routes to your internal networks to your ISP, since the ISP should be using static routing tables for traffic going to you. Likewise, you should never need to receive routing information from outside your network.
- ✦ Disable SNMP access across your firewall. Don't let a hacker see into your routers and network structure.
- ✦ Register as little information as possible with the InterNIC (or other Internet registration organization). Put as few computers as practical in any DNS (Domain Name System) database visible to the outside world. For example, you'll want to have your WWW server listed as www.company.com and will probably have your e-mail servers listed as well. However, internal computers need not be listed. (Doesn't credit-card-server.company.com sound like an appealing target?) Consider using a HOSTS file or an internal DNS server for internal computers, blocked from outside access by your firewall.

Implementing Active Resistance

After removing security risks that simply aren't necessary, you must build a defense for the remaining risks. Actually, it's not as hard as it sounds, as long as you remember to "block everything first, then allow as required," rather than the other way around.

Using Firewalls to Block Traffic

The single most effective tool to secure your network from attack is a firewall. As I've mentioned before, a firewall enables you to focus your security efforts in just one place — the point of contact with the Internet. Using a firewall gives you control over exactly what kind of traffic enters and leaves your network. Firewalls can perform either or both of two main functions — filtering and proxying.

Filtering is the process of permitting or denying passage to the data packets entering and leaving your network. When you install a filtering router, you set up a table of allowed packet types and source and destination addresses. Whenever a packet arrives at one side of the router, the router examines its table to decide whether to

- ✦ Permit the packet to pass in or out.
- ✦ Silently drop (ignore) the packet.
- ✦ Drop the packet and return an error message to its sender.
- ✦ Let the packet's passage go unrecorded.
- ✦ Log the packet's details in an error log.
- ✦ Send a warning message to the network administrator.

Understanding how to set up a filter requires understanding the details of the TCP/IP protocol. This is a fairly complicated topic. I'll go over the basic concepts later in this chapter, in the section called "Firewall Filtering and TCP/IP Services." For more details, consult a book on Internet security and the documentation that came with your router.

Firewalls can be built into an NT server or can be part of an external router device. The guiding principles of "least access" and "simplest for the job" dictate that it should be safer to rely on a separate special-purpose program or device to do this very important job. External routers may also contain the hardware necessary to establish a connection to an ISP via modem, ISDN, Frame Relay, or other data communication service. When using a dial-up ISDN or modem connection, they can be configured to "dial-on-demand" automatically only when outgoing traffic is present. (NT 4.0's RAS AutoDial feature provides similar functionality.)

A firewall can also provide a tunneling service, which encapsulates and encrypts data sent between two networks. Figure 24-4 shows how a tunnel works. In this illustration, Networks A and B are private networks, neither directly reachable from the Internet. Only firewall routers *b* and *c* have valid IP addresses. When computer *a* sends a data packet to computer *d*, router *b* encrypts it and inserts it into a packet addressed from *b* to router *c*. Router *c* removes the enclosed encrypted packet, decodes it, and passes it along to computer *d*. This technique enables you to use the Internet to connect two private networks securely, which users on the Internet at large can't access. Windows NT Server 4.0 contains tunneling software called PPTP (point-to-point tunneling protocol), discussed in Chapter 11. Alternatively, you can use the tunneling features of an external router.

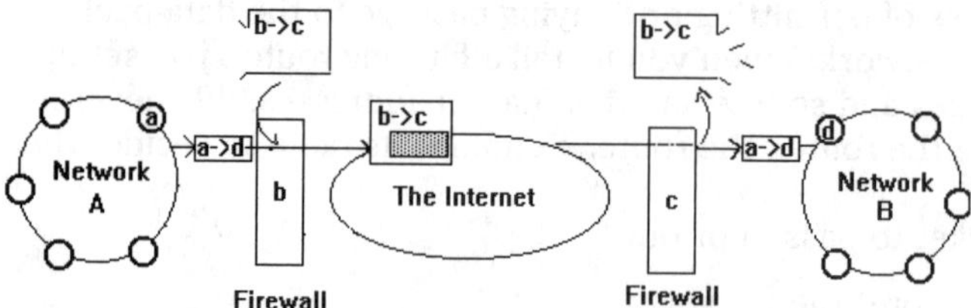

Figure 24-4: You can use an IP tunnel to connect two private networks securely via the Internet.

Using Proxies and Gateways

Models B and C in Figure 24-1 use firewalls and proxies to keep most of your network hidden from the outside world, exposing only those computers or services that are absolutely required. The gateway model (B) physically puts only one computer within reach of the Internet, whereas the remainder of your network is hidden.

The proxy model (C) uses a firewall with proxy software or an address translation feature to carry out Internet transactions on behalf of an inside user, passing back the obtained information. Proxies can work at one of two levels — the application level or the circuit level. At the application level, the proxy actually understands the information that it's processing. At the circuit level, the proxy passes packets and simply changes the source and destination IP addresses on behalf of its inside clients. Address translating routers use the circuit level approach and can be the basis of a very secure Internet connection.

Be sure to consider the availability of these features when you select your routers and network hardware.

Using Encryption and Authentication

As I mentioned earlier in this chapter, hackers with physical access to an Internet data cable or who have hacked their way into computers in an ISP's office can monitor network traffic and read unencrypted passwords.

NT's FTP server and most mail servers use the NT accounts database (the SAM database, discussed in Chapters 2 and 10) to authenticate user names and passwords. Since FTP and POP mail protocols don't encrypt their passwords, an eavesdropping hacker can use these protocols to obtain valid user names and passwords for your computers. This bears repeating: I strongly suggest that if you permit TCP/IP file-sharing over the Internet that you *don't* install FTP or POP mail services accessible from the outside world. If these services aren't installed or reachable from the Internet, your users won't be enticed by them to expose their user names and passwords. Conversely, if you install a POP or FTP server that will use actual NT user names and passwords, restrict access by these programs to separate volumes containing no sensitive files.

Microsoft's IIS includes an encryption feature called the Secure Sockets Layer, or SSL, which is compatible with Microsoft's Internet Explorer. Look up SSL in Internet Service Manager's online Help for details on how to configure it to encrypt your transmitted data.

If you don't enable encryption on your Web server, you can still opt to encrypt files before sending them using powerful cryptographic software such as PGP, which stands for Pretty Good Privacy. PGP is available for distribution in the U.S. and Canada from MIT. For details on how to obtain it, see the `http://web.mit.edu/network/pgp.html` Web page.

Keeping Yourself Current

One final active step that you can take to prevent break-ins is to keep yourself informed of security developments in the Internet world. You'll want to hear about new ways of protecting your network and of newly discovered security risks as soon as possible.

Here are some Internet locations that you can visit to find up-to-date information on Internet security issues:

```
http://www.cert.org
http://www.first.org
ftp://www.first.org/pub/first
http://cs-www.ncsl.nist.gov
http://www.cs.purdue.edu/coast/coast.html
ftp://coast.cs.purdue.edu/pub/aux/documents.abstract
ftp://coast.cs.purdue.edu/pub/aux/tools.abstract
http://www.greatcircle.com
```

Some of these sites will point you toward security-related mailing lists. You should at least subscribe to CERT-CC advisories, and perhaps to other lists in digest form.

In addition, you can monitor the following Internet newsgroups:

```
comp.security.*
comp.risks
```

Watching for Security Breaches

It's not enough to install firewalls and limit access rights and just hope that it all works. Try breaking into your own network. Do this before you connect your network to the Internet, immediately after you've connected to the Internet, and periodically thereafter. Test your defenses before the hackers do. You'll also need to have monitoring procedures in place so that you can detect problems with your security methods as the problems occur.

Testing before You Connect

Before you connect that line to your ISP, be sure to test as many of your internal security features as you can. For example, use NT's built-in FTP command to see what you can accomplish by logging on anonymously, as a regular network user, and as an administrator. Try to change to the Windows NT SystemRoot directory (C:\WINNT, for example) — you shouldn't be able to access it. Try to write to directories that you expect to be read-only. It's best to find out if there are any problems now, before anyone else gets a shot! Similarly, test your Web server for inappropriate access. Many organizations use their internal intranet first to test their security precautions before connecting their network to the outside world.

If you have a firewall and can set up a workstation on the outside network (you'll have to change the computer's IP address to an outside Internet network address), it's well worth the effort. By doing this, you can test your packet-filtering scheme without any outside exposure. Try to access shared volumes and access your Web and mail services. Try everything that should and shouldn't be allowed. This is also a good time to check your logging and monitoring methods. You should be able see logged traces of all of your failed attempts to access your network.

Monitor Internet Traffic

A few days ago while I was connected by modem to my ISP via my desktop computer, my hard disk light and the modem activity lights started flashing, even though I wasn't doing anything. What was going on? I wasn't able to find out. The dialer and Winsock software that I was using has no tracing feature enabling me to view the actual data going to and from my Internet connection. (This alone should scare you away from using a direct connection from the Internet to your NT server.)

If you aren't using a router with a packet-tracing feature, it's wise to have a software or hardware protocol monitor available to hook up to your network. These tools enable you to debug problems by displaying packets coming from unexpected sources or viewing interactions between computers on and off your internal network.

Soon after your network is installed and running, I suggest that you test out the packet-tracing features on your network to watch a simple network transaction, just to get an idea of what you're looking at *before* it's an issue of urgency and security. For example, learn what a domain name lookup looks like. Understand the transactions involved in viewing a simple Web page.

Also, learn about the TCP/IP command-line utilities provided with Windows NT Server. You'll find them listed and briefly described in Appendix A.

Recording and Detecting Suspicious Activity

Your router should also provide the means of displaying and recording information about blocked access attempts, discarded packets, and so on. The display will show you the source and destination IP addresses of the rejected packets, and you can use Internet tools such as NSLOOKUP or DIG to find the names of the offending hosts.

In most cases, you'll find that the packets are innocuous. For example, if you're using a dial-up connection to your ISP, sometimes you'll receive packets that are very-long-overdue replies to connections established by the person previously using the same dial-up connection. A filtering router might detect that these packets don't belong to a connection which originated from inside your network and will log and discard them.

These logs must, of course, go to a printer or to a disk volume separate from other volumes on your network, or a prolonged attack on your network will fill up a disk needed for other purposes. Some routers can also send log events via the network. If you find an NT version of the UNIX utility SYSLOG, it can be installed as a service and directed to a small volume for storage on an NT server. (If you do this, however, be sure to block SYSLOG packets at the firewall from coming in through the Internet.)

It's a good idea to configure all NT Server software to log failed logon and service requests. Monitor the logs frequently for signs of probing and attack.

Planning for Security Disasters

What if the worst happens? If someone does break into your system and causes a crash, deletes files, or damages data, how are you going to examine the server that's been compromised? Like a live bomb or a box of poison, that's how!

If your server security has been breached, you can't take any chances that the perpetrator didn't leave behind some way of getting back in. Perhaps he or she left a virus that will compromise other computers on your network. You'll want to reformat the disks, install from pristine distribution CD-ROMs or floppy disks, and make a clean start. Then, you can look at recent backups to determine if you have any that you're sure aren't compromised. If you have them, restore them, and then go on. It's not going to be a happy time for anyone. Besides the pressure on you to get the server up, you're going to be busy trying to find out what went wrong with your security measures so that you can fix them. A little planning now will go a long way toward helping you through this crisis. (I discussed how to back up and restore your server in Chapter 18. I hope this little scenario helps drive home the point that being connected to the Internet makes it even more important to be prepared.)

Backing Up before You're Connected

Always make a permanent backup of a computer *before* you put it on the Internet. This way, you'll be able to check files for corruption in the event of an attack. It does no good to restore a computer from a backup made *after* an attack has damaged or compromised it. Never recycle these pre-Internet backups. Keep them as permanent archival copies. You can use them in file comparison mode to check files for damage after a crash or attack.

Backing Up after You're Connected

As discussed in Chapter 6 and again in Chapter 18, have a backup plan and stick to it. This is even more vitally important when you're connected to the Internet. Make backups at sensible intervals and always after a session of extensive or significant changes (for example, installing new software, adding user accounts, and so forth). Be sure to keep a few tapes out of your reuse cycle; if it takes a while to discover loss or damage, you'll be pretty unhappy if you've overwritten all of the tapes made before a file was lost or corrupted.

Having a Security Incident Plan

If you detect or suspect a break-in, your first course of action should be to secure your site by disconnecting from the Internet, if this is feasible. Second, consider reporting the incident to appropriate authorities. Criminal issues may be involved, and even without the criminal aspect, computer security organizations such as CERT-CC (the Computer Emergency Response Team Coordination Center) may be able to help you or to use information from your break-in to protect others. For information about CERT-CC, see `ftp://info.cert.org` or, in an emergency, call (412) 268-7090. Also, FIRST (the Forum of Incident Response and Security Teams) can tell you which agencies might best be able to help you in the event of a security incident. Contact them at (301) 975-3359.

Firewall Filtering and TCP/IP Services

In this section, I'll present a brief primer on TCP/IP networking and packet filtering. This isn't going to be a complete treatment of the topic. It should, however, give you enough information to be able to absorb a more advanced book more quickly than I did the first time. Before proceeding with this section, you should be familiar with the terms and concepts introduced in Chapter 11, in the section entitled "Understanding the World of TCP/IP."

For a good introduction to firewalls and Internet security in general, I recommend *Building Internet Firewalls* by D. Brent Chapman and Elizabeth D. Zwicky (O'Reilly & Associates, ISBN 1-56592-124-0). *Firewalls and Internet Security: Repelling the Wily Hacker* by William R. Cheswick and Steven M. Bellovin of AT&T Bell Labs (Addison & Wesley, ISBN 0-201-63357-4) is a more thorough, academic treatment.

Understanding Packets and Ports

Data sent over the Internet, or over any TCP/IP network, is broken into packets that are usually 20 to 1500 bytes long. Each packet contains values that indicate its protocol type, source and destination IP addresses, and sometimes a port number that identifies the type of service to receive the packet. The main protocol types are ICMP (Internet Control Message Protocol), UDP (User Datagram Protocol), and TCP (Transmission Control Protocol). ICMP packets are usually used to report error conditions. For example, if an Internet connection is down, the router before the failed connection will return an "ICMP Destination Unreachable" packet to anyone trying to send data across the failed line. UDP packets are used for brief, simple Internet services such as Domain Name lookup. TCP is used by all heavy-duty services, since it provides a stable pipeline, almost like a phone call connection. TCP packets also contain a special mark indicating whether they're part of a brand-new connection (analogous to the ringing of a telephone) or an already established connection.

Each standard TCP/IP service such as FTP uses a standard protocol type and port number to receive requests. For example, an FTP server waits for someone to send TCP packets to it at port 20.

Creating Filtering Rules

Writing rules for a packet filter involves specifying which packets are allowed to pass through and which are to be blocked. The rules are based on the packets' protocol types, source and destination IP addresses, and port numbers. Let's consider an example. Suppose you're using the standard firewall model (C), shown in Figure 24-1. You want to give your internal users access to any outside site and service that they want, but you want to block all outside access to your internal servers. Your packet-filtering rules for TCP packets may be

- ✦ Allow in any TCP packet that's part of an established connection.
- ✦ Block any other incoming TCP packets and log them to the router's display.

What does this do? If any outside user attempts to make contact with any server inside your network, it won't be considered by the first rule (since it's not part of an already established connection), and it will then be blocked by the second. An alert message may appear on a screen, printer, or terminal attached to the router telling you to investigate a potential break-in attempt.

What about outgoing packets? If an internal user establishes contact with an outside server (say, with www.microsoft.com), the returned packets will be part of an established connection, so they'll be allowed in. Just these two rules enforce your desired Internet policy.

What about a hacker who tries to fool you by sending packets that appear to be part of an established conversation? TCP/IP software will (usually) ignore these packets, since it keeps track of each established connection. (You can see this by typing **NETSTAT** on your NT server while it's servicing TCP/IP requests).

Remember earlier in this chapter when I discussed spoofing, where a hacker sends in packets that look as if they came from inside your network? You can revise your filter rules to eliminate this possibility outright:

✦ Block any incoming packet of any type that has an internal IP address as its source address.

✦ Allow in any TCP packet that's part of an established connection.

✦ Block any other incoming TCP packets and log them to the router's display.

Now, allow the outside world access to your Web server at IP address 012.34.56.79, and only to that address. Add one more rule:

✦ Block any incoming packet of any type that has an internal IP address as its source address.

✦ Allow in any TCP packet that's part of an established connection.

✦ Allow in any TCP packet that's explicitly addressed to 012.34.56.79 on port 80.

✦ Block any other incoming TCP packets and log them to the router's display.

Initial attempts to contact your Web server are allowed in by the new third rule. Any further communication over established connections between an outside user and your Web server are allowed in by the second rule.

Of course, you'll need some additional rules for UDP and ICMP. UDP is more difficult to filter, because the packets are all independent of each other and there's no way to tell whether they're part of an incoming or outgoing connection. (Proxying firewalls generally do a better job of handling this, because they must keep track of who has made a request in order to send the response to the correct computer on your network.)

Check with your ISP to make sure that they're taking care of security, too. Be sure that they're using static routing for all of their customers' subnets. Also, make sure that they're using anti-spoofing filters on all customer connections. If they're not, a hacker with a connection to your ISP can try to tell their routers to send your traffic to him or her instead of to you.

Filtering in the Real World

Each router manufacturer uses a different format for specifying filtering rules. I use a shareware program called IPROUTE as my Internet site's router and firewall. See `http://www.mischler.com/iproute` for details. Using IPROUTE, the four filtering rules discussed earlier in this section look something like

```
filter outside log drop in * 012.34.56.78/28 *
filter outside permit in tcp-xsyn * *
filter outside permit in tcp * 012.34.56.79:80
filter outside log drop in tcp * *
```

IPROUTE can turn an old 386 into a nifty Internet firewall router, adequate for Internet connection speeds of T1 or less, plus it has many other features that I've mentioned. It provides network translation (proxying) to protect a private network, supports both dial-in and demand-dial-out connections using PPP, and offers encrypted tunneling. It's a nice tool for small offices, nonprofit organizations, schools, and so on. Corporate MIS groups are likely to be more interested in a name-brand hardware router. These cost around $1500 and up, but the name-brand confidence and support that they offer is well worth it.

Filtering TCP/IP Services

Now, let's look at what kind of TCP services are available, in order to know what you may want to permit or block. Remember, you're probably going to block all incoming connections by default. You'll only enable incoming access to specific ports that correspond to services that you want to provide to the world (for example, your Web site and your FTP server). You probably want to permit all types of outgoing connections, but you may want to block some of them, based on your security and computer-use policies.

When you install TCP/IP on a Windows NT Server computer, the Simple TCP/IP Services package activates several services of which you might not be aware. Table 24-2 describes these services.

Table 24-2
Simple TCP/IP Services and Their TCP/IP Ports

TCP/IP Service	*Port Number*	*Description*
ECHO	7	Echoes whatever data it is sent.
DISCARD	9	Discards whatever data it is sent.
DAYTIME	13	Returns the time and date as a character string.

(continued)

Table 24-2 (continued)

TCP/IP Service	*Port Number*	*Description*
QOTD	17	Returns a brief quotation ("quote of the day"). It's similar to fortune cookie services on other operating systems.
CHARGEN	19	Sends a stream of ASCII characters as fast as it can.

Although these services may be useful for internal testing and debugging on your network, ECHO, DISCARD, and CHARGEN are just the ticket for denial of service attacks from the outside. They can easily use up all of the bandwidth of your server or Internet connection. You can see this for yourself. On an NT computer with TCP/IP installed, at a Command Prompt, type:

```
TELNET LOCALHOST CHARGEN
```

and watch what happens. Figure 24-5 shows how this utility eats up your CPU bandwidth locally. I don't recommend allowing access to these services across your firewall.

FTP uses ports 20 (for commands) and 21 (for data) on the server. You'll need to allow access to these ports if you want outside access to your FTP server. If you're using a proxy router, you'll specify that packets for ports 20 and 21 be forwarded to the computer running your FTP server.

A firewall also has an impact on your internal FTP users. FTP transfers normally create a TCP connection from the FTP server to the client for data transfers. By default, when an internal user attempts to use an FTP server outside your firewall, the remote FTP server will try to establish an incoming connection to the user. Because you block incoming TCP connections by default, your FTP users won't be able to connect to FTP servers outside your firewall. Instruct your users to set their FTP client programs to *passive mode* when contacting external FTP servers. In passive mode, the FTP client initiates data connections and your firewall will permit the file transfer.

TELNET, which uses port 23, is a remote terminal protocol. Several NT-based Telnet servers are available. They allow remote users to connect to an NT server and execute commands from their terminal screen. Since the Telnet protocol sends clear text passwords without encryption, I recommend that you avoid installing Telnet servers and that you prevent incoming connections to port 23 through the firewall.

DNS (Domain Name Server), which uses port 53, is the name server protocol used to resolve a name such as www.microsoft.com to its IP address 207.68.137.40. Generally, you must permit UDP packets for port 53 to pass through your gateway.

These packets represent your users' requests working their way through the Internet's DNS. TCP connections on port 53, however, are used by one name server to back up another or by hackers hunting for interesting node names. Unless you have a primary name server inside your firewall and a secondary one outside, I recommend that you don't permit any incoming TCP connections on port 53.

BOOTP and TFTP, which use ports 67 and 69, are used on some systems to start up diskless computers. TFTP (Trivial File Transfer Protocol) is quite dangerous, because it will transfer files without passwords of any sort. Although I don't know of any available NT-based TFTP servers, don't enable TFTP across your firewall.

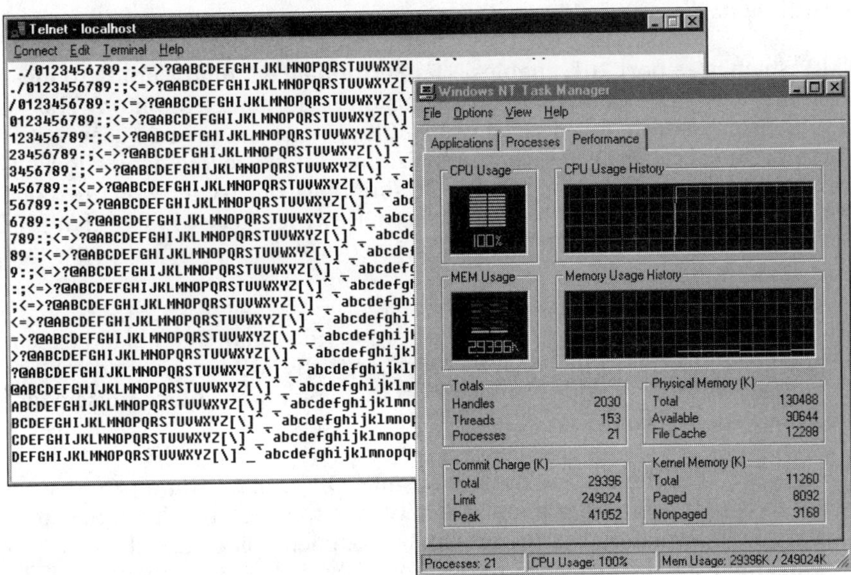

Figure 24-5: Built-in TCP/IP services can be used to consume your CPU and Internet connection bandwidth.

FINGER, on port 79, allows people to retrieve user names on your network. If you install a third-party Finger server on your network, don't allow finger packets to cross the firewall. It violates the policy of hiding information that's not really necessary to the outside world.

HTTP, on port 80, is used by Web servers. You'll probably want to permit incoming connections to port 80, at least for those servers that contain public Web pages. You'll probably want to leave port 80 blocked for any other internal (intranet) Web servers containing confidential company information.

POP3, on port 110, is used to read mail. However, as mentioned earlier, it sends passwords without encryption. This can be a great security risk, since FTP and NT file sharing usually use these same passwords. If your internal users want to be able to read e-mail from home, I suggest letting them dial into your internal network as in model D in Figure 24-1. This is probably going to be the trickiest case of having to balance the needs and desires of users against your security needs. If you do permit POP3 across the firewall, be sure that the FTP server, if installed, is configured to prevent reading any sensitive volumes readable by your internal users.

NNTP uses port 119 on the server. It's used to transfer News messages. You only need to allow NNTP into your network if you're running a News server. Otherwise, block these packets at the firewall.

SNMP, which uses port 161, enables NT's Performance Monitor utility to measure TCP/IP services. (See Chapter 19 for details on Performance Monitor.) This is a very important feature for internal use, but it provides an outside user quite a bit of information about your network organization. I don't recommend allowing incoming SNMP to cross your firewall. Be sure that your router won't respond to SNMP commands from its outside interfaces. However, keep in mind that SNMP can be very useful inside your network, to record system error messages from servers and routers.

RSH and RCMD use ports 513 and 514. They provide remote command execution. As I mentioned earlier in this chapter, because the RCMD server sends clear text passwords over the network, I recommend that you always block these connections from crossing your firewall.

RIP, on port 520, is the routing protocol using UDP packets. Routers and servers use RIP to inform each other about the networks to which they're connected and how to route information between them. I recommend blocking RIP packets from entering or leaving through the firewall. You should also verify that your ISP blocks these packets as well. Why? Between you and the outside world, they convey no useful information, and there's a risk that a hacker could manage to have your router redirect network traffic from the intended recipients.

You can find many of the standard TCP/IP port numbers that are assigned to well-known services by looking in the SERVICES file in the SystemRoot\SYSTEM32\DRIVERS\ETC directory. SERVICES is a text file, so you can view it with Notepad.

Summary

In this chapter, you've learned that connecting your network to the Internet brings much more than just great opportunities for new types of communication. It also gives tens of millions of computer users around the world the potential to reach right into your network in ways that you never expected. You can protect your servers and network from unauthorized use, damage, or worse by applying one basic theme to every aspect of your network installation — "Block access to everything by default, and only permit access to things that you know are necessary, that you understand, and for which you've prepared." This will be the path of least security surprises.

Summary

[illegible]

Appendixes

✦ ✦ ✦ ✦

In This Part

✦ ✦ ✦ ✦

Windows NT Command Reference

This appendix provides you with a handy reference to the Windows NT commands, including descriptions of all commands accepted by NT and some tips on using command line utilities. Although you can start any of NT's graphical applications from an NT Command Prompt, this appendix focuses only on command-line utilities that don't have a graphical user interface. See the section called "Console Application" in Chapter 17 for details on configuring the NT Command Prompt.

To find detailed syntax information on each of the Windows NT Server 4.0 commands, click Start ➪ Help and click the Contents tab. Double-click the Windows NT Commands book icon, then double-click the Windows NT Commands document icon. Search for a specific command by scrolling down the alphabetized list or click a letter to jump directly to the desired section.

You can also get online Help on commands from the Command Prompt itself. Typing HELP displays a list of one-line descriptions of several (but not all) available NT commands. If a command appears on this list, you can type HELP followed by the command name to see detailed syntax information. Most commands also accept a /? parameter. Just type the command name followed by /? to see a detailed syntax description.

Windows NT Command Descriptions

Table A-1 presents a comprehensive alphabetical list of all commands accepted by Windows NT, along with brief descriptions of each one. Refer to online Help (as described earlier in this appendix) for detailed syntax information.

Table A-1
Windows NT Command Descriptions

Command	*Description*
APPEND	Fools applications and the command interpreter into thinking that files in the specified directories are actually in the current directory. Applications can open files without specifying the actual directories where the files reside. (This is a 16-bit DOS command.)
ARP	Modifies and displays the translation tables that map IP addresses to physical network adapter addresses, used by the Address Resolution Protocol (ARP). This command is available only with the TCP/IP protocol.
ASSOC	Assigns, displays, and deletes associations between file extensions and file types. FTYPE associates file types with actual applications. NT Explorer also allows you to do this, as described in Chapter 14.
AT	Schedules commands to run unattended at specific times, dates, and frequencies. Requires the NT Schedule service. See Chapter 21 for details.
ATTRIB	Modifies and displays file attributes (read-only, archive, system, hidden) associated with a file. Doesn't manage the compress attribute on NTFS objects. See the COMPACT command.
BACKUP	Performs backups of files from hard disk to floppy or hard disk. Data can be retrieved using the RESTORE command. BACKUP doesn't support tape backup. Use NTBACKUP for this. (This is a 16-bit DOS command.)
BREAK	This command is ignored by Windows NT and is accepted only for compatibility with existing batch files.
BUFFERS	This command is ignored by Windows NT and is accepted only for compatibility with existing batch files.
CACLS	Modifies and displays the Access Control List (ACL) associated with an NTFS file. You can specify multiple files and users in a single command. NT Explorer also enables you to do this, as described in Chapter 18.

Command	Description
CALL	Runs a batch program from within another batch program without terminating the calling program.
CD	Modifies or displays the current directory in a Command Prompt window.
CHCP	Modifies or displays the currently active codepage for the Command Prompt. Modifies the codepage for full-screen mode or Command Prompt windows using TrueType fonts only.
CHDIR	See the CD command.
CHKDSK	Performs an integrity check of FAT or NTFS file system structures on hard disk or floppy disk, displays a report, and optionally corrects detected errors. Requires administrative privileges to run on hard disk.
CLS	Clears the contents of the Command Prompt window or full screen, leaving only the prompt and cursor in the upper left corner.
CMD	Starts a new instance of the Windows NT command interpreter. (CMD is the NT replacement for DOS's COMMAND.COM.) You can nest multiple instances and return to the previous instance using the EXIT command.
CODEPAGE	Specifies the codepage to be used by the OS/2 subsystem. This command is used in the OS/2 CONFIG.SYS file.
COLOR	Modifies the default text foreground and background colors. The Console application in Control Panel and the Properties command in the Command Prompt's window menu also enable you to do this, as described in Chapter 17.
COMP	Performs a byte-by-byte comparison of two files or sets of files and reports the first 10 differences between them, if any.
COMPACT	Modifies and displays the compress attribute of NTFS files and directories. Performs the appropriate compression or decompression when the compress attribute is modified. NT Explorer also enables you to do this, as described in Chapter 19.
CONVERT	Performs an in-place conversion of an existing FAT volume to an NTFS volume, leaving all data on the volume intact. (No longer supports conversion from HPFS to NTFS in Windows NT 4.0.)
COPY	Copies files to and from files and devices. Concatenates files.
COUNTRY	Specifies the country code for DOS applications to use the appropriate conventions for time, date, currency, capitalization, and decimal separators. The Regional Settings application in Control Panel enables you to specify these settings for Windows programs.
DATE	Modifies the system date stored in CMOS. The Date/Time application in Control Panel also enables you to do this, as described in Chapter 17.

(continued)

Table A-1 *(continued)*	
Command	***Description***
DEBUG	Starts the DOS debugger, allowing you to debug DOS applications. (This is a 16-bit DOS command.)
DEL	Performs a delete of specified files. The NT version has additional features.
DEVICE	Loads a DOS device driver for use with DOS applications. This command is used in the CONFIG.NT file.
DEVICEHIGH	Loads a DOS device driver into high memory for use with DOS applications, leaving more conventional memory for the application itself. This command is used in the CONFIG.NT file.
DEVINFO	Prepares a device to use codepages under the OS/2 subsystem. This command is used in the OS/2 CONFIG.SYS file.
DIR	Displays a list of the contents of a directory. The NT version has additional features.
DISKCOMP	Performs a track-by-track comparison of two floppy disks. Some switches supported in DOS aren't supported in NT.
DISKCOPY	Creates a track-by-track copy from one floppy disk to another. Some switches supported in DOS aren't supported in NT.
DISKPERF	Enables and disables updates of disk performance counters, reported by Performance Monitor. See Chapter 19.
DOS	Links DOS to high memory and controls whether portions of DOS itself are loaded into high memory. This command is used in the CONFIG.NT file.
DOSKEY	Maintains a history of commands which can be selected, edited, and reused. The Console application in Control Panel and the Properties command in the Command Prompt's window menu also enable you to do this, as described in Chapter 17.
DOSONLY	Prevents running a non-DOS application from COMMAND.COM when running a DOS TSR or temporarily suspending a DOS application. This command is used in the CONFIG.NT file.
DRIVEPARM	This command is ignored by Windows NT and is accepted only for compatibility with existing batch files.
ECHO	Displays a text string and turns batch command echoing on and off.
ECHOCONFIG	Displays progress messages during the processing of CONFIG.NT and AUTOEXEC.NT when a DOS application starts. This command is used in the CONFIG.NT file.

Command	Description
EDIT	Starts the DOS editor, allowing you to edit text files. Notepad also allows you to do this. (This is a 16-bit DOS command.)
EDLIN	Starts the now-pathetic DOS line-oriented editor, allowing you to edit text files. Use EDIT or Notepad to perform your text editing. (This is a 16-bit DOS command.)
ENDLOCAL	Within a batch file, reverts to the previous set of environment variables in effect before the last SETLOCAL command was executed.
ERASE	See the DEL command.
EXE2BIN	Converts DOS executable files to binary format. This command is useful only to software developers creating DOS applications. (This is a 16-bit DOS command.)
EXIT	Terminates the current instance of the Windows NT command interpreter and returns to the instance that executed the CMD command. If the current instance is the only instance in the Command Prompt window, the window is closed.
EXPAND	Decompresses compressed distribution files, typically provided on software distribution disks. Most files on the Windows NT Server CD-ROM are in this compressed form. (This is a 16-bit DOS command.)
FASTOPEN	This command is ignored by Windows NT and is accepted only for compatibility with existing batch files.
FC	Performs a binary or ASCII comparison of two files and displays the differences between them.
FCBS	Specifies the maximum number of file control blocks (FCBs) that a DOS application can have open at one time. This command, used in the CONFIG.NT file, is typically not required by newer DOS applications.
FILES	Specifies the maximum number of files that a DOS application can have open at one time. This command is used in the CONFIG.NT file.
FIND	Performs a line-by-line search of a file or set of files for a specified text string and displays the results. Typically used as a filter.
FINDSTR	A more powerful version of FIND. FINDSTR performs a search for multiple text strings within files, allowing wildcards in the strings.
FINGER	Displays information about a specified user on a computer running the Finger service. This command is available only with the TCP/IP protocol.
FOR	Within a batch file, executes a specified command repeatedly, once for each member of a set of files or text strings.

(continued)

Table A-1 *(continued)*

Command	***Description***
FORCEDOS	Forces a command to be executed as a DOS application, even if the program isn't recognized as DOS. Typically used to force execute of bound OS/2 applications as DOS commands. See Chapter 17 for more details.
FORMAT	Formats a hard disk (FAT or NTFS) or floppy disk (FAT only). Requires administrative privileges to run on hard disk. Also requires exclusive access to the volume.
FTP	Transfers files to and from a server running the FTP service. This command is available only with the TCP/IP protocol.
FTYPE	Modifies and displays file types used in file associations. Maps the file type specified in the ASSOC command with the application used to open files of a specific type. NT Explorer also enables you to do this, as described in Chapter 14.
GOTO	Transfers control within a batch file to the line with the specified label.
GRAFTABL	Enables a Command Prompt running in full-screen mode to display the extended characters of a specified codepage.
GRAPHICS	Enables NT to print color screen graphics to a printer using appropriate gray scales and orientation. (This is a 16-bit DOS command.)
HELP	Displays a syntax description of the specified command. Doesn't provide Help on all commands. Click Start ➪ Help ➪ Contents ➪ Windows NT Commands ➪ Windows NT Commands comprehensive online Help.
HOSTNAME	Displays the name of the current host (computer). This command is available only with the TCP/IP protocol.
IF	Within a batch file, executes a specified command if the specified conditional expression is true. If the condition is false, no action is taken.
INSTALL	Loads a memory-resident program immediately before executing a DOS application that requires it.
IPCONFIG	Displays all TCP/IP network configuration information, including assignments made automatically by DHCP. This command is available only with the TCP/IP protocol.
IPXROUTE	Modifies and displays routing table information used by the IPX protocol.

Command	Description
KEYB	Configures the keyboard for a specific language. This command is used in the CONFIG.NT file. The Keyboard application in Control Panel also enables you to do this.
LABEL	Modifies the volume label of a hard disk or floppy disk. NT Explorer and the Disk Administrator utility also allow you to do this. See Chapter 18 for details.
LASTDRIVE	This command is ignored by Windows NT and is accepted only for compatibility with existing batch files. Windows NT always sets LAST-DRIVE to Z.
LH	Loads a DOS application into high memory, leaving more conventional memory for other applications. (This is a 16-bit DOS command.)
LIBPATH	Specifies the set of paths that the OS/2 subsystem uses to search for dynamic link libraries (DLLs). This command is used in the OS/2 CON-FIG.SYS file.
LOADFIX	Loads a DOS application above the first 64K of conventional memory and executes the application. Used to overcome the "Packed file cor-rupt" error message. (This is a 16-bit DOS command.)
LOADHIGH	See the LH command.
LPQ	Displays status of a print queue on a computer running the LPD server. This command is available only with the TCP/IP protocol.
LPR	Prints a file to a print queue on a computer running the LPD server. This command is available only with the TCP/IP protocol.
MD	Creates a new directory or subdirectory on disk.
MEM	Displays information about allocated memory, free memory, and appli-cations that are currently loaded in the DOS environment. (This is a 16-bit DOS command.)
MKDIR	See the MD command.
MODE	Configures several PC devices including keyboard, video mode, serial, and printer ports. This command has changed significantly from the DOS version.
MORE	A filter that displays one screen (or window) of output at a time, paus-ing between each screen. The NT version of MORE has more features than the DOS version.
MOVE	Moves files from a source directory to a destination directory.

(continued)

Table A-1 (continued)

Command	***Description***
NBTSTAT	Displays protocol statistics and connections using NBT (NetBIOS over TCP/IP). This command is available only with the TCP/IP protocol.
NET ACCOUNTS	Modifies account policies for behavior of logons and passwords. The User Manager for Domains option under Policies ➪ Account enables you to make similar changes.
NET COMPUTER	Adds or removes a computer account from a domain. This command is available only on Windows NT Server. Server Manager provides similar functionality under Computer ➪ Add to Domain or Remove from Domain.
NET CONFIG	Displays a list of configurable services that are currently running (typically server and workstation) and optionally modifies their configuration.
NET CONTINUE	Resumes a paused service that was paused by the NET PAUSE command. The Services application in Control Panel provides similar functionality.
NET FILE	Displays a list of all open shared files and their file locks. Optionally closes specified files and removes their locks. Server Manager under Computer ➪ Properties ➪ In Use provides similar functionality.
NET GROUP	Modifies, displays, adds, and deletes global groups in an NT domain. This command is available only on Windows NT Server. You can perform the same functions in User Manager for Domains, as described in Chapter 18.
NET HELP	Displays online Help on the specified NET command.
NET HELPMSG	Displays more detailed information on a specified Windows NT message number.
NET LOCALGROUP	Modifies, displays, adds, and deletes local groups. You can perform the same functions in User Manager for Domains, as described in Chapter 18.
NET NAME	Adds or deletes a name, used by the Messenger service, on a computer.
NET PAUSE	Pauses a service temporarily. You can resume the service using the NET CONTINUE command. The Services application in Control Panel provides similar functionality.
NET PRINT	Controls and displays print jobs and printer queues. The Printers folder, described in Chapter 18, provides similar functionality.

Command	Description
NET SEND	Sends a short, pop-up message to other computers on the network by specifying their computer names, user names, or messaging names added with the NET NAME command. Optionally sends a message to all names in a domain or all computers connected to a server.
NET SESSION	Displays or disconnects all sessions between a server and its clients. Server Manager under Computer ⇨ Properties ⇨ Users provides similar functionality.
NET SHARE	Displays, creates, and deletes shared resources on a server. NT Explorer can be used to perform these functions.
NET START	Displays a list of running services or starts a specified service. The Services application in Control Panel provides similar functionality.
NET STATISTICS	Displays statistics associated with server or workstation services.
NET STOP	Stops a specified running service. The Services application in Control Panel provides similar functionality.
NET TIME	Synchronizes the local computer's clock with that of another computer.
NET USE	Displays information about computer connections and creates or deletes connections to shared resources.
NET USER	Modifies or displays user account information. User Manager for Domains provides similar functionality.
NET VIEW	Displays a list of domains, computers, or resources shared by servers.
NETSTAT	Displays protocol statistics and connections. This command is available only with the TCP/IP protocol.
NLSFUNC	This command is ignored by Windows NT and is accepted only for compatibility with existing batch files.
NSLOOKUP	Displays Domain Name System (DNS) name servers. This command is available only with the TCP/IP protocol.
NTBOOKS	Accesses Windows NT Server and Windows NT Workstation online manuals.
NTCMDPROMPT	Forces starting the Windows NT command interpreter CMD.EXE even after starting a DOS TSR or from within a DOS application.
PATH	Modifies the set of directories used to search for executable files. You can use the %PATH% environment variable to add directories to an existing set.
PAUSE	Stops execution of a batch program, waits for the user to press a key, then continues execution.

(continued)

Table A-1 *(continued)*

Command	***Description***
PAX	Starts the Portable Archive Interchange (PAX) utility, which reads and writes POSIX-compliant archive files. (Note that POSIX applications cannot access NT tape devices.)
PENTNT	Detects the Pentium floating-point error. If the error is present, it disables the floating-point hardware and enables floating-point software emulation.
PING	Verifies a network connection between two computers by specifying either IP addresses or host names. This command is available only with the TCP/IP protocol.
POPD	Changes back to the directory stored by the previous PUSHD command.
PORTUAS	Migrates an existing LAN Manager 2.x accounts database to a Windows NT accounts database.
PRINT	Sends a file to the print queue, to be printed in background. Some switches available in DOS don't make sense on NT.
PROMPT	Modifies the contents of the prompt within a Command Prompt window.
PROTSHELL	This command is ignored by Windows NT, and is accepted only for compatibility with existing OS/2 batch files.
PUSHD	Saves the current directory and changes to the specified directory. The POPD command restores the directory saved by PUSHD.
QBASIC	Starts the Quick Basic interpreter. (This is a 16-bit DOS command.)
RCP	Copies files between a Windows NT computer and a computer running RSHD (remote shell daemon) or between two computers running RSHD. This command is available only with the TCP/IP protocol.
RD	Deletes an existing directory. The NT version can delete a non-empty directory (with the /S parameter).
RECOVER	Attempts to restore data from a partially defective disk, by reading a file sector-by-sector and recovering data from the readable sectors.
REM	Allows inclusion of comments in batch files and configuration files. REM comments are ignored during execution of the batch or configuration file.
REN	Modifies the names of files within a single directory.
RENAME	See the REN command.
REPLACE	Replaces files in a destination directory with files of the same name in a source directory. Typically used to update only those files that have changed.

Command	*Description*
RESTORE	Restores files that were backed up using the BACKUP command. (This is a 16-bit DOS command.)
REXEC	Executes commands on remote computers that are running the REXEC service. This command is available only with the TCP/IP protocol.
RMDIR	See the RD command.
ROUTE	Modifies network routing tables. This command is available only with the TCP/IP protocol.
RSH	Executes commands on remote computers that are running the RSH service. This command is available only with the TCP/IP protocol.
SET	Assigns a value to a specified environment variable, removes a variable from the environment, or lists the currently defined environment variables.
SETLOCAL	Within a batch file, begins a section in which subsequent changes to environment variables are in effect only temporarily, until an ENDLOCAL command is executed. Must have a corresponding subsequent ENDLOCAL command to restore environment variables to their previous state.
SETVER	Fools DOS applications into thinking that they're running on earlier versions of DOS, for those applications that require a DOS version earlier than 5.0. (This is a 16-bit DOS command.)
SHARE	This command is ignored by Windows NT and is accepted only for compatibility with existing batch files.
SHELL	Specifies a custom DOS command interpreter other than the special COMMAND.COM version that's included in Windows NT. Since the included COMMAND.COM is designed to interact correctly with other NT subsystems, use of a custom DOS command interpreter isn't recommended.
SHIFT	Changes the position of command-line parameters (%0, %1, %2, and so on) within a batch file.
SORT	A filter that reads the input stream, sorts it according to specified criteria, and displays the sorted output. The NT version of SORT has more features than the DOS version.
STACKS	Specifies the number and size of stacks for handling hardware interrupts in the DOS environment.
START	Starts a separate Command Prompt window to launch the specified application.
SUBST	Associates a new drive letter with an existing path.

(continued)

Table A-1 *(continued)*

Command	***Description***
SWITCHES	Causes an enhanced (newer) keyboard to behave as a conventional (older) keyboard, for DOS applications that don't behave correctly with an enhanced keyboard.
TFTP	Transfers files to and from a server running the TFTP service. This command is available only with the TCP/IP protocol.
TIME	Modifies the system time stored in CMOS. The Date/Time application in Control Panel also enables you to do this, as described in Chapter 17.
TITLE	Modifies the title of the Command Prompt window to a specified text string.
TRACERT	Displays the route taken between source and destination by an Internet Control Message Protocol (ICMP) echo packet with various router hop counts. This command is available only with the TCP/IP protocol.
TREE	Displays the directory tree structure of a disk or directory in graphical form.
TYPE	Displays the contents of a specified text file.
VER	Displays the Windows NT version number. On both Server and Workstation products, VER displays "Windows NT Version 4.0."
VERIFY	This command is ignored by Windows NT and is accepted only for compatibility with existing batch files.
VOL	Displays the disk volume label and serial number assigned when the disk was formatted. These same two lines are displayed at the beginning of the output of the DIR command.
WINNT	Starts a Windows NT 4.0 installation or upgrade while running DOS on an Intel computer. See Chapter 9 for details.
WINNT32	Starts a Windows NT 4.0 installation or upgrade while running a version of Windows NT on an Intel or RISC platform. See Chapter 9 for details.
XCOPY	Copies files, directories, and subdirectories from a specified source to a specified destination. The NT version of XCOPY has more features than the DOS version.

Volume, Directory, and File Manipulation Commands

The bulk of NT commands are designed to manipulate disk volumes, directories, and files. From formatting a volume to setting attribute bits on individual files, most of your command-line work will probably involve these commands. See Table A-1 for a description of each command and refer to online Help for specific command syntax information.

When specifying long file and directory names, either on FAT or NTFS, you need to surround the entire name in quotes if it contains any spaces.

Here are the volume, directory, and file manipulation commands:

ASSOC	ATTRIB	CACLS	CD	CHDIR
CHKDSK	COMP	COMPACT	CONVERT	COPY
DEL	DIR	DISKCOMP	DISKCOPY	ERASE
FC	FINDSTR	FORMAT	FTYPE	LABEL
MD	MKDIR	MOVE	RD	RECOVER
REN	RENAME	REPLACE	RMDIR	TREE
TYPEVOL	XCOPY			

Both CHKDSK and CONVERT require exclusive use of the volume on which they're operating. If the volume can't be locked for exclusive use (say, because it contains a paging file or because a database application has a file open), these utilities offer to schedule the operation to be performed at the next restart of the computer. CHKDSK causes AUTOCHK.EXE, a native NT version of CHKDSK, to scan the volume when the operating system boots the next time. Likewise, CONVERT causes AUTOCONV.EXE, a native NT version of CONVERT, to convert the volume to NTFS when the operating system boots the next time. AUTOCHK and AUTOCONV aren't designed to be used from the Command Prompt — they're meant to run early in the operating system boot sequence, before the system is completely running.

Network Commands

The second largest collection of commands in NT enables you to control networking functions. The NET command is at the heart of these features. It provides such a wide variety of functions, many folks consider it a language unto itself. See Table A-1 for a description of each command and refer to online Help for specific command syntax information. (Additional network commands are provided specifically for the TCP/IP protocol. See the section called "TCP/IP Commands" later in this appendix.)

If you're already familiar with LAN Manager 2.x, you'll see many similarities between the NT and the LAN Manager network commands. However, there are quite a few differences. Click Start ⇨ Help, click the Contents tab, double-click Windows NT Commands, and double-click What's New or Different from LAN Manager? for details on what has changed in NT.

Here are the NT network commands:

IPXROUTE	NET ACCOUNTS	NET COMPUTER	NET CONFIG
NET CONTINUE	NET FILE	NET GROUP	NET HELP
NET HELPMSG	NET LOCALGROUP	NET NAME	NET PAUSE
NET PRINT	NET SEND	NET SESSION	NET SHARE
NET START	NET STATISTICS	NET STOP	NET TIME
NET USE	NET USER		

NET START and NET STOP are used to start and stop NT services. The service names that you use will often consist of several words separated by spaces. For example, the file-serving portion of SFM is called "File Server for Macintosh." When you specify services in NET commands, you need to surround any names that contain spaces in quotation marks. Services also have short names that don't include spaces. You can opt to use these short names with the NET START and NET STOP commands.

Filter Commands

SORT, MORE, and FIND are filter commands that enable you to sort input and output, cause output to be displayed one screen at a time, and search for specified text within a file. They are different from typical NT commands in that they expect text input from the keyboard or from a file, process that input, and generate resulting output. In this sense, they act as filters for textual data.

The most common approach to using these filters involves piping the output of other utilities into the input of the filters. See the section later in this appendix called "Using Windows NT Command Symbols" for details on how to do this.

DOS-Oriented Commands

A number of DOS utilities have been brought into Windows NT completely untouched. In fact, they're still implemented as 16-bit DOS code. In addition, several commands have been modified or added to configure the DOS VDM environment correctly for execution of DOS applications on NT. See Table A-1 for a description of each command and refer to online Help for specific command syntax information. Here are the DOS-oriented commands:

APPEND	BACKUP	COUNTRY	DEBUG
DEVICE	DEVICEHIGH	DOS	DOSONLY
ECHOCONFIG	EDIT	EDLIN	EXE2BIN
EXPAND	FCBS	FILES	GRAPHICS
INSTALL	LH	LOADFIX	LOADHIGH
MEM	NTCMDPROMPT	QBASIC	RESTORE
SETVER	SHELL	STACKS	SWITCHES

Environment Commands

Several NT commands are designed to control the command interpreter environment, including handling nested command interpreters and manipulating search paths and environment variables. See Table A-1 for a description of each command and refer to online Help for specific command syntax information. Here are the environment commands:

CMD	EXIT	FORCEDOS	PATH	POPD
PROMPT	PUSHD	SET	SUBST	

Batch Commands

Several commands built into the Windows NT command interpreter are designed specifically for use within batch files. See Table A-1 for a description of each command and refer to online Help for specific command syntax information.

PUSHD AND POPD

Sounds like some sort of puppet show, doesn't it? Actually, this handy pair of commands lets you quickly perform a very common operation that used to take multiple steps. PUSHD saves the current directory and changes to a new current directory that you specify. Later, you can execute POPD to retrieve the directory that PUSHD saved, restoring it as the current directory. These commands are especially useful in batch files but can be used at the command line as well.

Although the names imply that a stack is being maintained, you can't nest these commands. Only one directory is stored by PUSHD, and it's overwritten by the next PUSHD. Moreover, POPD clears the saved directory.

SETLOCAL AND ENDLOCAL

No, these aren't labor unions, but they can be labor savers in your batch files. With them, you can change environment variables within a batch file and later restore your previous environment as if nothing changed.

When you execute SETLOCAL in a batch file, all subsequent changes to environment variables will remain in effect until an ENDLOCAL is executed. At that point, the changes made since SETLOCAL are discarded, and the environment is restored to its state before SETLOCAL was executed. If you exit the batch file without executing the corresponding ENDLOCAL, the environment changes remain in effect outside of the batch file. As a standard practice, some administrators place SETLOCAL and ENDLOCAL commands at the beginning and end of all of their batch files to prevent side-effect changes to the user's environment variables.

You can nest SETLOCAL and ENDLOCAL pairs, since these commands can internally save and restore multiple environments. So, you can create scopes in which certain environment changes are active within the batch file.

Files with either .BAT or .CMD extensions are recognized by Windows NT as batch files. The syntax rules within these files are identical. The .CMD extension was put in place back when NT was going to have an OS/2 2.x user interface. Although both extensions are accepted, I recommend using the .BAT extension for your batch files.

Here are the batch file commands:

CALL	ECHO	ENDLOCAL	FOR	GOTO
IF	PAUSE	REM	SETLOCAL	SHIFT

TCP/IP Commands

Several commands supplied with Windows NT are specific to the TCP/IP network transport protocol. When you install the TCP/IP protocol, as described in Chapter 11, these additional network commands are installed as well. See Table A-1 for a description of each command and refer to online Help for specific command syntax information. Here are the TCP/IP commands:

ARP	FINGER	FTP	HOSTNAME	IPCONFIG
LPQ	LPR	NBTSTAT	NETSTAT	NSLOOKUP
PING	RCP	REXEC	ROUTE	RSH
TFTP	TRACERT			

Obsolete DOS and OS/2 Commands

Several commands are ignored by Windows NT but are still accepted for compatibility with existing DOS and OS/2 batch and configuration files. No action is taken when NT encounters these commands:

BREAK	BUFFERS	DRIVEPARM	FASTOPEN	LASTDRIVE
NLSFUNC	PROTSHELL	SHARE	VERIFY	

Using Windows NT Command Symbols

Windows NT reserves several special symbols that you can use in a Command Prompt window and in batch files to manipulate input and output of commands and control their conditional execution. Table A-2 presents the symbols reserved by the Windows NT command interpreter. You're probably already familiar with some of these symbols, which are defined by the DOS command interpreter. Others in the table are unique to Windows NT.

Table A-2
Windows NT Reserved Command Symbols

Command Symbol	*Available under DOS?*	*Definition and Usage*
> or 1>	✓	Directs the output of a command to a specified destination file or device. If the destination file exists, it's replaced. Example: DIR > DIRECTRY.TXT sends the output of DIR to a file called DIRECTRY.TXT.
>> or 1>>	✓	Directs the output of a command to a specified destination file. If the destination file already exists, it appends the new data to the end of the file. Example: DIR >> DIRLOG.TXT appends the output of DIR to the file DIRLOG.TXT.
2>	✓	Directs the *error* output of a command to a specified destination file or device. If the destination file exists, it's replaced. Example: DIR 2> DIRECTRY.ERR sends the error output of DIR to a file called DIRECTRY.ERR.

(continued)

<table>
<tr><th colspan="3">Table A-2 (continued)</th></tr>
<tr><th>Command Symbol</th><th>Available under DOS?</th><th>Definition and Usage</th></tr>
<tr><td>2>></td><td>✓</td><td>Directs the error output of a command to a specified destination file. If the destination file already exists, it appends the new data to the end of the file.

Example: DIR 2>> DIRLOG.ERR
appends the error output of DIR to the file DIRLOG.ERR.</td></tr>
<tr><td><</td><td>✓</td><td>Directs input from a specified source file into a command. Information normally read by the command from the keyboard is read from the file instead.

Example: SORT < DIRECTRY.TXT
sorts the contents of DIRECTRY.TXT, which is taken as input to SORT.</td></tr>
<tr><td>|
or
0></td><td>✓</td><td>Pipes the output of one command to the input of another command. Information normally read by the second command from the keyboard is read from the output of the first command instead.

Example: TYPE DIRECTRY.TXT | MORE
which sends the output of TYPE to the input of MORE, displaying the contents of DIRECTRY.TXT one screen at a time.</td></tr>
<tr><td>||</td><td></td><td>Executes the command following the || symbol only if the command preceding the || symbol fails.

Example: DIR A: || ECHO FAILED
"FAILED" is displayed only if DIR A: fails.</td></tr>
<tr><td>&</td><td></td><td>Separates multiple commands on the command line. Commands are executed in sequence, from left to right.

Example: DIR A: & DIR B: & DIR C:
performs a sequence of three DIR operations.</td></tr>
<tr><td>&&</td><td></td><td>Executes the command following the && symbol only if the command preceding the && symbol succeeds.

Example: DIR A: && ECHO SUCCEEDED
"SUCCEEDED" is displayed only if DIR A: succeeds.</td></tr>
<tr><td>()</td><td></td><td>Groups commands together. Commands are still executed in sequence, from left to right.

Example: DIR A: & (DIR B: & DIR C:)
performs a sequence of three DIR operations.</td></tr>
</table>

Command Symbol	*Available under DOS?*	*Definition and Usage*
^		Escape character that enables you to use command symbols within command line text. The command interpreter doesn't interpret the character following the ^ symbol. Example: MYEXE ^<BILL^&TED^> passes "<BILL&TED>" as a command-line parameter to MYEXE.
;		Separates command line parameters. Example: MYEXE 12;BILL;TED passes 12, BILL, and TED as command-line parameters to MYEXE.
,		Separates command line parameters. Example: MYEXE 12,BILL,TED passes 12, BILL, and TED as command-line parameters to MYEXE.

Are you experiencing unexplained behavior in the Windows NT Command Prompt window that you don't see under DOS? If you have a DOS command line utility that uses the ampersand (&) character for one of its switches, you'll need to take an extra step to make it work properly. The PKZIP shareware utility is a classic example of this.

The problem is that the ampersand symbol is a reserved symbol, as shown in Table A-2. If your utility requires an ampersand on the command line, you must tell the command interpreter to take the ampersand as a literal use of the character. Do this by placing a carat (^) symbol before the ampersand. For example, in the PKZIP case, the DOS command line

```
PKZIP -& DOCS.ZIP *.DOC
```

would need to be entered on NT as

```
PKZIP -^& DOCS.ZIP *.DOC
```

When a command fails, the error messages generated are often displayed in the Command Prompt window, even if you've redirected the command's output to a file. Most commands write their normal output to one place and their error messages to another. The > symbol only takes care of redirecting normal output to a file, but you can capture the error messages to a file using the 2> symbol. For example:

```
MYEXE > OUTPUT.TXT 2> ERRORS.TXT
```

writes the MYEXE command's normal output to OUTPUT.TXT and any error messages to ERRORS.TXT. Most of the commands supplied with Windows NT conform to this standard, but some just write everything (error messages and all) to the same place where they write regular output.

Deleted Commands

Unlike obsolete commands that are still recognized for compatibility but don't actually do anything, a number of commands available under DOS aren't available at all in Windows NT. In many cases, the deleted commands just don't make any sense in the Windows NT environment. In others, execution of the command would violate NT security, or the functionality is superseded by another NT feature. Table A-3 presents a list of the DOS commands that aren't available in Windows NT.

GETTING A HANDLE ON REDIRECTION

If you've been exposed to C programming, you know that most applications write their normal output to a file handle called STDOUT. They usually write their error messages to STDERR. The values of these two file handles are 1 and 2, respectively. So the 2> symbol tells the command interpreter to redirect output meant for handle 2 (STDERR, the destination of error message output) to a specified file. Likewise, the 1> symbol can be used in place of the simpler > symbol to redirect output meant for handle 1 (STDOUT, the destination of normal output text) to a file. For example,

```
MYEXE > OUTPUT.TXT 2> ERRORS.TXT
```

is identical to

```
MYEXE 1> OUTPUT.TXT 2> ERRORS.TXT
```

Another file handle, STDIN, is typically used for keyboard input. Its file handle happens to be 0. Using the 0> symbol, you can get the same effect as piping output to another application. For example,

```
TYPE DIRECTRY.TXT | SORT
```

is equivalent to

```
TYPE DIRECTRY.TXT 0> SORT
```

Both use the output of the TYPE command to replace the input that SORT is expecting from the keyboard.

The 2> symbol is actually useful for gathering error output, but for clarity in your batch files, use the > and | symbols instead of 1> and 0>.

Table A-3
DOS Commands Not Available in Windows NT

Deleted Command	*Comment*
ASSIGN	Windows NT doesn't support this utility.
CHOICE	Windows NT doesn't support this utility.
CTTY	Windows NT doesn't support this utility.
DBLSPACE	DriveSpace compression isn't supported on NT. Use file compression on NTFS instead. See Chapter 19 for details.
DEFRAG	Windows NT does a more optimal job of using disk space than DOS does. Third-party defragmentation utilities are available.
DOSSHELL	Windows NT doesn't support this utility.
DRVSPACE	DriveSpace compression isn't supported on NT. Use file compression on NTFS instead. See Chapter 19 for details.
EMM386	Windows NT automatically provides this functionality to DOS applications.
FASTHELP	Use the HELP command instead.
FDISK	Use the Disk Administrator utility instead.
INCLUDE	Windows NT doesn't support multiple configurations of DOS.
INTERLNK	Windows NT doesn't support this utility.
INTERSRV	Windows NT doesn't support this utility.
JOIN	Larger partition sizes, better file systems, and volume sets make JOIN obsolete on NT.
MEMMAKER	Windows NT automatically optimizes memory usage in DOS VDMs.
MENUCOLOR	Windows NT doesn't support multiple configurations of DOS.
MENUDEFAULT	Windows NT doesn't support multiple configurations of DOS.
MENUITEM	Windows NT doesn't support multiple configurations of DOS.
MIRROR	Windows NT doesn't support this utility.
MSAV	Windows NT doesn't support this utility. Virus scanners for NT are available from third parties.
MSBACKUP	Windows NT doesn't support this utility. For backup to tape, use NT Backup. For backup to disk, use the BACKUP and RESTORE commands.

(continued)

Table A-3 (continued)

Deleted Command	***Comment***
MSCDEX	Windows NT automatically provides CD-ROM access to DOS and Win16 programs.
MSD	Use the Windows NT Diagnostics utility, described in Chapter 21.
NUMLOCK	Windows NT doesn't support this utility.
POWER	Windows NT doesn't support this utility.
SCANDISK	Windows NT doesn't support this utility.
SMARTDRV	Windows NT automatically and dynamically manages caching of disk data, including that for DOS applications.
SUBMENU	Windows NT doesn't support multiple configurations of DOS.
SYS	Windows NT won't fit on a single floppy disk. To create an NT boot floppy that boots from an existing NT installation, see Chapter 9.
UNDELETE	Windows NT doesn't support this utility. You can undo deletes from NT Explorer or retrieve deleted items from the Recycle Bin. Objects deleted from the Command Prompt are gone for good.
UNFORMAT	Windows NT doesn't support this utility.
VSAFE	Windows NT doesn't support this utility.

In Windows NT 3.x, the ACLCONV command was used to convert OS/2 HPFS386 permissions to NTFS permissions. Since the HPFS file system is no longer supported in Windows NT 4.0, the ACLCONV command isn't supported in 4.0 either.

Glossary of Windows NT Server Terms

Numeric

10Base2 Thin coaxial cable running at 10Mbps, with a distance limit of 185 meters per segment, as specified in the IEEE 802.3 standard.

10Base5 Thick coaxial cable running at 10Mbps, with a distance limit of 500 meters per segment, as specified in the IEEE 802.3 standard.

10BaseT Unshielded twisted-pair running at 10Mbps, typically used in a star topology. Specified in the IEEE 802.3 standard. See also UTP.

16-bit A memory model in application and operating system code that uses 16-bit addresses, segments, and offsets as provided in the Intel CPU architecture. DOS and Windows 3.x are 16-bit operating systems.

32-bit A memory model in application and operating system code that uses a flat 32-bit-wide address as provided in Intel and RISC CPU architectures. Windows NT is a full 32-bit operating system. Windows 95 is a combination of 16- and 32-bit code.

A

access method The approach used by a network technology to allow a node to gain access to the network medium for transmission of information.

account See user account.

account database See SAM database.

account policy A set of rules defining how passwords and other attributes of accounts behave. Managed via the User Manager for Domains utility.

ACE Access Control Entry. An element of an ACL that maps a user account to specific access permissions.

ACK Acknowledgment.

ACL Access Control List. A list of ACEs associated with a specific object that controls user account access permissions to the object.

active hub See hub.

active monitor A network node responsible for managing a Token Ring to ensure that tokens aren't lost or data doesn't circulate indefinitely.

active partition A system partition from which an operating system will boot when the computer is restarted. Managed by the Disk Administrator utility.

administrative alerts Informational messages sent to specific accounts, groups, or computers announcing security events, performance problems, loss of server power, printer errors, and other events.

Alerter service The Windows NT service that processes administrative alerts. The Messenger service is also required on both the sending and receiving computers for the Alerter to work.

Alpha AXP A RISC CPU architecture developed and offered by DEC which runs Windows NT 3.x and later versions.

AMP See asymmetric multiprocessing.

ANSI American National Standards Institute. An organization in the U.S. that coordinates voluntary standards groups. ANSI is a member of the ISO.

API Application Programming Interface. A set of callable software functions that applications use to make requests of the operating system. Windows NT supports applications that call the following API sets: Win32, Win16, POSIX (IEEE 1003.1), and OS/2 1.x.

applet A term sometimes used to refer to any of the small utility applications included in Control Panel.

AppleTalk A set of communication protocols developed by Apple Computer and used by Macintosh computers for network communication.

application layer The seventh or highest layer of the OSI reference model, responsible for providing high-level network services to applications.

ARC Advanced RISC Computing. A design standard that specifies the hardware and firmware interfaces on RISC computers on which Windows NT runs.

arcname An ARC path name, specifying a particular device on the computer. Arcnames are used to specify devices on both RISC and Intel architectures.

archive attribute A bit associated with a file that indicates whether the file has changed since it was last backed up. A normal (full) backup using the NT Backup utility clears a file's archive bit. Modification of the file sets it. Incremental backups copy only those files whose archive attribute is set.

ARCnet Attached Resource Computer Network. A token-passing network technology introduced by Datapoint Corporation in 1968, characterized by simplicity and low cost.

ASCII American Standard Code for Information Interchange. An 8-bit character coding scheme used for simple text files.

asymmetric multiprocessing (AMP) An approach to multiprocessor hardware design which dedicates specific CPUs within the computer to fixed application or operating system tasks. Windows NT doesn't support AMP. See also symmetric multiprocessing.

asynchronous I/O An approach to performing I/O operations in which the requesting process is allowed to continue executing while the I/O operation is being handled by the operating system. Used by applications to improve performance by doing useful work on the CPU during relatively slow I/O operations. See also synchronous I/O.

ATM Asynchronous Transfer Mode. A high-bandwidth network switching technology, ranging in speed from 1Mbps to 1Gbps.

attenuation The loss of communication signal strength due to internal cable resistance and external EMI interference.

audit policy A set of rules defining the set of events that are audited and how those events are reported. Managed via the User Manager for Domains utility.

auditing An approach to collecting and reporting information on security-related events, including failed attempts to log on, successful or failed attempts to access resources, and so on. Audited events are recorded in the security log, which can be reviewed using the Event Viewer utility.

AUI Attachment Unit Interface. A device sometimes used to connect a node to a thick Ethernet network transceiver. See also DIX.

authentication The procedure used by Windows NT to determine whether a user is authorized to access the computer or network. When the user supplies an account name and password, the access is authenticated by the local computer or by a domain controller.

autoplay A feature of Windows NT (and Windows 95) that automatically plays an audio CD or executes an application on a CD-ROM when a disc is inserted into the CD-ROM drive. CD-ROM discs must be equipped with the appropriate autoplay files for this feature to work.

autorun See autoplay.

AVIO Advanced Video I/O. A low-level graphical interface on the OS/2 operating system. OS/2 1.x AVIO applications are supported on NT only with the addition of the Windows NT Add-on Subsystem for Presentation Manager.

B

backbone network A network primarily designed as a high-speed conduit for data transmitted between other networks.

back end See server.

BackOffice A suite of Microsoft server products including Windows NT Server, SQL Server, Systems Management Server, SNA Server, Exchange Server, and Internet Information Server.

backup browser A computer that maintains a backup copy of available servers and resources used in browsing the network. Backup browsers request database updates from the master browser every 15 minutes.

backup domain controller (BDC) A computer running Windows NT Server that maintains a backup copy of the SAM database so that it can share the load of authenticating users when they attempt to log on to the domain. Changes to the SAM database on the primary domain controller are automatically replicated to all BDCs in the domain.

backup set A separate set of data created on tape by the NT Backup utility for each disk volume included in a backup.

basic rate interface (BRI) The ISDN interface consisting of two B channels and one D channel for communication of voice, data, and video.

batch program A text file with a .BAT or .CMD filename extension that instructs the Windows NT command interpreter to perform one or more tasks. Batch programs are typically used to automate common administrative tasks using command-line utilities.

Bcc See blind carbon copy.

BDC See backup domain controller.

beta An early version of software released for testing purposes before it is commercially available.

bindery The NetWare account database, functionally equivalent to the Windows NT SAM database. The Migration Tool for NetWare utility converts account information in a NetWare bindery to SAM database format.

binding An association between layered network components to create a path between network adapter hardware drivers and transport protocols, and between transport protocols and higher-level network components (such as the server and redirector). The Network application in Control Panel manages network bindings.

binding path The chain of bindings linking the highest-level network component to the lowest.

blind carbon copy (Bcc) An e-mail feature that allows mailing a copy of a message to one or more users without those users appearing on the list of recipients.

Blue Screen of Death The affectionate name for the screen that appears when the Windows NT operating system halts due to a critical error. NT displays information about the failure and may perform a memory dump and automatic restart of the computer.

BootP A protocol used by a network node to discover the IP addresses of its Ethernet adapters, used to accomplish booting the operating system across the network.

boot partition The hard disk drive partition that contains the Windows NT Server operating system files (that is, the SystemRoot directory). The boot partition may or may not be the same as the system partition.

BRI See basic rate interface.

bridge A device that passes network data between two segments of a network.

broadcast A message sent to all nodes on a network.

broadcast address A special network address reserved for specifying all nodes on a network.

broadcast storm A network condition in which many broadcasts are sent at one time, consuming a large percentage of network bandwidth and often causing network time-out conditions and slow response at network nodes.

browse master See master browser.

browsing The act of reviewing and choosing from lists of available files within a directory, directories on disk, resources offered by servers, and servers within domains.

bus mastering An adapter architecture that includes its own intelligence to perform all data transfers between the device and RAM without involving the CPU. Bus mastering adapters don't suffer from the potential performance penalties imposed by PIO and DMA adapters.

bus topology A network topology that connects each node along a single cable called a bus. The cable is terminated at both ends of the network.

C

C2-level certifiable security A computer security specification established by the National Computer Security Center (NCSC), a department of the U.S. National Security Agency (NSA). Windows NT meets this specification by providing discretionary access and auditing capabilities on objects.

Cairo Microsoft's code name for a future version of the Windows NT operating system which may include an object file system (OFS), network directory services, and other advanced enterprise features.

CAL Client Access License.

CAPI See Cryptography API.

carrier sensing An access method in which a node listens on the shared network medium to determine if another node is already transmitting before starting a new transmission. Ethernet uses this approach as part of its CSMA/CD access method.

cell A small, uniformly sized chunk of data transmitted on an ATM network.

CGI Common Gateway Interface.

Cheapernet See 10Base2.

checksum See CRC.

Chicago Microsoft's code name for the Windows 95 project before it was named Windows 95.

CISC Complex Instruction Set Computer. A computer technology based on a CPU designed with a relatively large number of complex and diverse built-in instructions. Relative to RISC, less code is required on a CISC processor to perform a complex task, but the individual instructions sometimes take longer to execute. Intel's 80486, Pentium, and Pentium Pro employ a combination of RISC and CISC technologies.

clear text Transmitted text data that's not encrypted in any way. Protocols which send clear text user names and passwords over a communication link are less secure than protocols which perform encryption.

client A computer that accesses resources shared on the network by another (server) computer. In the context of processes, a client process accesses resources and services offered by another (server) process which may or may not run on the same computer.

client/server model In Windows NT internals, the architecture of environment subsystems (server processes) providing operating system services to client applications. For example, the Win32 environment subsystem is the server to all Win32 client processes. In networking, the distribution of processing between a client application on one network node and a server application on another.

Clipboard An internal temporary storage area on the local computer used for transferring data of various types between applications. The ClipBook application manages the contents of the Clipboard and can be used to share data from the Clipboard over the network.

ClipBook An NT application that manages storage and sharing of Clipboard data over the network.

ClipBook service The Windows NT service that allows you to share ClipBook pages over the network. The Network DDE service is also required for this feature to work.

cluster A unit of disk allocation, typically consisting of one or more disk sectors. When referring to a collection of computers, a set of computers that are interconnected to provide fault-tolerant access to resources, even if some members of the cluster become unavailable.

CMD.EXE The 32-bit Windows NT command interpreter that provides a character-based interface, a batch language interpreter, and the ability to execute any supported Windows NT application type.

coaxial cable (coax) A transmission medium consisting of a single inner wire conductor surrounded by a hollow outer cylindrical conductor.

collision The condition that occurs on a network when two nodes attempt to communicate over a shared network medium at the same time. Such networks (including Ethernet) require collision detection logic to arbitrate the use of the shared network medium.

collision detection A design element of network technologies that rely on a shared network medium to detect the collision of two nodes attempting to communicate at the same time.

command interpreter The portion of the Windows NT CMD.EXE application that translates commands and batch programs into actions on the computer.

Command Prompt A window or full-screen session running CMD.EXE which accepts commands and allows you to execute applications.

compound document A document file that consists of more than one type of document (for example, a spreadsheet document embedded within a word processing document). OLE is used to link or embed documents, and to start the appropriate applications to edit them.

computer account An object in the SAM database that describes a specific computer within a Windows NT network domain. A computer account is created for each NT node added to the domain. Each computer account consumes 0.5KB of SAM database space.

Computer Browser service A Windows NT service that maintains a list of servers and resources on the network. See also master browser, backup browser.

computer name A unique name assigned to each computer on the network, consisting of up to 15 characters. Names are assigned during NT installation, must be unique within a domain or workgroup, and can be changed via the Network application in Control Panel.

concentrator See hub.

context switch The action that an operating system takes when it assigns a CPU to execute a different thread from the one currently executing. A context switch typically requires overhead of saving the current state (context) of the old thread before executing the new one.

control set The portion of the NT registry under the HKEY_LOCAL_MACHINE\SYSTEM key that contains information required to boot the operating system and restore the last known good configuration.

cooperative multitasking An approach to coordinating multiple running processes by having each process yield control to allow other processes to run. The processes themselves determine how much time is spent on each task. Windows 3.x uses cooperative multitasking. See also preemptive multitasking.

copy backup A type of backup similar to a normal backup, except that the archive attribute bit is not cleared on files included in the backup.

CRC Cyclic redundancy code or cyclic redundancy check. An error-checking technique in which the sender calculates a value based on the remaining data and appends the value to the data. The receiver recalculates the value based on the data received to determine if the data arrived intact.

Cryptography API (CAPI) A programming interface that provides data encryption and decryption functions for application developers, first introduced in Windows NT 4.0.

CSD Customer Service Disk. See service pack.

CSMA/CD Carrier Sense Multiple Access/Collision Detection. A collision detection method used by Ethernet network technology.

cyclic redundancy check See CRC.

cyclic redundancy code See CRC.

D

daily backup A backup type that includes only those files that are created or modified on the current calendar date.

Data Link Control (DLC) A low-level network protocol at the data link layer of the OSI model. DLC is required by HP JetDirect network-connected printers.

data link layer The second layer of the OSI model, which transmits data in frames and performs error detection on them.

DCOM See Distributed Component Object Model.

DDE Dynamic Data Exchange. An approach to sharing data between applications. DDE-enabled applications transmit data by cooperatively conversing with each other. OLE is quickly supplanting DDE.

dedicated server A computer whose sole purpose is to share resources or run server-based portions of client/server network applications.

dedicated server network A network designed around one or more server nodes which are dedicated to acting as servers to the client nodes on the network.

default gateway A computer attached to each network running TCP/IP that knows how to route data to other networks.

dependent service An NT service that requires the presence of another service or driver already running on the computer.

destination document The compound OLE document in which data objects are placed. For example, a compound Word document is an instance of a destination document. Data objects from source documents can be embedded or linked into destination documents.

device driver A kernel-mode software component that provides an interface between a hardware device and the NT I/O system.

DHCP See Dynamic Host Configuration Protocol.

DHCP scope A set of IP addresses from which a DHCP server can dynamically assign addresses to other nodes on the network. The pool of addresses can consist of a range which explicitly excludes addresses that are already statically assigned.

differential backup A backup type that includes all files whose archive attribute bit is set. Unlike incremental backup, differential backup doesn't clear the archive attribute bits after backing up the files.

differential SCSI A SCSI bus wiring scheme that uses two wires for each signal transmitted on the bus. One wire carries the signal; the other carries its inverse. Minimizes the effect of external interference, allowing longer SCSI cable lengths. See also single-ended SCSI.

DIMM Dual In-line Memory Module.

directory An object within a file system containing files or other directories. In Windows NT 4.0, the term *folder* is used synonymously with the term *directory.*

directory replication A method of distributing data within a network by storing files on centralized (export) servers and automatically updating copies of the files on other (import) computers. The Directory Replicator service synchronizes all of the replicated files to match the master files whenever they're modified.

Directory Replicator service A Windows NT service that's responsible for performing directory replication.

disabled user account A user account that has temporarily been disabled via User Manager for Domains, preventing a user from logging on and using that account.

discretionary access control The ability to assign access permissions at the discretion of the owner of an object. A required capability of a C2-certifiable operating system.

disk duplexing An approach to fault tolerance (RAID 1) that is identical to disk mirroring, except that the two drives participating in the mirror set are attached to separate disk controllers. See also disk mirroring.

disk mirroring An approach to fault tolerance (RAID 1) that provides data redundancy by writing two copies of all data to two different disk drives. Two identical partitions are established as a mirror set, where one partition is the primary member and one is the shadow member. All writes go to both primary and shadow, and all reads are done from the primary. If the primary fails, all reads are done from the shadow. See also disk duplexing.

disk striping An approach to fault tolerance that provides improved performance (RAID 0 and 5) and data redundancy (RAID 5 only). Data is distributed across partitions on multiple disk drives, which are treated collectively as a single logical volume. If RAID 5 (stripes with parity) is used, parity information is distributed across the disks as well, allowing automatic recovery of data if one drive fails.

Distributed Component Object Model (DCOM) Formerly known as Network OLE, a new feature of Windows NT 4.0 that allows software developers to create robust, distributed applications based on OLE. DCOM uses RPC, caching of objects, and other techniques to create a reliable approach to OLE over the network. Microsoft plans to support DCOM on Windows 95 and Macintosh in the future.

DIX Digital-Intel-Xerox. A connector sometimes used to connect a node to a thick Ethernet network transceiver. See also AUI.

DLC See Data Link Control.

DLL Dynamic Link Library.

DMA Direct memory access. An adapter architecture that allows the adapter to transfer data between the device and RAM without involving the CPU. ISA DMA adapters can only address 16MB of system RAM. If the data to be transferred happens to be above the 16MB line, performance is degraded since data must be copied to and from high memory. PCI, EISA, and VLB adapters don't suffer from this performance penalty.

DNS See Domain Name System.

domain A group of networked computers, centered around Windows NT Server, that share a common user account database. A domain provides a single user account and password for each user in the domain and offers centralized account and security administration. On the Internet, a domain is a portion of a name hierarchy tree. See also trust relationship, primary domain controller, backup domain controller.

domain database See SAM database.

domain extension In TCP/IP networks, the three-letter extension following an organization name, indicating the type of organization. For example, the domain extension of .COM in microsoft.com indicates that Microsoft is a commercial enterprise.

domain model A group of one or more Windows NT Server domains along with the trust relationships established between them. The standard domain models include single domain, single master domain, and multiple master domain.

domain name A unique name assigned to each Windows NT domain on the network. A domain name is established during NT Server installation. In the context of TCP/IP, the name of an organization followed by its domain type extension (for example, microsoft.com).

Domain Name System (DNS) A distributed database of mappings between host names (actually FQDNs) and IP addresses. DNS is a static database, requiring manual updating when changes are made to the network. Windows NT Server 4.0 provides a DNS Server. (DNS is sometimes called Domain Name Service or Domain Name Server in the Windows NT Server documentation.)

domain synchronization The act of keeping copies of the SAM database stored on multiple BDCs updated with changes applied to the central PDC.

dotted-decimal notation The notation used to express IP addresses. Each of the four bytes of a 32-bit IP address is represented by a decimal number. The numbers are separated by period (.) characters (for example, 129.37.15.6).

DoubleSpace A technology used to create and maintain compressed disk volumes on DOS. Windows NT doesn't support DoubleSpace compression.

DRAM Dynamic Random Access Memory.

DriveSpace A technology used to create and maintain compressed disk volumes on DOS. Windows NT doesn't support DriveSpace compression.

DSN Data Source Name.

dual-attached nodes Nodes attached to both FDDI rings, providing maximum network fault tolerance if a link fails on one of the rings. See also single-attached nodes.

dual-boot The ability to boot the computer using two or more different operating systems or two or more versions of the same operating system. The System application in Control Panel enables you to control which operating system boots by default.

duplexing See disk duplexing.

DWORD A 4-byte (32-bit) data structure.

dynamic data exchange See DDE.

Dynamic Host Configuration Protocol (DHCP) A feature of Windows NT Server that automatically assigns IP addresses to computers running TCP/IP whenever they start up. Addresses are selected dynamically from a pool (DHCP scope) of available IP addresses.

E

EDO RAM Extended Data Out RAM.

EIDE Enhanced Integrated Drive Electronics.

EISA Extended Industry Standard Architecture. A 32-bit computer bus architecture introduced by several PC vendors to compete with MCA and to maintain compatibility with ISA adapters.

embedded object A component (source) OLE document within a compound (destination) document. The data is actually stored within the compound document rather than in its own file on disk. See also linked object.

EMI Electromagnetic interference.

EMS See Expanded Memory Specification.

environment subsystem A user-mode process that emulates the behavior and programming interface of a specific operating system. Windows NT includes environment subsystems for Win32, OS/2, and POSIX.

environment variable A symbolic identifier used to define aspects of the environment. Can be defined at the system scope or specific to a user. Able to be set from the System applet in Control Panel or from the NT Command Prompt.

error-correcting code (ECC) A code, calculated based on the contents of a message, containing enough information to allow the receiver of the message to detect and correct most errors in transmission.

error-detecting code (EDC) A code, calculated based on the contents of a message, containing enough information to allow the receiver of the message to detect most errors in transmission.

Ethernet A network technology invented by Xerox Corporation and developed jointly by Xerox, DEC, and Intel. Ethernet uses a logical bus topology and a CSMA/CD access method and is partially defined in the IEEE 802.3 standard.

EtherTalk AppleTalk protocols running on Ethernet network technology.

EULA End User License Agreement.

event A network message or log entry indicating a significant occurrence, such as a physical network problem, completion of a requested task, or a security breach.

Event Log service A Windows NT service responsible for logging important system, application, and security events to the event log. The Event Viewer lets you review and manage the log.

Exchange Server A server application included in the BackOffice suite that provides e-mail, group scheduling, and message integration in a client/server environment.

Expanded Memory Specification (EMS) A standard that allows Intel CPUs (8088 and later) to access more than 640K of physical RAM. Developed jointly by Lotus, Intel, and Microsoft. Sometimes called LIM EMS. Widely used in older DOS applications but has been largely supplanted by XMS and Windows.

export server A computer running Windows NT Server from which data is copied during directory replication. Data is replicated to computers running either Windows NT Server or Windows NT Workstation. See also import computer.

Extended Memory Specification (XMS) An industry standard for allowing Intel 80286 and higher processors to access memory above 1MB. Windows 3.x and Windows NT both use extended memory but don't require XMS.

extended partition A disk partition that can be further subdivided into logical drives, which can be individually formatted and accessed. A physical hard disk can contain no more than one extended partition. See also partition, primary partition.

F

FAT See file allocation table.

fault tolerance The ability of the operating system to respond gracefully to severe error conditions, such as the failure of a hard disk or a power failure. Typically implies the ability to continue operation without loss of data or interruption of service.

file allocation table (FAT) The file system originally used on DOS that utilizes a table to store information about the sizes, locations, and properties of files stored on disk. Windows NT supports FAT on both floppy and hard disks.

FDDI Fiber Distributed Data Interface. A network technology specifying a 100Mbps, token-passing, dual-ring network that uses fiber-optic cables as the transmission medium.

fiber A lightweight thread that's manually scheduled by an application, intended to ease porting of applications that are designed to schedule their own threads. The term is also used as a shortened form of fiber-optic cable. See also multithreading.

fiber-optic cable A transmission medium consisting of a thin, flexible cable capable of transmitting data via modulated light. Characterized by higher cost, higher data rates, and very little susceptibility to EMI.

firewall A hardware or software component in the data path between the Internet and an internal network which filters packets by examining them on one side and deciding what to pass along to the other side.

folder The term used for a directory in the new Windows NT 4.0 user interface. The term *folder* is used synonymously and interchangeably with the term *directory.*

FQDN Fully qualified domain name.

frame A chunk of information transmitted at the data link layer of the OSI model that contains data as well as error-detection information.

Frame Relay A protocol used to communicate across the interface between user devices (such as servers and routers) and network equipment (such as switching nodes). Designed as a more efficient replacement for the X.25 protocol.

free space A region of a disk that's not yet partitioned or a region within an extended partition that hasn't yet been organized into a logical drive within that partition.

FTP File Transfer Protocol. A member of the TCP/IP protocol suite, designed to transfer files between network nodes.

full backup See normal backup.

G

gateway A computer that acts as a translator on the network, as a router between two network technologies, a translator between two different network protocols, or a translator between data formats of incompatible network applications.

Gateway Services for NetWare (GSNW) A gateway provided with Windows NT server that allows network clients to access resources on a NetWare server as if those resources were shared on an NT Server computer. GSNW translates between the Windows NT SMB and the NetWare NCP protocols.

GDI Graphics Device Interface. The component of Windows NT (specifically, the kernel-mode portion of the Win32 subsystem) that manages low-level graphical elements on a display or other output device. Moved from user mode to kernel mode in Windows NT 4.0 to improve performance.

global group A list of user accounts within a specific domain, providing a convenient means of setting up a list of users that can be utilized both in and out of the domain in which the group was created.

group A collection of user accounts managed through the User Manager for Domains utility to allow convenient assignment of rights and permissions.

GSNW See Gateway Services for NetWare.

H

HAL See hardware abstraction layer.

handle A data structure used to refer to an object.

hardware abstraction layer (HAL) A low-level component of the Windows NT operating system that provides an interface between the operating system kernel and aspects of the computer's hardware.

headless server A server computer that has no video monitor attached. Windows NT Server doesn't directly support headless servers, but a single video monitor can be shared among multiple servers using appropriate video switching hardware.

heterogeneous network A network consisting of dissimilar nodes running different network technologies, protocols, operating systems, or hardware platforms.

High Performance File System (HPFS) A file system developed by Microsoft and IBM for use under the OS/2 operating system to provide better security, disk capacity, and speed than that of the FAT file system. Starting with Windows NT 4.0, NT no longer supports reading from, writing to, or converting volumes formatted as HPFS.

hive A portion of the NT registry that's stored in a physical disk file. Hives are edited using the Registry Editor utility.

home directory A directory associated with each user account, used for storing personal files either on the user's local computer or on a central server.

homogeneous network A network consisting of nodes running identical network technologies, protocols, and often the same operating systems and hardware platforms.

hop The transmission of a data packet through one router, enroute to its final destination.

hop count A metric used to measure the distance (number of routers) between a source node and destination node.

host A node (including clients, servers, and network-connected printers) connected to a network running the TCP/IP protocol. If the node contains more than one network adapter, each adapter is considered a separate host.

host name The name of the computer assigned when you installed the NT operating system. The host name is used by the TCP/IP protocol.

HPFS See High Performance File System.

HTML Hyper Text Markup Language.

HTTP Hyper Text Transfer Protocol.

hub A device that serves as the center of a physical star topology. Hubs can implement different logical topologies, including bus and ring. Passive hubs simply split received signals among other connected nodes. Active hubs amplify or repeat incoming signals before distributing them.

I

ICMP Internet Control Message Protocol.

IDC Internet Database Connector.

IDE Integrated Drive Electronics.

idle thread A special thread that's assigned to a CPU when no other operating system or application threads are available to run on it.

IEEE Institute of Electrical and Electronic Engineers. A professional organization that establishes standards, including networking standards.

IIS Microsoft Internet Information Server.

import computer A computer running either Windows NT Server or Windows NT Workstation that acts as the destination for data replicated from directories on export servers. See also directory replication.

in-place editing The ability to change dynamically the application menus and toolbars between the destination OLE application and the source OLE application, if both applications are OLE 2.x compliant.

in-place file system conversion The process of converting from one file system to another without disturbing the files on the existing file system. The CONVERT utility allows you to convert a FAT volume to an NTFS volume while leaving the existing data intact.

incremental backup A backup type that includes all files whose archive attributes are set. Unlike differential backup, incremental backup clears the archive attribute bit on each file that it includes in the backup.

input queue A storage area that receives messages representing input events such as mouse movements, mouse button clicks, or key presses. Events are then routed to the appropriate application to be read and processed.

internal fragmentation A condition of wasted disk space in which small files or file fragments consume an entire disk cluster, even though the space required to store the data is much smaller than the cluster size.

Internet The world's largest internetwork, connecting over 20,000 networks in 132 countries, with nearly 35 million users worldwide.

internet See internetwork.

Internet Protocol (IP) See TCP/IP.

internetwork A collection of interconnected networks, linked by routers, and designed to operate as a single, larger network. Sometimes called *internet,* of which the Internet is one example.

Internetwork Packet Exchange/Sequenced Packet Exchange (IPX/SPX) The native transport protocols used to communicate with computers running Novell NetWare.

InterNIC Internet Network Information Center. The organization responsible for assigning Internet network addresses and domain names.

interoperability The ability of network nodes to communicate with each other over the network using compatible network technologies and communication protocols.

interrupt request line (IRQ) A hardware line within the computer over which devices can send signals to get the attention of the processor when the device has completed an operation and is ready to transmit or receive data. In most cases, each device attached to the computer uses its own IRQ.

intranet A network within an enterprise that makes use of Internet tools for internal communications to employees connected to the corporate LAN. The LAN may or may not be connected to the Internet.

I/O address A channel through which data is transferred between the CPU and a device. The address is either mapped into the 64K I/O address space (on an Intel processor) or into a RAM address.

I/O request packet (IRP) An internal data structure used to communicate information about an I/O request between layered drivers in the operating system.

IP Internet Protocol. See TCP/IP.

IP address A unique 32-bit address assigned to each network adapter in each computer attached to the network. An IP address specifies both the network and the host address. See also dotted-decimal notation.

IPX Internetwork Packet Exchange.

IPX/SPX See Internetwork Packet Exchange/Sequenced Packet Exchange.

IRP See I/O request packet.

IRQ See interrupt request line.

ISA Industry Standard Architecture.

ISAPI Internet Server Application Programming Interface.

ISDN Integrated Services Digital Network. A set of communication protocols that permit telephone networks to carry voice, data, and video.

ISO International Standards Organization.

ISO/OSI Reference Model See OSI Reference Model.

ISP Internet Service Provider.

ITG Information Technology Group. The name of the internal MIS organization at Microsoft Corporation.

K

kernel The core component of the Windows NT operating system that schedules threads to run on each available CPU, manages thread priorities, handles hardware device interrupts, and deals with exception conditions.

kernel mode The most privileged processor mode, has unrestricted access to memory, hardware devices, and privileged instructions. Used by trusted components of the operating system, including device drivers and file systems. On Intel CPUs, kernel mode is Ring 0. See also user mode.

key A node within the tree of the NT registry. Keys can have subkeys, and subkeys can have their own subkeys. The root of a registry subtree is called a key, and the nodes below it are typically called subkeys.

keyboard buffer An area of memory used to store keystrokes as they're entered from the keyboard. Keystrokes are translated to input messages, which are then distributed to the input queue of the appropriate application.

L

LAN See local area network.

LAN Manager A network operating system product line developed by Microsoft and 3Com for OS/2 and UNIX. LAN Manager is interoperable with Windows NT Server, Windows for Workgroups, Windows 95, PC-NET, and MS-NET. On an NT Server network, LAN Manager can act as a BDC but can't act as a PDC.

LAN Server A version of LAN Manager offered by IBM specifically designed for use on the OS/2 operating system.

last known good configuration The last bootable configuration that you successfully used on the computer. NT saves this configuration and offers it as an option during the boot process.

least recently used (LRU) A method of determining which pages should be removed from physical memory when additional space is required to read pages from disk. The least recently accessed pages are the first candidates for removal, since they're less likely to be needed immediately.

linked object A component (source) OLE document within a compound (destination) document. An icon is stored in the destination document, and the source document exists as a separate file on disk. See also embedded object.

LLC See logical link control.

local area network (LAN) A collection of computers connected using high-speed cable or wireless transmission for sharing data and resources. A LAN typically covers a limited area such as an office or building. See also wide area network.

local group A group that describes access permissions to resources that are local to a domain. You can't see or use a local group outside of its home domain, but you can include user accounts and global groups from other domains within a local group, as long as the other domain is trusted by the local domain.

local printer A printer connected directly to the local computer.

local procedure call (LPC) An interprocess communication mechanism used to transmit data efficiently between processes on the same computer. LPC is used to communicate between applications and environment subsystems.

Local Security Authority (LSA) A user-mode security subsystem component of Windows NT that manages the security policy on the local computer and provides user authentication services to other operating system components.

LocalTalk The primary network technology used by Apple Macintosh computers, on which AppleTalk protocols run. See also EtherTalk and TokenTalk.

local user profile A user profile that's local to the computer on which it's created. It doesn't follow the user if he or she logs on to another computer. See also roaming user profile, mandatory user profile.

logical drive A separately formattable and accessible area of a hard disk that lies within an extended partition. A logical drive is assigned a drive letter and can be accessed as if it were a separate physical hard disk.

logical link control (LLC) One of two sublayers within the data link layer of the OSI model, it manages node-to-node communication flow.

logical printer See print queue.

logical topology See topology.

logon hours The time periods during which a user account is allowed to log on and access the network.

logon process A user-mode process that's part of the security subsystem. It accepts logon requests at the local computer, displays the logon dialogs, and communicates with other security components to authenticate the user by communicating with the LSA.

logon script A batch file that's automatically run when you log on to the Windows NT Server network from an NT, DOS, Windows for Workgroups, or OS/2 computer.

logon workstations The set of computers from which a particular user account is permitted to log on to the network.

LRU See least recently used.

long-haul network See wide area network.

LUN Logical unit number. The logical address of a SCSI device if multiple devices are attached to a single SCSI device ID. The LUN is typically zero, unless the SCSI adapter supports multiple LUNs on a single SCSI device ID.

M

MAC sublayer Media Access Control sublayer. The lower portion of the OSI reference model data link layer, responsible for implementing the network technology access method.

Mach An operating system design that influenced the Windows NT kernel architecture design. It provides robustness and flexibility by isolating the kernel from protected subsystems that provide interfaces to applications.

machine account See computer account.

Mailslot File System (MSFS) The Windows NT file system that manages mailslot access and connections.

mailslots An interprocess communication mechanism that provides one-to-many and many-to-one communication, ideal for broadcasting a message to multiple processes. Implemented on NT via the Mailslot File System.

MAN Metropolitan area network. Used to refer to a network that is neither contained enough to be a LAN nor spread out enough to be a WAN. The term *WAN* is now typically used to describe these networks.

mandatory user profile A user profile that's created and managed by the network administrator. It's stored on a server and is downloaded to the local computer whenever the user attempts to log on to the network. See also roaming user profile, local user profile.

master account domain In a multiple domain model, a domain used specifically for maintenance and authentication of user accounts on the network. The master account domain is trusted by one or more resource domains that share network resources.

master browser A computer that maintains a master list of available servers and resources used in browsing the network. It designates one or more other computers as backup browsers, which are updated with changes to the browse list every 15 minutes.

MAU See multistation access unit.

maximum password age The oldest that an account password can get before NT forces the user to change it. More frequent password changes provide increased security. An account policy set in User Manager for Domains.

MCA Microchannel Architecture. A 32-bit computer bus architecture introduced by IBM in its PS/2 models.

media access control (MAC) See MAC sublayer.

medium See network medium.

message queue See input queue.

Messenger service A Windows NT service that's required in order to send and receive alert messages between computers. See also Alerter service.

MIB variables Management Information Base variables. A database of information on objects that can be accessed and managed via network management protocols such as SNMP.

minimum password age The shortest time allowed between changes to a user account password. An account policy set in User Manager for Domains.

minimum password length The minimum number of characters that a user account can have in its password. Longer passwords are more secure. An account policy set in User Manager for Domains.

MIPS RX000 A RISC CPU architecture developed and offered by MIPS and Silicon Graphics which runs Windows NT 3.x and later versions.

mirror set See disk mirroring.

mirroring See disk mirroring.

MLID See Multiple Link Interface Driver.

MMTA Multitasking Message Transfer Agent.

MPR MultiProtocol Routing. Also see Multiple Provider Router.

MSAU See multistation access unit.

MSFS See Mailslot File System.

MTA Message Transfer Agent.

MTBF Mean Time Between Failure. A measurement of reliability typically associated with hardware components and expressed as the number of hours expected between failures.

MTF Microsoft Tape Format. The layout of data on backup tapes generated by the NT Backup utility supplied with Windows NT. Some third-party tape backup packages also use this tape format.

multihomed computer A networked computer containing more than one active network adapter.

multiple access A characteristic of a network technology in which a single cable is shared by all nodes on the network. An Ethernet bus is an example of a multiple access network technology.

Multiple Link Interface Driver (MLID) A network driver standard used in NetWare. NDIS on NT provides similar functionality.

Multiple Provider Router (MPR) A user-mode Windows NT network component that polls each of the network provider DLLs to determine which network provider should deal with a request.

Multiple UNC Provider (MUP) A kernel-mode Windows NT network component that simultaneously shows a UNC name to all network providers on the local system until one of them claims that it can process the name.

multiprocessor computer See symmetric multiprocessing.

multiprocessing See symmetric multiprocessing.

multistation access unit (MAU or MSAU) A device used to connect nodes to a logical ring topology network using a physical star topology.

multitasking An approach to coordinating the execution of multiple processes by dividing the CPU time among them. See also cooperative multitasking, preemptive multitasking.

multithreading An approach to software design that breaks application or system processes into smaller executable functions called threads. Each thread performs a specific portion of the work, and threads are executed simultaneously by the operating system. Applications are by default single-threaded and must be designed explicitly to take advantage of multithreading. The Windows NT operating system itself is multithreaded. Windows NT and Windows 95 both support multithreaded applications. Windows 3.x does not support multithreading.

MUP See Multiple UNC Provider.

N

named pipes An interprocess communication mechanism that allows applications to pass data easily back and forth between two processes, whether or not they're on the same computer. Implemented on NT via the Named Pipe File System.

Named Pipe File System (NPFS) The Windows NT file system that manages named pipe access and connections.

name resolution The activity of translating between computer names and IP addresses, typically performed by WINS on Windows NT.

NBF See NetBEUI Frame.

NBT NetBIOS over TCP/IP.

NCP See NetWare Core Protocol.

NCSC National Computer Security Center.

NDIS See Network Driver Interface Specification.

NDIS wrapper A library of standard functions available to NDIS device drivers to make them more independent of operating system details.

Net Logon service The Windows NT service that authenticates user account logons to the domain and manages synchronization of the SAM database between the PDC and its BDCs.

NetBEUI NetBIOS Extended User Interface. The transport protocol used by all of Microsoft's network systems, including Windows 95, MS-NET, LAN Manager, Windows for Workgroups, Windows NT Workstation and Server, and Microsoft OS/2 1.x, as well as IBM's LAN Server-based networks. See also NetBEUI Frame.

NetBEUI Frame (NBF). The name of the implementation of the NetBEUI transport protocol on Windows NT.

NetBIOS Network Basic I/O System. An API that provides an interface to basic network system services, allowing networked computers to send, receive, and process I/O requests from each other over the network. NetBIOS has become an industry standard API for network operating systems.

NetWare A network operating system developed and offered by Novell. The current market share leader in dedicated file and print server markets.

NetWare Core Protocol (NCP) A high-level network protocol that's equivalent in function to Microsoft's SMB. It communicates between the requester and server components over the network.

NetWare Link (NWLink) Microsoft's version of Novell's IPX/SPX protocol, allowing communication with Novell NetWare networks.

network Two or more computers connected together allowing them to communicate. The hardware and software required to permit this communication.

network adapter The physical device that plugs into the computer and acts as an interface between the computer and the network.

network analyzer (sniffer) A device composed of hardware and software designed to troubleshoot network problems by examining data transmitted on the network and by performing network diagnostics. The Network Monitor utility included with Windows NT Server performs this function.

Network Driver Interface Specification (NDIS). A standard low-level device driver interface that decouples the transport protocols in the upper layers from network adapter-specific functions. Windows NT network adapter drivers and transport protocol drivers are written to the NDIS 3.0 interface. See also Open Datalink Interface.

network interface card (NIC) See network adapter.

network layer The third layer of the OSI model. It handles routing between network nodes and breaking large messages into manageable packet sizes.

network medium The physical network path through which data is transmitted, ranging from cable to radio waves.

Network OLE See Distributed Component Object Model.

network operating system (NOS) Software that controls network functions, manages resource sharing, and provides security and administrative tools. Can run on top of an existing general-purpose operating system or can be an operating system that integrally provides network functionality.

network technology A specific set of standards for addressing, accessing, arbitrating, and transmitting between nodes on the network. The two most common network technologies in use today are Ethernet and Token Ring.

network topology The physical wiring scheme of the network (the physical topology) and the logical path taken by the data within the network (the logical topology).

NIC Network interface card. See network adapter.

NMI Non-Maskable Interrupt. A hardware signal generated to indicate that a hardware failure (such as a parity error) has occurred. The NMI signal causes Windows NT Server to halt to avoid potential corruption of data.

node Any device directly connected to the network, including client computers, server computers, network-connected printers, and other network-ready devices.

node address A unique number programmed into the network adapter by its manufacturer, providing a unique way of identifying each node on the network.

nondedicated server A server computer that's not completely dedicated to sharing resources or running the server portion of client/server applications. You can use the computer to run local applications or act as a network client, while the server functions take place in the background. See also dedicated server.

normal backup A backup type that copies all of the files that you specify to tape, then clears the archive attribute bit to signal that the files have been archived.

NOS See network operating system.

NPFS See Named Pipe File System.

NT New Technology. Used as a shorthand reference to Windows NT, which includes both Windows NT Server and Windows NT Workstation products.

NT executive A set of kernel-mode operating system components. User mode processes interact with the NT executive by calling system service APIs.

NT File System (NTFS) The file system of choice for Windows NT Server, offering improved recoverability, security, disk space efficiency, file compression, long filenames, and support for POSIX and Macintosh environments.

NT native services A set of APIs, comprising the system services layer, that provides an interface between user-mode processes (such as environment subsystems) and kernel-mode components.

NTAS Windows NT Advanced Server version 3.1. Subsequent versions of the product are called Windows NT Server.

NTFS See NT File System.

NTLDR The name of the Windows NT operating system loader on the Intel platform.

NWLink See NetWare Link.

O

object linking and embedding (OLE) A data-sharing method that creates functional links between documents such as spreadsheets, charts, and word processing documents. OLE makes it easy to mix different types of data within a single document, even if those pieces are created and edited by a wide variety of applications.

octet Archaic term for byte.

ODBC See Open Database Connectivity.

ODI See Open Datalink Interface.

OLE See object linking and embedding.

OLE client An application that accepts an object (source document) as part of a compound (destination) document.

OLE server An application that creates and edits an object (source document) that can be embedded or linked in other (destination) documents.

Open Database Connectivity (ODBC) A software interface that allows applications to access data in database management systems using SQL as a standard method of access.

Open Datalink Interface (ODI) NetWare's device driver interface standard that achieves protocol independence from network adapter device drivers. Performs a similar function to NDIS on Windows NT.

orphan A single failed drive that's a member of an NT fault-tolerance set, either a mirror set or a stripe set with parity.

OS Operating system.

OS/2 An operating system (dubbed "Operating System/2," to accompany the IBM PS/2 computer) originally developed jointly by Microsoft and IBM, and now exclusively by IBM. Versions 1.x are 16-bit operating systems, whereas version 2.x and Warp products are 32-bit operating systems. All are multitasking and multithreaded.

OS/2 subsystem The environment subsystem in Windows NT that provides services to 16-bit OS/2 1.x applications via the OS/2 1.x APIs.

OSI Open Systems Interconnect. An international standardization program designed to create network standards to promote interoperability between network vendors' products. Developed the OSI seven-layer reference model.

OSI Reference Model A seven-layer model for network communication developed by the OSI program. It's used for design of networks and for study of existing network designs.

P

packet A chunk of information that contains the original data to be transmitted, along with some additional addressing information. If a packet is too large to be transmitted by the data link layer, the network layer breaks it into multiple pieces, sends them through the data link layer, and reassembles the packet at the receiving end.

page A 4KB block of storage used to implement virtual memory. At any given time, a page might be somewhere in RAM, or it might be in a file on disk. The virtual memory manager keeps track of the location of each page of memory.

page fault An exception triggered by a process attempting to access a page that currently doesn't reside in RAM. As a result, the page is read into RAM from disk.

paging file A file named PAGEFILE.SYS that's used to store pages on disk that don't fit in memory. One paging file is automatically created during NT installation in the root directory of the partition where you installed the operating system.

partition A portion of a hard disk drive that functions as if it were a physically separate drive, with its own drive letter. A hard disk can be divided into up to a total of four partitions. Extended partitions can be used to create additional logical drives. See also primary partition.

passive hub See hub.

PC Card Formerly called PCMCIA, a type of adapter card typically used in laptop computers. Windows NT supports PC Card adapters but doesn't support dynamic addition or deletion of PC Card adapters without restarting the operating system.

PCI Peripheral Computer Interface. A 64-bit-wide, high-speed bus architecture.

PCMCIA See PC Card.

PDC See primary domain controller.

peer NOS A network operating system that allows all nodes on the network to act as both clients and servers. See also peer-to-peer network.

peer-to-peer network A type of network in which no computer has more control over the network than another, since each can act as both a client and a server. As compared with dedicated server networks, peer-to-peer is characterized by lower cost, more difficult administration (especially of large networks), and less security.

permission A rule that governs which users have access to an object and how they can access it. Permissions can be assigned to folders, files, network share points, printers, shared ClipBook pages, and other objects.

PGP Pretty Good Privacy

physical layer The first, lowest layer of the OSI model, defining the specifications for physical data transmission on the network medium, including electrical, mechanical, distances, and so forth.

physical-layer-service-data-unit See frame.

physical topology See topology.

PIF See program information file.

Pinball In Windows NT 3.x, the internal Microsoft code name for the HPFS driver on Windows NT 3.x. PINBALL.SYS was the name of the file system driver, which is no longer present in Windows NT 4.0. In Windows NT 4.0, the name of a 3D game included with the operating system.

PIO Programmed I/O. An adapter architecture that requires the CPU itself to transfer data between the device and system RAM. PIO adapters are less expensive than DMA or bus master adapters and may offer similar throughput. However, some PIO adapters can consume 40 percent or more of CPU bandwidth, causing significant overall performance degradation, especially on large data transfers.

PM See Presentation Manager.

Point-to-Point Protocol (PPP) An industry standard set of protocols that negotiate various aspects of a remote node network connection. Windows NT RAS clients can dial in to existing non-NT servers running PPP, and non-NT clients running PPP can dial in to a Windows NT RAS Server. You can run any combination of TCP/IP, IPX/SPX, and NetBEUI on PPP clients. See also SLIP.

Point-to-Point Tunneling Protocol (PPTP) A new feature of Windows NT Server 4.0 that enables you to create virtual private networks (VPNs) over the Internet. You can create a completely secure connection between remote client computers and your corporate network, running any combination of protocols.

POP Post Office Protocol.

POSIX Portable Operating System Interface based on UNIX. A standard (IEEE Standard 1003.1-1990) that provides a set of APIs and rules which UNIX operating system vendors follow to provide better application portability between UNIX implementations. Windows NT supports character-based POSIX application source code that's compliant with 1003.1.

POSIX subsystem The environment subsystem in Windows NT that provides services to 32-bit POSIX-compliant character-based applications via the POSIX APIs.

Postoffice Microsoft Mail's central database repository for e-mail.

PowerPC (PPC) A RISC CPU architecture developed by Motorola, IBM, and Apple which runs Windows NT 3.51 and later versions. Windows NT will run only on

PowerPC computers that are designed according to the PREP reference standard. Current Macintosh PowerPC computers are not designed to this standard and, therefore, can't run Windows NT. Future Macintosh versions may be designed for Windows NT compatibility.

PPC See PowerPC.

PPP See Point-to-Point Protocol.

PPTP See Point-to-Point Tunneling Protocol.

preemptive multitasking An approach to coordinating multiple running processes by providing each process with a slice of CPU time. Higher-priority processes preempt lower-priority processes. The operating system determines how much time is spent on each task. See also cooperative multitasking.

presentation layer The sixth layer of the OSI reference model, responsible for encryption, compression, and translation of data between applications in differing environments.

Presentation Manager (PM) The graphical user interface associated with the OS/2 operating system. OS/2 1.x PM applications are supported on NT via the Windows NT Add-on Subsystem for Presentation Manager.

PRI Primary Rate Interface. The ISDN interface to primary rate access, which consists of one 64Kbps D channel and 30 B channels for voice and data transmission.

primary domain controller (PDC) A computer running Windows NT Server that maintains the centralized SAM database for the domain, used to authenticate users when they attempt to log on to the domain. Changes in the SAM database are automatically replicated to backup domain controllers. Domains have only one PDC. See also backup domain controller.

primary member One of two members of a mirror set. The primary member is the disk being mirrored, whereas the shadow member refers to the mirror copy. See also disk mirroring.

primary partition A disk partition that can be used by the operating system as a bootable volume. Each physical disk drive can have up to four primary partitions, although DOS can recognize only one. If the disk includes an extended partition, only three primary partitions are allowed.

print queue A prioritized list of print jobs maintained by the Windows NT print spooler. Sometimes called a logical printer.

print spooler See spooler.

printer pool A single logical printer (print queue) that operates a collection of physical printers. The physical printers are identical to each other in every respect. Print jobs are dispatched to the first available printer in the pool, maximizing throughput.

privilege See right.

process An executable program with its own address space and one or more threads of execution. An application typically consists of one process but can include multiple processes.

processor A physical CPU. Windows NT supports one or more physical CPUs within a computer. See also symmetric multiprocessing.

program information file (PIF) A file that provides environmental information on how best to run a specific DOS application. PIF settings override settings in configuration files. In Windows NT 4.0, defining a PIF is no longer necessary. You can provide this environmental information using the Properties dialog box associated with a DOS application.

protected subsystem See environment subsystem.

protocol A formal set of communication conventions used by two network nodes to communicate properly with each other.

provider An add-on client network component, which establishes Windows NT as a client of a remote server. The NT redirector is a provider, as is Novell's client requester for NT.

provider interface A DLL that implements a standard set of the WNet APIs for a specific provider (for example, the NT redirector or the NetWare requester for NT).

Q

quick format A fast way to format or reformat a floppy disk or hard disk volume. Unlike regular format, quick format doesn't erase the entire contents of the disk or scan the disk for bad sectors. It rewrites the FAT or NTFS data structures to their initial state, with no files present. All files are effectively erased.

R

RAID See redundant array of inexpensive disks.

RAS See Remote Access Service.

redirector The component of a network operating system that intercepts and handles requests for shared resources on the network from the local computer and directs those requests to the correct server. For example, a request to read a file from a server on the network is handled by the redirector. A similar component in the NetWare environment is called a requester.

redundant array of inexpensive disks (RAID) A technology that employs multiple disks to increase overall disk throughput, data reliability, or a combination of both. RAID is defined in terms of levels, in which each level represents a different combination of redundancy and recoverability.

registration database See registry.

registry A hierarchical database containing virtually all operating system and application configuration information. Usually, applications in Control Panel and other utilities are used to alter the contents of the registry. In some cases, you need to edit the registry directly using the Registry Editor (REGEDT32) utility.

registry database See registry.

remote access A generic term referring to either remote control or remote node technologies. In the case of Windows NT Server, remote access refers to the remote node capability offered by RAS.

Remote Access Service (RAS) A multiprotocol router in which the server is dedicated to handling communications between multiple remote nodes and the local network. RAS provides remote node capability — each remote computer has full access as if it were directly attached to the network.

remote control An approach to remote access in which the remote computer takes over control of a single computer's keyboard and screen. Each remote control computer requires a counterpart host computer on the network.

remote node An approach to remote access in which the remote computer acts as a node on the network, connecting via a centralized remote access server.

remote procedure call (RPC) An industry standard mechanism for making calls from client processes on one computer to server processes on another computer. Client and server processes can also be on the same computer.

Remote Procedure Call service A Windows NT service that must be running on both NT computers before an RPC conversation between client and server processes can be established.

repeater A device that amplifies incoming transmission signals before regenerating them on its output. See also hub.

replication See directory replication.

Request for Comments (RFC) A set of documents, maintained by InterNIC, specifying various aspects of the Internet.

requester The Novell equivalent of the Windows NT redirector, responsible for the client side of network connections.

resource A physical part of a computer that a process, application, or user might access, including disks, memory, printers, and so on. Network resources are computer resources such as disks and printers that are shared across the network for use by other computers.

resource domain In a multiple domain model, a domain responsible only for sharing network resources. Resource domains don't perform user authentication. They trust other (master account) domains that are responsible for user accounts and authentication.

retensioning An operation periodically performed on some types of backup tape media to ensure proper tape tension within the cartridge. Retensioning fast-forwards and rewinds the entire tape.

RFC See Request for Comments.

right Authorization for a user to perform specific actions on the Windows NT computer. Sometimes called a privilege. NT prevents you from performing certain actions if the account that you use to log on doesn't have rights to perform those actions.

Ring A privilege mode or level on Intel x86 processors, ranging from 0 to 3. Ring 0 (NT's kernel mode) is the most privileged mode. Ring 3 (NT's user mode) is the least privileged mode.

ring topology A network topology that forms a single data path from one node to the next, with the first and last nodes in the path connected to each other. In other words, the network is an unbroken circle or ring of nodes.

RISC Reduced Instruction Set Computer. A computer technology based on a CPU designed with a relatively small number of built-in instructions. The intended advantage of RISC CPUs is increased speed, since very simple instructions execute faster than more complex instructions. Although more instructions are required to perform complex tasks, the execution of those additional instructions are highly optimized. By keeping the instructions simple and uniform, RISC processors can execute portions of multiple instructions simultaneously using instruction pipelines. The DEC Alpha AXP, MIPS R4000, Motorola/IBM PowerPC, Hewlett-Packard HP-PA, Intel i860, and Sun SPARC processors are all examples of RISC CPUs. Although they're not considered RISC processors, Intel's 80486, Pentium, and Pentium Pro employ a combination of RISC and CISC technologies.

roaming user profile A user profile that follows the user from one computer to the next. It's stored on a server and is downloaded to the local computer when a user attempts to log on to the network. See also local user profile, mandatory user profile.

router A device that forwards data packets from one network to another, often between two different network technologies. Routing is performed based on a static table or based on dynamic performance information. See also gateway.

roving profile See roaming user profile.

RPC See remote procedure call.

S

SAM See Security Accounts Manager.

SAM database The database that contains all of the user accounts, groups, policies, and other information related to the domain. The database is accessed internally through the Security Accounts Manager component and is maintained via the User Manager for Domains utility.

Schedule service A Windows NT service required to allow a computer to perform an automated task at a scheduled time using the AT command.

SCSI See Small Computer Systems Interface.

secure attention sequence A keyboard input sequence that prevents malicious programs from impersonating the NT logon process to steal passwords. Because CTRL+ALT+DEL is reserved for system use in DOS and Windows, it's used as NT's secure attention sequence. The operating system always intercepts this sequence.

security access token An internal data structure generated by the LSA whenever a user logs on, used to validate access to computer and network resources.

Security Accounts Manager (SAM) A user-mode security subsystem component of Windows NT that manages and provides access to the account database (the SAM database).

security database See SAM database.

security ID A password-like value internally assigned by Windows NT to a computer whenever NT is installed, or to a domain, user account, or group. When you delete and reinstall or recreate an object that has a SID attached, a new SID is generated even if you use the same name when creating the new object.

security identifier See security ID.

security log A log file that houses security auditing events based on the auditing settings that you specify in User Manager for Domains. Only administrators have access to the security log, using the Event Viewer utility.

security reference monitor (SRM) A Windows NT kernel-mode component that validates each request to access an object before allowing access. SRM also audits object accesses.

security subsystem A user-mode component of Windows NT that includes the local security authority (LSA), security account manager (SAM), and the logon process.

Sequenced Packet Exchange (SPX) See Internetwork Packet Exchange/Sequenced Packet Exchange.

server A computer that shares resources on the network with other (client) computers. In the context of processes, a server process offers resources and services to other (client) processes, which may or may not run on the same computer.

Server Manager A Windows NT Server utility used for managing domains, workgroups, and computers.

Server Message Block (SMB) A high-level protocol between redirector and server used in Windows NT, LAN Manager, LAN Server, Windows for Workgroups, Windows 95, MS-NET, and PC-LAN.

Server service The Windows NT service that manages sharing of and access to local resources shared over the network.

service A Windows NT program that provides a specific function to applications. Services typically run in the background, without a user interface. NT services are designed around RPC, so they can be used by other computers on the network. The Services application in Control Panel lets you manage services.

service pack An update to the Windows NT operating system, released approximately quarterly by Microsoft. Service packs include fixes for any critical problems found by Microsoft or its customers.

Services for Macintosh (SFM) A feature of Windows NT Server that allows it to share files and printers with Macintosh clients, centralize network administration, provide improved password security, and connect multiple AppleTalk networks together.

session layer The fifth layer of the OSI model, negotiates and maintains connections between processes on different nodes. Conversations between processes on different nodes are established, maintained, and terminated by the session layer.

SFM See Services for Macintosh.

shadow member One of two members of a mirror set that acts as the mirror image of a primary member. Duplicate data is written to the shadow member and is read only when the primary member cannot be read. See also disk mirroring.

share name The name of a shared resource on a server.

share point A directory or device to which other network users can connect, typically expressed as a UNC name consisting of the server name and the share name.

shared pages Pages of Clipboard data shared over the network by the ClipBook application.

shared resource See resource.

shell The Windows NT 4.0 user interface.

Shell Update Release (SUR) Understated name of the Windows NT 4.0 release, referring to its new Windows 95-like user interface.

shortcut A pointer to an item that can be located anywhere on the local computer or on the network. When you double-click a shortcut icon, NT runs the application or opens the folder or file — just as if it were the item's original icon.

SID See security ID.

SIMM Single In-line Memory Module.

single network logon The ability of a user to log on to the network once, by specifying one user account name and password, to gain access to all network resources. The user doesn't need to log on to each individual server that offers resources.

single-attached nodes Nodes attached to one of the two FDDI rings, providing less fault tolerance than dual-attached nodes if a link fails.

single-ended SCSI A SCSI bus wiring scheme that uses a single wire for each signal transmitted on the bus. More commonly used than differential SCSI.

SLIP Serial Line Internet Protocol. A RAS protocol designed to run the IP protocol over serial communication lines. See also Point-to-Point Protocol.

Small Computer Systems Interface (SCSI) Pronounced "scuzzy." An interface standard used to connect hard disks, CD-ROM drives, tape drives, printers, scanners, and other devices to computers. A SCSI host adapter is used to control and connect SCSI devices.

SMB See Server Message Block.

SMP See symmetric multiprocessing.

SMS See Systems Management Server.

SMTP Simple Mail Transfer Protocol. A member of the TCP/IP protocol suite used for transmission of electronic mail.

sniffer See network analyzer.

SNA Systems Network Architecture.

SNMP Simple Network Management Protocol. A member of the TCP/IP protocol suite used for monitoring and setting network parameters. Required for gathering TCP/IP counters using the Performance Monitor utility.

source document The OLE document in which a data object is originally created. For example, source documents include spreadsheets, graphs, and sound clips that can be linked or embedded within other (destination) documents.

special group A group created automatically by Windows NT whose membership is predefined and automatically updated. Special groups provide a convenient way to describe sets of users that might dynamically change over time. For example, the Everyone group always includes all domain users and is automatically updated as user accounts are added and deleted.

special identity See special group.

spin lock A critical section mechanism used by kernel-mode components to ensure proper synchronization between multiple CPUs in an SMP computer.

spooler An operating system component that manages and services jobs stored in a print queue. The bulk of the Windows NT 4.0 print spooler now runs in kernel mode.

SPX See Sequenced Packet Exchange.

SQL Structured Query Language.

SQL Server The database server member of the BackOffice suite of server applications.

SSL Secrue Sockets Layer.

standard permissions Common combinations of individual permissions that define a specific type of access. For example, Full Control provides the full range of available access permissions.

star topology A network topology that connects each node to a central device called a hub. Depending on how the hub is wired, a physical star topology can be used to implement a logical bus or ring topology.

sticky drive lettering The ability to assign drive letters to partitions and logical drives and have those assignments remain in effect across reboots.

STP Shielded twisted-pair.

stripe set See disk striping.

stripe set with parity See disk striping.

stub function An API function that doesn't perform the requested operation itself, but rather packages the request, sends it to a server process for execution, and transparently returns the result to the calling application. This approach is used by LPC and RPC.

subkey A key within the Windows NT registry that is stored within another key. Subkeys can have their own subkeys. Typically, the root of a subtree is called a key, and the nodes below it are called subkeys.

subnet A subset of a LAN defined as a logical network for purposes of IP addressing. See subnet mask.

subnet layers Layers 3 through 5 of the OSI model, including the network, transport, and session layers. Network protocols are often implemented completely within these three layers.

subnet mask A data structure that looks like an IP address but describes a mask that defines which part of the IP address is used for the network address and which part is used for the host address. Bits set to 1 in the subnet mask indicate the bits of the IP address that make up the network address.

subtree A portion of the NT registry tree. Subtrees can be nested within other subtrees.

SUR See Shell Update Release.

swap file See paging file.

switching hub See hub.

symmetric multiprocessing (SMP) An approach to multiprocessor hardware design that gives multiple CPUs in a single computer equal access to system memory and hardware devices. Windows NT supports SMP computers containing multiple processors.

synchronous I/O An approach to performing I/O operations in which the requesting process is blocked until the I/O operation has been completed by the operating system. See also asynchronous I/O.

System DSN System Data Source Name.

system partition The volume that contains the hardware-specific files required to load Windows NT. On RISC platforms, the system partition must be formatted using FAT. The system partition may or may not be the same as the boot partition.

Systems Management Server (SMS) A server application in the BackOffice suite that enables you to inventory hardware and software over the network and manage software upgrades automatically.

T

T1 A digital carrier facility used for transmission of data through the telephone network at 1.5Mbps. The monthly cost to lease and use a T1 line is approximately $1,500 to $2,000.

T3 A WAN digital carrier facility used for transmission of data at 45Mbps. The monthly cost to lease and use a T3 line is approximately $65,000 to $85,000.

tape retensioning See retensioning.

TAPI See Telephony API.

TCP Transmission Control Protocol. See TCP/IP.

TCP/IP Transmission Control Protocol/Internet Protocol. A set of network protocols and associated tools that gained popularity in the UNIX and Internet environments. It has become the protocol of choice in many organizations (including Microsoft's ITG), even though it can be more complex to administer than other protocols.

TDI See Transport Driver Interface.

Telephony API (TAPI) A set of functions provided for development of applications involving telephone call processing. The Novell NetWare equivalent is TSAPI.

Telnet A member of the TCP/IP protocol suite used to perform terminal emulation.

terminator A device that provides resistance at the end of a transmission line to absorb the signal and prevent it from bouncing back to nodes that have already seen the transmission. Used at the ends of Ethernet cables and SCSI cables, for example.

TFTP Trivial File Transfer Protocol.

thread See multithreading.

Thinnet See 10Base2.

token A special data frame used to pass access control of the network from one node to the next. Possession of the token allows a node to transmit data on the network. See also token passing, Token Ring.

token passing An access method in which nodes take turns obtaining access to the network by taking possession of a special data frame called a token, as it passes by on the network. See also token, Token Ring.

Token Ring A network technology developed by IBM that's now an industry standard. It relies on token passing as an access method. The logical topology is always a ring, but the physical topology is typically a star.

TokenTalk AppleTalk protocols running on Token Ring network technology.

topology The physical or logical arrangement of network nodes and connections between nodes on a network. The physical topology is determined by the actual physical layout of network components (nodes, cables, hubs). The logical topology is determined by the actual path taken by the data as it travels through the network.

transceiver See multistation access unit.

Transmission Control Protocol (TCP) See TCP/IP.

Transport Driver Interface (TDI) A standard interface between transport protocol drivers and the OSI session layer components (redirector and server) above them. Windows NT transport protocols present the TDI interface, and session layer components make calls into the TDI interface.

transport layer The fourth layer of the OSI reference model, responsible for reliable communication of data between source and destination network nodes.

trust relationship An association between two domains that allows users to cross domain boundaries without having to log on multiple times and be authenticated in both domains. A user needs only one account in one domain. If that user's domain is trusted by the other domain, the other domain will accept the user's initial logon as valid. See also single network logon.

trusted domain A domain that a trusting domain will allow to authenticate logons. In multiple domain models, the trusted domain is typically a master domain that performs user authentication.

trusting domain The domain that relies on another domain to perform at least some user authentication. In multiple domain models, the trusting domain is typically a resource domain that relies solely on a master domain to perform authentication.

twisted-pair A type of network cabling consisting of two insulated wires arranged in a regular spiral pattern. The wires may be shielded (STP) or unshielded (UTP).

U

UAM See User Authentication Module.

UDP User Diagram Protocol.

UNC See Uniform Naming Convention.

Unicode A 16-bit computer encoding scheme that can represent 64K different characters, enough for all world languages that are currently involved in computing, plus a few others.

Uniform Naming Convention (UNC) An approach to referring to shared resources that doesn't require an existing connection to the resource. The name typically includes the name of the server, the share point, and any subdirectories on the shared resource.

Unimodem An NT driver that supports standard modem commands compatible with the Hayes AT command set.

uninterruptible power supply (UPS) A device containing a battery that can survive a power outage and keep a computer running long enough to shut it down gracefully. Some UPSs include a serial port to signal the server when a power outage has taken place. The UPS application in Control Panel enables you to control how these signals are processed.

UPS See uninterruptible power supply.

UPS service A Windows NT service that processes messages between a UPS device and the computer.

URL Uniform Resource Locator.

User The component of Windows NT (specifically the kernel portion of the Win32 subsystem) that manages windows and other user interface components. Moved from user mode to kernel mode in Windows NT 4.0 to improve performance.

user account The information, stored in the SAM database, that defines a user to Windows NT. This includes user name, password, group memberships, rights to perform tasks, and permissions to access resources. Managed with User Manager for Domains.

user account database See SAM database.

User Authentication Module (UAM) An optional Macintosh client component that provides password encryption across the network and the ability to use passwords containing up to 14 characters.

User Manager for Domains An administrative tool, primarily accessible only to administrators, used to manage user accounts, groups, and security policies for Windows NT domains and systems.

user mode The most restricted processor mode, which can only access its own virtual address space. User-mode code must rely on code running in kernel mode to access hardware or perform privileged operations. On Intel CPUs, user mode is at Ring 3. See also kernel mode.

user profile The personal settings that a user has established in his or her Windows NT environment, including desktop settings, network connections, Explorer settings, and so forth. See also roaming user profile, local user profile, mandatory user profile.

UTP Unshielded twisted-pair.

V

value entry The actual data within the NT registry, stored within keys. Each value entry has a name, a data type, and the value itself. The length and format of the value depend on its data type.

vampire tap A connector that clamps onto the network cable, forcing metal prongs through the insulation to make contact with the conductors inside.

VDM See virtual DOS machine.

VESA Local Bus (VLB) A high-speed bus architecture designed for 486-based motherboards and fast video adapters.

VFAT The variant of the FAT file system introduced with Windows 95 and supported by Windows NT. VFAT offers long filenames and performance improvements over the FAT file system.

VGA Video Graphics Array. A standard PC video adapter, first introduced by IBM in 1987, with a display resolution of 640x480.

VINES Virtual Network System. A network operating system developed by Banyan.

virtual DOS machine (VDM) An environment provided to each DOS application on Windows NT to simulate the hardware and software present on a standard PC. A single WOW VDM is provided for all Win16 applications running on NT. If a Win16 application is set to run in its own memory space, it's given its own VDM.

virtual memory (VM) A technique that allows the operating system to supplement physical RAM by using available disk space. NT provides the illusion of a large physical address space by swapping pages of applications and data between RAM and disk.

Virtual Memory Manager (VMM) A kernel-mode component of the Windows NT operating system that manages paging, memory allocation, and other virtual memory functions.

VLB See VESA Local Bus.

VM See virtual memory.

VMM See Virtual Memory Manager.

volatile key An NT registry key whose contents are dynamically reconstructed at boot time, rather than being stored in a hive file.

volume A hard disk partition or logical drive formatted with a file system (either FAT or NTFS) and available for use by the operating system. In the context of SFM, a Macintosh volume refers to an NTFS or CD-ROM directory that's been designated as accessible by Macintosh clients.

volume set A collection of two or more areas of hard disk free space that have been logically connected to form a larger volume. Volume sets can be formatted as FAT or NTFS. Existing NTFS volumes and volume sets can be extended. FAT volumes can't be extended.

volume spanning See volume set.

W

WAN See wide area network.

WfW See Windows for Workgroups.

wide area network (WAN) A network spanning a wide geographic area, involving multiple buildings, cities, states, or countries. See also local area network.

Win16 application A 16-bit Windows program, designed to run on Windows 3.1 or Windows for Workgroups. It uses the 16-bit Windows API to request services from the operating system. Most Win16 applications can be run on Windows NT through the WOW VDM.

Win32 application A 32-bit Windows program, designed to run on Windows NT, Windows 95, Win32s on Windows 3.1, or some combination of these. It uses the Win32 API to request services from the operating system. Most Win32 applications can be run on both Windows NT and Windows 95, unless they require features unique to only one of these operating systems.

Win32 subsystem The environment subsystem in Windows NT that provides services to 32-bit Windows applications via the Win32 APIs.

Win32s application A 32-bit Windows program, designed to run on Win32s on Windows 3.1, using the Win32s libraries. It uses a limited set of the Win32 API to allow execution on Win32s, Windows NT, and Windows 95.

Windows 95 A desktop operating system released by Microsoft in 1995, containing a new user interface, Plug-and-Play, and several architectural features from NT. Windows 95 is a combination of 32-bit and 16-bit code. Windows NT 4.0 sports the new user interface that Windows 95 introduced.

Windows for Workgroups A version of 16-bit Windows 3.x that added built-in peer-to-peer networking, improved file access performance, and groupware features.

Windows Internet Name Service (WINS) A facility that performs dynamic translation of computer names to IP addresses. WINS works closely with DHCP to keep these translations up to date at all times.

Windows Messaging Starting with Windows 95 and Windows NT 4.0, the name Microsoft has chosen for its communication and groupware technology.

Windows NT The generic name for the operating system architecture common to both Windows NT Workstation and Windows NT Server products. If referring to the NT operating system version 3.1, Windows NT was the name of the workstation product. Starting with version 3.5, the product was renamed Windows NT Workstation.

Windows NT Advanced Server The name of Microsoft's server version of the Windows NT operating system version 3.1. Starting with version 3.5, the product was renamed Windows NT Server.

Windows NT Server The name of Microsoft's server version of the Windows NT operating system version 3.5 and later. Called Windows NT Advanced Server in version 3.1. Windows NT Server uses the same core operating system as Windows NT Workstation and adds centralized management and security, fault tolerance, additional connectivity, and other features.

Windows NT Workstation The name of Microsoft's workstation version of the Windows NT operating system version 3.5 and later. Called Windows NT in version 3.1.

Windows Sockets An API for Windows-based operating systems, specifically designed to provide TCP/IP and Internet communication facilities to Windows-based programs. Commonly called Winsock.

WINS See Windows Internet Name Service.

Winsock See Windows Sockets.

wiring closet A specially designed room that serves as a central junction point for network wiring and wiring equipment.

workgroup A collection of networked computers grouped together to facilitate work that users tend to perform together. Computers running Windows NT, Windows 95, or Windows for Workgroups can participate in a workgroup. See also peer-to-peer network.

workstation See Windows NT Workstation.

Workstation service A Windows NT service that implements the redirector network functions.

workstation operating system (WOS) Obsolete term referring to a NOS running on a workstation computer.

WOS See workstation operating system.

WOSA Windows Open Services Architecture.

WOW Win16 on Win32, or Windows on Windows. The Win32 process on Windows NT that provides a VDM environment to Win16 applications and emulates the 16-bit Windows environment. By default, a single WOW process runs all Win16 applications, protecting the rest of the NT operating system from them, but not protecting them from each other. You can optionally set an individual Win16 application to run in its own WOW process, isolating it from other Win16 applications.

WOW VDM The single virtual DOS machine used by Windows NT to emulate the 16-bit Windows 3.x environment for all Win16 applications. Optionally, the VDM provided exclusively to a Win16 application running in its own address space.

WWW World Wide Web.

WYSIWYG What you see is what you get.

X

X.25 A standard that defines the packet format for data transfers on a public network. See also Frame Relay.

XMS See Extended Memory Specification.

Z

zone A logical group of network devices in an AppleTalk network.

Workstation service A Windows NT service that implements the redirector [illegible] working tools.

workstation operating system (WOS) Obsolete term [illegible] running on a workstation computer.

WOS See workstation operating system.

WQS Windows Quest Services [illegible]

WOW Win16 on Win32 or Windows on Windows. The Win32 process on Windows NT that provides a VDM environment to Win16 applications and emulates the 16-bit Windows environment. By default, a single WOW process runs all Win16 applications, protecting the rest of the NT operating system from them, but not protecting them from each other. You can optionally set an individual Win16 application to run in its own WOW process, isolating it from other Win16 applications.

WOW VDM The single virtual DOS machine used by Windows NT to emulate the 16-bit Windows 3.x environment for all Win16 applications. Optionally, the VDM provided exclusively to a Win16 application running in its own address space.

WWW World Wide Web.

WYSIWYG What you see is what you get.

X

X.25 A standard that defines the packet format for data transfers on a public network. See also Frame Relay.

XMS See Extended Memory Specification.

Z

zone A logical group of network devices in an AppleTalk network.

Windows NT Server Information Resources

The key to your success as a Windows NT network administrator is having the right information at the right time. Knowing where to look for it is more than half the battle. In this appendix, you'll find several Windows NT Server information resources that I recommend.

Using Technical Support

This is probably the most expensive source of information available to you, both in terms of dollar cost and your time on the phone. Whether you pay by the amount of time that you spend with a support representative or by the number of incidents that you open, it seems as though the meter is always running.

I recommend using technical support as a last resort, when you've exhausted the other sources discussed in this section. There are times, however, when calling technical support is the right thing. When you do, be prepared with all of the details of your computer and network configurations, specifics of the problem that you're having, and any serial numbers or other information required to prove that you're entitled to support.

Whenever you contact technical support, always keep track of the date, time, issue, person with whom you spoke, and resolution or next steps. You'll be given an "SR" number to keep track of each issue. Be sure to record it as well. If you ever have to reconstruct what happened or bring a new support person up to speed on what's transpired so far, this information will be very valuable and will save time for everyone.

Microsoft has a Fast Tips service that allows you to order detailed information by phone, 24 hours a day, 7 days a week. When you first call one of the Fast Tips phone numbers, select the options that let you order the Fast Tips catalog. With this in hand, you'll be able to order specific documents by number and have them immediately mailed or faxed to you. Here are the Microsoft Fast Tips phone numbers:

Business Systems (NT, BackOffice)	1-800-936-4400
Personal OSs (DOS, Windows, Windows 95)	1-800-936-4200
Desktop Applications (Office)	1-800-936-4100
Development Tools	1-800-936-4300

For the live technical support phone number, as well as other support options available to you, see the technical support and registration materials included in your Windows NT Server package. If you received Windows NT Server preinstalled on your computer and didn't receive Microsoft technical support information, contact your computer vendor for details on how to obtain live support.

Getting Trained and Certified

Now that Microsoft has a professional certification program, a wide range of training kits and live courses are available from a variety of local sources. Some of the live NT courses are expensive (costing in the $2000 range for a five-day workshop), but Microsoft maintains good quality control of the instructors and training materials. Many of these courses are quite worthwhile, especially the ones that specialize in a specific area of the product, such as TCP/IP.

Be careful with mail-order, self-paced training courses. Some vendors charge high prices and offer little useful information. Your best bet is to stick with vendors who display the *Microsoft Certified Professional — Approved Study Guide* logo. Here are a couple of vendors that currently produce approved self-paced materials:

CBT Systems
400 Oyster Point Blvd. #401
South San Francisco, CA 94080
(800) 929-9050

NETG
1751 West Diehl Road
Naperville, IL 60563-9009
(708) 369-3000

If you have multiple people in your network administration group, it's typically cost effective to get one of your group members formally trained. This person can come back and share their knowledge with the rest of the team.

Storage Technology References

If you're interested in the internals of the NTFS file system, you can find lots of detail in *Inside the Windows NT File System* by Helen Custer, published by Microsoft Press. This fairly short read covers how structures are laid out on an NTFS volume and explains how NTFS interacts with other components of the operating system.

Chapter 19 discusses setting up RAID fault tolerance on your Windows NT server. You can find additional background on RAID technology in *The RAIDbook — A Source Book for Disk Array Technology,* published by the RAID Advisory Board, St. Peter, Minnesota.

Windows NT Resource Kit

Microsoft publishes a multiple-volume set of books collectively called the *Windows NT Resource Kit.* It includes a CD-ROM and is updated periodically, typically every six months. This kit contains vast amounts of valuable information about Windows NT and enterprise networking. At the time of this writing, the kit includes the following volumes:

- ✦ Volume 1: Windows NT Resource Guide
- ✦ Volume 2: Windows NT Networking Guide
- ✦ Volume 3: Windows NT Messages
- ✦ Volume 4: Optimizing Windows NT

As new versions of Windows NT are released, Microsoft either reissues the entire kit (as they did for NT 3.5) or publishes update volumes (as they did for NT 3.51). Microsoft is releasing a completely new resource kit for Windows NT 4.0.

The CD-ROM that is included contains an array of generally useful utilities. Unfortunately, these programs aren't officially supported by Microsoft. However, some of the more useful ones do find their way into the supported NT product in subsequent releases. (The DNS Server is an example of an NT feature that started as a freebie in the resource kit.) I highly recommend having a copy of the kit available in any organization basing its network on Windows NT Server. The retail cost is approximately $199, or about $150 street price.

Before you run out and buy a resource kit, check out the next section that talks about Microsoft TechNet. The TechNet subscription includes an electronic version of the *Windows NT Resource Kit* for free. Also, if all you're after are the resource kit utilities, they're available free from Microsoft's ftp site. Check out `ftp.microsoft.com/bussys/winnt/winnt-public/reskit/nt4`. (Microsoft's policy of giving away the resource kit with TechNet and on the Internet may change in the near future.)

Microsoft TechNet

Microsoft offers an annual subscription to TechNet, a monthly pair of CD-ROMs that contain vast amounts of information on all Microsoft products. One CD-ROM includes product documentation, white papers, resource kits, and Microsoft's product support knowledge base. This last piece is the same database used by Microsoft staff to support customers over the phone. If you're involved in your organization's Help desk operations or you need to provide support internally for one or more Microsoft products (including Windows NT Server), this CD-ROM can be an extremely valuable tool. By avoiding costly support calls to Microsoft, the subscription can pay for itself very quickly. All of the information is easily searchable.

The other monthly CD-ROM contains drivers, code samples, utilities, and product patches, including service packs for Windows NT products. In my view, this is a much more convenient way of obtaining NT service packs, since you don't have to download a huge file over the Internet. In TechNet, just click MS BackOffice ➪ MS Windows NT Server ➪ Windows NT 4.0 Service Packs, then click the button for your CPU platform, and you're in business. Keep in mind, however, that the version on the CD-ROM can lag a few weeks, depending on when the NT service pack is actually released.

At the time of this writing, a one-year TechNet subscription costs $299 for a single user or $699 for a license that allows you to install it on a single server with unlimited users. I highly recommend the TechNet subscription. It's an extremely valuable tool for MIS departments and anyone integrating or supporting a range of Microsoft products. To order, call 1-800-344-2121 during Microsoft business hours, which are 6:30 a.m. to 5:30 p.m. PST.

Microsoft Developer Network

If you're involved in developing in-house or commercial software products based on Microsoft operating system platforms, Microsoft offers a quarterly subscription to its Developer Network, called MSDN. This subscription provides you with all of the latest operating systems, development kits, and developer knowledge base. You also get online versions of documentation and several programming-related books and periodicals covering Microsoft products. As shown in Table C-1, three levels of MSDN membership are available: Library, Professional, and Enterprise.

Table C-1
The Three Levels of MSDN Membership

MSDN Includes	***Level 1 "Library"***	***Level 2 "Professional"***	***Level 3 "Enterprise"***
Quarterly Development Library CD-ROM	✓	✓	✓
Bimonthly MSDN Newsletter	✓	✓	✓
Two free product support telephone incidents	✓	✓	✓
Full access to CompuServe member forums	✓	✓	✓
Quarterly Development Platform CD-ROMs (operating systems including NT Workstation, SDKs, DDKs)		✓	✓
Interim CD-ROMs containing new tools and operating system beta releases		✓	✓
Quarterly BackOffice CD-ROMs containing products for development and testing purposes (including NT Server)			✓
Interim CD-ROMs containing new BackOffice tools and product beta releases			✓
Two additional free product support telephone incidents			✓
Multiple user licenses	Available	Not available	Included
Annual subscription cost	$195	$495	$1495

The development platform kits don't include key tools such as Visual C++ or Visual Basic. (Visual C++ has its own subscription program, if you want the latest compiler features hot off the CD-ROM press.) You must purchase these separately to make use of the tools provided in MSDN. If you're doing software development for Microsoft platforms or if you need to evaluate beta versions of Microsoft's operating system or BackOffice products, MSDN provides a ton of useful information.

Microsoft has started offering beta versions of its operating system products in less expensive venues. For example, you could obtain the Windows 95 beta for about $30, and one of the Windows NT 4.0 betas was made available free of charge. So, I don't recommend investing in MSDN unless you're doing software development.

A Web of NT Pages

Assuming that you have Internet access, you can use your favorite World Wide Web browser to gather information from Microsoft and other sources on the Web. Since content and locations change continuously, I won't pinpoint many specific areas to go within these pages. I'll leave the navigation to you.

A recent set of searches that I did on Windows NT-related topics using Yahoo's default search engine (`http://www.yahoo.com`) yielded 424 pages mentioning Windows NT, 77 pages mentioning Windows NT Server, and 27 pages that touch on BackOffice. There's more out there, but doing a search like this can be a good starting point in identifying some useful NT Web sites.

To find out what's going on with Microsoft and its products, visit its home page at `http://www.microsoft.com`. From this page, you can navigate into online support, gather information on any of Microsoft's products, or download free software updates.

You can focus on NT Server and BackOffice by visiting `http://www.microsoft.com/BackOffice`. This page typically links to all sorts of useful information about current and future trends, case studies, and so on.

You can find an up-to-date Windows NT Server Hardware Compatibility List (HCL) by visiting `http://www.microsoft.com/BackOffice/ntserver/hcl`. I highly recommend checking this updated list before you purchase hardware to be used with Windows NT. Chances are this list will have more information than the one included with your Windows NT Server package.

Digital Equipment Corporation (DEC) hosts a Windows NT resources page at `http://www.windowsnt.digital.com`. This page includes lots of links to useful information. As you might expect, it leans a bit toward information about NT on the Alpha RISC platform.

Visit `http://www.ntadvantage.com`, run by Beverly Hills Software. There you'll find interesting NT-related material in electronic magazine article form.

Online NT Newsletters

Several mailing lists exist on the Internet that are dedicated to discussion of Windows NT Server and Workstation topics. I've included the more popular ones here, along with information on how to get on each mailing list. If you have more than one e-mail account, be sure to request the subscription from the e-mail account where you want to receive the mailings.

Microsoft and Beverly Hills Software publish an NT newsletter called *WINNTNEWS*. Subscribe by sending e-mail with "SUBSCRIBE WINNTNEWS" as the first line of your message to the Internet address `winntnews-admin@microsoft.bhs.com`.

Microsoft and Beverly Hills Software also publish a BackOffice newsletter called *BACKOFFICENEWS*. Subscribe by sending e-mail with "SUBSCRIBE BACKOFFICENEWS" as the first line of your message to the Internet address `backofficenews-admin@microsoft.bhs.com`.

Microsoft publishes a newsletter that covers all Windows products (including Windows NT) called *WINNEWS*. Subscribe by sending e-mail with a blank subject line and only the words "SUBSCRIBE WINNEWS" in the message body to the Internet address `admin@winnews.microsoft.com`.

You can also subscribe to *Win NTools News,* a biweekly newsletter designed for administrators who are using NT in a production environment. Send e-mail to `listproc@intnet.net` with "SUBSCRIBE NT-LIST <your first name> <your last name>" as the first line of the message body.

Online NT Discussion Groups

The International Windows NT Users Group is designed to allow Windows NT professionals to ask questions and share information related to Windows NT products. Members expect you to exhaust other resources such as the NT product documentation and the NT resource kit before asking for help. Join the list by sending e-mail with only the words "join iwntug" in the message body to the Internet address `list@bhs.com`.

EmeraldNET sponsors an unmoderated group that discusses Windows NT and the Internet. Join the list by sending e-mail with the subject line "SUBSCRIBE" to the Internet address `http_winnt@Emerald.NET`.

You can join a Windows NT Server discussion list by sending e-mail to `mailbase@mailbase.ac.uk`. The body of your message must contain the single line "join windows-nt <your first name> <your last name>."

To join a list that discusses Microsoft BackOffice, send e-mail to ms-backoffice-request@go.net. The body of your message must contain the single line "join ms-backoffice <your first name> <your last name>." To join yet another group that discusses Windows NT Server, send e-mail to listserv@peach.ease.lsoft.com with the one-line body of the message "sub winnt-l <your first name> <your last name>." You'll get an e-mail message back with instructions on how to confirm and complete your subscription.

Online NT Newsgroups

There are several Windows NT newsgroups active at the time of this writing. The two most active ones are comp.os.ms-windows.nt.setup, which focuses on installation and configuration issues, and comp.os.ms-windows.nt.misc, dealing with just about everything else NT-ish. Here are some newsgroups that you may want to visit:

comp.os.ms-windows.nt.admin.misc

comp.os.ms-windows.nt.admin.networking

comp.os.ms-windows.nt.misc

comp.os.ms-windows.nt.setup.misc

comp.os.ms-windows.nt.setup.hardware

comp.os.ms-windows.nt.software.backoffice

NT CompuServe Forums

If you're a CompuServe user, there are several forums available where Windows NT is discussed among users and representatives from Microsoft. You can sometimes save expensive support calls by searching these forums for discussions of whatever ails your network. Table C-2 lists a few good forums available at the time of this writing.

Table C-2
CompuServe Forums That Discuss Windows NT

CompuServe Forum	*Description*
GO WINNT	This forum is used to discuss general Windows NT topics, typically common to both Server and Workstation products.
GO NTWORK	This forum is used to discuss Windows NT Workstation topics, although many of the discussions are generally applicable to NT.
GO NTSERVER	This forum is used to specifically discuss Windows NT Server.
GO MSWIN32	If you're doing software development for Windows NT, you'll be interested in this forum that discusses Win32 programming issues.
GO MICROSOFT	This is a good starting place for finding discussion groups on all of Microsoft's products.

Index

(continued)

(continued)

D

(continued)

E

F

(continued)

M

(continued)

O

P

Q

R

S

(continued)

(continued)

U

V

W

IDG BOOKS WORLDWIDE, INC. END-USER LICENSE AGREEMENT

Read This. You should carefully read these terms and conditions before opening the software packet(s) included with this book ("Book"). This is a license agreement ("Agreement") between you and IDG Books Worldwide, Inc. ("IDGB"). By opening the accompanying software packet(s), you acknowledge that you have read and accept the following terms and conditions. If you do not agree and do not want to be bound by such terms and conditions, promptly return the Book and the unopened software packet(s) to the place you obtained them for a full refund.

License Grant. IDGB grants to you (either an individual or entity) a nonexclusive license to use one copy of the enclosed software program(s) (collectively, the "Software") solely for your own personal or business purposes on a single computer (whether a standard computer or a workstation component of a multi-user network). The Software is in use on a computer when it is loaded into temporary memory (i.e., RAM) or installed into permanent memory (e.g., hard disk, CD-ROM or other storage device). IDGB reserves all rights not expressly granted herein.

Ownership. IDGB is the owner of all right, title and interest, including copyright, in and to the compilation of the Software recorded on the disk(s)/CD-ROM. Copyright to the individual programs on the disk(s)/CD-ROM is owned by the author or other authorized copyright owner of each program. Ownership of the Software and all proprietary rights relating thereto remain with IDGB and its licensors.

Restrictions On Use and Transfer.

(a) You may only (i) make one copy of the Software for backup or archival purposes, or (ii) transfer the Software to a single hard disk, provided that you keep the original for backup or archival purposes. You may not (i) rent or lease the Software, (ii) copy or reproduce the Software through a LAN or other network system or through any computer subscriber system or bulletin-board system, or (iii) modify, adapt or create derivative works based on the Software.

(b) You may not reverse engineer, decompile, or disassemble the Software. You may transfer the Software and user documentation on a permanent basis, provided that the transferee agrees to accept the terms and conditions of this Agreement and you retain no copies. If the Software is an update or has been updated, any transfer must include the most recent update and all prior versions.

Restrictions on Use of Individual Programs. You must follow the individual requirements and restrictions detailed for each individual program in Appendix C of this Book. These limitations are contained in the individual license agreements recorded on the disk(s)/CD-ROM. These restrictions include a requirement that after using the program for the period of time specified in its text, the user must pay a registration fee or discontinue use. By opening the Software packet(s), you will be agreeing to abide by the licenses and restrictions for these individual programs. None of the material on this disk(s) or listed in this Book may ever be distributed, in original or modified form, for commercial purposes.

Limited Warranty.

(a) IDGB warrants that the Software and disk(s)/CD-ROM are free from defects in materials and workmanship under normal use for a period of sixty (60) days from the date of purchase of this Book. If IDGB receives notification within the warranty period of defects in materials or workmanship, IDGB will replace the defective disk(s)/CD-ROM.

(b) **IDGB AND THE AUTHOR OF THE BOOK DISCLAIM ALL OTHER WARRANTIES, EXPRESS OR IMPLIED, INCLUDING WITHOUT LIMITATION IMPLIED WARRANTIES OF MERCHANTABILITY AND FITNESS FOR A PARTICULAR PURPOSE, WITH RESPECT TO THE SOFTWARE, THE PROGRAMS, THE SOURCE CODE CONTAINED THEREIN, AND/OR THE TECHNIQUES DESCRIBED IN THIS BOOK. IDGB DOES NOT WARRANT THAT THE FUNCTIONS CONTAINED IN THE SOFTWARE WILL MEET YOUR REQUIREMENTS OR THAT THE OPERATION OF THE SOFTWARE WILL BE ERROR FREE.**

(c) This limited warranty gives you specific legal rights, and you may have other rights which vary from jurisdiction to jurisdiction.

Remedies.

(a) IDGB's entire liability and your exclusive remedy for defects in materials and workmanship shall be limited to replacement of the Software, which is returned to IDGB at the address set forth below with a copy of your receipt. This Limited Warranty is void if failure of the Software has resulted from accident, abuse, or misapplication. Any replacement Software will be warranted for the remainder of the original warranty period or thirty (30) days, whichever is longer.

(b) In no event shall IDGB or the author be liable for any damages whatsoever (including without limitation damages for loss of business profits, business interruption, loss of business information, or any other pecuniary loss) arising out of the use of or inability to use the Book or the Software, even if IDGB has been advised of the possibility of such damages.

(c) Because some jurisdictions do not allow the exclusion or limitation of liability for consequential or incidental damages, the above limitation or exclusion may not apply to you.

U.S. Government Restricted Rights. Use, duplication, or disclosure of the Software by the U.S. Government is subject to restrictions stated in paragraph (c) (1) (ii) of the Rights in Technical Data and Computer Software clause of DFARS 252.227-7013, and in subparagraphs (a) through (d) of the Commercial Computer—Restricted Rights clause at FAR 52.227-19, and in similar clauses in the NASA FAR supplement, when applicable.

General. This Agreement constitutes the entire understanding of the parties, and revokes and supersedes all prior agreements, oral or written, between them and may not be modified or amended except in a writing signed by both parties hereto which specifically refers to this Agreement. This Agreement shall take precedence over any other documents that may be in conflict herewith. If any one or more provisions contained in this Agreement are held by any court or tribunal to be invalid, illegal or otherwise unenforceable, each and every other provision shall remain in full force and effect.

IDG BOOKS WORLDWIDE REGISTRATION CARD

RETURN THIS REGISTRATION CARD FOR FREE CATALOG

Title of this book: Windows NT™ Server 4.0 Administrator's Bible

My overall rating of this book: ❑ Very good [1] ❑ Good [2] ❑ Satisfactory [3] ❑ Fair [4] ❑ Poor [5]

How I first heard about this book:

❑ Found in bookstore; name: [6] ____ ❑ Book review: [7] ____

❑ Advertisement: [8] ____ ❑ Catalog: [9] ____

❑ Word of mouth; heard about book from friend, co-worker, etc.: [10] ____ ❑ Other: [11] ____

What I liked most about this book: ____

What I would change, add, delete, etc., in future editions of this book: ____

Other comments: ____

Number of computer books I purchase in a year: ❑ 1 [12] ❑ 2-5 [13] ❑ 6-10 [14] ❑ More than 10 [15]

I would characterize my computer skills as: ❑ Beginner [16] ❑ Intermediate [17] ❑ Advanced [18] ❑ Professional [19]

I use ❑ DOS [20] ❑ Windows [21] ❑ OS/2 [22] ❑ Unix [23] ❑ Macintosh [24] ❑ Other: [25] ____ (please specify)

I would be interested in new books on the following subjects:
(please check all that apply, and use the spaces provided to identify specific software)

❑ Word processing: [26] ____ ❑ Spreadsheets: [27] ____

❑ Data bases: [28] ____ ❑ Desktop publishing: [29] ____

❑ File Utilities: [30] ____ ❑ Money management: [31] ____

❑ Networking: [32] ____ ❑ Programming languages: [33] ____

❑ Other: [34] ____

I use a PC at (please check all that apply): ❑ home [35] ❑ work [36] ❑ school [37] ❑ other: [38] ____

The disks I prefer to use are ❑ 5.25 [39] ❑ 3.5 [40] ❑ other: [41] ____

I have a CD ROM: ❑ yes [42] ❑ no [43]

I plan to buy or upgrade computer hardware this year: ❑ yes [44] ❑ no [45]

I plan to buy or upgrade computer software this year: ❑ yes [46] ❑ no [47]

Name: ____ Business title: [48] ____ Type of Business: [49] ____

Address (❑ home [50] ❑ work [51]/Company name: ____)

Street/Suite# ____

City [52]/State [53]/Zipcode [54]: ____ Country [55] ____

❑ **I liked this book!** You may quote me by name in future IDG Books Worldwide promotional materials.

My daytime phone number is ____

IDG BOOKS®
THE WORLD OF COMPUTER KNOWLEDGE

YES!

Please keep me informed about IDG's World of Computer Knowledge.
Send me the latest IDG Books catalog.

BUSINESS REPLY MAIL

FIRST CLASS MAIL PERMIT NO. 2605 FOSTER CITY, CALIFORNIA

IDG Books Worldwide
919 E Hillsdale Blvd, STE 400
Foster City, CA 94404-9691